RESEARCH HANDBOOK ON INTERNATIONAL CONFLICT AND SECURITY LAW

RESEARCH HANDBOOKS IN INTERNATIONAL LAW

This highly original series offers a unique appraisal of the state-of-the-art research and thinking in international law. Taking a thematic approach, each volume, edited by a prominent expert, covers a specific aspect of international law or examines the international legal dimension of a particular strand of the law. A wide range of sub-disciplines in the spheres of both public and private law are considered; from international environmental law to international criminal law, from international economic law to the law of international organisations, and from international commercial law to international human rights law. The *Research Handbooks* comprise carefully commissioned chapters from leading academics as well as those with an emerging reputation. Taking a genuinely international approach to the law, and addressing current and sometimes controversial legal issues, as well as affording a clear substantive analysis of the law, these *Handbooks* are designed to inform as well as to contribute to current debates.

Equally useful as reference tools or introductions to specific topics, issues and debates, the *Handbooks* will be used by academic researchers, post-graduate students, practising lawyers and lawyers in policy circles.

Titles in this series include:

Research Handbook on International Criminal Law
Edited by Bartram S. Brown

Research Handbook on the Law of International Organizations
Edited by Jan Klabbers and Åsa Wallendahl

Research Handbook on the Theory and History of International Law
Edited by Alexander Orakhelashvili

Research Handbook on International Sports Law
Edited by James A.R. Nafziger and Stephen F. Ross

Research Handbook on International Conflict and Security Law
Jus ad Bellum, Jus in Bello, and *Jus post Bellum*
Edited by Nigel D. White and Christian Henderson

Research Handbook on International Conflict and Security Law

Jus ad Bellum, Jus in Bello, and *Jus post Bellum*

Edited by

Nigel D. White
University of Nottingham, UK

Christian Henderson
University of Liverpool, UK

RESEARCH HANDBOOKS IN INTERNATIONAL LAW

Edward Elgar
Cheltenham, UK • Northampton, MA, USA

© The Editors and Contributors Severally 2013

All rights reserved. No part of this publication may be reproduced, stored in a retrieval system or transmitted in any form or by any means, electronic, mechanical or photocopying, recording, or otherwise without the prior permission of the publisher.

Published by
Edward Elgar Publishing Limited
The Lypiatts
15 Lansdown Road
Cheltenham
Glos GL50 2JA
UK

Edward Elgar Publishing, Inc.
William Pratt House
9 Dewey Court
Northampton
Massachusetts 01060
USA

A catalogue record for this book
is available from the British Library

Library of Congress Control Number: 2012954978

This book is available electronically in the ElgarOnline.com Law Subject Collection,
E-ISBN 978 1 84980 857 6

ISBN 978 1 84980 856 9 (cased)

Typeset by Columns Design XML Ltd, Reading
Printed and bound in Great Britain by T.J. International Ltd, Padstow

Contents

List of contributors	vii
Introduction: international conflict and security law *Christian Henderson and Nigel D. White*	1
1 Conflict prevention *Kenneth Manusama*	4
2 Disarmament and non-proliferation *Mirko Sossai*	41
3 The prohibition of threats of force *Nicholas Tsagourias*	67
4 The prohibition of the use of force *Mary Ellen O'Connell*	89
5 The centrality of the United Nations Security Council in the legal regime governing the use of force *Christian Henderson*	120
6 A study of the scope and operation of the rights of individual and collective self-defence under international law *Dino Kritsiotis*	170
7 The use of force for humanitarian purposes *Christine Gray*	229
8 A taxonomy of armed conflict *Marko Milanovic and Vidan Hadzi-Vidanovic*	256
9 Weapons *Karen Hulme*	315
10 Targets *David Turns*	342
11 Protected persons in international armed conflicts *Tom Ruys and Christian De Cock*	375
12 Private military companies *Chia Lehnardt*	421
13 International humanitarian law and human rights law *Matthew Happold*	444
14 War crimes *Robert Cryer*	467
15 Peace settlements and international law: from *lex pacificatoria* to *jus post bellum* *Christine Bell*	499

16 Foreign territorial administration and international trusteeship over people: colonialism, occupation, the mandates and trusteeship arrangements, and international territorial administration 547
    Ralph Wilde
17 Peacekeeping or war-fighting? 572
    Nigel D. White
18 Human rights protection during extra-territorial military operations: perspectives at international and English law 598
    Alexander Orakhelashvili
19 Reparation and compensation 638
    Natalino Ronzitti

Index 661

Contributors

Christine Bell is Professor of Constitutional Law, University of Edinburgh. She read law at Selwyn College, Cambridge (1988) and gained an LLM in Law from Harvard Law School (1990), supported by a Harkness Fellowship. She is a former Director of the Human Rights Centre, Queen's University Belfast, and of the Transitional Justice Institute, University of Ulster. Her research interests lie in the interface between constitutional and international law, gender and conflict, and legal theory, with a particular interest in peace processes and their agreements. She has participated in a number of peace negotiations. In 2007 Christine won the American Society of International Law's Francis Deake Prize for her article on 'Peace Agreements: Their Nature and Legal Status' which was published in the *American Journal of International Law*. She has authored two books: *On the Law of Peace: Peace Agreements and the Lex Pacificatoria* (Oxford: Oxford University Press, 2008), which won the Hart Socio-legal Book Prize, awarded by the Socio-legal Studies Association UK, and *Peace Agreements and Human Rights* (Oxford: Oxford University Press, 2000).

Robert Cryer obtained his undergraduate law degree at Cardiff Law School, then moved to the School of Law in Nottingham, where he obtained his LLM and PhD degrees in 1996 and 2000 respectively. He was a Lecturer at the University of Manchester from 1999–2001 before returning to the School of Law, University of Nottingham in September 2001. He moved to Birmingham in April 2007 as Professor of International and Criminal Law. In addition to a number of articles and book chapters he is the author of *Prosecuting International Crimes: Selectivity and the International Criminal Law Regime* (Cambridge: Cambridge University Press, 2005) and co-author (with Hakan Friman, Darryl Robinson and Elizabeth Wilmshurst) of *An Introduction to International Criminal Law and Procedure*, 2nd edn (Cambridge: Cambridge University Press, 2010) and (with Neil Boister) of *The Tokyo International Military Tribunal: A Reappraisal* (Oxford: Oxford University Press, 2008). He is co-editor of the *Journal of Conflict and Security Law* and a member of the editorial board of the *Journal of International Criminal Justice*.

Christian De Cock holds Master's degrees in the fields of Aeronautical and Military Sciences, Law, Political Sciences, Public Management, Security and Defence. After graduating from the Belgian Royal Military School, he served in the Belgian air force as Platoon and Company Commander for the Force Protection Units (1990–1996). After two years as a Military Instructor (1996–1998), he taught at the Law Department of the Belgian Royal Military School for five years (1998–2003). He became Legal Adviser at the Belgian Ministry of Defence from 2004 to 2007, prior to which he joined a course at the Royal Defence College, Belgium, and after which he participated in an Advanced Staff and Command Course at the National Defence College in the Netherlands. Since 2004, Lieutenant-Colonel De Cock has participated in several operational deployments: ISAF, counter-piracy, counter-narcotics, and Unified Protector (2011). In 2008, he took up the position of Head of the International Law Section at the Belgian Ministry of Defence. He is also a member of the visiting teaching staff at the International Institute of Humanitarian Law (San Remo) and Lecturer at the Royal Military School (Brussels).

Christine Gray is Professor of International Law at the University of Cambridge and a Fellow of St John's College. She has written widely on the use of force. Her main publications are *International Law and the Use of Force*, 3rd edn (Oxford: Oxford University Press, 2008) and *Judicial Remedies in International Law* (Oxford: Clarendon Press, 1987). She is a member of the editorial board of several journals, including the *British Yearbook of International Law*, the *European Journal of International Law*, the *Journal of Conflict and Security Law* and the *Cambridge Law Journal*. She has been a Visiting Fellow at the Max Planck Institute in Heidelberg, as well as Visiting Professor at Duke and other US universities.

Vidan Hadzi-Vidanovic is a PhD candidate at the University of Nottingham School of Law. He holds a Bachelor degree in Law from the University of Belgrade Faculty of Law and an LLM in Human Rights Law from the University of Nottingham. He is an Associate of the Belgrade Centre for Human Rights and was previously a research assistant at the Human Rights Law Centre of the University of Nottingham.

Matthew Happold is Professor of Public International Law at the University of Luxembourg. He previously taught at several UK universities, and has been a Visiting Fellow at the Human Rights Program, Harvard Law School and a Visiting Professional in the Office of the Prosecutor of the International Criminal Court. A general international lawyer, Matthew has published widely across the field. His recent publications include *Settlement of Investment Disputes under the Energy Charter Treaty* (Cambridge: Cambridge University Press, 2011) (co-authored with Thomas Roe) and *International Law in a Multipolar World* (Abingdon: Routledge, 2012) (editor). Matthew is also an associate tenant at 3 Hare Court, London.

Christian Henderson is Senior Lecturer in Law and Director of the Human Rights and International Law Unit at the University of Liverpool, where he teaches public international law, international peace and security and the law of armed conflict. He obtained his LLM from the University of Liverpool and his PhD from the University of Nottingham. As well as being the author of several articles and book reviews he published *The Persistent Advocate and the Use of Force: The Impact of the United States upon the* Jus ad Bellum *in the Post-Cold War Era* in 2010. He is General Editor of the *Journal of International Humanitarian Legal Studies* and Book Review Editor of the *Journal of Conflict and Security Law*. He is a member of the ILA Committee on the Use of Force.

Karen Hulme is Senior Lecturer at the School of Law, University of Essex. Karen's book entitled, *War Torn Environment: Interpreting the Legal Threshold* won the ASIL Francis Lieber Prize for 2004. Karen has written on the legality of cluster munitions and depleted uranium weapons, and ecocentrising the laws of armed conflict, and authored the chapter commenting on the environmental rules of the Customary Humanitarian Law Study in Wilmshurst and Breau, *Perspectives on the ICRC Customary International Humanitarian Law Study* (Cambridge: Cambridge University Press, 2007). She has recently worked with UNEP and ICRC, contributing comments on the report, *Protecting the Environment during Armed Conflict: An Inventory and Analysis of International Law*.

Dino Kritsiotis is Professor of Public International Law at the University of Nottingham, where he teaches, amongst other things, international law on the use of force and international humanitarian law. He gained his undergraduate degree from the University of Wales College at Cardiff before obtaining an LLM from the University of Cambridge. He also holds a Diploma of International Humanitarian Law from the International Committee of the Red Cross. His research interests concern international law and the use of force, international humanitarian law and general international law, as well as the history and theory of international law. He is widely published in these fields. He sits on the editorial boards of the *Journal of Conflict and Security Law*, the *Human Rights Law Review*, *Human Rights & Human Welfare* and the *African Yearbook of International Humanitarian Law*.

Chia Lehnardt is an Associate with the international arbitration group Hengeler Mueller. Previously she was a doctoral fellow with the research training group Multilevel Constitutionalism at Humboldt University Berlin, an Institute Fellow and Program Officer with the Institute for International Law and Justice, NYU Law School, and an assistant to the legal adviser to the Social Democratic parliamentary group in the German Bundestag. She is co-editor, along with Simon Chesterman, of *From Mercenaries to Market: The Rise and Regulation of Private Military Companies* (Oxford: Oxford University Press, 2007), and author of *Private Militärfirmen und Völkerrechtliche Verantwortlichkeit* ('Private Military Companies and International Responsibility') (Tübingen: Mohr Siebeck, 2011).

Kenneth Manusama is Assistant Professor of International Law at the Vrije Universiteit Amsterdam, where he also obtained his PhD. He has taught public international law at several Dutch universities, Amsterdam University College, and New York University. Dr Manusama also gained practical experience at a law firm in New York and served as interim legal counsel at the Dutch Ministry of Foreign Affairs. His research activities are in the fields of international peace and security, and the role of international law in foreign policy decision-making.

Marko Milanovic is Lecturer in Law at the University of Nottingham School of Law. He obtained his first degree in law from the University of Belgrade Faculty of Law, his LLM from the University of Michigan Law School, and his PhD in international law from the University of Cambridge. He is Secretary-General and member of the Executive Board of the European Society of International Law, an Associate of the

Belgrade Centre for Human Rights, and co-editor of *EJIL: Talk!*, the blog of the *European Journal of International Law*.

Mary Ellen O'Connell holds the Robert and Marion Short Chair in Law and is Research Professor of International Dispute Resolution, Kroc Institute for Peace Studies at the University of Notre Dame. Her research is in the areas of international legal theory, international law on the use of force and international dispute resolution. She is the author or editor of numerous books and articles on these subjects, including, *What is War? An Investigation in the Wake of 9/11* (Leiden: Martinus Nijhof, 2012) and *The Power and Purpose of International Law: Insights from the Theory and Practice of Enforcement* (Oxford: Oxford University Press, 2008, paperback 2011).

Alexander Orakhelashvili is Lecturer in Law at the University of Birmingham. He obtained his Master's degree (LLM *cum laude*) from Leiden University in 2000 and his PhD from Cambridge University in 2005. He has been a fellow of Jesus College Oxford (2005–2008), and has for several years taught public international law at the universities of Oxford, Cambridge and London. His research interests encompass all areas of public international law. He is the author of *Peremptory Norms in International Law* (Oxford: Oxford University Press, 2006); *The Interpretation of Acts and Rules in Public International Law* (Oxford: Oxford University Press, 2008); and *Collective Security* (Oxford: Oxford University Press, 2011), as well as a number of articles in leading international law periodicals in Britain, Europe and the US. He has provided legal advice on international law matters arising in litigation before English and American courts, and is an editor of the *Journal of International Peacekeeping*.

Natalino Ronzitti is Professor of International Law (former Chair of International Law at LUISS University, Rome) and member of the Institut de Droit International. He is also an advisory expert for the Istituto Affari Internazionali, Rome. He has authored and edited numerous books, in both Italian and English. He has been a legal adviser for the Italian Government to several diplomatic conferences and to the Italian Mission at the Conference on Disarmament, Geneva (1991–1995). He is chairing the International Law Association Committee on Reparation for Victims of Armed Conflict. He is a member of the Italian Bar (Corte di Cassazione).

Tom Ruys (LLM, PhD) studied law and international relations at the universities of Ghent, Nottingham and Leuven. From 2004 to 2009 he worked as full-time doctoral fellow (FWO-aspirant) at the Institute for International Law at the University of Leuven. He was a visiting researcher at Yale Law School in Spring 2008 and defended his doctoral thesis in Leuven in 2009. Tom is the author of *'Armed Attack' and Article 51 UN Charter* (Cambridge: Cambridge University Press, 2010), which was awarded the 2010 Lieber Prize of the American Society of International Law, as well as co-editor of two books on EU external relations (The Hague: TMC Asser Press, 2006 and 2010) and of the Competition Law Handbook 2012 (London: Sweet & Maxwell, 2011). Tom is currently practising law at the Brussels Bar (Stibbe, PG European and Competition Law). He is also a senior member of the Leuven Centre for Global

Governance Studies and teaches the course on public international law at the University of Leuven. He is a member of the ILA Committee on the Use of Force.

Mirko Sossai is Lecturer in International Law at the University of Rome III, Italy. He holds a PhD in international law from the University of Sienna. His recent publications include *La prevenzione del terrorismo nel diritto internazionale* ('The prevention of terrorism in international law') (Turin: Giappichelli, 2012) and *Multilevel Regulation of Military and Security Contractors: The Interplay between International, European and Domestic Norms* (co-edited with C. Bakker) (Oxford: Hart Publishing, 2012).

Nicholas Tsagourias (LLM, PhD) is Professor of International Law at the University of Sheffield. His main research interests are in the areas of the law of armed conflict, international criminal law, and international and European constitutional theories. He is on the editorial board of the *Journal of Conflict and Security Law* and member of the Use of Force Committee of the ILA. He has published widely in scholarly publications. Among his publications are the books *Jurisprudence of International Law: The Humanitarian Dimension* (Manchester: Manchester University Press, 2000) and the edited book *Transnational Constitutionalism: International and European Models* (Cambridge: Cambridge University Press, 2007).

David Turns is Senior Lecturer in International Laws of Armed Conflict at the Defence Academy of the United Kingdom (Cranfield University). He was previously Lecturer in Law at the University of Liverpool (1994–2007) and taught at the London School of Economics. In 2002 he was Visiting Professor at the Institute for International Law and International Relations, University of Vienna. Since 2008 he has been the Chairman of the UK National Group of the International Society for Military Law and the Law of War. He has extensive experience of teaching international law to military officers and has published widely in international law.

Nigel D. White is Professor of Public International Law at the University of Nottingham, and formerly Professor of International Law at the University of Sheffield. He has held a Chair since 2000 and an academic post since 1987. In addition to publishing over 50 articles and essays, many in leading journals and collections, he is author of a number of books, including *Keeping the Peace* (Manchester: Manchester University Press, 1997), *The UN System: Toward International Justice* (Boulder, CO: Lynne Reiner, 2002), *The Law of International Organisations* (Manchester: Manchester University Press, 2005) and *Democracy Goes to War: British Military Deployments under International Law* (Oxford: Oxford University Press, 2009). He is also editor and co-editor of a number of collections, including *The UN, Human Rights and Post-Conflict Situations* (Manchester: Manchester University Press, 2005), *European Security Law* (Oxford: Oxford University Press, 2007), *International Law and Dispute Settlement* (Oxford: Hart, 2010), *International Organizations and the Idea of Autonomy* (Abingdon: Routledge, 2011) and *Counter-Terrorism: International Law and Practice* (Oxford: Oxford University Press, 2012). He is editor of the *Journal of Conflict and Security Law* published by Oxford University Press, which is in its seventeenth year.

Ralph Wilde is a member of the Faculty of Laws at University College London, University of London. His current research focuses on the extraterritorial application of international human rights law. His book, *International Territorial Administration: How Trusteeship and the Civilizing Mission Never Went Away* (Oxford: Oxford University Press, 2008) was awarded the Certificate of Merit of the American Society of International Law in 2009. At the International Law Association Ralph is Co-Rapporteur of the Human Rights Committee, and previously served as one of the UK representatives on the International Executive Council, Rapporteur of the Study Group on UN Reform, and Joint Honorary Secretary of the British Branch. Ralph has held visiting positions at the CEU in Budapest, Melbourne University, NYU, Texas University, UCLA and Yale Law School, and served on the Executive Council of the American Society of International Law.

Introduction: international conflict and security law
Christian Henderson and Nigel D. White

It has perhaps become something of a truism to say that the attacks of 11 September 2001 (hereinafter '9/11') and subsequent events led to a reconsideration of the fundamental rules that govern international security and armed conflicts. Yet, as this *Research Handbook on International Conflict and Security Law* aims to demonstrate, the results of this reconsideration are still not altogether clear. What is clear, however, is that the relevant debates as to what the current state of the law is – or ought to be – stretch right across the boundaries of international conflict and security law.

The direct response to the attacks of 9/11 asked fundamental questions of the legal rules and principles governing the use of force, otherwise known as the *jus ad bellum*. In particular, questions were asked as to when actions in self-defence can lawfully take place, and, perhaps most importantly, against whom they may be taken and the weapons and tactics that may be employed in doing so. However, subsequent uses of force by the United States and its allies, particularly in Iraq in 2003 and Libya in 2011, raised important questions as to the role and relevance of the United Nations Security Council, including where the authority in deciding upon the necessity for enforcement action employing the use of force and in interpreting its resolutions is positioned. Similarly, the normative debates concerning the relevance of the prohibition of the use of force were, as ever, lively and often polarised. However, as an undercurrent to these debates – and largely missed but no less important – was the question as to the continuing role of the norm prohibiting *threats* of force of both an express and implied nature, a question which is, of course, of current importance given the raft of threats made against Iran and North Korea in relation to their nuclear capabilities.

Yet even these continuing debates are only the first port of call when considering the relevant legal issues that have been fervently debated more than ever over the past decade. Indeed, the uses of force and armed conflicts that have been engaged in during this period raise particular questions as to the typology of armed conflict. The outcome to this debate has an impact upon the relevant legal rules and principles that are applicable in an armed conflict, otherwise known as the *jus in bello*. This branch of international law seeks to regulate the way in which armed conflicts are fought so as to enable states to achieve their military objectives while protecting civilians. In this respect, but also more broadly, legal issues regarding the use of weapons, targeting practices, the use of private contractors to engage in armed combat on behalf of states, and concern regarding protected persons during these conflicts have never been far away from both the pages of the international law literature and newspapers across the globe. The violation of the law governing these areas not only gives rise to issues of state responsibility but also war crimes, the latter being particularly topical given the prominence of the now functioning International Criminal Court and the establishment of various *ad hoc* courts, tribunals and fact-finding commissions.

While the protection of civilians during armed conflict is key to realising the aims of the *jus in bello*, questions as to the role of international human rights law in such conflicts have also arisen. The regime interaction between these two branches of international law, but also their interaction with the *jus ad bellum*, is a topic that is particularly relevant given the realities and complexities of what have become known as 'targeted killings'. Though the traditional separation of the *jus ad bellum* from the *jus in bello* still holds sway, there are increasing signs of it coming under greater strain. Violations of the *jus in bello* may be a justification for using force; and in Libya in 2011 the law governing military operations was not simply the rules and principles of the *jus in bello*, but also the Security Council Resolution authorising the use of force.

Despite the unavoidable prominence of global terrorism in recent years and its potential impact upon traditional understandings of international law, there are other equally pressing issues that come under the umbrella of international conflict and security law. Indeed, since the intervention in Kosovo in 1999 – which many perceived as being 'legitimate yet unlawful' – there has been much discussion and debate regarding the legal concept of humanitarian intervention, and in particular where the authority lies in determining the necessity for such interventions. As a consequence of this debate – and in many respects still fuelled by it – the concept of a 'responsibility to protect' emerged, the boundaries of which are currently being tested in the context of the Arab Spring.

Yet issues of international security are broader than just when and how the use of armed force is permitted. Indeed, pre-conflict issues in respect to conflict prevention, arms control and disarmament, as well as the concerns regarding nuclear weapons development and proliferation, are, as they were for much of the 20th century, on the agendas of states and international lawyers. However, the conceptual separation of 'preventive' security from other areas of conflict and security law is not always convincing as it remains that arms control measures may be applied during all stages, and of course diplomacy should never be ruled out as a means of heading off or stopping conflict, or of peace-building. Also, issues of a post-conflict nature (featured in the contemporary discussion over the emergence of a possible *jus post bellum*, which incorporates those legal issues that arise in the transition from war to peace) cannot be forgotten in any treatment of international conflict and security law. Indeed, the consensual imposition of peacekeeping forces – and their 'muscularisation' – into areas which are witnessing the transition from war to peace are a large part of the function of the UN and other organisations. Furthermore, it is also often in this context that territories are administered externally, raising issues of the law applicable to the components of peace – the peace agreements themselves and the international actors whose presence guarantees the peace. Issues as to compensation and reparations for the wrongs that have been committed remain areas that are underdeveloped despite the existence of a number of historical precedents.

Ultimately, though we can say that the various components of international conflict and security law are identifiable, and indeed within those components detailed substantive laws exist, their interpretation and application are often disputed. As the above, albeit brief, introduction has thus far attempted to demonstrate, the relationships between the various components are still changing and unclear.

This *Research Handbook* brings together 21 leading international law scholars from around the world. The authors are experts in the field of international conflict and security law which, as highlighted above, is the term used in this volume as an umbrella for many issues of international law that affect in one way or another international peace and security, as well as the regulation of the conduct of hostilities. In this context, the authors introduce, analyse and discuss the contemporary debates regarding various topics drawn from across the conceptual and legal divides of the *jus ad bellum*, *jus in bello* and *jus post bellum*. Although it was originally intended that the various chapters would be neatly divided along the lines of these three branches of international conflict and security law, the resulting chapters made such a divide almost impossible to achieve. However, this was a positive result as it simply highlighted the need for such topics to be addressed together as well as the overall success of the resulting project (we hope that readers agree with our assessment!). This is also down to the skill and deftness of approach of the individual authors who kindly agreed to write on a topic on which they have notable expertise. Consequently, while the chapters are organised in the book in a logical sequence, they can equally be read and referred to in any order. Although the book aims to cover many of the controversial issues highlighted above regarding conflict prevention and the legality of resorting to the use of armed force through to those arising during armed conflict and in the phase between conflict and peace, the breadth and scope of the subject preclude coverage, or at least dedicated coverage, of all topics. However, being the first to examine many of the most relevant topics under these areas in one volume, the book will be of interest to scholars from various disciplinary backgrounds looking for a contemporary grounding in issues under the broad theme of international conflict and security law.

CH
NDW
August 2012

1. Conflict prevention
Kenneth Manusama

1. INTRODUCTION

The general purpose of this first chapter is to ascertain and outline the law of conflict prevention through peaceful means with a focus on the role of the United Nations Security Council (hereinafter 'UNSC'). As such, it is a prelude to the bulk of this volume on the law applicable to armed conflict, albeit a very necessary one, because it is clear that it is better to prepare and prevent, than to repair and repent.

Two overriding considerations dictate the scope of the inquiry. First, the study of conflict prevention could comprise various scholarly disciplines such as political science, economics and international law, but also anthropology and theology. Conflict prevention entails more than the enforcement of international law, as a legal rule may have yet to be broken, and sub-topics may vary from the root causes of conflicts to the effectiveness of shuttle diplomacy on the brink of conflict eruption.[1] However, to an extent this chapter approaches conflict prevention in a manner that could be viewed as formalistic and legalistic, as the inquiry is conducted on the basis of public international law that provides relevant norms for, and allocates competences to, different actors. Secondly, conflict prevention is squarely placed within the context and institutions of the international collective security system. In doing so, it covers a few areas of the collective security system that are dealt with in far greater substance elsewhere in this volume, but which have a distinct preventive feature in them.

As a preliminary matter, section 2 defines some of the core concepts of 'collective security', 'conflict' and 'conflict prevention' for the purposes of this chapter, as well as the most relevant legal norms related to conflict prevention. Sections 3 and 4 form the nucleus of the chapter as they examine in more detail how the relevant mechanisms and institutional powers of the UN collective security system aim to prevent armed conflicts, with the UNSC at its core. Section 5 examines coercive conflict prevention under Chapter VII of the UN Charter while section 6 offers some general conclusions.

---

[1] M. Lund, 'From Lessons to Action', in F.O. Hampson and D.M. Malone (eds), *From Reaction to Conflict Prevention: Opportunities for the UN System* (Boulder, CO: Lynne Rienner, 2002), at 160.

2. COLLECTIVE SECURITY AND CONFLICT PREVENTION IN THE 21ST CENTURY

A. The Preventive Function of Collective Security

Based on the available descriptions,[2] 'collective security' is understood here as the threat and use of institutionalized collective action to deter, prevent and correct violations of community values and prevent the escalation of ongoing conflicts. Nevertheless, despite its broad scope, collective security is most equated with collective *action*, meaning forcible measures to be taken by the UNSC under Chapter VII of the UN Charter,[3] that is the use of force by the UN as a response to a threat to or breach of the peace.[4] Yet, the system of collective security also has a clear preventive function. First of all, the very existence of the system is a preventive measure, because of the threat of collective action against a state that endangers international peace and security. As Article 1 of the Charter states, the prevention of threats to the peace is the primary purpose and promise of the UN.[5] Predicated on the notion of one against all[6] and the institutionalization of international power in and for the sake of collective aims,[7] states are largely deterred from violating certain international norms, such as the

---

[2] Cf. H. Kelsen, *Collective Security under International Law* (Washington, DC: Naval War College, 1957), at 9; D. Sarooshi, *The United Nations and the Development of Collective Security* (Oxford: Oxford University Press, 1999), at 5; Y. Dinstein, *War, Aggression and Self-Defence*, 4th edn (Cambridge: Cambridge University Press, 2005), at 278; A. Orakhelashvili, *Collective Security* (Oxford: Oxford University Press, 2011), at 11–16.

[3] See, for example, Dinstein, *ibid.*, at 278; S.R. Ratner, 'Image and Reality in the UN's Peaceful Settlement of Disputes', (1995) *Eur J Int'l L* 426, at 428–431. See the chapter by Christian Henderson in this volume for more on the forcible measures by the UNSC under Chapter VII of the UN Charter.

[4] See, for example, N.D. White, 'On the Brink of Lawlessness: The State of Collective Security Law', (2002) 13 *Ind Int'l & Comp L Rev* 237, at 237.

[5] Article 1(1) of the UN Charter provides:

To maintain international peace and security, and to that end: to take effective collective measures for the prevention and removal of threats to the peace, and for the suppression of acts of aggression or other breaches of the peace, and to bring about by peaceful means, and in conformity with the principles of justice and international law, adjustment or settlement of international disputes or situations which might lead to a breach of the peace.

See F.O. Hampson *et al.*, 'Introduction: Making Conflict Prevention a Priority', in Hampson and Malone, *supra* n.1, at 1; *Report of the UN Secretary-General, 'Prevention of Armed Conflict' (2001)* UN Doc A/55/985-S/2001/574, 7 June 2001, at paras 17–18 (hereafter 'Prevention of Armed Conflict').

[6] R. Wolfrum, 'Purposes and Principles', in B. Simma (ed.), *The Charter of the United Nations: A Commentary*, 2nd edn (Oxford: Oxford University Press, 2002), at 42; C.A. Kupchan and C.A. Kupchan, 'Concerts, Collective Security, and Europe', (1991) 16 *International Security* 114, at 119; L.H. Miller, 'The Idea and the Reality of Collective Security', (1999) 5 *Global Governance* 303, at 303.

[7] Orakhelashvili, *supra* n.2, at 6, 8.

prohibition of the use of force against other states.[8] Secondly, the institutionalization of diplomacy to prevent armed conflict has created a permanent forum for international negotiations and the establishment of the principle of accountability[9] that enables the development of common interests and shared values.[10] Thirdly, conflict prevention must be considered an element of collective security, because without preliminary preventive procedures 'it would be impossible to ascertain whether a coercive collective security action was warranted'.[11]

The original idea or ideal type of collective security system foresaw a system that offered 'the certainty, backed by legal obligation, that any aggressor would be confronted with collective sanctions'.[12] However, it has been widely observed and lamented that the UN system is a far cry from an ideal system of collective security.[13] Considered as a realist improvement over the idealistic League of Nations, as it is more based on Great Power dynamics,[14] the UN Charter does not adopt wholesale 'the philosophy of legalistic monism', but preserves to a large extent 'the methods of traditional diplomacy.'[15] The Charter lays down some fundamental legal obligations for Member States, but aims to have disputes resolved peacefully by states themselves through traditional diplomatic means, as reflected by Article 33(1).[16] The UNSC may only get involved as a subsidiary matter[17] through the use of its recommendatory, that is non-legally binding, 'power' under Chapter VI, or take non-forcible enforcement measures under Chapter VII when the dispute reaches a certain level of intensity.[18] Even then, however, the UN system lacks automaticity in its response to a threat to peace and security.[19] On the contrary, the use of the UNSC's powers is contingent on a political and discretionary decision by the Council, and therefore much criticized for being highly selective in determining and acting upon dangers or even threats to the peace.[20] A collective and forceful response is made uncertain by the discretionary nature of the Council's powers and the institutionalized balance of power between its permanent members, mitigating the deterrent effect of collective security. In the eyes of

---

[8] Kupchan and Kupchan, *supra* n.6, at 125–129; Dinstein, *supra* n.2, at 280. See chapter 4 by Mary Ellen O'Connell in this volume for more on the prohibition of the use of force norm.

[9] I.L. Claude Jr., *Swords into Plowshares: The Problems and Process of International Organization*, 3rd revised edn (London: Random House, 1964), at 231.

[10] See, for example, Kupchan and Kupchan, *supra* n.6, at 132.

[11] Orakhelashvili, *supra* n.2, at 15.

[12] I.L. Claude Jr., as quoted in Kupchan and Kupchan, *supra* n.6, at 119; Miller, *supra* n.6, at 303.

[13] Kupchan and Kupchan, *supra* n.6, at 120.

[14] K. Anderson, 'United Nations Collective Security and the United States Security Guarantee in an Age of Rising Multipolarity: The Security Council as the Talking Shop of the Nations', (2009) 10 *Chi J Int'l L* 55, at 59–61.

[15] H.J. Morgenthau, 'Diplomacy', (1946) *Yale LJ* 1067, at 1071.

[16] *Ibid*. See also *infra* section 2C(i).

[17] C. Tomuschat, 'Article 33', in Simma (ed.), *supra* n.6, at 584–585.

[18] See *infra* section 3A.

[19] Kupchan and Kupchan, *supra* n.6, at 122; M. Koskenniemi, 'The Place of Law in Collective Security', (1996) 17 *Mich J Int'l L* 455, at 457; Orakhelashvili, *supra* n.2, at 8.

[20] Koskenniemi, *ibid*., at 460.

an ever-expanding, critical and changing world, UNSC legitimacy is further undermined by its unrepresentative composition and failure to reform despite persistent efforts over the last decades.[21]

Although collective security is grounded in some core legal obligations, the answers to the question of what community values the collective security seeks to defend are not necessarily couched in legal terms. In the use of its powers, the UNSC is not obliged to become involved only when there is a breach of international law. What one may call UNSC jurisdiction depends on what the Council's understanding is of key requirements in the Charter such as 'danger to the peace' and 'threat to peace'. Determinations as to what situations cross these thresholds will reflect to a great extent what values the Council and the international community seek to uphold. Originally, the UN's collective security system was aimed at addressing the fundamental national security concerns of states,[22] that is a sovereignty-centred approach.[23] However, the UN has supplemented – and to a certain extent, replaced – these concerns with concepts like 'human security' and the 'responsibility to protect', as the basis for collective action.[24] One may debate whether this constitutes a move by states to act beyond their self-interest on the basis of common values, or whether the protection of those values is in the self-interests of states.[25] In any case, with this notion of comprehensive collective security, the international community has re-defined concepts such as 'peace', 'security' and 'conflict', with important implications for conflict prevention.

B. Conflict in the 21st Century

It could be argued that the catalogue of community values that the collective security system aims to uphold, which arose from World War II, has now become indeterminate and is therefore a source of uncertainty about the system as well. Nevertheless, it has become a truism that the nature of conflict and the perception of what is a matter of international concern or threatens international peace have significantly shifted since the end of the Cold War in 1990. While focused on and originally designed to prevent and respond to (armed) conflicts between states, the international community has been increasingly confronted with violent conflicts *within* states.[26] Already in the UN

---

[21] See generally, K. Manusama, *The United Nations Security Council in the Post-Cold War Era – Applying the Principle of Legality* (Leiden: Martinus Nijhoff, 2006), at 3–12.
[22] Orakhelashvili, *supra* n.2, at 4.
[23] M.-F. Cuéllar, 'Reflections on Sovereignty and Collective Security', (2004) 40 *Stan J Int'l L* 211, at 215.
[24] Hampson *et al.*, *supra* n.5, at 3.
[25] Orakhelashvili, *supra* n.2, at 6, 9.
[26] According to the Uppsala Conflict Data Project (UCPD), available at http://www.pcr.uu.se/research/ucdp/, using definitions from an earlier project, an 'interstate armed conflict occurs between two or more states', and an 'internal armed conflict between the government of a state and internal opposition groups without intervention from other states'. The Project also distinguishes between 'extrastate armed conflict' and 'internationalized armed conflict', but the refinement is irrelevant here. N.P. Gleditsch *et al.*, 'Armed Conflict 1946–2001: A New Dataset', (2002) 39 *J Peace Res* 615, at 619.

Secretary-General's *Agenda for Peace* of 1992 those new conflicts were signalled,[27] but the 1994 intrastate Rwandan genocide set a moral benchmark. It exemplified the changed nature and sources of armed conflict, and subsequently changed perceptions of international security, after which more concrete measures were contemplated.[28] The power of identity politics was unleashed by the 'conclusion' of the Cold War and accelerated globalization,[29] bringing increased international focus on the plight and interests of individuals within states and the so-called non-military sources of conflict.[30] Moreover, modern internal conflicts are often fed by international connections and have international repercussions.[31] For all these reasons, the Secretary-General concluded in 2001 that the UN had to move to a culture of prevention, because '[i]n the twenty-first century, collective security should imply an obligation for all of us to strive to address tensions, grievances, inequality, injustice, intolerance and hostilities at the earliest stage possible, before peace and security are endangered'.[32]

With the recognition that conflicts originate in economic and political grievances of individuals and local communities,[33] conflict prevention has been greatly expanded to include measures to 'address the institutional, socio-economic, and global environment within which conflicting actors operate'.[34] In order to determine the proper role of the UNSC in conflict prevention, reference is made to the different stages that are commonly discerned in a conflict cycle and the type of preventive measures associated with them. Thus, following Lund, one may position the concept of conflict prevention in the stage of 'unstable peace',[35] 'a situation in which tension and suspicion among parties run high, but violence is either absent or only sporadic'.[36] The measures

---

[27] Report of the Secretary-General, 'An Agenda for Peace: Preventive Diplomacy, Peace-making and Peace-Keeping', (1992) UN Doc. A/47/277-S/24111, 17 June 1992 (hereinafter 'Agenda for Peace'). See also, for example, 2005 World Summit Outcome, UN Doc. A/RES/60/1, 24 October 2005, at paras 69–72.

[28] Carnegie Commission on Preventing Deadly Conflict, *Preventing Deadly Conflict* (1997), at 3–7.

[29] See, generally, M. Kaldor, *New & Old Wars: Organized Violence in a Global Era*, 2nd edn (Cambridge: Polity, 2006), at 73–94. Cf. S.N. Kalyvas, '"New" and "Old" Civil Wars: A Valid Distinction', (2001) 54 *World Politics* 99.

[30] Carnegie Commission, *supra* n.28, at 25–37; R. Thakur, *The United Nations and Peace and Security* (Cambridge: Cambridge University Press, 2006), at 79–80.

[31] Thakur, *ibid.*, at 16; *A More Secure World: Our Shared Responsibility: Report of the High Level Panel on Threats, Challenges and Change* (United Nations, 2004) (hereinafter 'High Level Panel Report'), at paras 1–16, 74–88.

[32] High Level Panel Report, *ibid.*, at para. 19.

[33] P. Wallensteen, 'Reassessing Recent Conflicts: Direct vs. Structural Prevention', in F.O. Hampson and D.M. Malone (eds), *From Reaction to Conflict Prevention: Opportunities for the UN System* (Boulder, CO: Lynne Rienner, 2002), at 213.

[34] M. Lund, 'Conflict Prevention: Theory in Pursuit of Policy and Practice', in J. Bercovitch et al. (eds), *The SAGE Handbook of Conflict Resolution* (London: Sage Publications, 2009), at 289.

[35] *Ibid.*, and graph 15.1 at 290.

[36] M. Lund, *Preventing Violent Conflicts: A Strategy for Preventive Diplomacy* (Washington, DC: USIP, 1996), at 39. Swanström and Weissmann distinguish this phase as 'open conflict', but also separate this from 'crisis', meaning a situation in which (larger scale) use of violence is likely and is the preferable option for the parties. N.L.P. Swanström and M.S.

associated with this stage and intensity of the conflict are authoritatively termed 'direct' or 'operational' prevention, to prevent an imminent crisis, reduce or eliminate violence, and reduce tensions between the parties. Based on the brief examination above, this chapter focuses on measures to prevent disputes, openly acknowledged non-violent conflicts and low-grade violent skirmishes from escalating into large-scale armed conflict by deploying operational and direct preventive measures.[37] Given the nature of modern conflict, such measures may now be deployed irrespective of whether they concern an international or internal situation. Moreover, to add to the conceptual confusion,[38] conflict prevention as used here denotes 'preventive diplomacy' – confidence-building measures, fact-finding and early warning systems[39] – but only as conducted by the UNSC. It is concerned with the law and practice of traditional methods of diplomacy as laid down in Chapter VI of the UN Charter, as well as the tools of coercive diplomacy granted to the UNSC in Chapter VII – sanctions, preventive deployment and the threat of the use of force.[40]

C. The Legal Framework of Conflict Prevention in Collective Security

The operationalization of the UN's preventive mission is grounded in several legal obligations incumbent on states that together, with the more general legal constraints upon the UNSC, form the legal framework for conflict prevention in the context of the UN collective security system. This chapter is concerned with the obligation to settle disputes peacefully, the regulation of armaments and collective 'measures' taken by the UNSC. As such, they form part of what Randelzhofer calls 'a system of war prevention in international law'.[41]

i. The obligation to settle disputes peacefully

A 'dispute' is 'a disagreement on a point of law or fact, a conflict of legal views or interests between two persons'.[42] Articles 2(3) and 33(1) of the UN Charter together establish an obligation for states to settle international disputes peacefully, that is

---

Weissmann, 'Conflict, Prevention and Conflict Management and Beyond: A Conceptual Exploration' (Central Asia-Caucasus Institute & Silk Road Studies Programs, 2005), at 11, available at http://www.silkroadstudies.org/new/docs/ConceptPapers/2005/concept_paper_ConfPrev.pdf.

[37] E.M. Cousens, 'Conflict Prevention', in D.M. Malone (ed.), *The UN Security Council: From the Cold War to the 21st Century* (Boulder, CO: Lynne Rienner, 2004), at 106. The UCDP defines 'armed conflict' as 'a contested incompatibility that concerns government or territory or both where the use of armed force between two parties results in 25 battle-related deaths. Of these two parties, at least one is the government of a state.' Gleditsch *et al.*, *supra* n.26, at 618–619.

[38] Swanström and Weissmann, *supra* n.36, at 5.

[39] Agenda for Peace, *supra* n.27, at para. 20.

[40] For the UNSC's role in the actual use of force see chapter 5 in this volume by Christian Henderson.

[41] A. Randelzhofer, 'Article 2(4)', in Simma (ed.), *supra* n.6, at 114.

[42] *The Mavrommatis Palestine Concessions (Greece v U.K.)* (Objection to the Jurisdiction of the Court) PCIJ Rep Series A No 2 (30 August 1924), at 11. For a more detailed discussion, see, for example, R.B. Bilder, 'An Overview of International Dispute Settlement', (1986) 1 *Emory J Intl Dispute Resolution* 1.

disputes 'in which the rivalling claims are based on international law',[43] although a clear difference between the two could be argued.[44] Article 2(3) entails a negative obligation not to undertake settlement of a dispute by means that would endanger peace and security.[45] In other words, Article 2(3) does not contain an obligation to settle disputes, but rather the obligation not to endanger peace and security when states nevertheless decide to attempt settlement. The language of Article 33 suggests a more positive or active obligation of states to seek peaceful settlement of those disputes 'the continuance of which is likely to endanger the maintenance of international peace and security'.[46] Thus, the difference in language suggests a gap in the obligations contained in these provisions, namely that states are not required to attempt to settle their dispute,[47] unless peace is endangered and then settlement must be pursued by peaceful means. Nevertheless, a more general obligation to settle disputes has been assumed.[48] With minor variations, this obligation can be found, *inter alia*, in the 1970 *Friendly Relations Declaration*[49] and the 1982 *Manila Declaration on the Peaceful Settlement of Disputes*,[50] as well as the various Secretary-General reports discussed in this chapter[51] and relevant UNSC resolutions.[52] In the *Nicaragua* case, the International Court of Justice (hereinafter 'ICJ') referred to Article 33(1) and restated the principle.[53] As with

---

[43] A. Peters, 'International Dispute Settlement: A Network of Cooperational Duties', (2003) 14 *Eur J Int'l L* 1, at 3.

[44] See, for example, A. Aust, *Handbook of International Law* (Cambridge: Cambridge University Press, 2005), at 431.

[45] Bilder, *supra* n.42, at 8; Cf. Goodrich and Hambro, who argue the opposite: L. Goodrich and E. Hambro, *Charter of the United Nations – Commentary and Documents*, rev. edn (Boston, MA: World Peace Foundation, 1949), at 102.

[46] N. Stürchler, *The Threat of Force in International Law* (Cambridge: Cambridge University Press, 2007), at 53; *North Sea Continental Shelf (Germany v Netherlands)* (Judgment) ICJ Rep 1969 3, paras 86–87.

[47] Bilder, *supra* n.42, at 7.

[48] See, for example, H. Kelsen, 'The Settlement of Disputes by the Security Council', (1948) 2 *ICLQ* 174, at 174; Goodrich and Hambro, *supra* n.45, at 102; Claude , *supra* n.9, at 205; A. Cassese, *International Law* (Oxford: Oxford University Press, 2001), at 217; J.G. Merrills, *International Dispute Settlement*, 5th edn (Cambridge: Cambridge University Press, 2011), at 220; C. Tomuschat, 'Article 2(3)', in Simma (ed.), *supra* n.6, at 105.

[49] *Declaration on Principles of International Law concerning Friendly Relations and Cooperation amongst States*, UNGA Res. 2625 (XXV) (24 October 1970) (hereinafter 'Friendly Relations Declaration'): 'Every State shall settle its international disputes with other States by peaceful means in such a manner that international peace and security and justice are not endangered. States shall accordingly seek early and just settlement of their disputes by [peaceful means].' See also V.S. Mani, 'The Role of Law and Legal Considerations in the Functioning of the United Nations', (1995) 35 *Indian J Int L* 91, 104, as reprinted in N.D. White (ed.), *Collective Security Law* (Aldershot: Ashgate Dartmouth, 2003).

[50] *Manila Declaration on the Peaceful Settlement of International Disputes*, UNGA Res. 37/10 (1982), para. 2: 'Every State shall settle its international disputes exclusively by peaceful means in such a manner that international peace and security, and justice, are not endangered.'

[51] For example, Prevention of Armed Conflict, *supra* n.5.

[52] For example, UNSC Res. 1366 (2001).

[53] *Military and Paramilitary Activities in and against Nicaragua (Nicaragua v USA)* (Merits) ICJ Rep 1986 14, para. 290.

the earlier *North Sea Continental Shelf* cases, the Court did not make a distinction between different disputes.[54] Thus, from Articles 2(3) and 33(1) and state practice emerges a general obligation to settle all disputes by peaceful means. However, the language used by the General Assembly (hereinafter 'UNGA') and the ICJ makes clear that the obligation is to *seek* a peaceful settlement and not reach a settlement of the dispute *per se*.[55] Yet, states are required to continue to seek peaceful settlement even though no resolution may be to hand.[56] To ensure continuation of settlement efforts there is the additional obligation for states in Article 37 to refer the dispute to the UNSC if they fail to settle it through the means listed in Article 33.

ii. The preventive function of disarmament obligations[57]

Article 26 of the UN Charter grants the UNSC a general power to involve itself in and promote disarmament.[58] 'Disarmament' – defined by Claude as 'the limitation, control and reduction of the human and material instrumentalities of warfare as well as their literal abolition'[59] – may not be the correct term as, *inter alia*, Article 26 talks about the *regulation* of armaments and not their reduction.[60] Thus, this focus on arms control instead of disarmament is far less ambitious than its League of Nations predecessor, but it shares the notion in the League Covenant[61] that either arms control or reduction of armaments is essential for the maintenance of peace and security.[62] It could be argued that arms control is part of structural prevention, as opposed to the focus on operational

---

[54] *Ibid.*, para. 86.
[55] Tomuschat, *supra* n.48, at 106.
[56] Friendly Relations Declaration, *supra* n.49; Cassese, *supra* n.48, at 217.
[57] See chapter 2 in this volume by Mirko Sossai for more on disarmament and non-proliferation.
[58] Article 26 reads:

In order to promote the establishment of international peace and security with the least diversion for armaments of the world's human and economic resources, the Security Council shall be responsible for formulating, with the assistance of the Military Staff Committee referred to in Article 47, plans to be submitted to the Members of the United Nations for the establishment of a system for the regulation of armaments.

See also Article 47, para. 1:

There shall be established a Military Staff Committee to advise and assist the Security Council on all questions relating to the Security Council's military requirements for the maintenance of international peace and security, the employment and command of forces placed at its disposal, the regulation of armaments, and possible disarmament.

[59] Claude, *supra* n.48, at 261.
[60] Goodrich and Hambro, *supra* n.45, at 210; H.-J. Schütz, 'Article 26', in Simma (ed.), *supra* n.6, at 469. See also Den Dekker on the definitions and difference between 'arms control' and 'disarmament', as well as the interrelationship between 'security' and 'arms control': G. Den Dekker, *The Law of Arms Control: International Supervision and Enforcement* (Leiden: Martinus Nijhoff, 2001), at 21–23, 27–32.
[61] See Article 8, Covenant of the League of Nations (1919).
[62] See, for example, Kelsen, *supra* n.2, at 197; Claude, *supra* n. 48, at 262–263; Den Dekker, *supra* n.60, at 18–19; Essentials of Peace, UNGA Res. 290 (IV), 1 December 1949, paras 12–13; Report of the Secretary-General, 'Supplement to an Agenda for Peace' (1995), UN Doc. A/50/60-S/1995/1, 3 January 1995, paras 57–65; High Level Panel Report, *supra* n.31, at

or direct prevention in this chapter. However, practice has shown that arms control is now perceived as being of far more immediate importance to international peace and security,[63] despite the fact that discussions within the UNSC in 1947 on nuclear disarmament proved that inspection in arms control was highly controversial.[64] Thus, no proposals or discussions within the Council bore any fruit.[65] Arms control law has, therefore, not developed by or within the UNSC, but rather outside of the collective security system, where states have no restrictions on their national armament policies unless such restrictions have been accepted by them.[66] Nevertheless, although the UNSC has not attempted to set up 'a system for the regulation of armaments', as called for in Article 26, it has in different negotiations paid attention to, for instance, the proliferation of small arms.[67] With respect to the proliferation of weapons of mass destruction (hereinafter 'WMD') the UN has become quite active indeed.[68]

3. THE DIPLOMATIC MEANS OF THE UNSC

The law of conflict prevention in collective security is formally established in Chapter VI of the UN Charter and is 'one of the most poorly drafted' parts of the Charter.[69] It has been called 'the neglected step-brother' of Chapter VII as any explicit reliance upon it was virtually non-existent during the Cold War.[70] Although many issues were referred to the UNSC in this period, there is relatively little actual discernable practice regarding Chapter VI because the Council often declined to even put them on its agenda.[71] This lack of practice is consequently reflected in the sparse legal scholarly work devoted to provisions of Chapter VI.[72] Nevertheless, the authority given to the Council is potentially great. It may only issue recommendations, but in the right political climate and depending on the regard in which the UNSC is held, these may carry great political

---

107–1044; *In larger Freedom: Towards Development, Security and Human Rights for All – Report of the Secretary-General* (United Nations, 2005), at 97–105.

[63] See *infra* section 5C; for example, K. Wellens, 'The UN Security Council and New Threats to the Peace: Back to the Future', (2003) 8 *J Confl & Sec L* 15, at 40–41; Carnegie Commission, *supra* n.28, at 16–19.

[64] Goodrich and Hambro, *supra* n.45, at 211–213; L.R. Sucharipa-Behrmann and T.M. Franck, 'Preventive Measures', (1998) 30 *NYU J Int'l L & Pol'y* 485, at 519.

[65] Goodrich and Hambro, *supra* n.45, at 211–212; Schütz, *supra* n.60, at 475.

[66] Den Dekker, *supra* n.60, at 37–38; *Nicaragua* case, *supra* n.53, at para. 135; *Legality of the Threat or Use of Nuclear Weapons* (Advisory Opinion), ICJ Rep 1996 226, para. 52.

[67] Since 2001, the Council has intermittently debated and issued presidential statements and resolutions on illicit small arms, and requested the Secretary-General to issue biannual reports on the matter. See, for example, Report of the Secretary-General, 'Small Arms' (2011), UN Doc. S/2011/255, 5 April 2011.

[68] See *infra* section 5C. See also chapter 2 by Mirko Sossai in this volume.

[69] C. Eagleton, 'The Jurisdiction of the Security Council over Disputes', (1946) 40 *AJIL* 513, at 513.

[70] Ratner, *supra* n.3 at 428.

[71] *Ibid.*; L.B. Sohn, 'Editorial Comment: The Security Council's Role in the Settlement of International Disputes', (1984) 78 *AJIL* 402, at 402–403.

[72] Ratner, *supra* n.3, at 427.

and legal weight.[73] A closer look at the principles, powers and procedures of Chapter VI is, and remains, therefore, justified.

A. UNSC Jurisdiction

At least from a textual perspective, the powers of the UNSC are linked to the gravity of the situation with which it is confronted. In more legal terms, the exercise of Council powers is dependent on the gravity of the situation, which is translated into a jurisdictional threshold – or 'objective pre-conditions'[74] – for the Council to cross.[75] Thus, Articles 34 and 35 formally require that there exists either a dispute, or a situation 'which might lead to international friction or give rise to a dispute', before the Council may exercise its power to investigate or be seized of a matter when referred to it by a Member State.[76] Articles 33 and 36–38 speak of a dispute or situation the continuance of which 'is likely to endanger the maintenance of international peace and security', which narrows the cases relevant to the UNSC significantly when compared with the general obligation to settle *any* dispute in Article 2(3).[77] Article 37 only refers to disputes of such nature.

The question naturally arises whether there is any difference between a 'dispute' and a 'situation'. The term 'dispute' has been defined above, and is mainly concerned with identified parties with claims and counter-claims,[78] while a 'situation' is a 'state of affairs',[79] a broader and rather indeterminate concept that is defined only by its potential to endanger international peace and security, and also covers disputes.[80] According to Conforti and Focarelli, any distinction made between the two, based on the presence or absence of a disagreement between states, is fleeting and of 'no practical use', despite the fact that the distinction is the prevalent view.[81] However, as Kelsen has shown, there are several important distinctions to make. The authority of the UNSC is indeed circumscribed by the nature of the situation, as it determines who may seize the Council, and what powers it may exercise.[82] In addition, the distinction between dispute and situation is of significance as permanent members of the UNSC

---

[73] For example, Eagleton, *supra* n.69, at 529; P. Hulsroj, 'The Legal Function of the Security Council', (2002) 59 *Chinese J Int'l L* 9.
[74] B. Conforti and C. Focarelli, *The Law and Practice of the United Nations* (Leiden: Martinus Nijhoff, 2010), at 188 and further.
[75] *Ibid.*, 192; Manusama, *supra* n.21, at 47–48.
[76] T. Schweisfurth, 'Article 34', in Simma (ed.), *supra* n.6, at 600.
[77] Tomuschat, *supra* n.17, at 584.
[78] Goodrich and Hambro, *supra* n.45, at 249; Schweisfurth, *supra* n.76, at 599; Merrills, *supra* n.48, at 1.
[79] Goodrich and Hambro, *supra* n.45, at 248; Schweisfurth, *supra* n.76, at 600.
[80] Conforti and Focarelli, *supra* n.74, at 190; Orakhelashvili, *supra* n.2, at 27.
[81] Conforti and Focarelli, *supra* n.74, at 191–192.
[82] As Kelsen demonstrates, close reading of Chapter VI reveals that the Security Council may be involved in any dispute between states, regardless of its possible effect on peace and security; situations which might lead to international friction or give rise to a dispute; situations, the continuance of which is likely to endanger the maintenance of international peace and security. Kelsen, *supra* n.48.

are barred from voting on decisions regarding disputes to which they are a party.[83] However, states and the Council itself in practice use the terms 'disputes' and 'situations' interchangeably, making any discussion of them largely irrelevant.

The procedures of Chapter VI reflect four principles. First, states are obliged to continue to seek peaceful settlement of their disputes, and states should make the effort to do so before the UNSC is involved.[84] Secondly, Chapter VI respects the legal principle found in customary international law that states are free to choose their own means in settling their disputes amicably. Thirdly, none of the Council's powers in Chapter VI authorize it to impose a settlement of the dispute on parties.[85] Fourthly, Chapter VI establishes a role for the UNSC only when disputes or situations reach a certain gravity, and then only a recommendatory role at that. These four principles determine when and to what extent the Council may become involved and thus reflect the subsidiary role that the UNSC plays in the peaceful settlement of disputes.[86] This is a logical consequence of the role and purpose of the collective security system and is highlighted in the context of conflict prevention by the primary responsibility of states to settle disputes peacefully.[87]

Depending on the nature of the entity and the situation or dispute the UNSC may:

- issue a general call to use the means of Article 33(1) on the basis of Article 33(2);
- conduct an investigation into 'any dispute, or any situation which might lead to international friction or give rise to a dispute' on the basis of Article 34;
- recommend appropriate procedures or methods of adjustment on the basis of Article 36(1) in the case of a dispute or situation 'which is likely to endanger the maintenance of international peace and security', or if so requested by the parties as provided for in Article 38; or
- recommend appropriate terms of settlement on the basis of Article 37(2) in the case of a dispute 'which is likely to endanger the maintenance of international peace and security' if the parties fail to settle it by the means indicated in Article 33(1), or on the basis of Article 38 if so requested by the parties.

---

[83] See Article 27(3), UN Charter (1945).

[84] See, for example, the *Declaration on the Prevention and Removal of Disputes and Situations Which May Threaten International Peace and Security and on the Role of the United Nations in this Field*, UNGA Res. 43/51 (1988), Annex, paras 11–13.

[85] See *Status of Eastern Carelia Case (Finland v USSR)* (Advisory Opinion) PCIJ Series B No 5 (23 July 1923), at 27: 'It is well established in international law that no State can, without its consent, be compelled to submit its disputes with other States either to mediation or to arbitration, or to any other kind of pacific settlement.'

[86] C. Eagleton, 'The Pacific Settlement of Disputes under the Charter', (1946) 246 *Ann. Am. Acad. Polit. Soc. Sci.* 24, at 25; Ratner, *supra* n.3, at 429; Orakhelashvili, *supra* n.2, at 28–30 and the 'adverse presumption' against Security Council involvement. See also Article 2(7) which states that '[n]othing (…) shall require the Members to submit [matters which are essentially in the domestic jurisdiction of any state] to settlement (…)'.

[87] Cf. UNSC Res. 1366 (2001), para. 2: 'The Security Council (…) [s]tresses that the essential responsibility for conflict prevention rests with national governments (…)'; Kelsen, *supra* n.48, at 174.

These procedures reflect a central role for the concept of endangerment of international peace and security, a situation that may or may not be determined to exist after an investigation by the UNSC under Article 34. Yet, the legal and practical significance of this criterion for UNSC jurisdiction can be questioned, as much depends on the discretion of the Council to make a determination in the first place[88] and the nebulous nature of the criteria themselves. Indeed, any such determination, as well as the difference between a 'danger to the peace' of Articles 33, 36, 37 and 38 on the one hand, and 'threat to peace' of Article 39 on the other, may only be a label 'put into resolutions to indicate the political climate in the Council'.[89]

The term 'situation' in Chapter VI is broad enough to include internal situations, that is situations that occur within the borders of a state, raising the question of the extent to which the domestic jurisdiction clause of Article 2(7) applies to Chapter VI. It stipulates:

- that the Charter does not in any way authorize the UN 'to intervene in matters which are essentially within the domestic jurisdiction of any state'; and
- that the Charter does not in any way 'require the Members to submit such matters to settlement under the Charter'.

What constitutes a matter 'essentially within the domestic jurisdiction of states' depends not merely on its international effect, but on the development of international relations and whether a state is subject to international legal obligations regarding the matter.[90] Article 2(7) only excludes Chapter VII enforcement measures from its scope, implying that any action taken by the UNSC under Chapter VI is indeed subject to Article 2(7), as was arguably intended by the drafters.[91] However, the clause seems of little legal or practical relevance given the subsidiary and recommendatory nature of Chapter VI and that the UNSC is not empowered to impose a binding settlement under Chapter VI. Moreover, although a decision under Article 34 may to some extent impose a duty to cooperate with a UNSC investigation, this does not signify 'intervention' or directly relate to the settlement of a dispute.

B. UNSC Investigations

A textual interpretation of Article 34 limits the Council's powers to the goal of determining 'whether the continuance of the dispute or situation is likely to endanger the maintenance of international peace and security'. However, this is sometimes refuted by reference to the rationale of the provision and the unreasonableness of

---

[88] Goodrich and Hambro, *supra* n.45, at 250: 'The Security Council has maintained that it is the master of its own agenda'; Schweisfurth, *supra* n.76, at 602.
[89] N.D. White, *Keeping the Peace* (Manchester: Manchester University Press, 1997), at 37.
[90] *Ibid.*, at 57–58; *Nationality Decrees issued in Tunis and Morocco on November 8th, 1921* (Advisory Opinion) PCIJ Series B No 4 (7 February 1923), at 23–24; Schweisfurth, *supra* n.76, at 601; Manusama, *supra* n.21, at 52–55; Conforti and Focarelli, *supra* n.74, at 158–159.
[91] For an overview of Article 2(7), see G. Nolte, 'Article 2(7)', in Simma (ed.), *supra* n.6, at 148–171, in particular 165–166; K. Ahmed, 'The Domestic Jurisdiction Clause in the United Nations Charter: A Historical View', (2006) 10 *Singapore YBIL* 195.

limiting its reach to the UNSC's role in the peaceful settlement of disputes.[92] A general, broader, implied investigative power of the Council is, therefore, widely assumed, including for the purpose of determining a threat to the peace or worse under Article 39, albeit probably under different provisions of the Charter, namely both Articles 34 and 39.[93] Regardless, when viewed in the limited context of the literal purpose of Article 34, it is clear that the UNSC does not necessarily need to employ an official investigation if the endangerment to peace and security is evident, at least to the Council.[94]

The investigatory power is not dependent on disputing parties raising the question whether a decision to undertake an investigation constitutes a binding decision on the UN membership, with which states must cooperate. Binding effect is attributed on the basis of the principle of effectiveness[95] and denied on the basis of its position in Chapter VI among other non-binding powers.[96] The 1991 *Declaration on Fact-Finding by the United Nations in the Field of the Maintenance of International Peace and Security* strongly suggests that a state must consent before a fact-finding mission can enter its territory, and that it must cooperate with the mission in general.[97] Conforti and Focarelli offer a convincing third option, namely that a decision under Article 34 is an operational decision, not leading to binding effect under Article 25, but rather to an obligation to cooperate as required by Article 2(5). Yet, this does not appear to resolve the issue of the extent of cooperation that states must give a UNSC fact-finding mission.[98]

C. Appropriate Procedures and Methods of Adjustment

Pursuant to Articles 36(1) and 37(2), the UNSC has the power to recommend those dispute settlement procedures and methods of adjustment that it deems appropriate to defuse the danger to peace and security. It can do so 'at any stage' and on its own initiative. The power to recommend specific procedures or methods distinguishes it from a more general call on states to use the dispute settlement mechanisms on the

---

[92] Conforti and Focarelli, *supra* n.74, at 182–183.
[93] *Ibid.*; J. Quiqley, 'The Security Council Fact-Finding: A Prerequisite to Effective Prevention of War', (1992) 7 *Fla J Int'l L* 191, 192; Orakhelashvili, *supra* n.2, at 31. Cf. Schweisfurth considers a general power to investigate matter to be an implied power, and not falling under Article 34: Schweisfurth, *supra* n.76, at 595. See also Kelsen, *supra* n.48, at 185–186. Rather, reference is made to Articles 22 and 29.
[94] E.L. Kerley, 'The Powers of Investigation of the United Nations Security Council', (1961) 55 *AJIL* 892, at 900–901; Schweisfurth, *supra* n.76, at 606.
[95] Goodrich and Hambro, *supra* n.45, at 247; Kerley, *supra* n.94, at 893–897; Kelsen, *supra* n.48, at 185; Conforti and Focarelli, *supra* n.74, at 186–187; Orakhelashvili, *supra* n.2, at 36.
[96] White, *supra* n.89, at 83–85; for example, E. de Wet, *The Chapter VII Powers of the United Nations Security Council* (Oxford: Hart, 2004), at 37–40.
[97] *Declaration on Fact-Finding by the United Nations in the Field of Maintenance of International Peace and Security*, UNGA Res. 46/59 (1991) UN Doc. A/RES/46/59, 9 December 1991. See also, A. Berg, 'The 1991 Declaration on Fact-Finding by the United Nations', (1993) 4 *Eur J Int'l L* 107.
[98] Conforti and Focarelli, *supra* n.74, at 187–188.

basis of Article 33(2).[99] Paragraphs 2 and 3 of Article 36, as well as the principle of 'free choice of means' mitigate this 'power', by having the Council take into account mechanisms adopted earlier by the parties and the principle that legal disputes should be referred to the ICJ. It could be argued that Article 36 repeats the obvious, as does Eagleton, as he laments that the power of recommendations under the provision 'can only be regarded as a device making the part of the UNSC in the settlement of disputes appear to be more important than it really is'.[100] While the Council is essentially free to involve itself in disputes under Article 36, its only task is facilitating and furthering peaceful settlement. On the other hand, it may be argued that for the UNSC to have added value in a dispute settlement process, that process must be failing along with the dispute endangering the peace.[101] In the same vein, it could be argued that the Council is not limited to recommending any of the procedures and mechanisms listed in Article 33, in line with the spirit of Chapter VI, which is to ensure that dangers to the peace are settled or adjusted peacefully,[102] and that it does not have to wait until efforts undertaken by the parties have failed.[103] Moreover, the UNSC can provide any such procedure or method itself, for instance through the creation of subsidiary organs under Article 29.[104] In any case, it is clear that the Council has a significant amount of discretion in deciding when to make its recommendation, or what to recommend,[105] limited only by the prohibition that it may not suggest procedures or methods that go to the merits of the case.[106]

D. Appropriate Terms of Settlement

Eagleton cynically called the power of the UNSC to recommend actual terms of settlement under Article 37(2) 'the height of the means provided by the Charter for the pacific settlement of disputes between nations'.[107] It follows after the fulfilment of the obligation of the parties, laid down in paragraph 1 of Article 37, to refer the dispute to the Council if the parties fail to settle it by any of the means of Article 33, and provided the dispute is a danger to peace and security. These pre-conditions poignantly reflect the subsidiary role of the UNSC in this area, despite the fact that these conditions may not have had much practical impact on the freedom of the Council to make recommendations.[108] On the other hand, when the parties to a dispute have failed to settle it, the UNSC is in turn obliged to make a decision, whether to recommend procedures for settlement or make recommendations regarding the merits of the dispute, or arguably decide not to act.[109] Article 37(2) is the ultimate transition point

---

[99] *Ibid.*, at 193.
[100] Eagleton, *supra* n.86, at 25.
[101] T. Stein, 'Article 36', in Simma (ed.), *supra* n.6, at 624; Orakhelashvili, *supra* n.2, at 28.
[102] Stein, *supra* n.101, at 622.
[103] Kelsen, *supra* n.48, at 192.
[104] Conforti and Focarelli, *supra* n.74, at 195.
[105] Goodrich and Hambro, *supra* n.45, at 256; Conforti and Focarelli, *supra* n.74, at 196.
[106] Stein, *supra* n.101, at 622; Conforti and Focarelli, *supra* n.74, at 195.
[107] Eagleton, *supra* n.86, at 26.
[108] Conforti and Focarelli, *supra* n.74, at 198; Cf. Stein, *supra* n.101, at 632–633.
[109] Stein, *supra* n.101, at 638.

from the bilateral settlement of disputes to non-coercive collective measures by the Council. Its distinguishing feature is that these recommendations may pertain to the controversies that make up the dispute between the parties.[110]

The UNSC has thus assumed a quasi-judicial role.[111] The main question regarding Article 37(2) is what the UNSC is allowed to recommend in terms of international law. The scholarly consensus characterizes the Council as a political, executive body bound by law, particularly in the peaceful settlement of disputes according to Article 1(1) of the Charter.[112] The non-binding nature of the recommendations does not mean that the UNSC is authorized to contravene international law. As Higgins argues, the term 'appropriate' in Article 37(2) means a 'broad discretion within the framework of the principles of international law',[113] meaning general compatibility with international law, although the recommendation may contradict existing law.[114] The Council may thus pronounce on legal issues, either raised by the parties or because it considers it pertinent to the dispute.

E. Citing Chapter VI Provisions

Only very early Council practice can be cited when discussing the provisions of Chapter VI. Thus, the Council mentioned Article 35 in the *Spanish Question* when it decided on the establishment of a sub-committee under Articles 34 and 29 'to determine whether the situation in Spain has led to international friction and does endanger international peace and security'.[115] However, with respect to the *Greek Question* the UNSC did mention Article 34, but invoked the provision to ascertain facts only, rather than to determine a danger to the peace.[116] This practice of interpreting Article 34 as a broader authority for investigation while not invoking it explicitly was repeated in subsequent practice throughout the history of the UN,[117] and is further supported by the 1991 *Declaration on Fact-Finding*.[118] In the *Repertoire of the Practice of the UNSC*, investigative practices are described as 'investigative and fact-finding activities that may be deemed to fall within the scope of Article 34 or be

---

[110] *Ibid.*, at 639.
[111] O. Schachter, 'The Quasi-judicial Role of the Security Council and the General Assembly', (1964) 58 *AJIL* 960–965; K. Harper, 'Does the United Nations Security Council have the Competence to Act as Court and Legislature?', (1994) 27 *NYU J Int'l L & Pol'y* 103.
[112] R. Higgins, 'The Place of Law in the Settlement of Disputes by the Security Council', (1970) 64 *AJIL* 1, at 9, disputing Kelsen, *supra* n.48, at 182; Stein, *supra* n.101, at 640; Manusama, *supra* n.21, at 9–10.
[113] Higgins, *supra* n.112, at 9.
[114] Stein, *supra* n.101, at 640.
[115] UNSC Res. 4 (1946); Schweisfurth, *supra* n.76, at 597.
[116] UNSC Res. 15 (1946).
[117] Goodrich and Hambro, *supra* n.45, at 345; Kelsen, *supra* n.48, at 184–185; White, *supra* n.89, at 84; Quigley, *supra* n.93, at 192; Conforti and Focarelli, *supra* n.74, at 183. Cf. Schweisfurth, who contends that the legal basis for such investigations and fact-finding efforts must be found elsewhere. Schweisfurth, *supra* n.76, at 600–601.
[118] Declaration on Fact-Finding, *supra* n.97; Berg, *supra* n.97.

related to its provisions'.[119] Similarly, most referrals of disputes or situations, ostensibly under Article 35, do not include any reference to that provision.[120] When procedures, methods or terms of settlement are recommended, no provisions of Chapter VI are cited as a basis, leading to the conclusion that 'the Council's powers as regards settlement have been amalgamated'.[121]

4. PRACTISING CONFLICT PREVENTION

Cousens rightly notes that the 'central preventive challenge of the Cold War – that of averting conflict between nuclear-armed superpowers – was clearly met'.[122] At the same time, however, it is commonly acknowledged that due to the Cold War, the proxy armed conflicts that often raged within states did not feature on the UNSC's agenda.[123] Ever since the Cold War, these disputes, situations and conflicts may have reached the Council's agenda, but the question remains whether the UNSC has exercised its proper role in conflict prevention. The sections below outline several trends in the practice of the UNSC in conflict prevention.

A. Timing: From Conflict Prevention to Conflict Management and Resolution

The legal analysis of Chapter VI shows that there is a presumption that the UNSC is empowered to involve itself or be involved before large-scale violence erupts. Yet, that presumption was largely abandoned after the Cold War. In his 1992 *Agenda for Peace*, the UN Secretary-General emphasized his role in preventive diplomacy, and only referred to the UNSC under Chapter VI in the context of 'peace-making', defined as 'action to bring hostile parties to agreement'.[124] The terms 'peace-making' and 'hostile' both imply that peace has already been violated at that stage and that the parties are engaged in armed hostilities. Moreover, the Secretary-General urged 'the Council to take full advantage of the provisions of the Charter under which it may recommend appropriate procedures or methods for dispute settlement'.[125] In effect, the Secretary-General acknowledged and confirmed previous practice, while at the same time expecting the UN to involve itself more and at an earlier stage of conflicts.[126] Yet, calls

---

[119] See, for example, United Nations Department for Political Affairs (UNDPA), *Repertoire of the Practice of the Security Council: 1989–1992*, at 852. Moreover, 'Article 34 does not (…) exclude other organs from performing investigative functions nor does it limit the Council's general competence to obtain knowledge of the relevant facts of any dispute or situation by dispatching a fact finding mission'.
[120] See, for example, *Repertoire 1989–1992, ibid.*, at 840–851. From 2000 on, the *Repertoire* overview stopped including a column entitled 'Article included in communication'.
[121] White, *supra* n.89, at 87. On very few occasions, the UNSC may invoke Chapter VI in general. See, for example, UNSC Res. 1495 (2003).
[122] Cousens, *supra* n.37, at 103.
[123] For example, Sucharipa-Behrmann and Franck, *supra* n.64, at 485.
[124] Agenda for Peace, *supra* n.27, at para. 20.
[125] *Ibid.*, para. 35.
[126] Cousens, *supra* n.37, at 103.

for peaceful settlement in the post-Cold War period were generally made during hostilities or a lull in hostilities,[127] despite the lip service paid to the UNSC's role in this process[128] and the fact that referrals under Articles 35(1) and (2) and 37(1) had been increasing.[129] The two most spectacular failures of the 1990s reflect this paradoxical stance. The civil war that led to the break-up of Yugoslavia did not become the subject of a UNSC resolution until after hostilities had broken out between the republics, and it did so on account of the heavy loss of life and consequences for the region.[130] In the case of Rwanda, which started as a regional issue in October 1990, the UNSC did not ask the Secretary-General to explore the possibility of deploying military observers until March 1993,[131] after a ceasefire was agreed and had collapsed, and after Rwanda and Uganda had requested an observer mission.[132]

After these experiences, Kofi Annan, the new UN Secretary-General, aimed to develop a 'culture of prevention', instead of bringing about institutional change.[133] In his 2001 report, he acknowledged, *inter alia*, the belated involvement of the UNSC in armed conflicts, but proposed only informal and flexible 'periodic reporting' by the Secretary-General to the Council, and the establishment of 'new mechanisms for discussing prevention'.[134] Presumably, the Secretary-General aimed to enable the UNSC to act preventively in a timely manner, yet the emphasis of the entire report was squarely on structural prevention, not operational prevention.[135] The adoption of the 2004 Report of the High-Level Panel on Threats, Challenges and Change[136] more or less codified or endorsed the timing of Council involvement and an enhanced role for the Secretary-General in both types of prevention. It acknowledged that '[i]n the past, the United Nations helped to reduce the threat of inter-state conflicts through the Secretary-General's "good offices"'[137] and emphasized more efforts towards 'envoys,

---

[127] White, *supra* n.89, at 197.
[128] UNSC Presidential Statement 34 (1999) UN Doc. S/PRST/1999/34, 2: 'The Security Council is aware of the importance of its early consideration of situations which might deteriorate into armed conflicts.' See also UNSC Presidential Statement 25 (2000) UN Doc. S/PRST/2000/25, 2; UNSC Res. 1327 (13 November 2000) UN Doc. S/RES/1327, at 4.
[129] UNDPA, *Repertoire of the Practice of the Security Council: 2000–2003*, Advance Version, Chapter X, at 5.
[130] UNSC Res. 713 (25 September 1991), UN Doc. S/RES/713.
[131] UNSC Res. 812 (12 March 1993), UN Doc. S/RES/812.
[132] *Letter dated 22 February 1993 from the Permanent Representative of Uganda to the United Nations addressed to the President of the Security Council, requesting establishment of a United Nations observer force on the Uganda side of the border with Rwanda*, UN Doc. S/25356.
[133] S. Chesterman et al. (eds), *Law and Practice of the United Nations – Documents and Commentary* (New York: Oxford University Press, 2008), at 246.
[134] Prevention of armed conflict, *supra* n.5, at paras 33–39. One of the ten principles that was to guide the move towards the culture of prevention reiterates the importance of Chapter VI, but points towards cultural instead of institutional change: para. 169.
[135] For example, *ibid.*, paras 6–16; see also Report of the Secretary-General, 'Progress Report on the Prevention of Armed Conflict', (2006) UN Doc. A/60/891, para. 7 (hereinafter 'Progress Report').
[136] High Level Panel Report, *supra* n.31.
[137] *Ibid.*, para. 76.

mediators and special representatives' with respect to internal conflicts.[138] Similar sentiments can be found in the Secretary-General's 2005 and 2006 reports,[139] the 2005 *World Summit Outcome* document,[140] and several UNSC resolutions and statements.[141]

In 2010 the UNSC invoked both the provisions and general terminology of Chapter VII while recalling its role in 'all stages of the conflict cycle'.[142] In the 2011 Secretary-General's report that was subsequently requested by the UNSC it was acknowledged that:

> [i]n the past, the Council focused largely on dealing with conflicts and emergencies after they occurred, but recent years have seen a push for greater engagement and flexibility in addressing emerging threats before they are placed on the Council's formal agenda.[143]

Moreover, the UNSC has made greater use of fact-finding missions by Council members to conflict areas.[144] Since 2008 the Council has resorted to so-called 'informal interactive dialogues' before an issue is formally placed on the agenda, as well as receiving monthly briefings from the Department of Political Affairs on current and emerging conflicts.[145]

Nevertheless, despite such cautious developments, the record since 2001 shows that, by and large, procedures and terms of settlement of disputes and situations have only been recommended or commended after armed conflicts have erupted. Thus, after failing to prevent the 2001 Afghanistan and 2003 Iraq conflicts the UNSC failed, for example, to prevent interstate violence between Djibouti and Eritrea in 2008[146] and the armed incidents in 2011 between Thailand and Cambodia over ownership of the *Preah Vihear* temple.[147] Yet, whether UNSC action with respect to internal conflicts is timely may depend on what one considers to constitute an internal armed conflict. It may be argued that UNSC involvement in internal disputes *after* an incident, but in which no

---

[138] *Ibid.*, para. 100.
[139] *In Larger Freedom*, *supra* n.62, at para. 106; Progress Report, *supra* n.135, at paras 31, 58.
[140] 2005 World Summit Outcome, *supra* n.27, at paras 73–76.
[141] For example, UNSC Res. 1366 (30 August 2001) UN Doc. S/RES/1366; UNSC Res. 1625 (14 September 2005) UN Doc. S/RES/1625, para. 2 under (a); UNSC Presidential Statement 1 (2007) UN Doc S/PRST/2007/1, 2. In another Presidential Statement, the UNSC acknowledged 'the importance of the settlement of disputes by peaceful means and promoting necessary preventive action in response to threats to international peace and security', apparently instead of doing so in response to dangers to international peace and security as authorized in Chapter VI. UNSC Presidential Statement 31 (2007), at 1; UNSC Presidential Statement 36 (2008), at 1; UNSC Presidential Statement 8 (2009), at 1.
[142] UNSC Presidential Statement 14 (2010), at 1. The Council invoked Articles 33, 34 and 35, as well as 99.
[143] Report of the Secretary-General, 'Preventive Diplomacy: Delivering Results' (2011) UN Doc. S/2011/552, para. 12 (hereafter 'Delivering Results').
[144] From 1946 to 1990, the Council undertook 10 missions; from 1991 to 1999, 7 missions; and from 2000 to 2010, 30 missions.
[145] Delivering Results, *supra* n.143, at para. 12.
[146] See, for example, UNSC Presidential Statement 20 (2008) UN Doc. S/PRST/2008/20.
[147] Tensions over this temple go back to even before the ruling of the ICJ in 1962. *Temple of Preah Vihear (Cambodia v Thailand)* (Merits) ICJ Rep. 1962 6.

large-scale violence has erupted, is timely. Thus, UNSC involvement in Haiti in 1993 after the 1991 *coup d'état* by a military junta and the measures that followed may still be considered a success in terms of timing and final result.[148] Moreover, an armed incident may create a dispute, or focus renewed attention to an existing one, possibly leading to a public response by the UNSC.[149] The speed with which internal violence may come about also arguably makes it difficult for the Council to respond in a timely fashion, as in the case of the violence in Kenya that erupted immediately after the 27 December 2007 election,[150] or the Libyan demonstrations in 2011 which the Gaddafi regime attempted to put down with brute force.[151] At the same time, involvement at a stage that cannot be deemed to be an armed conflict may be considered as an inappropriate interference in to internal affairs.

Generally, direct UNSC involvement in an internal situation will only be provoked when Council members are willing to hear and/or take up the matter, and the situation is internationalized, that it is a matter of international concern because of the nature of the situation (occurrence of international crimes) and/or has international repercussions (spill-over effect),[152] or because the incident occurs in the context of a conflict in which violence has abated but which is still of concern to the UNSC.[153]

B. The Role of the UN Secretary-General

It already emerges from the previous section that 'UN activities in conflict prevention have centered on the preventive diplomacy and mediating functions of the Secretary-General's office and the Department of Political Affairs'.[154] Originally created as a principal organ and the 'chief administrative officer' of the UN, the Secretary-General has evolved into the world's highest-ranking diplomat with commensurate prestige and

---

[148] See also *infra* section 5B.

[149] For example, in October 2003 Syria requested an emergency meeting of the UNSC to consider the violation of Lebanese and Syrian airspace, and the attack on an civilian site within Syria later that day, UN Doc. S/2003/939, 5 October 2003. The Council did convene, but did not adopt any decision on the matter. See UNSC Verbatim Record (5 October 2003) UN Doc. S/PV.4836.

[150] The UNSC spoke out two months after the election, welcoming the agreement between the parties and expressing appreciation for the efforts of the African Union and the Secretary-General. *Security Council Press Statement on Kenya Agreement*, UN Doc. SC/9265, 29 February 2008.

[151] The Council nevertheless issued a press statement only a week after the demonstrations began, calling for an end to the violence and *inter alia* 'steps to address the legitimate demands of the population, including through national dialogue', which may be interpreted as a recommendation under Article 36(1). *Security Council Press Statement on Libya*, UN Doc. SC/10180-AFR/2120, 22 February 2011.

[152] See, for example, Manusama, *supra* n.21, at 47–117.

[153] See, for example, *Repertoire*, *supra* n.129, at 61.

[154] B.R. Rubin and B.D. Jones, 'Prevention of Violent Conflict: Tasks and Challenges for the United Nations', (2007) 13 *Global Governance* 391, at 391; See also P. Szasz, 'The Role of the U.N. Secretary-General: Some Legal Aspects', (1991) 24 *NYU J Int'l L & Pol'y* 161, at 185–186; T.M. Franck, 'The Secretary-General's Role in Conflict Resolution: Past, Present and Pure Conjecture', (1995) 6 *Eur J Int'l L* 360, at 360; Thakur, *supra* n.30, at 322–326.

responsibilities.[155] This is due in part to UNSC paralysis during the Cold War[156] and its post-Cold War involvement in internal conflicts.[157] The greater than envisaged reliance on the Secretary-General in conflict prevention has expressed itself also in a continuing call for greater resources for the Secretary-General and the Secretariat, resulting in, for instance, the Department for Political Affairs (hereinafter 'UNDPA') within the Secretariat.[158] Similar calls, appeals and recommendations to further strengthen the capacity of the Secretariat to collect, analyse and report on relevant information as part of the UN early warning system[159] are a recurring theme in the Secretary-General's, as well as other, reports.[160] Next to establishing an information-gathering and early warning system, the Secretary-General has several key functions in operational conflict prevention, as identified by Lavalle,[161] namely referring disputes and situations to the UNSC under Articles 35 and 99; conducting fact-finding missions on request by a state, his own authority or as mandated by, *inter alia*, the UNSC; providing his 'good offices' when requested by the parties to a dispute, on his own authority or as mandated by the UNSC; and, where appropriate, encouraging efforts undertaken at the regional level to prevent or remove a dispute or situation in the region concerned.[162]

The legal basis for exercising certain powers in conflict prevention is not unambiguous. Only Article 99 directly grants the Secretary-General an explicit political power in this respect, namely to 'bring to the attention of the Security Council any matter which in his opinion may threaten the maintenance of international peace and security'. This power is of a procedural nature[163] but offers the Secretary-General an 'important behind-the-scenes diplomatic role'.[164] On the basis of Article 98 the Secretary-General may have certain functions and powers delegated to him, as designated by the words 'entrusted to him', including operating and coordinating peacekeeping operations, albeit within the legal limits of the powers of the delegating organ and the Charter in

---

[155] Article, 97 UN Charter (1945); Chesterman *et al.*, *supra* n.133, at 133; E. Newman, 'The Post-Cold War Secretary-General: Opportunities and Constraints', (2000) 2 *Global Dialogue* 96, at 97.

[156] For example, Franck, *supra* n.154, at 362–363.

[157] Newman, *supra* n.155, at 102; Thakur, *supra* n.30, at 320.

[158] Supplement to an Agenda for Peace, *supra* n.62, at para. 26. See generally on the UNDPA and early warning, S Rakita, 'Early Warning as a Tool of Conflict Prevention', (1998) 30 *NYU J Int'l L & Pol'y* 539.

[159] Orakhelashvili, *supra* n.2, at 14–15.

[160] For example, prevention of armed conflict, *supra* n.5, at paras 73–80; Progress Report, *supra* n.135, at paras 86–97.

[161] Lavalle calls this Declaration a 'minicode' for the Secretary-General's activities in this field: R. Lavalle, 'The "Inherent" Power of the UN Secretary-General in the Political Sphere: A Legal Analysis', (1990) 37 *NILR* 22, at 32.

[162] *Declaration on the Prevention and Removal of Disputes and Situations Which May Threaten International Peace and Security and on the Role of the United Nations in this Field*, UNGA Res. 43/51 (1998), Annex, in particular paras 20–24.

[163] Conforti and Focarelli, *supra* n.74, at 321.

[164] P.R. Baehr and L. Gordenker, *The United Nations at the End of the 1990s*, 3rd edn (New York: St. Martin's Press, 1999), at 32. See also E. Newman, *supra* n.155, at 98; W. Fiedler, 'Article 99', in Simma (ed.), *supra* n.6.

general.¹⁶⁵ No explicit basis can be found for the political activities of the Secretary-General that are not mandated or delegated by the Charter, the Security Council or General Assembly,¹⁶⁶ and some disagreement exists whether, for instance, a formal fact-finding power of the Secretary-General can be found to be implicit in Article 99.¹⁶⁷ Lavalle concludes that these activities do not contradict the Charter, but 'the direct legal basis for [this] practice would be a permissive rule of customary international law'.¹⁶⁸ Moreover, despite this disagreement, the independent authority to conduct investigations and fact-finding missions has been acknowledged, 'codified' and relied on as part of preventive diplomacy as conducted by the Secretary-General.¹⁶⁹ Consequently, 'in effect it has become pointless to try to locate the precise source of authority of each of the Secretary-General's political actions'.¹⁷⁰

The political activities of the Secretary-General that are relevant here are those concerning or mandated by the UNSC to prevent large-scale armed conflict¹⁷¹ at a time when overall UNSC preventive efforts are increasing.¹⁷² Yet, despite, or because of, the enhanced role of the Secretary-General with respect to conflict prevention, the Secretary-General has not implicitly or explicitly referred a situation to the UNSC under Articles 35 and 99 in the 2000s,¹⁷³ but has instead drawn 'the attention of the Security Council to a number of deteriorating situations which were already on the Council's agenda, and requested the Council to consider taking appropriate action'.¹⁷⁴ The UNSC requested the Secretary-General to undertake a number of investigations and fact-finding missions, but these were all requested after armed conflict on a significant scale had already erupted,¹⁷⁵ to investigate violations of international law during an ongoing armed conflict¹⁷⁶ or regarding a possible UN mission for an ongoing

---

¹⁶⁵ See, for example, Szasz, *supra* n.154, at 188; Conforti and Focarelli, *supra* n.74, at 318–319; D. Sarooshi, *supra* n.2, at 51–53.

¹⁶⁶ Lavalle, *supra* n.161, at 29; Conforti and Focarelli, *supra* n.74, at 321.

¹⁶⁷ Cf. C. Bourloyannis, 'Fact-Finding by the Secretary-General of the United Nations', (1990) 22 *NYU J Int'l L & Pol'y* 641, at 647, 660; Szasz, *supra* n.154, at 187; Conforti and Focarelli, *supra* n.74, at 322.

¹⁶⁸ Lavalle, *supra* n.161, at 29.

¹⁶⁹ Declaration on Fact-Finding, *supra* n.97, at paras 7, 12–15; Agenda for Peace, *supra* n.27, at para. 25; Prevention of Armed Conflict, *supra* n.5, at paras 54–55.

¹⁷⁰ Szasz, *supra* n.154, at 191.

¹⁷¹ As has been noted previously, in most instances the UNSC does not engage with a situation unless armed conflict has already broken out. However, as the UCDP shows, conflicts drag out over time, particularly internal conflicts. What may be designated as a 'conflict' may see only intermittent violence with significant time lapses between incidents. Whether a potential armed incident is 'new' depends in part on the length of such lapses and the source of the 'new' tensions endangering peace. The cases mentioned in this section are selected on that basis.

¹⁷² *Repertoire 2000–2003*, *supra* n.129, at 1; UNDPA, *Repertoire of the Practice of the Security Council: 2004–2007*, Advance Version, Chapter X, at 3.

¹⁷³ The Secretary-General has invoked Article 99 to refer a situation to the UNSC twice in history: in the Congo crisis and the hostage situation in Tehran in 1979. See, for example, Fiedler, *supra* n.164, at 1220–1223.

¹⁷⁴ *Repertoire 2000–2003*, *supra* n.129, at 16; *Repertoire 2004–2007*, *supra* n.172, at 17.

¹⁷⁵ For example, UNSC Presidential Statement 27 (2002) (DRC); UNSC Presidential Statement 17 (2004) (Ivory Coast).

¹⁷⁶ For example, UNSC Res. 1564 (2004) (Sudan).

armed conflict.[177] In addition, the UNSC may request the Secretary-General to present it with options and recommendations regarding a particular situation,[178] which the Council may act upon. Indeed, when the UNSC formally requests the Secretary-General to take certain action, it mostly does so on the basis of the Secretary-General's recommendations.

The term 'good offices' generally refers to 'the independent political role of the Secretary-General in preventing or mediating conflicts among, and more recently within, States'[179] and nowadays covers different things, such as conciliation and mediation.[180] The Secretary-General's good offices function is implied in Article 99 and can be exercised independently from any other UN organ. Although it is difficult to measure the exact impact of good offices, it is generally considered the most important conflict prevention tool, which the Secretary-General tends to use more frequently, precisely because of the ability to exercise it independently.[181] The UNSC has frequently commended the Secretary-General's role in conflict prevention;[182] called upon the parties to cooperate with the Secretary-General's efforts;[183] welcomed, commended, endorsed and requested continuing efforts by the Secretary-General that the Secretary-General had commenced independently in particular situations; and requested the Secretary-General to (continue to) use his good offices as a dispute settlement mechanism in both interstate and intrastate conflict, ostensibly under Article 36(1).[184]

C. The Role of Regional Arrangements and Initiatives

The *Repertoires of the Practice of the Security Council* since 2000 note in the context of UNSC recommendations that 'the Council has increasingly demonstrated a regional

---

[177] For example, UNSC Res. 1744 (2007) (Somalia).

[178] For example, UNSC Res. 1918 (2010) (prosecution of persons responsible for acts of piracy or armed robbery at sea).

[179] Franck, *supra* n.154, at 361.

[180] *Handbook on the Peaceful Settlement of Disputes Between States*, UNGA 'Report of the Special Committee on the Charter of the United Nations and on the Strengthening of the Role of the Organizations' UNGAOR 46th Session (1991) Supp No. 33 UN Doc. A/46/33, Annex, para. 104; Sucharipa-Behrmann and Franck, *supra* n.63, at 488–489; A. Brehio, 'Good Offices of the Secretary-General as Preventive Measures', (1998) 30 *NYU J Int'l L & Pol'y* 592; Merrills, *supra* n.48, at 26. For a general historical overview of the 'good offices' practice before the 2000s that includes the use of the tool in all circumstances, see T.M. Franck, *Fairness in International Law and Institutions* (Oxford: Oxford University Press, 1997), at 173–217.

[181] See, for example, Prevention of Armed Conflict, *supra* n.5, at para. 52; Brehio, *supra* n.180, at 599–600.

[182] See, for example, UNSC Res. 1366 (2001), preamble; UNSC Presidential Statement 31 (2007); UNSC Presidential Statement 18 (2011).

[183] UNSC Res. 1398 (2002).

[184] See, for example, *Repertoire 2000–2003*, *supra* n.129, at 68; *Repertoire 2004–2007*, *supra* n.172, at 28, 72; UNSC Res. 1268 (1999) (Angola); UNSC Presidential Statement 42 (2002) (Ivory Coast); UNSC Res. 1475 (2003); UNSC Presidential Statement 38 (2007) (Guinea Bissau); UNSC Res. 1806 (2008) (Afghanistan); UNSC Res. 1872 (2009) (Somalia); UNSC Res. 1944 (2010) (Haiti); UNSC Res. 2014 (2011) (Yemen).

approach to the prevention and resolution of conflicts'.[185] However, the relationship between the UNSC and regional arrangements[186] in the peaceful settlement of disputes is a complex one and some disagreement exists as to the proper interpretation of Article 52 on regional arrangements. The Charter embodies a compromise between the universalist and regionalist approaches to international peace and security,[187] and the question is what model governs the role of the UNSC *vis-à-vis* regional arrangements. Article 52 – considered by Conforti as 'an almost superfluous provision'[188] – strongly suggests in paragraph 2 that, at first instance, states have an obligation to revert to regional mechanisms as a means of fulfilling the obligation of Article 33(1), before referring the dispute to the UNSC. As such, it reflects the general subsidiary nature of the UN's system for peaceful settlement, and Article 52 can be considered *lex specialis* in its relationship with Article 33 in that system.[189] The core question is to what extent the UNSC may involve itself in a matter when a regional procedure is being used. It is argued that there can be no concurrent jurisdiction and that Article 52(4) in effect blocks the Council from exercising its prerogatives under Articles 36(1) and 37(2).[190] With respect to Article 36 it is also argued that the UNSC may only make recommendations on that basis if regional efforts fail.[191] This is not entirely convincing. First of all, the text of Article 36(1) does not support it. Secondly, although it is implied from paragraphs 2 and 3 of the same provision that the UNSC must take into account the means for settlement employed by the parties themselves, including international adjudication, and must prove the necessity of intervening, it is not blocked from making recommendations. Rather, the relationship between Article 52(3) and 36(1) must be interpreted differently, namely that the UNSC can recommend that states which are locked in a dispute engage regional arrangements under these provisions, which adds to the legally binding force of Article 52(3). Thus, the UN Charter gives priority to bilateral and regional dispute settlements, and the UN system is subsidiary to these mechanisms, with the ultimate primary responsibility for international peace and security in the hands of the UNSC in which disputes threaten peace and security.

As a matter of policy, it is widely acknowledged in theory and practice that preference should be given to regional dispute settlement.[192] Since 1991, the importance of regional organizations has been stressed by the UNSC on different

---

[185] *Repertoire 2000–2003, supra* n.129, at 34; *Repertoire 2004–2007, supra* n.172, at 37.
[186] There is no official definition, but see the pragmatic definition by Hummer and Schweitzer: W. Hummer and M. Schweitzer, 'Article 52' in Simma (ed.), *supra* n.6, at 819.
[187] *Ibid.*, at 812–820; Orakhelashvili, *supra* n.2, at 97–98.
[188] Conforti and Focarelli, *supra* n.74, at 325.
[189] Hummer and Schweitzer, *supra* n.186, at 841 and the sources cited therein. See also C. Schreuer, 'Regionalism v. Universalism', (1995) 6 *Eur J Int'l L* 477, at 478, 490; Orakhelashvili, *supra* n.2, at 107.
[190] Hummer and Schweitzer, *supra* n.186, at 838–841; Orakhelashvili, *supra* n.2, at 130–134.
[191] Hummer and Schweitzer, *supra* n.186, at 841; Orakhelashvili, *supra* n.2, at 133.
[192] See generally Orakhelashvili, *supra* n.2, at 89–106.

occasions.[193] As recognized by the UNSC and Secretary-General, regional arrangements have the advantage of proximity to the situation,[194] leverage, credibility and familiarity with local actors and the issues involved,[195] as well as an interest in the matter.[196] Noted already in the *Agenda for Peace*, 'regional action as a matter of decentralization, delegation and cooperation with United Nations efforts could not only lighten the burden of the Council but also contribute to a deeper sense of participation, consensus and democratization in international affairs'.[197] Since the *Agenda for Peace*, regional organizations have assumed an increasingly prominent role in conflict prevention,[198] leading the UN to work 'increasingly in tandem with regional actors in a variety of ways: in a lead role, in a supporting role, in a burden-sharing role, in sequential deployments and in several joint operations'.[199] In light of the Charter system on the peaceful settlement of disputes, the relationship between the UN and regional arrangements has become not a matter of primacy or supremacy[200] but of subsidiarity and complementarity,[201] a relationship that 'will need to be based on a clearer definition of the basis and processes of (...) cooperation'.[202] It must be noted, however, that the increased use of and reliance on regional organizations has also often highlighted their lack of capacity and resources to shoulder a heavier preventive burden, focusing the partnership on building such capacity and increasing resources.[203]

The question for this section is how this increase in the utilization of regional organizations has taken shape in UNSC practice. In the 2000s the Council 'on various occasions, expressed encouragement [and support] for efforts undertaken by regional organizations in the pacific settlement of disputes'.[204] As the different regional organizations enhanced conflict prevention capabilities in close coordination with the

---

[193] UNSC Res. 1366 (2001), para. 3; UNSC Res. 1625 (2005), preamble, para. 2; UNSC Presidential Statement 42 (2007), preambular paras 3 and 6; UNSC Presidential Statement 14 (2010), preambular para. 9.

[194] For example, Prevention of Armed Conflict, *supra* n.5, at para. 137.

[195] For example, Progress Report, *supra* n.135, at para.63; Delivering Results, *supra* n.143, at para. 51.

[196] Relationship between the United Nations and regional organizations, in particular the African Union, in the maintenance of international peace and security (2008), UN Doc. S/2008/186, para. 9.

[197] Agenda for Peace, *supra* n.27, at 64.

[198] Relationship between the United Nations and regional organizations, *supra* n.196, at para. 4.

[199] Delivering Results, *supra* n.143, at 49.

[200] Cf. White, *supra* n.89, at 20.

[201] Orakhelashvili, *supra* n.2, at 124–125, 129–130; Schreuer, *supra* n.189, at 494.

[202] Relationship between the United Nations and regional organizations, *supra* n.196, at para. 8.

[203] For example, UNSC Res. 1366 (2001), paras 19, 20; UNSC Res. 1625 (2005), para. 11.

[204] UNDPA, *Repertoire of the Practice of the Security Council: 2000–2003*, Advance Version, Chapter XII – Millennium Supp (2000–2003) 81; UNDPA, *Repertoire of the Practice of the Security Council: 2004–2007*, as of 19 January 2010, Chapter XII, at 92.

Secretary-General,[205] the role of the UNSC *vis-à-vis* regional arrangements closely resembles that of the Secretary-General. Generally, as the Council was increasingly confronted with potential internal conflicts, the regional arrangements took the lead in conflict prevention efforts as violence threatened to erupt or escalate, often due to crisis in government. In the 1993 case of Haiti, as mentioned earlier, the Council of the Organization of American States (hereinafter 'OAS') reacted 'with speed and decisiveness' to the 1991 military coup against the democratically elected president.[206] The government of Haiti referred the situation to the UNSC under Article 35, although no action was taken.[207] Not until two years later did the Council convene to impose mandatory sanctions, which partially copied those the OAS had imposed earlier.[208] Similarly, the UNSC was involved in Haiti in 2004 only when the OAS and the Caribbean Community were not able to convince local parties to accept a plan for the formation of a government and a humanitarian crisis started to unfold.[209] In the case of Zimbabwe in 2008 and 2009, the UNSC adopted a Presidential Statement condemning pre-election violence while efforts of the Southern Africa Development Community (hereinafter 'SADC') were under way, and which the Council welcomed.[210] In light of continued post-election violence, a draft resolution was floated among UNSC members that sought to declare the situation a threat to peace and impose targeted sanctions on Zimbabwe.[211] The African Union adopted a condemnatory resolution, and the UNSC failed to adopt the draft resolution. Subsequently, focus on preventing the escalation of violence reverted back to the SADC.

D. Preventive Deployment: UNPREDEP

In the 1992 *Agenda for Peace*, the Secretary-General promoted the concept of 'preventive deployment' of military forces as a tool of preventive diplomacy:

> [I]n conditions of national crisis there could be preventive deployment at the request of the Government or all parties concerned, or with their consent; in inter-State disputes such deployment could take place when two countries feel that a United Nations presence on both sides of their border can discourage hostilities; furthermore, preventive deployment could take place when a country feels threatened and requests the deployment of an appropriate United Nations presence along its side of the border alone.[212]

---

[205] See, for example, the establishment of the Peace and Security Council of the African Union, regional early warning systems and other developments. Progress R, *supra* n.135, at paras 63–68; Relationship between the United Nations and regional organizations, *supra* n.196, at para. 45.
[206] D.M. Malone, *Decision-Making in the UN Security Council: The Case of Haiti* (Oxford: Clarendon Press, 1998), at 62.
[207] *Ibid.*, at 63.
[208] UNSC Res. 841 (1993).
[209] See, for example, the account by Orakhelashvili, *supra* n.2, at 126–127; UNSC Presidential Statement 4 (2004); UNSC Res. 1529 (2004).
[210] UNSC Presidential Statement 23 (2008).
[211] Available at http://www.securitycouncilreport.org/chronology/zimbabwe.php.
[212] Agenda for Peace, *supra* n.27, at 28.

The UN Operation in the Former Yugoslav Republic of Macedonia is generally seen as the only clear example of preventive deployment.[213] The 2001 report of the UN Secretary-General, *Prevention of Armed Conflict*, mentions operations in the Central African Republic and Haiti,[214] but the timing of the Macedonian mission – before a situation occurs, instead of having to resolve it – sets it apart. As such, it reflects the basic principles of traditional peacekeeping, state consent, non-use of force and impartiality,[215] but the purpose and timing of preventive deployment arguably point to a different legal basis. In the absence of an explicit basis in the Charter, the legal basis for peacekeeping is often found in Chapter 'VI ½',[216] or implied powers.[217] Preventive deployment, however, could be more squarely placed conceptually in Chapter VI as a method of adjustment of a dispute by the UNSC itself of a situation that endangers peace, because of the combination of timing and nature of preventive deployment.

At the same time, however, the Macedonian mission was a part and continuation of the peace operation in other parts of the former Yugoslavia, United Nations Protection Force (UNPROFOR), which gradually displayed elements of Chapter VII.[218] Yet, before and at the time of the establishment of the presence in Macedonia, UNPROFOR was not mandated to exercise enforcement powers either implicitly or explicitly under Chapter VII. Neither UNSC Resolution 795 (1992)[219] or the Secretary-General report[220] referred to Chapter VII. Moreover, the mission was based on an original request made by Macedonia itself[221] and the objectives of the mission did not require any coercive action by UNPROFOR.[222] Before the Dayton Accords of November 1995, the mission in Macedonia was separated from UNPROFOR to form the United Nations

---

[213] S.T. Ostrowski, 'Preventive Deployment of Troops as Preventive Measures: Macedonia and Beyond', (1998) 30 *NYU J Int'l L & Pol'y* 793, at 795; High Level Panel report, *supra* n.31, at para. 104. For a succinct overview of the Macedonian case, see D.J. Ludlow, 'Preventive Peacemaking in Macedonia: An Assessment of U.N. Good Offices Diplomacy', (2003) *BYU L Rev* 761, at 764–767.

[214] Prevention of Armed Conflict, *supra* n.5, at para. 81.

[215] For example, *Report of the Panel on United Nations Peace Operations*, UN Doc. S/2000/809, 21 August 2000; *Comprehensive Review of the whole question of peacekeeping in all their aspects – Report of the Special Committee on Peacekeeping Operations*, UN Doc. A/56/83, 11 March 2002.

[216] For example, White, *supra* n.89, at 227–228; T.M. Franck, *Recourse to Force* (Cambridge: Cambridge University Press, 2003), at 39–40.

[217] For a discussion of the legal basis of UN peacekeeping operations, see A. Orakhelashvili, 'The Legal Basis of United Nations Peace-keeping Operations', (2003) 43 *Va J Int'l L* 485. See also chapter 17 by Nigel White in this volume.

[218] Orakhelashvili, *ibid.*

[219] UNSC Res. 795 (1992).

[220] *Report of the Secretary-General*, UN Doc. S/24923, 9 December 1992.

[221] *Letter dated 23 November 1992 from the Secretary-General addressed to the President of the Security Council*, UN Doc. S/24851, 25 November 1992.

[222] The objectives of the proposed mission were outlined in the 'Report of the UNPROFOR Exploratory Mission to Macedonia', para. 17, annexed to the report of the Secretary-General, *supra* n.220, at para. 17:

(a) 'To monitor the border areas and report to the Secretary-General, through the Force Commander, any developments which could pose a threat to Macedonia;

(b) By its presence, to deter such threats from any source, as well as help prevent clashes

Preventive Deployment Force (UNPREDEP).[223] With reference to a Secretary-General report, the UNSC endowed UNPREDEP 'with the same responsibilities and composition as UNPROFOR has at present in [Macedonia]'.[224] Moreover, the Secretary-General recommended '[t]he transfer to [UNPREDEP] of the applicability of all relevant Security Council resolutions and authorities relating to the functioning of UNPROFOR in [Macedonia]'.[225]

The UNPREDEP mandate was aimed at preventing external factors from threatening the territorial integrity and stability of Macedonia,[226] and UNPREDEP succeeded in doing so.[227] However, already in 1994 the Secretary-General and UNPREDEP had become involved in the internal factors that also constituted a threat to Macedonia's stability, as 'the more likely sources of violence and instability are internal and thus beyond the mandate of [UNPROFOR]'.[228] Based on his recommendation, the UNSC encouraged the Secretary-General, 'in cooperation with the authorities of the former Yugoslav Republic of Macedonia, to use his good offices as appropriate to contribute to the maintenance of peace and stability in that Republic'.[229] In contrast to its role with respect to the external threats, the UN was unable to cooperate effectively with local authorities due to local resistance.[230] UNPREDEP's mandate was not renewed in 1999 by the UNSC due to a veto from a permanent member. In 2001 ethnic tensions led to violence.[231]

In contemporary times, the UNPREDEP mission is also viewed as the first mission that practised one element of the concept of 'the responsibility to protect', that is the responsibility to prevent.[232] While the mission's success may be acknowledged, its legal basis – the consent of the state involved – is solid and uncontroversial once established but may be politically hard to establish in the first place. The preventive deployment of military forces requires on the one hand either a request by the relevant state or the political persuasion of that state, and on the other hand the political willingness of states that would supply the military forces, all in the absence of an imminent armed conflict. UNPREDEP was established at the request of a state to

---

which could otherwise occur between external elements and Macedonian forces, thus helping to strengthen security and confidence in Macedonia.'

[223] UNSC Res. 983 (1995).
[224] *Report of the Secretary-General pursuant to Security Council Resolution 947 (1994)*, UN Doc. S/1995/222, para. 85(c).
[225] *Ibid.*, at para. 85(e).
[226] *Letter Dated 23 November 1992 from the Secretary-General addressed to the President of the Security Council*, UN Doc. S/24851, 25 November 1992; Secretary-General report, *supra* n.220, at paras 6–10.
[227] For example, Ostrowski, *supra* n.213, at 818–821.
[228] *Report of the Secretary-General Pursuant to Resolution 871 (1993)*, UN Doc. S/1994/300, 42.
[229] UN Res. 908 (1994), para. 12.
[230] Ostrowski, *supra* n.213, at 824–825; O.P. Lefkon, 'Culture Shock: Obstacles to Bringing Conflict Prevention under the Wing of U.N. Development … and Vice Versa', (2003) 35 *NYU J Int'l L & Pol'y* 671, at 683–685; Ludlow, *supra* n.213, at 772–773.
[231] Ludlow, *supra* n.213, at 761.
[232] S. Breau, 'The Impact of the Responsibility to Protect on Peacekeeping', (2006) 11 *J Confl & Sec L* 429, at 431, 443–444. See also chapter 7 by Christine Gray in this volume.

counter the threat of spill-over effects from a neighbouring conflict in which a UN peacekeeping mission was already present, with substantial American involvement.[233] The 'fortuitous convergence of circumstances'[234] and other identified factors for success – timing, evolution of the UNPREDEP mandate, and sustained cooperation and commitment – are hard to duplicate politically and may explain why UNPREDEP has been the only mission of its kind.

5. COERCIVE CONFLICT PREVENTION UNDER CHAPTER VII

In theory, Chapter VII is of interest in the context of conflict prevention with respect to those disputes or situations that have not reached the stage of large-scale armed conflict, but which were deemed a threat to peace under Article 39 and on the basis of which subsequent non-forcible binding measures were taken by the UNSC. Particular attention is paid to arms control in the context of the role of arms control obligations in conflict prevention.[235]

A. Article 39: Of Threats, Demands and Recommendations

Article 39 of the UN Charter plays a pivotal role in collective security as it unlocks the power of the UNSC to take mandatory enforcement action. Furthermore, the Council may make recommendations under Article 39.[236] In light of early UNSC practice after the Cold War, the essential question regarding the UNSC became to what extent the Council is bound by principles and rules of (international) law – *legibus alligatus* – including in its determinations under Article 39, although such determination need not be based or include a violation of international law.[237] At a minimum, it is agreed that UNSC discretion in this matter is limited by the Purposes and Principles of the United

---

[233] Ostrowski, *supra* n.213, at 822.

[234] Ibid., at 818.

[235] See also *supra* section 2Cii. See also chapter 2 in this volume by Mirko Sossai on disarmament and non-proliferation.

[236] As Conforti and Focarelli note, the only difference with Chapter VI recommendations is the absence of the procedural requirement of Article 27. Conforti and Focarelli, *supra* n.74, at 220–223.

[237] For example, T. Gill, 'Legal and Some Political Limitations on the Powers of the UN Security Council to Exercise its Enforcement Powers under Chapter VII of the Charter', (1995) 33 *NED YIL* 46; I. Österdahl, *Threat to the Peace* (Stockholm: Iustus, 1998); G.H. Oosthuizen, 'Playing the Devil's Advocate: The United Nations Security Council is Unbound by Law', (1999) 12 *LJIL* 521; D. Schweigman, *The Authority of the Security Council under Chapter VII of the UN Charter: Legal Limits and the Role of the International Court of Justice* (The Hague: Springer, 2001); J. Frowein and N. Krisch, 'Introduction to Chapter VII' in Simma (ed.), *supra* n.6, at 710–712; de Wet, *supra* n.96, at 133–177; Manusama, *supra* n.21, at 47–117; Wellens, *supra* n.63, at 15–70; A. Orakhaleshvili, 'The Power of the UN Security Council to Determine the Existence of a "Threat to the Peace"', (2006) 1 *Irish YIL* 61; P. Johansson, 'The Humdrum Use of Ultimate Authority', (2009) 78 *Nordic J Int'l L* 309; Orakhelashvili, *supra* n.2, at 149–175.

Nations.[238] Article 2(7) still plays a particularly important role in guarding core elements of sovereignty and independent statehood,[239] and an Article 39 determination must be made 'in relation to such facts, events, and situations as justify adopting enforcement measures', 'so that these measures will then be both necessary and proportionate to address their object'.[240]

It was noted in section 4A above that the role of the UNSC has gradually changed from conflict prevention to conflict management and conflict resolution. Next to the focus on internal conflicts, the main development after the Cold War, however, has been the expansion of acts and elements that may constitute or contribute to a threat to the peace according to the UNSC. In internal conflicts, the gross violations of human rights and international humanitarian law have become an important factor in making a determination under Article 39,[241] as they did for instance in the conflict of the former Yugoslavia,[242] Rwanda[243] and Sudan.[244] Subsequent developments, such as piracy off the coast of Somalia, may be considered to aggravate the existing threat to the peace as determined by the UNSC.[245]

Outside of the context of armed conflict, and in the absence of any immediate risk to the eruption of armed conflict, three developments in the UNSC stand out. First, the non-compliance with or non-implementation of UNSC resolutions has triggered Article 39 determinations, particularly with respect to incidents of (international) terrorism. Thus, the refusal of both Libya and the Taliban regime to apprehend and extradite suspected terrorists was grounds for finding a threat to the peace after the cooperation regarding such persons was initially urged and insisted upon under Chapter VI.[246] Controversially, the UNSC consequently made such requests mandatory with the

---

[238] See also the Appeals Chamber decision in the *Tadić* case: '[T]he determination that there exists [a threat to peace] is not a totally unfettered discretion, as it has to remain, at the very least, within the limits of the Purposes and Principles of the Charter.' *Prosecutor v Tadić* (Jurisdiction) ICTY-94-1-AR72 (2 October 1995); see also, for example, Wellens, *supra* n.63, at 32; Orakhelashvili, *supra* n.2, at 155. See also chapter 5 by Christian Henderson in this volume.

[239] Manusama, *supra* n.21, at 55. But cf. Österdahl, *supra* n.236, at 31–32; Wellens, *supra* n.63, at 56. As argued elsewhere, the involvement of the UNSC in situations within states is always linked to some international effect or consequences. Manusama, *supra* n.21, at 47–117.

[240] Orakhelashvili, *supra* n.2, at 155.

[241] For example, Frowein and Krisch, *supra* n.237, at 724–725. See the general UNSC resolutions on the protection of civilians and children in armed conflict: UNSC Res. 1296 (2000) and UNSC Res. 1314 (2000).

[242] UNSC Res. 771 (1992).

[243] UNSC Res. 929 (1994).

[244] UNSC Res. 1556 (2004).

[245] UNSC Res. 1816 (2008) and subsequent resolutions on this topic: 'The Security Council, (…) Determining that the incidents of piracy and armed robbery against vessels in the territorial waters of Somalia and the high seas off the coast of Somalia *exacerbate* the situation in Somalia which continues to constitute a threat to international peace and security in the region' [emphasis added].

[246] Regarding Libya see UNSC Res. 713 (1992) and UNSC Res. 748 (1992); regarding the Taliban see UNSC Res. 1214 (1998) and UNSC Res. 1267 (1999).

accompanying enforcement measures imposed on the states.[247] Secondly, an important development is the UNSC response to the overthrow of freely elected governments. Starting with the 1993 case of Haiti, the Council has in essence assisted the efforts of third states and regional organizations to resolve these internal political crises when these efforts were not effective.[248] On the basis of early cases, it was debated whether there was emerging a 'right to democratic governance'.[249] UNSC practice shows that the Council stops short of imposing a form of government on states, unless the UN or the international community at large is directly involved in the administration of a state, such as in Kosovo. Nevertheless, that practice strongly suggests that the UNSC is partial to democratic governance, which it will promote at every opportunity.

Lastly, 'a complex of multiple facts, events and incidents [may give] rise to one single all-encompassing qualification in a particular dispute or situation',[250] but which may not involve an imminent use of large-scale armed force. The qualification of such a 'generic threat' as a threat to peace under Article 39 may be much more akin to structural prevention than operational prevention.[251] The UNSC has discussed HIV/AIDS,[252] the proliferation of small arms[253] and climate change,[254] but did not find a threat to peace.[255] However, in the post-9/11 world, any act of international terrorism is now considered a threat to the peace and security.[256] Moreover, as is discussed further below, the proliferation of small and light arms, as well as WMD, is a threat to the peace under certain circumstances.

---

[247] White, *supra* n.89, at 45–47; Wellens, *supra* n.63, at 39; Orakhelashvili, *supra* n.2, at 159–163.

[248] UNSC Res. 1464 (2003). See also the general concerns on unconstitutional changes in Africa, UNSC Presidential Statement 11 (2009); Frowein and Krisch, *supra* n.237, at 725.

[249] For example, T.M. Franck, 'The Emerging Right to Democratic Governance', (1992) 86 *AJIL* 46; G.H. Fox, 'Democratization', in Malone (ed.), *supra* n.37, at 69–84.

[250] Wellens, *supra* n.63, at 27; see also the 1992 Presidential Statement which stated that '[t]he non-military sources of instability in the economic, social, humanitarian and ecological fields have become threats to peace and security'. UNSC Presidential Statement of 31 January 1992, UN Doc. S/23500. The essence of the High Level Panel report is identifying new threats outside of the context of armed conflict. High Level Panel Report, *supra* n.31.

[251] Orakhelashvili, *supra* n.2, at 162.

[252] For example, UNSC Verbatim Record, 10 January 2000, UN Doc. S/PV.4087; UNSC Res. 1983 (2011).

[253] For example, UNSC Verbatim Record, 24 September 1999, UN Doc. S/PV.4084; UNSC Verbatim Record, 18 January 2004, UN Doc. S/PV.4896; UNSC Verbatim Record, 19 March 2010, UN Doc. S/PV.6288.

[254] For example, UNSC Verbatim Record, 17 April 2007, UN Doc. S/PV.5663; UNSC Verbatim Record, 20 July 2011, UN Doc. S/PRST/2011/15.

[255] For an interesting analysis of UNSC jurisdiction in economic and financial issues see K. Boon, 'Coining a New Jurisdiction: The Security Council as Economic Peacekeeper', (2008) 41 *Vand JTL* 991.

[256] See UNSC Res. 1373 (2001); UNSC Res. 1456 (2003).

B. Preventive Enforcement Measures

Non-forcible enforcement measures under Article 41 have generally been used by the UNSC:

- as a conflict management tool;
- as a subsidiary means to the efforts of the Secretary-General and/or regional arrangements in cases of operational conflict prevention; or
- in unique cases of structural prevention, like disarmament[257] and terrorism.

This chapter and section are only concerned with the latter two. Article 41 measures, most often referred to as 'sanctions', have also been part of the legality debate, along with Article 39 determinations,[258] because of the potentially grave human rights consequences as demonstrated, for instance, by the experience of twelve years of sanctions against Iraq. Non-forcible enforcement measures aim 'to give effect to [UNSC] decisions'.[259] Based on either Article 39 or 41,[260] the UNSC makes demands on states and non-state actors in order to maintain or restore international peace and security. The UNSC has demanded *inter alia* the immediate and unconditional withdrawal of troops,[261] disarmament,[262] compliance with human rights and international humanitarian law,[263] cessation of the use of force,[264] and cessation of arming, training or sheltering armed bands.[265] In cases of conflict prevention, the Council has demanded the restoration of constitutional government[266] and the extradition of individuals suspected of terrorism.[267]

To enforce these 'decisions' or demands, the UNSC has imposed import and export bans, and more limited measures such as arms embargoes, air embargoes, travel bans, targeted financial sanctions and embargoes on conflict-related natural resources, and has even created international criminal tribunals. Comprehensive economic sanctions have essentially not been repeated since the Iraq case in the early 1990s. The deployment of Article 41 sanctions in conflict prevention, particularly in response to terrorism, is characterized by the development of targeted and smart sanctions, the targeting of non-state actors[268] and the rise of UNSC 'legislation'. In the case of Libya, the UNSC imposed an embargo on all flights and arms sales to Libya, followed by

---

[257] See *supra* section 5C.
[258] See the sources cited in n.237.
[259] Article 41, UN Charter (1945).
[260] See the discussion in Conforti and Focarelli, *supra* n.74, at 235–236.
[261] For example, UNSC Res. 660, 2 August 1990, UN Doc. S/RES/660 (Iraq); UNSC Res. 1862, 14 January 2009, UNSC Res.1862 (Djibouti and Eritrea).
[262] For example, UNSC Res. 687 (1991) (Iraq); see *infra* section 5C.
[263] For example, UNSC Res. 764 (1992) (Bosnia and Herzegovina).
[264] For example, UNSC Res. 1970 (2011) (Libya).
[265] For example, UNSC Res. 1267 (1999) (Afghanistan).
[266] For example, UNSC Res. 1132 (1997) (Sierra Leone).
[267] For example, UNSC Res. 748 (1992) (Libya); UNSC Res. 1054 (1996) (Sudan); UNSC Res. 1267 (1999) (Afghanistan).
[268] See, generally, A. Franco, 'Armed Nonstate Actors', in Malone (ed.), *supra* n.37, at 117–130.

financial sanctions to force Libya to hand over terrorist suspects.[269] It repeated the use of Article 41 enforcement measures to enforce similar demands in the case of Sudan[270] and the Taliban in Afghanistan.[271] The enforcement of Chapter VI demands through Chapter VII measures is highly controversial as it suggests the artificial creation of a threat to peace.[272] Moreover, the UNSC arguably contravened the *aut dedere aut judicare* principle of anti-terrorism treaties and *jus cogens* right of states not to extradite one's own national by compelling states (unsuccessfully) to transfer individuals.[273]

The Council aimed to affect non-state actors and individuals suspected of terrorism directly and indirectly through non-forcible enforcement measures. In relation to the involvement of the Taliban faction in Afghanistan and the Al Qaeda organization in terrorist bombings, the UNSC first imposed an air embargo and financial sanctions on the Taliban.[274] It expanded the sanctions to the Al Qaeda organization by obliging states to *inter alia* freeze 'funds and other financial assets of Usama bin Laden and individuals and entities associated with him as designated by the [Sanctions Committee]'.[275] The 1267 Sanctions Committee was tasked with maintaining a list of individuals suspected of terrorism against whom states are to take intrusive measures, giving rise to many human rights concerns and efforts to modify the procedure of listing and de-listing individuals.[276] In the *Yusuf* and *Kadi* cases before the European Court of Justice,[277] these human rights concerns were adjudicated, in the midst of more calls and recommendations for modifications and adjustments.[278] In combating terrorism, the UNSC also reverted to so-called 'legislative' resolutions that created obligations for all states with respect to the phenomenon of terrorism that threatens international peace and security, 'regardless of concrete crises and without time

---

[269] UNSC Res. 748 (1992); UNSC Res. 883 (1993).
[270] UNSC Res. 1054 (1996) (Sudan).
[271] UNSC Res. 1267 (1999) (Afghanistan).
[272] See n.242 and accompanying text.
[273] Manusama, *supra* n.21, at 175–176.
[274] UNSC Res. 1267 (1999) (Afghanistan).
[275] UNSC Res. 1333 (2000), para. 8(c).
[276] UNSC Res. 1390 (2002), para. 2.
[277] Joined cases C-402/05P and C-415/05P, *Kadi and Al Barakaat v Council* [2008] ECR I-6351; see also J.S. Vara, 'The Consequences of Kadi: Where the Divergence of Opinion between EU and International Lawyers Lies?', (2011) 17 *ELJ* 252.
[278] See, for example, L. van den Herik and N. Schrijver, 'Human Rights Concerns in Current Targeted Sanctions Regimes from the Perspective of International and European Law', in T.J. Biersteker and S.E. Eckert (eds), *Strengthening Targeted Sanctions Through Fair and Clear Procedures* (Watson Institute for International Studies 2006), available at http://www.watsoninstitute.org/pub/Strengthening Targeted Sanctions.pdf; L. van den Herik and N. Schrijver, 'Delisting Challenges in the Context of UN Targeted Sanctions Regimes: A Legal Perspective', in T.J. Biersteker and S.E. Eckert (eds), *Addressing Challenges to Targeted Sanctions: An Update to the 'Watson Report'* (Watson Institute for International Studies 2009), available at http://www.watsoninstitute.org/pub/2009_10_targeted_sanctions.pdf; M. Bothe, 'Security Council's Targeted Sanctions against Presumed Terrorists: The Need to Comply with Human Rights Standards', (2008) 6 *J Int'l Crim Just* 541.

limits'.²⁷⁹ Resolution 1373 (2001) imposes on states the obligation to take comprehensive measures relating to terrorism financing and obliges states to adopt criminal legislation related to terrorism and terrorists.²⁸⁰ Resolution 1540 (2004) aims to prevent the proliferation of WMD to terrorists by imposing a basic obligation to refrain from aiding non-state actors attempting to 'develop, acquire, manufacture, possess, transport, transfer or use nuclear, chemical or biological weapons and their means of delivery'.²⁸¹ The power of the UNSC to adopt these legislative resolutions was debatable,²⁸² but they were ultimately justified by the perceived nature of the terrorist threat and the inadequacies of existing international law. These inadequacies consisted of the lack of universal implementation of existing treaties in the case of Resolution 1373 (2001), or the lack of any general obligations in existing international law with respect to WMD in Resolution 1540 (2004).²⁸³

C. Disarmament

It was noted earlier that any disarmament or arms control arrangements have developed outside of the collective security system, but that disarmament issues are vital to international security and therefore clearly within the purview of the UNSC.²⁸⁴ Therefore, the UNSC has involved itself in general terms with such issues. Moreover, 'given the magnitude of the WMD threat, it is not surprising that the Security Council largely has skipped over its Chapter VI powers in this context and has gone right for its coercive powers under Chapter VII'.²⁸⁵ Under these Chapter VII powers, the UNSC is able to address disarmament issues irrespective of the disarmament treaties and whether these have been violated in any way.

Several disarmament treaties and conventions acknowledge the central role of the UNSC. Article VIII, paragraph 36 of the Chemical Weapons Convention (hereinafter 'CWC') authorizes the Conference of the States Parties and the Executive Council of the Organization for the Prohibition of Chemical Weapons (hereinafter 'OPCW') to, 'in cases of particular gravity and urgency, bring the issue or matter, including relevant information and conclusions, directly to the attention of the United Nations General Assembly and the United Nations Security Council'.²⁸⁶ The Statute of the International Atomic Energy Agency (hereinafter 'IAEA'), charged with a verification role with

---

²⁷⁹ Conforti and Focarelli, *supra* n.74, at 240.
²⁸⁰ UNSC Res. 1373 (2001).
²⁸¹ UNSC Res. 1540 (2004), para. 1.
²⁸² See the discussion on legality in Conforti and Focarelli, *supra* n.74, at 240–242.
²⁸³ Manusama, *supra* n.21, at 184–189.
²⁸⁴ See *supra* section 2Cii.
²⁸⁵ J.D. Fry, 'Dionysian Disarmament: Security Council WMD Coercive Disarmament Measures and Their Legal Implications', (2008) 29 *Mich J Int'l L* 197, at 212–213.
²⁸⁶ Article VIII(36), *Convention on the Prohibition of the Development, Production, Stockpiling and Use of Chemical Weapons and on their Destruction*, 13 January 1993, 32 ILM 800; see also Article XII(4) CWC, and Article II(2)(a) and (b) of the *Agreement concerning the Relationship between the UN and the OPCW*, 17 October 2000, 2160 UNTS 209.

respect to the Non-Proliferation Treaty (hereinafter 'NPT'),[287] states, 'if in connection with the activities of the Agency there should arise questions that are within the competence of the Security Council, the Agency shall notify the Security Council, as the organ bearing the main responsibility for the maintenance of international peace and security'.[288] In the absence of a supervisory body, the Biological Weapons Convention states that any state party 'which finds that any other State Party is acting in breach of obligations deriving from the provisions of the Convention may lodge a complaint with the Security Council of the United Nations'.[289]

In general, the UNSC acknowledges the vital role of disarmament in maintaining peace and security[290] and its own position, 'where international treaties provide for recourse to the Council when their provisions are violated'.[291] In the aftermath of 9/11, WMD proliferation to terrorists became an urgent matter, ancillary to the threat to peace caused by terrorist acts in general, leading to Resolution 1540 (2004) discussed above. The UNSC has also frequently been occupied with small arms in the context of the protection of civilians in armed conflict. Small arms have an adverse and destabilizing effect on humanitarian assistance, the length of conflicts and civilians.[292] Moreover, next to calling for control and general reduction in the availability of small arms and light weapons[293] the Council has included programmes for disarmament, demobilization and reintegration in specific peacekeeping missions.[294]

Coercive arms control is 'the use or threatened use of military force (as opposed to other types of diplomatic measures or economic sanctions) to either eliminate or restrict the production or deployment of certain classes of weapon systems'.[295] In the case of Iraq, the UNSC had already responded to actual uses of WMD in the Iran–Iraq conflict,[296] before imposing comprehensive sanctions to enforce comprehensive disarmament obligations in Resolution 687 (1991).[297] Based on its past behaviour regarding WMD and its eviction from Kuwait, Iraq was forced to dismantle its WMD programmes and allow an intrusive inspection regime, arguably setting a precedent for future coercive arms control.[298] While the intention of North Korea to withdraw from

---

[287] Article III, *Treaty on the Non-Proliferation of Nuclear Weapons*, 1 July 1968, 729 UNTS 161.
[288] Article III(B)(4), *Statute of the International Atomic Energy Agency*, 26 October 1956, 276 UNTS 4.
[289] Article VI(1), *Convention on the Prohibition of the Development, Production and Stockpiling of Bacteriological (Biological) and Toxin Weapons and on their Destruction*, 10 April 1972, 1015 UNTS 163.
[290] UNSC Presidential Statement (1992), 4; UNSC Presidential Statement 1 (2007), 2.
[291] UNSC Presidential Statement 9 (1995), 3; see also UNSC Presidential Statement 43 (2008).
[292] For example, UNSC Res. 1674 (2006); UNSC Presidential Statement 24 (2007); UNSC Res. 1894 (2009).
[293] For example, UNSC Presidential Statement 1 (2009).
[294] For example, UNSC Res. 1296 (2000); UNSC Res. 1509 (2003).
[295] R.K. Smith, 'The Legality of Coercive Arms Control' (1994) 19 *Yale J Int'l L* 455, at 457.
[296] UNSC Res. 612 (1988); UNSC Res. 620 (1988).
[297] UNSC Res. 687 (1991).
[298] Smith, *supra* n.295, at 501; Fry, *supra* n.285, at 240–241.

the NPT in 1993 did not elicit a Chapter VII response,[299] the 2006 test-firing of a second ballistic missile that followed its actual withdrawal in 2003 and the announcement that it possessed nuclear weapons in 2005 finally culminated in a condemnation. Resolution 1695 (2006) was not adopted under either Chapter VI or VII. Instead, the Council was '[a]cting under its special responsibility for the maintenance of international peace and security'.[300] After North Korea conducted an underground nuclear test, the UNSC determined that the increased tension in the region was a threat to peace and subsequently imposed different kinds of sanctions to force it to comply with all NPT obligations, inspection and verification regimes.[301] In light of North Korea's continued defiance of UNSC resolutions and underground test and firing of ballistic missiles, these sanctions were expanded.[302]

Iran remained party to the NPT when suspected nuclear facilities were discovered, but which set off a process in which Iran, the IAEA and the UNSC squared off with respect to uncovering the exact nature of these facilities.[303] The IAEA determined that Iran had violated the NPT[304] and reported it to the Council.[305] The Council's call on Iran to halt all enrichment activities and cooperate with the IAEA did not have the desired effect,[306] prompting it to act 'under Article 40 of Chapter VII of the Charter of the United Nations in order to make mandatory the suspension required by the IAEA' – without explicitly determining the existence of a threat to peace under Article 39 – and demand suspension of all enrichment activities.[307] In light of continued intransigence by Iran, the UNSC imposed an import and export ban on certain goods and services related to enrichment and other nuclear activities.[308] The efforts by the IAEA and the UNSC were aimed at all times at verifying the claim that Iran was indeed intending to use nuclear technology for peaceful purposes as allowed by the NPT, and not a weapons programme. For that purpose, the Council sought to enforce, as it were, the obligations of Iran under the NPT, as well as the Additional Protocol despite the fact that Iran had signed, but not ratified, this Protocol. Thus, whereas heightened tensions in the region due to the evidently advanced nature of the North Korean nuclear programme were justification for UNSC involvement, the lack of verification of Iran's intentions was the prime concern and motivation for UNSC enforcement measures.

---

[299] UNSC Res. 825 (1993). For a more detailed account, see Fry, *supra* n.285, at 265–271.
[300] UNSC Res. 1695 (2006), preamble.
[301] UNSC Res. 1718 (2006).
[302] UNSC Res. 1874 (2009).
[303] For a more detailed account, see Fry, *supra* n.283, at 271–276.
[304] IAEA Board of Governors, *Implementation of the NPT Safeguards Agreement in the Islamic Republic of Iran – Resolution adopted on 24 September 2005* (GOV/2005/70).
[305] IAEA Board of Governors, *Implementation of the NPT Safeguards Agreement in the Islamic Republic of Iran – Resolution adopted on 4 February 2006* (GOV/2006/14); *Letter dated 6 February 2006 from the Secretary-General addressed to the President of the Security Council*, UN Doc. S/2006/80, 7 February 2006.
[306] UNSC Presidential Statement 15 (2006).
[307] UNSC Res. 1696 (2006), preamble, para. 2.
[308] UNSC Res. 1737 (2006). The sanctions were later expanded to include *inter alia* an arms embargo and travel ban. See UNSC Res. 1747 (2007); UNSC Res. 1803 (2008); UNSC Res. 1929 (2010).

6. CONCLUSION

While the original collective security scheme as laid down in the Charter was meant to ensure the possibility of UNSC involvement at every stage of a conflict cycle, the UN system has suffered from increased polarization in the exercise of its preventive function. The role of the UNSC has been confined to a threat of Council action based on the very existence of the system of collective security, and peaceful settlement recommendations and limited coercive enforcement measures for conflict management and resolution purposes, rather than conflict prevention. The UNSC has largely outsourced the preventive function to the Secretary-General and regional organizations, although a modest increase in Council activity may be discerned with respect to fact-finding. It has largely 'moved on' to tackling hard security issues, such as WMD proliferation and terrorism *in abstracto* through legislative resolutions. The lack of willingness of the UNSC to engage in conflict prevention seems to be based in part on the prevalent internal nature of contemporary armed conflicts. UNSC involvement is blocked by still prevailing state sensibilities as '[p]reventive measures awaken the dogs of sovereignty', and the fear of creating precedents for interference in their own affairs by the United Nations.[309] In addition, there is an institutional reluctance built into the UN to involve itself in disputes between states. This subsidiary character of the UN system, exemplified by Chapter VI, has not placated the fears for interference in the domestic jurisdiction of states, or the undermining of the primary role of the state in the creation of international law, as well as in international dispute settlement. That also explains why a similar reluctance does not exist on the part of the UNSC to engage individual states on questions of disarmament and WMD, in addition to the changed international psychology after 9/11, outside the context of an imminent armed conflict. When singling out a state regarding such questions, the UNSC does not impose a settlement on disputing states and act as an enforcer of prior existing international legal obligations. The internal nature of contemporary armed conflict also increased the involvement of the Secretary-General as his involvement does not necessarily require a mandate by the UNSC or UNGA. The UN system as a whole has increasingly focused on structural prevention instead of operational prevention, which involves other UN organs and international organizations that are better positioned to gauge internal conflicts.

True conflict prevention, and the proper role of the UNSC in it, remains neglected in practice and academic literature because of a polarization of focus on structural prevention and the Secretary-General on the one hand, and conflict management and UNSC legislation on the other. Moreover, when the function is outsourced, successful prevention becomes immeasurable or indiscernible as preventive activities increasingly move behind the diplomatic scenes. The question then becomes whether the continued decline in the number of armed conflicts[310] may be attributable to this polarization. In addition, is it appropriate, desirable or possible for the UNSC to intervene in internal

---

[309] Sucharipa-Behrmann and Franck, *supra* n.64, at 493; Lefkon, *supra* n.230, at 680–681; High Level Panel Report, *supra* n.31, at para. 100.

[310] L. Themnér and P. Wallensteen, 'Armed Conflict 1946–2010', (2011) 48 *J Peace Res* 525.

situations with the speed required to stop armed conflict from erupting? At the same time, the Council's role in dispute resolution and conflict management has only increased in which it has combined Chapter VI recommendations with Chapter VII enforcement measures, with the effect of imposing a binding dispute settlement on disputing parties. It lends the Council's still significant weight to the efforts of the Secretary-General when it delegates involvement in internal disputes, in effect leading to indirect, yet increased involvement in such disputes. Thus, although it may be correct to conclude that the UNSC has largely abdicated its direct role in conflict prevention, it would be too simple to conclude that the UN collective security system is failing.

2. Disarmament and non-proliferation
Mirko Sossai

1. INTRODUCTION

This chapter is aimed at assessing the law governing disarmament as one of the pillars constituting the overall framework for the maintenance of international peace and security. The objective of disarmament efforts is a negotiated reduction in armaments as a means to avoid the recourse to the use of force in international relations, although exigencies connected with the maintenance of international peace and security require the continued existence of efficient armed forces. It is significant that in the Presidential Statement issued at the end of a thematic debate held on this subject in 2008, the UN Security Council (hereinafter 'UNSC') stressed 'the importance of appropriate levels of military expenditure, in order to achieve undiminished security for all at the lowest appropriate level of armaments'.[1]

The modern law on weaponry is characterized by a close relationship between disarmament law and the law of armed conflict (*jus in bello*). In principle, their regulatory approach is different: whereas disarmament treaties introduce a ban on the development, production and stockpiling of weapons, international humanitarian law disciplines their use. However, recent disarmament treaties do take into account humanitarian concerns:[2] the paradigmatic example is the 1993 Convention on the Prohibition of the Development, Production, Stockpiling and the Use of Chemical Weapons and on their Destruction (hereinafter 'CWC'). Nevertheless it should be borne in mind that disarmament treaties and international humanitarian law on weaponry seek to achieve different objectives: both branches of law are aimed at reducing the destructive potential of war, but while the former serves the purpose of lessening the probability of the outbreak of war, the primary aim of the law of armed conflict is to preserve certain core humanitarian values during hostilities.[3]

The focus of the present analysis is the content of the relevant conventions on disarmament and non-proliferation, in order to individuate which features are recurrent in most of them. It would be impossible to understand the function they perform without first situating the issue of armaments regulation against the background of the

---

[1] UN Doc. S/PRST/2008/43, 19 November 2008.

[2] E.P.J. Myjer, 'Means and Methods of Warfare and the Coincidence of Norms between the Humanitarian Law of Armed Conflict and the Law of Arms Control', in W.P. Heere (ed.), *International Law and the Hague's 750th Anniversary* (The Hague: TMC Asser Press, 1999), 371, at 374.

[3] C. Greenwood, 'The Law of Weaponry at the Start of the New Millennium', in M. Schmitt and L.C. Green (eds), *The Law of Armed Conflict: Into the New Millennium* (Newport, RI: US Naval War College Studies Vol. 71, 1998) 185, at 190; W.H. Boothby, *Weapons and the Law of Armed Conflict* (Oxford: Oxford University Press, 2009).

UN Charter. This will permit consideration of the role played by the UN political organs in this field. By way of premise, and touching upon the *jus post bellum* element of disarmament, it is also important to enucleate the dimension of local disarmament, demobilization of the fighting groups and their reintegration (hereinafter 'DDR'), which has constituted an essential element in most of the peace agreements concluded since 1990 to terminate civil wars and has been included in the peace-building mandate of various multilateral missions operating in such post-conflict scenarios. After the Brahimi Report of 2000 recognized the importance of missions mandated to support peace processes,[4] all recent peacekeeping operations established by the Security Council have included DDR as part of their mandate.[5]

2. DISARMAMENT, NON-PROLIFERATION AND ARMS CONTROL

Disarmament needs to be differentiated from non-proliferation and arms control respectively.[6] As for the latter, whereas the concept of disarmament is related to the reduction and even the total abolition of a category of weapons, the notion of arms control was developed in the 1950s and 1960s in the context of nuclear dissuasion, which characterized the bipolar confrontation of the Cold War: since the aim was the stabilization of the security context, arms control instruments usually included measures consisting of mutual limitations of armaments or the freeze of their number at a given level.[7] In this context, the adoption of the Treaty on Conventional Armed Forces in Europe (hereinafter 'CFE Treaty') was aimed at reducing the conventional armaments and military equipment to agreed levels.

The same purpose of avoiding the alteration of the power balance characterizes the non-proliferation regimes of the 20th century, which were designed to maintain the *status quo* by preventing the spread of certain weapons. In this respect, the 1968 Non-Proliferation Treaty (hereinafter 'NPT') is the cornerstone of international efforts to address the problem of the horizontal proliferation of nuclear weapons. On the basis of the distinction between nuclear-weapons states and non-nuclear-weapons states, the balance of duties and rights included therein is usually considered under three pillars, which constitute the 'Grand Bargain' of the NPT: non-proliferation, the peaceful use of nuclear energy and disarmament.

At the beginning of the 21st century the international security scenario has dramatically changed. This is, of course, due to several factors: the end of the bipolar confrontation of the Cold War; the deployment of troops within the framework of

---

[4] *Report of the Panel on United Nations Peace Operations* (2000), UN Doc. A/55/305–S/2000/809.

[5] United Nations, *Second Generation Disarmament, Demobilization and Reintegration (DDR) Practices in Peace Operations: A Contribution to the New Horizon Discussion on Challenges and Opportunities for UN Peacekeeping* (2010).

[6] N. Ronzitti, *Diritto internazionale dei conflitti armati*, 4th edn (Torino: Giappichelli, 2011), at 361.

[7] J.H. Barton, 'Disarmament', (1992) *EPIL*, Vol. I, 1072–1076.

complex multilateral peace-support missions in situations of internal armed conflicts;[8] the rise of non-state armed groups; but also the evolution of science and military technology. The risk of a nuclear black market has also become a major concern, while the most frightening scenario has been identified in the acquisition of nuclear materials and technology by non-state actors or state sponsors of terrorism.

Such a change raised much concern about the adequacy of disarmament and non-proliferation law, since mutual deterrence is a redundant strategy in the context of terrorist groups or rogue states. Many commentators have made the point about a system in crisis, due to its structural defects. As a reaction, in the last decade several initiatives have been taken by states individually or collectively, representing a move towards a reconfiguration of the paradigm developed during the Cold War. In an attempt to classify these developments, some authors have employed the notion of counter-proliferation, which encompasses all the initiatives taken to ensure that weapons of mass destruction (hereinafter 'WMD') do not fall into the hands of non-state actors, including terrorists, or irresponsible governments.[9] Though treaties have been adopted to address such a threat, including the 2005 International Convention for the Suppression of Acts of Nuclear Terrorism,[10] the major actors of this paradigm shift have been, on the one hand, the UNSC and, on the other hand, the multilateral *fora* created within the framework of informal cooperative initiatives launched particularly after 11 September 2001: the Proliferation Security Initiative, aimed at countering the illicit trafficking of WMD, is just one example of them.[11]

3. DISARMAMENT AND THE UNITED NATIONS CHARTER

The first issue to be considered is the place of disarmament within the UN Charter: the relevant provisions are found in Articles 11, 26 and 47.[12] They confer a role in this field to both the General Assembly and the Security Council: while the former is entrusted with the mandate of formulating general principles of disarmament and regulation of armaments, the latter is directed to formulate concrete plans.[13]

It is significant that the UN Charter, while affirming the relationship between the level of armaments and the establishment and maintenance of international peace and security, focuses on the issue of their regulation more than on their disarmament. This testifies to the fact that in the UN framework the goal of disarmament does not have the

---

[8] For more on the concept of peacekeeping see chapter 17 in this volume by Nigel White.

[9] D. Joyner, *International Law and the Proliferation of Weapons of Mass Destruction* (Oxford: Oxford University Press, 2009); M. Bothe, 'Weapons of Mass Destruction, Counter-proliferation', in *Max Planck Encyclopedia of Public International Law*, available at www.m-pepil.com.

[10] UN Doc. A/RES/59/290, 13 April 2005. 2445 *UNTS* 89.

[11] See below in the text, section 7.

[12] D.S. Cheever, 'The UN and the Disarmament', (1965) 19 *International Organisation* 463; N. Elaraby, 'Some Reflections on Disarmament', in C. Tomuschat (ed.), *The United Nations at Age Fifty* (The Hague: Nijhoff, 1995), 9, at 10.

[13] See O.V. Bogdanov, 'Outlawry of War and Disarmament', (1971-II) 133 *Collected Courses of the Hague Academy of International Law* 15, at 25.

central position it had held in the League of Nations Covenant, where Article 8 strongly emphasized that the maintenance of international peace required a reduction in armaments.[14] It is important to situate the drafting process of the Charter provisions in their historical context, at a time when the negotiating parties were still at war and nuclear weapons had not yet revealed all their destructive potential. The content of Articles 11 and 26 has reflected the view that it was necessary to keep a certain level of armaments for the purposes of the collective security system envisaged in Chapter VII of the Charter.[15]

Notwithstanding the limited acknowledgement of disarmament issues within the UN Charter, the very first General Assembly resolution was devoted to the 'establishment of a Commission to deal with the problems raised by the discovery of atomic energy'.[16] It is not by chance that its approval came just a few months after the two atomic bombings of the cities of Hiroshima and Nagasaki in Japan. Analysis of the subsequent efforts by the General Assembly demonstrates that it has interpreted broadly its functions under the Charter,[17] by dealing not only with 'general principles' governing disarmament but also with specific questions. In this way, the General Assembly achieved a monopoly position in this area within the UN framework. In the course of its regular sessions, it passed various resolutions on different issues, ranging from the regulation of WMD, to military expenditures and disarmament and development.[18] In addition to the Atomic Energy Commission, established already with GA Res. 1 (1946), other bodies were created, such as the UN Disarmament Commission,[19] and the recommendations of the General Assembly represented landmarks in the drafting processes, as they preceded and contributed to promoting the successful conclusion of the three main conventions on WMD.[20] But the multiplication of resolutions on disarmament issues resulted in a reduction in their efficacy: the approval of several recommendations on similar topics, supported by different groups of states, impaired the clarity of the message they intended to convey and diminished their political impact.[21] The General Assembly also dedicated three special sessions to disarmament and arms control: the 1978 Final Document constitutes a sort of 'Disarmament Charter', as it identified a number of principles and guidelines which formed the basis of the subsequent programme of action within the framework of the Conference on

---

[14] L.M. Goodrich, E. Hambro and A.P. Simmons, *Charter of the United Nations* (New York: Columbia University Press, 1969), at 118.

[15] H. Gross-Espiell, 'Article 26', in J.-P. Cot and A. Pellet (eds), *La Charte des Nations Unies: Commentaire article par article* (Paris: Economica, 2005), 919, at 922.

[16] UNGA Res. 1 (I) (1946).

[17] See K. Hailbronner and E. Klein, 'Article 11', in B. Simma (ed.), *The Charter of the United Nations: A Commentary*, 2nd edn (Oxford: Oxford University Press, 2002), 276, at 278.

[18] For the text of the 55 resolutions and 3 decisions related to disarmament and arms control adopted by the UN General Assembly at its 65th session, see *The United Nations Disarmament Yearbook*, Vol. 35 (Part I) (New York: United Nations, 2010).

[19] UNGA Res. 502 (VI) (1952).

[20] See below in the text, section 5. See also J. Goldblat, 'Contribution of the UN to Arms Control', in D. Bourantonis and M. Evriviades (eds), *A United Nations for the Twenty-first Century* (The Hague: Kluwer Law International, 1996), 243, at 247.

[21] Hailbronner and Klein, *supra* n.17, at 280.

Disarmament (hereinafter 'CD').[22] Though not formally a UN organ, this body, initially created by the General Assembly in 1959, represents the only multilateral disarmament negotiating forum of the international community. Most of the disarmament treaties were negotiated in that framework, but the CD has remained in a state of stagnation in recent times: the members continue to disagree over its priorities, so that in the decade between 1999 and 2009 it was not even able to adopt a programme of work.[23]

While it was designed to be the focal point of all disarmament measures,[24] the Security Council has not fulfilled the mandate entrusted to it by Article 26.[25] The reasons for this are mainly related to the failure to fully implement the collective security system under Chapter VII, which also entrusted the Military Staff Committee with the duty of advising and assisting the Security Council.[26] However, since 1992 the Security Council has recognized that the proliferation of WMD, including their means of delivery, constitutes a threat to the peace under Article 39 of the Charter.[27] Different types of measures have been adopted under Chapter VII of the Charter, including economic sanctions targeted towards states deemed to be pursuing nuclear programmes.[28] Furthermore, in recent years Resolution 1540 (2004) has imposed on member states an obligation to enact domestic measures to prohibit the manufacturing, acquisition, possession and transfer of WMD by non-state actors, and to establish effective national controls. Whether such a determination of a threat to the peace is in conformity with Article 39 of the Charter and whether the measures adopted by the resolution are within the scope of the powers conferred to the Council by the UN Charter have been particularly controversial. It has been argued that the Council has no legislative power and therefore Resolution 1540 is unequivocally *ultra vires*.[29] But Article 39 does not exclude the possibility of the Security Council taking action in relation to certain activities in general, due to the global nature of the threat they pose, and when their very existence is held to be incompatible with the fundamental interests of the international community.[30] Article 41 of the Charter provides a non-exhaustive list of measures not involving the use of force: in the view of some authors, it represents an adequate legal basis for the adoption of measures such as those included

---

[22] J. Goldblat, *Arms Control: The New Guide to Negotiations and Agreements*, 2nd edn (London: Sage, 2002), 34.

[23] T. Galli, 'The Conference on Disarmament: Its Glorious History, Non-existent Present and Uncertain Future', in B. Vukas and T. Šošić (eds), *International Law, New Actors, New Concepts, Continuing Dilemmas: Liber amicorum Božidar Bakotić* (Leiden: Brill, 2010), 479.

[24] Elaraby, *supra* n.12, at 11.

[25] H.-J. Schütz, 'Article 26', in B. Simma (ed.), *supra* n.17, 464, at 474.

[26] See B.-O. Bryde and A. Reinisch, 'Article 47', in B. Simma (ed.), *supra* n.17, 769.

[27] UN Doc. S/23500 (1992).

[28] See below in the text, section 8.

[29] B. Elberling, 'The *Ultra Vires* Character of Legislative Action by the Security Council', (2005) 2 *International Organizations Law Review* 337, at 343.

[30] C. Tomuschat, 'Obligations Arising for States Without or Against Their Will', (1993-IV) 241 *Collected Courses of the Hague Academy of International Law* 195, at 344.

in Resolution 1540.[31] Others have recently made recourse to the doctrine of implied powers.[32]

The Security Council has clearly identified the relationship between collective security and disarmament. Not only has it held an open thematic debate on strengthening collective security through general regulation and reduction of armaments, but the adoption of Resolution 1887 (2009) marked a significant reorientation of its work, particularly in regards to nuclear disarmament:[33] the goal explicitly envisaged in the preamble is 'to seek a safer world for all and to create the conditions for a world without nuclear weapons'. Member states of the NPT are called upon to negotiate 'a Treaty on general and complete disarmament under strict and effective international control'. Resolution 1887 paved the way for further developments in 2010: the conclusion of the new START Treaty between the US and Russia and the positive outcome of the NPT Review Conference.[34]

4. SOURCES OF THE LAW ON DISARMAMENT

Through the lens of the *jus in bello*, there is little doubt that customary international law prohibits the use of certain weapons. The study of the International Committee of the Red Cross identifies a number which fall within this category: this is the case for both biological and chemical weapons.[35] It should be stressed that the use of prohibited weapons not only constitutes an international wrongful act, but might also involve the criminal liability of the individual: several conventions require states to consider the employment of a given weapon as a criminal offence under their domestic law.[36] In addition, the use of such weapons might constitute an international crime: under the 1998 Rome Statute, crimes of employing poison or poisoned weapons; of employing asphyxiating, poisonous or other gases, and all analogous liquids, materials or devices; and of employing bullets which expand or flatten easily in the human body, fall within the jurisdiction of the International Criminal Court, as serious violations of the laws and customs applicable in international armed conflict and, after the Kampala Review Conference, in armed conflicts not of an international character.[37]

---

[31] See, for example, S. Talmon, 'The Security Council as World Legislature', (2005) 99 *AJIL* 175, at 181.

[32] N. Tsagourias, 'Security Council Legislation, Article 2(7) of the UN Charter and the Principle of Subsidiarity', (2011) 24 *LJIL* 539. See also chapter 5 in this volume by Christian Henderson for more on the UN Security Council's implied powers.

[33] D.H. Joyner, 'Recent Developments in International Law Regarding Nuclear Weapons', (2011) 60 *ICLQ* 209, at 211.

[34] For further details, see below, section 5.

[35] J.-M. Henckaerts and L. Doswald-Beck (eds), *Customary International Humanitarian Law*, Vol. I (Cambridge: Cambridge University Press, 2005), at 259.

[36] Cf. for example Article 9 of both the 1997 Convention on the Prohibition of the Use, Stockpiling, Production and Transfer of Anti-Personnel Mines and on their Destruction, and the 2008 Convention on Cluster Munitions.

[37] RC/Res.5, *Amendments to Article 8 of the Rome Statute*, 10 June 2010. See chapter 14 in this volume by Robert Cryer for more on war crimes.

As for the customary international law on disarmament, the International Court of Justice (hereinafter 'ICJ') famously stated in the *Nicaragua* case, 'in international law there are no rules, other than such rules as may be accepted by the State concerned, by treaty or otherwise, whereby the level of armaments of a sovereign State can be limited'.[38] In its 1996 Advisory Opinion, the Court affirmed that 'there exists an obligation to pursue in good faith and bring to a conclusion negotiations leading to nuclear disarmament in all its aspects under strict and effective international control'.[39] In the Court's view, there is not only an obligation of conduct, a *pactum de negotiando*, but also an obligation to achieve the desired result, a *pactum de contrahendo*.[40] Less clear is the position of the Court on whether this obligation forms part of customary international law. However, it has been pointed out that such a duty derives from Article VI of the NPT and that it simply belongs to treaty law.[41]

Disarmament law is in essence treaty law. In order to present both the characteristics and the content of the main conventions, different classifications can be created on the basis of various criteria: the type of weapon, the scope of the content, the forum of negotiation or the number of states parties. A basic distinction is between conventional weapons and WMD. The latter 'include atomic explosive weapons, radio-active material weapons, lethal chemical and biological weapons'.[42] A different classification identifies those treaties which are aimed at eliminating an entire category of weapons by prohibiting the development, production, acquisition, stockpiling, retention, transfer or use of them, and by imposing their destruction. Along with the 1993 CWC, both the 1997 Anti-Personnel Landmines Convention[43] and the 2008 Convention on Cluster Munitions (hereinafter 'CCM')[44] belong to this category.

Furthermore, disarmament treaties could imply the de-militarized status of certain areas, as is the case of the 1959 Antarctic Treaty[45] and the 1967 Outer Space Treaty.[46] Furthermore, regional groups of states have established in their own territories

---

[38] *Military and Paramilitary Activities in and against Nicaragua (Nicaragua v. United States of America), Merits*, Judgment, [1986] ICJ Rep. 14, at 135. See G. Den Dekker, *The Law of Arms Control* (The Hague: Martinus Nijhoff, 2001), at 62.

[39] *Legality of the Threat or Use of Nuclear Weapons*, Advisory Opinion, [1996] ICJ Rep. 226, at 267.

[40] Bothe, *supra* n.9, at para. 12.

[41] Ronzitti, *supra* n.6, at 357.

[42] UN Department of Political and Security Council Affairs, *The United Nations and Disarmament 1945–1970* (New York: United Nations, 1970), at 28.

[43] Convention on the Prohibition of the Use, Stockpiling, Production and Transfer of Anti-personnel Mines and on their Destruction, 18 September 1997, 2056 *UNTS* 211.

[44] Convention on Cluster Munitions, 30 May 2008. The initiative of Norway to convene an international conference in Oslo to start a process towards the ban of cluster munitions was criticized in particular by the United States, which strongly supported negotiations on this topic within the framework of the 1980 Convention on Certain Conventional Weapons. See K. Hulme, 'The 2008 Cluster Munitions Convention: Stepping Outside the CCW Framework (Again)', (2009) 58 *ICLQ* 219.

[45] The Antarctic Treaty, 1 December 1959, 402 *UNTS* 71.

[46] Treaty on Principles Governing the Activities of States in the Exploration and Use of Outer Space, including the Moon and Other Celestial Bodies, 27 January 1967, 610 *UNTS* 205.

nuclear-weapon-free zones (hereinafter 'NWFZ') as means to consolidate international peace and security. The UN General Assembly defined them as:

> any zone recognized as such by the General Assembly of the United Nations, which any group of States, in the free exercise of their sovereignty, has established by virtue of a treaty or convention whereby: (a) the statute of total absence of nuclear weapons to which the zone shall be subject, including the procedure for the delimitation of the zone, is defined; (b) an international system of verification and control is established to guarantee compliance with the obligations deriving from that statute.[47]

Five regions are currently covered by NWFZ agreements: Latin America (the 1967 Treaty of Tlatelolco[48]); the South Pacific (the 1985 Treaty of Rarotonga[49]); Southeast Asia (the 1995 Treaty of Bangkok[50]); Africa (the 1996 Treaty of Pelindaba[51]); and Central Asia (the 2006 Treaty of Semipalatinsk[52]). A zone free of WMD in the Middle East has been proposed by Egypt since 1990: the Final Document of the 2010 NPT Review Conference eventually included reference to the convening of a Conference in 2012 on the establishment of such a zone, 'on the basis of arrangements freely arrived at by the states of the region, and with the full support and engagement of the nuclear-weapon states'.[53]

Another set of treaties introduce prohibitions or restrictions on nuclear testing. The 1963 Partial Test Ban Treaty[54] prohibits the carrying out of nuclear test explosions in the atmosphere, in outer space and under water. Bilateral treaties between the United States and the Soviet Union were concluded during the period of *détente* and entered into force in 1990: the 1974 Threshold Test Ban Treaty[55] and the 1976 Peaceful Nuclear Explosions Treaty[56] committed the two superpowers not to conduct any underground testing having a yield exceeding 150 kilotons. Despite all the efforts to promote the entry into force of the 1996 Comprehensive Test Ban Treaty (hereinafter 'CTBT'), 9 of the 44 designated 'nuclear-capable states' have not yet deposited their instruments of ratification.

Finally, as for conventional weapons, the 1990 CFE Treaty is an example of arms limitation, as it binds groups of states parties to reduce five categories of their conventional armaments and military equipment to agreed levels. An Adaptation Agreement was concluded in 1999, which updated the treaty structure in order to take into account the shifting security environment in Europe. But the Agreement has not yet entered into force, since NATO members decided not to ratify it until Russia

---

[47] GA Res. 3472 (XXX) B (1975).
[48] Treaty for the Prohibition of Nuclear Weapons in Latin America and the Caribbean, 14 February 1967.
[49] South Pacific Nuclear Free Zone Treaty, 6 August 1985.
[50] Southeast Asia Nuclear-Weapon-Free Zone Treaty, 15 December 1995.
[51] African Nuclear-Weapon-Free Zone Treaty, 11 April 1996.
[52] Treaty on a Nuclear-Weapon-Free Zone in Central Asia, 8 September 2006.
[53] Final Document – Volume I, NPT/CONF.2010/50 (Vol. I), para. 98.
[54] Treaty Banning Nuclear Weapon Tests in the Atmosphere, in Outer Space and Under Water, 5 August 1963.
[55] Threshold Test Ban Treaty, 3 July 1974, in (1974) 13 *ILM* 906.
[56] Peaceful Nuclear Explosions Treaty, 28 May 1976, in (1976) 15 *ILM* 891.

honoured its commitment to withdraw its military deployments in Moldova and Georgia. Also in response to that, Russia suspended its participation in the CFE Treaty in 2007.[57]

5. WEAPONS OF MASS DESTRUCTION

The three foundational treaties which address the issue of horizontal proliferation of WMD are the 1968 NPT; the 1972 Biological Weapons Convention[58] and the 1993 CWC. It has been questioned whether these three types of weapon could be in the same category. Their common denominator lies in the fact that the consequences of their use cannot be determined and controlled.[59] However, their 'possession prestige' is nowadays different: there is more interest in nuclear weapons than in bio-chemical weapons on the part of states. However, it does not follow that there is no potential for diversion and misuse of biological or chemical agents, including their use for terrorist purposes.

A. Nuclear Weapons

The question whether the use of nuclear weapons is wrongful notoriously represents one of the most challenging issues.[60] The *dispositif* of the Advisory Opinion on the *Legality of the Threat or Use of Nuclear Weapons*, given by the ICJ in 1996, constitutes one of the most controversial and commented upon judicial pronouncements by international legal scholars. In particular, attention has turned towards the problematic sentence which sets the relationship between *jus in bello* and *jus ad bellum*: although the Court stated that the use of nuclear weapons 'would generally be contrary to the rules of … armed conflicts', it could not reach a final conclusion on their legality 'in an extreme situation of self-defence, in which the very survival of a State would be at stake'.[61] The NPT crystallizes the situation in 1968 in regards to the number of declared Nuclear Weapon States (hereinafter 'NWS'). The instrument, which the parties decided to indefinitely extend in 1995,[62] is founded on a basic distinction between those five countries (China, France, Russia, United Kingdom, United States) and the

---

[57] The underlying reason is related to the Russian objection to the US plans to station elements of a missile defence system in Poland and the Czech Republic. In response to Russia's non-performance, in November 2011 the United States announced that it would cease carrying out certain obligations under the CFE Treaty with regard to Russia. See (2012) 106 *AJIL* 166.

[58] Convention on the Prohibition of the Development, Production and Stockpiling of Bacteriological (Biological) and Toxin Weapons and on Their Destruction, 10 April 1972, 1015 *UNTS* 163.

[59] H.A. Strydom, 'Weapons of Mass Destruction', in *Max Planck Encyclopedia of Public International Law*, available at www.mpepil.com, at para. 2.

[60] Cf. Y. Dinstein, 'Customary International Law and the Prohibition of Use of Weapons of Mass Destruction', in G. Gasparini and N. Ronzitti (eds), *The Tenth Anniversary of the CWC's Entry into Force: Achievements and Problems*, Vol. 10 (Rome: Quaderni IAI, English Series, 2007), 87.

[61] *Legality of the Threat or Use of Nuclear Weapons*, supra n. 39, at 266.

[62] NPT/ Conf. 1995/32 (Part I), 11 May 1995, in (1995) 34 *ILM* 959.

other non-nuclear-weapons states (hereinafter 'NNWS'): the former are under a duty 'not to transfer to any recipient whatsoever nuclear weapons or other nuclear explosive devices or control over such weapons or explosive devices directly, or indirectly' (Article I); the latter are obliged not to manufacture or otherwise acquire nuclear arms or other nuclear explosive devices (Article II), in return for which they receive access to nuclear technology and energy for peaceful purposes (Article IV). The NPT has been revealed to be an effective non-proliferation tool after the dissolution of the Soviet Union: all the former federal Republics except Russia adhered to the treaty as NNWS. Nonetheless, the effectiveness of the non-proliferation regime is undermined by the lack of universality, in particular because of the factual importance of the absentees. India, Israel and Pakistan have not yet ratified the NPT and North Korea withdrew from it in 2003: there is evidence that all these countries have nuclear-weapon capabilities, and this cannot but affect the security and stability of their respective regions.

The disarmament pillar of the NPT is represented by Article VI: it was included as a concession to the NNWS to balance the essential discriminatory nature of the rights and obligations under the treaty. As has been discussed above, Article VI contains a duty 'to pursue negotiations in good faith on effective measures relating to cessation of the nuclear arms race at an early date and to nuclear disarmament, and on a Treaty on general and complete disarmament'. Various commentators have emphasized that, particularly in the last decade, NWS prioritized nuclear non-proliferation principles over disarmament.[63] It needs to be emphasized that UN Secretary-General Ban Ki-moon is strongly committed to promoting the 'zero option' in regards to nuclear disarmament: in 2008, he launched a five-point proposal for achieving a world free of nuclear weapons, which included the negotiation of a nuclear-weapons convention.[64] There has indeed been a recent significant change in US policy and strategy regarding the role of nuclear weapons. Not only does the 2010 Nuclear Posture Review recognize the inherent link between non-proliferation and disarmament,[65] but it also contains a revision of its negative security assurance: it declared that 'the United States will not use or threaten to use nuclear weapons against non-nuclear weapons states that are party to the NPT and in compliance with their nuclear non-proliferation obligations'.[66] As a consequence, 'any state eligible for the assurance that uses [chemical or biological weapons] against the United States or its allies and partners would face the prospect of a devastating conventional military response',[67] but not the use of nuclear weapons.

Furthermore, the current US administration has taken various initiatives in the field of nuclear disarmament: President Obama chaired an historical meeting of the Security

---

[63] Joyner, *supra* n.9, at 66.

[64] Ban Ki-moon, Address to the East–West Institute entitled 'The United Nations and Security in a Nuclear-Weapon-Free World', 24 October 2008, available at www.un.org/apps/news/infocus/sgspeeches/search_full.asp?statID=351.

[65] Joyner, *supra* n.33, at 213.

[66] 2010 Nuclear Posture Review Report, at 15. On the security assurances, see H. Krieger, 'Disarmament Obligations of and Assurances of Non-use by Nuclear Weapon States', in T. Giegerich (ed.), *A Wiser Century? Judicial Dispute Settlement, Disarmament and the Laws of War 100 Years after the Second Hague Peace Conference* (Berlin: Duncker & Humbolt, 2009), 107.

[67] 2010 Nuclear Posture Review Report, at 16.

Council on nuclear security which led to the adoption of Resolution 1887 (2009) and convened a Nuclear Security Summit in 2010.[68] The new political scenario facilitated both the conclusion of the new START Treaty in April 2010, which committed Russia and the US to substantially reducing the number of deployed strategic warheads, and the positive outcome of the 2010 NPT Review Conference. After the failure of the 2005 Review Conference to produce a consensus Final Document, the one adopted in 2010 contains substantive language on the interpretation of Article VI: it notes 'the reaffirmation by the nuclear-weapon States of their unequivocal undertaking to accomplish, in accordance with the principle of irreversibility, the total elimination of their nuclear arsenals leading to nuclear disarmament'.[69] Furthermore, in the Action Plan the NWS 'commit to accelerate concrete progress on the steps leading to nuclear disarmament, contained in the Final Document of the 2000 NPT Review Conference, in a way that promotes international stability, peace and undiminished and increased security'.[70] Indeed, the 'thirteen practical steps for the systematic and progressive efforts to implement Article VI',[71] adopted in 2000, included a comprehensive list of commitments, such as the entry into force of the CTBT, the drafting of a fissile material cut-off treaty, and the principle of irreversibility to apply to nuclear disarmament, nuclear and other related arms control and reduction measures.

B. Biological and Chemical Weapons

Both the 1972 Biological and Toxic Weapons Convention (hereinafter 'BTWC') and the 1993 CWC are based on the 'General Purpose Criterion' (hereinafter 'GPC'), contained in Articles I and II respectively, which affirms their comprehensive approach towards chemical and biological disarmament. In other words, all the biological and toxic chemical agents, irrespective of their production method, are by definition weapons and, therefore, subject to the ban, unless they are used in a manner not prohibited by the Conventions. The GPC represents an extraordinary achievement, as it prevents both Conventions from becoming 'locked into the technology prevailing at the time that [they were] negotiated'.[72] The precise definition of what constitutes a 'non-prohibited purpose' under both Conventions becomes crucial. Whereas the BTWC employs the rather generic expression of 'prophylactic, protective or other peaceful purposes', Article II (9) of the CWC is more specific, by identifying certain civilian uses ('industrial, agricultural, research, medical, pharmaceutical or other peaceful purposes'), protective and military purposes not connected with the use of chemical weapons, and finally law enforcement, including domestic riot control.

As far as this latter purpose is concerned, the issue of the permitted uses of both riot control agents and incapacitants was much debated in the CWC 2008 Second Review

---

[68] For the Communiqué and other final documents of the Summit held in Washington on 12–13 April 2010, see www.thenuclearsecuritysummit.org. The Second Nuclear Security Summit was hosted in Seoul in March 2012.
[69] NPT/CONF.2010/50 (Vol. I), para. 79.
[70] *Ibid.*, Action 5.
[71] UN Doc. NPT/CONF.2000/28 (Part I and II), para. 15.
[72] D. Feakes, 'General Purpose Criterion', in *Open Forum on the Chemical Weapons Convention* (2003), 25, at 26, available at www.sussex.ac.uk/spru/hsp/publications.

Conference. It is important to stress that they belong to different classes of agents: while the former are designed to produce local sensory irritant effects, the latter target the human nervous system and other physiological systems. Given that states parties undertake 'not to use riot control agents as a method of warfare',[73] the first problem is whether the armed forces may use extraterritorially such chemicals against civilians for law enforcement. On the basis of the general rules of interpretation under Article 31 of the 1969 Vienna Convention on the Law of Treaties, one might conclude that the CWC allows states to employ tear gas for the maintenance of public order and safety both in situations of belligerent occupation and in the course of peace-support operations, provided that the quantity and the delivery system are consistent with such purpose.[74] The other crucial question is whether other chemical agents, apart from riot control agents, can be lawfully used for law enforcement: various commentators have held that incapacitating agents do not satisfy the qualitative and quantitative requirements for that specific purpose.[75]

Unlike the NPT, the CWC has created a non-discriminatory disarmament and non-proliferation regime. Unlike the BTWC, its Verification Annex details a comprehensive mechanism, based on the work of the Organization for the Prohibition of Chemical Weapons (hereinafter 'OPCW'), and characterized by a mix of cooperative and more forceful verification techniques. Since its entry into force in 1997, the CWC has been successful in making an inventory of the chemical weapons stockpiles in the world, ensuring the physical security of the sites, and promoting an effective destruction programme, although the possessors of the largest stockpiles – the United States and the Russian Federation – and Libya were not able to meet the envisaged deadline of 29 April 2012.[76] Financial constraints, technical difficulties and political resistance have been the main reasons for the slow progress in destruction activities. Therefore, in December 2011 the Conference of the States Parties decided that the possessor states should complete the destruction 'in the shortest time possible': they were required 'to submit a detailed plan', specifying the 'planned completion date'.[77] Finally, the decision provides for a reporting and monitoring system to review the progress towards total chemical disarmament.

There was an expectation that the CWC, thanks to its effective verification regime, would constitute a model for new disarmament efforts. However, it should be borne in

---

[73] Article 1 (5), CWC (1993).

[74] M. Sossai, 'Drugs as Weapons: Disarmament Treaties Facing the Advances in Biochemistry and Non-lethal Weapons Technology', (2010) 15 *JCSL* 5.

[75] D. Fidler, 'The Meaning of Moscow: "Non-lethal" Weapons and International Law in the Early 21st Century', (2005) 87 *IRRC* 525; W. Krutzsch and A. von Wagner, 'Law Enforcement Including Domestic Riot Control: The Interpretation of Article II, Paragraph 9 (d)', (2008) paper presented at the 28th Workshop of the Pugwash Study Group on the Implementation of the Chemical and Biological Weapons Conventions, available at www.pugwash.org/reports/nw/noordwijkAPR2008/papers.htm.

[76] Under Part IV (A) of the CWC's Annex on Implementation and Verification, each state party undertakes to destroy its chemical weapons stockpiles within the final deadline of the 15th anniversary of the treaty's entry into force.

[77] *Decision: Final Extended Deadline of 29 April 2012*, 1 December 2011, Doc. C-16/DEC.11.

mind that the CWC and the OPCW were products of the final phase of the Cold War and have taken advantage of a unique moment in the history of international relations: as a matter of fact, the CTBT has been far from entering into force.

6. RECURRENT ELEMENTS OF DISARMAMENT AND ARMS CONTROL TREATIES

As regards to the main characteristics of disarmament and arms control treaties, the essential elements of most of them constitute the existence of a verification system, the practice of the Review Conferences and the possibility of withdrawal.

A. Verification Mechanisms

Verification forms the basis for the evaluation of states' compliance with disarmament treaties. It has been defined as a 'process covering the entire set of measures aimed at enabling the Parties to an agreement to establish that the conduct of the other Parties is not incompatible with the obligations they have assumed under that agreement'.[78] Various means and methods can be employed, sometimes in combination: voluntary or compulsory declarations; national technical means; verification by international institutions; and on-site inspections.[79]

Three steps characterize any verification process: the gathering of information relating to the fulfilment of disarmament obligations by states parties; the analysis and evaluation of collected data from a technical and legal point of view; and the assessment of the observance of obligations through the legal qualification of state conduct.[80] Significantly, the UN Panel of Government Experts on Verification in all its Aspects refers to verification as 'a tool to strengthen international security. It involves the collection, collation and analysis of information in order to make a judgement as to whether a party is complying with its obligations.'[81]

Verification arrangements, like any other form of international control over state action, take into account the delicate balance of interests between the intrusive character of verification measures and the respect for both state sovereignty and national security, particularly as regards the protection of classified information.[82] The

---

[78] S. Sur (ed.), *Verification of Current Disarmament and Arms Limitation Agreements: Ways, Means and Practices* (Aldershot: Dartmouth, 1991), 13.

[79] B. Tuzmukhamedov, 'Disarmament', in *Max Planck Encyclopedia of Public International Law*, available at www.mpepil.com, at para. 43.

[80] S. Sur, 'Vérification en matière de désarmement', in (1999) 273 *Collected Courses of the Hague Academy of International Law* 9.

[81] *Report of the Panel of Government Experts on Verification in all its Aspects, including the Role of the United Nations in the Field of Verification*, UN Doc. A/61/1028 (2007), at para. 9.

[82] R. Hanski, 'On-site Inspection as a Form of Verification in Arms Control Agreements', in M. Bothe, N. Ronzitti and A. Rosas (eds), *The New Chemical Weapons Convention: Implementation and Prospects* (The Hague: Kluwer Law International, 1998), 37, at 42.

question has been framed in the following terms: how much verification is enough?[83] In order to guarantee an adequate balance of interests, the following key elements need to be considered:[84] the scope of access, that is the precise definition of items and sites under control; the scope and means of fact-finding, which implies both a determination of the relevant information and the identification of the available technical and procedural tools; the respect for the principle of confidentiality in the disclosure of sensitive information; and finally, while it is not in itself an integral part of verification, the type of possible reactions in the case of alleged violations.

It should be emphasized that there is a close relationship between the verification methods and the nature of disarmament and non-proliferation obligations.[85] Those contained in multilateral conventions are deemed as falling within the category of integral (or interdependent) obligations:[86] 'each party's performance is effectively conditioned upon and requires the performance of each of the others'.[87] Though such treaties usually entrust an international body – the OPCW or the International Atomic Energy Agency (hereinafter 'IAEA') – with the task of conducting verification activities, occasionally 'each State Party to the Treaty shall have the right to verify through observations the activities of the other States Parties of the Treaty'.[88] However, the parties to bilateral treaties are those who tend to rely primarily on their own national technical means, which encompass methods like photoreconnaissance satellites, radar installations and electronic surveillance capabilities, in order to assess whether the other party is in compliance with the treaty obligations. Monitoring can be exercised at a distance also in the context of collective mechanisms: the most comprehensive one is the system envisaged by the CTBT, which consists of 337 monitoring stations in more than 90 countries.[89]

It remains that the basic element of the monitoring and verification activities in most international instruments is represented by a voluntary method: the exchange of information and notification among the parties.[90] They often represent the starting point of more intrusive fact-finding means. Both Articles III and VI of the 1993 CWC require states to make various declarations regarding chemical weapons, including production

---

[83] A.S. Krass, *Verification: How Much is Enough?* (London: Taylor and Francis, 1985).

[84] M. Bothe, 'Verification of Disarmament Treaties', in Gasparini and Ronzitti (eds), *supra* n. 60, 45, at 48.

[85] See recently M. Happold, 'The "Injured State" in Case of a Non-proliferation Treaty and the Legal Consequences of Such a Breach', in D.H. Joyner and M. Roscini (eds), *Non-proliferation Law as a Special Regime* (Cambridge: Cambridge University Press, 2012) 175.

[86] The notion was developed by G. Fitzmaurice, 'Second Report on the Law of Treaties', in *Yearbook of the International Law Commission 1957*, Vol. II, at 54.

[87] Commentary to Article 42 of Draft Articles on the Responsibility of States for internationally wrongful acts, in *Yearbook of the International Law Commission 2001*, Vol. II, Part Two, at 119.

[88] Article III (1) of the Treaty on the Prohibition of the Emplacement of Nuclear Weapons and Other Weapons of Mass Destruction on the Sea-Bed and the Ocean Floor and in the Subsoil Thereof (Sea-bed Treaty), 11 February 1971, 955 *UNTS* 115.

[89] For further information see CTBTO Preparatory Commission, *The CTBT Verification Regime: Monitoring the Earth for Nuclear Explosions* (2011), available at www.ctbto.org/fileadmin/user_upload/public_information/2011/2011_Verification_Regime_web.pdf.

[90] Den Dekker, *supra* n.38, at 118–120.

facilities, and any chemical industry. On the basis of the collected data, on-site inspections are routinely carried out by the OPCW.[91] It is significant that inspections under the CWC now cover a major industrial sector: the issue of the disclosure of business information also arises in this context.[92] The text of the CWC sets out general principles of confidentiality relating to the conduct of verification measures by the OPCW. This is guaranteed by the combined effects of three factors: the precise definition of the data required; the conduct of the OPCW staff when acquiring the information; and a regime governing the handling of the information by the OPCW Technical Secretariat.[93]

Article III of the NPT entrusts an external body, the IAEA, with the task of verifying compliance and in particular to detect diversions of nuclear materials from peaceful uses to the production of nuclear weapons. Each NNWS concludes a bilateral safeguards agreement with the IAEA, as defined in the document INFCIRC/153: on the basis of the declarations on nuclear materials for peaceful uses, inspectors of the Agency are engaged in routine inspections of the relevant facilities. The right of access to the sites of a declared facility has been expanded: some 100 states concluded new agreements, according to the Model Additional Protocol, adopted by the IAEA Board of Governors in 1997.[94] At present, the safeguards system should be able to 'provide credible assurance not only about the non-diversion of nuclear material declared by a state but also about the absence of undeclared material and activities'.[95] However, the Additional Protocol is far from becoming universal.[96]

On-site inspections are also provided in bilateral treaties: Article XI of the new START Treaty between Russia and the United States, which entered into force on 5 February 2011, confers the right of the parties to carry out such an activity to confirm the accuracy of the information shared during data exchanges.[97]

Whereas the BTWC has no formal verification regime,[98] the CWC has established the most effective system of inspections. In addition to routine activities, Article IX

---

[91] T. Marauhn, 'Routine Verification under the Chemical Weapons Conventions', in Bothe, Ronzitti and Rosas (eds), *supra* n.82, 219, at 222.

[92] Confidential business information covers 'any information that gives its holder a commercial advantage because it is not widely known to competitors or the general public'. See B. Kellman, D.S. Gualtieri and E.A. Tanzman, 'Disarmament and Disclosure: How Arms Control Verification Can Proceed without Threatening Confidential Business Information', (1995) 36 *Harvard ILJ* 71.

[93] W. Krutzsch and R. Trapp (eds), *Verification Practice under the Chemical Weapons Convention: A Commentary* (The Hague: Kluwer Law, 1999), at 148.

[94] Doc. INFCIRC/540, *Model Protocol Additional to the Agreement(s) between State(s) and the International Atomic Energy Agency for the Application of Safeguards.*

[95] M. El-Baradei, 'Foreword', in *IAEA Safeguards Agreements and Additional Protocols: Verifying Compliance with Nuclear Non-proliferation Undertakings* (Vienna: IAEA, 2008), 2.

[96] M. Asada, 'The Treaty on the Non-proliferation of Nuclear Weapons and the Universalization of the Additional Protocol', (2011) 16 *JCSL* 3.

[97] Treaty between the United States of America and the Russian Federation on Measures for the Further Reduction and Limitation of Strategic Offensive Arms, 8 April 2010, available at www.state.gov/t/avc/newstart/index.htm.

[98] See J.M. Beard, 'The Shortcomings of Indeterminacy in Arms Control Regimes: The Case of the Biological Weapons Convention', (2007) 101 *AJIL* 271.

grants a member state the right to request a 'challenge' inspection of any facility, declared or undeclared, on the territory of another state party that the requesting state suspects of a treaty violation. Various reasons can be found to explain the reluctance of the states parties to use such a radical verification tool, including a lack of confidence in the ability of OPCW inspectors and the fear of retaliatory challenge inspections. Despite the fact that verification mechanisms are of a technical nature, there remains a risk that they are deemed as a substitute for the settlement of political disputes.[99]

Finally, the situation of Iraq after the adoption of Resolution 687 (1991) falls outside this taxonomy. There is a fundamental difference between the practice of inspections under disarmament treaties and the *ad hoc* coercive regime established by the Security Council: the United Nations Special Commission for Iraq (hereinafter 'UNSCOM') had the right to designate any site whatsoever for inspection and to use all the means at its disposal.[100] It has been pointed out that while treaty-based inspections are viewed as an opportunity for the parties to demonstrate compliance to each other, in the context of coercive regimes 'the inspection team is authorized to look for evidence of non-compliance'.[101]

On a broader perspective, one of the main challenges of any verification regime in the field of disarmament is that, apart from the case of a manifest violation, that is the 'smoking gun' scenario, it is difficult to remove all doubts about whether a state is adhering to its obligations. In particular, the evaluation is made more difficult by the dual-use character of relevant goods and technologies, as they can be used for both civil and military purposes. Nonetheless, it is important to discuss the ultimate purpose of verification tools. They serve three essential functions: not only to detect evidence of treaty violations, but also to prevent any risk of cheating and to build confidence. In other words, the very existence of verification mechanisms and procedures should deter violations of a disarmament treaty: a party does not consider the unilateral advantage of shirking treaty commitments, because it is aware that the benefits deriving from that conduct are outweighed by the costs, including the possible consequences if the activity were detected.[102] In addition, by providing states with clear and timely information about the other parties' commitment to the disarmament process, verification regimes contribute to improving transparency and predictability, reducing the risk of accidental war and preventing a surprise attack. Therefore, they play a role similar to the confidence-building measures (hereinafter 'CBMs'), which, nonetheless, remain conceptually distinct: the objective of the CBMs is to translate certain principles of international law, that is the ban on the use of force in international relations, into positive action so as to provide credibility to states' affirmations.[103] CBMs include:

---

[99] J. Hart and V. Fedchenko, 'WMD Inspection and Verification Regimes: Political and Technical Challenges', in N.E. Busch and D.H. Joyner (eds), *Combating Weapons of Mass Destruction: The Future of International Non-proliferation Policy* (Athens, GA: University of Georgia Press, 2009), 95, at 113.

[100] Sur, *supra* n.80, at 82; H. Ruiz Fabri, 'The UNSCOM Experience: Lessons from an Experiment', (2002) 13 *EJIL* 153. See also below, section 7.

[101] Hart and Fedchenko, *supra* n.99, at 99.

[102] See K.W. Abbott, '"Trust but Verify": The Production of Information in Arms Control Treaties and other International Agreements', (1993) 26 *Cornell Intl LJ* 1.

[103] Goldblat, *supra* n.22, at 10.

exchange of information about military expenditures; prior notifications of military manoeuvres; and the presence of foreign observers. A paradigmatic example of such measures is those adopted in the context of the CSCE/OSCE process.[104]

B. Review Conferences

Arms control and disarmament treaties generally include a clause which establishes a time-frame for convening a Review Conference on a regular basis. There are differences among the treaties as regards to the procedure, as a comparison between Article VIII (3) of the NPT, Article 12 of the BTWC and Article VIII (22) of the CWC makes clear. However, an analysis of the practice records that Review Conferences are convened every five years and constitute a regular element of the implementation process within the framework of all the three WMD regimes.[105] Furthermore, the review mechanism has become a sort of permanent process, thanks to the work of preparatory committees which discuss both procedural and substantive issues to be included in the final agenda. This preparatory activity is a key element of the successful outcome of a Conference. It should be borne in mind that Review Conferences are distinct from revision and amendment procedures. During the former, states parties take stock of developments in the implementation of treaty obligations, by way of a systematic analysis of each provision. Article VIII of the CWC makes clear that the Review Conference is a special session of the Conference of the States Parties and therefore enjoys the same powers of this organ; it considers 'any questions, matters or issues within the scope of this Convention', oversees the implementation of it, and undertakes 'reviews of the operation' every five years. Although the Review Conference might formulate revision recommendations, the amendment procedure is governed by special provisions included in Article XV of the CWC. One cannot exclude that in specific circumstances, a Review Conference may take decisions affecting the content or the scope of application of the relevant agreement. This was the case of the NPT Review Conference held in 1995, which decided upon the indefinite extension of the treaty.

The outcome of the Review Conference is a final document. It is usually composed of a political declaration, which may be complemented by a more elaborate instrument on substantive issues. From a strictly legal perspective, these texts as such are not legally binding. In any case, they reflect state practice and may be invoked for the interpretation of the Convention, as provided by Article 31 of the 1969 Vienna Convention on the Law of Treaties.

The assessment of the implementation steps undertaken by states parties constitutes the primary function of the review process. An essential element is its multilateral character: the Conference may adopt guidelines to assist states in fulfilling effectively their obligations, and, on a broader perspective, to keep the balance within the treaty

---

[104] See Z. Lachowski, 'Confidence-Building Measures', in *Max Planck Encyclopedia of Public International Law*, available at www.mpepil.com.

[105] S. Sur, 'A Comparison between NPT, BWC and CWC Provisions and Practices', in Institute of International Humanitarian Law (IIHL), *The Chemical Weapons Convention between Disarmament and International Humanitarian Law* (Sanremo: IIHL, 2008), 35.

between the various provisions, which may be perceived by the parties in a different way. A further function is assessing the effectiveness of the verification system: this does not mean that the Conference is entrusted with the task of solving specific country-related problems; rather, it should suggest ways to improve the mechanism. Finally, as a forum of cooperation and consultations among the parties at various levels, the Review Conference performs the function of a CBM, which may contribute to prevent or solve possible disputes. However, irreconcilable positions could undermine the whole review process: tensions were so acute within the 2005 NPT Review Conference that the parties were completely unable to find a final compromise and the outcome was a complete failure.

C. Withdrawal Clauses

Some commentators have raised questions relating to the effects of war on disarmament agreements: whether an armed conflict may cause their suspension is not clear.[106] In any case, under the three global WMD treaties, member states have the right to withdraw, subject to a requirement to provide some advance notice to all other parties and to the Security Council, when supreme interests are jeopardized by extraordinary events.[107] Though the mere fact of the outbreak of a conflict would not be a sufficient reason for withdrawal, a state may invoke a grave breach of the treaty or even the acquisition of the relevant category of weapons by a hostile non-party neighbour.[108]

There is no doubt that withdrawal is not a tool at states' disposal in order merely to absolve themselves of their obligations. After numerous allegations that North Korea was pursuing a nuclear programme, this country eventually announced its decision to withdraw from the NPT in 2003. The Security Council in Resolution 1718 (2006) demanded that North Korea 'immediately retract its announcement of withdrawal from the Treaty' and 'act strictly in accordance with' the NPT. Assuming that eliminating the right of withdrawal would not be desirable as it would discourage ratification by additional states, various proposals have been advanced to make withdrawal more difficult, such as providing the convening of a special Conference of the States Parties upon the announcement of an intent to withdraw; or obliging any state that implements a withdrawal to forfeit the right to retain or to use any of the technology or goods it acquired as a treaty party.[109] Interestingly, Resolution 1887 goes in the same direction when it encourages states 'to require as a condition of nuclear exports that the recipient State agree that [in case of withdrawal] the supplier State would have the right to

---

[106] See N. Ronzitti, 'Assessment of the 1993 Chemical Convention: Light and Shadow', in Gasparini and Ronzitti (eds), *supra* n.60, 33, at 36.

[107] Cf. Article X of the NPT; Article XIII of the BTWC; Article XVI of the CWC; see J.D. Fry, 'Sovereign Equality under the Chemical Weapons Convention: Doughnuts over Holes', (2010) 15 *JCSL* 45, at 63.

[108] Cf. A. Gioia, 'The Chemical Weapons Convention and its Application in Time of Armed Conflict', in Bothe, Ronzitti and Rosas (eds), *supra* n.82, 379, at 393. See recently G. den Dekker and T. Coppen, 'Termination and Suspension of, and Withdrawal from, WMD Arms Control Agreements in Light of the General Law of Treaties', (2012) 17 *JCSL* 25.

[109] The Weapons of Mass Destruction Commission, *Weapons of Terror: Freeing the World of Nuclear, Biological, and Chemical Arms* (Stockholm, 1 June 2006), 51.

require the return of nuclear material and equipment provided prior to such ... withdrawal'.[110]

In any case, it remains true that states could not withdraw from the obligations deriving from international humanitarian law, provided that they are either of a customary nature or contained within a treaty binding on them, as is the case of the 1925 Geneva Protocol for the Prohibition of the Use in War of Asphyxiating, Poisonous or other Gases, and of Bacteriological Methods of Warfare.

7. TRANSFER CONTROLS AS A TOOL FOR INTERNATIONAL SECURITY

Recent global trends pose new challenges to non-proliferation: a wider class of dual-use items is now available, partly due to technological innovations and partly as a result of the changes in the relevant marketplace.[111] In addition, the black market network created by A.Q. Khan, that delivered nuclear capabilities to various countries, revealed all the dangers resulting from the illicit trafficking.[112] There is a growing risk that proliferation-relevant technologies will continue to be spread more widely:[113] not only because 'countries remain interested in the illicit acquisition of weapons of mass destruction'[114] but also because non-state actors might be potential customers.

State export controls continue to play a fundamental role in preventing the transfer of materials and technologies which would assist other states or terrorist groups in acquiring WMD. An increasing number of states have joined the various informal, voluntary, non-treaty-based arrangements, which are complementary to treaty regimes, to improve the export controls on dual-use materials related to WMD: while the Australia Group covers biological and chemical agents, the Zangger Committee and Nuclear Suppliers Group (hereinafter 'NSG') establish standards and guidelines governing nuclear transfers. Other relevant export control regimes, covering for instance WMD delivery systems, include the Missile Technology Control Regime, and the Wassenaar Arrangement on Export Controls for Conventional Arms and Dual-Use Goods and Technologies.

In relation to the arms trade, a significant soft law initiative is the UN Register on Conventional Arms,[115] which collects information provided by states on a voluntary

---

[110] UNSC Res. 1887 (2009), at para. 18. Such a condition is applicable in the event the recipient state should not only withdraw but also 'be found by the IAEA Board of Governors to be in non-compliance with its IAEA safeguards agreement'.

[111] See *inter alia* S. Bauer, A. Dunne and I. Mićić, 'Strategic Trade Controls: Countering the Proliferation of Weapons of Mass Destruction', in *SIPRI Yearbook 2011* (Oxford: Oxford University Press, 2011), 431.

[112] See M. Fitzpatrick, *Nuclear Black Markets: Pakistan, A.Q. Khan and the Rise of Proliferation Networks* (London: The International Institute for Strategic Studies, 2007).

[113] S.A. Jones, M.D. Beck and S. Gahlaut, 'Trade Controls and International Security', in Busch and Joyner (eds), *supra* n.99, 118, at 121.

[114] M. El-Baradei, 'Saving Ourselves From Self-Destruction', *New York Times*, 12 February 2004.

[115] UNGA Res. 46/36 L (1991).

basis regarding the transfer of seven military equipment categories: battle tanks, armoured combat vehicles, large calibre artillery systems, combat aircraft, attack helicopters, warships, and missiles or missile systems. A key issue is the future interaction between the UN Register and the reporting mechanisms under a possible Arms Trade Treaty.[116]

In recent years, one of the most delicate issues in the context of export controls has been the revision of the NSG Guidelines for the export of nuclear materials, equipment and technology. In 2008, on the basis of a proposal made by the United States, which had previously concluded a bilateral nuclear cooperation agreement with India,[117] the NSG members granted India an exemption from some of the export guidelines, that is those requiring the recipient states to have full-scope IAEA safeguards. The waiver allowed nuclear trade with India for peaceful purposes, with the exception of enrichment and reprocessing transfers.[118] This is confirmed by the revised guidelines for the export of uranium-enrichment and spent-fuel reprocessing equipment and technology, approved at the NSG meeting in June 2011, that bar the transfer of such sensitive technologies to a state, unless it is 'a Party to the Treaty on the Non-Proliferation of Nuclear Weapons and is in full compliance with its obligations under the Treaty'.[119]

Finally, a major concern has been that terrorist groups might build a device with illegally acquired WMD-related materials, either purchased on the black market or stolen from vulnerable sites. The IAEA Illicit Trafficking Database contains 399 confirmed incidents involving nuclear 'unauthorized possession and related criminal activities'.[120] A crucial aspect of the Bush administration was its preference to react through coalitions of the willing: its response to such a threat was the creation of various multilateral initiatives and partnerships, which are not based on legally binding instruments. Announced in 2004 as an additional step to improve physical security, the Global Threat Reduction Initiative has been shown to be an effective tool aimed at

---

[116] See P. Holtom and M. Bromley, *Implementing an Arms Trade Treaty: Lessons on Reporting and Monitoring from Existing Mechanisms*, SIPRI Policy Paper No. 28, July 2011. The United Nations Conference on the Arms Trade Treaty (hereinafter 'ATT'), which was held from 2 to 27 July 2012 in New York, failed to reach agreement on a treaty text. Nevertheless, a group of over 90 countries expressed in a joint statement their determination 'to secure an ATT as soon as possible – one that will bring about a safer world for the sake of all humanity'. The statement read by Mexico on 27 July 2012 is available at www.acronym.org.uk/sites/default/files/ATT_27July_jointstatement.pdf. A renewed conference was convened in New York in March 2013 and the Arms Trade Treaty was finally adopted by the General Assembly on 2 April 2013.

[117] F.Z. Ntoubandi, 'Reflections on the USA–India Atomic Energy Cooperation', (2008) 13 *JCSL* 273.

[118] See the text of the NSG statement in D.G. Kimball, 'Text, Analysis, and Response to NSG Statement on Civil Nuclear Cooperation with India', (2008), available at www.armscontrol.org/node/3345.

[119] INFCIRC/254/Rev.10, *Communication Received from the Permanent Mission of the Netherlands regarding Certain Member States' Guidelines for the Export of Nuclear Material, Equipment and Technology*, 26 July 2011.

[120] *The IAEA Illicit Trafficking Database*, Factsheet, 2011, available at www-ns.iaea.org/downloads/security/itdb-fact-sheet.pdf.

securing, removing, relocating or disposing of vulnerable materials worldwide, in particular highly enriched uranium.[121] But the most well-known and controversial partnership is the Proliferation Security Initiative (hereinafter 'PSI'). Launched in May 2003, the PSI was meant as an association of like-minded countries, committed to strengthening the necessary capabilities to detect and interdict vessels and aircrafts suspected to be trafficking WMD, their delivery systems and related materials. It has been widely discussed whether the Statement of Interdiction Principles, that is the soft law document, which lies at the heart of this initiative, is in conformity with international law.[122]

As for maritime interdiction, the main question relates to the measures that states are allowed to take on the high seas. WMD proliferation activities do not constitute an exception to the general rule included in Article 110 of the UN Convention on the Law of the Sea (hereinafter 'UNCLOS'),[123] which provides that a warship that encounters on the high seas a foreign ship, is not justified in boarding it. Consent is therefore essential: the PSI principles indeed refer to this customary rule, asking states 'to seriously consider providing consent under the appropriate circumstances to the boarding and searching of its own flag vessels by other states'.[124] Article 110 UNCLOS leaves open the possibility that acts of interference might derive from powers conferred by treaty. The United States has concluded several bilateral boarding agreements with significant flag states: Liberia, Panama, the Marshall Islands, Cyprus, Croatia and Belize. The treaties confer reciprocal rights and duties, even though only the United States has the power to arrest and inspect suspected vessels on the high seas. Finally, the 2005 Protocol to the 1988 SUA Convention[125] also establishes a boarding regime in relation to ships suspected of transporting WMD or radioactive or fissile material, based on a simplified system of authorizations.

---

[121] R. Alcaro, N. Pirozzi and N. Ronzitti, 'The Global Initiative and Other Multilateral Initiatives and Partnerships against Nuclear Terrorism', in N. Ronzitti (ed.), *Coordinating Global and Regional Efforts to Combat WMD Terrorism*, Vol. 15 (Rome: Quaderni IAI, English Series, 2009), 75, at 99.

[122] D. Guilfoyle, *Shipping Interdiction and the Law of the Sea* (Cambridge: Cambridge University Press, 2009); N. Ronzitti, 'The Proliferation Security Initiative and International Law', in A. Fischer Lescano, H.-P. Gasser, T. Marauhn and N. Ronzitti (eds), *Frieden in Freiheit: Festschrift für Michael Bothe zum 70. Geburtstag* (Baden Baden: Nomos, 2008), 269; M. Malirsch and F. Prill, 'The Proliferation Security Initiative and the 2005 Protocol to the SUA Convention', (2007) 67 *ZaöRV* 229; W. Heintschel von Heinegg, 'The Proliferation Security Initiative: Security vs. Freedom of Navigation?', (2005) 35 *Israel YB Hum Rts* 181; M. Byers, 'Policing the High Seas: The Proliferation Security Initiative', (2004) 98 *AJIL* 526.

[123] United Nations Convention on the Law of the Sea, 10 December 1982, 1833 *UNTS* 396.

[124] PSI, Statement of Interdiction Principles, available at www.state.gov/t/isn/c27726.htm.

[125] IMO Doc. LEG/CONF.15/21, Protocol of 2005 to the Convention for the Suppression of Unlawful Acts Against the Safety of Maritime Navigation, 1 November 2005.

8. THE ROLE OF THE UN SECURITY COUNCIL

Given the failure to fulfil its mandate under Article 26 of the UN Charter, the role of the Security Council in the field of disarmament and non-proliferation is related to its functions under Chapter VII of the UN Charter. The measures which have been taken by this body under this provision can be classified under three different typologies. First, the Security Council has created a coercive regime for a specific situation, as in the case of Iraq. It has already been pointed out that Resolution 687 (1991), whose substance is that of a peace treaty,[126] imposed strict disarmament obligations involving the destruction or removal of all biological and chemical weapons as well as of all ballistic missiles with a range greater than 150 kilometres and related materials and sites. Moreover, the Security Council decided on a system of monitoring and verification based on the work of UNSCOM, with the cooperation of the IAEA.[127] Due to the failure of Iraq to cooperate, by denying full access to sites until the economic sanctions were lifted, the inspectors were withdrawn in December 1998: a few days later the United States and the United Kingdom launched military strikes against selected targets in Iraq. The inspections regime was then reintroduced by the Security Council with the adoption of Resolution 1284 (1999), which replaced UNSCOM with the United Nations Monitoring, Verifications and Inspections Commission, whose functions were renovated and strengthened through Resolution 1441 (2002). Secondly, all of the major disarmament and non-proliferation agreements recognize a role for the Security Council in enforcing compliance.[128] Under Article VI of the BTWC, the Security Council may receive a complaint from any state 'which finds that any other ... Party is acting in breach of obligations deriving from the provisions of the Convention'. The procedure under the CWC is more elaborate, since it first involves the organs of the OPCW, that is the Executive Council and the Conference, which, only in cases of particular gravity and urgency, may bring the matter directly to the attention of the UN General Assembly or the Security Council.[129] As far as the NPT is concerned, Article XII (C) of the Statute of the IAEA provides that the Board of Governors 'shall report the non-compliance to all members and to the Security Council and General Assembly of the United Nations'. The IAEA reported various cases to the Security Council, including Iraq in 1991,[130] Romania in 1992, Libya in 2004,[131] Syria in 2011[132] and, most notably, North Korea and Iran.

The North Korean nuclear crisis erupted when it announced its intention to withdraw from the NPT in 1993 but it reached its climax between October 2002 and January 2003, when the government of Pyongyang first admitted the existence of a clandestine

---

[126] C. Gray, 'After the Ceasefire: Iraq, the Security Council and the Use of Force', (1994) 65 *BYIL* 135, at 144.

[127] T. Marauhn, 'The Implementation of Disarmament and Arms Control Obligations Imposed upon Iraq by the Security Council', (1992) 52 *ZaöRV* 781; D. Fleck, 'Developments of the Law of Arms Control as a Result of the Iraq–Kuwait Conflict', (2002) 13 *EJIL* 105.

[128] Goldblat, *supra* n.22, at 342.

[129] Article VIII (36); Article XII (4) of the CWC.

[130] IAEA Doc. GC(XXXV)/RES/568, 20 September 1991.

[131] IAEA Doc. GOV/2004/18, 10 March 2004.

[132] IAEA Doc. GOV/2011/41, 9 June 2011.

programme to enrich uranium for nuclear weapons and then communicated its decision to eventually withdraw from the treaty.[133] The IAEA Board of Governors referred the case to the Security Council on the ground that the country had violated its safeguards agreement.[134] But it was only after North Korea conducted nuclear tests that the Security Council intervened by imposing sanctions measures.[135]

As for their content, it is useful to look at similar measures which have been adopted with regard to Iran. The Security Council initially adopted Resolution 1696 under Article 40 of the UN Charter, demanding that the government of Tehran 'suspend all enrichment-related and reprocessing activities, including research and development' as requested by the resolution of the IAEA Board of Governors that reported the matter to the Security Council.[136] Since 2002, following revelations which indicated that Iran was building a large underground nuclear-related facility and a heavy water production plant, the IAEA Director General has systematically reported to the Board of Governors on the concerns about the possible military dimension of Iran's nuclear programme.[137] After a period of cooperation between 2003 and 2005, in which Iran admitted its past contacts with clandestine nuclear supply networks and provided design information with respect to facilities where undeclared activities had taken place, Iran announced that it would resume uranium enrichment and cease abiding by the terms of the Additional Protocol, which was signed in 2003 but never ratified. While the IAEA continues to verify the non-diversion of declared nuclear material at the nuclear facilities declared by Iran under its Safeguards Agreement, it is unable to provide credible assurance about the absence of undeclared nuclear material and activities in Iran, due to a lack of transparency by the Tehran authorities, including by not implementing the Additional Protocol. Therefore the IAEA cannot 'conclude that all nuclear material in Iran is in peaceful activities'.[138]

In December 2006, Resolution 1737 imposed sanctions designed to 'constrain Iran's development of sensitive technologies in support of its nuclear and missile programmes'. It provided for an embargo on the export to and import from Iran of certain goods and technology related to nuclear weapons. Subsequent resolutions of the Security Council reaffirmed Iran's obligation 'to suspend all reprocessing, heavy water-related and enrichment-related activities' and strengthened the measures, by introducing *inter alia* a ban on the export of all arms and related materials from Iran and a ban on the supply of the seven categories of conventional weapons identified in

---

[133] Letter, dated 10 January 2003, from the North Korean Ministry of Foreign Affairs to the French Presidency of the United Nations Security Council and the States Parties of the Nuclear Non-proliferation Treaty, UN Doc. S/2003/91.

[134] IAEA Doc. GOV/2003/14, 12 February 2003. See M. Asada, 'Arms Control Law in Crisis – A Study of the North Korean Nuclear Issue', (2004) 9 *JCSL* 331.

[135] UNSC Res. 1718 (2006); 1874 (2009); 1928 (2010); 1985 (2011).

[136] IAEA Doc. GOV/2006/14, Implementation of the NPT Safeguards Agreement in the Islamic Republic of Iran, Resolution of the Board of Governors adopted on 4 February 2006. See Y. Ronen, *The Iran Nuclear Issue* (Oxford: Hart Publishing, 2010).

[137] IAEA Doc. GOV/2004/83, Implementation of the IAEA Safeguards Agreement in the Islamic Republic of Iran, 15 November 2004.

[138] IAEA Doc. GOV/2011/65, 8 November 2011; see W.Q. Bowen and J. Brewer, 'Iran's Nuclear Challenge: Nine Years and Counting', (2011) 87 *International Affairs* 923.

the UN Register.¹³⁹ It is noteworthy that the Security Council, having recognized Iran's failure to carry out its NPT-based obligations and requiring Iran to act in conformity with them, has actually introduced more extensive obligations,¹⁴⁰ including the duty not to acquire 'an interest in any commercial activity in another State involving uranium mining, production or use of nuclear materials and technology'.¹⁴¹

The third typology of Security Council measures covers those addressing the threat represented by the use of WMD by non-state actors. Resolution 1540 is aimed at filling the lacunae in the disarmament and non-proliferation treaties and in the export control regimes: their focus on horizontal state-to-state proliferation; the lack of universalization of the existing treaties; the lack of an organization having the task of addressing the proliferation of biological weapons and agents; and the difficulties under the current regimes in taking enforcement measures against noncompliant countries. As regards the relationship between Resolution 1540 and the existing legal framework, the Council affirmed that 'none of the obligations ... shall be interpreted so as to conflict with or alter the rights and obligations of States Parties to the Nuclear Non-Proliferation Treaty, the Chemical Weapons Convention and the Biological and Toxin Weapons Convention or alter the responsibilities of the International Atomic Energy Agency or the Organization for the Prohibition of Chemical Weapons'.¹⁴² There is no doubt that Resolution 1540 plays a complementary role with respect to the existing treaties. Its paragraph 2 states that all states must 'adopt and enforce appropriate effective laws which prohibit any non-State actor to manufacture, acquire, possess, develop, transport, transfer or use nuclear, chemical or biological weapons and their means of delivery': which implies that states are required to enact 'specific legislation that also penalizes prohibited activities of non-State actors'.¹⁴³ Furthermore, the resolution addresses the problem of the lack of universal standards for trade controls,¹⁴⁴ by imposing various binding measures, including the obligation '[to] establish, develop, review and maintain appropriate effective national export and trans-shipment controls over [WMD-related] items'. Finally, a Committee has been established to oversee the implementation of Resolution 1540, initially for a period of two years. Its mandate has been extended by subsequent resolutions until 25 April 2021.¹⁴⁵

9. CONCLUSION

As disarmament law is in essence treaty law, its efficacy is strictly related to the achievement of the goal of universality. While the non-adherence of India, Israel and

---

¹³⁹ UNSC Res. 1747 (2007); 1803 (2008); 1835 (2008); 1887 (2009); 1929 (2010).
¹⁴⁰ See J. Calamita, 'Sanctions, Countermeasures, and the Iranian Nuclear Issue', (2009) 42 *Vanderbilt JTL* 1393, at 1407.
¹⁴¹ UNSC Res. 1929 (2010), para. 7.
¹⁴² UNSC Res. 1540 (2004), para. 5.
¹⁴³ Report of the Committee Established Pursuant to Resolution 1540 (2004), UN Doc. S/2006/257 (2006), at 12.
¹⁴⁴ Jones, Beck and Gahlaut, *supra* n.113, at 127.
¹⁴⁵ UNSC Res. 1673 (2006); 1810 (2008); 1977 (2011).

Pakistan constitutes real limitations on the crucial aims of the NPT,[146] the CWC represents a successful example of quasi-universal ratification. A high price has sometimes been paid to attain that objective, even during the negotiation process. For example, at the very last moment of the Dublin Conference on the CCM, a compromise formula was reached as regards to the relations with states not party to the Convention, in order to take into account the concerns of the NATO countries about effects of the Convention on their military relationships with the United States, which was deemed unlikely to join the Convention. Article 21(3) allows states parties to 'engage in military cooperation and operations with States not party to this Convention that might engage in activities prohibited to a State Party'.[147] The provision simply appears to address an issue of legal interoperability in the context of a coalition force,[148] but it also introduces some elements of ambiguity that could undermine the comprehensive character of the CCM. To give just one example, it is unclear whether an aircraft equipped with cluster munitions may be stored within the jurisdiction of a state party.

The CCM follows the model of all the recent disarmament treaties, since the adoption of the CWC in 1993, which contain norms of *jus in bello*. Article 1 of the CCM, for example, prohibits the production and the stockpiling of cluster munitions as well as their use. But disarmament law and international humanitarian law serve different, though related purposes: as for the former, lessening the probability of the outbreak of war, while with the latter preserving certain core humanitarian values during hostilities. In post-conflict situations, disarmament activities involve the collection, control and disposal of small arms, ammunition, explosives, and light and heavy weapons from both combatants and the civilian population.[149] This task has been performed by various UN peacekeeping operations, including MONUSCO in the Democratic Republic of Congo, as an essential element of the peace-building efforts.[150] In the immediate aftermath of conflict, landmines and explosive remnants of war pose a serious threat to the population; suffice here to recall that Article 4 (1) of the CCM requires states parties to clear and destroy failed or abandoned munitions and unexploded sub-munitions and bomblets in areas under their jurisdiction or *de facto* control.

The above analysis has investigated the place of disarmament in the maintenance of international peace and security. The principal organs of the United Nations have performed various functions, that have been summarized as follows:[151] (a) *faire le*

---

[146] See also The Weapons of Mass Destruction Commission, *supra* n.109, at 50.

[147] T. Arntsen, 'Article 21', in G. Nystuen (ed.), *The Convention on Cluster Munitions: A Commentary* (Oxford: Oxford University Press, 2010), 541, at 571 *et seq.*; T. Di Ruzza, 'The Convention on Cluster Munitions: Towards a Balance between Humanitarian and Military Considerations?', (2008) 47 *Military Law and the Law of War Review* 405.

[148] Cf. Rule 164 of the HPCR Manual on International Law Applicable to Air and Missile Warfare (2009), at http://ihlresearch.org/amw/HPCR%20Manual.pdf.

[149] See C. Bell, 'Peace Agreements: Their Nature and Legal Status', (2006) 100 *AJIL* 373.

[150] See J.N. Clark, 'UN Peacekeeping in the Democratic Republic of Congo: Reflections on MONUSCO and its Contradictory Mandate', (2011) 15 *Journal of International Peacekeeping* 363.

[151] S. Sur, 'Conclusion générale', in R. Medhi (ed.), *Le Nations Unies face aux armes de destruction massive* (Paris: Pedone, 2004), 167, at 174.

droit, as contributed by the General Assembly, in particular with its first special session by creating the Conference on Disarmament; (b) *dire le droit*, as mainly undertaken by the Security Council when it qualified the proliferation of WMD as a threat to peace, or when the ICJ gave its advisory opinion on the legality of the threat or use of nuclear weapons; (c) *contribuer à la verification du respect du droit*, as the coercive regime established by the Security Council in Iraq sought to achieve; finally, (d) *faire respecter le droit*, which is the purpose of the sanctions measures adopted under Chapter VII of the Charter in recent years. It is, of course, within the powers of the Security Council to authorize the use of force to counter the threat posed by the proliferation of WMD, though it has yet to do so.

The vision of a world free of WMD is at the core of the commitment to disarmament of Secretary-General Ban Ki-moon.[152] If positive momentum has been created by the initiatives taken by the Obama administration, little progress has been achieved in relation to the controversial nuclear programmes of North Korea and Iran.[153] These contrasting results are a consequence of the radical change in the approach to non-proliferation issues. Rather than the product of a negotiation process, arms control has increasingly become, 'a *coercive* process designed to produce capitulation',[154] based on demands and pressures to get states to comply. Such a complex scenario has constituted a hard challenge for the organizers of a conference on the establishment of a Middle East zone free of WMD.[155]

---

[152] See recently 'Remarks to Nuclear Disarmament Conference', 24 October 2011, available at www.un.org/apps/news/infocus/sgspeeches/search_full.asp?statID=1353.

[153] The P5+1 (China, France, Germany, Russia, the United Kingdom and the United States) resumed the negotiations with Iran on its nuclear programme in 2012, with a view to agreeing confidence-building measures.

[154] S.M. Walt, 'Whatever Happened to Arms Control?', 29 March 2012, available at http://walt.foreignpolicy.com/posts/2012/03/29/whatever_happened_to_arms_control.

[155] Jaakko Laajava was appointed as 'facilitator' by a joint statement issued by Ban Ki-moon and the Governments of the Russian Federation, the United Kingdom and the United States. UN Doc. SG/2180, 14 October 2011.

3. The prohibition of threats of force
Nicholas Tsagourias

1. INTRODUCTION

Article 2(4) of the United Nations Charter sets out the rule prohibiting not just the use of force, but also the threat of force in international relations.[1] This twin prohibition is presented as one of the main pillars of the international system.[2] Although Article 2(4) dissects the threat of force from its actual use, treating them as independent legal proscriptions, little attention has been paid to the meaning and content of the notion of 'threat of force' or to the legal scope of its prohibition.[3] In contrast, the prohibition of the use of force has received extended scholarly and juridical attention even if its scope is still contested. This chapter proposes to examine the meaning and scope of the prohibition of the threat of force by looking into relevant case law and international practice before assessing the legal authority of the rule.

2. THE LEGAL STIPULATION OF THE PROHIBITION OF THE THREAT OF FORCE

As was said above, the prohibition of the threat or use of force set out in Article 2(4) of the UN Charter is one of the guiding principles and norms of international law, because it is the pre-requisite for maintaining international peace and security; one of the principal, perhaps the most important, objectives of the international system. The importance of this norm becomes apparent if it is compared with the pre-1945 rules on the use of force. The regime of the League of Nations (hereinafter 'LoN') did not prohibit the use of force but, instead, introduced certain procedural mechanisms to delay and perhaps prevent the outbreak of war among its members.[4] Since the term

---

[1] Article 2(4) reads as follows: 'All Members shall refrain in their international relations from the threat or use of force against the territorial integrity or political independence of any state, or in any other manner inconsistent with the Purposes of the United Nations.'

[2] As Judge Weeramantry observed, 'the principle of non-use of threats is thus as firmly grounded as the principle of non-use of force and, in its many formulations, it has not been made subject to any exceptions'. Dissenting Opinion, Judge Weeramantry in Legality of the *Threat or Use of Nuclear Weapons* (Advisory Opinion) [1996] ICJ Rep. 226, 526 (hereinafter referred to as *Nuclear Weapons*).

[3] R. Sadurska, 'Threats of Force', (1988) 82 *AJIL* 239; M. Roscini, 'Threats of Armed Force and Contemporary International Law', (2007) 54 *Neth. ILRev.* 229; N. Stürchler, *The Threat of Force in International Law* (Cambridge: Cambridge University Press, 2009); D. Kritsiotis, 'Close Encounters of a Sovereign Kind', (2009) 20 *EJIL* 299.

[4] Articles 10–16, Covenant of the League of Nations (1919).

'war' was also given a technical meaning, uses of force as well as threats of force fell outside the LoN's regime. In fact, demonstrations of force, ultimata and other intimidating acts were recurrent events in that era.

That said, the Council of the LoN had the power to advise members on the measures they should take in order to protect a state in case of a threat or danger of aggression,[5] and Article 11 of the LoN's Covenant declared that any war or threat of war was a matter of concern to the whole League. However, the aforementioned article did not prohibit war or the threat of war, as such, but formed the basis of the LoN's collective security system which, in any case, remained underused. The Pact of Paris (1928), which was the next major development in this area, curbed the freedom of states to wage war as an instrument of national policy but did not prohibit the threat of war, or indeed the threat or the use of force in any form.[6]

Attitudes, however, towards threats of force hardened after World War II, due to the fact that in the preceding era states were not only at liberty to issue such threats (setting off many adverse consequences) but had often brought them to fruition by resorting to war. One could mention, in this respect, the Italian ultimatum to Greece in 1940 to allow free passage to Italian forces and the occupation of certain Greek areas. Its rejection by Greece led to the outbreak of war between Greece and Italy.[7] Equally indicative are German threats towards Czechoslovakia and Austria which led to the invasion and annexation of Czechoslovakia, and the *Anschluss* with Austria.[8]

In light of such experiences, Article 2(4) was introduced which, breaking with the past, prohibits not only the use of force but also the threat of force. The *travaux préparatoires* reveal little about the content of the prohibition; instead, they demonstrate an overwhelming consensus among the delegates to the San Francisco conference that the twin prohibition was necessary in order to maintain international peace and order.[9] That objective was also supported by the obligation introduced in Article 2(3) to settle disputes peacefully and by the establishment of a collective security mechanism in Chapter VII of the UN Charter.

Since 1945, the prohibition of the threat of force has been restated and reaffirmed quite frequently,[10] but this rather mechanical repetition of the rule has deflected

---

[5] Article 10, Covenant of the League of Nations (1919).
[6] Indeed, the full title of the Pact was the General Treaty for the Renunciation of War as an Instrument of National Policy (1928).
[7] *Greece 1940–1949: A Documentary History*, edited and translated by Richard Clogg (Houndmills, Basingstoke: Palgrave Macmillan, 2002), at 34–36.
[8] Judgment of the International Military Tribunal for the Trial of German Major War Criminals, (1946) 41 *AJIL* 172, at 192–197.
[9] Stürchler, *supra* n.3, at 19–25.
[10] *Case Concerning Military and Paramilitary Activities in and against Nicaragua (Nicaragua v. United States of America)*, Merits, Judgment of 27 June 1986, [1986] ICJ Rep. 14, paras 187–190 (hereinafter referred to as the *Nicaragua Case*); *Legal Consequences of the Construction of a Wall in the Occupied Palestinian Territory*, Advisory Opinion of 9 July 2004, [2004] ICJ Rep. 200, para. 87 (hereinafter referred to as *Wall*); Declaration on Principles of International Law Concerning Friendly Relations and Co-operation Among States in Accordance with the Charter of the United Nations (1970), G.A Res. 2625 (XXV); On the Definition of Aggression (1974), G.A. Res. 3314 (XXIX); Declaration on the Enhancement of the Effectiveness of the Principle of Refraining from the Threat or Use of Force in International Relations

attention from the need to clarify its content and scope or to appraise its actual legal authority. In the sections that follow this chapter will examine these issues, starting in the next section with an indicative examination of international jurisprudence and practice relating to threats of force.

3. INTERNATIONAL JURISPRUDENCE AND PRACTICE

A. Case Law

The International Court of Justice (hereinafter 'ICJ') has had the opportunity to examine the legality of threats of force in a number of cases. The first instance was that of the *Corfu Channel Case* brought by the UK against Albania.[11] The case concerned two incidents, the first involving the passage of British ships through the Corfu Channel (over which Albania asserted territorial rights) and the second concerning a minesweeping operation conducted by the UK in the Corfu Channel. Prior to these two incidents, Albanian coastal batteries had fired on passing British ships. In response to such attacks, the British Government informed Albania that 'should Albanian coastal batteries in future open fire on any of His Majesty's vessels passing through the Corfu Channel force will be returned by his Majesty's ships',[12] which was interpreted by Albania as a threat.[13] With regard to the passage of British ships through the Corfu Channel – which for the Albanian Government confirmed the threat conveyed by the British note mentioned above[14] – the Court held that it was an innocent passage, notwithstanding the diamond formation of the ships and the number of them involved, because 'the intention must have been, not only to test Albania's attitude, but at the same time to demonstrate such force that she would abstain from firing again on passing ships'.[15] With regard to the minesweeping operation, the ICJ held that this action amounted to unlawful intervention and violation of Albanian sovereignty.[16]

Another case where the ICJ had the opportunity to examine and pronounce on the issue of threats of force is the *Nicaragua Case*, brought before the ICJ by Nicaragua, which complained, among other things, that the 'continuous US military and naval manoeuvres adjacent to Nicaraguan borders' formed part of a 'general and sustained policy of force, publicly expounded, intended to intimidate the lawful Government of Nicaragua into accepting the political demands of the United States Government, and resulting in substantial infringements of the political independence of Nicaragua'.[17]

(1987), GA Res. 42/22, UN Doc. A/42/22/766 (1987); Article 1 of North Atlantic Treaty (1949); Article 4, Constitutive Act of the African Union (2002).

[11] *Corfu Channel (United Kingdom v. Albania)*, Merits, Judgment of 9 April 1949, [1949] ICJ Rep. 9 (hereinafter referred to as the *Corfu Channel Case*).
[12] *Ibid.*, at 27.
[13] *Contre-Mémoire soumise par le gouvernement de la République Populaire d'Albanie*, 15 juin 1948, at 54.
[14] *Ibid.*, at 60, 124.
[15] *Corfu Channel Case*, supra n.11, at para. 32.
[16] *Ibid.*, at para. 35.
[17] *Nicaragua Case*, supra n.10, at para. 92.

Nicaragua referred more specifically to the military exercises and manoeuvres by the US and its allies near the Nicaraguan borders.

The Court was not 'satisfied that the manoeuvres complained of, in the circumstances in which they were held, constituted on the part of the United States a breach, as against Nicaragua, of the principle forbidding recourse to the threat or use of force'.[18] However, as Judge Schwebel, the US judge, admitted in his Dissenting Opinion, 'the United States decided to exert military pressure upon Nicaragua in order to force it to do what it would not agree to do'.[19] Concerning Nicaragua's complaint about US assistance to opposition groups in the form of weapons or logistical and other support, the Court held that such action might be 'a threat or use of force, or ... intervention in the internal or external affairs of other States'.[20] With regard to the US claims that the militarization of Nicaragua proved its aggressive intentions towards its neighbours, the Court opined that 'in international law there are no rules, other than such rules as may be accepted by the State concerned, by treaty or otherwise, whereby the level of armaments of a sovereign State can be limited'.[21] All in all, the Court found that none of the parties resorted to illegal threats of force; however, it reached its decision without indicating any standard against which certain events may or may not constitute a prohibited threat of force.

The ICJ was presented with the opportunity to examine in more detail the issue of the lawfulness of threats of force when the General Assembly requested an Advisory Opinion as to whether 'the threat or use of nuclear weapons in any circumstances [is] permitted under international law'.[22] For the Court,

> the notions of 'threat' and 'use' of force under Article 2, paragraph 4, of the Charter stand together in the sense that if the use of force itself in a given case is illegal – for whatever reason – the threat to use such force will likewise be illegal. In short, if it is to be lawful, the declared readiness of a State to use force must be a use of force that is in conformity with the Charter.[23]

Concerning the question of whether the possession of nuclear weapons constitutes in itself a prohibited threat of force, as some parties claimed, the ICJ said that:

> whether this is a 'threat' contrary to Article 2, paragraph 4, depends upon whether the particular use of force envisaged would be directed against the territorial integrity or political independence of a State, or against the Purposes of the United Nations, or whether, in the event that it were intended as a means of self-defence, it would necessarily violate the principles of necessity and proportionality. In any of these circumstances the use of force, and the threat to use it, would be unlawful under the law of the Charter.[24]

---

[18] *Ibid.*, at para. 227.
[19] Dissenting Opinion, Judge Schwebel, *Nicaragua Case*, *supra* n.10, at para. 34.
[20] *Nicaragua Case*, *supra* n.10, at para. 195.
[21] *Ibid.*, at para. 269.
[22] UN Doc. A/RES/49/75K (1994).
[23] *Nuclear Weapons*, *supra* n.2, at para. 47.
[24] *Ibid.*, at para. 2C of the dispositive and para. 48.

This led to the next finding that it 'cannot conclude definitely whether the threat or use of nuclear weapons would be lawful or unlawful in an extreme circumstance of self-defence, in which the very survival of the State would be at issue'.[25]

Although the Court's opinion (or lack thereof) raised more questions than it answered, its headline message was that the lawfulness of a threat of force is contingent on the lawfulness of the projected use of force, assessed by the standard of the UN Charter, which permits uses of force only in self-defence or as enforcement. This was reaffirmed later by the Independent International Fact-Finding Mission on the Conflict in Georgia which, however, went on to opine that in situations of severe tension, even the threat of lawful force should be avoided.[26]

B. State Practice

Although threats of force are quite frequent, this chapter will present two cases where such threats were not only visible but also central to the legal and political discourse that these cases generated: the Kosovo crisis of 1998–1999 and Iraq in the period following the end of the 1991 UN-authorized operation to liberate Kuwait.[27]

i. Kosovo (1998–1999)

Following Yugoslavia's aggressive response to the demand by the Kosovo Albanians for further autonomy and in view of the impeding humanitarian catastrophe, the Security Council adopted a number of resolutions which qualified the situation in Kosovo as a threat to the peace and demanded specific action by both parties in order to secure a peaceful conclusion of the crisis.[28] Consequently, both the US and NATO, among others, declared their readiness to use force. This led to the conclusion of agreements between Yugoslavia, on the one hand, and the Organization for Security and Cooperation in Europe (hereinafter 'OSCE') and NATO, on the other, allowing for verification missions to be deployed in Kosovo.[29] In the meantime, more pressure was exerted on the parties to reach agreement. NATO declared that it was ready to:

> take whatever measures are necessary ... [to] compel compliance with the demands of the international community and the achievement of a political settlement. The Council has therefore agreed today that the NATO Secretary-General may authorise air strikes against targets on FRY [Federal Republic of Yugoslavia] territory.[30]

---

[25] *Ibid.*, at para. 2E of the dispositive and paras 96–97.

[26] The Independent International Fact-Finding Mission on the Conflict in Georgia, Report, Volume II, at 237–238, available at www.ceiig.ch/report.html.

[27] For more on NATO's intervention in Kosovo see chapter 7 in this volume by Christine Gray on the use of force for humanitarian purposes.

[28] UNSC Res. 1199 (1998).

[29] As Madeleine Albright said, 'it [agreement with NATO] would not have happened if we had not combined diplomacy with the threat by NATO to use force'. M. Weller, *The Crisis in Kosovo 1989–1999, International Documents and Analysis*, Volume I (Cambridge: Documents and Analysis Publishing Ltd, 1999), at 284. Text of the agreements can be found in UN Doc. S/1998/978 and UN Doc. S/1998/991.

[30] Statement of the North Atlantic Council on Kosovo, Press Release (99) 12 (30 January 1999), at para. 5, available at http://www.nato.int/docu/pr/1999/p99-012e.htm.

A similar message was conveyed by NATO's Secretary-General to the Yugoslav Government, labelled as a 'final warning'.[31] At the same time, NATO engaged in building up its military capabilities in the region.

Yielding to such pressure, the parties agreed to participate in talks held at Rambouillet in France. Force was still threatened in order to convince them to produce a negotiated agreement. As the French Minister of Foreign Affairs declared:

> Nous avons donc décidé d'émettre une injonction. En général, l'ultimatum a un sens purement militaire. Nous fixons des dates, des délais et nous rappelons les responsabilités de chacun des deux camps, ce qu'ils doivent faire et ce qu'ils ne doivent pas faire. Appelez cela comme vous voulez mais on ne peut pas être plus pressant.[32]

Following the failure of the talks, for which Yugoslavia was blamed, NATO launched an air campaign against Yugoslavia which gave way to the post-conflict settlement of the crisis on the basis of Security Council Resolution 1244 (1999).

The international response to NATO's actions mainly focused on the legality of its use of force, rather than on the legality of the preceding threats of force.[33] Reactions also varied depending on the views states or legal analysts entertained about the legality of humanitarian intervention, the right to self-determination and the principle of state sovereignty. As far as the UN and the ICJ were concerned, they did not opine on the legality of NATO's threat and eventual use of force; although Yugoslavia complained to the Security Council that NATO's threat of air strikes represented 'an open and clear threat of aggression'[34] and later launched a complaint with the ICJ which was rejected on procedural grounds.[35] In view of the paucity of reactions to NATO's threats of force, it seems reasonable to assume that they were accepted as part of the diplomatic effort to secure a negotiated agreement in view of the issues that were at stake in Kosovo, which included denial of the right to self-determination and of basic human rights. Perhaps the views expressed by the UN Secretary-General Kofi Annan that the 'combination of force and diplomacy ... is the key to peace in the Balkans, as everywhere',[36] are indicative.

---

[31] UN Doc. S/1999/107 (2 February 1999), at 3.

[32] 'We decided to issue an injunction. Generally, the ultimatum has a strictly military meaning. We set the dates, deadlines and we remind both sides of their responsibilities, what they may and may not do. Call it what you want but one cannot be more pressing' (translation provided by the author), 'Pratique française du droit international', (1999) 45 *AFDI* 883.

[33] B. Simma, 'NATO, the UN and the Use of Force: Legal Aspects', (1999) 10 *EJIL* 1; 'Editorial Comments: NATO's Kosovo Intervention', (1999) 93 *AJIL* 824ff.

[34] Letter dated 1 February 1999 from the Minister for Foreign Affairs of the Federal Republic of Yugoslavia addressed to the President of the Security Council, S/1999/107 (2 February 1999).

[35] *Case Concerning the Legality of Use of Force (Yugoslavia v. Belgium and others)*, available at www.icj-cij.org.

[36] Available at http://www.nato.int/docu/speech/1999/s990128a.htm. See also Simma, *supra* n.33, at 8.

ii. Iraq (1991–2003)

Following Iraq's invasion of Kuwait in 1990, the Security Council authorized states cooperating with the Government of Kuwait to use 'all necessary means' to eject Iraq from Kuwait and to restore peace and security in the region.[37] The forcible action that followed was terminated with a cease-fire which was contained in Security Council Resolution 687 (1991), this resolution also setting out the post-conflict regime to apply to Iraq. One of its terms was the elimination (under international inspection and verification) of all 'weapons of mass destruction' possessed by Iraq.[38] For this reason, a UN Commission (hereinafter 'UNSCOM') was created, whose mandate was to monitor the destruction and dismantling of such weapons in coordination with the International Atomic Energy Agency (hereinafter 'IAEA').

At the same time, Resolution 687 reaffirmed Security Council Resolution 678 (1990), which contained the initial authorization to use force. Since 1991, a number of states that took part in the action to evict Iraq from Kuwait, particularly the US and the UK, had threatened Iraq with the use of force in order to induce compliance with the terms of Resolution 687. Such threats were not just verbal but were also accompanied by demonstrations of force, movement of troops, over-flights and military build-up in the region. Often threats materialized. One such incident took place from 16 to 20 December 1998 when US and UK forces carried out air attacks on Iraqi military facilities, following the report to the Security Council by Richard Butler, Head of UNSCOM, which blamed Iraq for obstructing the inspection of certain strategic sites. In his 15 December 1998 report to the Security Council, Butler concluded that 'UNSCOM had not been able to conduct the substantial disarmament work mandated to it by the UN Security Council'.[39] The raid was preceded by warnings from the US and the UK Governments that they intended to use force[40] in order to compel cooperation with the weapons inspectors and more specifically to allow inspections of the so-called 'presidential' sites, as provided for in the Memorandum of Understanding signed between Iraq and the UN Secretary-General.[41] Iraq's signing of the Memorandum was induced by the threats of force levelled by the US and the UK against Iraq, following Iraq's refusal to cooperate fully with the UN inspectors the previous year. The UN Secretary-General publicly thanked the US and the UK for their previous efforts leading to the signing of the Memorandum and commented that 'you can do a lot with diplomacy but of course you can do a lot more with diplomacy backed by fairness and force'.[42]

---

[37] UNSC Res. 678 (1990).
[38] *Ibid.*, at paras 8, 12.
[39] *Keesing's Record of World Events* (1998) 42697 (hereinafter referred to as *Keesing's*).
[40] For example, on 14 November 1998 the US and UK Governments authorized substantial military action against Iraq which was averted at that time by Iraq's statement that it would comply with the inspections requirement. 'Iraq: "Desert Fox" and Policy Developments', House of Commons Library, Research Paper 99/13, 18.
[41] Memorandum of Understanding between the United Nations and the Republic of Iraq (23 February 1998) (1998) 37 *ILM* 501.
[42] Quoted by Hon. Carl Levin in the Senate, 9 October 1998, available at http://www.iraqwatch.org/government/US/Letters,%20reports%20and%20statements/levin-10-9-98.html.

The Memorandum, which provided for 'immediate, unconditional and unrestricted access' to all sites, was endorsed by Security Council Resolution 1154 (1998), which also made compliance by Iraq 'necessary for the implementation of Resolution 687 (1991)' and warned that any violation thereof 'would have severest consequences for Iraq'. Legal commentaries on the December incident, as well as states' reactions, focused mainly on the legality of the actual use of force and more specifically on whether previous Security Council resolutions (including Resolutions 678 and 687) provided the legal basis for such action or, failing that, whether the US and UK had an independent right to take action based on self-defence, or as reprisals.[43] Although many states condemned the actual use of force, such condemnations were often guarded, placing blame also on Saddam Hussein's regime.[44] The League of Arab States, in its turn, failed to adopt a resolution condemning the action.[45] As for the UN Secretary-General, he condemned the actual use of force.[46] The preceding threats of force did not generate any considerable reaction by states, but the Secretary-General's expression of gratitude for the US and UK's efforts, involving threats of force, to secure the signing of the Memorandum of Understanding and the endorsement of the latter by the Security Council indicate acceptance of such threats.[47]

Attitudes towards Iraq and its continuous brinkmanship with the UN changed after the events of 11 September 2001, when pre-emptive action (broadly defined) against the threats that terrorism or Weapons of Mass Destruction (hereinafter 'WMD') represent was elevated to the pinnacle of US policy.[48] Following the action against Afghanistan, the US set its eyes on Iraq and the threat it posed by the perceived development and possession of WMD, a threat that was made more credible and urgent by Iraq's refusal to submit to inspections or to comply with previous Security Council resolutions, and in particular Resolution 687 (1991). The US piled the pressure on Iraq by placing it on the so-called 'axis of evil' list;[49] by stating that 'the purposes of the United States should not be doubted. The Security Council resolutions will be enforced

---

[43] R. Wedgwood, 'The Enforcement of Security Council Resolution 687: The Threat of Force Against Iraq's Weapons of Mass Destruction', (1998) 92 *AJIL* 724; N.D. White and R. Cryer, 'Unilateral Enforcement of Resolution 687: A Threat too Far?', (1999) 29 *Cal. W.I.L.J.* 243.

[44] UN Doc. S/PV.3955, 16 December 1998; House of Commons Library, Research Paper 99/13, 32.

[45] House of Commons Library, Research Paper 99/13, 33–34.

[46] 'This is a sad day for the United Nations and for the world ... It is also a sad day for me personally. Throughout this year I have done everything in my power to ensure peaceful compliance with Security Council resolutions, and so to avert the use of force ... . I deeply regret that today these efforts have proven insufficient.' House of Commons Library, Research Paper 99/13, 32.

[47] UNSC Res. 1154 (1998).

[48] *The National Security Strategy of the United States of America*, September 2002, 15, available at http://georgewbush-whitehouse.archives.gov/nsc/nss/2002/ (last visited 23 January 2012).

[49] George W. Bush, 'Address Before the Joint Session of the Congress on the State of the Union' 38 *Wkly Comp. Pres. Doc.* 133–139 (29 January 2002).

... or action will be unavoidable';⁵⁰ by getting Congressional authorization to use force;⁵¹ and by engaging in military build-up in the region. The Security Council also adopted Resolution 1441 (2002), which introduced an enhanced regime of inspections and gave Iraq a final opportunity to comply with its terms under the threat of serious consequences for failure to do so.

Following these events, Iraq allowed the return of inspectors, who finally entered the country on 18 November 2002. Their mandate was to present to the UN Security Council periodic progress reports. The first was on 27 January 2003 criticizing Iraq's failure to actively comply with Resolution 1441;⁵² the second report on 14 February⁵³ was less critical; and their final report before the war commenced contained a mixed assessment.⁵⁴ Notwithstanding the inspectors' reports and the failure to secure a second Security Council resolution explicitly authorizing the use of force, on 17 March 2002 President Bush in a televised address gave Saddam Hussein and his sons 48 hours to leave Iraq and warned that 'refusal to do so will result in military conflict commenced at a time of our choosing'.⁵⁵

Eventually the US, the UK and their allies launched 'Operation Iraqi Freedom' on 20 March 2002. As with Kosovo, reactions were more vociferous with regard to the actual use of force, the legality of which has been challenged on many grounds and in many quarters.⁵⁶ The threat of force received less attention. There is no doubt however that most states believed that threats played an important role in the usual brinkmanship between Iraq and the international community, and were often necessary to induce compliance by Iraq with its international obligations. What states resented, however, and felt uncomfortable with, was that, often, the US threats of force did not serve the interests of the international community, but served instead narrowly defined US interests. That was exemplified in the attitudes of the Non-Aligned Movement – which welcomed the return of the inspectors, secured by the threat of force, but rejected any type of unilateral action⁵⁷ – and the fact that the draft resolution introduced by the US, UK and Spain on 24 February 2003 authorizing the use of force failed, because it did not give more time to inspectors; those inspectors whose presence and operation in Iraq were, in any case, thanks to the threats of force.

---

⁵⁰ George W. Bush, 'Address to the United Nations General Assembly in New York City' 38 *Wkly Comp. Pres. Doc.* 1529–1533 (12 September 2002).
⁵¹ Authorisation for Use of Military Force Against Iraq Resolution of 2002, Pub.L.No. 107-243, 116 Stat. 1498–1502 (16 October 2002).
⁵² *Keesing's* (2003) 45218.
⁵³ *Ibid.*, at 45266.
⁵⁴ *Ibid.*, at 45314.
⁵⁵ President George W. Bush's Address to the Nation on Developments in Iraq, 17 March 2003, available at www.whitehouse.gov/news/releases/2003/03/20030317-7html.
⁵⁶ Indicatively see N.D. White and E.P.J. Myjer, 'Editorial: The Use of Force Against Iraq' (2003) 8 *JCSL* 1. For various views see 'Agora: Future Implications of the Iraq Conflict' (2003) 97 *AJIL* 553ff.
⁵⁷ Letter dated 10 October 2002 from the Permanent Representative of South Africa to the United Nations addressed to the President of the Security Council (on behalf of the Non-Aligned Movement), UN Doc. S/2002/1132, 10 October 2002, and his speech to the Security Council in UN Doc. S/PV. 2625 (2002).

76   *Research handbook on international conflict and security law*

4. PHYSIOGNOMY OF PROHIBITED THREATS OF FORCE

Although Article 2(4) does not define the notion of a threat of force, according to a classic definition adopted also by the ICJ, a 'threat of force' is 'an express or implied promise by a government of a resort to force conditional on non-acceptance of certain demands of that government'.[58] This definition seems to describe a threat in terms of a negative *quid pro quo* exchange between two states. Put differently, a threat of force exists when a demand is made, upon which the eventual use of force is contingent. Such a demand can be specific or general, for example a demand that a state changes its political or economic direction,[59] and can involve actions or omissions. An example of the latter is the 1994 resolution of the Turkish Parliament granting the Turkish Government 'all powers, including those deemed necessary in the military field, for safeguarding and defending the vital interests of Turkey'[60] in the eventuality of Greece extending its territorial waters in the Aegean Sea to 12 nautical miles, as provided by the 1982 Law of the Sea Convention. As the Greek Representative to the UN noted, 'it is beyond any doubt that [the Turkish Parliament's resolution] constitutes a direct violation of article 2, paragraph 4, of the Charter of the United Nations' because 'what Turkey is in fact attempting to do is to intimidate Greece into forfeiting an acknowledged right'.[61]

A threat of force contingent on a more general demand is the 2005 Chinese Law against the Separation of Taiwan, according to which:

> In the event that the 'Taiwan independence' secessionist forces should act under any name or by any means to cause the fact of Taiwan's secession from China, or that major incidents entailing Taiwan's secession from China should occur, or that possibilities for a peaceful reunification should be completely exhausted, the state shall employ non-peaceful means and other necessary measures to protect China's sovereignty and territorial integrity.[62]

The immediate question is whether threats which are not contingent upon any demand are also prohibited by Article 2(4). This is, for example, the case with Iran's threat to

---

[58] I. Brownlie, *International Law and the Use of Force by States* (Oxford: Oxford University Press, 1963), at 364; Sadurska, *supra* n.3, at 242; Lettre en date du 20 juin 1995 du Ministre des affaires étrangères de la République française, accompagnée de l'exposé écrit du Gouvernement de la République française, in *Nuclear Weapons*, *supra* n.2, at 25.

[59] *Nuclear Weapons*, *ibid.*, at para. 47.

[60] Text of the Turkish Grand National Assembly's Unanimous Declaration of 8 June 1995, available in LEXIS, News Library, Bbcswc file. See also *Financial Times*, 9 June 1995, at 3.

[61] UN Doc. S/1995/47 (12 June 1995). The Turkish Government has not as yet withdrawn the threat. See European Parliament Resolution of 9 March 2011 on Turkey's 2010 Progress Report, at para. 45: '… considers it regrettable, however, that the *casus belli* threat declared by the Turkish Grand National Assembly against Greece has not yet been withdrawn' (Res. P7_TA(2011)0090).

[62] Anti-Secession Law (adopted at the Third Session of the 10th National People's Congress on 14 March 2005), at para. 8, in (2005) 4 *Chinese JIL*, at 461–463. That law has been criticized by many states including the US and the UK. See *Keesing's* (2005) 46520–46521.

wipe Israel off the face of the Earth and other similar statements by Iranian officials.[63] Although the Iranian threat derives from ideological and religious beliefs, it constitutes a threat nonetheless, because it conveys a message that it is part of state policy to inflict harm on Israel.

What thus defines a threat is the element of coercion deduced from the explicit or implicit promise inherent in the threat to inflict certain injury on its recipient. It transpires then that a 'threat of force' belongs to the wider genre of unlawful intervention.[64] As the ICJ stated in the *Nicaragua Case*, 'the element of coercion, which defines, and indeed forms the very essence of prohibited intervention, is particularly obvious in the case of intervention which uses force'.[65] The reason why the use of force and indeed the threat of force are treated separately is because, individually or in combination, they constitute one of the most grave forms of intervention in view of the instruments used, their direct effects on the target state and the consequences for international peace and security.

That having been said, which specific conditions a threat of force should fulfil in order to fall within the meaning of Article 2(4) is not evident. More specifically, should it reach a certain threshold of gravity or imminence to be prohibited, or is it sufficient for it to be credible that force will be used at some point, irrespective of imminence or gravity? In the latter case what makes it credible? The Independent International Fact-Finding Mission on the Conflict in Georgia relied on the element of credibility in order to assess the threats issued by all parties in the Russian–Georgian war of 2008. As it noted, 'the emphasis of the practice of states is on credibility. A threat is credible when it appears rational that it may be implemented, when there is a sufficient commitment to run the risk of armed encounter.'[66] Also, is it any threat of force that meets the criteria, however they are defined, that is prohibited – or only threats directed against certain values of the international society?

This leads us to the next question, which is whether the assessment of the existence and lawfulness of a threat of force can be subjective or objective. It has been contended in this respect that assessment of the existence of a threat cannot be purely subjective, but that there must be some objective criteria and verification from an impartial third party.[67] This describes an ideal situation where criteria exist to identify or measure the seriousness of a threat and impartial third parties can immediately provide their services to the parties concerned. Alas, the international system is far from being ideal in this regard.

Assessments of threats are in most cases self-judging without any agreed or objective criteria. For example, it was Iran that interpreted statements by US officials to 'use all tools at our disposal' or to inflict 'tangible and painful consequences' as constituting

---

[63] Such threats have been widely criticized. For Security Council criticisms see SC/8542, 28 October 2005 and SC/8576, 9 December 2005. See, for others: http://english.aljazeera.net/archive/2005/10/2008410141649646492.html.

[64] R. Jennings and A. Watts (eds), *Oppenheim's International Law*, Vol. 1, 'Peace', 9th edn (London: Longman, 1992), at para. 128.

[65] *Nicaragua Case, supra* n.10, at para. 205.

[66] Independent International Fact-Finding Mission on the Conflict in Georgia, Report, Volume II, at 232, available at www.ceiig.ch/report.html.

[67] White and Cryer, *supra* n.43, at 253.

'unlawful, unacceptable and dangerous threats to use force'.[68] Iran's inference of a threat of force was made in the context of international opprobrium for its atomic programme, US declarations that force could be used against those possessing WMD and the precedent of US/UK action in Iraq. Did these events constitute objective indicators of a threat that gave good reason to believe that force was contemplated? Was such a threat perception credible and could it be verified by an impartial third party? Answers to the above questions can be debated *ad infinitum* but the crux of the matter is that Iran felt threatened and as a result it might have been forced to change its policy, in which case the threat would have succeeded, or it might have responded in kind – aggravating an already tense situation. As for third party assessment, the Security Council, to which Iran complained, did not deal with the complaint. As the Iranian Ambassador said on a different occasion, the Security Council 'should be held accountable … for its repeated failures to act against threats to international peace and security'.[69] Neither could the impartiality of the Council, had it taken up the complaint, be assumed.

To give another example, Iran's call for the annihilation of the state of Israel should be assessed also in light of Iran's active development of conventional and nuclear capabilities and the Jewish experience of the Holocaust. For the Israeli Prime Minister, 'the threat to our existence, to our future, is not theoretical. It cannot be swept under the carpet; it cannot be reduced. It faces us and all humanity and it must be thwarted. So the first lesson is to take those who threaten our existence seriously.'[70]

Neither are judicial assessments of the existence or lawfulness of a threat of force more enlightening or conclusive. In the preceding section the ICJ jurisprudence was presented which, as was indicated there, is sufficiently muddled to fail to provide clear guidance. The Guyana/Suriname Arbitral Award is also indicative in this respect. One issue the Arbitral Tribunal had to grapple with was that of the lawfulness of a warning issued by Surinamese gunboats to Guyana's exploratory and drill ship *C.E. Thornton* to leave Suriname's waters within 12 hours or face the consequences. Guyana understood this to mean that force would be used but Suriname denied this and claimed that no such instructions were given and neither had the gunboats the weapons to do so.[71] The Tribunal admitted that 'no unanimity as to what these "consequences" might have been' existed. Nevertheless, it concluded by relying exclusively on the testimonies of Guyana's officials and without giving any further explanation that it constituted 'an explicit threat that force might be used if the order was not complied with'.[72]

Even if third party assessment was available and criteria were to be agreed, their interpretation would definitely be 'lost in translation' due to the imprecise or faulty

---

[68] Letter dated 17 March 2006 from M. Zavad Zarif, Permanent Representative of the Islamic Republic of Iran to the UN addressed to the Secretary-General. UN Doc. A/60/730-S/2006/178, 22 March 2006.

[69] UN Doc. S/PV. 5647 (2007), at 15.

[70] Prime Minister Netanyahu at the Opening Ceremony of Holocaust and Heroism Remembrance Day (1 May 2011), available at: http://www.mfa.gov.il/MFA/The+Iranian+Threat/Statements+by+Israeli+leaders/Iran_Statements_Israeli_leaders-May_2011.

[71] Guyana and Suriname Award of the Arbitral Tribunal of 17 September 2007, paras 425–438.

[72] *Ibid.*, at para. 439.

nature of intelligence or other evidence that proves the existence or not of a threat; the confidential nature of such evidence which states prefer to keep secret; the inadequacy of intelligence assessments; the difficulty in predicting future state action; the difficulty of third party appraisal of the ideological, political or other assumptions that the target state makes with regard to the threat; the difficulty in appraising how the consequences of a threat play out in the specific state; and the difficulty in appraising the behaviour and intent of the threatening state, or the credibility of the threat (unless it materializes). Moreover, although states are rational actors, there is no hypothetical 'reasonable state', as there is a 'reasonable man' (in English law) to help us determine state conduct on the basis of objective tests.

It follows from the above that a threat of force is incapable of being determined objectively, but that assessment by individual states or institutions of the existence of a threat is subjective and contextual; each actor trying to predict and project within a limited, imprecise and uncertain analytical framework. It is in such a context that states have to make decisions being also cognizant of the possible costs of an unwarranted action – which may precipitate or even further aggravate a crisis – as well as of the costs of remaining inactive and suffering greater injury. As a result, states contemplate their range of options to forestall a threat directed against them, and such options may include institutional or unilateral, peaceful or forceful courses of action; but they cannot be prescribed in advance. Moreover, it should not be forgotten that states represent people; they are accountable to domestic audiences, and their legitimacy, and above all their existence, depend on their capacity to protect effectively the community they represent. On the other hand, institutional assessments take place within institutional settings, are not accountable to domestic audiences and decisions are made according to institutional interests, which may conflict with state interests.

5. LEGAL INDETERMINACY IN ASSESSING THREATS OF FORCE

The uncertainty and indeterminacy in the identification of a threat of force affect the legal treatment of such threats, because facts feed into the legal assessment; but the legal assessment of threats of force is further complicated by rule indeterminacy, notwithstanding the Court's valiant efforts to construct a minimalistic legal regime on the use of force.

A. Threats to Avert Humanitarian Catastrophe

One problematic area concerns the threat of force in order to avert a humanitarian disaster.[73] Following the ICJ formula mentioned above of pairing threats with the actual use of force, if humanitarian uses of force are lawful, threats of force will be equally lawful and vice versa. The answer is not, however, clear. For those who subscribe to the view that Article 2(4) contains an absolute prohibition of the use of force, such uses as

---

[73] For analysis of the use of force for humanitarian purposes see chapter 7 by Christine Gray in this volume.

well as threats of force will be unlawful; whereas for those who view the prohibition in Article 2(4) as being conditional, humanitarian uses and threats of force will be legal. For others, humanitarian uses of force are lawful as part of the customary law that survived the Charter, which means that threats of force will also be lawful; but this raises the question of whether the lawfulness of threats of force is assessed only according to the law of the Charter, as the ICJ has often said, or, additionally, according to customary law. From this brief and rather sketchy exposition of the law, it becomes apparent that the lawfulness of humanitarian uses of force is still debated and consequently the threat of force to attain humanitarian objectives is equally uncertain. What the Kosovo case demonstrates, however, is that when massacres or egregious human rights violations occur and the Security Council fails to act, threats of force will be accepted or at least tolerated in view of their objective, which is to put an end to such violations by using less disruptive means than the actual use of force.

B. Defensive Threats

Another area strained by legal uncertainty is that of defensive threats of force.[74] Although self-defence is a well-established right, its scope is hotly debated and this inevitably affects judgments about the lawfulness of defensive threats of force. According to international jurisprudence, self-defence is lawful when it is preceded by an 'armed attack' (defined by the scale and effects of the underlying use of force) and when it satisfies the criteria of necessity and proportionality.[75] It thus follows that a defensive threat of force, for example a message by a state to another state that force will be used to repel an armed attack, will in principle be lawful. Yet this amounts to a presumptive legality, because the requirements that self-defence should meet – necessity, proportionality and armed attack – are not present or tangible at the time when the defensive threat is uttered. This means that a situation may arise where assessments of the legality of a threat of force – and those on the subsequent use of force – may vary, unless legal assessment of the threat of force is suspended until the actual use of force occurs. In this case, the legality of the initial threat will be incidental to the legality of the actual use of force but the prohibition of the threat of force will then lose its character as an independent title.

The next question is whether a threat to use force in order to forestall an imminent attack or to deter a future attack would be lawful. This depends on the lawfulness of pre-emptive and preventive self-defence. Pre-emptive self-defence refers to situations where force is used by way of self-defence against an imminent attack; whereas preventive self-defence refers to situations where force is used by way of self-defence against a speculative attack. The ICJ has not as yet opined on the lawfulness of

---

[74] See chapter 6 by Dino Kritsiotis in this volume for analysis of the use of force in self-defence.
[75] Article 51, UN Charter (1945). *Nicaragua Case, supra* n.10, at paras 195, 210; *Case Concerning Oil Platforms (Islamic Republic of Iran v. United States of America)*, [2003] ICJ Rep. 161, at paras 51, 64, 77 (hereinafter referred to as *Oil Platforms*); *Wall, supra* n.10, at para. 139; *Case Concerning Armed Activities on the Territory of the Congo (Democratic Republic of Congo v. Uganda)* [2005] ICJ Rep., para. 147.

pre-emptive or preventive self-defence, although a case can be made that both versions of self-defence are unlawful under the Charter. Yet there is a strong corpus of legal opinion and practice supporting these versions of self-defence, particularly after the events of 11 September 2001.[76] The current position can be summed up by the UN report *A More Secure World*, according to which pre-emptive self-defence is permissible when the threat of an attack is imminent;[77] whereas with regard to 'non-proximate' and 'non-imminent' threats, states should not take unilateral action but put their evidence to the Security Council, which can then authorize the use of force.[78] It thus transpires from the above that a threat of pre-emptive self-defence will be lawful whereas a preventive threat of force will be unlawful unless it is in anticipation of Security Council authorization.

Be that as it may, the most intriguing question is whether defensive counter-threats of force should be removed from the scope of Article 2(4) and be treated as self-defence actions proper, albeit non-forcible ones.[79] More specifically, the question is whether defensive countervailing threats such as messages, military build-ups, movement of troops, acquisition of weapons and military exercises, instead of being viewed as lawful or unlawful *threats of force* should instead be treated as non-forcible *self-defence actions, simpliciter*. This is because, as one commentator put it, threats of force are often 'ritualised substitutes for violence'.[80] In this case we can speak of inchoate self-defence.

What comes to mind in the first place, in terms of non-forcible self-defence actions, are those defensive actions taking place between an armed attack and the actual use of force in self-defence. For example, following the Argentinean invasion of the Falkland Islands and before despatching its expedition force, the UK promised to remove Argentinean troops from the islands and military preparations were put in train.[81] The UK also established a maritime exclusion zone around the islands.[82] Likewise, the US and its allies engaged in demonstrations of force coupled with warnings, following the invasion of Kuwait by Iraq. Although the legal status of such acts is often absorbed by the self-defence action that follows, in those cases where no self-defence action is taken or when such demonstrations of force succeed in themselves to reverse the initial attack, the legal status of such threats should be considered independently and in isolation. In the opinion of the present writer, verbal or material 'threats' of defensive force following a prior armed attack should be removed from the category of threats

---

[76] The *Caroline Case* (1841) 29 BFSP 1137–1138; *The National Security Strategy of the United States*, supra n.45, at 15.

[77] *A More Secure World: Our Shared Responsibility*, Report of the Secretary-General's High-Level Panel on Threats, Challenges and Change, UN Doc. A/59/565 (2004), at para. 188.

[78] *Ibid.*, at paras 189–191.

[79] J.A. Green and F. Grimal, 'The Threat of Force as an Action in Self-Defense Under International Law', (2011) 44 *Vanderbilt J Transnational L.* 285.

[80] Sadurska, *supra* n.3, at 246.

[81] Margaret Thatcher, *The Downing Street Years* (London: HarperCollins, 1993), at 173–185, available at http://www.margaretthatcher.org/search/displaydocument.asp?docid=109110&doctype=1.

[82] United Kingdom Materials on International Law, (1982) 53 *BYIL* 539–541.

and be treated either as part of a protracted self-defence action culminating in the actual use of force or as inchoate self-defence action.

Inchoate self-defence is even more pertinent in the case of an imminent or future threat of an armed attack. In such cases, the threatened attack is countered by a verbal or material threat of defensive force. As the ICJ admitted, 'in order to lessen or eliminate the risk of unlawful attack, States sometimes signal that they possess certain weapons to use in self-defence against any state violating their territorial integrity or political independence'.[83] Inchoate self-defence is more palatable in such cases because it is less destructive than the actual use of force. To give an example, the deployment of troops in Kuwait in 1994 and the determined language used by the US and the UK averted a possible attack by Iraq on Kuwait following Iraq's large-scale military build-up on its border with Kuwait.[84] The Iraqi actions were viewed by the US and the UK as demonstration of Iraq's *animus aggressionis*, in view of its previous invasion of Kuwait and its subsequent refusal to recognize Kuwait's sovereignty.[85] In the same vein, the deployment of US warships near the Taiwan Strait from 1995 to 1996, as well as official statements that the US would defend Taiwan,[86] were factors that contributed to the de-escalation of the crisis between China and Taiwan; a crisis that had included demonstrations of force, military exercises and the firing of missiles, the aim of which was to force Taiwan into abandoning what, in China's view, were Taiwan's assertions of independence.[87]

The problem that arises in situations where threats of force are met by defensive counter-threats, but no armed attack is launched, is how to distinguish between genuine defensive threats and aggressive ones, when the initial threat which is supposedly met by a defensive counter-threat is also clothed in defensive language. There is in this instance a sequence of threats where one threat pre-empts another threat and none can be qualified properly without tracing and qualifying the original threat. For example, when the Cypriot Government decided to purchase and install on the island Russian S-300 missiles, it justified this action as being part of its defence against Turkey's air superiority over Cyprus.[88] Turkey threatened to use force to stop their deployment and verbal threats were accompanied by demonstrations of force.[89] Although Turkey did not argue its case in the context of self-defence but on the basis of geopolitical interests, more specifically that the deployment of the missiles would disturb the balance of power between Greece and Turkey, had it claimed self-defence against a threat of an armed attack, it would have been difficult to decipher which claim or counterclaim (Cyprus's or Turkey's) genuinely qualified as self-defence.

---

[83] *Nuclear Weapons*, *supra* n.2, at para. 47.
[84] UNSC Res. 949 (1994), at para. 3: 'demands that Iraq not again utilise its military or any other forces in a hostile or provocative manner to threaten either its neighbours or United Nations operations in Iraq'. See also Stürchler, *supra* n.3, at 206–212.
[85] S/PV.3438, 15 October 1994, at 9, 11; S/PV.3439, 17 October 1994, at 7.
[86] H.R. Con. Res. 140, 104th Cong (1996).
[87] Stürchler, *supra* n.3, at 240–245.
[88] SCOR Supp. S/1997/739, 26 September 1997; SCOR Supp. S/1997/762, 29 September 1997.
[89] Stürchler, *supra* n.3, at 146–150.

Similarly, the military build-up preceding the 2003 action against Iraq was partially justified as being defensive (particularly by the US) but the Arab League condemned it as a threat of aggression to Iraq, and a threat to the national security of all Arab states.[90] Likewise Iran viewed a series of 'vulgar' US statements and publications as constituting a threat of force. Such 'threats' were, however, levelled by the US in the context of self-defence against WMD, as provided for in the US National Security Strategy of 2006[91] (as well as in its predecessor of 2002). It is in that context that the declaration by Iran's Supreme Leader, Ayatollah Ali Khamenei, that any aggression against Iran would 'have a response from all sides by Iranian people' should be seen: that is, either as a defensive threat of force or as an initial threat.[92]

Moving some years back, the installation of strategic missiles in Cuba was treated by the US as a threat of force,[93] to which it responded by imposing a defensive quarantine, interdicting ships destined for Cuba.[94] The aim was to 'prevent the use of missiles against this [the US] or any other country'.[95] However, the installation of the missiles in Cuba could primarily be justified as a self-defence measure, in light of the US policies and actions against it.[96] Above all, the policy of nuclear deterrence is based on maintaining a mutually credible chain of threats and counter-threats of defensive force.[97]

C. Threats under Chapter VII of the UN Charter

This chapter now examines the other basis upon which a threat of force may become lawful according to the ICJ, which would be when it falls within Chapter VII of the UN Charter. There are two issues that deserve further explanation in this regard: the first concerns the legality of institutional threats of force and the second concerns the legality of unilateral threats in order to enforce collective security obligations.

i. Institutional threats of force

With regard to the first issue, the Security Council can adopt non-coercive as well as forcible measures in order to deal with threats to the peace, breaches of the peace or acts of aggression.[98] The Council can also issue threats in order to secure compliance with its decisions. For example, with regard to Iraq, Resolution 678 (1990):

---

[90] S/PV.4625 (Resumption 1), 26 October 2002, at 7.
[91] Available at http://georgewbush-whitehouse.archives.gov/nsc/nss/2006/.
[92] N. Fathi, 'Iran's Leader Warns the U.S. About Carrying Out Any Attack', *New York Times*, 9 February 2007, at A10.
[93] According to President Kennedy, their purpose was to provide a nuclear strike capability against the Western Hemisphere, and they were a threat to the peace. 47 *Dep't State Bull*, 12 November 1962, 715–716.
[94] 'Interdiction of the Delivery of Offensive Weapons to Cuba', (1963) 57 *AJIL* 512.
[95] *Supra* n. 93.
[96] Q. Wright, 'The Cuban Quarantine', (1963) 57 *AJIL* 547, at 548–553.
[97] '[I]f a threat of possible use did not inhere in deterrence, deterrence would not deter.' See Dissenting Opinion, Judge Schwebel in *Nuclear Weapons*, supra n.2, at 314.
[98] Articles 39–42, UN Charter (1945).

[a]uthorizes Member States co-operating with the Government of Kuwait, unless Iraq on or before 15 January 1991 fully implements, [the stated] resolutions, to use all necessary means to uphold and implement resolution 660 (1990) and all subsequent relevant resolutions and to restore international peace and security in the area.

This was presented to Iraq as a final opportunity before military action would commence. Some years later, in order to enforce compliance with the Memorandum of Understanding signed by Iraq and the UN Secretary-General, Resolution 1154 (1998) warned Iraq that any violation thereof 'would have severest consequences' for it. In Resolution 1199 (1998), the Council demanded that Yugoslavia implement a number of measures to bring to a peaceful solution the Kosovo crisis and warned that it would take further action and additional measures if Yugoslavia failed to do so. In November 2002, the Security Council in Resolution 1441 threatened Iraq with serious consequences if it failed to comply with its terms. In Resolution 1696 (2006), and clearly outside of the realms of threats of force, the Council gave Iran one month to comply with the obligation imposed by the resolution to cease nuclear enrichment and reprocessing activities and comply with the IAEA transparency procedures to avoid sanctions.[99] Such threats issued by the Security Council are lawful because they fall within its competence under the UN collective security system. The Charter, in other words, centralizes and institutionalizes not only the use of force but also threats of force as part of the collective security system's preventive, reactive and remedial aims.

ii. Unilateral threats in the enforcement of collective security obligations

What is more controversial, though, is the legality of unilateral threats of force to enforce resolutions of the Security Council. Using Iraq again as a case study, the US and the UK openly and directly threatened Iraq with the use of force in order to enforce its disarmament obligations, as imposed by Resolution 687 (1991).[100] Such threats led to the Memorandum of Understanding which allowed the resumption of inspections and was adopted in Resolution 1154 (1998). Still, the US was quite open about the possibility of using force unilaterally in order to enforce that resolution. The US Representative to the Security Council, Bill Richardson, stated that Resolution 1154 'did not preclude the unilateral use of force'[101] to enforce its provisions, and US President Bill Clinton said that the resolution provided authority to act if Iraq did not comply with the Memorandum of Understanding signed with the UN Secretary-General.[102] Threats of force by the US and the UK, in order to enforce compliance with previous Council resolutions, and in particular the cease-fire resolution, were also central to the diplomatic tug of war that preceded the 2003 US/UK action against Iraq. Even after the adoption of Resolution 1441 (2002) that reinstated the inspectors in Iraq, the US and UK used bellicose language and declared that there was no need for a second resolution to sanction the use of force if Iraq failed to honour the terms of

---

[99] UNSC Res. 1696 (2006), at paras 7, 9. Iran refused to comply and sanctions were imposed by UNSC Res. 1737 (2006), UNSC Res. 1747 (2007), UNSC Res. 1803 (2008) and UNSC Res. 1919 (2010).
[100] See *supra* section 3B.ii.
[101] *Keesing's* (1998) 42163.
[102] Ibid.

Resolution 687 (1991) because the authorization under Resolution 678 (1990) would be revived.[103] It is also in the context of Iraq that the US, UK and certain other states used force in order to enforce the no-fly zone over Kurdistan authorized by Resolution 688 (1991) in order to protect the Kurdish population from Sadam's wrath. As the British Secretary of Defence stated, the UK was 'entitled to patrol the no-fly zones to prevent a grave humanitarian crisis. That is the legal justification in international law'.[104]

If a threat of force is paired with the actual use of force as the ICJ stated, the issue of the lawfulness of such threats boils down to whether the actual use of force is legal. As far as the 2003 action against Iraq is concerned, its legality has been dealt with exhaustively in the literature and there is no need to rehearse again the arguments for or against the action. It is sufficient for present purposes to note that the UK put forward a strong argument grounding the legality of the 2003 action on Security Council resolutions.[105] If the UK's line of reasoning is correct, then the preceding threats of force are also legal. Would threats of force made in anticipation of a Security Council authorization be equally legal? For example, the US and UK, having made the threats, often said that the matter should be decided by the Council and tried but failed to secure a second resolution authorizing the use of force. By analogy with the case of threats of defensive force which are deemed to be legal – even if when they are made not all of their conditions are present – one may say that threats of force in anticipation of Security Council authorization are equally legal.

The crucial question, however, is whether the US and UK had legal authority to issue such threats. If Iraq's counterparty was the UN, neither the US nor the UK were justified in issuing unilateral threats on the basis of UN resolutions. That notwithstanding, threats of force by the US and UK clothed in institutional language and aiming to promote UN interests were tolerated or accepted as a means of enforcing compliance by Iraq with its UN obligations. When the UK Representative to the Security Council said that 'the only way that we can achieve [Iraq's] disarmament of weapons of mass destruction [...] is by backing our diplomacy with the credible threat of force'[106] he expressed a widely held view based on previous practice. Also to be recalled in this respect is Kofi Annan's public expression of gratitude towards the US and the UK for facilitating, through the threat of force, the conclusion of the Memorandum of Understanding that ended the 1997–1998 inspection crisis with Iraq and Annan's view that UN diplomacy can be backed with the threat of force to be more effective.

The same holds true for NATO's threat to use force against Yugoslavia in order to enforce compliance with its Security Council obligations regarding Kosovo. Such

---

[103] *Keesing's* (2002) 45115–45117.

[104] *Hansard House of Commons Debates*, vol. 363, col. 625, 26 February 2001.

[105] Statement by the Attorney General, Lord Goldsmith, in Answer to a Parliamentary Question, Tuesday 18 March 2003, www.fco.gov.uk. See (2005) 54 *ICLQ* 767–778. See also Remarks of the Honorable William Howard Taft, IV, Legal Adviser, U.S. Department of State Before the National Association of Attorneys General, 20 March 2003, available at http://usinfo.state.gov/regional/nea/iraqtext2003/032129taft.htm. See also W.H. Taft IV and T.F. Buchwald, 'Preemption, Iraq, and International Law', (2003) 97 *AJIL* 557.

[106] UN Doc. S/PV.4714, 7 March 2003, at 27. Also see UN Doc. S/PV.4707, 14 February 2003, at 18, 21.

threats played an important role in securing Yugoslavia's agreement to permit the deployment of OSCE and NATO verification missions. As the US Representative to the Security Council observed, 'a credible threat of force was key to achieving the OSCE and NATO agreements and remains key to ensuring full implementation'.[107] The Council then went on to endorse these agreements[108] and Kofi Annan, as pointed out above, commended NATO's action but condemned the unilateral use of force.

The Iraqi saga as well as the Kosovo case thus demonstrates that unilateral threats of force to enforce institutional interests are more or less accepted, whereas threats of force to promote national interests are frowned upon. The downside of unilateral threats, even for worthy purposes, is that they may spiral out of control. On the one hand, a state that issues such threats and succeeds in attaining the sought-after result may be emboldened even further and thus act always on the basis of threats. This is an exact element of Iran's complaint to the Security Council against the US. It complained that US officials were emboldened by the Council's past failures to deal properly with US threats or uses of force, 'both of which are specifically rejected by Article 2(4) of the Charter as violations of one of the most fundamental principles of the Organization'.[109] On the other hand, a state may be caught in a credibility dilemma where the actual use of force is the only credible outcome of the threat, particularly if the threat has been hyped. For example, it would have harmed the credibility of the US in 2003 if it had backed away from acting against Iraq.[110]

A threat of force in support of the UN collective security system brings us to another issue, which is the relationship between a unilateral threat – or even a unilateral use – of force on the one hand, and the UN collective security system on the other. More specifically, the question is whether such unilateral threats of force fill in gaps in the UN system, gaps in the law or gaps in its enforcement. The Charter regime on the use of force has its own logic and dynamic in that an all-inclusive prohibition of the unilateral threat or use of force is supported by a collective security mechanism whose mandate is to deal in a timely manner and effectively with events that endanger international peace and security.[111] It is, however, well known that the UN collective security mechanism suffers from two drawbacks – it is inherently selective and it

---

[107] UN Doc. S/PV.3937, 24 October 1998, at 15.
[108] UNSC Res. 1203 (1998).
[109] Letter dated 17 March 2006 from M. Zavad Zarif, Permanent Representative of the Islamic Republic of Iran to the UN addressed to the Secretary-General, UN Doc. A/60/730-S/2006/178, 22 March 2006.
[110] As the UK Foreign Minster Jack Straw put it with regard to Iraq: 'If we back away from that – if we decide to give unlimited time for little or no cooperation on substance – then the disarmament of Iraq and the peace and security of the international community, for which we are responsible, will get not easier, but very much harder.' UN Doc. S/PV.4707, 14 February 2003, at 18.
[111] R. Jennings, 'General Course on Principles of International Law', 121 *R.C.*, (1967 II), 325, at 584; B. Asrat, *Prohibition of Force under the U.N. Charter. A Study of Article 2(4)* (Uppsala: *Iustus forlag*, 1991), at 43: 'obligations were obviously consented to in anticipation of benefit from an organised and lawfully functioning system. It would hence be scarcely possible not to acknowledge the governing role of the *quid pro quo*'.

malfunctions in practice.¹¹² As a result, there is often no countervailing mechanism to deal with the complaints of individual states which are thus left without institutional protection or redress. Consequently, a unilateral *jus ad bellum* has been revived,¹¹³ which compensates for the weaknesses of the collective security system. Such a *jus ad bellum* includes threats of force as well as uses of force that act as a unilateral or institutional deterrence or sanction, or protect values.

6. CONCLUSION

From the preceding discussion it becomes apparent that notwithstanding the frequent and abstract reaffirmation of the rule prohibiting the threat of force, legal and political attitudes towards such threats of force are nuanced.

On the one hand stands the juridical treatment of threats of force. The ICJ admitted that not all threats of force are unlawful and, even more, that (un)lawfulness is a contextual issue depending on the surrounding circumstances; without, however, explaining its decisions or spelling out any concrete criteria according to which threats of force can be judged.¹¹⁴ Thus Judge Simma's observation that the failure to assess the nature of the UN principles on the use of force in the contemporary context as regrettable is particularly true with regard to threats of force.¹¹⁵ In the *Nuclear Weapons* Advisory Opinion the ICJ tried, for purposes of clarity and simplicity, to pair in legal terms threats of force with the use of force. However, disputes about the lawfulness of the actual use of force – as in the case of pre-emptive or preventive self-defence, as well as disputes about the available evidence – affect legal assessments of threats of force.

On the other hand, in the real world of international politics where standards and criteria are quite elastic and not exclusively legal, and where the UN collective security mechanism malfunctions and is unpredictable, states have to make decisions about the capabilities or intentions of the other party to realize the threat which has been uttered in situations of evidential uncertainty. Such decisions can never be accurate or perfect but are made on the understanding that a threat may materialize and inflict the intended harm, or that a premature reaction may aggravate the conflict. Thus states pursue different courses of action to forestall such threats, from issuing countervailing threats, to involving the Security Council, to using force themselves.

Other actors' attitudes towards threats of force are also qualified. Instead of being debilitated by legal absolutes, states or other relevant international actors take a macroscopic view of threats of force, trying to assess their gravity as well as their role in securing or denying important international values such as peace, security and human dignity. This position is exemplified by the toleration and approval of unilateral threats of force by NATO against Yugoslavia, or threats by the US and the UK against

---

¹¹² See chapter 5 in this volume by Christian Henderson.
¹¹³ M.W. Reisman, 'Criteria for the Lawful Use of Force in International Law', (1985) 10 *Yale J.I.L.* 279, at 281.
¹¹⁴ *Nuclear Weapons*, *supra* n.2, at para. 47.
¹¹⁵ Separate Opinion, Judge Simma, *Oil Platforms*, *supra* n.75, at para. 6.

Iraq, whereas the actual uses of force in both cases have been contested and criticized in some quarters. The critical question that is often asked is to what extent a threat of force can be used in order to counter other threats of force, or to enforce international values without challenging the established minimum international normative order. The case of 'threats of force' thus demonstrates that there are many other parameters than law within which threats of force operate, and in which legal and political attitudes towards them are formed. Contrary to what Article 2(4) of the UN Charter implies, law cannot just extinguish or outright condemn threats of force or even the eventual use of force, because often it is just those threats and uses of force that, in the end, uphold the law.

4. The prohibition of the use of force
Mary Ellen O'Connell

1. INTRODUCTION

H.L.A. Hart, the renowned Oxford scholar of jurisprudence, described legal rules that 'restrict the free use of violence' as 'obviously essential … to the maintenance of social life'.[1] Some may believe that the international legal system lacks such essential rules, and, therefore, fails to qualify as a true legal system. In fact, principles for the control of violence have been a feature of international law at all stages of the system's development. This observation will likely not satisfy critics of international law who believe that while international legal rules on the control of violence may exist in theory, they have no impact in the real world. These critics would conclude that international law *in reality* has no rules to restrict violence. A similar charge could, however, be levelled at domestic law. Murder, rape, robbery and assault are common in every city of the world and are even rampant in places where, nevertheless, no one doubts that a legal system is in place.[2] Still, the charge against international law should be taken seriously. While it is not the case that international law has no rules against violence or that the rules work any better or worse than domestic anti-violence rules, it is the case that failures to control violence at the international level impose far greater suffering than analogous failures at the national level. Humanity can and should demand more effective and extensive legal controls of international violence.

This chapter concerns the central international legal rule against violence: Article 2(4) of the United Nations Charter. Article 2(4) generally prohibits the use of force by states.[3] It is a treaty rule that is also widely regarded as a rule of customary international law and, indeed, in certain respects, as a peremptory rule or rule of *jus cogens*.[4] Article 2(4) was adopted along with the rest of the Charter in 1945 after the catastrophe of the Second World War in which an estimated 60 million people died. Despite its relatively recent adoption, Article 2(4) has ancient roots, dating back to the emergence of the Just War Doctrine in the fifth century AD and earlier. Moral philosophers, theologians, ethicists and legal scholars held for centuries before 1945

---

[1] H.L.A Hart, *The Concept of Law*, 2nd edn (Oxford: Oxford University Press, 1994), at 87ff., 91.
[2] Honduras was the most violent state in the world in early 2012. A. Murphy, 'Who Rules in Honduras: Coup's Legacy of Violence' (National Public Radio, 2012), available at http://www.npr.org/2012/02/12/146758628/who-rules-in-honduras-a-coups-lasting-impact.
[3] For its prohibition of the threat of force see chapter 3 by Nicholas Tsagourias in this volume.
[4] See n.141 and accompanying text.

that war is prohibited unless it meets the conditions of the Just War Doctrine.[5] Under the Doctrine war is justified only when fought for certain just causes and then only when the war is a last resort that has a reasonable chance of succeeding. Even when resort to force meets these criteria the cost of achieving success through force must not be disproportionate to the value of the aim in terms of civilian lives lost and property destroyed.[6]

These principles of the Just War Doctrine began to take more precise form in positive law in 1899 with the adoption of the Hague Convention for the Pacific Settlement of Disputes.[7] The Hague Convention requires that states attempt peaceful settlement of inter-state disputes before resorting to war. In 1907, states agreed to the first multilateral treaty prohibiting resort to war for the collection of contract debts.[8] Resort to war was further restricted in the Covenant of the League of Nations adopted in 1919[9] and in the 1928 Kellogg–Briand Pact.[10] In 1945, a fully elaborated peace regime was created through another multilateral treaty, the United Nations Charter. At the heart of the Charter is the general prohibition on the use of force in Article 2(4):

> All Members shall refrain in their international relations from the threat or use of force against the territorial integrity or political independence of any State, or in any other manner inconsistent with the Purposes of the United Nations.

In September 2005, the vast majority of UN members, or in other words, virtually all sovereign states in the world, gathered in New York to reconfirm their commitment to strict compliance with Article 2(4) and the Charter's other provisions regulating the resort to force.[11]

Despite this overwhelming support for Article 2(4) and its status as a *jus cogens* norm, the prohibition on the use of force has been under pressure from certain quarters since its adoption.[12] Article 2(4) is regularly challenged by those – governments and scholars – interested in broader rights to resort to armed force.[13] Perhaps worse than the persistent pressure to selectively dilute the prohibition has been the frequent and serious disregard by states of their obligation to refrain from resort to force. These challenges to Article 2(4) suggest that the most humanity can hope for in the future is

---

[5] See, for example, B. Conforti, 'The Doctrine of Just War and Contemporary International Law', (2002) XII *It. Yrbk Int'l* 3.

[6] See nn.152–154 and accompanying text.

[7] 1899 Convention for the Pacific Settlement of Disputes (adopted 29 July 1899), available at pca-cpa.org/showpage.asp?pag_id+1187.

[8] Convention Respecting the Limitation of the Employment of Force for the Recovery of Contract Debts (adopted 18 October 1907, entered into force 26 January 1910) Stat. 36: 2241, Malloy's TS 2:2248 (hereinafter '1907 Convention').

[9] The Covenant of the League of Nations (signed 28 June 1919, entered into force 10 January 1920), available at http://avalon.law.yale.edu/20th_century/leagcov.asp#art12.

[10] The Pact may be found at http://www.yale.edu/lawweb/avalon/imt/kbpact.htm.

[11] 2005 World Summit Outcome, UN Doc. A/RES/60/1, 24 October 2005, 22–23.

[12] For an account of the United States' arguments on greater rights to resort to force see, generally, C. Henderson, *The Persistent Advocate and the Use of Force: The Impact of the United States upon the* Jus ad Bellum *in the Post-Cold War Era* (Farnham: Ashgate, 2010).

[13] See nn.71–122 and accompanying text.

to hold the line at the current rule. Yet, history also demonstrates that such challenges may be rebutted and progress may well be possible towards a broader and more respected prohibition on violence in inter-communal relations.

More details of the long history of the prohibition on force in international law are provided in the next section of the chapter. The discussion then turns in section 3 to contemporary interpretations of the prohibition on force, including the widely held view that serious violations of Article 2(4) are prohibited by the *jus cogens* norm, barring aggression.[14] Section 4 discusses attempts to weaken the prohibition on force but concludes that those attempts have largely failed. The international legal community should be credited for preserving the prohibition on force. Nevertheless, after almost 70 years with Article 2(4) in place, it seems time to do more than merely defend the current prohibition. The chapter postscript points to the possibilities of both improving enforcement of Article 2(4) as well as expanding the current international legal obligation to reject violence in favour of peaceful means of settling disputes.

2. THE HISTORY OF ARTICLE 2(4)[15]

Histories of Article 2(4) classically begin as this chapter has with the Christian Just War Doctrine.[16] The Just War Doctrine has played a major role in the development of Article 2(4), but prohibition on resort to force is a common feature of most major religious, ethical and philosophical traditions. Indeed, Stephen Neff points to Confucianism as the first tradition to develop the concept that peace is the normal condition of social life,[17] in contrast to traditions that, while possibly embracing some restraints in war, nevertheless accept major inter-communal violence as inevitable. Neff points to only one other ancient community as having developed a similar view: Christianity.[18] According to Ian Brownlie, the 'early Christian Church refused to accept war as moral in any circumstances and until A.D. 170 Christians were forbidden to enlist. This period of extreme pacifism lasted for three centuries after Christ'.[19]

Christians mostly abandoned pacifism as Christianity spread throughout the Roman Empire, an entity built and maintained by war. Christians rose to positions of power within the Empire, and then faced the question of whether they would hold on to pacifism at the potential cost of temporal power.[20] St. Augustine of Hippo offered an

---

[14] O. Corten, *The Law Against War: The Prohibition on the Use of Force in Contemporary International Law* (Oxford: Hart, 2010), at 200–213.

[15] M.E. O'Connell, 'Peace and War', in B. Fassbender and A. Peters (eds), The Oxford Handbook of the History of International Law, ch. 11 (Oxford: Oxford University Press, 2012), at 272ff. See also, generally, M.E. O'Connell, The Power and Purpose of International Law (Oxford: Oxford University Press, 2008, 2011).

[16] See, for example, S.C. Neff, *War and the Law of Nations: A General History* (Cambridge: Cambridge University Press, 2005), 46; Conforti, *supra* n.5.

[17] Neff, *supra* n.16, at 31.

[18] *Ibid.*, at 39.

[19] I. Brownlie, *International Law and the Use of Force by States* (Oxford: Clarendon, 1963), at 5 (citation omitted).

[20] R. Gill, *A Textbook of Christian Ethics*, 3rd edn (London: T&T Clark, 2006), at 194.

apparent way out of the dilemma – Christians could fight for peace. They could fight to end fighting. Building on the work of earlier Church scholars,[21] Augustine sought to move Christians away from the strict pacifism of the beatitudes and the commandment to love one's enemy.[22] Augustine retained a focus on peace but separated it from passive conduct, citing insights from Roman and Greek philosophy and law. The Roman Cicero had argued that it could be just to fight a war with the aim of establishing peace.[23] Aristotle similarly taught that peace was the ultimate just cause of war.[24] Given the Christian commitment to peace, Augustine argued that Christians, too, could fight for peace. He concluded that using limited war when necessary as 'a means of preserving or restoring peace' is acceptable for Christians who desire to conform their conduct to their religious belief.[25] St. Augustine considered it just to fight in self-defence, to recover stolen property and to respond to other wrongs. He also thought that war to deter future wrongdoing could be just. Most notably, perhaps, he wrote that it was just to wage war to promote Christianity.[26]

This last cause, the promotion of Christianity, helped to convert Christianity generally from a pacifist system to one that extolled war.[27] Crusades were fought for control of the Holy Land or to otherwise thwart the spread of Islam; some Crusaders became saints. By AD 800, as a result of wars waged by Christians, the Holy Roman Empire had been built. It lasted from the crowning of Charlemagne[28] to the end of the Thirty Years' War in 1648. During this long period, scholars continued to develop the Just War Doctrine. The most influential Just War scholar of the Middle Ages, St. Thomas Aquinas, working in the 13th century, systematized St. Augustine's work, emphasizing core conditions for a just war: a war may only be declared by a leader with proper authority to do so; the cause of the war must be just, and the leader's intention in waging it must be right.[29] After Aquinas, scholars conceived that princes could justifiably use war to respond to violations of sovereign territory, to treaty breaches and to violations of diplomatic immunity – many of the principles that would come to form the core of international law.

---

[21] Brownlie, *supra* n.19 at 5. See also Neff, *supra* n.16, at 3–5, 10–11.

[22] W.G. Grewe, *The Epochs of International Law* (trans. & rev'd, Michael Byers) (Berlin: DeGruyter, 2000), at 108–111; A. Nussbaum, *A Concise History of the Law of Nations*, revised edn (London: Macmillan, 1962), at 35.

[23] Neff recounts similar but earlier ideas in Confucianism: 'War was seen as a last resort, to counteract antisocial conduct and reinforce the norms which integrated the society into a harmonious whole.' Neff, *supra* n.16, at 10.

[24] J. Von Elbe, 'The Evolution of the Concept of the Just War in International Law', (1939) 33 *AJIL* 665, at 666 (n.9), citing *Aristotle's Nicomachean Ethics*, Book X, Ch. VI XVII, 6; *Politics*, VII, 14.

[25] Grewe, *supra* n.22, at 107 (Latin re-phrasing omitted).

[26] Von Elbe, *supra* n.24, at 665.

[27] G. Parker, 'Early Modern Europe', in M. Howard *et al.* (eds), *The Laws of War: Constraints on Warfare in the Western World* (New Haven, CT: Yale University Press, 1994), 40, 43.

[28] Nussbaum, *supra* n.22, at 20.

[29] Grewe, *supra* n.22, at 109. See also Von Elbe, *supra* n.24, at 669; Brownlie, *supra* n.19, at 6.

The Just War Doctrine was, however, challenged at each stage of its development. Some Christians never lost their commitment to pacifism and continued to reject as immoral any resort to war. From a very different perspective, political realists such as Niccolo Machiavelli (1469–1527) challenged the concept that there could be any restriction on a sovereign's right to resort to war. Machiavelli famously wrote '"that war is just which is necessary" and every sovereign entity may decide on the occasion for war'.[30]

Machiavelli's views gained ascendency – it was certainly not the pacifist Christians who prevailed. The mainstream Church was itself declining as a political force in the face of 'well-organized political units, monarchic and national in form, secular in government, and commercial, dynastic, and colonizing' that were replacing smaller principalities and less-well-defined entities.[31] Thinkers interested in suppressing war were aware of what these developments would mean. Francisco Vitoria, a Dominican monk and member of a group known as the Spanish scholastics, began to promote the idea that the law itself could be used as the governor of human action as a substitute for the Pope or the Holy Roman Emperors.[32] Vitoria also, however, promoted the idea that all parties to a conflict could be fighting with the right intentions and, therefore, doing nothing morally wrong, not unlike Machiavelli's view.[33]

Vitoria's emphasis on individual intention appealed to Protestants owing to its acceptance of individual conscience, separate from the judgements of the Pope and clergy of the Catholic Church. Alberico Gentili, an Italian Protestant who fled Italy for England and taught law at Oxford University, is particularly associated with the idea that an individual leader should have the right to decide on the justice of a cause of war.[34] Hugo Grotius, another Protestant scholar and diplomat, understood the pitfall of the view that all sides in war could make a good faith claim to a just cause. Grotius was a witness to the opening of the brutal Thirty Years' War, a war between Protestants and Catholics for dominance in Europe. Everyone was fighting in a subjectively just cause; indeed, each could argue that he was fighting for the right to follow his conscience in the practice of his faith. Grotius, however, insisted that any just cause of war must be tested objectively – no allowance could be spared for a prince acting in good faith if that prince was acting without a just cause as defined objectively in law. According to Von Elbe, '[t]he demise of the concept of the just war to which the idea of the *bellum*

---

[30] Brownlie, *supra* n.19, at 11.
[31] *Ibid*.
[32] Von Elbe, *supra* n.24, at 674–675; Nussbaum, *supra* n.22, at 79–91. Vitoria may be even better known for arguing that the Just War Doctrine applied to non-Christians. This argument arose in Vitoria's defence of the Native Americans. He argued that in their fear and ignorance they misunderstood the intentions of the Spaniards and attacked them. The Spaniards used force in response in justifiable self-defence. This argument was considered highly progressive when contrasted with other extent arguments holding that non-European people were barbarians, without souls, and therefore not entitled to the constraints of the Just War Doctrine. Nussbaum, *supra* n.22, at 81. For a particular focus on Vitoria, his view of Native Americans and the origins of international law, see A. Anghie, *Imperialism, Sovereignty, and the Making of International Law* (Cambridge: Cambridge University Press, 2005).
[33] Nussbaum, *supra* n.22, at 80.
[34] Von Elbe, *supra* n.24, at 678.

justum ex utraque parte seemed to lead was averted by Grotius who made of it an issue of modern international law'.[35]

Grotius made his just war argument in his seminal work, *On the Law of War and Peace* (1625), written to help end the Thirty Years' War and mitigate its horrors. Grotius believed in the Christian law of love and the optimistic view of people's nature and capacity contained in Christianity.[36] He wanted to inspire greater humanity in the conduct of the war and encourage the establishment of a legal order for Western Europe after the War.[37] Building on the Spanish Scholastics, he proposed that people could understand what law required through reason rather than divine revelation or clerical interpretation. Nevertheless, God remained the ultimate law giver, meaning law remained superior to the wishes of individuals or communities.

The Thirty Years' War ended more than 20 years after *On the Law of War and Peace* was first published. It is difficult to conclude that the book had much influence on ending the War, but it did appear to influence the peace.[38] The 1648 treaties of Osnabrück and Muenster, known as the Peace of Westphalia, included many of Grotius's ideas, from respect for territorial boundaries to tolerance for religious difference to the use of arbitration to settle disputes.[39] Parties to any dispute had to try peaceful settlement prior to any resort to force.[40] Arthur Nussbaum called this the 'first attempt at international organization for peace'.[41]

The new peace order in Europe may have been necessary to end the war, but as a secular legal regime establishing equal, sovereign states, it undermined the conception of community and community law. '[T]he Peace of Westphalia, while paying lip service to the idea of a Christian commonwealth, merely ushers in the era of sovereign absolutist states which recognized no superior authority.'[42] Emmerich de Vattel helped cement the view within international law of co-equal states, unable to judge the conduct of others, especially respecting resort to force. In his book, *The Law of Nations* published in 1758, Vattel shifted the focus in international law from the law above states to the law made by states – it was a decided shift from natural law theory to the theory of positive law.

Yet, neither Vattel nor his successors succeeded in completely eliminating the Just War Doctrine, a product of natural law theory, from consideration by states when

---

[35] Ibid., at 678. '*Ex utraque parte*' refers to all sides in a conflict potentially having a just cause.

[36] H. Lauterpacht, 'The Grotian Tradition in International Law', (1946) 23 *BYIL* 31, citing Grotius, *De Jure Beli ac Pacis*, Prolegomena, 23.

[37] Nussbaum, supra n.22, at 105.

[38] L. Gross, 'The Peace of Westphalia', in *I Essays on International Law and Organization* (Dobbs Ferry: Transnational Publishers, 1984), at 9, citing P.H. Winfield, *The Foundations and the Future of International Law* (Cambridge: Cambridge University Press, 1941), at 20 and W. Van der Vlugt, *L'Oeuvre de Grotius et son Influence sur le Développement du Droit International* (Paris: Hachette, 1925), at 448.

[39] Nussbaum, supra n.22, at 115.

[40] Ibid., at 117.

[41] Ibid. See also Gross, supra n.38, citing D.J. Hill *II A History of Diplomacy in the International Development of Europe* (Buffalo: W.E. Hein, 1925), at 625.

[42] Gross, supra n.38 at 18–19.

resorting to war. The Doctrine was too deeply entrenched in Western thought to fade away completely. Despite the lack of positive law restricting resort to war, national leaders did continue to declare the justice of their causes;[43] to declare that the resort to war was a last resort, necessitated when peaceful means had failed,[44] or that there was no resort to war at all but to measures short of war.

Indeed, even those international law scholars who contend that no law existed on resort to war in the 19th century because no positive law existed do admit there was plenty of international law relevant to resort to war. This fact should raise doubts about the core proposition that with the rise of positivism in the 18th and 19th centuries, restraints on war faded. Measures short of war were subject to a restrictive legal regime of their own as the 1841–1842 correspondence between British and American officials over the scuttling of the ship *Caroline* in 1837 indicates.[45] British forces suppressing a rebellion in Canada that was being supported by groups in the United States had sent the *Caroline* over Niagara Falls, resulting in loss of life as well as the ship. The *Caroline* was being used to ferry weapons to anti-British rebels in Canada. US Secretary of State Daniel Webster wrote to British Foreign Minister Lord Ashburton:

> The President sees with pleasure that your Lordship fully admits those great principles of public law, applicable to cases of this kind, which this government has expressed; and that on your part, as on ours, respect for the inviolable character of the territory of independent states is the most essential foundation of civilization. And while it is admitted on both sides that there are exceptions to this rule, he is gratified to find that your Lordship admits that such exceptions must come within the limitations stated and the terms used in a former communication from this department to the British plenipotentiary here. Undoubtedly it is just, that while it is admitted that exceptions growing out of the great law of self-defence do exist, those exceptions should be confined to cases in which the 'necessity of that self-defence is instant, overwhelming and leaving no choice of means, and no moment for deliberation'.[46]

In addition to the limits on measures short of war, states recognized and developed rules for the conduct of war that were adjunct to the rules on resort to war, such as the formalities for declaring war and the rules on remaining neutral from the wars of other states. In 1856, states adopted the Paris Declaration Respecting Maritime Law, which spelled out principles respecting maritime neutrality. The Paris Declaration also prohibited state exercise of force through contracts with privateers.[47] In 1863, President Lincoln issued General Orders 100, also known as the Lieber Code, for governing the conduct of Union forces in the American Civil War.[48] In 1864, the first Geneva

---

[43] Von Elbe *supra* n.24, at 684.
[44] Brownlie, *supra* n.19, at 22.
[45] J. Noyes, 'The Caroline', in J. Noyes *et al.* (eds), *International Law Stories* (New York: Foundation, 2007).
[46] Letter from Webster to Lord Ashburton (6 August 1842), available at http://www.yale.edu/lawweb/avalon/diplomacy/britain/br-1842d.htm.
[47] Paris Declaration Respecting Maritime Law, 16 April 1856, ICRC, available at www.icrc.org/ihl.nsf/INTRO/105?OpenDocument.
[48] *Instructions for the Government of Armies of the United States in the Field*, ICRC, available at http://www.icrc.org/ihl.nsf/FULL/110?OpenDocument.

Convention for the protection of war victims was adopted.[49] From this period forward, regulation of the conduct of force in positive law became an important part of the restrictions on the use of force.

By the 1870s and 1880s, the organized peace movements of the United Kingdom and United States had renewed calls for alternatives to war following the 1872 *Alabama Claims* arbitration between the US and Britain.[50] The arbitration concerned the US claim that Britain had failed to observe its neutral duties during the American Civil War. The British had failed to prevent the Confederacy from purchasing three naval ships from a shipbuilder in Liverpool during the War. The ships did significant damage and, the US argued, had extended the War. The US won the case, and Britain paid sizeable damages. The *Alabama Claims* arbitration became an iconic example of how peaceful methods of dispute settlement could be substituted for war. By the end of the 19th century, peace organizations, such as the American Peace Society and the Universal Peace Union, had successfully lobbied for treaties obligating states to go to arbitration in the case of certain kinds of disputes. In the course of this effort, the discussion began to shift from arbitration to judicial settlement in courts, in particular, a world court.[51] The United States Supreme Court was cited as an example of how a court could successfully resolve disputes between at least semi-sovereign states. Peaceful settlement of disputes had become so accepted that by the 1880s both major US political parties included commitments to inter-state arbitration in their party platforms.[52] It came as a terrible shock to the peace movements when, in 1898, President McKinley declared war on Spain. McKinley had been a champion of arbitration and had repeatedly affirmed his opposition to war with Spain. He changed position under pressure from pro-war advocates such as the newspaper editor William Randolph Hearst and the politician Theodore Roosevelt. Roosevelt helped to ensure that the war would occur by interfering with the investigation into the explosion of the *USS Maine* docked at Havana, Cuba. Cuba was a Spanish colony at the time. The US had shown sympathy for the militant independence movement on the island. When the *Maine* exploded, Hearst, Roosevelt and hawks pointed to Spain. Roosevelt even saw to it that evidence of the more likely cause of the disaster – the poor design of the coal fuelled ship – never made it into the investigation.[53]

The US quickly won the war and acquired its first colonies. The peace movements saw the whole episode as a denial of America's highest values of democracy, the rule of law and the peaceful settlement of disputes. Just at this moment, Tsar Nicholas II called an international conference on disarmament for 1899. American and European peace

---

[49] *Introduction*, ICRC, available at http://www.icrc.org/ihl.nsf/INTRO/110?OpenDocument; *Convention for the Amelioration of the Condition of the Wounded in Armies in the Field*, ICRC, available at http://www.icrc.org/ihl.nsf/full/120?opendocument, available at icrc.org.

[50] See E.C. Bruggink, 'The Alabama Claims', (1996) 57 *Ala. L. Rev.* 339.

[51] *The Court: History*, International Court of Justice, http://www.icj-cij.org/court/index.php?p1=1&p2=1.

[52] *Republican Party Platform, 1884*, available at http://www.presidency.ucsb.edu/ws/index.php?pid=29626#axzz1ncXfZObp; *Democratic Party Platform, 1888*, available at http://www.presidency.ucsb.edu/ws/index.php?pid=29584#axzz1ncXfZObp.

[53] E. Thomas, *The War Lovers: Roosevelt, Lodge, Hearst, and the Rush to Empire* (London: Little Brown, 2010), at 213–224.

advocates lobbied to get the subject of peaceful settlement of disputes on the agenda as well. The delegates agreed to attempt to settle disputes peacefully before resort to war. They also agreed to the establishment of the Permanent Court of Arbitration. The PCA is a secretariat that assists in the formation of *ad hoc* arbitral tribunals.[54] The Hague Convention (I) for the Pacific Settlement of International Disputes (1899) provides:

Article 1

With a view to obviating, as far as possible, recourse to force in the relations between States, the Signatory Powers agree to use their best efforts to insure the pacific settlement of international differences.

Article 2

In case of serious disagreement or conflict, before an appeal to arms, the Signatory Powers agree to have recourse, as far as circumstances allow to the good offices or mediation of one or more friendly Powers.[55]

In 1905, President Theodore Roosevelt mediated the end of the Russo-Japanese War, a very popular accomplishment with the peace movement for which he won the Nobel Peace Prize in 1906. Also in 1906, the mechanism of inquiry was used by the United Kingdom and Russia to resolve the dangerous Dogger Bank dispute. Russian naval vessels had opened fire on six British fishing vessels. The incident nearly sparked a war, but the Commission of Inquiry reported that the Russians mistook the vessels for submarines.[56]

The success defusing the Dogger Bank incident led to further development of inquiry at the Second Hague Peace Conference held in 1907, when states gathered a second time, with a more ambitious agenda and larger group of states. Roosevelt sent his trusted Secretary of State, Elihu Root, who, in 1906, became the founding president of the American Society of International Law. Root believed strongly in the promise of international law and a world court as mechanisms to avoid war.[57] He arrived in The Hague with a blueprint for a court, as did the British delegation.[58] The Germans, however, had only just begun to establish an overseas empire and wanted no limits on their right to wage war.[59] They effectively blocked the move to establish a court in 1907, but the delegates did manage to outlaw war in a particular cause, namely to collect contract debts.[60]

None of the treaty obligations agreed to at The Hague Peace Conferences to prevent or delay war played any role, however, in impeding the outbreak of the First World War. The War was triggered by the assassination of the Austro-Hungarian Empire's heir

---

[54] See the website of the Permanent Court of Arbitration, at www.pca-cpa.org.
[55] *Ibid.*
[56] R.N. Lebow, 'Accidents and Crises: The Dogger Bank Affair', (1978) 31 *Nav. War. Col. Rev.* 66–75.
[57] P.C. Jessup, *Elihu Root* (New York: Dodd, Mead, 1938).
[58] M. Pomerance, *The United States and the World Court as a 'Supreme Court of the Nations': Dreams, Illusions and Delusions* (Heidelberg: Springer, 1996), at 54–55.
[59] K. Schlichtmann, 'Japan, Germany and the Idea of the Hague Peace Conference', (2003) JPR 377, at 390–392.
[60] 1907 Convention, *supra* n.8.

to the throne by a secret pro-Serbian nationalist group, the Black Hand. Many peace activists in the United States and Europe urged world leaders to try mediation or other alternatives to resort to war, but others, such as Elihu Root, believed war with Germany was inevitable.[61]

As Europe emerged from the carnage of the War, the peace movement appeared vindicated. Statesmen gathering in Paris arrived committed to new institutions and new rules to avoid another such war.[62] The resulting Treaty of Versailles took a multi-faceted approach to ensuring peace. It provided for a new international organization devoted to peace – the League of Nations, a world court, the break-up of the German, Ottoman and Austro-Hungarian Empires, and the prosecution of the Kaiser for waging war in violation of treaties.[63] The Covenant of the League of Nations, concluded as part of the Treaty of Versailles, built upon the obligation of the Hague Conventions to attempt peaceful settlement of disputes before resort to war, with Article 12 stating that:

> The Members of the League agree that, if there should arise between them any dispute likely to lead to a rupture they will submit the matter either to arbitration or judicial settlement or to enquiry by the Council, and they agree in no case to resort to war until three months after the award by the arbitrators or the judicial decision, or the report by the Council.

One of the League's first actions was to appoint a Committee of Jurists to draft a statute for the Permanent Court of International Justice (hereinafter 'PCIJ'). The PCIJ heard its first cases by 1922. It was the first international court open to all states for the resolution of disputes through the application of international law.[64]

The United States, despite its central role in the formation of both the League of Nations and the PCIJ, did not join either institution. The League's failure to enforce the peace in the inter-war period is often linked with the absence of the US. The American peace movement, however, did persuade American officials to show that the country supported peace, despite the prevailing isolationist mood. Secretary of State Frank Kellogg joined with his French counterpart and drafted the 1928 Kellogg–Briand Pact or Pact of Paris, which, in Article I, outlawed war as an instrument of national policy:

> The High Contracting Parties solemnly declare in the names of their respective peoples that they condemn recourse to war for the solution of international controversies, and renounce it, as an instrument of national policy in their relations with one another.[65]

---

[61] M.E. O'Connell, 'Elihu Root and Crisis Prevention', (2001) 95 *Proceedings of the ASIL* 115.
[62] For an excellent account of the post-First World War peace negotiations, see M. Macmillan, *Peacemakers, Six Months that Changed the World: The Paris Peace Conference of 1919 and its Attempt to End War* (Abingdon: Hachette UK Co., 2001).
[63] The Treaty of Versailles, 28 June 1919. League of Nations Covenant (1919), available at http://avalon.law.yale.edu/20th_century/leagcov.asp#art12. See also Brownlie, *supra* n.19, at chapter IV.
[64] International Court of Justice, *History*, http://www.icj-cij.org/court/index.php?p1=1&p2=1.
[65] Kellogg–Briand Pact (1928), available at www.yale.edu/lawweb/avalon/imt/kbpact.htm.

The parties to the Kellogg–Briand Pact understood that the agreement did not prohibit force in self-defence. The parties were divided, however, as to whether states could still use force to enforce other types of rights.[66]

Germany, Italy and Japan all claimed to have rights under international law to invade and conquer other states despite the Kellogg–Briand Pact, the League Covenant, the Hague Conventions and numerous bilateral treaties requiring peaceful resolution of disputes. The three Axis powers argued they had rights of conquest principally based on self-defensive claims, such as the need for *Lebensraum* or critical natural resources. They also claimed to be acting to defend the rights of minorities, such as the Sudeten Germans. It was apparent to US President Franklin Roosevelt that the weakness of the post-war order lay not in the rules prohibiting resort to force but in the institution intended to interpret and enforce the rules. Thus, as early as 1938, Roosevelt tasked US government officials with designing a new organization to ensure the peace.[67]

3. THE MEANING OF ARTICLE 2(4)

Roosevelt is thought to have sacrificed his health in the waning days of the Second World War to get the agreement of the United Kingdom and the Soviet Union to his basic plan for the United Nations.[68] In June 1945, Roosevelt's successor, Harry Truman, oversaw a conference of 50 national delegations in San Francisco to finalize the United Nations Charter. At the heart of the Charter is the general prohibition on the use of force by states in Article 2(4). A new organ, the Security Council, was created to enforce Article 2(4). Only one narrow exception is provided for states to use force without Security Council authorization.[69] Article 51 permits individual and collective self-defence if an armed attack occurs, but, even then, only until the Security Council takes 'measures necessary to maintain international peace and security'.[70]

The discussion below looks at Article 2(4) setting out, first, its intended scope and, secondly, its two levels of prohibited force: aggression, which is a serious violation of Article 2(4), and all other force in violation of the prohibition. The conclusion of this section is that under the best interpretation, Article 2(4) prohibits any use of armed force or armed force equivalent by a state against another state when the force involved is more than *de minimis*. Further, serious violations of Article 2(4) are considered acts

---

[66] Brownlie, *supra* n.19, at 218.
[67] S.C. Schlesinger, *Act of Creation: The Founding of the United Nations* (Boulder, CO: Westview, 2003), at 33.
[68] *Ibid.*, at 57.
[69] Article 2(4), UN Charter (1945).
[70] Article 51 of the UN Charter provides: 'Nothing in the present Charter shall impair the inherent right of individual or collective self-defense if an armed attack occurs against a member of the United Nations, until the Security Council has taken measures necessary to maintain international peace and security. Measures taken by members in the exercise of this right of self-defense shall be immediately reported to the Security Council and shall not in any way affect the authority and responsibility of the Security Council under the present Charter to take at any time such action as it deems necessary in order to maintain or restore international peace and security.'

of aggression that may result in the individual accountability of a state leader responsible for the decision to engage in aggression.

A. The Scope of Article 2(4)

The records of the 1945 San Francisco Conference confirm that the delegations intended Article 2(4) to have a broad scope; in other words, that it would prohibit almost every use of inter-state armed violence. Nevertheless, at the time of the Conference and periodically since, the argument has been made that Article 2(4) only restricts force aimed at the 'territorial integrity' and 'political independence' of another state.[71] Those making this argument typically assert that force for other purposes, such as ending atrocities in another state, instituting democracy, instituting communism or pre-empting future attacks, would not violate the Article 2(4) prohibition.[72] The negotiating history from San Francisco is clear, however, that the references in Article 2(4) to 'territorial integrity', 'political independence' and, especially, 'in any other manner inconsistent with the Purposes of the United Nations' were intended to broaden the prohibition on force, not narrow it. A member of the US delegation responded to a question from the Brazilian delegation on the intended scope of Article 2(4) by saying: '[T]he intention of the authors of the original text was to state in the broadest terms an absolute all-inclusive prohibition; the phrase "or in any other manner" was designed to insure that there should be no loopholes.'[73] Brownlie emphasizes that the delegations agreed that '[t]here was a presumption against self-help and even action in self-defence within Article 51 was made subject to control by the Security Council'.[74]

The overall structure of the Charter that emerged in San Francisco also supports the interpretation that the prohibition on the use of force was to apply widely. The UN Security Council was given explicit, broad authority in Articles 39 and 42 to use force against threats, as well as breaches of the peace and acts of aggression. By contrast, states acting without Security Council authority have only one express possibility to engage in force and that is restricted to self-defence under the stringent terms of Article 51. Article 51 permits force in individual and collective self-defence 'if an armed attack occurs' until the Security Council takes action. If Article 2(4) only prohibited force aimed at territorial integrity and political independence, Article 51 would be unnecessary since force in self-defence would not be aimed at the territorial integrity or political independence of the attacking state, but instead at repulsing a use of force aimed at the defender's territorial integrity or political independence.

---

[71] R. Lillich, 'Humanitarian Intervention: A Reply to Ian Brownlie and a Plea for Constructive Alternatives', in J.N. Moore (ed.), *Law and Civil War in the Modern World* (Baltimore, MD: The Johns Hopkins University Press, 1974), 229, at 235–251.

[72] *Ibid.*; F.R. Tesón, 'The Liberal Case for Humanitarian Intervention', in J.L. Holzgrefe and R.O. Keohane (eds), *Humanitarian Intervention: Ethical, Legal, and Political Dilemmas* (Cambridge: Cambridge University Press, 2003), 94; A. D'Amato, 'Israel's Air Strike Upon the Iraqi Nuclear Reactor', (1983) 77 *AJIL* 584.

[73] Documents of the United Nations Conference on International Organization, vol. 6 (San Francisco, 25 April 1945), at 334–335.

[74] Brownlie, *supra* n.19, at 275.

Despite the broad nature of the Charter's prohibition on force, in the almost 70 years since its adoption, four limits on Article 2(4) are discernible, each of which will be discussed in some detail below. First, states and commentators indicate that the type of force prohibited in Article 2(4) is armed force or the equivalent of armed force, in distinction to other types of coercive conduct. Secondly, very minimal uses of armed force are not covered by Article 2(4). States engaged in the minimal use of armed force, for example to affect an arrest, will not violate Article 2(4). Thirdly and more controversially, is the right of states to use major armed force on the territory of another state with the invitation of that other state. Finally, Article 2(4) currently prohibits force against another sovereign state, in distinction to force against non-state actor groups resorting to force within states or even against non-state actors based outside the state, if there is no attribution of the force used by the non-state actor to a *de facto* or *de jure* state.

i. Force other than armed force

Article 2(4) prohibits armed force, not *all* forceful conduct. Over the years, it has become clear, particularly from observing state practice, that states see Article 2(4) as applying to forms of force that are categorized as armed force or the equivalent of armed force. The records from San Francisco as well as decisions of the International Court of Justice (hereinafter 'ICJ') also support this view.[75] Excluded from the scope of Article 2(4) are such coercive measures as economic sanctions; diplomatic protest; physical force not involving weapons, such as cutting the nets of fishing vessels; disrupting internet service by denial of service attacks; and unconsented presence of official vessels or vehicles within another state's jurisdiction. While these and many other possible examples will not as a general matter fall within Article 2(4), most are nevertheless prohibited by other principles of international law. The principle of non-intervention would prohibit the unconsented presence of vessels or vehicles within another state's jurisdiction. Disrupting fishing or internet use might violate economic rights or property rights – to name just a few prohibitory rules.[76]

---

[75] Documents of the United Nations Conference on International Organization (25 April–26 April 1945), 334 (discussing the rejection of a proposal by Brazil to extend the prohibition on force to economic coercion). The Simma commentary points to paragraph 7 of the preamble of the Charter – which states that 'armed force shall not be used, save in the common interest' – and to Article 44 of the Charter – which refers to 'armed force' for instances wherein the Council decides to use force – to support the view that the general prohibition on the use of force under Article 2(4) refers solely to military force. B. Simma *et al.* (eds), *The Charter of the United Nations: A Commentary*, 2nd edn (Oxford: Oxford University Press, 2002), 118.

[76] Declaration on Principles of International Law Concerning Friendly Relations and Cooperation Among States in Accordance with the Charter of the United Nations, GA Res. 2625 (XXV) (1970) (hereinafter 'Declaration on Friendly Relations') ('No State may use or encourage the use of economic political or any other type of measures to coerce another State in order to obtain from it the subordination of the exercise of its sovereign rights and to secure from it advantages of any kind.').

ii. Minimal force

Even within the category of armed force, Article 2(4) is narrower than it might appear on its face. Minimal or *de minimis* uses of force are likely to fall below the threshold of the Article 2(4) prohibition.[77] For example, in the case of a fishing enforcement vessel firing bullets across the bow of a foreign vessel suspected of illicit fishing, the enforcement vessel is clearly using armed force. Nevertheless, the type of force associated with law enforcement does not come within the Article 2(4) prohibition. Shooting across the bow of a ship, shooting at the legs of a person evading arrest and dropping a bomb on an oil tanker to prevent coastal pollution are all examples of such minimal or *de minimis* armed force.[78] Such minimal force has been used to arrest pirates,[79] hijackers, terrorists and smugglers, and in the physical prevention of damage to the environment. If the force used is not sufficient for the purpose, the enforcing state is nevertheless required to stop short of force that would violate Article 2(4).

This conclusion about minimal uses of force falling outside the scope of Article 2(4) is based on observation of state practice, the implications of certain judgments of the ICJ and commentary. There is no express authority on the point, in contrast to the authority reviewed above supporting the interpretation that Article 2(4) concerns armed force and not all types of forceful action.

The ICJ indicated that minimal force falls outside of Article 2(4) in one of its earliest decisions, the *Corfu Channel* case.[80] The case arose following several incidents in the Strait of Corfu, a waterway formed by the island of Corfu and the coasts of Albania and Greece. In May 1946, two British Navy vessels, the *Orion* and *Superb*, were passing through the North Corfu Channel when they came under fire from an Albanian shore battery. The British vessels were not struck. The British protested; Albania replied that under its view of international law warships must give notice and receive permission before transiting a strait like the Corfu Channel. Britain replied that in its view, warships have a right of innocent passage through straits connecting two areas of high seas. In October 1946, British vessels returned to the Corfu Channel. Two ships struck maritime mines, suffering extensive damage and the loss of 44 sailors' lives.

In November 1946, Britain carried out a mine-sweeping operation in the Channel. It had informed the International Central Mine Clearance Board of its intentions. The

---

[77] T.D. Gill, 'The Forcible Protection, Affirmation and Exercise of Rights by States Under Contemporary International Law', (1992) 23 *Neth. Y.B. Int'l L.* 105, at 125.

[78] In 1967, the UK bombed the *Torrey Canyon*, an oil tanker that had run aground in international waters and threatened serious oil pollution damage to the UK coast. *In Re Barracuda Tanker Corp.*, 409 F.2d 1013 (1968). The action was universally approved and codified at Article 216 of the United Nations Convention on the Law of the Sea (III). UN Convention on the Law of the Sea (opened for signature 10 December 1982), UN Doc. A/Conf.62/122, Article 216, reprinted in UN, Official Text of the United Nations Convention on the Law of the Sea with Annexes and Index, UN Sales No. E.83.v.5 (1983), 21 ILM 1261 (1982) (hereinafter 'UNCLOS'). The *Torrey Canyon* incident is said to have led to an international 'right of intervention when a threat of pollution of a State's coastal zone presents a grave and imminent danger'. L.A. Malone, 'Discussion in the Security Council on Environmental Intervention in Ukraine', (1994) 27 *Loy. L.A. L. Rev.* 893, 905.

[79] UNCLOS, *ibid.*, at Art. 107.

[80] *Corfu Channel Case* (UK v. Albania) (Judgment) [1949] ICJ Rep. 4.

Board supported the operation but conditioned it on the UK receiving Albania's consent. Albania did not give its consent. Nevertheless, the sweep went forward. In a case brought by Britain against Albania before the ICJ, Britain argued that the sweep was legally justified even without Albania's consent both to collect evidence and as lawful self-help. The Court ruled in favour of the UK's principal arguments in the case that warships had, under the rule then in place, a right of innocent passage through straits connecting two areas of high seas. Albania also had a fundamental duty to warn ships transiting the Channel of the danger posed by the maritime mines. Britain did not, however, have a right to sweep the Channel without Albania's permission on either basis that it argued in the case. The critical point for this chapter is the legal principle cited by the ICJ in ruling on Britain's action. The Court does not mention Article 2(4); rather, it said that the:

> Court can only regard the alleged right of intervention as the manifestation of a policy of force, such as has, in the past, given rise to most serious abuses and such as cannot, whatever be the present defects in international organization, find a place in international law. Intervention is perhaps still less admissible in the particular form it would take here; for, from the nature of things, it would be reserved for the most powerful States, and might easily lead to perverting the administration of international justice itself. ... Between independent States, respect for territorial sovereignty is an essential foundation of international relations. ... [T]he Court must declare that the action of the British Navy constituted a violation of Albanian sovereignty.[81]

In subsequent cases involving claims by states of a right to resort to major military force in accord with the right of self-defence as provided in Article 51 of the UN Charter, and its customary law equivalent, the ICJ has indicated the importance of assessing the amount of force that a defending state alleges has been used against it. In the 1986 *Nicaragua* case, the Court explained the importance of distinguishing 'the most grave forms of the use of force (those constituting an armed attack) from other less grave forms'.[82] States resorting to less grave forms may violate the principle of non-intervention (as was the case of the UK in *Corfu Channel*) but do not trigger rights of a victim state under Article 51. To support its ruling the ICJ cited the principle of non-intervention, not Article 2(4). It referenced the UN General Assembly's Declaration on Friendly Relations,[83] the Organization of American States (hereinafter 'OAS') Convention on the Rights and Duties of States in the Event of Civil Strife,[84] and the Declaration on Non-Intervention.[85]

---

[81] *Ibid.*, at 35 (paragraph break omitted).
[82] *Military and Paramilitary Activities in and Against Nicaragua* (Nicaragua v. United States of America) (Judgment) [1986] ICJ Rep. 14, at 101–103 (hereinafter '*Nicaragua*').
[83] Declaration on Friendly Relations, *supra* n.76.
[84] OAS Convention on the Rights and Duties of States in the Event of Civil Strife (entered into force 21 May 1929) 134 LNTS 45.
[85] Declaration on the Inadmissibility of Intervention in the Domestic Affairs of States and the Protection of Their Independence and Sovereignty, UNGA Res. 2131 (XX) (1981), UN Doc. A/RES/36/103.

The Court has gone into detail to explain in the *Nicaragua* case and subsequent cases that the type of attack that triggers the right of self-defence must involve a significant use of force:

> [T]he prohibition of armed attacks may apply to the sending by a State of armed bands to the territory of another State, if such an operation, because of its scale and effects would have been classified as an armed attack rather than a mere frontier incident had it been carried out by regular armed forces.[86]

The ICJ made similar assessments of 'scale and effects' of violent action in the *Oil Platforms* case,[87] the *Wall* advisory opinion[88] and the *DRC v. Uganda* case.[89]

In *Oil Platforms*, the United States indicated in its pleadings the need to prove that a use of force or pattern of force was grave enough to justify a response in self-defence. The United States contended that the fact its ship, the *USS Samuel B. Roberts*, struck a maritime mine *together* with the pattern of Iranian uses of force 'added to the gravity of the specific attacks, reinforced the necessity of action in self-defense, and helped to shape the appropriate response'. The ICJ, however, held that the US did not prove its case as to the mining incident in several important respects. The Court did not need to analyse the US's legal theory as to whether a cumulated series of attacks could amount to a sufficiently grave attack to trigger the right of self-defence.

> The question is therefore whether that incident sufficed in itself to justify action in self-defence, as amounting to an 'armed attack'. The Court does not exclude the possibility that the mining of a single military vessel might be sufficient to bring into play the 'inherent right of self-defence'; but in view of all the circumstances, including the inconclusiveness of the evidence of Iran's responsibility for the mining of the USS *Samuel B. Roberts*, the Court is unable to hold that the attacks on the Salman and Nasr platforms have been shown to have been justifiably made in response to an 'armed attack' on the United States by Iran, in the form of the mining of the *USS Samuel B. Roberts*.[90]

In addition to these ICJ decisions in cases involving aspects of self-defence, the ICJ, other courts and investigative commissions have assessed uses of armed force in a variety of maritime enforcement cases. The decisions in these cases do not refer to the use of force as violating Article 2(4), even when, as in the case of the *Red Crusader* inquiry, a Danish fishing protection vessel was found to have used excessive force against a British fishing vessel.[91] The ICJ heard arguments in cases brought by the UK and Germany against Iceland that involved Icelandic coast guard vessels firing at British and German fishing vessels. The fishing vessels were subsequently escorted by British and German Navy vessels. No reference is made to Article 2(4) by the Court in

---

[86] *Nicaragua*, supra n.82, at 103–104.
[87] *Oil Platforms* (Iran v. USA) (Judgment) [2003] ICJ Rep. 161, 191.
[88] *Legal Consequences of the Construction of a Wall in the Occupied Palestinian Territory* (Advisory Opinion) [2004] ICJ Rep. 136, at 195 (hereinafter '*Wall* opinion').
[89] *Armed Activities on the Territory of the Democratic Republic of the Congo* (DRC v. Uganda) (Judgment) [2005] ICJ Rep. 168, at 301 (hereinafter 'DRC v. Uganda').
[90] *Oil Platforms*, supra n.87, at 195–196.
[91] *Report of the Commission of Inquiry into the Red Crusader Incident* (1962) 35 ILR 485.

these cases.[92] In the mid-1990s, Canada attempted to prevent overfishing of halibut by cutting the nets of Spanish fishing vessels and, in one case, arresting a vessel by firing across the bow of the *Estai*.[93] Spain attempted to bring a case against Canada to the ICJ, complaining about Canada's 'measures of coercion and the exercise of jurisdiction over [the *Estai*] and its captain'. Spain also claimed that Canada's actions violated Article 2(4).[94] The ICJ did not find jurisdiction in the case. It is a rare example of state practice against the position taken in this chapter that the Article 2(4) prohibition on the use of force does not reach minimal uses of force.

This point respecting Article 2(4)'s lower threshold becomes particularly important with respect to terrorism. Terrorist attacks perpetrated by states and non-state actors have almost without exception been treated as crimes under the national criminal law of the state where the injuries were suffered and not as violations of Article 2(4). The major exception is 9/11. The UN Security Council found in Resolution 1368 (2001) that the 9/11 attacks triggered the right of self-defence.[95] Otherwise, terrorist attacks sponsored by a state have been treated as violating the obligation of non-intervention owed to the state where the violence is perpetrated. Such attacks are also treated as violating the human rights of the victims. Individuals carrying out terrorist attacks, whether as the agent of a state, a non-state actor or acting independently, are treated as having carried out a crime. In the *Nicaragua* case, the ICJ pointed out that the General Assembly's reference to state obligations in respect to terrorism in the Declaration on Friendly Relations are included in the Declaration's section devoted to the principle of non-intervention.[96] One high-profile example of this point is the Libyan-sponsored attack on a Pan Am flight while over Lockerbie, Scotland, that resulted in criminal trials of the agents who carried out the attacks in a civilian, not a military court.[97]

The remainder of the examples in this section are not the subject of deliberation by a court or other bodies such as the Security Council. They are, nevertheless, included here as additional instances of state practice that are consistent with the decisions just

---

[92] *Fisheries Jurisdiction Case* (UK v. Iceland) (Judgment) [1974] ICJ Rep. 56; *Fisheries Jurisdiction Case* (Federal Republic of Germany v. Iceland) (Judgment) [1973] ICJ Rep. 49.

[93] P.G.G. Davies, 'The EC/Canadian Fisheries Dispute in the Northwest', (1995) 44 *Atlantic Int. and Comp. L. Quarterly* 927, at 927.

[94] *Fisheries Jurisdiction* (Spain v. Canada) (Judgment) [1995] ICJ Rep. 87.

[95] Trying to fit even such serious terrorist attacks into the Article 51 self-defence paradigm has raised significant legal issues as predicted by a number of scholars soon after the adoption of Security Council Resolution 1368. M.E. O'Connell, 'Ad Hoc War', in H. Fischer *et al.* (eds), *Krisensicherung und Humanitärer Schutz: Crisis Management and Humanitarian Protection* (Berlin: Berliner Wissenschafts-Verlag, 2004), 399; M.A. Drumbl, 'Victimhood in Our Neighborhood: Terrorist Crime, Taliban Guilt and the Asymmetries of the International Legal Order', (2002) 81 *N. C. L. Rev.* 1; E.P.J. Myjer and N.D. White, 'The Twin Towers Attack: An Unlimited Right to Self-Defence?', (2002) 7 *JCSL* 5.

[96] Declaration on the Inadmissibility of Intervention in the Domestic Affairs of States and the Protection of their Independence and Sovereignty, UNGA Res. 2131 (XX) of 21 Dec. 1965, available at http://www.un-documents.net/a20r2131.htm.

[97] D.G. McNeil, Jr., 'The Lockerbie Verdict: The Overview; Libyan Convicted By Scottish Court in '88 Pan Am Blast', *New York Times*, 1 February 2001, available at http://www.nytimes.com/2001/02/01/world/lockerbie-verdict-overview-libyan-convicted-scottish-court-88-pan-am-blast.html?.

surveyed. The US, for example, has for years implemented a programme challenging extensive maritime boundary claims by sending Navy vessels into disputed zones. In August 1981, the US sent ships into the Gulf of Sidra to challenge Libya's claim that the Gulf is a historic bay. In response, Libya sent attack planes against the ships. The Libyans fired on the US planes that were coming to meet them; the Americans returned fire, shooting down the Libyans.[98] Shooting at the attackers was arguably lawful in the specific defence of the US planes, rather than as an exercise of the right of self-defence under Article 51. As such, the case is not one of an Article 2(4) violation by the US. On 31 March 1999 three US soldiers patrolling the Serbia–Macedonia border apparently strayed into Serbia (then still called Yugoslavia) and were detained.[99] Despite the fact that NATO had already begun bombing Serbia to force Serb troops out of Kosovo, the border incursion by the three was not part of the armed conflict then underway and is best categorized as a use of force below the Article 2(4) threshold. Serbia freed the three in response to a mediation effort by the Reverend Jesse Jackson.[100] A similar incident occurred when British sailors apparently strayed into Iranian territorial waters in 2007 during the Iraq War. Iran detained the crew, treating the matter as one of illegal entry and suggesting it might put the crew on trial.[101] The British claimed the crew was in Iraqi, not Iranian, waters. Neither side mentioned Article 2(4). More serious violations of maritime space have occurred than that just described, but, consistently, Article 2(4) has not been invoked. North Korean Navy submarines have been detected in Japanese territorial waters, not in transit and not on the surface – two violations of the right to be in the zone.[102] These submarines are small and have not used armed force. In 1982, in a similar incident, Sweden detected a submerged submarine in a restricted area. There was an attempt to get the sub to surface using depth charges and to arrest it by blocking it into an area using a metal barrier and mines.[103] Plainly the use of depth charges and mines constitutes armed force, but in this case the use did not violate Article 2(4) because it was a minimal use to detain the submarine.

Limited armed force to pluck hostages away from armed captors would also appear to be outside of the Article 2(4) prohibition. In two well-known cases excessive force was likely used and, therefore, Article 2(4) was implicated. In 1976, Israel rescued over 100 Israeli nationals who were on board a hijacked Air France flight forced to land by hijackers at Entebbe Airport in Uganda. Some 100 Israeli commandos managed to

---

[98] A.M. Weisburd, *Use of Force: The Practice of States Since World War II* (University Park, PA: The Pennsylvania State University Press, 1997), at 276–277.

[99] W. Branigin, 'Release of 3 Soldiers is Sought; Cypriot Leader Going to Belgrade, *Washington Post*, 8 April 1999.

[100] S. Sachs, 'Crisis in the Balkans: Prisoners; Serbs Release 3 Captured U.S. Soldiers', *New York Times*, 2 May 1999.

[101] M. Stannard, 'What Law Did Tehran Break? Capture of British Sailors a Gray Area in Application of Geneva Conventions', *San Francisco Chronicle*, 1 April 2007.

[102] 'The Call to Arms', *Economist*, 27 February 1999, at 23; 'The Koreas: The Money Factor', *Economist*, 31 October 1998, at 45.

[103] R. Sadurska, 'Foreign Submarines in Swedish Waters: The Erosion of an International Norm', in W.M. Reisman and A.R. Willard (eds) *International Incidents: The Law that Counts in World Politics* (Princeton: Princeton University Press, 1998), 40.

rescue almost all of the hostages in a daring night raid.[104] In doing so, three hostages were killed, as well as one Israeli soldier, 45 Ugandan soldiers and all of the hijackers. Thirty Ugandan Air Force planes were destroyed on the ground. UN Secretary-General Kurt Waldheim denounced Israel's action as a violation of Uganda's territory. The Security Council, however, took no action beyond hearing Uganda's charges and Israel's defence.[105]

On 11 September 2000, over 150 British troops rescued five British soldiers and their interpreter taken captive by rebel forces, called the West Side Boys, in Sierra Leone. Again, as in Entebbe, the rescue appeared to involve excessive force. The six hostages were successfully freed from their captors within about 90 minutes, but the British rescuers continued battling the West Side Boys for hours to retrieve equipment and, apparently, to weaken the militants as a fighting force. The West Side Boys' putative leader was captured. One British soldier was killed but over 70 militants died.[106] Cyberspace is another area where some writers try to equate crime with armed attack for the purposes of triggering a right to resort to force under Article 51. The internet is a zone of communications and commerce where a good deal of crime occurs. Enhancing cyber security, however, should be the job of the police, not the military.[107]

iii. Invitation

The Charter provides no express guidance on the right of a state to use major military force on the territory of another state at the invitation of the government of the other state. It is possible to interpret the Charter as prohibiting such force. Article 2(4) is a general prohibition on the use of force by states that allows for only one exception for the unauthorized use of force: self-defence under Article 51. Article 51 provides that states may join in collective self-defence, so the one exception to Article 2(4) deals expressly with the case of assistance. The law preceding the Charter provides some support for this interpretation. It held that when a rebel movement acquired sufficient strength to challenge a government, a status known as belligerency, all states wishing to retain neutral rights had to withdraw assistance even to the government.[108]

---

[104] Weisburd, *supra* n.98, at 289–290.

[105] T.M. Franck, *State Action Against Threats and Armed Attacks* (Cambridge: Cambridge University Press, 2002), at 85; C. Gray, *International Law and the Use of Force*, 3rd edn (Oxford: Oxford University Press, 2008), at 32–33.

[106] K. Sengupta, 'British Soldier Killed in Sierra Leone', *Independent*, 23 April 2000. See also W. Fowler, *Operation Barras: The SAS Rescue Mission, Sierra Leone 2000* (London: Cassell Military, 2005). The United States attempted a rescue mission in 1980 of the 53 persons being held hostage in the US embassy in Tehran, Iran. In principle, the US had the right to try to rescue its nationals, even using military force. Yet, the operation to rescue the US hostages had a number of practical issues associated with it. The commandos sent to execute the rescue never made it to Tehran, however, owing to two transport helicopters crashing and a third helicopter returning to the aircraft carrier after encountering a sand storm.

[107] See M.E. O'Connell, 'Cyber Security without Cyber War', (2012) 17 *JCSL* 187.

[108] H. Lauterpacht, *Oppenheim's International Law: Vol. II, Disputes, War and Neutrality* (London: Longmans, 1944), 490.

The Soviet intervention in Hungary in 1956 is probably the first significant use of force on the basis of an invitation following the adoption of the Charter. In that year, the Soviet Union sent 60,000 troops into Hungary to crush a popular revolution aimed at moving Hungary out of the Eastern Bloc. To obtain the invitation from Hungary, the Soviet Union plotted with a high-ranking member of the Hungarian government, Janos Kadar, to represent himself as the true government, moving aside the choice of the reformers, Imre Nagy.[109] The critical reaction to the intervention generally focused on the treatment of Nagy and the suppression of popular will, more than the basis of the intervention being an invitation. The Soviet Union followed a very similar pattern in obtaining invitations to intervene in Czechoslovakia in 1968[110] and Afghanistan in 1979.[111] The US also obtained a questionable invitation to intervene in Grenada in 1983.[112]

In 1985, however, Louise Doswald-Beck wrote:

> It is submitted that there is, at the least, a very serious doubt whether a State may validly aid another government to suppress a rebellion, particularly if the rebellion is widespread and seriously aimed at the overthrow of the incumbent regime. ... [S]tatements [of governments] stressing true independence, self-determination and non-intervention in internal affairs, provide[s] substantial evidence to support a theory that intervention to prop up a beleaguered government is illegal.[113]

Olivier Corten, writing in 2010, throws doubt on Doswald-Beck's conclusion. He finds that 'all the commentators who have dealt with the question share one point in common: in principle, no one denies that validly given consent can make a military operation lawful'.[114] Yet, the conclusions of these commentators are more likely based on their subjective assessment of what the rule should be rather than on valid state practice. With few exceptions, consent to intervene was either obtained through manipulation or came from a beleaguered government that had very questionable authority to invite assistance. This was the case in respect of the Economic Community of West African States' (ECOWAS) intervention in Liberia,[115] the US intervention in Panama[116] and many of the French interventions in its former

---

[109] C. Gati, *Failed Illusions: Moscow, Budapest, and the 1956 Hungarian Revolt* (Palo Alto, CA: Stanford University Press, 2006), at 17ff., 233.

[110] P. Windsor and A. Roberts, *Czechoslovakia 1968: Reform, Repression and Resistance* (London: Chatto & Windus, 1969).

[111] M.E. O'Connell, 'Soviet Prisoners in the Afghan Conflict', (1985) 23 *Col. J. Trans. L.* 483.

[112] C.C. Joyner, 'Reflections on the Lawfulness of Invasion', (1984) 78 *AJIL* 131.

[113] L. Doswald-Beck, 'The Legal Validity of Military Intervention by Invitation of the Government', (1989) 56 *BYIL* 189, at 251.

[114] Corten, *supra* n.14, at 249.

[115] M. Gestri, 'The ECOWAS Operations in Liberia and Sierra Leone: Amnesty for Past Unlawful Actions or Progress Towards Future Rules?', in M. Bothe *et al.* (eds), *Redefining Sovereignty* (New York: Transnational, 2005), 211–250.

[116] The Panamanian Revolution: Diplomacy, War and Self-Determination in Panama, (1990) 84 *Proc. Am. Soc'y Int'l L.* 182–189.

colonies.¹¹⁷ These interventions and others like them support the argument that even if Article 2(4) does not expressly prohibit intervention by invitation, other principles of international law, such as the principle of self-determination, raise important questions about the legality of such uses of force. Doswald-Beck, in fact, partly supports her position respecting invitation by pointing to the inconsistency with self-determination of propping up weak governments through external military intervention.

iv. Rebellion

Compared with intervention by invitation, there is even less support for any application of Article 2(4) to resort to force by governments against insurgents or insurgents against governments wholly within one state. Domestic law generally prohibits violent overthrow of a government or killing by any unauthorized persons. International human rights law applies to governments in respect to how much force may be applied in any particular situation.¹¹⁸ State parties to certain human rights treaties must formally derogate from those treaties to be able to lawfully detain without trial or use lethal force at the more flexible level applicable in armed conflict. Most human rights continue to apply in armed conflict or peace, but the content of rights, such as the right to life, may differ depending on the situation in which it is invoked. The right to life will be violated if military force is used with lethal consequences in a situation less than armed conflict. However, during armed conflict governments may employ lethal force if reasonably necessary.¹¹⁹ Lives may lawfully be taken in circumstances that would be unlawful outside such situations.¹²⁰ Governments reacting to violence in circumstances less than armed conflict may only lawfully use lethal force in situations of absolute necessity.¹²¹ Domestic police forces may, for example, kill a hostage-taker

---

¹¹⁷ France intervened in Africa no fewer than 19 times between 1962 and 1995. A. Hansen, 'The French Military in Africa, Council on Foreign Relations', 8 February 2008, available at http://www.cfr.org/france/french-military-africa/p12578#5.

¹¹⁸ Every human being has a right to life. This right is affirmed in the International Civil and Political Rights Covenant in Article 6: 'Every human being has the inherent right to life. This right shall be protected by law. No one shall be arbitrarily deprived of his right to life.' The law governing when human life may be intentionally ended, when the limitation on 'arbitrary' deprivation is avoided, falls into two categories: peacetime rules and rules within the law of armed conflict. In peace, a state may only take a human life when 'absolutely necessary in the defence of persons from unlawful violence'. *McCann & Others v. United Kingdom*, app, no. 324, app no. 18984/91 (ECtHR, 1995). See also Inter-American Court of Human Rights, *Montero-Aranguren et al. (Detention Center of Catia) v. Venezuela* (2006), at para. 69 and the United Nations Basic Principles for the Use of Force and Firearms by Law Enforcement Officials, Adopted by the Eighth United Nations Congress on the Prevention of Crime and the Treatment of Offenders, Havana, Cuba, 27 August to 7 September 1990, Article 9, available at http://www2ohchr.org/english/law/firearms.htm.

¹¹⁹ These customary international law rights may be deduced from the customary international law duties respecting targeting and detention. See J.-M. Henckaerts and L. Doswald-Beck, *Customary International Humanitarian Law*, vol. I (Cambridge: Cambridge University Press, 2005).

¹²⁰ N. Melzer, *Targeted Killing in International Law* (Oxford: Oxford University Press, 2008), at xiii.

¹²¹ See *supra* nn.118–119 and accompanying text.

on the verge of killing a hostage if there is no reasonable alternative for saving the hostage's life.[122]

B. The Two Categories of Article 2(4)

The armed force that is forbidden by Article 2(4) falls into at least two categories: aggression, which constitutes a 'serious' violation of Article 2(4), and all other violations. Article 39 of the UN Charter provides the first indication that aggression is a separate category within the larger category of force prohibited by the Charter. Article 39 provides authority for the Security Council to take measures to respond to threats to the peace, breaches of the peace and acts of aggression. In 1974, the United Nations General Assembly adopted a resolution defining aggression,[123] the preamble of which refers to aggression as 'the most serious and dangerous form of the illegal use of force'.[124]

It is not easy to discern and distinguish in the abstract a minor use of force and a use of force that is not minor but is less than 'the most serious and dangerous' form of illegal force. The General Assembly's Definition does provide a definition of aggression, along with several important examples of uses of force that meet the definition.[125]

---

[122] Ibid.
[123] Article 3(g), Definition of Aggression, UNGA Res. 3314 (XXIX) (1974).
[124] Articles 1–3 provide the most relevant details of the definition:

Article 1: Aggression is the use of armed force by a State against the sovereignty, territorial integrity or political independence of another State, or in any other manner inconsistent with the Charter of the United Nations, as set out in this Definition.

Article 2: The First use of armed force by a State in contravention of the Charter shall constitute prima facie evidence of an act of aggression although the Security Council may, in conformity with the Charter, conclude that a determination that an act of aggression has been committed would not be justified in the light of other relevant circumstances, including the fact that the acts concerned or their consequences are not of sufficient gravity.

Ibid.

[125]
Article 3: Any of the following acts, regardless of a declaration of war, shall, subject to and in accordance with the provisions of article 2, qualify as an act of aggression:
(a) the invasion, attack, military occupation or annexation by the armed forces of one State of the territory of another State;
(b) bombardment or the use of any weapons by a State against the territory of another State;
(c) blockade of the ports or coasts of a State by the armed forces of another State;
(d) an attack by the armed forces of a State on the land, sea or air forces, or marine and air fleets of another State;
(e) the use of armed forces of one State which are within the territory of another State with the agreement of the receiving State, in contravention of the conditions provided for in the agreement or any extension of their presence in such territory beyond the termination of the agreement;
(f) the action of a State in allowing its territory, which it has placed at the disposal of another State, to be used by that other State for perpetrating an act of aggression against a third State;

Yet, it is questionable whether all of the examples would be included today if the list were to be revised. The Definition, for instance, lists blockade, although until a blockade is challenged militarily it is similar to the category of wrongs described above that violate the non-intervention principle. The same can be said about military forces remaining after the host state withdraws consent for their presence. The presence of unconsented-to forces would violate the non-intervention principle unless the visiting forces fight to remain on the host state's territory or carry out some other form of significant military force while remaining on the host state's territory. In the *DRC v. Uganda* case, the ICJ found that Uganda had violated Article 2(4) by fighting in the DRC and occupying part of its territory. Initially, the DRC authorities had agreed to Uganda's presence, but when Uganda continued to fight after the DRC had made it clear that Uganda should leave, Uganda committed a violation of Article 2(4).[126]

In 2010, the parties to the Rome Statute added the crime of aggression to the list of crimes that would come within the International Criminal Court's (hereinafter 'ICC's') jurisdiction.[127] The ICC crime of aggression concerns individual accountability for aggression. It is not clear whether the parties to the Rome Statute intended to include that the crime of aggression prosecutable under the Rome Statute would be the same *jus ad bellum* violation, described in the General Assembly's Definition of Aggression.[128] Regardless of the intention, aggression as defined in the Rome Statute is plainly different in significant respects from the conduct discussed in the General Assembly's Definition. In analysing the ICC version of the crime of aggression, Elizabeth Wilmshurst suggests that certain conduct falls into a 'grey area' that is between clear cases of aggression and conduct that is not aggression. She lists as examples of these ambiguous cases: 'anticipatory self-defence, forcible reactions to a "minor" use of force of another State, armed interventions to rescue nationals, the extraterritorial use of force against a massive non-state armed attack, and genuine humanitarian intervention'.[129] While there is a good deal of discussion among commentators about all of the conduct on this list, the only conduct that at least a few governments officially support is anticipatory self-defence in the case of an imminent armed attack.[130] Even this example runs counter to the express terms of Article 51,

---

(g) the sending by or on behalf of a State of armed bands, groups, irregulars or mercenaries, which carry out acts of armed force against another State of such gravity as to amount to the acts listed above, or its substantial involvement therein.

Ibid.

[126] DRC v. Uganda, at 213, para. 106.

[127] Amendments to the Elements of Crimes, Annex II, Review Conference of the Rome Statute of the International Criminal Court, RC/Res 6, 11 June 2010.

[128] For a detailed comparison of the ICC crime of aggression and *jus ad bellum* aggression more generally, see M.E. O'Connell and M. Niyazmatov, 'What is Aggression?', (2012) 10 *J. Int'l Crim. Just.* 189.

[129] See C. Kress, 'Time for Decision: Some Thoughts on the Immediate Future of the Crime of Aggression: A Reply to Andreas Paulus', (2010) 20 *Eur. J. of Int'l L.* 1129, at 1140, citing E. Wilmshurst, 'Aggression' in R. Cryer *et al.*, *An Introduction to International Criminal Law and Procedure* (Cambridge: Cambridge University Press, 2007) 262, at 268ff.

[130] In 2004, the UK Attorney-General rejected any right of pre-emptive force but did indicate that the UK believed the 1841 *Caroline* correspondence set out the contemporary test for anticipatory self-defence. See the debate in the House of Lords, 21 April 2004, cols. 369–371.

which conditions self-defence on an armed attack occurring. The ICJ has not ruled on the question of anticipatory self-defence. The closest authoritative support for the right to act prior to an attack occurring is the UN Security Council's failure to clearly condemn Israel for attacking Egypt in the 1967 Six Day War.[131] This is at best equivocal support for the proposition, however. Many assume that Israel acted in anticipation of an imminent invasion by Egypt. In fact, when Israel argued before the Security Council in 1967, it stated that it had been attacked by Egypt *before* it responded. In 2005 when states came together at the UN World Summit in New York, they reaffirmed the obligation of strict compliance with the Charter rules on the use of force.[132] No amendments to the UN Charter were suggested allowing for anticipatory self-defence, let alone the far more controversial exceptions to Article 2(4) that have been proposed, in particular humanitarian intervention without Security Council authorization and self-defence against a state that is not responsible for an armed attack originating from its territory.

As for Wilmshurst's other 'grey areas', both 'minor' uses of force and limited force to rescue hostages are discussed above as falling below the Article 2(4) threshold.[133] Finally, no state has to date confronted a 'massive non-state armed attack' where the host state of the non-state actor bore no responsibility for the armed attack. In the case of attacks on Israel from the Occupied Palestinian Territories, as the ICJ determined in the *Wall* case, Israel is the responsible state for the territories as the occupying power.[134] The ICJ found in the *DRC v. Uganda* case that the attacks by non-state actors on Uganda did not amount to 'massive' attacks.[135] The ICJ did indicate, however, that Uganda might have had the right to intervene in the DRC if the attacks had been more significant – presumably of a kind that could only be carried out if the militant groups were supported by the *de facto* government of an area.

The situation the ICJ seems to be referring to would be like the Taliban's control of most of Afghanistan in 2001 or the Kurds' control of northern Iraq. Afghanistan under the *de facto* government of the Taliban bore state responsibility for the 9/11 attacks and could thus be the target of force in self-defence under Article 51.[136] Ethnic Kurdish groups have controlled northern Iraq since 1991. The groups have supported an effort by Kurds in Turkey to wrest control of Turkish regions through military force. Turkey has responded by incursions into northern Iraq citing Article 51.[137] As these cases show, launching an attack serious enough to trigger Article 51 indicates the ability to

---

[131] For a discussion of the legal arguments surrounding the Six Day War, see M.E. O'Connell, 'The Myth of Preemptive Self-Defense' (ASIL Task Force on Terrorism, 6 August 2002), available at http://www.asil.org/taskforce/oconnell.pdf.

[132] *Supra* n.11.

[133] *Supra* nn.77–107 and accompanying text.

[134] *Wall* opinion, *supra* n.88.

[135] DRC v. Uganda, at 223, para. 146. See also J.T. Gathii, 'Irregular Forces and Self-Defense Under the UN Charter', in M.E. O'Connell (ed.), *What is War? An Investigation in the Wake of 9/11* (Leiden: Martinus Nijhoff, 2012).

[136] T.M. Franck, 'Terrorism and the Right of Self Defense', (2001) 95 *AJIL* 839, at 842; M.E. O'Connell, 'Lawful Self-Defense to Terrorism', (2002) 63 *U. Pitt. L. Rev.* 889, at 889–904.

[137] See 'Turkey Invades Northern Iraq', *Economist*, 28 February 2008, available at http://www.economicst.com/world/africa/displaystory.cfrm?stroy_id=10766808.

control enough territory to be able to stage such an attack or receive enough support from a *de facto* or *de jure* state to do so, meaning that a massive non-state actor attack inevitably implicates a state in aggression.[138]

In brief, the prohibition on the use of force, as codified in Article 2(4) of the UN Charter, bars resort to armed force or conduct that is the equivalent of armed force by one state against another state. Other forceful conduct, such as economic sanctions, is beyond the scope of Article 2(4). Certain minimal uses of force are also outside the scope of Article 2(4). Intervention by invitation when the intervening state has a legitimate invitation from a government in control with the authority to request assistance is rarely condemned as unlawful. International law does not yet control the use of force within states under the prohibition on the use of force – civil war is subject to the law of human rights but not the *jus ad bellum*. While not all uses of military force are subject to the *jus ad bellum*, any serious violation of the prohibition on the use of force as found in Article 2(4) is considered aggression. Persons responsible for certain forms of aggression may be subject to criminal prosecution before the ICC.

4. THE IMPACT OF ARTICLE 2(4)

Article 2(4) has been violated so often since its adoption in 1945 that it is difficult to have an accurate count.[139] Such violations have induced a handful of scholars beginning in the 1970s to declare it a 'dead letter', an example of desuetude in the law.[140] Most scholars, however, have agreed with the ICJ that this conclusion is likely derived from a poor understanding of how rules work in the international community. The greater weight of authority not only supports the current validity of Article 2(4), but also its status as a *jus cogens* norm,[141] indicating that the prohibition does not change, let alone cease to exist, through the processes of customary international law or treaty law creation and extinction.[142] Categorization as a *jus cogens* norm is clearly an important development respecting the contemporary normative force of Article 2(4). There have been other important developments since 1945. These will be discussed in

---

[138] *Ibid*.

[139] Cherif Bassiouni has conducted a study finding 300 internal and international armed conflicts since 1945. M. Cherif Bassiouni, 'Assessing Conflict Outcomes: Accountability and Impunity', in M. Cherif Bassiouni (ed.), *The Pursuit of International Criminal Justice: A World Study on Conflicts, Victimization, and Post-Conflict Justice* (Cambridge: Intersentia, 2010), 11.

[140] T.M. Franck, 'Who Killed Article 2(4)?', (1970) 64 *AJIL* 809. But see T.M. Franck, 'Terrorism and the Right of Self-Defense', (2001) 95 *AJIL* 839; M.J. Glennon, 'The Fog of Law: Self-Defense, Inherence, and Incoherence in Article 51 of the United Nations Charter', (2002) 25 *Harv. J. L. & Pub. Pol'y* 539, at 546. See also M.J. Glennon, 'Pre-empting Terrorism: The Case for Anticipatory Self-Defense', *Wkly. Standard*, 28 January 2002, 24.

[141] For a detailed discussion of *jus cogens* norms, including the prohibition of aggression, see M.E. O'Connell, '*Jus Cogens*, International Law's Higher Ethical Norms', in D.E. Childress III (ed.), *The Role of Ethics in International Law* (Cambridge: Cambridge University Press, 2011), 78.

[142] L. Henkin, 'The Reports of the Death of Article 2(4) Are Greatly Exaggerated', (1971) 65 *AJIL* 544; Y. Dinstein, *War, Aggression, and Self-Defence*, 5th edn (Cambridge: Cambridge University Press, 2011); Gray, *supra* n.105.

the first part of this section. The second part will discuss the constant challenges to Article 2(4) from a few governments and international law scholars, especially in the US and UK. The vast majority of governments, however, have resisted these attempts and agreed in 2005 to keep the Charter rules on the use of force as adopted in 1945. Scholars looking to the sources of international law, as opposed to certain policy positions, conclude that Article 2(4) is unchanged. Yet, that also means that Article 2(4) has not expanded. The original limits on its scope remain. One is hard-pressed to find even a discussion of proposals for greater restrictions on the use of major military force.

A. The Challenges to Article 2(4)

As just mentioned, the provisions of the Charter prohibiting force have been upheld over the decades since their adoption, but little evidence exists of interest in expanding those provisions or making them more effective. Indeed, the major efforts in respect of Article 2(4) have been to limit it by expanding the right to use force in self-defence or to accomplish other goals through the application of armed force. Efforts at promoting peace are few, in contrast to, for example, efforts to expand the right to use force to promote democracy, human rights and arms control. Indeed, the inclusion of the crime of genocide in the Rome Statute exemplifies the contrast between concern for protecting human rights and concern for ensuring peace. Little or no controversy surrounded the inclusion of war crimes or crimes against humanity in the Rome Statute. Respecting aggression, however, the US Legal Advisor to the State Department, Harold Koh, lobbied against adding the crime of aggression to the Rome Statute in part because 'every U.S. president' could be accused of aggression.[143] This is in fact not true as neither Dwight Eisenhower nor Jimmy Carter ordered uses of force in violation of Article 2(4). Nevertheless, it is difficult to conceive that Koh would lobby against including any other *jus cogens* norm in the Rome Statute – torture, slavery, genocide, apartheid and widespread extrajudicial killing. Rather than argue for expanding the prohibition on force, as mentioned at the outset of this chapter, most of the action has been towards diluting Article 2(4). The discussion about aggression and the Rome Statute is part of a long-running debate between those who support a strict reading of the Charter on use of force questions, and those who either support a relaxed reading of the restrictions or who want outright expansion of the right to use force in international relations.[144]

The debate over strict versus relaxed reading of the Charter began soon after the Suez Crisis erupted in 1956.[145] Egypt nationalized the Suez Canal and the United Kingdom and France decided to use force to return control of the canal to the British–French company that owned it. In order to avoid a blatant violation of the Charter, the two European states colluded with Israel. Israel would attack Egypt first,

---

[143] H.H. Koh, 'Statement Regarding the Crime of Aggression at the Resumed Eighth Session of the Assembly of States Parties of the International Criminal Court', 23 March 2010, available at http://usun.state.gov/briefing/statements/2010/139000.htm.
[144] Kress, *supra* n.129; Corten, *supra* n.14.
[145] See, generally, R. Bowie, *Suez 1956* (Oxford: Oxford University Press, 1974).

claiming that it was acting in self-defence at a critical moment when Egypt was building its military capability but before it became too powerful for Israel to defeat. Britain and France would then intervene in the conflict to stop the fighting between Egypt and Israel. Both the US and the Soviet Union, however, condemned the use of force by Israel, Britain and France.[146]

Two years later, Derek Bowett published a book that sought to justify the use of force by the interveners in the Suez case as lawful self-defence under Article 51 of the Charter.[147] Bowett, who would become the Whewell professor of international law at Cambridge University, created an elaborate account of the term 'inherent right' of self-defence in Article 51. He argued that the term was a reference back to the standard for self-defence discussed in 1841 by the US and Britain following the sinking of the ship *Caroline* in 1837.[148] In the mid-19th century a state could justify resort to force as lawful self-defence if it was facing a situation of necessity. Necessity existed if there was a threat of force that was 'instant, overwhelming, leaving no moment of deliberation'.[149] In Bowett's view, the *Caroline* test supported the use of force in self-defence, even if an armed attack had not occurred. Only such an argument could justify Israel's attack at the behest of the UK and France following the nationalization of the canal. Since the publication of the book, Bowett's 'inherent right' has been a persistent feature of the scholarship on the *jus ad bellum*,[150] and governments have put forward a variety of defence policies based on that scholarship, including policies claiming rights to use force in anticipatory self-defence, pre-emptive self-defence, self-defence against terrorists, and more.[151] Five years after the publication of *Self-Defence in International Law*, Ian Brownlie, who would become the Chichele professor of public international law at Oxford University, responded with a detailed refutation of Bowett's *Caroline* thesis.[152] Brownlie made his case based on the plain meaning and negotiating history of Article 51, concluding that the drafters of the Charter clearly intended that use of major military force in self-defence must respond to an armed attack. Brownlie argued that the requirements of Article 51 could not be eliminated through re-interpretation. Article 51's reference to 'inherent right' did indicate customary international legal rules on the right to resort to force, as Bowett indicated, but rather those customary rules providing additional restrictions beyond the restrictions expressly included in Article 51. Customary international law restricts resort to force to situations of necessity, and even then the principle of proportionality requires that a resort to force not cause disproportionate injury. Brownlie further supported his position, pointing out that 'the dominant policy of the law and of the United Nations is

---

[146] L. Henkin, 'Use of Force: Law and U.S. Policy', in L. Henkin *et al.* (eds), *Might v. Right: International Law and the Use of Force* (New York: Council on Foreign Relations, 1989), 45.

[147] D. Bowett, *Self-Defence in International Law* (Manchester: Manchester University Press, 1958).

[148] *Ibid*.

[149] *Supra* n.46.

[150] See, for example, D.B. Rivkin, Jr. *et al.*, 'War, International Law, and Sovereignty: Reevaluating the Rules of the Game in a New Century; Preemption and Law in the Twenty-First Century', (2005) 5 *Chi. J. Int'l L.* 467.

[151] *Ibid*. For a discussion of a number of these claims, see O'Connell, *supra* n.131.

[152] Brownlie, *supra* n.19, at 428–436.

to maintain international peace and to avoid creating possibilities of breaches of the peace, in the form of vague and extensive justifications for resort to force or otherwise'.[153] Brownlie, too, has his followers, so that scholars today refer to the 'restrictivists' and 'anti-restrictivists' or the 'narrow' and 'broad' interpreters of the UN Charter provisions on the use of force.[154]

This review of the Bowett–Brownlie debate might indicate that the greatest challenge to the Charter has been in the area of the right of self-defence.[155] In actual practice, however, another justification for resort to force is probably invoked more often than self-defence: intervention by invitation. Occasionally, an invitation will be issued that is characterized as collective self-defence under Article 51. The US claimed it was invited to join in collective self-defence to defend South Vietnam from aggression launched by North Vietnam in the 1960s–1970s.[156] The US gave the same argument for using force on behalf of El Salvador against Nicaragua in the 1980s.[157] These cases involved alleged attacks by one sovereign state upon another. The more typical reason for a government to invite intervention is to respond to internal violence. Sometimes this form of collective force is known as 'humanitarian intervention', although 'humanitarian intervention' is an argument for using force that goes beyond intervention by invitation.[158] A variety of purposes have been linked to the designation of 'humanitarian', from spreading communism, to supporting democracy, to ending weapons programmes,[159] to ending the commission of atrocities.[160] In one of the first discussions of the right to use force beyond the clear terms of the Charter for humanitarian purposes, Richard Lillich debated Ian Brownlie in the 1970s.[161] Brownlie again defended the Charter's terms restricting force to self-defence or force authorized by the Security Council.[162]

Humanitarian intervention was officially invoked as a justification by some members of NATO in that organization's resort to force against Serbia during the 1999 Kosovo Crisis.[163] In a case brought to the ICJ by Serbia against ten NATO members for the

---

[153] *Ibid.*, at 436.

[154] Corten, *supra* n.14.

[155] M.E. O'Connell, 'Self-Defence', in *Oxford Bibliographies Online* (Oxford: Oxford University Press, 2011).

[156] J.N. Moore, *Law and the Indo-China War* (Princeton, NJ: Princeton University Press, 1972).

[157] *Nicaragua*, *supra* n.82, at 22, 27.

[158] An early prominent work advocating a right of humanitarian intervention is F. Tesón, *Humanitarian Intervention: An Inquiry into Law and Morality* (Dobbs Ferry, NY: Transnational, 1988). See also F. Tesón, 'The Liberal Case for Humanitarian Intervention', *supra* n.72.

[159] L. Feinstein and A.-M. Slaughter, 'A Duty to Prevent', (2004) *Foreign Affairs* 83.

[160] For a general critique of humanitarian intervention, see R. Falk, 'Can Humanitarian Intervention ever be Humanitarian?', 4 August 2011, available at http://mwcnews.net/focus/editorial/12577-humanitarian-intervention.html?tmpl=component. See also S. Chesterman, *Just War or Just Peace? Humanitarian Intervention and International Law* (Oxford: Oxford University Press, 2001).

[161] Lillich, *supra* n.71 and Brownlie, 'Humanitarian Intervention', in Moore (ed.), *supra* n.71, 217–228.

[162] Brownlie, *supra* n.161, at 159.

[163] Gray, *supra* n.105, at 38.

unlawful use of force, however, only Belgium argued the right of humanitarian intervention had crystallized as a right beyond the Charter.[164] Until then states consistently took the position that force could not be used lawfully for humanitarian reasons except through the collective decision-making of the Security Council. Following the end of NATO's Kosovo intervention, the Canadian government created the International Commission on Intervention and State Sovereignty (hereinafter 'ICISS') to study the concept of humanitarian intervention. The ICISS produced a report in December 2001, asserting a right to intervene militarily if a state failed to protect its population from atrocities.[165] The ICISS report became known as 'R2P' and received wide publicity. As a result, despite developments such as the 2005 World Summit Outcome discussed above, many commentators continue to write about the need for or existence of a right of humanitarian intervention.

B. Achievements of Article 2(4)

Given the decades of challenges to the prohibition on the use of force, the fact that Article 2(4) received an overwhelming endorsement in 2005 is a notable achievement. In terms of actually impacting state conduct, the record is generally poor, but in one significant area Article 2(4) has been singularly successful. Since the adoption of the UN Charter no state has succeeded in conquering a member of the United Nations and extinguishing its existence.[166] The kind of aggression practised by Germany, Italy and Japan in the 1930s is today clearly beyond the pale, effectively outlawed as egregious crime. When the dictator of Iraq, Saddam Hussein, attempted to conquer Kuwait in 1990, the world came together in a near-unanimous coalition to oppose him. After months of negotiation and economic sanctions, military force was finally used to push the Iraqi army out of Kuwait.[167] The effort not only succeeded in liberating Kuwait, it also reinforced the Charter's core norm against the use of force and against aggression in particular. In addition, Article 2(4) and the exceptions for self-defence in Article 51 and collective security in Articles 39–42 remain the law around which all resort to major force is judged in the world.

---

[164] *Legality of the Use of Force* (Serbia and Montenegro v. Belgium) (Memorials) [2004] ICJ Rep. 279.

[165] The term used to indicate both a state's obligation to its population and a state's right to intervene is known as 'responsibility to protect' or 'R2P'. See, generally, ICISS, *The Responsibility to Protect* (2001), available at responsibilitytoprotect.org/ICISS%20Report.pdf.

[166] Some argue that the 1956 Soviet invasion of Hungary was, in effect, conquest. See *supra* n.109. Hungary did, however, keep its sovereign statehood, remained a member of the United Nations and was in a position to completely free itself of Soviet domination by the late 1980s. Others might cite cases of a similar kind, but it should be recognized that the sort of conquest that Germany was seeking respecting Poland and other neighbours, or that Japan sought respecting Manchuria, Korea, the Philippines and others, has not occurred since the adoption of the Charter. That is a victory for law.

[167] For a discussion of the facts and law surrounding the 1990–1991 Gulf War, see M.E. O'Connell, 'Enforcing the Prohibition on the Use of Force: The U.N.'s Response to Iraq's Invasion of Kuwait', (1991) 15 *S. Ill. U. L.J.* 453, at 479–480.

Since the drafting of the Charter, numerous decisions of the ICJ, resolutions of the Security Council and UN General Assembly, and official government statements have confirmed the binding nature of these rules and their meaning.[168] Indeed, the international community has repeatedly confirmed its support for the regime of peace and the prohibition on war between states. We often hear from some quarters that these rules became obsolete after 9/11,[169] but it was in 2005 – four years after the 9/11 attacks – that the world re-affirmed the rules. Indeed, the World Summit Outcome document stated that:

> 78. We reiterate the importance of promoting and strengthening the multilateral process and of addressing international challenges and problems by strictly abiding by the Charter and the principles of international law, and further stress our commitment to multilateralism.
>
> 79. We reaffirm that the relevant provisions of the Charter are sufficient to address the full range of threats to international peace and security. We further reaffirm the authority of the Security Council to mandate coercive action to maintain and restore international peace and security. We stress the importance of acting in accordance with the purposes and principles of the Charter.[170]

These paragraphs reflect a true achievement with respect to maintaining the law prohibiting force in international relations.

5. POSTSCRIPT: EXPANDING THE PROHIBITION ON THE USE OF FORCE

The prohibition on the use of force found in Article 2(4) has been maintained since 1945. Almost 70 years after its drafting it might finally be time to address expanding the prohibition. During this long period, the law of human rights has grown dramatically; few doubt that states owe respect for the human rights of their nationals, that international law reaches into the domestic sphere to protect individuals. Since the Nuremberg Tribunal, international law has recognized individual and non-state actor group obligations with respect to human rights and international humanitarian law. With changes associated with the Arab Spring, the time may be ripe to extend the *jus ad bellum* to the use of force within states.

Throughout the Arab Spring of 2011–2012, governments have been criticized for excessive force against peaceful protesters. Little is said about any obligations on the part of protestors when they choose to resort to military force as in Libya and Syria. Tunisians, Egyptians, Bahrainis and others chose *not* to resort to force. These examples from the Arab Spring invite a discussion of a future rule in which the international community prohibits those opposing governments from resort to violence to achieve

---

[168] *Supra* n.11 and accompanying text.
[169] See, for example, D.B. Rivkin, Jr. *et al.*, *supra* n.150. A blog called 'Lawfare' regularly features books and articles by advocates of aggressive use of military force beyond the limits of international law. See http//www.lawfareblog.com/.
[170] 2005 World Summit Outcome document, UN Doc. A/RES/60/1, 24 October 2005.

change – as a matter of international law. This would be a *jus ad bellum* rule applicable to non-state actors as other international law rules are applicable, such as human rights and international humanitarian law rules.[171] The international community could demand the same progress within states respecting the use of force that it has seen for human rights.

A more modest step forward would be a return to a stricter understanding of the right to intervene by invitation. The international community could at least return to a version of the rule that existed prior to the adoption of the Charter that limited the right to intervene once a rebel group reached the stage of belligerency.[172] A government that is being seriously challenged such as that in Liberia in the 1990s or Afghanistan after 2002 would not have the right to invite in outside military assistance. If such a rule were re-instated, escalation to civil war might not occur or might end sooner than the long-running brutal civil wars fuelled by outside intervention, such as those in the DRC, Sri Lanka, El Salvador, Afghanistan, Iraq, Libya, Somalia, and so many other places.

It is a great achievement of the international legal community that Article 2(4) of the UN Charter has remained a valid and binding rule and is even in some respects a *jus cogens* norm. Humanity could achieve much more, however, than only preserving Article 2(4). Greater effort could be expended in getting compliance with the prohibition on the use of force, and the prohibition could well be expanded. Extending the prohibition on the use of force to resort to armed force within states could save thousands of lives every year. Limiting the right to intervene by invitation could do the same. It is to protect life, health, property and the natural world that people of good will have worked for millennia to prohibit the use of force. There is no reason to stop now.

---

[171] A number of commentators believe that a non-state actor attack on a foreign sovereign state triggers the Article 51 right of self-defence by the victim state against the state from where the attack was launched or members of the non-state actor group exist, even where there is no attribution to a state for the acts of the non-state actor group. See *supra* nn.134–136 and accompanying text. While this position is not consistent with the ICJ's interpretation of Article 51, it does suggest that scholars are prepared to extend some UN Charter rules respecting the use of force to non-state actor groups.

[172] *Supra* n.108.

5. The centrality of the United Nations Security Council in the legal regime governing the use of force

*Christian Henderson**

1. INTRODUCTION

The United Nations Security Council (hereinafter 'UNSC') is the organ of the United Nations bestowed with 'primary responsibility for the maintenance of international peace and security'.[1] The possession of such a responsibility has led to the notable presence of this particular organ of the UN across the divides of international conflict and security law. For example, the UN Charter expressly provides the UNSC with a key role in the peaceful settlement of disputes and conflict prevention[2] in addition to its role in actions taken by states in self-defence.[3] It also in this context acts as perhaps the primary forum for the discussion and presentation of legal arguments regarding the use of force. Furthermore, it issues ceasefires,[4] plays a key role in foreign territorial administration,[5] establishes and implements peacekeeping operations under what some have described as its 'Chapter VI ½' powers,[6] and has now an important responsibility in referring individuals suspected of international crimes to the International Criminal Court.[7]

---

* The author wishes to thank Aurel Sari, James Green, Nigel White and Meagen Wong for providing comments on previous drafts of this chapter. Any errors remain those of the author.

[1] Article 24(1), UN Charter (1945). For an account of the general activities of the UNSC under the theme of 'war' see V. Lowe *et al.*, *The United Nations Security Council and War: The Evolution of Thought and Practice since 1945* (Oxford: Oxford University Press, 2008).

[2] See Chapter VI of the UN Charter (1945). For more on the UNSC's role in conflict prevention see the chapter by Kenneth Manusama (Chapter 1) in this volume.

[3] See Article 51 of Chapter VII of the UN Charter. For more on the UNSC's role in self-defence see *infra* section 2B of this chapter and the chapter by Dino Kritsiotis (Chapter 6) in this volume.

[4] See, for example, UNSC Resolution 1860 (2009), para. 1. For more on the UNSC's role in this respect see C. Henderson and N. Lubell, 'The Contemporary Legal Nature of UN Security Council Ceasefire Resolutions', (2013) 26 *LJIL* 369.

[5] See Ralph Wilde's chapter (Chapter 16) in this volume for more on the issue of foreign territorial administration.

[6] This phrase was first employed by Dag Hammarskjöld, the second UN Secretary-General. For more on the UNSC's role in peacekeeping operations see Nigel White's chapter (Chapter 17) in this volume.

[7] See Article 13(b) of the Rome Statute of the International Criminal Court (1998). As an example of this in practice see UNSC Resolution 1970 (2011), paras 4–8. For more on war crimes see Robert Cryer's chapter (Chapter 14) in this volume.

However, arguably the most important element of this responsibility for the maintenance of international peace and security – and the one under focus in this chapter – is its unique position in the realm of forcible measures. Indeed, this importance is manifested in the fact that the UNSC is the only entity today with the unique competence to decide to employ forcible measures outside of the context of a state's inherent right of self-defence. The aim of this chapter is thus to provide an integrated conceptual and empirical analysis of the contemporary role and relevance of the UNSC in the regime governing the use of force. In particular, the modern challenges it faces to its authority in the realm of forcible measures will be assessed. This chapter, however, begins with an analysis of the conceptual basis of the UNSC and its specific role and forcible powers as envisaged in the Charter of the United Nations (section 2). The intention is for this to lay the foundations for an analysis of the impediments to its functioning during the Cold War (section 3) and its functional transformation witnessed in the post-Cold War era (section 4), followed by a focus upon the contemporary challenges that it faces (section 5). Lastly a conclusion is offered as to the UNSC's contemporary and future role in the regime governing the use of force (section 6).

2. THE UN CHARTER AND THE ENFORCEMENT POWERS OF THE UN SECURITY COUNCIL

Collective security regimes have existed in one form or another for two centuries with the Concert of Europe (1815–1914) being the earliest notable example. This was, however, a regime of political convenience between the great powers at the time, whereby the ambitions of each power were curbed by the other powers, as opposed to one that was in any true sense governed by law.[8] The League of Nations (1919–1946) was therefore the first attempt at such a 'legal' regime established as it was under a Covenant and consisting of a formal structure with certain powers. It was in many respects the first permanent international organisation with the principal aim of maintaining world peace through collective security. In particular, the Covenant established that '[a]ny war or threat of war ... is hereby declared a matter of concern to the whole League, and the League shall take any action that may be deemed wise and effectual to safeguard the peace of nations'.[9] However, the weaknesses of the League and its Covenant, in particular the various loopholes in the obligation not to resort to war,[10] led to its relatively quick demise and ultimately to the calamity of the Second World War.

---

[8] For a good account of the 'balance of power' during this era see G. Simpson, *Great Powers and Outlaw States: Unequal Sovereigns in the International Legal Order* (Cambridge: Cambridge University Press, 2004), at 96–102.

[9] Article 11, League of Nations Covenant (1919).

[10] The Preamble of the Covenant stated that '[t]he High Contracting Parties, [i]n order to promote international co-operation and to achieve international peace and security, by *acceptance of obligations not to resort to war* ... [a]gree to this Covenant of the League of Nations' (emphasis added). However, the loopholes to this general obligation included the fact that Members agreed not to resort to war only for three months after an award by the arbitrators or a report by the League Council (Article 12(1)); if the Council failed to reach a report which was unanimously agreed the Members of the League reserved the right to take such action as they

A. The Institutional Division of Competence in the Maintenance of International Peace and Security within the UN

Due to the widespread recognition that the international community could not afford a third world war, the UN was established in 1945 to replace the flawed League of Nations. As the opening words of the UN Charter declare: 'We the peoples of the United Nations determined ... to save succeeding generations from the scourge of war, which twice in our lifetime has brought untold sorrow to mankind.'[11] In its efforts to achieve this aim the first operative paragraph of the Charter states that:

> The Purposes of the United Nations are ... [t]o maintain international peace and security, and to that end: to take effective collective measures for the prevention and removal of threats to the peace, and for the suppression of acts of aggression or other breaches of the peace.[12]

As such, the ideal of collective security and, significantly, the aim of taking 'effective' measures – something that was so dismally lacking in the League of Nations – is at the heart of the UN organisation. While the UN was established with six organs,[13] and has since established many of a subsidiary nature,[14] powers to maintain international peace and security fell to the two which can be regarded as the most important. The Charter first provides for a limited role in this respect for the General Assembly (hereinafter 'UNGA'), the largest of the organs of the UN. In this role the UNGA 'may discuss any questions or any matters within the scope of the present Charter or relating to the powers and functions of any organs provided for in the present Charter'.[15] As such, it may consider 'the general principles of co-operation in the maintenance of international peace and security'[16] or 'discuss any questions relating to the maintenance of

---

considered necessary for the maintenance of right and justice (Article 15(7)); in addition there was an obligation upon the arbitrators to make their award within a reasonable time, and on the Council to issue its report within six months (Article 12(2)), the implication being that if they failed to do so then Members had the right to resort to war.

[11] Preamble, UN Charter (1945).

[12] Article 1(1), UN Charter (1945).

[13] The General Assembly; the Security Council; the Economic and Social Council; the Secretariat; the International Court of Justice; and the United Nations Trusteeship Council.

[14] Other prominent UN agencies include the World Health Organisation, the World Food Programme and the United Nations Children's Fund.

[15] Article 10, UN Charter (1945). This should not be interpreted, however, as a power of review by the UNGA. Nevertheless, while each organ of the UN can at first instance interpret those parts of the Charter that apply to its activities, if an interpretation of its powers by the UNSC is not found to be generally acceptable to the UN membership it will arguably be without binding force. The UNGA, being fully representative of the Membership of the UN, is the ideal forum in which such general acceptability can be discerned. See A. Orakhelashvili, *Collective Security* (Oxford: Oxford University Press, 2011), at 53–54. Furthermore, while the International Court of Justice does not have a specific power of review of the actions of the other organs of the UN, it is the sole judicial organ of the UN and, as such, is ultimately responsible for interpretation of the Charter as a treaty. See Article 36(2), Statute of the International Court of Justice (1945).

[16] Article 11(1), UN Charter (1945).

international peace and security brought before it'.[17] Nevertheless, while in either case appropriate 'recommendations' may be made by the UNGA, this is in contrast to the more prominent role and powers of the UNSC.

In the UN Charter the Member States of the UN conferred upon the UNSC *'primary responsibility for the maintenance of international peace and security'*.[18] In reflecting the embodiment of collective security they 'agree[d] that in carrying out its duties under this responsibility the Security Council acts on their behalf'.[19] Furthermore, this responsibility was provided to this relatively uncrowded organ of the UN, consisting as it does today of only 15 Members,[20] '[i]n order to ensure prompt and effective action by the United Nations'.[21] It could thus be argued that the perceived necessity of 'prompt and effective' action was the *raison d'être* underlying the creation of such a small organ for the purposes of collective security.[22] It should also be pointed out that the UNSC was not envisaged as a law enforcer. As Kelsen has noted, '[t]he purpose of enforcement action … is not to maintain or restore law, but to maintain and restore peace, which is not necessarily identical with the law'.[23] Indeed, enforcement of the law and maintenance of the peace are not synonymous. While both may often be accomplished by the same action, the UNSC does not shoulder any express responsibility under the original scheme of the Charter to ensure that international law is upheld.

The institutional primacy of the UNSC in the maintenance of international peace and security was expressly preserved in the Charter through two means. First, Members of the UN as a whole are obliged to accept and carry out its decisions.[24] Although the UNSC is a political body[25] it is at the same time unique within the UN as possessing the power to adopt legally binding decisions of general applicability.[26] Secondly, the Charter provides that so long as the UNSC 'is exercising in respect of any dispute or situation the functions assigned to it in the present Charter, the General Assembly shall not make any recommendation with regard to that dispute or situation unless the

---

[17] Article 11(2), UN Charter (1945).
[18] Article 24(1), UN Charter (1945) (emphasis added).
[19] Article 24(1), UN Charter (1945); although the wording of this provision has been criticised on the basis that the UNSC acts on behalf of the UN, not its Member States. See F. Seyersted, *Common Law of International Organisations* (Leiden: Brill, 2008), at 372.
[20] This was expanded in 1963 from 11. This can be contrasted with that of the UNGA which, while originally composed of 51 Members, now has 193.
[21] Article 24(1), UN Charter (1945).
[22] While smaller organs are perhaps considered more effective, the relatively small size of the UNSC, given that membership of the UN as a whole has grown from 51 in 1945 to 193 today, is an incentive for reform. For more on reform of the UNSC see *infra* section 6.
[23] H. Kelsen, *The Law of the United Nations: A Critical Analysis of its Fundamental Problems* (London: Stevens, 1950), at 736.
[24] Article 25, UN Charter (1945).
[25] Orakhelashvili, *supra* n. 15, at 23. See also Kelsen, *supra* n. 23, at 735.
[26] Furthermore, Article 103 of the Charter provides that: 'In the event of a conflict between the obligations of the Members of the United Nations under the present Charter and their obligations under any other international agreement, their obligations under the present Charter shall prevail.'

Security Council so requests'.[27] Consequently, even the rather limited power of the UNGA to issue recommendations in this area is restricted to those circumstances where the UNSC is not actively engaged with a matter.

B. Specific Enforcement Functions and Powers of the UN Security Council under the UN Charter

The specific powers granted to the UNSC for the discharge of its duties in regards to the maintenance of international peace and security 'are laid down in Chapters VI, VII, VIII, and XII'.[28] While Chapter XII is essentially redundant, having as its concern the International Trusteeship System, and Chapter VI deals with the pacific settlement of disputes,[29] Chapters VII and VIII concern the enforcement measures that are available to the UNSC.

Chapter VII of the Charter arguably contains the most important – not to mention controversial – provisions of the Charter. The first provision of this Chapter, Article 39, provides at the outset that '[t]he Security Council shall determine the existence of any threat to the peace, breach of the peace, or act of aggression'. It is possible to interpret this apparently prescriptive phrase in two ways. It may, on the one hand, indicate that if there is an objectively identifiable threat to the peace then the UNSC *must* determine it to be so. On the other hand, it could be an indication as to the division of constitutional responsibilities in the context of the maintenance of international peace and security, in that it is expressly stated to be the UNSC – to the exclusion of the other organs – that shall make such a determination for the purposes of enforcement action. While some argue that the UNSC is under an obligation to make such a determination,[30] as per the first interpretative option above, others have argued that '[n]owhere is the Security Council under less strictures that in its determination that a threat to the peace exists'[31] so that 'it is completely within the discretion of the Security Council to decide what constitutes a "threat to the peace"'.[32] This latter view, it is submitted, is the correct one, particularly in the absence of any express qualification in the UN Charter itself as to the responsibilities and obligations of the UNSC in this respect. As long as

---

[27] Article 12(1), UN Charter (1945). Although see *infra* section 3 on the *Uniting for Peace* resolution. Furthermore, both the UNGA and the UN Secretary-General are able to bring to the attention of the UNSC situations that may threaten or endanger international peace and security (Articles 11(3) and 99 of the UN Charter respectively). Given that it is the UNSC, rather than the UNGA, that the Secretary-General shall refer matters to, under the provisions of the UN Charter the UNSC was clearly envisaged as the most significant of the organs of the UN in the realms of the maintenance of peace and security.

[28] Article 24(2), UN Charter (1945).

[29] For more on the pacific settlement of disputes see Kenneth Manusama's chapter (Chapter 1) in this volume.

[30] See, for example, A. Tzanakopoulos, *Disobeying the Security Council: Countermeasures Against Wrongful Sanctions* (Oxford: Oxford University Press, 2011), at 60–64; A. Orakhelashvili, 'The Power of the UN Security Council to Determine the Existence of a Threat to the Peace', (2006) 1 *Irish Yearbook of International Law* 61.

[31] Y. Dinstein, *War, Aggression, and Self-Defence*, 5th edn (Cambridge: Cambridge University Press, 2011), at 309.

[32] Kelsen, *supra* n. 23, at 727.

any determination, or absence thereof, remains within the broad Purposes and Principles of the Charter[33] then it has a wide discretion as to the determination of such a threat. Furthermore, no reasons are required to be given for such a determination, even though it might appear arbitrary for the Council to fail to do so.[34] Consequently, and as Akehurst summarises, 'a threat to the peace in the sense of Article 39 seems to be whatever the Security Council says is a threat to the peace'.[35]

Upon such a determination, Article 39 of the Charter goes on to provide that the UNSC then 'shall make recommendations, or decide what measures shall be taken in accordance with Articles 41 and 42, to maintain or restore international peace and security'. Under Article 25 of the UN Charter, it is the decisions of the UNSC that are binding and, therefore, given that Chapter VII provides also for the possibility of recommendations, not all action taken under an Article 39 determination is legally binding upon other Member States. However, once such a determination is made 'the door is automatically opened to enforcement measures of a non-military or military kind'[36] if the UNSC decides that these are necessary.

Non-forceful measures under Article 41 'may include complete or partial interruption of economic relations and of rail, sea, air, postal, telegraphic, radio, and other means of communication, and the severance of diplomatic relations'. Alternatively, if the UNSC decides that these would be inadequate, or have proved to be inadequate, it may, under Article 42:

> take such action by air, sea, or land forces as may be necessary to maintain or restore international peace and security. Such action may include demonstrations, blockade, and other operations by air, sea, or land forces of Members of the United Nations.

In reading Article 42, Article 43 is of significance, if only historically.[37] This provides that all Members of the UN 'undertake to make available to the Security Council, on its call and in accordance with a special agreement or agreements, armed forces, assistance, and facilities, including rights of passage, necessary for the purpose of maintaining international peace and security'.[38] It was thus originally intended that

---

[33] Article 24(2) of the UN Charter (1945) states that '[i]n discharging [its] duties the Security Council shall act in accordance with the Purposes and Principles of the United Nations'. As the ICTY stated in the *Tadić* case, 'the determination that there exists such a threat is not a totally unfettered discretion, as it has to remain, at the very least, within the limits of the Purposes and Principles of the Charter'. *Prosecutor v. Tadić*, Jurisdiction, ICTY, Appeals Chamber, 1995, at para. 29.

[34] Cf. Orakhelashvili, *supra* n. 15, at 155. See also E. de Wet, *The Chapter VII Powers of the United Nations Security Council* (Oxford: Hart Publishing, 2004), at 134–144.

[35] M. Akehurst, *Akehurst's Modern Introduction to International Law*, 7th edn (P. Malanczuk (ed.)), (London: Routledge, 1997), at 426. However, this is not to say that the UNSC is *legibus solutus*. See *infra* section 2C.

[36] I. Osterdahl, *Threats to the Peace: The Interpretation by the Security Council of Article 39 of the UN Charter* (Uppsala: Och Justus Forlag, 1998), at 28.

[37] See *infra* sections 3 and 4 of this chapter.

[38] Article 43(1), UN Charter (1945). Article 43(2) goes on to provide that '[s]uch agreement or agreements shall govern the numbers and types of forces, their degree of readiness and general location, and the nature of the facilities and assistance to be provided'.

through such agreements the UNSC was to possess something akin to a standing army at its disposal to be composed of forces from Member States of the UN.[39] Furthermore, a 'Military Staff Committee' comprising the Chiefs of Staff of the Permanent Members was to be established[40] and was:

> to advise and assist the Security Council on all questions relating to the Security Council's military requirements for the maintenance of international peace and security, the employment and command of forces placed at its disposal, the regulation of armaments, and possible disarmament.[41]

Nevertheless, despite a certain level of control envisaged by the UNSC over the forcible action concerned, it was still the case that ultimately the decisions would 'be carried out by the Members of the United Nations *directly* and through their action in the appropriate *international agencies* of which they are members'.[42] If the forces of Member States were to be utilised 'directly' in implementing the decisions of the UNSC, the action was to be taken 'by *all* the Members of the United Nations or by *some of them*, as the Security Council may determine'.[43] Yet the reference here to action also possibly being taken by 'international agencies' is recognition within the Charter of the existence of other organisations possessing a security mandate. Indeed, in the envisaged collective security system 'international agencies' and 'regional organisations' were expressly recognised as possessing a level of competence in this area.[44] It was furthermore envisaged that these organisations would in certain circumstances be a state's primary point of contact.[45]

The issue is then how one is to determine whether a particular dispute falls within the jurisdiction of the UN or another organisation. In the absence of a central treaty or instrument providing for a regime of competence allocation in collective security law any attempt at the division of competence between collective security organisations should first be made through an examination of their relevant constituent instruments.[46] As has been emphasised above, the UN Charter provides the UNSC with *primary* responsibility for the maintenance of international peace and security. Yet this primacy takes on a different meaning depending upon the context of a particular dispute.[47] In the context of disputes that have developed as, and remain, purely peaceful, the UN and

---

[39] See, generally, A. Roberts, 'Proposals for UN Standing Forces: A Critical History', in Lowe *et al.*, *supra* n. 1, 99.
[40] Article 47(1), UN Charter (1945).
[41] Article 47(2), UN Charter (1945).
[42] Article 48(2), UN Charter (1945) (emphasis added).
[43] Article 48(1), UN Charter (1945) (emphasis added).
[44] See, generally, Chapter VIII of the UN Charter (1945).
[45] Article 52(2), UN Charter (1945).
[46] Orakhelashvili, *supra* n. 15, at 109.
[47] One may question whether this primacy was only intended to reflect the relations between the organs of the UN. However, Chapter VIII of the UN Charter highlights the meaning of this primacy in the context of regional organisations. See *infra* in this section.

regional organisations possess concurrent competence.[48] However, there is a presumption within the Charter in favour of regional organisations settling local disputes before the UNSC becomes directly involved,[49] with Article 52(2) stating that:

> The Members of the United Nations entering into [regional] arrangements or constituting [regional] agencies shall make every effort to achieve *pacific settlement* of local disputes through such regional arrangements or by such regional agencies *before* referring them to the Security Council. (Emphasis added)

If the dispute is then referred to the UNSC it has various powers under Chapter VI of the Charter to resolve it.[50] However, if the dispute gives rise to a necessity for enforcement measures employing the use of force the competence of the UN then becomes exclusive. To be sure, while the principle of subsidiarity has a role to play in determining competence in settling disputes using non-forcible measures,[51] '[s]ubsidiarity does not apply where competence is exclusive under the constituent instruments, for instance under Article 53 of the UN Charter which makes the use of force part of the exclusive competence of the Security Council'.[52] Indeed, Article 53 provides that '[t]he Security Council shall, where appropriate, utilize such regional arrangements or agencies for *enforcement action under its authority. But no enforcement action shall be taken under regional arrangements or by regional agencies without the authorization of the Security Council*' (emphasis added).[53] Therefore, it is not the use of enforcement action itself in which the UNSC has exclusive competence, but rather in making the decision that such measures are necessary, and Article 53 clearly telegraphs the hierarchical relationship that the UNSC is to have with other organisations in this respect.[54]

Furthermore, those organisations that were not designated, at least not originally, as regional organisations but instead as collective defence organisations, were still kept under the wings of the UNSC by the inclusion of Article 51 in Chapter VII of the Charter.[55] This provision, which enshrines the 'inherent right of individual or collective self-defence',[56] states that this right is only exercisable upon the occurrence of an 'armed attack' and:

---

[48] Orakhelashvili, *supra* n. 15, at 107.
[49] *Ibid.*, at 124.
[50] Chapter VI is concerned with the 'Pacific Settlement of Disputes'. See Kenneth Manusama's chapter (Chapter 1) in this volume for more on the UNSC's role in settling such disputes.
[51] Orakhelashvili, *supra* n.15, at 130.
[52] *Ibid.*
[53] As Orakhelashvili notes, '[t]he primary responsibility of the Security Council necessarily includes its primacy over regional organizations in the area of enforcement'. See Orakhelashvili, *ibid.*, at 120.
[54] See *infra* section 5A. Enforcing this view is the stipulation contained in Article 103 of the Charter. See *supra* n. 26.
[55] For more on self-defence as an exception to the general prohibition of the use of force see *infra* sections 5Bii and 5Ci and the chapter by Dino Kritsiotis in this volume (Chapter 6).
[56] Collective self-defence was included in Article 51 through the insistence of the Latin American states to make clear the compatibility of the existing American system and the new

until the Security Council has taken measures necessary to maintain international peace and security. Measures taken by Members in the exercise of this right of self-defence shall be immediately reported to the Security Council and shall not in any way affect the authority and responsibility of the Security Council under the present Charter to take at any time such action as it deems necessary in order to maintain or restore international peace and security.

While there has been some academic debate as to when it can be said that 'necessary' measures have been taken by the UNSC, thus extinguishing the right of self-defence,[57] not to mention who is to determine this, the fact remains that the UNSC was designated as possessing ultimate control and primacy as far as the use of force is concerned.[58] This focus on the ultimate authority of the UNSC in the provision on *self*-defence indicates that rather than simply being lumped in at the end of Chapter VII this article represents a significant element in the regime governing collective security.[59] The UN Charter system, and in particular the UNSC's overarching authority, is thus envisaged as an integrated and conceptually unique system for collective security.

C Limits upon the Forcible Powers of the UN Security Council

While the UNSC is at the apex of the collective security system, there are limits of both an internal and external nature upon its functioning and powers. As the International Criminal Tribunal for the former Yugoslavia stated in the *Tadić* case, 'neither the text nor the spirit of the Charter conceives of the Security Council as *legibus solutus* (unbound by law)'.[60] Consequently, '[b]road as the Security Council's powers are, they still are grounded in the Charter through which they have been delegated to it by states'.[61]

Perhaps the greatest constraint, and one of a procedural nature, is that in adopting any substantive measures there is the necessity of securing the 'concurring votes' of the five Permanent Members.[62] This procedural requirement thus means that action is by no means guaranteed should, for whatever reason, a Permanent Member decide against action being taken. In addition, Article 25 of the UN Charter states that '[t]he Members of the United Nations agree to accept and carry out the decisions of the Security

---

UN system. See C. Gray, *International Law and the Use of Force*, 3rd edn (Oxford: Oxford University Press, 2008), at 170.

[57] See Dinstein, *supra* n. 31, at 238–239; generally, D.W. Greig, 'Self-Defence and the Security Council: What Does Article 51 Require?', (1991) 40 *ICLQ* 366.

[58] K. Okimoto, *The Distinction and Relationship between* Jus ad Bellum *and* Jus in Bello (Oxford: Hart Publishing, 2011), at 80. For challenges to this state of affairs see, generally, *infra* section 5.

[59] For more on self-defence in connection with collective security see Orakhelashvili, *supra* n. 15, at 277–287. See also, generally, H. Kelsen, 'Collective Security and Collective Self-Defence under the Charter of the United Nations', (1948) 41 *AJIL* 783; M. Halberstam, 'The Right to Self-Defence Once the Security Council Takes Action', (1995–96) 17 *MJIL* 229.

[60] *Tadić*, *supra* n. 33, at para. 28.

[61] Orakhelashvili, *supra* n. 15, at 51. Cf. Dinstein, who talks of them being 'exceedingly wide' and 'well-nigh unlimited'. Dinstein, *supra* n. 31, at 308.

[62] Article 27(3), UN Charter (1945). See *infra* section 2 on how this has subsequently been interpreted.

Council *in accordance with the present Charter*' (emphasis added). This reference to only carrying out decisions that are in accordance with the Charter could, of course, be read as a reference to the fact that decisions should be adopted under the procedural requirements of Article 27, with no intentional reference to the substantive standards under which they should be adopted.[63] Nevertheless, the preponderant view among scholars is that this phrase indicates that the decisions should not only be procedurally correct in terms of the Charter, but also substantively in accordance with its Purposes and Principles.[64] More fundamentally, it is also clear that the UNSC is subject to peremptory norms of international law.[65] Such fundamental norms often seek to prevent the occurrence of specific acts with horrific consequences, for example genocide and torture, and are not restricted in application *ratione personae* to states or individuals.[66] Consequently, the UNSC is similarly prohibited from adopting decisions which produce such consequences.[67]

It has been argued by some scholars that the decisions and actions of the UNSC must satisfy the requirements of necessity and proportionality.[68] These conditions are typically associated with the right of self-defence.[69] However, Dinstein argues against the transposition of these constraining principles as 'the conflation of unilateral self-defence and collective security has no leg to stand on, either in theory or in practice'.[70] Yet the UNSC *is* expressly limited in Article 42 of the UN Charter to only 'tak[ing] such action by air, sea, or land forces *as may be necessary*' (emphasis added). Furthermore, given that the UNSC is also under an obligation to act in accordance with the Purposes and Principles of the UN Charter, the overarching one being the elimination of armed conflict, it could conceivably be argued that if it were to undertake action of a forcible nature that was either unnecessary or disproportionate

---

[63] This is the implied assertion by Dinstein. See Dinstein, *supra* n. 31, at 345–348.

[64] See Tzanakopoulos, *supra* n. 30, at 58. See also *supra* section 2B on the UNSC's power of determination of the existence of a threat to the peace.

[65] The International Law Commission, for example, has accepted this in Article 26 of its Draft Articles on the Responsibility of International Organisations: 'Nothing in this Chapter precludes the wrongfulness of any act of an international organization which is not in conformity with an obligation arising under a peremptory norm of general international law.' See further, for example, A. Bianchi, 'Assessing the Effectiveness of the UN Security Council's Anti-terrorism Measures: The Quest for Legitimacy and Cohesion', (2007) 17 *EJIL* 881, at 887; Orakhelashvili, *supra* n. 15, at 57–58.

[66] Indeed, in the *Kadi* case the Court of First Instance of the European Communities declared that *jus cogens* was 'a body of higher rules of public international law binding on all subjects of international law, including the bodies of the United Nations'. *Kadi v. Council of the European Union and Commission of the European Communities*, Court of First Instance of the European Communities, 2005, at para. 226.

[67] D. Akande, 'The International Court of Justice and the Security Council: Is There Room for Judicial Control of Decisions of the Political Organs of the United Nations?', (1997) 46 *ICLQ* 309, at 322.

[68] See, for example, J. Gardam, *Necessity, Proportionality and the Use of Force by States* (Cambridge: Cambridge University Press, 2004), at 188–212.

[69] While not expressly stipulated in Article 51 of the UN Charter their existence is most often referred back to customary international law and the *Caroline* incident of 1837. For more on this see the chapter by Dino Kritsiotis in this volume (Chapter 6).

[70] Dinstein, *supra* n. 31, at 309.

then this, rather than furthering those Purposes and Principles, would rather seem to act against them.

Lastly, if forcible measures are to be taken by the UNSC through it utilising the forces that have been placed at its disposal through the conclusion of Article 43 agreements – as envisaged in the UN Charter – it will often lead to it becoming a party to an armed conflict.[71] Given the historical nature of the rules of international humanitarian law, which have traditionally been perceived as applying between states, or more recently between states and certain non-state actors, the emergence of the UNSC as a body with forcible capabilities would not seem to fit within the traditional paradigm of intended subjects of this branch of international law. Neither the Geneva Conventions nor the Additional Protocols, both of which emerged after the establishment of the UN, expressly make provision for the UNSC as a subject. However, given that international force was envisaged as being undertaken under the auspices of the UNSC with its own standing army, in addition to the fact that shortly after the adoption of the UN Charter the UN was recognised as possessing international legal personality,[72] an effective interpretation of them leads to the conclusion that forcible actions taken directly by the UNSC are indeed covered, a conclusion affirmed by the UN Secretary-General some years later.[73]

3. THE MANIFESTATION OF COLD WAR IDEOLOGICAL CONFLICT IN THE SECURITY COUNCIL CHAMBER

Given the grand designs for the UNSC as the central organ of an institutionalised collective security system, it was something of an ironic twist of fate that within just a few years of its establishment – with the onset of the Cold War – the ideological differences that existed between its founding Members should cause the UNSC to begin and live much of its life partially paralysed.[74] In particular, one of the casualties of the unforeseen onset of superpower rivalry was the making of the 'special agreements' of Article 43.[75] Consequently, the UNSC to this day has never possessed any of the forces at its disposal that was initially envisaged. Additionally, the

---

[71] Although this may not be the case if the UNSC was to simply take action that amounted to, for example, a blockade or demonstration, as also expressly envisaged in Article 42. See *infra* sections 3 and 4 for the problems associated with implementing the mechanism as found in the Charter and the way in which the UNSC uses force today.

[72] See *Reparations for Injuries Suffered in the Service of the United Nations* (Advisory Opinion) 1949 ICJ Reports 174.

[73] See UN Secretary-General's Bulletin, *Observance by United Nations Forces of International Humanitarian Law*, UN Doc. ST/SGB/1999/13, 6 August 1999. Although this was adopted in the context of UN peacekeeping missions, it would similarly apply in the context of forcible missions under the command and control of the Council, as opposed to those 'authorised' by the Council, as addressed in the following sections of this chapter.

[74] See, for example, N.D. White, *Keeping the Peace: The United Nations and the Maintenance of International Peace and Security*, 2nd edn (Manchester: Manchester University Press, 1997), at 7; Gray, *supra* n. 56, at 254.

[75] See *supra* text accompanying nn 37–39.

ideological divide that defined the Cold War era had other collateral effects, such as the Military Staff Committee never fully functioning as was intended,[76] along with the emergence of other collective self-defence or collective security organisations, in particular NATO and the Warsaw Pact.

However, this period was perhaps most notably – not to mention negatively – associated with the use of the veto, or more commonly the threat of its invocation, which the five Permanent Members wielded.[77] The veto, as noted above, was a legitimate part of the collective security system of the UN Charter and could be invoked by a Permanent Member if its interests were negatively affected or, indeed, for any other reason. Although the edge was in a sense taken off the stringencies of the veto, in that the necessity of securing the 'concurring votes' of the Permanent Members in adopting resolutions on substantive issues was subsequently watered down to mean the absence of a negative vote,[78] this was not sufficient to heal the gaping fissure in the functioning of the UNSC. As a result, the model collective forcible measures system was not fully realised during the Cold War.[79]

The first major test for the UNSC during this period, which it arguably passed but only through a rather fortuitous set of circumstances, was North Korea's invasion of the Republic of Korea in 1950. Indeed, it was only as a result of the absence of the Soviet ambassador in the chamber of the UNSC – due to a dispute over the rightful representation of China at the UN – that permitted the UNSC to take action in connection with the Korean situation.[80] Nevertheless, given the lack of Article 43 agreements the UNSC did not have any forces at its own disposal. Instead, the UNSC, after '*determin*[ing] that the *armed attack* upon the Republic of Korea by forces from North Korea constitute[d] a *breach of the peace*',[81] went on to '*recommend* that the Members of the United Nations furnish such assistance to the Republic of Korea as may be necessary to repel the armed attack and to restore international peace and

---

[76] See *supra* text accompanying nn 40–41. Although the Committee does occasionally meet, its role is far less prominent than that envisioned within the UN Charter.

[77] C. Gray, 'The Charter Limitations on the Use of Force: Theory and Practice', in Lowe *et al.*, *supra* n. 1, 86, at 87.

[78] See, generally, C.A. Stavropoulos, 'The Practice of Voluntary Abstentions by Permanent Members of the Security Council under Article 27, Paragraph 3, of the Charter of the United Nations', (1967) 61 *AJIL* 737. This practice of the UNSC has been endorsed by the International Court of Justice in *Legal Consequences for States of the Continued Presence of South Africa in Namibia (South-West Africa) notwithstanding Security Council Resolution 276* (Advisory Opinion) [1971] ICJ Rep. 17, at 22.

[79] C. Henderson, *The Persistent Advocate and the Use of Force: The Impact of the United States Upon the* Jus ad Bellum *in the Post-Cold War Era* (Farnham: Ashgate, 2010), at 41. Dinstein describes this as a period that was 'disappointing in the extreme'. Dinstein, *supra* n. 31, at 317.

[80] M.J. Matheson, *Council Unbound: The Growth of UN Decision Making on Conflict and Postconflict Issues after the Cold War* (Washington, DC: United States Institute of Peace Press, 2006), at 144.

[81] UNSC Res. 83 (1950) (emphasis added). See also UNSC Res. 84 (1950), Preamble.

security in the area'.[82] This mandate was, as Nigel White has described, 'ambiguous',[83] in that the language used and the subsequent action taken under it could be interpreted as either an example of the UNSC bestowing its blessing upon states to act in collective self-defence,[84] or alternatively as an example of it exercising its authority under Chapter VII, albeit rather differently from that intended.[85] Either way, the UNSC was involved in an action which proved a success to the extent that it eventually led to a return to the status quo in the Korean Peninsula.[86]

However, the Soviet Union's return to the UNSC chamber during the Korean affair starkly highlighted the UNSC's fragility and vulnerability to being held hostage to power politics. Consequently, focus shifted to the UNGA as a possible substitute for the ailing UNSC, leading to the adoption by the UNGA of the *Uniting for Peace* resolution (hereinafter '*UfP*') on 3 November 1950.[87] The salient paragraph of this resolution provides that:

> if the Security Council, because of lack of unanimity of the permanent members, fails to exercise its primary responsibility for the maintenance of international peace and security in any case where there appears to be a threat to the peace, breach of the peace, or act of aggression, the General Assembly shall consider the matter immediately with a view to making appropriate recommendations to Members for collective measures, including in the case of a breach of the peace or act of aggression the use of armed force if necessary, to maintain or restore international peace and security.[88]

This resolution, while not placing question marks over the UNSC's primary responsibility in the area of maintaining international peace and security, does at first glance appear to implicitly provide the UNGA with a sort of 'secondary' responsibility, including in the area of enforcement measures. Indeed, despite the rather limited

---

[82] UNSC Res. 83 (1950) (emphasis added). The reference to recommending only such assistance as may be 'necessary' to repel North Korea is an example of the UNSC adhering to the principle of necessity. For more on this principle see *supra* section 2C.

[83] N.D. White, *The United Nations System: Toward International Justice* (Boulder, CO: Lynne Rienner, 2002), at 153.

[84] For example, the UNSC made constant reference to the action by North Korea constituting an 'armed attack'; it welcomed the support that UN Member States had given 'to assist the Republic of Korea in *defending itself against armed attack*' (UNSC Res. 84 (1950), para. 1 (emphasis added)); it only passively recommended assistance and did not do so in an operative paragraph of a resolution; and it merely requested the US to keep it informed of its progress, perhaps in a similar way as the reporting requirement in Article 51 was envisaged (UNSC Res. 84 (1950), para. 6).

[85] For example, the UNSC determined that there had been a 'breach of the peace' and that there was a necessity to 'restore international peace and security in the area', thus implicitly opening the door to Chapter VII measures (UNSC Res. 83 (1950), Preamble). Furthermore, while only making a 'recommendation' to Member States to furnish assistance to the Republic of Korea, such recommendations by the Council are nonetheless envisaged under Article 39 of the UN Charter. Lastly, it authorised the acting forces to use the UN flag in its operations, a symbolic gesture indicative of it being a UN mission (UNSC Res. 84 (1950), para. 5).

[86] White, *supra* n. 83, at 153.

[87] UNGA Res. 377 A (1950).

[88] *Ibid.*, para. 1.

powers of the UNGA in the maintenance of international peace and security as described above,[89] the progressive element of the *UfP* resolution was its apparent breakaway from Article 12 of the UN Charter with the possibility for the UNGA now to consider a matter even if the UNSC is seized of it.

Nevertheless, with the *UfP*'s reference to the UNGA making 'appropriate recommendations' it only confirmed the UNGA's existing Charter-based recommendatory powers in the field of peace and security, with the UNSC remaining the sole organ with the capacity to take obligatory action.[90] The UNGA's powers under the *UfP* resolution are also limited to recommending the use of armed force 'in the case of a breach of the peace or act of aggression', and not in the case of a threat to the peace, as lies within the remit of the UNSC. While a breach of the peace or act of aggression cannot necessarily be assimilated with an 'armed attack',[91] it is nonetheless arguable that the *UfP* resolution limits the UNGA to encouraging states to invoke, and by doing so endorsing, their right of individual and collective self-defence in a particular situation.[92] These issues are, though, in many respects restricted to academic interest, as while the *UfP* resolution 'was envisaged as the main pathway for the General Assembly to address issues of war and conflict'[93] it has not recommended the use of enforcement measures to this day and is instead traditionally more associated with the establishment of consensual peacekeeping missions, something which the UNSC has in any case taken over the administration of.[94]

However, with this knock to its confidence the UNSC limped through the following decades still not fully functioning or utilising the forcible powers that it possesses under the Charter in any true sense. Indeed, other than in Korea, it can only be said to have been involved in the use of force on two other occasions and, as with Korea, instead of using force itself through the model system described above, it again bestowed its blessing upon Member States to do so. In the Congo in 1960 the UNSC 'authorised' the UN Secretary-General to establish the UN Operation in the Congo and 'to take the necessary steps ... to provide such military assistance as may be necessary'[95] to the Congolese Government so as to enable it to establish security in the country, while in 1966 it 'called upon' Great Britain 'to prevent, by the use of force if necessary', oil from reaching Southern Rhodesia in an act to enforce the sanctions

---

[89] See *supra* section 2A.

[90] Indeed, the Charter is clear that '[a]ny such question on which action is necessary shall be referred to the Security Council by the General Assembly either before or after discussion'. Article 11(2), UN Charter (1945).

[91] As found in Article 51 of the UN Charter, which is the provision of the Charter providing for the right of individual or collective self-defence. See the chapter in this volume by Dino Kritsiotis for more on self-defence (Chapter 6).

[92] Dinstein, *supra* n. 31, at 341.

[93] D. Zaum, 'The Security Council, the General Assembly, and War: The Uniting for Peace Resolution', in Lowe, *supra* n. 1, 154, at 155.

[94] For more on the institution of peacekeeping see the chapter by Nigel White (Chapter 17) in this volume.

[95] UNSC Res. 143 (1960), para. 2. Although in the *Certain Expenses* Advisory Opinion the International Court of Justice perceived this force as a peacekeeping operation, as opposed to an enforcement operation. See *Certain Expenses of the United Nations* (Advisory Opinion) [1962] ICJ Rep. 151.

imposed against it.[96] These incidents again demonstrate that while 'the UNSC was involved in the collective use of force and clothed certain actions with its unique legitimacy, ... the full extent of its powers was never exhibited'.[97]

Given this state of partial paralysis, arguments of a systemic nature were made during the Cold War that respect for the prohibition of the use of force norm and the exceptions to it were conditional upon the effective functioning of the collective security system. The predicament that the UNSC found itself in led some scholars – who were mainly based within the US – to argue that states had forsaken their right to use force upon the condition that this system was to be operational.[98] Consequently, it was argued, states should not be precluded from unilaterally using force, either to defend themselves in circumstances beyond the direct occurrence of an 'armed attack' or for the protection of others, given the implausibility of the issue being effectively addressed by the UNSC. Thomas Franck, for example, (in)famously proclaimed the 'death' of the prohibition of the use of force norm on the basis that violations of Article 2(4) were so rife that its existence could no longer be presumed.[99] If the norm no longer existed then, under this argument, neither could the purposely restrictive exceptions to it. One of Franck's 'factors undermining Article 2(4)' was the disagreement between the Permanent Member States of the UNSC which meant that 'despite some one hundred separate outbreaks of hostility between states' only one – and this was by chance – had been responded to forcibly by this organ.[100] This state of affairs, Franck argued, 'indicates why, for security, nations have increasingly fallen back on their own resources and on military and regional alliances'.[101] It should, of course, be noted that while there was some truth to this argument, which was undoubtedly a damning indictment of the fragility of the UN Charter collective security apparatus at the time, it was of some significance that states themselves did not similarly proclaim the end of the UN system – either in the abstract or in justifying their actions – and it was instead an argument that was largely confined to the writings of certain scholars.

In more nuanced tones, other scholars offered the more tightly construed argument that while the norm in Article 2(4) was not dead, given the pertaining predicament it 'should be read to allow the use of force to further "world public order" or the principles and purposes of the UN'.[102] Consequently, arguments were advanced that actions that did not encroach upon the 'territorial integrity' or 'political independence' of any other state or did not defeat the purposes of the UN, or perhaps were seen

---

[96] UNSC Res. 221 (1966), para. 5.
[97] Henderson, *supra* n. 79, at 41.
[98] See, for example, W.M. Reisman, 'Coercion and Self-Determination: Construing Charter Article 2(4)', (1984) 78 *AJIL* 642.
[99] See T.M. Franck, 'Who Killed Article 2(4)? or: Changing Norms Governing the Use of Force by States', (1970) 64 *AJIL* 809.
[100] *Ibid.*, at 810–811.
[101] *Ibid.*, at 811.
[102] As described by Christine Gray. See Gray, *supra* n. 56, at 31. For an example of such an argument being made see Reisman, *supra* n. 98.

instead to be furthering those purposes, were, or at least should be, permitted.[103] However, these arguments were, again, mostly confined to the work of scholars, not states themselves, with exceptions being the arguments made by the UK in the *Corfu Channel* case in 1949, which were implicitly rejected by the International Court of Justice (hereinafter 'ICJ'),[104] and by Israel in justifying its intervention to rescue hostages in Entebbe in 1976,[105] which were dismissed by other states within the UNSC.[106] Nevertheless, as the next section illustrates, the UNSC began to invoke its forcible powers in the post-Cold War era, thus shifting from an 'episodic and tentative'[107] record during the Cold War to a more consistent and effective one and thus rendering such arguments more difficult to plausibly make.

4. POST-COLD WAR REVITALISATION OF THE FORCIBLE POWERS OF THE UN SECURITY COUNCIL

With the end of the Cold War in 1989 came the possibility of consensus between Member States within the chamber of the UNSC.[108] Consequently, as Gray notes, '[t]he end of the Cold War brought with it a steep decline in the use of the veto and a massive increase in the activity of the Security Council'.[109] Nevertheless, the UNSC still did not go on to function as originally intended, and did not implement the procedure for using force inscribed within the UN Charter. Instead, it came to firmly embed within its practice – in drawing upon elements of the language of the Cold War permissions to use force – the method of 'authorising' states to use 'all necessary means'.[110] The initiation of such a practice came with Iraq's aggressive invasion of Kuwait in the final stages of the Cold War.

On 2 August 1990 Iraqi tanks rolled over the border into Kuwaiti territory.[111] The UNSC immediately condemned this action as a 'breach of international peace and security'[112] and demanded an immediate and unconditional withdrawal of Iraqi forces from Kuwait.[113] However, the most significant action by the UNSC came on 29 November 1990 when it adopted Resolution 678 (1990). The key paragraph of this resolution, which was adopted under Chapter VII of the UN Charter,

---

[103] See, for example, D. Bowett, *Self-Defence in International Law* (Manchester: Manchester University Press, 1958), at 152; A. D'Amato, 'Israel's Air Strike Upon the Iraqi Nuclear Reactor', (1983) 77 *AJIL* 584, 585.
[104] *Corfu Channel Case* (United Kingdom v. Albania) [1949] ICJ Rep. 4, at 35.
[105] See UN Doc. S/PV.1939, 9 July 1976, paras 105–121.
[106] See, generally, UN Docs S/PV.1939–1943, 9–14 July 1976.
[107] Matheson, *supra* n. 80, at 144.
[108] N. Blokker, 'Is the Authorization Authorized? Powers and Practice of the UN Security Council to Authorize the Use of Force by "Coalitions of the Able and Willing"', (2000) 11 *EJIL* 541, at 542.
[109] See Gray, *supra* n. 56, at 264.
[110] Henderson, *supra* n. 79, at 42.
[111] See *Keesing's Record of World Events* (hereinafter '*Keesing's*') (1990) 37632.
[112] UNSC Res. 660 (1990), Preamble.
[113] *Ibid.*, para. 2.

Authorize[d] Member States co-operating with the Government of Kuwait, unless Iraq on or before 15 January 1991, fully implement[ed] … the foregoing resolutions, to use all necessary means to uphold and implement resolution 660 and all subsequent resolutions and to restore international peace and security in the area.[114]

Subsequently, after giving Iraq a pause of goodwill to vacate Kuwait, a US-led 'coalition of the willing', acting under the authority of Resolution 678 (1990),[115] launched an air offensive against Iraq (code-named Operation Desert Storm) on 16 January 1991 followed by a ground invasion.[116]

The rather euphemistic 'authorisation' to use 'all necessary means' employed in Resolution 678 (1990) was virtually universally accepted and supported by those within the UNSC as amounting to a permission to use armed force.[117] While not in itself vastly different from the relatively rare permissions to use force provided by the UNSC in the Cold War era, the adoption of the resolution was accompanied by an unprecedented revolutionary wind of cooperation that swept through the chamber of the UNSC. The reasons for this cooperation arguably lay in a confluence of factors pertaining at that particular moment. Indeed, Iraq's brazen invasion of Kuwait, which was the first time in the UN era that a Member State had sought to completely annex another,[118] occurred at approximately the same time as Cold War politics had finally relinquished their grip in predetermining the actions of the Permanent Members of the UNSC. Consequently, Iraq's clear transgression of the prohibition of the use of force,[119] coming as it did at the very end of the Cold War and with the emergence of a 'New World Order', galvanised the members of the UNSC in a way that had not been possible during the previous 45 years of the Council's life.[120]

---

[114] UNSC Res. 678 (1990), para. 2.

[115] Although Dinstein argues that this was an action in collective self-defence. See Dinstein, *supra* n. 31, at 299–300. While this is a tenable argument, the action at the time and subsequently has been framed as an authorisation by the UNSC. In any event, if the coalition forces were acting in self-defence there would have been no need to seek UNSC authorisation for such a use of force. See also generally E.V. Rostow, 'Until What? Enforcement Action or Collective Self-Defense?', (1991) 85 *AJIL* 506.

[116] *Keesing's* (1991) 37936–37939.

[117] See, generally, UN Doc. S/PV.2963, 29 November 1990. The authorisation was only directly challenged by Iraq which, although referring to the cases 'in which the use of force may legally be *authorized* by the Security Council', went on to elaborate that this meant 'collective action under the command and control of the Security Council, in coordination with the Military Staff Committee'. *Ibid.*, at 21 (emphasis added). However, Blokker has termed this a 'case related' critique, since Iraq was the state towards which the authorisation was targeted. See Blokker, *supra* n. 108, at 567.

[118] See C. Greenwood, 'New World Order or Old? The Invasion of Kuwait and the Rule of Law', (1992) 55 *MLR* 153, at 153.

[119] Although the UNSC did not condemn the invasion as a violation of Article 2(4), as an act of aggression or as an 'armed attack'.

[120] Although a not uncommon position has been adopted that while the resolution and the resulting use of force may arguably have been legal, due to the great-power pressure diplomacy behind the adoption of the resolution, the rejection of economic sanctions and other nonviolent options as well as the resolution's unrestricted character rendered its legitimacy '[a] borderline

Furthermore, at the meeting when Resolution 678 (1990) was adopted there was a clear belief among the Members of the UNSC that it would have precedential value. The US, for example, correctly predicted that '[i]t will surely do much to determine the future of the body'.[121] Although the US has continued to be authorised to lead operations,[122] the technique has also been employed to provide authorisations to other states, such as France,[123] Italy[124] and Australia.[125] It has also been used to authorise organisations such as NATO,[126] the Economic Community of West African States,[127] the African Union (hereinafter 'AU')[128] and the EU[129] to conduct various forcible operations.

What is particularly notable about these authorisations, however, is that while undoubtedly the original Charter scheme for the use of collective force under the auspices of the UNSC was framed in the *inter*-state context,[130] and indeed this was the context of the authorisation provided in Resolution 678 (1990), these subsequent authorisations have almost exclusively been provided to combat threats to the peace emanating from an *intra*-state situation.[131] Indeed, force has been used under the auspices of the UNSC to make conditions suitable for humanitarian aid operations to take place,[132] to enforce no-fly zones,[133] to protect designated safe havens,[134] to disarm factions within a civil war,[135] to arrest those responsible for the deaths of UN

---

proposition at best'. See B.H. Weston, 'Security Council Resolution 678 and Persian Gulf Decision Making: Precarious Legitimacy', (1991) 85 *AJIL* 516, at 533.

[121] UN Doc. S/PV.2963, *supra* n.117, at 6. See also Kuwait at 18, Yemen at 32, Malaysia at 76, Cuba at 59–60 and Romania at 97. Christine Gray describes the adoption of Resolution 678 (1990) and Operation Desert Storm as a 'revolutionary development' and the 'catalyst for fundamental change in the international regulation of the use of force' (Gray, *supra* n. 56, at 357) while Olivier Corten notes that 'the Gulf War was to be a turning point, with the Security Council thereafter being presented as an effective player, able to circumscribe the use of force in the name of the international community'. O. Corten, *The Law Against War: The Prohibition on the Use of Force in Contemporary International Law* (Oxford: Hart Publishing, 2010), at 350.

[122] For example in Somalia (UNSC Res. 794 (1992), para.10).
[123] For example in Rwanda (UNSC Res. 929 (1994), paras 2 and 3).
[124] For example in Albania (UNSC Res. 1101 (1997), para. 4).
[125] For example in East Timor (UNSC Res. 1264 (1999), para. 3).
[126] For example in Bosnia (UNSC Res. 816 (1993), para. 4). Although note that the UNSC does not identify the organisation concerned, just Member States 'acting nationally or through regional organizations or arrangements'.
[127] For example in Côte d'Ivoire (UNSC Res. 1464 (2003), para. 9).
[128] For example in Somalia (UNSC Res. 1744 (2007), para. 4).
[129] For example in Chad (UNSC Res. 1778 (2007), para. 6(a)).
[130] Indeed, the UNSC was given primary responsibility in Article 24(1) of the UN Charter for maintaining *international* peace and security.
[131] Although this was not exactly novel, as witnessed in the Congo and Southern Rhodesia, and arguably also the Korea episodes described *supra* in section 3.
[132] For example in Somalia (UNSC Res. 794 (1992), para. 10).
[133] For example in Bosnia (UNSC Res. 816 (1993), para. 4) and Libya (UNSC Res. 1973 (2011), para. 8).
[134] For example in Bosnia (UNSC Res. 836 (1993), para. 10).
[135] For example in Somalia (UNSC Res. 814 (1993), paras 5–7).

peacekeepers,[136] to stabilise post-conflict situations[137] and, perhaps as the high-water mark of the UNSC's intervention in the internal affairs of states, to impose democracy.[138] The problem with such interventions is that the UN is expressly prohibited under Article 2(7) of the UN Charter from intervening 'in matters which are essentially within the domestic jurisdiction of any state'. Nonetheless, this 'principle shall not prejudice the application of enforcement measures under Chapter VII'. Thus, if the measures have been adopted under Chapter VII, 'the broad powers conferred on the Council in the province of collective security override, where necessary, the sovereignty of any Member of the United Nations'.[139]

While the UNSC has never specified precisely the provision under which it was acting when it has provided such authorisations, it has nonetheless consistently stated to be adopting such resolutions under Chapter VII. Whether one takes the view that Chapter VII has been consequently disingenuously invoked in an attempt to depict the particular situation as a threat to *international* peace and security, when in actual fact it posed no such threat,[140] it remains the case that the contextual shift of the interventions has elicited little in the way of general condemnation, arguably representing an acknowledgment of the fact that intra-state security issues now outweigh those of an inter-state nature. The very fact that they have been adopted means that even states of a traditionally non-interventionist nature – particularly Russia and China – have provided their support. In this respect, whether or not such forcible interventions were the original intention of the drafters of the Charter, subsequent practice has demonstrated that '[a] threat to the peace may be determined by the Security Council even in the face of mere violations of human rights not entailing the use of force'.[141] In any case, apart from the instances of Iraq (1990) and Haiti (1994), authorised missions have been undertaken with the consent of, or even at the request of, the territorial state,[142] with the authorisation and backing of the UNSC playing a support role in an operation that could have been undertaken unilaterally. The reason for the authorisation has thus been to make the forcible action independent of the existence and scope of the state's consent should this, for whatever reason, be revoked at any point.[143]

This set of events clearly breathed new life into the UNSC realising its role in forcibly maintaining international peace and security. Yet it also breathed new life more

---

[136] For example in Somalia (UNSC Res. 837 (1993), para. 5).
[137] For example in Afghanistan (UNSC Res. 1386 (2001), paras 1–3).
[138] For example in Haiti (UNSC Res. 940 (1994), para. 4).
[139] Dinstein, *supra* n. 31, at 314.
[140] Although it should be noted that while the UNSC has primary responsibility for the maintenance of international peace and security, Chapter VII is concerned with 'threats to the peace, breaches of the peace and acts of aggression', not explicitly being located in the international context. Cf. R. Cryer, 'The Security Council and Article 39: A Threat to Coherence?', (1996) 1 *JACL* 161, at 188. ('This [practice of the Council] can only be justified by a reference to the redefinition of international peace to include the more positive aspects of common interests of humanity, there being a threat to the peace if there are violations of these interests, irrespective of where they occur.') See also, generally, K. Wellens, 'The UN Security Council and New Threats to the Peace: Back to the Future', (2003) 9 *JCSL* 15.
[141] Dinstein, *supra* n. 31, at 313.
[142] Corten, *supra* n. 121, at 314. See also Gray, *supra* n. 56, at 328.
[143] Corten, *ibid*.

specifically into the provisions of the UN Charter. However, the result was a rather more modest interpretation of the UNSC's forcible powers than contended by some.[144] As noted above,[145] Chapter VII of the UN Charter was framed in such a way that once a decision that forcible measures were necessary had been taken by the UNSC there were to be no question marks as to whether force was ultimately to be deployed. Such a decision was binding and the action required to carry it out was envisaged as being undertaken by the standing army of forces that had been provided by Member States under the Article 43 agreements, and that the UNSC was to have at its disposal. In contrast, and in light of the absence of the Article 43 agreements, the new and embedded 'authorisation' mechanism is permissive in nature. That is to say no state is under an obligation to deploy its armed forces in the realisation of the aims of the resolution.[146] In fact, in the absence of such agreements this was arguably a necessary compromise, given the obvious difficulties in the UNSC making *ad hoc* demands for a state to use its armed forces and put its military personnel at risk for a mission with no direct national interest for the contributing state concerned.[147]

Nevertheless, while the UN Secretary-General has claimed that the authorisation technique 'provides the Organization with an enforcement capacity it would not otherwise have and is greatly preferable to the unilateral use of force by Member States without reference to the United Nations',[148] others have discounted the legality of the mechanism altogether given the obvious contrast between it and the strictures prescribed within the UN Charter. Tsagourias, for example, has argued that 'the Charter contains specific enforcement procedures. The [Security Council] has no choice in enforcement mechanisms and indeed authorisations as a practice cannot be assumed from either the letter or the purposes of the intentions of the UN members.'[149] Yet while the UNSC has never been specific in stating the precise legal basis for the mechanism, this claim can be refuted.

---

[144] See, generally, N. Tsagourias, 'The Shifting Laws on the Use of Force and the Trivialization of the UN Collective Security System: The Need to Reconstitute It', (2003) 34 *NYIL* 55.

[145] See *supra* section 2.

[146] It is in this respect that Sarooshi describes the authorisation technique as a 'delegation' of the powers of the UNSC. However, while the power to use force to achieve the aims of the authorising resolution may be delegated, the competence to either decide the existence of a threat to the peace or possess unrestricted power of command and control over a force carrying out authorised military enforcement action cannot be. See D. Sarooshi, *The United Nations and the Development of Collective Security: The Delegation by the UN Security Council of its Chapter VII Powers* (Oxford: Clarendon Press, 1999), generally and, in particular, at 32–35. See also, generally, H. Freudenshuß, 'Between Unilateralism and Collective Security: Authorizations of the Use of Force by the UN Security Council', (1994) 5 *EJIL* 492. For a critical dismissal of the delegation technique see J. Quigley, 'The United Nations Security Council: Promethean Protector or Helpless Hostage?', (2000) 35 *Texas ILJ* 129, at 156–161.

[147] This is arguably the reason why, with a few exceptions, the contributing states have had some connection with the state in which force has been authorised.

[148] Report of the UN Secretary-General, 'Supplement to an Agenda for Peace', (1995) UN Doc. A/50/60, at para. 80.

[149] Tsagourias, *supra* n. 144, at 63–64.

It has, for example, been suggested that Article 43 agreements are a condition precedent to the taking of collective military action by the UNSC under Article 42.[150] While it must be conceded that this argument has some merit to it, it is also true that 'no explicit language in Article 42 or in Articles 43, 44, and 45 ... precludes states from voluntarily making armed forces available to carry out the resolutions of the Council adopted under Chapter VII'.[151] Furthermore, '[w]hile the Charter appears to envisage the Council taking military action through forces under its own command, nothing in the Charter precludes the Council authorizing military action by others and Articles 48 and 53 clearly envisage it'.[152] Indeed, the facility for the UNSC to 'authorise' regional organisations to carry out enforcement action on its behalf but under its supervision and authority already exists in Article 53 of the Charter.[153] As such, the authorisation technique is not exactly alien to the powers of the UNSC.

In this context, the only thing that we know for certain from the practice of the UNSC is that it regularly expressly states to be acting under Chapter VII in adopting authorising resolutions, a practice which even the doubters of the authorisation technique's legality would have to acknowledge has been generally accepted by other states and become embedded into UNSC practice. Therefore, while one may speculate as to the exact legal basis upon which the authorisation technique sits, without more it is safest to conclude that the UNSC acts 'on a liberal construction of its authority derived from its general powers to maintain and restore international peace and security'.[154] In this respect, the *Reparations for Injuries* Advisory Opinion of 1949 provides support to the assertion that powers of the UN can be implied from the provisions of the UN Charter. Indeed, the ICJ provided the Charter with an effective interpretation so that 'the Organization must be deemed to have those powers which, though not expressly provided for in the Charter, are conferred upon it by necessary implication as being essential to the performance of its duties'.[155] More specifically, the ICJ followed this Opinion 13 years later in the *Certain Expenses* Advisory Opinion by rejecting the proposition that authorisation for the use of armed force by the UNSC must be based upon Article 42. Instead, it stated that it could not assume such 'a limited ... view of the powers of the Security Council'.[156] Indeed, the Court was clear that '[i]t cannot be said that the Charter has left the Security Council impotent in the

---

[150] L. Goodrich and A. Simons, *The United Nations and the Maintenance of International Peace and Security* (Washington, DC: Brookings Institution, 1955), at 398–405; Kelsen, *supra* n. 23, at 756; Weston, *supra* n. 120, at 510; K.P. Saksena, *The United Nations and Collective Security* (Delhi: DK Publishing House, 1974), at 93. See also the Report of the Secretary-General, 'An Agenda for Peace', (1992) UN Doc. A/47/277, para. 43. Article 106 of the UN Charter also suggests this.

[151] O. Schachter, 'United Nations Law in the Gulf Conflict', (1991) 85 *AJIL* 452, at 464. White notes that 'it would be incorrect to say that there is an inextricable link between Articles 42 and 43'. See White, *supra* n. 74, at 117. See also Greenwood, *supra* n. 118, at 167.

[152] C. Greenwood, 'Humanitarian Intervention: The Case of Kosovo', (1999) 10 *Finnish Yearbook of International Law* 141, at 154.

[153] See *supra* section 2.

[154] Schachter, *supra* n. 151, at 461.

[155] *Reparations* Advisory Opinion, *supra* n. 72, at para. 182.

[156] *Certain Expenses* Advisory Opinion, *supra* n. 95, at para. 167.

face of an emergency situation when agreements under Article 43 have not been concluded'.[157] As a result, '[i]n the *Certain Expenses* Opinion the International Court admitted the exercise of implied powers by principal organs to the extent that this serves the purposes of the UN'.[158] Consequently, '[t]he implied powers doctrine is reinforced by the principle of effective interpretation of the Charter as a treaty' and '[t]he rationale of effective interpretation is that, if the organ in question is to discharge its responsibilities under the Charter effectively, then it should be able to adopt such decisions as are necessary for and antecedent to that'.[159]

However, it is also the case that '[i]mplied powers can only be those that correspond to the overall character of an organ under the constituent instrument and enable it to carry out functions conferred on it'.[160] As has been noted above, not only does the UN Charter clearly state that the central purpose of the UN is '[t]o maintain international peace and security' – and to that end 'to take *effective* collective measures for the prevention and removal of threats to the peace, and for the suppression of acts of aggression or other breaches of the peace'[161] – but also that the UNSC is specifically designated with primary responsibility for this task. Consequently, '[e]ven if the authorisation given to States to use force is not explicitly taken up in [the provisions of the UN Charter], it seems difficult to contest that such a mechanism is consistent with both their spirit and their letter'.[162]

There have, nonetheless, been accusations that the authorisation mechanism in effect 'privatised' the collective security system, and is thus incongruent with the collective nature of the measures to be taken under Chapter VII.[163] As mentioned above, this mechanism is already found in Chapter VIII of the Charter concerning regional organisations. Yet there does not seem to be any more to fear in authorising individual states or 'coalitions of the willing' than regional organisations; under the authorisation mechanism both act under the general authority and strategic control of the UNSC. In any case, while Chapter VII envisages the UNSC as having forces at its disposal, the actual command and control of these forces was not necessarily to fall to the UNSC itself. Indeed, Article 47(2) expressly notes that '[q]uestions relating to the command of such forces shall be worked out subsequently'. In fact, Chapter VII does not provide for the UNSC to have any more command over the forces at its disposal than as provided under the authorisation mechanism. As such, while command of authorised forces of Member States under Chapter VII has thus far been by the authorised states or international organisations themselves, this is something that was equally feasible under

---

[157] *Ibid.* The ICJ also noted in the *Namibia* Advisory Opinion that 'the Members of the United Nations have conferred upon the Security Council powers commensurate with its responsibility for the maintenance of peace and security'. *Namibia* Advisory Opinion, *supra* n. 78, at 52.
[158] Orakhelashvili, *supra* n. 15, at 51.
[159] *Ibid.*
[160] *Ibid.*
[161] Article 1(1), UN Charter (1945) (emphasis added).
[162] Corten, *supra* n. 121, at 315.
[163] See, generally, J. Quigley, 'The "Privatization" of Security Council Enforcement Action: A Threat to Multilateralism', (1996) 17 *MJIL* 249.

the envisaged system. In either case, the UNSC would possess 'overall' and not 'effective' control of the forces deployed under its auspices.[164]

Ultimately, the drafters of the Charter did not anticipate the superpower disagreements that characterised the Cold War, but their eventual realisation – and their lasting impact which gave rise to the authorisation technique – did not result in a *rebus sic stantibus*, thus rendering the UN Charter, or at least Chapter VII, inapplicable due to a fundamental change of circumstances.[165] On the contrary, these events and the now established practice of the authorisation technique are 'subsequent practice' in the interpretation of the UN Charter.[166] Today, the authorisation technique's general use outside of the Chapter VIII context can be viewed 'as a necessary incremental shift regarding the competence of the organ'.[167] Indeed, this subsequent practice is now so clear that '[e]arly questions about the procedural legality of this adaptation of the Council's role now appear moot in light of state practice over the past decade'.[168] As such, '[e]ven if it is not covered by explicit regulations in the UN Charter, no one contests the lawfulness of the principle of military intervention authorised by the Security Council'[169] so that it is today perhaps of little 'practical significance' upon which basis the UNSC acts when it decides to do so.[170]

5. CONTEMPORARY CHALLENGES TO THE EXCLUSIVE COMPETENCE OF THE UN SECURITY COUNCIL

As described above, the dawn of the post-Cold War era, and the almost simultaneous eviction of Iraq from Kuwait, witnessed the heavy cloud of the assured threat of the veto drifting out of the Council chamber. The associated rise in the activity of the UNSC did not, however, dampen the appetite for challenges to its authority. Nevertheless, there were two noticeable differences associated with these compared with those witnessed during the Cold War. First, the now comparatively revived functioning of the UNSC meant that such fundamental systemic arguments were not as easily made. The

---

[164] Although in terms of allocating responsibility for the actions of the authorised forces this would remain with the individual Member States as they would be in effective control of them.

[165] See Article 62, Vienna Convention on the Law of Treaties (1969).

[166] Article 31(3)(b), *ibid*.

[167] Henderson, *supra* n. 79, at 47. In the debates over the possible use of force in Somalia, Zimbabwe noted that 'in this new era – the post-cold-war era – it is not unreasonable to expect individual states or a group of states to provide the necessary resources, both human and material, to help resolve such a crisis as part of the international effort'. UN Doc. S/PV.3145, 3 December 1992, at 7.

[168] S. Chesterman, *Just War or Just Peace? Humanitarian Intervention and International Law* (Oxford: Oxford University Press, 2001), at 164.

[169] Corten, *supra* n. 121, at 312; Kohen has also observed that 'the practice of Security Council authorizations to member states to use force is today too well established to be contested'. M.G. Kohen, 'The Use of Force by the United States After the End of the Cold War, and its Impact Upon International Law', in M. Byers and G. Nolte (eds), *United States Hegemony and the Foundations of International Law* (Cambridge: Cambridge University Press, 2003), 197, at 215.

[170] Gray, *supra* n. 56, at 259.

reality was that the UNSC *was* functioning, albeit differently from the scheme originally set out in the UN Charter. Instead, and arguably as a consequence of this rise in activity and the realisation of the threat it posed to the possibilities for unilateral action, challenges were increasingly being made by states, as opposed to being made almost exclusively by scholars, as was witnessed during the Cold War. Secondly, the challenges have taken on a different shape, as they have not been able to exclude the possibility of the UNSC acting with such confidence given its revitalised functioning. Now, instead of existential challenges to the authority of the UNSC, the challenges have been made more in connection with competence allocation in dealing with particular threats and issues affecting international peace and security.

In an attempt to clearly present the basis of the challenges to the UN Charter system of collective security, they will be conceptualised here in the form of their *ratione personae*, *ratione materiae* and *ratione temporis* nature. This is not to say that they can necessarily be neatly divided in this way, neither that there are no overlaps between these categories, but that this division highlights the underlying nature of the challenges in the context of the particular area of competence possessed by the UNSC.

A. *Ratione personae*

The *ratione personae* competence of the UNSC has been challenged through specific interpretations that have on occasion been given to the constitutive instruments of other organisations. These have sought to provide the organisation concerned with autonomy in decisions to resort to enforcement measures either against their own members or as a result of the location of the state causing the particular threat to, or breach of, the peace. Orakhelashvili helpfully describes the 'autonomy thesis' in the following terms:

> Unlike the concept of subsidiarity, which applies only to areas in which the competence of different organizations is concurrent not exclusive, the autonomy thesis essentially aims to rearrange the allocation of competence under organizations' constituent instruments – including exclusive competence – and thus enable a regional organization to undertake an action that otherwise needs UN authorization.[171]

The UNSC's exclusive competence is in taking decisions that force is necessary; decisions that would otherwise be a breach of the prohibition of the use of force. Other than in self-defence, and in the absence of a civil war, the only clear possibility that states or other organisations possess to lawfully use force unilaterally is with the consent of the state concerned.[172] However, forcible action under these circumstances is not enforcement action *per se* as there is no measure of coercion on the state upon

---

[171] Orakhelashvili, *supra* n. 15, at 141–142. Indeed, 'when the Charter was adopted the idea of allocating regional zones of responsibility was rejected'. *Ibid.*, at 142.

[172] It has been argued by some scholars that when a civil war is in progress states are prohibited from providing any forcible assistance to any of the forces involved, including those of the government. See Gray, *supra* n. 56, at 81. However, this is far from universally accepted. See, for example, D. Akande, 'Would it be Lawful for European (or Other) States to Provide Arms to the Syrian Opposition?', *EJIL Talk!*, 17 January 2013, available at http://www.ejiltalk.org/would-it-be-lawful-for-european-or-other-states-to-provide-arms-to-the-syrian-opposition/.

whose territory the action is being taken. These types of intervention based upon *ad hoc* consent should thus be distinguished from those arrangements which appear to be similar to the UN Charter's scheme for collective security; that is, those in which a state has ostensibly provided advance consent to forcible intervention through becoming a party to a constitutive treaty which provides the organisation with the authority to forcibly intervene in particular circumstances, despite there being the possibility that the state will subsequently disagree with the forcible enforcement action being taken against it.[173]

While in its Constitutive Act of 2000 the AU reaffirmed the principle of the 'peaceful resolution of disputes' and the 'prohibition of the use of force or the threat to use force',[174] it also provided somewhat ambiguously in Article 4(h) for 'the right of the Union to intervene in a Member State pursuant to a decision of the Assembly in respect of grave circumstances, namely war crimes, genocide and crimes against humanity'.[175] Although the Constitutive Act also reaffirmed in Article 4(j) 'the right of Member states to request intervention from the Union in order to restore peace and security',[176] it has been argued that the absence of a request will not prevent the AU from acting under Article 4(h).[177] In other words, it has been contended that the AU has claimed autonomy (though not necessarily of an exclusive nature) in making decisions regarding enforcement action of a forcible kind, albeit in the limited circumstances of a humanitarian crisis, in one of its Member States.[178]

Of equal significance has been the particular interpretation given by the US to NATO's new strategic direction in the post-Cold War era. In its founding North Atlantic Treaty NATO expressly categorised itself as a collective defence alliance as opposed to a regional organisation,[179] apparently to avoid the constraints of Chapter VIII,[180] while at the same time expressly recognising that the UNSC had primary responsibility for

---

[173] For example, Iraq was a party to the UN Charter in 1991 and had thus accepted the UNSC's exclusive competence to use force against it should it deem it necessary but did not accept Operation Desert Storm, which was authorised against it in November 1990 and which commenced in January 1991. That is, there was no consent by Iraq to the operation at the time it was launched. For more on this operation see *supra* section 4.

[174] Articles 4(e) and 4(f) respectively, Constitutive Act of the African Union (2000). Also included was 'non-interference by any Member state in the internal affairs of another' (Article 4(g)) and 'peaceful co-existence of Member states and their right to live in peace and security' (Article 4(i)).

[175] Article 4(h), *ibid*.

[176] Article 4(j), *ibid*.

[177] A. Abass, *Regional Organisations and the Development of Collective Security: Beyond Chapter VIII of the UN Charter* (Oxford: Hart Publishing, 2004), at 165.

[178] J. Levitt, 'The Peace and Security Council of the African Union and the United Nations Security Council: The Case of Darfur, Sudan', in N. Blokker and N. Schrijver (eds), *The Security Council and the Use of Force* (Leiden: Martinus Nijhoff, 2005), 211, at 229. Gray refers to this as 'a regional right of humanitarian intervention'. Gray, *supra* n. 56, at 53.

[179] See Preamble and Article 5, The North Atlantic Treaty (1949). Orakhelashvili has commented that '[t]he Article 5 commitment to collective defence remains the principal *raison d'être* of NATO'. Orakhelashvili, *supra* n. 15, at 80. It is not within the purview of this chapter to discuss whether NATO is a regional organisation. For a useful discussion see Orakhelashvili, *ibid.*, at 95–96.

the maintenance of international peace and security.[181] As such, it was clearly intended that forcible action would be taken externally in the defence of the Alliance and its members. However, with the end of the Cold War and the associated security risks the Organisation sought to redefine its role.[182] While its strategic concept of 1991 still emphasised that 'the Alliance is purely defensive in purpose',[183] NATO's involvement in the conflict in Yugoslavia in 1991–1995 bore witness to it beginning to shift away from being a purely external defence alliance to adopting a broader constitutional mandate which incorporated a distinct internal crisis management role, particularly within the Euro-Atlantic region. Consequently, its 1999 strategic concept emphasised that the role of the Organisation was not simply defensive but was also to maintain peace and security within the 'Euro-Atlantic region'.[184] Indeed, it emphasised that the Alliance 'not only ensures the defence of its members but contributes to peace and stability in this region'.[185] As Orakhelashvili notes, it is possible for such organisations to extend their constitutional mandate[186] and '[i]t seems that these new fields of competence relate, not to NATO's implied powers (which can only exist on the basis of enabling the Alliance to effectively carry out its defensive function), but as a consensually agreed expansion to cover tasks qualitatively different from those set out in Article 5'.[187] As a result, even if it is argued that NATO was not a regional organisation for the purposes of Chapter VIII of the UN Charter at the time of its formation, it appears that by 1999 it had, through redefinition, arguably become one.[188] While this redefinition in itself did not pose a challenge to the UNSC's exclusive competence in the field of enforcement measures, at the time of the Kosovo intervention in 1999 some within the administration of US President Bill Clinton began to argue that NATO had autonomy in decisions to resort to force. Indeed, in conjunction with the adoption of the new Strategic Concept in 1999, the autonomy of NATO in the

---

[180] D. Leurdijk, 'The UN and NATO: The Logic of Primacy', in M. Pugh and W.P.S. Sidhu (eds), *The United Nations and Regional Security: Europe and Beyond* (Boulder, CO: Lynne Rienner, 2003), 32, at 57. However, this is inherently illogical as regardless of how it characterised itself, if the circumstances for collective self-defence arose its constituent states would nonetheless be permitted to act.

[181] Article 7, The North Atlantic Treaty (1949) ('This Treaty does not affect, and shall not be interpreted as affecting in any way the rights and obligations under the Charter of the Parties which are members of the United Nations, or the primary responsibility of the Security Council for the maintenance of international peace and security').

[182] On this redefinition see, generally, B. Simma, 'NATO, the UN and the Use of Force: Legal Aspects', (1999) 10 *EJIL* 1.

[183] Paragraph 35, 1991 NATO Strategic Concept, available at http://www.nato.int/cps/en/natolive/official_texts_23847.htm?selectedLocale=en.

[184] NATO's 1999 Strategic Concept makes 39 references to its operations in the 'Euro-Atlantic' region. See 1999 NATO Strategic Concept, available at http://www.nato.int/cps/en/natolive/official_texts_27433.htm.

[185] Paragraph 6, *ibid*.

[186] See Orakhelashvili, *supra* n. 15, at 96–97.

[187] *Ibid.*, at 80–81.

[188] Although it regularly engages in 'out of area' missions, for example in the form of the International Security Assistance Force in Afghanistan.

realms of enforcement decision making and its non-subordination to any other organisation, including the UN, were asserted.[189]

On the basis of both of these challenges, which sought to offer a particular interpretation regarding the powers of the respective organisations, it appeared that a normative conflict had arisen between their constitutive documents and that of the UN Charter. Yet, any claims to autonomy bump up against the clear Chapter VIII establishment of the UNSC's exclusive competence in the realm of forcible measures and the necessity for authorisation to use force, as outlined above.[190] Indeed, if the constitutive instrument of an organisation is interpreted as providing it with powers of enforcement action similar to the UNSC then this is in direct conflict with the UN Charter. In this respect, Article 103 of the UN Charter can be seen as the final word on such a perceived conflict. Although not exactly of the nature of a Kelsenian 'grundnorm' it nevertheless provides that in the face of such a normative conflict the obligations under the Charter shall prevail.[191] It could, of course, be argued that the obligations under Chapter VIII and Article 103 were only intended to bind states, not other international organisations. This was the result – or 'systemic inconsistency'[192] – that the European Court of Justice essentially endorsed in the *Kadi* case.[193] However, in reality any claims as to the autonomy of international organisations can only be viewed through the prism of the obligations imposed upon the individual Member States of which they are comprised.[194] Therefore, such arguments asserting the autonomy of an organisation to take a decision to resort to enforcement action involving the use of force, even against a state within the organisation's particular region of activity, can be doubted.

Furthermore, in the context of the US's assertions regarding NATO not only were these statements as to autonomy not shared by other NATO Member States but they have also been countered in repeated declarations by NATO affirming the primacy of

---

[189] Orakhelashvili, *supra* n. 15, at 143. See also M. Zwarenburg, 'NATO, its Member States and the Security Council', in Blokker and Schrijver, *supra* n. 178, 197, at 204. Although it can be presumed that this assertion as to the autonomy of NATO only arose within the Euro-Atlantic region, it was not explicit as to any delimitation of this nature. Outside of this region, it was noticeable that prior to the adoption of UNSC Resolution 1973 (2011) certain Member States (for example the UK) equivocally stated the need for 'lawful authority' to use force in Libya, while NATO's Secretary-General was adamant that authorisation from the UNSC was required. See C. Henderson, 'International Measures for the Protection of Civilians in Libya and Côte d'Ivoire', (2011) 60 *ICLQ* 767, at 778. For more on the Libya conflict see *infra* section 5Ciii.

[190] See *supra* section 2B.

[191] See *supra* n. 26.

[192] Orakhelashvili, *supra* n. 15, at 143.

[193] Joined Cases C-402/05 P and C-415/05 P *Yassin Abdullah Kadi and Al Barakaat International Foundation v. Council of the European Union and Commission of the European Communities*, Judgment of the European Court of Justice (Grand Chamber), 3 September 2008, available at http://eur-lex.europa.eu/LexUriServ/LexUriServ.do?uri=CELEX:62005J0402:EN:HTML.

[194] See, generally, A. Sari, 'The Relationship between Community Law and International Law after Kadi: Did the ECJ Slam the Door on Effective Multilateralism?', in M. Happold (ed.), *International Law in a Multipolar World* (Abingdon: Routledge, 2011), 303.

the UNSC in matters of enforcement.[195] In the context of the arguments made regarding Article 4(h) of the AU's Constitutive Act, without any helpful additional explanation from the AU and little in the way of practice in connection with this provision, it could equally be argued that the relevant provisions were in fact not an 'assertion of a right to use of force against states without the Security Council's authorization; instead, they contemplate[d] action with the government's consent' on each occasion.[196] It was, for example, only upon this basis that the AU was willing to act in Darfur.[197] If this provision is interpreted as providing not a general predetermined right for the organisation to intervene as and when it decides it is necessary, but instead for the right to do so upon the consent of the state concerned on a case-by-case basis, this would not in principle create a conflict with the provisions of the UN Charter. As such, it can be presumed that neither potential challenge has been sustained thereby giving rise to a breach of Article 2(4) and thus a normative conflict with the multilateral exception to it of authorisation by the UNSC.

It is also perhaps of some significance that similar claims have not been expressly made by other regional organisations and neither have there been interpretations of their particular constitutive instruments by Member States or scholars so as to provide such autonomy. For example, the Arab League does not consider itself to possess autonomous powers of enforcement within its sphere of influence. Article 11 of the Treaty of Joint Defense and Economic Cooperation Between the States of the Arab League (1950) unequivocally states that:

> No provision of this Treaty shall in any way affect, or is intended to affect, any of the rights or obligations devolving upon the Contracting States from the United Nations Charter or the responsibilities borne by the United Nations Security Council for the maintenance of international peace and security.

While the EU's Cologne Summit Document (1999) states that the EU has the 'capacity for autonomous action' this is 'not the same as autonomous decision making; in this area, the EU does not claim competence to make decisions autonomously. Its relevant documents reveal no intention to that effect.'[198] The Rio Treaty of the OAS submits to the UN Charter in its Preamble, Article 1 (on the non-use of force contrary to the

---

[195] See Final Communiqué, Brussels Ministerial Meeting, 17 December 1992, paras 4–5; Declaration of the Heads of State and Government, Ministerial Meeting of the North Atlantic Council/North Atlantic Cooperation Council, NATO Headquarters, Brussels, 10–11 January 1994, para. 7; Founding Act on Mutual Relations, Cooperation and Security between NATO and the Russian Federation, Paris, 27 May 1997, Section III; NATO Strategic Concept (1999), para. 31. Adding to this was the former UN Secretary-General, Kofi Annan, who at the time of the Kosovo intervention asserted the primary responsibility of the UNSC for the maintenance of international peace and security, although adding, rather equivocally, that 'the Council should be *involved* in any decision to resort to force'. See UN Doc. SG/SM/6938, 24 March 1999 (emphasis added).
[196] Orakhelashvili, *supra* n. 15, at 270.
[197] Gray, *supra* n. 56, at 55.
[198] Orakhelashvili, *supra* n. 15, at 144. Article 21(1) of the Treaty on European Union states that '[t]he Union's action on the international scene shall be guided by … respect for the United Nations Charter and international law'.

provisions of the Charter) and Article 5 (reference to reporting under Articles 51 and 54 of the Charter). Ultimately, as Orakhelashvili notes, 'organisations which have developed the idea of crisis management, such as NATO and the EU, have committed themselves to act within the broader framework of the UN's collective security'.[199]

B. Ratione materiae

i. Humanitarian crises

The claim that individual states have a right of unilateral humanitarian intervention was one that was occasionally made during the Cold War.[200] However, any enthusiasm from commentators for such a claim generated by the practice of a handful of states on a handful of occasions was dampened by the lack of any *opinio juris* for such a right from those very same acting states. In the paradigm Cold War incidents which are often drawn upon in support of a claim of a right of humanitarian intervention – India's intervention in East Pakistan (1971), Vietnam's intervention in Cambodia (1978–1979) and Tanzania's intervention in Uganda (1979) – the acting states did not make a claim to be acting under a right of humanitarian intervention, but instead used claims of self-defence to justify their actions.[201] Furthermore, the enthusiasm for a right of humanitarian intervention was similarly dampened by the lack of enthusiasm from states pontificating in the abstract. For example, in 1986 the UK was open in its belief that 'the overwhelming majority of contemporary legal opinion [came] down against the existence of a right of humanitarian intervention' so that 'the best case that [could] be made in support of humanitarian intervention is that it [could not] be said to be unambiguously illegal'.[202]

In the post-Cold War era, the claim has been made only occasionally by states themselves. This is arguably due to the fact that, as highlighted above, the use of force for humanitarian purposes is something in which the UNSC has shown it is willing and able to engage.[203] Consequently, claims by states that they possess a form of concurrent jurisdiction with the UNSC in taking forcible measures to prevent, or respond to, a humanitarian catastrophe have been rare. Rather ironically, given its rejectionist position towards the end of the Cold War in 1986, the UK has been the lead proponent

---

[199] Orakhelashvili, *supra* n. 15, at 66. Although, as the intervention in Kosovo in 1999 demonstrates, such commitment may be asserted in word but may not always be observed in deed.

[200] See, for example, R.B. Lillich, 'Forcible Self-Help by States to Protect Human Rights', (1967–1968) 53 *Iowa L.Rev.* 325. For more on the use of force for humanitarian purposes see Chapter 7 by Christine Gray in this volume.

[201] See Henderson, *supra* n. 79, at 120. See also, in general, N.J. Wheeler, *Saving Strangers: Humanitarian Intervention in International Society* (Oxford: Oxford University Press, 2002).

[202] UK Foreign Office Policy Document No. 148. See 'UK Materials in International Law', (1986) 57 *BYIL* 614, at 619.

[203] See *supra* section 4. As Murphy clearly highlights, 'human rights atrocities are … fair game for enforcement action under Chapter VII'. S.D. Murphy, 'The Security Council, Legitimacy, and the Concept of Collective Security After the Cold War', (1994–1995) 32 *Colum. J. Transnat'l L.* 201, at 286.

– or 'norm entrepreneur'[204] – in this respect in the post-Cold War era. In particular, in 1992, and in light of the establishment of the no-fly zones in Iraq in protection of the Kurds in the north and the Shias in the south, it argued that the use of force 'can be justified in cases of extreme humanitarian need'.[205] However, even if this was a claim that intervention can be *legally* justified on such a basis, and this is not altogether clear,[206] it remains a rather isolated example of a *state* claiming such a right.[207] For example, at the time of NATO's intervention in Kosovo in 1999, arguments that a unilateral right of humanitarian intervention existed were restricted to the UK and Belgium.[208] Other acting or supporting states, including the US, did not make explicit arguments of a legal right of humanitarian intervention.[209] Indeed, such arguments were exceptional. Consequently, while challenges have been witnessed, few states – or indeed scholars – argued for, or claimed there was, a new defined legal right of unilateral humanitarian intervention for states or coalitions of states.[210]

---

[204] A term used by D. Armstrong, T. Farrell and H. Lambert in *International Law and International Relations*, 2nd edn (Cambridge: Cambridge University Press, 2012), at 104.

[205] See 'UK Materials on International Law', (1992) 63 *BYIL* 824. This was quite a turnaround from its position in 1986. Yet, as Gray points out, 'it did not explain *how* this alleged change in the law had come about. If Article 2(4) of the UN Charter is a dynamic provision open to changing interpretation over time, what developments in fact justified a new interpretation?' See Gray, *supra* n. 56, at 37.

[206] For example, a 'right of humanitarian intervention' was not expressly invoked and it is not clear whether its claims of being 'justified' in acting in these circumstances were on a moral or legal level, or indeed both. Furthermore, its claims as to be justified in acting were also based upon the fact that the UNSC had become involved with the situation and condemned Iraq's suppression of the Kurds and Shias in Resolution 688 (1991). For more on this argument see *infra* text accompanying nn 221–227.

[207] Effort has been made by the key actors in the Kosovo intervention to limit its precedential value. See J.F. Murphy, 'Is US Adherence to the Rule of Law in International Affairs Feasible?', in M.N. Schmitt and J. Pejic (eds), *International Law and Armed Conflict: Exploring the Faultlines (Essays in Honour of Yoram Dinstein)* (The Hague: Martinus Nijhoff, 2007), 197, at 226.

[208] This was most notable in their arguments before the ICJ in the *Legality of Use of Force Case* (Provisional Measures) [1999] ICJ Rep. 124. See also C. Gray, 'The Legality of NATO's Military Action in Kosovo: Is there a Right of Humanitarian Intervention?', in W. Tieva and S. Yee (eds), *International Law in the Post-Cold War World* (Abingdon: Routledge, 2000), 240, at 248–250.

[209] Cf. D. Kritsiotis, 'The Kosovo Crisis and NATO's Application of Armed Force Against the Federal Republic of Yugoslavia', (2000) 49 *ICLQ* 330, at 357–358, where it is claimed that '[t]he NATO intervention, controversial and regrettable though it was in certain quarters, witnessed an important and undeniable invocation of the so-called right of humanitarian intervention in state practice, and it now remains for the wider implications of this development to be calculated'. In respect to the latter part of this statement Peter Hilpold was adamant shortly after the intervention that '[u]ltimately, a new consensus between international subjects giving shape to this new rule has to be proved. This proof is totally lacking.' P. Hilpold, 'Humanitarian Intervention: Is There a Need for a Legal Reappraisal?', (2001) 12 *EJIL* 437, at 452.

[210] Instead the notion that the intervention in Kosovo was an 'illegal but justified' intervention appeared to be the predominant view of legal scholars and commentators. See, for example, A. Roberts, 'Legality vs Legitimacy: Can Uses of Force be Illegal but Justified?', in P. Alston and E. Macdonald (eds), *Human Rights, Intervention, and the Use of Force* (Oxford:

a. Inter-organisational challenges to the UN Security Council's exclusive competence

The greater challenge to the exclusive competence of the UNSC to forcefully intervene in humanitarian situations has instead been made at the inter-organisational level. For instance, during the intervention in Kosovo it was argued by certain NATO Member States that while institutionally the UNSC has *primary* responsibility for the maintenance of international peace and security, it does not have *exclusive* responsibility and is thus not the only organisation with competence to act in the face of a humanitarian crisis. This general claim, which was not intended to completely displace or disavow the role of the UNSC, manifested itself in various forms with varying degrees of severity for the authority of the UNSC.

The most extreme form of this challenge came from some of the US administration's claims regarding NATO's possession of autonomy to act during the humanitarian crisis in Kosovo, as described above.[211] Yet this was very much an isolated argument. Instead, the milder proposition that NATO has a 'secondary responsibility' to intervene for humanitarian purposes should the UNSC fail to act had more support within NATO. Slovenia, for example, argued that '[t]he responsibility of the Security Council for international peace and security is a primary responsibility ... not an exclusive responsibility' so that the Council's authority in this field depended 'on its ability to develop policies that will make it worthy of the authority it has under the Charter'.[212] However, in addition to the fact that other states, notably Russia and China, took issue with this argument, there is also no authority for suggesting that other organisations can just pick up the tab when the UNSC does not authorise, or indeed look likely to authorise, force when a state or group of states within the particular organisation is of the opinion that it should.[213] As noted above, the UNSC has exclusive responsibility when it comes to enforcement measures. While it is not beyond the realms of possibility that the Charter could be reinterpreted through clear and consistent subsequent practice to permit secondary responsibility to be invoked by others in these circumstances,[214] such practice has simply not been evident.

Oxford University Press, 2008), 179, at 182–183; Simma, *supra* n. 182; A. Cassese, '*Ex iniuria ius oritur*: Are We Moving towards International Legitimization of Forcible Humanitarian Countermeasures in the World Community?', (1999) 10 *EJIL* 23. In a slightly later article, Cassese made the argument that while there had been little consistent *usus* or *opinio juris* regarding unilateral humanitarian intervention, there had by contrast been noticeable '*opinio necessitatis*' in the justifications of acting states. See, generally, A. Cassese, 'A Follow-Up: Forcible Humanitarian Countermeasures and *Opinio Necessitatis*', (1999) 10 *EJIL* 791.

[211] See *supra* section 5A.

[212] UN Doc. S/PV.3988, 24 March 1999, at 19. For a more restrained version of this argument see the Netherlands Ambassador's statement at 8. Some scholars have previously argued that a failure by the UNSC to act provides grounds for states to take unilateral action. See, for example, Reisman, *supra* n. 98.

[213] While a draft resolution authorising the use of 'all necessary means' was not put to the UNSC for adoption during the Kosovo crisis this is not necessarily of great significance as there were strong indications that any such resolution would be vetoed by Russia and China.

[214] Article 31(3)(b) of the Vienna Convention on the Law of Treaties (1969) states that 'any subsequent practice in the application of the treaty which establishes the agreement of the parties regarding its interpretation' is a relevant factor in its interpretation.

In any event, even if the UNSC's exclusive enforcement competence in the realm of forcible measures is not accepted, NATO did not in this case possess a subsidiary competence to forcibly intervene in the Federal Republic of Yugoslavia (hereinafter 'FRY') under the principle of subsidiarity.[215] This principle 'normally applies only to organizations in the relevant crisis region *which benefit from the knowledge of root causes of conflicts in their own region*'.[216] While NATO had concerns regarding the 'powder keg at the heart of Europe',[217] it simply could not claim to have greater knowledge of the root causes of the situation in the FRY – a non-Member of NATO – than the UN, of which the FRY was a Member. In any case, it is arguable that if the UNSC was perceived as not living up to its primary responsibility for the maintenance of international peace and security by failing to halt the humanitarian catastrophe, then, rather than a secondary responsibility falling to an organisation or coalition of states outside of the UN, it would instead fall to the UNGA under the *UfP*.[218] The problem this argument poses, however, is that the recommendation of forcible measures by the UNGA was only envisaged if there was a breach of the peace or act of aggression.[219] Neither of these could be discerned in the Kosovo crisis, with the actions of the FRY and the Kosovo Liberation Army being categorised by the UNSC as a lesser 'threat' to the peace and thus restricted to possible action by the Council.[220]

b.   Unilateral enforcement of the collective will   In many respects the arguments, as set out above, made by some states as to other organisations possessing a secondary responsibility should the UNSC fail to invoke its primary responsibility, or fail to invoke it responsibly, miss the point. The UNSC *had* invoked its primary responsibility prior to the establishment and enforcement of the no-fly zones in Iraq in 1991–2003 and the forcible intervention in Kosovo in 1999, leaving no room to argue that a secondary responsibility could be invoked. Indeed, on both occasions prior to the unilateral uses of force the UNSC had become actively engaged with the situations by taking steps, albeit non-forcible ones.[221] In such circumstances caution should be taken in equating a lack of authorisation of forcible measures with a lack of action and thus a failure to invoke its primary responsibility, or at least invoke it responsibly.

---

[215]   For more discussion on this principle see *supra* section 2B.
[216]   Orakhelashvili, *supra* n. 15, at 130 (emphasis added).
[217]   BBC News, 'Clinton's Statement: Stabilising Europe', 25 March 1999, available at http://news.bbc.co.uk/1/hi/world/americas/303693.stm.
[218]   See N.D. White, 'Bombing in the Name of Humanity', (2000) 5 *JCSL* 27, at 40; Roberts, *supra* n. 210, at 187–188. For more on the *UfP* resolution see *supra* section 3.
[219]   See *supra* section 3.
[220]   *Ibid*. However, the categorisation of such humanitarian crises as constituting even a 'threat' to international peace and security is not at first sight obvious, given that they essentially occur within the territorial confines of a single state. While 'breaches of the peace' and acts of 'aggression' continue to be viewed strictly in the inter-state context this is not to say that, as with threats to the peace, they could not in the future be interpreted so as to incorporate such humanitarian crises, thus opening up the possibility for the *UfP* resolution to be invoked.
[221]   See UNSC Res. 688 (1991) on Iraq and Resolutions 1160 (1998), 1199 (1998) and 1205 (1998) on Kosovo.

In fact, the UNSC's non-forcible involvement turned out to be of some significance as most states, as opposed to making arguments of pure autonomy or secondary responsibility in the absence of any action by the UNSC, instead placed great emphasis upon the fact that the UNSC had already expressed concern regarding the situation, deemed it a threat to the peace and demanded certain action by the parties concerned.[222] Indeed, the general claim appeared to be that any right to forcibly intervene for humanitarian purposes required the prior involvement of the UNSC. For example, Baroness Symons stated in the House of Lords in 1998 that:

> [t]here is no general doctrine of humanitarian intervention in international law. Cases have nevertheless arisen (as in northern Iraq in 1991) when, in the light of all the circumstances, a limited use of force was justifiable *in support of purposes laid down by the Security Council but without the Council's express authorisation* when that was the only means to avert an immediate and overwhelming humanitarian catastrophe. Such cases would in the nature of things be exceptional and would depend on an objective assessment of the factual circumstances at the time and *on the terms of relevant decisions of the Security Council bearing on the situation in question.*[223]

The states making such an argument were, in essence, arguing that a right to use force was only invocable given the prior engagement of the UNSC, although in claiming not that the action concerned was lawful but rather 'justifiable' the argument being expounded was more that there was a certain legitimacy in unilaterally enforcing the collectively expressed will of the UNSC. Ultimately, this meant that neither the exclusive competence of the UNSC to authorise such action nor a pure right of unilateral humanitarian intervention were being advanced.[224] Yet such a doctrine of unilateral enforcement of the collective will has no place within international law. Indeed, as Dinstein correctly summarises:

> as long as there was no express authorization by the Council to take enforcement action, no State or group of States was entitled to resort to forcible measures in response to a mere threat to the peace. It is the exclusive prerogative of the Security Council to decide or recommend when and how to respond to a threat to the peace. And ... when authorization of enforcement action is issued by the Security Council, the mandate allowing States or regional organizations to take action must be clear and not merely implicit.[225]

---

[222] See, for example, UNSC Res. 688 (1991), paras 1 and 2.

[223] Baroness Symons, Hansard HL Debates, WA 139–140, 16 November 1998 (1998) 69 *BYIL* 593 (emphasis added).

[224] As Nico Krisch has described it, '[t]hese claims to a right to use force in order to ensure compliance with Security Council resolutions imply the rejection of a legal necessity to obtain clear authorization, but likewise that of a purely unilateral right of action.' N. Krisch, 'Unilateral Enforcement of the Collective Will: Kosovo, Iraq and the Security Council', (1999) 3 *Max Planck Yrbk UN L* 59, at 91.

[225] Dinstein, *supra* n. 31, at 337. See also Krisch, *ibid.*, at 86–89; N. Ronzitti, 'The Current Status of Legal Principles Prohibiting the Use of Force and Legal Justifications of the Use of Force', in M. Bothe, M.E. O'Connell and N. Ronzitti (eds), *Redefining Sovereignty: The Use of Force after the Cold War* (New York: Transnational Publishers, 2005), 91, at 107.

The main risk associated with such a doctrine is that if force is witnessed as being taken to enforce the common will of the UNSC in the absence of an express authorisation to do so, then the members of the Council will become wary in adopting any resolution that could conceivably be used to subsequently justify forcible measures. As Wood notes, 'there is surely a risk that, if this were accepted, the Council's work could be inhibited because of fears that if it laid down a "common purpose" this could be interpreted as indirectly sanctioning the unilateral use of force.'[226] Indeed, while in 2011 NATO Member States were in possession of an *express* authorisation to use force to protect civilians in Libya, it was, however, arguably NATO's broad interpretation of the mandate[227] that ultimately led to both Russia and China vetoing any resolution which expressed anything other than mild condemnation of the Assad regime's suppression of civilians in Syria in 2011–2012 for fear that it would subsequently be used to justify forcible intervention.

c. Reconsidering humanitarian intervention: R2P The upshot of these various attempts by states and organisations to establish competence to forcibly intervene for humanitarian purposes is a reconsideration of when, how and by whom forcible intervention can be taken in furtherance of such purposes. Indeed, the UN Secretary-General (hereinafter 'UNSG') noted at the end of the NATO campaign in Kosovo that 'emerging slowly, but I believe surely, is an international norm against the violent repression of minorities that will and must take precedence over concerns of State sovereignty'[228] The question was what form this international norm would take.

An answer to this question began to emerge in the form of the concept 'responsibility to protect' (hereinafter 'R2P') which was 'stimulated by concern at the unilateralism inherent in the Kosovo action'.[229] While initially devised by the International Commission on Intervention and State Sovereignty in 2001[230] the concept was subsequently endorsed by the High-Level Panel on Threats, Challenges and Change in 2004[231] and the UN Secretary-General in 2005,[232] and was finally adopted by states at the 2005 UN World Summit Outcome document.[233] In essence, R2P posits that there is first and

---

[226] M. Wood, 'The Law on the Use of Force: Current Challenges', (2007) 11 *Singapore Yrbk Int'l L* 1, at 10.

[227] See, generally, Henderson, *supra* n. 189 and Chapter 7 by Christine Gray in this volume.

[228] See Gray, *supra* n. 56, at 46.

[229] Wood, *supra* n. 226, at 12. See Chapter 7 in this volume by Christine Gray for more on R2P and its implementation.

[230] See Report of the International Commission on Intervention and State Sovereignty, *The Responsibility to Protect*, December 2001, available at http://responsibilitytoprotect.org/ICISS %20Report.pdf (hereinafter 'ICISS report').

[231] High-Level Panel on Threats, Challenges and Change, *A more secure world: Our shared responsibility*, 2 December 2004, UN Doc. A/59/565, at paras 199–203 (hereinafter '*A more secure world*'). See, in general, M. Odello, 'Commentary on the United Nations' High-Level Panel on Threats, Challenges and Change', (2005) 10 *JCSL* 231.

[232] Report of the UN Secretary-General, *In Larger Freedom: Towards Security, Development and Human Rights for All*, 21 March 2005, UN Doc. A/59/205, at paras 132–135 (hereinafter '*In Larger Freedom*').

[233] 2005 World Summit Outcome document, 15 September 2005, UN Doc. A/60/L.1, at paras 138–139.

foremost a responsibility upon the leaders of domestic states to protect their citizens. However, where this responsibility is not met it is one that then falls to the international community.[234] It is significant, however, that this responsibility has subsequently been placed in the hands of the UNSC. For example, in the 2005 UN World Summit Outcome document states expressed their preparedness:

> to take collective action, in a timely and decisive manner, *through the Security Council, in accordance with the Charter, including Chapter VII*, on a case-by-case basis and in cooperation with relevant regional organizations as appropriate, should peaceful means be inadequate and national authorities are manifestly failing to protect their populations from genocide, war crimes, ethnic cleansing and crimes against humanity.[235]

Nevertheless, the innovation in the R2P concept was not that there was now a duty upon the UNSC to act. Indeed, Member States, and 'particularly those who bear the main burden of action, are unlikely to be willing to agree to a legal obligation to act to achieve objectives that may require huge resources and where, depending on the circumstances, success may be uncertain'.[236] Instead, the innovation in the R2P doctrine was that now Member States of the UN 'clearly ... expected the Security Council to take action in appropriate cases'.[237]

It could, of course, be argued that while the role of the UNSC under this responsibility has been confirmed in theory, in practice it has failed to meet expectations. Its failure to intervene in Burma in 2007[238] and 2008[239] along with its continuous failure to fully implement the responsibility in Darfur[240] are but a few examples. Nevertheless, while these examples might be perceived as a gaping failure by the UNSC to take forcible action under this responsibility, events in 2011 in Libya are evidence that the UNSC is capable, at least, in meeting the responsibility placed upon it.[241] Indeed, while there was ambiguity in the statements of some NATO states as to

---

[234] See ICISS report, *supra* n. 230, at VIII.
[235] 2005 World Summit Outcome document, *supra* n. 233, at para. 139 (emphasis added). See also ICISS report, *ibid.*, at para. 6.38; *A more secure world, supra* n. 231, at para. 203; *In Larger Freedom, supra* n. 232, at para. 125.
[236] Wood, *supra* n. 226, at 12.
[237] *Ibid.*, at 13.
[238] See the UNSC's 5619th meeting on 12 January 2007 (UN Doc. S/PV.5619) where China and Russia vetoed a draft non-Chapter VII resolution which had been proposed by the UK and US in response to the violent crackdown by the Burmese authorities in response to anti-government protests.
[239] This was in response to the restrictions imposed by the government of Myanmar on the delivery of humanitarian aid in the aftermath of Cyclone Nargis. See, generally, R. Barber, 'The Responsibility to Protect the Survivors of Natural Disaster: Cyclone Nargis, a Case Study', (2009) 14 *JCSL* 3.
[240] The Council was only willing to intervene with Sudan's consent. See Gray, *supra* n. 56, at 53.
[241] Although the authorising resolution, SC Res. 1973 (2001), only talked of the responsibility of the state concerned in protecting its civilians rather than that of the international community as a whole or any particular body or organisation.

how forcible action was to proceed,[242] it is significant that NATO itself, through the statements of its Secretary-General, was adamant that UNSC authorisation was required before enforcement action could be undertaken.[243] As Dinstein points out, '[i]t speaks volumes about the new state of mind prevailing in NATO ... that there was no dissent from the view that any humanitarian intervention in Libya, in early 2011 ... must be firmly embedded in Security Council authorization'.[244] However, the conflict in Syria in 2011–2012 is the latest example of the UNSC refraining from taking action in precisely the sort of situation in which the R2P concept was designed to be invoked. The question is what is to happen when there are calls from within the international community for an intervention of a forcible nature after a state has clearly failed to protect its citizens but, as a result of one or more states within the Council, the collective security system cannot formally sanction it? The answer to this question will provide the next instalment as to whether R2P, or at least the responsibility to react to a humanitarian crisis, becomes a fully functioning international legal norm or remains an aspirational code of conduct.[245] Provocations towards finding an answer were provided in the context of the Syrian conflict when, in light of the Russian and Chinese vetoes to a resolution on the situation in the UNSC, the Arab League claimed to have a 'special responsibility'[246] and US Senator John McCain called for US-led air strikes for humanitarian purposes in light of the prolonged attacks on civilians by the Assad regime.[247] Yet, while challenges to the UNSC's authority persist, it remains significant that at the time of writing the UNSC and the UN in general remain at the forefront of

---

[242] The UK, for example, claimed ambiguously that there was a necessity for 'lawful authority' to take forcible action to protect the Libyans. See *supra* n. 189.

[243] *Ibid*. Although the controversy was surrounding the limits of the mandate to 'protect civilians', which has no doubt had negative knock-on effects in terms of the invocation of R2P in Syria, despite the Free Syrian Army expressly calling for outside intervention to protect civilians within the state.

[244] Dinstein, *supra* n. 31, at 338.

[245] On this point, Focarelli claims that while 'some consensus on the principle does exist, ... disagreement is still considerable on the specific question of a general legal regime allowing military intervention'. C. Focarelli, 'The Responsibility to Protect Doctrine and Humanitarian Intervention: Too Many Ambiguities for a Working Doctrine', (2008) 13 *JCSL* 191, at 210. See also, generally, C. Stahn, 'Responsibility to Protect: Political Rhetoric or Emerging Legal Norm?', (2007) 101 *AJIL* 99. Hilpold has observed that:

> the norm creation process leading to R2P can be compared with that characterizing the development of the law of self-determination. In both cases, at the beginning we have a political slogan of uncertain meaning. Nonetheless, as the case of self-determination demonstrates, political rhetoric can solidify to legal principles and even if they remain vague and prone to be abused by opposed camps some consensual lines will emerge over time.

P. Hilpold, 'Intervening in the Name of Humanity: R2P and the Power of Ideas', (2012) 17 *JCSL* 49, at 79.

[246] Although this has not been interpreted to mean in the context of forcible measures. Indeed, as noted above, the Arab League has expressed its commitment to the UNSC. See *supra* section 5A.

[247] See BBC News, 'US Senator John McCain Calls for Air Strikes on Syria', 6 March 2012, available at http://www.bbc.co.uk/news/world-us-canada-17266798.

efforts to resolve the crisis with states continuing to disavow any solution to the crisis through unilateral forcible measures and action.[248]

ii. The phenomenon of 'global' terrorism

Prior to the events of 9/11 states reserved the right to use force in self-defence against discrete acts of terrorism.[249] Given that these individual acts of terrorism were generally carried out by non-state actors and targeted specifically towards a certain state, often in furtherance of a particular ideological cause, they were identified more as a threat to the security of the victim state concerned than as a broader threat to international peace and security, and were thus not always referred to or addressed by the UNSC.[250] States wished to assert the right to defend themselves in these circumstances and, today, arguably possess such a right, even if they have not always been perceived as doing so.[251]

Yet in the wake of the events of 9/11, rather than continuing to view acts of terrorism as a succession of isolated incidents, the general perception seemed to shift to viewing the new breed of terrorism, in particular that perpetrated by the al-Qaida organisation, as a global phenomenon.[252] Indeed, the notion that the civilised world was engaged in a global 'war on terror' became a prevalent one, particularly in the US, albeit that it was one that was discredited by, among others, many international lawyers.[253] However, although the threat was now being portrayed as constituting more of a threat to *international* peace and security given its global nature, the means of combating it forcibly were, at first, seen through the prism of *self*-defence. Indeed, while the UNSC was immediately involved, with its Member States – along with virtually the entire

---

[248] See 'Kofi Annan's Six-Point Plan for Syria', *Al Jazeera*, 27 March 2012, available at http://www.aljazeera.com/news/middleeast/2012/03/2012327153111767387.html. However, Kofi Annan resigned from his position as UN–Arab League Peace Envoy on 2 August 2012, citing a 'clear lack of unity' within the UNSC as one of the reasons for his departure. See BBC News, 'Syria Crisis: Kofi Annan Quits as UN–Arab League Envoy', 2 August 2012, available at http://www.bbc.co.uk/news/world-middle-east-19099676. Lakhdar Brahimi has since been appointed as the new UN–Arab League Peace Envoy. See BBC News, 'Syria Envoy Lakhdar Brahimi on First Visit to Damascus', 13 September 2012, available at http://www.bbc.co.uk/news/world-middle-east-19590084.

[249] See Chapter 6 in this volume by Dino Kritsiotis for more on the legal notion of self-defence.

[250] More often it was the victim state's response to the terrorist attack which was addressed by the Council.

[251] See N. Lubell, *Extraterritorial Use of Force against Non-State Actors* (Oxford: Oxford University Press, 2010), at 25–84.

[252] See, for example, UN High Commissioner for Refugees, 'Terrorism as a Global Phenomenon', UNHCR presentation to the Joint Seminar of the Strategic Committee on Immigration, Frontiers and Asylum (SCIFA) and Committee on Article 36 (CATS), 17 January 2008, available at: http://www.unhcr.org/refworld/docid/4794c7ff2.html.

[253] A. Sofaer, 'Terrorism as War', (2002) *ASIL Proceedings* 254. Cf. F. Megret, '"War"? Legal Semantics and the Move to Violence', (2002) 13 *EJIL* 361. While the previous Legal Advisor to the US State Department, Harold Koh, did not claim that there was a 'war' with al-Qaida, he did describe the situation as constituting an 'armed conflict'. See H.H. Koh, 'The Obama Administration and International Law', Speech at the ASIL 104th Meeting, 25 March 2010, available at http://www.state.gov/s/l/releases/remarks/139119.htm.

international community – supportive of a response to the attacks,[254] the US opted to respond by invoking its legal right of self-defence even with a resolution from the Council authorising the use of all necessary means all but assured.[255] This invocation could thus be interpreted as a challenge to the *ratione materiae* competence of the UNSC, as with the 'armed attack' of 9/11 over, and with forcible measures taken by the US justified upon the necessity to 'prevent and deter' further attacks,[256] this was arguably a situation squarely within the competence of the UNSC.[257] Indeed, determinations under Article 39 are not restricted to individual or discrete incidents or threats, with those of a more systemic nature – including climate change and, in this case, global terrorism – equally coming within the purview of the limits of the UNSC's powers under Chapter VII.[258]

Nevertheless, subsequent events could be interpreted as militating against the initial severity of this challenge to the competence of the UNSC to forcibly address global terrorism. The UNSC has arguably met its primary responsibility in combating this particular threat to the peace through a number of non-forcible actions.[259] In fact, several of the measures that it has adopted in the fight against global terrorism have given rise to accusations that it has overstepped its constitutional limits.[260] Furthermore, while the UNSC has not as yet authorised the use of forcible measures as part of its strategy to combat global terrorism, there are various indicators that it has not relinquished its competence to do so. Indeed, the attacks of 9/11, the US's response to them, and the UNSC's response and reaffirmation of the right of self-defence should be seen for a number of reasons as exceptional rather than precedent setting.

---

[254] See, generally, UNSC Res. 1368 (2001), adopted on 12 September 2001. See Henderson, *supra* n. 79, at 154–158.

[255] See UN Doc. S/2001/946, 7 October 2001.

[256] *Ibid.* See also *infra* section 5Ci on threats to the peace.

[257] See *infra* sections 5Ci and ii on challenges *ratione temporis*. Yet the invocation of self-defence on this occasion was something that the UNSC itself arguably endorsed, when immediately after the tragic attacks of 9/11 it reaffirmed this right despite it being an ideal situation in which resort to the UNSC could have – and arguably should have – been made. See UNSC Res. 1368 (2001), Preamble, in which the UNSC '[r]ecogniz[ed] the inherent right of individual or collective self-defence in accordance with the Charter'.

[258] There has been, for example, some support for climate change being considered as a threat to the peace. See the debate in UN Doc. S/PV.5663, 17 April 2007. The fact that the UNSC could take action under Chapter VII in response to the 9/11 attacks was highlighted by the fact that UNSC Res. 1368 (2001) was titled 'Threats to international peace and security caused by terrorist acts'.

[259] For example, it has set up an anti-terrorism committee (UNSC Res. 1267 (1999)), requested that Member States freeze the bank accounts of terror suspects (UNSC Res. 1373 (2001), para. 1c), requested that Member States prosecute the perpetrators of specific terrorist acts (UNSC Res. 1373 (2001), para. 2e), and acted as a *de facto* legislator in this area of concern (see, generally, UNSC Res. 1373 (2001)).

[260] As Tams writes, the UNSC's 'new activism is based on enforcement measures of a non-military character. In fact, with respect to Article 41 [of the UN Charter], there is very little the Council has *not* done, and it may have exceeded its competences more than once in the process.' See C.J. Tams, 'The Use of Force against Terrorists', (2009) 20 *EJIL* 359, at 376.

First, despite many terrorist attacks since, including by al-Qaida, the UNSC has not subsequently reaffirmed the right of self-defence by states.[261] Secondly, despite the occurrence of terrorist attacks by al-Qaida, states have not invoked their right of self-defence in the same way.[262] Thirdly, where action has been taken by states to forcibly respond to attacks by non-state actors, this has either generally been outside of what may be seen as the global terrorism context,[263] received the consent of the territorial state,[264] the action has been undertaken in a situation where there has been no government to request consent from which has had control of the areas in which the terrorist actors are located,[265] or the acting states have not adopted the wide 'harbouring' standard of attribution that the US invoked in Operation Enduring Freedom, permitting action against the terrorist groups *and* the infrastructure of the state 'harbouring' them.[266] Fourthly, even in Afghanistan after the launching of the response to the 9/11 attacks, forcible action to maintain security in Kabul was ultimately taken under the authority of the UNSC.[267] Lastly, the High-Level Panel's report *A More Secure World*, the UN Secretary-General's report *In Larger Freedom* and the 2005 World Summit Outcome document have not stated the need for any changes to the UN Charter-based system of collective security to combat this phenomenon.[268] Taken together, these observations do not necessarily specifically and conclusively reaffirm the role of the UNSC as such, but they do provide something of a defence to accusations that its competence in forcibly combating global terrorism has been made secondary to that of individual states or other organisations.

---

[261] See, for example, UNSC Res. 1450 (2002) in which the UNSC deplored the claims of responsibility by al-Qaida for terrorist attacks in Kenya but made no reference to self-defence.

[262] Although in the context of those in which al-Qaida was involved this could be because military action was already being undertaken against it in the form of Operation Enduring Freedom in Afghanistan.

[263] That is, they have been linked to historical grievances by a non-state actor towards a particular state. This was the case, for example, in the context of Israel's response to attacks by Hezbollah in 2006, Turkey's responses to attacks by the PKK based in Iraq, and Columbia's forcible response to attacks by FARC based in Ecuador.

[264] This is the case, for example, with the US's actions against al-Qaida in the Arabian Peninsula in Yemen.

[265] This was the case with Kenya's incursion into Somali territory in response to attacks by the Al-Shabaab group in 2011.

[266] In fact, this standard of attribution has received very little support in the aftermath of Operation Enduring Freedom. See Henderson, *supra* n. 79, at 159–169; K.N. Trapp, *State Responsibility for International Terrorism* (Oxford: Oxford University Press, 2011), at 51–61.

[267] This was with the establishment of the International Security Assistance Force to assist the Afghan Interim Authority in the maintenance of security in Kabul and its surrounding areas. See UNSC Res. 1386 (2001), para. 1.

[268] See *supra* nn 231–233. The World Summit Outcome document specifically reaffirmed that 'the relevant provisions of the Charter are sufficient to address the full range of threats to international peace and security'. *Supra* n. 233, at para. 79.

C. *Ratione temporis*

i. Competence in responding to 'threats' to the peace

The above section addressed the UNSC's competence to respond to the phenomenon of global terrorism which, in the context of Chapter VII, can be deemed a 'threat' to the peace. While the Council was somewhat side-lined by the US as a result of its actions in self-defence after the 9/11 attacks, the overwhelming acceptance by the international community of the forcible actions in Afghanistan was arguably at least in part due to the fact that they were in response to what was widely considered to be an 'armed attack' for the purposes of Article 51 of the UN Charter.[269] The fact that these actions were also expressly taken to 'prevent and deter' future attacks was, importantly, seen in the context of this prior attack having taken place. However, it was of significance that the US went on to make claims that the use of force in self-defence can be taken in the *absence* of a prior armed attack.

Although anticipatory self-defence, that is the use of force to respond to an imminent armed attack, continues to invoke controversy in some quarters,[270] it has also received a large degree of acceptance.[271] Indeed, it has been argued to be reconcilable with the right of self-defence as contained in Article 51 and its requirement for the occurrence of 'an armed attack' as, if there is a high level of certainty that the threat of an armed attack is to be imminently realised unless action is taken to prevent it, then, so the argument goes, the armed attack can be said to have already commenced.[272]

Pre-emptive self-defence, on the other hand, is a forcible action in response to a non-imminent, or temporally remote, threat of an armed attack that the acting state perceives as possibly coming to fruition at some point in the future.[273] While the making of claims regarding the existence of a right of pre-emptive self-defence was by no means new, they were asserted in their most prominent and legalistic – not to mention infamous – form in the 2002 *National Security Strategy of the United States of America* (hereinafter '2002 NSS') where it was argued that the concept of imminence in self-defence should be widened to take into account the *modus operandi* of contemporary enemies, in particular the threat of weapons of mass destruction in the

---

[269] See *infra* section 5Cii.
[270] See, for example, C. Gray, 'A Crisis of Legitimacy for the UN Collective Security System?', (2007) 56 *ICLQ* 157, at 160.
[271] For example, the UK Attorney-General stated in his advice on the war in Iraq that '[f]orce may be used in self-defence if there is an actual or imminent threat of an armed attack ... It is now widely accepted that an imminent armed attack will justify the use of force.' See 'Attorney General's Advice on the Iraq War: Resolution 1441', (2005) 54 *ICLQ* 767, at 768. The reports of both the High-Level Panel and the UN Secretary-General were also supportive of this form of self-defence. See *A more secure world*, *supra* n. 231, at paras 188–192 and *In Larger Freedom*, *supra* n. 232, at paras 122–126.
[272] For more on the notion of anticipatory self-defence see Chapter 6 by Dino Kritsiotis in this volume.
[273] However, it should be noted that the terms pre-emptive, anticipatory and preventive are used interchangeably by states and commentators.

hands of rogue states and global terrorists.[274] This was an attempt to legitimise a claim of pre-emptive self-defence by dressing it up in the language of the more acceptable anticipatory self-defence.

While such claims bent beyond breaking point the legal limits *lex lata* of the right of self-defence and the requirement for an armed attack,[275] it is also clear that with no reference to the UNSC in the 2002 NSS these claims also presented an attempted usurpation of the authority and role of this organ. This was for the reason that, as Article 39 of the UN Charter makes clear, the UNSC is the only entity that is permitted to forcibly act in the face of a mere 'threat to the peace'.[276] Indeed, as Dinstein points out:

> The notion of maintaining international peace and security has a preemptive thrust. The purpose is to ensure, before it is too late, that no breach of the peace will in fact occur. Measures taken by the Council to forestall a breach of the peace have deterrence and prevention as their goals.[277]

In this light, it is significant that while the claim of pre-emption was persisted with by the Bush administration in its 2006 NSS[278] and, in a more subtle way, in the Obama administration's NSS of 2010,[279] it has received very little support from other states. Indeed, the only states to openly accept this claim of the US have been Australia and North Korea,[280] while Israel – which has a history of engaging in such pre-emptive strikes[281] – appeared to implicitly accept such an expansive right that usurped the competence of the UNSC in dealing with such threats to the peace.[282] Even the former UK Attorney-General, Lord Goldsmith, not one known to be shy in expressing support

---

[274] See The White House, *The National Security Strategy of the United States of America*, 20 September 2002, 15, available at http://www.commondreams.org/headlines02/0920-05.htm.

[275] See Henderson, *supra* n. 79, at 183–190.

[276] See *supra* section 2B. Article 50 of the UN Charter also talks of the UNSC taking 'preventative … measures'.

[277] Dinstein, *supra* n. 31, at 305. Dinstein continues: 'Patently, the Council may initiate a preventive war in anticipation of a future breach of the peace – figuring only as a threat to the peace at the time of action – a privilege that the Charter withholds from any individual State or group of states acting alone.' *Ibid.*, at 309.

[278] See, generally, C. Gray, 'The Bush Doctrine Revisited: The 2006 National Security Strategy of the USA', (2006) 5 *Chinese JIL* 555; C. Henderson, 'The 2006 National Security Strategy of the United States: The Pre-emptive Use of Force and the Persistent Advocate', (2007) 15 *Tulsa J. of Comp. & Int'l L.* 1.

[279] See, generally, C. Gray, 'President Obama's 2010 National Security Strategy and International Law on the Use of Force', (2011) 10 *Chinese JIL* 35; C. Henderson, 'The 2010 National Security Strategy of the United States and the Obama Doctrine of "Necessary Force"', (2010) 15 *JCSL* 403.

[280] See Henderson, *supra* n. 79, at 183–184.

[281] In 1981 Israel attacked the Osiraq nuclear reactor in Iraq, an action that was condemned by both the UNGA (UNGA Res. 36/27 (1981)) and the UNSC (UNSC Res. 487 (1981)).

[282] In 2007 Israel carried out air strikes against the al-Kibar nuclear facility in Syria. However, this was a covert operation with no justification of a pre-emptive nature forthcoming from Israel, thus perhaps demonstrating a lack of *opinio juris* that such a right existed. See, generally, A. Garwood-Gowers, 'Israel's Airstrike on Syria's Al-Kibar Facility: A Test Case for

for US-led forcible actions, was clear that 'this is not a doctrine which, in [his] opinion, exists or is recognized in international law'.[283]

However, the overwhelming response to such a claim was not so much to assert the narrowness of the right of self-defence but to positively reaffirm the authority of the UNSC and its role as principal guarantor and guardian of international peace and security. Indeed, the general reaction, as the High-Level Panel's report *A more secure world* put it, was that 'if there are good arguments for preventive military action, with good evidence to support them, they should be put to the Security Council, which can authorize such action if it chooses to'.[284] Furthermore, in emphasising the UNSC's exclusive competence in the taking of pre-emptive action, the report was clear that '[t]he Security Council is fully empowered under Chapter VII of the Charter of the United Nations to address the full range of security threats with which States are concerned'[285] so that '[t]he question is not whether such action can be taken: it can, by the Security Council as the international community's collective security voice, at any time it deems that there is a threat to international peace and security'.[286] Supporting this view, the UN Secretary-General, in his report *In Larger Freedom*, stated that '[w]here threats are not imminent but latent, the Charter gives *full authority* to the Security Council to use military force, including preventively, to preserve international peace and security'.[287] Additionally, while the 2005 World Summit Outcome document did not comment directly upon the right of pre-emptive self-defence, it did recognise that 'many of today's threats ... must be tackled ... in accordance with the Charter and international law,'[288] and that '[s]tates must ensure that any measures taken to combat terrorism comply with their obligations under international law'.[289] This general position has also received support from the ICJ which, in the *DRC v. Uganda* case of 2005, stated that:

> Article 51 of the Charter may justify a use of force in self-defence only within the strict confines there laid down. It does not allow the use of force by a state to protect perceived security interests beyond these parameters. Other means are available to a concerned state, including, in particular, recourse to the Security Council.[290]

The exclusive authority of the UNSC to address these temporally remote threats has thus been continuously reaffirmed in different forums and by different actors. This

---

the Doctrine of Pre-emptive Self-Defence?', (2011) 16 *JCSL* 263. See *infra* text accompanying nn 291–292 on Iran.
[283] See 'Attorney General's Advice on the Iraq War: Resolution 1441', *supra* n. 271, at para. 3.
[284] *A more secure world*, *supra* n. 232, at paras 190–191.
[285] *Ibid.*, at para. 198.
[286] *Ibid.*, at para. 194.
[287] *In Larger Freedom*, *supra* n. 232, at para. 125 (emphasis added).
[288] 2005 World Summit Outcome document, *supra* n. 233, at para. 71.
[289] *Ibid.*, at 85.
[290] *Armed Activities on the Territory of the Congo* (Democratic Republic of Congo v. Uganda), Judgment, [2005] ICJ Rep. 168, at para. 148. However, while specific emphasis was placed upon the UNSC the Court did not go into detail as to what the 'other means' it referred to were.

reaffirmation appears to be also witnessed in the current dispute regarding Iran's development of a nuclear capability. Israel has been forthright in its assertions that it would, if it felt it necessary, use force to pre-empt the threat posed by Iran's development of nuclear weapons.[291] However, the UNSC has not even discussed the prospect of military action either by itself or any other state or organisation; a sign, no doubt, that aside from Israel there is simply no appetite for a pre-emptive strike within the international community.[292] As such, the illegality of such a strike in the absence of a threat of an imminent armed attack is beyond doubt, with the UNSC, at the time of writing, continuing to take the lead in responding to this particular threat to international peace and security.

ii. Reprisals

A more understated challenge to the *ratione temporis* competence of the UNSC has come in the form of unilateral armed reprisal action. It is continuously repeated, and is at least in this respect a well-established principle of international law, that armed reprisals, which are 'measures of counter-force, "short of war", undertaken by one State against another in response to an earlier violation of international law',[293] are unlawful *stricto sensu*.[294] Yet state practice is replete with examples of them justified, and sometimes accepted, as self-defence.[295] Indeed, very rarely do actions justified as self-defence occur during the paradigmatic situation in which a state forcibly defends itself against an armed attack that is currently physically taking place against it. Instead, they more often than not occur *after* the specific armed attack has ceased. However, it is in these circumstances difficult to accept such an armed response as having a purely defensive character as after the armed attack has ended there is no longer an immediate need to resort to forcible self-defence, unless there is a threat of imminent further attack or the initial attack has resulted in an occupation.[296] Indeed, outside of these circumstances the armed response would be deemed an unlawful

---

[291] See Wyre Davies, 'How will Israel Try to Stop Iran's Nuclear Progress?', BBC News, 9 November 2011, available at http://www.bbc.co.uk/news/world-middle-east-15662122.

[292] See, for example, BBC News, 'Obama Warns against Pre-emptive Iran Strike', 2 March 2012, available at http://www.bbc.co.uk/news/world-us-canada-17236549.

[293] Dinstein, *supra* n. 31, at 244–245.

[294] For example, Principle 1 of the UNGA's *Friendly Relations Declaration* of 1970 is clear that 'States have a duty to refrain from acts of reprisal involving the use of force'.

[295] For example, the US's forcible actions in self-defence on 26 June 1993 in response to an assassination attempt on former US President George H.W. Bush which took place in April 1993 more than two months before the armed response, as well as its strikes against Libya on 15 April 1986 in response to the bombing of a discotheque in Berlin ten days before. On these incidents see, respectively, D. Kritsiotis, 'The Legality of the 1993 US Missile Strike on Iraq and the Right of Self-Defence in International Law', (1996) 45 *ICLQ* 162; and C. Greenwood, 'International Law and the United States' Air Operations Against Libya', (1986–1987) 89 *W. Va. L. Rev.* 933.

[296] However, Dinstein employs the terminology of 'defensive armed reprisals' in an attempt to distinguish those reprisals with defence as their aim from their punishment-oriented counterparts. See Dinstein, *supra* n. 31, at 244–245. Although not synonymous with a use of force, the UNGA's Definition of Aggression includes occupation as an example of aggression. See Article 3(a), Definition of Aggression, UNGA Resolution 3314 (XXIX) (1974).

reprisal with the expectation instead being that the victim state selects peaceful means to settle the dispute,[297] including by taking any dispute to the UNSC which can, if deemed necessary, authorise the use of force.

However, the acceptability of uses of force which have the hallmarks of reprisal action is heightened in the context of terrorist attacks where the identity of the perpetrator of the armed attack is not immediately clear. Indeed, the investigation as to the perpetrator might need to be taken into account in judging the 'immediacy' of the action,[298] while in the context of attacks undertaken by non-state actors negotiation with the host state may need to be taken into consideration when judging its 'necessity'. Perhaps the paradigm example of this can be seen in the actions of the US after the attacks of 9/11 in which over a month had passed before the US finally embarked upon its operation in self-defence. Nevertheless, while the response was ostensibly taken to 'prevent and deter' further attacks,[299] its retributive element and the simple need to do something appeared to be just as important as, if not more important than, any clearly defined defensive purpose.[300]

Ultimately, when states act in these circumstances the purpose behind such actions must always be questioned: self-defence or punishment? While actions taken with the latter as their aim are unlawful, even those taken with an ostensibly clear defensive aim have to be scrutinised. Indeed, while it may be argued that although the armed attack has ceased there remains an ongoing threat to the security of the attacked state,[301] in these circumstances the UNSC has exclusive competence in regards to enforcement action. However, given the prevalence of states acting in such circumstances, for example the US's response to the attacks upon its embassies in Kenya and Tanzania in 1998 and Turkey's frequent incursions into Iraq in response to attacks which have been attributed to the PKK, along with the frequent acquiescence of the international community to them, it has to be acknowledged that this is a challenge to the authority of the exclusive competence of the UNSC which has been sustained.

iii. Post-authorisation control of forcible actions

A final challenge to the *ratione temporis* competence of the UNSC can be found in the disagreements within the Council chamber as to where ultimate authority lies in determining the continuing validity or breadth and scope of an authorisation. In terms of determining the continuing validity of an authorisation, this challenge to the competence of the UNSC arose exclusively within the context of forcible measures against Iraq during the period 1990–2003. While the initial authorisation to use 'all necessary means' provided in Resolution 678 (1990) was, as described above,[302] a

---

[297] See Article 2(3), UN Charter (1945).
[298] Immediacy is often included along with necessity and proportionality as a customary law requirement of self-defence. See Dinstein, *supra* n. 31, at 249.
[299] See UN Doc. S/2001/946, 7 October 2001.
[300] For example, in his statement on 7 October 2001 President Bush was clear that the Taliban would 'pay a price' for harbouring members of al-Qaida. See http://www.johnstons archive.net/terrorism/bush911d.html.
[301] M.E. O'Connell, 'Evidence of Terror', (2002) 7 *JCSL* 19, at 30.
[302] See *supra* section 4.

turning point in the contemporary significance of the UNSC, this particular authorisation was to provide the vehicle for a very particular challenge to the authority of this body.

The authorisation provided in Resolution 678 (1990) was expressly stated to be for the purposes of implementing resolutions which demanded the eviction of Iraq from Kuwait and which sought to restore international peace and security in the area.[303] With these aims seemingly achieved and with a 'formal ceasefire' adopted by the UNSC in Resolution 687 (1991),[304] this appeared to be an end to the authorisation. Yet the US, the UK and, at least initially, France and Russia, began to take more limited military action against Iraq which was justified, albeit not always consistently and clearly, upon the authorisation provided in Resolution 678 (1990).[305] This was despite the fact that Iraq had not launched a new offensive against Kuwait or any other state. Instead, these actions were ostensibly taken to enforce the regime of weapons inspection that was set out in Resolution 687 (1991).[306] The revival of authority for these purposes, it has to be acknowledged, did not receive a large amount of dissent, at least initially, from other states.[307] Nevertheless, murmurings of discontent with such actions gained momentum over the course of the decade, with France and Russia ultimately ceasing their cooperation in the operations.[308] Indeed, while getting the weapons inspectors into Iraq with the freedom to conduct effective inspections was of clear importance to the Members of the UNSC and the international community, the use of force to punish Iraq for non-compliance was by the end of the decade firmly outside of the general consensus within the UNSC as to what constituted acceptable action.[309]

However, the US and the UK were not to acknowledge the unacceptability of the 'revival' argument.[310] Instead, with the adoption of Resolution 1441 in 2002 and the determination that Iraq was in 'material breach' of its disarmament obligations, along with the provision of a 'final opportunity' to comply and the threat of 'serious consequences' if compliance was not forthcoming, it received its greatest exposure. Indeed, the argument was employed by these two states that due to Iraq continuing to be in 'material breach' of its disarmament obligations, even though no 'smoking gun'

---

[303] UNSC Res. 678 (1990), para. 2.
[304] UNSC Res. 687 (1991), paras 1 and 33.
[305] See, for example, 'US Press Release: Attack Shows U.S. Fully Backs U.N. Mandate', 17 January 1993, reprinted in M. Weller (ed.), *Iraq and Kuwait: The Hostilities and Their Aftermath* (Cambridge: Grotius, 1993), at 746; UN Doc. S/1998/1181, 16 December 1998. See, generally, C. Gray, 'After the Ceasefire: Iraq, the Security Council and the Use of Force', (1994) 65 *BYIL* 135.
[306] *Ibid*. The inspection regime was set out in UNSC Res. 687 (1991), paras 7–14.
[307] See Henderson, *supra* n. 79, at 67–71.
[308] *Ibid*.
[309] *Ibid*.
[310] The 'revival' argument, and the eventful period between the authorisation to use force to evict Iraq from Kuwait in 1990 to the final assault on Iraq in 2003 which forms its context, has been exhaustively discussed elsewhere so will not be covered in any detail here. See, for example, S.D. Murphy, 'Assessing the Legality of Invading Iraq', (2004) 92 *GeoLJ* 173; M. Weller, *Iraq and the Use of Force in International Law* (Oxford: Oxford University Press, 2010), at 132–188; Henderson, *supra* n. 79, at 63–95.

was said to exist by the weapons inspectors themselves,[311] the authorisation to use all necessary means in Resolution 678 was revived. The crucial element to this argument was the proposition that only a meeting of the UNSC to discuss the matter was required in Resolution 1441 (2002) and not a further decision authorising force.[312] This argument was made to the chagrin of other states within the UNSC as, although ultimately acknowledging that the use of force should be under the authority of the UNSC,[313] the US and the UK effectively displaced the Council's exclusive competence as a collective body in determining the necessity of forcible action by placing such competence in their own hands.

The 'revival' argument was limited to the *sui generis* context of Iraq. However, a second challenge along similar lines has been seen on more than one occasion. Under the argument associated with this challenge, while contemporary authorisation has been provided to use force, and so does not depend upon states attempting to revive previous authorisations, the breadth and scope of the enforcement measures provided for under the particular mandate are disputed among the Member States of the UNSC. While certain controls were developed by the UNSC in the years following the authorisation technique's initial use in Operation Desert Storm in 1991 so as to try and limit the possibilities for individual states to subsequently unilaterally determine elements of the mandate,[314] arguably most concern was expressed over providing limits upon the possibility for unilateral determinations as to the scope of the mandates of the authorisations.[315] This concern has not been addressed by the Council, at least not consistently. Indeed, the interpretation of enforcement mandates came starkly into focus during NATO's operation in Libya in 2011. On this occasion, authorisation was provided in Resolution 1973 (2011) for the use of all necessary measures 'to protect civilians and civilian populated areas under threat of attack in the Libyan Arab Jamahiriya'.[316] However, a subsequent dispute as to the interpretation of this mandate arose between the US, the UK and France on the one hand and other members of the UNSC, particularly Russia, China and Germany, on the other.[317]

This interpretive dispute was initially about the *type* of force to be employed in enforcing the mandate. As was stated by the ICJ in the *Nicaragua* case, force can be either direct, using a state's armed forces or those sent on its behalf, or indirect,

---

[311] See H. Blix, 'An Update on Inspection', UN Doc. S/PV.4692, 27 January 2003, at 1.

[312] This referred to the notion of 'automaticity' that was key to understanding the revival argument. While the UK and US understood this to mean that at the least a meeting would be held before resorting to force, other states interpreted this so as to mean that a further decision from the UNSC would be necessary. See Henderson, *supra* n. 79, at 86–92.

[313] Although the final paragraph of the US's letter to the UNSC in commencing Operation Iraqi Freedom did refer to the action being necessary 'to defend the United States and the international community from the threat posed by Iraq and to restore international peace and security in the area'. See UN Doc. S/2003/351, 20 March 2003.

[314] These essentially included the involvement of the UN Secretary-General (e.g. UNSC Res. 794 (1992), para. 10; UNSC Res. 908 (1994), para. 8), time limits (e.g. UNSC Res. 929 (1994), para. 4), and reporting requirements (e.g. UNSC Res. 794 (1992), para. 18).

[315] See, for example, the concerns of Zimbabwe at the adoption of UNSC Res. 794 (1992) in UN Doc. S/PV.3145, 3 December 1992, at 7–8.

[316] UNSC Res. 1973 (2011), para. 4.

[317] See the discussion in Henderson, *supra* n. 189.

through a state supplying arms to rebels located in another state.[318] While NATO busily bombed key sites of the Gaddafi regime within Libya, ostensibly in the protection of civilians, the US and the UK also reserved the right under the mandate to supply non-lethal military equipment to the rebels, while France supplied arms.[319] Indeed, it was argued that although there had been an arms embargo imposed in Resolution 1970 (2011), this was overridden by the authorisation contained in Resolution 1973 (2011) as it expressly provided for the use of all necessary measures to protect civilians and civilian populated areas under threat of attack 'notwithstanding paragraph 9 of resolution 1970 (2011)' in which the arms embargo was imposed.[320] Thus 'all necessary measures' meant *all* necessary measures.

However, this ties very much into the second dispute which arose between the UNSC Member States as to the *scope* of the authorisation. If equipment and weapons were being supplied to the rebel forces in this civil war surely this action, which many saw as an unlawful intervention, had the potential – intended or otherwise – of leading to the toppling of the government. There was thus some ambiguity in the statements of the US, UK and France, as while they paid lip service to the unlawful aim of regime change, the underlying argument was that civilians were only ever going to be protected if Gaddafi was no longer in power.

In this respect the issue arose as to whether Gaddafi could also be directly targeted by the NATO strikes.[321] During a conventional international armed conflict between two states the armed forces of the opposing party to the conflict are legitimate targets at all times, as long as they have not been rendered *hors de combat*.[322] However, this was not a traditional armed conflict as the NATO forces acting in Libya were acting under the specific mandate of the UNSC and were thus not entitled to simply target the opposing party's armed forces with the aim of military defeat, but instead were limited to what was necessary in fulfilling the particular mandate provided.[323] As noted above, however, the argument that directly targeting Gaddafi was necessary in order to offer long-term protection to civilians and civilian populated areas perhaps had some legs, given what was known of Gaddafi's general treatment of his own citizens.

---

[318] See *Case Concerning Military and Paramilitary Activities in and against Nicaragua* (Nicaragua v. United States of America) [1986] ICJ Rep. 14.

[319] See H. Mulholland, 'UK Providing "Non-lethal Equipment" to Libyan Rebels, says Hague', *The Guardian*, 4 April 2011, available at http://www.guardian.co.uk/politics/2011/apr/04/uk-libyan-rebels-william-hague; 'U.S. to Give Libyan Rebels Non-lethal Aid', *CBS News*, 20 April 2011, available at http://www.cbsnews.com/2100-202_162-20055686.html; BBC News, 'Libyan Conflict: France Air-Dropped Arms to Rebels', 29 June 2011, available at http://www.bbc.co.uk/news/world-africa-13955751.

[320] UNSC Res. 1973 (2011), para. 4.

[321] For more on the issue of targeting under the law of armed conflict see David Turns's chapter (Chapter 10) and that by Tom Ruys and Christian De Cock (Chapter 11).

[322] Article 43(2), Protocol Additional to the Geneva Conventions of 12 August 1949, and relating to the Protection of Victims of International Armed Conflicts (Protocol I), 8 June 1977; Geneva Convention (I) for the Amelioration of the Condition of the Wounded and Sick in Armed Forces in the Field, Geneva, 12 August 1949; Geneva Convention (II) for the Amelioration of the Condition of Wounded, Sick and Shipwrecked Members of Armed Forces at Sea, Geneva, 12 August 1949.

[323] Henderson, *supra* n. 189, at 775.

In assessing these two *ratio temporis* challenges, that is, the type of force to be deployed under an authorisation as well as the overall scope of the mandated actions, one must bear in mind that UNSC resolutions are the product of a negotiated agreement. This, of course, means that it is not feasible to rule out both the possibility of ambiguity – intended or otherwise – or that the resolution at the point of adoption will not mean different things to different states. While these two challenges exhibit states acknowledging the primacy of the UNSC and the necessity for its authorisation for the use of armed force which is not in self-defence, they at the same time undermine the 'collective' in collective security and pay total disregard to the fact that when dealing with each threat to the peace the UNSC consistently stresses to be as a collective unit 'seized of the matter'.[324] Indeed, just as a resolution is not simply adopted by the positive votes of a handful of Member States the interpretation of these resolutions as to how they will be implemented on the ground similarly does not fall to a minority within the Council, particularly when the proffered interpretations widely differ and have potentially devastating consequences.[325]

While the set of events regarding Iraq are arguably *sui generis*, and thus an occasion for the revival argument to be invoked may never arise again, the unilateral interpretations regarding the breadth and scope of the UNSC's mandate will almost certainly be witnessed again in the future. However, the level of distrust that currently exists among some states as to the intentions of other Council Members may mean that not only is more caution being exercised, as witnessed in the context of Syria, but that the UNSC is deadlocked when it is perhaps needed most.

6. CONCLUSION

With the end of the Cold War the UNSC has taken pronounced strides in realising its potential. The great-power politics of the Cold War have given way to a more subtle interplay of influences within the Council chamber that although continue to prevent it from fully functioning as envisaged in the UN Charter have nonetheless resulted in it finding an equilibrium in regards to its role within the legal regime governing forcible measures. In the post-Cold War era the Council is thus exhibiting an established capacity to authorise forcible measures; something in which it was only able to tentatively engage in before. However, as discussed in this chapter, the Council continues to face challenges to its exclusive competence to use force outside of the realms of self-defence, albeit often of a different nature from those witnessed during the Cold War. While the UNSC has withstood – and, as argued here, is so far

---

[324] For example, para. 34 of UNSC Resolution 687 (1991) states that the UNSC '[d]ecid[ed] to remain seized of the matter and to take such further steps as may be required for the implementation of the present resolution and to secure peace and security in the region' while para. 29 of UNSC Resolution 1973 (2011) states that the UNSC '[d]ecid[ed] to remain actively seized of the matter'.

[325] N.D. White, 'The Will and Authority of the Security Council after Iraq', (2004) 17 *LJIL* 645, at 656–657; F. Berman, 'The Authorization Model: Resolution 678 and Its Effects', in D.M. Malone (ed.), *The UN Security Council: From the Cold War to the 21st Century* (Boulder, CO: Lynne Rienner, 2004), 153, at 158.

withstanding – many of these challenges, there is the perennial question of reform in order to enable it to operate more efficiently and legitimately, thus arguably rendering such challenges less frequent and significant.

The issue of reform of the UNSC has been on the agenda of the UNGA since the 1970s.[326] However, the institutional momentum for reform of the UNSC has increased since the early 1990s when the issue began to be seriously discussed.[327] Most of the discussions and proposals since have called for equitable representation on, and an increase in, the membership of the Council, as well as reform of the voting procedures and an increase in the transparency and accountability of the Council.[328] Most recently, the High-Level Panel on Threats, Challenges and Change recommended in 2004 an enlargement of the composition of the Council membership to improve its credibility through an increased involvement by those states that contribute financially, militarily and diplomatically to its decision making and through broader membership so as to include more states from the developing world.[329] Indeed, while the composition and sheer size of the international community have changed, and the problems affecting international peace and security have evolved, the body remains structurally and compositionally more or less as it did in 1945. However, despite the reports and documents that have been generated in this respect, all of which have noted the need to make the UNSC work more efficiently and to improve representation within the Council chamber, none have found universal favour, including in the 2005 World

---

[326] S. Daws, 'The Reform of the UN Security Council: Introduction', in P. Taylor, S. Daws and U.T.E. Adamczick-Gerteis (eds), *Documents on Reform of the United Nations* (Aldershot: Dartmouth, 1997), 415, at 415.

[327] *Ibid.*, at 415.

[328] *Ibid.*, at 415–418.

[329] *A more secure world*, supra n. 231, at para. 249. The Panel floated two plans: Model A, which proposed six new permanent seats but without vetoes and three additional non-permanent seats, and Model B, which envisaged eight new semi-permanent seats with four-year renewable terms and only one additional non-permanent seat. The Council would thus be enlarged to 24 but with no provision of veto powers to any of the new Members but also no alteration to the veto powers of the existing Members. These proposals, and other similar ones, have nonetheless been criticised as not increasing the effectiveness of the Council. See N. Schrijver, 'Reforming the UN Security Council in Pursuance of Collective Security', (2007) 12 *JCSL* 127. See also E.C. Luck, 'How Not to Reform the United Nations', (2005) 11 *Global Governance* 412. Murphy, on the other hand, advocates more modest reforms: 'Efforts to achieve greater involvement of states capable of providing significant military or economic support for Chapter VII enforcement actions should be explored, but more extensive reforms of the process do not at this stage seem warranted', adding that areas where the UNSC needs 'improvement' – and not necessarily reform – is 'in the deterrence of aggressors from pursuing either armed conflict or widespread human rights atrocities', as well as in the development of Article 43 agreements, the greater utilisation of regional organisations, and finally the pursuance of 'initiatives that foster the creation and development of rule of law institutions within countries as a process of "deterrence from within"'. Murphy, *supra* n. 203, at 287–288. However, a sustained argument has been advanced by some, particularly within the US, that reform, not to mention mere improvement, of the Council is not a sufficient or realistic move, arguing instead for complete institutional replacement. See, for example, M.J. Glennon, 'The UN Security Council in a Unipolar World', (2003–2004) 44 *VJIL* 91.

Summit Outcome document which did not address any of the recommendations and remained silent on the possibility of reform. The issue, as such, remains a sticking point.

While the exclusive competence of the UNSC has arguably thus far been reaffirmed with an – albeit occasionally tentative – rebuttal of the various challenges to its authority, unless action is taken to reform in the long term its legitimacy and role as the key global forum for dealing with issues of peace and security will be put in jeopardy.[330] Indeed, other forums and organisations that are perceived to be more effective, efficient and modern, whether or not currently in existence, may prove to be a challenge to the UNSC's authority which will be difficult to fend off.[331] If, and if so how, this will occur is not clear at the current time, but any sustained challenge will be a momentous occasion not only for international conflict and security law, but for the maintenance of international peace and security more generally.

---

[330] For a discussion of the legitimacy of the UNSC with proposals for reform that is 20 years old but of continuing validity and relevance see, generally, D.D. Caron, 'The Legitimacy of the Collective Authority of the Security Council', (1993) 87 *AJIL* 552.

[331] UN News Centre, 'Without Security Council Reform, UN will Lose Credibility – General Assembly Chief', 16 May 2011, available at http://www.un.org/apps/news/story.asp?NewsID=38390. Cf. D. Malone, 'The Security Council in the Post-Cold War Era: A Study in the Creative Interpretation of the UN Charter', (2003) 35 *NYU J. Int'l L. & Pol.* 487, at 516. ('Even in its darkest hours [in the mid-1990s], no alternative international institution was mooted to supplant the Council. Indeed, the degree of consensus that would be required to create a different multilateral structure to promote collective security is inconceivable in the absence of a global cataclysm. Thus, the Council is fated to muster on.')

6. A study of the scope and operation of the rights of individual and collective self-defence under international law

Dino Kritsiotis

1. INTRODUCTION

Article 51 of the Charter of the United Nations assures to all Member States of that Organization their 'inherent' right of self-defence, and provides in part that:

> [n]othing in the present Charter shall impair the inherent right of individual or collective self-defence if an armed attack occurs against a Member of the United Nations, until the Security Council has taken measures necessary to maintain international peace and security.

This provision, which appears under the rubric concerning action with respect to threats to the peace, breaches of the peace and acts of aggression, is the solitary article in Chapter VII of the Charter to identify an entitlement of Member States to take action independent of authorization from the Security Council,[1] although this is then hemmed in by the so-called 'until clause' of Article 51, which provides that the right of self-defence may be exercised 'until the Security Council has taken measures necessary to maintain international peace and security'. Additionally, Article 51 imposes a reporting requirement whereby '[m]easures taken by Members in the exercise of this right of self-defence shall be immediately reported to the Security Council', but the provision concludes by stating that these measures 'shall not in any way affect the authority and responsibility of the Security Council under the present Charter to take at any time such action as it deems necessary in order to maintain or restore international peace and security'.[2]

The Charter, therefore, never sought to inaugurate the right of self-defence for states as a matter of international law; indeed, it could not be clearer in conveying the fact that Article 51 was connecting with an *existing* – or an inherent – legal right of states,

---

[1] Under Chapter XVII of the Charter, on Transitional Security Arrangements, Article 107 provides that '[n]othing in the present Charter shall invalidate or preclude action, in relation to any state which during the Second World War has been an enemy of any signatory to the present Charter, taken or authorized as a result of that war by the Governments having responsibility for such action'. For further discussion on the significance of this so-called 'enemy state clause', see H. Kelsen, 'Limitations on the Functions of the United Nations', (1946) 55 *Yale LJ* 997, at 1012–1015.

[2] See, generally, A. Randelzhofer, 'Article 51', in B. Simma (ed.), *The Charter of the United Nations: A Commentary* (Vol. I), 2nd edn (Oxford: Oxford University Press, 2002), at 788–806.

though that provision is frequently credited with introducing the language of 'collective self-defence' into the *jus ad bellum*.³ Be this as it may, the essential commitment of Article 51 was therefore neither to initiate nor (as it so fulsomely professes with its opening words) to *impair* the right of self-defence – but, rather, to adapt its application to a more modern age marked by the taking of 'effective collective measures' against threats to the peace, breaches of the peace and acts of aggression.⁴ Such collective measures would occur through the political organ of the Security Council, entrusted as it is under Article 24 of the Charter with the 'primary responsibility'⁵ of maintaining international peace and security, and, to this end, the Charter demarcated 'specific powers'⁶ for the Council to discharge its duties – powers to be found in Chapters VI (pacific settlement of disputes), VIII (regional arrangements) and XII (international trusteeship system) of the Charter, but, also, as we have mentioned, under Chapter VII (action with respect to threats to the peace, breaches of the peace and acts of aggression).⁷

Considered from this context, Article 51 is best understood as accommodating the right of self-defence within the institutional design of collective security contained in the Charter and the emerging reality of the 'authority and responsibility'⁸ of the Security Council – an interpretation very much reinforced by the fact that the provision in question did not actually feature in the original draft of the Charter.⁹ Indeed, it appears that, in significant measure, Article 51 found its way into the Charter following the concern expressed by those states who had concluded the Act of Chapultepec in March 1945 that, without more, their arrangement¹⁰ might somehow be considered to

---

³ For what it is worth, Kelsen regards the Charter as having 'established' the right of collective self-defence. See H. Kelsen, *The Law of the United Nations: A Critical Analysis of its Fundamental Problems* (New York: Frederick A. Praeger, 1950), at 918.

⁴ Article 1(1), UN Charter (1945). See, further, I. Brownlie, *International Law and the Use of Force by States* (Oxford: Clarendon Press, 1963), at 272, and S.A. Alexandrov, *Self-Defence Against the Use of Force in International Law* (The Hague: Kluwer Law International, 1996), at 79 (regarding China's concern of the relationship between the right of self-defence and the powers of the Security Council).

⁵ Article 24(1). For more on the centrality of the Council in the regime governing the use of force see the chapter by Christian Henderson (chapter 5) in this volume.

⁶ Article 24(2).

⁷ For a full and detailed discussion of this matter, consider T.M. Franck, *Recourse to Force: State Action Against Threats and Armed Attacks* (Cambridge: Cambridge University Press, 2002), at 29–44.

⁸ As *per* the concluding statement of Article 51: *supra* n.2.

⁹ D.W. Bowett, *Self-Defence in International Law* (Manchester: Manchester University Press, 1958), at 182. See, also, J.L. Kunz, 'Individual and Collective Self-Defense in Article 51 of the Charter of the United Nations', (1947) 41 *AJIL* 872.

¹⁰ Which provided that 'every attack of a State against the integrity of the inviolability of the territory, or against the sovereignty or political independence of an American State, shall ... be considered as an act of aggression against the other States which sign this Act': Resolution VIII on Inter-American Reciprocal Assistance and Solidarity of the Inter-American Conference on Problems of War and Peace ('Act of Chapultepec'), Part I (para. 3).

be at odds with the new legal order set out in the Charter.[11] They were not alone in this regard.[12]

That system of collective security was anchored in the Charter's organizing principle of Article 2(4) that Member States of the United Nations are to 'refrain in their international relations from the threat or use of force against the territorial integrity or political independence of any State, or in any other manner inconsistent with the Purposes of the United Nations'. The Charter, however, made no immediate effort to explain how these various propositions of the new system – the threat or use of force, armed attack, threat to the peace, breach of the peace, act of aggression – would or should relate with one another.[13] Still, the general understanding that came to pass amongst states in the practice of the United Nations was that, in appropriate circumstances and under recognized conditions, the right of self-defence was to be considered as an instance of *permissible* force under international law, one that is *exceptional* to the prohibition of force contained in the Charter.[14] Positions have not been unanimous on this point, for some have argued for a much broader provenance for the right of self-defence in practice so as to encompass the taking of 'unilateral

---

[11] This was known as the 'Latin-American crisis': Kunz, *supra* n.9, at 872. For the Declaration, of Part I of the Act, was accompanied by the Recommendation of Part II of the Act, which provided '[t]hat for the purpose of meeting threats or acts of aggression against any American Republic following the establishment of peace', the Governments of the American Republics may consider, amongst other things, the 'use of armed force to prevent or repel aggression'. See, further, M.S. Canyes, 'The Inter-American System and the Conference of Chapultepec', (1945) 39 *AJIL* 504 and, also, W.W. Kulski, 'The Soviet System of Collective Security Compared with the Western System', (1950) 44 *AJIL* 453.

[12] See Kunz, *supra* n.9, at 873. Amongst other states, Bowett mentions those members of League of Arab States: *supra* n.9, at 183. They concluded their Pact on 22 March 1945, which provided in Article 6(1) that '[i]n case of aggression or threat of aggression by a State against a member State, the State attacked or threatened with attack may request an immediate meeting of the Council', which was to be composed of the representatives of each of its Member States (Article 3). According to Article 6(2) of the Pact, '[t]he Council shall determine the necessary measures to repel this aggression' by way of unanimous decision, where the vote of the aggressor state 'will not be counted in determining the unanimity'. See, further, Alexandrov, *supra* n.4, at 91.

[13] R. Higgins, *The Development of International Law through the Political Organs of the United Nations* (London, New York, Toronto: Oxford University Press, 1963), at 173.

[14] See J. Combacau, 'The Exception of Self-Defence in U.N. Practice', in A. Cassese (ed.), *The Current Legal Regulation of Force* (Dordrecht: Martinus Nijhoff Publishers, 1986), 9. See, also, G.M. Badr, 'The Exculpatory Effect of Self-Defense in State Responsibility', (1980) 10 *Georgia JICL* 1. This is quite apart from the demarcation of powers set forth in Chapter VII of the Charter for the Security Council: according to Article 39 of the Charter, the Security Council must determine 'the existence of any threat to the peace, breach of the peace, or act of aggression' as a precursor to the making of a recommendation or decision as to 'what measures shall be taken in accordance with Articles 41 and 42, to maintain or restore international peace and security'. I emphasize the distinct qualities of these – often overlapping – components of the Charter's framework in D. Kritsiotis, 'Topographies of Force', in M.N. Schmitt and J. Pejic (eds), *International Law and Armed Conflict: Exploring the Faultlines* (Leiden, Boston: Martinus Nijhoff Publishers, 2007), 29, at 45–63.

economic interests' against offending states,[15] and, in an apparent extension of this logic and thinking, we find that Israel has formed the view that its construction of a wall or security barrier in the occupied territories constituted 'a measure wholly consistent with the right of States to self-defence [as] enshrined in Article 51 of the Charter'.[16] In her separate opinion in *Legal Consequences of the Construction of A Wall in the Occupied Palestinian Territory* (2004), Judge Rosalyn Higgins remained 'unconvinced' that 'non-forcible measures (such as the building of a wall) fall within self-defence under Article 51 of the Charter as that provision is normally understood'.[17] The right of self-defence was there to justify the application – that is, the threat or the use – of force in international law; it was not there as a default argument for all manner of actions that states may devise or deem necessary to ensure their greater safety and well-being.[18] This chapter will thus seek to articulate how the diverse interpretations and invocations of the right of self-defence have occurred over time, especially with reference to the United Nations and its system of collective security, and in particular view of the evolving jurisprudence of the International Court of Justice. As will be appreciated, not every episode of this practice has been litigated before the Court,[19] but, in the analysis that follows, we shall wish to concentrate to an appreciable extent on the findings and insights that the Court has shared in the *Nicaragua Case* (1986),[20] the *Oil Platforms Case* (2003)[21] and *Case Concerning Armed Activities in the Territory of the*

---

[15] In other words, those responsible for a delict against the self-defending state, 'posing an immediate danger to its security or independence in a situation affording no alternative means of protection and, lastly, that the reaction was proportionate to the harm threatened'. See D.W. Bowett, 'Economic Coercion and Reprisals by States', (1972) 13 *Virginia JIL* 1, at 7. See, further, Bowett, *supra* n.9, at 186 and R.W. Tucker, 'Reprisals and Self-Defense: The Customary Law', (1972) 66 *AJIL* 586, at 587 ('[a] state's security and independence may be impaired by the behavior of another state, although the latter does not employ force or even the threat of force') and 589 ('measures of self-defense are, in principle ... permitted by the customary law in response to acts threatening a very wide range of interests roughly identified with the state's security and independence. Nor must these acts involve the use or even the threat of force in order to justify self-defense').

[16] The position argued by the Permanent Representative of Israel to the United Nations before the General Assembly. See UN Doc. A/ES-10/PV.21 (20 October 2003), at 6.

[17] (2004) ICJ Rep. 136, at 215–216 (para. 35). The reference to the building of a wall relates to what the International Court of Justice called 'a complex construction' by Israel in its advisory opinion (*ibid.*, at 164 (para. 67)), involving some 8.5 kilometres of concrete wall of the approximately 180 kilometres completed or under construction. See *ibid.*, at 170 (para. 82). See, further, C.J. Tams, 'Light Treatment of a Complex Problem: The Law of Self-Defence in the Wall Case', (2005) 16 *EJIL* 963, at 967.

[18] Although these may of course find legal mooring elsewhere in the discipline of public international law – for example, at some other point in the laws of peace, or, conceivably, in the laws of armed conflict (including the law of belligerent occupation).

[19] See, generally, J.A. Green, *The International Court of Justice and Self-Defence in International Law* (Oxford and Portland: Hart Publishing, 2009).

[20] *Case Concerning Military and Paramilitary Activities in and Against Nicaragua* (Nicaragua v. United States of America) (Merits) (1986) ICJ Rep. 14.

[21] *Oil Platforms Case* (Islamic Republic of Iran v. United States of America) (Judgment) (2003) ICJ Rep. 161.

Congo (2005).[22] There shall be reflection, too, on the Court's contributions arising from its advisory proceedings, where the focus shall be on *Legal Consequences of the Construction of A Wall in the Occupied Palestinian Territory* and on *Legality of the Threat or Use of Nuclear Weapons* (1996).[23] At the same time, we shall want to cast a firm eye on the state of the law on the right of self-defence *prior* to the conclusion of the Charter of the United Nations in June 1945 – after all, the right of self-defence was an existing right of states that the Charter did not wish to impair[24] – and as refracted through the practices of states *subsequent* to the Charter's entry into force in October 1945.

The chapter shall therefore proceed according to the following structure: it will commence in section 2 by examining the 'inherent' nature of the right of self-defence by specific reference to the famous *Caroline* correspondence of 1838–1842 between the United States and Great Britain. Section 3 will then etch the common ground and the differences that exist between the 'rights' of individual and collective self-defence, for, as we shall see, the latter carries with it its own set of tailored particulars, a sort of *lex specialis* for collective self-defence. Section 4 will proceed to explore the possibilities for a right of anticipatory self-defence, that is whether the right of self-defence exists in the absence of an armed attack – or, in the more acute framing of the International Court of Justice in the *Nicaragua Case* of June 1986, an 'imminent threat of armed attack'.[25] Then, in section 5, the meaning of the concept of an 'armed attack' will be explored in some detail, for this holds implications for both individual and collective self-defence. In section 6, the critical question of the proportionality of an action undertaken in self-defence will be considered, before, in section 7, the relationship between the right of self-defence and the Security Council is assessed. This will be foretold through the 'until clause' and reporting requirement of Article 51 of the Charter. In section 8, a general summation shall be given of the contents of the chapter, together with some concluding reflections on the nature of the rights of individual and collective self-defence in international law.

2. THE 'INHERENT' RIGHT OF SELF-DEFENCE

A. Origins: Self-Preservation, Self-defence and Necessity

On its most obvious reading, the 'inherent' character of the right of self-defence could refer to the fact that the right *inheres* in, and is thus inseparable from, the right-holder – which in this instance would be the state.[26] This understanding takes us back to the

---

[22] *Case Concerning Armed Activities in the Territory of the Congo* (Democratic Republic of the Congo v. Uganda) (Judgment) (2005) ICJ Rep. 168.
[23] (1996) ICJ Rep. 226.
[24] Consider Brownlie, *supra* n.4, at 235–250 and 257–261.
[25] *Nicaragua Case*, *supra* n.20, at 103 (para. 194).
[26] *See*, for example, the discussion of M.J. Glennon, 'The Fog of Law: Self-Defense, Inherence, and Incoherence in Article 51 of the United Nations Charter', (2002) 25 *Harvard JLPP* 539, at 553–556.

actual origins of the right within international law, or, perhaps at a much more abstract level of engagement, to the beginning of the state as a form of political organization and as a unit of social relations,[27] though it is clear from various earlier assessments the extent to which the right of self-defence had an intricate association with the notion of self-preservation: for Emer de Vattel in his *The Law of Nations, or Principles of the Law of Nature Applied to the Conduct and Affairs of Nations and Sovereigns* (1758), '[s]elf-defence against unjust violence is not only the right', he wrote, 'but the duty of a nation, and one of her most sacred duties',[28] where nature awarded men the entitlement to employ force 'when it becomes necessary for self-defence and the preservation of their rights'.[29] Some two centuries later, Sir Humphrey Waldock wrote of an apparent 'right' of self-preservation that was external to the system of positive law and its predicates, where '[t]he truth is that self-preservation in the case of a State as of an individual is not a legal right but an instinct; and even if it may often happen that the instinct prevails over the legal duty not to do violence to others, international law ought not to admit that it is lawful that it should do so.'[30] Others, too, have very much emphasized the foundations of such a right of self-preservation within the encomium of natural law,[31] and of self-defence being 'swallowed up by more general rights, variously designated "self-preservation" or "self-help," which States are alleged to possess'.[32] According to another account, '[f]rom the earliest time of the existence of the Law of Nations' – note the actual commitment here to trace the origins of the legal right and relate it to 'the law of nations' – 'self-preservation was considered sufficient

---

[27] Brownlie, *supra* n.4, at 42. And, as such, has been regarded as singularly unhelpful: '[t]he phrase "inherent right" can only serve to obscure legal meaning. As a legal right, granted by positive international law, it has to be defined by this positive law.' See Kunz, *supra* n.9, at 876. See, also, M.A. Weightman, 'Self-Defense in International Law', (1951) 31 *Virginia LR* 1095, at 1108 ('["inherent"] can only suggest that self-defense is a natural right, i.e., one above and apart from rules, treaties, and conventions of positive international law. Thus casually was a natural-law concept revived after lying two centuries in a juridical coma'). Consider, too, the Note of the United States appended to the 1928 Kellogg–Briand Pact, that 'there is nothing in the American draft ... to restrict or impair in any way the right of self-defense. That right is inherent in every sovereign State and is implicit in every Treaty'. See *The General Pact for the Renunciation of War: Text of the Pact as Signed, Notes, and Other Papers* (Washington, DC: Govt. Printing Office, 1928). See, further, Address of the Hon. Frank B. Kellogg, 28 April 1928 (1928) 22 *Proceedings ASIL* 141, at 142.

[28] Book III, Ch. I, §35.

[29] Book III, Ch. I, §4 (and *ibid.*, at §201, '[t]he whole right of the conqueror is derived from justifiable self-defence ... which comprehends the support and prosecution of his rights'). And, at Book II, Ch. IV, Book II, §49: 'Every nation, as well as every man, has, therefore, a right to prevent other nations from obstructing her preservation, her perfection, and happiness.'

[30] J.L. Brierly, *The Law of Nations: An Introduction to the International Law of Peace*, 6th edn, (C.H.M. Waldock ed, Oxford: Clarendon Press, 1963), at 405.

[31] See S.C. Neff, *War and the Law of Nations: A General History* (Cambridge: Cambridge University Press, 2005), at 133, and Brownlie, *supra* n.4, at 41.

[32] Weightman, *supra* n.27, at 1103. See, also, A. Cassese, *International Law*, 2nd edn (Oxford: Oxford University Press, 2005), at 359, and N. Rostow, 'Nicaragua and the Law of Self-Defense Revisited', (1986) 11 *Yale JIL* 437, at 451–452.

justification for many acts of a State which violate other States',[33] though it is also true that the right of self-defence has been regarded as one of the earliest mechanisms for the actual enforcement of international law, and has been labelled as a 'remedial' right that 'presuppose[s] a breach of some duty' by another state.[34]

This connection that self-preservation shares with self-defence in international law has also been developed for the relationship between necessity and self-defence, so that self-preservation has been 'asserted parallel to, or as a form of, a doctrine of necessity'.[35] In this, it is important to emphasize the *function* that appears to have been allocated to each of these propositions in classical law and practice, where:

> [t]here would seem analytically to be no distinction between the two [*i.e.* self-preservation and necessity] and the discussions in works of international law certainly treat them as identical except in so far as necessity is a wider legal category and may, for example, appear in the context of the laws of war. In many cases necessity thus appears merely as an aspect of the right of self-preservation. When 'necessity' is defined it appears to be applicable when action is necessary for the security or safety of the state. As the state taking such action was regarded as the judge of the situation, necessity, like preservation, usually appears as the window dressing of *raison d'état*.[36]

This reasoning might now be thought to have greater resonance for the right of self-defence given the finding of the International Court of Justice in its advisory opinion in *Legality of the Threat or Use of Nuclear Weapons* – that 'in view of the current state of international law, and of the elements of fact at its disposal, the Court cannot conclude definitively whether the threat or use of nuclear weapons would be lawful or unlawful in an extreme circumstance of self-defence, in which the very survival of a State would be at stake'.[37] Equally important to observe is the fact that

---

[33] L. Oppenheim, *International Law: A Treatise* (Vol. I) (Peace) (London, New York, Bombay: Longmans, Green & Co., 1905), at 177. Consider, too, the following formulation in the latest edition of Oppenheim's treatise:

> As a rule, all States are under a mutual duty to respect one another's sovereignty, and are bound not to violate one another's independence. Exceptionally, however, a state may in certain circumstances violate another state's territory. One such exception occurs in those few cases in which intervention is permitted. The other principal exception was formerly regarded as covering violations for the purpose of self-preservation, it being widely maintained that every state had a fundamental right of self-preservation. But this alleged right, if it ever existed, was often a barely colourable excuse for violations of another state's sovereignty.

R.Y. Jennings and A.D. Watts (eds), *Oppenheim's International Law* (Vol. I: Peace) 9th edn (London and New York: Longman, 1992), at 416 (§126). See, further, H. Kelsen, *Principles of International Law* (New York: Rinehart & Co., 1952), at 59.

[34] D.W. Bowett, 'The Interrelation of Theories of Intervention and Self-Defence', in J.N. Moore (ed.), *Law and Civil War in the Modern World* (Baltimore, MD: JHU Press, 1974), 38. See, also, Cassese, *supra* n.32, at 355. ('Since aggression constitutes a violation of the sovereign rights of the victim, in resorting to self-defence the latter engages in legal enforcement.') Cf. Kunz, *supra* n.9, at 876.

[35] Brownlie, *supra* n.4, at 42.

[36] *Ibid.*

[37] *Supra* n.23, at 266 (para. 105 (2) (E)). This framing of the Court by seven votes to seven (by the President's casting vote) is interesting because it suggests the Court on that occasion was

while self-preservation does not appear today as a circumstance precluding the wrongfulness of an internationally wrongful act in the law of state responsibility, both self-defence and necessity *do* feature in these terms towards the identical end of providing 'a shield against an otherwise well-founded claim for the breach of an international obligation'[38] but they are explicitly *not* treated as one and the same thing.[39]

B. The *Caroline* Correspondence 1838–1842

It is from the correspondence between the United States and Great Britain coming out of the celebrated *Caroline* episode of December 1837 that a much keener sense developed of the distinction between the right of self-preservation and that of self-defence within international law, for 'whereas self-defence presupposes an attack, self-preservation has no such limitation, and, broadly applied, would serve to cloak with an appearance of legality almost any unwarranted act of violence on the part of the State'.[40] The episode is, in fact, renowned as the *locus classicus* of the law on self-defence,[41] although it should be observed that in the earlier iterations of the correspondence that lasted from January 1838 until August 1842, it was the position of Great Britain that its destruction of the *Caroline* (which had been hired to ferry arms, men and other supplies from the United States to Navy Island, on the Canadian side of

---

minded to distinguish between ordinary invocations of the right of self-defence and those involving 'extreme circumstance', that is where 'the very survival of a State would be at stake'. See, further, M.G. Kohen, 'The Notion of "State Survival" in International Law', in L. Boisson de Chazournes and P. Sands (eds), *International Law, the International Court of Justice and Nuclear Weapons* (Cambridge: Cambridge University Press, 1999), 293.

[38] J.R. Crawford, *The International Law Commission's Articles on State Responsibility: Introduction, Text and Commentaries* (Cambridge: Cambridge University Press, 2001), at 160.

[39] So, whereas Article 21 of the 2001 International Law Commission Draft Articles on State Responsibility provides (without more) that '[t]he wrongfulness of an act of a State is precluded if the act constitutes a lawful measure of self-defence taken in conformity with the Charter of the United Nations', Article 25(1) of the Draft Articles stipulates that '[n]ecessity may not be invoked by a State as a ground for precluding the wrongfulness of an act not in conformity with an international obligation of that State unless the act: (*a*) is the only way for the State to safeguard an essential interest against a grave and imminent peril; and (*b*) does not seriously impair an essential interest of the State or States towards which the obligation exists, or of the international community as a whole'. See *ibid.*, at 166 and 178. One can surely appreciate the possibilities of overlap between the right of self-defence and the doctrine of necessity as articulated here – especially in respect of the safeguarding of 'an essential interest against a grave and imminent peril' – but it is worth noting that the *Caroline* correspondence is cited in the commentary for Article 25 – and not that of Article 21 – of the Draft Articles: Crawford, *ibid.*, at 179–180.

[40] R.Y. Jennings, 'The Caroline and McLeod Cases', (1938) 32 *AJIL* 82, at 91 (though admitting, *ibid.*, that 'it is to be doubted whether this distinction, which appears so obvious to the modern lawyer, was at all appreciated in the earlier stages in the development of international law').

[41] *Ibid.*, at 92.

the border, to assist rebels fighting British rule) on the territory of the United States was undertaken on the basis of 'the necessity of self-defence and self-preservation'.[42]

However, as the correspondence took substantive shape and drew to its eventual close, it is noticeable how much the focus purposefully shifted towards the concept of a right of self-defence, with the United States Secretary of State Daniel Webster setting out the legal principles for those claims made in its name. This he did in a letter dated 24 April 1841:

> Under these circumstances, and under those immediately connected with the transaction itself, it will be for Her Majesty's Government to show, upon what state of facts, and what rules of national law, the destruction of the *Caroline* is to be defended. It will be for that Government to show a necessity of self-defence, instant, overwhelming, leaving no choice of means, and no moment for deliberation. It will be for it to show, also, that the local authorities of Canada, – even supposing the necessity of the moment authorized them to enter the territories of the United States at all, – did nothing unreasonable or excessive; since the act justified by the necessity of self-defense, must be limited by that necessity, and kept clearly within it. It must be shewn that admonition or remonstrance to the persons on board the *Caroline* was impracticable, or would have been unavailing; it must be shewn that daylight could not be waited for; that there could be no attempt at discrimination, between the innocent and the guilty; that it would not have been enough to seize and detain the vessel; but that there was a necessity, present and inevitable, for attacking her, in the darkness of the night, while moored to the shore, and while unarmed men were asleep on board, killing some, and wound[ing] others, and then drawing her into the current, above the cataract, setting her on fire, and careless to know whether there might not be in her the innocent with the guilty, or the living with the dead, committing her to a fate, which fills the imagination with horror. A necessity for all of this, the Government of the United States cannot believe to have existed.[43]

---

[42] W.R. Manning, *Diplomatic Correspondence of the United States, Canadian Relations, 1784–1860* (Vol. III: 1836–1848; Documents 1193–1853) (Washington, DC: Carnegie Endowment for International Peace, 1943), at 422 (Doc. No. 1426) (letter of Henry S. Fox, British Minister at Washington DC, to United States Secretary of State John Forsyth of 6 February, 1838). As Jennings wrote, 'Fox continually uses the phrase "self-defence and self-preservation" as if the two were synonymous terms' (*ibid.*, at 91). A helpful summary of the factual background is provided in V. Lowe, *International Law* (Oxford: Oxford University Press, 2007), at 275–276. Selections from the correspondence – including the seminal letter of Secretary Webster from April 1841, whose main formulation was repeated by Secretary Webster in a letter dated 27 July 1842, to Lord Ashburton, special envoy of Great Britain to the United States – have been made available by the Avalon Project (Documents in Law, History and Diplomacy) of Yale Law School at http://avalon.law.yale.edu/19th_century/br-1842d.asp. See, further, the excellent treatment of J.E. Noyes, 'The Caroline: International Law Limits on Resort to Force', in J.E. Noyes, L.A. Dickinson and M.W. Janis (eds), *International Law Stories* (New York: Foundation Press, 2007), 263, and of J.A. Green, 'Docking the *Caroline*: Understanding the Relevance of the Formula in Contemporary Customary International Law Concerning Self-Defense', (2006) 14 *Cardozo JICL* 429; T. Kearley, 'Raising the *Caroline*', (1999) 17 *Wisconsin ILJ* 325; M.B. Occelli, '"Sinking" the *Caroline*: Why the *Caroline*'s Restrictions on Self-Defense Should Not Be Regarded As Customary International Law', (2003) 4 *San Diego JIL* 467 and M.A. Rogoff and E. Collins, Jr., 'The *Caroline* Incident and the Development of International Law', (1990) 16 *Brooklyn JIL* 493.

[43] See Manning, *supra* n.42, at 145 (Doc. No. 1269).

It is from this passage that we are able to deduce the two – rather than three[44] – principles from the *Caroline* correspondence designed to regulate the right of self-defence in international law: the principles of necessity and proportionality,[45] which have been credited for making it no longer possible for Great Britain, or indeed, any other state, 'to talk vaguely of self-defence and self-preservation as if the mere utterance of the words excused any and every sin'.[46]

Through a close reading of this formulation from April 1841,[47] it will be appreciated that Secretary Webster intended to establish a framework for the rendering of *both* the official legal argumentation and requisite evidence by the British Government for its invocation of the right of self-defence as justification for its action of December 1837, where, first and foremost, a 'necessity' of self-defence would have to be shown, which would implicate a series of factual considerations ('instant, overwhelming, leaving no choice of means, and no moment for deliberation'). Satisfaction of this principle would entitle one state to initiate force against another state (as Secretary Webster then wrote, 'the necessity of the moment' would have 'authorized [the local authorities of Canada] to enter the territories of the United States at all');[48] then, and only then, would the principle of proportionality become legally relevant, for the British Government would then need to demonstrate in addition to the necessity of its action that its officers had done 'nothing unreasonable or excessive' in terms of their overall response.[49] An intricate relationship was therefore intended for the principles of necessity and proportionality within this framework, whereby any lawful exercise of the right of self-defence could not occur without *both* of these principles being redeemed or obliged by the self-defending state, as the proportionality of a given action could only be calculated and measured as against its necessity ('the act justified by the necessity of self-defence, must be limited by that necessity, and kept clearly within it').[50]

C. An Inherent Right and Custom

All of this presents us with a second possible meaning of the 'inherent' right of self-defence as proclaimed in Article 51 of the Charter, and it is the one adopted by the International Court of Justice in its judgment in the *Nicaragua Case* in June 1986, where the Court used the inherent nature of the right as the reference-point for the legal

---

[44] As maintained by Yoram Dinstein, that is, that 'the two conditions of necessity and proportionality are accompanied by a third condition of immediacy'. See Y. Dinstein, *War, Aggression and Self-Defence*, 5th edn (Cambridge: Cambridge University Press, 2011), at 230 ('these three conditions are distilled from yardsticks set out by [Secretary Webster] some 170 years ago').

[45] See Lowe, *supra* n.42, at 276 ('[t]here are two critical elements in the *Caroline* formula').

[46] Jennings, *supra* n.40, at 89. Also: '[i]t was in the *Caroline case* that self-defence was changed from a political excuse into a legal doctrine': *ibid.*, at 82.

[47] Repeated in subsequent correspondence of Secretary Webster, for example in his letters to Lord Ashburton dated 27 July 1842 and 6 August 1842.

[48] *Supra* n.43.

[49] *Ibid.*

[50] *Ibid.*

regulation of self-defence prior to the adoption of the Charter: 'this reference to customary law', the Court reasoned,

> is contained in the actual text of Article 51, which mentions the 'inherent right' (in the French text 'droit naturel') of individual or collective self-defence, which 'nothing in the present Charter shall impair' and which applies in the event of an armed attack.[51]

In other words, the Court's interest in the 'inherent' nature of the right of self-defence stemmed from the state of the law – the *lex lata* as it were – on the right of self-defence in the period prior to the Charter of the United Nations and how this customary dimension evolved subsequent to the adoption of the Charter.[52] There is, to be sure, some coincidence of these ideas in the reflection the Court makes in the *Nicaragua Case* that:

> Article 51 of the Charter is only meaningful on the basis that there is a 'natural' or 'inherent' right of self-defence, and it is hard to see how this can be other than of a customary nature, even if its present content has been confirmed and influenced by the Charter.[53]

This proved an important statement for the Court to have made in the context of the case before it, since the United States had entered a reservation to the application of multilateral treaties in cases with which it was involved before the Court,[54] but it also affirms the more general position which the Court took in its judgment on the relationship between treaty and customary law:

> On a number of points, the areas governed by the two sources of law do not exactly overlap, and the substantive rules in which they are framed are not identical in content. But in addition, even if a treaty norm and a customary norm relevant to the present dispute were to have exactly the same content, this would not be a reason for the Court to take the view that the operation of the treaty process must necessarily deprive the customary norm of its separate applicability. Nor can the multilateral treaty reservation be interpreted as meaning that, once applicable to a given dispute, it would exclude the application of any rule of customary international law the content of which was the same as, or analogous to, that of the treaty-law rule which had caused the reservation to become effective.[55]

With these words, the Court was therefore making clear that there in fact exists a totality of rules – or, better, a totality of principles and rules – which comprise the regulation of the right of self-defence in contemporary international law and that this law derives from *both* convention and custom. The Court was precluded by virtue of

---

[51] *Nicaragua Case*, supra n.20, at 94 (para. 176).
[52] See C. Gray, *International Law and the Use of Force*, 3rd edn (Oxford: Oxford University Press, 2008), at 117.
[53] *Nicaragua Case*, supra n.20, at 94 (para. 176).
[54] According to the Vandenberg Reservation of 26 August 1946, the United States accepted the jurisdiction of the Court on the proviso that 'disputes aris[e] under a multilateral treaty, unless (1) all parties to the treaty affected by the decision are also parties to the case before the Court, or (2) the United States of America specially agrees to jurisdiction'. (The Reservation is reproduced in the *Nicaragua Case*, supra n.20, at 31 (para. 42).)
[55] *Nicaragua Case*, supra n.20, at 94 (para. 175).

the Vandenberg Reservation from applying *any* aspect of the conventional law – or of 'treaty-law' rules, as the Court put it in this excerpt from its judgment – that was not reflected or assured by custom,[56] and the Court did go on to provide an example of custom that pre-existed, and therefore was wholly independent from, the Charter: the Charter, the Court said by way of example, 'does not contain any specific rule whereby self-defence would warrant only measures which are proportional to the armed attack and necessary to respond to it, a rule well established in customary international law'.[57] This, of course, recalls and relates the second of the principles from the *Caroline* correspondence raised and discussed in general terms above,[58] but, for the Court, the length and breadth of the customary law on self-defence was not confined to the *Caroline* correspondence but extended to include the Charter's 'influence'[59] on the content of custom beyond 1945: on this front, the Court mentioned the concept of an armed attack as set out in Article 51 of the Charter, noting that the Charter fails to define the concept and that, as such, any definition of an armed attack could not be said to form 'part of treaty law'.[60]

3. THE RIGHTS OF INDIVIDUAL AND COLLECTIVE SELF-DEFENCE

A. Bifurcation: The Rights of Individual and Collective Self-defence

It will be appreciated that, in its specifications regarding the concept of an armed attack in the *Nicaragua Case*, the Court detected a common denominator for the rights of *individual* and *collective* self-defence, but it is also clear that the Court articulated a separate and additional schemata for the regulation of the right of collective self-defence in international law. Indeed, in the *Oil Platforms Case* of November 2003, the Court made a point of recalling that the United States had *not* claimed the right of collective self-defence before it in the context of 'attacks on vessels and aircraft of *other* nationalities',[61] since the first of the two incidents giving rise to that case

---

[56] Indeed, the Court had formed the view that 'the effect of the reservation in question is confined to barring the applicability of the United Nations Charter and Organization of American States Charter as multilateral treaty law, and has no further impact on the sources of international law which Article of the Statute [of the International Court of Justice] requires the Court to apply': *Nicaragua Case, supra* n.20, at 38 (para. 56).
[57] *Nicaragua Case, supra* n.20, at 94 (para. 176).
[58] And the subject of more extended treatment *infra* in section 6.
[59] See *supra* n.53.
[60] *Nicaragua Case, supra* n.20, at 94 (para. 176). The 1969 Vienna Convention on the Law of Treaties does, however, provide that, for all treaties coming within its temporal remit, together with the context of the terms of a given treaty, there shall also be taken into account 'any subsequent practice in the application of the treaty which establishes the agreement of the parties regarding its interpretation'. See Article 31(3)(b), Vienna Convention on the Law of Treaties (23 May 1969).
[61] *Oil Platforms Case, supra* n.21, at 186 (para. 51) (i.e. 'on behalf of the neutral vessels engaged in shipping in the Persian Gulf') (emphasis added). For further discussion of

involved the missile strike of a Kuwaiti tanker, *Sea Isle City*, on 16 October 1987, that had been reflagged by the United States.[62] In making this observation, the Court nevertheless adverted to some of the peculiarities of the law governing the exercise of the right of collective self-defence.[63] As we shall see, these peculiarities coincided with the Court's jurisprudence from its earlier decision in the *Nicaragua Case*,[64] and we shall spend this section detailing what these laws are and the reasons underpinning them, as well as reflecting upon their actual application in practice.

B. The Nature of Collective Self-defence

Article 51, of course, does not restrict itself to the right of 'individual' self-defence alone, the subject of the *Caroline* correspondence of 1838–1842: it also concerns the right of 'collective' self-defence,[65] which for some time has been regarded as an 'inaccurate' turn-of-phrase on account of the fact that '[d]efence of the self cannot be collective; though there may exist collective security or mutual aid'.[66] The idea being put forward here on this reading of the right of collective self-defence is that it involves the simultaneous exercise or 'pooling' of individual *rights* of self-defence,[67] all permissibly invoked under international law for the 'right to intervene' in such circumstances ultimately 'stems from the threat to [each] state's *own* security'.[68] Collective self-defence on this account therefore amounts to no more than the collective exercise of these individual rights of self-defence: it has been argued that 'some sort of proximate relationship' must exist as the right of collective self-defence 'extends to the defence of one's family, one's servants, and to those persons whom one is under a recognized duty to protect'.[69] This approach, which owes its existence to certain constructions occurring within and drawn from private law, does 'seem to presuppose

---

the background to these episodes, consider Gray, *supra* n.52, at 143–148. See, also, R. Leckow, 'The Iran–Iraq Conflict in the Gulf: The Law of War Zones', (1988) 37 *ICLQ* 629; C. Gray, 'The British Position in Regard to the Gulf Conflict', (1988) 37 *ICLQ* 420 and C. Gray, 'The British Position with Regard to the Gulf Conflict (Iran–Iraq): Part 2', (1991) 40 *ICLQ* 464.

[62] The second incident, on 14 April 1988, involved the *Samuel B. Roberts*, a warship of the United States, that had struck a mine in international waters. See, further, D. Raab, '"Armed Attack" After the Oil Platforms Case', (2004) 17 *Leiden JIL* 719.

[63] *Oil Platforms Case*, *supra* n.21, at 186 (para. 51).

[64] *Infra* nn.79–85 (and accompanying text).

[65] See H. Kelsen, 'Collective Security and Collective Self-Defense under the Charter of the United Nations', (1948) 42 *AJIL* 783.

[66] *Supra* n.13, at 208–209. For Kunz, the term 'collective self-defence' is 'not a happy one' for '[i]t is not self-defence, but defence of another state'. See Kunz, *supra* n.9, at 875. Elsewhere, it has been regarded as 'ambiguous': M. Shaw, *International Law*, 6th edn (Cambridge: Cambridge University Press, 2008), at 1146. This is not to mention the complication it raises for an 'inherent' right of *collective* self-defence. See Weightman, *supra* n.27, at 1111 ('It is hardly possible to regard the right or duty of a state to go to the assistance of another state as "inherent", in a natural law-sense').

[67] Shaw, *supra* n.66, at 1146.

[68] Bowett, *supra* n.34, at 47 (emphasis added). *See*, further, Cassese, *supra* n.32, at 365.

[69] Bowett, *supra* n.9, at 201–202. *See*, also, D.W. Bowett, 'Collective Self-Defence under the Charter of the United Nations', (1955–1956) 32 *BYBIL* 130.

an interest which the person has a right to defend, for example his interest in the integrity and well-being of his family or his servants' in setting down the threshold as to when the right of self-defence could be activated,[70] and is set against the theory of collective self-defence as based on 'the concept of a duty to maintain international peace and to redress a violation of the rules of international law'.[71]

In the *Nicaragua Case*, which involved the invocation of the United States of its right of collective self-defence on behalf of El Salvador, Costa Rica and Honduras, against each of the armed attacks alleged to have been committed against these three states by Nicaragua, there was some support for this particular understanding of the right of collective self-defence. In his dissenting opinion in that case, Sir Robert Y. Jennings advised that, whatever else might be entailed by a right of collective self-defence in international law, it was not and could not be regarded as a 'vicarious defence of champions':

> The assisting State is not an authorized champion, permitted under certain conditions to go to the aid of a favoured State. The assisting State surely must, by going to the victim State's assistance, be also, and in *addition* to other requirements, in some measure defending itself. There should even in 'collective self-defence' be some real element of self involved with the notion of defence. This is presumably also the philosophy which underlies mutual security arrangements, such as the system of the Organization of American States, for which indeed Article 51 was specifically designed. By such a system of collective security, the security of each member State is meant to be involved with the security of the others; not merely as a result of a contractual arrangement but by the real consequences of the system and its organization. ... [The Charter of the Organization of American States] should not be regarded as a mere contractual arrangement for collective defence – a legal fiction used as a device for arranging for mutual defence – ; it is to be regarded as an organized system of collective security by which the security of each member is made really and truly to have become involved with the security of the others, thus providing a true basis for a system of collective self-defence.[72]

From this passage, it is clear how much perceptions of collective self-defence have been shaped by 'mutual security arrangements'[73] of the order of the Organization of American States. Another, formed shortly after the Second World War, was the North

---

[70] Bowett, *supra* n.9, at 202 (although Bowett observed that, in Roman law, 'the interest was confined to those cases where the "protector" had rights of dominion over the persons he sought to protect in self-defence'). See, also, Kunz, *supra* n.9, at 875.

[71] Bowett, *supra* n.9, at 203 (which Bowett received with some scepticism, 'for the existence of such duties in international law is highly questionable'). *See*, also, *supra* n.34.

[72] *Nicaragua Case*, *supra* n.20, at 545–546. In describing the 'self', Judge Jennings entered the following annotation: 'It may be objected that the very term "self-defence" is a common law notion, and that, for instance, the French version is for once, merely unhelpful; it does no more than beg the question of what is "légitime".' *Ibid.*, at 545.

[73] *Ibid. See*, also, the discussion of Kunz, *supra* n.9, at 874. Article 5(f) of the Charter of the Organization of American States – also known as the Bogota Pact of May 1948 – provides that '[a]n act of aggression against one American State is an act of aggression against all other American States'. As amended by the Protocols of Buenos Aires (27 February 1967), Cartagena de Indias (5 December 1985), Washington (14 December 1992) and Managua (10 June 1993), this stipulation now appears as Article 3(h) of the Charter.

Atlantic Treaty Organization (hereinafter 'NATO'), where parties agreed in Article 5 of the Washington Treaty of April 1949:

> that an armed attack against one or more of them in Europe or North America shall be considered an attack against them all and consequently they agree that, if such an armed attack occurs, each of them, in exercise of the right of individual or collective self-defence recognized by Article 51 of the Charter of the United Nations, will assist the Party or Parties so attacked by taking forthwith, individually and in concert with other Parties, such actions as it deems necessary, including the use of armed force, to restore and maintain the security of the North Atlantic area.[74]

This provision has the character more of an *obligation* of collective self-defence,[75] although it happens to be cast in the language of a soft obligation ('such action as [each member of NATO] deems necessary') – one which would then presumably connect to the *right* to take action in collective self-defence as is deemed appropriate by each of the treaty partners to that organization.[76]

---

[74] Another arrangement in this very mould is Article 4 of the Treaty of Friendship, Cooperation and Mutual Assistance Between the People's Republic of Albania, the People's Republic of Bulgaria, the Hungarian People's Republic, the German Democratic Republic, the Polish People's Republic, the Rumanian People's Republic, the Union of Soviet Socialist Republics and the Czechoslovak Republic (the 'Warsaw Pact') of May 1955:

> In the event of armed attack in Europe on one or more of the Parties to the Treaty by any state or group of states, each of the Parties to the Treaty, in the exercise of its right to individual or collective self-defence in accordance with Article 51 of the Charter of the United Nations Organization, shall immediately, either individually or in agreement with other Parties to the Treaty, come to the assistance of the state or states attacked with all such means as it deems necessary, including armed force. The Parties to the Treaty shall immediately consult concerning the necessary measures to be taken by them jointly in order to restore and maintain international peace and security.
> Measures taken on the basis of this Article shall be reported to the Security Council in conformity with the provisions of the Charter of the United Nations Organization. These measures shall be discontinued immediately the Security Council adopts the necessary measures to restore and maintain international peace and security.

[75] Kunz, *supra* n.9, at 875.

[76] It is useful to set these earlier examples against the terms of Article IV of the South East Asia Collective Defence Treaty of September 1954:

> 1. Each party recognizes that aggression by means of armed attack in the treaty area against any of the parties or against any state or territory which the parties by unanimous agreement may hereafter designate, would endanger its own peace and safety, and agrees that it will in that event act to meet the common danger in accordance with its constitutional processes. Measures taken under this paragraph shall be immediately reported to the Security Council of the United Nations.
> 2. If, in the opinion of any of the parties, the inviolability or the integrity of the territory or the sovereignty or political independence of any party in the treaty area or of any other state or territory to which the provisions of Paragraph I of this Article from time to time apply is threatened in any way other than by armed attack or is affected or threatened by any fact or situation which might endanger the peace of the area, the parties shall consult immediately in order to agree on the measures which would be taken for the common defence.

C. The Regulation of Collective Self-defence

At the heart of Judge Jennings' conceptualization of the right of collective self-defence was his concern that, if it were at all otherwise, the right would very much be 'open to abuse',[77] but, though the full Court would share this concern of their much-respected colleague, it departed from his view on the precise nature of the right and on how international law should approach the matter of its regulation. The Court offered what Judge Jennings went on to describe as 'a somewhat formalistic view of the conditions for the exercise of collective self-defence'[78] which, as far as the Court was concerned, would operate as mechanisms that would check such possibilities for abuse. These may be identified as follows:

First, that, as with the right of individual self-defence, the state concerned must have been the victim of an armed attack, and that '[r]eliance on collective self-defence of course does not remove the need for this'.[79] In other words, the occurrence of an armed attack as opposed to other forms of force is central to any permissible exercise of the right of collective self-defence under international law; it is in this context that the Court later ventured that an armed attack constitutes 'the condition *sine qua non* required for the exercise of the right of collective self-defence'.[80]

Secondly, that a declaration of an armed attack must be issued by the state that is the victim of an armed attack: 'it is to be expected,' said the Court, 'that the State for whose benefit this right [of collective self-defence] is used will have declared itself to be the victim of an armed attack.'[81] Later on in its ruling, the Court maintained that 'it is evident that it is the victim State, being the most directly aware of that fact [that an armed attack has occurred], which is likely to draw general attention to its plight.'[82]

Thirdly and finally, that an actual request for collective self-defence must be made by the victim state to the states purporting to act in collective self-defence: 'there is no rule,' concluded the Court, 'permitting the exercise of collective self-defence in the absence of a request by the State which regards itself as the victim of an armed

---

3. It is understood that no action on the territory of any state designated by unanimous agreement under Paragraph I of this Article or on any territory so designated shall be taken except at the invitation or with the consent of the government concerned.

To similar effect, consider Article IV of the Security Treaty between Australia, New Zealand and the United States of America (hereinafter 'ANZUS') of September 1951. Consider, further, Article 6 of the Pact of the League of Arab States of March 1945 (which entitles a Member State of the League which becomes the victim of aggression or threat of aggression to 'request an immediate meeting' of the Council of the League; it is the Council that 'shall determine the necessary measures to repel this aggression', with its decision to be taken unanimously – but 'if the aggression is committed by a Member State [of the League] the vote of that State will not be counted in determining unanimity'). *Supra* n.12.

[77] *Nicaragua Case, supra* n.20, at 545.
[78] *Ibid.*, at 544.
[79] *Ibid.*, at 103 (para. 195).
[80] Not in existence on the facts before it in that case: *ibid.*, at 122 (para. 237). Consider, however, the conventional approaches discussed at *supra* n.76.
[81] *Ibid.*, at 104 (para. 195).
[82] *Ibid.*, at 120 (para. 232). The Court drew attention to this fact when it examined the behaviour of Honduras and Costa Rica. See *ibid.*, at 119–120 (para. 231).

attack,'[83] or, as the Court then immediately put it, 'the requirement of a request by the State which is the victim of the alleged attack is additional to the requirement that such a State should have declared itself to have been attacked.'[84] The Court later said that it was 'evident' that 'if the victim State wishes another State to come to its help in the exercise of the right of self-defence, it will normally make an express request to that effect' – and that, in consequence, the Court was:

> entitled to take account, in judging the asserted justification of the exercise of collective self-defence by the United States, of the actual conduct of El Salvador, Honduras and Costa Rica at the relevant time, as indicative of a belief by the State in question that it was the victim of an armed attack by Nicaragua, and of the making of a request by the victim State to the United States for help in the exercise of collective self-defence.[85]

In the application of these latter two requirements – the issuance of a declaration of an armed attack and the request for assistance in terms of collective self-defence by the victim state – it is instructive to note that the Court considered the timing of their occurrence to be of some relevance:

> while no strict legal conclusion may be drawn from the date of El Salvador's announcement that it was the victim of an armed attack, and the date of its official request addressed to the United States concerning the exercise of collective self-defence, those dates have a significance as evidence of El Salvador's view of the situation. The declaration and the request of El Salvador, made publicly for the first time in August 1984, do not support the contention that in 1981 there was an armed attack capable of serving as a legal foundation for United States activities which began in the second half of that year. The States concerned [i.e. El Salvador, Costa Rica and Honduras] did not behave as though there were an armed attack at the time when the activities attributed by the United States to Nicaragua, without actually constituting such an attack, were nevertheless the most accentuated; they did so behave only at a time when these facts fell furthest short of what would be required for the Court to take the view that an armed attack existed on the part of Nicaragua against El Salvador.[86]

The ultimate approach taken by the Court in its jurisprudence to the matter of the regulation of the right of collective self-defence might be thought to inject an unrealistic and undesirable bureaucracy into the law at a time when compliance with such technicalities is not likely to register high on the list of priorities of the victim state of an armed attack or on those states seeking to intervene on its behalf.[87] The appeal of such legal niceties might well not shine through the raw realities or emergencies of the application of force and the need for counter-force. Be this as it

---

[83] *Ibid.*, at 105 (para. 199).
[84] *Ibid.* A statement to the same effect – recalling this aspect of the *Nicaragua* judgment – is made in the *Oil Platforms Case*: the right of collective self-defence 'would have required the existence of a request made to the United States "by the State which regards itself as the victim of an armed attack"': *supra* n.21, at 186 (para. 51).
[85] *Nicaragua Case*, *supra* n.20, at 120 (para. 232). And *ibid.*, at 120 (para. 234).
[86] *Ibid.*, at 122 (para. 236).
[87] The Court repeated the availability of the right of collective self-defence in the event of an invitation for assistance by the victim state in *Case Concerning Armed Activities in the Territory of the Congo*, *supra* n.22, at 218 (para. 128).

may, the obligations as recalled and outlined here were no doubt indicators that the Court found useful in testing the veracity of claims made before it by states,[88] and, in the main, states do not seem to have found these procedures to be either onerous or inconvenient to their actions:[89] this can be maintained for the period both *before* the Court's judgment[90] as well as afterwards, where Kuwait was quick off the mark to announce to the world in August 1990 that 'Iraqi forces [have] crossed Kuwait's internationally recognized boundaries, penetrated Kuwait's territory and reached its populated area';[91] it followed this statement by informing the Security Council that – in the name of individual and collective self-defence – it had requested some states 'to take such military or other steps as are necessary to ensure the effective and prompt implementation' of the economic sanctions that had been adopted by the Security Council.[92]

4. THE POSSIBILITIES FOR ANTICIPATORY SELF-DEFENCE

A. Introduction

Two crucial questions arise from the Court's preoccupation with the concept of an armed attack in its jurisprudence in the *Nicaragua Case* and in the *Oil Platforms Case*. The first of these questions concerns whether the right of self-defence is permissible in the instance of an imminent (rather than an actual) armed attack – whether, that is, it admits of a right of anticipatory self-defence, or whether Article 51 of the Charter should be read so as to state that the right of self-defence exists *if and only if an armed attack occurs*.[93] The second pertains to the meaning of an armed attack for the purposes

---

[88] Such as the timing of the declaration of an armed attack and the request for assistance issued by El Salvador in August 1984 as *per supra* n.86.

[89] Note that the Court nowhere specified the *form* that this request or declaration must take.

[90] Where some evidence exists of these procedures in action: the United States conceived of its action of collective self-defence in respect of South Vietnam as a response to *requests* from the Government in Saigon: L.C. Meeker, 'The Legality of United States Participation in the Defense of Viet-Nam', (1966) 54 *Dept. St. Bull.* 474.

[91] See UN Doc. S/PV. 2932 (2 August 1990), at 6 (the term 'armed attack' was not in fact used by Kuwait; that of 'invasion' repeatedly so).

[92] UN Doc. S/21498 (13 August 1990).

[93] As formulated by Judge Stephen M. Schwebel in his dissenting opinion in the *Nicaragua Case*: *supra* n.20, at 347 (para. 173). Judge Schwebel recognized the 'controversial' character of this question (*ibid.*, at 348 (para. 173)), but he cited the position of Sir Humphrey Waldock as the most convincing:

It would be a misreading of the whole intention of Article 51 to interpret it by mere implication as forbidding forcible self-defence in resistance to an illegal use of force not constituting an 'armed attack'. Thus, it would, in my view, be no breach of the Charter if Denmark or Sweden used armed force to prevent the illegal arrest of one of their fishing vessels on the high seas in the Baltic. The judgment in the *Corfu Channel Case* is entirely consistent with this view.

See C.H.M. Waldock, 'The Regulation of the Use of Force by Individual States in International Law', (1952–II) *Hague Recueil*, at 451, at 496–497. It would appear that the example provided

of calculating the exact perimeters of the right of self-defence as understood by the Charter.[94] The latter of these questions forms the basis of the analysis of the next section of this chapter; for now, we shall turn to the possibilities that exist for any right of *anticipatory* self-defence in international law.

B. The Concept of Anticipatory Self-defence

In the *Nicaragua Case*, the Court specifically reserved its judgment on the question of the lawfulness of anticipatory self-defence in customary international law, since, as it said, 'reliance is placed by the Parties only on the right of self-defence in the case of an armed attack which has already occurred, and the issue of the lawfulness of a response to the imminent threat of armed attack has not been raised [so that] the Court expresses no view on that issue'.[95] This seems to be a rather definitive statement of the Court sequestering the 'issue' (as the Court called it) of anticipatory self-defence and setting it aside for some future jurisprudential intervention of the Court, although the manner in which the Court framed its appreciation of an armed attack in the remainder of its judgment – where, as we have seen, the Court depicted an armed attack as a legal requirement for the right of (collective) self-defence,[96] and went on to refer to it as the 'condition *sine qua non* required for the exercise of the right of collective self-defence'[97] – could well be taken to suggest the foreclosure of any possibility for the right of anticipatory self-defence to be held permissible in international law: the Court spoke in such forthright terms and used such direct language in setting down the *need* for an armed attack in its conceptualization of the right of self-defence that its jurisprudence might well be thought to rule out once and for all the possibilities for any right of anticipatory self-defence in international law.

It would seem to stretch the reality of this jurisprudence to say that the Court ruled out all such possibilities, for both present and future purposes, of a right of anticipatory self-defence, and that it did so by implication. What the Court did seem to do, and to do in the most subtle of manners, was to frame the parameters of the debate on

---

by Waldock in this excerpted passage from his lectures at the Hague Academy of International Law – and cited with approval by Judge Schwebel in the *Nicaragua Case* – goes more to the point of an illegal use of force not amounting to an armed attack, rather than to an imminent threat of an armed attack.

[94] And the consequences of a use of force falling short of an armed attack, on which consider *infra* n.225.

[95] *Nicaragua Case*, *supra* n.20, at 103 (para. 194). Also, *ibid.*, at 27–28 (para. 35).

[96] As the Court appeared to do at *supra* n.20, at 119 (para. 229): 'For the Court to conclude that the United States was lawfully exercising its right of collective self-defence, it must find that Nicaragua engaged in an armed attack against El Salvador, Honduras or Costa Rica.' See, also, its statement at *ibid.*, 36 (para. 51): 'If the Court found that no armed attack had occurred [against El Salvador], then not only would action by the United States in purported exercise of the right of collective self-defence prove to be unjustified, but so also would action which El Salvador might take or might have taken on the asserted ground of individual self-defence.'

[97] *Ibid.*, at 122 (para. 237).

'anticipatory self-defence' by making reference in its jurisprudence to armed action taken against *the imminent threat of an armed attack*.[98] This does suggest that, in the Court's view, should the right of anticipatory self-defence exist at all in international law, it would do so within the limited but identifiable confines of the imminent threat of an armed attack – a threshold that is somehow reminiscent of the approach of the *Caroline* correspondence in presenting the principle of necessity – but which here, quite clearly, is anchored to the concept of an armed attack. If this interpretation is correct, it will have involved the Court in discriminating between certain threats of force in international law and all others since not all 'threats of force' as that term is used in Article 2(4) of the Charter presumably constitute an 'imminent threat of armed attack' (in the words of the Court).[99] Indeed, the concept of the threat of force was not in actual fact far from the mind of the Court in the *Nicaragua Case*,[100] and the idea of ranking threats of force according to their level of seriousness would have done for this aspect of the prohibition contained in Article 2(4) of the Charter what the Court did for *uses* of force when it distinguished, again in the *Nicaragua Case*, 'the most grave forms of the use of force (those constituting an armed attack) from other less grave forms'.[101]

C. Historical and Contemporary Practices

It remains the case that the classic authority for the right of self-defence in international law – namely the *Caroline* correspondence – resulted from an anticipatory action taken

---

[98] *Supra* n.25.

[99] Consider the assessment of R. Sadurska, 'Threats of Force', (1988) 82 *AJIL* 239 and, more recently on this topic, N. Stürchler, *The Threat of Force in International Law* (Cambridge: Cambridge University Press, 2007). See, also, the chapter by Nicholas Tsagourias (chapter 3) in this volume.

[100] Indeed, Nicaragua had 'made some suggestion' to the Court that the military manoeuvres the United States had undertaken 'near the Nicaraguan borders' had amounted to a threat of force under international law – and an unlawful one at that (*Nicaragua Case, supra* n.20, at 118 (para. 227)). The Court, however, was 'not satisfied that the manoeuvres complained of, in the circumstances in which they were held, constituted on the part of the United States a breach, as against Nicaragua, of the principle forbidding recourse to the threat or use of force' (*ibid.*). For consideration of threats of force as lawful measures of self-defence see J.A. Green and F. Grimal, 'The Threat of Force as An Action in Self-Defense in International Law', (2011) 44 *Vanderbilt JTL* 285, and, also, J. Suri, 'Bomb North Korea, Before It's Too Late', *NY Times*, 12 April 2013. The quarantine of Cuba by the United States in October and November 1962 might well have matured into an instance of a threat of force undertaken in self-defence *were it not for the fact that the United States entered a justification on other grounds for its actual response*: A. Chayes, *The Cuban Missile Crisis: International Crisis and the Role of Law* (Oxford: Oxford University Press, 1974), at 62–64. See, however, W.T. Mallison Jr., 'Limited Naval Blockade or Quarantine Interdiction: National or Collective Defense Claims Valid under International Law', (1962) 31 *Geo. W. Law Rev.* 335.

[101] *Nicaragua Case, supra* n.20, at 101 (para. 191): see *infra* n.132.

by Great Britain in December 1837,[102] an action that was not regarded as impermissible *ab initio* by either the enactment or the content of the principles of necessity and proportionality: if anything, the idea behind those principles, as set forth by Secretary Webster in April 1841,[103] was to afford Great Britain with an opportunity to argue as well as adduce evidence for the perceived 'necessity' of self-defence – that is, to demonstrate that it was faced with a threat that was, in Secretary Webster's words, 'instant, overwhelming, leaving no choice of means, and no moment for deliberation'.[104] And it is these principles which, at their root, seemed to accommodate the possibilities for anticipatory self-defence given the right factual circumstances that Secretary Webster resolved, in a letter of August 1842, both governments had committed to '[u]nderstanding these principles alike, the difference between the two Governments is only whether the facts in the case of the *Caroline* make out a case of such necessity for the purposes of self-defence'.[105] It transpires, then, that 'within the

---

[102] Against any future attack, as per the letter of Lord Ashburton of July 1842 (*infra* n.186) – but it is worthwhile reading this against the factual background he outlined in the same letter: 'the persons criminally concerned in [some tumultuous proceedings in Upper Canada] took refuge in the neighbouring state of New York, and with a very large addition to their numbers openly collected, *invaded the Canadian territory taking possession of Navy Island*' (emphasis added). This 'invasion' occurred on 16 December 1837, according to Lord Ashburton, and:

a gradual accession of numbers and of military ammunition continued openly, and though under the sanction of no public authority, at least with no public hindrance until the 29th of the same month, when several hundred men were collected, and twelve pieces of ordnance, which could only have been procured from some public store or arsenal, were actually mounted on Navy Island and were used to fire within easy range upon the unoffending inhabitants of the opposite shore. Remonstrances, wholly ineffectual were made; so ineffectual indeed that a Militia regiment, stationed on the neighbouring American island, looked on without any attempt at interference, while shots were fired from the American island itself. ... This force, formed of all the reckless and mischievous people of the border, formidable from their numbers and from their armament, had in their pay and as part of their establishment this steamboat *Caroline*, the important means and instrument by which numbers and arms were hourly increasing. I might safely put it to any candid man acquainted with the existing state of things, to say whether the military commander in Canada had the remotest reason on the 29th of December to expect to be relieved from this state of suffering by the protective intervention of any American authority. How long could a Government, having the paramount duty of protecting its own people be reasonably expected to wait for what they had then no reason to expect? What would have been the conduct of American officers – what has been their conduct under circumstances much less aggravated? I would appeal to you, Sir, to say whether the facts which you say would alone justify this act, *viz*: 'a necessity of self defence, instant, overwhelming, leaving no choice of means and no moment for deliberation', were not applicable to this case in as high a degree as they ever were to any case of a similar description in the history of nations.

See Avalon Project (Documents in Law, History and Diplomacy), *supra* n.42.

[103] *Supra* n.43.

[104] *Ibid*. According to Rostow, 'the *Caroline* standard' was much more specific than allowing for the right of self-defence in the event of 'a prior breach of international law of a forceful character', where 'a responsive use of force under [A]rticle 51 must aim to cure the breach that gave rise to the exercise of the right of self-defense'. *Supra* n.32, at 453.

[105] See Manning, *supra* n.42, at 188 (Doc. No. 1298).

terms of the *Caroline* [correspondence], there has always been recognized an "anticipatory" right of self-defence' in international law,[106] even though for some the bar that was set was far too high.[107]

Well over a century later, in June 1981, it was these self-same principles that were invoked by Israel to underpin its claim for exercising its right of self-defence against Iraq, after it had used force to destroy a nuclear reactor under construction at Osiraq, some 17 kilometres southeast of Baghdad. Israel argued that '[a] threat of nuclear obliteration' was being developed against it by Iraq,[108] and that it 'was exercising its inherent right of self-defence as understood in general international law and as preserved in Article 51 of the [United Nations] Charter'.[109] Importantly, while the Security Council issued a strong condemnation of Israel's action for being 'in clear violation of the Charter of the United Nations and the norms of international conduct' in Resolution 487 (1981),[110] it is useful to consider how states differed in challenging the lawfulness of force on that occasion: not all adopted the line that the right of anticipatory self-defence had not survived the advent of the Charter and that it therefore no longer continued to be a lawful proposition;[111] the more moderate and in many ways the more persuasive view was that the right of anticipatory self-defence very much continued to exist within the framework of the Charter of the United Nations but that Israel had not satisfactorily discharged the argumentative or the evidential burden of proving *imminence* in its invocation of this right.[112]

---

[106] Higgins, *supra* n.13, at 199. See, also, N.D. White, *Democracy Goes to War: British Military Deployments under International Law* (Oxford: Oxford University Press, 2009), at 41.

[107] For McDougal and Feliciano, the *Caroline* principles were 'cast in language so abstractly restrictive as almost, if read literally, to impose paralysis'. See M.S. McDougal and F.P. Feliciano, *Law and Minimum World Public Order: The Legal Regulation of International Coercion* (New Haven and London: Yale University Press, 1961), at 217. See, further, the discussion of M.E. O'Connell, 'The Myth of Pre-emptive Self-Defense', American Society of International Law Task Force on Terrorism (August 2002).

[108] UN Doc S/PV. 2280 (12 June 1981), at 38.

[109] *Ibid.*, at 37. Importantly, in its presentation of the 'legalities' of its position, Israel recited the observation of D.W. Bowett from *Self-Defence in International Law* (Manchester: Manchester University Press, 1958): 'No state can be expected to await an initial attack, which in the present state of armaments, may well destroy the state's capacity for further resistance and so jeopardize its very existence.' *Supra* n.9, at 191–92. See, further, Government of Israel, *The Iraqi Nuclear Threat: Why Israel Had to Act* (Jerusalem: Government of Israel, 1981), and, also, N.J. Kaplan, 'The Attack on Osirak: Delimitation of Self-Defense under International Law', (1982) 4 *NY Law Sch. JICL* 131.

[110] First operative paragraph – a resolution in which the Security Council also called upon Israel 'to refrain in the future from any such acts or threats thereof' (second operative paragraph).

[111] Algeria exemplified this approach with its statement that '[t]he Israeli action has the monstrous characteristic of introducing into international relations new and frightening forms of action based on aggression, baptized "preventive" in order to make the unacceptable acceptable.' UN Doc. S/PV.2280 (12 June 1981), at 78–80. Consider, too, India's position that '[t]o cite Article 51 of the Charter in support of this indefensible action is a travesty of the very provisions of the Charter': UN Doc. S/PV.2281 (13 June 1981), at 17.

[112] As represented by the United Kingdom before the Security Council: '[t]here was no instant or overwhelming necessity of self-defence'. See UN Doc. S/PV.2288 (19 June 1981), at 42. See, further, J. Gardam, *Necessity, Proportionality and the Use of Force by States*

D. Imminence and the Proposed Right of Pre-emptive Self-defence

It is this criterion of imminence that proved problematic for the Bush Administration and its intentions after the tragic events in the United States on 11 September 2001, and, after a considerable commitment to developing the rhetoric of a right of pre-emptive (as opposed to anticipatory) self-defence,[113] the United States published its National Security Strategy on 17 September 2002, in which it posited:

> For centuries, international law recognized that nations need not suffer an attack before they can lawfully take action to defend themselves against forces that present an imminent danger of attack. Legal scholars and international jurists often conditioned the legitimacy of pre-emption on the existence of an imminent threat – most often a visible mobilization of armies, navies, and air forces preparing to attack. We must adapt the concept of imminent threat to the capabilities and objectives of today's adversaries. Rogue states and terrorists do not seek to attack us using conventional means. They know such attacks would fail. Instead they rely on acts of terror and, potentially, the use of weapons of mass destruction – weapons that can be easily concealed, delivered covertly, and used without warning. ... The United States has long maintained the option of preemptive actions to counter a sufficient threat to

---

(Cambridge: Cambridge University Press, 2006), at 154, and the discussion of the Security Council deliberations in A.C. and R.J. Beck, *International Law and the Use of Force* (London and New York: Routledge, 1993), at 78–79 (reporting on the position of Ambassador Koroma for Sierra Leone, that 'the plea of self-defence is untenable where no armed attack has taken place or is imminent'). However, consider the position of W. Michael Reisman – that Israel's action of June 1981 'was widely condemned as a violation of international law' but that, '[s]carcely a decade later, after the legal and aggressive character of the regime in Baghdad was exposed, opinions about the preemptive action of 1981 underwent revision in many quarters, suggesting that there may be unarticulated, but operative, criteria for assessing the lawfulness of preemptive actions': 'Assessing Claims to Revise the Laws of War', (2003) 97 *AJIL* 82, at 88. That said, Israel's strike on an alleged nuclear facility at Al-Kibar in September 2007 did not elicit anywhere near the same level of criticism – and nor did it find Syria vocalized in response: J. Borger, 'Israeli Airstrike Hit Military Site, Syria Confirms', *The Guardian*, 2 October 2007, at 18. See, further, A. Garwood-Gowers, 'Israel's Airstrike on Syria's Al-Kibar Facility: A Test Case for the Doctrine of Pre-emptive Self-Defence', (2011) 16 *JCSL* 263.

[113] As represented by President George W. Bush's State of the Union Address of January 2003, in which he said:

> Some have said we must not act until the threat is imminent. Since when have terrorists and tyrants announced their intentions, politely putting us on notice before they strike? If this threat is permitted to fully and suddenly emerge, all actions, all words, and all recriminations could come too late. Trusting in the sanity and restraint of Saddam Hussein is not a strategy, and it is not an option.

President Bush's public speeches very much seem to cohere with the 'One Percent Doctrine' outlined by Vice President Dick Cheney and recounted in R. Suskind, *The One Percent Doctrine: Deep Inside America's Pursuit of Its Enemies* (New York: Simon & Schuster, 2006), at 62 (according to which, in November 2001, Vice President Cheney concluded: 'If there's a one percent chance that Pakistani scientists are helping al Qaeda build or develop a nuclear weapon, we have to treat it as a certainty in terms of response. ... It's not about our analysis, or finding a preponderance of evidence. It's about our response.') See, further, M.W. Boyle, *Striking First: Preemption and Prevention in International Conflict* (Princeton, NJ: Princeton University Press, 2008) and 'Personality, Ideology and Bush's Terror Wars', *N.Y. Times*, 20 June 2006.

our national security. The greater the threat, the greater the risk of inaction – and the more compelling the case for taking anticipatory action to defend ourselves, even if uncertainty remains as to the time and place of the enemy's attack. To forestall or prevent such hostile acts by our adversaries, the United States will, if necessary, act preemptively.[114]

This statement is important to dissect because, at least at the beginning of the excerpted passage, there appears to be a clear sense of distinguishing between *lex lata* and *lex desiderata*: that there is a certain type of normative practice amongst states that is in existence and readily identifiable – and which pertains to the right of self-defence against 'an imminent danger of attack' – but which is separate to the law as it ought to now be or the *lex desiderata* (at least in the view of the Bush Administration). Hence the need for *change* in the law, or, as it is sublimely put in the above passage, the need to *adapt* the concept of imminent threat to the capabilities and objectives of today's adversaries. However, quickly after these positions are made, the prescriptions of *lex lata* and *lex desiderata* somehow meld together and become indistinguishable from one another,[115] since we learn that, at least as far as the United States is now concerned, it has 'long maintained the option of preemptive actions to counter a sufficient threat to our national security'.[116] Coupled with this factor is the oscillation of language as between 'preemptive actions' and the 'taking [of] anticipatory action', when it is clear from the doctrine as well as the literature that the concept of imminence has affixed to the right of *anticipatory* self-defence.[117] Yet, here, 'anticipatory action' is taken to include situations where 'uncertainty remains as to the time and place of the enemy's attack',[118] so that it is on the disingenuous side to claim that the concept of imminence must (or should) be *adapted*: what is evidently intended by this approach ('uncertainty remains as to the time and place of the enemy's attack') is that there be *no* need whatsoever for imminence for the operation of the new right of pre-emptive self-defence that is being proclaimed in the 2002 National Security Strategy – that, for these purposes, the concept of imminence is to be effectively removed or banished – even though (we can presume) it would still obtain for the regulation of the right of *anticipatory* self-defence in international law.[119]

---

[114] See, *The National Security Strategy of the United States* (Washington, DC: Office of the White House, 2002), at 15. *See,* further, C. Gray, 'The US *National Security Strategy* and the New "Bush Doctrine" on Preemptive Self-Defence', (2002) 1 *Chinese JIL* 437.

[115] The document has been interpreted to assert 'an evolving right under international law for the United States to use military force pre-emptively against the threat posed by "rogue States" possessing weapons of mass destruction': S.D. Murphy, 'Contemporary Practice of the United States', (2003) 97 *AJIL* 179, at 203.

[116] *Supra* n.114. For the possibilities of this history, consider A.D. Sofaer, 'On the Necessity of Pre-emption', (2003) 14 *EJIL* 209, at 210.

[117] See, generally, S.D. Murphy, 'The Doctrine of Pre-emptive Self-Defense', (2005) 50 *Villanova LR* 699.

[118] And where pre-emptive action (in the final sentence of this excerpt) is discussed in the same breath as 'anticipatory action'.

[119] See C. Greenwood, 'International Law and the Pre-emptive Use of Force: Afghanistan, Al-Qaida and Iraq', (2003) 4 *San Diego JIL* 7. In its National Security Strategy of March 2006, the Bush Administration announced that '[t]he place of pre-emption in our national security strategy remains the same. We will always proceed deliberately, weighing the consequences of

This suggestion by the United States was most critically received by states as a whole – including by the closest of allies of the United States. Prime Minister Tony Blair of the United Kingdom, for instance, advised the Liaison Committee of the House of Commons in January 2003 that the United Kingdom had chosen 'a particular way' of dealing with Iraq given its recalcitrance on the issue of weapons inspection, and that:

> we did that *precisely because we recognize [that] this was not a situation where we could say there is an immediate threat to Britain of a nuclear strike from Iraq. I have never made that case. I have never said that is the case.*[120]

What is of significant importance here is that the British Prime Minister is steering clear of any and all references to self-defence – whether in its individual or collective form – as the legal justification for Operation Iraqi Freedom (which ensued in March 2003), and he immediately followed this statement by informing the Liaison Committee that:

> there is an issue about weapons of mass destruction, the Iraqis have to disarm, and the best way of doing that is through the United Nations process, and we have given that process the time to work. ... if you end up in a situation where there is a fresh UN Resolution authorizing

---

our actions. The reasons for our actions will be clear, the force measured and the cause just.' See *National Security Strategy of the United States of America* (Washington, DC: Office of the White House, 2006), at 23. The National Security Strategy of May 2010, issued by the Obama Administration, struck an altogether different tone:

> The United States must reserve the right to act unilaterally if necessary to defend our nation and our interests, yet we will also seek to adhere to standards that govern the use of force. Doing so strengthens those who act in line with international standards, while isolating and weakening those who do not. We will also outline a clear mandate and specific objectives and thoroughly consider the consequences – intended and unintended – of our actions.

See *National Security Strategy* (Washington, DC: Office of the White House, 2010), at 22 (where the notion of pre-emptive self-defence was not even mentioned). See, further, C. Henderson, 'The 2010 United States National Security Strategy and the Obama Doctrine of "Necessary Force"', (2010) 15 *JCSL* 403.

[120] United Kingdom Parliament: Liaison Committee of the House of Commons (21 January 2003), Question 58 of the Examination of Witness, available at www.publications.parliament.uk/pa/cm200203/cmselect/cmliaisn/334-i/3012104.htm (emphasis added). It is worth reciting in this respect the third paragraph of the advice provided by the United Kingdom's Attorney-General Goldsmith to Prime Minister Blair on 7 March 2003:

> Force may be used in self-defence if there is an actual or imminent threat of an armed attack ... The concept of what is imminent may depend on the circumstances. Different considerations may apply, for example, where the risk is of attack from terrorists sponsored or harboured by a particular State, or where there is a threat of an attack by nuclear weapons. *However, in my opinion there must be some degree of imminence*. I am aware that the USA has been arguing for recognition of a broad doctrine of a right to use force to pre-empt danger in the future. If this means more than a right to respond proportionately to an imminent attack (and I understand that the doctrine is intended to carry that connotation) *this is not a doctrine which, in my opinion, exists or is recognized in international law*.

The advice is reproduced at www.ico.gov.uk/upload/documents/library/freedom_of_information/notices/annex_a_-_attorney_general's_advice_070303.pdf (emphases added).

action, surely that must be the circumstances in which it is right for the international community to act?[121]

Prime Minister Blair was thus placing the issue of justification in the domain of the collective security system of the Charter of the United Nations, and it is rather telling that, when hostilities commenced against Iraq in March 2003, the United States informed the Security Council that '[t]he actions being taken are authorized under existing [Security] Council resolutions, including its resolutions 678 (1990) and 687 (1991).'[122] According to the United Kingdom, therefore, the right of self-defence was not therefore being engaged.

This seemed to put to rest – at least for the time being – the proposition of any right of pre-emptive self-defence, or self-defence action taken in the *absence* of any condition of imminence. Subsequently the United Nations Secretary-General's High-Level Panel on Threats, Challenges and Change concluded in December 2004 that 'a threatened State, according to long established international law, can take military action as long as the threatened attack is *imminent*, no other means would deflect it and the action is proportionate'.[123] This eventuality was set apart from 'where the threat in question is not imminent but still claimed to be real',[124] which the Panel addressed in terminologies different from those used in this section:

> 189. Can a State, without going to the Security Council, claim in these circumstances the right to act, in anticipatory self-defence, not just pre-emptively (against an imminent or proximate threat) but preventively (against a non-imminent or non-proximate one)? Those who say 'yes' argue that the potential harm from some threats (e.g., terrorists armed with a nuclear weapon) is so great that one simply cannot risk waiting until they become imminent, and that less harm may be done (e.g., avoiding a nuclear exchange or radioactive fallout from a reactor destruction by acting earlier).
>
> 190. The short answer is that if there are good arguments for preventive military action, with good evidence to support them, they should be put to the Security Council, which can

---

[121] *Ibid.*

[122] UN Doc. S/351 (21 March 2003). See, further, D. Kritsiotis, 'Arguments of Mass Confusion', (2004) 15 *EJIL* 233.

[123] Report of the Secretary-General's High-Level Panel on Threats, Challenges and Change, *A More Secure World: Our Shared Responsibility*, UN Doc. A/59/565 (2 December 2004), at 54 (para. 188). The Panel was chaired by Anand Panyarachun, former Prime Minister of Thailand, and was asked by United Nations Secretary-General Kofi A. Annan to 'assess current threats to international peace and security; to evaluate how our existing policies and institutions have done in addressing those threats; and to make recommendations for strengthening the United Nations so that it can provide collective security for all in the twenty-first century' following his speech to the General Assembly in September 2003: *ibid.*, at 1. The findings of the High-Level Panel are available at www.un.org.secureworld/. See, further, C. Gray, 'A Crisis of Legitimacy for the UN Collective Security System?', (2007) 56 *ICLQ* 157, at 160–164, and P. Hilpold, 'The Duty to Protect and the Reform of the United Nations – A Step in the Development of International Law?', (2006) 10 *Max Planck Yrbk. UN Law* 35, at 56–61.

[124] Report of the Secretary-General's High-Level Panel, *ibid.*, at 54 (para. 188): for example, the acquisition, with allegedly hostile intent, of nuclear weapons-making capability. This is certainly the position Israel has argued with respect to Iran and its development of a nuclear arsenal. See C. McGreal, 'Netanyahu Tells Obama: Israel Must Have Right to Remain "Master of Its Fate"', *The Guardian*, 5 March 2012.

authorize such an action if it chooses to. If it does not so choose, there will be, by definition, time to pursue other strategies, including persuasion, negotiation, deterrence and containment – and to visit again the military option.

191. For those impatient with such a response, the answer must be that, in a world full of perceived potential threats, the risk to the global order and the norm of non-intervention on which it continues to be based is simply too great for the legality of unilateral preventive action, as distinct from collectively endorsed action, to be accepted. Allowing one to so act is to allow all.

192. *We do not favour the rewriting or reinterpretation of Article 51.*[125]

The High-Level Panel's separate treatment of the permissibility of *anticipatory* and *pre-emptive* self-defence as those terms have been used and developed here has not been accepted in all quarters,[126] and, in his report *In Larger Freedom: Towards Development, Security and Human Rights for All* in March 2005, United Nations Secretary-General Kofi A. Annan took account of the fact that states have disagreed on whether they have a 'right' to use force for pre-emptive self-defence – but also as to whether they can take action against 'imminent threats'.[127] States have, it is true, disagreed on many propositions involving the application of force within the framework of the Charter, and Secretary-General Annan made great play in his report of the need for agreement on these high matters of state and security.[128] Nevertheless, he felt able to conclude – and to conclude with some conviction it must be said – that '[i]mminent threats are fully covered by Article 51' of the Charter,[129] where the tradition of accommodating a right of anticipatory self-defence within international law was recognized,[130] and it is a tradition that can be traced back at least as far as the terms of the *Caroline* correspondence.[131]

5. THE CONCEPT OF AN 'ARMED ATTACK'

We have already observed that, in its judgment in the *Nicaragua Case*, the International Court of Justice distinguished between 'the most grave forms of the use of force' – in

---

[125] Report of the Secretary-General's High-Level Panel, *supra* n.123, at 54–55 (emphasis in original). The importance of terminological clarification has been emphasized by, amongst others, Christopher Greenwood: *supra* n.119, at 9. The terms that have been adopted in this chapter follow the reception of the *Caroline* correspondence in the literature, and the advent of 'pre-emptive self-defence' in the language of President Bush. See, further, Sofaer, *supra* n.116.

[126] Gray notes how it 'controversially accepted anticipatory self-defence against an imminent attack', *supra* n.52, at 212. Consider further C. Gray, 'The Charter Limitations on the Use of Force: Theory and Practice', in V. Lowe, A. Roberts, J. Welsh and D. Zaum (eds), *United Nations Security Council and War: The Evolution of Thought and Practice Since 1945* (Oxford: Oxford University Press, 2008), 86, at 97.

[127] UN Doc. A/59/2005 (21 March 2005), at 33 (para. 122). Further details of this report are available from www.un.org/largerfreedom/.

[128] *Ibid.*, at 33 (para. 123).

[129] *Ibid.*, at 33 (para. 124). See, further, *supra* n.99 (and accompanying text).

[130] *Ibid.*

[131] *Supra* nn. 104–106 (and accompanying text).

other words, those amounting to an armed attack – and 'other less grave forms'.[132] The Court did so in order to delimit the significance of the right of self-defence as understood from the terms of the United Nations Charter, without prejudice to any position it might have held on the permissibility of the right of *anticipatory* self-defence under international law.[133] If the right of self-defence turns on the occurrence of an armed attack, then, as the Court went on to indicate in paragraph 195 of its judgment in the *Nicaragua Case*, an armed attack will turn on the facts of a given case. For the Court:

> There appears now to be general agreement on the nature of the acts which can be treated as constituting armed attacks. In particular, it may be considered to be agreed that an armed attack must be understood as including not merely action by regular armed forces across an international border, but also 'the sending by or on behalf of a State of armed bands, groups, irregulars or mercenaries, which carry out acts of armed force against another State of such gravity as to amount to' (*inter alia*) actual armed attack conducted by regular forces, 'or its substantial involvement therein'. This description, contained in Article 3, paragraph (g), of the Definition of Aggression annexed to General Assembly resolution 3314 (XXIX), may be taken to reflect customary international law. The Court sees no reason to deny that, in customary law, the prohibition of armed attacks may apply to the sending by a State of armed bands to the territory of another State, if such an operation, because of its scale and effects, would have been classified as an armed attack rather than as a mere frontier incident had it been carried out by regular armed forces. But the Court does not believe that the concept of 'armed attack' includes not only acts by armed bands where such acts occur on a significant scale but also assistance to rebels in the form of the provision of weapons or logistical or other support. Such assistance may be regarded as a threat or use of force, or amount to intervention in the internal or external affairs of other States.[134]

Three observations seem apposite in view of the definition of an armed attack set out by the Court in the above passage. The first is that the Court is here setting out a definition of the concept of armed attack *as it pertains in customary international law*: indeed, the Court twice makes reference to custom in this excerpt from its jurisprudence, but it also speaks of 'general agreement' – presumably the general agreement of states 'on the nature of the acts which can be treated as constituting armed attacks'[135] – so that what follows enjoins with the earlier remark of the Court that the definition of an armed attack 'is not provided [for] in the Charter, and is not part of treaty law'.[136] The definition of an armed attack as devised in custom is then provided, even though the Court nowhere in its reasoning identifies or makes explicit what these specific

---

[132] *Nicaragua Case*, *supra* n.20, at 101 (para. 191) – an approach that the Court dutifully followed in the *Oil Platforms Case*: *supra* n.21, at 186–187 (para. 51); see, also, *infra* n.161.
[133] *Supra* n.95.
[134] *Nicaragua Case*, *supra* n.20, at 103–104 (para. 195). See, also, T.D. Gill, 'The Law of Armed Attack in the Context of the *Nicaragua Case*', (1988) 1 *Hague YBIL* 30; N.M. Feder, 'Reading the U.N. Charter Connotatively: Toward A New Definition of An Armed Attack', (1987) 19 *NYUJILP* 395; and A.A. Yusuf, 'The Notion of "Armed Attack" in the *Nicaragua* Judgment and Its Influence on Subsequent Case Law', (2012) 25 *Leiden JIL* 461.
[135] *Supra* n.134.
[136] *Nicaragua Case*, *supra* n.20, at 94 (para. 176).

practices of states were or how any of them came to pass.[137] To be sure, the Court does have recourse to the Definition of Aggression annexed to General Assembly Resolution 3314 (XXIX) in its formulations, and this might well be regarded as consonant with the guarded attention that the Court had earlier paid to General Assembly resolutions.[138] However, one ought to proceed with considerable care down this route for it does need to be recalled that the General Assembly had set itself the task of defining the concept of aggression as it appeared in the Charter's arrangements for collective security and had not attempted to define the scope of an armed attack – even though there is sure to be some coincidence between both of these propositions.[139]

The second observation we should make concerns the actual *substance* of an armed attack as far as the Court was concerned – and the fact that this was not confined to 'action by regular armed forces across an international border'[140] but can include 'the sending by or on behalf of a State of armed bands, groups, irregulars or mercenaries, which carry out acts of armed force against another State of such gravity as to amount to' (*inter alia*) actual armed attack conducted by regular forces, 'or its substantial involvement therein'.[141] The latter formulation does seem to suggest that the Court introduced an unspecified threshold for the *quantum* of force required for an action of irregular armed forces (i.e. 'armed bands, groups, irregulars or mercenaries') for that to be quantified as an armed attack: the Court mentions the need for 'such gravity' of these acts, and proceeds to speak of 'acts by armed bands where such acts occur on a significant scale,'[142] terms which are not explicitly invoked for the actions of regular

---

[137] R. Higgins, *Problems and Process: International Law and How We Use It* (Oxford: Oxford University Press, 1994), at 250.

[138] Where it claimed that *opinio juris sive necessitatis*:

> may, though with all due caution, be deduced from, *inter alia*, the attitude of States towards certain General Assembly resolutions, and particularly resolution 2625 (XXV) ... The effect of consent to the text of such resolutions cannot be understood as merely that of a 'reiteration or elucidation' of the treaty commitment undertaken in the Charter. On the contrary, it may be understood as an acceptance of the validity of the rule or set of rules declared by the resolution by themselves ... It would therefore seem apparent that the attitude referred to expresses an *opinio juris* respecting such rule (or set of rules), to be thenceforth treated separately from the provisions, especially those of an institutional kind, to which it is subject on the treaty-law plane of the Charter.

Nicaragua Case, supra n.20, at 99–100 (para. 188).

[139] See Alexandrov, *supra* n.4, at 105–120. See, further, Higgins, *supra* n.13, at 178–180; S.M. Schwebel, 'Aggression, Intervention and Self-Defence in Modern International Law', (1972–II) 139 *Hague Recueil* 411 and V. Cassin, W. Debevoise, H. Kailes and T.W. Thompson, 'The Definition of Aggression', (1975) 16 *Harvard ILJ* 589.

[140] Of the order witnessed on 2 August 1990, when Iraq invaded Kuwait. See C. Greenwood, 'New World Order or Old? The Invasion of Kuwait and the Rule of Law', (1992) 55 *MLR* 153, at 164.

[141] The aspect adopted from General Assembly Resolution 3314 (XXIX) on the Definition of Aggression. Whereas both of these actions came within the fray of the concept of an armed attack, the same could not be said of 'assistance to rebels in the form of the provision of weapons or logistical or other support'. *Supra* n.134.

[142] To cohere, we can presume, with the Court's schemata of grave and less grave uses of force: *supra* nn.101 and 132. For further discussion, see Green, *supra* n.19, at 34–38.

armed forces as armed attacks. However, as one reads deeper into the analysis of the Court, it is clear that it has in mind an identical (although equally unspecified) threshold for the actions of regular armed forces, for it goes on to distinguish an 'actual'[143] armed attack from 'a mere frontier incident'[144] when conducted by regular armed forces. The former would meet the threshold of an armed attack;[145] evidently, in the view of the Court, the latter would not.[146]

The matter of the action of irregular armed forces arose again for consideration of the Court in the *Case Concerning Armed Activities* between the Democratic Republic of the Congo and Uganda, where Uganda claimed that it had exercised its right of self-defence in September 1998 against the Alliance des forces démocratiques pour la libération du Congo (hereinafter 'ADF') who were based in the Congo and who had carried out activities against Uganda from May 1998 onwards. According to Uganda, these developments had occurred with the support of both the Congo and the Sudan, but the Court found against this claim on the ground that '[t]he "armed attacks" to

---

[143] In so doing, the Court does draw a direct equation between aggression and armed attack because, *in toto*, Article 3(g) of the Definition of Aggression includes '[t]he sending by or on behalf of a State of armed bands, groups, irregulars or mercenaries, which carry out acts of armed force against another State of such gravity *as to amount to the acts listed above*, or its substantial involvement therein', that is the acts of aggression itemized in Article 3(a)–(f) of the definition (emphasis added).

[144] *Supra* n.134 – to cohere, again we can presume, with the Court's distinction between 'the most grave forms of the use of force' and 'other less grave forms'. See *supra* nn. 101 and 132. For an excellent assessment of frontier incidents, consider Gray, *supra* n.52, at 177–183. It has been contended that '[t]he assumption that "a mere frontier incident" can have no "scale and effects" is quite bothersome'. See Dinstein, *supra* n.44, at 210.

[145] And would appear to encompass the possibility of an 'accumulation of events', each of which is not able to cross the required threshold but can be interpreted cumulatively. On the relevant state practice and the (implied) jurisprudence of the Court, consider T. Ruys, *'Armed Attack' and Article 51 of the UN Charter: Evolutions in Customary Law and Practice* (Cambridge: Cambridge University Press, 2010), at 172–173. See, also, T. Reinold, 'State Weakness, Irregular Warfare, and the Right to Self-Defense Post-9/11', (2001) 105 *AJIL* 244, at 259 and 285, and, further *infra* n.172.

[146] A point that has brought the Court in for considerable criticism:

When a state has to decide whether it can repel incessant low-level irregular military activity, does it really have to decide whether that activity is the equivalent of an armed attack by a foreign army – and, anyway, is not *any* use of force by a foreign army entitled to be met by sufficient force to require it to withdraw? Or is that now in doubt also? Is the question of *level* of violence by regular armed forces not really an issue of *proportionality*, rather than a question of determining what is 'an armed attack'?

See Higgins, *supra* n.137, at 250–251. The approach of the Court must also put in question whether it is true to claim – as so many have for so many years – that the right of self-defence is actually an exception to Article 2(4) of the Charter *in toto* (on which, see *supra* n.14), or whether it is more accurate to contend that the right of self-defence is only an exception to *certain* violations of this provision of the Charter. See, further, S.R. Ratner, 'Self Defense Against Terrorists: The Meaning of Armed Attack', in N. Schrijver and L. van den Herik (eds), *The Leiden Policy Recommendations on Counter-terrorism and International Law* (Cambridge: Cambridge University Press, forthcoming; on file with the author), at 6.

which reference was made came from the ADF' and not the Democratic Republic of the Congo. It then went on to observe that:

> there is no satisfactory proof of the involvement in these attacks, direct or indirect, of the Government of the DRC. The attacks did not emanate from armed bands or irregulars sent by the DRC or on behalf of the DRC, within the sense of Article 3 (g) of General Assembly Resolution 3314 (XXIX) on the definition of aggression ... The Court is of the view that, on the evidence before it, even if this series of deplorable attacks could be regarded as cumulative in character, they still remained non-attributable to the DRC.[147]

This *dictum* carries potent echoes of the *Nicaragua Case*, where the Court had drawn a very clear dividing line between actions of irregular armed forces that are 'attributable' – in the language of the *Case Concerning Armed Activities* – to a given state, and situations where a state provides 'assistance to rebels in the form of the provision of weapons or logistical or other support'.[148] For the Court, the latter could only ever count as 'a threat or use of force, or amount to intervention in the internal or external affairs of other States',[149] and not as an armed attack which entitled a state to exercise its right of self-defence (or seek other states to exercise *their* right or rights of collective self-defence). It is for this reason that the claim of self-defence argued by the United States before the Court in the *Nicaragua Case* did not meet with success.

The third and final observation to be made in respect of the definition of an armed attack in the *Nicaragua Case* concerns the extent to which this definition in the jurisprudence of the Court might be thought to be comprehensive: lest it be thought that the Court was setting out an exhaustive definition of the concept of an armed attack once and for all, it should be clear that the Court's conclusions could only ever be as good as their empirical underpinnings, so that what might have passed for custom in June 1986 might no longer hold true. Perhaps much more critical is the fact that, as we have discovered from other moments in the same jurisprudence,[150] the Court held back on issues not before it in that case – and 'what [was] in issue' in the *Nicaragua Case* was 'the purported exercise by the United States of a right of collective self-defence in response to an armed attack on another State'.[151] The definition given by the Court was therefore induced by the very facts before it, and these facts act as a controlling device on what the Court was prepared to venture forth in terms of the *scope* of an armed attack: its definition, then, is by no means to be treated as complete and conclusive or as immune to change.

---

[147] *Case Concerning Armed Activities*, supra n.22, at 223 (para. 146). For Judge Kooijmans in his separate opinion to this judgment, '[b]y drawing this conclusion, the Court ... implicitly rejects Uganda's argument that mere tolerance of irregulars "creates a susceptibility to action in self-defence by neighbouring States"'. *Ibid.*, at 312 (para. 22). See, further, S.A. Barbour and Z.A. Salzman, '"The Tangled Web": The Right of Self-Defense Against Non-State Actors in the *Armed Activities Case*', (2008) 40 *NYUJILP* 53 and P.N. Okowa, 'Case Concerning Armed Activities on the Territory of the Congo (Democratic Republic of the Congo v. Uganda)', (2006) 55 *ICLQ* 742.

[148] *Supra* n.134.
[149] *Ibid.*
[150] *Supra* n.95.
[151] *Nicaragua Case*, supra n.20, at 27 (para. 35).

If one steps back and assesses the broader points of coincidence between the Definition of Aggression as provided by the General Assembly in December 1974 and the *possibilities* for an armed attack under the Charter of the United Nations, one discovers that the International Court of Justice might have found additional agreement amongst states since the Definition of Aggression includes '[t]he invasion or attack by the armed forces of a State of the territory of another State'[152] – the formulation with which the Court commences its definition of an armed attack in the *Nicaragua Case*.[153] For the reason already given, this definition of the Court is as focused on the territory of states as it is on the attributability of an armed attack to a state,[154] but the Definition of Aggression also includes within its ambit the '[b]ombardment by the armed forces of a State against the territory of another State or the use of any weapons by a State against the territory of another State'.[155] This, of course, was not mentioned by the Court in its definition of an armed attack as the United States had not levelled this particular accusation against Nicaragua – and nor was any 'blockade of the ports or coasts of a State by the armed forces of another State' brought forward.[156]

We do, however, find that, all things told, subsequent jurisprudence of the Court has begun to sketch a broader definition of an armed attack that responds to the factual circumstances presented to the Court *differently* from those appearing in the *Nicaragua Case*: Article 3(d) of General Assembly Resolution 3314 (XXIX) includes within the Definition of Aggression '[a]n attack by the armed forces of a State on the land, sea or air forces, or marine and air fleets of another State',[157] and in the *Oil Platforms Case*, the Court was called upon to assess whether an armed attack had occurred against the United States since the Kuwaiti tanker, the *Sea Isle City*, which had been reflagged to the United States, was hit by a Silkworm missile near Kuwait harbour (i.e. in the territorial waters of Kuwait) on 16 October 1987.[158] According to the Court,

---

[152] Article 3(a) of the Definition of Aggression (which continues: 'or any military occupation, however temporary, resulting from such invasion or attack, or any annexation by the use of force of the territory of another State or part thereof').
[153] *Supra* n.134.
[154] Note, too, the explanatory note to Article 1 of General Assembly Resolution 3314 (XXIX) (which defines aggression as 'the use of armed force *by a State against the sovereignty, territorial integrity or political independence of another State*, or in any other manner inconsistent with the Charter of the United Nations, as set out in this Definition' (emphasis added)): 'the term "State": (a) is used without prejudice to questions of recognition or to whether a State is a member of the United Nations; (b) includes the concept of a "group of States" where appropriate.'
[155] Article 3(b) of General Assembly Resolution 3314 (XXIX).
[156] Article 3(c) of General Assembly Resolution 3314 (XXIX).
[157] In this respect, it is worth referring back to Article V of the ANZUS Treaty, *supra* n.76, that 'an armed attack on any of the Parties is deemed to include an armed attack on the metropolitan territory of any of the Parties, or on the island territories under its jurisdiction in the Pacific or on its armed forces, public vessels or aircraft in the Pacific'.
[158] According to the United States, the firing of the missile had been the work of the Iranian armed forces, and on 19 October 1987, the United States reported to the Security Council that 'United States forces have exercised the inherent right of self-defence under international law by taking defensive action in response to attacks by the Islamic Republic of Iran against *United*

the evidence indicative of Iranian responsibility for the attack on the *Sea Isle City* is not sufficient to support the contentions of the United States [and] [t]he conclusion to which the Court has come on this aspect of the case is thus that the burden of proof of the existence of an armed attack by Iran on the United States, in the form of the missile attack on the *Sea Isle City*, has not been discharged.[159]

What is instructive about this approach of the Court is that it does not rule out *per se* the potential of this particular target to be amenable to an armed attack as a matter of law, and it is useful to take account of how the Court responded to the surrounding incidents that – in the view of the United States[160] – Iran had been responsible for, and that provided the context for the alleged armed attack on the *Sea Isle City* in October 1987:

> On the hypothesis that all the incidents complained of are to be attributed to Iran, and thus setting aside the question ... of attribution to Iran of the specific attack on the *Sea Isle City*, the question is whether the attack, either in itself or in combination with the rest of the 'series of ... attacks' cited by the United States justifying self-defence. The Court notes first that the *Sea Isle City* was in Kuwaiti waters at the time of the attack on it, and that a Silkworm missile fired from (it is alleged) more than 100 [kilometres] away could not have been aimed at the specific vessel, but simply programmed to hit some target in Kuwaiti waters. Secondly, the *Texaco Caribbean*, whatever its ownership, was not flying a United States flag, so that an attack on the vessel is not in itself to be equated with an attack on that State. As regard the alleged firing on United States helicopters from Iranian gunboats and from the Reshadat oil platform, no persuasive evidence has been supplied to support this allegation. There is no evidence that the minelaying alleged to have been carried out by the *Iran Ajr*, at a time when Iran was at war with Iraq, was aimed specifically at the United States; and similarly it has not been established that the mine struck by the *Bridgeton* was laid with the specific intention of harming that ship, or other United States vessels. Even taken cumulatively, and reserving ... the question of Iranian responsibility, these incidents do not seem to the Court to constitute an armed attack on the United States, of the kind that the Court, in the case concerning *Military and Paramilitary Activities in and against Nicaragua*, qualified as a 'most grave' form of the use of force.[161]

In the *Oil Platforms Case*, the Court also had to consider whether an armed attack had occurred on the United States when one of its naval warships, the USS *Samuel B.*

States vessels in the Persian Gulf'. See UN Doc. S/19219 (emphasis added). Elsewhere in the same communication, the United States described the *Sea Isle City* as 'a United States flag vessel'.

[159] *Oil Platforms Case, supra* n.21, at 190 (para. 61).
[160] *Ibid.*, at 191 (para. 63).
[161] *Ibid.*, at 191–192 (para. 64). The requirement – that the most grave form of the use of force must be 'aimed specifically' at the target state – has been criticized on the basis that '[s]uch a proposition ... is not supported by international law, and it would undermine, rather than maintain, international peace and security. States have a right of self-defense so that they can protect their national security and deter attacks against them, concerns that are implicated just as much when states are subjected to indiscriminate attacks as when they are subjected to targeted attacks.' See W.H. Taft IV, 'Self-Defense and the *Oil Platforms* Decision', (2004) 29 *Yale JIL* 295, at 302.

Roberts,[162] struck a mine in the Persian Gulf in April 1988 – which the United States believed to be the work of Iran. Once again, the Court found the evidence placed before it wanting – 'highly suggestive', it said, 'but not conclusive'[163] – but the Court nevertheless proceeded to entertain the question of whether such an action would be sufficient in principle to constitute an armed attack in international law (assuming all other factors were equal):

> No attacks on United States-flagged vessels (as distinct from United States-owned vessels), additional to those cited as justification for the earlier attacks on the Reshadat platforms, have been brought to the Court's attention, other than the mining of the USS *Samuel B. Roberts* itself. The question is therefore whether that incident sufficed in itself to justify action in self-defence, as amounting to an 'armed attack'. The Court does not exclude the possibility that the mining of a single military vessel might be sufficient to bring into play the 'inherent right of self-defence'; but in view of all circumstances, including the inconclusiveness of the evidence of Iran's responsibility for the mining of the USS *Samuel B. Roberts*, the Court is unable to hold that the attacks on the Salman and Nasr platforms have been shown to have been justifiably in response to an 'armed attack' on the United States by Iran, in the form of the mining of the USS *Samuel B. Roberts*.[164]

This approach of the Court must raise questions as to whether there are other possible representations of that state that can be designated as appropriate targets for an armed attack for the purposes of the right of self-defence, such as embassies and diplomatic premises,[165] as well as the nationals of a state.[166] This latter point has proved a recurrent and controversial theme in the practice of states, as well as in the *scope* they have afforded to their right of self-defence over the years, ranging from the Israeli raid

---

[162] *Ibid.*, at 194 (para. 69). The Court observed that in its communication to the Security Council, the United States claimed to have been exercising the right of self-defence in response to the 'attack' on the USS *Samuel B. Roberts*, 'linking it also with "a series of offensive attacks and provocations Iranian naval forces have taken against neutral shipping in the international waters of the Persian Gulf"' – but that, before the Court, the United States contended that 'the mining was itself an armed attack giving rise to the right of self-defence and that the alleged pattern of Iranian use of force "added to the gravity of the specific attacks, [and] reinforced the necessity of action in self-defense, and helped to shape the appropriate response"': *Oil Platforms Case, supra* n.21, at 195 (para. 72).

[163] *Ibid.*, at 195 (para. 71).

[164] *Ibid.*, at 195–196 (para. 72).

[165] Such as the attacks on the US embassies in Nairobi and Dar es Salaam in August 1998. See UN Doc. S/1998/780 (20 August 1998). See, further, R. Wedgwood, 'Responding to Terrorism: The Strikes Against Bin Laden', (1999) 24 *Yale JIL* 599 and L.M. Campbell, 'Defending Against Terrorism: A Legal Analysis of the Decision to Strike Sudan and Afghanistan', (2000) 74 *Tulane LR* 1067.

[166] Consider N. Ronzitti, *Rescuing Nationals Abroad through Military Coercion and Intervention on the Grounds of Humanity* (Dordrecht, Boston, Lancaster: Martinus Nijhoff Publishers, 1985). See, also, R.J. Zedalis, 'Protection of Nationals Abroad: Is Consent the Basis of Legal Obligation?', (1990) 25 *Texas ILJ* 211; T. Ruys, 'The "Protection of Nationals" Doctrine Revisited', (2008) 13 *JCSL* 233; K.E. Eichensehr, 'Defending Nationals Abroad: Assessing the Lawfulness of Forcible Hostage Rescues', (2007–2008) 48 *Virginia JIL* 451, and F. Grimal and G. Melling, 'The Protection of Nationals Abroad: Lawfulness or Toleration? A Commentary', (2011) 16 *JCSL* 541.

on Entebbe Airport in Uganda in July 1976[167] to the aborted attempt of the United States to rescue hostages at its seized embassy in Tehran, Iran, in April 1980.[168] This issue rests on an expansive understanding of the state as the governing framework for scope of the right of self-defence – and of the unit of the *self* that is ultimately being defended by the exercise of this right:

> While it has often been argued that the notion of an armed attack is confined to attacks upon the territory and, perhaps, the ships and aircraft, of a State, the better view is that an attack upon a State's nationals outside its territory also constitutes an armed attack, or at least amounts to a use of force sufficient to allow the victim State to invoke the right of self-defence. There is little doubt that customary international law in the period before 1945 recognized a right to use force in defence of nationals who were attacked abroad and there is no indication that Article 51 [of the Charter] was intended to remove that aspect of the customary right. On the contrary, Article 51 refers to an armed attack upon a member State; since population is one of the attributes of statehood, an attack upon a State's population would seem to be just as much an attack upon that State as would an attack upon its territory. There is something inherently unattractive about a view of self-defence which would allow a State to use force to protect uninhabited territory but not in defence of its nationals. State practice in protecting nationals abroad since 1945 also supports this interpretation of Article 51.[169]

Our consideration of the concept of an armed attack thus far has assumed that the perpetrators of an armed attack are state actors or representatives of the state, although (as we have seen) the General Assembly's definition of aggression as endorsed by the International Court of Justice in June 1986 allowed for splitting the *author* from the *perpetrator* of an armed attack,[170] so that these need not be one and the same actor. However, in so doing, the Court bound these two propositions together with its reference to 'the sending by a State of armed bands to the territory of another State, if such an operation, because of its scale and effects, would have been classified as an armed attack rather than as a mere frontier incident had it been carried out by regular

---

[167] See UN Doc. S/PV.1939 (9 July 1976), at 14 (para. 115). See, further, D.J. Gordon, 'Use of Force for the Protection of Nationals Abroad: The Entebbe Incident', (1977) 9 *Case Western Reserve JIL* 117 and J.J. Paust, 'Entebbe and Self-Help: The Israeli Response to Terrorism', (1978) 2 *Fletcher F. World Aff.* 86.

[168] See UN Doc. S/13908 (25 April 1980). In its consideration of the legal proceedings instituted by the United States in November 1979 in respect of Iran's obligations under (*inter alia*) the 1961 Vienna Convention on Diplomatic Relations and the 1963 Vienna Convention on Consular Relations, the International Court of Justice referred to 'the armed attack on the United States Embassy by militants on 4 November 1979' (*ibid.*, at 29 (para. 57)), as well as the earlier 'armed attack' on the United States Embassy in Tehran on 14 February 1979 (*ibid.*, at 31 (para. 64)). See, further, B.V.A. Röling, 'Aspects of the Case Concerning United States Diplomatic and Consular Staff in Tehran', (1980) 11 *Netherlands YBIL* 125; A. Jeffery, 'The American Hostages in Tehran: The I.C.J. and the Legality of Rescue Missions', (1981) 30 *ICLQ* 717; and J.R. D'Angelo, 'Resort to Force by States to Protect Nationals: The U.S. Rescue Mission to Iran and Its Legality under International Law', (1980–1981) 21 *Virginia JIL* 485.

[169] C. Greenwood, 'International Law and the United States' Air Operation Against Libya', (1986–1987) 89 *West Virginia LR* 933, at 940–941.

[170] Without any prejudice to making a direct comparison between the concepts of aggression and armed attack. See *supra* n.139.

armed forces'.[171] It is this formulation that has given rise to the notion of attribution within the jurisprudence of the Court, and is surely responsible for the subsequent statement of the Court, delivered in the course of its advisory opinion in *Legal Consequences of the Construction of A Wall* in July 2004, that Article 51 of the Charter 'recognizes the existence of an inherent right of self-defence in the case of armed attack by one State against another State'.[172] This position brought an immediate retort from *within* the Court, for Judge Rosalyn Higgins argued in her separate opinion in that very case that '[t]here is, with respect, nothing in the text of Article 51 that *thus* stipulates that self-defence is available only when an armed attack is made by a State'.[173]

The Court had formulated its position on this point of law in the shadow of the events occurring in the United States on 11 September 2001,[174] where the Security Council wasted little time in adopting a resolution that unequivocally condemned in the strongest of terms 'the horrifying terrorist attacks' which had occurred the previous day in New York, Washington DC and Pennsylvania[175] – a resolution that had recognized in the text of its preamble 'the inherent right of individual or collective self-defence in

---

[171] The other manner in which the Court described its second situation of an armed attack in the *Nicaragua Case*, that is further to its articulations at *supra* n.142 (and accompanying text).

[172] *Legal Consequences of the Construction of A Wall in the Occupied Palestinian Territory* (Advisory Opinion), *supra* n.17, at 194 (para. 139) (and that Israel 'does not claim that the attacks against it are imputable to a foreign State': *ibid*.). See, also, the Court's position in *Case Concerning Armed Activities in the Territory of the Congo* – that:

> there is no satisfactory proof of the involvement in these attacks, direct or indirect, of the Government of the [Democratic Republic of Congo] [on Uganda]. The attacks did not emanate from armed bands or irregulars sent by the DRC or on behalf of the DRC ... The Court is of the view that, on the evidence before it, even if this series of deplorable attacks could be regarded as cumulative in character, they still remained non-attributable to the DRC.

Supra n.22, at 223 (para. 146).

[173] *Ibid*., at 215 (para. 33). Indeed, it was Judge Higgins who connected the Court's thinking to its articulations in the *Nicaragua Case*:

> *That* qualification is rather a result of the Court so determining in *Military and Paramilitary Activities in and against Nicaragua (Nicaragua v. United States of America) (Merits, Judgment, I.C.J. Reports 1986,* p. 14). It there held that military action by irregulars could constitute an armed attack if these were sent by or on behalf of the State and if the activity 'because of its scale and effects, would have been classified as an armed attack ... had it been carried out by regular armed forces' (*ibid*., p. 103, para. 195). While accepting, as I must, that this is to be regarded as a statement of the law as it now stands, I maintain all the reservations as to this proposition that I have expressed elsewhere (R. Higgins, *Problems and Process: International Law and How We Use It*, pp. 250–251).

Ibid (emphasis in original). See, further, I. Scobbie, 'Words My Mother Never Taught Me – "In Defense of the International Court"', (2005) 99 *AJIL* 76.

[174] See, in particular, C.J. Tams, 'The Use of Force Against Terrorists', (2009) 20 *EJIL* 359; K.N. Trapp, 'Back to Basics: Necessity, Proportionality, and the Right of Self-Defence Against Non-State Terrorist Actors', (2007) 56 *ICLQ* 141 and T. Ruys and S. Verhoeven, 'Attacks by Private Actors and the Right of Self-Defence', (2005) 10 *JCSL* 289.

[175] Security Council Resolution 1368 (2001) (12 September 2001), first operative paragraph (where the Council regarded those acts 'like any acts of international terrorism as a threat to international peace and security': *ibid*.).

accordance with the Charter'.[176] There are difficulties in reading this statement as saying anything other than the opportunities for exercising the right of self-defence now existed and existed pursuant to the armed attack – or, possibly, the *armed attacks* – of 11 September 2001,[177] perhaps enhanced by the fact that the Security Council then twice referred to the 'terrorist attacks' that had occurred on that date.[178] The Council also called on 'all States to work together urgently to bring to justice the perpetrators, organizers and sponsors of these terrorist attacks' and it 'stresse[d] that those responsible for aiding, supporting or harbouring the perpetrators, organizers and sponsors of these acts will be held accountable',[179] although the Council in no way specified whether the form this accountability would take was somehow connected with the parameters and exercise of the right of self-defence, or whether this would be achieved through other avenues of action.

To be sure, one way of viewing the subsequent application of force in individual and collective self-defence by the United States and its allies – against Afghanistan on 7 October 2001 – is to regard the armed attack (or attacks) of the previous month as the work of al-Qaeda, as well as to regard al-Qaeda and the Taliban (as the Government of Afghanistan) as 'two sides of the same coin', the phrase of an Afghan official that the British Government cited in its dossier entitled *Responsibility for the Terrorist Atrocities in the United States, 11 September 2001* (2001).[180] For the legal purposes of the right of self-defence, this would have the effect of treating the two actors as identical – as one and the same concern. However, the position of the United States in informing the Council that it and other states had 'initiated actions in the exercise of its inherent right of individual and collective self-defence following the armed attacks' – plural – 'that were carried out against the United States on 11 September 2001' was that separate responsibilities had been born of both al-Qaeda and the Taliban from these developments.[181] For the United States, 'clear and compelling information' had come to light that 'the al-Qaeda organization, which is supported by the Taliban regime in

---

[176] *Ibid.* Ditto the fourth preambular paragraph of Security Council Resolution 1373, adopted on 28 September 2001 (where the Security Council reaffirmed 'the inherent right of individual or collective self-defence as recognized by the Charter of the United Nations as reiterated in Resolution 1368 (2001)').

[177] Though cf. in particular E.P.J. Mjyer and N.D. White, 'The Twin Towers Attack: An Unlimited Right to Self-Defence?', (2002) 7 *JCSL* 5.

[178] Third and fifth operative paragraphs respectively on Resolution 1368 (2001): *supra* n.175. Although in addressing the meeting of the Council that adopted this resolution, United Nations Secretary-General Kofi A. Annan said that everyone felt 'deep shock and revulsion at the cold-blooded viciousness of this attack'. See UN Doc. SC/7143 (12 September 2001). See, further, S.D. Murphy, 'Terrorism and the Concept of "Armed Attack" in Article 51 of the U.N. Charter', (2002) 43 *Harvard ILJ* 41; C. Stahn, 'Terrorist Attacks as "Armed Attack": The Right to Self-Defence, Article 51½ of the UN Charter, and International Terrorism', (2003) 27 *Fletcher F. World Aff.* 35; and T.M. Franck, 'Terrorism and the Right of Self-Defense', (2001) 95 *AJIL* 839.

[179] Third operative paragraph of Resolution 1368 (2001).

[180] Available at http://www.fas.org/irp/news/2001/11/ukreport.html (para. 19).

[181] UN Doc. S/2001/946 (7 October 2001).

Afghanistan, had a central role in the attacks',[182] where the support was described in the following terms:

> The attacks on 11 September 2001 and the ongoing threat to the United States and its nationals posed by the al-Qaeda organization have been made possible by the decision of the Taliban regime to allow the parts of Afghanistan that it controls to be used by this organization as a base operation. Despite every effort by the United States and the international community, the Taliban regime has refused to change its policy. From the territory of Afghanistan, the al-Qaeda organization continues to train and support agents of terror who attack innocent people throughout the world and target United States nationals and interests in the United States and abroad.[183]

It will be appreciated that this method of reasoning does not coincide with the formula for an armed attack invoked and used by the International Court of Justice in the *Nicaragua Case* in June 1986, but it does us well to recall that the law of self-defence has long acknowledged the possibilities of *differing* configurations for the relationship between the state and the non-state actor in order to consummate any entitlement to the right of self-defence: in short, it is not confined to the 'sending' of the latter by the former so long as a particular threshold of force is attained,[184] an approach that is better or best regarded as informed by the very facts that gave rise to the relevant litigation.[185] The *Caroline* correspondence bears this point out to an appreciable extent, because, on behalf of Great Britain, Lord Ashburton responded to Secretary Webster's template for the right of self-defence in July 1842 by marshalling the facts towards satisfaction of the principle of necessity:

> Supposing a man standing on ground where you have no legal right to follow him has a weapon long enough to reach you, and is striking you down and endangering your life, how

---

[182] *Ibid*.

[183] *Ibid*. This report to the Council was much more explicit in terms of describing the 'support' of the Taliban than the communication of the United Kingdom, which stated simply: '[t]his military action has been carefully planned, and is directed against Usama bin Laden's al-Qaeda terrorist organization and the Taliban regime that is supporting it.' UN Doc. S/2001/947 (7 October 2001). The emphasis was very much on the responsibility and capabilities of al-Qaeda: *ibid*. However, the British Government subsequently provided further details on this point to the Council in *Responsibility for the Terrorist Atrocities in the United States, 11 September 2001*:

> Usama Bin Laden's al-Qaeda and the Taleban régime have a close and mutually dependent alliance. Usama Bin Laden and al-Qaeda provide the Taleban régime with material, financial and military support. They jointly exploit the drugs trade. The Taleban régime allows Bin Laden to operate his terrorist training camps and activities from Afghanistan, protects him from attacks from outside, and protects the drug stockpiles. Usama Bin Laden could not operate his terrorist activities without the alliance and support of the Taleban régime. The Taleban's strength would be seriously weakened without Usama Bin Laden's military and financial support.

See Annex to UN Doc. S/2001/949 (8 October 2001).

[184] See S.D. Murphy, 'Self-Defence and the Israeli Wall Advisory Opinion: An *Ipse Dixit* from the ICJ?', (2005) 99 *AJIL* 62, 65.

[185] See Trapp, *supra* n.174, at 141–142.

long are you bound to wait for the assistance of the authority having the legal power to relieve you or, to bring the facts more immediately home to the case, if cannon are moving and setting up in a battery which can reach you and are actually destroying life and property by their fire, if you have remonstrated for some time without effect and see no prospect of relief, when begins your right to defend yourself, should you have no other means of doing so, than by seizing your assailant on the verge of a neutral territory?[186]

In other words, in that instance the United States was implicated for its failure to act – or to act more adequately than it had done – where an imminent threat of attack did not stem from the United States itself.[187] We have also already referred to the Israeli rescue mission at Entebbe Airport in July 1976, which involved the hijacking of a commercial airliner with 250 passengers on board at the hands of non-state actors, when members of the Popular Front for the Liberation of Palestine and from the Baader-Meinhof Gang (Germany) seized control of a commercial flight and redirected its path – where the Government of Uganda had no role in authorising the hijacking but was 'directly implicated in keeping the hostages under detention'.[188] The action taken in self-defence was justifiable – and might even have been *justified* – since 'the local powers-that-be collaborate[d] with the terrorists',[189] and Israel argued before the Security Council that Uganda had either co-operated with the hijackers or it did not 'exercise sovereignty over its territory and was incapable of dealing with half a dozen terrorists'.[190] This proved central to the claim of activating its right of self-defence that Israel sought to make within the United Nations,[191] and, in more recent times, some have suggested that the relationship of the United States with Pakistan in the context of the operation of May 2011 concerning Osama bin Laden was based on a test of the 'unwilling or unable' stance of Pakistan.[192]

Compare and contrast Israel's invocation of its right of self-defence against Lebanon in July 2006 in response to what it had labelled a 'belligerent act of war': on the morning of 12 July 2006, it advised the Security Council that 'Hezbollah terrorists [had] unleashed a barrage of heavy artillery and rockets into Israel, causing a number of deaths [and that] [i]n the midst of this horrific and unprovoked act, the terrorists infiltrated Israel and kidnapped two Israeli soldiers, taking them into Lebanon'.[193] For Israel, this became the *casus belli* for the hostilities it entered into with Lebanon over

---

[186] See Manning, *supra* n.42, at 766 (Doc. No. 1593) (28 July 1842).
[187] Murphy, *supra* n.178, at 50.
[188] Dinstein, *supra* n.44, at 257.
[189] *Ibid.*, at 258. The fact that the debate had moved to the proportionality of Israel's use of force might be sufficient to suggest that Israel was justified in its initiation of force against Uganda. See, also, Franck, *supra* n.7, at 85 ('the considerable support Israel aroused … demonstrates the persuasive power of a well-presented and factually demonstrated case').
[190] UN Doc. S/PV.1939 (9 July 1976), at 12 (para. 98).
[191] UN Doc. S/12123 (4 July 1976).
[192] A.S. Deeks, '"Unwilling or Unable": Toward A Normative Framework for Extraterritorial Self-Defense', (2012) 52 *Virginia JIL* 483, at 499–501. On this standard, see, further, Reinold, *supra* n.145, at 257, and Trapp, *supra* n.174, at 147.
[193] UN Doc. A/60/937-S/2006/515 (12 July 2006).

the period of the next 33 days,[194] but, in legal terms, it maintained before the Council that it reserved the right to act in self-defence in accordance with Article 51 of the United Nations Charter – and to do so 'when an armed attack is launched against a Member of the United Nations'.[195] This, Israel believed, had happened with the events of 12 July 2006 and it advised the Council that it would take 'the appropriate actions to secure the release of the kidnapped soldiers and bring an end to the shelling that terrorizes our citizens'.[196] What interests us for present purposes is how Israel conceived – and how it presented to the Council – the issue of the responsibility for the armed attack it had adverted:

> Responsibility for this belligerent act of war lies with the Government of Lebanon, from whose territory these acts have been launched into Israel. Responsibility also lies with the Government of the Islamic Republic of Iran and the Syrian Arab Republic, which support and embrace those who carried out this attack. ... The ineptitude and inaction of the Government of Lebanon has led to a situation in which it has not exercised jurisdiction over its own territory for many years. The Security Council has addressed this situation time and time again in its debates and resolutions. Let me remind you also that Israel has repeatedly warned the international community about this dangerous and potentially volatile situation. In this vacuum festers the Axis of Terror: Hezbollah and the terrorist States of Iran and Syria, which have today opened another chapter in their war of terror.[197]

This formulation, then, very much seems to echo the reasoning that permeated some of the *Caroline* correspondence, where, on that occasion, the omissions of a state were factored into the decision by Great Britain to activate its right of self-defence. Central to the thinking is that another state has either fallen incompetent or it has proved unwilling to rise to the tasks associated with its 'jurisdiction', as Israel presented it in the above legal position.[198] However, speaking on the very same day as these developments, Prime Minister Ehud Olmert of Israel seemed to articulate a very different line of reasoning for the exercise of the right of self-defence, when he declared that '[t]his morning's events were not a terrorist attack, *but the act of a*

---

[194] See G. Achar and M. Warschawski, *The 33-Day War: Israel's War on Hezbollah in Lebanon and Its Consequences* (London: Paradigm Publishers, 2007) – where the end of hostilities has been perceived to coincide with the cease-fire of 14 August 2006, though the formal conclusion of conflict was reached with Israel's lifting of its naval blockade against Lebanon on 8 September 2006.

[195] UN Doc. A/60/937-S/2006/515 (12 July 2006). See, further, M.N. Schmitt, '"Change Direction" 2006: Israeli Operations in Lebanon and the International Law of Self-Defence', (2008) 29 *Michigan JIL* 127; A. Zimmermann, 'The Second Lebanon War: *jus ad bellum, jus in bello* and the Issue of Proportionality', (2007) 11 *Max Planck Yrbk UN Law* 99; T. Ruys, 'Crossing the Thin Blue Line: An Inquiry Into Israel's Recourse to Self-Defence Against Hezbollah', (2007) 45 *Stanford JIL* 272; and Y. Ronen, 'Israel, Hizbollah, and the Second Lebanon War', (2006) 9 *Yrbk. IHL* 362.

[196] UN Doc. A/60/937-S/2006/515 (12 July 2006).

[197] *Ibid.*

[198] *Ibid.* For a fuller exposition of the origins and activities of Hezbollah, see A.R. Norton, *Hezbollah: A Short History* (Princeton, NJ: Princeton University Press, 2007). See, also, Reinold, *supra* n.145, at 264.

sovereign State that attacked Israel for no reason and without provocation'.[199] He continued: 'The Lebanese Government, *of which Hizbullah is a member*, is trying to undermine regional stability. Lebanon is responsible and Lebanon will bear the consequences of its actions.'[200] According to this reasoning, for all legal intents and purposes, Hezbollah were to be considered members of the Government of Lebanon such that its acts could be directly equated with those of the Government,[201] and, *in ultimo*, the state of Lebanon. They would thus stand to be counted as part of the regular armed forces of Lebanon, or quite possibly to associated 'militia and volunteer corps',[202] and Lebanon's responsibility for the armed attack (or attacks) would have flowed from that fact – rather than from any *de facto* allowance or acquiescence in the use of its territory for such activities.

6. THE QUESTION OF PROPORTIONALITY

Assuming that the right of individual or collective self-defence has been lawfully invoked in a given situation, the state (or states) exercising that right of individual or collective self-defence do not have a free rein to use force without limitation; the force that is used must accord with the necessity for action – or, as it was put in the *Caroline* correspondence, 'the act justified by the necessity of self-defence ... must be limited by that necessity, and kept clearly within it'.[203] The International Court of Justice was alert to this criterion for any lawful exercise of the right of self-defence in its judgment in the *Nicaragua Case*, for, as we have earlier observed, the Court noted that Article 51 of the Charter 'does not contain any specific rule whereby self-defence would warrant only measures which are proportional to the armed attack and necessary to respond to it'[204] – a rule, the Court said, that is 'well established in customary international law'.[205] The idea is that once a state has determined that there is a necessity to act in self-defence, international law does not grant that state a

---

[199] Israel Ministry of Foreign Affairs, P.M. Olmert: Lebanon is Responsible and Will Bear the Consequences, Communiqué of 12 July 2006, available at www.mfa.gov.il/MFA/Government/Communiques/2006/PM+Olmert+-+Lebanon+is+responsible+and+will+bear+the+consequences+12-Jul-2006.htm (emphasis added).

[200] *Ibid* (emphasis added).

[201] Though the Government of Lebanon denied knowledge and responsibility of these acts: 'The Lebanese Government was not aware of the events that occurred and are occurring on the international Lebanese border. The Lebanese Government is not responsible for these acts and does not endorse them.' See UN Doc. S/2006/518 (13 July 2006).

[202] As it is put in Article 1 of the Regulations annexed to the 1907 Hague Convention (IV) Respecting the Laws and Customs of War on Land. Article 4(A)(1) of the 1949 Geneva Convention (III) Relative to the Treatment of Prisoners of War refers to '[m]embers of the armed forces of a Party to the conflict, *as well as members of militias or volunteer corps forming part of such forces*' (emphasis added).

[203] *Supra* n.43.

[204] *Nicaragua Case, supra* n.20, at 94 (para. 176). *Supra* n.57.

[205] *Ibid*. See, further, *Legality of the Threat or Use of Nuclear Weapons* (advisory opinion), *supra* n.23, at 254 (para. 41) and *Oil Platforms Case, supra* n.21, at 198 (para. 76).

blank cheque to use as much force as it chooses;[206] indeed, the requirement of proportionality seems to be one of the constraints that 'are inherent in the very concept of self-defence'.[207]

The difficulty is how to measure the proportionality of a given instance of force, including force taken against the threat of an armed attack.[208] This, of course, is where the facts underpinning the *Caroline* correspondence enter the discussion, and it is useful to learn from those written exchanges that the idea was that the self-defending state or states would do 'nothing unreasonable or excessive' once the principle of necessity 'authorized' them to enter (or use force) in the territories of the opposing state.[209] The *Caroline* correspondence therefore established an essential dynamic between the principles of necessity and proportionality,[210] whereby the principle of necessity would attend to the forcible response by one state (or set of states acting in collective self-defence) against another in the first instance, and the principle of proportionality would stand to measure all of the force that ensues in the name of self-defence – where it would measure the quantum of force in its totality.

Understood from this angle, the calculation of proportionality under the *jus ad bellum* is of a different order from that which occurs under the *jus in bello*;[211] whereas the former intends to measure the force used in an operation of self-defence in its entirety, the latter considers the force applied as against a specific military target as

---

[206] Though the response in self-defence could conceivably encompass the *threat* as well as the *use* of force on the thinking of the International Court of Justice in its *Nuclear Weapons* advisory opinion: '[t]he notions of "threat" and "use" of force under Article 2, paragraph 4, of the Charter stand together in the sense that if the use of force itself in a given case is illegal – for whatever reason – the threat to use such force will likewise be illegal. In short, if it is to be lawful, the declared readiness of a State to use force must be a use of force that is in conformity with the Charter.' *Supra* n.23, at 246 (para. 47). While this may be so, one can envisage the difficulties in calculating the proportionality of a threat of force undertaken in self-defence. See, in particular, Green and Grimal, *supra* n.100.

[207] As found by the Court in its *Nuclear Weapons* (advisory opinion): *supra* n.23, at 244 (para. 40).

[208] As *per* the previous discussion accompanying *supra* nn.106–112.

[209] *Supra* n.43.

[210] In its *Nuclear Weapons* advisory opinion, the Court referred to '[t]his dual condition' of necessity and proportionality – which, the Court said, 'applies equally to Article 51 of the Charter, whatever the means of force employed' (*supra* n.23, at 245 (para. 41)). However, notice how, in its judgment in the *Nicaragua Case*, the International Court of Justice orientates the principle of proportionality around 'the armed attack and necessary to respond to it'. See *supra* n.57. See, further, Trapp, *supra* n.174, at 146.

[211] Or laws applicable in the context of international and non-international armed conflicts. See, further, D. Kretzmer, 'The Inherent Right to Self-Defence and Proportionality in *Jus ad Bellum*', (2013) 24 *EJIL* 235. The International Court of Justice appears to have viewed the operation of the principle of proportionality at two levels of its analysis in the *Nuclear Weapons* advisory opinion where it said that 'a use of force that is proportionate under the law of self-defence, must in order to be lawful, also meet the requirements of the law applicable in an armed conflict which comprise in particular the principles and rules of international humanitarian law'. See *supra* n.23, at 245 (para. 42). See, further, Dinstein, *supra* n.44, at 233.

defined by international law at any given point during that operation.[212] According to Article 51(5)(b) of the 1977 First Additional Protocol to the four Geneva Conventions of August 1949, within the context of hostilities amounting to an international armed conflict,[213] an attack will be considered indiscriminate if, *inter alia*, it 'may be expected to cause incidental loss of civilian life, injury to civilians, damage to civilian objects, or a combination thereof, *which would be excessive in relation to the concrete and direct military advantage anticipated*'.[214] This point came into sharp relief in the *Oil Platforms Case*, where the International Court of Justice emphasized that the full scale of force used for an operation was necessary in order to determine its proportionality as a matter of the *jus ad bellum* – it is just that, in that case, it was difficult for the Court to demarcate where the United States' exercise of its right of self-defence had begun. Four days after the mining of the *Samuel B. Roberts*, the United States had responded with force against Iranian oil platforms on 18 April 1988, but, as far as the Court was concerned:

> [i]n the case of [these] attacks … they were conceived and executed as part of a more extensive operation entitled 'Operation Praying Mantis' … [and] the Court cannot assess in isolation the proportionality of that action to the attack to which it was said to be a response; it cannot close its eyes to the scale of the whole operation, which involved, *inter alia*, the destruction of two Iranian frigates and a number of other naval vessels and aircraft. As a response to the mining, by an unidentified agency, of a single United States warship, which was severely damaged but not sunk, and without loss of life, neither 'Operation Praying Mantis' as a whole, nor even that part of it that destroyed the Salman and Nasr platforms, can

---

[212] Wedgwood refers to these (respectively) as the strategic and tactical applications of the principle of proportionality. See R. Wedgwood, 'Proportionality and Necessity in American National Security Decision Making', (1992) 86 *Proceedings ASIL* 58, at 59. According to Article 52(2) of the First Additional Protocol, '[a]ttacks shall be limited strictly to military objectives' and '[i]n so far as objects are concerned, military objectives are limited to those objects which by their nature, location, purpose or use make an effective contribution to military action and whose total or partial destruction, capture or neutralization, in the circumstances ruling at the time, offers a definite military advantage'.

[213] This rule – or principle – does not appear as such and in these terms in the Second Additional Protocol; although consider Rule 14 of the International Committee of the Red Cross's study on international humanitarian law – '[l]aunching an attack which may be expected to cause incidental loss of civilian life, injury to civilians, damage to civilian objects, or a combination thereof, which would be excessive in relation to the concrete and direct military advantage anticipated, is prohibited' – which is regarded as applicable to *both* international and non-international armed conflicts alike. See J.-M. Henckaerts and L. Doswald-Beck (eds), *Customary International Humanitarian Law* (Vol. I: Rules) (Cambridge: Cambridge University Press, 2005), at 46–50. See, also, J.-M. Henckaerts, 'Study on Customary International Humanitarian Law: A Contribution to the Understanding and Respect for the Rule of Law in Armed Conflict', (2005) 87 *Int'l Rev. Red Cross* 175, at 189.

[214] Emphasis added. For a discussion of the meaning of the provision, as well as an emphasis on the notion of 'excessive' damage, consider Y. Dinstein, *The Conduct of Hostilities under the Law of International Armed Conflict*, 2nd edn (Cambridge: Cambridge University Press, 2010), at 130–133. See, further, W.J. Fenrick, 'The Rule of Proportionality and Protocol I in Conventional Warfare', (1982) 98 *Military LR* 91, and, also, David Turns' chapter in this volume (chapter 10).

be regarded, in the circumstances of this case, as a proportionate use of force in self-defence.[215]

By comparing the principle of proportionality in these separate contexts,[216] we are able to gather a much better sense of the kinds of considerations entailed by these distinct frameworks for legal analysis – even though the precise parameters of the principle of proportionality might not be able to be configured exactly or with the kind of precision that would be expected from the law.[217] In addition, it might do us well to recall that, as part of the framework for analysing invocations of the right of self-defence, the broader *purpose* of the right is rather distinct in terms of 'protecting the security of the state and the essential rights – in particular the rights of territorial integrity and political independence – upon which that security depends',[218] and differs from the purpose of armed reprisals (whose function was 'punitive in character: they [sought] to impose reparation for the harm done, or to compel a satisfactory settlement of the dispute created by the initial illegal act, or to compel the delinquent state to abide by the law in the future').[219] That said, some have contended that '[t]he action needed to halt and repulse [an] attack may well have to assume dimensions *disproportionate* to those of the attack suffered'.[220]

---

[215] *Oil Platforms Case*, supra n.21, at 198–199 (para. 77).

[216] Of course, these are not the only instances where the principle of proportionality makes itself felt in the discipline of international law. See T.M. Franck, 'On Proportionality of Countermeasures in International Law', (2008) 102 *AJIL* 715, at 719.

[217] Tucker, *supra* n.15, at 588 ('[f]or these restraints – necessity and proportionality – themselves permit a substantial uncertainty, and consequently a considerable latitude, in application').

[218] D. Bowett, 'Reprisals Involving Recourse to Armed Force', (1972) 66 *AJIL* 1, at 3. See, also, Tucker, *supra* n.15, at 588 ('it is precisely the purpose of self-defense to prevent, if possible, the commission of such injurious action') and Randelzhofer, *supra* n.2, at 805 ('lawful self-defence is restricted to the repulse of an armed attack and must not entail retaliatory or punitive actions').

[219] Bowett, *ibid*.,, at 3 (while admitting, *ibid*., at 2, that reprisals as self-defence 'are forms of the same generic remedy, self-help'). Armed reprisals – or reprisals involving recourse to armed force – are now, however, considered unlawful *per se*. See General Assembly Resolution 2625 (XXV) Declaration on Principles of International Law Concerning Friendly Relations and Co-operation Among States in accordance with the Charter of the United Nations ('States have a duty to refrain from acts of reprisal involving the use of force'). See Tucker, *supra* n.15, at 594. Countermeasures, on the other hand, are acts of reprisal not involving recourse to armed force and are considered lawful as a matter of principle in the 2001 Articles on State Responsibility of the International Law Commission: Article 22. See Crawford, *supra* n.38, at 168. One of these criteria is that of proportionality: according to Article 51 of the Articles, '[c]ountermeasures must be commensurate with the injury suffered, taking into account the gravity of the internationally wrongful act and the rights in question'. See Crawford, *ibid.*, at 294–296.

[220] R. Ago, *Addendum to the Eighth Report on State Responsibility*, (1980) 2 *Yrbk. ILC* 13, at 69–70 (emphasis added). Consider, too, Tucker, *supra* n.15, at 589. This is not to mention what 'disproportionality' might be involved for the exercise of an anticipatory right of self-defence. See Gardam, *supra* n.112, at 179–180.

The usefulness of the principle of proportionality thus comes not in its capacities for providing exactitude, but, rather, in its endeavour 'to achieve [its] dispute-resolving project by deliberately creating a space for "second opinions" to which claims of disputants can be referred'.[221] 'The principle,' Thomas M. Franck has argued,

> does not create a rule for conflict resolution so much as it creates an institutional process to which a dispute can be referred for a credible opinion to trump and supplant the rival opinions expressed by the disputants. These second opinions are rendered in many contexts but appear primarily after a person, government, or institution has taken an action against another in response to what is believed to be a detrimental and unlawful provocation.[222]

One perhaps obtains a better appreciation of this approach from reading further into the *Caroline* correspondence, where Lord Ashburton engaged the point of the proportionality of the action in a letter to Secretary Webster in July 1842 where he wrote:

> Some importance is attached to the attack having been made in the night and the vessel having been set on fire and floated down the falls of the river, and it is insinuated rather than asserted that there was carelessness as to the lives of the persons on board. The account given by the distinguished officer who commanded the expedition distinctly refutes or satisfactorily explains these assertions. The time of night was purposely selected as most likely to ensure the execution with the least loss of life, and it is expressly stated that, the strength of the current not permitting the vessel to be carried off, and it being necessary to destroy her by fire, she was drawn into the stream for the express purpose of preventing injury to persons or property of the inhabitants of Schlosser.[223]

In terms of the practical operation of the principle of proportionality, in the *Nicaragua Case* the Court found that since no armed attack had been committed by Nicaragua as against El Salvador, the United States was not entitled to resort to force in collective self-defence. For the Court, since the condition *sine qua non* for the lawful exercise of the right of self-defence – that is, the existence of an armed attack – was not 'fulfilled' in that case, the Court was of the view that 'the appraisal of the United States activities in relation to the criteria of necessity and proportionality takes on a different significance'.[224] The Court then attended to the facts in view of both of the principles and necessity in order to test the possibilities of 'an additional ground of wrongfulness',[225] though its assessment could, however, shed some light on how it would have

---

[221] Franck, *supra* n.216, at 717.
[222] *Ibid.*
[223] *Supra* n.43 (referring to House Doc. No. 302, 25th Congress, 2d. session, serial 329).
[224] *Nicaragua Case*, *supra* n.20, at 122 (para. 237). What this means, or could mean, is not it must be said entirely clear: the Court followed this statement by saying that 'even if the United States activities in question had been carried on in strict compliance with the canons of necessity and proportionality, they would not thereby become lawful. If however they were not, this may constitute an additional ground of wrongfulness.' *Ibid.*
[225] *Ibid.* Since, according to the Court, the United States could not invoke collective armed countermeasures: '[t]he acts of which Nicaragua is accused, even assuming them to have been established and imputable to the State, could only have justified proportionate counter-measures on the part of the State which had been the victim of these acts, namely El Salvador, Honduras or Costa Rica. They could not justify counter-measures taken by a third State, the United States,

approached the question of proportionality had it found that El Salvador had been faced with an *actual* armed attack by Nicaragua:

> Whether or not the assistance to the *contras* might meet the criterion of proportionality, the Court cannot regard the United States activities ... relating to the mining of the Nicaraguan ports and the attacks on ports, oil installations, etc., as satisfying that criterion. Whatever uncertainty may exist as to the exact scale of the aid received by the Salvadoran armed opposition from Nicaragua, it is clear that these latter United States activities in question could not have been proportionate to that aid. Finally on this point, the Court must also observe that the reaction of the United States in the context of what it regarded as self-defence was continued long after the period in which any presumed armed attack by Nicaragua could reasonably be contemplated.[226]

The Court's calibrations on this score indicate that the principle of proportionality can, and perhaps should, be applied in general terms, so that even though the 'exact scale' of the Nicaraguan assistance to the rebels of El Salvador was not then known,[227] the Court could still hazard that the response of the United States – the mining of ports as well as attacks on ports and oil installations, amongst other things – could not have been brought within the remit of the principle of proportionality given all of the circumstances of that case.[228] In so doing, it appears that one of the guiding considerations of the Court was the *function* of the right of self-defence as a defensive (rather than punitive) measure of action taken by states: the Court remained mindful of how the 'reaction' of the United States needed to be defined by 'the period in which any presumed armed attack by Nicaragua could reasonably be contemplated'.[229] To similar effect, in the *Case Concerning Armed Activities*, the Court advised that:

> since the preconditions for the exercise of self-defence do not exist in the circumstances of the present case, the Court has no need to enquire whether such an entitlement to self-defence was in fact exercised in circumstances of necessity and a manner that was proportionate. The Court cannot fail to observe, however, that the taking of airports and towns many hundreds of

---

and *particularly could not justify intervention involving the use of force.*' See *Nicaragua Case*, supra n.20, at 127 (para. 249) (emphasis added). See, further, J.L. Hargrove, 'The *Nicaragua* Judgment and the Future of the Law of Force and Self-Defense', (1987) 81 *AJIL* 135, at 138.

[226] *Nicaragua Case*, supra n.20, at 122–123 (para. 237). In so doing, the Court made reference to paras 80, 81 and 86 of its judgment.

[227] *Ibid.* For the Court, Nicaragua's actions in El Salvador could not amount to an armed attack as that term had been understood in international law, but this did not mean that they did not infringe the prohibition of force: '[s]uch assistance [to rebel force, i.e. in the form of the provision of weapons or logistical or other support] may be regarded as a threat or use of force, or amount to intervention in the internal or external affairs of other States'. *Nicaragua Case*, supra n.20, at 104 (para. 195).

[228] See, further, C. Greenwood, 'Self-Defence and the Conduct of International Armed Conflict', in Y. Dinstein and M. Tabory (eds), *International Law at a Time of Perplexity: Essays in Honour of Shabtai Rosenne* (Dordrecht: Martinus Nijhoff Publishers 1989), 273.

[229] *Supra* n.226.

kilometers from Uganda's border would not seem proportionate to the series of transborder attacks it claimed had given rise to the right of self-defence, nor to be necessary to that end.[230]

Where there may be no question that an armed attack has occurred, the assessment of the proportionality of an action undertaken in self-defence stands to be defined from the animating reason or 'provocation'[231] for the exercise of that right of self-defence – and in the instance of Iraq's invasion of Kuwait, this would have entailed the eviction of any (and all) Iraqi forces from the territory of Kuwait.[232] In short, the actual act and immediate effects of the invasion – or the armed attack, to put it in the language of the *jus ad bellum* – needed to be reversed and the 'authority of the legitimate power' returned to the rightful sovereign of Kuwait.[233] Naturally, the principle of proportionality would accommodate the application of military force towards this end, though some question was raised at the relevant time as to how much further it could go – and would stretch – beyond that point.[234] Importantly, the operation of the principle of proportionality would define the permissible amount of force in self-defence in a much more limited and constraining manner than had the same operation been undertaken with the authorization of the Security Council since, at that stage, it would assume a new point of focus and purpose. The emphasis of Resolution 678 (1990) was not only on the upholding and implementation of Resolution 660 (1990) and all subsequent relevant resolutions of the Security Council – but *also on the restoration of international peace and security in the area*.[235] This reason, amongst others, explains why it was so significant to determine whether the application of force occurred pursuant to the right of individual and collective self-defence or whether it occurred with the institutional imprimatur of the Security Council.[236]

---

[230] *Case Concerning Armed Activities in the Territory of the Congo*, *supra* n.22, at 223 (para. 147).

[231] The term used by Wedgwood, *supra* n.212, at 59.

[232] Separate to the application of the principle of proportionality as a matter of the *jus in bello*. See Greenwood, *supra* n.140, at 173, and, further, F.J. Hampson, 'Proportionality and Necessity in the Gulf Conflict', (1992) 86 *Proceedings ASIL* 45.

[233] This is not the terminology of the *jus ad bellum* – but, rather, of the *jus in bello*. Article 43 of the Hague Regulations provides that '[t]he authority of the legitimate power having in fact passed into the hands of the occupant, the latter shall take all the measures in his power to restore, and ensure, as far as possible, public order and safety, while respecting, unless absolutely prevented, the laws in force in the country'. This comes after the Regulations provide (in Article 42) that '[t]erritory is considered occupied when it is actually placed under the authority of the hostile army'. See, further, Gardam, *supra* n.112, at 159.

[234] For example, the stopping of shipping of states other than Iraq bound to or from ports not under Iraqi control. See Greenwood, *supra* n.140, at 162.

[235] As *per* the second operative paragraph of Resolution 678 (1990).

[236] See Gray, *supra* n.52, at 265 ('[t]he question is only of practical significance if the legal basis affects the scope of the permissible action that could be taken by States'). See, though, the concern regarding proportionality of D.P. Wood in 'Debate: Adjudicating Operation Iraqi Freedom', (2006) 100 *Proceedings ASIL* 179, at 199.

In Operation Change Direction, the action of self-defence undertaken by Israel against Lebanon for Hezbollah's activities in July and August 2006,[237] there was no issue of an authorization forthcoming from the Security Council. As such, the matter was to rest, for better or for worse, on Israel's invocation of its right of self-defence,[238] including (as we can now appreciate) the quantum of its response to the events of 12 July 2006.[239] Within the Security Council, what is striking is the frequency with which those states which fashioned criticism of the behaviour of Israel in terms of its response to these earlier events did so on the premise of proportionality – but also how soon they felt able to do so after Israel initiated its response; these claims were made within a matter of days of Israel's recourse to force against Lebanon.[240] The importance of these criticisms is their implication that a right of self-defence was admitted in the circumstances in which Israel found itself,[241] and that the extent of its force (or, more properly, its early intensity) did not bode well for any satisfaction of the principle or expectations of proportionality by Israel: Russia condemned the actions of Hezbollah, but regarded Israel's response as 'a disproportionate and inappropriate use of force that threatens the sovereignty and territorial integrity of Lebanon and peace and security throughout the region';[242] Argentina believed that Israel had to exercise its right of self-defence 'in accordance with international law and in particular with the provisions of international humanitarian law';[243] for Qatar, '[w]hile we recognize the right of all States, including Lebanon, to defend themselves, the waging of a wide-spread military campaign directly targeting civilians and hitting their infrastructure, such as in the current campaign by the Israeli forces, can in no way be consonant with that objective';[244] China denounced the 'armed aggression' of Israel against Lebanon, arguing that '[t]he Israeli military force have used disproportionate force and have

---

[237] *Supra* nn.193–201 (and accompanying text).

[238] See, though, the Security Council's determination of Israel's 'offensive military operations' in Resolution 1701 (11 August 2006), first operative paragraph. See, also, Schmitt, *supra* n.195, at 128–129.

[239] As framed in the claim of Israel: *supra* n.195 (notwithstanding the considerable evidence that the events of 12 July 2006 themselves occurred within a broader context. See Gray, *supra* n.52, at 239). This means that, for legal purposes, this further context of circumstances had not given rise to an (international) armed conflict, and that the appropriate framework of analysis on this occasion is – first and foremost – the laws of the *jus ad bellum*, followed by the laws of the *jus in bello*. See, further, F.L. Kirgis, 'Some Proportionality Issues Raised by Israel's Use of Force in Lebanon', *ASIL Insights*, Vol. 10, Issue 20 (17 August 2006) and E. Cannizzaro, 'Contextualizing Proportionality: *jus ad bellum* and *jus in bello* in the Lebanese War', (2006) 88 *IRRC* 779.

[240] See, for example, M. Walzer, 'On Proportionality', *The New Republic*, 8 January 2009, and Cannizzaro, *supra* n.239, at 782–783. See, also, the position of the Human Rights Council's Commission of Inquiry, which delivered its report in November 2006: Human Rights Council, Commission of Inquiry on Lebanon, *Report of the Commission of Inquiry on Lebanon Pursuant to Human Rights Council Resolution S-2/1*, UN Doc. A/HRC/3/2 (23 November 2006), para. 61.

[241] Cannizzaro, *supra* n.239, at 780 and also at 782–783.

[242] UN Doc. S/PV.5489 (14 July 2006), at 7.

[243] *Ibid.*, at 9.

[244] *Ibid.*, at 10.

caused massive destruction of infrastructure in Lebanon';[245] Japan acknowledged what it called 'the legitimate security concerns of Israel', but strongly urged Israel 'to refrain from excessive use of force and, in particular, from actions that endanger the civilian population and the infrastructure';[246] the United Kingdom argued that Israel has 'every right to act in self-defence', but that 'it must exercise restraint and ensure that its actions are proportionate and measured, conform to international law and avoid civilian death and suffering';[247] the Democratic Republic of the Congo condemned 'the disproportionate reprisals by the Israeli army, which did not hesitate to bomb Beirut intensively, to launch incursions into southern Lebanon and to impose a land, sea and air blockade of Lebanon';[248] Tanzania expressed grave concern at 'the intensity of the fighting and the disproportionate use of force';[249] Peru recognized Israel's 'right to self-defence and security', but argued that 'it must exercise that right in accordance with the principles and norms of the Charter';[250] Denmark accepted Israel's right of self-defence, though 'care must be taken to ensure that the exercise of that right is proportional and measured';[251] Slovakia, too, recognized and acknowledged the right of each and every state to act in self-defence, '[b]ut that right cannot, and should not, be confused with counterattacks or acts of military provocation';[252] and, for Greece, 'while preserving the right of self-defence, Israel must respect is obligations under international law, including international humanitarian law, as well as the sovereignty and territorial integrity of Lebanon'.[253]

When the Security Council convened a week later, Lebanon concentrated on the theme of the proportionality – or disproportionality – of the ongoing hostilities which, it was reported to the Council, had claimed the lives of 300 Lebanese and 34 Israelis, with over 500 Lebanese and approximately 200 Israelis injured.[254] Lebanon was of the

---

[245] *Ibid.*, at 11.
[246] *Ibid.*, at 12 (Japan made reference to the Israeli military operations of 13 July 2006, 'which caused many civilian casualties and the destruction of the airport facilities in Lebanon').
[247] *Ibid.* ('Disproportionate action will only escalate an already dangerous situation.')
[248] *Ibid.*, at 13 (described as 'acts of war that endanger the civilian population and that destroy socio-economic infrastructure and seriously weaken the Lebanon authorities, who are embarked upon a national dialogue that we have encouraged').
[249] *Ibid.*
[250] *Ibid.*, at 14.
[251] *Ibid.*, at 15.
[252] *Ibid.*, at 16.
[253] *Ibid.*, at 17.
[254] According to Vijay Nambiar, Special Adviser to the Secretary-General. See UN Doc.S/PV.5493 (21 July 2006), at 4; who also advised, *ibid.* at 5, that:

> Israel had decided that military operations would continue until Hizbollah was seriously weakened; this was not, as in the past, a response to a particular incident – the abduction of two soldiers – but was a definitive response to an unacceptable strategic threat posed by Hizbollah and a message to Iran and Syria that threats by proxies would no longer be tolerated. It was stated [by Israel] that the Israeli captives must be unconditionally released and that, this time, Israel was not prepared to negotiate with Hizbollah through third parties, which in the past had led to prisoner exchanges.

view that Israel was 'betting on its excessive force to settle its problems with its neighbours',[255] advising the Council:

> [s]ince the beginning of its military operations [ten] days ago, Israel destroyed Lebanon's infrastructure and targeted its civilians, destroying their livelihoods and disrupting their movements. The death toll has risen to well over 350, with more than 1,000 injured and half a million displaced and without shelter. Tens of thousands of foreigners have fled the country – foreigners that Lebanon had succeeded in attracting over the past 15 years after it was able to rebuild itself and rise from the wreckage to play a constructive role in the region and the world.[256]

This recounting of the debates and positions held within the Security Council ultimately reveals a test of the parameters of the principle of proportionality, and its function and utility in practice for defining the scope of the right of self-defence: the principle, it is clear, emphasizes the importance of defining the yardstick for the right of self-defence whether in terms of the imminence of an armed attack or the occurrence of an actual armed attack, at the same time that it recalls the general purpose of each act of self-defence.[257] However, difficulties also soon surface as to which considerations are to be deemed relevant to the calculation of proportionality – whether this is to be measured in terms of lives lost, injuries sustained, or further humanitarian consequences such as displacement and disruption of food and medical supplies – and, of course, its relationship in actual terms with the principle of proportionality when operating as part of the *jus in bello*.[258]

7. SELF-DEFENCE AND THE UN SECURITY COUNCIL

A. The Until Clause and the Duration of the Right of Self-defence

If the principle of proportionality is designed to mark out the extent of the permissible exercise of the right of self-defence under international law, Article 51 of the Charter of the United Nations introduces what might be termed an institutional dimension to the duration of this right with the stipulation of its 'until clause',[259] which provides that the right of self-defence remains available to states 'until the Security Council has taken measures necessary to maintain international peace and security'.[260] This stands to reason, for:

---

[255] *Ibid.*, at 13.
[256] *Ibid.* These sentiments also found expression in the report of Jan Egland, Under-Secretary General for Humanitarian Affairs and Emergency Relief Co-ordinator, to the Council. *Ibid.*, at 6.
[257] See the discussion in Schmitt, *supra* n.195, at 153; and, also, at 154. See, also, *supra* n.219.
[258] Cannizzaro, *supra* n.239, at 781.
[259] See Randelzhofer, *supra* n.2, at 804–805.
[260] For a fuller exploration of the background history to this aspect of Article 51, see Alexandrov, *supra* n.4, at 87–88.

[w]ithin a system of collective security organized on the basis of a complete centralization of the legitimate use of force, self-defense as a case of decentralized use of force is an exceptional and provisional interlude between an act of illegal use of force ... and the collective enforcement action which the community, through its central organ, is to take as a sanction against the illegal use of force.[261]

And this fact is recognized by those conventional arrangements devoted to collective self-defence that we have canvassed earlier in the chapter. For example, the Warsaw Pact provided that measures undertaken in collective self-defence 'shall be discontinued immediately [when] the Security Council adopts the necessary measures to restore and maintain international peace and security',[262] and, for the North Atlantic Treaty Organization, such measures 'shall be terminated when the Security Council has taken the measures necessary to maintain international peace and security'.[263]

To be sure, Article 51 does not elaborate further as to *when* this moment will occur *in stricto sensu*, but, in setting out the terms of the reporting requirement for self-defence (which we shall soon come to consider), it should be observed that this aspect of Article 51 actually adverts to 'the authority and responsibility of the Security Council under the present Charter to take at any time such action as it deems necessary in order to *maintain* or *restore* international peace and security'.[264] These contrasting formulations within Article 51 begin to hint at potential difficulties at giving concrete meaning to the until clause because, on the one hand, the mention of measures *necessary* to maintain international peace and security suggests that these measures need to be proven, or, at the very least, they need to be amenable to objective

---

[261] Kelsen, *supra* n.65, at 785.

[262] *Supra* n.74, Article 4.

[263] *Ibid.*, Article 5. Ditto Article V of the ANZUS Treaty: 'Such measures shall be terminated when the Security Council has taken the measures necessary to restore and maintain international peace and security.' *Supra* n.76.

[264] *Supra* nn.2, 265 and 290 (emphasis added). Indeed, an earlier version of the 'until clause' provided for the right of self-defence 'until the Security Council has taken measures necessary to maintain or restore international peace and security', but the USSR considered that the word 'maintain' encompassed the notion of the *restoring* of international peace and security; the United Kingdom, the United States, China and France had all expressed a preference for retaining the word 'restore' in the context of the 'until clause', but it was thought that the final formulation presented the possibility for a united front of all putative permanent members of the Security Council. This legislative background of Article 51 is helpfully recalled by M. Halberstam, 'The Right to Self-Defense Once the Security Council Takes Action', (1996) 17 *Michigan JIL* 229, at 243–244. On three separate occasions – Article 39, Article 42 and Article 51 itself – does the Charter invoke the notion of the maintenance *or* restoration of international peace and security. Article 51 is unique in this set of provisions because it additionally addresses itself (in the form of the until clause) to the *maintenance* of international peace and security, a form of words that also occurs in the preamble ('to unite our strength and to maintain international peace and security'); Article 1 ('[t]o maintain international peace and security'); Article 43 ('necessary for the purpose of maintaining international peace and security'); and Article 106 ('as may be necessary for the purpose of maintaining international peace and security'). These linguistic variations, however, only lead to positions of 'possible conjecture', according to D.W. Greig, 'Self-Defence and the Security Council: What Does Article 51 Require?', (1991) 40 *ICLQ* 366, at 389.

identification – a process that could conceivably reduce the overall effect of the until clause if the general idea is to wait until *adequate* and *effective* measures have indeed been taken by the Security Council;[265] on the other hand, it cannot go unnoticed that, with its reference to 'such action as [the Security Council] deems necessary in order to maintain or restore international peace and security', the reporting requirement of Article 51 injects a subjective element into its appraisal of things, one very different from that signalled in the context of the until clause of the very same provision of the Charter. It is a formulation that indicates that, at various points of its engagement with the maintenance or restoration of international peace and security, the Security Council may be of the view that *multiple* measures may be called for – 'such action as *it* deems necessary' – each of which might well not coincide with the measures that are actually necessary for the purposes of interpreting or activating the until clause.

These different possibilities all came to the fore following Iraq's invasion of Kuwait in August 1990,[266] when the Security Council adopted a series of measures through resolutions adopted under Chapter VII of the Charter,[267] commencing with its condemnation of the invasion and its demand that Iraq 'withdraw immediately and unconditionally' all of its forces to their positions the day before the invasion (Resolution 660).[268] Amongst other measures taken, the Security Council also adopted comprehensive economic sanctions against Iraq (Resolution 661),[269] as well as a naval interdiction

---

[265] The emphasis of Halberstam, *supra* n.264, at 242. See, also, Bowett, *supra* n.9, at 196 and Franck, *supra* n.178, at 841. The Permanent Representative of Argentina claimed that the right of self-defence of the United Kingdom 'cannot be invoked when the Security Council had adopted measures for the maintenance of international peace and security, the first provision of which demands precisely the immediate cessation of hostilities'. UN Doc. S/15014 (29 April 1982). This was a reference to Resolution 502 (1982), which the Security Council had adopted on 3 April 1982 (*infra* n.283). The United Kingdom rejected this assertion of Argentina – '[i]t hardly lies in the mouth of Argentina to invoke the terms of ... Resolution 502 (1982) when it is Argentina which has persistently refused by word and deed to comply with the terms of that resolution for no less than 27 days' (UN Doc. S/15017 (30 April 1982)) – and it also argued before the Council that the until clause of Article 51 could be taken to refer to measures which were 'actually effective to bring about the stated objective'. Since Resolution 502 (1982) had not proved effective, the right of self-defence remained unimpaired. See UN Doc. S/PV.2360.

[266] See, in particular, E.V. Rostow, 'Until What? Enforcement Action or Collective Self-Defense?', (1991) 86 *AJIL* 506 and T.M. Franck and F. Patel, 'UN Police Action in Lieu of War: "The Old Order Changeth"', (1991) 85 *AJIL* 63. See, further, K.S. Elliott, 'The New World Order and the Right of Self-Defense in the United Nations Charter', (1992) 15 *Hastings ICLR* 55 and T.K. Plofchan, Jr., 'Article 51: Limits on Self-Defense?', (1992) 13 *Michigan JIL* 336.

[267] Consider Randelzhofer, *supra* n.2, at 804.

[268] A resolution in which the Security Council determined that 'there exists a breach of international peace and security as regards the Iraqi invasion of Kuwait', and in which it acted under Articles 39 and 40 of the Charter of the United Nations.

[269] A resolution in which the Security Council, acting under Chapter VII of the Charter, determined that Iraq had failed to comply with its demand for the immediate and unconditional withdrawal of Iraqi forces from Kuwait and decided '*as a consequence* to take ... measures to secure compliance of Iraq with ... Resolution 660 (1990) *and to restore the authority of the legitimate government of Kuwait*' (emphases added). This resolution ended with the Council deciding 'to keep this item on its agenda and to continue to put an early end to the invasion by Iraq' (eleventh operative paragraph).

that would 'halt all inward and outward maritime shipping in order to inspect and verify their cargoes and destinations' (Resolution 665).[270] Finally, and *in ultimo*, the Council authorized Member States of the United Nations which were co-operating with the Government of Kuwait 'to use all necessary means to uphold and implement Resolution 660 (1990) and all subsequent relevant resolutions *and to restore international peace and security in the area*'.[271]

The *restoration* of international peace and security therefore seems to be a recurrent theme with all of these resolutions,[272] although the Security Council did announce in Resolution 678 (1990) that it was '[m]indful of its duties and responsibilities under the Charter of the United Nations for the maintenance and preservation of international peace and security',[273] as if it were setting down the foundation for the argument that the restoration of international peace and security was an essential first step towards ensuring its maintenance and preservation.[274] Be this as it may, Iraq was of the view that with its 'hasty and unjust' adoption of Resolution 661 on 6 August 1990, the Council had in fact taken the measures envisaged in the first sentence of Article 51 and that the until clause had thereby been activated.[275] In making this argument, it is clear that Iraq had not adopted or chosen to pursue the more extreme interpretation of the until clause – that as soon as the Security Council became seized of an issue, that fact alone is sufficient to set the consequences of the until clause in motion.[276] Nevertheless, the United States wasted no time in pointing to the specific terms of Resolution 661 (1990) – in which the Security Council actually affirmed 'the inherent right of individual or collective self-defence, in response to the armed attack by Iraq against

---

[270] Again, in the final (fifth) operative paragraph of the resolution, the Security Council decided to 'remain actively seized of the matter'. Notably, the preamble to this resolution announced the Council's determination 'to bring an end to the occupation of Kuwait by Iraq which imperils the existence of a Member State *and to restore the legitimate authority, and the sovereignty, independence and territorial integrity of Kuwait which requires the speedy implementation of the ... resolutions [660 (1990), 661 (1990), 662 (1990) and 664 (1990)]*' (emphasis added).

[271] Second operative paragraph of Resolution 678 (1990) (emphasis added). See, further, B.H. Weston, 'Security Council Resolution 678 and Persian Gulf Decision Making: Precarious Legitimacy', (1991) 86 *AJIL* 516. The qualification of member states co-operating with the Government of Kuwait is emphasized by V. Lowe, 'The Iraq Crisis: What Now?', (2003) 52 *ICLQ* 859, at 866.

[272] In Resolution 662 (1990), third and fourth preambular paragraphs; in Resolution 674 (1990), second and eleventh preambular paragraphs. Consider, too, the fifth and seventh preambular paragraphs of Resolution 83 (1950).

[273] Third preambular paragraph.

[274] Ditto Resolution 674, *ibid.*, which, in the ninth preambular paragraph, reaffirmed 'the goal of the international community of maintaining international peace and security by seeking to resolve international disputes and conflicts through peaceful means'. Indeed, in the eighth (and final) operative paragraph of Resolution 686 (1991), the Security Council announced that it would remain actively seized of the matter 'in order to secure the rapid establishment of a definitive end to the hostilities'.

[275] UN Doc. S/PV.2937 (18 August 1990), at 42.

[276] As *per* the apparent interpretation of Professor Rein Mullerson (as cited by Rostow, *supra* n.266, at 511).

Kuwait, in accordance with Article 51 of the Charter'[277] – to underscore its position that the lawfulness of the exercise of collective self-defence continued beyond the adoption of Resolution 661 (1990).[278]

This approach accords, too, with the general interpretation we should attach to the until clause's reference to measures taken by the Security Council 'necessary to maintain international peace and security',[279] since, it is clear, economic sanctions in and of themselves would not have been able to reverse Iraq's action (as well as its ensuing consolidation of this action) of 2 August 1990.[280] That said, it is unclear what measures might be 'necessary' in this very sense in which the until clause intends that term absent the Security Council's capacities to assert or apply its *own* force in international relations,[281] or whether the political realities of the foreseeable future are such that the Security Council is confined to providing authorizations of force in accordance with the terms of Chapter VII of the Charter.[282] Still, it is instructive how varied the responses of the Security Council have been in situations in which the right of self-defence has been claimed. During the hostilities over the Falkland Islands, the Security Council demanded an immediate cessation of hostilities in the same breath that it also demanded 'an immediate withdrawal of all Argentine forces from the Falkland Islands (Islas Malvinas)';[283] following the successful reversal of the Iraqi invasion and occupation of Kuwait in February 1991, the Security Council adopted a comprehensive cease-fire resolution which declared that 'upon official notification by Iraq to the Secretary-General and to the Security Council of its acceptance of [these] provisions ... a formal cease-fire is effective between Iraq and Kuwait and the Member States cooperating with Kuwait in accordance with Resolution 678 (1990)';[284] in

---

[277] *Supra* n.269 (seventh preambular paragraph).
[278] Importantly, the ninth operative paragraph of the same resolution made clear that 'nothing in the present resolution shall prohibit assistance to the legitimate Government of Kuwait'. See, also, Greenwood, *supra* n.140, at 164.
[279] *See* Greenwood, *supra* n.140, at 164 ('[i]t is very doubtful ... that economic measures will have the same effect [as the use of force]').
[280] See J. Simpson, *From the House of War* (London: Arrow Books, 1991), at 380.
[281] As was to be provided under Article 43(1) of the Charter. See J.A. Frowein and N. Krisch, 'Article 43', in Simma (ed.), *supra* n.2, 760, at 763. See, further, J.E. Rossman, 'Article 43: Arming the United Nations Security Council', (1994) 27 *NYUJILP* 227. See, also, Christian Henderson's chapter in this volume (chapter 5).
[282] Though it has of course been mooted that Resolution 678 might have been 'merely a case of the [Security] Council giving its blessing to action based upon the right of self-defence': Greenwood, *supra* n.140, at 167. See, also Rossman, *supra* n.281, at 231 and Rostow, *supra* n.267, at 508–509. The exhortatory character of this authorization – cast as it was in recommendatory terms, and not as an institutional obligation – led Rostow to conclude (*ibid.*, at 510) that the Security Council 'conceived of its actions as supplementing the programs of collective self-defence organized by the United States, not as supplanting them'.
[283] First and second operative paragraphs, respectively, of Resolution 502 (1982) (3 April 1982). Curiously, the Government of Argentina put more store on the former of these demands than it did on the latter: it emphasized '[r]espect for the cessation of hostilities is something to be demanded of both parties. Its violation originates with the United Kingdom, which has already sent a large fleet of war to the zone and initiated a naval blockade of the islands. This fleet also includes nuclear submarines.' See UN Doc. S/14968 (12 April 1982).
[284] Resolution 687 (1991) (3 April 1991), thirty-third operative paragraph.

August 2006, almost one month to the day since Israel invoked its right of self-defence as against Lebanon, the Security Council called for 'a full cessation of hostilities based upon, in particular, the immediate cessation by Hizbollah of all attacks and the immediate cessation by Israel of all offensive military operations'.[285] Each of these representations by the Security Council suggests how conscious the Council has been of 'its responsibilities to help secure a permanent ceasefire and a long-term solution to the conflict',[286] but the effect of each of these interventions is more uncertain in terms of any significance they yield for the purposes of the until clause of Article 51 of the Charter. To *call upon* states to do something, including to cease their respective fires with one another, is very different from *demanding* that they do the very same thing,[287] and it perhaps remains appropriate, in particular view of the inherent character of the right of self-defence, to conclude that '[o]nce action in self-defence is in motion, it requires an affirmative decision of the Council, including the concurring votes of the Permanent Members, to order the cessation of defensive action'.[288]

B. The Reporting Requirement

Finally, and as we have already mentioned, Article 51 requires that those measures taken by Member States of the United Nations in the exercise of the right of individual or collective self-defence 'shall be immediately reported to the Security Council',[289] so that a reporting requirement is appended to each invocation of this right in practice.[290] There is no stipulation in Article 51 as to the actual form or contents that such a report should entail,[291] and there is a marked variance in what states have chosen to report (and not to report) to the Council and the frequency with which reports have made their way to the Council over the entire period of an operation undertaken in self-defence. Consider and contrast the extent of the reporting of the United States to the Council in respect of its right of collective self-defence in Vietnam[292] with the reports filed by the

---

[285] Security Council Resolution 1701 (2006) (11 August 2006), first operative paragraph.

[286] As the Security Council has itself put it – in the ninth preambular paragraph to Resolution 1701 (2006).

[287] Hence, in Resolution 660 (1990) – adopted on the very day that Iraq's armed forces invaded Kuwait – the Security Council demanded that Iraq 'withdraw immediately and unconditionally all its forces to the positions in which they were located on 1 August 1990' (second operative paragraph), but it also called upon Iraq and Kuwait 'to begin immediately intensive negotiations for the resolution of their differences and support all efforts in this regard, and especially those of the League of Arab States' (third operative paragraph).

[288] See Waldock, *supra* n.93, at 495–496.

[289] As *per* the text accompanying *supra* n.2.

[290] For further examination, consider Gray, *supra* n.52, at 121–124 and Greig, *supra* n.264, at 367–388. Greig draws a distinction between a requirement that is 'mandatory' (so that a claim of self-defence would 'lose its validity if the action is not reported in accordance with Article 51') as opposed to 'directory' in character ('in the sense that non-compliance with the requirement does not invalidate the plea of self-defence'): *ibid.*, at 367.

[291] Cf. *supra* n.89 (regarding the procedural requirements for collective self-defence).

[292] See Gray, *supra* n.52, at 188. Following the request by the United States for an urgent meeting of the Security Council in August 1964 (UN Doc. S/5849 (5 August 1964)), Ambassador Stevenson of the United States noted before the Council that 'a series of deliberate

United Kingdom following Argentina's use of force in the Falkland Islands in April 1982.[293]

In the *Nicaragua Case*, the International Court of Justice found that:

> in customary international law it is not a condition of the lawfulness of the use of force in self-defence that a procedure so closely dependent on the content of a treaty commitment and of the institution established by it, should have been followed.[294]

---

hostile actions have already taken place' – those occurring in the Gulf of Tonkin – and that 'the Charter of the United Nations provides not for deliberate consideration, but explicitly calls for immediate reporting to the Council, of measures taken by Members in the exercise of their right of self-defence'. See UN Doc. S/PV.1140 (5 August 1964), at 3. In a letter dated 7 February 1965, Stevenson informed the Council of 'acts which have further disturbed the peace in Viet-Nam' committed by the Viet Cong – or so it was alleged – and advised of the 'prompt defensive action' that was taken from the air 'against certain military facilities in the southern area of North Viet-Nam' that same day. According to Stevenson, '[t]he Republic of Viet-Nam and, at its request, the Government of the United States and other Governments are resisting this systematic and continuing aggression. Since reinforcement of the Viet Cong by infiltrators from North Viet-Nam is essential to this continuing aggression, counter-measures to arrest such reinforcement from the outside are a justified measure of self-defence.' See UN Doc. S/6174 (8 February 1965). This report of the United States was therefore used as much to convey the exercise of the right of collective self-defence – together with the particularities that attend that designation – as well as to provide details of the actual operation ('an attack was carried through against Dong Hoi, which is a military installation and one of the major staging areas for the infiltration of armed cadres of North Viet-Namese troops into South Viet-Nam in violation of international law and of the Geneva Agreements of 1954'). See, further, R.A. Falk, 'International Law and the United States Role in the Viet Nam War', (1966) 75 *Yale LJ* 1122.

[293] See, for example, UN Doc. S/14961 (9 April 1982); UN Doc. S/14963 (10 April 1982); UN Doc. S/14964 (11 April 1982); UN Doc. S/14973 (13 April 1982); UN Doc. S/14997 (24 April 1982); UN Doc. S/15002 (26 April 1982); UN Doc. S/15006 (28 April 1982); UN Doc. S/15010 (29 April 1982); UN Doc. S/15016 (30 April 1982); UN Doc. S/15031 (4 May 1982); UN Doc. S/15058 (8 May 1982); UN Doc. S/15063 (10 May 1982); UN Doc. S/15098 (20 May 1982); UN Doc. S/15104 (23 May 1982); UN Doc. S/15134 (28 May 1982); and UN Doc. S/15307 (22 July 1982). Since Argentina also claimed that it was exercising its right of self-defence, it, too, reported that claim to the Security Council. See UN Doc. S/14961 (9 April 1982); UN Doc. S/15018 (30 April 1982); and UN Doc. S/15059 (8 May 1982). See, further, UN Doc. S/14968 (12 April 1982) and UN Doc. S/14999 (25 April 1982). Consider, further, S. Korman, *The Right of Conquest: The Acquisition of Territory by Force in International Law and Practice* (Oxford: Oxford University Press, 1996), at 275–280 and T.M. Franck, '*Dulce et Decorum Est*: The Strategic Role of Legal Principles in the Falklands War', (1983) 77 *AJIL* 109.

[294] *Nicaragua Case*, supra n.20, at 105 (para. 200). In this, the Court was very much influenced by the correspondence of the given rule with the institutional design of the Charter; it had earlier concluded that '[t]he principle of non-use of force ... may thus be regarded as a principle of customary international law, not as such conditioned by provisions relating to collective security, or to the facilities of armed contingents to be provided under Article 43 of the Charter. It would therefore seem apparent that the attitude referred to expresses an *opinio juris* respecting such rule (or set of rules), to be thenceforth treated separately from the provisions, especially those of an institutional kind, to which it is subject on the treaty-plane of the Charter.' *Ibid.*, at 100 (para. 188). The Court later referred to 'a principle enshrined in a treaty [that] may well be so unencumbered with the conditions and modalities surrounding it in the treaty.' *Ibid.*, at 105 (para. 200).

The Court followed this up by saying that it would therefore not treat the absence of a report on the part of the United States 'as the breach of an undertaking forming part of the customary international law applicable to the present dispute'.[295] Taken together, these representations of the Court might well be taken to suggest that, as a matter of the strict letter of the law of the Charter as opposed to the position in custom, compliance with the reporting requirement *is* indeed very much indispensible to any successful claim of self-defence being made – or, as it has been put elsewhere, 'the duty of reporting becomes a substantive condition and a limitation on the exercise of self-defence'.[296] That conclusion could have far-reaching resonance if one considers that the vast majority of states are now members of the United Nations, and that the reason for the Court's observation in that case was the jurisdictional reservation of the United States[297] – and *not* because one of the states appearing before it was not a high contracting party to the United Nations Charter.

Having considered the comparative status of this requirement as a matter of both convention and of custom, the Court then proceeded to observe that it was 'justified' in 'observing that this conduct of the United States' – in other words, its failure to report its military and paramilitary activities in Nicaragua as an exercise of its right of collective self-defence – 'hardly conforms with the [United States'] avowed conviction that it was acting in the context of collective self-defence as consecrated by Article 51 of the Charter'.[298] The Court therefore seized on the absence of a report from the United States as evidence of the veracity of its claim in self-defence, and this was made all the more noteworthy (the Court said) because 'in the Security Council, the United States has itself taken the view that failure to observe the requirement to make a report contradicted a State's claim to be acting on the basis of collective self-defence'.[299] This was a reference to the position held by the United States in the context of the Soviet Union's intervention in Afghanistan in November 1979:

---

[295] *Nicaragua Case, supra* n.20, at 121 (para. 235). The failure of the United States to report the exercise of its right of collective self-defence in respect of Nicaragua deserves to be contrasted with the report it filed with the Council in respect of its action to assist the Government of Kuwait: the United States informed the Council that, 'in accordance with Article 51 of the Charter', it moved 'to report that the United States has deployed military forces to the Persian Gulf region' and that '[t]hese forces have been dispatched in exercise of the inherent right of individual and collective self-defence, recognized in Article 51, in response to developments and requests from the Government in the region, including requests from Kuwait and Saudi Arabia, for assistance'. See UN Doc S/21492.

[296] Dinstein, *supra* n.44, at 240 – or, to fashion it in Greig's terms, the requirement is of a mandatory as opposed to directory kind (*supra* n.290).

[297] Which, as *per supra* n.56, requires that all parties to a multilateral treaty that would be affected by a decision of the Court on the treaty must be parties to the case. See US Declaration of 14 August 1946, 61 Stat. 1218 (1947).

[298] *Nicaragua Case, supra* n.20, at 121 (para. 235).

[299] *Ibid.*, at 121–122 (para. 235).

[t]hat neither the Soviet Union nor the puppet régime it has installed in Afghanistan has given the required notice to the Security Council under Article 51 is itself evidence of the hollowness of the Soviet Union's refuge in the Charter.[300]

For the Court, then, as for the United States, the *reporting* of the exercise of the right of self-defence to the Security Council had important probative value, quite apart from any substantive significance that one might wish to award it.

The Court remains mindful of occasions in which states have – for whatever reason – failed to report the exercise of their right of self-defence,[301] even though, in the *Nicaragua Case*, Judge Stephen M. Schwebel outlined the difficulties he had with the value the Court seemed to attach to the reporting requirement under international law. According to Judge Schwebel:

> Defensive measures may be overt or covert, and have been in wars fought before and after the entry into force of the United Nations Charter. In the Korean War, United Nations support for paramilitary and covert operations was not regarded as illegal by the United Nations. During the covert hostilities conducted by Indonesia against Malaysia in 1965, the United Kingdom not only provided covert assistance to Malaysia but also reportedly provided covert assistance to guerrilla and insurgent forces operating against President Sukarno's forces within Indonesia. Any such measures were not reported to the Security Council, but they would not appear to have been any less defensive for that. Thus it appears that, in resisting aggression, covert measures have been and legitimately may be used, which could not, by their nature, be reported to the Security Council without prejudicing the security and effectiveness of those measures.[302]

Notwithstanding this set of observations, Article 51 does not discriminate between the different invocations of self-defence that occur in practice – individual or collective; overt versus covert operations; presumably anticipatory as well as all other forms of self-defence – and we can appreciate that its effort in respect of the reporting requirement is to preserve the right of self-defence as well as adapt it to the modern context of the universal collective security system of which it forms so profound and fitting a part.

---

[300] UN Doc. S/PV.2187 (6 January 1980), at 3. Had the Court enquired further into these deliberations of the Security Council, it would have found that Liberia asked certain questions regarding 'the clear stipulations of Article 51' (*ibid.*, at 12), one of which concerned the second sentence of that provision: 'Far from having had a report of these supposed acts of self-defence [by the Soviet Union] to the Security Council, we have heard both the Soviet representative and the Foreign Minister of Afghanistan declare that the Security Council has no competence to discuss this issue. Accordingly, even in the view of those Governments, Article 51 does not apply in this case. If Article 51 does not apply, then it seems to us that the Charter has been violated' (*ibid.*, at 13).

[301] In the *Armed Activities Case*, the Court did not lose sight of the fact that Uganda had not reported to the Security Council that it had exercised its right of self-defence as against the Democratic Republic of Congo in August and September 1998: *Case Concerning Armed Activities in the Territory of the Congo*, supra n.22, at 222 (para. 145).

[302] *Nicaragua Case*, supra n.20, at 374 (para. 223).

8. CONCLUSION

This chapter has sought to provide a detailed account – but, also, an appropriate amount of empirical data – on the right of self-defence in international law: its history, the various interpretations and practices of states, the meaning and significance of Article 51 of the Charter of the United Nations and its relation to the seminal *Caroline* correspondence of 1838–1842. Throughout, we have been alert to the 'inherent' character of the right as described by the Charter, which must mean that it is for states in the first instance to determine whether their right of self-defence could be invoked as a matter of international law. However, the articulation of the principles of necessity and proportionality from the *Caroline* correspondence must also mean that claims made in respect of the invocation and application of the right of self-defence become the subject of critical assessment by other states and, even on occasion, by a court of law. States which claim that they have acted pursuant to their right of individual or collective self-defence cannot therefore have the last say on the lawfulness of their actions; such an approach would reduce the concept of self-defence to no more than a self-serving justification for each and every military action that is taken, one that carries no continuous or coherent meaning from one precedent or moment of application to the next.

The Charter has built upon this framework of the *Caroline* correspondence with its reference to an armed attack, but also with its specification of the 'until clause' and its reporting requirement – developments that clearly seek to align this traditional right of states with the evolving collective security system of the Charter, and, specifically, the powers and responsibilities of the Security Council under Chapter VII of the Charter.[303] We have observed how the right of individual and collective self-defence has been used in a fascinating span of circumstances – ranging from the invasion and occupation of an entire country (Kuwait in August 1990) to the concerted actions of terrorist actors (in the United States in September 2001) – and how states, time and time and time again, have found it necessary to reflect on the legal positions that have been put forward by states having recourse to this right. The International Court of Justice, too, has acted as an occasional interpreter of the right of self-defence, but its interpretations have been forthcoming on a much less regular basis than those of states,[304] and have very much served to highlight how the right of self-defence is regulated as a matter of conventional *and* customary international law – where its significance has not been confined to instances of regular and irregular force committed on the territory of a state. Plainly, this all speaks to the versatility of application of the rights of individual and collective self-defence in international law, but it is also the case, as we have so often seen, that not every invocation of the right earns the favour of other states or of the Court – and it is these practices that have come to inform the content of the *lex lata* for individual and collective self-defence.

---

[303] *Supra* nn.8 and 9 (and accompanying text).
[304] *Supra* n.19.

7. The use of force for humanitarian purposes
Christine Gray

1. INTRODUCTION

Humanitarian intervention remains a very controversial area of international law. For many commentators the paradigm case is that of NATO's 1999 operation over Kosovo, but states are still divided on the legality of this use of force. As Kosovo pursues independence today the question whether it was created by the unlawful use of force is still important. The doctrine of humanitarian intervention is strongly opposed by the Non-Aligned Movement, which regards it as a pretext for intervention by powerful states. It is not acceptable to Russia or China. Few states openly support the legal doctrine; even fewer have relied on it to justify their use of force. The African Union (hereinafter 'AU') has provision for humanitarian intervention in its Constitutive Act, but there are some questions about the interpretation of this provision. Perhaps of equal importance, the scope of the doctrine remains unclear. What is the threshold for humanitarian intervention? Does the situation have to constitute a threat to international peace and security? Can an air campaign constitute humanitarian action? In recent years the focus has shifted from the controversial doctrine of humanitarian intervention to the more appealing but still problematic 'responsibility to protect' (hereinafter 'R2P'). The interventions in Libya and Côte d'Ivoire have been hailed as the implementation of the R2P doctrine, but this practice has led to divisions between states and between commentators as to the future of this doctrine.

2. LEGAL BASIS OF HUMANITARIAN INTERVENTION

For supporters of humanitarian intervention – that is, the unilateral use of force in a third state for humanitarian aims – the legal basis is essentially an interpretation of Article 2(4) of the UN Charter which allows the use of force to further the purposes of the UN, in particular the protection of human rights.[1] Article 2(4) provides: 'All Members shall refrain in their international relations from the threat or use of force against the territorial integrity or political independence of any state, or in any other manner inconsistent with the Purposes of the United Nations.' Supporters of the doctrine of humanitarian intervention argue that the last section of this article means that states may use force to intervene for humanitarian purposes because this does not harm the state's territorial integrity or political independence. Initially this type of argument on the interpretation of Article 2(4) was based on the deadlock in the UN

---

[1] F.R. Teson, *Humanitarian Intervention: An Inquiry into Law and Morality*, 2nd edn (Dobbs Ferry, NY: Transnational Publishers, 1997), at 151.

Security Council during the Cold War: because the UN collective security system under Chapter VII of the Charter could not operate as originally planned, member states could reinterpret Article 2(4) to allow the use of force to further the purposes of the UN.[2] Today the argument for the legality of humanitarian intervention is more likely to be based on the growth in importance of human rights and the restrictions on state sovereignty. It is claimed that since the protection of human rights is no longer a purely domestic matter, a use of force for humanitarian purposes overrides the prohibition of the use of force.[3]

However, there is a fundamental division on this issue of the interpretation of Article 2(4) and the legality of humanitarian intervention. For those states and commentators who oppose humanitarian intervention the position is simple. Article 2(4) is an absolute prohibition of the use of force; its concluding words are not to be construed as a loophole allowing the use of force for what states may claim to be benign purposes.[4] These words limit rather than enable the use of force.[5] Since the prohibition of the use of force is also *jus cogens*, the creation of new exceptions to the prohibition would need universal support, and maybe even revision of the UN Charter.[6] It is not enough that human rights law has (at least in part) now also achieved this status of *jus cogens*; that in itself is not enough to override the *jus cogens* prohibition of the use of force. This interpretation of Article 2(4) is confirmed by the most important General Assembly resolutions on the prohibition of the use of force and on the principle of non-intervention. The *Declaration on Friendly Relations* contains a blanket prohibition of forcible intervention and makes no provision for humanitarian intervention.[7] The *Definition of Aggression* is even more categorical; it provides that 'No consideration of whatever nature, whether political, economic, military or otherwise, may serve as a justification for aggression.'[8]

Those who deny the legality of humanitarian intervention also invoke the statements by the International Court of Justice (hereinafter 'ICJ') in the *Corfu Channel* and *Nicaragua* cases which can be seen as adopting a strict interpretation of Article 2(4). In *Corfu Channel* the Court rejected the UK's alleged right of forcible intervention to

---

[2] See, generally, M. Reisman, 'Coercion and Self-determination', (1984) 78 *AJIL* 642.

[3] C. Greenwood, *Essays on War in International Law* (London: Cameron May, 2006), at 593.

[4] I. Brownlie, *International Law and the Use of Force by States* (Oxford: Oxford University Press, 1963), at 267; O. Corten, *The Law Against War: The Prohibition of the Use of Force in Contemporary International Law* (Oxford: Hart Publishing, 2010), at 495.

[5] This is revealed in the *travaux préparatoires*. See A. Randelzhofer, 'Article 2(4)', in B. Simma (ed.), *The Charter of the United Nations: A Commentary*, 2nd edn (Oxford: Oxford University Press, 2002), 112, at paras 37–39.

[6] Indeed, under Article 53 of the Vienna Convention of the Law of Treaties (1969) 'a peremptory norm of general international law is a norm accepted and recognized by the international community of States as a whole as a norm from which no derogation is permitted and which can be modified only by a subsequent norm of general international law having the same character'.

[7] Declaration on Principles of International Law Concerning Friendly Relations and Co-operation Among States in Accordance with the Charter of the United Nations, 24 October 1970, GA Res. 2625 (XXV) (1970).

[8] Definition of Aggression, 14 December 1974, GA Res. 3314 (XXIX) (1974).

rescue evidence from Albania's territorial waters.⁹ One of the UK's arguments was that its military action was lawful as it did not threaten the territorial integrity or political independence of Albania. The Court held that the UK's claim to a right of intervention was based on a policy of force 'such as has, in the past, given rise to most serious abuses and such as cannot, whatever be the present defects in international organization, find a place in international law'. In *Nicaragua* the Court interpreted this ruling as a blanket condemnation of intervention.[10] The USA did not expressly put forward the doctrine of humanitarian intervention to justify its support for the armed opposition (the contras) in their attempt to overthrow the government of Nicaragua. Nevertheless the Court considered whether US action could be legally justified in protection of human rights. It said:

> the use of force could not be the appropriate method to monitor or ensure such respect. With regard to the steps actually taken, the protection of human rights, a strictly humanitarian objective, cannot be compatible with the mining of ports, the destruction of oil installations, or again with the training, arming and equipping of the contras.[11]

Thus, the Court directly addressed the question of the legality of the use of force to protect human rights, and seemed to affirm a strict interpretation of Article 2(4). Nevertheless some have argued that its statement is only a rejection of the legality of the US use of force on the particular facts.[12]

3. STATE PRACTICE

The controversy as to the interpretation of Article 2(4) makes it necessary to consider whether states have in practice claimed a right of humanitarian intervention, and what they say about the scope of the doctrine.

A. The Enforcement of the No-Fly Zones Over Iraq (1991–2003)[13]

The UK is one of the foremost state supporters of the doctrine. It was the first state in the UN era expressly to rely on a version of this doctrine to justify its use of force. It did so in Iraq in the aftermath of *Operation Desert Storm*. The 'coalition of the willing' had been authorized under Security Council Resolution 678 (1990) to drive Iraqi troops out of Kuwait, but had left Saddam Hussein in power in Iraq. His government then

---

⁹ *Corfu Channel Case*, Merits, [1949] ICJ Rep. 4.
[10] *Case Concerning Military and Paramilitary Activities in and against Nicaragua (Nicaragua v. United States of America)*, Merits, Judgment of 27 June 1986, [1986] ICJ Rep. 14, at para. 202.
[11] *Ibid.*, at para. 268.
[12] S. Murphy, *Humanitarian Intervention: The UN in an Evolving World Order* (Philadelphia, PA: University of Philadelphia Press, 1996), at 129.
[13] See, generally, C. Gray, 'From Unity to Polarization: International Law and the Use of Force against Iraq', (2001) 13 EJIL 1.

turned on those who had risen up against him during *Operation Desert Storm*; the Kurds in the north and the Shiites in the south. The UN Security Council, in Resolution 688 (1991), called on Iraq to end the repression of its civilian population and to allow access to international humanitarian organizations, but it did not pass this resolution under Chapter VII and it did not authorize forcible intervention to protect the Kurds and Shiites.[14]

The USA, the UK and France subsequently proclaimed no-fly zones over Iraq, first in the north and then in the south. They patrolled Iraqi airspace to prevent government bombardment of civilians. However, they initially did not offer a public legal justification for their use of force. They did not report to the UN that they were acting in humanitarian intervention. This may be seen as evidence that there was no well-established doctrine of humanitarian intervention at that time. Although some commentators claimed that there had been earlier state practice which supported a customary international law right of humanitarian intervention, states themselves had not clearly made such a claim.[15] Thus, India had intervened in Bangladesh to help to secure its independence and to stop the repression by the Pakistani armed force (1971); Tanzania had intervened in Uganda to drive out the repressive ruler Idi Amin (1979); Vietnam had used force to overthrow the Khmer Rouge regime of Pol Pot in Cambodia (1978). But in these cases the states using force offered other legal justifications,[16] such as self-defence, and did not rely on humanitarian intervention. Moreover, France and the UK expressly rejected the legality of the last intervention by Vietnam, saying that violations of human rights could not justify the use of force. However, the UK did develop a doctrine to justify its actions over the Iraqi no-fly zones. It abandoned its earlier equivocation and moved toward support for an emerging doctrine of unilateral humanitarian intervention.[17] In a working document, published with Foreign and Commonwealth Office approval in 1992, it said that international law develops to meet new situations: 'We believe that international intervention without the invitation of the country concerned can be justified in cases of extreme humanitarian need.'[18] But the UK did not provide any further explanation of how this was compatible with Article 2(4). This seems to have been the first explicit invocation of humanitarian intervention in practice by a state; the USA and France did not adopt even this level of support for humanitarian intervention.

The enforcement of the no-fly zones over Iraq continued for over a decade and came to be openly opposed by other states. There was a gradual widening of the military targets and the rules of engagement.[19] This pattern was to be repeated in subsequent 'humanitarian' operations. When Iraq protested to the Security Council in 1999,[20] the USA and the UK did not offer any clear legal justification. Russia condemned the

---

[14] The resolution was nevertheless controversial; it passed by 10–3 (Cuba, Yemen, Zimbabwe) – 2 (China, India).
[15] S. Chesterman, *Just War or Just Peace? Humanitarian Intervention and International Law* (Oxford: Oxford University Press, 2001), at chapters 1 and 2.
[16] 1979 UNYB 271, at 274.
[17] UK Materials on International Law, (1986) 57 *BYIL* 614.
[18] UK Materials on International Law, (1992) 63 *BYIL* 824.
[19] 2002 UNYB 315, 2003 UNYB 370.
[20] 1999 UNYB 254.

continuing aerial bombing of Iraqi civilian and military facilities by the USA and the UK 'under the illegal pretext of the no-fly zones which were created unilaterally, in circumvention of the Security Council'; China said that it was strongly opposed to the bombing of civilian targets and demanded an immediate halt to the bombing missions in the so-called no-fly zone.[21] In the lead-up to *Operation Iraqi Freedom* (2003) the US and UK operations in the no-fly zones seemed to be aimed at the destruction of Iraqi air defences rather than for purely humanitarian purposes. The USA and the UK seem to have been motivated by the desire to secure regime change in Iraq. Ultimately, this prolonged use of force was controversial, and it was not relied on as a precedent for NATO's action in Kosovo.

B. Kosovo (1999)

A few more states did expressly invoke humanitarian intervention to justify the NATO operation in Kosovo.[22] However, NATO itself did not offer a clear legal justification of its use of force. The operation was a response to the increasing repression and 'ethnic cleansing' of the Kosovo Albanians by the federal government of Yugoslavia under President Milošević. He had abolished the special status of Kosovo under the federal constitution. Some of those seeking independence for Kosovo turned to violence through the Kosovo Liberation Army, and the federal government used violent measures against them. The Security Council passed a series of resolutions calling for a peaceful settlement of the dispute over the future of Kosovo.[23] But when Yugoslavia refused to accept the Rambouillet Agreement with Kosovo, NATO turned to the use of force. This refusal by Yugoslavia was understandable given the terms of the proposed agreement; Yugoslavia would have been required to concede almost unlimited autonomy to Kosovo and to allow free movement for NATO troops throughout the whole of Yugoslavia.[24]

In March 1999 NATO began its 78-day high-level air campaign to stop the repression. It used 1,000 aircraft in 38,000 combat missions.[25] It destroyed Yugoslav military infrastructure, bridges, military and government facilities, power plants and radio stations. In the short term Yugoslavia took the opportunity to increase its repressive actions on the ground, and there was a massive increase in the displacement of Kosovo Albanians. The International Criminal Tribunal for the Former Yugoslavia (hereinafter 'ICTY') found that the deliberate actions of the Yugoslav forces caused the departure of at least 700,000 Kosovo Albanians from Kosovo during the conflict.[26] A

---

[21] SC 4008th meeting, 21 May 1999, UN Doc. S/PV.4008 (1999).
[22] See C. Gray, *International Law and the Use of Force*, 3rd edn (Oxford: Oxford University Press, 2008), at 39. See also, generally, N.D. White, 'The Legality of Bombing in the Name of Humanity', (2000) 5 *JCSL* 27.
[23] SC Res 1160 (1998), 1199 (1998), 1203 (1998).
[24] 1999 UNYB 340.
[25] UK House of Commons Defence Committee, 'Fourteenth Report – Lessons of Kosovo', Session 1999–2000, at Section III: The Conduct of the Campaign, available at www.publications.parliament.uk/pa/cm199900/cmselect/cmdfence/347/34702.htm.
[26] *Prosecutor v. Milutinović et al.*, ICTY Case No. IT-05-87, Trial Chamber Judgment, 26 February 2009.

report commissioned by the ICTY estimated that 10,356 ethnic Albanians were killed in Kosovo during the conflict; the figures for the casualties of NATO raids vary from 2,500 to 5,000.[27]

NATO itself did not expressly rely on humanitarian intervention to justify its use of force. In fact, it offered no clear legal explanation. The NATO Council's authorization of air-strikes said that the crisis in Kosovo was a threat to the peace and security of the region. NATO's strategy was to halt the violence and avert a humanitarian catastrophe.[28] It justified its resort to force as intended to halt the violence and bring an end to the humanitarian catastrophe. However, NATO also claimed to be acting to further the aims of the international community; this language seemed to indicate that it was relying on the doctrine of implied Security Council authorization.[29]

Opinion was divided as to the legality of the NATO action.[30] States supporting the action offered a mainly moral and political justification for the operation. In the Security Council meetings after the start of the campaign the USA's position was that NATO had acted to avert a humanitarian catastrophe and to deter future aggression and repression in Kosovo. It did not offer a full legal argument. The UK offered a more expressly legal justification, specifically asserting that the action taken was legal. It was an exceptional measure to prevent an overwhelming humanitarian catastrophe. Every means short of force had been tried. Military intervention was legally justifiable as an exceptional measure on grounds of overwhelming humanitarian necessity. The Netherlands simply asserted that the use of force was lawful on the basis of the protection of human rights.

In contrast, those opposing the use of force challenged it on legal grounds. Yugoslavia, Russia and China all condemned the action as a violation of the UN Charter. However, a Russian draft resolution condemning the NATO action as a violation of Article 2(4) and of Article 24 on the primacy of the Security Council failed to secure the necessary majority of the Security Council to pass.[31] Only China, Russia and Namibia voted for the resolution;[32] 12 member states voted against. This cannot necessarily be taken as support for a legal doctrine of humanitarian intervention. Those who voted against the resolution generally stopped short of expressly putting forward such a doctrine. Some of those who defended the legality of the operation did so in terms of implied Security Council authorization. This was apparently the position of France. Some offered a purely political justification. The USA simply denied that the operation was a violation of the UN Charter and said that the Charter did not imply that the international community should turn a blind eye to a growing humanitarian disaster.

---

[27] 'Hague Tribunal Publishes Balkan War Statistics', *Wien International*, 13 April 2011, available at www.wieninternational.at/en/content/hague-tribunal-publishes-balkan-war-statistics-en.

[28] NATO Press Release 99/12, 30 January 1999, available at www.nato.int/docu/pr/1999/p99-012e.htm.

[29] For more see chapter 5 in this volume by Christian Henderson.

[30] SC 3988th meeting, 24 March 1999, UN Doc. S/PV.3988 (1999); SC 4011th meeting, 10 June 1999, UN Doc. S/PV.4011 (1999).

[31] SC 3989th meeting, 26 March 1999, UN Doc. S/PV.3989 (1999).

[32] India also spoke in favour of the resolution. See *ibid*.

The UK said that military intervention was justified as an exceptional measure to prevent an overwhelming humanitarian catastrophe.

i. Security Council Resolution 1244 (1999)

When the NATO operation concluded, the Security Council passed Resolution 1244 (1999) by 14–0–1, with China abstaining. This resolution set out the general principles for a political solution to the Kosovo crisis. Some commentators have argued that it constituted a retrospective endorsement of the legality of the NATO military campaign, and thus conceivably also of the doctrine of humanitarian intervention. But this does not seem convincing.[33] It is common for the Security Council to endorse peace settlements concluded after conflicts and to make arrangements for UN or member state forces to be deployed in the conflict area. It is difficult to see how such resolutions could be interpreted as approving the use of force by one side in the conflict in the absence of any clear provision. On policy grounds also this seems an unattractive argument as governments might be reluctant to accept UN involvement in a peace settlement if this could be construed as an acknowledgment of the legality of the use of force against them in the preceding conflict. There is also nothing in the Security Council debate to support the argument that Resolution 1244 was an acceptance of the legality of the NATO operation. Even those who had supported the NATO campaign did not claim that Resolution 1244 endorsed the use of force.[34] Russia repeated its view that NATO's military actions against Yugoslavia were unlawful, and strongly condemned the NATO aggression against a sovereign state. China spoke of NATO's serious violation of the UN Charter and said that its actions had undermined the authority of the Security Council. It said that respect for sovereignty and non-interference in internal affairs are basic principles of the UN Charter. Since the end of the Cold War, the international system had undergone major changes, but those principles were by no means outdated. The resolution made no mention of the disaster caused by NATO bombing and did not fully reflect China's principled stand, but China abstained rather than veto the resolution because Yugoslavia had accepted the peace plan, NATO had suspended its bombing, and the resolution reaffirmed the purposes and principles of the UN Charter, the primary responsibility of the Security Council, and the commitment of all member states to the sovereignty and territorial integrity of Yugoslavia. Russia and China both argued that the intervention was counterproductive; thus, China said: 'This war, waged in the name of humanitarianism, has in fact produced the greatest humanitarian catastrophe in post-Second World War Europe and has seriously undermined peace and stability in the Balkans.'[35]

---

[33] See, generally, T. Franck, 'Interpretation and Change in the Law of Humanitarian Intervention', in J.L. Holzgrefe and R.O. Keohane (eds), *Humanitarian Intervention: Ethical, Legal, and Political Dilemmas* (Cambridge: Cambridge University Press, 2003), 204. For an opposing view, see P. Hilpold, 'Humanitarian Intervention: Is There a Need for a Legal Reappraisal?', (2001) 12 *EJIL* 437.
[34] UN Doc. S/PV.4011, *supra* n. 30.
[35] *Ibid.*

ii. Legality of the use of force at the ICJ

The issue of the legality of the NATO use of force was also referred to the ICJ when Yugoslavia brought actions against ten NATO member states.[36] Yugoslavia claimed that they had violated the obligations not to use force and not to intervene in Yugoslavia. It argued first that there was no right of humanitarian intervention in international law; the prohibition of the use of force in Article 2(4) was unqualified and subsequent practice did not show any departure from this. Secondly, Yugoslavia argued that even if there were such a right it would not justify high-level air-strikes; that is, the modalities employed by NATO could not constitute humanitarian intervention. The Court decided that it did not have jurisdiction to hear the case, but Yugoslavia and Belgium set out their views on the substance of the case in their pleadings.[37]

Thus, Belgium offered a legal justification for the NATO action. In part it relied on implied Security Council authorization, but it also expressly invoked humanitarian intervention. It relied on a narrow interpretation of Article 2(4), saying that NATO was not intervening against the territorial integrity or political independence of Yugoslavia. It was acting to save a population in danger and so its action was compatible with Article 2(4). It even asserted that there was an obligation to intervene to prevent the humanitarian catastrophe which had been established by the Security Council in order to protect those essential human rights which had achieved the status of *jus cogens*. Belgium referred to the interventions in Bangladesh, Uganda and Cambodia as precedents, and also the regional action by the Economic Community of West African States (hereinafter 'ECOWAS') in Liberia and Sierra Leone. It is striking that Belgium did not mention the US and UK action over the Iraqi no-fly zones as a precedent.

Divisions persist as to the legality of NATO's Kosovo campaign and the existence of a doctrine of humanitarian intervention.[38] There have been repeated statements on behalf of the Non-Aligned Movement denying the existence of such a doctrine. Russia and China continue to express their opposition. NATO members Germany and the USA made statements that the Kosovo operation was not to be seen as a precedent for future action.[39] Even the UK had private doubts. In his Memorandum on the 2003 use of force against Iraq the UK Attorney-General acknowledged that the doctrine was controversial.[40] He said that:

---

[36] *Legality of Use of Force*, Provisional Measures, Order of 2 June 1999, [1999] ICJ Rep. 124. Yugoslavia brought actions against ten states. For current purposes the difference between the Court's Orders and Judgments are not significant and reference will be made to the case against Belgium.

[37] *Legality of Use of Force (Serbia and Montenegro v. Belgium)*, Preliminary Objections, Judgment, [1999] ICJ Rep. 279.

[38] See Corten, *supra* n. 4, at 527.

[39] S. Talmon, 'Changing Views on the Use of Force: The German Position', (2005) 5 *BaltYIL* 41; M. Byers and S. Chesterman, 'Changing the Rules About Rules? Unilateral Humanitarian Intervention', in Holzgrefe and Keohane (eds), *supra* n. 33, 177, at 199.

[40] 'Attorney General's Advice on the Iraq War: Resolution 1441', (2005) *ICLQ* 767, at para. 4. The UK Foreign Affairs Committee was also doubtful about the doctrine. In its report on Kosovo it concluded that the NATO operation was contrary to the specific terms of the UN Charter. It said that the doctrine had a tenuous basis in current international customary law, and that this rendered NATO action legally questionable. However, it concluded that the military

[t]he use of force to avert an overwhelming humanitarian catastrophe has been emerging as a further, and exceptional, basis for the use of force. It was relied on by the UK in the Kosovo crisis and is the underlying justification for the No-Fly Zones. The doctrine remains controversial, however.

He thus saw no reason why it would be an appropriate basis for action against Saddam Hussein.

C. The African Union Constitutive Act

The AU, in a striking reversal of its earlier suspicion of intervention and commitment to state sovereignty, included provision for humanitarian intervention in its 2000 Constitutive Act.[41] The traditional principles of the prohibition on the use of force and of non-intervention in the internal affairs of another member are spelled out in Article 4. However, Article 4(h) provides for 'the right of the Union to intervene in a Member State pursuant to a decision of the Assembly in respect of grave circumstances, namely: war crimes, genocide and crimes against humanity'. It is not explicit that this means forcible intervention; if it does, then member states may be taken to have consented to such action. Whatever the correct interpretation of Article 4(h), it is clear under Article 103 that the UN Charter prevails over obligations under any other international agreement, and so it is the interpretation of Article 2(4) of the UN Charter which is the crucial question. In practice the AU has not proved enthusiastic about forcible intervention. In Darfur it sent in a peacekeeping force only with the consent of the government of Sudan.[42] Most strikingly, the AU was not only unwilling itself to undertake humanitarian intervention in Libya, but it also opposed the military action by other states, even though they were acting under the cover of a Security Council resolution.[43]

4. ATTEMPTS AT DEVELOPING A FRAMEWORK FOR HUMANITARIAN INTERVENTION

The Kosovo operation left many questions unresolved. If there is a right of humanitarian intervention – and it is extremely doubtful whether state practice supports such a conclusion – what is the scope of the right? What is the threshold for intervention: is it mass violations of human rights or threatened violations? Does the Security Council play a role in this regard: is it necessary that it should have determined that there is a threat to international peace and security under Chapter VII; should it have made binding demands on the territorial state, demands which have then been ignored? Does the right to intervene only arise when the Security Council has decided not to act, or failed to act because of the veto? Could one state acting on its own carry out a

---

action was justified on moral grounds. UK House of Commons Foreign Affairs Committee, 'Fourth Report – Kosovo', Session 1999–2000, available at http://www.publications.parliament.uk/pa/cm199900/cmselect/cmfaff/28/2802.htm.

[41] 2158 UNTS 3.
[42] 2003 UNYB 256; 2004 UNYB 233.
[43] See *infra* section 5Bi.

humanitarian intervention? What are the appropriate modalities: can a high-level bombing campaign constitute humanitarian action? The UK government first invoked the doctrine to justify the no-fly zones over Iraq. It has subsequently made attempts to draw up a legal framework to govern the use of force on behalf of the international community to prevent humanitarian catastrophes. In its early consideration of this doctrine it deliberately did not attempt to establish a precise threshold for intervention. Thus, in 1992, in answer to questions by the UK Foreign Affairs Committee, the government said:

> We do not have a formal set of criteria to apply in assessing whether or not the level of suffering in a particular emergency justifies intervention for humanitarian purposes ... It would be wrong to try to set parameters for human suffering. The application of a set of criteria would inhibit the decision-making process and limit the flexibility of our response. We firmly believe that the nature of the response should be matched to the scale of the problem. It was on this basis that we deployed troops to Northern Iraq last year.[44]

However, the UK continued to try to produce a framework for humanitarian intervention.[45] During the NATO operation, Prime Minister Tony Blair developed the doctrine of the 'international community' in a key speech given in Chicago.[46] He listed five factors to be taken into account in deciding whether to intervene. First, are we sure of our case; secondly, have we exhausted all diplomatic options; thirdly, are there military options we can sensibly and prudently undertake; fourthly, are we prepared for the long term? And, finally, do we have national interest involved? Again this does not set out a threshold for intervention.

In 2000 the UK Foreign Secretary set out a more elaborate framework for intervention.[47] This was based on six principles. First, there is a need for a stronger culture of conflict prevention. Secondly, armed force should only be used as a last resort. Thirdly, the immediate responsibility for halting the violence is with the territorial state. Fourthly, when the government is not willing or able to prevent an overwhelming humanitarian catastrophe or is actively promoting it, the international community should intervene. There should be convincing evidence of extreme humanitarian distress on a large scale requiring urgent relief. There should be no practicable alternative to the use of force to save lives. Fifthly, the use of force should be proportionate to the humanitarian purpose and be carried out in accordance with international law. The military action should be likely to achieve its objectives. Sixthly,

---

[44] UK Materials on International Law, (1992) 63 *BYIL* 825, at 826.

[45] The Netherlands also asked the Advisory Committee on Issues of Public International law and the Advisory Council on International Affairs to produce an advisory report on humanitarian intervention. See Advisory Council on International Affairs, Advisory Committee on Issues of Public International Law, *Humanitarian Intervention*, Report No. 13, The Hague (April 2000). The English version of the report is available at www.aiv-advice.nl. For analysis of the report see I.F. Dekker, 'Illegality and Legitimacy of Humanitarian Intervention: Synopsis of and Comments on a Dutch Report', (2001) 6 *JCSL* 115.

[46] It was later made public during the Chilcot Inquiry into Iraq that the Prime Minister had relied heavily on a draft by a member of the Inquiry Panel, Professor Lawrence Freedman, to assist with this speech. See www.iraqinquiry.org.uk/media/42661/freedman-chilcot-letter.pdf.

[47] (2000) 71 *BYIL* 646.

any use of force should be collective. No one state could reserve to itself the right to act on behalf of the international community. However, this framework did not attract wider support. Subsequently the UK's main focus turned to the development of guidelines for Security Council action.[48] Its 2008 *National Security Strategy* repeated the UK's commitment to building a better rules-based framework for intervention and in this context it referred to the responsibility to protect the international community.[49] In contrast, the UK's 2010 *National Security Strategy*, in its section on 'An international military crisis', makes no reference to a responsibility to protect; it merely says that '[t]here will also be occasions when it is in our interests to take part in humanitarian interventions.'[50] This choice of language seems to indicate that the UK maintains its right to undertake unilateral humanitarian intervention, and this has recently been confirmed with regard to Libya.[51]

In contrast, the USA has been cautious. It did not invoke humanitarian intervention to justify its military action over the Iraqi no-fly zones. It claimed that the NATO action over Kosovo was not a precedent. President Bush also left this question open in his 2006 *National Security Strategy*. The section on 'Genocide' included the statement that '[w]here perpetrators of mass killing defy all attempts at peaceful intervention, armed intervention may be required, preferably by the forces of several nations working together under appropriate regional or international auspices'.[52] But President Obama's 2010 *National Security Strategy* may mark a new departure, although it is equivocal to say the least.[53] This states that force can be justified on humanitarian grounds: 'Military force, at times, may be necessary … to preserve broader peace and security, including by protecting civilians facing a grave humanitarian crisis.'[54] It is not entirely clear what

---

[48] (2001) 72 *BYIL* 694.

[49] See *infra* section 5.

[50] The Cabinet Office, 'A Strong Britain in an Age of Uncertainty: The National Security Strategy', Cm 7953, 18 October 2010, available at http://www.official-documents.gov.uk/document/cm79/7953/7953.asp.

[51] See *infra* section 5Bi.

[52] The White House, 'The 2006 National Security Strategy of the United States of America' (16 March 2006), at 17, available at http://georgewbush-whitehouse.archives.gov/nsc/nss/2006/. The 2008 French White Paper on Defence and National Security was similarly equivocal on this question, available at merln.ndu.edu/whitepapers/france_english2008.pdf.

[53] The White House, 'The 2010 National Security Strategy of the United States of America' (27 May 2010), available at http://www.whitehouse.gov/sites/default/files/rss_viewer/national_security_strategy.pdf (hereinafter '2010 USNSS'). Henderson has argued that this supports unilateral humanitarian intervention. See C. Henderson, 'The 2010 United States National Security Strategy and the Obama Doctrine of "Necessary Force"', (2010) 15 *JCSL* 403, at 429.

[54] 2010 USNSS, *ibid.*, at 22. The Nobel Peace Prize acceptance speech said that force could be justified on humanitarian grounds as it was in the Balkans. It is not clear whether this is a reference to the 1999 NATO action over Kosovo. See White House Press Office, 'Remarks by the President at the Acceptance of the Nobel Peace Prize' (10 December 2009), available at http://www.whitehouse.gov/the-press-office/remarks-president-acceptance-nobel-peace-prize. President Obama later issued the *Presidential Study Directive on Mass Atrocities* on 4 August 2011. This begins: 'Preventing mass atrocities is a core national security interest and a core moral responsibility for the US.' It directs the establishment of an inter-agency Atrocities Prevention Board to coordinate the government's approach to preventing mass atrocities and

this involves, and in particular it is not clear whether this amounts to a claim to a right of unilateral military action rather than collective humanitarian intervention through the United Nations. If so, this would mark a change of approach by the USA, which had previously taken a rather non-committal stance on the controversial right to humanitarian intervention.

5. RESPONSIBILITY TO PROTECT

In the last ten years a new concept of Responsibility to Protect (hereinafter 'R2P') has emerged. Does this mean the end of claims to a legal right of unilateral humanitarian intervention? Supporters of R2P hope that it will be less controversial and more effective than humanitarian intervention. It was initially devised by an independent panel set up by the Canadian government, the International Commission on Intervention and State Sovereignty.[55] The Commission's idea that there is a duty on states to act in cases of humanitarian crisis – a responsibility to protect – has proved more widely acceptable than the doctrine of humanitarian intervention. It was supported by the High-Level Panel set up by the UN Secretary-General to consider the future of the UN collective security system after the divisions over the use of force against Iraq in 2003. The Panel's report, *A More Secure World*, claimed that there was an emerging norm of a collective responsibility to protect in cases of genocide, ethnic cleansing or serious violation of international humanitarian law.[56] It dealt with R2P in its section on 'Using force: rules and guidelines'. The UN Secretary-General himself then considered the question in his report *In Larger Freedom*.[57] However, he considered this, not in the section on the use of force, but in Section IV of the report on 'Freedom to live in dignity', which covers the rule of law, human rights and democracy. He acknowledged that states had in the past disagreed over whether there was a right or even an obligation to use force to protect citizens of foreign states from genocide or other international crimes. Nevertheless, he said that states should now be willing to embrace the responsibility to protect in cases where the territorial state was unwilling or unable to act.

This responsibility was unanimously supported by the member states of the UN in the *World Summit Outcome Document* of the UN Millennium Summit. This included provision on R2P in its section on 'Human rights and the rule of law'.[58] The primary

---

genocide. See The White House, 'Presidential Study Directive on Mass Atrocities' (4 August 2011), available at http://www.whitehouse.gov/the-press-office/2011/08/04/presidential-study-directive-mass-atrocities. The UN Secretary-General welcomed this on 9 August 2011. See UN Doc. SG/SM/13739 (9 August 2011), available at http://www.un.org/News/Press/docs/2011/sgsm13739.doc.htm.

[55] International Commission on Intervention and State Sovereignty, *The Responsibility to Protect*, December 2001, available at http://responsibilitytoprotect.org/ICISS%20Report.pdf.

[56] High-Level Panel on Threats, Challenges and Change, *A More Secure World: Our Shared Responsibility*, 2 December 2004, UN Doc. A/59/565, at paras 199–203.

[57] Report of the UN Secretary-General, *In Larger Freedom: Towards Security, Development and Human Rights for All*, 21 March 2005, UN Doc. A/59/205, at paras 132–135.

[58] *2005 World Summit Outcome Document*, 15 September 2005, UN Doc. A/60/L.1, at paras 138–139.

responsibility was on each state to protect its own population from genocide, war crimes, ethnic cleansing and crimes against humanity. There was also a responsibility on the international community to use diplomatic, humanitarian and other peaceful means in accordance with Chapter VI of the Charter to help to protect populations. When peaceful means are inadequate and national authorities are manifestly failing to protect their populations from genocide, ethnic cleansing and crimes against humanity, then the *Outcome Document* asserted that 'we are prepared to take collective action, in a timely and decisive manner, through the Security Council in accordance with the UN Charter, including Chapter VII, on a case-by-case basis, and in cooperation with relevant regional organizations as appropriate.' While this brief provision was hailed as a major advance at the time there has since been some controversy as to whether R2P is actually a new legal concept or a framework for political action. The UN Secretary-General's Special Adviser on R2P takes the line that it is not a new legal concept, but is based on well-established international law and the provisions of the UN Charter.[59] States are divided on this point, with those which are suspicious of the doctrine tending to claim that it is a new legal concept.[60]

The Security Council has passed several resolutions referring to the provision for R2P in the *World Summit Outcome Document*. The first was Resolution 1674 (2006) on the protection of civilians in armed conflict.[61] The Security Council has also included reference to R2P in its resolutions on Darfur (Sudan).[62] The conflict which broke out between government and rebels in 2003 led to an estimated 200,000 dead and massive displacement of civilians.[63] In Resolutions 1556 and 1564 (2004) the Security Council affirmed that the primary responsibility to protect was with the government of Sudan. The Security Council referred the situation to the International Criminal Court in 2005. However, there was no willingness by states to intervene without the consent of the government of Sudan. In its first resolution on the situation in Darfur, the Security Council stressed that the primary R2P lay with the government. The UN Security Council left it to the AU to take the lead, although the AU was not willing to send in a

---

[59] UN Press Release, GA/10847, 23 July 2009, 'Delegates Seek to End Global Paralysis in Face of Atrocities', available at www.un.org/News/Press/docs/2009/ga10847.doc.htm.

[60] See General Assembly Plenary Debates, 63rd session, 97th–101st meetings, UN Press Releases GA/10848, GA/10849, GA/10850 (23, 24, 28 July 2009); General Assembly Annual General Debate, 66th session, 11th–24th meetings, UN Press Releases GA/11147–GA/11153 (21–24 September 2011). See C. Stahn, 'Responsibility to Protect: Political Rhetoric or Emerging Legal Norm', (2007) 101 *AJIL* 99.

[61] See www.un.org/en/peacekeeping/issues/civilian.shtml on the UN's work on protection of civilians. There is a close relationship between protection of civilians and R2P: they overlap but are not identical. The main differences are that R2P is not limited to armed conflict, and is only triggered by genocide, war crimes, ethnic cleansing and crimes against humanity. See the discussion by the Netherlands in the May 2011 Security Council debate on the protection of civilians, UN Doc. S/PV.6531 (Res. 1) (10 May 2011), at 23. See also J. Welsh, 'Civilian Protection in Libya: Putting Coercion and Controversy Back into RtoP', (2011) *Ethics and International Affairs* 1, at 3.

[62] UNSC Resolutions 1706 (2006), 1755 (2007), 1784 (2007).

[63] Report of the Secretary-General, UN Doc. S/2004/703, 30 August 2004.

peacekeeping force without government consent; it did not rely on the provision on humanitarian intervention in the AU Constitutive Act.[64]

There is some disagreement among commentators as to whether the use of force in the name of R2P can be carried out only by the UN Security Council and, as such, rules out the unilateral use of force by states. The Canadian Commission envisaged unilateral action if the Security Council failed to act,[65] but the various UN reports and the *World Summit Outcome Document* which supported the concept of R2P did not make any provision for this. There is today very little state support for a unilateral right to use force in the name of the international community and R2P. Many developing states are still suspicious of the concept of R2P and fear that the doctrine will be used as a pretext for intervention by powerful states.[66] Although China accepted R2P in the *World Summit Outcome Document*, it has consistently stressed the need for prevention and peaceful settlement and rejected forcible interventions not authorized by the Security Council.[67] Russia also supported the adoption of R2P, but emphasizes that it is governed by the rules of the UN Charter.[68]

The USA's position is not entirely clear. It did not use the phrase 'responsibility to protect' in the section of the 2010 *National Security Strategy* which dealt with the 'Use of force'. But in the section on 'Peacekeeping and armed conflict', after a brief statement on the US role with regard to Sudan, R2P is mentioned as having been endorsed by the USA and all member states of the UN.[69] The international community has a responsibility when governments themselves commit genocide or mass atrocities, or when they are unable or unwilling to take necessary action to prevent or respond to such crimes inside their borders. But when prevention by the international community fails, the USA will work multilaterally and bilaterally to mobilize diplomatic, humanitarian, financial and – in certain instances – military means to prevent and respond to genocide and mass atrocities. This could conceivably be read as endorsing unilateral action – that is, action not authorized by the UN Security Council – but the meaning is not entirely clear. Similarly, Susan Rice, the US Ambassador to the UN, in her first speech to the Security Council, spoke in support of R2P, but did not expressly claim any unilateral rights.[70]

---

[64] See *supra* section 3C.
[65] *The Responsibility to Protect*, *supra* n. 55, at 107.
[66] See *infra* pages 15–16.
[67] S. Teitt, 'The Responsibility to Protect and China's Peacekeeping Policy', (2011) 18 *International Peacekeeping* 298.
[68] For example, UN Press Release GA/10850, 28 July 2009.
[69] 2010 USNSS, *supra* n. 53, at 48. See Henderson, *supra* n. 53; C. Gray, 'President Obama's 2010 National Security Strategy and International Law on the Use of Force', (2011) 10 *Chinese JIL* 35.
[70] US Mission to the UN, Statement of Ambassador Susan E. Rice, 29 January 2009, available at usun.state.gov/briefing/statements/2009/january/127018.htm.

A. The UN Secretary-General's Reports on R2P

The UN Secretary-General has produced three reports on R2P. The first and most important was his 2009 report, *Implementing the Responsibility to Protect*.[71] The second report was *Early Warning, Assessment and the Responsibility to Protect* in 2010,[72] and the third was on *The Role of Regional and Sub-regional Arrangements in Implementing the Responsibility to Protect* in 2011.[73] These were prepared for informal interactive dialogue in the General Assembly. The first report outlined a three-pillar strategy. First, the responsibility of each state to protect its own people from mass atrocities. Secondly, international assistance and capacity building. Thirdly, 'timely and decisive response', which included the use of force. The Secretary-General underscored that the provisions of the *2005 World Summit Outcome Document* on R2P were firmly anchored in well-established principles of international law.

With regard to the use of force, the Secretary-General said that during the final years of the twentieth century humanitarian intervention had posed a false choice between two extremes: either standing by in the face of mounting civilian deaths or deploying coercive military force to protect the vulnerable and threatened populations.[74] He urged the five permanent members of the Security Council not to use or threaten to use the veto power in situations where a state had manifestly failed to meet its obligations with regard to R2P. The credibility, authority and hence effectiveness of the UN in advancing the principles relating to R2P depend in large part on the consistency with which they are applied. This was particularly true when military force was used to enforce them. In that regard states may want to consider the principles, rules and doctrine that should guide the application of coercive force in extreme situations relating to R2P. The General Assembly also had a role with regard to military action under the *Uniting for Peace* resolution where the Security Council fails to exercise its responsibility with regard to international peace and security because of the lack of unanimity among its five permanent members. He noted that Assembly measures were not legally binding on members. On a practical level, he recognized that the UN was far from developing an adequate rapid-response military capacity to handle rapidly unfolding atrocity crimes. Better modes of collaboration between the UN and regional arrangements were also needed.

This report was discussed by the General Assembly in July 2009,[75] the first General Assembly discussion of R2P since the adoption of the *World Summit Outcome Document*. The President of the General Assembly took a sceptical approach, but

---

[71] *Implementing the Responsibility to Protect*, Report of the UN Secretary-General, UN Doc. A/63/677, 12 January 2009.
[72] *Early Warning, Assessment and the Responsibility to Protect*, Report of the UN Secretary-General, UN Doc. A/64/864, 14 July 2010.
[73] *The Role of Regional and Sub-regional Arrangements in Implementing the Responsibility to Protect*, Report of the UN Secretary-General, UN Doc. A/65/877-S/2011/393, 28 June 2011.
[74] UN Doc. A/63/677, *supra* n. 71, at para. 7.
[75] UN Press Releases GA/10848, GA/10849, GA/10850 (23, 24, 28 July 2009). See discussion by Global Centre for the Responsibility to Protect, *Implementing the Responsibility to Protect. The 2009 General Assembly Debate: An Assessment*, August 2009, available at http://globalr2p.org/media/pdf/GCR2P_General_Assembly_Debate_Assessment.pdf.

member states generally reaffirmed their commitment to R2P. Only four states – Cuba, Nicaragua, Sudan and Venezuela – said that it should be renegotiated. However, many states expressed concern about R2P, and especially about its third pillar. Some were still concerned about the use of coercive action for humanitarian ends; many were concerned about the possibility of abuse and the danger of selective application. Some commented on the failure to respond to other conflicts, in particular the 2009 Gaza conflict. In reply, some said that it would be wrong to conclude that because the international community could not act everywhere it therefore should act nowhere.[76] Several states expressed concern that R2P would lead to unilateral intervention; these included Pakistan and states hostile to the USA such as Venezuela, North Korea and Iran. The Non-Aligned Movement statement also said it feared that R2P would be used to claim legitimacy for unilateral coercive measures. Others replied that R2P did not allow unilateral action. No state unequivocally claimed any right of unilateral action. The UK was silent on this issue. France said that 'importantly, the responsibility should not be limited exclusively to the Security Council', but it is not entirely clear what this means.[77] Some of those in favour of R2P supported the call in the Secretary-General's Report for the five permanent members of the Security Council not to use the veto in R2P situations. There were the usual calls for reform of the composition of the Security Council, and some debate as to whether it should be the Security Council or the General Assembly which should authorize action.

B. Implementing R2P

i. Libya (2011)

The 2011 military operation in Libya has been hailed by many as a landmark in the successful implementation of R2P, but difficult questions arise out of its invocation in this conflict. Some commentators have suggested that the manner of the implementation of R2P in the Libyan conflict has fundamentally undermined the concept, and has made it likely that future claims to act in the name of R2P (or humanitarian intervention) will be met by greater suspicion.[78] In particular, it has been asked whether the real goal of the military operation was regime change rather than protection of the population of Libya against international crimes.

The conflict in Libya began in February 2011 when anti-government protests were met with violent repression by Colonel Gaddafi's regime. It used heavy weapons against unarmed protesters.[79] The Security Council's initial response was the unanimous adoption of Resolution 1970 (2011). The preamble expressed grave concern at the situation in Libya and condemned the violence and use of force against civilians; it also deplored the gross and systematic violation of human rights, including the repression of peaceful demonstrators. The Security Council did not specifically

---

[76] For example Chile. See UN Press Release GA/10849, 24 July 2009.
[77] See UN Press Release GA/10848, 23 July 2009.
[78] For example, *Accidental Heroes: Britain, France and the Libya Operation*, an Interim RUSI Campaign Report (September 2011), available at http://www.voltairenet.org/IMG/pdf/Accidental_Heroes.pdf.
[79] *Keesing's Record of World Events* (2011) 50309, 50365 (hereinafter '*Keesing's*').

determine that the situation in Libya was a threat to international peace and security under Chapter VII of the Charter. However, it was 'mindful of its primary responsibility for the maintenance of international peace and security', and expressly stated that it was acting under Chapter VII of the Charter and taking measures under Article 41 in imposing an arms embargo, a travel ban and an assets freeze. The Security Council also referred the situation to the Prosecutor of the International Criminal Court; the Court subsequently issued warrants for the arrest of Colonel Gaddafi, his son, Saif al Islam Gaddafi, and the Head of Intelligence for crimes against humanity.[80]

The violence quickly turned into a civil war involving significant loss of life and massive displacement of civilians.[81] The rebel forces were initially successful in seizing control of towns and cities, but these initial successes were reversed by government counter-offensives. Pro-Gaddafi forces now turned on the opposition-held city of Benghazi with tanks and aircraft. Colonel Gaddafi issued violent threats against the rebels; no mercy would be shown to the inhabitants of Benghazi who resisted him.[82] There was prolonged discussion by other states of the appropriate response.

The first thing to note is that states did not assert a right of unilateral humanitarian intervention. The UK was a striking exception in this regard.[83] NATO laid down three conditions for intervention: there should be a demonstrable need, broad regional support and a clear legal basis.[84] With regard to the legal basis, the NATO Secretary-General insisted that a Security Council resolution was necessary for military action.[85] The UK accepted the three conditions laid down by NATO, but claimed that there was 'a clear legal basis' for unilateral action. Thus, the UK Foreign Secretary said: 'in cases of great overwhelming humanitarian need nations are able to act under international law, even without a resolution of the Security Council'.[86] This reaffirmed the position the UK had taken with regard to the unilateral use of force for humanitarian intervention in the Iraqi no-fly zones and Kosovo.[87]

---

[80] *The Prosecutor v. Muammar Gaddafi, Saif Al-Islam Gaddafi and Abdullah Al-Senussi*, ICC-01/11-01/11, 27 June 2011.

[81] See UN Docs S/PV 6505 (24 March 2011), 6509 (4 April 2011), 6527 (3 May 2011), 6530 (9 May 2011), 6541 (31 May 2011); *Keesing's* (2011) 50366.

[82] *Keesing's* (2011) 50365.

[83] There were newspaper reports that France also contemplated unilateral action: 'Victory for US as Defence Ministers Agree on Minimal Intervention', *The Guardian*, 11 March 2011, at 21.

[84] 'NATO Ready to Support International Efforts on Libya', 10 March 2011, available at http://www.nato.int/cps/en/natolive/news_71446.htm; 'Libya's War Intensifies as the West Holds Fire', *The Guardian*, 10 March 2011, at 24.

[85] 'No-Fly Zone Plan Goes Nowhere as US, Russia and NATO Urge Caution', *The Guardian*, 2 March 2011, at 10.

[86] BBC News, 'G8 Leaders Consider Libya No-Fly Zone', 14 March 2011, available at http://www.bbc.co.uk/news/world-africa-12735491.

[87] However, because the Security Council subsequently adopted Resolution 1973 (2011) authorizing the use of force it was not necessary for the UK to rely on a right of unilateral humanitarian intervention, and the UK government referred only to the Security Council resolution in its subsequent justification of the use of force. See HM Government's Note on Legal Basis for Deployment of UK Forces and Military Assets, 21 March 2011, available at http://www.guardian.co.uk/law/2011/mar/21/government-legal-military-action-libya.

The caution of the AU was also very notable in this regard, especially given the provision in Article 4(h) of its Constitutive Act for 'the right of the Union to intervene in a Member State pursuant to a decision of the Assembly in respect of grave circumstances, namely: war crimes, genocide and crimes against humanity'.[88] The AU rejected foreign military intervention in Libya, and pursued a negotiated solution.[89] It did not even mention a right of humanitarian intervention, despite the International Criminal Court's issue of arrest warrants for crimes against humanity, a threshold for the right to intervene under the Constitutive Act.

The crucial turning point came when the Council of the League of Arab States passed a resolution 'having considered the crimes and violations that have been committed by the Libyan authorities against the Libyan people, and, in particular, the use of military aircraft, cannons and heavy weaponry against the population'. It rejected all forms of foreign intervention, but decided:

> to call on the Security Council, in view of the deterioration in the situation, to shoulder its responsibilities and take the measures necessary to immediately impose a no-fly zone on Libyan military aircraft and establish safe havens in areas that are exposed to bombardment, as precautionary measures that will provide protection for the Libyan people ... while respecting the sovereignty and territorial integrity of neighbouring States.[90]

It also said that Gaddafi's government was illegitimate and suspended Libya's membership. Support for a no-fly zone came also from the Organization of the Islamic Conference and the Gulf Cooperation Council.[91] There was no such support from the AU, though the African Court of Human and Peoples' Rights ordered the government of Libya to halt its attacks on civilians: Libya should immediately refrain from any action that would result in a loss of life or violation of physical integrity of persons.[92]

In response to the Arab League resolution, the UN Security Council adopted Resolution 1973 (2011) by 10–0–5 (Brazil, China, Germany, India, Russia). The three African states on the Security Council (Gabon, Nigeria and South Africa[93]) all voted for the resolution. Resolution 1973 expressly determined that the situation in Libya

---

[88] See *supra* section 3C.

[89] African Union Peace and Security Council, 265th meeting, AU Doc. PSC/PR/COMM.2(CCLXV), 10 March 2011, available at http://www.au.int/en/sites/default/files/COMMUNIQUE_EN_10_MARCH_2011_PSD_THE_265TH_MEETING_OF_THE_PEACE_AND_SECURITY_COUNCIL_ADOPTED_FOLLOWING_DECISION_SITUATION_LIBYA.pdf.

[90] 'Letter dated 14 March 2011 from the Permanent Observer of the League of Arab States to the United Nations addressed to the President of the Security Council', UN Doc. S/2011/137, 15 March 2011. There is no official record of the vote, but newspaper reports say that only Syria and Algeria voted against this resolution.

[91] 'NATO Prepares the Case for a No-Fly Zone', *The Guardian*, 9 March 2011, at 17.

[92] *African Commission on Human and Peoples' Rights v. Great Socialist People's Libyan Arab Jamahiriya*, African Court on Human and Peoples' Rights, Order for Provisional Measures, Application No. 004/2011, 25 March 2011, available at http://www.worldcourts.com/acthpr/eng/decisions/2011.03.25_ACmHPR_v_Libya.pdf.

[93] South Africa later backed away from this support. It repeatedly expressed concern that the military operation had gone beyond its lawful mandate. See, for example, UN Security Council 6566th meeting, 27 June 2011, UN Doc. S/PV.6566 (2011) and 6595th meeting, 28 July 2011, UN Doc. S/PV.6595 (2011).

'continued to be a threat to international peace and security'. Acting under Chapter VII, the Security Council authorized member states that notified the Secretary-General, acting nationally or through regional organizations, and in cooperation with the Secretary-General to take 'all necessary measures'. This formula has been understood to constitute an authorization of the use of force since it was first employed in Resolution 678 (1990).[94] The Security Council authorized the use of force for three purposes. First, 'to protect civilians and civilian populated areas under threat of attack in the Libyan Arab Jamahiriya, including Benghazi'. This authorization expressly excluded 'a foreign occupation force of any form on any part of Libyan territory'. Secondly, to enforce compliance with a no-fly zone over the whole of Libya. Thirdly, to enforce the arms embargo. No time limit was imposed on the authorization to take all necessary measures.

The Security Council for the first time cited R2P in the preamble of a Chapter VII resolution. However, it only referred to the R2P of *Libya*. In the preamble to Resolution 1970 (2011) it 'recall[ed] the Libyan authorities' responsibility to protect its population', and in the preamble to Resolution 1973 (2011) it reiterated 'the responsibility of the Libyan authorities to protect the Libyan population'. It made no express reference to any R2P on the part of the international community. The legal basis for the subsequent military intervention was an authorization under Chapter VII of the UN Charter, as it had been earlier when the Security Council authorized the use of all necessary measures for the delivery of humanitarian aid in Somalia (1992) and Bosnia-Herzegovina (1992), and for the establishment of no-fly zones and safe havens in Bosnia-Herzegovina (1993). But Resolution 1973 provided a much wider authorization of force than these earlier resolutions.[95]

In the Security Council meeting which led to the adoption of Resolution 1973 (2011) the abstaining states expressed doubts about the wide scope of the authorization to use force.[96] Thus, India was concerned about the relatively little credible information on the situation on the ground in Libya and the lack of clarity about the details of enforcement measures. Brazil abstained because the text of Resolution 1973 (2011) contemplated measures that went far beyond the call of the League of Arab States for a no-fly zone. Russia said that a whole range of legitimate and concrete questions remained unanswered: how would the no-fly zone be enforced; what would the rules of engagement be; and what were the limits on the use of force? The draft had transcended the initial concept as stated by the League of Arab States and provisions had been introduced into the text that would potentially open the door to large-scale military intervention. China also regretted that specific questions had not been clarified.

Military action began on 19 March 2011 under US command (codenamed *Operation Odyssey Dawn*). The USA, France and the UK took the lead with assistance from Canada, Denmark, Norway, Belgium, Spain and Italy. Among Arab states, Qatar and

---

[94] See Gray, *supra* n. 22, at 264.
[95] Regarding the breadth of the mandate provided in Resolution 1973 (2011) see, generally, C. Henderson, 'International Measures for the Protection of Civilians in Libya and Côte d'Ivoire', (2011) 60 *ICLQ* 767.
[96] UN Security Council 6498th meeting, 17 March 2011, UN Doc. S/PV.6498 (2011).

the UAE took part in the operations.[97] The UK in the summary of its legal justification for the military action in Libya did not refer to R2P. The legal basis it relied on was the authorization in Security Council Resolution 1973 (2011).[98] In contrast, the US State Department Legal Advisor did make a passing reference to R2P in his *Statement Regarding Use of Force in Libya*. Like the UK he said that the operation was based on the authorization in Security Council Resolution 1973 (2011). He also said that 'Qaddafi has forfeited his responsibility to protect his own citizens, and created a serious need for immediate humanitarian assistance and protection'[99] and that the mission would be time limited, well defined, discrete and aimed at preventing an imminent humanitarian catastrophe that directly implicates the national security and foreign policy interests of the United States. On 31 March 2011 NATO took over command in *Operation Unified Protector*.[100] It flew over 25,000 sorties, including over 9,000 air-strikes. The NATO operation finally came to an end in October 2011 after the rebels took control of the Gaddafi stronghold (and birthplace) of Sirte with NATO air support.[101]

Supporters of R2P assert that this operation was carried out under the R2P umbrella; they hail this use of force as a successful implementation of R2P. The new government of Libya in its first appearance at the UN Security Council said: '[f]or the very first time, we witnessed in Libya the operationalization of the responsibility to protect, which was carried out in a reasonable manner, saving the lives of thousands of Libyans and maintaining the sovereignty and territorial integrity of Libya.'[102] However, many doubts remain, and for some commentators they undermine not just this operation but the whole concept of R2P.[103] The Arab League, which had initially called on the UN Security Council to establish a no-fly zone and safe havens, seemed to back away.[104]

---

[97] *Keesing's* (2011) 50366. See also *Accidental Heroes, supra* n. 78.

[98] HM Government's Note on Legal Basis for Deployment of UK Forces and Military Assets, *supra* n. 87.

[99] US Department of State Legal Advisor, 'Statement Regarding Use of Force in Libya', 27 March 2011, available at www.america.gov/st/texttrans-english/2011/March/20110327160858 su0.4296992.html.

[100] NATO, 'NATO Takes Command in Libya Air Operations', 31 March 2011, available at www.nato.int/cps/en/natolive/news_71867.htm.

[101] See, for example, NATO, 'NATO Strikes Protect Civilians in Sirte', 24 September 2011, available at www.nato.int/cps/en/natolive/news_78493.htm; NATO, 'Operational Media Update: NATO and Libya', 25 October 2011, available at www.nato.int/cps/en/natolive/news_71994.htm. See also 'NATO Chief Hails End of Military Operation in Libya', *The Guardian*, 1 November 2011, at 1. On the death of Gaddafi, see *Keesing's* (2011) 50735.

[102] UN Security Council 6620th meeting, 16 September 2011, UN Doc. S/PV.6620 (2011).

[103] R. Falk, 'Preliminary Libyan Scorecard: Acting Beyond the UN Mandate', available at www.foreignpolicyjournal.com/2011/09/08/preliminary-libyan-scorecard-acting-beyond-the-u-n-mandate/; M.W. Doyle, 'The Folly of Protection', *Foreign Affairs*, 20 March 2011, available at www.foreignaffairs.com/articles/67666/michael-w-doyle/the-folly-of-protection; A.J. Bellamy, 'The Responsibility to Protect and the Problem of Regime Change', 27 September 2011, available at www.e-ir.info/?p=14350.

[104] 'Britain and France Appear Ever More Isolated as World Opinion Turns Hostile', *The Guardian*, 22 March 2011, at 6; 'Arab League Chief Admits Doubts about Air Strikes', *The Guardian*, 22 June 2011, at 16.

Russia and China, having abstained on Resolution 1973 (2011), also expressed doubts immediately after the start of the military operation.[105]

The AU never supported the military action. It consistently called for a cease-fire and a negotiated solution.[106] It attempted mediation between the opposing parties and proposed a Road Map for peace which would have left Colonel Gaddafi in power.[107] The AU also said it would not cooperate with the International Criminal Court to execute the arrest warrants for Colonel Gaddafi.[108] On 25 May the AU Assembly issued a *Decision on the Peaceful Resolution of the Libyan Crisis*. This stressed the obligation of all UN member states to fully comply with the letter and spirit of Security Council Resolutions 1970 and 1973. It 'expressed deep concern that a dangerous precedence [sic] was being set by one-sided interpretations of these resolutions, in an attempt to provide a legal authority for military and other actions on the ground that were clearly outside the scope of these resolutions'.[109] Many questioned whether the NATO-led action had exceeded the authorization by the Security Council. They asked whether R2P, like humanitarian intervention, carries a serious, perhaps an inescapable, danger of mission creep. The military operation to establish the no-fly zone and to protect civilians and civilian populated areas began by destroying the regime's air defences. The inhabitants of Benghazi were saved from the onslaught of Gaddafi's troops. Then NATO's air-strikes were directed at a wider range of targets; they bombed columns of troops, tanks, command and control centres, supply lines to Gaddafi's troops, telephone exchanges and other communications centres. In the capital, Tripoli, NATO struck military command and control centres in order to paralyse the Gaddafi regime's ability to give orders to its forces.[110] The rebels took control of Tripoli in August 2011 and prepared to establish a new government.[111] As the NATO operation continued it seemed to many that its air campaign was more in support of the rebels than directly to stop harm to civilians. In particular, the final stages of the conflict seemed to stretch the Security Council mandate. As a newspaper report put it, the rebel breakthrough in the west – armed by the French, trained by the UK, led by Qatari special forces – advanced on the capital, and rebel supporters in Tripoli rose up. NATO air support had stopped Gaddafi's advance, eroded his power to resist the rebels and wiped out his tanks and

---

[105] UN Doc. S/2011/209; UN Press Release GA/11155, 27 September 2011; 'Britain and France Appear Ever More Isolated as World Opinion Turns Hostile', *The Guardian*, 22 March 2011.

[106] See, for example, African Union Peace and Security Council 291st meeting, AU Doc. PSC/AHG/COMM(CCXCI).

[107] See, for example, African Union Peace and Security Council 265th meeting, AU Doc. PSC/PR/COMM.2/(CCLXV); 268th meeting, AU Doc. PSC/PR/BR.1(CCLXVIII); AU Consultative Meeting on the Situation in Libya, 25 March 2011, Communiqué; UN Security Council 6555th meeting, 15 June 2011, UN Doc. S/PV.6555 (2011).

[108] Decisions adopted during the 17th AU Summit, Malabo, 1 July 2011.

[109] Extraordinary Session of the Assembly of the Union, 25 May 2011, AU Doc. EXT/ASSEMBLY/AU/DEC/(01.2011).

[110] NATO, 'Operation Unified Protector: Protection of Civilians and Civilian-Populated Areas', June 2011, available at www.nato.int/nato_static/assets/pdf/pdf_2011_06/2011 0608_Factsheet-UP_Protection_Civilians.pdf.

[111] *Keesing's* (2011) 50620.

heavy weapons.¹¹² The authorization contained in Resolution 1973 (2011) expressly precluded the deployment of *occupying* forces, but this clever choice of language – designed to allay suspicions that the military operation would lead to occupation as in the case of Iraq – did not exclude the deployment of (non-occupying) ground troops, and there were newspaper reports that the special forces of several states, including the UK, France, the UAE and Qatar, played a crucial role in the military operation.¹¹³

NATO's position was that operations would continue until all attacks on civilians and civilian populated areas had ended, the Gaddafi regime had withdrawn all military and paramilitary forces to bases, and the regime had permitted access to humanitarian aid for the Libyan people.¹¹⁴ The AU Peace and Security Council, however, on 21 September 2011 called on the UN Security Council 'to lift the measures imposed with respect to no-fly zones and ban on flights and to terminate the authorization given to member states in this respect, bearing in mind the very purpose for which resolution 1973 was adopted'.¹¹⁵

It has been suggested that NATO became the air arm (and possibly also the intelligence and special operations arms) of the rebel forces.¹¹⁶ Venezuela said: 'it is deplorable that NATO forces are acting as an army in the service of an insurgent group against the Government of Libya, thereby detracting from the humanitarian character of the protection of civilians in armed conflict.'¹¹⁷ But the wide drafting of Resolution 1973 (2011) allowed the use of all necessary measures to protect civilians and civilian populated areas against 'threat of attack'; this could conceivably be interpreted as flexible enough to cover NATO's use of force so long as pro-Gaddafi forces continued to fight and even to overthrow Gaddafi if this was necessary to protect civilians from the threat of attack.¹¹⁸ As Russia and China and the other states that had abstained on Resolution 1973 had pointed out, the scope of the authorization of force was not clear. The legal basis of *Operation Unified Protector* was clearly stronger than that for the operations over Kosovo (1999) and against Iraq (2003), where there was no express authorization by the Security Council.

The most fundamental concern about *Operation Unified Protector* was that its aim was not just to stop atrocities, but to secure regime change. It was clear that the rebel forces were not capable of winning on their own. The USA, the UK and France openly and repeatedly called for Colonel Gaddafi to go; President Obama, President Sarkozy and Prime Minister Cameron set out their position in a letter to several newspapers.¹¹⁹

---

¹¹² 'Gaddafi's End', *The Observer*, 28 August 2011, at 21; *Accidental Heroes*, *supra* n. 78.

¹¹³ *The Observer*, *supra* n. 112.

¹¹⁴ NATO, 'NATO and Libya – Operation Unified Protector', 25 October 2011, available at www.nato.int/cps/en/natolive/topics_71652.htm; NATO, 'Ministers Determined to Pursue Operation in Libya as Long as Threats Persist', 6 October 2011, available at www.nato.int/cps/en/natolive/news_78934.htm. See also 'NATO Meets to Discuss Ending Libyan Air War', *The Guardian*, 6 October 2011, at 32.

¹¹⁵ African Union Peace and Security Council 294th meeting, AU Doc. PSC/PR/COMM(CCXCIV).

¹¹⁶ *Accidental Heroes*, *supra* n. 78; Falk, *supra* n. 103.

¹¹⁷ UN Security Council 6531st meeting, 10 May 2011, UN Doc. S/PV 6531 (Res. 1), at 19.

¹¹⁸ Henderson, *supra* n.95, at 775.

¹¹⁹ 'Libya's Pathway to Peace', *International Herald Tribune*, 15 April 2011.

Their language was careful, but inevitably gave rise to concerns about their true motives. They said that so long as Gaddafi was in power, NATO and its coalition partners must maintain their operations so that civilians remained protected and the pressure on the regime built. For the transition from dictatorship to an inclusive constitutional process 'Colonel Gaddafi must go, and go for good.' They confirmed that their mandate under Security Council Resolution 1973 (2011) was to protect civilians. It was not to remove Gaddafi by force. But it was impossible to imagine a future for Libya with Gaddafi in power. Later Russia also declared that Gaddafi must step down as his government had failed to fulfil its responsibility to protect the Libyan population and had lost all legitimacy.[120] The rebels entered Colonel Gaddafi's compound in Tripoli on 23 August 2011, and this brought an end to the Gaddafi regime. The UN General Assembly accredited delegates from the Transitional National Council on 16 September,[121] and the AU recognized the new representatives of Libya on 20 September.[122] The Security Council terminated its authorization of force in Resolution 2016 (2011), passed unanimously.

But divisions persist. Should this operation be seen as a model of R2P by the international community after the failure of the government to protect its population from international crimes? Or was it rather a self-interested intervention in pursuit of regime change? In the General Assembly's 2011 informal debate on R2P several states voiced their doubts about the manner in which NATO was implementing Resolution 1973 (2011) in Libya.[123] The fears that they had expressed in earlier discussions of R2P had now been realized; their concerns about possible abuse had been justified. Some states asked whether it would be possible to develop criteria to determine when it was justified to turn to force. They were concerned that Libya showed the danger of a selective response as this would undermine the general acceptability of R2P. In the General Assembly's Annual General Debate in September 2011 most states that addressed the issue welcomed the outcome of the operation in Libya.[124] However, a few states again repeated their earlier doubts. Zimbabwe and Cuba expressed the suspicion that this operation, like that in Iraq, had been fundamentally a war about oil and regime change.[125] Many African states regretted that the Security Council rather than the AU had taken the lead.

ii. Côte d'Ivoire

Less attention has been paid to recent events in Côte d'Ivoire, but some cite this too as an instance of military action under the R2P.[126] In this case, like that of Libya, there was also concern that the implementation of R2P involved regime change. The

---

[120] *Keesing's* (2011) 50485.
[121] (114–17–15), UN Press Release GA/11137, 16 September 2011.
[122] BBC News, 'Libyan War: African Union Recognises NTC as Leaders', 21 September 2011, available at www.bbc.co.uk/news/world-africa-14986442.
[123] International Coalition for the Responsibility to Protect, 'Interactive Dialogue of the UNGA on the Regional and Sub-regional Arrangements in Implementing the RtoP', August 2011; UN Press Release GA/11112, 12 July 2011.
[124] UN Press Releases GA/11147–11155, 21–27 September 2011.
[125] UN Press Releases GA/11151, 22 September 2011, and GA/11154, 26 September 2011.
[126] Henderson, *supra* n.95, at 768–769.

Secretary-General's Special Advisers on the R2P and on Prevention of Genocide warned in January 2011 that urgent steps should be taken in accordance with R2P to prevent possible genocide, crimes against humanity, war crimes and ethnic cleansing.[127] Here, as with Libya, the UN Security Council did refer to R2P, but, as with Libya, the reference was only to the R2P of Côte d'Ivoire rather than that of the international community. In Resolution 1975 (2011) the Security Council reaffirmed 'the primary responsibility of each state to protect civilians'. The International Criminal Court Prosecutor subsequently requested permission to open an investigation into international crimes committed in Côte d'Ivoire.[128]

Conflict broke out in Côte d'Ivoire when President Gbagbo refused to accept his defeat by opposition leader Allassane Ouattara in the October 2011 elections. The Special Representative of the UN Secretary-General certified Ouattara's victory, and this was endorsed by ECOWAS, the AU and the UN Security Council.[129] Gbagbo's forces used heavy weapons against peaceful demonstrations. They also carried out violent attacks on areas which supported Ouattara. The conflict escalated and there were direct confrontations between the troops of both sides. Once again, as in Libya, the AU did not turn to military force; it did not advocate humanitarian intervention under the AU Constitutive Act.[130] It attempted to reach a peaceful compromise.[131] In contrast, ECOWAS called on the Security Council to facilitate the transfer of power to Ouattara and to strengthen the mandate of UNOCI, including the use of force against Gbagbo.[132]

UNOCI, the UN force which had been in Côte d'Ivoire since 2004 after the end of an earlier conflict, was already authorized under Chapter VII to 'use all necessary means' to carry out its mandate within its capabilities and its areas of deployment. Its mandate included the monitoring of the cease-fire and the protection of civilians under imminent threat of physical violence.[133] It was supported by French troops initially present in Côte d'Ivoire at the request of the government, and subsequently authorized by the UN Security Council 'to use all necessary means in order to support UNOCI'.[134] When Gbagbo refused to step down the Security Council passed Resolution 1962 (2010). This urged all parties to respect the outcome of the election and the AU's recognition of Ouattara, recalled its authorization to UNOCI to use all necessary means

---

[127] Press Conference by Secretary-General's Special Advisers on Responsibility to Protect, Genocide, in connection with situation in Côte d'Ivoire, 19 January 2011, available at www.un.org/News/briefings/docs/2011/110119_Guest.doc.htm.

[128] ICC-OTP-20110623-PR686, 23 June 2011. The International Criminal Court later authorized the launch of the investigation. See ICC-CPI-20111003-PR730, 3 October 2011.

[129] UN Secretary-General's 27th Report on Côte d'Ivoire, 30 March 2011, UN Doc. S/2011/211 (2011).

[130] See *supra* section 3C.

[131] Secretary-General's 27th Report on Côte d'Ivoire, *supra* n.129, and UN Secretary-General's 28th Report on Côte d'Ivoire, 24 June 2011, UN Doc. S/2011/387 (2011).

[132] Resolution A/Res.1/03/11 of the Authority of Heads of State and Government of ECOWAS on the Situation in Côte d'Ivoire, ECOWAS Press Release 043/2011, 25 March 2011, available at http://news.ecowas.int/presseshow.php?nb=043&lang=en&annee=2011.

[133] SC Res. 1528 (2004), as modified in SC Resns 1609 (2005), 1739 (2007).

[134] SC Res. 1527 (2004); SC Res. 1528 (2004), at para. 16.

to carry out its mandate, and reiterated the importance for UNOCI to implement its 'protection of civilians' mandate, particularly in the light of the current risks for human rights and civilians in the country. The Security Council later authorized an increase in the size of UNOCI.[135] But violence continued and Gbagbo forces carried out attacks on UNOCI and on opposition supporters. The Security Council then passed a further resolution elaborating on its authorization of the use of all necessary means. Resolution 1975 (2011):

> *recall*[*ed*] its authorization ... to the UNOCI ... to use all necessary means to carry out its mandate to protect civilians under imminent threat of physical violence, within its capabilities and its areas of deployment, *including to prevent the use of heavy weapons against the civilian population.*[136]

UNOCI, with the crucial support of the French forces, took military action in April 2011 to stop Gbagbo using mortars, rocket-propelled grenades and machine guns against civilians; they attacked his Presidential palace and military barracks. Gbagbo was arrested and Ouattara was sworn in as President.[137]

The UN Secretary-General hailed this as a success for R2P. He said: '[w]hat is happening in Libya, Côte d'Ivoire and elsewhere is a historic precedent, a watershed in the emerging doctrine of the responsibility to protect. Never again, world leaders resolved in 2005 after the tragedies in Rwanda and Srebrenica. They enunciated this new doctrine: the responsibility to protect.'[138] Others, however, remain more sceptical.

6. CONCLUSION

It is difficult, if not impossible, to make a legal case for the existence of a right of unilateral humanitarian intervention today. Even if there is such a legal right its scope remains undefined. In so far as the legal case is based on a restrictive interpretation of Article 2(4) of the UN Charter, which disregards the *jus cogens* status of that prohibition, in order to allow the use of force in protection of human rights, such an interpretation has been adopted by a tiny number of states.[139] There is very little unequivocal support for a right of unilateral humanitarian intervention, and widespread express rejection – as was apparent in the General Assembly debates on R2P. Even with regard to Kosovo there was little invocation of a right of unilateral intervention by the states taking part in the military operations. Moreover, states and commentators are divided as to whether the NATO intervention in Kosovo should be counted as a success: does intervention save lives or prolong conflict? Can intervention ever be genuinely humanitarian?

---

[135] UNSC Res. 1967 (2011).
[136] UNSC Res. 1975 (2011), at para. 6.
[137] Secretary-General's 28th Report on Côte d'Ivoire, *supra* n. 131.
[138] UN Press Release SG/SM/13548, 6 May 2011, available at un.org/News/Press/docs/2011/sgsm13548.doc.htm. See also UN Press Release SG/SM/13838, 23 September 2011.
[139] See Corten, *supra* n. 4, at 515.

The subsequent shift of focus to R2P has attracted an enormous amount of discussion. R2P was unanimously accepted in the *2005 World Summit Outcome Document* when states accepted the responsibility of the international community to take collective action through the Security Council, including military action, in cases where the territorial state was unable to protect its population from international crimes. This does not seem to be a new legal right, but rather a new label for existing international law. Although many states continue to speak out in favour of R2P, others have expressed their concerns about the abuse of the right and about the inevitable selectivity in the choice of where to intervene. The military operations in Libya and Côte d'Ivoire have brought increased suspicion of R2P in some quarters. The actual legal justification for these operations lay in Chapter VII of the UN Charter, and even though the Security Council referred to R2P it referred only to the responsibility of the state and not to that of the international community. But some states and officials, and many commentators, did use the rhetoric of R2P in relation to *Operation Unified Protector* in Libya and to the use of force in Côte d'Ivoire.

The increased suspicion was manifest in the failure to secure a Security Council resolution on the situation in Syria in October 2011. A draft resolution was put forward by France, Germany, Portugal and the UK. It recalled 'the Syrian government's primary responsibility to protect its population', strongly condemned the continued grave and systematic human rights violations and the use of force against civilians by the Syrian authorities, demanded an immediate end to all violence and that the Syrian authorities cease violations of human rights, cease the use of force against civilians, and alleviate the humanitarian situation in crisis areas.[140] The draft resolution was not based on Chapter VII and made no determination that there was a threat to international peace and security. The text was defeated by the vetoes of China and Russia. Brazil, India, Lebanon and South Africa abstained. That is, the BRICS states were not ready to accept the invocation of R2P with regard to Syria.[141]

Russia said that the situation could not be considered separately from the Libyan experience: 'The international community was alarmed by statements that compliance with Security Council Resolutions on Libya in the NATO interpretation is a model for the future actions of NATO in implementing the responsibility to protect.'[142] It was important to see how that model had been implemented. The demand for a quick cease-fire had turned into a civil war, the humanitarian, social and military consequences of which had spilled beyond Libya. The arms embargo had turned into a naval blockade on west Libya. Such models should be excluded from global practice. Russia's proposals that the resolution should include express provision on the non-acceptability of foreign military intervention had not been taken into account, and based on the well-known events in North Africa 'that can only put us on our guard'.[143] South Africa was also concerned that the resolution's sponsors had rejected language that opposed military intervention in Syria. Council texts had been abused and

---

[140] France, Germany, Portugal and United Kingdom of Great Britain and Northern Ireland: Draft Resolution, UN Doc. S/2011/612, 4 October 2011.
[141] UN Security Council 6627th meeting, 4 October 2011, UN Doc. S/PV 6627 (2011).
[142] *Ibid.*
[143] *Ibid.*

implementation of mandates had gone far beyond that intended. The Council should not be part of any hidden agenda for regime change. China also stressed the importance of respecting Syria's sovereignty and territorial integrity. Any action should comply with the UN Charter principles of non-interference in internal affairs.

Those supporting the resolution argued that it made clear that any steps taken would be non-military. The USA, in unusually strong language, expressed outrage that the Security Council had not addressed the situation in Syria. It said that the draft was not about Libya or about military intervention; that suggestion was 'a cheap ruse by those who would rather sell arms to the Syrian regime than stand with the Syrian people'.[144] Russia and China may well have been disingenuous in their arguments to justify the use of the veto, but the experience of Iraq and Kosovo had shown that such assurances in Security Council debates cannot necessarily be relied on. Initially R2P was seen as a more attractive alternative to humanitarian intervention. However, it seems that some of the suspicion that had been attached to that doctrine had now transferred to R2P, following the use of force in Libya and Côte d'Ivoire.

---

[144] *Ibid.*

8. A taxonomy of armed conflict
*Marko Milanovic and Vidan Hadzi-Vidanovic**

1. INTRODUCTION

With some relatively minor exceptions international humanitarian law (hereinafter 'IHL') applies only when a certain threshold is met: the existence of an armed conflict or belligerent occupation. The purpose of this chapter is to explore the many difficulties surrounding the classification of armed conflicts in modern IHL.[1] While the two main archetypes – international armed conflict (hereinafter 'IAC') and non-international armed conflict (hereinafter 'NIAC') – are reasonably clear in their basic forms, their boundaries are complex and obscure. Many recent conflicts do not fit the classical archetypes well, provoking debates on spillover, internationalized, mixed or hybrid and even transnational armed conflicts.

The qualification exercise is often deliberately avoided, for several reasons. First, politically, the classification of armed conflict may have an impact on the *perceptions* of the legitimacy of the warring parties. Secondly, pragmatically, the qualification exercise can be so complex and indeterminate that dwelling on it overlong would threaten to bog down the implementation of basic rules of IHL and undermine the whole purpose of the regime. Thirdly, normatively, for the last two decades or so IHL has developed along the lines of a reasonably coherent project of bringing together the *substantive* law applicable in IACs and NIACs. Largely influenced by considerations of morality and the impact of human rights on IHL, or by the humanization of international law more generally,[2] and spearheaded by diverse actors – academics, non-governmental organizations, international tribunals,[3] the International Committee

---

* We would like to thank Charles Garraway, Robin Geiss, Douglas Guilfoyle, Monica Hakimi, Kevin Jon Heller, Christian Henderson, Robert Kolb, Claus Kress, Dino Kritsiotis, Marty Lederman, Naz Modirzadeh, Steven Ratner, Sandesh Sivakumaran and Nigel White for their most helpful comments.

[1] We will not be dealing with the threshold of belligerent occupation, on which see, for example, Y. Dinstein, *The International Law of Belligerent Occupation* (Cambridge: Cambridge University Press, 2009).

[2] See T. Meron, 'The Humanization of Humanitarian Law', (2000) 94 *AJIL* 239.

[3] As most famously articulated in *Prosecutor v. Tadić*, Decision on the Defence Motion for Interlocutory Appeal on Jurisdiction, IT-94-1- AR72, 2 October 1995, at para. 119: '[w]hat is inhumane, and consequently proscribed, in international wars, cannot but be inhumane and inadmissible in civil strife.' See also T. Hoffmann, 'The Gentle Humanizer of International Law – Antonio Cassese and the Creation of the Customary Law of Non-International Armed Conflicts', in C. Stahn and L. van den Herik (eds), *Future Perspectives on International Criminal Justice* (The Hague: TMC Asser Press, 2010), 58.

of the Red Cross (hereinafter 'ICRC')[4] and finally even states[5] – this project has been remarkably successful. In a relatively short time-span, it transformed the received wisdom from the pre-*Tadić* standpoint that in NIACs there are no war crimes under international law[6] to the ICRC Customary IHL Study view that the law in IACs and the law in NIACs have largely converged.[7]

From the perspective of this project, the question of classification of armed conflict is at best redundant and at worst dangerous.[8] Redundant, because if nothing hinges on the classification of conflict, since the substantive law that applies in all armed conflicts is always the same, then it is enough to label a particular situation as 'armed conflict' *simpliciter*; there is no need to say what *kind* of conflict it is. Dangerous, as insisting on the classification exercise implicitly threatens the foundations of the project as it invariably emphasizes the differences, rather than the similarities, between the two kinds of armed conflict.[9] While fully accepting the normative desirability and indeed the considerable results of this project, our aim here is to test its limits. We will show that the time will shortly come, if it has not come already, when that project will have exhausted its potential, and there are *some* differences between IACs and NIACs that *cannot* be erased simply by reasoning from analogy or from moral imperative.[10] Therefore, the classification of armed conflict is an issue that matters and will continue to matter for the considerable future.

Our purpose in this chapter is not to produce some earth-shatteringly original account of the various types of armed conflict in contemporary international law. Rather, our goal is above all *clarity*, clarity in a conceptual and doctrinal framework which can enable legal and policy debates to be properly had and argued without their

---

[4] See J.-M. Henckaerts and L. Doswald-Beck, *Customary International Humanitarian Law* (Cambridge: Cambridge University Press, 2005).

[5] For instance, by accepting and developing in the Rome Statute of the International Criminal Court (hereinafter 'ICC') the *Tadić* holding that war crimes were criminalized at the international level even in internal armed conflicts.

[6] See, for example, C. Greenwood, 'International Humanitarian Law and the *Tadić* Case', (1996) 7 *EJIL* 265, at 280 (citing *inter alia* ICRC comments on the proposal to establish the International Criminal Tribunal for the Former Yugoslavia (hereinafter 'ICTY'), stating that 'according to international humanitarian law as it stands today [in 1993], the notion of war crimes is limited to situations of international armed conflict'). See also C. Kress, 'Some Reflections on the International Legal Framework Governing Transnational Armed Conflicts', (2010) 15 *JCSL* 245, at 273. For more on war crimes see chapter 14 by Robert Cryer in this volume.

[7] *Supra* n.4. The study thus posits that out of the total of 161 customary rules binding in IACs 148 also apply in NIACs. See J. Pejic, 'The Protective Scope of Common Article 3: More than Meets the Eye', (2011) 93 *IRRC* 189, at 205–206.

[8] On the dangers of the project itself see esp. N. Modirzadeh, 'The Dark Sides of Convergence: A Pro-civilian Critique of the Extraterritorial Application of Human Rights Law in Armed Conflict', (2010) 86 *U.S. Naval War College International Law Studies (Blue Book) Series* 349.

[9] Cf. J. Stewart, 'Towards a Single Definition of Armed Conflict in International Humanitarian Law: A Critique of Internationalized Armed Conflict', (2003) 83 *IRRC* 313.

[10] In that regard see especially S. Sivakumaran, 'Re-envisaging the International Law of Internal Armed Conflicts', (2011) 22 *EJIL* 219; G. Blum, 'Re-envisaging the International Law of Internal Armed Conflict: A Reply to Sandesh Sivakumaran', (2011) 22 *EJIL* 265.

participants talking past each other.[11] Thus, while we are confident that those reading this chapter are aware, and indeed take part, in the current debates on the classification of armed conflicts, we still need to cover some familiar ground. Although the main topic of our inquiry is the controversies of today, to get there we must provide some context; it is impossible to comprehend the categories and concepts of modern IHL in clinical isolation, without understanding how and why they evolved. So bear with us – in section 2 we will be briefly examining the framework of war and peace in classical international law, while in section 3 we will be looking at the conceptual revolution brought about by the aftermath of the Second World War, namely the separation of the *jus ad bellum* from the *jus in bello*, and the rejection of 'war' as an operative legal concept. Section 4 will finally bring us to the modern law and to developing a comprehensive taxonomy of armed conflict, while we will be discussing the practical consequences of classification throughout.

2. WAR AND PEACE IN CLASSICAL INTERNATIONAL LAW

A. The Law of War and the Law of Peace

International law developed in parallel with the emergence and subsequent domination of the modern state in organized human society.[12] A horizontal system designed to regulate relations between sovereign units with their own means of coercion but without such authority over them had no choice but to accept inter-state violence as an unavoidable reality.[13] Since that violence, however, had significant consequences on the application of the rules designed to govern 'normal'[14] or 'peaceful' relations between the states, two separate regimes evolved in parallel – the law of war and the law of peace.

Classical international law was compartmentalized. Like war and peace, the law of war and the law of peace excluded each other.[15] It was considered that the moment 'war enters on the scene, all law that was previously concerned with the dispute retires, and the new law steps in, directed only to secure fair and not too inhumane fighting'.[16] The general rule of classical international law was that war abrogates treaties between

---

[11] For the purposes of clarity we also include as an annex to the chapter a schema of armed conflict, which we hope will be useful to the reader.

[12] What follows is an admittedly simplified account of the international legal regulation of war. For a sophisticated one, see S. Neff, *War and the Law of Nations: A General History* (Cambridge: Cambridge University Press, 2005).

[13] See L. Oppenheim, *International Law: A Treatise: Vol. II – War and Neutrality*, 3rd edn (London: Longmans, 1920), at 66; W.E. Hall, *International Law* (Oxford: Clarendon Press, 1880), at 51.

[14] See Hall, *supra* n.13, at 36; J.S. Risley, *The Law of War* (London: A.D. Innes and Co, 1897), at 1.

[15] See Neff, *supra* n.12, at 178 ff.; I. Detter, *The Law of War*, 2nd edn (Cambridge: Cambridge University Press, 2000), at 6.

[16] J. Westlake, *International Law: Part II – War*, 2nd edn (Cambridge: Cambridge University Press, 1913), at 4.

the belligerents and that their revival had to be determined through a peace treaty once the war was over.[17] This wartime suspension of peacetime rights and obligations included even the most fundamental of principles upon which pacific international relations were built, such as respect for the sovereignty, territorial integrity and independence of a state.[18] Into the void left by the law of peace stepped in the law of war.[19] These rules were primarily concerned with the rights and obligations of belligerents concerning their subjects, armies and property, and gradually started including some rudimentary rules on the means of warfare.[20] The outbreak of war also triggered the laws of neutrality that governed the relations between the belligerents and third states. These special rights and obligations came into effect once the outbreak of war was notified or otherwise made known to the neutral states and expired with the cessation of the war.[21] The laws of neutrality were thus designed to preserve the relations of third states with the belligerents as far as the circumstances allowed it.

For most of the classical period international law did not regulate when states could resort to war. While war was perhaps not considered a right, since there was no corresponding obligation,[22] it was seen simply as an expression of a state's sovereignty. The power to wage war was inherent to the state as the sole legitimate monopoly of force. Naturalist just war theories were rejected by classical positivists.[23] War did not even need to be a measure of last resort, however loosely defined.[24] Rudimentary limitations on the unlimited freedom of states to wage war started to emerge only after the Hague peace conferences, while war itself was finally renounced as an instrument of national policy under the terms of the 1928 Kellogg–Briand Pact.[25] This prohibition on war, however, ultimately unveiled all of the shortcomings of 'war' as a legal term of art, to which we now turn.[26]

B. War as a Subjective Legal Concept

Because its outbreak had far-reaching legal consequences on inter-state relations, 'war' was not merely a state of fact, but a full-fledged legal institution.[27] And since the waging of war was an expression of the sovereign will of a state, war could not legally

---

[17] *Ibid.*, at 32.
[18] Oppenheim, *supra* n.13, at 66, 145 ff.
[19] Some pacific rules would, however, continue to apply if they were specifically designed to continue during the war. See Hall, *supra* n. 13, at 322 ff.; Oppenheim, *supra* n.13, at 145 ff.
[20] See, for the discussion on the evolution of the rules regulating warfare, R. Kolb and R. Hyde, *An Introduction to the International Law of Armed Conflicts* (Oxford: Hart Publishing, 2008), at 37 ff.
[21] Article 2 of the Hague Convention III relative to the Opening of Hostilities, 18 October 1907.
[22] Oppenheim, *supra* n.13, at 99.
[23] *Ibid.*, at 79, 81–82.
[24] *Ibid.*, at 67.
[25] See, generally, Y. Dinstein, *War, Aggression and Self-Defence*, 5th edn (Cambridge: Cambridge University Press, 2011), at 84 ff.
[26] See also Neff, *supra* n.12, at 293–296.
[27] A.D. McNair, 'The Legal Meaning of War, and the Relation of War and Reprisals', (1926) 11 *Tr. Grotius Sc.* 29, at 33.

exist without an *animus belligerendi*, or at least many so argued.[28] This subjective *animus* could be proven, or not, by reference to criteria such as the severance of diplomatic relations between belligerents, the existence of a declaration of war or of a notification of the state of war to neutral powers, recognition of the state of war by these neutral powers, and so on.

In search of this *animus* more objective criteria such as the intensity of any clashes between states' armies often fell by the wayside. This in turn opened the way to situations of widespread and protracted fighting in which the states concerned for political reasons refused to recognize the existence of war. A gap opened up between a common sense, factual understanding of 'war' and one derived from the niceties of international law, a gap to be exploited when it served state interests. It not only introduced a large degree of uncertainty with regard to the rights of private citizens,[29] but more importantly created a major obstacle to the application of any humanitarian rules of the law of war. All a state had to do to avoid the law of war was to deny the existence of war *in the legal sense*, no matter how much blood was being shed in a very real sense. One of the most notorious historical examples in which belligerents (as well as third states and even the League of Nations Commission of Inquiry)[30] refused to recognize a state of war despite all evidence to the contrary was the 'Manchurian crisis' or the Sino-Japanese war.[31] The 'crisis' started with the full-scale Japanese invasion and the occupation of Manchuria, a Chinese province. It involved heavy military clashes with great loss of life.[32] Eventually, Japan renamed Manchuria as Manchukuo and established it as a puppet state. Yet both China and Japan refused to recognize that a state of war existed between them. Japan did so in order to preserve its good standing as a founder of the League of Nations and a signatory of the Kellogg–Briand Pact.[33] China did not want to disturb its trade with the United States by activating the laws of neutrality.[34] As the existence of war was denied by both parties, the law of war could not apply.

It was precisely the rigidity of the law of peace/law of war framework and the strict consequences that followed the transition from one to the other that provided the incentive for states to avoid recognizing the existence of war. This led some scholars of the period to argue for the legal recognition of a third, middle category between war

---

[28] See Hall, *supra* n.13, at 63; more recently, C. Greenwood, 'War, Terrorism and International Law', (2003) 56 *CLP* 505, at 513, 515. For discussion see Dinstein, *supra* n.25, at 14; Neff, *supra* n.12, at 172 ff.

[29] One of the most famous discussions on the subject occurred on private lawsuit in the case of *Kawasaki Kisen Kabushiki Kaisha of Kobe v. Bantham Steamship Company, Ltd*, [1939] 2 K.B. 544 (Court of Appeal).

[30] The Report of the Commission of Inquiry appointed by the Council of the League of Nations, Lytton Report, Series League of Nations Publications, VII, Political, 1932, 12.

[31] For a detailed legal and factual account of the Sino-Japanese war see A. Carty and R.A. Smith, *Sir Gerald Fitzmaurice and the World Crisis: A Legal Adviser in the Foreign Office 1932–1945* (The Hague: Martinus Nijhoff, 2000), at 41 et seq.

[32] See J.L. Brierly, 'International Law and Resort to Armed Force', (1932)4 *CLJ* 308, at 312.

[33] See D. Kritsiotis, 'When States Use Armed Force', in C. Reus-Smit (ed.), *The Politics of International Law* (Cambridge: Cambridge University Press, 2004), 45, at 53.

[34] *Ibid.*

and peace – a *status mixtus*.³⁵ Others, in turn, wanted to objectivize war.³⁶ But what the humanity-minded lawyers may have wanted and what states thought to be in their interest was not necessarily one and the same. Rather than bringing some resolution the controversies on the legal nature of war brought even more uncertainty.³⁷

C. War as Inter-state Conflict

With one exception, which we will address below, war as a legal concept denoted solely inter-state armed conflict.³⁸ Although from the modern perspective this looks like an excessively rigid, formalistic position, a system built upon the presumption that sovereign states are the sole legitimate bearers of the monopoly of force could not initially do anything but dismiss non-state violence as illegitimate and hence irrelevant in international law.³⁹ It was thought that only modern states with their trained, disciplined standing armies could observe and create the laws of war; non-state armed groups were not only undeserving of protection, but could not comply with rules designed to regulate the conduct of states.⁴⁰

This state-centric conception of war was not entirely without humanitarian benefits. Burdened with notions of collective responsibility, pre-classical international law made no distinction between combatants and civilians.⁴¹ The belligerents' populations were seen as participants in the conflict and 'every subject of a belligerent, whether an armed and fighting individual or not, whether man or woman, adult or infant, could be killed or enslaved by the other belligerent at will'.⁴² Warfare was essentially unrestrained, and it was precisely the emergence of the 'civilized' state, possessed with 'absolute sovereignty' and 'ordered diplomacy', with 'lawful bearers of arms' embodied in its standing army, that enabled a measure of restraint.⁴³

The narrow state-centric approach to war completely excluded conflicts waged by European empires at the margins of the 'civilized world.' This, however, was precisely the point of this approach – the laws of war applied only to those belonging to the 'civilized family of nations' for which they were designed,⁴⁴ thus enabling European

---

³⁵ See G. Schwarzenberger, 'Jus Pacis ac Belli?', (1943) 37 *AJIL* 460, at 470; P.C. Jessup, 'Should International Law Recognize an Intermediate Status between Peace and War?', (1954) 48 *AJIL* 98, at 100.
³⁶ See Brierly, *supra* n.32; T.S. Woolsey, 'The Beginning of a War', (1900) 9 *Yale LJ* 153.
³⁷ For a discussion see M.S. McDougal and F.P. Feliciano, *The International Law of War: Transnational Coercion and World Public Order* (The Hague: Martinus Nijhoff Publishers, 1994), at 99–101.
³⁸ See, for example, Dinstein, *supra* n.25, at 5–6.
³⁹ The tradition of such thinking in Western legal thought is a long one – see Neff, *supra* n.12, at 250 ff.
⁴⁰ See Oppenheim, *supra* n.13, at 86.
⁴¹ See T. Becker, *Terrorism and the State: Rethinking the Rules of State Responsibility* (Oxford: Hart Publishing, 2006), at 13–14.
⁴² Oppenheim, *supra* n.13, at 70.
⁴³ J. Keegan, *A History of Warfare*, 2nd edn (London: Pimlico, 2004), at 12, 23.
⁴⁴ See, generally, Oppenheim, *supra* n.13, at 108; M. Koskenniemi, *Gentle Civilizer of Nations: The Rise and Fall of International Law* (Cambridge: Cambridge University Press, 2001), at 98 ff.; D. Pendas, '"The Magical Scent of the Savage": Colonial Violence, the Crisis of

imperialism against the not-so-civilized in all its brutality. As the German nationalist writer Heinrich von Treitschke so openly put it at the close of the nineteenth century:

> There is nothing in international law more beautiful, or showing more unmistakably the continual progress of mankind, than a whole series of principles, grounded only upon *universalis consensus* and yet as firmly established as those of the Common Law of any country. ... Still, the whole trend of political life has come into the open to such a degree that any gross breach of international law immediately causes great irritation in every civilized country. ... It is mere mockery, however, to apply these principles [of international law] to warfare against savages. A Negro tribe must be punished by the burning of their villages, for it is the only kind of example which will avail. If the German Empire has abandoned this principle to-day it has done so out of disgraceful weakness, and for no reasons of humanity or high respect for law.[45]

Similarly, even in the 'civilized world' the state-centred approach excluded organized violence between a state and its own subjects from international regulation; the peculiar 'sporting outlook'[46] that sovereigns applied to limiting warfare among themselves did not have the same sway when it came to maintaining their own power internally. We will now briefly turn to the *ad hoc* attempts to regulate internal conflicts in the classical, rigid framework of the laws of war and peace.

D. Civil War: Rebellion, Insurgency and Belligerency

The exclusion of internal conflicts from the scope of international legal regulation may have been the rule, but it was not an absolute rule.[47] The need to regulate at least some internal conflicts gradually became apparent, first in order to protect the interests of third states and then for interests of humanity. As already explained, within the purview of the classical law of war were not only the relations between the belligerents, but also those between belligerents and neutrals. The latter were of pivotal importance in developing the notion of the recognition of belligerency.[48] It was first accepted that once an internal conflict endangered the 'normal' relations of a third state with the state embroiled in civil strife, 'the law of nations will step in to define and to fix the rights and duties of belligerents relatively to neutrals'.[49] Subsequently, the law of nations was also allowed to step in and define the relations between the (civil) belligerents

---

Civilization and the Origins of the Legalist Paradigm of War', (2007) 30 *BC Intl & Comp LRev* 29; G. Gong, *The Standard of 'Civilization' in International Society* (Oxford: Clarendon Press, 1984); L. Arimatsu, 'Territory, Boundaries and the Law of Armed Conflict', (2009) 12 *Y Intl HL* 157, at 162–165.

[45] H. von Treitschke, *Politics* (Hans Kohn ed., 1963) (1898), at 300–301, 306, quoted according to Pendas, *supra* n.44.

[46] Neff, *supra* n.12, at 189.

[47] See esp. A. Cassese, 'The Spanish Civil War and the Development of Customary Law Concerning Internal Armed Conflicts', in A. Cassese, *The Human Dimension of International Law: Selected Papers* (Oxford: Oxford University Press, 2008), 128 (arguing that customary law started regulating internal conflicts as such even before the Second World War).

[48] Neff, *supra* n.12, at 251.

[49] J.F. Macqueen, *Chief Points in the Laws of War and Neutrality* (London and Edinburgh: William and Robert Chambers, 1862), at 15.

themselves. This interference of international law in internal conflicts was, however, of a limited character, with regulation being of an *ad hoc*, inconsistent and even arbitrary character.

Internal armed struggles came to be seen through three legal categories – rebellion, insurgency and belligerency. Any one of these could have been characterized in common parlance as a civil war. A rebellion was an uprising of limited duration and intensity which could have been successfully resolved with regular police action.[50] Insurgency involved 'the existence of an armed revolt of grave character and the incapacity, at least temporarily, of the lawful Government to maintain public order and exercise authority over all parts of the national territory'.[51] The two were outside the scope of international law unless the insurgency ultimately proved to be successful, whether in replacing the prior government of the country or in managing to effect secession of part of its territory.

Belligerency, in contrast, was regulated by international law if a number of conditions were met. As canonically summarized by Wheaton, these were 'the existence of a *de facto* political organization of the insurgents, sufficient in character, population and resources, to constitute it, if left to itself, a State among the nations, reasonably capable of discharging the duties of a State; the actual employment of military forces on each side, acting in accordance with the rules and customs of war'.[52] While these criteria seemed objective, they were much debated due to their openness to different interpretations. The malleability and vagueness of the criteria suggested that the recognition of belligerency was always more a matter of political expediency than a matter of law.[53]

Despite the existence, *vel non*, of these objective requirements, belligerency had to be recognized either by the state fighting the insurgency or by third states.[54] These recognitions did not have the same legal effect. Recognition of belligerency by third states led to the application of the rules of neutrality, but it made no difference with regard to the relations of belligerents themselves. The legitimate government, which was in conflict with its own subjects, was perfectly free to decide whether or not to treat the insurgency as a belligerency, whatever the attitude of third states.[55] If it did

---

[50] See S. Sivakumaran, *The Law of Non-International Armed Conflict* (Oxford: Oxford University Press, forthcoming 2012) (manuscript on file with the authors); R. Falk, 'Janus Tormented: The International Law of Internal War', in J.N. Rosenau (ed.), *International Aspects of Civil Strife* (Princeton, NJ: Princeton University Press, 1964), at 185, 197; L. Kotzsch, *The Concept of War in Contemporary History and International Law* (Geneva: Droz, 1956), at 230.

[51] Sivakumaran, *supra* n.50; E Castrén, *Civil War* (Helsinki: Suomalainen Tiedeakatemia, 1966), at 211.

[52] C. Phillipson, *Wheaton's Elements of International Law*, 5th edn (London: Stevens and Sons Ltd, 1916), at 411.

[53] See Sivakumaran, *supra* n.50; E. Luard, 'Civil Conflicts in Modern International Relations', in E. Luard (ed.), *The International Regulation of Civil Wars* (London: Thames and Hudson, 1972), 20; H.A. Wilson, *International Law and the Use of Force* (Oxford: Clarendon Press, 1988), at 26; D.A. Elder, 'The Historical Background of Common Article 3 of the Geneva Conventions of 1949', (1979) 11 *Case W Res J Intl L* 37.

[54] See Neff, *supra* n.12, at 258 ff.; D. Schindler, 'The Different Types of Armed Conflicts According to the Geneva Conventions and Protocols', (1979-II) 163 *Rd C* 131, at 145–146.

[55] See Oppenheim, *supra* n.13, at 76.

recognize belligerency, third states could be notified thereof in order to activate the rules of neutrality. Hence, depending on its originator, the effect of recognition of belligerency was the transformation of a civil war into a 'war' proper, regulated by the international law of war.[56] With recognition, the insurgents acquired international personality *vis-à-vis* those who recognized them to the extent necessary for the regulation of the hostilities, thus being effectively admitted as putative members into the family of 'civilized' nations. Recognition of belligerency, however, did not prevent the lawful and ultimately successful government from treating the insurgents as traitors once the conflict was over.[57]

Despite some notable examples, such as the United States Civil War and the Boer War,[58] recognitions of belligerency were rarely granted. Third states were reluctant to recognize belligerency in order to avoid the restrictions on commerce and all other consequences that the rules of neutrality imposed, and in order to avoid causing great offence to governments embroiled in civil strife.[59] On the other hand, for such governments recognizing belligerency would invariably be seen as an admission of weakness and a legitimization of the insurgents. The most notable example of the doctrine's failure was the Spanish Civil War of 1936–1939, in which belligerency was not recognized despite the conflict's intensity and duration.[60] The *ad hoc* attempts to regulate internal armed conflict were thus structurally prone to failure.

3. A CONCEPTUAL REVOLUTION: IMPACT OF THE SECOND WORLD WAR

A. Separation of the *jus ad bellum* and the *jus in bello*

The Second World War was the crucible that shaped the modern law of armed conflict and broke the rigid, formalist framework of classical international law. Its aftermath brought about two sets of conceptual changes in the law, as a reaction to the inadequacies of the classical legal regime of war and peace as applied in the first half of the twentieth century. The first was the separation of the *jus ad bellum* and the *jus in bello*; the second the rejection of the concept of 'war' in both the *ad bellum* and the *in bello* contexts. We will briefly deal with each in turn.

Despite the Latin veneer of antiquity, the two terms were first used only in the interwar period, in the early 1930s.[61] This is not to say that the law of nations, as it stood before, could not distinguish between *ad bellum* and *in bello* issues and

---

[56] See Macqueen, *supra* n.49, at 15.
[57] See Oppenheim, *supra* n.13, at 76.
[58] See L. Moir, *The Law of Internal Armed Conflict* (Cambridge: Cambridge University Press, 2002), at 19.
[59] *Ibid.*; Neff, *supra* n.12, at 268.
[60] See also H. Lauterpacht, *Recognition in International Law* (Cambridge: Cambridge University Press, 1978), at 272 ff.; Cassese, *supra* n.47.
[61] See, generally, R. Kolb, 'Origin of the Twin Terms *Jus ad Bellum/Jus in Bello*', (1997) 37 (320) *IRRC* 553.

considerations, but that there was little practical point in doing so as the two types of questions were considered to be inextricably linked. In the naturalist tradition the principal issue was whether a war was *just*, primarily by reference to considerations of the *ad bellum* variety, and only a just war was legally regulated. In the classical positivist tradition *ad bellum* considerations almost evaporated together with just war theory. War was now seen as the ultimate prerogative and a matter of discretion of any sovereign – and it was only then that the *jus in bello*, equally applied between sovereigns, naturally started to emerge as a fully fledged corpus of rules and institutions. While any state could resort to force any time it wished, the *manner* in which force was used required some basic legal regulation, resting on the reciprocity and mutuality of obligations; it took the devastation of the two world wars to bring *ad bellum* considerations fully back into the picture.[62]

With the entry into force of the UN Charter in 1945 and the four Geneva Conventions in 1949, the separation between the *jus ad bellum* and the *jus in bello* was complete – though it has never been safe from challenge. Separation has become a cardinal principle of those seeking to preserve the humanitarian integrity of the *jus in bello*, now rebranded as IHL.[63] It is because we know from experience that every party to a conflict will portray itself as having a just cause that we cannot accept a principle by which a 'just' party would have to abide by fewer obligations, as that would invariably lead to a spiral of law-breaking that the law and the humanitarian interests it seeks to protect could not survive.[64] For the purposes of the present chapter, we will leave the question of separation aside.[65] More pertinent for our analysis of thresholds of IHL is the second principal conceptual shift after the Second World War – that of the rejection of 'war' itself as an operative legal concept.

B. Discarding the Concept of War in both the *jus ad bellum* and the *jus in bello*

Although 'war' was used in common parlance and as an operative legal concept before the Second World War, in both (as yet formally undivided) *in bello* and *ad bellum* contexts,[66] states decided to discard it in both. In the *jus ad bellum*, war was replaced

---

[62] *Ibid*. See also J. Moussa, 'Can *Jus ad Bellum* Override *Jus in Bello*? Reaffirming the Separation of the Two Bodies of Law', (2008) 872 *IRRC* 963.

[63] See, for example, Neff, *supra* n.12, at 342.

[64] See Dinstein, *supra* n.25, at 167–170.

[65] For strong defences of the separation between the *jus ad bellum* and the *jus in bello*, and the concomitant principle of equal application of the *jus in bello* to all parties to a conflict, see especially R. Sloane, 'The Cost of Conflation: Preserving the Dualism of *Jus ad Bellum* and *Jus in Bello* in the Contemporary Law of War', (2009) 34 *Yale J Intl L* 47;A. Roberts, 'The Equal Application of the Laws of War: A Principle Under Pressure', (2008) 90 *IRRC* 931; M. Sassoli, '*Ius ad Bellum* and *Ius in Bello* – the Separation between the Legality of the Use of Force and Humanitarian Rules to be Respected in Warfare: Crucial or Outdated?', in M. Schmitt and J. Pejic (eds), *International Law and Armed Conflict: Exploring the Faultlines: Essays in Honour of Yoram Dinstein* (Leiden: Martinus Nijhoff, 2007), 241.

[66] See, for example, J. Pictet (ed.), *Commentary on the Geneva Conventions of 12 August 1949*, 4 vols., (Geneva: ICRC, 1952–1959; the full text of the Commentary is available at www.icrc.org), at 19: 'The Hague Convention of 1899, in Article 2, stated that the annexed Regulations concerning the Laws and Customs of War on Land were applicable "in case of war".

with the more general concept of the use of (armed) *force*, with Article 2(4) of the UN Charter providing that '[a]ll Members shall refrain in their international relations from the threat or use of force against the territorial integrity or political independence of any state, or in any other manner inconsistent with the Purposes of the United Nations'.[67] In the *jus in bello*, war was replaced with the notion of international armed conflict, as provided for in Common Article 2 of the 1949 Geneva Conventions.[68]

There were four basic reasons for discarding war as an operative concept. First, it was much too rigid in its consequences. As we have seen, the classical division between the law of peace and the law of war assigned to the existence of war effects such as the rupture of diplomatic and treaty relations, rights and obligations of neutrality for third parties, and so on. In some situations, however, while being perfectly content with fighting one another states did not want such consequences to ensue, thus leading them to deny the existence of war as the applicable legal condition.[69] Secondly, war was much too contested as a concept, with significantly diverging views being offered as to its elements. Thirdly, and relatedly, war was regarded by many as being *subjective* in nature, as requiring a specific *animus belligerendi* for its existence. Finally, and consequently, a significant number of instances of inter-state use of armed force went legally unregulated, since the law of war could not apply where there legally was no war.

Additional to these concerns in the inter-state context was the lack of any systemic regulation of internal conflict. The concept of war thus outlived its usefulness, while in the post-UN Charter world the word itself became politically unpalatable, with formal declarations of war falling into disuse. The principal purpose in replacing it was to provide *objective* thresholds to describe inter-state violence that was subject to legal regulation.[70] In the *jus ad bellum*, politically more controversial and hence legally more open to indeterminacy, that endeavour was less successful. Article 2(4) of the Charter is famously open to interpretation due to its reference to a particular purpose for the use of force,[71] while the scope of the self-defence exception in its Article 51 is similarly

---

This definition was not repeated either in 1907 at The Hague or in 1929 at Geneva; the very title and purpose of the Conventions made it clear that they were intended for use in war-time, and the meaning of war seemed to require no defining.' As for the nascent *jus ad bellum*, in Article I of the 1928 Kellogg–Briand Pact the states parties 'condemn[ed] recourse to *war* for the solution of international controversies, and renounce[d] it, as an instrument of national policy in their relations with one another' (emphasis added).

[67] See chapter 3 by Nicholas Tsagourias and chapter 4 by Mary Ellen O'Connell in this volume for more on the threat and use of force.

[68] For a detailed account see D. Kritsiotis, 'Topographies of Force', in Schmitt and Pejic, *supra* n.65, at 29.

[69] See, for example, Neff, *supra* n.12, at 286, 296 ff. (on the 'art of avoiding war'); Schindler, *supra* n.54, at 125.

[70] See, for example, E. Holland, 'The Qualification Framework of International Humanitarian Law: Too Rigid to Accommodate Contemporary Conflicts?', (2011) 34 *Suffolk Trans L Rev* 145, at 149–151; Stewart, *supra* n.9, at 316–318; S. Vité, 'Typology of Armed Conflicts in International Humanitarian Law: Legal Concepts and Actual Situations', (2009) 91 *IRRC* 69, at 72.

[71] See, generally, Dinstein, *supra* n.25, at 88–94.

contested.[72] The *jus in bello* concepts of IAC and NIAC are more stable and explicitly objective and factual,[73] although of course far from crystal clear – their apparent firmness when compared with the *jus ad bellum* is thus more one of degree than one of kind. Most importantly, as a matter of *general* international law neither the *ad bellum* use of force nor the *in bello* armed conflict produce overarching legal effects as war did in classical international law. The law is no longer strictly divided into the law of peace and law of war;[74] neither treaty nor diplomatic relations are ruptured *ipso facto* merely because the *ad bellum* or *in bello* thresholds are crossed. Thus, for example, in Article 3 of its Draft Articles on the Effects of Armed Conflict on Treaties that it recently adopted on second reading, the International Law Commission (hereinafter 'ILC') reverses the classical presumption by stipulating the general principle that the 'existence of an armed conflict does not *ipso facto* terminate or suspend the operation of treaties'.[75] Modern IHL is now simply one of a number of interlocking and overlapping legal sub-regimes applying simultaneously to the same situation.[76] The rigidity of the legal regime that the concept of war once brought to bear, and accordingly the incentive for states to avoid recognizing the existence of war with the consequent lack of legal regulation of hostilities, are thereby avoided.[77]

C. Outline of the Thresholds of Armed Conflict

The Geneva Conventions set out three distinct thresholds for their applicability. First, Common Article 2 (hereinafter 'CA2'), paras 1 and 2, provides that:

> In addition to the provisions which shall be implemented in peace time, the present Convention shall apply to all cases of declared war or of any other armed conflict which may arise between two or more of the High Contracting Parties, even if the state of war is not recognized by one of them.
>
> The Convention shall also apply to all cases of partial or total occupation of the territory of a High Contracting Party, even if the said occupation meets with no armed resistance.

---

[72] See, for example, Neff, *supra* n.12, at 317 ff., esp. at 328 ('Self-defence claims blossomed so luxuriantly, and expanded in so many directions as effectively to encompass *any* arguably justifiable resort to force'). See also chapter 6 by Dino Kritsiotis in this volume.

[73] See, for example, Pictet, *supra* n.66, at 23: 'It remains to ascertain what is meant by "armed conflict". The substitution of this much more general expression for the word "war" was deliberate. It is possible to argue almost endlessly about the legal definition of "war". A State which uses arms to commit a hostile act against another State can always maintain that it is not making war, but merely engaging in a police action, or acting in legitimate self-defence. The expression "armed conflict" makes such arguments less easy.'

[74] See, especially, C. Stahn, '"*Jus ad bellum*", "*jus in bello*"... "*jus post bellum*"? – Rethinking the Conception of the Law of Armed Force', (2007) 17 *EJIL* 921. For more on the *jus post bellum* see chapter 15 by Bell in this volume.

[75] UN Doc. A/CN.4/L.777, 11 May 2011.

[76] See also Stahn, *supra* n.74, at 926.

[77] The question to what extent the concept of 'war' has continuing relevance regarding issues such as neutrality is a difficult one, and we will leave it aside. See, generally, Dinstein, *supra* n.25, and Neff, *supra* n.12, at 347–356. Suffice it to say that it has no bearing on the application of modern IHL. See, for example, N. Lubell, *Extraterritorial Use of Force against Non-State Actors* (Oxford: Oxford University Press, 2010), at 87–88.

Paragraph 1 defines international armed conflict as a conflict between two or more high contracting parties, which could be definition only be states. A declaration of war automatically creates an IAC even before the start of hostilities,[78] but as we have seen they have fallen into disuse. The fact that a state of war is not recognized by a party or indeed *both* parties is made irrelevant, thereby removing the subjectivity that plagued the earlier regime and making IAC a purely factual threshold.[79] Paragraph 2 sets out belligerent occupation as a distinct threshold of application.

Common Article 3 (hereinafter 'CA3') of the Conventions provides for NIAC, the third threshold of application, by stipulating that '[i]n the case of armed conflict not of an international character occurring in the territory of one of the High Contracting Parties, each Party to the conflict shall be bound to apply, as a minimum' a number of humanitarian provisions with respect to persons who are *hors de combat*. While CA2 is the threshold of application for *all* of the Conventions but for CA3, CA3 is the threshold only for its own applicability.[80] As is well known, during the drafting of the Convention the original proposal by the ICRC was to apply most of the Conventions to internal or non-international armed conflicts, but that proposal was met with overwhelming opposition from states.[81]

CA3 was the first true attempt at regulating internal armed conflict systematically, rather than arbitrarily and *ad hoc* through recognitions of belligerency as in the classical law of war. It grew precisely out of a moral need to regulate such type of conflict which could be just as devastating as inter-state wars. But that moral imperative went only so far in 1949. It is easy to forget from the standpoint of our modern project of humanizing IHL and creating substantive law in NIACs by analogy to IACs that at the time of its drafting there was *no law* in internal armed conflicts but CA3. Together with the 1948 Genocide Convention, whose prohibitions were so narrow that even Stalin was perfectly happy with the final product, CA3 was the first substantial limitation that states have accepted with regard to their own population. Human rights law was barely embryonic, and for many decades the law of internal armed conflict contained no rules on the conduct of hostilities nor were serious violations of CA3 considered as creating individual criminal responsibility at the international level, that is as constituting war crimes.

In short, states saw CA3 as a major constraint on their sovereignty and their ability to effectively suppress rebellions, and thus minimized its scope as much as they could, in tension with moral considerations under which distinctions between IACs and NIACs made no sense. They accordingly elevated the threshold of internal armed conflict so that it required a level of intensity that the ICTY Appeals Chamber in *Tadić* was later to characterize as 'protracted armed violence', which rose above the level of mere riots

---

[78] See Schindler, *supra* n.54, at 131–132.

[79] See Pictet, *supra* n.66, at 23; D. Akande, 'Classification of Armed Conflicts: Relevant Legal Concepts' (forthcoming in a Chatham House collection edited by Elizabeth Wilmshurst, manuscript on file with the authors), at 9–10.

[80] Although the substantive *content* of CA3 applies as a matter of custom to both NIACs and IACs.

[81] See, for example, Stewart, *supra* n.9, at 313–314; Akande, *supra* n.79, at 3.

or disturbances.[82] Similarly, CA3 carefully provided that the existence of a NIAC would not affect the legal status of the parties to the conflict, that is would not legitimize rebellion against the lawful (or at least extant) authority. And when further rules were added to regulate NIACs in response to the humanitarian imperative and the growing influence of human rights, as in the 1977 Additional Protocol II to the Geneva Convention, the price to be paid for these additional rules was the heightening of the applicability threshold.[83]

With the 1949 Geneva Conventions being the only treaties to achieve universal ratification, the CA2 and CA3 thresholds have undoubtedly long achieved customary status.[84] New states, as they spring up from time to time, would be bound by customary IHL that would apply on the basis of the CA2 and CA3 thresholds, regardless of their accession or succession to the Conventions. New thresholds and new rules can of course be created, whether by treaty, as with Additional Protocols I and II (hereinafter 'AP I' and 'AP II', or under custom, with the treaty threshold applying only *inter partes* so long as they, in turn, do not reach customary status. For the time being, however, CA2 and CA3 remain the baselines and the principal thresholds of IHL's applicability.

D. Is there a Generic Concept of Armed Conflict?

Before turning to the typology of armed conflicts, it is necessary to ask ourselves whether there is a *generic* concept of armed conflict. Looking at the text of CA2 and CA3, it seems as if the concept of NIAC is defined *residually* from or in opposition to IAC, that is a NIAC would be an armed conflict which is *not* an IAC.[85] The analytical approach to qualifying a particular situation would then be as follows: (1) Is it an armed conflict? (2) If so, is it an IAC? (3) If not, it must be a NIAC. 'Armed conflict' would then be a generic term, whose definitional elements could logically be met *before* making the further step of qualifying it in kind either as an IAC or a NIAC.[86] Indeed, not only does this reasoning follow textually from CA2 and CA3, but it is frequently resorted to in practice, if implicitly. A good example is the *Hamdan* case before the US Supreme Court,[87] in which the Court found that (1) there was an armed conflict between the US and Al-Qaeda;[88] (2) that this conflict could not be international in character, as IACs are defined as conflicts between states, which Al-Qaeda was

---

[82] See, for example, Pejic, *supra* n.7, at 192.

[83] See *infra* section 4B.

[84] As rules of general international law, both CA2 and CA3 would necessarily be reformulated so that the reference to 'high contracting parties' is changed to (any) states. Note, of course, the general difficulty in deriving custom from widely accepted treaties.

[85] Cf. Holland, *supra* n.70, at 155; Vité, *supra* n.70, at 75–76.

[86] Perhaps most notably, this is now the view of the International Law Association (hereinafter 'ILA') Use of Force Committee, chaired by Mary Ellen O'Connell, in its Final Report on the Meaning of Armed Conflict in International Law (2010).

[87] *Hamdan v. Rumsfeld*, 548 U.S. 557 (2006).

[88] This was admittedly more of an unchallenged assumption than a true legal and factual finding. See also M. Ramsden, 'Targeted Killings and International Human Rights Law: The Case of Anwar Al-Awlaki', (2011) 16 *JCSL* 385, at 390.

not;[89] and consequently (3) that the conflict was a NIAC.[90] The Court was not entirely clear on whether this conflict was a NIAC in Afghanistan or in some other locale, or was rather *global* in character.[91]

That particular ambiguity aside, however, the Court's logic is flawed. While it is certainly correct that the US 'war on terror' against Al-Qaeda cannot be an IAC under the CA2 definition, it does *not* follow from that conclusion that it must be a NIAC. Despite the textual impulse to define NIACs negatively or residually from IACs and a broader notion of armed conflict this is *not* how the thresholds work.[92] In mathematical terms, if you will, the two are not subsets of the same set. 'Armed conflict' cannot be defined generically.[93] Any such definition requires an inquiry into the *party structure* of the conflict,[94] which is the most important, but not the *only*, distinguishing criterion between IACs and NIACs. Rather, unlike IACs, NIACs require a level of sustained hostilities between a state and a non-state actor, or between two or more non-state actors, the continued existence of 'protracted armed violence' taking place within a certain defined area.[95] Only once this threshold is crossed would a NIAC legally exist, since states did not and do not want every outburst of internal violence to be regulated by IHL, seeing this as a potential intrusion upon their sovereignty.[96]

Rather than being a generic concept, 'armed conflict' is merely shorthand for an IAC or a NIAC and all their descriptive sub-types. If a third category of armed conflict were to develop through treaty or custom, for example transnational armed conflict,[97] then 'armed conflict' would be shorthand for that as well. But one *cannot* first say that a

---

[89] *Hamdan, supra* n.87 at 630: 'The Court of Appeals thought, and the Government asserts, that Common Article 3 does not apply to Hamdan because the conflict with al Qaeda, being "international in scope," does not qualify as a "conflict not of an international character." 415 F. 3d, at 41. That reasoning is erroneous. The term "conflict not of an international character" is used here in contradistinction to a conflict between nations.'

[90] *Ibid.*: 'The latter kind of conflict [NIAC] is distinguishable from the conflict described in Common Article 2 chiefly because it does not involve a clash between nations (whether signatories or not). In context, then, the phrase "not of an international character" bears its literal meaning.'

[91] See, for more, M. Milanovic, 'Lessons for Human Rights and Humanitarian Law in the War on Terror: Comparing *Hamdan* and the Israeli *Targeted Killings* Case', (2007) 89 *IRRC* 373; N. Balendra, 'Defining Armed Conflict', (2008) 29 *Cardozo L Rev* 2461, at 2474; Holland, *supra* n.70, at 167–169.

[92] See, generally, the incisive analysis by D. Kritsiotis, 'The Tremors of *Tadić*', (2010) 43 *Is L R* 262.

[93] Cf. Schindler, *supra* n.54, at 131: 'the term "armed conflict" is not understood in exactly the same way in the case of international and of non-international conflicts'.

[94] See, for example, Y. Sandoz et al. (eds), *Commentary on the Additional Protocols of 8 June 1977 to the Geneva Conventions of 12 August 1949* (Geneva: ICRC, 1987), at 1319: '[A] non-international armed conflict is distinct from an international armed conflict because of the legal status of the entities opposing each other: the parties to the conflict are not sovereign States, but the government of a single State in conflict with one or more armed factions within its territory.'

[95] Cf. Stewart, *supra* n.9, at 435 (noting how the intensity threshold poses a problem for a generic definition); Lubell, *supra* n.77, at 87, 89.

[96] See, for example, Sandoz, *supra* n.94, at 1320.

[97] See *infra* section 4E.

particular situation *clearly* constitutes an armed conflict and then proceed to classify or qualify that conflict. That is not how the concepts legally work, since NIACs are not defined simply as not being IACs.[98] We can see this from how the Appeals Chamber used the term 'armed conflict' in *Tadić*, when it found that 'an armed conflict exists whenever there is a resort to armed force between States or protracted armed violence between governmental authorities and organized armed groups or between such groups within a State'[99] – or, in other words, an armed conflict exists whenever there is an IAC or a NIAC, not the other way around.[100] As well explained by Kritsiotis, while at first glance:

> by its choice and use of words, the Appeals Chamber might be taken to have been defining the concept of an 'armed conflict' as a generic proposition… nothing could be further from the truth for it becomes immediately apparent upon reading this *dictum* in full that the Appeals Chamber was in fact committing itself to the provision of not one but *two* definitions.[101]

Its otherwise abundant references to 'armed conflict' were not to some generic term, but were again shorthand for 'IAC or a NIAC'.[102]

'Armed conflict' is particularly convenient as shorthand when one wants to deliberately avoid qualifying the conflict, either because the qualification would be politically

---

[98] As well put by Sivakumaran:

I find the descriptor 'non-international' to be somewhat misleading as it unhelpfully defines the category by what it is not. It suggests that there is but one armed conflict and, if it is not international in character, by default it is non-international. However, in practice, an internal/non-international armed conflict is identified in a rather different manner. For example, in order for an internal/non-international armed conflict to exist, the violence must reach a certain level of intensity; yet, for an international armed conflict to exist one dominant view is that there is no such requirement. The category of internal/non-international armed conflict is thus in no way a default category which serves to catch those conflicts which are excluded from the international category. Yet this is what is suggested through the use of the terminology of 'non-international' armed conflict.

S. Sivakumaran, 'Re-envisaging the International Law of Internal Armed Conflict: A Rejoinder to Gabriella Blum', (2011) 22 *EJIL* 273.

[99] *Prosecutor v. Tadić*, IT-94-1, Appeals Chamber, Decision on Jurisdiction, 2 October 1995, at para. 70.

[100] Similarly, see Article 2(b) of the ILC Draft Articles on Effects of Armed Conflict on Treaties, *supra* n.75, which takes up the *Tadić* definition.

[101] Kritsiotis, *supra* n.92, at 267.

[102] *Ibid.*, at 268: 'We should therefore be alert to, and most cautious of, the littering of references to "armed conflict" that occur within the *Tadić* jurisprudence of the sort recalled here; these should be regarded as a convenient form of abbreviation for pluralized references to both international and non-international armed conflicts – but only as and where such references are appropriate and make genuine and accurate legal sense.' Similarly, the Appeals Chamber itself said: '[t]he definition of "armed conflict" varies depending on whether the hostilities are international or internal', *Tadić*, at para. 67, thus 'suggesting that the quantum of hostilities is intrinsic to the very definition of each of the concepts of international and non-international armed conflicts as the Appeals Chamber understood them'. Kritsiotis, *supra* n.92, at 292.

or legally difficult,[103] or even because we feel that qualification is unnecessary since the substantive law applicable in both kinds of conflicts is (now) the same.[104] But that this approach is at times appealing does not mean that the identification of an 'armed conflict' is possible *without* qualifying it – it is not, because IACs and NIACs are categorically different rather than defined residually from each other. It is as inappropriate to conceive of NIACs as *non*-IACs as it is for IACs to be seen as *non*-NIACs.

E. Why the Distinction Persists, and Why it Matters

Despite all the successes of the IAC/NIAC unification project in the past two decades, the distinction between the two persists, and will continue to be enormously important in the foreseeable future. While the modern law has managed to gradually elide the differences between the two regimes when these were *morally* unsustainable, for example so that rape would be a war crime in both internal and international armed conflict, others are not susceptible to the same kind of normative pressure. This elision has come – if it has indeed come – through custom; the difference between the conventional law applicable in IACs and NIACs is as vast as ever.

The persistence of the IAC/NIAC dichotomy despite these customary developments is a function of state interest. IACs rest on the fundamental presupposition that these are equal actors who have the authority, if not the right, to engage in organized violence in a state-ordered and centred international system. It is for this reason, and not simply considerations of humanitarianism, that those lawfully fighting on behalf of sovereign parties are entitled to the combatant's privilege – they may take life, limb and property consistently with IHL, and they may be prosecuted for such acts only insofar as they violate IHL.[105] It is also for this reason that captured combatants are entitled to the elaborate and detailed protections granted to prisoners of war. A soldier should not be

---

[103] Thus, for example, the ICRC frequently does not disclose its own qualification of a particular armed conflict publicly (for example with respect to the 2006 Israel/Hezbollah/Lebanon conflict), and indeed its internal doctrine pursuant to which it makes the qualification remains confidential. See S. Ratner, 'Law Promotion Beyond Law Talk: The Red Cross, Persuasion, and the Laws of War', (2011) 22 *EJIL* 459, at 474–477 (arguing that the ICRC worries that states may react adversely enough to the ICRC's opinions that they will withhold cooperation from it).

[104] See, for example, Report of the United Nations Fact-Finding Mission on the Gaza Conflict ('Goldstone Report'), UN Doc. A/HRC/12/48, 25 September 2009, at paras 281–283, especially para. 282 ('as the Government of Israel suggests, the classification of the armed conflict in question as international or non-international, may not be too important'). Similarly, in the *Gotovina* case before the ICTY, dealing mainly with crimes against the Serbs in Croatia, the Prosecution explicitly argued that it was not necessary to qualify the armed conflict as the crimes charged existed in both IAC and NIAC. The Trial Chamber accepted that an 'armed conflict' existed, but then proceeded to qualify it as an IAC, based on the Federal Republic of Yugoslavia's (hereinafter 'FRY's') overall control over the Croatian Serbs. See *Prosecutor v. Gotovina et al.*, IT-06-90-T, Judgment, 15 April 2011, at paras 1679–1682, 1693.

[105] See, for example, K. Dörmann, 'Combatants, Unlawful', in *Max Planck Encyclopedia of Public International Law*, available at www.mpepil.com, at para. 4: 'In international armed conflicts, the term "combatants" denotes the right to participate directly in hostilities (Art. 43(2) Additional Protocol I). Consequently, (lawful) combatants cannot be prosecuted for lawful acts

punished simply for fighting on the losing side. In NIACs, however, the fighter of a rebel armed group can be prosecuted merely for rising against the lawful, or at least the winning, government, even if he is guilty of no war crimes.[106] So long as this difference remains NIACs can never become truly equal to IACs.

IACs are thus predicated on the existence of combatants and civilians as formal statuses, which cannot operate in NIACs. These statuses, in turn, have ripple effects on targeting and detention rules,[107] which are often difficult to apply by analogy in NIACs. Similarly, belligerent reprisals, although greatly limited in scope, are available as lawful measures only in IACs, since states would never recognize the right of non-state actors to take such measures against them, while in turn the principle of equal application of IHL mandates that states likewise cannot resort to reprisals against non-state actors. Finally, the grave breaches regime of the Geneva Conventions is explicitly confined to IACs, with important consequences for any duty to suppress international crimes.[108] In short, even assuming the existence of some non-state actors which are organizationally so well developed that they can effectively comply with the detailed obligations that IHL imposes on states in IACs, some differences between the two kinds of armed conflict are structurally embedded and cannot be overcome simply on the basis of humanitarian or human rights-protective impulses.[109]

4. THRESHOLDS IN THE MODERN LAW OF ARMED CONFLICT

A. International Armed Conflict

i. Generally

As we have seen, IAC was crafted as an explicit replacement for the concept of war. As with war, IAC as defined in CA2 is of an exclusively inter-state nature, a conflict between two equal sovereigns. In the words of the authoritative Pictet *Commentary*:

> Any difference arising between two States and leading to the intervention of members of the armed forces is an armed conflict within the meaning of [Common] Article 2, even if one of

---

of war in the course of military operations even if their behaviour would constitute a serious crime in peacetime. They can be prosecuted only for violations of IHL, in particular for war crimes.'

[106] See, for example, Dörmann, *supra* n.105, at para. 36: 'The law applicable in non-international armed conflicts does not foresee a combatant's privilege (ie the right to participate in hostilities and impunity for lawful acts of hostility)'; Stewart, *supra* n.9, at 320; M. Sassoli, 'Combatants', in *Max Planck Encyclopedia of Public International Law*, available at www.m-pepil.com, at paras 35–38.

[107] See, for example, J. Pejic, '"Unlawful/Enemy Combatants:" Interpretations and Consequences', in Schmitt and Pejic (eds), *supra* n.65, at 335; Akande, *supra* n.79, at 6–9. See also, in a different vein, E. Crawford, *The Treatment of Combatants under the Law of Armed Conflict* (Oxford: Oxford University Press, 2010).

[108] See also J. Stewart, 'The Future of the Grave Breaches Regime: Segregate, Assimilate or Abandon?', (2009) 7 *JICJ* 855.

[109] Cf. R. Bartels, 'Timelines, Borderlines and Conflicts: The Historical Evolution of the Legal Divide between International and Non-International Armed Conflicts', (2009) 91 *IRRC* 35.

the Parties denies the existence of a state of war. It makes no difference how long the conflict lasts, how much slaughter takes place, or how numerous are the participating forces; it suffices for the armed forces of one Power to have captured adversaries falling within the scope of Article 4 [of the Third Geneva Convention]. Even if there has been no fighting, the fact that persons covered by the Convention are detained is sufficient for its application.[110]

The CA2 threshold is thus remarkably low – all it needs is a difference between two states leading to the intervention of their armed forces.[111] Whether Pictet is indeed correct in this, or whether a *de minimis* level of violence needs to occur in order to avoid mere border incidents being classified as IACs, is not the object of our inquiry at this time. Opinions and practice on this point seem to be conflicted.[112] What we *do* wish to emphasize is that, however exactly defined, the IAC threshold is far lower than the NIAC 'protracted armed violence',[113] as it is not subject to the same sovereignty concerns as NIACs. The exact same amount of violence may produce an IAC if perpetrated between states, but might not qualify as a NIAC if committed by non-state actors.[114]

It is simply not correct to assert, as the Supreme Court of Israel did in the *Targeted Killings* case,[115] that the defining criterion of IACs is their *cross-border* nature.[116] That position finds no support either in the text of the treaties or in state practice; it is certainly not true, for example, that any NIAC which crosses a state border is thereby *ipso facto* internationalized.[117] While it is true that hostilities in IACs will cross state borders, it is not the *locale* of the fighting, but the identity of the actors – states – which defines international conflicts. The policy that drives the definition is not statehood as such, but the *legitimacy* that international law confers upon states,

---

[110] Pictet, *supra* n.66, at 23.

[111] See also Schindler, *supra* n.54, at 128, 131.

[112] See, for example, Kritsiotis, *supra* n.92, at 279–280; Lubell, *supra* n.77, at 94–95; Akande, *supra* n.79, at 12; G. Solis, *The Law of Armed Conflict* (Cambridge: Cambridge University Press, 2010), at 151–152.

[113] See, for example, Vité, *supra* n.70, at 72, 76.

[114] See, for example, Kritsiotis, *supra* n.92, at 296: 'if, *arguendo*, the tragic acts that transpired in the United States on September 11, 2001, had been committed by members of the regular armed forces of Afghanistan, there is no question that an international armed conflict would have been inaugurated between Afghanistan and the United States by virtue of those events. However, if the same set of events had occurred at the instigation of members of an organized armed group, all of whom, *arguendo*, had carried the nationality of the United States, it cannot be assumed that as a matter of international law, those acts would have constituted a non-international armed conflict within the United States.'

[115] *The Public Committee against Torture in Israel et al. v. The Government of Israel et al.*, Supreme Court of Israel sitting as the High Court of Justice, Judgment, 11 December 2006, HCJ 769/02, available at http://elyon1.court.gov.il/Files_ENG/02/690/007/a34/02007690.a34.HTM (hereinafter '*Targeted Killings*').

[116] *Ibid.*, at para. 18: 'This law applies in any case of an armed conflict of international character – in other words, one that crosses the borders of the state – whether or not the place in which the armed conflict occurs is subject to belligerent occupation.'

[117] See also Milanovic, *supra* n.91, at 382–386.

primarily but not exclusively.[118] Statehood remains the baseline against which other potential actors should be measured, and it will remain such so long as statehood is the fundamental ordering principle of the international system. In other words, the fact that the hostilities between a non-state actor and a state cross state borders does not justify treating that non-state actor as being on par with the state in terms of the IAC/NIAC distinction. The contours of IACs are thus reasonably clear, but for three main sets of definitional problems. The first is that of possible internationalization of *prima facie* NIACs, which we will deal with in detail further below. The second and the third are problems of international personality and state representation that we will address now.

ii. Problems of international personality

If IACs are under CA2 defined as conflicts between states parties to the Geneva Convention, and defined under its customary equivalent as conflicts between any two states, the most basic problem that can arise is whether a specific entity which claims statehood is, in fact, a state. The paradigmatic example would be that of a secessionist territory claiming independence from its mother country. Consider Kosovo, which declared independence from Serbia in 2008 but which Serbia still claims as a part of its own territory. If a new conflict were to erupt between them, it would be an IAC only if Kosovo does in fact fulfil the criteria for statehood under international law.[119] This is obviously a matter which remains highly controversial. Similarly, consider a hypothetical conflict between China and Taiwan in which the latter formally renounced the authority of Beijing and claimed independence, or indeed possible resurgence of conflict between Georgia and its separatist territories of Abkhazia and South Ossetia. In all these scenarios the qualification of the conflict would depend on a *renvoi* to general international law and its criteria for statehood, which carry their own difficulties and complexities. In principle, it is quite difficult for a secessionist entity to gain statehood on the basis of force alone; while international law does not prescribe a duty of loyalty to one's state nor prohibit secession as such, it does not favour it either.[120]

The second possible problem of international personality arises when an IAC is *multilateral*, that is when a number of states join alliances and coalitions and then proceed to fight one another. Such alliances are of course as old as war itself and in and of themselves pose no difficulties. A single IAC can have many states on opposite sides, as the text of CA2 itself allows. In effect, such an IAC is reducible to a network of bilateral relationships. Any single state can pursue a separate peace or change sides, and the legal framework is perfectly capable of accommodating that.

---

[118] See *supra* section 2D on recognition of belligerency; *infra* section 4Ciii on wars of national liberation.

[119] At least under the (unlikely) assumption that the international forces deployed in Kosovo took no part in the conflict. If they did so, the question is whether the conflict would be internationalized even if Kosovo did not fulfil the criteria for statehood (we think not), or whether there would be an IAC between Serbia and third states and a NIAC between Serbia and Kosovo running in parallel, that is a mixed IAC/NIAC (the better view). See also *infra* sections 4C and D.

[120] See, generally, J. Crawford, *The Creation of States in International Law*, 2nd edn (Oxford: Oxford University Press, 2006), at 374 ff.

The real problem is when states act jointly with or through separate, distinct international legal persons, above all international organizations (hereinafter 'IOs'), and place their forces under the command of other actors. Consider the 2011 campaign of allied forces against Libya, which was complicated by the involvement of two IOs – the UN and NATO. In early 2011, a rebellion was underway against the Gaddafi regime, to which the regime responded with a military crackdown, ostensibly committing crimes against humanity.[121] The insurgency became centred on the area of Benghazi and at some point the hostilities reached the level of 'protracted armed violence', thereby initiating a NIAC. On 17 March 2011 the UN Security Council adopted Resolution 1973, authorizing the use of force against Libya in order 'to protect civilians and civilian populated areas under threat of attack'. Immediately thereafter US and allied forces launched air strikes against Libyan state forces, while on 31 March NATO took command over the coalition operations. We will turn to the example of Libya once more when we discuss internationalized and mixed armed conflicts. Now, however, we wish to examine the role of IOs.

When a UK aircraft operating under UN authorization and NATO command engages in hostilities against Libya, the question arises whether the UK is engaged in an IAC with Libya or rather whether IOs as separate international legal persons themselves participate in the conflict and perhaps even remove the UK out of the equation. Note, in that regard, that IOs are not parties to the major IHL treaties, simply because it was never really foreseen that IOs as such could directly participate in armed conflicts.[122] In short, whose aircraft is it – the UK's, the UN's, NATO's, or indeed everyone's? In answering that question we may either find IHL-specific solutions or approach it from the standpoint of attribution under the general international law of responsibility.[123] The same problem arises with regard to the possible internationalization of a NIAC due to the intervention of a third state, an issue that we will address below.[124] For now, however, we will proceed on the assumption that attribution may be the appropriate conceptual framework in this particular context as all relevant actors are international legal persons in their own right.

If so, we can distinguish between three different legal and factual situations. In the first scenario the conduct of a military asset would be attributable exclusively to the state, despite some involvement on the part of the IO. In the second the conduct would

---

[121] In Resolution 1970 the UN Security Council referred the situation in Libya to the International Criminal Court, acting under Chapter VII of the UN Charter and pursuant to Article 13(b) of the Rome Statute. On 27 June 2011 the Court issued warrants of arrest for Muammar Gaddafi and several associates, finding that there are reasonable grounds to believe that crimes against humanity have been committed in Libya – see Warrant of Arrest for Muammar Mohammed Abu Minyar Gaddafi, No.ICC-01/11.

[122] Despite the fact that the original scheme of UN collective security essentially envisaged a standing army at the disposal of the Security Council. See also Schindler, *supra* n.54, at 127 and chapter 5 by Christian Henderson in this volume.

[123] On which the ILC recently completed a major codification project, the Draft Articles on the Responsibility of International Organizations (2011), available at http://untreaty.un.org/ilc/texts/instruments/english/draft%20articles/9_11_2011.pdf. See esp. Art. 7 and commentary thereto.

[124] Section 4Cii.

be attributable *both* to the state and to the IO or IOs, that is this would be a scenario of dual or multiple attribution and accordingly of shared responsibility. In the third, and the most problematic as far as the applicability of IHL is concerned, the conduct would be attributable only to the IO.

We can see these eventualities at play in our Libyan example. First, the fact that the UN Security Council authorized the use of force against Libya does *not* make the conduct of military assets deployed by states for that purpose *ipso facto* attributable to the UN since the UN lacked effective control over these forces, contrary to the lamentable admissibility decision of the European Court of Human Rights in the *Behrami and Saramati* case.[125] At least at the initial stages of the operation, it is clear that the conduct of US, UK, French and other coalition forces was attributable to these states, and that there was an IAC between Libya on the one hand and the US, UK, France and other states on the other, which ran in parallel with the NIAC between the Libyan government and the rebels.[126]

Secondly, because NATO is a separate international legal person the situation becomes more complicated after 31 March 2001, when it assumed command of the operation. A reasonable argument can be made that the acts of forces under NATO command are attributable only to NATO.[127] However, we submit that the better view is that in such cases attribution becomes *dual* – the conduct of these forces is attributable both to NATO and to states whose forces are put under NATO command. It is a general principle of the law of state responsibility that the acts of state organs are attributable to the state so long as they act in their official capacity.[128] Putting these organs under the operational command of a third party does not by itself change this legal position; something more is required for their acts to *cease* being attributable to their own state.[129] Particularly bearing in mind the institutional make-up of NATO, which receives both political direction and troop contribution from states which remain its

---

[125] *Behrami and Behrami v. France, Saramati v. France, Germany and Norway* [GC] (dec.), App. Nos. 71412/01 and 78166/01, 2 May 2007. For critiques of the decision see, for example, M. Milanovic and T. Papic, 'As Bad As It Gets: The European Court of Human Rights' *Behrami and Saramati* Decision and General International Law', (2009) 58 *ICLQ* 267; A. Sari, 'Jurisdiction and International Responsibility in Peace Support Operations: The Behrami and Saramati Cases', (2008) 8 *HRLR* 151; K. Mujezinovic Larsen, 'Attribution of Conduct in Peace Operations: The "Ultimate Authority and Control" Test', (2008) 19 *EJIL* 509; L.A. Sicilianos, 'Entre multilatéralisme et unilatéralisme: l'autorisation par le Conseil de sécurité de recourir à la force', (2009) 339 *Rd C*13, at 377 ff.

[126] See also Akande, *supra* n.79, at 39–40.

[127] As an example with the acts of KFOR troops in Kosovo. See, generally, A. Pellet, 'L'imputabilité d'éventuels actesillicites – Responsabilite' de l'OTAN ou des Etats membres', in C. Tomuschat (ed.), *Kosovo and the International Community: A Legal Assessment* (The Hague: Kluwer, 2002), 193.

[128] See Article 4 of the International Law Commission's Draft Articles on State Responsibility.

[129] As the European Court of Human Rights now acknowledged in *Al-Jedda v. UK*, App. No. 27021/08, 7 July 2011, at para. 80: '[The Court] does not consider that, as a result of the authorisation contained in Resolution 1511, the acts of soldiers within the Multi-National Force became attributable to the United Nations or – *more importantly, for the purposes of this case – ceased to be attributable to the troop-contributing nations*' (emphasis added).

ultimate masters and which always retain the final decision to contribute or withdraw troops, there are sound considerations of policy against attributing the acts of NATO-led troops exclusively to NATO.

So long as the conduct of armed forces remains attributable to the troop contributing states, whether exclusively or jointly with an IO, no serious qualification issue will arise under IHL, since an IAC would exist between all relevant states. A qualification problem would arise only if the conduct of (some of) the troops were to be attributable *exclusively* to an IO, as in our third scenario, since the major IHL treaties do not allow for the eventuality that IOs as such can be parties to an IAC, nor to the treaties themselves. What is clear is that as a matter of policy states cannot be permitted to evade the application of IHL by acting through IOs as proxies. Whether the evolution of a customary rule that IOs have the capacity to be parties to IACs just like states would be appropriate and necessary is a difficult question that we will leave aside at this point, except to say that the only alternative to such a rule would be to treat IOs like any other non-state actors, despite them being established by states, and to qualify conflicts in which forces exclusively belonging to IOs fight with those of some state as NIACs.[130]

Problems of personality and qualification are particularly acute in one specific area – peacekeeping, especially under UN auspices. It was long in doubt whether IHL can apply to UN forces as such, precisely because of the UN's separate legal personality and the fact that it is not a party to the relevant treaties. Today, after developments in practice and the UN's own self-regulation, it can be taken for granted that IHL can in principle apply to peacekeeping forces.[131] That, however, does not resolve the difficulties we can have in terms of qualifying an armed conflict. Our starting point is that IHL has opted to treat peacekeepers as *civilians* with regard to an *existing* armed conflict between some other parties, even though they are professional soldiers.[132] From the criminal law standpoint, the Rome Statute of the ICC provides that '[i]ntentionally directing attacks against personnel, installations, material, units or vehicles involved in a humanitarian assistance or peacekeeping mission in accordance with the Charter of the United Nations, as long as they are entitled to the protection given to civilians or civilian objects under the international law of armed conflict' is a war crime in both IACs and NIACs.[133] So long as this situation persists, that is so long as the peacekeepers are essentially passive observers in the conflict, using force only on a

---

[130] See also Akande, *supra* n.79, at 43–44.

[131] See, generally, C. Greenwood, 'International Humanitarian Law and United Nations Military Operations', (1998) 1 *Y Intl HL* 3; D. Shraga, 'The Secretary-General's Bulletin on the Observance by United Nations Forces of International Humanitarian Law: A Decade Later', (2009) 39 *Israel YB Hum Rts* 357; M. Zwanenburg, 'United Nations and International Humanitarian Law', in *Max Planck Encyclopedia of Public International Law*, available at www.mpepil.com, and the references cited therein.

[132] This is admittedly a bit bizarre. One can, however, analogize members of peace operations to other armed individuals who do not normally take part in hostilities, for example police forces.

[133] Articles 8(2)(b)(iii) and 8(2)(e)(iii) of the Rome Statute.

very limited basis, the nature of the conflict would remain the same.[134] If, on the other hand, peacekeepers start directly participating in hostilities, not only would they lose protection from attack, but the nature of the conflict itself may be at issue, as the peacekeepers may *themselves* become parties to the conflict.[135] To the extent the existing conflict is a NIAC it is hard to see how or why it could be internationalized as a whole (although the matter is admittedly controversial); at the very least any component of the conflict which involves engagements with rebel armed groups would have to remain a NIAC, as the status of rebels could not be upgraded merely because they are fighting international forces.[136]

iii. Problems of state representation

This brings us to problems of state representation. It may be easy to say that IACs are fought between states and statehood may even be uncontested in a given case, but who gets to *represent* the state may turn out to be a very difficult issue. Not only is this question important for the initial qualification of a conflict, but it may also prove to be crucial for its requalification or transition from one type to another.

Consider, first, the invasion of Afghanistan by US-led coalition forces in 2001. The first representational difficulty we encounter in qualifying the conflict is that the Taliban regime was not recognized as the lawful government of Afghanistan by the states that launched the invasion or by the international community generally. That difficulty is however reasonably easy to deal with. It is precisely because historically the recognition of states and governments was a way to avoid the application of the law of war that the position in modern IHL is that it is *de facto* government and not recognition that matters.[137] While they never controlled all of Afghanistan, at the time the Taliban were in effective power in most of the country, including the capital Kabul, and they had established institutions of government. Accordingly, there was an IAC between the US and other coalition states on one side and the state of Afghanistan, represented *de facto* by the Taliban regime, on the other, while there was also a NIAC running in parallel between the Taliban and the forces of the Northern Alliance.

But then the Taliban were defeated; their institutional rule over Afghanistan could not survive the joint coalition–Northern Alliance assault. Today we of course know that the defeat of the Taliban was far from complete, but it is still true to say that they lost territorial control of the kind that denotes a government rather than simply an armed group. That vacuum was filled through a long transitional process, lasting from the end of 2001 up until 2003, which was approved by the UN Security Council and ultimately resulted in the establishment of a new Afghan government. The new government not only consented to the presence of international forces in Afghanistan, but together with the international forces continued to fight the growing Taliban insurgency.[138]

---

[134] For a thoughtful discussion see O. Engdahl, 'The Status of Peace Operations Personnel under International Humanitarian Law', (2008) 11 *Y Intl HL* 109.
[135] See, for example, Pejic, *supra* n.7, at 194–195.
[136] See also Vité, *supra* n.70, at 87–88; Engdahl, *supra* n.134, at 120.
[137] See Schindler, *supra* n.54, at 128–130.
[138] For a general overview see, for example, A. Bellal, G. Giacca and S. Casey-Maslen, 'International Law and Armed Non-State Actors in Afghanistan', (2011) 93 *IRRC* 47, and S.

The question thus is whether and at what point the conflict transitioned from a mixed IAC/NIAC to a NIAC pure and simple, that is at what point the Taliban lost the capacity to represent the state of Afghanistan, and accordingly lost belligerent rights *vis-à-vis* third states intervening in Afghanistan. At the heart of this question lies a tension between competing policy considerations. On one hand, we do not want the mere fact of military defeat to allow the intervening states to transform the character of the conflict simply by setting up a quisling administration that could then 'consent' to their presence in the country[139] – think only of the Third Reich's *modus operandi* throughout Europe during the Second World War. At the same time, however, in some cases we want to enable the situation to move forward and allow a transition from an authoritarian regime to a more representative one under some level of international supervision. Such introduction of considerations of *legitimacy*, while perhaps inevitable both politically and legally, poses a particular danger for IHL as it smacks of the *jus ad bellum* that we for good reason wish to keep IHL insulated from.[140]

We can observe the same dynamics at play in the case of Iraq post-2003, where there was initially undoubtedly an IAC which resulted in belligerent occupation; following a transitional process under international supervision a new Iraqi government was formed which provided its consent to the presence of coalition forces, thereby terminating the IAC and the occupation; as this process was underway, an insurgency erupted which for a substantial period crossed the threshold of 'protracted armed violence', thereby creating a NIAC.[141]

The most recent examples of such problems of state representation are the conflicts in the Côte d'Ivoire and Libya.[142] As for the former, the story of the disputed Ivorian elections in 2010 and the ensuing crisis is well known. According to international observers, the incumbent president Laurent Gbagbo lost the elections to his challenger Alassane Ouattara, but the results were overturned by a Gbagbo-appointed commission. After a number of unsuccessful attempts at resolving the crisis, Ouattara was formally recognized as the lawful president of the Côte d'Ivoire by the UN, ECOWAS, the African Union and many countries. A conflict erupted between state forces loyal to Gbagbo and various armed groups supporting Ouattara, in which the latter was the ultimate winner. This conflict was at all times undoubtedly a NIAC. But what complicates matters is the intervention near the end of this conflict by UN and French

---

Wills, 'The Legal Characterization of the Armed Conflicts in Afghanistan and Iraq: Implications for Protection', (2011) 58 *NILR* 173.

[139] See, in that vein, D. Turns, 'The International Humanitarian Law Classification of Armed Conflicts in Iraq Since 2003', (2010) 86 *US Naval War College International Law Studies* 97, esp. at 113–114.

[140] Cf. Stewart, *supra* n.9, at 342–344 (discussing Soviet intervention in Afghanistan starting in 1979), and W.M. Reisman and J. Silk, 'Which Law Applies to the Afghan Conflict?', (1988) 82 *AJIL* 459.

[141] See, generally, Turns, *supra* n.139.

[142] See, for example, C. Henderson, 'International Measures for the Protection of Civilians in Libya and Côte d'Ivoire', (2011) 60 *ICLQ* 767.

peacekeepers in support of Ouattara.[143] Leaving the involvement of UN forces aside, when the French forces attacked Gbagbo's compound and military assets, was this an IAC between France and the Côte d'Ivoire, or was it rather a NIAC since the French forces acted with the consent of Ouattara, the lawful and legitimate president of the country?

Similarly, in Libya, as we have already said, the conflict was initially a mixed one: an IAC between Libya and the coalition states, and a NIAC between the Gaddafi regime and the Benghazi rebels. However, as the conflict intensified and the rebels became better organized, forming a National Transitional Council, a number of states recognized this Council as the legitimate government of Libya.[144] Together with the crumbling of the Gaddafi regime, did such recognition lead to the transformation of the IAC into a NIAC, with the coalition at some point intervening on behalf of the legitimate government of the country?

What is at stake here is a process of internalization, or de-internationalization, of a conflict, that is its transformation from an IAC into a NIAC. Looking at the competing policy considerations, we can see what is *not* enough for such internalization to occur. That the incumbent government of a country is defeated cannot by itself transform the conflict, nor can the establishment of a proxy government by the victors, as this would allow them to effectively strip by force the protections granted in IACs to the remaining combatants of the defeated state, turning them into unprivileged belligerents. Similarly, that a rebel group is recognized as the new legitimate government of the country cannot of itself transform the character of the conflict, as this would again allow the intervening states to unilaterally do what they will.[145]

When would the transformation of the conflict then occur? In our opinion, both considerations of policy and recent practice support a rule consisting of the following three elements: the conflict would transform from an IAC into a NIAC only when (1) the old regime has lost control over most of the country, and the likelihood of it regaining such control in the short to medium term is small or none (negative element); (2) the new regime has established control over a significant part of the country, and is legitimized in an inclusive process[146] that makes it broadly representative of the people (positive element); and (3) the new regime achieves broad international recognition (external element). None of these elements is enough by itself, but jointly they take into account both questions of legitimacy and factual developments on the ground while providing safeguards against abuse. With regard to both the positive and the negative elements, the degree of control would be looked at holistically, taking into account not

---

[143] See, for example, 'Strikes by U.N. and France Corner Leader of Ivory Coast', *New York Times*, 4 April 2011, available at http://www.nytimes.com/2011/04/05/world/africa/05ivory.html?_r=3.

[144] See, for example, S. Talmon, 'Recognition of the Libyan National Transitional Council', *ASIL Insights*, 16 June 2011, available at http://www.asil.org/insights110616.cfm. Note that the process of recognition was somewhat more complicated, with some recognitions perhaps capable of being conceptualized as recognitions of belligerency. For our purposes, however, we are interested at this point only in recognitions of the (former) rebels as *the* government of the country.

[145] See also Akande, *supra* n.79, at 36–37.

[146] Not necessarily requiring democratic elections, but certainly favouring them.

just troops on the ground but also direction over state institutions more generally, its economic assets, the media, and the like.

Thus, there is at least a strong majority view that the transitional processes in Iraq and Afghanistan at some point led to the transformation of the conflicts from IACs or mixed IACs/NIACs into NIACs pure and simple.[147] Similarly, looking at the Ivorian example, when the Gbagbo regime was effectively reduced to Abidjan, with the forces of the internationally recognized president Ouattara holding the remainder of the country, the intervention by French troops cannot be said to have constituted an IAC. When it comes to Libya, the tipping point probably came with the National Transitional Council's takeover of Tripoli, the acceptance of its representatives by the UN General Assembly's credentials committee, and the endorsement of the new government by the Security Council. Obviously, it is hard to pinpoint the exact moment of internalization in any given case, and thankfully in most cases it may be unnecessary to do so, but it *is* necessary for us to be aware of the relevant elements and their interplay. And while fully acknowledging the fluid nature of these elements, we must also be aware that the internalization of a conflict has as its consequence a possible reduction of various protections under IHL.[148]

B. Non-international Armed Conflict

i. Generally

The evolution of the NIAC definition was not linear, but has been the object of a process of long duration that included the adoption of successive treaties, such as AP II and the Rome Statute of the ICC, as well as major judicial developments, above all *Tadić* and its progeny. This process has ultimately produced a certain level of clarity, clarity that is all the more necessary because the incidence of NIACs today by far surpasses the incidence of IACs.

A number of controversial issues of course still remain. None of the major treaties actually contains a comprehensive definition of NIACs. They speak generally of 'conflicts not of an international character', as if the phrase was self-explanatory, its purpose being less to define a concept and more to accommodate fundamental disagreements between the drafters. Some do not even operate within the same legal framework or regime. CA3 and AP II are parts of IHL, and the provisions on their material application are contextual bases for the application of this body of law. The Rome Statute is an instrument of international criminal law, and the provisions of its Articles 8(2)(c) and 8(2)(e) seek to determine the field of applicability of war crimes committed in NIAC that are within the ICC's jurisdiction, rather than directly prescribe rules of IHL.

As it stands today, NIAC is a plural legal concept, defined differently under different treaty regimes. The basic definition of NIAC, which encompasses all others, is that in

---

[147] See, for example, Bellal *et al*, *supra* n.138, at 51–53, and the works cited therein; R. Geiss and M. Siegrist, 'Has the Armed Conflict in Afghanistan Affected the Rules on the Conduct of Hostilities?', (2011) 93 *IRRC* 11, at 13–16; Turns, *supra* n.139 (stating that this is the majority view despite disliking it as a matter of policy); Pejic, *supra* n.7, at 196.

[148] See Wills, *supra* n.138. See chapter 14 in this volume by Robert Cryer.

CA3. Its terms were famously elaborated by the ICTY Appeal Chamber in the *Tadić* Interlocutory Decision on Jurisdiction,[149] which has been widely accepted as reflecting custom[150] by the *ad hoc* international criminal tribunals[151] and the ICC,[152] other international bodies,[153] national legislation[154] and the ICRC.[155]

Uncertainties regarding the exact contours of NIAC must be observed against the political context, at the centre of which is sovereignty as the legal expression of a legitimate monopoly on violence that rests solely, or mainly, with states.[156] IACs are conflicts in which this monopoly is expressed, NIACs those in which it is challenged. As the first systematic attempt at regulating internal violence by international law, CA3 was a remarkable breakthrough. Prior to the 1949 Geneva negotiations, proposals for such regulation were vigorously opposed by most states. When in 1912 the ICRC tried to introduce a convention which would merely define its role in situations of civil war, this attempt was firmly dismissed by states claiming that any assistance offered by the Red Cross to insurgents would be 'aiding and abetting ... common criminals and traitors'.[157] The proposal simply stood too far from the established, state-centred and 'regimental' world that states at the time wished to preserve.[158]

Both the sparse content of CA3 and its lack of a precise definition of NIAC, as well as the restrictive requirements in Article 1 AP II were consequences of interminable battles between the advocates of humanitarianism and those concerned with the

---

[149] *Prosecutor v. Tadić*, IT-94-1-AR72, Decision on the Defence Motion for Interlocutory Appeal on Jurisdiction (Appeals Chamber), 2 October 1995), at para. 70.

[150] See, for example, Kritsiotis, *supra* n.92, at 262–263.

[151] For the International Criminal Tribunal for Rwanda (hereinafter 'ICTR') see, for example, *Prosecutor v. Akayesu*, ICTR-96-4, Trial Chamber Judgment, 2 September 1998, at para. 619; *Prosecutor v. Rutaganda*, ICTR-96-3, Trial Chamber Judgment, 6 December 1999, at para. 92. For the Special Court for Sierra Leone see *Prosecutor v. Fofana et al.*, Decision on Appeal against 'Decision on Prosecution's Motion for Judicial Notice and Admission of Evidence', Appeals Chamber Decision of the Special Court for Sierra Leone, Separate Opinion of Justice Robertson, 16 May 2005, at para. 32.

[152] *Prosecutor v. Lubanga*, ICC-01/04-01/06, Decision on the Confirmation of Charges, 29 January 2007, at para. 233; *Prosecutor v. Bemba Gombo*, ICC-01/05-01/08, Decision on the Confirmation of Charges, 15 June 2006, at para. 229.

[153] Report of the Mapping Exercise documenting the most serious violations of human rights and international humanitarian law committed within the territory of the Democratic Republic of the Congo between March 1993 and June 2003, August 2010, at paras 470–471; Report of the Secretary-General's Panel of Experts on Accountability in Sri Lanka, 31 March 2011, at para. 181; Children and Armed Conflict: Report of the Secretary-General, A/62/609-S/2007/757, 21 December 2007, at para. 5, n.2; ILC First Report on the Effects of Armed Conflicts on Treaties, A/CN.4/627, 22 March 2010, at para. 30 (Draft Article 2(b)).

[154] See, for example, Philippines Act on Crimes against International Humanitarian Law, Genocide, and Other Crimes against Humanity, Section 3(c).

[155] 'How is the Term "Armed Conflict" Defined in International Humanitarian Law?: International Committee of the Red Cross (ICRC) Opinion Paper', March 2008, at 4, available at http://www.icrc.org/eng/assets/files/other/opinion-paper-armed-conflict.pdf.

[156] See, for example, Pejic, *supra* n.7, at 200.

[157] D.A. Elder, 'The Historical Background of Common Article 3 of the Geneva Conventions of 1949', (1979) 11 *Case W Res J Intl L* 37, at 41.

[158] See Keegan, *supra* n.43, at 12, 23.

realities of a state-centred system of institutionalized violence, with the humanizing impulse eventually leading to the regime of the Rome Statute and the formulation of a fairly inclusive customary rule. We will first look at some of the most notable differences with regard to the NIAC threshold between these diverse regimes. We will then concentrate on one specific aspect of the threshold requirement which is most relevant for contemporary conflicts led by states against transnational armed (terrorist) groups – the geographical scope of NIACs, with NIACs commonly understood as being synonymous with internal armed conflicts. We will then address the applicability of the existing concepts of NIAC to two basic scenarios of cross-border non-international violence, spillover and foreign intervention.

ii. Plurality of non-international armed conflicts

The text of CA3 gives few clues as to what a NIAC actually is, despite introducing the concept into the legal vocabulary. This lack of a clear definition was deliberate on the part of the drafters,[159] and for long presented a significant challenge to the effective applicability of IHL.[160] An effort in the authoritative Pictet *Commentary* to elaborate on the (non-)definition was little more than a rather unselective compilation of rejected proposals during the drafting process.[161] Some elements of NIACs, however, are apparent from the outset. In terms of party structure, being 'not of an international character' NIACs are conflicts in which at least one party is a non-state armed group, and indeed all of the parties might be such armed groups.[162] The group must have a sufficient level of organization that would enable it to effectively implement IHL.[163]

The text of CA3 also *prima facie* delineates the geographical scope of the conflict, which must occur 'in the territory of one of the High Contracting Party'. This particular requirement has been given several different interpretations to which we will turn shortly. No other element can be conclusively inferred from the text while the *travaux* provide only limited guidance. While CA3 was not intended to regulate situations of 'disorder, anarchy or brigandage'[164] and 'mere riot or disturbances caused by bandits',[165] it does not explain how to distinguish these situations from an armed conflict.[166] As a result, although CA3 was a significant breakthrough in regulating

---

[159] See Sivakumaran, *supra* n.50.
[160] See D.P. Forsythe, 'Legal Management of Internal War: The 1977 Protocol on Non-International Armed Conflicts', (1978) 72 *AJIL* 272, at 273.
[161] Pictet, *supra* n.66, at 49–52.
[162] This raises the difficult question as to how exactly a treaty provision created binding rules for non-state actors who did not and could not agree to it – see especially A. Cassese, 'The Status of Rebels under the 1977 Geneva Protocol on Non-International Armed Conflicts', (1981) 30 *ICLQ* 416; S. Sivakumaran, 'Binding Armed Opposition Groups', (2006) 55 *ICLQ* 369; L. Zegveld, *The Accountability of Armed Opposition Groups in International Humanitarian Law* (Cambridge: Cambridge University Press, 2002), at 134 ff.; see also M. Milanovic, 'Is the Rome Statute Binding on Individuals? (And Why We Should Care)', (2011) 9 *JICJ* 25.
[163] See, for example, Pejic, *supra* n.7, at 191–192; Schindler, *supra* n.54, at 147.
[164] E. La Haye, *War Crimes in Internal Armed Conflicts* (Cambridge: Cambridge University Press, 2008), at 7.
[165] *Ibid*.
[166] On which see, for example, Vité, *supra* n.70, at 76–77.

NIACs it was by design of limited success.[167] The lack of clarity in defining NIAC enabled governments to often avoid implementing IHL by simply refusing to characterize violence as an armed conflict, which was the whole point of the ambiguous definition.[168]

At the time of its adoption CA3 was the sum total of all the law regulating NIACs; there was no other treaty or custom complementing it.[169] The need for a more comprehensive instrument became evident soon thereafter, but it took some thirty years until AP II was adopted in 1977. The added regulation came at a price. On one side, AP II provided wider protection in NIACs and defined a subset thereof with more precision. On the other, AP II's definition of NIAC significantly reduced its field application when compared with CA3.[170]

The AP II NIAC threshold consists of two major elements – intensity of the violence and the quality of the parties. While a requirement of organization is presumed with regard to governmental armed forces,[171] due to the informal nature of non-state armed groups Article 1(1) AP II requires an organizational structure with a responsible command, control of a part of state territory, the ability to conduct sustained and concerted military operations and the ability to implement the Protocol. The requirements are cumulative. Article 1(2) further specifies that AP II 'shall not apply to situations of internal disturbances and tensions, such as riots, isolated and sporadic acts of violence and other acts of a similar nature, as not being armed conflicts'.

The requirement that an armed group must control a part of the territory of a state with which it is in conflict is specific to AP II. How much territory a group should control is uncertain, but it has been suggested that the territory does not have to be substantial nor the control stable.[172] AP II is, moreover, applicable only to conflicts in which one of the parties is a state.[173] Unlike CA3, AP II cannot govern hostilities between two non-state armed groups.[174] Finally, an AP II NIAC can only occur

---

[167] Minimum Humanitarian Standards: Analytical Report of the Secretary-General Submitted Pursuant to Commission on Human Rights Resolution 1997/21, E/CN.4/1998/87, 5 January 1988, at para. 74; Moir, *supra* n.58, at 34; A. Cullen, *The Concept of Non-International Armed Conflict in International Humanitarian Law* (Cambridge: Cambridge University Press, 2010), at 57.

[168] *Conference of Government Experts on the Reaffirmation and Development of International Humanitarian Law Applicable in Armed Conflicts (Geneva, 24 May–12 June 1971): Submitted by the International Committee of the* Red *Cross* (Geneva: ICRC, 1971) Part V: Protection of Victims of Non-International Armed Conflicts, at 43; K.E. Kilgore, 'Geneva Conventions Signatories Clarify Applicability of Laws of War to Internal Armed Conflicts', (1978) 8 *Ga J Intl & Comp L* 945.

[169] But see Cassese, *supra* n.47.

[170] See, for example, Vité, *supra* n.70, at 79–80.

[171] AP II does not require a formal military structure. According to the ICRC Commentary of AP II, governmental armed forces can include such formations as customs, police forces, national guard and so on. See ICRC Commentary AP II, at para. 4462, available at http://www.icrc.org/ihl.nsf/COM/475-760004?OpenDocument.

[172] ICRC Commentary, *ibid.*, at para. 4464–4467; *Akayesu*, Trial Judgment, *supra* n.151, at para. 626.

[173] Schindler, *supra* n.54, at 148–149.

[174] *Ibid.*

between the armed forces of a state on whose territory the conflict is ongoing and an armed group which controls a part of that state's territory.[175] For example, AP II cannot govern a conflict between Turkey and Kurdish rebels controlling only parts of *Iraqi* territory and occurring solely on Iraqi soil, or between the intervening states assisting the Afghan government and the Taliban.[176]

The AP II regime and its NIAC definition do not modify the CA3 definition, but exist simultaneously and in parallel. However, it could be said that since *Tadić* the two thresholds have been brought closer together and that their differences are not as great. It is today generally accepted that some level of organization of an armed group is also required for the application of CA3,[177] although this requirement 'should not be exaggerated'.[178] Similarly, even CA3 requires 'protracted armed violence'. While, as suggested by the ICTY in the *Boškovski* case,[179] this might be a lower threshold than that of 'sustained and concerted military operations' the two are not necessarily far apart. Finally, it is also generally accepted that Article 1(2) AP II analogously applies to CA3 conflicts.[180]

That said, CA3 NIAC and AP II NIAC remain two distinct thresholds as a matter of conventional IHL. To what extent exactly that distinction remains practically relevant is a different and difficult matter. First, it can be argued that the difference in thresholds is rendered largely irrelevant because most, if not all, of the rules under AP II have been transposed to CA3 NIACs under customary law. Thus, for example, in its customary IHL study the ICRC not only claims that most rules applicable in IACs are today also applicable in NIACs, but in doing so it does not distinguish between CA3 and AP II NIACs, opting rather to apply all these rules to CA3 conflicts.[181] Whether practice in fact supports this claim is a matter of some disagreement; the possibility that several NIAC thresholds exist in custom cannot be excluded.[182]

---

[175] Under Article 1(1) AP II the conflict must 'take place in the territory of a High Contracting Party between *its* armed forces and dissident armed forces or other organized armed groups' (emphasis added). See also Lubell, *supra* n.77, at 100.

[176] See Geiss and Siegrist, *supra* n.147, at 16.

[177] Schindler, *supra* n.54, at 147; R.J. Wilhelm, 'Problèmes relatifs à la protection de la personne humaine par le droit international dans les conflits armés ne présentant pas un caractère international', (1972)137 *Rd C*, at 347–348.

[178] C. Kress, 'The 1999 Crisis in East Timor and the Threshold of the Law on War Crimes', (2002) 13 *Crim L F* 409, at 416.

[179] For the different view see: *Boškoski and Tarčulovski*, Case no. IT-04-82, Trial Judgment, 10 July 2008, at para. 197. See also: A. Zimmerman, 'War Crimes', in O Triffterer (ed.), *Commentary on the Rome Statute of the International Criminal Court: Observers' Notes, Article by Article* (München: Beck, 1999), at 501; Cullen, *supra* n.167, at 128, 142.

[180] G. Abi-Saab, 'Non-International Armed Conflicts', in R. Baxter and C. Pilloud (eds), *International Dimensions of Humanitarian Law* (Paris: UNESCO, 1988), at 229; ICRC, *supra* n.155, at 5; Holland, *supra* n.70, at 156.

[181] The stated basis for this approach is that states do not distinguish between the two thresholds in practice – see Pejic, *supra* n.7, at 191.

[182] See, for example, J. Pejic, 'Status of Armed Conflicts', in E. Wilmshurst and S. Breau (eds), *Perspectives on the ICRC Study on Customary International Humanitarian Law* (Cambridge: Cambridge University Press, 2007), 88; Bellal *et al.*, *supra* n.138, at 62; J. Bellinger and

Secondly, and also subject to reasonable disagreement, the adoption of the Rome Statute arguably further eroded the gap between the two concepts of NIAC, at least in the context of international criminal law. Views are divided as to whether the Statute introduced a single threshold for all war crimes applicable in NIACs in Articles 8(2)(d) and (f), or whether it sets a higher threshold for crimes derived from AP II when compared with serious violations of CA3.[183]

Article 8(2)(d), which sets the threshold of NIAC for serious violations of CA3 in Article 8(2)(c), only distinguishes armed conflict from internal disturbances and tensions. Article 8(2)(f), defining the scope of 'other serious violations of laws and customs applicable' in NIAC under Article 8(2)(e), makes the same distinction but adds that it applies to armed conflicts that 'take place in the territory of a State when there is protracted armed conflict between governmental authorities and organized armed groups or between such groups'. Both the text and the drafting history of this provision show that it was derived from the *Tadić* formula, itself defining CA3 rather than AP II conflicts.[184] Does, therefore, Article 8(2)(f) set a higher threshold than Article 8(2)(d), or are they in fact one and the same, their artificial separation merely a consequence of convoluted drafting?[185]

It is certain that Article 8(2)(f) did not integrate the strict AP II threshold into the Rome Statute. Such a proposal was rejected during the drafting process,[186] and the Court in its case law made clear that the requirement of territorial control by an armed group is not a part of the Statute.[187] The requirement for (a level of) organizational structure of an armed group, as already said, has become an integral part of CA3 NIAC, and the ICC accepted it as such.[188] The sole potential discrepancy is, therefore, in the requirement of 'protracted armed conflict' for AP II crimes and the (textual) absence of such a requirement for CA3 crimes, an issue that the Court has so far managed to avoid.[189] The Court, however, did integrate most of the requirements from Article 8(2)(f) into Article 8(2)(d) through the interpretation of requirements intrinsic to

---

V. Padmanabhan, 'Detention Operations in Contemporary Conflicts: Four Challenges for the Geneva Conventions and Other Existing Law', (2011) 105 *AJIL* 201, at 208–209.

[183] See Vité, *supra* n.70, at 82–83; A. Bouvier and M. Sassoli (eds), *How Does Law Protect in War?* Vol. I (Geneva: ICRC, 2006), at 110; R. Provost, *International Human Rights and Humanitarian Law*(Cambridge: Cambridge University Press, 2002), at 268; W. Schabas, *An Introduction to the International Criminal Court*, 3rd edn (Cambridge: Cambridge University Press, 2007), at 116.

[184] See S. Sivakumaran, 'Identifying an Armed Conflict Not of an International Character', in C. Stahn and G. Sluiter (eds), *The Emerging Practice of the International Criminal Court* (Leiden: Martinus Nijhoff, 2009), at 374–375; Kress, *supra* n.178, at 419.

[185] See Kritsiotis, *supra* n.92, at 286–290; Akande, *supra* n.79, at 28–29.

[186] See A. Cullen, 'The Definition of Non-International Armed Conflict in the Rome Statute of the International Criminal Court: An Analysis of the Threshold Contained in Article 8(2)(f)', (2007) 12 *JCSL* 419, at 429.

[187] *Prosecutor v. Bemba Gombo*, ICC-01/05-01/08, Decision on Confirmation of Charges, 15 June 2006, at para. 236.

[188] *Ibid.*, at paras 227, 232.

[189] *Ibid.*, at para. 235.

CA3 and it is quite possible that if it is ever forced to do so[190] it will take the same route in integrating the temporal requirement as well.

It is hence entirely possible that the law regulating NIACs went through a process of unification and that the plurality of NIACs has been lost for all purposes but the applicability of AP II as a treaty. If, after all, soldiers must comply with AP II requirements even if the AP II threshold is not met because they would be subjected to criminal sanction under the Rome Statute if they did not do so, then the applicability of AP II as such becomes a rather moot point as far as parties to the Rome Statute are concerned.[191] That said, we will for the time being continue to treat AP II as a distinct NIAC threshold. Similarly, and crucially, whether or not a plurality of NIACs exists in terms of applicable law it certainly exists *descriptively*, so as to help us better understand the various factual situations that are legally to be characterized as NIACs. It is also possible that an entirely new kind of legally cognizable armed conflict between states and non-state actors has evolved or is evolving post-9/11, and we will deal with this eventuality further below.[192] Now, however, we must first address the question of geographical scope of NIACs and the further question of whether NIACs are confined to purely internal situations, or indeed whether the law recognizes some varieties of non-internal non-international armed conflicts or cross-border NIACs.

iii. Are NIACs exclusively internal?

All definitions of NIAC are closely bound up with the question of its geographical scope. CA3 talks about conflicts 'occurring in the territory of one of the High Contracting Parties'; Article 1(1) AP II similarly about conflicts 'which take place in the territory of a High Contracting Party'; the ICTY in *Tadić* about conflicts 'within a state';[193] and the Rome Statute about conflicts 'that take place in the territory of a State'.[194] The natural interpretation of all these texts would confine the meaning of NIAC to conflicts which take place within the territory of a single state.[195] In other words, NIAC would equal internal armed conflict.

There is little (if any) historical evidence that the drafters of the major IHL instruments had anything other than purely internal conflicts in mind when formulating the relevant provisions. After all, the overwhelming concerns about the possible impact

---

[190] The Court might never come into a situation to deal with the borderline instances considering the gravity threshold from Article 17(1)(d) of the ICC Statute. In addition, most of the conduct which can be categorized as a war crime in NIAC can also be qualified as a crime against humanity which can be perpetrated in the time of peace. Accordingly, the ICC Prosecutor is likely to opt for the latter qualification if the fact of the existence of armed conflict is not fairly easy to prove. As an example of such an approach see: *Prosecutor v. Gaddafi et al.*, issued on 27 June 2011 (the charges enlisted in the warrant are all concerned with the crimes against humanity).

[191] Note, however, that not *every* rule in AP II is subject to criminal punishment for a violation as a war crime under the Rome Statute.

[192] See *infra* section 4E.

[193] *Tadić*, *supra* n.99, at para. 70.

[194] Article 8(2)(f) of the ICC Statute.

[195] See, for example, Pejic, *supra* n.7, at 199 (citing further commentary to that effect); Lubell, *supra* n.77, at 100.

of these instruments on state sovereignty and the freedom of states to deal with their own problems as they see fit make sense only in the context of internal insurrections and rebellions. Of course, cross-border incursions of armed groups were occurring even prior to the adoption of the Geneva Conventions.[196] While these occurrences did raise significant questions with regard to state responsibility for revolutionary acts and within the *jus ad bellum* framework, they were rarely, if ever, perceived as requiring specific regulation in the *jus in bello*. Even as spillovers of internal conflicts became more frequent, as in the developing world during anti-colonial struggles, the primary concern was legitimization (or not) of national liberation movements which was the object of Article 1(4) AP I.[197] The sporadic nature and low intensity of cross-border incursions by armed groups meant that the issue was politically hardly one of global concern, and it was largely off the legal radar. For all intents and purposes, NIACs were synonymous with purely internal conflicts, and that was that, for states and scholars alike.[198]

Things have since changed. Al-Qaeda's 9/11 attacks and the ensuing US 'war on terror' and conflicts in Iraq and Afghanistan (and Pakistan and Yemen) raised serious issues of conflict qualification and the continuing desirability of the exclusively binary IAC/NIAC mould. Nor was this the only such example. The conflict between Israel and Hezbollah in Lebanon,[199] the situation in the Democratic Republic of the Congo and constant spillovers of multiple NIACs occurring there to the territories of neighbouring countries, the incursions of Ogaden militias from Ethiopia and Al-Shabaab militia from lawless Somalia onto Kenyan territory,[200] and the Kurdish fight for independence against Turkey and Iran[201] all pose serious challenges to the binary framework and NIAC's narrow geographical scope. These conflicts are not IACs as they are not inter-state; nor are they purely internal in character as they cross the borders of several states. What, then, are they?

Can the text of CA3 accommodate a cross-border dimension? There are two ways in which the CA3 reference to conflicts 'occurring in the territory of one of the High Contracting Parties' can be interpreted. The first, and perhaps more natural, is to say that the territory referred to is that of a state actually taking part in the conflict – in other words, CA3 would inherently be limited to conflicts which are purely internal in scope. The second would be to say that the reference is to the territory of *any* high contracting party, not necessarily that of a state actually a party to the conflict.[202] The

---

[196] See, for example, H. Lauterpacht, 'Revolutionary Activities by Private Persons against Foreign States', (1928) 22 *AJIL* 105; I. Brownlie, 'International Law and Armed Bands', (1958)7 *ICLQ* 720.
[197] See, generally, A. Cassese, 'Wars of National Liberation and Humanitarian Law', in Cassese, *supra* n.162, at 99 ff.
[198] But see D. Jinks, 'September 11 and the Laws of War', (2003) 28 *Yale JIL* 1.
[199] For more see Lubell, *supra* n.77, at 250.
[200] See V. Hadzi-Vidanovic, 'Kenya Invades Somalia Invoking the Right to Self-Defence', *EJIL: Talk!*, 18 October 2011, available at http://www.ejiltalk.org/kenya-invades-somalia-invoking-the-right-of-self-defence/.
[201] See T. Franck, *Recourse to Force: State Practice against Threats and Armed Attack* (Cambridge: Cambridge University Press, 2002), at 63 ff.
[202] In other words, CA3, just like any other treaty provision, applies *qua* treaty only for the parties to the treaty – see Vité, *supra* n.70, at 88–89; M. Sassoli, 'Transnational Armed Groups

latter interpretation allows CA3 NIACs to encompass situations which are not confined within the borders of a single state, and should in our view be preferred.[203]

While NIACs have historically certainly been treated as synonymous with purely internal conflicts, and while such internal conflicts remain the paradigmatic examples of NIACs, NIACs can today also be seen as a somewhat wider category. Interpreted evolutively and in accordance with contemporary practice, the CA3 threshold textually allows for non-internal or cross-border NIACs, to which we will now turn while continuing our discussion of NIACs' territorial scope. We will distinguish (if not very rigidly) between two major sub-types of cross-border NIAC – spillover and foreign intervention[204] – and then see how the definitions of NIAC, as explained above, would apply to these factual situations.

iv. Cross-border or non-internal NIACs: spillover conflicts and foreign intervention

The first sub-type of cross-border or non-internal NIAC, and perhaps the easier to deal with, is the spillover scenario. Initially, an ordinary, internal NIAC is fought on the territory of state A, either between the armed forces of state A and armed group X, or between armed groups X and Y. Then, however, fighting crosses the border and spills over onto the territory of state B (normally, but not necessarily, adjacent to A), which itself may or may not join in the fighting; combat operations on B's territory may be either sporadic or intense and protracted.

Examples of such spillover conflicts are legion. One of the most recent would be the situation along the Somali border with Kenya. There is an ongoing internal NIAC between Al-Shabaab militants and the Transitional Federal Government of Somalia on the territory of Somalia. The Al-Shabaab militants, however, frequently cross onto the territory of Kenya and conduct sporadic attacks there. Kenyan forces respond to these attacks in order to expel the group from Kenyan territory, at times crossing over the Somali border.[205]

How does the law qualify such spillover scenarios? Two basic approaches seem to be appropriate. First, if the spilled-over component of the conflict taking place on the territory of state B by itself satisfies the 'protracted armed violence' threshold, then we can speak of two separate NIACs, one in state A and the other in state B. But what if the conflict on the territory of state B never independently reaches the CA3 threshold of NIAC as it is lacking the needed duration and intensity? Would, in other words, a *sporadic* spillover scenario that fails to reach the NIAC threshold thereby leave those particular instances of violence unregulated by IHL? While domestic law could to an extent fill the regulatory gap, in some cases at least such a result would morally be

---

and International Humanitarian Law', *HPCR Occasional Paper Series*, Winter 2006, No. 6, at 8–9; Pejic, *supra* n.7, at 200–201.

[203] See also Holland, *supra* n.70, at 159–160; Lubell, *supra* n.77, at 101–104; Akande, *supra* n.79, at 46–47.

[204] See also Holland, *supra* n.70, at 161.

[205] In October 2011, however, Kenya commenced a full-scale invasion of the Somali territory intervening against Al-Shabaab with the consent of the transitional Somali government. See Letter dated 17 October 2011 from the Permanent Representative of Kenya to the United Nations addressed to the President of the Security Council, UN Doc. S/2011/646.

completely arbitrary; a rape by a rebel soldier on one side of the border would constitute a war crime, but not on the other.

Such a gap can in our view be largely avoided. Recall how in its analysis of the geographic scope of NIACs *within* the state the ICTY Appeal Chamber in *Tadić* held that it is sufficient to show that certain military operations 'were closely related to the hostilities occurring in other parts of the territories controlled by the parties to the conflict' to subsume these events under the ongoing NIAC.[206] In other words, if there is a sufficient nexus between an ongoing NIAC and military operations that are occurring outside the areas in which the conflict and 'protracted armed violence' normally take place, these military operations will nevertheless be understood as part of the overall armed conflict. This reasoning can be extended by analogy to military operations *outside* the state.[207] Thus, IHL would be applicable to sporadic military clashes between Colombian forces and Fuerzas Armadas Revolucionarias de Colombia (hereinafter 'FARC') spilling over onto Ecuadorian territory if a sufficient nexus with the ongoing NIAC between the two entities in Colombia could be established, that is if the spilled-over component was still clearly between the forces of Colombia and FARC that are engaged in the core part of the NIAC and the hostilities in the two territories were not completely unconnected.

Simply put, while NIAC requires 'protracted armed violence' within the territory of a state, it does not necessarily need *all* of that violence to take place within that state, so long as there is an organic or structural link between the sporadic extraterritorial outbreaks of violence and the main body of the conflict. The application of this nexus requirement would of course depend on the facts of each particular case of sporadic spillover. In cases in which either the nexus was lacking and thus the violence could not be tied to an existing NIAC or the spilled-over violence failed to independently reach a level of intensity and duration, the spilled-over violence would not be part of any legally cognizable NIAC and would be unregulated by IHL. The geographical scope of NIACs would accordingly largely resemble the geographical scope of IACs; just like the fighting between, say, France and Germany could spill over onto Italian territory, with the IAC not being confined exclusively to French and German sovereign territory, so could a NIAC expand into something more than a purely internal conflict.

The second sub-type of cross-border NIAC is that of foreign intervention: state A is engaged in internal conflict with armed group X on its own territory, and then invites state B to help it in the conflict against X, which B does on A's territory. The paradigmatic example is of course the US involvement in Afghanistan after the ousting of the Taliban regime, the establishment of a new Afghan government of Afghanistan and its invitation to the United States to assist it in its armed conflict against Al-Qaeda and the Taliban.[208] The ongoing conflict between the Afghan government and the Taliban is an internal NIAC. As we will see below, a foreign intervention on behalf of the country's government does not *ipso facto* internationalize the NIAC. The United States is, therefore, involved in a cross-border NIAC taking place in Afghanistan and not on its own soil.

---

[206] *Tadić, supra* n.99, at para. 70.
[207] See also Kress, *supra* n.6, at 265.
[208] See, for example, Vité, *supra* n.70, at 73.

Another variant of a foreign intervention scenario is when state B enters into protracted armed violence against armed group X on the territory of state A, but this time *without* A's invitation, as when Israel intervened in Lebanon against Hezbollah in 2006. Depending on whether the lack of state A's consent is to be given normative relevance in internationalizing the conflict, the conflict could be characterized either as a cross-border NIAC or as an IAC, as we will explain below.

Not only is a combination of spillover and foreign intervention scenarios possible, but *any* spillover conflict which involves the forces of one state crossing onto the territory of another state is also a case of foreign intervention, with or without the territorial state's consent. Similarly, a foreign intervention may itself spill over, for example if state B intervenes in the conflict between state A and armed group X, but that conflict crosses onto the territory of state C, or even onto the territory of more than one state. This is very much the case with the current engagement of the United States in Afghanistan and the wider region. In Afghanistan, the US is involved in a NIAC between the Afghan government and the Taliban. Frequently, however, the United States conducts attacks, particularly drone strikes, against Al-Qaeda and Taliban targets on Pakistani territory, with or without the permission of Pakistani authorities. One such attack was the operation of US special forces which led to the death of Osama bin Laden. For its part, Pakistan also fights its own militants, whose connections with the Afghan Taliban are not always clear, while the US has been using drone strikes against various Al-Qaeda affiliated groups in Yemen and Somalia.

Legally characterizing this politically undeniably connected jumble of conflicts is a difficult exercise. First, it should be borne in mind that it is entirely possible to have multiple and distinct parallel conflicts even in the same territory.[209] Secondly, if the United States engagement with armed groups in Pakistan reaches a level of protracted armed violence, it could be characterized as an independent NIAC, as would any such fighting between Pakistani forces and the armed groups. Alternatively, these operations could be considered as parts of the Afghan NIAC if the nexus criteria outlined above are met.

C. Internationalized Non-international Armed Conflict

i. Generally

Now we need to look at one of the most complex and discussed topics of contemporary IHL: internationalized armed conflicts. Before this discussion can advance any further, we believe it crucial to clarify, first, the *concept* of internationalized armed conflict, and, secondly, the *mechanism* or mechanisms of internationalization.

In our view, the concept of internationalization is only truly useful if it is defined as the transformation of a *prima facie* NIAC into an IAC, thereby applying to this conflict the more comprehensive IAC legal regime.[210] The most important of these legal

---

[209] See *infra* section 4D.
[210] Note that one can use the term 'internationalized armed conflict' in a different, descriptive sense, as any NIAC in which there is some type of foreign intervention – see, for example, Geiss and Siegrist, *supra* n.147, at 14, n.8. This is again, *not* how we will be using the term, in order to maximize both its utility and precision.

consequences is the grant, in principle, of privileged belligerency to combatants on both sides of the conflict. As for the mechanism of internationalization, we have seen that under CA2 IACs are defined as differences leading to the use of armed force *between two states*. Accordingly, there are two basic ways of internationalizing a NIAC. First, a *prima facie* NIAC can be subsumed under the *existing* CA2 definition. In other words, what at first glance looks like a conflict between a state and a non-state actor is on a deeper look actually a conflict between two states. Secondly, a NIAC can be internationalized through the *redefinition* of IAC in terms of its party structure, so that the CA2 definition is exceptionally expanded under a treaty or customary rule so as to potentially include some non-state parties. Internationalization under this heading would clearly require proof of a specific rule to that effect. We will now deal in turn with both types of internationalization.

ii. Internationalization under the existing definition

We have already mentioned one way in which internationalization can occur under the CA2 definition – if a non-state actor embroiled in a CA3 conflict with a state manages to create a new state in the course of the conflict.[211] Think only of the dissolution of the former Yugoslavia, or the possible emergence of a state of Palestine; as we have said above, statehood is to be measured by the rules of general international law. From the moment of the new state's creation, any conflict with the other state would become an IAC.[212]

Other than through the process of state creation internationalization can occur under the CA2 definition in two basic scenarios: (1) if state A intervenes on the territory of state B in support of non-state actor C against state B; and (2) if state A intervenes on the territory of state B against non-state actor C without B's consent. In both cases what at first glance appears to be a NIAC between (1) B and C, and (2) A and C may actually amount to an IAC between A and B.

In the first scenario, the intervening state must use the non-state actor as a proxy against the territorial state, that is A acts through C to attack B. It is generally not disputed in doctrine that internationalization can occur in such circumstances; what is in dispute is the precise nature of the link between the intervening state and the non-state actor that suffices for internationalization.[213] On one view, this link must be that of attribution as a matter of the secondary rules of state responsibility.[214] This, of course, was famously the approach of the ICTY Appeals Chamber in the *Tadić* appeals judgment,[215] where it considered that the acts of the Bosnian Serbs had to be attributable to the FRY/Serbia in order for the conflict to become international in character, and fashioned the 'overall control' test of responsibility in order to do so,

---

[211] See, for example, Akande, *supra* n.79, at 14.
[212] See also *supra* section 4Aii.
[213] See, for example, Arimatsu, *supra* n.44, at 174–175; Holland, *supra* n.70, at 162–163; Vité, *supra* n.70, at 90–92; Lubell, *supra* n.77, at 97–99; Akande, *supra* n.79, at 30; Solis, *supra* n.112, at 155.
[214] See also our discussion of problems of international personality in IACs in *supra* section 4Aiii.
[215] *Prosecutor v. Tadić*, IT-94-1, Appeals Chamber, Judgment, 15 July 1999.

thereby rejecting the reasoning of the International Court of Justice (hereinafter 'ICJ') on attribution in the *Nicaragua* case.[216]

There is an intuitive appeal to the *Tadić* approach. After all, what else could it mean for a non-state actor to be acting on behalf of a state than for its acts to be attributable to the state? However, as one of us has argued at length elsewhere,[217] the Appeals Chamber's approach was erroneous for two basic reasons. First, it actually misinterpreted the ICJ's *Nicaragua* judgment as setting out only *one* test of attribution, that of effective control, and thought that this single test was unreasonable and impracticable. Indeed, it would be so, had the ICJ not set out *two* tests of attribution in its judgment – that of complete dependence and control, operating at a general level and seeking to attribute *all* of the acts of a non-state actor to a state, and that of effective control, seeking to attribute *specific* acts controlled by the state.[218] Secondly, and more importantly for our purposes, it is conceptually inappropriate for secondary rules of attribution to determine the scope of application of the primary rules of IHL. Rather, it is upon IHL to fashion a test which determines when the relationship between a state and a non-state actor is such that a NIAC is to be internationalized – and that test may well be that of overall control.[219]

In its 2007 *Bosnian Genocide* merits judgment,[220] the ICJ rejected the overall control test in the context of attribution, finding that it was too loose to fit that particular purpose. However, the Court left open the possibility that the test is valid for the IHL-specific purposes of qualifying a conflict:

> This is the case of the doctrine laid down in the *Tadić* Judgment. Insofar as the 'overall control' test is employed to determine whether or not an armed conflict is international, which was the sole question which the Appeals Chamber was called upon to decide, it may well be that the test is applicable and suitable; the Court does not however think it appropriate to take a position on the point in the present case, as there is no need to resolve it for purposes of the present Judgment. On the other hand, the ICTY presented the 'overall control' test as equally applicable under the law of State responsibility for the purpose of determining – as the Court is required to do in the present case – when a State is responsible for acts committed by paramilitary units, armed forces which are not among its official organs. In this context, the argument in favour of that test is unpersuasive.
>
> It should first be observed that logic does not require the same test to be adopted in resolving the two issues, which are very different in nature: the degree and nature of a State's involvement in an armed conflict on another State's territory which is required for the conflict to be characterized as international, can very well, and without logical inconsistency, differ

---

[216] *Military and Paramilitary Activities in and Against Nicaragua (Nicaragua v. United States)*, Judgment (Merits), 27 June 1986, [1986] ICJ Rep. 14 (hereinafter '*Nicaragua*').

[217] See M. Milanovic, 'State Responsibility for Genocide', (2006) 17 *EJIL* 553, at 575 ff.

[218] See also S. Talmon, 'The Responsibility of Outside Powers for Acts of Secessionist Entities', (2009) 58 *ICLQ* 493.

[219] For more see Milanovic, *supra* n.217, at 584–585, as well as M. Milanovic, 'State Responsibility for Genocide: A Follow-Up', (2007) 18 *EJIL* 669.

[220] *Application of the Convention on the Prevention and Punishment of the Crime of Genocide (Bosnia and Herzegovina v. Serbia and Montenegro)*, 26 February 2007, [2007] ICJ Rep. 43.

from the degree and nature of involvement required to give rise to that State's responsibility for a specific act committed in the course of the conflict.[221]

We submit that the ICJ has the better of this argument.[222] Again, we do not disagree that there is an intuitive appeal to the *Tadić* approach; for example, the ICJ's holding to the contrary was criticized by Marina Spinedi in an excellent article.[223] However, in our view, *Tadić* is right only to the extent that if the acts of the Bosnian Serbs were attributable to Serbia then the conflict would surely have been international in nature, since the Bosnian Serbs would not have been a non-state actor at all, but agents of Serbia. In other words, attribution *suffices*, but it need not be *necessary*, for internationalization.[224] IHL, as a distinct body of primary rules, can adopt its own solution regarding the link between a state and a non-state actor that would suffice for internationalization of a conflict, and that link need not be attribution as a matter of state responsibility.[225]

In short, the internationalization of a *prima facie* NIAC in the first scenario set out above – an intervention into a civil conflict by a third state – depends on the nature of the relationship between the intervening state and a non-state actor. That relationship may, but need not be, attribution. A relationship of overall control, which does not suffice for attribution, may suffice for internationalization, as the ICJ itself allows.[226]

What, then, of our second scenario, where state A intervenes on the territory of state B against the non-state actor C? As we have seen above,[227] if state B actually consents to the intervention the conflict can only be qualified as a NIAC. For the intervening state or states this is a cross-border NIAC, for the territorial state it is simply internal in nature. Conflicts in Iraq and Afghanistan after the establishment of their new governments, which gave consent to the participation of foreign troops in the conflict, provide good examples. Hence, when it comes to internationalization the only additional situation is one in which the territorial state does *not* give its consent to the foreign intervention. Consider in that regard the Israel/Hezbollah/Lebanon conflict in 2006 – how is it to be qualified?

We can initially treat this second scenario exactly like the first: so long as non-state actor C is under B's overall control or C's acts are attributable to B, there would be an

---

[221] *Ibid.*, at paras 404–405.
[222] See also Akande, *supra* n.79, at 31–33.
[223] M. Spinedi, 'On the Non-Attribution of the Bosnian Serbs' Conduct to Serbia', (2007) 5 *JICJ* 829.
[224] See also Akande, *supra* n.79, at 33–35.
[225] To clarify, we are not arguing for an IHL-specific set of *secondary* rules of attribution that would regulate state responsibility for violations of IHL. Rather, we are arguing for a set of *primary* rules of IHL that would better define IHL's own scope of application. In short, if an IAC is defined as a use of force between two states, the primary rules of IHL would further develop this definition by saying that if state A exercises overall control over non-state actor B which is directly engaged in hostilities with state C, such control would qualify as an inter-state use of force for IHL classification of conflict purposes.
[226] The *Tadić* overall control test was endorsed for the purposes of conflict qualification by the ICC Pre-Trial Chamber in *Prosecutor v. Thomas Lubanga Dyilo*, Decision on the Confirmation of Charges, ICC-01/04-01/06, 29 January 2007, at para. 211.
[227] See *supra* sections 4Biii and iv.

IAC between states A and B. What first looks like a non-state actor is really a state actor, and what first looks like a NIAC is really an IAC. Thus, if the acts of Hezbollah were attributable to the state of Lebanon, for example because Hezbollah acted in the absence or default of official authorities in Southern Lebanon or because of the participation of Hezbollah in the Lebanese government,[228] or if regardless of attribution Lebanon exercised overall control over Hezbollah,[229] then the 2006 Israel/Hezbollah/ Lebanon conflict would in fact simply have been an IAC between Israel and Lebanon.

But what if Hezbollah was not fighting on behalf of Lebanon? How would the conflict be characterized then? One solution would be to say that the conflict was then a mixed one: an IAC between Israel and Lebanon and a cross-border NIAC between Israel and Hezbollah (so long as there was 'protracted armed violence' between the two in Lebanon). Another view would be to say that the territorial state's *consent* to the foreign intervention, or lack thereof, would have bearing on the matter.[230] Note that there is little doubt that the very fact that state A uses force on the territory of state B without its consent creates an IAC between the two states, at least in addition to any separate conflict with the non-state actor.[231] Again, an IAC is *any* 'difference arising between two States and leading to the intervention of members of the armed forces'.[232] Israel's invasion of Lebanon initiated a conflict with Lebanon, *inter alia* by imposing a maritime blockade, not just with Hezbollah.[233] This would have remained the case even if Israel limited itself strictly to attacking Hezbollah targets (which it did not), and Hezbollah fighters could perhaps be classified as civilians taking a direct part in hostilities in the IAC between Lebanon and Israel. Similarly, the 2008 incursions by Colombia into Ecuador in order to attack the FARC rebels could be qualified as an IAC

---

[228] See Articles 4, 5 and 9 of the ILC Articles on State Responsibility. Note that at the time of the conflict the Israel government made conflicting statements as to whether it considered the acts of Hezbollah to be attributable to Lebanon. On 12 July 2006 it thought that 'the Lebanese government, of which Hizbullah is a member, is trying to undermine regional stability. Lebanon is responsible and Lebanon will bear the consequences of its actions.' On 16 July 2006, 'Prime Minister Olmert emphasized that Israel is not fighting Lebanon but the terrorist element there, led by Nasrallah and his cohorts, who have made Lebanon a hostage and created Syrian- and Iranian-sponsored terrorist enclaves of murder.' See M. Milanovic, 'Self-Defense and Non-State Actors: Indeterminacy and the *Jus ad Bellum*', *EJIL: Talk!*, 21 February 2010, available at http://www.ejiltalk.org/self-defense-and-non-state-actors-indeterminacy-and-the-jus-ad-bellum/.

[229] This conclusion is unlikely on the facts, but there is also the possibility that some third state may have exercised such control, for example Syria or Iran, thereby complicating the qualification issue even further.

[230] See, for example, Arimatsu, *supra* n.44, at 177, 184; Akande, *supra* n.79, at 48–51.

[231] See, for example, Kritsiotis, *supra* n.92, at 280–281.

[232] Pictet, *supra* n.66, at 23.

[233] Note that this does not mean that we would be introducing *ad bellum* considerations into the *in bello* qualification framework. What matters is not the *lawfulness* of the use of inter-state force, but only whether the territorial state *consented* to the use of force; the two are not necessarily one and the same. For example, it may well be that Israel had the right to self-defence under Article 51 of the UN Charter to engage Hezbollah in Lebanon. Considerations of proportionality aside, this would have made its invasion of Lebanon lawful under the *jus ad bellum*. But for IHL qualification purposes, all that would matter is that Lebanon did not consent to the intervention, with the use of force thereby initiating an IAC between the two states.

between Colombia and Ecuador in which the FARC were civilians taking a direct part in hostilities, regardless of any institutional link between FARC and Ecuador; all that would matter is that Ecuador did not consent to the deployment of Colombian troops.

Relying on consent as an additional criterion for internationalization in our second scenario could greatly simplify the qualification analysis. We would only have a single IAC to deal with. It would not, however, be entirely without its problems. There are cases in which it is hard to say whether the territorial state consented to the foreign intervention or not because for political reasons that state wishes to maintain an ambiguous position. The best current example is that of the use of drones by the US military against Taliban assets on Pakistani territory, which the Pakistani government expressly neither condemns nor endorses. There can also be cases in which consent is given by the territorial state, but the intervening state exceeds the boundaries of that consent.

Moreover, the greater the cohesion of the armed group and its organizational independence from the government of the territorial state, the more artificial it would seem to label the conflict as a single IAC, even if the territorial state does not consent.[234] For instance, while the Israeli intervention against Hezbollah in Lebanon significantly affected Lebanon itself, Colombia targeted FARC in the jungle, far away from any assets or the population of Ecuador. One could wonder whether the quality of the territory affected and the potential targets could also play a role in deciding on internationalization. What would be the use of the application of the rules of IAC in the Colombia/FARC/Ecuador scenario when the only potential addressees of those rules on one side of the conflict would be FARC irregulars? The NIAC regime would appear to be more appropriate, and would govern the hostilities between Colombia and FARC, while a parallel IAC between Colombia and Ecuador, while formally in effect, would have very little practical relevance.[235] In the Israel/Hezbollah/Lebanon scenario, however, the exposure of the Lebanese civilian population and infrastructure to the fighting would make internationalization a more viable option, and if not the conflict would at the very least be a mixed IAC/NIAC.[236]

Thus, whether consent should be a distinct criterion of internationalization in our second scenario, or whether that scenario should be treated exactly like the first, will be a matter of some controversy. In any event, we would caution against relying exclusively on the secondary rules of attribution in either scenario, as these general rules are not suited for this purpose and do not necessarily take into account IHL-specific policy considerations. Limiting internationalization strictly to those cases where the acts of a non-state actor could be attributed to a state would have a number of adverse consequences. Since the general rules of attribution are strict precisely because they need to be of general application, this would either greatly limit the number of possible cases of internationalized NIACs, or would lead to fragmentationist jurisprudential conflicts on attribution of the *Nicaragua/Tadić/Genocide* variety;[237] it is

---

[234] See Kress, *supra* n.6, at 253–254.
[235] Cf. Lubell, *supra* n.77, at 110–111.
[236] See also Akande, *supra* n.79, at 52–53.
[237] *Tadić* was, for instance, driven by a very strong double dynamic: in order to maximize international criminalization and the possibility of effective prosecution, the ICTY Appeals

good both for IHL and for general international law to separate internationalization from attribution.[238]

iii. Internationalization through redefinition

We have now dealt with internationalization of NIACs under the existing CA2 definition of IACs as conflicts between states. The other broad rubric of internationalization is that of IACs *redefined* as something other than conflicts between states, with the status of a non-state actor upgraded, so that the same privileges that international law recognizes to states and their agents are exceptionally extended to some other type of actor. This type of internationalization of necessity requires proof of some additional rule, whether based in treaty or custom; CA2 is not enough. There are several possible candidates for such a rule.

First, the only such rule which exists beyond any doubt is Article 1(4) AP I, on wars of national liberation.[239] The rationale behind this rule is that a people fighting against racist foreign domination is legitimately entitled to be prospectively treated as a state, even if it is yet to realize external self-determination and create a new state. When AP I was drafted such conflicts were mostly a historical relic, as decolonization had already largely been completed. The only conflicts that could potentially qualify as such today are the Israeli–Palestinian one and the one in Western Sahara. However, this redefinition of IACs in AP I proved to be very controversial and was objected to by a number of states, which for that reason either refused to ratify AP I or did so with reservations.[240] Accordingly, Article 1(4) has not achieved customary status.[241] Internationalization under this rule can occur *only* with respect to *prima facie* NIACs

---

Chamber both held that war crimes exist in internal armed conflicts and wanted to allow as much as possible for the internationalization of these conflicts through the overall control test, thus hedging its bets in case the success of its first strategy was limited. It is precisely because of such a specific policy-driven context that the application of general rules of attribution is inappropriate, as the same dynamic might not replicate itself in other contexts, with international criminal law and IHL demanding their own sets of rules tailored to their particular needs.

[238] The same argument can be made for the *jus ad bellum* context. See M. Milanovic, 'State Responsibility for Acts of Non-State Actors: A Comment on Griebel and Plücken', (2009) 22 *LJIL* 307.

[239] See, generally, Schindler, *supra* n.54, at 133 ff.

[240] This was for example the position of the US government. In his Message to the Senate Transmitting a Protocol to the 1949 Geneva Conventions, dated 29 January 1987 and reproduced in (1987) 81 *AJIL* 910–912, President Reagan refused to submit Protocol I to the Senate for ratification, stating that:

> Protocol I is fundamentally and irreconcilably flawed. It contains provisions that would undermine humanitarian law and endanger civilians in war. One of its provisions, for example, would automatically treat as an international conflict any so-called 'war of national liberation.' Whether such wars are international or non-international should turn exclusively on objective reality, not on one's view of the moral qualities of each conflict. To rest on such subjective distinctions based on a war's alleged purposes would politicize humanitarian law and eliminate the distinction between international and non-international conflicts. It would give special status to 'wars of national liberation,' an ill-defined concept expressed in vague, subjective, politicized terminology.

[241] See, for example, Akande, *supra* n.79, at 21.

occurring in the territory of one of AP I's contracting parties which has not made a reservation to this provision.

Secondly, despite having fallen into disuse the recognition of belligerency did not necessarily fall into desuetude and may still have relevance in modern law.[242] Even historically such recognition was rarely explicit, that is made as such in a formal declaration, but was made implicitly, for example through the invocation of neutrality by third states. It is possible that such implicit recognition can operate today as well, if the relevant non-state actor is sufficiently state-like in its qualities and exercises institutional control over territory, thereby upgrading a NIAC into an IAC.[243] One possible such recent example is that of the maritime blockade imposed by Israel on Hamas-controlled Gaza, resulting *inter alia* in the 2010 Mavi Marmara incident. A reasonable argument can be made that a maritime blockade, which involves the interdiction of the shipping on third states on the high seas, can only be effected in an IAC; it traditionally took place only in wars, and it necessarily involves a relinquishment by third states of their rights to the belligerents. Both the imposition of the blockade by Israel and any acquiescence by third states in it may be interpreted as recognitions of Hamas' belligerent status,[244] accordingly transforming a *prima facie* cross-border NIAC between Israel and Hamas into an IAC.[245] From the Israeli perspective, the problem here would be that the principle of equal application of IHL would grant Hamas the equal right to blockade Israel, if it had the factual ability to do so, not to mention that from a political standpoint its legitimacy may be perceived as having been accepted by Israel. This is at least one of the reasons why Israel argues that it is engaged in an 'armed conflict' with Hamas while studiously avoiding to qualify this conflict.[246] For our present purposes we do not wish to claim conclusively

---

[242] See, in that regard, Y. Lootsteen, 'The Concept of Belligerency in International Law', (2000) 166 *Mil L Rev* 109; Akande, *supra* n.79, at 22.

[243] One should also bear in mind in that regard the possibility of *ad hoc* agreements under CA3, which do not amount to a recognition of belligerency but can bring IAC rules to bear.

[244] See, for example, Lauterpacht, *supra* n.60, at 177: 'In particular, acquiescence in the exercise of the right of blockade may, in the absence of indications to the contrary, not improperly be regarded as recognition of belligerency'; Sandoz, *ICRC Commentary to Additional Protocols*, *supra* n.94, at 1320–1321: 'Tacit recognition of belligerency, which covers the majority of cases, can be deduced from government measures or attitudes towards an internal situation of conflict (for example, a blockade)'; Neff, *supra* n.12, at 267.

[245] See also in that regard, D. Akande, 'Legal Issues Raised by Israel's Blockade of Gaza', *EJIL: Talk!*, 2 June 2010, at http://www.ejiltalk.org/legal-issues-raised-by-israels-blockade-of-gaza/; K. Heller, 'Why is Israel's Blockade of Gaza Legal?', *Opinio Juris*, 2 June 2010, available at http://opiniojuris.org/2010/06/02/why-is-israels-blockade-of-gaza-legal/; K. Heller, 'The Civil War and the Blockade of Gaza (a Response to Posner)', *Opinio Juris*, 4 June 2010, available at http://opiniojuris.org/2010/06/04/eric-posners-incomplete-editorial-on-the-blockade-of-gaza/, and comments thereto.

[246] See, for example, Israeli Ministry of Foreign Affairs, 'The Gaza Flotilla and the Maritime Blockade of Gaza – Legal Background', 31 May 2010, available at http://www.mfa.gov.il/MFA/Government/Law/Legal+Issues+and+Rulings/Gaza_flotilla_maritime_blockade_Gaza-Legal_background_31-May-2010.htm.

that the Gaza blockade constitutes recognition of belligerency,[247] but merely to point out that a reasonable argument can be made to that effect and that the recognition of belligerency doctrine may still have some life to it.[248]

Thirdly, as we have also seen above it is possible that a special rule of IHL has evolved that transforms armed conflicts in which international organizations (hereinafter 'IOs') directly participate as parties into IACs when fighting states, even though IOs are not states themselves and would thus presumably be covered by default by the NIAC regime. This is a difficult and complex question that we for reasons of space cannot develop here any further.

iv. Circumstances which do not lead to internationalization

Having now defined the circumstances which *do* lead to internationalization, we can briefly dispense with those that do not. Indeed, we have already dealt with all or some

---

[247] Note that the argument presumes that NIAC requirements of intensity and duration would already be independently met. For a critique of the belligerency argument, see especially D. Guilfoyle, 'The *Mavi Marmara* Incident and Blockade in Armed Conflict', (2010) 81 *BYIL* 171, at 21–24. See also R. Buchan, 'The International Law of Naval Blockade and Israel's Interception of the *Mavi Marmara*', (2011) 58 *NILR* 209.

[248] Note in that regard the Report of the Secretary-General's Panel of Inquiry on the 31 May 2010 Flotilla Incident (Palmer Committee Report), leaked by the *New York Times* and available at http://graphics8.nytimes.com/packages/pdf/world/Palmer-Committee-Final-report.pdf, which in para. 73 qualifies the conflict between Israel and Hamas as an IAC with a more-or-less political justification, but perhaps implicitly taking the recognition of belligerency route:

> The Panel now turns to consider whether the other components of a lawful blockade under international law are met. Traditionally, naval blockades have most commonly been imposed in situations where there is an international armed conflict. While it is uncontested that there has been protracted violence taking the form of an armed conflict between Israel and armed groups in Hamas-controlled Gaza, the characterization of this conflict as international is disputed. The conclusion of the Panel in this regard rests upon the facts as they exist on the ground. The specific circumstances of Gaza are unique and are not replicated anywhere in the world. Nor are they likely to be. Gaza and Israel are both distinct territorial and political areas. Hamas is the de facto political and administrative authority in Gaza and to a large extent has control over events on the ground there. It is Hamas that is firing the projectiles into Israel or is permitting others to do so. The Panel considers the conflict should be treated as an international one for the purposes of the law of blockade. This takes foremost into account Israel's right to self-defence against armed attacks from outside its territory. In this context, the debate on Gaza's status, in particular its relationship to Israel, should not obscure the realities. The law does not operate in a political vacuum, and it is implausible to deny that the nature of the armed violence between Israel and Hamas goes beyond purely domestic matters. In fact, it has all the trappings of an international armed conflict. This conclusion goes no further than is necessary for the Panel to carry out its mandate. *What other implications may or may not flow from it are not before us, even though the Panel is mindful that under the law of armed conflict a State can hardly rely on some of its provisions but not pay heed to others.* (Emphasis added)

The italicized sentence is crucial here – if this is indeed an IAC, then Hamas fighters are presumptively combatants. This is obviously not a conclusion that Israel would like, or indeed would be likely to accept, as it essentially upgrades the status of Hamas from that of a terrorist organization to that of a government.

of them implicitly in our preceding discussion. First, the mere fact that hostilities cross state borders does not lead to internationalization. In terms of the CA2 definition it is not the location of the hostilities but the identity of the actors that creates an IAC.[249] Outside of that definition there does not seem to be any practice in support of a rule that a conflict between a state and a non-state actor that crosses a border *ipso facto* becomes internationalized. On the contrary, there is no good reason of policy to grant privileged status to non-state actors merely because of the transnational element, and as we have seen the existing framework is perfectly capable of accommodating various kinds of cross-border NIACs.

Similarly, the fact that a conflict erupts in an occupied territory between the occupying state and a non-state actor does not mean that this *prima facie* NIAC becomes internationalized. It is true that the Israeli Supreme Court in the *Targeted Killings* case, relying on the opinion of Professor Cassese, held to the contrary,[250] as did the ICC Pre-Trial Chamber in *Lubanga*.[251] However, not only do these decisions not provide adequate reasoning for their holding, but there does not seem to be any relevant practice to support it.[252] Nor is it somehow warranted by logic. The occupation may well outlive the conflict that created it, as it did in the Israeli–Palestinian case.

---

[249] See also Guilfoyle, *supra* n.247, at 16–17; Holland, *supra* n.70, at 160.

[250] *Targeted Killings supra* n.115, at para. 18:

> The normative system which applies to the armed conflict between Israel and the terrorist organizations in the *area* is complex. In its centre stands the international law regarding international armed conflict. Professor Cassese discussed the international character of an armed conflict between the occupying state in an area subject to belligerent occupation and the terrorists who come from the same area, including the armed conflict between Israel and the terrorist organizations in the *area*, stating:
>
>> An armed conflict which takes place between an Occupying Power and rebel or insurgent groups – whether or not they are terrorist in character – in an occupied territory, amounts to an international armed conflict (A. Cassese, International Law 420 (2nd ed. 2005), hereinafter Cassese).
>
> This law includes the laws of belligerent occupation. However, it is not restricted only to them. This law applies in any case of an armed conflict of international character – in other words, one that crosses the borders of the state – whether or not the place in which the armed conflict occurs is subject to belligerent occupation. This law constitutes a part of *ius in bello*. From the humanitarian perspective, it is part of international humanitarian law. That humanitarian law is the *lex specialis* which applies in the case of an armed conflict. When there is a gap (*lacuna*) in that law, it can be supplemented by human rights law.

[251] In *Lubanga*, the Chamber seemed to consider that occupation internationalizes any other conflict – see *Lubanga* Confirmation Decision, para. 220. In *Katanga*, the Chamber characterized the conflict as international without making explicit the legal basis for doing so; it considered the intervention by Ugandan troops in the Congo to have internationalized the conflict, but it is unclear whether it considered the relevant non-state armed groups to have been under Uganda's overall control, or whether the mere presence of foreign troops led to internationalization. The possibility of parallel conflicts was not discussed. See *Prosecutor v. Germain Katanga and Mathieu Ngudjolo Chui*, Decision on the Confirmation of Charges, ICC-01/04-01/07, 30 September 2008, at para. 240.

[252] For more see Milanovic, *supra* n.91, at 382–386. See also Guilfoyle, *supra* n.247, at 11–17.

Why should a more or less unrelated outbreak of violence, whose actors are completely different, be treated as an IAC? Unless we follow the controversial logic of Article 1(4) AP I, why should the status of a non-state actor be upgraded to full belligerent rights if the actor is not fighting on behalf of any state? That two legal regimes would apply in parallel is not reason enough. As with cases of mixed or parallel armed conflicts, IHL can allow for the possibility of the simultaneous existence of occupation and of a NIAC in occupied territory.[253]

Finally, the mere fact that international or foreign forces are deployed in a certain territory does not of itself suffice for the internationalization of the whole conflict.[254] As we have seen, the qualification of such situations depends on the existence, *vel non*, of the consent of the territorial state to the presence of the international forces and of their relationship with the relevant non-state actors.[255] Thus, for instance, the fact that NATO intervened against Serbia in 1999, which was at the time fighting the KLA insurgency in Kosovo, does not mean that the whole conflict was internationalized. There was certainly an IAC between the NATO states and Serbia, but the NIAC between Serbia and the KLA would have been internationalized only if the NATO states exerted the necessary degree of control over the non-state actor.

D. Parallel or Mixed Armed Conflicts

We have already dealt extensively with parallel or mixed armed conflicts throughout the preceding analysis. In complex conflicts fought between a variety of state and non-state actors a mixed characterization may be unavoidable, as for example in Bosnia, Afghanistan or Libya. Internationalizing the whole lot may be an appetizing prospect, as the whole structure and accordingly the applicable law are simplified.[256] That, however, may not always be possible, considering the criteria for internationalization that we have just examined. Similarly, as a matter of policy, treating a complex conflict purely as an IAC may risk imposing obligations that were made for and fit states on non-state actors, obligations that they may well feel to be overburdensome and hence simply ignore. Consequently, rather than treating a particular situation as a singular IAC there may be sound reasons to treat it as a network of separate conflicts or bilateral relationships, whose characterization would depend foremost on the identity of the actors.[257]

The possibility of mixed or parallel conflict is generally accepted in the case law, as for instance in *Tadić*. Perhaps the first such example was given by the ICJ in *Nicaragua*, when it stated that:

---

[253] For a contrary view see Akande, *supra* n.79, at 18–19.
[254] See, for example, Pejic, *supra* n.7, at 194.
[255] See also Stewart, *supra* n.9, at 328–335 (discussing relevant ICTY case law).
[256] Cf. Holland, *supra* n.70, at 177–180.
[257] See Schindler, *supra* n.54, at 150; Greenwood, *supra* n.6, at 270 ff.; Kress, *supra* n.6, at 256–257; Guilfoyle, *supra* n.247, at 17–18.

The conflict between the *contras*' forces and those of the Government of Nicaragua is an armed conflict which is 'not of an international character'. The acts of the *contras* towards the Nicaraguan Government are therefore governed by the law applicable to conflicts of that character, whereas the actions of the United States in and against Nicaragua fall under the legal rules relating to international conflicts.[258]

While acknowledging that it has not been without its opponents,[259] we think the category of mixed conflicts to be so well established that we will not belabour it in detail beyond the analysis that we have already provided. Suffice it to say that mixed or parallel conflicts serve as a fall-back category of sorts in cases in which arguments in favour of internationalization fail. Accordingly, those authors who see the process of internationalization in much broader terms than we do will also see the category of mixed conflicts as either misplaced or undesirable. But if we are correct about the current scope of the two main processes of internationalization – under the basic IAC definition or through redefinition – then the incidence of mixed conflicts will invariably be relatively high.[260]

E. Transnational Armed Conflict

This brings us to our final topic. The increased political relevance of the activities of transnational armed or terrorist groups, frequent cross-border interventions of states against such groups, and particularly the controversies regarding the legal characterization of the US 'global war on terror' prompted some authors to contemplate a reform of the IAC/NIAC duopoly of armed conflict by introducing a third category, variously called transnational armed conflict (hereinafter 'TAC') or extra-state armed conflict.[261] Different authors offer different reasons for and different conceptions of this third category. Lumping them all together, as we are about to do, comes at the cost of diminishing the sophistication of some of their arguments. That said, we believe that this can be safely done for our present taxonomical purposes, and that the purported third category of armed conflict raises two basic questions that we will try briefly to address. First, *de lege lata*, does it exist in the modern *jus in bello*? Secondly, *de lege ferenda*, should it exist even if we do not already have it?

i. Does TAC exist *de lege lata*?

The first of these questions is easier to answer. Hardly anybody suggests that this new type of conflict already exists as a distinct threshold in positive IHL. It would not, in

---

[258] *Nicaragua*, supra n. 216, at para. 219.
[259] See, for example, T. Meron, 'Classification of Armed Conflict in the Former Yugoslavia: *Nicaragua's* Fallout', (1998) 92 *AJIL* 236.
[260] See also Akande, *supra* n.79, at 37–38.
[261] See, for example, G. Corn, 'Making the Case for Conflict Bifurcation in Afghanistan: Transnational Armed Conflict, Al Qaida, and the Limits of the Associated Militia Concept', (2009) 85 *US Naval War College International Law Studies* 181; G. Corn and E. Talbot, 'Transnational Armed Conflict: A Principled Approach to the Regulation of Counter-Terror Combat Operations', (2009) 42 *Is L R* 46; R. Schondorf, 'Extra-State Armed Conflicts: Is there a Need for a New Legal Regime?', (2003) 37 *NYU J Intl L & Pol* 61; E. Posner, 'Terrorism and the Laws of War', (2005) 5 *Chi J Intl L* 421.

our opinion, be reasonably possible to argue differently. A third category cannot be inferred from the treaty rules of IHL.[262] None of the conventions mentions or regulates it. There is no state practice or *opinio juris* which would suggest that such a category of conflicts emerged in customary international law independently of conventional IHL or that the states actually desire the emergence of such a category. This is, of course, not to deny the controversies regarding the qualification of the 'war on terror' or other recent conflicts between states and non-state actors. But, as far as states have formally expressed their positions regarding these controversies, they have exclusively limited themselves to arguing about qualification under the existing IAC/NIAC framework, as is well shown in the example of the United States, to which we will turn shortly. One cannot impute to states legal positions that they have themselves not taken.[263] Hence, at least for the time being, any discussion about TAC or some other third category can be had only at the level of *de lege ferenda* policy arguments either in favour or against its emergence.

Note, however, that one can speak of 'transnational armed conflict' in a different sense, as a purely *descriptive* category rather than as a *legal* concept.[264] Just like we have used the notion of 'cross-border NIAC' to better describe a complex factual situation to which the existing law can still apply, so can one deploy the idea of TAC to advance our understanding of a peculiar modern phenomenon. Such use of the term may or may not be useful, but it is certainly legitimate, so long as one avoids any confusion with a purported third legal threshold of armed conflict. One can, in short, pin the TAC label on any given situation, but if that situation cannot be qualified as either an IAC or a NIAC it is not an armed conflict in the legal sense of the word.[265]

ii. Should TAC exist as a separate legal category of armed conflict?

This brings us to the second, more complex question regarding TAC or some other third legal category of armed conflict – do we need it? This question is clearly far more open to disagreement than the first. There are two related and overlapping reasons, or groups of reasons, for arguing in favour of such a category. First, if the existing regime has gaps in coverage, that is if there are some situations that look like armed conflict, walk like armed conflict and quack like armed conflict, yet legally are *not* armed conflict, this is something that we need to remedy, if nothing else then for humanitarian reasons.[266] Secondly, even if there are no gaps in coverage, the transnational context may warrant the modification of existing substantive rules so as to provide a better fit with reality and/or remove some of the constraints of the IAC/NIAC duopoly.

a. Is there a gap that TAC could fill? It is likely that cross-border conflicts between states and non-state armed groups were not envisioned by the drafters of the Geneva

---

[262] Thus, the ICRC's official position is that 'no other type of armed conflict exists' but for IAC and NIAC. See ICRC, *supra* n.155.

[263] *Nicaragua*, *supra* n.216, para. 207. For a discussion see D. Kritsiotis, 'Arguments of Mass Confusion', (2004) 15 *EJIL* 233, at 238.

[264] For works which use the TAC label in this descriptive sense, see, for example, Kress, *supra* n.6.

[265] See *supra* section 3D.

[266] See, for example, Pejic, *supra* n.7, at 203 (discussing the 'gap theory').

Conventions and their Protocols simply because of their rarity and lack of political relevance at the time. Accordingly, it can be reasonably argued that the specific circumstances under which these conflicts are waged largely escape the binary Geneva framework of IHL or do not fit it well.[267] And, since cross-border armed conflicts are a factual novelty, they should be followed by legal innovation. Authors advocating for TAC point out that the responsiveness of IHL to new realities is precisely what has kept this body of law current and relevant.[268]

While it is probably true that the drafters of the Conventions and Protocols did not have cross-border armed conflicts between states and non-state armed groups in mind, their novelty is exaggerated; their incidence has been growing for at least 30 years.[269] States have had plenty of time to create special treaty or customary rules governing these conflicts if they deemed it necessary. What *is* relatively new is the increasing political relevance of these conflicts, which now have bearing on the interests of the most powerful members of the international community. But, as we have seen, even in the past decade states have not shown a particular desire for a third legal category.

In that regard, although the CA3 notion of NIAC was clearly intended to cover situations of internal strife and it would be ahistorical to claim otherwise, this does not mean that the text of the treaty, its object and purpose, and its customary gloss cannot reasonably apply to cross-border situations.[270] The direction of both state practice and scholarship has indeed been towards such stretching of the idea of NIAC, the historical intentions of the drafters notwithstanding. And this *is* new. Admittedly, it is somewhat artificial to call a situation in which the United States fights the Taliban in Afghanistan, or Israel fights Hezbollah in Lebanon, a non-international armed conflict. But this does not mean that the category does not do the job, together with the remainder of the IAC/NIAC conceptual apparatus, that is internationalized and mixed conflicts.[271] If this apparatus is applied as we have suggested in this chapter, few if any gaps will remain, particularly when it comes to more orthodox or large-scale instances of violence, as in our Israel/Hezbollah/Lebanon and Colombia/FARC/Ecuador examples. But this serves only to better delineate the two lines of inquiry that we have identified: even accepting all the varieties of cross-border NIAC, will there still be situations which will not be but should be characterized as an armed conflict? And even if not, could TAC introduce new rules that would overcome any substantive deficiencies in treating these situations as NIACs?

b. Shifting dynamics of the perception of IHL In order to proceed along these two lines of inquiry we must first understand some relatively recent shifts in the underlying legal and political dynamics. As originally designed and through most of its history

---

[267] See Schondorf, *supra* n.261, at 51.
[268] See Corn, *supra* n.261, at 184.
[269] For the enumeration of the most prominent examples prior to 9/11 seeSchondorf, *supra* n.261, at 9; H.P. Gasser, 'Internationalized Non-International Armed Conflicts: Case Studies of Afghanistan, Kampuchea and Lebanon', (1983) 33 *Am U L Rev* 145, at 155–156; C. Le Mon, 'Unilateral Intervention by Invitation in Civil War: The Effective Control Test Tested', (2003) 35 *NYUJ Intl L & Pol* 741.
[270] See also Lubell, *supra* n.77, at 122–123.
[271] See also Pejic, *supra* n.7, at 204–205.

IHL was seen by states as a system of *limitations* on their sovereignty and freedom of action, particularly so when it comes to the law of internal armed conflict. In other words, the *baseline* for international regulation from the classical period onwards was that states had the unrestrained freedom to wage war, both against each other and internally, and the law of war evolved precisely to impose such restraints, first and foremost in the inter-state context. As we have seen, states resisted the regulation of internal conflict because of the fear – founded or not – that it would impose limits on how they could deal with rebels, and confer on these rebels some rights in international law. It is this sovereignty-induced concern of states that explains the IAC/NIAC dichotomy in modern law and the principal features of NIACs, such as the *Tadić* intensity and duration criteria and the distinction between NIACs and mere riots or disturbances. Hence, it was rarely if ever in the interest of a state embroiled in internal conflict to recognize the existence of such conflict – it simply *did not want* IHL to apply.[272] This is why, for instance, the United Kingdom consistently denied the existence of a NIAC in Northern Ireland, or why it made a reservation to Article 1(4) AP I which explicitly excluded acts of terrorism, whether concerted or in isolation, from the scope of armed conflict.[273]

Now, however, human rights have gradually replaced, or are in the process of replacing, the idea of unrestrained freedom of action as the baseline for regulation, as much *culturally* as formally. Instead of IHL being the only set of limitations on states, a more rigid, demanding and legalistic set of limitations has emerged, particularly in the internal context. States, or at least some states, have accordingly stopped seeing IHL as a constraining body of rules whose application they want to avoid in their engagements with non-state actors.[274] Rather, they have progressively started seeing IHL as an *authorizing* body of rules liberating them or derogating from human rights or other constraints, often on the dubious basis of the *lex specialis* principle.[275] For example, while IHL targeting or detention rules evolved as limitations (for example you must not deliberately target civilians),[276] they are now seen as permissive rules authorizing departures from human rights (for example you may kill an enemy fighter

---

[272] See Sassoli, *supra* n.202, at 7–8.

[273] 'It is the understanding of the United Kingdom that the term "armed conflict" of itself and in its context denotes a situation of a kind which is not constituted by the commission of ordinary crimes including acts of terrorism whether concerted or in isolation. The United Kingdom will not, in relation to any situation in which it is itself involved, consider itself bound in consequence of any declaration purporting to be made under paragraph 3 of Article 96 unless the United Kingdom shall have expressly recognised that it has been made by a body which is genuinely an authority representing a people engaged in an armed conflict of the type to which Article 1, paragraph 4, applies.' Reservation of 28 January 1998, available at http://www.icrc.org/ihl.nsf/NORM/0A9E03F0F2EE757CC1256402003FB6D2?OpenDocument.

[274] Cf. Lubell, *supra* n.77, at 123–124.

[275] For more see M. Milanovic, 'Norm Conflicts, International Humanitarian Law and Human Rights Law', in O. Ben-Naftali (ed.), *International Humanitarian Law and International Human Rights Law* (Oxford: Oxford University Press, 2011), 95.

[276] See chapter 10 by David Turns in this volume.

even if he does not pose an imminent threat; you may detain preventively for reasons of security even if human rights law generally prohibits preventive detention).[277]

To see how these dynamics evolved we need only look at US policy post-9/11.[278] The US government from the outset decided to cast the Al-Qaeda threat and US response as a 'war' for both domestic and international purposes, in order to get the detention and targeting authority that it thought it needed and thus derogate from any applicable rules of domestic constitutional law as well as international human rights law. The moniker 'global war on terror' denoted a supposed IHL conflict between the US on one side and Al-Qaeda and its affiliates on the other. Initially, the US characterized this conflict as an IAC, albeit a strange sort of IAC which transcended the Geneva CA2 definition as one of its parties was not a state. In the US government's view, the CA2 definition did not create 'field pre-emption', that is was not all-encompassing; put in more traditional international legalese, the notion of IAC was wider under customary law.[279] This, as we have seen, was a completely ahistorical argument; the notion of IAC was *invented* in Geneva and replaced the equally inter-state notion of war, while there was no evidence that it was redefined either through treaty or through custom in this particular fashion.[280] The administration also considered that the conflict could not be a NIAC as it transcended the borders of a single state.[281] In *Hamdan*, the US Supreme Court rejected the government's arguments and found that the conflict with Al-Qaeda could not be an IAC, and in an ambiguous holding that we have already examined qualified it as a NIAC.[282] The position of both the Bush and Obama administrations post-*Hamdan* has hence been that the conflict with Al-Qaeda is some sort of *global* NIAC, which is territorially unlimited in scope.

Even under the framework that we have outlined above, which allows for various kinds of cross-border NIACs, the idea of a global NIAC makes sense only as an oxymoron. Any NIAC requires the existence of protracted armed violence which by definition has to take place *somewhere*, that is has to be localized at least to the territory of one state. As we have seen, that violence can spill over to the territory of another state (which need not necessarily be adjacent to the primary state), but there has to be a *nexus* to the protracted violence in the primary state. Thus, while one can safely speak of a NIAC between the United States and the Taliban and other armed

---

[277] See, for example, Bellinger and Padmanabhan, *supra* n.182 (repeatedly referring to targeting and detention authority under IHL, and identifying gaps of such authority in NIACs, which they feel is needed). See also Kress, *supra* n.6, at 260 (speaking of states 'availing themselves of the wider powers they can derive from the application of the law of non-international armed conflict (compared with international human rights law) than they are concerned by the restraining effect of the ensuing obligations.').

[278] In that regard, see especially K. Anderson, 'Targeted Killing and Drone Warfare: How We Came to Debate Whether There Is a "Legal Geography of War"', Hoover Institution (2011), available at http://ssrn.com/abstract=1824783.

[279] *Hamdan v. Rumsfeld*, Government Brief on the Merits, available at http://www.hamdanvrumsfeld.com/HamdanSGmeritsbrief.pdf, at 26.

[280] See also Kress, *supra* n.6, at 255; Pejic, *supra* n.107, at 344–347; Sassoli, *supra* n.202, at 4–5; Lubell, *supra* n.77, at 96.

[281] See Pejic, *supra* n.7, at 195.

[282] See *supra* section 3D.

groups in Afghanistan and once in Iraq, and while that conflict can spill over into, say, Pakistan or any other country, the existing legal framework does not seem to allow for a construction as amorphous as a global NIAC,[283] particularly one in which a loose terrorist network such as Al-Qaeda is treated as a single organizational entity and belligerent party.[284]

The US position has had little traction outside the US itself. Within it, however, the conversation is very different. Bearing in mind that all branches of the US government and all major groups within the two main political parties accept the premise of a global war, denying this premise is pretty much a non-starter, even in academic circles, to the extent that academics want their work to have practical relevance and exert some influence on US policy. Despite the low quality of the reasoning of the major US Supreme Court cases on point – indeed the lack of *any* real reasoning or meaningful engagement with modern IHL – they all either hold or assume the existence of an armed conflict with Al-Qaeda, however defined.[285] That assumption now seems to be set in stone, and has been built upon by a multitude of lower courts deciding *habeas corpus* cases from Guantanamo or elsewhere. To the extent that those of us outside the United States want to engage in the legal conversation within it, accepting or at least not continuously challenging that assumption may seem the most expedient course. The divergence of views has become so insurmountable that for some, at least, creating a new threshold of TAC may provide a viable mediating option.

c. *The 'costs' in recognizing a NIAC*   This new preparedness of the US not only to accept, but to positively *desire* the legal recognition of an armed conflict with a non-state actor does not come only from the shift in perception of IHL from a limiting to an authorizing body of rules. While in traditional, purely internal NIACs it is in the state's interest to deny the existence of the NIAC as IHL can be perceived as legitimizing rebels fighting against its authority and as an admission of its weakness and inability to exert a monopoly on physical force throughout its territory, such sovereignty concerns can have much less relevance in a cross-border context. When the US fights the Taliban in Afghanistan, the Taliban are challenging or trying to topple the Afghan government, but they obviously have no such impact on US soil. When Israel fights Hezbollah in Lebanon, Hezbollah is not a direct threat to its own sovereignty, whatever it may be to Lebanon's. And when the US targets Osama bin Laden in

---

[283] See Y. Dinstein, *The Conduct of Hostilities under the Law of International Armed Conflict*, 2nd edn (Cambridge: Cambridge University Press, 2010), at 56: 'from the vantage point of international law … a non-international armed conflict cannot possibly assume global dimensions'.

[284] See also Kress, *supra* n.6, at 261; Ramsden, *supra* n.88, at 390; Vité, *supra* n.70, at 92–93; Pejic, *supra* n.7, at 196; Lubell, *supra* n.77, at 114–121.

[285] See, for example, Bellinger and Padmanabhan, *supra* n.182, who do not seriously even entertain the idea that there is no global armed conflict with Al-Qaeda as such, and in a similar vein L. Blank, 'Defining the Battlefield in Contemporary Conflict and Counterterrorism: Understanding the Parameters of the Zone of Combat', (2010) 39 *Ga J Intl & Comp L* 1.

Pakistan, or Anwar Al-Awlaki in Yemen,[286] it is the sovereignty of these states rather than that of the US itself that is at issue. In other words, in a foreign intervention scenario it is politically far less costly for the intervening state to recognize the existence of a NIAC – or, perhaps, some third category of armed conflict.

d. Evaluating TAC Bearing these policy considerations in mind we can better evaluate any benefits that TAC could bring to the existing framework of armed conflict. First, there are few, if any, good reasons to create a new category for larger-scale cross-border conflicts between states and non-state actors, as, for example, with the US against the Taliban in Afghanistan or Israel against Hezbollah in Lebanon. The cross-border NIAC sub-type seems perfectly capable of handling such a scenario, particularly bearing in mind that all or some parts of the conflict may become internationalized, and that an IAC would exist at least in parallel in cases where one state intervenes on the territory of another without its permission, protecting the latter state's civilians, infrastructure and cultural objects, while the law of belligerent occupation would also apply if such an occupation were established. This admittedly eclectic mix of overlapping regimes is messy but not inadequate, and nor would putting a TAC label on it somehow significantly improve it.[287] Moreover, in the era of convergence of IAC and NIAC one can question the desirability of the emergence of yet another type of armed conflict with its own set of norms which would fragment rather than unify this area of law, even if the convergence projects has already (over?) reached its safe limits. Whether one fully accepts the ICRC's contention that most of the customary rules are now the same in both IAC and NIAC, the necessity of creating an entirely new type of conflict with its own set of rules is doubtful, while introducing an additional category of conflicts (except, again, in a purely descriptive sense) would necessarily bring even more uncertainty into the conflict qualification exercise.[288]

There is, however, one particular factual scenario in which the possible utility of TAC might be at its highest – that of a relatively isolated or sporadic use of force by a state against a diffuse and decentralized transnational non-state group. Consider, again, the targeted killings of Osama bin Laden and Anwar Al-Awlaki, that the United States sees through the prism of armed conflict. As we have explained above, unless a nexus can be shown between these individuals and uses of force to an established NIAC, that is protracted armed violence in Afghanistan, Pakistan or Yemen, the targeted killings cannot be said to have taken course in a NIAC. Let us assume *arguendo* that no such

---

[286] See, generally, Ramsden, *supra* n.88; R. Chesney, 'Who May Be Killed? Anwar al-Awlaki as a Case Study in the International Legal Regulation of Lethal Force', (2010) 13 *Y Intl H L* 3.

[287] Note, for instance, Schondorf's argument that in TACs civilians could be protected under rules applicable in IACs, while fighters should be treated as they are in NIACs, in essence making TACs more protective for the civilian population than NIACs. See Schondorf, *supra* n.261. Again, however, for reasons that we give above, this potential increase in protection does not seem to be all that large. More importantly, to the extent that TAC might be appealing for states this is *not* because it would be *more* protective than NIAC. See Sassoli, *supra* n.202, at 22–23.

[288] See also Kress, *supra* n.6, at 257–258; Sassoli, *supra* n.202, at 25.

nexus existed on the facts of those particular cases.[289] If so, the killings – at least that of Al-Awlaki, to which Yemen consented – did not take place in any legally cognizable armed conflict, within the framework that we suggest in this chapter. Hence, the only two applicable bodies of international law would have been the *jus ad bellum* and human rights law, which in our view applies extraterritorially.[290] From the *jus ad bellum* standpoint, the lawfulness of each killing would depend on whether the territorial state gave its consent to the use of force, and, if not, whether the US could make a valid self-defence claim in justification.[291] From the human rights standpoint, the lawfulness of the killing would depend above all on whether the US exhausted all practicable non-lethal means in order to capture the dangerous individual in question before resorting to deadly force.[292]

That is not, of course, how the United States sees the matter. It consistently denies that human rights treaties can apply extraterritorially. But – perhaps paradoxically considering its formal rejection of a human rights baseline in this scenario – it both sees IHL as a grant of authority and sees no downside to its application as its own sovereignty is unaffected, and hence deploys the notion of a global NIAC. Moreover, it sees this grant of authority as relevant not only for the *jus in bello* but also for the *jus ad bellum*. As John Brennan, President Obama's chief advisor on terrorism, stated in a recent speech:

> As the President has said many times, we are at war with al-Qa'ida. In an indisputable act of aggression, al-Qa'ida attacked our nation and killed nearly 3,000 innocent people. And as we were reminded just last weekend, al-Qa'ida seeks to attack us again. *Our ongoing armed conflict with al-Qa'ida stems from our right – recognized under international law – to self defense.*
>
> An area in which there is some disagreement is the geographic scope of the conflict. The United States does not view our authority to use military force against al-Qa'ida as being restricted solely to 'hot' battlefields like Afghanistan. Because we are engaged in an armed conflict with al-Qa'ida, the United States takes the legal position that – in accordance with international law – we have the authority to take action against al-Qa'ida and its associated forces *without doing a separate self-defense analysis each time*. And as President Obama has stated on numerous occasions, we reserve the right to take unilateral action if or when other governments *are unwilling or unable to take the necessary actions themselves*.[293]

---

[289] For a detailed argument that Al-Awlaki was killed in the context of a NIAC in Yemen, see Chesney, *supra* n.286, at 31–34.

[290] See, generally, M. Milanovic, *Extraterritorial Application of Human Rights Treaties: Law, Principles, and Policy* (Oxford: Oxford University Press, 2011).

[291] See chapter 6 by Dino Kritsiotis in this volume.

[292] Cf. Leiden Policy Recommendations on Counter-Terrorism and International Law, 1 April 2010, available at http://www.grotiuscentre.org/resources/1/Leiden%20Policy%20Recommendations%201%20April%202010.pdf, paras 38–48, 75–77.

[293] Remarks of John O. Brennan – As Prepared for Delivery, Assistant to the President for Homeland Security and Counterterrorism, Program on Law and Security, Harvard Law School, 16 September 2011 (emphasis added), quoted in full in M. Lederman, 'John Brennan Speech on Obama Administration Antiterrorism Policies and Practices', *Opinio Juris*, 16 September 2011, available at http://opiniojuris.org/2011/09/16/john-brennan-speech-on-obama-administration-antiterrorism-policies-and-practices/.

While acknowledging that Mr Brennan is himself not a lawyer, this is in fact the fullest articulation to date of the Obama administration's legal position on extraterritorial uses of force against Al-Qaeda members and affiliates.[294] And it is here – even if we dismiss as mere rhetorical flourish some legally truly dubious points, for example that the US is at 'war' with a non-state actor which committed an 'act of aggression' – that we can see the work that the idea of global armed conflict does as a matter of US policy. Note the persistent conflation between the *jus ad bellum* and the *jus in bello*. The armed conflict thus *stems* from the right to self-defence, even though the two are neither legally nor logically interrelated; whether the US and Al-Qaeda are *factually* in armed conflict does not depend one bit on whether the US has the *right* to pursue Al-Qaeda, or has exceeded that right. But there is a policy behind this conflation – the US needs this idea of persistent armed conflict in order to have 'the authority to take action against al-Qa'ida and its associated forces *without doing a separate self-defense analysis each time*'. Thus, if Anwar Al-Awlaki was a member of Al-Qaeda he could have been killed by the US, even if Yemen had not consented, and even if Al-Awlaki was not himself involved in any ongoing or imminent armed attack against the US, so long as Yemen was unwilling or unable to apprehend him. Note also how the unwilling or unable test is imported from self-defence analysis, even though this is an analysis that the US supposedly does not have to make![295]

This is, we believe, a deeply flawed, and even dangerous position for the US government to take. It is flawed because even if an armed conflict is 'global' in scope this does not obviate the need for a *jus ad bellum* justification if a particular use of force infringes on the territory of some other state without its consent. It is dangerous because its conflation of the *jus ad bellum* and the *jus in bello* can have unintended ripple consequences and undermine the whole structure of the modern law of war.[296]

That said, and the *jus ad bellum* aside, a case could be made that IHL should cover even such isolated targeted killings. Especially if the argument that human rights treaties apply extraterritorially is rejected, IHL could not merely provide states with authorization to use deadly force that they desire, but also some meaningful humanitarian protection.[297] And it is perhaps precisely TAC that could fill this gap, in essence serving the same purpose as the current US construction of a global NIAC while explicitly dispensing with the *Tadić* criteria of intensity and duration.[298] A TAC could

---

[294] This speech elaborates on a prior statement by Harold Koh, the State Department Legal Adviser, on which see especially Ramsden, *supra* n.88, at 388–389.

[295] The unwilling and unable test has generally been applied in the literature as part of the necessity analysis to situations in which a non-state actor has committed or is committing an armed attack, but its acts are not attributable to any state. But the test is *not* generally applied in situations in which there is no armed attack, and no consequent specific self-defence claim. See, generally, Kress, *supra* n.6, at 248–252; K. Trapp, 'Back to Basics: Necessity, Proportionality, and the Right of Self-Defence against Non-State Terrorist Actors', (2007) 56 *ICLQ* 142; M. Schmitt, 'Responding to Transnational Terrorism under the *Jus ad Bellum*: A Normative Framework', in Schmitt and Pejic, *supra* n.65, 157, at 176 ff.

[296] See *supra* section 3A.

[297] Cf. Chesney, *supra* n.286, at 36–38.

[298] See, for example, comments by M. Lederman to A. Margalit, 'The Bin Laden Killing: Clarifying the Normative Framework(s) Governing the "War on Terror"?', *EJIL: Talk!*, 12

thus be defined as any use of force between a state and a non-state actor outside that state's borders.

The desirability of such a low threshold of TAC is ultimately a matter of policy and value judgment. For our part, we remain unpersuaded. To the extent that there are any gaps in need of filling, human rights – applied flexibly – appear to be far better suited to the task,[299] as do other branches of international and municipal law.[300] Similarly, while it is easy to see why a low threshold of TAC would be in the interest of states wishing to use force extraterritorially against non-state actors, it is also hard to see any principled reason why the higher *Tadić* threshold should remain for instances of larger-scale violence, external or internal, and how one could prevent the collapse of any NIAC threshold altogether.[301]

In sum, we maintain that the existing binary framework of IHL is capable of responding to the challenges posed by modern conflicts. We say so without making an appeal to some sort of overly defensive conservatism. While the character of modern armed conflicts has changed significantly, and the political, technological, strategic and tactical changes may have been great, they do not *ipso facto* require radical changes to the existing legal framework as it has evolved through state practice.[302] Despite some viable policy arguments in favour of recognizing TAC as a third type of conflict, the arguments against it are stronger, even if reasonable people can disagree. We do not think, however, that there can be reasonable disagreement with regard to the non-existence of TAC *de lege lata*, unless TAC is seen purely as a descriptive category.

5. CONCLUSION

The apparent simplicity of the IAC/NIAC dichotomy belies the true complexity of the conflict classification exercise in modern IHL. Again, our main purpose in writing this chapter was to clarify as much as possible the conceptual foundations of the taxonomy of armed conflict, rather than advocate for one particular position or the other. We hope to have succeeded in pointing out areas of reasonable disagreement, as well as those in which such disagreement does not seem to be possible. This, we also hope, will allow discussions on the classification of specific problematic situations to progress further, as clarifying our common vocabulary lessens the odds of us speaking past each other. And while these taxonomical arguments are often formalistic and sterile, they are with us to stay for the foreseeable future, despite all of the successes of the humanity-driven

---

October 2011, available at http://www.ejiltalk.org/the-bin-laden-killing-clarifying-the-normative-frameworks-governing-the-war-on-terror/; M. Lewis, 'Drones and the Boundaries of the Battlefield', (2011) 47 *Tex Intl L J*(forthcoming), draft available at http://ssrn.com/abstract=1917461, at 7–8, 11 ff.

[299] For more see Milanovic, *supra* n.290.

[300] See also Sassoli, *supra* n.202, at 25–27.

[301] See also R. Geiss, 'Asymmetric Conflict Structures', (2006) 88 *IRRC* 757; Lubell, *supra* n.77, at 129–131.

[302] For a similar conclusion regarding substantive rather than threshold issues, see especially Geiss and Siegrist, *supra* n.147.

project of unifying the substantive laws of IAC and NIAC.[303] Because classification still crucially affects the status of the parties to the conflict and their perceived legitimacy, it remains a function of states' interests and their particular policy preferences which may differ in any given situation.[304] In principle, however, so long as states remain unwilling to extend the same belligerent rights to organized non-state actors that they claim for themselves, the dichotomy remains, and with it the need to approach threshold questions of application in a coherent and systematic way.

---

[303] As acknowledged, for example, by one of the main authors of the ICRC customary IHL study: 'The divide between law on international and non-international armed conflicts, in particular concerning the conduct of hostilities, the use of means and methods of warfare and the treatment of persons in the power of a party to a conflict, has largely been bridged. But this is not to say that the law on international and non-international armed conflicts is now the same. Indeed, concepts such as occupation and the entitlement to combatant and prisoner-of-war status still belong exclusively to the domain of international armed conflicts.' J.-M. Henckaerts, 'Customary International Humanitarian Law: A Response to US Comments', (2007) 89 *IRRC* 473, 487.

[304] See also N. Berman, 'Privileging Combat? Contemporary Conflict and the Legal Construction of War', (2004) 43 *Columbia JTL* 1.

ANNEX: SCHEMA OF ARMED CONFLICT

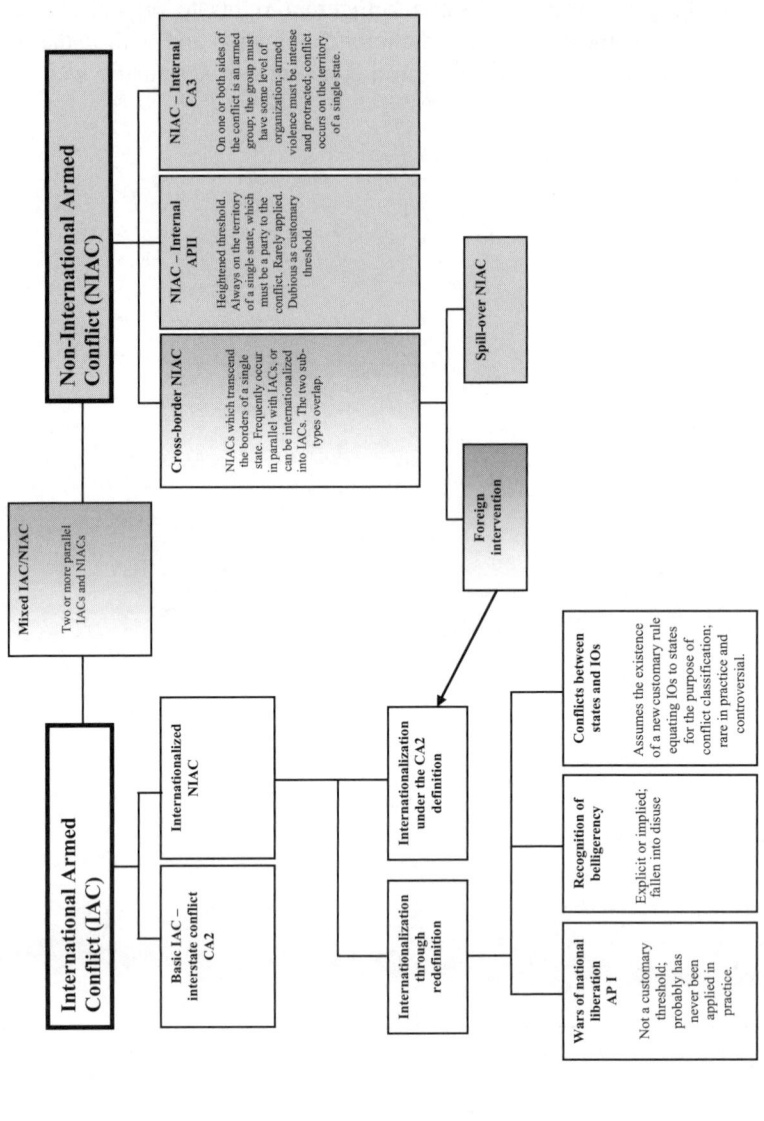

314

9. Weapons
Karen Hulme

1. INTRODUCTION

Weapons have a clear strategic and security dimension; most patently epitomized by nuclear weapons and the Cold War strategy of 'mutual assured destruction' (hereinafter 'MAD'). They also play a broader role in the lead-up to war; in arms races, military preparations for war and, of course, in the opening throes of battle. During armed conflict itself the laws attempt to humanize warfare and the instruments with which it can be fought, limiting the crueller and more barbaric forms of weaponry and those unable to distinguish between soldier and civilian. Yet, it is the continuing threat that weapons leave on the battlefield after the conflict that has drawn most attention in recent years. With the adoption of numerous instruments requiring the post-conflict removal of weapons and weapons debris, as well as the care of weapons-affected victims, a *jus post bellum* of weaponry already exists.

In 1975 Richard Baxter wrote of the legal regulation of weaponry that it was 'either pitched on a very high level of abstraction or was directed to specific weapons or projectiles of marginal military utility'.[1] By comparison, said Baxter, were the 'enormous technological developments that had taken place in the art of warfare'.[2] Such views are arguably not sustainable today, as the most recent prohibition on cluster munitions demonstrates.[3] Yet, as enormous technological developments continue apace, for example in the development and use of drones, will we be able to come to this same judgement in the near future? The core principles of the laws of armed conflict have endured for centuries. Yet, just how robust do *jus in bello* principles continue to be in regulating the good, the bad and the ugly (or drones, Improvised Explosive Devices (hereinafter 'IEDs') and white phosphorus (hereinafter 'WP')) of modern weaponry? How willing are states in limiting the means available to them to win in war?

This chapter will commence in section 2 with a spectrum-wide look at weapons, ranging from their *jus ad bellum* to their *jus post bellum* relevance before moving to more specific analysis of the *jus in bello* rules in section 3. Section 4 briefly examines other models of arms control, with special focus on the regulation of weapons of mass destruction (hereinafter 'WMD'), including the most vexing of weapons issues: the legality and regulation of nuclear weapons. In the final substantive section the analysis moves to consideration of five of the most interesting and legally contentious

---

[1] R.R. Baxter, 'Conventional Weapons under Legal Prohibitions', (1977) 1 *Int. Security* 42, at 45.
[2] *Ibid.*
[3] See the 2008 Convention on Cluster Munitions, (2009) 48 *ILM* 357–369.

contemporary weapons developments; namely, cluster munitions, IEDs, WP, weaponized drones and robots, and cyber warfare.

2. THE SIGNIFICANCE OF WEAPONS ACROSS THE SPECTRUM OF *JUS AD BELLUM*, *JUS IN BELLO* AND *JUS POST BELLUM*

Clearly the *jus in bello*, or the laws of armed conflict, imposes limits to the choice of weaponry in conflict, but so too might the *jus ad bellum*. The much trumpeted, at least at the time, 'Responsibility to Protect' (hereinafter 'R2P') doctrine inspired the mandate of the operations in Libya in 2011[4] which excluded a 'foreign occupation force',[5] thus limiting military actions and weaponry during the conflict. In a similar vein, the so-called 'transformational' conflicts in Afghanistan (2001), Iraq (2003) and Kosovo (1999) demonstrated how limitations at the policy level could restrict how the war was waged, specifically to achieve the democratizing or humanitarian objectives of the *jus ad bellum*. For example, in targeting, and thus in weaponry policy too, military planners were mindful from an early stage of the conflict to limit the level of post-conflict reconstruction that would be needed, and hence at the strategic command level restrictions were imposed on the targeting of electrical power grids, roads and industry.[6] The use of precision weapons, on the other hand, allowed states to gain the moral high ground, and helped in the battle to win 'hearts and minds', as well as to limit post-conflict reconstruction. The 2003 invasion of Iraq, on the other hand, which was premised on the disarmament of a regional tyrant, illustrates the more classic interplay between the *jus ad bellum* and international security issues. Key to the *jus ad bellum* for the 2003 Iraq invasion was the notion of international security, the ever-present fear of the proliferation of WMD and verification of Iraqi compliance with the 1991 UN ceasefire terms.[7] Nuclear weapons proliferation has plagued the *jus ad bellum* since the Israeli bombings of reactors in Iraq (1981) and Syria (2007)[8] to the demilitarization and denuclearization of Outer Space.[9] And so clearly, nothing evidences the strategic or security dimension of weapons development and acquisition

---

[4] UN Security Council Resolution 1973 (2011), preambular para. 4.

[5] *Ibid.*, para. 4.

[6] N.A. Canestaro, 'Legal and Policy Constraints on the Conduct of Aerial Precision Warfare', (2004) 37 *Vand. J. Transn'l L.* 431, at 475, quoting CENTCOM (US Central Command) Commander General Tommy Franks and William M. Arkin, 'An Old Fashioned Fight', *Los Angeles Times*, 12 January 2003. Note the use of carbon-graphite filaments by US forces in Kosovo in 1999 to temporarily knock out the power lines instead of using heavier bombs; H. Shue and D. Wippman, 'Limiting Attacks on Dual-Use Facilities Performing Indispensable Civilian Functions', (2001–2002) 35 *Cornell Int'l L.J.* 559, at 565.

[7] Security Council Resolutions 687 (1991) and 1441 (2002).

[8] G. Solis, *The Law of Armed Conflict: International Humanitarian Law in War* (Cambridge: Cambridge University Press, 2010), 180–185.

[9] 1967 Treaty on Principles Governing the Activities of States in the Exploration and Use of Outer Space, Including the Moon and Other Celestial Bodies, (1967) 610 *UNTS* 205.

more than nuclear weapons: the stalwart of Cold War strategies of brinkmanship and MAD, meaning that the first nuclear strike would inevitably lead to a response in kind.[10]

On the issue of the strategic nuclear deterrent, while it remains central to the US' national security strategy today, including its National Missile Defence policy, the US, also seeks battlefield supremacy; principally domination in battlefield technology such as hi-tech computerized and robotic weapons and weaponized drones, as well as information and surveillance superiority. On this point, press reports of a new 21,000 lbs US (GPS-guided) Massive Ordnance Air Blast (nicknamed 'MOAB') bomb released just days before the 2003 invasion of Iraq were clearly designed as a psychological show of firepower. Quickly followed by the US' opening offensive of 'shock and awe', with the idea of overwhelming 24/7 aerial firepower, and the battle for the psychological advantage in the Iraq conflict was undoubtedly won in the first week of battle.

Yet, in addition to overwhelming firepower and battlefield superiority, US weapons use has also managed a very carefully constructed moral posturing. As Smith observes, after having heavy criticism levelled at its tactics and weaponry employed in the Vietnam War, the US managed the media portrayal of the 1991 Gulf Conflict as the war of smart weapons and as 'the most discriminate air campaign in history', at least until it could make the same claim for the conflict in Afghanistan ten years later.[11] Since their first outing in Iraq 1990, therefore, precision-guided munitions (hereinafter 'PGMs') gained the US the moral and legal high-ground.[12] The development of PGMs revolutionized warfare and perfectly suited the legal and policy objectives of humanitarian or R2P motivations, exemplified by interventions in Kosovo and Iraq 2003. The arrival of smarter, more precise weaponry also impacted upon the *post bellum* context by reducing collateral civilian damage and, hence, the need for post-conflict reconstruction. Oddly, the development of precision weapons also gave momentum to the increasingly influential anti-landmine and anti-cluster bomb campaigns – viewed more and more as imprecise, non-discriminating weapons. A stalwart in arsenals for decades, first landmines in the 1980–1990s and then cluster bombs in the 2000s became the

---

[10] Arguably, the very notion of an 'extreme circumstance of self-defence' referred to in the 1996 *Legality of the Threat or Use of Nuclear Weapons*, Advisory Opinion, [1996] ICJ Rep. 226, at 263.

[11] See T.W. Smith, 'The New Law of War: Legitimizing Hi-Tech and Infrastructural Violence', in T. Farrell (ed.), *Security Studies: Critical Concepts in International Relations* (London: Routledge, 2010), chapter 42, 327–351, at 337, 346; *Conduct of the Persian Gulf War, Final Report to Congress Pursuant to Title V of the Persian Gulf Conflict Supplemental Authorization and Personnel Benefits Act of 1991* (Public Law 102–25), April 1992, Appendix O (1992) 31 *ILM* 615, at 623; comments of General Franks, see E. Schmitt, 'A Nation Challenged: The Military; After January Raid, Gen. Franks Promises To Do Better', *New York Times*, 8 February 2002, available at http://www.nytimes.com/2002/02/08/world/nation-challenged-military-after-january-raid-gen-franks-promises-better.html?pagewanted=all&src=pm.

[12] D.D. Jividen, '*Jus in Bello* in the Twenty First Century: Reaping the Benefits and Facing the Challenges of Modern Weaponry and Military Strategy', (2005) 8 *YIHL* 113, at 118–134; C.J. Dunlap, *Technology and the 21st Century Battlefield: Recomplicating Moral Life for the Statesman and the Soldier* (Strategic Studies Institute, US Army War College, Carlisle, 1999), at 5, available at http://www.strategicstudiesinstitute.army.mil/pubs/display.cfm?pubID=229.

subject of intense criticism leading eventually to their comprehensive prohibition; in large part due to their continuing post-deployment (and, hence, more often than not, post-conflict) civilian impact.

Weapons, therefore, play a multitude of roles even before the conflict commences, but especially as a psychological force-multiplier or strategic deterrent, as well as provocateur of arms races. During the conflict, weapons use can be portrayed as restrained, moral, superior and decisive, as well as treacherous, terrorizing, will-destroying and battle-ending (such as the US' use of nuclear weapons on Japan in 1945). But after the conflict, unexploded and toxic weapons, as well as weapons debris, remain on the battlefield as a reminder of the bloodshed, and often pose a future, continuing threat, both to the civilian population and the environment. And, as the Iraqi case (1990–2003) aptly demonstrates, issues of weapons acquisition, development and retention, viewed as a core tenet of state sovereignty, have throughout history remained central to the *jus post bellum* in the sense of disarming a defeated foe.[13]

States have traditionally maintained the monopoly on the possession of hi-tech and high-expense weapons, while non-state armed groups tend to resort to low-tech, more primitive means of warfare such as IEDs and landmines. Yet, while non-state armed groups may now boast ever more impressive arms, such as rockets, cluster bombs and even micro-drones, we should not underestimate the effectiveness of weapons such as IEDs in the asymmetries of civil wars. Probably the most worrying proliferation issue at present, however, is the weaponization of cyberspace, shifting the traditional weapons paradigm involving state versus armed group acquisition, to acquisition by anyone with a computer and sufficient technological know-how. But at the low-tech end of the spectrum, too, recent attacks have called into question existing perceptions of weapons, notably whether the aeroplanes used in the 9/11 attacks could be classified as 'weapons' for the notion of *armed* attack?

As demonstrated, weapons illustrate perfectly an impact across the full spectrum of the *jus ad*, *jus in* and *jus post bellum* as well as the notion of international peace and security. Thus, many of these issues will be returned to throughout the remainder of the chapter. The next section, however, will focus on the humanitarian principles underpinning the central *jus in bello* weapons limitations.

3. THE *JUS IN BELLO*

A. Defining 'Weapons' for the *Jus in Bello*

In the laws of armed conflict reference is made to 'weapons', but more common is the notion of 'means and methods of warfare'.[14] There would appear to be general

---

[13] Note the disarming of defeated Germany, Part V, Military, Naval and Air Clauses, 1919 Treaty of Versailles (1919) 13 *AJIL* 151 Supp.; and Roman disarmament of Carthage as a security measure in the Rome–Carthage Treaty of Peace 202 BC. See R.D. Burns, *The Evolution of Arms Control* (Santa Barbara, CA: Praeger Security International/ABC CLIO, 2009), at 20.

[14] See Article 35, 1977 Protocol Additional to the Geneva Conventions of 12 August 1949, and Relating to the Protection of Victims of International Armed Conflicts (1979) 1125 *UNTS*

consensus that 'means' of warfare refers to weapons, as well as weapons launch and delivery systems.[15] To this list Dinstein adds 'means of communications and signalling devices'.[16] Thus, 'weapons' generally refers to such things as arms, munitions, projectiles and materiel (such as chemicals in chemical weapons). 'Methods of warfare' generally refers to tactics, such as starvation, or to the way in which weapons are used'.[17] Furthermore, the draft US Law of War Manual specifies that 'means' of warfare refers only to the 'intended effects of weapons in their normal and expected use', leaving unintended uses – or 'weapons employment in a broader sense' – to the notion of 'methods of warfare'.[18] There is also the question of the weapons platform in the form of ships, tanks and aircraft. Most definitions of 'means of warfare' do not appear to include these.[19] However, for McClelland the issue is whether the equipment has 'an offensive capability that can be applied to a military object or enemy combatant'.[20] Consequently, he suggests that even a mine clearance vehicle could fall within the definition of 'means and methods of warfare'.[21]

Ultimately, while there is no definitive meaning to the various terms this vagueness does not in practice seem to cause too many problems. The combined definition of 'weapons, means and methods' thus appears sufficiently flexible to encompass new ways of harming the enemy, such as cyber weaponry or manipulations of the environment, which are clearly methods of warfare even if not means. Consequently, the notion of 'weapons' will be used here as shorthand to connote the broader notion of 'weapons, means and methods of warfare', which more accurately defines the topic under the *jus in bello*.

3-608. Note for civil wars see 1977 Protocol Additional to the Geneva Conventions of 12 August 1949, and Relating to the Protection of Victims of Non-International Armed Conflicts (1979) 1125 *UNTS* 609–699.

[15] W.H. Parks, 'Conventional Weapons and Weapons Reviews', (2006) 9 *YIHL* 55, at 118; I. Daoust, R. Coupland and R. Ishoey, 'New Wars, New Weapons? The Obligation of States to Assess the Legality of Means and Methods of Warfare', (2002) 846 *IRRC* 345, at 352; J. McClelland, 'The Review of Weapons in Accordance with Article 36 of Additional Protocol I', (2003) 850 *IRRC* 397, at 405.

[16] Y. Dinstein, *The Conduct of Hostilities Under the Law of International Armed Conflict*, 2nd edn (Cambridge: Cambridge University Press, 2010), at 1.

[17] Y. Sandoz, C. Swinarski and B. Zimmermann (eds), *International Committee of the Red Cross Commentary on the Additional Protocols of 8 June, 1977, to the Geneva Conventions of 12 August, 1949: In Collaboration with Jean Pictet* (Geneva: Martinus Nijhoff, 1987), at 621. See also Daoust *et al.*, *supra* n. 15, at 352; C. Greenwood, 'The Law of Weaponry at the Start of the New Millennium', in C. Greenwood (ed.), *Essays on War in International Law* (London: Cameron May, 2006), 223, at 223; McClelland, *supra* n. 15, at 404–405; W.H. Boothby, *Weapons and the Law of Armed Conflict* (Oxford: Oxford University Press, 2009), at 4; Parks, *supra* n. 15, at 118.

[18] As quoted in Parks, *supra* n. 15, at 118–119. The UK defines 'means' as weapons and 'methods' as tactics; see UK Ministry of Defence, *The Manual of the Law of Armed Conflict* (Oxford: Oxford University Press, 2004) (hereinafter 'UK Military Manual'), §.5.32.4.

[19] *Supra* n. 15.

[20] McClelland, *supra* n. 15, at 404–405.

[21] *Ibid.*

B. The *Jus in Bello* Rationales for Weapons Regulation

This section analyses the main *jus in bello* principles governing the legality of weapons: the rule of distinction, the prohibition on the causing of 'unnecessary suffering' and the environmental protections applicable during armed conflict. Long before states prohibited the resort to war itself, they regulated its horrors and barbarity, including limiting the destructiveness of the weapons with which war could be fought. And so Article 22 of the 1899 Second Hague Convention With Respect to the Laws and Customs of War on Land declared, albeit rather vaguely, that the right of parties in their choice of means and methods of warfare was 'not unlimited'.[22] Infamous examples of ancient weapons regulation include the attempt in 1139 by the Second Lateran Council to ban (except for use against infidels) the use of crossbows, including longbows, due to their perceived barbarity,[23] the Koran's (632) prohibition on the use of fire (except against non-believers),[24] and the Laws of Manu's (c.200 BC) prohibition on the use of barbed projectiles as 'weapons of the wicked'.[25] This fundamental concept of limiting weaponry continues today to occupy a central position within the *jus in bello*, its basis being the notion of humanity and the collective will of states to humanize warfare. Yet, the history of warfare is clearly also one characterized by some very barbaric methods of inflicting cruelty upon fellow human beings.

The following sub-sections will analyse the main *jus in bello* rules limiting weaponry design; namely, the rule of distinction (and proportionality), the prohibition on weapons causing 'unnecessary suffering or superfluous injury' and the rules governing protection of the natural environment.

i. The obligation of distinction

The rule is simply stated, as requiring that parties to a conflict must at all times distinguish between military objectives and civilian persons and objects.[26] Thus, the rule of distinction or 'discriminate warfare' requires that weapons must be designed with the capability of their effects being sufficiently targetable, meaning capable of being limited to a specific military objective (spatially and temporally). Obvious examples of indiscriminate weapons are chemical and biological weapons. This customary prohibition is echoed in Rule 71 of the Customary Humanitarian Law Study, thus '[t]he use of weapons which are by nature indiscriminate is prohibited',[27] drawn

---

[22] 26 *Martens Nouveau Recueil (ser. 2)* 949. See also Article 35(1), API.
[23] Parks, *supra* n. 15, at 62, where he recognizes that the Lateran Council lacked the authority to issue the 'ban', thus it was ignored.
[24] Burns, *supra* n. 13, at 65.
[25] L.C. Green, 'What One May Do in Combat: Then and Now', in A.J.M. Delissen and G.J. Tanja (eds), *Humanitarian Law of Armed Conflict: Challenges Ahead* (Dordrecht: Martinus Nijhoff, 1991), 269, at 269.
[26] Article 48, API. The rule undoubtedly forms part of customary international law even in non-international armed conflict. See Rule 1 in J. Henckaerts and L. Doswald-Beck, *Customary International Humanitarian Law* (Cambridge: Cambridge University Press, 2005), at 3.
[27] Henckaerts and Doswald-Beck, *supra* n. 26, at 244.

from Article 51(4) of the 1977 Additional Protocol I to the Geneva Conventions of 1949 (hereinafter 'API').[28]

It is on this rule that most treaty prohibitions are founded, many such provisions being located within the 1980 UN Convention on Prohibitions or Restrictions on the Use of Certain Conventional Weapons Which May be Deemed to Be Excessively Injurious or to Have Indiscriminate Effects (hereinafter 'CCW') and its five Protocols.[29] Examples of such civilian protections include measures limiting the use of landmines contained in Protocol II on Mines[30] and the 1996 Amended Mines Protocol,[31] as well as those mandating the removal of explosive remnants of war in Protocol V.[32] Beyond the 1980 CCW, two treaties guaranteeing significant civilian protection are the 1997 Ottawa Convention on the Prohibition of the Use, Stockpiling, Production and Transfer of Anti-Personnel Mines and on Their Destruction[33] (hereinafter 'Ottawa APM Treaty') and the 2008 Cluster Munitions Convention (hereinafter 'CMC'). However, these instruments do not specifically designate a particular weapon as 'indiscriminate' since such a determination would seem to tie the hands of non-parties under the customary rule of distinction.[34] Furthermore, few conventional weapons could be viewed as inherently indiscriminate, since most could legitimately target a distinct, clearly separate military objective.

The more pertinent question, therefore, concerns the discriminate use of weapons.[35] It is this aspect that has sparked most controversy for states using landmines and cluster munitions. When technological improvements and self-imposed buffer zones (sometimes of up to 500 metres from civilian areas[36]) failed to reduce the level of civilian casualties, it was hard to avoid the conclusion – for certain, older varieties of cluster munitions with a very high failure rate – that there had been a blurring of the

---

[28] Breach of the rule is also a war crime: Articles 8(2)(b)(i)(ii) and 8(2)(e)(i)(ii), 1998 Statute of the International Criminal Court, (1998) 37 *ILM* 999.

[29] (1980) 19 *ILM* 1523. Protocol on Non-Detectable Fragments (1980) 19 *ILM* 1529; Protocol on Prohibitions or Restrictions on the Use of Mines, Booby-Traps and Other Devices (1980) 19 *ILM* 1529; and Protocol on Prohibitions or Restrictions on the Use of Incendiary Weapons (1980) 19 *ILM* 1534; Protocol on Blinding Laser Weapons (1996) 35 *ILM* 1218; 1996 Amended Protocol II on Prohibitions or Restrictions on the Use of Mines, Booby-Traps and Other Devices (1996) 35 *ILM* 1206; and Protocol on Explosive Remnants of War, available at http://www.icrc.org/ihl.nsf/FULL/610?OpenDocument.

[30] See especially Articles 4(2), and 5–7, Protocol II on Mines.

[31] See especially Articles 3–7, Amended Mines Protocol.

[32] See especially Articles 5 and 9, Protocol V.

[33] (1997) 36 *ILM* 1507.

[34] Parks, *supra* n. 15, at 137 emphasizes that the determination is one for each state under Article 36, API.

[35] Note the Trial Chamber found the M-87 Orkan cluster munition to be an indiscriminate weapon in *Prosecutor of the Tribunal v. Milan Martic*, 12 June 2007 (IT-95-10), at para. 463, available at http://www.icty.org/x/cases/martic/tjug/en/070612.pdf; and the bombardment of the town of Tskhinvali by Georgian MLRS GRAD rockets to be an indiscriminate attack, see *Independent International Fact-Finding Mission on the Conflict in Georgia*, December 2009, Volume II, 339, available at http://www.ceiig.ch/Report.html.

[36] Human Rights Watch, *Off Target: The Conduct of the War and Civilian Casualties in Iraq* (New York: Human Rights Watch, 2003), at 80.

distinction between weapons that are inherently indiscriminate (that is however they are used) and indiscriminate use of an otherwise lawful weapon.

One step beyond the rule of distinction is the rule prohibiting excessive collateral harm to civilians and civilian property, namely the rule of proportionality.[37] Clearly, the choice of weapon used for a particular attack will be relevant to increasing or decreasing the scale of collateral harm. In this regard, technological developments, such as PGMs, have revolutionized warfare and bolstered the efficacy of the notion of proportionality: an otherwise rather vague, lop-sided rule, overly favourable to arguments of military necessity.

ii. Prohibition on 'superfluous injury or unnecessary suffering'

The prohibition on the use of weapons causing 'unnecessary suffering' reflects the aspiration of humanity in warfare, of treating one's enemy with respect even in warfare, in shunning cruel means and methods in battle. Thus, if observed, the rule should produce less animosity and revenge-mentality and so aid the transition from the *jus post bellum* to peace. The rule works by limiting unnecessary, usually crueller, effects of weapons on combatants.[38] Thus if a bullet would kill or wound the combatant the poison tip would only ensure that he suffers a cruel death.[39]

The 1868 St. Petersburg Declaration[40] captures the rationale for the rule that states had 'by common agreement fixed the technical limits at which the necessities of war ought to yield to the requirements of humanity'.[41] Those limits were set such that the objective, notably to weaken the military forces of the enemy, 'would be exceeded by the employment of arms which uselessly aggravate the sufferings of disabled men'.[42] Today the rule is found in Article 35(2) of API, such that '[i]t is prohibited to employ weapons, projectiles and material and methods of warfare of a nature to cause superfluous injury or unnecessary suffering.'[43] Recognized as the 'Guiding Principle'[44] regarding weapons use by the 2004 UK Military Manual, the rule is undoubtedly customary law in international armed conflicts.[45] Unfortunately, the rule's applicability to non-international armed conflicts remains debatable. The Customary Humanitarian

---

[37] See Article 51(5)(b), API.

[38] See General Orders No. 100, Instructions for the Government of Armies of the United States in the Field, 1863, reprinted in R.S. Hartigen, *Lieber's Code and the Law of War* (Chicago: Precedent, 1983).

[39] The UK Military Manual, *supra* n. 18, at §6.6, gives as examples of weapons causing unnecessary suffering, lances with barbed heads and bayonets with serrated edges.

[40] 1868 St. Petersburg Declaration Renouncing the Use, in Time of War, of Explosive Projectiles Under 400 Grammes Weight (1907) 1 *AJIL Supplement* 95.

[41] Ibid.

[42] Ibid.

[43] See also Article 23(e) of both the 1899 Second Hague Convention and the 1907 Hague Regulations Respecting the Laws and Customs of War on Land (1910) UKTS 9, Cd.5030.

[44] UK Military Manual, *supra* n. 18, at §6.1.

[45] The Customary Humanitarian Law Study lists the principle (in a slightly re-worded formulation to that of Article 35(2), API) as Rule 70, Henckaerts and Doswald-Beck, *supra* n. 26, at 237. See also Article 8(2)(b)(xx), 1998 ICC Statute. Note the rule was not included in APII.

Law Study suggests that the rule is customary also in non-international conflicts.[46] However, Turns and Parks both point to the lack of evidence for such a proposition, as well as disputing the *obiter dicta* proposition in the *Tadić* case[47] of the International Criminal Tribunal for the former Yugoslavia that weapons considered to be inhumane in international armed conflict must surely also be inhumane in non-international conflicts.[48] That such debate continues in the twenty-first century is surely lamentable. In applying the rule it is the designed, or intended, effects of the weapon in its normal usage that are key, since all weapons can be misused to cause additional suffering.[49] The UK Military Manual suggests that in calculating the 'legality of use of a specific weapon, it is necessary to assess; (a) its effects in battle; (b) the military task it is required to perform; and (c) the proportionality between factors (a) and (b)'.[50] In this approach it is clear that the effects of the weapon (that is the suffering) are only one factor, one part of the calculation; thus particularly horrific injuries of themselves (for example burns and blinding) are not 'unnecessary' suffering.[51] However, the prohibition is easier to state than to apply in practice. For example, what degree of additional suffering would be too high where the military utility provided by the innovation was very weighty? An additional dimension, albeit a practically impossible one for observers to apply in practice, involves a comparison between alternative available weapons. According to the rule, the use of a weapon could cause unnecessary suffering if the humanitarian *disadvantages* of using a particular weapon clearly outweigh the military advantages of using *that* weapon over any other weapon, practically available for use.[52]

Poison is subject to an ancient prohibition due to its treachery and the additional, superfluous suffering it causes.[53] Chemical and biological weapons prohibitions are

---

[46] Rule 70, Henckaerts and Doswald-Beck, *supra* n. 26, at 239. Rather erroneously the European Union's Fact-Finding Mission to Georgia considers that classification of conflicts is irrelevant, see *Fact-Finding Mission, supra* n. 35, 304. See also chapter 8 in this volume by Marko Milanovic and Hadzi-Vidanovic.

[47] *Prosecutor v. Dusko Tadić* (1996), Case no. IT-94-1 (ICTY), (1996) 35 *ILM* 32, at 64.

[48] See Parks, *supra* n. 15, at 121, who indicates the application in non-international conflict is a policy rather than law, and D. Turns, 'Weapons in the ICRC Study on Customary International Humanitarian Law', (2006) 11 *JCSL* 201, at 208–210. But see Greenwood, *supra* n. 17, at 270.

[49] UK Military Manual, *supra* n. 18, at §6.2.2.

[50] *Ibid.*

[51] Here the ICRC SIrUS project proved to be useful, at least in the sense of confirming that injuries alone are not a judge of 'unnecessary suffering'. See R.M. Coupland, 'The SIrUS Project: Towards a Determination of which Weapons Cause "Superfluous Injury or Unnecessary Suffering"', in H. Durham and T.L.H. McCormack (eds), *The Changing Face of Conflict and the Efficacy of International Humanitarian Law* (London: Martinus Nijhoff Publishers, 1999), at 99–118.

[52] See *Weapons That May Cause Unnecessary Suffering or Have Indiscriminate Effects: Report on the Work of Experts*, International Committee of the Red Cross (Geneva: ICRC, 1973), 13.

[53] Principle 16, 1863 Lieber Code. See Article 8(2)(b)(xvii)(xviii), 1998 ICC Statute.

also based on this rule.[54] There are strong arguments for including nuclear weapons too, although smaller, tactical devices may be less objectionable depending on the strength of the military utility of particular weapons. Anti-personnel exploding bullets[55] and bullets that easily deform, flatten or expand within the body are also prohibited.[56] Within the category also fall the prohibitions in Protocol I to the 1980 CCW on non-detectable fragments (such as glass), and Protocol IV on blinding laser weapons.[57] Interestingly, neither weapon actually existed at the time of its prohibition.[58] In fact, as is often the case in arms control, it is the weapons that states have little or no intention of developing and using that are subject to easy bans.[59] Finally, is the issue of anti-materiel weapons such as incendiary weapons, designed for use against armoured vehicles and fortifications, but which cause horrific burn injuries to personnel. Here the rule seems to have had mixed application by states, with some prohibiting anti-personnel use of incendiaries either specifically on the basis of the 'unnecessary suffering' rule[60] or more generally restricting use against combatants only when inside armoured vehicles.[61] Thus for anti-materiel use the rule is of more limited application, since the suffering, though inevitable to those inside the target, is balanced against a much weightier military advantage, for example in defeating an armoured tank.[62] Furthermore, Protocol III to the 1980 CCW on incendiary weapons does not prohibit anti-personnel use of incendiary weapons. Yet, the issue remains a controversial one, especially in light of recent usages of WP by the US against enemy personnel in Iraq.[63]

iii. Environmental protection

A core development in the 1970s was the recognition that weapons effects endure, often long after the conflict demanding their use has ended. Thus, steadily the *jus in*

---

[54] See, for example, the 1925 Geneva Protocol for the Prohibition of the Use in War of Asphyxiating, Poisonous or Other Gases, and of Bacteriological Methods of Warfare (1930) UKTS 24. See Article 8(2)(b)(xviii), 1998 ICC Statute.

[55] First outlawed in the now outdated St. Petersburg Declaration. See also Rule 78, Henckaerts and Doswald-Beck, *supra* n. 26, at 272.

[56] 1899 Hague Declaration (IV, 3) Concerning Expanding Bullets (1907) UKTS 32, Cd. 3751; Rule 77, Henckaerts and Doswald-Beck, *supra* n. 26, at 272. Haines queries whether their use against suicide bombers, to ensure that such persons do not survive, might remain lawful. See S. Haines, 'Weapons of Warfare', in E. Wilmshurst and S. Breau (eds), *Perspectives on the ICRC Customary International Humanitarian Law Study* (Cambridge: Cambridge University Press, 2007), 258, at 272. See Article 8(2)(b)(xix), 1998 ICC Statute.

[57] Note Parks again, that no treaty determines the weapon to cause unnecessary suffering, *supra* n. 15, at 79, and UK Military Manual, *supra* n. 18, at §6.1.2.

[58] Parks, *supra* n. 15, at 76.

[59] Note Protocol I to the 1980 CCW on non-detectable fragments, and Protocol IV on blinding laser weapons.

[60] Henckaerts and Doswald-Beck, *supra* n. 26, at 290, reporting the practice of Belgium, Colombia, Sweden and Norway.

[61] UK Military Manual, *supra* n. 18, at §6.12.6, and Henckaerts and Doswald-Beck, *supra* n. 26, at 290.

[62] For a good insight see Greenwood, *supra* n. 17, at 238–243.

[63] Captain J.T. Cobb, First Lieutenant C.A. LaCour and Sergeant First Class W.H. Hight, 'TF 2-2 IN FSE AAR: Indirect Fires in the Battle of Fallujah', *Field Artillery*, March–April 2005, 23, at 26, available at http://www.tradoc.army.mil/pao/ProfWriting/2-2AARlow.pdf.

bello rule of distinction evolved a time dimension, that weapons might be indiscriminate as to time; with landmines and cluster munitions being obvious examples. With heightened environmental awareness in the 1970s also, partly a result of US defoliation tactics in the Vietnam War, it became accepted that states should consider the longer-term consequences of weapons in and on the natural environment. Taking this point one stage further in 2003, Protocol V to the 1980 CCW tackled the issue of explosive remnants of war; imposing reliability specifications for weapons to reduce the number of unexploded remnants, as well as removal obligations.[64] Weapons law has, therefore, recognized a *jus post bellum* for some time.[65]

In the 1977 API, states included, in Articles 35(3) and 55, two provisions limiting the effects of weapons in the natural environment. These provisions impose an absolute ceiling of harm (that is even if a higher level of damage would otherwise be proportionate) on the use of methods or means of warfare intended or expected to cause 'widespread, long-term and severe' environmental damage. The 2005 Customary Humanitarian Law Study concluded that a customary rule protecting the environment during international armed conflict had formed, but this conclusion is doubted.[66] In reality, however, the specific threshold of harm has raised too many questions of application and the provisions have, as a consequence, achieved little. With the terms nominally defined to mean environmental damage on a scale of several hundred square kilometres lasting for decades, many states believe that the provisions have no application to conventional weapons.[67] Add to this the restrictions imposed by nuclear possessor states at the 1977 treaty negotiations of the non-applicability of such new rules to nuclear weapons[68] and the environmental provisions appear to be of little practical effect in prohibiting the use of any weapon.[69]

In rather poor phraseology, the Customary Humanitarian Law Study stipulates that 'destruction of the natural environment may not be used as a *weapon*'.[70] Presumably the provision is a reference to methods of warfare involving environmental modification techniques falling within the 1976 United Nations Convention on the Prohibition of Military or Any Other Hostile Use of Environmental Modification Techniques

---

[64] Articles 3, 7, 8, 9 and the Technical Annex to Protocol V.

[65] Note the removal and clean-up undertaken by states of depleted uranium ammunition; see United Kingdom Ministry of Defence, 'Depleted Uranium and the Environment', available at http://www.mod.uk/DefenceInternet/AboutDefence/WhatWeDo/HealthandSafety/Depleted Uranium/DepletedUraniumAndTheEnvironment.htm.

[66] See Rules 43–45, Henckaerts and Doswald-Beck, *supra* n. 26, at 143–158. The Study suggested it had only 'arguably' formed for non-international armed conflict.

[67] 2010 *Operational Law Handbook*, International and Operational Law Department, Judge Advocate General's Legal Center and School, United States, at 352, available at http://www.loc.gov/rr/frd/Military_Law/pdf/operational-law-handbook_2010.pdf.

[68] See the reservations of the UK and France to API, available at http://www.icrc.org/ihl.nsf/WebSign?ReadForm&id=470&ps=P.

[69] The Study concluded that the nuclear possessor states were persistent objectors to Rule 45 in its application to nuclear weapons; Henckaerts and Doswald-Beck, *supra* n. 26, at 153–155. For criticism of this view see K. Hulme, 'Natural Environment', in Wilmshurst and Breau (eds), *supra* n. 56, 204, at 233.

[70] Emphasis added. Rule 45, Henckaerts and Doswald-Beck, *supra* n. 26, at 151–158.

(hereinafter 'ENMOD').[71] Pioneered in the 1960s and 1970s during the Vietnam War, so-called rain-making techniques were prohibited if of sufficient magnitude to breach ENMOD's low scale of harm; notably 'widespread, long-lasting or serious' environmental damage.[72] Other mooted applications of ENMOD techniques in the 1970s included the rather far-fetched use of nuclear weapons to trigger earthquakes, tsunamis and volcanic eruptions to cause damage to the enemy. Consequently, while ENMOD has had little or no practical utility on the battlefield, its real significance may have been in the realm of ensuring 'superpower' security, the Soviet Union and the US being its sponsors.

C. The Effectiveness of *Jus in Bello* Weapons Regulation

That the two central rationales for limiting weapons during conflict, the rule of distinction and the prohibition on causing unnecessary suffering, continue to be fundamental to the laws of armed conflict is beyond doubt. However, are these customary rules sufficient to prohibit the use of a specific weapon? The US view appears to be that the rules are insufficient in themselves to prohibit a weapon, but that instead a specifically negotiated treaty is required, for example the 2008 CMC. Thus, under this theory, the rules are reduced to providing merely rationales for action regarding any particular weapon.[73] The effectiveness and rigour of the rules are further reduced when one considers the cumbersome procedural mechanisms created under the main weapons regime – the 1980 CCW. Indeed, it was only outside this mechanism that adoption of the 1997 Ottawa APM Treaty and the 2008 CMC were possible.

Strictly speaking, the *jus in bello* is limited to regulating conduct, including the use of weapons, during conflict.[74] Consequently, this body of law is not generally concerned with the possession and transfer of weapons.[75] However, it is usually these aspects, including the wide-scale proliferation and the misuse of weapons by such recipients, such as non-state armed groups, that causes real problems for the overarching principle of humanity. To address these pivotal issues states instead turn to more general, multilateral arms control measures, which are the subject of the following section.

---

[71] (1978) 1108 UNTS 151.

[72] Note the Understandings adopted contemporaneously with the treaty: 'widespread' means 'an area of several hundred square kilometres', 'long-lasting' means 'several months or more, or approximately a season', and 'severe' means 'severe or significant disruption or harm to human life, natural or economic resources, or other assets'. P. Fauteux, 'The Gulf War, the ENMOD Convention and the Review Conference', (1992) 18 *UNIDIR Newsl.* 6.

[73] Turns, *supra* n. 48, at 212, but see Greenwood, *supra* n. 17, at 235, and Henckaerts and Doswald-Beck, *supra* n. 26, at 242–243.

[74] With the exception being occupied territory, Article 3(b), API; Article 6, 1949 Geneva Convention Relative to the Protection of the Civilian Persons in Time of War, (1950) 75 UNTS 287.

[75] Note that states are required by Article 36, API to determine if their weaponry would breach the applicable law, but there is no further requirement on their destruction or non-acquisition once so determined.

4. WEAPONS REGULATION MORE BROADLY

A. The Evolution of Weapons Regulation

Among Burns' list of arms control categories the third refers to bilateral and multilateral reciprocal measures of seeking security through group disarmament.[76] It is here that most weapons prohibitions truly lie. Although most treaty prohibitions are based on humanitarian principles, the laws of armed conflict have little interest in weapons beyond limiting the effects of their use. Aspects of acquisition, possession or transfer of weapons are then instead perceived as arms control. On the other hand, there is more clearly a *jus post bellum* dimension even to the *jus in bello* rules, with the inclusion of environmental protections in API and the notion of conflict and its effects being a temporary phenomenon, thus eschewing longer-term impacts in general.

In Burns' third category of multilateral arms control could therefore be included the 1899 Hague Declarations prohibiting the use of balloon warfare,[77] asphyxiating gases[78] and expanding bullets,[79] weapons limitations in the 1899 and 1907 Hague Conventions on the Laws and Customs of War on Land,[80] the 1868 St. Petersburg Declaration on exploding bullets and the 1925 Geneva Gas Protocol. Giving a rather negative view of early arms control, however, is the realization that most of these treaty obligations were all too quickly abandoned when states deemed it militarily expedient to do so. States refused to adopt further obligations on balloon warfare and limitations on air warfare, for fear of losing out on such valuable weapons.[81] And all too quickly states abandoned the prohibition on poisons and gas warfare in the First World War. Not until the final years of the Vietnam War did states return to the negotiating table keen to discuss multilateral weapons prohibitions. But when they did, they now did it in a comprehensive way, such as the 1972 Convention on the Prohibition and Development, Production and Stockpiling of Bacteriological (Biological) and Toxin Weapons and Their Destruction.[82] The trend for multilateral treaty limitations clearly continues to be strong today, with similarly comprehensive prohibitions on the stockpiling and use of chemical

---

[76] Burns, *supra* n. 13, at 11–12.
[77] 1899 Declaration (IV, 1) to Prohibit, for the Term of Five Years, the Launching of Projectiles and Explosives from Balloons, and Other Methods of Similar Nature, available at http://www.icrc.org/ihl.nsf/FULL/160?OpenDocument.
[78] 1899 Hague Declaration (IV, 2) Concerning Asphyxiating Gases (1907) UKTS 32, Cd. 3751.
[79] For the 1899 Declaration (IV, 3), see *supra* n. 56.
[80] 1899 Hague Convention (II) with Respect to the Laws and Customs of War on Land and its annex: Regulations concerning the Laws and Customs of War on Land 26 Martens Nouveau Recueil (ser. 2) 949; for the 1907 Hague Convention IV, see *supra* n. 43.
[81] D.C. Watt, 'Restraints on War in the Air Before 1945', in M. Howard (ed.), *Restraints on War: Studies in the Limitation of Armed Conflict* (Oxford: Oxford University Press, 1979), 57, at 60–61.
[82] (1972) 11 *ILM* 309. Use is not specifically prohibited, but is arguably implicit in the comprehensive prohibition.

weapons,[83] anti-personnel landmines (1997 Ottawa APM Treaty) and cluster munitions (2008 CMC), in addition to the prohibitions and limitations contained in the 1980 CCW and its protocols. The 1997 Ottawa APM Treaty was a particularly important development. While the civilian harm from anti-personnel landmines (hereinafter 'APMs') had become clear in the 1990s, so too had the limitations of the CCW forum for adopting meaningful weapons limitations. Stepping outside the Geneva forum was a gamble but one that paid off, and now the use of APMs has been almost eliminated.[84] Landmines were an inexpensive, low-tech weapon and in 1994 the US estimated there to be 80–110 million littered in 64 countries 'which maim or kill an estimated 500 people every week, mostly innocent civilians'.[85] Where arms control treaties have added benefits, beyond the *jus in bello* regulations, is in the aspect of verification regimes to ensure compliance with treaty obligations. It is with this aspect firmly in mind that the next section turns to the regulation of WMD.

i. Chemical and biological weapons

Mutual distrust during the Second World War, of course, led to participating states stockpiling chemical weapons as a defensive measure. Yet, such weapons were not used. International consideration of a ban on biological and chemical weapons began again in 1968, with the final adoption of the two texts in 1972 for bioweapons and 1993 for chemical weapons.[86] While both biological and chemical weapons would today clearly fall foul of the rules of distinction and unnecessary suffering, the comprehensive treaty prohibitions go much further. The pinnacle of verification measures is provided in the 1993 Chemical Weapons Convention, which includes mandatory on-site inspections of chemical facilities to ensure that toxic chemicals are not used for prohibited purposes.[87] Of equal humanitarian concern are biological weapons, although here compliance measures are much weaker, with the US blocking verification measures at the time of adoption and despite 25 years of negotiations to strengthen the treaty. Both conventions allow for recourse to the Security Council when suspicions are raised regarding the actions of a state party,[88] clearly a valuable tool in the fight against WMD proliferation and, hence, for global security.

---

[83] 1993 Convention on the Prohibition of the Development, Production, Stockpiling and Use of Chemical Weapons and on Their Destruction, (1993) 32 *ILM* 800.

[84] International Campaign to Ban Landmines, *Landmine Monitor 2010* (Mines Action Canada, 2010), Major Findings, 1, available at http://www.the-monitor.org/lm/2010/resources/Landmine_Monitor_2010_lowres.pdf. The 2009–2010 Monitor recorded the smallest total ever of new landmine laying.

[85] *Hidden Killers: The Global Landmine Crisis 1994*, Report to the U.S. Congress on the Problem with Uncleared Landmines and the United States Strategy for Demining and Landmine Control Prepared by the Office of International Security and Peacekeeping Operations, U.S. Department of State, Washington, DC, January 1994, Executive Summary.

[86] At August 2012 the Biological Weapons Convention has 163 state parties, and the Chemical Weapons Convention 188.

[87] Articles VI and IX and the Verification Annex to the 1993 Chemical Weapons Convention. For a weaker regime see Article 8(8), 1997 Ottawa APM Treaty, and note the CMC does not contain provisions for verification.

[88] Article XII, Chemical Weapons Convention and Article VI, Biological Weapons Convention.

ii. Nuclear weapons

The limitations of the laws of armed conflict to regulate nuclear weapons use became evident when key possessor states kept them off the agenda when negotiating the 1977 API. Thus, while existing customary rules governing civilian protections, such as the rule of distinction, would continue to apply to the use of nuclear weapons,[89] new rules in the 1977 Protocol would not, including those designed to protect the environment. As a consequence, despite the use of such tactics at the negotiating conference, the use of megaton strategic nuclear weapons would generally constitute a breach of the civilian protections afforded by the customary rule of distinction. A relatively small-scale tactical device, on the other hand, might be sufficiently discriminating to remain lawful with regards to this rule, especially in naval warfare, although questions remain regarding possible breach of the rule prohibiting weapons causing 'unnecessary suffering'. If one takes the view that these rules alone are sufficient for weapons limitations, then, even in the absence of a specific treaty banning the use of nuclear weapons, most uses of nuclear weapons must surely be unlawful.

What distinguishes nuclear weapons from other WMD, therefore, is the absence of a comprehensive treaty prohibition. And following the 1996 Advisory Opinion of the International Court of Justice, which held that it could not 'reach a definitive conclusion as to the legality or illegality of the use of nuclear weapons by a State in an extreme circumstance of self-defence, in which its very survival would be at stake',[90] it cannot be said that there is a clear customary rule prohibiting all possession and uses.[91] However, arms control is not completely absent for nuclear weapons. Proliferation, that is, the transfer, acquisition and new possession of nuclear weapons, is prohibited under the 1968 Treaty on the Non-Proliferation of Nuclear Weapons.[92] Yet, the treaty's goal appears ever more illusory with North Korea's withdrawal from the treaty, key non-parties acquiring nuclear weapons (Israel, Pakistan and India), and the discovery of nuclear weapons programmes in Iraq (1991) and Libya (2003). Certainly more effective verification procedures, including environmental sampling to confirm the absence of undeclared nuclear material, are helping to create a stricter, more transparent system,[93] but with suspected programmes in Syria and Iran the regime of nuclear 'haves' and 'have-nots' is looking set to create a new arms race, this time in the Middle East.[94]

---

[89] See the *Legality of Nuclear Weapons*, supra n. 10, at 259; Sandoz *et al.*, supra n. 17, at 592–593.

[90] *Legality of Nuclear Weapons*, supra n. 10, at 263.

[91] The Customary Humanitarian Law Study's analysis of the issue is rather disappointingly short, see Henckaerts and Doswald-Beck, supra n. 26, at 255.

[92] (1968) 729 UNTS 161. See UN Security Council Resolution 1540 (2004), concerning the non-proliferation of WMD, notably to non-state actors.

[93] The International Atomic Energy Agency adopted a Model Additional Protocol to the Safeguard Agreements in 1997.

[94] See UN Security Council Resolution 1696 (2006) regarding the issue of the potential acquisition of nuclear weapons by Iran, and with regard to Syria see *Implementation of the NPT Safeguards Agreement in the Syrian Arab Republic*, GOV/2011/41, 9 June 2011, available at http://www.iaea.org/Publications/Documents/Board/2011/gov2011-41.pdf.

While international concern focuses on the global security dimension of nuclear weapons proliferation to pariah states and terrorist organizations, the bilateral relationship between the Cold War superpower rivals has remained relatively stable. Decades of bilateral negotiations, declarations and treaties have fostered a unique situation of disarmament. The most recent New START (Strategic Arms Reduction) Treaty[95] of 2010 built on previous strategic weapons limitations by further reducing stockpiles of strategic warheads,[96] but in a major advance New START contains an enhanced, on-site verification and inspection regime.[97] A major cause of confrontation, however, continues to be the US policy of National Missile Defence, viewed by Russia as a violation of the MAD strategic principle.[98] Ultimately, despite US assurances of a 'thin' shield principally designed to counteract the perceived Iranian threat, Russia fears an inevitable thickening of the shield to counter any Russian nuclear missiles.[99]

5. CONTEMPORARY WEAPONS ISSUES

For Greenwood weapons law is one of the most established areas of the laws of armed conflict, but, he suggests, it is one of the least effective.[100] The reason proffered for this position is again the failure of the law to keep pace with technological developments in weaponry.[101] Accordingly, this section will analyse five weapons of contemporary relevance to gauge the effectiveness, or otherwise, of current weapons law.

A. Cluster Munitions

Cluster munitions undoubtedly have military utility, being especially effective against mixed (hard and soft) and moving targets. However, the combination of their multiple sub-munition composition and high failure-rates led to the comprehensive prohibition in the 2008 CMC[102] of those munitions that 'cause unacceptable harm to civilians'.[103] Modelled on the 1997 Ottawa Treaty, the CMC goes far beyond the imposition of

---

[95] 2010 Treaty Between the United States of America and the Russian Federation on Measures For the Further Reduction and Limitation of Strategic Offensive Arms, US Department of State, available at http://www.state.gov/t/avc/newstart/c44126.htm. See also the Protocol and Annexes.
[96] P. Rusman, 'New START, A Preliminary Analysis', (2010) 15 *JCSL* 557, at 564.
[97] Article XI, New START, and the Protocol at Part 5, Section VI, Article 2 (for type one inspections) and Part 5, Section VII, Article 2 (for type two inspections).
[98] The US effectively terminated the 1972 Anti-Ballistic Missile Treaty ((1972) 11 *ILM* 784) when it withdrew in 2002 in order to proceed with its plans for National Missile Defence.
[99] Rusman, *supra* n. 96, at 570; Russia Activates Missile Early Warning Radar System, *BBC News*, 29 November 2011, available at http://www.bbc.co.uk/news/world-europe-15938494.
[100] Greenwood, *supra* n. 17, at 223.
[101] *Ibid*.
[102] The Convention entered into force in August 2010, and has 75 state parties, as at August 2012.
[103] Declaration, Oslo Conference on Cluster Munitions, 22–23 February 2007, available at http://www.regjeringen.no/upload/UD/Vedlegg/Oslo%20Declaration%20(final)%2023%20February%202007.pdf.

technical specifications for cluster munitions, such as those contained in the 2003 Protocol V to the 1980 CCW on Explosive Remnants of War, and self-imposed 'non-use zones'.[104] Yet, the CMC is also far more than a comprehensive arms control treaty; it focuses on the protection of cluster munition victims: a true *jus post bellum* weapons issue.

Relevant to the *jus post bellum* debate is the continuing threat of injury to civilians caused by legacy weapons: unexploded weapons and toxic[105] debris remaining in harm's way after the conflict has ended. Consequently, post-conflict rehabilitation and reconstruction was a core aim of the CMC, which achieves this in two pivotal ways: first, back-dating the clearance obligations for user states to cover weapons used by those states even before the adoption of the treaty,[106] and, secondly, mandatory state assistance to victims. The definition of 'cluster munition victims' is broad, and includes those suffering psychological as well as physical injury, those killed and those suffering economic loss, social marginalization or substantial impairment of their rights caused by the use of cluster munitions, as well as affected families and communities.[107] Article 5 requires a national plan and budget for victim assistance, with consultation of victim groups on policies to be developed to meet their needs. International assistance is also required of those states 'in a position to do so', which are to 'adequately provide age- and gender-sensitive assistance' including medical care, rehabilitation and psychological support, as well as for their social and economic inclusion.[108] Consequently, demonstrating a continual, shifting approach in arms control treaties, the language used in the CMC is more emotional and personal to the victims, and the obligations more stringent, than that found in the earlier 1997 Ottawa APM Treaty. Although certain hi-tech munitions remain permissible under the CMC,[109] the definitional minefield has not been so successfully negotiated in the parallel CCW discussions. Since core user states refuse to ratify the CMC, the parallel, slower negotiations under the CCW regime could prove vital in ensuring cluster munitions use is more widely prohibited. Yet, disappointingly, the latest CCW draft protocol omits from its definition of cluster munitions those with a failure rate of 1 per cent or below 'across the range of intended operational environments'.[110] Thus, even the draft protocol's comprehensive prohibition on older cluster munitions (that is those that pre-date 1980) is subject to this major

---

[104] Human Rights Watch, *supra* n. 36.
[105] Note the continuing controversy over the use of depleted uranium ammunition by NATO in the 2011 Libyan intervention.
[106] Article 4(4), CMC.
[107] See Article 2, CMC.
[108] Article 6(7), CMC.
[109] See Article 2(3)(9)(10), CMC and M. Hiznay, 'Operational and Technical Aspects of Cluster Munitions', United Nations Institute for Disarmament Research, Disarmament Forum, No. 4, 2006, available at http://www.unidir.org/pdf/articles/pdf-art2530.pdf for existing weapons which may remain lawful. J. Borrie, 'The "Long Year": Emerging International Efforts to Address the Humanitarian Impacts of Cluster Munitions, 2006–2007', (2007) 10 *YIHL* 251, at 270.
[110] Draft Protocol VI to the 1980 CCW on cluster Munitions, 21 August 2011, available at http://www.unog.ch/80256EDD006B8954/%28httpAssets%29/65A1309ABEE8EF50C125792C0033A369/$file/ConfIV_PVI+draft_110826-B.pdf, Technical Annex A, para. 5.

limitation.[111] Clearly, while proving such a low operational failure rate could be problematic for user states, particularly since previous official figures have been shown to be false,[112] there is also concern that such a lower standard of reliability might contradict 'norms enshrined in the CMC'.[113] Ultimately, however, the problem remains of reluctant states such as Russia, which argues that stockpile destruction would be too expensive to implement,[114] and the US and others that view cluster munitions as having clear military utility.[115]

B. Improvised Explosive Devices

IEDs are certainly not a new phenomenon in warfare. Deployed since the Second World War, today their use is largely confined to insurgent, or non-state armed groups such as the Viet Cong in the Vietnam War, the Irish Republican Army in Northern Ireland and the Tamil Tigers in Sri Lanka.[116] In the Afghanistan conflict which commenced in 2001, the use of anti-vehicle IEDs (so-called 'roadside bombs') has caused more casualties among US troops than any other weapon,[117] making them an effective and inexpensive weapon, as well as causing high numbers of civilian casualties.[118]

An IED is simply a 'home made' explosive device; it can, for example, involve an explosive device strapped to an existing munition, possibly an abandoned munition or one that failed to explode (so-called explosive remnants of war).[119] Such bombs can therefore be extremely diverse in design, including car and truck bombs, roadside bombs, fertilizer bombs, pipe bombs and even so-called dirty bombs, containing chemical and nuclear material. They can be 'victim activated' – and so are akin to mines or booby traps – 'time activated' or 'command activated', usually by remote

---

[111] Draft Articles 4(1) and 7(1) comprehensively prohibit those manufactured before 1980.

[112] C. King, O. Dullum and G. Østern, 'M85 – An Analysis of Reliability', Norwegian People's Aid, Norway, 2007, available at http://www.stopclustermunitions.org/wp/wp-content/uploads/2008/07/m85-analysis-of-reliability-npa.pdf, the study suggests consistent evidence of a failure rate of about 10%.

[113] As suggested in the Alternative Protocol text put forward by Norway, Mexico and Austria in August 2011, CCW/GGE/2011-III/WP.1/Rev.1, available at http://daccess-dds-ny.un.org/doc/UNDOC/GEN/G11/632/80/PDF/G1163280.pdf?OpenElement.

[114] Cluster Munition Monitor 2010 (Mines Action Canada 2010), at 240.

[115] Ibid., 260–266.

[116] C. Kopp, 'Technology of Improvised Explosive Devices', Defence Today, 46–49, available at http://www.ausairpower.net/DT-IED-1007.pdf .

[117] T. Vanden Brook, 'IED Attacks Increase Outside of Afghanistan, Iraq', USA Today, 19 October 2011, available at http://www.usatoday.com/news/military/story/2011-10-19/ied-use-increasing/50831988/1.

[118] 'Afghan Civilian Deaths Rise, Insurgents Responsible for Most Casualties – UN', UN News Centre, 14 July 2011, available at http://www.un.org/apps/news/story.asp?NewsID=39036.

[119] Mr. Reto Wollenmann, Food-for-Thought Paper, Discussion Paper 1, Improvised Explosive Devices (IEDs), 2009 Group of Experts of the States Parties to the CCW Amended Protocol II, available at http://www.unog.ch/80256EDD006B8954/(httpAssets)/073D1F307686E69CC12575830049422B/$file/DP1+IED+food+for+thought.pdf.

control using a mobile phone or detonator. And recent developments in IED design have produced armour-piercing capability in Explosively Formed Penetrator IEDs (hereinafter 'EFPs') which fire a shaped charge at high velocity when detonated. Accordingly, EFPs remain effective at greater distances (apparently up to 50 metres) from the target.[120]

Improvised explosive devices are not a prohibited weapon *per se*. Thus, it is not their 'improvised' or homemade character that causes legality issues, but their specific design and targeting. As regards the use of manually emplaced IEDs, these fall within the definition of 'other devices' for Protocol II on mines[121] and the Amended Mines Protocol.[122] Depending on their design and construction, IEDs could also fall within the definition of 'booby traps'[123] and mines (either anti-vehicle or anti-personnel mines) and thus are regulated by the 1997 Ottawa Treaty ban and both Protocol II of the CCW and the Amended Mines Protocol. Vitally all three instruments are applicable in non-international armed conflicts, where non-state armed groups will be the predominant users.[124] The definition of mines was purposefully drafted to be broad, and stipulates that 'any munition' may be a mine provided that it is 'placed under, on or near the ground or other surface area' and if its design is to be 'exploded by the presence, proximity or contact of a person or vehicle'.[125]

Thus, if the IED fulfils the definition of APMs their use will be prohibited by the 1997 Ottawa Treaty, while the Amended Mines Protocol requires that they be detectable,[126] comply with self-deactivation and self-destruction requirements,[127] and their location recorded. Finally, parties laying such devices bear the obligation to clear, remove and destroy them.[128] Unfortunately such compliance is highly unlikely for an improvised weapon. Furthermore, for civilians, the general prohibition on indiscriminate use of such devices remains applicable, and regarding 'booby traps' the Amended Mines Protocol rules out the use of, *inter alia*, animal carcasses, 'apparently harmless portable objects' such as the cola cans used in Vietnam and children's toys.[129] More likely, however, is the use of roadside bombs, otherwise known as anti-vehicle IEDs (akin to anti-vehicle mines (hereinafter 'AVMs')). Here, however, regulation is sparse, limiting only the use of remotely delivered AVMs.[130] Of course, the general prohibition on weapons causing unnecessary suffering would clearly prohibit the use of IEDs containing such things as particles of broken glass (as non-detectable fragments) and,

---

[120] Kopp, *supra* n. 116, at 2.
[121] Article 2(3), Protocol II on mines.
[122] Article 2(5), Amended Mines Protocol.
[123] Article 2(4), Amended Mines Protocol, and Article 2(2), Protocol II.
[124] Article 2(1), Amended Mines Protocol, Article 1(1), Ottawa Treaty, and 2001 Amendment Article 1 to the 1980 CCW, available at http://www.icrc.org/ihl.nsf/FULL/600?OpenDocument.
[125] Article 2(1), Amended Mines Protocol.
[126] Article 4, Amended Mines Protocol.
[127] Articles 4 and 5, and the Technical Annex, to Amended Mines Protocol.
[128] Articles 3(2), 9 and 10, Amended Mines Protocol.
[129] Article 7, Amended Mines Protocol.
[130] See Article 6, Amended Mines Protocol.

of course, toxic and poisonous chemicals such as IEDs reportedly used in Iraq (2003).[131]

If states are unwilling to regulate AVMs (and therefore anti-vehicle IEDs), reducing the access of armed groups to key components of IEDs could clearly go a long way to reducing the threat of IEDs.[132] Thus, delegates in the CCW forum have placed emphasis on existing obligations requiring the clearance, removal and destruction of unexploded and abandoned ordnance,[133] as well as tightening controls over unsecured weapons stockpiles.[134]

C. White Phosphorus

The chemical known as white phosphorus burns at approximately 815°C.[135] It burns intensely and on contact with human skin causes severe and persistent chemical burning.[136] However, the military utility of WP is argued not to be its incendiary capability of setting fire to other objects, but its capability of setting fire to itself (its pyrophoric properties) to act as an illuminant (a flare) to mark a target, or to create a dense white smoke which acts as an obscurant to provide cover for troops in daylight.[137] This point is known as the 'primary purpose' argument and its intended effect is to keep WP shells beyond the remit of Protocol III to the 1980 CCW on incendiary weapons.[138]

The added value of WP is that it blocks infra-red optics and weapons-tracking systems whereas ordinary smoke munitions do not, thus increasing WP's military utility in evading enemy tracing mechanisms.[139] Even used legitimately as an obscurant or illuminant, however, its use in populated areas of Gaza in 2009 by Israeli forces

---

[131] Article 3(3), Amended Mines Protocol. See the reported use of chlorine IEDs in Iraq in C. Parsons, 'Chlorine Bombs Mark New Guerrilla Tactics: U.S.', *Reuters*, 22 February 2007, available at http://www.reuters.com/article/2007/02/22/us-iraq-idUSKRA14854020070222.

[132] R. Wollenmann, *Improvised Explosive Devices (IEDs)*, Report by the Friend of the President, 19 October 2009, CCW/AP.II/CONF.11/2, at para. 13, available at http://daccess-dds-ny.un.org/doc/UNDOC/GEN/G09/641/76/PDF/G0964176.pdf?OpenElement; R. Wollenmann, *Improvised Explosive Devices*, CCW/AP.II/CONF.12/3, at para. 6, available at http://www.unog.ch/80256EDD006B8954/(httpAssets)/9D351066DC9A78B4C12577E00064355C/$file/Report+APII+Coordinator+on+IED+(Draft).pdf.

[133] Articles 3, 7 and 8, 2003 Protocol V to the 1980 CCW on Explosive Remnants of War.

[134] See Human Rights Watch, 'Libya: Transitional Council Failing to Secure Weapons, Stockpiles of Surface-to-Air Missiles, Other Arms Found Unguarded', 25 October 2011, available at http://www.hrw.org/news/2011/10/25/libya-transitional-council-failing-secure-weapons?tr=y&auid=9766287.

[135] It is difficult to place WP within the prohibition on chemical weapons. See I.J. MacLeod and A.P.V. Rogers, 'The Use of White Phosphorus and the Law of War', (2007) 10 *YIHL* 75, and the Chemical Weapons Convention, Article II for the definition.

[136] Human Rights Watch, *Rain of Fire: Israel's Unlawful Use of White Phosphorus in Gaza*, 2009, at 3, available at http://www.hrw.org/reports/2009/03/25/rain-fire-0.

[137] MacLeod and Rogers, *supra* n. 135, at 76. See also Boothby, *supra* n. 17, at 244–246, and D.P. Fidler, 'The Use of White Phosphorus Munitions by U.S. Military Forces in Iraq', *ASIL Insight*, 2005, available at http://www.asil.org/insights051206.cfm.

[138] Note the definition of incendiary weapon for Protocol III at Article 1(1)(b)(i).

[139] Human Rights Watch, *supra* n. 136, at 4.

sparked severe controversy, particularly its use during the day when there would be little need to block night vision capabilities.[140] During *Operation Cast Lead* the Israeli WP smoke projectile shells contained 116 felt wedges dipped in white phosphorus.[141] Thus, hundreds of burning fragments were scattered over Gaza,[142] prompting accusations of the use of indiscriminate weapons as two hospitals and a UN compound were set on fire.[143] Even without the 'reckless use' of WP,[144] certainly in air-delivered or artillery form, its use in built-up areas surely calls into question observance of fundamental rules of distinction. Israel argues that WP is not a weapon but an obscurant, and thus not subject to the rules of targeting.[145] However, some definitions of means and methods would appear broad enough to include obscurants due to their offensive capability, and certainly the use of WP obscurants in a heavily populated area would appear to violate civilian protections demanded by the rules on 'precautions in attack'.[146] Since alternative obscurants are available with no similar civilian threat, its use in populated areas must be highly questionable. The 2009 Goldstone Report of the UN Fact-Finding Mission on the Gaza Conflict called for a complete ban on the use of WP.[147] On the other hand, Human Rights Watch advocates an alternative, effects-based approach to WP, and has urged state parties to the CCW to re-visit Protocol III on incendiary weapons with an amendment to this effect.[148]

Yet, what of the use of white phosphorus in a clear-cut military setting with no civilian presence? The first question is whether WP is an incendiary weapon. The US argues that it is not, since it is not 'primarily designed to set fire to objects or to cause burn injury to persons'.[149] Furthermore, that Protocol III to the 1980 CCW should include restrictions on uses against military personnel was not the subject of agreement

---

[140] *Ibid.*

[141] *Ibid.*; the figure was said to be 160 wedges per shell according to *Human Rights in Palestine and Other Occupied Arab Territories: Report of the United Nations Fact-Finding Mission on the Gaza Conflict*, Human Rights Council, A/HRC.12/48, 25 September 2009, at 194 (hereinafter 'Goldstone Report').

[142] Human Rights Watch estimates the footprint to be of the magnitude of a 125 metre radius, see Human Rights Watch *supra* n. 136, at 3.

[143] Goldstone Report, *supra* n. 141 at 194–196. See also the response by the Israeli Defence Force that targeting was undertaken in line with the necessary precautions, see *The Operation in Gaza, 27 December 2008–18 January 2009: Factual and Legal Aspects*, Israeli Ministry of Foreign Affairs, July 2009, at paras 330–335, 341–355, 370–376, 405–430, available at http://www.mfa.gov.il/MFA/Terrorism-+Obstacle+to+Peace/Hamas+war+against+Israel/Operation_in_Gaza-Factual_and_Legal_Aspects.htm.

[144] This was the opinion expressed in the Goldstone Report, *supra* n. 141, at 195.

[145] Israeli Ministry of Foreign Affairs Report, *supra* n. 143, at 416.

[146] Article 57, API, states that '[i]n the conduct of military operations, constant care shall be taken to spare the civilian population, civilians and civilian objects'.

[147] The Goldstone Report, *supra* n. 141, at 196, refers to a prohibition on its use as an obscurant. Note recent uses also in Lebanon and Somalia.

[148] Human Rights Watch, *Strengthening the Humanitarian Protection of Protocol III on Incendiary Weapons: Memorandum to Convention on Conventional Weapons (CCW) Delegates*, 22 August 2011, available at http://www.hrw.org/news/2011/08/22/strengthening-humanitarian-protections-protocol-iii-incendiary-weapons.

[149] Article 1(1), PIII, 1980 CCW.

at the negotiations.[150] Thus, the US, among others, does not absolutely rule out the anti-personnel use of WP even as an incendiary weapon, for example on the grounds of 'unnecessary suffering'.[151] The authors of the Customary Humanitarian Law Study partly concur in this conclusion, evidencing a customary prohibition on the anti-personnel use of incendiary weapons 'unless it is not feasible to use a less harmful weapon to render a person *hors de combat*'.[152] Thus, while it proved to be an embarrassing climb-down for the US having to correct its previous denials of use against Iraqi personnel, the use of WP by US forces in smoking insurgents out of trenches in Fallujah in 2004 would not appear to have been unlawful.[153] Consequently, the UK's position in prohibiting the use of WP 'directly against personnel' is arguably going beyond the current requirements of the law[154] although it raises questions as to whether the US and Israeli positions will remain tenable for much longer.[155]

D. Drones and Robots

Computerization of weapons and surveillance systems has revolutionized war-fighting. From unmanned aerial vehicles (so-called UAVs or drones) with mere surveillance capability to weaponized drones (unmanned combat aerial vehicles) and automated weapons systems (robots) that can act as sentry, there is criticism that hi-tech warfare is becoming too detached from the theatre of battle.[156] The psychological and physical distance from the battlefield of the operators of these robots and drones, able to extinguish human life from thousands of miles away safe from harm, is a concern. Fears centre on this perceived psychological 'impersonalization of battle'[157] for the

---

[150] Parks, *supra* n. 15, at 78.

[151] *Ibid.*

[152] Rule 85, Henckaerts and Doswald-Beck, *supra* n. 26, at 289. For criticism of this conclusion see Haines, *supra* n. 56, at 276.

[153] The US had to retract an earlier denial of anti-personnel use of WP in Iraq when its officers wrote an account of such use in an army magazine. See Cobb *et al.*, *supra* n. 63, at 26.

[154] UK Military Manual, *supra* n. 18, at §6.12.6, although use against armoured vehicles, for example, with persons inside, is acceptable.

[155] The US ratified Protocol III in 2009 but its reservation allowing the use of incendiary weapons 'against military objectives located in concentrations of civilians where it is judged that such use would cause fewer casualties and/or less collateral damage than alternative weapons' has courted incompatibility objections by 16 states, and a narrow reading by the UK regarding use only against biological weapons facilities where the extremely high temperatures of incendiary weapons are required to destroy the toxins. See the UN Treaty Database, available at http://treaties.un.org/pages/ViewDetails.aspx?src=TREATY&mtdsg_no=XXVI-2&chapter=26&lang=en.

[156] See P.W. Singer, *Wired For War: The Robotics Revolution and Conflict in the 21st Century* (London: Penguin Books, 2009).

[157] The notion was first coined by historian John Keegan. See J. Keegan, *The Face of Battle* (London: Jonathan Cape, 1976), at 320. See also D. Grossman, *On Killing: The Psychological Cost of Learning to Kill in War and Society* (Boston: Little, Brown and Company, 1996), and Statement by Dr. Jacob Kellenberger, 'International Humanitarian Law and New Weapon Technologies', 34th Round Table on Current Issues of International Humanitarian Law, San Remo, 8 September 2011, available at http://www.icrc.org/eng/resources/documents/statement/new-weapon-technologies-statement-2011-09-08.htm.

distant operators and the potential for greater abuses of humanitarian law.[158] On the other hand, Lewis posits that the 'sanitary environment' in the drone control room, far removed from the stressful life-threatening pressures of flying in the airspace above hostile territory, actually allows for a calmer assessment and better decision-making and thus compliance with the rules on distinction and proportionality.[159] However, questions remain as to when there is a systems error or glitch, common among computerized technology, that leads a drone or robot to malfunction, killing civilians.[160] Furthermore, it is unclear as to whether machines can commit war crimes or whether new war crimes need to be designed for those that employ such weapons.

Robots, or unmanned ground vehicles, are increasingly being deployed in combat zones to perform a multitude of functions, including a large dog-like robot to carry equipment and machines that perform reconnaissance and surveillance tasks, chemical detection, IED detection and bomb disposal, as well as weaponized robots. As for robotic weapons systems such as those that stand guard or sentry and fire on approaching enemies, concerns have been raised regarding their ability to comply with the rules on distinction. Yet, it could be questioned whether this is simply another example of hi-tech systems coming in for greater scrutiny than their dumber counterparts. It surely all boils down to the role assigned to them. If robotic sentries are nothing more than hi-tech booby traps, then the limited regulations applicable would prohibit their utilization of a perfidious or otherwise inappropriate 'apparently harmless object'.[161] And so if such robotic sentries are capable of issuing warnings and requests for surrender, can shoot to wound, can use non-lethal bullets, and can refrain from firing in some circumstances (for example when they detect a non-threatening presence such as an unarmed person), then they seem far removed from the brutal simplicity of a perfectly legal booby trap. Consequently, here the key to legality would be in the precautions in attack undertaken to ensure that the positioning or locating of the sentries was such as to ensure against disproportionate civilian casualties.[162] Before such robots could be used in a greater combat role, including in scenarios more akin to a real soldier where the robot makes the determination of distinction, then certainly the ability of acting in a discriminating manner becomes vital. Accordingly, Jacob Kellenberger, President of the International Committee of the Red Cross, has suggested that the deployment of such robotic systems would entail a 'paradigm shift and a major qualitative change in the conduct of hostilities'.[163] Again he expresses similar ethical and societal concerns raised by the use of robots as previously for drones.[164]

The physical separation of the operator from the theatre of battle also raises concerns regarding the limits of the battlespace, effectively turning the US operator into a

---

[158] Kellenberger, *supra* n. 157.
[159] M.W. Lewis, 'Drones and the Boundaries of the Battlefield', (2012) 47(2) *TILJ* 293–413, at 298.
[160] R. Norton-Taylor and R. Evans, 'The Terminators: Drone Strikes Prompt MoD to Ponder Ethics of Killer Robots', *The Guardian*, 17 April 2011, available at http://www.guardian.co.uk/world/2011/apr/17/terminators-drone-strikes-mod-ethics.
[161] Articles 2(2) and 6, Amended Mines Protocol.
[162] Article 57, API and Article 3(7)–(11), Amended Mines Protocol.
[163] Kellenberger, *supra* n. 157.
[164] *Ibid.*

legitimate military target in the control room in the Nevada Desert.[165] Additional, *jus ad bellum* issues are raised where a state targets persons or objectives inside another (presumably neutral) state. This issue is, of course, probably the most controversial international law topic of the past few years, namely that of targeted killings. Drones have undoubtedly made such attacks easier, being extremely effective in both surveillance and targeting.[166] Thus, in both the *jus ad bellum* and *jus in bello* senses, drones appear to be causing the 'hot battlefield' zone to expand geographically, meaning that the battlefield is becoming much more of a movable target.[167] Such a development will undoubtedly impact upon human rights law and the *jus ad bellum*, especially when non-state armed groups and terrorists acquire such technology.

E. Cyber Warfare

With global incidents of cybercrime on the increase and notions of cyber security and cyber terrorism infiltrating the language of Governments, it was only a matter of time before cyber warfare became a reality.[168] However, hacking into government files or systems could fit within any of the above scenarios. The question is when it becomes a means or method of warfare.

Clearly if an armed conflict is on-going any belligerent use of cyberspace would need to fulfil the criteria for a lawful attack, including compliance with the principles of distinction and proportionality. Knocking out military information or surveillance systems, or power to a military facility, would clearly fulfil the notion of attacking a military objective, but there are concerns that much of the computer and information servers in use by the military are also heavily reliant on and linked with civilian usage.[169] Of particular concern as potential collateral harm are civilian chemical and energy industries, for example nuclear power stations and dams.[170]

Carried out in a controlled way a computerized attack on a nuclear power plant could fulfil the promise of a 'bloodless' weapon, as many perceive cyberwarfare to be,[171] in

---

[165] Article 52(2), API.

[166] Certain drones can remain in flight for 30 hours, making them very effective in following moving targets such as a person. See Lewis, *supra* n. 159, at 296–297.

[167] This is not to suggest that military objectives could not be targeted in a state not taking part in the armed conflict, see Lewis, *ibid.*, at 312–313, and ICRC, 'Interpretative Guidance on the Notion of Direct Participation in Hostilities under International Humanitarian Law', for the notions of 'direct participation in hostilities' (Sections IV–VII) and 'continuous combat functions', available at http://www.icrc.org/eng/resources/documents/publication/p0990.htm.

[168] According to some sources, Russia used cyber-weapons in its conflicts against Chechen insurgents during 1999–2000 and with Georgia in 2008. See M. Roscini, 'World Wide Warfare – Jus Ad Bellum and the Use of Cyber Force', (2010) 14 *Max Planck Yearbook of United Nations Law* 85, at 90.

[169] Note the concept of the 'reverberating effects' of attacks on so-called 'dual use' facilities. See M.N. Schmitt, 'Future War and the Principle of Discrimination', (1999) *ISR. Y.B. ON HUM. RTS.* 51, at 80.

[170] Note Articles 56, API and 15, APII on the protection of dams, dykes and nuclear electrical generating facilities.

[171] Dunlap, *supra* n. 12, at 10.

that it could be extremely precise in cutting the electrical energy output to the grid.[172] Thus, such weapons could clearly be advantageous to both defending and attacking parties, reducing or eliminating the number of military and civilian casualties. Of greater concern, therefore, is probably the situation in non-international armed conflict where a non-state armed group might gain great advantage over government forces in using relatively cheap cyber 'weaponry'. The concern is clearly driven by the realization that cyber weaponry could cause large-scale civilian harm (for example the release of poisonous gases from industrial facilities) coupled with the generalization that non-state groups tend to have little regard for civilian life or the laws of armed conflict.

The ICRC has warned that self-replicating 'worms' that cannot be controlled may not be sufficiently discriminatory in their effects, in terms of both time and spatial impacts.[173] In consequence some have suggested similar technological fixes for cyber weapons as exist for their tangible brethren, notably self-destruct and self-deactivation features as mandated for landmines and cluster munitions.[174] However, General Michael V. Hayden (retired) of the US Airforce questions whether cyber arms control will ever be possible.[175] On the other hand, he also asks whether certain methods of attack are ever justified.[176] He specifically refers to 'distributed denial of service attacks' and botnets.[177]

How soon cyber arms control agreements, prohibiting the use of a specific cyber method or weapon, will become a reality is not clear at present, but there is little reason to believe that such weapons will escape regulation. States may prefer at present to shore up their defensive capability, particularly while they figure out the capabilities of such techniques. Yet, as with all new weapons, battlefield advantage is often fleeting and quite quickly gives way to insecurity or stalemate. On one level cyber weaponry could be analogized alongside many other weapons, capable of being discriminate and possibly precision guided. On the other hand, it is also possible to envisage cyber weaponry as more akin to nuclear weapons, having a greater strategic security dimension rather than a mere battlefield presence. Developments may be slow as these potentialities are worked through. Certainly one expert, Major General Charles Dunlap (retired) formerly of the US Airforce, has expressed his hesitancy for a new instrument

---

[172] In 2010 the Stuxnet worm was reportedly used to target the Iranian nuclear programme. See C.C. Demchak and P. Dombrowski, 'Rise of a Cybered Westphalian Age', (2011) 5 *SSQ* 32, at 32.
[173] C. Droege, 'No Legal Vacuum in Cyber Space', 16 August 2011, available at http://www.icrc.org/eng/resources/documents/interview/2011/cyber-warfare-interview-2011-08-16.htm. The ICRC also reminds states of the requirements of Article 36, API and the necessary precautions in attack under Article 57, API.
[174] B. Schneier, 'It Will Soon Be Too Late To Stop The Cyberwars', *Financial Times*, 2 December 2010, available at http://www.ft.com/cms/s/0/f863fb4c-fe53-11df-abac-00144feab49a.html#axzz1uNpVREwm.
[175] M.V. Hayden, 'The Future of Things "Cyber"', (2011) 5 *SSQ* 3, at 6.
[176] *Ibid.*
[177] *Ibid.* A botnet is a network of infected computers which carry the bot author's malware and usually engage in stealing passwords, logging keystrokes or diffusing viruses to other linked machines or accounts.

or even definitional guidance, fearing that any such move will create a 'legal impediment' for US forces, and thus the possibility of losing the cyber arms race.[178]

While the established rules of the *jus in bello* appear to be more than capable of dealing with cyber weaponry, the more vexing legal issues pertain to the *jus ad bellum*, and especially the notion of when an *armed* attack can be said to have occurred for Articles 2(4) and 51 of the UN Charter.[179] Problematic for the law will be the question of the commencement of an 'attack', its 'armed' nature, its 'scale and effects' and, ultimately, its perpetrator.[180] Clearly, without attribution to a state (or to persons within the territory of a state) for such an attack, Article 2(4) is not activated.[181] Worrying, therefore, is the fact that, unlike any other weapon, the perpetrators of cyber attacks can be almost impossible to trace.

6. CONCLUSIONS

The 1868 St. Petersburg Declaration is the epitome of arms control. Based on the cruelty of that weapon's (notably explosive projectiles under 400g in weight) effects on combatants, as well as more practical reasons of affordability of the weapon by Russia and the broader, balance of power dimension, the treaty prohibited a weapon which quickly became outdated due to technological developments on the battlefield. Yet, the humanitarian principles enshrined in the treaty have stood the test of time.

All three dimensions of *jus in*, *jus ad* and *jus post bellum* clearly influence and are influenced by the topic of weapons. While the Cold War period emphasized the *jus ad bellum* and the broader security dimension of nuclear weapons and nuclear deterrence (including in Outer Space and the notion of National Missile Defence), over the last few years the *jus in bello* emphasis has been firmly rooted at the other end of the spectrum – on the lingering post-conflict effects of weapons and weapons debris. Such longer-term concerns have altered the rule on distinction, broadening the range of weapons effects beyond the immediate, and have generated humanitarian protections for the natural environment. Yet, there is much room for criticism of the *jus in bello* principles. Baxter's reference to the principles being vague is particularly true for the 'unnecessary suffering' rule, which as a consequence forms the basis of very few weapons bans.[182] While civilian protection, in the form of the rule of distinction, forms a much more solid basis of weapons limitation, it too has proven dependent upon the will of states to prohibit a militarily useful weapon in the face of overwhelming civilian harm. In an age of hi-tech, low-casualty warfare, of precision weaponry and so-called

---

[178] C.J. Dunlap, 'Perspectives for Cyber Strategists on Law for Cyberwar', (2011) 5 *SSQ* 81, at 83.

[179] See Roscini, *supra* n. 168.

[180] See M.N. Schmitt, 'Computer Network Attack and the Use of Force in International Law: Thoughts on a Normative Framework', (1998–1999) 37 *Colum. J. Transnat'l L.* 885; M.C. Waxman, 'Cyber-attacks and the Use of Force: Back to the Future of Article 2(4)', (2011) 36 *Yale J. Int'l L.* 421. See also chapter 6 in this volume by Dino Kritsiotis on self-defence.

[181] Article 11, 2001 Articles on Responsibility of States for Internationally Wrongful Acts, annexed to General Assembly Resolution 56/83, 12 December 2001.

[182] Baxter, *supra* n. 1.

'bloodless' warfare, one weapon stands out as being wholly inconsistent with a 21st century notion of humanity in warfare: white phosphorus. Here, the central principles of the *jus in bello*, especially the balancing exercise demanded by the 'unnecessary suffering' rule, as well as the protections afforded to civilians, appear at their weakest in the face of such clear cruelty. And so the limits and compromises of treaty negotiations are most evident when user states are able to dictate the terms of any resultant prohibition. Ultimately, then, the real tensions in this area of the law are not between weapons and the rules regulating their use, but between the views of states (or at least their militaries) and the views of civil society as regards the true effects of a weapon, and how it should consequently be categorized.

With landmines and cluster munitions great legal advances were achieved in the form of comprehensive treaty prohibitions, not only on use but also acquisition, retention and, most importantly, transfer to non-party states and non-state armed groups. Such achievements were only possible outside the established CCW forum, where key sponsoring states were able to avoid some of the negative influences of recalcitrant user states on the treaty text. And evident again was the value of civil society in driving these debates forward, as it has so often done since Solferino; witnessing firsthand the cruelty of weapons on the battlefield, collecting the evidence and, ultimately, of holding those to justice who breach the rules. Of course, weapons laws need to be realistic, as states will not ratify if they are not, but, as many authors observe, much time and energy has been expended to date negotiating treaty prohibitions for weapons that did not exist and were never going to exist. Thus, weapons regulation is often a very fine balance to be struck. How it will develop in the future is probably not so difficult to predict: future weapons are as likely to test the application of core humanitarian principles as current weapons, but so too the will of states, and civil society will undoubtedly meet the challenge with further regulation.

10. Targets

*David Turns**

> The Prime Minister: The difficulty [with military objectives] arises when one of the forces engaged in aerial warfare, being accused of deliberate bombing of civilians, deny that they were bombing civilians or that it was deliberate, and allege that they were in pursuit of military objectives. Again, what is a military objective? Surely these are not matters which can be passed over as if they were of no importance. Suppose a church is used as the headquarters of a division. Is that a military objective or is it not?
>
> S.O. Davies: It depends upon what side it is on.[1]

1. INTRODUCTION

It is entirely uncontroversial to assert, in the early 21st century, that the principles and rules of the *jus in bello* relating to the selection of targets and the prosecution of attacks during armed conflict are in practical terms among the most important in the entire corpus of contemporary international humanitarian law (hereinafter 'IHL'). From sustained airstrikes on hostile territory to individual targeted killings of identified hostile leaders, the definition and identification of targets are a vital aspect of contemporary military operations. Yet this now-indisputable proposition is very much a product of certain historical trends in the evolution of means and methods of warfare and of weapons technology that have only manifested themselves in the last hundred years;[2] the relevant detailed substantive rules of treaty law – although admittedly not the relevant general principles of customary law – are less than four decades old,[3] while it was a mere twenty years ago[4] that it first became evident in practice that the military legal adviser's daily functions on the battlefield included the operationally crucial task

---

* All opinions stated herein are those of the author and do not necessarily represent the views of the Government or Ministry of Defence of the United Kingdom.

[1] *Hansard*, HC Debs, vol. 337, col. 938 (21 June 1938).

[2] It was the advent of aircraft in modern warfare that eventually prompted the elaboration and development of detailed legal rules concerning the choice of targets. For more see chapter 9 in this volume by Karen Hulme.

[3] The first – indeed, to date, the only – general treaty in force to deal in any detail with choice of targets and precautions in attack was the Protocol Additional to the Geneva Conventions of 12 August 1949, and relating to the Protection of Victims of International Armed Conflicts (Protocol I) (8 June 1977), *UNTS*, 1125, 3-608. Until its adoption, the term 'military objective' remained legally undefined.

[4] The first Gulf War (1991) was the first modern international armed conflict to be completely dominated by strategic airstrikes conducted by the militarily stronger party to the conflict; these had such an overwhelming adverse effect on Iraq's overall ability to conduct military operations that the outcome of the conflict was never seriously in doubt.

of giving legal advice to commanders as to the lawfulness of attacking particular targets. These timelines are minuscule in the context of the millennia of history behind the laws of war.

The targeting aspect of the modern international law of armed conflict (hereinafter 'LOAC') is simultaneously very widely discussed in contemporary Western liberal-democratic societies engaged in such conflicts – thanks to the modern prevalence of continuous media reporting from battle zones – and very widely misunderstood, thanks to the subtlety of its intricate provisions on the delicate balance between the pursuit of military necessity and the preservation of humanity. Indeed, in technologically disadvantaged societies on the receiving end of Western targeting operations, the strictures of the law are widely abused in order to place the militarily stronger party at a moral (though not necessarily legal) disadvantage in the eyes of public opinion.[5] On the other hand, since at least the Kosovo War (1999), that same public opinion, in Western liberal democracies, has become increasingly averse to the idea that people actually get killed in war, which in turn has encouraged commanders to attach ever-greater importance to 'force protection' (that is, avoiding exposure of their own troops to unnecessary risk),[6] as well as applying the highest possible standards of precautions in attack, as required by the law. These trends have become particularly evident in the contemporary reality of urban and/or counterinsurgency operations, wherein it is exceedingly difficult to identify in advance those persons and objects that may legitimately be subjected to attack. In an age of seemingly routine reports of 'collateral damage' arising from military operations, the technologically advanced nations that conduct warfare in this fashion are increasingly pilloried in the court of public opinion for their armed forces' actions, with a correspondingly negative effect on perceptions of the legitimacy of a particular conflict: thus, failure to demonstrate compliance to the utmost extent feasible with the *jus in bello* rules of targeting is doubly important, because it adversely affects perceptions as to compliance with the *jus ad bellum* also.

The legality of attacking specific targets during an armed conflict lies at the intersection of the four fundamental, core principles of modern IHL: military necessity, humanity, distinction and proportionality. The first of these essentially permits the use of force – up to and including the infliction of death and destruction – to the extent that is necessary for the attainment of legitimate military objectives and as long as it is not otherwise contrary to the laws and customs of war.[7] For example, military necessity would legitimate the sinking of an enemy merchant ship transporting war *matériel*, but

---

[5] A strategy that has been characterised as 'lawfare'. See Colonel C.J. Dunlap Jr, 'Law and Military Interventions: Preserving Humanitarian Values in 21st [Century] Conflicts', available at http://www.duke.edu/~pfeaver/dunlap.pdf; Major General C.J. Dunlap Jr, 'Lawfare Today: A Perspective', (2008) 3 *YJIA* 146; 'Is Lawfare Worth Defining? Report of the Cleveland Experts Meeting September 11, 2010', (2010) 43 *CaseWRes J Intern'l L* 11. See also The Lawfare Project, available at http://www.thelawfareproject.org.

[6] See A.P.V. Rogers, 'Zero-Casualty Warfare', (2000) 837 *IRRC* 165.

[7] *The Hostages Trial (Trial of Wilhelm List and Others)* [1948] VIII Law Reports of Trials of War Criminals 34, at 66. This statement of the principle, while basically correct, has been subject to variations of interpretation; for an overview of the different approaches, see D. Turns, 'Military Necessity', Oxford Bibliographies Online: International Law, available at http://about obo.com/international-law/.

not the massacre of survivors in the water, which constitutes the war crime of wilfully murdering persons protected under the Geneva Conventions.[8]

The principle of humanity is, so to speak, the other side of the coin: it counterbalances military necessity by decreeing that the horrors of war must, to the extent possible and without unduly hindering the attainment of lawful military objectives, be alleviated by considerations of humanitarianism (such as the protection of enemy soldiers who have surrendered). The balance between military necessity and humanity is not always easy to strike – the examples just cited are clear and beyond doubt, perhaps even unusually so – and it has been aptly characterised as 'a subtle equilibrium between two diametrically opposed impulses', namely '[minimising] human suffering without undermining the effectiveness of military operations', resulting in a 'compromise formula'.[9]

The principle of distinction has been described by the International Court of Justice as the first of the 'cardinal principles' of IHL, as it is 'aimed at the protection of the civilian population and civilian objects and establishes the distinction between combatants and non-combatants; States must never make civilians the object of attack'.[10] This rule is said to have emerged clearly as such by the 18th Century at the latest, although it undoubtedly existed previously in customary international law;[11] today it is included in the compendium of customary rules of humanitarian law produced by the International Committee of the Red Cross (hereinafter 'ICRC').[12] Its first conventional expression came in the late 19th Century[13] and today it is elaborated principally in the 1977 Protocol I Additional to the Geneva Conventions.[14] An important corollary of the principle of distinction, worth noting as a separate rule in its own right, is the ban on indiscriminate weapons.[15]

---

[8] *Heinz Eck and Others (The Peleus Trial)* [1945] I Law Reports of Trials of War Criminals 1.

[9] Y. Dinstein, *The Conduct of Hostilities under the Law of International Armed Conflict* (Cambridge: Cambridge University Press, 2004), at 16–17. See also M.N. Schmitt, 'Military Necessity and Humanity in International Humanitarian Law: Preserving the Delicate Balance', (2010) 50 *Va J Int'l L* 795.

[10] *Legality of the Threat or Use of Nuclear Weapons*, Advisory Opinion, [1996] ICJ Rep. 226, at 257.

[11] See A.P.V. Rogers, *Law on the Battlefield*, 2nd edn (Manchester: Manchester University Press, 2004), at 8. By the mid-19th Century the principle was said to be 'more and more acknowledged': US War Department, *General Orders No. 100 – Instructions for the Government of Armies of the United States in the Field*, 24 April 1863 ('the Lieber Code'), Art. 22, reprinted in D. Schindler and J. Toman, *The Laws of Armed Conflicts* (Leiden: Martinus Nijhoff Publishers, 1998), at 3–23.

[12] J.-M. Henckaerts and L. Doswald-Beck, *Customary International Humanitarian Law, Volume I: Rules*, (Cambridge: Cambridge University Press, 2005) (hereinafter 'CIHL'), Rules 1 and 7, 3–8 and 25–29.

[13] St Petersburg Declaration Renouncing the Use, in Time of War, of Explosive Projectiles Under 400 Grammes Weight, 11 December 1868, reprinted in Schindler and Toman, *supra* n.11, at 102.

[14] Article 48, API.

[15] *Ibid.*, Article 51(4)(b)–(c); CIHL, Rule 71.

Proportionality goes hand in hand with distinction. Although usually referred to as a fundamental principle of IHL in its own right,[16] arguably it is better viewed as a *procedural method* whereby distinction is achieved, rather than as a discrete *substantive rule*: it is the mechanism which provides the fulcrum on which the balance between military necessity and humanity oscillates. Briefly stated, the principle of proportionality operates to ensure that the negative effect of an attack on the civilian population and/or civilian objects is broadly proportionate to the positive military advantage to be gained from that attack.

Given the sophistication and subtlety of the interaction of these rules and principles and the fact that they lie at the very core of modern IHL, it is instructive to consider the historical context within which they evolved, before proceeding to examine their substantive detail and contemporary challenges in their application on the battlefield. The chapter will conclude with a basic description – to the extent that unclassified sources make possible – of the typical targeting process in contemporary military operations as conducted by the United Kingdom and allies within the North Atlantic Treaty Organisation (hereinafter 'NATO') or *ad hoc* coalitions.

2. HISTORICAL DEVELOPMENT OF THE RULES ON TARGETING

A. Persons

Through much of their history, there was little or no need for the development of special rules in the laws of war relating to the selection of targets. This was so until at least the late 19th Century, principally for two reasons, which, as military history has shown, were interrelated: the actors in war, and the means by which war was carried on. From the advent of the nation-state in the mid-17th Century onwards, war was recognised as an essentially public activity, which was carried on by professional or semi-professional, regularly constituted, uniformed armies, acting under a hierarchy of command responsible to the government of the state.[17] Even in earlier times, soldiers – whether through the wearing of distinctive items of clothing such as tunics embroidered with the emblems of their feudal lords, chain mail or armour, or the bearing of arms – were in general easily distinguishable from civilians. Most war-fighting took place between men who could see each other directly face to face, with weapons of limited range; even field artillery was used tactically against enemy military formations on the battlefield, rather than as a strategic weapon against objects or installations in the enemy's rear. Battles were fought mostly by rival armies[18] in open countryside, far from major civilian population centres; local civilians such as farmers would generally

---

[16] *Ibid.*, Articles 51(5)(b) and 57(2)(a)–(b); CIHL, Rule 14, 46–50.

[17] This is not to say that irregular forces or militias could not be used: during the American War of Independence (1775–1783) the rebels relied very heavily on the colonial militias (known as 'Minutemen'), while the British made extensive use of Indian irregulars, particularly from the Iroquois Nations, and the Creek and Seminole tribes.

[18] Rogers, *supra* n.11, at 58–59.

leave the area at the first sign of an approaching army, did not usually take up arms to support one side or the other and consequently were simply not generally involved in hostilities. The main exception was in the context of siege warfare, in the event that the civilian population of a fortified town remained *in situ*; although they might be offered a chance to leave the town so as to escape the effects of a siege, there was no legal obligation either on them to accept such an offer, nor indeed upon the besieging force to make it. If an offer of safe conduct were made and the civilian population failed to avail itself thereof, it was understood that they ran the risks entailed in the siege, just as the military defenders did.[19] Since civilians from rural areas surrounding a fortified town would often take refuge therein from an invading army, it came to be accepted that they would suffer the effects of war along with the garrison; indeed, customary law before 1977 had long permitted the commander of a besieging force to drive fleeing civilians back into the city in order to increase the burden on the defending commander and hasten his surrender.[20]

It having traditionally been relatively clear who was and who was not a soldier, the question of defining lawful combatant status only really arose as a result of the Franco-Prussian War (1870–1871), in which the French made use of certain irregular formations, made up of (mostly) local farmers who belonged to 'rifle clubs or unofficial military societies',[21] which had been popular before the war in the eastern French districts which were now being occupied by the Germans. These units emerged from nowhere to carry out acts of sabotage, ambushes and sniping activities against the occupying troops; although nominally under the authority of the French Ministry of War (which expected them to act as light troops and skirmishers in the event of an invasion) they wore no uniforms, elected their own officers and failed to respond to any military discipline at all. As a result, the Germans termed them *francs-tireurs* ('free-shooters', that is, in the sense of being civilians using weapons without the responsibility of the state) and tended to execute them, often without trial.[22] By the end of the 19th Century it was clear that, while it was universally accepted that belligerent acts in wartime *should* be committed only by members of regular state armed forces,

---

[19] See J. Bradbury, *The Medieval Siege* (Woodbridge: The Boydell Press, 1992), at 308–309 and 317–322.

[20] In World War II ordering artillery to fire on Soviet civilians attempting to escape from the besieged city of Leningrad was not considered criminal under customary law: *The German High Command Trial (Trial of Wilhelm von Leeb and Thirteen Others)* [1948] XII Law Reports of Trials of War Criminals 1, at 84. On the customary law of siege warfare generally, see C.C. Hyde, *International Law Chiefly as Interpreted and Applied by the United States* (Boston: Little, Brown and Company, 1922), Vol. 2, at 302–305. The rather harsh customary legal position has not survived in the modern law: see Article 54, API, although for criticism, see Dinstein, *supra* n.9, at 135–136.

[21] *The Encyclopaedia Britannica*, 11th edn (Cambridge: Cambridge University Press, 1910), at 15.

[22] The Germans' experience in France in 1870–1871 was to have a seminal influence on their attitude to the civilian population in occupied areas of that country and in Belgium some 40 years later in World War I, when they tended to regard all local civilians as at least potential enemies and instituted a policy of brutal reprisals for any attacks on the occupying forces. See *ibid.*, at 16; M.R. Stoneman, 'The Bavarian Army and French Civilians in the War of 1870–1871: A Cultural Interpretation', (2001) 8 *War in Hist* 271, at 272–277; A.P.V. Rogers,

the *actual* use of irregular forces in certain types of warfare was not only inevitable, but increasing. During the Second Boer War (1899–1902), the British treated all members of the Boer Commandos as legitimate belligerents, and consequently as prisoners of war (hereinafter 'POW') – despite their distinctly unconventional military structure, lack of uniforms and (after the occupation and formal annexation of the Orange Free State and the South African Republic by the British Empire) use of exclusively guerrilla tactics, they were indisputably the 'official' armed forces of the Boer Republics.[23] Interestingly, the British maintained this approach even after publicly designating as 'rebels' any who refused to surrender after the annexation, by which time technically the Boer Republics had ceased to exist as states in international law. The confusion and contradictions in the British attitude[24] may be explained, at least in part, by the fact that neither Boer Republic was party to Hague Convention (hereinafter 'HC') II of 1899; therefore the Regulations were formally inapplicable to the conduct of hostilities and both sides could only make reference to customary law.[25]

The first adoption of a legally binding definition of those persons who were entitled to the 'combatant's privilege' – that is, the right to take part in armed hostilities and consequently to have the status of POW upon capture – was made in The Hague Regulations, which recognised that,

> The laws, rights and duties of war apply not only to armies, but also to militia and volunteer corps fulfilling the following conditions:
>
> 1. To be commanded by a person responsible for his subordinates;
> 2. To have a fixed distinctive sign recognizable at a distance;
> 3. To carry arms openly; and
> 4. To conduct their operations in accordance with the laws and customs of war.[26]

'Combatant Status', in E. Wilmshurst and S. Breau (eds), *Perspectives on the ICRC Study on Customary International Humanitarian Law* (Cambridge: Cambridge University Press, 2007), 101, at 104.

[23] See H. Vincent, 'The Juridical Basis of the Distinction between Lawful Combatant and Unprivileged Belligerent', US Army TJAGLCS: Selected Theses (1959), at 52–59, available at http://www.loc.gov/rr/frd/Military_Law/theses.html; J. Dugard, 'The Treatment of Rebels in Conflicts of a Disputed Character: The Anglo-Boer War and the "ANC-Boer War" Compared', in A.J.M. Delissen and G.J. Tanja (eds), *Humanitarian Law of Armed Conflict: Challenges Ahead: Essays in Honour of Frits Kalshoven* (Dordrecht: Martinus Nijhoff, 1991), 447, at 448–450.

[24] Compare various *Proclamations issued by Field-Marshal Lord Roberts in South Africa* 1900 [Cd. 426], notably at 8, 14, 15 and 18.

[25] For example, see *Telegrams from Field-Marshal Lord Roberts to the Secretary of State for War* 1900 [Cd. 122], reproducing mutual accusations of abusing the white flag, in violation of customary international law.

[26] Regulations Respecting the Laws and Customs of War on Land, Annex to The Hague Convention (IV) Respecting the Laws and Customs of War on Land (18 October 1907), (1908) 2 *AJIL*, (Supplement), 90, Article 1 (hereinafter 'H Regs'). The original version of the Regulations had been adopted in 1899; the wording of this article can be traced back to the *Oxford Manual of the Laws of War on Land*, adopted by the Institute of International Law (1880) and the Brussels Declaration Concerning the Laws and Customs of War (1874); both documents are reprinted in Schindler and Toman, *supra* n.11.

Although the above definition has been revisited over the years since 1907,[27] and notwithstanding some debate as to whether its conditions attach only to 'militia and volunteer corps' or also to members of regular state armed forces,[28] The Hague Regulations in their entirety were accepted as expressing customary international law by 1939 at the latest.[29]

The significance of the definition of a combatant, for the purposes of a discussion of permissible targets under IHL, is twofold: first, it assists in the identification of the legal category of civilians, since the latter are negatively defined (under IHL, a civilian is basically anyone who is not a combatant)[30] – this is crucial for the effective operation of the principle of distinction outlined earlier. Secondly, having combatant status cuts both ways: not only does it grant the bearer the right to participate in hostilities and to have POW status upon capture, it also means that s/he can lawfully be attacked – that is, all combatants in an armed conflict are by definition lawful targets who may in principle be attacked at any time and in any place. Thus, the sinking of the Argentine cruiser *General Belgrano* some 35 miles outside the Total Exclusion Zone during the Falklands War (1982)[31] was perfectly lawful, since she was a warship (therefore, a military objective) and her crew were all sailors in the Argentine Navy (therefore, combatants): the fact of their being outside the Total Exclusion Zone at the time renders questions of distinction and proportionality redundant.

B. Objects

The elaboration of any concept of lawful targets under the laws of war was inextricably bound up with the rise of a particular new means of warfare: the aeroplane. When this new-fangled invention was first conceived of as having military uses, it was originally restricted to reconnaissance;[32] however, the second decade of the 20th Century saw

---

[27] Principally in the Geneva Convention (III) Relative to the Treatment of Prisoners of War of August 12, 1949, 75 UNTS 135–285 (hereinafter 'GC III'), and API in 1977. GC III defined POWs by reference to Article 1 H Regs (for members of armed forces and other militia and volunteer corps) and added as lawful combatants the category of *levée en masse* – inhabitants of unoccupied territory who spontaneously take up arms to resist an approaching invader without being organised as regular armed units, but who carry arms openly and respect the laws and customs of war – Article 4(A)(6). It may also be inferred from Art. 4 that combatants forming part of irregular forces must belong to a party to the conflict. See Dinstein, *supra* n.9, at 39–40.

[28] Dinstein suggests that this is no more than a 'presumption [which] can definitely be rebutted', as 'regular forces are not absolved from meeting the cumulative conditions binding irregular forces'. See Dinstein, *ibid.*, at 36. Rogers, on the other hand, assumes that mere membership of armed forces entitles one to combatant status without the need to comply with any further conditions. See Rogers, *supra* n.11, at 32. The present author agrees with Rogers' interpretation, on the basis of history and the relevant treaty texts.

[29] *Trial of the Major War Criminals Before the International Military Tribunal*, Nuremberg, 14 November 1945–1 October 1946, *Proceedings 27 August 1946–1 October 1946*, XXII, 497.

[30] Article 50, API.

[31] See *Hansard*, HC Debs, vol. 23, cols. 29–37 (4 May 1982).

[32] Observers had been sent aloft in balloons as early as the American Civil War (1861–1865) in order to ascertain movements of enemy forces on the battlefield.

three separate conflicts in which aircraft were used to bomb enemy targets, developments which led directly to the articulation of air power doctrines in all the major military powers of the time. The very first country to deploy powered aircraft in battle was Italy, during the Italian-Turkish War in Libya (1911–1912): although nine aircraft were used in the anticipated reconnaissance role (and also as spotters to correct inaccurate artillery fire) from 23 October 1911, the truly historic event for targeting purposes occurred on 1 November, when pilot Lieutenant Giulio Gavotti threw four Cipelli hand grenades, which he held between his knees in a leather bag with a detonator in his pocket, out of his open cockpit at a Turkish infantry camp at Ain Zara on the Tripoli front.[33] Further similar missions followed, which probably had more effect on the local civilians than on the enemy soldiers since accuracy in these conditions was hardly possible, but already there was a foretaste of the bitterness every subsequent aerial bombing campaign has provoked: on several occasions, in December 1911 and April, May and August 1912, the Ottoman Red Crescent formally protested that its clearly marked field hospitals at several locations, as well as a cemetery at Al-Aziziyah, had been illegally attacked by both aeroplanes and airships of the Italian forces. Each such allegation was summarily denied by the Italian authorities, who accused the Turks of deliberately propagating malicious falsehoods;[34] the pattern for 'lawfare' was thus clearly established well before the advent of rolling news reporting.

The first known attempt to bomb a city from the air occurred during the First Balkan War (1912–1913), when Bulgarian aircraft dropped primitive 22-pound bombs on the fortified Turkish city of Adrianople, after leafleting the city from the air with threats that it would be destroyed if it did not surrender.[35] However, it was in World War I that the bombing of cities was first used as a systematic tactic to induce an enemy to make peace (as opposed to the accomplishment of a tactical military objective like the capture of a city). In 1915 Captain Peter Strasser of the German Imperial Naval Airship Division began bombing civilian targets in Great Britain with his Zeppelins, for, as he put it: 'England can be overcome by means of airships ... through increasingly extensive destruction of cities, factory complexes, dockyards, harbour works with war and merchant ships lying therein, railroads, etc.'[36] He was interested primarily in

---

[33] See Air Vice Marshal T. Mason, *Air Power: A Centennial Appraisal* (London: Brassey's, 1994), at 10–12; Commodore W.H. Beehler, *The History of the Italian-Turkish War, September 29, 1911, to October 18, 1912* (Annapolis: The Advertiser-Republican, 1913), at 31, 34 and 98.

[34] For the exchange of correspondence, see *'La Guerre en Tripolitaine'*, (1912) 43 (169) *Bulletin International des Sociétés de la Croix-Rouge* 75; *ibid.*, 43 (170), at 174–180; *ibid.*, 43 (171), at 268–272; and *ibid.*, 43 (172), at 330–333.

[35] M. Paris, *Winged Warfare: The Literature and Theory of Aerial Warfare in Britain, 1859–1917* (Manchester: Manchester University Press, 1992), at 110–111.

[36] Quoted in E. Lawson and J. Lawson, *The First Air Campaign, August 1914–November 1918* (Cambridge: Da Capo Press, 1996), at 79. Similar attacks on enemy civilian infrastructure and morale were carried out in land warfare during the 'March to the Sea' in the later stages of the American Civil War, when US forces marched through Georgia and the Carolinas with the strategic aim of cutting the Confederacy in half and destroying its willingness and capacity to make war (albeit not targeting the civilian *population* as such). See W.T. Sherman, *Orders to the Mayor and City Council of Atlanta, 12 September 1864*, and *Special Field Orders, No. 120, 9 November 1864*, available at http://www.sewanee.edu/faculty/Willis/Civil_War/documents.html. For a modern perspective, see T.G. Robisch, 'General William T. Sherman: Would the Georgia

harming civilian morale and was not in the least bit squeamish about causing civilian casualties:

> We who strike the enemy where his heart beats have been slandered as 'baby killers' and 'murderers of women'. What we do is ... but necessary. Very necessary. Nowadays there is no such animal as a non-combatant. Modern warfare is total warfare. ... If what we do is frightful, then may frightfulness be Germany's salvation.[37]

The Zeppelin raids continued until 1918 and certainly caused some hysteria among the British civilian population, but their physical effects were relatively unimpressive and as a decisive weapon to win the war – Strasser's objective – they were unsuccessful. In 1917 the German Imperial Air Service commenced strategic bombing raids against British cities using the Gotha G.IV heavy bombers, but these incurred disproportionately heavy losses and within 12 months the campaign was suspended. The British, for their part, were not inactive: in late 1917 the Royal Flying Corps and the Royal Naval Air Service were directed by the War Cabinet to commence strategic bombing of industrial targets (including those located in urban areas) in Germany, at least in part as a reprisal for the German bombing raids mentioned above.[38]

The experience of World War I was to have an enormous impact on the rise of strategic bombing doctrines in the interwar period and during World War II, not least on the seminal work of the Italian air power theorist General Giulio Douhet, who in 1921 published one of the most influential works on aerial warfare doctrine: *The Command of the Air*. Douhet was one of the very first air power theorists to emphasise the importance of targeting in order to realise the potential of this new weapon – not, it must be said, out of any legalistic concerns, but out of a desire for maximising its effect in winning a war. By the same token, Douhet was not overly concerned with accuracy: the whole point of the area bombing that he advocated was to have as widespread an effect on the enemy civilian population as possible, rather than to limit such effects as the modern law requires. He identified five basic target sets as the vital centres of any modern country: industry, transportation infrastructure, communication nodes, government buildings and the will of the people.[39] It was the last of these that Douhet thought the most important – with a reasoning strikingly similar to Strasser's in rejecting the idea that the mass population were non-combatants in modern war – and that would indeed come to dominate targeting in bombing campaigns during the 1930s and 1940s. Douhet believed that if a civilian population's morale were to be broken by aerial bombardment, that population would exert irresistible pressure on its government to end the war.[40] He was hostile to limitations imposed by law and morality and openly

---

Campaigns of the First Commander of the Modern Era Comply with Current Law of War Standards?', (1995) 9 *Emory Int'l L Rev* 459.

[37] Lawson and Lawson, *ibid.*, at 79.

[38] See T. Biddle, 'Learning in Real Time: The Development and Implementation of Air Power in the First World War', in S. Cox and P. Gray (eds), *Air Power History: Turning Points from Kitty Hawk to Kosovo* (Abingdon: Frank Cass Publishers, 2002), 3, at 8–14.

[39] See P.S. Meilinger, *Airwar: Theory and Practice* (London: Frank Cass Publishers, 2003), at 12–30.

[40] *Ibid.*, at 21.

advocated attacking cities with chemical bombs, even after Italy had ratified the 1925 Geneva Gas Protocol;[41] indeed, the Italians were to use chemical warfare shamelessly, mostly from the air, against a largely defenceless civilian population during their invasion of Ethiopia (1935–1936),[42] and the deliberate aerial bombardment of major cities like Barcelona and Madrid with the specific intention of shattering civilian morale, mostly by the Italian and German air contingents supporting the Nationalist Air Force, was to be a significant feature of the Spanish Civil War (1936–1939).[43] Strategic bombing doctrine was developed during the interwar period in the Royal Air Force by the post-World War I Chief of Air Staff, Air Chief Marshal Hugh Trenchard, who advocated attacks on enemy industry in order to break the will of factory workers directly supporting the enemy's war effort.[44] This was described as 'morale bombing', but, taken to its extreme in World War II by Air Chief Marshal Arthur Harris, it became better known as 'area bombardment' or 'carpet bombing' (or, in German propaganda, 'terror bombing'):[45] the designation of entire areas (often encompassing urban centres) of Germany for aerial destruction by massive and sustained bombing raids, with a view to destroying both Germany's capacity for war (in the form of its industrial plant and transport infrastructure) and its people's will to fight.[46] The nadir of this type of policy was reached with the American dropping of the atomic bombs on the Japanese cities of Hiroshima and Nagasaki in August 1945, in order to force Japan to surrender quickly.

Nevertheless, to adapt Cicero's celebrated aphorism, *inter arma non silent leges*:[47] even at this embryonic stage in the development of a concept of targets, some legal standards had been formulated. The principal rules relevant to targets concerned bombardment and were all contained in the instruments that emerged from the 1899 and 1907 Peace Conferences held at The Hague; these were essentially divided into

---

[41] Geneva Protocol for the Prohibition of the Use in War of Asphyxiating, Poisonous or Other Gases, and of Bacteriological Methods of Warfare (17 June 1925), (1931) 25 *AJIL* (Supplement) 94.

[42] For the formal notification by the Ethiopian Red Cross of the Italian use of mustard gas, see '*Conflit italo-éthiopien*', (1936) 18 *Revue Internationale de la Croix-Rouge et Bulletin International des Sociétés de la Croix-Rouge* 326. The Italian Delegate to the League of Nations, Baron Aloisi, inferred obliquely in a debate in that forum that the Italian use of gas was by way of belligerent reprisal for various alleged atrocities to which it had been claimed Italian soldiers and POWs had been subjected: see 91st Session of the Council, Ninth Meeting (20 April 1936) 17 *League of Nations – Official Journal* 375.

[43] See J.S. Corum, 'The *Luftwaffe* and Lessons Learned in the Spanish Civil War', in Cox and Gray, *supra* n.38, 66, at 78–80; C.C. Locksley, 'Condor Over Spain: The Civil War, Combat Experience and the Development of Luftwaffe Airpower Doctrine', (1999) 2 *Civil Wars* 69, at 80–84.

[44] See Meilinger, *supra* n.39, 36–63.

[45] Thereby providing an early illustration of the truth of the statement that, '[w]hether a particular operation was regarded as "illegal" or "immoral" depended entirely upon whether the person was the bomber or the "bombee", that is, the recipient of the bombs': W.H. Parks, 'Air War and the Law of War', (1990) 32 *AF L Rev* 1, at 21.

[46] For a contemporary (and highly polemical) account, see J.M. Spaight, *Bombing Vindicated* (London: Geoffrey Bles, 1944).

[47] Often rendered in English as 'laws are silent 'midst the clash of arms', the correct original phrase (*silent enim leges inter arma*) is attributed to Marcus Tullius Cicero's oration *Pro milone* (52 BCE).

rules relating to land warfare and maritime warfare. In respect of the former, Article 25 of The Hague Regulations stipulated, 'The attack or bombardment, by whatever means, of towns, villages, dwellings, or buildings which are undefended is prohibited'; reciprocal duties of attacking and defending forces' commanders, in terms of providing advance warning of a bombardment and indicating the presence of certain buildings such as hospitals and cultural property respectively, are outlined in subsequent provisions.[48] Maritime warfare was the subject of an entire (albeit short) convention,[49] the essence of whose rules was mostly similar to those pertaining to land warfare,[50] with the notable exception that '[m]ilitary works, military or naval establishments, depots of arms or war *matériel*, workshops or plant which could be utilized for the needs of the hostile fleet or army, and the ships of war in the harbor' of an undefended port could lawfully be attacked, without the attacking commander incurring legal responsibility 'for any unavoidable damage [to the town] which may be caused by a bombardment'.[51] Whereas the general customary prohibition on attacking undefended towns was recognised before 1907,[52] the great innovation of HC IX was to introduce the concepts of military objectives and collateral damage – despite those phrases not being used in the text of the Convention. The list of objects not exempt from attack even in an otherwise undefended locality constituted the first example in international law of specified military objectives.[53] Articles 6 of HC IX and 27 of the Regulations, moreover, constituted the first (oblique) acknowledgement of the concept of collateral damage in the law of armed conflict, albeit only in respect of damage to civilian objects, not civilian casualties.[54] The addition of the phrase 'by whatever means' to Article 25 of the Regulations suggested that both naval and, eventually, aerial bombardments were being contemplated at the time.[55]

The single most important legal development relevant to targeting in armed conflicts, although it was never adopted as a legally binding treaty, was Part II of the General Report of the Commission of Jurists which met in The Hague in 1922–1923. Until the adoption of API in 1977, The Hague Rules of Aerial Warfare[56] were the only international legal provisions specifically to address issues of target selection in armed conflicts – and to this day they remain the only such provisions exclusively to address aerial warfare. The Hague Rules reaffirmed the basic principle of distinction by stating that, 'Any air bombardment for the purpose of terrorizing the civilian population or

---

[48] H Regs, *supra* n.26, at Articles 26 and 27.
[49] The Hague Convention (IX) Concerning Bombardment by Naval Forces in Time of War (18 October 1907), (1908) 2 *AJIL* (Supplement), 146 (hereinafter 'HC IX').
[50] Articles 5 and 6 of the Convention, for example, are almost *verbatim* identical to Articles 26 and 27 of the Regulations.
[51] HC IX, *supra* n.49, at Article 2.
[52] See Brussels Declaration, *supra* n.26, at Article 15; *Oxford Manual*, *supra* n.26, at Article 32(c).
[53] This was largely confirmed by state practice in strategic bombing operations during World War I. See Parks, *supra* n.45, at 21; J.M. Spaight, 'Air Bombardment', (1923–1924) 4 *BYIL* 21, at 23–25.
[54] See Parks, *ibid.*, at 15–16 and 18.
[55] See Spaight, *supra* n.53, at 21–22.
[56] (1923), 17 *AJIL* (Supplement), 245 (hereinafter 'H Rules').

destroying or damaging private property without military character or injuring non-combatants, is prohibited.'[57] The most significant development contained in the Rules, however, was their explicit adoption of the notion of 'military objective' as a legal concept.[58] Article 24(1) provided that in order for aerial bombardment to be legitimate, it had to be directed at a military objective; paragraph (2) then provided what the wording implies was an exhaustive list of such objectives, namely: 'military forces; military works; military establishments or depots; factories constituting important and well-known centres engaged in the manufacture of arms, ammunition or distinctively military supplies; lines of communication or transportation used for military purposes'. The article went on to prohibit the bombardment of civilian objects not in the immediate vicinity of land forces and their bombardment (when in such vicinity) if indiscriminate bombardment of the civilian population was unavoidable.[59] It also introduced the earliest formulation of the rule of proportionality: bombardment of civilian objects (where located in the immediate vicinity of land operations) was legitimate, 'provided that there exists a reasonable presumption that the military concentration [targeted] is sufficiently important to justify such bombardment, having regard to the danger thus caused to the civilian population'.[60]

Parks' summary dismissal of The Hague Rules as 'an immediate and total failure ... totally at odds with state practice, technological advances, and military thinking'[61] is rather unfair and evinces a one-dimensional perspective; the listing of military objectives (albeit in a short and patently non-exhaustive list) and the formulation of proportionality were very significant pointers to the future. State practice evidenced their partial acceptance, even if not as strictly binding legal obligations,[62] and many of the provisions pioneered in the Rules have since been revisited in later instruments.[63] The International Law Association prepared in 1938 a Draft Convention for the Protection of Civilian Populations Against New Engines of War,[64] which sought to prohibit attacks on undefended localities,[65] but it defined these in such restricted terms that in practice hardly any cities in Europe would have benefited from its protection:

---

[57] *Ibid.*, at Article 22.

[58] Parks notes that the British and American delegations (whose countries would in 20 years' time be bombing Germany and Japan) fundamentally differed in their approach to this concept, the British attaching great importance to the term 'military objective' without actually defining it, while the Americans preferred to list designated specific objects which could be bombed, while avoiding use of the term 'military objective'. Parks, *supra* n.45, at 28.

[59] H Rules, *supra* n.56, at Article 24(3).

[60] *Ibid.*, at Article 24(4).

[61] Parks, *supra* n.45, at 31.

[62] For example, both sides during World War II cited the Rules when accusing each other of violating international law concerning aerial warfare. See A. Roberts and R. Guelff, *Documents on the Laws of War*, 3rd edn (Oxford: Oxford University Press, 2000), at 140.

[63] *Ibid.*, at 141.

[64] Amsterdam, 2 September 1938, reprinted in Schindler and Toman, *supra* n.11, at 223–229.

[65] It also prohibited making the civilian population the object of attack (Article 1), bombardment of defended towns when military objectives could not be 'clearly recognized' (Article 3), aerial bombardment for the purpose of terrorising the civilian population (Article 4),

A town, port, village or isolated building shall be considered undefended provided that not only (a) no combatant troops, but also (b) no military, naval or air establishment, or barracks, arsenal, munition stores or factories, aerodromes or aeroplane workshops or ships of war, naval dockyards, forts, or fortifications for defensive or offensive purposes, or entrenchments ... exist within its boundaries or within a radius of 'x' kilometres from such boundaries.[66]

The Draft Amsterdam Convention was never even opened for signature. Thus, at the start of World War II, there was no binding treaty in force specifically governing aerial warfare and only the most general principles governing aerial bombardment could be said to have passed into customary international law, as enunciated by British Prime Minister Neville Chamberlain in the House of Commons,[67] and subsequently adopted in a unanimous resolution of the Assembly of the League of Nations,[68] namely:

1. direct bombardment of the civilian population was unlawful;
2. targets for aerial bombardment had to be legitimate, identifiable military objectives; and
3. reasonable care had to be taken to avoid bombardment of a civilian population in the vicinity of such military objectives.

All of these principles were violated by both sides at various stages of the conflict that followed, from the German bombings of Warsaw, Rotterdam and Coventry[69] to the Anglo-American mass raids on Hamburg, Dresden and Tokyo.[70]

3. THE MODERN LAW OF TARGETING: RULES

The modern rules of targeting in the law of armed conflict were not formulated until the adoption of API in 1977, but after the relatively indiscriminate aerial bombing campaigns of World War II and the subsequent three decades of legal silence, they represent a clear revival and endorsement of the fundamental IHL principles of military necessity, humanity, distinction and proportionality. The Protocol is currently binding on 171 states[71] – that is, a very large majority of states in the world – and it is

---

and aerial bombardment not directed at 'combatant forces or belligerent establishments [as defined in Article 2] or lines of communication or transportation used for military purposes' (Article 5(1)).

[66] *Ibid.*, Article 2.
[67] *Hansard*, HC Debs, vol. 337, cols. 937–938 (21 June 1938).
[68] 'Protection of Civilian Populations Against Bombing From the Air in Case of War', 30 September 1938, available at http://www.dannen.com/decision/int-law.html#D.
[69] The first two of these were deliberately carried out with no other purpose than to terrorise the Polish and Dutch populations (successfully, in both cases) into surrendering; the destruction of Coventry, notorious epitome of German barbarism as it was held up to be at the time, was actually a belligerent reprisal for the first British air raids on Berlin.
[70] See C.S. Maier, 'Targeting the City: Debates and Silences about the Aerial Bombing of World War II', (2005) 859 *IRRC* 429.
[71] International Committee of the Red Cross, 'International Humanitarian Law – Treaties and Documents', available at http://www.icrc.org/ihl.nsf/INTRO?OpenView.

important to note that its rules on targeting, in particular, are generally accepted as reflecting customary international law.[72] This is true to at least some extent even of states, like the USA[73] and Israel,[74] which have refused to become parties to the Protocol as a whole.

First, the 'Basic Rule' of distinction is stated: 'In order to ensure respect for and protection of the civilian population and civilian objects, the Parties to the conflict shall at all times distinguish between the civilian population and combatants and between civilian objects and military objectives and accordingly shall direct their operations only against military objectives.'[75] Next, specific protections are provided for the civilian population, which may not be attacked or terrorised, as such.[76] Civilians (that is, persons who are not combatants) are protected, 'unless and for such time as they take a direct part in hostilities'.[77] Indiscriminate attacks – that is, those that are not directed at a specific military objective,[78] or which employ a method or means of warfare which cannot be so directed,[79] or whose effects cannot be limited as required by the Protocol,[80] and which consequently fail to observe the basic rule of distinction – are prohibited. Belligerent reprisals against civilians are prohibited,[81] as is the use of the latter, by a party to an armed conflict, as human shields, 'to render certain points or areas immune from military operations'.[82]

Similar general protection is provided for civilian objects. Like civilians, these benefit only from a negative definition: a civilian object is anything which is not a military objective.[83] The definition of such objectives therefore becomes absolutely crucial to the interpretation and application of the law, just as the definition of combatant status has been essential in determining civilian (that is, protected) status. Certain types of object benefit additionally from specific protection from attack under

---

[72] *Western Front, Aerial Bombardment and Related Claims – Eritrea's Claims 1, 3, 5, 9–13, 14, 21, 25 & 26*, Eritrea-Ethiopia Claims Commission, Partial Award, 19 December 2005, para. 14, available at http://www.pca-cpa.org/upload/files/FINAL%20ER%20FRONT%20CLAIMS.pdf.

[73] It should be noted that US acceptance of the API rules on targeting is neither wholesale nor unrestricted by caveats and variations in interpretation of some of those rules; nevertheless, the US broadly accepts the principles restated in the Protocol as expressive of customary international law. See M.J. Matheson, 'The United States Position on the Relation of Customary International Law to the 1977 Protocols Additional to the 1949 Geneva Conventions', (1987) 2 *Am U J Int'l L & Pol* 419, at 426–427; US Department of the Navy, *The Commander's Handbook on the Law of Naval Operations*, (2007) NWP 1-14M, chapter 8, available at http://www.usnwc.edu/getattachment/a9b8e92d-2c8d-4779-9925-0defea93325c/1-14M_(Jul_2007)_(NWP) (hereinafter '*Commander's Handbook*').

[74] See *Public Committee against Torture in Israel v. Government of Israel* [2006], (2007) 46 *ILM* 375 (hereinafter '*Targeted Killings Case*').

[75] Article 48, API.
[76] *Ibid.*, Article 51(2).
[77] *Ibid.*, Article 51(3).
[78] *Ibid.*, Article 51(4)(a).
[79] *Ibid.*, Article 51(4)(b).
[80] *Ibid.*, Article 51(4)(c).
[81] *Ibid.*, Article 51(6).
[82] *Ibid.*, Article 51(7).
[83] *Ibid.*, Article 52(1).

the terms of the Protocol: cultural property,[84] objects indispensable to the survival of the civilian population (such as foodstuffs, crops, livestock and drinking water installations),[85] and works and installations containing dangerous forces ('namely dams, dykes and nuclear electrical generating stations').[86] Finally, the parts of the Protocol specifically concerned with targeting operations place extensive obligations on an attacking force to take stringent precautions in both the selection of targets and the prosecution of attacks thereon,[87] while also requiring a defending force to take rather minimalist and generic precautions against the effects of attacks.[88]

4. THE MODERN LAW OF TARGETING: CONTROVERSIES

Although the large majority of states in the world are now parties to API, and many of its substantive provisions have directly influenced the formulation of customary rules of IHL espoused by the ICRC in recent years,[89] it would be fair to say that many states had (and some continue to have) strong reservations about various aspects of the Protocol. Some were accordingly very slow to ratify; the UK, for example, signed in 1977 but did not ratify until 1998.[90] Others have never done so: these include, for example, such substantial military powers as the USA, Morocco, Sudan, Israel, Turkey, Iran, Pakistan, India, Sri Lanka, Burma, Indonesia and the Philippines. As has been observed, the list of non-parties amounts to a veritable roll-call of states that have been actively engaged in armed conflicts since the 1980s.[91] It is no secret that among the most ardent supporters of the Additional Protocols figure most prominently states which never become embroiled in armed conflicts, such as Ireland, Sweden, Switzerland and Austria. On the other hand, it is equally true to say that the large majority of states in the world have no great objection to many of API's substantive provisions. Indeed, in the case of the targeting rules, many states accept that these constitute customary law[92] and some even apply them, as a matter of policy if not of legal obligation, in non-international (as well as international) armed conflicts.[93] Moreover,

---

[84] *Ibid.*, Article 53.
[85] *Ibid.*, Article 54(2).
[86] *Ibid.*, Article 56(1).
[87] *Ibid.*, Article 57.
[88] *Ibid.*, Article 58.
[89] See, generally, CIHL, *supra* n.12; D. Bethlehem, 'The Methodological Framework of the Study', in Wilmshurst and Breau, *supra* n.22, 3, at 8–13.
[90] In the UK's case this reticence was due to concerns that it might, in light of its expanded scope of application, cause the characterisation of 'the Troubles' in Northern Ireland as an international armed conflict.
[91] Bethlehem, *supra* n.89, at 7.
[92] Thus, US and Coalition/NATO forces applied them during the first Gulf (1991) and Kosovo (1999) Wars. See M.N. Schmitt, 'The Law of Targeting', in Wilmshurst and Breau, *supra* n.22, 131, at 131–132 and 134.
[93] For example, UK Ministry of Defence, *Joint Doctrine Publication 3-46: Legal Support to Joint Operations*, 2nd edn (2010), at para. 130, available at http://www.mod.uk/DefenceInternet/MicroSite/DCDC/OurPublications/JDWP/Jdp346LegalSupportToJointOperations2ndEdition.htm (hereinafter '*Legal Support*').

the same rules are also generally considered to apply, *mutatis mutandis*, to targeting in both the maritime[94] and aerial[95] warfare operational environments.[96] That said, there are several aspects of the rules that require particularly careful explanation in order to understand how they actually affect operations on the battlefield. Following the structure of the rules as they are contained in the Protocol, these may be grouped into four principal topics, as follows:

- the direct participation of civilians in hostilities;
- the use of human shields;
- the concept and definition of military objectives;
- collateral damage and the rule of proportionality.

A. Direct Participation in Hostilities (Hereinafter 'DPH')

The most obvious consequence of the basic rule of distinction in practice has been the prohibition on attacking civilians and civilian objects: such attacks are now listed as war crimes in the Statute of the International Criminal Court[97] and have – at least in the case of attacks on civilians – been unequivocally prohibited in customary international law at least since the time of the American Civil War.[98] However, the experience of conflicts over a century, from the Franco-Prussian War to the Vietnam War (1955–1975), demonstrated that civilians increasingly participated in hostilities in one way or another. The practice of belligerents during that period equally demonstrated that states tended to treat such civilians as 'unlawful combatants' (to use the infelicitous American phrase applied to Taliban, Al-Qaeda and other irregular enemies of the USA after the terrorist attacks of 11 September 2001) or 'unprivileged belligerents' – a legally more accurate, albeit older, term since it emphasises such persons' *conduct* (which can change their entitlement to protection under IHL) rather than their *status* (which cannot change as such unless they formally join or leave the armed forces).[99] The immediate consequence of such behaviour was that civilians acting in this way lost their

---

[94] See L. Doswald-Beck (ed.), *San Remo Manual on International Law Applicable to Armed Conflicts at Sea* (Cambridge: Cambridge University Press, 1995), Part III.

[95] See Program on Humanitarian Policy and Conflict Research, *Manual on International Law Applicable to Air and Missile Warfare* (Cambridge, MA: Harvard University Press, 2009), Sections D–H.

[96] The Protocol itself also provides for the application of its rules on protection of the civilian population in respect of 'any land, air or sea warfare' and 'all attacks from the sea or from the air against objectives on land'. See Article 49(3), API.

[97] Rome Statute of the International Criminal Court (1998), (1998) 37 *ILM*, 999, at Article 8(2)(b)(i)–(ii).

[98] See C. Byron, *War Crimes and Crimes Against Humanity in the Rome Statute of the International Criminal Court* (Manchester: Manchester University Press, 2009), at 61.

[99] See Major R.R. Baxter, 'So-Called "Unprivileged Belligerency": Spies, Guerrillas and Saboteurs', (1951) 28 *BYIL* 323.

entitlement to protection under IHL and became targetable as if they were combatants.[100] API recognised this state of affairs with its Article 51(3): 'Civilians shall enjoy the protection of this Section, unless and for such time as they take a direct part in hostilities.' This bland statement begs several questions: what are 'hostilities'? What is 'a direct part'? What is the temporal scope of DPH – is protection lost during preparations for, or redeployment from, an attack? What about the typical insurgency scenario, wherein a person may be a 'farmer by day, fighter by night' – the so-called 'revolving-door of combatancy': does he regain protection every day while engaged in his normal peaceful work? What are the precise consequences of the loss of protection stipulated in the event of DPH?

The authoritative *Commentary* to API purports to answer only some of these questions, and then only in minimalist fashion, which has made the provision exceedingly hard to apply in practice. The concept and duration of hostilities are described as 'acts which by their nature and purpose are *intended* to cause actual harm to the personnel and equipment of the armed forces';[101] these extend to 'preparations for combat and return from combat', including 'not only the time that the civilian actually makes use of a weapon, but also … the time that he is carrying it, as well as situations in which he undertakes hostile acts without using a weapon'.[102] 'Direct' participation is characterised as 'acts of war which by their nature or purpose are *likely* to cause actual harm to the personnel and equipment of the enemy armed forces'.[103] The *Commentary* states that, '[o]nce he ceases to participate, the civilian regains his right to protection',[104] but does not elaborate on how such cessation could be measured and verified. In view of the lacunae and discrepancies apparent in the *Commentary*, and the dawning realisation that DPH would be more likely, not less so, in contemporary conflicts, the ICRC in 2003 convened an international Group of Experts to clarify the whole concept of DPH. The result, after a 'clarification process' lasting six years, was the ICRC's *Interpretive Guidance on the Notion of Direct Participation in Hostilities under International Humanitarian Law*.[105] The document has not been free from controversy – a substantial number of the Experts expressly disassociated themselves from the final product – and, crucially, major military powers have yet to signal in any discernibly official manner the extent to which they agree or disagree with its

---

[100] Among its most controversial provisions, the Protocol expanded the possibility of irregular fighters being entitled to combatant (and POW) status while simultaneously loosening the requirements for them to comply with previous restrictions on such entitlement. See Articles 43–45, API. For criticism, see Dinstein, *supra* n.9, at 44–47.

[101] Y. Sandoz, C. Swinarski and B. Zimmermann (eds), *Commentary on the Additional Protocols of 8 June 1977 to the Geneva Conventions of 12 August 1949* (Geneva: ICRC/Martinus Nijhoff Publishers, 1987), at para. 1942 (hereinafter '*ICRC Commentary*') (emphasis added).

[102] *Ibid.*, at para. 1943.

[103] *Ibid.*, at para. 1944 (emphasis added). Note the discrepancy with the similar phrase in para. 1942, which describes hostile acts, as opposed to direct participation therein. It seems illogical that hostile acts require specific intention but 'direct' participation therein does not.

[104] *Ibid.*

[105] (2008) 872 *International Review of the Red Cross* 991 (hereinafter 'IGDPH').

conclusions.¹⁰⁶ Although the process has undeniably been useful in enabling matters of controversy to be aired and elaborated, uncertainties remain and it is not at all clear how the guidance might be applied in practice on the battlefield, since it can be very difficult for troops on the ground to identify whom exactly they may attack (except in cases of self-defence, which are relatively obvious). This is especially true in urban operations, where civilians who are and those who are not directly participating in hostilities may be confusingly intermingled.

The IGDPH stipulates three cumulative constitutive elements of DPH (on which there was general agreement among the Experts):

1. the act must be likely to adversely affect the military operations of a party to an armed conflict or, alternatively, to inflict death, injury or destruction on persons or objects protected against direct attack (threshold of harm);
2. there must be a direct causal link between the act and the harm likely to result either from that act, or from a coordinated military operation of which that act constitutes an integral part (direct causation);
3. the act must be specifically designed to directly cause the required threshold of harm in support of a party to the conflict and to the detriment of another (belligerent nexus).¹⁰⁷

As regards the threshold of harm, it has for some time been understood that the concept of DPH involves a spectrum of possible activities, not necessarily limited to actual combat,¹⁰⁸ and that acts at either end of the spectrum can easily be characterised as DPH or not DPH. It is beyond dispute that (for example) actually ordering or executing a direct attack on hostile forces constitutes DPH, while selling medicines to or cooking food for combatants does not.¹⁰⁹ Picking up a weapon and using it to inflict death or injury on an enemy soldier is evidently an act of DPH, while manufacturing weapon components in an arms factory is not (although the civilian worker in the factory could not lawfully be targeted individually as his actions would not constitute DPH, he would be collateral damage in the event of targeting *the factory*, since the latter would be a legitimate military target, as discussed below). The difficult cases lie in the grey area between two such extremes, and such as have been proposed as constituting or not

---

¹⁰⁶ Although many of the Experts were serving members of national armed forces or defence ministry officials, it was made clear from the beginning that they were involved only in their personal capacities and were not formally representing the views of their respective states. Several of the dissenting Experts have since written scholarly articles in academic journals, setting out their views to the extent that they differed from those expressed in the IGDPH. See, for example, Forum, 'Direct Participation in Hostilities: Perspectives on the ICRC Interpretive Guidance', (2010) 42 *NYU J Int'l L& Pol* 637.

¹⁰⁷ IGDPH, *supra* n.105, at 995. For detailed analysis and discussion, see M.N. Schmitt, 'Deconstructing Direct Participation in Hostilities: The Constitutive Elements', (2010) 42 *NYU J Int'l L & Pol* 697.

¹⁰⁸ *Prosecutor v. Strugar* [2008], ICTY Appeals Chamber Judgment, Case No.IT-01-42-A, para. 176, available at http://www.icty.org/x/cases/strugar/acjug/en/080717.pdf. However, DPH 'cannot be held to embrace all activities in support of one party's military operations or war effort ... to hold [so] would in practice render the principle of distinction meaningless' *(ibid.)*.

¹⁰⁹ *Targeted Killings Case*, *supra* n.74, at para. 35.

constituting DPH have been so described on an *ad hoc*, case-by-case basis.[110] Uncertainty remains as to whether, for example, providing 'spiritual' leadership and general political or motivational guidance to (without having specific operational authority over) an armed group really constitutes DPH or not.[111]

The targeting of a civilian (or apparently civilian) Head of State who is somehow implicated in military operations has also given rise to differing interpretations, as was illustrated by the case of Colonel Muammar Gaddafi during the 2011 Libyan Civil War: despite his military background and habitual use of a military title, Gaddafi throughout the conflict appeared in civilian dress and was apparently unarmed. However, it was clear that he was effectively directing the operations of the Libyan Armed Forces to a greater or lesser extent and much speculation focused on whether NATO was targeting him directly, even before an airstrike on his compound in Tripoli killed his youngest son and three of his grandchildren.[112] Within a 24-hour period earlier in the campaign, two British Cabinet ministers and the country's senior serving military officer had expressed quite different views on the subject: Defence Secretary Liam Fox opined that specifically targeting Gaddafi 'would potentially be a possibility',[113] while Foreign Secretary William Hague refused to rule it out in all circumstances.[114] The British Chief of the Defence Staff, General Sir David Richards, on the other hand, stated unequivocally that it was 'absolutely not' allowed under UN Security Council Resolution 1973 (which had provided NATO with the authority to use force in Libya).[115] On the same day, US General Carter Ham also said that it was not part of the mission in Libya.[116] Unfortunately, the parameters of this debate were not set under the *jus in bello*, but under the *jus ad bellum* – targeting Gaddafi was seen by politicians and generals alike in terms of whether it was authorised by the terms of the mandate to use force. An analysis conducted correctly under IHL would have focused on whether Gaddafi was a civilian or not, and, if so, whether he was DPH. If he was, he would in any case have been a lawful target. Subsequently in the conflict the view developed that, while NATO was not attempting to kill him deliberately as such, 'if it happened that he was in a command and control centre that was hit by Nato [*sic*] and he was

---

[110] For examples, see *Strugar*, *supra* n.108, at para. 177; Dinstein, *supra* n.9, at 27–28; Rogers, *supra* n.11, at 10–12; IGDPH, *supra* n.105, at 1017–1018.

[111] In 2004 Israel justified the targeted killing of Sheikh Ahmed Yassin, the 'spiritual leader' of Hamas, on the basis that he was 'the head' of a terrorist organisation. See UN Security Council 4934th meeting, 25 March 2004, UN Doc. S/PV.4934, at 6 (statement of Mr Gillerman). The Israeli representative also implied that a reason for targeting Yassin was that he had not only planned terrorist attacks in the past, but would have done so again in the future.

[112] Reuters Africa, 'NATO says Airstrikes Not Targeting Gaddafi', 1 May 2011, available at http://af.reuters.com/article/libyaNews/idAFLDE73T0CW20110501.

[113] BBC News, 'Liam Fox Says Targeting Gaddafi "Would Potentially be a Possibility"', 21 March 2011, available at http://www.bbc.co.uk/news/uk-politics-12805378.

[114] BBC Radio 4 Today, '"No Weakening" in Arab Support for Libya Air Strikes', 21 March 2011, available at http://news.bbc.co.uk/today/hi/today/newsid_9431000/9431064.stm.

[115] BBC News, 'Richards: "Targeting Gaddafi Not Allowed under UN"', 21 March 2011, available at http://www.bbc.co.uk/news/uk-12803224.

[116] Reuters, 'Targeting Gaddafi Not Part of Mission – US General', 21 March 2011, available at http://www.reuters.com/article/2011/03/21/libya-usa-gaddafi-idUSWAT01499620110321.

killed, then that is within the rules'.[117] It is submitted that this was an unnecessarily cautious attitude to take in respect of IHL: if Gaddafi had retained his full military rank and functions, then he was a combatant and could in any event be targeted. Even had it been determined that Gaddafi was not a member of the Libyan Armed Forces (which arguably he still was), if he was actually directing their operations – of which there seems to have been at least some evidence – then he was DPH and liable to be targeted.

To qualify as DPH, the harm which must be caused may be either an adverse effect on the enemy[118] or an attack on protected persons or objects; in the case of the former, the quantum of harm caused is irrelevant and it is not necessary for the harm to rise to the level of an 'attack' as defined in Article 49(1) of API, since it need not involve acts of violence.[119] Thus, an individual broadcasting negative propaganda to undermine the morale of the enemy civilian population would not be DPH, but one who broadcast a direct appeal or instruction to undertake a specific action adversely affecting the military capacity of the enemy (for example, directing an attack on a patrol in a given district) would be DPH.[120]

The second constitutive element requires that there be a direct causal link between the act and the harm, notably in a single causal step. Indirect causation (more than one step between the act and the harm) is therefore excluded, as are acts that benefit one party to the conflict without *per se* harming the other.[121] The problems associated with this approach are demonstrated by the case of the maker of an improvised explosive device (hereinafter 'IED'). A civilian who purchases or supplies materials to be used in the construction of an IED would undoubtedly be contributing to the military capacity of his/her party to the conflict, but according to the ICRC's approach, even though the act would be 'connected with the resulting harm through an uninterrupted causal chain of events', it does not cause the harm directly, 'unlike the planting and detonation of [the] device', and therefore would not amount to DPH.[122] It has been suggested, no doubt correctly, that 'few states would hesitate, on the basis that the action is not "direct enough", to attack those in the process of assembling IEDs'.[123]

The third constitutive element requires that the act be in some way connected to the situation of armed conflict, thereby excluding from DPH opportunistic actions that may be permitted to flourish in conditions created by armed conflict, such as looting

---

[117] 'Nato [sic] must Target Gaddafi Regime, Says Armed Forces Chief Gen Sir David Richards', *The Telegraph*, 14 May 2011, available at http://www.telegraph.co.uk/news/world news/africaandindianocean/libya/8514034/Nato-must-target-Gaddafi-regime-says-Armed-Forces-chief-Gen-Sir-David-Richards.html.

[118] This has been criticised for under-inclusiveness. See Schmitt, *supra* n.107, at 718–720.

[119] See *ibid.*, at 713–716.

[120] By analogy, it is submitted that the same would probably be true of broadcasting incitement to criminal activity, such as direct and public incitement to commit genocide, so long as it was connected to the armed conflict. See *The Prosecutor v. Ruggiu* [2000], ICTR Trial Chamber I, Judgment and Sentence, Case No.ICTR-97-32-I, available at http://www.unictr.org/Portals/0/Case/English/Ruggiu/judgement/rug010600.pdf. See also Schmitt, *supra* n.107, at 721–724.

[121] Schmitt, *ibid.*, at 727–729.

[122] IGDPH, *supra* n.105, at 1022.

[123] Schmitt, *supra* n.107, at 731.

abandoned homes.[124] In the International Criminal Tribunal for the Former Yugoslavia (hereinafter 'ICTY') a conviction for the war crime of deliberately targeting a civilian staff driver (on the assumption that he was DPH) has been upheld on the basis that the victim was merely on his way to work at the time of the attack and was not in fact DPH, because there was no belligerent nexus between his activity at the time and any possible belligerent activity by the officials whom he would have driven.[125]

Apart from a dissection of its constitutive elements, the notion of DPH as interpreted by the ICRC has been subject to criticism on various other grounds relevant to targeting, *inter alia*, its apparent creation of a 'third category' of persons in armed conflicts (members of 'organized armed groups') defined by reference to criteria ('continuous combat function') not otherwise found in either treaty or customary IHL, the adoption of which places persons who perform similar tasks for regular state armed forces at a significant disadvantage.[126] Doubt also persists as to the temporal scope of loss of protection due to DPH, since the IGDPH takes a restrictive view of what acts may constitute preparation for, deployment to and return from an attack; in so doing, it has been criticised for reinforcing the perceived 'revolving-door' of combatancy and the imbalance of protections, since civilians regularly undertaking DPH (unless they are members of organised armed groups) are only subject to attack during limited time-windows for each of these activities, whereas members of regular armed forces undertaking the same activities are subject to attack continuously.[127]

B. Human Shields

Although the issue of human shields in IHL is dealt with separately in API, it has come to be regarded as an aspect of the notion of DPH. The Protocol stipulates that:

> The presence or movements of the civilian population or individual civilians shall not be used to render certain points or areas immune from military operations, in particular in attempts to shield military objectives from attacks or to shield, favour or impede military operations. The Parties to the conflict shall not direct the movement of the civilian population or individual civilians in order to attempt to shield military objectives from attacks or to shield military operations.[128]

In itself, the provision is not difficult to understand or apply. Thus, Saddam Hussein's repeated use of Kuwaiti and Iraqi civilians to shield military objectives from lawful Coalition attack during the first Gulf War was clearly illegal,[129] and in 2005 the Supreme Court of Israel unequivocally banned the practice of the Israel Defence Force (hereinafter 'IDF') of using Palestinian civilians in the so-called 'early warning

---

[124] *Ibid.*, at 735.
[125] *Strugar, supra* n.108, at paras 180–186.
[126] See K. Watkin, 'Opportunity Lost: Organized Armed Groups and the ICRC "Direct Participation in Hostilities" Interpretive Guidance', (2010) 42 *NYU J Int'l L & Pol* 641.
[127] See B. Boothby, '"And For Such Time As": The Time Dimension to Direct Participation in Hostilities', (2010) 42 *NYU J Int'l L & Pol* 741.
[128] Article 51(7), API.
[129] See US Department of Defense, 'Final Report to Congress on the Conduct of the Persian Gulf War – Appendix O: The Role of the Law of War', (1992) 31 *ILM* 615, at 624–627

procedure' during operations to arrest terrorist suspects.[130] The questions arise when the issue of human shields is considered in conjunction with the notion of DPH: namely, are human shields regarded as civilians who are DPH and, if so, does it make a difference if the human shields are voluntary or involuntary? Should human shields, as civilians, be counted towards the proportionality assessment in planning and executing an attack on a lawful military objective?

Involuntary human shields are civilians who are coerced into going to certain places in order to prevent or discourage an enemy from attacking them; to the extent that their actions are forced upon them and they therefore lack the requisite autonomous intention to inflict harm on the adverse party's forces, the correct view is that they are not DPH and therefore count in full towards the collateral damage estimate in the proportionality assessment of whether an attack on a shielded target would be lawful.[131] It should be remembered that although the use of human shields is illegal, the fact of such use by a defender does not release the attacker from his legal obligations regarding precautions in attack in order to spare the civilian population.[132] This approach is borne out by state practice: for example, Coalition aircraft in the first Gulf War on several such occasions suspended their attacks, diverted to alternative targets or returned to base with their weapons unused.[133]

There is less certainty in respect of voluntary human shields, that is, civilians who 'voluntarily and deliberately position themselves to create a physical obstacle to military operations of a party to the conflict'.[134] The IGDPH posits a difference between civilians who act as voluntary human shields in ground operations, such as urban warfare, and those who do so in operations involving artillery bombardment or airstrikes, in the sense that in the former type of operation they constitute a physical obstacle to (for example) advancing troops. In such cases, it is generally agreed that such civilians are DPH.[135] But in the latter type of scenario, the IGDPH suggests that the civilians are a *legal* rather than a *physical* obstacle, as the attacker with modern weaponry may still be able to identify and destroy the shielded objective (unlike in ground operations, where the attacker would putatively be able to advance but for the civilians). Therefore, the suggestion is that civilians in such cases are not DPH but increase the probability of the expected collateral damage being regarded as too high.[136] The IGDPH, in requiring that such civilians do more than merely be physically present and regarding such presence as being only *indirect* participation in hostilities,

---

(hereinafter '*Appendix O*'); also condemnations of the practice, expressed in official correspondence with the UN by the Governments of Kuwait (22 January 1991, UN Doc. S/22128) and Senegal (31 January 1991, UN Doc. S/22181).

[130] *Adalah – The Legal Center for Arab Minority Rights in Israel et al. v. GOC Central Command, IDF, et al.* [2006], (2006) 45 *ILM* 491.
[131] IGDPH, *supra* n.105, at 1027.
[132] Article 51(8), API.
[133] See *Appendix O*, *supra* n.129, at 622; *Letter dated 13 February 1991 from the Permanent Representative of the United Kingdom of Great Britain and Northern Ireland to the United Nations addressed to the President of the Security Council*, UN Doc. S/22218.
[134] IGDPH, *supra* n.105, at 1024.
[135] *Ibid.*
[136] *Ibid.*, at 1024–1025.

shifts the parameters of the proportionality assessment in executing attacks in such cases very much to the detriment of the attacker and is most unlikely to be regarded by military forces as realistic in practice.[137] Nevertheless, again, what state practice has been reported tends to show that armed forces will abort airstrikes in the face of voluntary human shields protecting the target, precisely because they feel that the level of collateral damage would cause unacceptable political, diplomatic and public relations harm.[138]

C. Military Objectives

A central feature of modern IHL is the limitation of attacks to military objectives, as required by the rule of distinction.[139] Since a civilian object is anything that is not a military objective,[140] the definition of such objectives is crucial to the operation of the law. They are defined as, 'those objects which by their nature, location, purpose or use make an effective contribution to military action and whose total or partial destruction, capture or neutralization, in the circumstances ruling at the time, offers a definite military advantage'.[141] Simply stated, this is a two-pronged test for determining whether a given object is in fact a military objective: (1) whether for one of the reasons listed it makes an effective contribution to military action, and (2) whether targeting it would offer the attacker a definite military advantage.

The 'nature' of an objective refers to its inherently belonging to or forming part of armed forces; examples would be military barracks, command and control installations, warships and missile launch sites.[142] A site, installation or geographical feature may by its 'location' become a military objective if it makes 'an effective contribution' to military action and needs to be captured or destroyed; thus, a strategically important bridge, mountain pass or canal could be viewed as a military objective.[143] The 'purpose' of an objective refers to its intended future use; a power plant under construction, which would on completion generate electricity for operating military facilities, for example, could be targeted if intelligence suggested that the enemy intended to use it in the future for military purposes.[144] The 'use' of an objective refers to its present use; it would therefore be justifiable to attack a house of worship if it

---

[137] For cogent criticism along these lines, see Schmitt, *supra* n.107, at 732–734.

[138] For example, 'Gaza: Use of Human Shields Continues', *The Jerusalem Post*, 19 November 2006, available at http://fr.jpost.com/servlet/Satellite?apage=1&cid=1162378435257&pagename=JPost/JPArticle/ShowFull.

[139] For general discussion, see C. Byron, 'International Humanitarian Law and Bombing Campaigns: Legitimate Military Objectives and Excessive Collateral Damage', (2010) 13 *YIHL*, 175.

[140] Article 52(1), API.

[141] *Ibid.*, Article 52(2). The ICRC considers this definition to be part of customary international law: CIHL, Rule 8. See also International Criminal Tribunal for the Former Yugoslavia, 'Final Report to the Prosecutor by the Committee Established to Review the NATO Bombing Campaign Against the Federal Republic of Yugoslavia', (2000) 39 *ILM*, 1257, at 1269 (hereinafter '*OTP Final Report*').

[142] See *ICRC Commentary*, *supra* n.101, at para. 2020.

[143] See *ibid.*, at para. 2021.

[144] See Byron, *supra* n.139, at 181–182.

were actually being used by the enemy's forces to store weapons,[145] or private forms of transport if commandeered to ferry troops to or from the combat zone.[146] The 'definite military advantage' expected to be gained from capturing, destroying or neutralising objectives that meet the above criteria must be concrete and noticeable, not hypothetical or speculative; it must also obtain 'in the circumstances ruling at the time' and not at some indeterminate point in the future.[147] In the event of any doubt arising as to whether a given, ostensibly civilian, object is actually making an effective contribution to military action, Article 52(3) of the Protocol requires the attacker to presume that it is not – in other words, to err on the side of caution. Various types of objects are afforded specific protection from attack: namely cultural objects and places of worship,[148] objects indispensable to the survival of the civilian population,[149] the natural environment,[150] and works and installations containing dangerous forces.[151] It is also forbidden to attack non-defended localities[152] and demilitarised zones.[153] It is forbidden (as an indiscriminate attack) to treat a number of 'clearly separated and distinct' military objectives co-located in an area with civilians or civilian objects as a single military objective:[154] thus, the type of 'area bombardment' witnessed in World War II is excluded by the modern law. The ICTY has recently convicted a Croatian general for, *inter alia*, ordering his artillery to treat the entire Serb-held town of Knin as a military objective, rather than directing fire at specific military objectives identified within it.[155]

The definition of military objectives, being entirely new to treaty law at the time of the adoption of API, was and remains subject to a number of reservations entered by various states parties at ratification of the Protocol, by which they preserve their military establishments' understanding of legitimate targets in armed conflict. For example, several NATO states entered 'statements of understanding' to the effect that 'an area of land' may by its location become a military objective, and that the military advantage anticipated must be understood in relation to the attack as a whole and not

---

[145] See Israeli Ministry of Foreign Affairs (2009), *The Operation in Gaza: Factual and Legal Aspects*, at paras. 164–166, available at http://www.mfa.gov.il/MFA/Terrorism-+Obstacle+to+Peace/Hamas+war+against+Israel/Operation_Gaza_factual_and_legal_aspects_use_of_force_Hamas_breaches_law_of_armed_conflict_5_Aug_200.htm (hereinafter '*IMFA Gaza Report*').
[146] Rogers, *supra* n.11, at 63.
[147] Byron, *supra* n.139, at 182.
[148] Article 53, API.
[149] Such as foodstuffs, crops, livestock or drinking water installations. See *ibid.*, Article 54(2).
[150] *Ibid.*, Article 55(1).
[151] Namely dams, dykes and nuclear electrical generating stations. See *ibid.*, Article 56(1).
[152] *Ibid.*, Article 59.
[153] *Ibid.*, Article 60.
[154] *Ibid.*, Article 51(5)(a).
[155] *Prosecutor v. Gotovina, Čermak & Markač*, [2011] ICTY Trial Chamber I Judgment, Case No.IT-06-90-T, at paras 1893–1911, available at http://www.icty.org/x/cases/gotovina/tjug/en/110415_judgement_vol2.pdf.

isolated or particular parts of the attack.[156] Probably the most significant divergence in national approaches to the definition of military objectives, however, lies in the US insistence that economic targets or those which support the 'war-sustaining capability' of an opponent fall within the definition. This approach has its origins in the US interdiction of the production of and trade in cotton during the American Civil War, on the basis that virtually the entire Confederate war effort was funded and sustained by the Southern States' reliance on that single crop;[157] it has been formally enunciated as part of American military doctrine since at least 1995.[158] A contemporary example of its use by US forces is seen in the targeting of drug laboratories, stockpiles and caches in Afghanistan, since the drug trade in that country generates funds for the purchase of weapons and supplies which sustain the continuing Taliban insurgency.[159] Consistent American usage to this effect notwithstanding, however, the view that 'war-sustaining' or purely economic targets are legitimate military objectives has not found acceptance in the military doctrine and practice of other states – the British position, for example, is that such objects do not of themselves make an *effective* contribution to *military* action and therefore fall outside the parameters of permissible targets under Article 52(2)[160] – and it would be correct to regard it as unlawful under IHL.[161]

Other prominent points of controversy in contemporary campaigns have included the targeting of broadcasting facilities as a source of propaganda for a hostile regime, and the whole concept of 'dual-use objects'. Both were highlighted by NATO's attack on the Serbian Radio and Television studios (hereinafter 'RTS') in Belgrade during the 1999 Kosovo War. To the extent that the RTS facility, although in itself a civilian object, was being used as part of the C3 (Command, Control and Communications) network of the Serbian military and security forces, as claimed by NATO, and was deliberately targeted on that basis, it is clear that by use it constituted a legitimate military objective that made an effective contribution to Serbian military action.[162] However, an additional justification presented for the attack was that RTS was part of the propaganda machinery sustaining the regime of President Slobodan Milošević and,

---

[156] See the statements of understanding/interpretation or declarations by Australia, Canada, Germany, Italy, the Netherlands, New Zealand, Spain and the UK. See Roberts and Guelff, *supra* n.62, at 500–511.

[157] Rogers, *supra* n.11, at 59; Hyde, *supra* n.20, at 375; *Mrs Alexander's Cotton*, [1864] 69 US 404, at 419–420; *Lamar v. Browne*, [1875] 92 US 187, at 194; *Young v. United States*, [1877] 97 US 39, at 59–61.

[158] See Byron, *supra* n.139, at 186–188; J. Holland, 'Military Objective and Collateral Damage: Their Relationship and Dynamics', (2004) 7 *YIHL* 35, at 44–46. An authoritative current statement of the position is in the *Commander's Handbook*, *supra* n.73, at para. 8.2.5.

[159] US Air Force Judge Advocate General's School (2009), *Air Operations and the Law – A Guide for Air, Space & Cyber Forces*, 2nd edn, at 250, available at http://www.afjag.af.mil/shared/media/document/AFD-100510-059.pdf (hereinafter '*Air Operations*').

[160] Rogers, *supra* n.11, at 70–71.

[161] Dinstein characterises the entire concept as a 'slippery-slope' and opines that it 'goes too far'. See Dinstein, *supra* n.9, at 87. Byron notes in this context that it could logically include banks and other financial institutions that fund a state's participation in an armed conflict and correctly states that 'the definition of military objectives in Article 52 would be stretched to breaking point' if this were to be correct. See Byron, *supra* n.139, at 188.

[162] *OTP Final Report*, *supra* n.141, at 1277–1278.

even more dubiously, that it failed to provide equal airtime for Western news broadcasts. The Committee of the ICTY's Office of the Prosecutor, charged with investigating the NATO campaign for possible violations of IHL, conceded that 'stopping ... propaganda may serve to demoralize the Yugoslav population and undermine the government's political support', but thought it 'unlikely that either of these purposes would offer the "concrete and direct" military advantage necessary to make them a legitimate military objective'.[163] The Committee's analysis suggested, however, that a media outlet broadcasting directions, appeals or incitement to commit criminal violations of international law during an armed conflict could be a legitimate military objective by use; this may or may not have been the approach taken by the Coalition in targeting Iraqi television stations during the second Gulf War after they broadcast footage of US POWs and dead soldiers in violation of GC III.[164] A similar ambivalence was apparent when Israel targeted the Al-Manar television station in Lebanon during its conflict with Hezbollah in 2006, claiming that it was 'used to relay messages to terrorists as well as incite acts of terrorism';[165] the UN Human Rights Council, on the other hand, thought its function more analogous to that of RTS in Serbia, namely that it was used by Hezbollah as a propaganda tool but did not make an effective contribution to military action such as to render it a military objective.[166]

Broadcasting facilities are the archetypal so-called 'dual-use object', that is, an object that is primarily civilian in character but has some military uses in armed conflict, such as to convert it into a military objective; other now-classic examples are national electricity grids, which power military communications and other facilities while also supporting many of the most basic necessities of daily civilian existence, such as water purification or sewage treatment plants. In a sense, *prima facie*, this should be a non-issue in IHL: the term 'dual-use object' as such is nowhere to be found in API and the rare mentions of it in the context of customary law only serve to emphasise its ambiguity and subjectivity.[167] It would not be at all illogical to conclude from the strict wording of API that either an object is a military objective, or it is not. Nevertheless, this 'harsh approach'[168] is not justified by the realities of modern societal and military infrastructures; it is also a fact that dual-use objects are explicitly acknowledged as such in the targeting practice of states.[169] It should be noted that the mere fact that a given civilian object has some potential or actual military uses does not automatically convert it into a military objective; ultimately, the test for whether or not

---

[163] *Ibid.*, 1278.
[164] Byron, *supra* n.139, 185.
[165] Israeli Ministry of Foreign Affairs (2006), *Responding to Hizbullah [sic] attacks from Lebanon – Issues of Proportionality*, available at http://www.mfa.gov.il/MFA/Government/Law/Legal+Issues+and+Rulings/Responding+to+Hizbullah+attacks+from+Lebanon-+Issues+of+proportionality+July+2006.htm (hereinafter '*IMFA Lebanon Report*').
[166] See *Report of the Commission of Inquiry on Lebanon pursuant to Human Rights Council Resolution S-2/1*, 23 November 2006, UN Doc. A/HRC/3/2, at paras. 140–143 (hereinafter '*UN Lebanon Report*').
[167] *OTP Final Report, supra* n.141, at 1266–1267; CIHL, *supra* n.12, at 32.
[168] Byron, *supra* n.139, at 183.
[169] *Appendix O, supra* n.129, at 623–624; UK Ministry of Defence, *The Manual of the Law of Armed Conflict* (Oxford: Oxford University Press, 2004), at para. 5.4.1.

it may lawfully be attacked is whether, in the circumstances ruling at the time, it makes an effective contribution to military action and its destruction would offer a definite military advantage to the attacker, as specified in Article 52(2) of API. The infamous Al-Firdus bunker in Baghdad, constructed as a multi-level civilian air-raid shelter during the Iran–Iraq War and subsequently converted to military use on some levels as a C2 command and control bunker while still used to shelter civilians on other levels, was deliberately targeted by the US Air Force in February 1991 using precision-guided munitions, which resulted in its destruction with the loss of an estimated 200–300 civilians. The American view of the bunker was that, since its conversion to primary military use, it was a legitimate military target despite its continued civilian use.[170]

D. Collateral Damage and Proportionality

The example of the Al-Firdus bunker is a good illustration of the concepts of collateral damage and proportionality, since even though the bunker was identified by the Coalition as a legitimate military objective because of its C2 function, the presence of civilians in or adjacent to the target must give the attacker pause for thought. In the event, the Americans did not know that the Iraqis were still using the bunker to shelter civilians, alongside its military role. The former chief attack planner in the Joint Forces Air Component Commander's targeting cell stated in this context that, 'had we known that there were civilians in the bunker, it never would have been attacked'.[171] In point of fact, such absolute restraint is not required by the LOAC: one of the most consistently misrepresented of the law's strictures is the recognition that civilian casualties may in any event occur as a result of the targeting process and will not necessarily be unlawful, provided that they are judged not to be disproportionate to the corresponding military advantage. Within these terms, collateral damage, far from being a callous fig-leaf for military carelessness at best or a war crime at worst, is not only permissible, but an actual legal doctrine. More than half a century before the adoption of API, a noted authority was able to write:

> An impressive, although unfortunate aspect of military arrangements respecting land warfare is the tendency to cause the operation of restrictions of acts regarded as normally improper, to be dependent on the judgment of the individuals whom they purport to restrain. This tendency breeds confusion of thought, inasmuch as it serves to give an appearance of lawlessness to acts which in reality conform to what is required. It allows too much to rest upon the character, temperament, and training of a commanding officer, and permits, in consequence, opposing armies, under similar circumstances, to resort to widely differing practices without exposing either to just charges of misconduct.[172]

To the extent that most states are now either parties to API or accept the main substance of its targeting rules as customary international law, the 'unfortunate aspect' of which

---

[170] See *Appendix O, supra* n.129, at 626–627; *Letter dated 14 February 1991 from the Permanent Representative of the United States of America to the United Nations addressed to the President of the Security Council*, UN Doc. S/22227; M.W. Lewis, 'The Law of Aerial Bombardment in the 1991 Gulf War', (2003) 97 *AJIL* 481, at 502–504.
[171] Quoted by Lewis, *ibid.*, at 503.
[172] Hyde, *supra* n.20, at 301.

Hyde complained in 1922 is universally accepted; however, it does appear that there is an – at least unofficial – standard of 'the reasonable military commander' when it comes to assessing the judgment of an attacker in relation to any given incident involving loss of civilian life and/or damage to civilian objects.[173]

Collateral damage is defined in the modern law as 'incidental loss of civilian life, injury to civilians, damage to civilian objects, or a combination thereof'[174] – the word 'incidental' clearly indicating that it is an undesired (but inevitable or accidental) corollary of an attack on a *legitimate military objective*. The concept of collateral damage is not relevant if an attack is deliberately directed against civilians or is indiscriminate: such attacks, as violations of Articles 51(2) and 51(4) respectively, automatically qualify as war crimes and the damage resulting therefrom would not in any sense be 'collateral'. But the civilian deaths in the Al-Firdus bunker constituted accidental collateral damage because the attacking force (a) did not know of civilians' presence in the legitimate military objective and (b) did not intend to target them. Collateral damage will only be unlawful if it 'may be expected' to cause death or injury to civilians or damage to civilian objects, 'which would be excessive *in relation to the concrete and direct military advantage anticipated* [from the attack]'.[175] As part of the targeting process, commanders are thus expected to engage in a calculation of the balancing act mentioned at the beginning of this chapter: they must weigh up the expected collateral damage incidental to an otherwise lawful attack, and decide (on the basis of all the available intelligence and with the benefit of legal advice) whether it would be disproportionate to the anticipated military advantage that would accrue from the attack; if it would, the law expects them to decide not to launch the attack,[176] or to cancel or suspend it if it is already in progress.[177]

There are other precautions to be taken in order to spare the civilian population, both in attack and in defence. Those who plan or decide upon an attack must do everything feasible to verify that the objectives to be attacked are in fact military objectives,[178] must 'take all feasible precautions in the choice of means and methods of attack with a view to avoiding, and in any event to minimizing' collateral damage,[179] and must give 'effective advance warning' of attacks which may affect the civilian population, 'unless circumstances do not permit'.[180] Where there is a choice between different targets which may be attacked to obtain a similar military advantage, the one expected to cause

---

[173] *OTP Final Report, supra* n.141, at 1271.
[174] Article 51(5)(b), API.
[175] *Ibid.*
[176] *Ibid.*, Article 57(2)(a)(iii).
[177] *Ibid.*, Article 57(2)(b).
[178] *Ibid.*, Article 57(2)(a)(i).
[179] *Ibid.*, Article 57(2)(a)(ii). This means that an attacking commander with a choice of weaponry at his disposal should choose the weapon(s) least likely to cause collateral damage.
[180] *Ibid.*, Article 57(2)(c). In the context of Israeli operations in Gaza in 2008–2009, the need for warnings to be 'effective' in order for an attacker to comply with the legal obligations, has been emphasised. See *Report of the United Nations Fact Finding Mission on the Gaza Conflict*, 15 September 2009, UN Doc. A/HRC/12/48, at paras 497–540 (hereinafter '*Goldstone Report*'). For the same point in relation to Israeli operations in Lebanon in 2006, see *UN Lebanon Report, supra* n.166, at paras 149–158.

the least collateral damage should be selected.[181] Defenders must take specific precautions to remove the civilian population under their control from the vicinity of military objectives and avoid locating such objectives within or adjacent to densely populated areas, along with other general necessary precautions.[182]

Although these provisions appear reasonable enough *in abstracto*, the experience of recent armed conflicts continues to demonstrate the limits of their practical application in many contemporary military operating environments. Urban warfare where the civilian population (for whatever reason) remains *in situ* and where the defending forces deliberately mingle with and operate from among that population, exemplified in recent years by Israel's incursions into Gaza, makes application of the rules of distinction and proportionality extraordinarily fraught with difficulties. It is important to understand that the notion of proportionality does not equate to a rigidly mathematical formula: there is no set number of civilians' lives considered to be 'worth' the destruction of any given military objective. The ICTY Office of the Prosecutor's review of the NATO bombing campaign against Serbia in 1999 considered that the civilian casualties (up to 17 civilians were killed) in the bombing of the RTS building in Belgrade 'were unfortunately high but do not appear to be clearly disproportionate';[183] yet in another case the Trial Chamber found that the shelling of Knin by Croatian artillery in 1995 (12 130-millimetre shells were fired at a single apartment where a military objective had been identified) 'created a significant risk of a high number of civilian casualties and injuries, as well as damage to civilian objects', which 'was excessive in relation to the anticipated military advantage', even in the absence of detailed statistics about the collateral damage caused.[184] Thus, in determining the proportionality of a given targeting operation, everything depends on the context and facts of the situation 'in the circumstances ruling at the time'. In any particular situation, theoretically, the incidental death of just one civilian might be considered too much; there are other situations in which, if a particularly important military advantage might be achieved from pressing home an attack, dozens or even hundreds of civilian casualties might theoretically be contemplated. Although it predated the adoption of API, the American use of atomic bombs against Hiroshima and Nagasaki in 1945, in order to force a quick Japanese surrender and obviate the need for a potentially very costly (in terms of lives as well as resources) ground invasion of Japan, was a case in point.[185] This has in effect been the ultimate question about proportionality: are the deaths of hundreds of thousands of civilians 'worth' the near-immediate surrender of an otherwise fiercely determined opponent, thereby avoiding heavy future casualties to the attacking military forces?

Questions of proportionality in the conduct of military operations are often intricately bound up with assessments of the legality of a conflict *ab initio*, due to the

---

[181] Article 57(3), API.
[182] *Ibid.*, Article 58.
[183] *OTP Final Report*, supra n.141, at 1279.
[184] *Gotovina*, supra n.155, at para. 1910.
[185] For a flavour of the arguments to this effect, see Henry Stimson (US Secretary of War) to Harry S. Truman (President of the USA), *Memorandum on Warning to Japan*, 2 July 1945, available at http://www.nuclearfiles.org/menu/library/correspondence/stimson-henry/corr_stimson_1945-07-02.htm.

widespread media reporting of civilian casualties in warfare and the negative effect that such reports have on popular opinion in Western liberal democracies. Following on from this approach a regrettable tendency has developed, in sections of the media and human rights organisations, whereby the legality of a given targeting operation is judged by the result alone and the fact of there being civilian casualties leads to a presumption of guilt. Press reports often state in absolute terms that civilian casualties are 'disproportionate', without any effort to identify *what* they are disproportionate *to*, that is, without attempting to comprehend the process whereby expected military advantage is weighed against anticipated collateral damage. This has the effect of creating a form of 'strict-liability' understanding of the law governing the conduct of hostilities, which is totally at odds with its actual provisions.[186]

Ultimately, it is often difficult to discern the objective truth about collateral damage and proportionality amid the 'fog of war'. Sober analysis and rational debate are all too often displaced by increasingly shrill denunciations and counter-denunciations, as evidenced by the Israeli operations in Lebanon (2006) and Gaza (2008–2009). In both cases, high-profile UN fact-finding missions issued reports which were heavily critical of Israeli targeting practices, in particular accusing the IDF of causing disproportionate casualties among the civilian population and destruction of civilian objects and infrastructure.[187] In both cases, Israel responded with its own reports, relying on its right of self-defence under the *jus ad bellum* as a catch-all justification for its operations, dismissing the UN's accusations as biased and asserting that the IDF had taken the fullest possible precautions in attacking its irregular enemies in a difficult urban environment.[188] A similarly unhelpful exchange of assertions and counter-assertions followed the Sri Lankan Armed Forces' victory over the Liberation Tigers of Tamil Eelam at the conclusion of the Sri Lankan Civil War in 2009.[189]

5. OUTLINE OF MODERN TARGETING PROCESSES

Methodologies of targeting have changed over time. From manually throwing bombs over the sides of aircraft in the early stages of World War I to drawing squares on maps and bombing entire areas thus delimited in World War II, pre-1949 practices were unsophisticated in the extreme. The then-prevalent view was expressed thus after the February 1945 fire-bombing of Dresden: 'Where bombing is necessary for the conduct of military affairs, with military objectives, it is just too bad if civilians and old women get their guts blown into tree tops, but there it is. That is war and has got to be put up

---

[186] See Y. Dinstein, 'Concluding Remarks: LOAC and Attempts to Abuse or Subvert It', (2011) 87 *Int'l L Studies: International Law and the Changing Character of War* 483.

[187] See *UN Lebanon Report*, supra n.166, at paras 93–148; *Goldstone Report*, supra n.180, at paras 651–701.

[188] See *IMFA Lebanon Report*, supra n.165 at 2–5; *IMFA Gaza Report*, supra n.145 at paras 151–170 and 249–261.

[189] See *Report of the Secretary-General's Panel of Experts on Accountability in Sri Lanka* (31 March 2011), at 23–36, available at http://www.un.org/News/dh/infocus/Sri_Lanka/POE_Report_Full.pdf; Sri Lankan Ministry of Defence, *Humanitarian Operation Factual Analysis: July 2006–May 2009*, at 52–68, available at http://www.defence.lk/news/20110801_Conf.pdf.

with.'[190] Strategic aerial bombing was not attempted again until – in a more limited context – it was used by the Americans against North Vietnam; on that occasion, owing to the political indefensibility of strategic bombing, the military targeting process was effectively replaced by an extremely restrictive political one, which was conducted with little regard for what was in fact permissible under the LOAC and arguably excessive attention to domestic public opinion and the propaganda reactions of the North Vietnamese.[191] The modern age of effects-based aerial operations conducted under the media spotlight of scrutiny by human rights organisations and the public at large effectively began with the first Gulf War in 1991. Since then there have been high-profile aerial campaigns that have been dissected for compliance with IHL in Serbia (1999), Afghanistan (2001 until the present), the second Gulf War (2003), Lebanon (2006), Gaza (2008–2009) and Libya (2011).[192] The powers that have conducted these campaigns keep the full operational details of their targeting decisions classified – for obvious reasons of military security – but some of them do publish their officially promulgated unclassified targeting doctrines, as does NATO; these contain generalised descriptions of the overall process which they follow in targeting operations. One legal adviser in the Royal Australian Air Force has even published his PhD thesis on the topic as an academic text.[193] These materials enable a reasonable picture of the legal framework within which targeting decisions are made to be presented.

As was recently explained in the context of the Libyan operations, there are two main types of targeting process: deliberate and 'dynamic'.[194] The former refers to the selection of installations and static, fixed-site targets before an operation actually starts; statistically, less collateral damage occurs with this type of targeting because the pre-operation planning has fully integrated legal considerations, including the identification of likely collateral damage, into the selection process. The main danger for the targeteer occurs during the latter type of targeting, which is where commanders must respond (often very quickly indeed) to moving targets and events as they develop on the battlefield. Thus, some of the worst incidents of collateral damage during Israeli operations in Gaza occurred when IDF troops were fired on from unexpected locations, to which they immediately returned fire.[195] On the other hand, it has become an absolute imperative for NATO forces – particularly when operating in Muslim countries

---

[190] *Hansard*, HC Debs, vol. 408, col. 1899 (6 March 1945). The Member of Parliament who made this comment, Richard Stokes, was a long-time opponent of strategic bombing and in the same debate went on to criticise trenchantly the raid on Dresden.

[191] See W.H. Parks, 'Rolling Thunder and the Law of War', (1982) *Air University Review*, available at http://www.airpower.au.af.mil/airchronicles/aureview/1982/jan-feb/parks.html.

[192] This list omits bombing campaigns conducted by states that seemingly make no attempt to apply IHL to their military operations, such as the two Russian campaigns against Chechnya in the 1990s (the first of which saw the carpet-bombing of the Chechen capital Grozny by the Russian Air Force).

[193] I. Henderson, *The Contemporary Law of Targeting: Military Objectives, Proportionality and Precautions in Attack under Additional Protocol I* (Leiden: Koninklijke Brill NV, 2009).

[194] See House of Commons Defence Committee, *Operations in Libya: Ninth Report of Session 2010–2012*, 8 February 2012, HC 950, Volume I, Evidence 7 and 30 (hereinafter '*Operations in Libya*'). See also NATO, *Allied Joint Doctrine for Joint Targeting*, (2008) AJP-3.9, at para. 0106 (hereinafter '*Allied Joint Doctrine*').

[195] For example, see *Goldstone Report*, *supra* n.180, at paras 651–701.

where there is usually substantial local hostility to their presence – to avoid civilian casualties almost at all costs.[196] This may lead to precautionary directions on matters of detail – for example, in operations in Afghanistan, requirements that all Afghans are to be presumed civilian, all compounds are to be presumed civilian objects, and civilian presence is to be presumed in all locations where there is any evidence of human habitation.[197] In individual operations, attacks are aborted at short notice if any expected civilians are located in the target area.[198] On a more general level, there is a debate about the consideration (morally and legally) which a commander is required to give to the protection of his own forces as a factor in deciding military advantage and corresponding proportionality.[199]

A preliminary issue in targeting will be whether a given target belongs to an authorised Target Set. These are categories of installations according to their type and function. NATO lists them as: Command, Control, Communication, Computers and Intelligence; Weapons of Mass Destruction; Ground Forces and Facilities; Air Forces and Airfields; Air Defence; Naval Forces and Ports; Space Forces; Ballistic Missiles; Electric Power; Petroleum Industry; Industry; Transportation/Lines of Communication; Military Supply and Storage; Special Category; Military Leadership; Political Leadership; Economic Leadership; General Public; and Adversary Media.[200]

The basic targeting process for deliberate targeting as applied by the UK is as follows: Directives issued by the Chief of the Defence Staff and the Joint Commander of a given operation set out objectives, priorities and general guidance as to the effects desired and the level and type of force authorised to achieve them.[201] All targets are placed on one of a number of specific Target Lists, namely: the No-Strike List, the Restricted Target List, the Joint Target List, the Joint Integrated Target List, the Joint Integrated Prioritised Target List and the Target Nomination List. The first and second contain objects which are protected from attack under international law, either permanently or provisionally. The third, fourth and fifth are progressively refined 'master lists' of potential targets authorised and prioritised for attack. The sixth is the final daily list of targets to be attacked.[202] Daily meetings are held throughout the campaign to continuously review and approve the daily attack lists.[203] Legal issues – whether an object is a military objective, what the military advantage to be gained is – are determined with the assistance of a military legal adviser (hereinafter 'LEGAD') at the time that an attack is authorised and based on the most up-to-date and relevant intelligence available.[204] The final decision – to attack or not to attack – is that of the

---

[196] See *Operations in Libya, supra* n.194 at 27–28, Evidence 8, 27 and 42.
[197] HQ International Security Assistance Force/US Forces-Afghanistan, *COMISAF's Tactical Directive*, 30 November 2011, at 2, available at http://www.isaf.nato.int/images/docs/20111105%20nuc%20tactical%20directive%20revision%204%20%28releaseable%20version%29%20r.pdf.
[198] *Operations in Libya, supra*, n.194, Evidence 21 and 27–29.
[199] See N. Neuman, 'Applying the Rule of Proportionality: Force Protection and Cumulative Assessment in International Law and Morality', (2004) 7 *YIHL* 79.
[200] *Allied Joint Doctrine, supra* n.194, at para. A001.
[201] *Legal Support, supra* n.93, at para. 224.
[202] *Ibid.*, at para. 225.
[203] *Ibid.*, at para. 226.
[204] *Ibid.*, at para. 229.

commander, not the LEGAD.[205] Complex, unforeseen or politically sensitive issues arising during targeting operations should be referred by the LEGAD for higher-level guidance from Permanent Joint Headquarters, which co-ordinates with the Ministry of Defence and the Government.[206]

The above procedure may be summarised in the American system as one of target development, vetting, validation, nomination and prioritisation.[207] Particular questions that will need to be answered, especially in the context of dynamic targeting, are whether the target is a valid military objective, whether there is positive identification, whether there are any restrictions on attacking the target, and whether there will be any expected collateral damage – and, if so, whether it will be proportionate to the military advantage expected.[208] Other factors that will be taken into account in the targeting process are: the desired point of impact, the desired level of damage or degradation, determination of the most appropriate types of weapon and munitions, and the effect of terrain and weather. An essential part of the process is determining the Collateral Damage Estimate (hereinafter 'CDE').[209] It is generally the practice that CDE up to a certain number of civilian casualties may be approved by the military commander on the ground, but anything above that level will require political approval – if necessary, even from the Head of Government or Head of State. A further issue is that of time-sensitive targeting: where an immediate decision is required in cases of fleeting targets of opportunity or those that do not currently pose a threat but will soon do so. Typical examples could be anything that is mobile: rocket launchers or missile systems, command posts or communication facilities.[210]

---

[205] *Ibid.*, at para. 230.
[206] *Ibid.*, at para. 231.
[207] *Air Operations*, supra n.159, at 257.
[208] *Ibid.*, at 260–261.
[209] *Ibid.*, at 255.
[210] *Allied Joint Doctrine*, supra n.194, at para. 0501.

11. Protected persons in international armed conflicts
Tom Ruys and Christian De Cock*

> The stillness of the night was broken by groans by stifled sighs of anguish and suffering. Heart-rending voices kept calling for help. Who could ever describe the agonies of that fearful night! (Henri Dunant, *A Memory of Solferino*, 1862)

1. INTRODUCTION

On 24 June 1859, a Swiss merchant, aged 31, was clearly what most would label 'in the wrong place, at the wrong time.' Having travelled to Italy on a business mission, the young Henri Dunant was journeying in Castiglione delta Pieve on the exact day when the French and Sardinian armies clashed with the troops of the Austrian Emperor at the nearby village of Solferino. As the town was flooded with casualties, the sceneries witnessed by Dunant changed his life forever. Shocked by the lack of adequate care for the sick and wounded – with so many young men simply left to die on the battlefield – Dunant embarked on a crusade for the protection of those *hors de combat*.

Dunant's quest resulted in the creation, in 1863, of an international movement that would eventually become the International Committee of the Red Cross (hereinafter 'ICRC'), as well as the adoption, one year later, of the Geneva Convention for the Amelioration of the Condition of the Wounded in Armies in the Field. This Convention became the first instrument of what is sometimes referred to as the 'Geneva Law', viz. the branch of the law of armed conflict (hereinafter 'LOAC') dealing with the protection of persons in the hands of the enemy, as opposed to the 'Hague Law', which developed mainly from the 1899 and 1907 Hague Conferences and which focuses on the actual conduct of hostilities as such. The distinction between two analytically separate branches of LOAC has rightly been criticized as a chimera, primarily because the two have always intersected.[1] However, for didactical purposes – and for didactical purposes only – the distinction probably serves its purpose. Thus, the two previous chapters, dealing respectively with weapons (Chapter 9) and targeting (Chapter 10), generally fall within the ambit of the Hague Law. By contrast, the present Chapter primarily addresses aspects of the 'Geneva Law'.

Ever since 1864, the body of 'Geneva Law' has developed considerably, by and large as a result of major armed conflicts revealing lacunae in the existing protective regimes.

---

* The views expressed in this chapter are those of the author in his personal capacity and do not intend to reflect the views of the DG or of the Ministry of Defence.

[1] Many treaties indeed contain both 'Geneva' and 'Hague' rules. This is particularly true for the two Additional Protocols of 1977, but also for older instruments, such as, for instance, the 1907 Hague Regulations (Annexed to Hague Convention IV regarding the laws and customs of war on land).

Thus, the First World War inspired a revision of the Convention on the Wounded and Sick (1929) as well as the adoption of a separate Geneva Convention relative to the Treatment of Prisoners of War (1929). The abuses and horrors of the Second World War inspired a further codification effort, leading to the adoption of the four 1949 Conventions, including a separate Convention dealing specifically with 'the protection of civilian persons in time of war' (GC IV) – a topic that had hitherto gone by and large unregulated under LOAC. The Four Geneva Conventions – all of which have been ratified universally[2] and may in any event be taken to reflect customary law – have in various ways been supplemented by the First Additional Protocol of 1977 (hereinafter 'AP I'). It is important to stress, however, that while many provisions of AP I are similarly reflective of customary international law, this is not necessarily true for all of its provisions. Thus, in any given international armed conflict, determining whether the Belligerent Parties have ratified AP I is and remains a crucial step in the analysis.[3]

The purpose of the present Chapter is twofold. First, it intends to give an overview of the personal scope of application of the protective regimes enshrined (primarily) in the four Geneva Conventions. At the same time, it intends to give a brief overview of the substantive rules of LOAC dealing with the protection of persons in the hands of the enemy. Thus, we will subsequently address the protection of the wounded, sick and shipwrecked (Section 2a), the treatment of prisoners of war (hereinafter 'POWs') (Section 2b) and the protection of civilians (Section 2c). A further Section (Section 2d) addresses some specific categories of persons, the protection of which has drawn particular attention in more recent decades, such as women, children, journalists, civilian contractors and personnel of international organizations. Two reservations are due, however. First, given the vast amalgam of rules enshrined in the Four Geneva Conventions and in AP I, the present Chapter clearly does not claim exhaustivity. The purpose is merely to offer a brief introduction to the 'Geneva Law' by addressing a number of 'capita selecta' and by flagging some interpretive difficulties in the law that have come to the fore as a result of the advance of irregular warfare and transnational terrorism, and the increased participation of civilians in hostilities.[4] Secondly, given the

---

[2] For an overview of existing LOAC treaty law and of statuses of ratification see the ICRC Treaty database, available at http://www.icrc.org/ihl.nsf/INTRO?OpenView. At the time of writing, the Four Geneva Conventions had been ratified by 194 States Parties.

[3] A useful overview of the rules that are deemed binding as customary international law in the view of the ICRC can be found in J.-M. Henckaerts and L. Doswald-Beck (eds.), *Customary International Humanitarian Law. Vol. I Rules* (Cambridge: Cambridge University Press, 2005) (hereinafter 'ICRC Customary Study'), 621. The findings of the ICRC Customary Study have, however, not gone without objections. See, for example, J.B. Bellinger III, W.J. Haynes II, 'A US Government Response to the International Committee of the Red Cross Study Customary International Humanitarian Law', (2007) 866 *IRRC* 462; E. Wilmshurst and S. Breau (eds.), *Perspectives on the ICRC Study on Customary International Humanitarian Law* (Cambridge: Cambridge University Press, 2007), 433.

[4] One particularly controversial aspect, notably the detention of persons other than POWs, is not tackled here. On this topic see J.B. Bellinger III and V.M. Padmanabhan, 'Detention Operations in Contemporary Conflicts: Four Challenges for the Geneva Conventions and Other Existing Law', (2011) 105 *AJIL* 201–243; J. Pejic, 'Procedural Principles and Safeguards for Internment/Administrative Detention in Armed Conflict and Other Situations Of Violence', (2005) 87 *IRRC* 375. See also the references under n.79.

scope of application of the Geneva Conventions and of AP I, the different sections of this Chapter deal exclusively with international armed conflicts.

Before embarking on an analysis of the substantive protective regimes applicable to the sick and wounded, POWs or civilians, the issue of qualification arises first. More in particular, it is crucial to familiarize oneself with the criteria that determine who qualifies as a POW, a person *hors de combat* or as a civilian. This vexing issue is at the heart of some of the most delicate and consequential controversies of LOAC.

2. INDIVIDUAL STATUS IN THE CONTEXT OF INTERNATIONAL ARMED CONFLICTS

A. Introduction

At its outset, the application of LOAC begs two foundational classification questions. The first concerns the classification of the armed conflict itself: is it international (or internationalized) in nature, or is it non-international? This question – which determines the body of (treaty and customary) law applicable in a given situation – was addressed above in Chapter 7 and will not be re-examined here. The second question concerns the individual status of persons participating in, or victim of, an ongoing conflict. In international armed conflicts, the individual status question is often narrowed down to the – at face value relatively easy – question of whether a given person is a 'combatant' or a 'civilian', the two categories being mutually exclusive. The truth, however, is far more complex. Indeed, those hoping to neatly fit together the relevant Treaty provisions of the Hague Regulations (hereinafter 'HagueReg'), the Geneva Conventions and the First Additional Protocol as different pieces of a single jigsaw puzzle are bound to come home empty-handed.

B. Individual Battlefield Status

i. The combatant privilege

The traditional approach to distinguish between 'combatants' and 'civilians' is to define 'combatants' as all persons that have the 'right to participate directly in hostilities', or, put differently, all persons endowed with the so-called 'combatant privilege'. This is the approach followed by the First Additional Protocol[5] and reflected in the writings of the ICRC. LOAC indeed recognizes that in international armed conflicts there are specific categories of individuals that – subject to certain conditions – may lawfully take direct part in hostilities. Such persons cannot be prosecuted merely for doing so; instead they can only be prosecuted insofar as they have committed specific war crimes. By contrast, individuals not falling within one of these categories can be prosecuted for any punishable acts they commit that are contrary to domestic law or international criminal law. For example, when John Doe, a civilian, shoots an enemy soldier, he may be tried for murder (save of course if he were acting in self-defence). If,

---

[5] See Article 43(2), API.

however, John Doe were a regular soldier in uniform, the killing of an enemy soldier would not give rise to any lawful conduct on his part (save, for example, if he were to engage in perfidy, use a prohibited weapon, ...).

In broad terms, three categories of 'combatants' can be discerned:

1. Members of the regular armed forces of a Party to the conflict.
2. Members of the irregular organized armed forces of a Party to the conflict.
3. Participants in a so-called *levée en masse*.

In accordance with Article 50(1) of AP I, any person not falling within one of these categories qualifies as a 'civilian', implying that the precise definition of the different categories of 'combatants' is the crux of the matter.[6] In case of doubt as to an individual's status, he or she shall also be considered as a civilian.

The first of the categories of combatants listed above is fairly straightforward. All members of the regular armed forces, including members of militias or volunteer corps forming part of such armed forces qualify as combatants and may in principle lawfully take part in hostilities. Article 43(2) of AP I clarifies that this only holds true for *organized* armed forces, groups and units 'belonging to'[7] a Party to the conflict which are under a *command responsible* to that Party for the conduct of its subordinates.[8] On the other hand, it is immaterial whether or not the Party is represented by a government or an authority *recognized* by the adverse Party.[9] Thus, the Taliban being in *de facto* control in the bulk of Afghan territory in 2001, the non-recognition of their regime by the majority of the international community had no impact on the Taliban fighters' individual status in the initial armed conflict with the United States.[10]

---

[6] The negative definition of the notion of 'civilian' is also reflected in Rule 5 of the ICRC Customary Study. ICRC Customary Study Vol. I, *supra* n.3, at 17. The Commentary makes clear that while not explicit in Rule 5 as such, participants in a *levée en masse* are also to be regarded as combatants (*ibid.*, at 18). See also ICRC, 'Interpretive Guidance on the Notion of Direct Participation in Hostilities Under International Humanitarian Law', adopted by the ICRC Assembly on 26 February 2009, at 21, available at http://www.icrc.org/eng/assets/files/other/irrc-872-reports-documents.pdf.

[7] See, for example, Israel, Military Court, *Military Prosecutor v. Kassem et al.* (1969) 42 *ILR* 470, at 476. See also ICTY, *Prosecutor v. Tadic*, IT-94-1-A, A. Ch., 15 July 1999 (1999) 38 *ILM* 1518, at 1537. The concept of 'belonging to' requires at least a *de facto* relationship between an organized armed group and a Party to the conflict. This relationship may be officially declared, but may also be expressed through tacit agreement or conclusive behaviour. See ICRC, Interpretive Guidance, *supra* n.6, at 23–24. See also on this requirement: K. Del Mar, 'The Requirement of "Belonging" under International Humanitarian Law' (2010) 21 *EJIL* 105–124.

[8] See also Rule 4 of the ICRC Customary Study *supra* n.3.

[9] See Article 4(A)(3) GC III; Article 43(1), AP I. This qualification was introduced in GC III in response to the denial of POW status by Nazi Germany to the *Forces françaises libres* of General de Gaulle (whose government in exile was not recognized by Berlin). See G.D. Solis, *The Law of Armed Conflict* (Cambridge: Cambridge University Press, 2010), at 198.

[10] Y. Dinstein, *The Conduct of Hostilities under the Law of International Armed Conflict*, 2nd edn (Cambridge: Cambridge University Press, 2010), at 55.

For the sake of completeness, it is noted that LOAC explicitly excludes from the first category medical personnel and chaplains.[11] Such persons are precluded from taking direct part in hostilities; they can only be lightly armed and may only use force in their own defence or in defence of the wounded and sick in their charge.[12] This (commonsensical) exception illustrates that the traditional dogma that every person is either a combatant or a civilian cannot be upheld in absolute terms. Insofar as they are members of the regular armed forces, doctors and chaplains cannot be considered as civilians. At the same time, insofar as they cannot take direct part in hostilities, they remain non-combatants. In a similar vein, it must be added that states may unilaterally decide to qualify other members of their regular armed forces, such as judges or blue-collar workers, as 'non-combatants' (prevented from taking direct part in hostilities).[13]

The terms 'combatant' and 'combatant privilege' are not confined to *regular* armed forces, but equally cover *irregular* armed forces belonging to a Party to the conflict, viz. 'other militias and members of other volunteer corps, including those of organized resistance movements'.[14] This is the second category of 'combatants'. As before, this category only covers '*organized* armed forces under a *command responsible* for the conduct of its subordinates'.[15] This does not imply that small irregular units are outlawed under LOAC, yet individual *francs-tireurs* acting on their own initiative are.

Otherwise, Article 1 of the Hague Regulations and Article 4(A)(2) of GC III spell out three further cumulative conditions that irregular armed forces should fulfil. First, they must have a fixed distinctive sign recognizable at a distance. The most obvious example consists in the wearing of a standard uniform, yet this requirement may also be fulfilled by wearing a particular headgear (e.g., a beret) – distinct from what ordinary civilians usually wear – an armband or certain insignia. It must be kept in mind that the gist of this rule is the principle that combatants should distinguish themselves from civilians. This principle is one of the normative pillars of the LOAC framework and is inspired

---

[11] See Articles 19 *et seq.*, GC I; Article 33, GC III; Article 43(2), AP I.

[12] See Article 22, GC I.

[13] Cf. Article 3, HagueReg: 'The armed forces of the belligerent parties may consist of combatants and non-combatants.' The presumption, however, is that all members of the armed forces, with exceptions of medical and religious personnel, are combatants permitted to take direct part in hostilities. See K. Ipsen, 'Combatants and Non-combatants', in D. Fleck *et al.* (eds), *The Handbook of International Humanitarian Law*, 2nd edn (Oxford: Oxford University Press, 2008), 79–117, at 82. Examples include Germany's Military Manual, which stresses that 'judges, government officials and blue-collar workers' shall be non-combatants; the US Naval Handbook states the same in respect of 'civil defense personnel' (see ICRC Customary Study Vol. I, *supra* n.3, at 13). Conversely, states sometimes incorporate paramilitary or armed law enforcement agencies into the armed forces (e.g., gendarmerie). Article 43(3), AP I demands that such incorporation be notified to the other Parties to the conflict. According to the ICRC, '[w]hile notification is not constitutive of the status of the units concerned, it does serve to avoid confusion and thus enhances respect for the principle of distinction'. ICRC Customary Study, Vol. I, *supra* n.3, at 17.

[14] Article 4(A)(2), GC III. Article 1, HagueReg similarly refers to 'militia and volunteer corps' fulfilling certain criteria. Article 43(1), AP I refers to 'armed forces' in general terms.

[15] Article 43(2), AP I. Article 43(1), AP I adds that 'armed forces shall be subject to an internal disciplinary system which, inter alia, shall enforce compliance' with the LOAC. This requirement supplements the need for command responsibility.

by the desire to minimize civilian exposure in armed conflict. Accordingly, it is clear that combatants are not required to wear fluorescent clothing at night and that nothing prohibits the use of a camouflaged battle dress.[16] In the *Kassem* case, for instance, an Israeli military court ruled that the wearing of mottled caps and green clothes fulfilled the requirement of distinction, as this was not the usual attire of inhabitants of the area in which the Palestinian partisans were operating.[17] Secondly, irregulars must carry their arms openly. For the same reason as before, this requirement must be construed reasonably. Clearly, carrying a sidearm in a holster is just as permitted as the use of camouflage.[18] Thirdly, irregular forces must conduct their operations in accordance with the laws and customs of war.

Although the cited treaty provisions only explicitly impose the latter three conditions on irregular forces, they must arguably also be complied with by *regular* armed forces.[19] Undeniably, regular forces have the same duty to abide by the rules of LOAC and to distinguish themselves from the civilian population as their irregular counterparts. By contrast with irregular troops, however, there is a – rebuttable – presumption that regular armed forces do fulfil the cited preconditions.

It is important to emphasize that the three requirements spelled out above are not 'constitutive' of combatant status.[20] Put differently, when a combatant exercises his combatant privilege in an unlawful manner by failing to comply with the cited standards, he may be tried and punished for doing so. More fundamentally, failure to comply may affect the application of the protective regimes of the GC III and GC IV.[21] By contrast, failure to comply does not result in the loss of combatant status which is inherently affixed to being a member of the armed forces.

The third category of persons endowed with the 'combatant privilege'[22] concerns the scenario of a *levée en masse*. Article 2 of the Hague Regulations and Article 4(1)(6) of GC III recognize that the inhabitants of a territory which has not been occupied may spontaneously take up arms to resist invading troops. This is the only category which is not subject to the requirement that combatants form part of an organized group under a responsible command. Indeed, a *levée en masse* is by nature conceived of as a spontaneous uprising, rather than an orchestrated operation. Still, participation to a *levée en masse* is subject to stringent criteria under LOAC. By analogy with categories 1 and 2, participants should carry their arms openly and respect the laws and customs of war. In addition, a *levée en masse* is only accepted prior to actual occupation; in

---

[16] See Dinstein, *supra* n. 10, at 44–45.
[17] See, for example, Israel, Military Court, *Kassem*, *supra* n. 7. See also T. Pfanner, 'Military Uniforms and the Law of War', (2004) 86 *IRRC* 93, at 107.
[18] See also *infra* n.46.
[19] See, for example, ICRC Customary Study, Vol. I, *supra* n.3, at 15. See also S.D. Murphy, 'Evolving Geneva Convention Paradigms in the "War on Terrorism": Applying the Core Rules to the Release of the Persons Deemed "Unprivileged Combatants"', (2007) 75 *George Washington L. Rev.* 1105, at 1125–1126. But see E.J. Wallach, 'Afghanistan, Quirin and Uchiyama: Does the Sauce Suit the Gander?', (2003) *Army Lawyer*, November 2003, at 18, 24.
[20] See also ICRC, Interpretive Guidance, *supra* n.6, at 22.
[21] See *infra* Section 2Ci.
[22] This category is oddly overlooked by Article 43 of AP I, but is nonetheless referred to in the mirroring provision of Article 50(1) of AP I.

other words, in the course of the (in principle rather brief) invasion phase.[23] LOAC does not legitimize guerrilla warfare in situations of occupation. Given the stringent criteria, the aversion towards civilian involvement in hostilities and the changed nature of modern-day warfare, this category is often thought to be mostly of historical importance.[24]

ii. (Presumed or actual) direct participation in hostilities and (direct) liability to attack

The distinction between 'combatants' and 'civilians' is sometimes framed in a different, more descriptive – or 'non-legal'[25] – manner. Indeed, the 'combatant' label can also be used to identify not only those persons that are endowed with the combatant privilege but also all others that are actually taking direct part in hostilities. Framed in such manner, the notion includes both 'lawful combatants' – that is, persons belonging to one of the three categories listed above – and so-called 'unprivileged' or 'unlawful' combatants,[26] viz. persons that are not permitted by LOAC to take part in hostilities. Both categories are directly liable to attack. Indeed, (presumed or actual) direct participation in hostilities and direct liability to attack are two sides of the same coin.

As far as 'lawful combatants' are concerned, it is in principle uncontroversial that (as a logical corollary of their 'combatant privilege') they are always liable to attack (1) irrespective of time and place, and (2) irrespective of their specific tasks within the armed forces.[27] First, the time and place of attack are immaterial: a member of the armed forces of a Party to the conflict can be targeted at any time, including when sleeping in his/her barracks. Such an attack, when otherwise conducted in conformity with the applicable prescripts, is not 'murder' but a lawful act under LOAC – 'targeted killing' is not as such prohibited under LOAC. In a similar vein, members of the armed forces can be targeted not only when engaging in combat at the frontline, but also when they are far removed from the actual locus of hostilities – albeit that the sudden broadening of the theatre of hostilities may exceptionally give rise to a breach of the

---

[23] Ipsen stresses that civilians involved in armed resistance may not have had the time to secure the authorization of their state by joining the armed forces, as a militia or a volunteer corps. Ipsen, *supra* n.13, at 93–94.

[24] See, for example, *ibid.*, at 94. But see also Solis, *supra* n.9, at 201 (referring to Georgian citizens taking up arms against Russian troops entering South Ossetia in 2008).

[25] Ipsen, *supra* n.13, at 98.

[26] The notion of 'unlawful combatancy' is generally traced back to Baxter. See R.R. Baxter, 'So-Called 'Unprivileged Belligerency: Spies, Guerrillas, and Saboteurs', (1951) 28 *BYIL* 323, at 328.

[27] Absent evidence in state practice and *opinio iuris* since the adoption of the Geneva Conventions it is not entirely clear whether this holds true, not only for regular and irregular armed forces (categories 1 and 2 described above), but also for participants in a *levée en masse* (category 3). The problem is of course that the latter are difficult to distinguish from ordinary civilians; they are not required under LOAC to carry a distinctive emblem/uniform, but only to carry their arms openly. The implication is that at least in practical, if not in legal, terms their direct liability should be construed by analogy with the liability to attack of civilians (unlawfully) taking direct part in hostilities. See on this *infra*.

proportionality principle under the *jus ad bellum* and/or the *jus in bello*.[28] Secondly, the role/task of the person concerned is immaterial: a cook or driver can be a lawful target of attack just as much as a paratrooper or other commando. As mentioned above, medical personnel and chaplains, although members of the armed forces, do not enjoy combatant privilege. As a corollary, they are not liable to direct attack (lest they (unlawfully) engage in direct participation in hostilities (cf. *infra*)). Whether this reasoning extends to other members of regular armed forces that are prohibited from taking part in hostilities, not because of a rule of LOAC but by unilateral decision of the state itself (cf. *supra* (e.g., legal advisors)), is open to debate.[29] Reservists are not lawful targets of attack: potential mobilization does not render the person concerned a combatant liable to attack.[30]

While lawful combatants can in principle be attacked in any place, at any time, this exposure to attack is not of a never-ending nature. First, combatants can 'withdraw' from hostilities by retiring or demobilizing, upon which they return to civilian status. Secondly, they can gain immunity from attack by becoming *hors de combat*, either on a voluntary basis (e.g., by surrendering) or by force. In the latter scenario, the question pops up what protective regime they are entitled to (cf. *infra*).

Persons that do not qualify under one of the three categories of 'lawful combatants' listed above are in principle protected from direct attack. Clearly, this does not mean that civilians enjoy absolute protection from the harmful consequences of hostilities. On the one hand, LOAC prohibits direct (and deliberate) as well as indiscriminate attacks against civilians or civilian objects, and imposes certain precautionary obligations[31] in order to spare civilians and civilian objects. On the other hand, LOAC does accept incidental injury to civilians as collateral damage resulting from attacks against military objectives, as long as the damage is 'proportional' to the military advantage sought by the attack. Exposure to incidental injury is of course strongly influenced by civilians' 'proximity' to military objectives. Thus, civilian contractors accompanying regular armed forces are more likely to get caught in the cross-fire (without such 'collateral damage' giving rise to an infringement of LOAC).

Furthermore, Article 51(3) AP I makes clear that protection from direct attack is granted 'unless and for such time as they take a direct part in hostilities'.[32] Indeed, *any* person that does not enjoy combatant privilege but nonetheless takes direct part in hostilities (whether he be a chaplain, a civilian contractor working for the armed forces,

---

[28] For an analysis of the role of the proportionality principle in the *jus ad bellum* and *jus in bello*, see J. Gardam, *Necessity, Proportionality and the Use of Force by States* (Cambridge: Cambridge University Press, 2004).

[29] Suffice to note that (a) a state party to an armed conflict cannot be expected to scrutinize the domestic regulations of its opponent to examine which members of the latter's armed forces are permitted to take part in hostilities, and that (b) the presence of 'non-combatant members of the armed forces' – chaplains, medical personnel or other – at a military objective does not require an attacking enemy to take any special precautionary measures, as would the presence of civilians. According to Ipsen, non-combatant members of armed forces can be directly targeted (Ipsen, *supra* n.13, at 99).

[30] ICRC Customary Study, Vol. I, *supra* n.3, at 14.

[31] See in particular Articles 48–58, AP I.

[32] Article 51(3), AP I.

a civilian inhabitant of occupied territory, …) can be directly attacked. Given the important consequences attached, the definition of 'direct participation in hostilities' has proven to be one of the most controversial questions of LOAC, and especially since 9/11. The question is essentially two-fold. First, what specific 'acts' qualify as 'direct participation'? It is uncontroversial that a farmer or other individual driving a truck of food supplies to a military camp does not by that conduct take 'direct' part in hostilities. By contrast, an 'insurgent' who takes up arms to attack occupying forces or who assembles improvised explosive devices undeniably meets the standard of 'direct participation'. Apart from a number of uncontested examples, many other situations are less clear-cut (one of the most debated scenarios concerns that of an individual driving an ammunitions truck to supply a Party to the conflict). The second aspect of the controversy concerns the time factor. It is recalled that Article 51(3) of AP I states that a person only loses immunity from attack 'for such time as' he or she takes direct part in hostilities. In light hereof, it is accepted that a civilian who takes direct part in hostilities only once (or even sporadically) does not lose protection from attack on a permanent basis.[33] What is much more controversial, however, is the extent to which persons that engage in a recurrent cycle of direct participation – for example, persons that engage in repeated raids at night while acting as innocent civilians by day – may or may not be immune to attack during the intervals in-between hostile acts (that is, the so-called 'revolving door' scenario).

The ICRC has sought to clarify the notion of direct participation by means of a series of expert meetings that began in 2003. In its Customary Study of 2005, the ICRC recognized that 'a clear and uniform definition … has not been developed in State practice'.[34] Eventually, in 2009, it published a lengthy 'Interpretive Guidance on the Notion of Direct Participation in Hostilities'.[35] The Interpretive Guidance distinguishes between 'members of organized groups belonging to a non-state party to an armed conflict', who lose protection against direct attack 'for as long as they assume their continuous combat function', and 'civilians', who, by contrast, only lose protection against direct attack 'for the duration of each specific act amounting to direct participation in hostilities'.[36] As for the type of 'specific acts' that qualify as 'direct participation', the Guidance identifies the following (cumulative) constitutive elements:

1. The act must be likely to adversely affect the military operations or military capacity of a Party to an armed conflict or, alternatively, to inflict death, injury, or destruction on persons or objects protected against direct attack (threshold of harm), and
2. there must be a direct causal link between the act and the harm likely to result either from that act, or from a coordinated military operation of which that act constitutes an integral part (direct causation);

---

[33] Dinstein, *supra* n.10, at 148.
[34] ICRC Customary Study, Vol. I, *supra* n.3, at 23.
[35] ICRC Interpretive Guidance, *supra* n.6.
[36] *Ibid.*, recommendation VII. Recommendation VI adds that '[m]easures preparatory to the execution of a specific act of direct participation in hostilities, as well as the deployment to and the return from the location of its execution, constitute an integral part of that act'.

3. the act must be specifically designed to directly cause the required threshold of harm in support of a Party to the conflict and to the detriment of another (belligerent nexus).

It must be observed, however, that the publication of the ICRC's Interpretive Guidance was met with strong criticism from various scholars.[37] The final word remains to be said.

An important catalyst of the controversy is the dangerous trend to confuse the criteria of individual battlefield status with the applicability of the different protective regimes laid down in the Geneva Conventions. Indeed, it is undeniable that in the tumultuous years following 9/11, attempts have been made (within and without the Bush administration) to present the labels of 'unlawful' or 'unprivileged' combatants as constituting a third category, apart from 'combatants' and 'civilians' – the underlying idea being that while the latter categories are respectively covered by GC I–III and GC IV, the former are bereft of all protection under LOAC, save perhaps with the minimum (customary) protection accorded by Common Article 3 of the Geneva Conventions and Article 75 AP I (cf. *infra*).[38] These generalized attempts to confuse the application of the protective regimes with a person's battlefield status must be rejected: the status, rights and protection of persons outside the conduct of hostilities do not depend on their generic qualification as 'lawful combatants', 'unlawful combatants' or 'civilians', but rest exclusively on the precise personal scope of application of the provisions conferring the relevant status, rights and protections, such as Articles 4 GC III, 4–5 GC IV, 13 GC I, 13 GC II and 75 AP I.[39] It is to the latter Articles that we must now turn.

C. Individual Status Beyond the Battlefield: Scope of Application of the Different Protective Regimes

i. POW status

a. Categories The linchpin provision establishing the personal scope of application of the POW regime is found in Article 4(A), GC III.[40] Article 4(A), GC III spells out several categories of persons – identical lists are found in Articles 13 GC I and 13 GC II – who, when having fallen into the power of the enemy, are entitled to POW status. Articles 4(A)(1)–(3) and (6) refer to those individuals endowed with the 'combatant privilege', or, put differently, to lawful combatants (see the three categories discussed above). As a general principle, any person entitled to lawfully take part in hostilities

---

[37] See in particular the contributions of B. Boothby, W. Hays Parks, M.N. Schmitt and K. Watkin, as well as the defence of N. Melzer in (2010) 42 *NYU J. of Int'l L. & Politics*. See also D. Akande, 'Clearing the Fog of War?: The ICRC's Interpretive Guidance on Direct Participation in Hostilities', (2010) 59 *ICLQ* 180; W.J. Fenrick, 'ICRC Guidance on Direct Participation in Hostilities', (2009) 12 *YIHL* 287; E. Christensen, 'The Dilemma of Direct Participation in Hostilities', (2010) 19 *J. of Transnat'l L. & Policy* 281; A.P.V. Rogers, 'Direct Participation in Hostilities: Some Personal Reflections', (2009) 48 *RDMDG* 143.
[38] The customary status of both Articles is uncontested.
[39] ICRC Interpretive Guidance, *supra* n.6, at 13 (n.5).
[40] See also Articles 1–3, 13, HagueReg.

will also, upon capture (or surrender), be entitled to POW protection. As will be seen below, however, this principle is not absolute.In addition, the provision adds two categories of non-combatants who may also benefit from POW status, provided they take no direct part in hostilities. The first category consists of 'persons who accompany the armed forces without actually being members thereof', such as journalists, technicians and various kinds of civilian contractors. Such persons will benefit from POW status, provided that they have received authorization from the armed forces which they accompany, 'who shall provide them for that purpose with an identity card'. While persons accompanying the armed forces often run increased risk of collateral injury, Parties to a conflict are required to take precautionary measures to limit such injury to a minimum and are prohibited from directly targeting these persons. The position of journalists and private military contractors (hereinafter 'PMCs') is tackled in greater detail in Section 2d below. The second category consists of merchant marine and civilian aircraft crews (e.g., the crew of a civilian aircraft transporting troops to the battlefield). Insofar as they do not benefit from more favourable treatment under international law, these persons should also be treated as POWs.

Finally, Article 4(B) GC III extends POW protection to retired or mobilized military personnel in occupied territory (where the Occupying Power deems it necessary to intern them), as well as to military internees in neutral countries.[41]

b. Loss of POW status As indicated above, for combatants to lawfully take part in hostilities, they must in principle fulfil three cumulative conditions: (1) they must have a fixed distinctive sign recognizable at a distance; (2) they must carry their arms openly; and (3) they must conduct their operations in accordance with the laws and customs of war.[42]

One of the most controversial questions of LOAC, however, is to what extent non-compliance with these criteria results in the loss of POW status.[43] The Third Geneva Convention does not provide a general answer to this question. It merely stresses that POWs prosecuted for acts committed prior to capture 'shall retain, even if convicted', the benefits of the GC III, thus indicating that infringements of LOAC normally do not deprive a person of POW status.[44] Article 44(2)–(3) of AP I, moreover, adds that combatants only lose POW status when they fail to 'distinguish themselves from the civilian population while they are engaged in an attack or in a military operation preparatory to an attack'.[45] This means that it is sufficient for armed forces to wear a military uniform, or to wear a fixed distinctive sign (recognizable at a distance)

---

[41] See on the origins of this Solis, *supra* n.9, at 202.

[42] As explained above, there is a presumption of compliance with the conditions on the part of regular troops.

[43] There is some discussion as to whether a state, party to a conflict, must accord POW status to an (enemy) combatant having the nationality of that state. Against this see, for example, Dinstein, *supra* n.10, at 46–47. Arguing that nationality does not affect POW status see H.S. Levie, *Prisoners of War in International Armed Conflict* (Newport International Law Studies, US Naval War College, 1978), at 174–177; Solis, *supra* n.9, at 197–198.

[44] Article 85 GC III. This principle finds affirmation in Article 44(2)–(3), AP I. But see Dinstein, *supra* n.10, at 50.

[45] In a similar vein see ICRC Customary Study, Vol. I, *supra* n.3, at 384 (Rule 106).

and to carry arms openly. At the same time, it is probably no exaggeration that most non-state armed groups fail to satisfy these requirements.

Two exceptions exist to the rule that the recognition of POW status requires the wearing of a fixed (and recognizable) distinctive sign. First, for participants in a *levée en masse*, it is sufficient that they carry their arms openly. Secondly, and far more controversially, Article 44(2)(3) AP I 'recognizes' that 'there are situations in armed conflicts where, owing to the nature of the hostilities an armed combatant cannot ... distinguish himself'. In such situations a person shall nonetheless retain his status as a combatant, provided that he carries his arms openly.[46] In the latter scenario, even if a combatant fails to carry his arms openly, he shall, nevertheless, be given 'protections equivalent in all respects' to those granted to POWs, including in the case of criminal prosecution (Article 44(4), AP I).

The inclusion of Article 44(3)–(4), AP I was the object of fierce debates at the 1977 Geneva Conference. Whereas some states advocated better protection for certain guerrilla liberation movements, others objected that the erosion of the obligation of combatants to distinguish themselves from civilians could only lead to greater exposure of civilians to the harmful effects of hostilities. Numerous states indicated that the exception should be confined to armed resistance in occupied territories or in wars of national liberation and insisted that the duty to carry arms openly be interpreted broadly.[47] While the United States originally voted in favour of the provision, it has since voiced strong opposition to the rule (as has Israel). This has led some authors to argue that the rule does not form part of customary international law, 'with the result that there are currently two different standards of what constitutes lawful combatancy' depending on whether Parties to a conflict have ratified AP I.[48]

c. *Doubt* Should 'any doubt arise' as to whether persons having fallen into the hands of the enemy qualify as POWs, such persons shall enjoy the protection of the GC III until their status has been determined 'by a competent tribunal' (Article 5 GC III). This rule may be of considerable importance to *inter alia* civilian contractors accompanying the armed forces or deserters who have lost their Geneva Convention ID card, as well as to irregular fighters. The need for status determination by a 'competent tribunal' arises not only when a person 'appears to be entitled' to POW status, or when 'the Party on which he depends claims such status on his behalf', but also when the person himself claims the status of POW (Article 45(1), AP I). A person who is not held as a POW and *who is to be tried* for an offence arising out of the hostilities, has the right to assert his entitlement to POW status before a *judicial* tribunal (Article 45(2), AP I). By contrast, if the person concerned is not prosecuted, it follows *a contrario* that the 'tribunal' competent for determining his status can potentially be military, civilian or

---

[46] Article 44(3) AP I more specifically requires that arms are carried openly: '(a) during each military engagement, and (b) during such time as [the person concerned] is visible to the adversary while he is engaged in a military deployment preceding the launching of an attack in which he is to participate'.

[47] See ICRC Customary Study, Vol. I, *supra* n.3, at 387–389.

[48] C. Greenwood, 'The Law of War (International Humanitarian Law)', in M.D. Evans (ed.), *International Law*, 2nd edn (Oxford: Oxford University Press, 2006), 783, at 790.

administrative. The lack of further guidance as to the adequacy of Article 5 proceedings leaves room for discussion on the applicable fair trial guarantees.[49]

The United States has set up hundreds of 'Article 5 hearings', *inter alia* in the Vietnam War and the First Gulf War. In the wake of the 9/11 attacks, however, the Bush administration initially refused to organize Article 5 hearings to determine the status of captured Al Qaeda or Taliban members because the President found that there could be no doubt that they did not deserve such status. This decision resulted in the detention of some apparently uninvolved civilians for years longer than necessary.[50] Eventually, following the US Supreme Court decisions in *Rasul v. Bush*[51] and *Hamdi v. Rumsfeld*,[52] the US began providing detainees with Combatant Status Review Tribunals.

d. Special categories Finally, reference must be made to a number of categories that are either granted a special status, distinct from POW status, or are explicitly excluded from POW protection.

First, as mentioned above, medical and religious personnel, in spite of being members of the armed forces, are not regarded as combatants. They cannot be held as POWs for the duration of hostilities, but may nonetheless be 'retained' with a view to assisting POWs (Article 4(C) *juncto* 33 GC III). Such 'retainees' may not be compelled to do work other than their medical or pastoral work and should normally be repatriated when there is no longer need for their services (albeit that such repatriation pending the armed conflict rarely occurs in practice).[53]

Secondly, members of the armed forces who would otherwise be entitled to POW status upon capture will lose this status when caught while engaging in spying.[54] This is a long-established rule of customary international law, although it may have lost some of its importance as a result of the development of modern-day electronic renaissance techniques. The rule applies to combatants wearing civilian clothing as well as those wearing the uniform of the adversary, but not to reconnaissance patrols wearing their own uniform. Spies caught in the act may be punished for their actions.

---

[49] See on this Bellinger III and Padmanabhan, *supra* n.4, at 221 *et seq*. Bellinger and Padmanabhan point out that Article 75 AP I provides procedural protections accompanying trials on criminal charges in an international armed conflict, but provides nothing regarding the procedures that must accompany the decision to detain the combatant. But see Y. Naqvi, 'Doubtful Prisoner-of-War Status', (2002) 847 *IRRC* 571 (arguing that core due process rights recognized as customary IHL are secured).

[50] See Bellinger III and Padmanabhan, *supra* n.4, at 223 *et seq*.

[51] US Supreme Court, *Rasul v. Bush*, 542 U.S. 466 (2004).

[52] US Supreme Court, *Hamdi v. Rumsfeld*, 542 U.S. 507 (2004).

[53] For a good general overview of the situation of retainees, see Solis, *supra* n.9, at 191–194.

[54] Spying refers to the gathering of information clandestinely or under false pretences in territory controlled/occupied by an adverse Party. Articles 46, AP I and 29–31 HagueReg. See also Rule 107 ICRC Customary Study, Vol. I, *supra* n.3, at 391. Remark: the customary status of Article 47, AP I is contested by the United States (see J.-M. Henckaerts and L. Doswald-Beck (eds), *Customary International Humanitarian Law. Vol. II* (Cambridge: Cambridge University Press, 2005), § 314). See on this: F. Lafouasse, 'L'espionnage en droit international', (2001) 47 *AFDI* 63; E. Chadwick, 'The Legal Position of Prisoners, Spies and Deserters during World War I', (1997) 36 *RDMDG* 73.

On the other hand, no such punishment can take place absent a trial corresponding to the minimum guarantees laid down in Article 75, AP I (thus ruling out summary executions). A spy that is caught after rejoining his armed forces shall retain his POW status and incurs no responsibility for previous acts of espionage.

On a final note, it may be observed that mercenaries, as defined in Article 47, AP I, do not have the right to POW status.[55] This rule finds its origin in the controversial involvement of mercenaries in armed conflicts on the African continent in the decolonization era, but may nowadays be relevant for certain private military companies or private security companies (cf. *infra*). It is noted, however, that the definition of 'mercenaries' in the Protocol is so narrow[56] that it has no direct impact on the scope of application of the POW regime of GC III: a person meeting the cumulative requirements of Article 47(2), AP I by definition does not fall within one of the categories of potential POWs listed above.[57] Like spies, mercenaries are punishable for their acts (subject to the basic guarantees of Article 75, AP I).

ii. Wounded, sick and shipwrecked

Having previously examined the POW regime, the scope of the protective regime for the wounded, sick and shipwrecked of a belligerent is fairly easy to summarize. In essence, Article 13, GC I (sick and wounded) and Article 13, GC II (shipwrecked) reiterate the personal scope of application of the GC III (Article 4(A), GC III), without, however, copying the reference to retired or mobilized military personnel in occupied territory, or to military internees in neutral countries (Article 4(B), GC III).[58]

When the wounded, sick or shipwrecked 'of a belligerent' fall into enemy hands, they shall be prisoners of war, and the provisions of international law concerning POWs will apply to them (Articles 14, GC I and 16, GC II). Hence the GC III only comes into operation gradually, as the wounded, sick or shipwrecked are transferred behind the lines or taken on board and interned in a POW camp. The protection of sick and wounded POWs is governed by the more detailed provisions concerning health and medical care of the Third Geneva Convention.

---

[55] Article 47, AP I moreover explicitly denies them combatant privilege. See, for example, on the position of mercenaries E. David, *Mercenaires et volontaires internationaux en droit des gens* (Brussels: ULB, 1978); J. Tercinet, 'Les mercenaires et le droit international', (1977) 23 *AFDI* 269; K. Fallah, 'Corporate Actors: The Legal Status of Mercenaries in Armed Conflict', (2006) 88 *IRRC* 599; L.C. Green, 'The Status of Mercenaries in International Law', (1978) 8 *Israel Yb. H.R.* 9; H.C. Burmester, 'The Recruitment and Use of Mercenaries in Armed Conflicts', (1978) 72 *AJIL* 37.

[56] For a critique, see F.J. Hampson, 'Mercenaries: Diagnosis Before Prescription', (1991) 22 *NYIL* 3, at 30.

[57] See in particular requirements (d) and (e) (which exclude members of the armed forces and participants in a *levée en masse*) and requirement (b) in Article 47(2), AP I. Accordingly, in practice, the provision may mainly be relevant for determining whether certain persons enjoy protection under GC IV or only benefit from the minimum guarantees of Article 75, AP I.

[58] From a practical perspective, militia, volunteer corps, resistance movements and mass levies are unlikely to be engaged in hostilities at sea and are therefore unlikely to come within the ambit of the GC II.

It may be observed that the GC IV also contains provisions concerning the protection of wounded, sick and shipwrecked 'civilians', albeit that the protection is more rudimentary than that granted by GC I and GC II.

In the meantime, however, the First Additional Protocol (Part II) has extended the protection granted to the sick, wounded and shipwrecked in Geneva Conventions I, II and IV, without maintaining a distinction between military persons or civilians. The result is a certain unification of the rules applicable to the wounded, sick and shipwrecked. Article 8 AP I now also provides for a definition of the notions of 'sick and wounded' (a concept which is understood broadly as including mental disorders) and 'shipwrecked'[59] – whereas the Geneva Conventions only defined the latter term.[60]

iii. Civilians

a. Article 4 GC IV The Fourth Geneva Convention contains a series of protective provisions that are of general application and cover 'the whole of the populations of the countries in conflict' (Part II, Articles 13–26). The thrust of the Convention is, however, found in Part III (Articles 27–141), which deals with the 'status and treatment of *protected persons*'. Just as the concept of 'civilian' is defined negatively for the purpose of determining individual battlefield status, the notion of 'protected person' (in the sense of the GC IV) is defined in part in a negative manner. Article 4§4 GC IV explicitly holds that persons protected by GC I, II or III shall not be considered as protected persons within the meaning of the Fourth Geneva Convention and are excluded from its scope of application.

In positive terms, there is a two-fold requirement to be regarded as a 'protected person': (a) the person should be 'in the hands of' a 'Party to the conflict or Occupying Power', and (b) he or she should not be a national of that Party or Occupying Power.[61]

The expression 'in the hands of' is used in an extremely general sense and need not necessarily be understood in the physical sense. It simply means that the person concerned is in the territory under the control of the power in question.[62] Consequently,

---

[59] For the purposes of the AP I, Article 8(a) defines 'wounded' and 'sick' as referring to 'persons, whether military or civilian, who, because of trauma, disease or other physical or mental disorder or disability, are in need of medical assistance or care and who refrain from any act of hostility', including maternity cases, new-born babies and expectant mothers. Article 8(b) defines 'shipwrecked' as referring to 'persons, whether military or civilian, who are in peril at sea or in other waters as a result of misfortune affecting them or the vessel or aircraft carrying them and who refrain from any act of hostility', including persons that are being rescued. Note that there is a small difference with GC II, which only applies to the 'shipwrecked at sea' (excluding those in peril in local waters).

[60] According to Article 12, GC II, the term 'shipwreck' includes forced landings at sea by or from aircraft.

[61] Article 4(1), GC IV.

[62] J. Pictet, *Commentary, Geneva Convention Relative to the Protection of Civilian Persons in Time of War, Convention IV* (Geneva: ICRC, 1958), at 47. See also ICTY, *Prosecutor v. Rajic*, IT-95-12-R61, paras 35–37: 'Because the Trial Chamber has already held that there are reasonable grounds for believing that Croatia controlled the Bosnian Croats, Croatia may be regarded as being in control of that area. Thus, although the residents of Stupni Do were not directly or physically in the hands of Croatia, a country of which they were not nationals. The

GC IV protects those civilians who find themselves in the territory of a Party to the conflict or in territory effectively occupied by a Party to the conflict of which they are not nationals.[63] Whether Part III of the GC IV also applies to the so-called invasion phase preceding actual occupation is subject to debate.[64] One approach holds that, since the concept of 'occupation' only extends to situations where territory is 'actually placed under the authority of the hostile army' (Article 42 HagueReg), contested areas (which are still embattled) generally fall beyond the scope of the regime of the GC IV pertaining to 'protected persons'.[65] According to this view, in the 'invasion' scenario, the invading force must respect the rules dealing with the 'General protection of populations against certain consequences of war' (GC IV Part II), as well as the provisions relating to means and methods of warfare (including targeting, for example, Articles 48–67, AP I), but not, for example, the detailed rules regarding the treatment (including trial) of internees (GC IV Part III). The implication is that so-called 'unlawful combatants' captured on the battlefield in enemy territory would (in terms of detention and trial) only enjoy minimal protection under Article 75 of AP I.[66] By contrast, the Commentary to the GC IV[67] puts forward a position – which is supported by the ICRC[68] and arguably also by the ICTY[69] – which aims at maximizing protection of affected persons. According to this approach, whenever, even during the invasion phase, persons come within the power or control of a hostile army, they should be guaranteed the protection of the Fourth Geneva Convention as a minimum.

The second requirement is that civilians are only protected persons under GC IV insofar as they are not nationals of the Party to the conflict into whose hands they have fallen.[70] As a consequence, in the course of the international armed conflict in Afghanistan following the attacks of 9/11, the legal status of a person differed depending on whether the person was captured by Afghan forces or by US troops. The validity of the 'nationality requirement' has been questioned by repeated holdings of

---

Trial Chamber therefore finds that the civilian residents of the village of Stupni Do were ... protected persons vis-à-vis the Bosnian Croats because the latter were controlled by Croatia.'

[63] Pictet, *supra* n.62, at 46.

[64] See, for example, K. Dörmann, 'The Legal Situation of Unlawful/Unprivileged Combatants', (2003) 85 *IRRC* 45, at 61–64.

[65] See, for example, H.-P. Gasser, 'Protection of the Civilian Population', in Fleck *et al.*, *supra* n.13, 237, at 276–277. See also the interpretation of occupation in UK Ministry of Defence, *The Manual of the Law of Armed Conflict* (Oxford: Oxford University Press, 2004), at 275–276; US Department of the Army, *Field Manual 27-10: The Law of Land Warfare* (18 July 1956), Rules 352–356, available at http://www.globalsecurity.org/military/library/policy/army/fm/27-10/.

[66] See, for example, Dinstein, *supra* n.10, at 36, 38.

[67] Pictet, *supra* n.62, at 67.

[68] See M. Sassoli and A.A. Bouvier (eds), *How Does Law Protect in War? Vol. I*, 3rd edn (Geneva: ICRC, 2011), Chapter 8, at 2. D. Thürer, 'Current Challenges to the Law of Occupation', *Proceedings of the Bruges Colloquium*, 20–21 October 2005, 9, at 11–13.

[69] ICTY, *Prosecutor v. Naletilic and Martinovic*, Judgment, Case No. IT-98-34-T, T.Ch. I, 31 March 2003, at 210–223.

[70] For the sake of completeness, it may be observed that the nationality requirement does not apply in case of a 'war of national liberation' in the sense of Article 1(4) of AP I – at least insofar as the First Additional Protocol is directly applicable to the conflict concerned.

the International Criminal Tribunal for the former Yugoslavia (hereinafter 'ICTY'). Thus, in *Tadic*, the Tribunal noted that:

> While previously wars were primarily between well-established States, in modern inter-ethnic armed conflicts such as that in the former Yugoslavia, new States are often created during the conflict and ethnicity rather than nationality may become the grounds for allegiance. Or, put another way, ethnicity may become determinative of national allegiance. Under these conditions, the requirement of nationality is even less adequate to define protected persons.[71]

Time will tell if the Tribunal's view will become state practice.[72]

Irrespective of the foregoing, the 'nationality of the agents' of the Party to the conflict does not affect the latter's responsibility for the treatment accorded to protected persons by these agents.[73] That is of particular importance in occupied territories, as it means that the occupying authorities are responsible for acts committed by their locally recruited agents of the nationality of the occupied territory – even if the foreign power 'occupies' or operates in certain territory solely through the acts of local *de facto* organs or agents.[74]

b. Article 5 GC IV A particular category of protected persons is those individuals who are definitely suspected of or engaged in activities hostile to the security of the state. Such individuals remain protected persons, although they shall not be entitled to claim such rights and privileges 'as would, if exercised in the favor of such individual person, be prejudicial to the security of the State' (Article 5 GC IV). As stated in the Commentaries,

> it might have been simpler to exclude them from the benefit of the Convention, if such a course had been possible, but the terms espionage, sabotage, terrorism, banditry and intelligence with the enemy, have so often been used lightly, and applied to so trivial offences, that it was not advisable to leave the accused at the mercy of those detaining them.[75]

---

[71] ICTY, *Prosecutor v. Tadic*, Judgment, *supra* n. 7, at 166.
[72] According to Solis '[f]or now, the ICTY's position remains a minority view, authoritative but not binding other courts and tribunals'. Solis, *supra* n.9, at 236.
[73] Pictet, *supra* n.62, at 212; Article 29, GC IV.
[74] In *Tadic*, the Appeals Chamber stated that:

the Bosnian Serbs, including the Appellant, had the same nationality as the victims, that is, they were nationals of Bosnia and Herzegovina. However, it has been shown above that the Bosnian Serb forces acted as de facto organs of another State, namely, the FRY. Thus the requirements set out in Article 4 of Geneva Convention IV are met: the victims were 'protected persons' as they found themselves in the hands of armed forces of a State of which they were not nationals.

ICTY, *Prosecutor v. Tadic*, *supra* n.7, at §167.
[75] Pictet, *supra* n.62, at 53.

Although states have discretion to decide whether a threat to the security exists, this decision must be made on an individual basis and does not provide 'blanket power to detain the entire civilian population'.[76]

Article 5§2 GC IV specifies that in occupied territory, persons definitely suspected of hostile activities can, where absolute military security so requires, be regarded as having forfeited rights of communication. In each case, such persons must nevertheless be treated with humanity and, in case of trial, shall not be deprived of the rights of fair and regular trial (Article 5(3) GC IV).[77] They shall, as a *minimum minimorum* enjoy the fundamental guarantees of Article 75 AP I. Restrictions imposed on the basis of Article 5 GC IV (e.g., incommunicado detention) must be lifted as soon as they are no longer justified by security reasons.[78]

c. The position of 'unlawful combatants' As mentioned above, persons protected by GC I, II or III are not regarded as protected persons in the sense of the Fourth Geneva Convention. An important question in this regard – and one of the most heated controversies of modern-day LOAC – is whether persons participating directly in hostilities, and who do not meet the requirements for POW status, can qualify as 'protected persons' in the sense of Article 4 GC IV. This question is particularly important in respect of members of organized irregular forces under a responsible command, who fail to distinguish themselves from the civilian population. The wager of the controversy is considerable. Whether 'unlawful combatants' are to be considered as 'protected persons' in the sense of the GC IV indeed has a crucial impact on the possibility for detaining them and the judicial guarantees applicable.[79] Thus, protected

---

[76] ICTY, *Prosecutor v. Delalic et al.*, Judgment, Case IT-96-21-A, A.Ch., 20 February 2001, at 327:

It is perfectly clear from the provisions of Geneva convention IV referred to above that there is no such blanket power to detain the entire civilian population of a party to the conflict in such circumstances, but there must be an assessment that each civilian taken into detention poses a particular risk to the security of the State.

[77] According to Dörmann,

[t]he two categories of non-derogable protections include: the right to 'humane treatment' as defined in Articles 27 and 37, and thus the prohibition of torture and ill-treatment; as well as the fair trial rights contained in Articles 71–76, which are made applicable to internees in non-occupied territory by Article 126 in the event of criminal proceedings.

Dörmann, *supra* n.64, at 66 *et seq.*

[78] Obviously, detention must not necessarily be lifted where a person is serving a sentence following trial.

[79] On the status and detention of enemy combatants, see, for example, D. Cassell, 'International Human Rights Law and Security Detention', (2009) 40 *Case W. Res .J. Int'l. L* 383; S. Camera, 'The Exploitation of Legal Loopholes in the Name of National Security: A Case Study on Extraordinary Renditions', (2006) 37 *California Western I.L.J.* 121; L.N. Sadat, 'A Presumption of Guilt: The Unlawful Enemy Combatant and the U.S. War on Terror', (2009) 37 *Denv. J. Int'l. L. & Pol'y.* 539; A. Roberts, 'Righting Wrongs or Wronging Rights? The United States and Human Rights Post-September 11', (2004) 15 *EJIL* 721; K. Watkin, 'Warriors Without Rights? Combatants, Unprivileged Belligerents, and the Struggle Over Legitimacy', *Hum. Pol'y & Conflict Research Occasional Paper Studies* (Harvard University, 2005); M.

persons may in principle only be detained on the basis of individualized determinations that the security of the detaining power makes detention absolutely necessary, and detention must cease when the need ends.[80]

The view expounded by the Commentary to the GC IV is that:

> every person in enemy hands must have some status under international law: he is either a prisoner of war and, as such, covered by the Third Geneva Convention, a civilian covered by the Fourth Convention, or again, a member of the medical personnel of the armed forces who is covered by the First Convention. There is no intermediate status; nobody in enemy hands can be outside the law.[81]

The Commentary explicitly adds that:

> [i]f members of a resistance movement who have fallen in to enemy hands do not fulfill [the] conditions [for POW status]; they must be considered protected persons within the meaning of [the GC IV]. That does not mean that they cannot be punished for their acts, but the trial and sentence must take place in accordance with the provisions of Article 64 and the Articles which follow it.[82]

This 'traditional' approach is adhered to by the ICRC,[83] as well as numerous legal scholars.[84] It finds support also in the fact that Article 5 GC IV suggests by negative inference that engaging in hostile activities does not automatically deprive an individual of protected person status, as well as in the rule that, in cases of doubt as to a person's status, he or she shall be considered to be a civilian (Article 50, AP I).[85] It might be argued that under the traditional approach, the title of GC IV ('Geneva Convention relative to the Protection of Civilian Persons in Time of War') is to some extent a misnomer, since protected person status is granted not only to *civilians* (sporadically) participating directly in hostilities, but also to actual *combatants* (members of organized armed forces acting under a responsible command) that do not meet the requirements for POW status. At the same time, it must be kept in mind that, for the purposes of the conduct of hostilities (e.g., direct liability to attack), a member of irregular armed forces failing to fulfil the requirements for POW status is still regarded as a combatant. In addition, in accordance with the parameters spelled out above, Article 5 GC IV can be invoked to limit the claims and privileges to which 'unlawful combatants' are entitled.[86]

The alternative approach holds that unlawful combatants are by definition not entitled to protection either under the GC III, or under the GC IV, but can at most enjoy

---

Sassoli, 'Transnational Armed Groups and International Humanitarian Law', *Hum. Pol'y & Conflict Research Occasional Paper Series* (Harvard University, 2006).
[80] Articles 42–43, GC IV. See Bellinger and Padmanabhan, *supra* n.4, at 215.
[81] Pictet, *supra* n.62, at 51.
[82] *Ibid.*
[83] See, for example, ICRC Interpretive Guidance, *supra* n.6, at 22 (n.15).
[84] See, for example, Ipsen, *supra* n.13, at 83; Solis, *supra* n.9, at 325. See also Dörmann, *supra* n.64 and the references cited in that article, sub-note 36.
[85] For a good overview see Dörmann, *supra* n.64, at 48 *et seq.*
[86] See, for example, ibid., at 50.

the minimum guarantees of Article 75, AP I. This was the approach followed by the Bush administration *vis-à-vis* Taliban and Al Qaeda fighters captured in Afghanistan.[87] In support of this view, it has been argued that the negotiation history of the GC IV calls into question the idea that protected person status was intended to be a safety net protecting those who took up arms illegally.[88] On the other hand, from a teleological perspective, it is feared that the concept of 'unlawful combatants' may be used as an easy escape category for detaining powers,[89] a concern that has been strengthened by the US position regarding individuals captured on the Afghan battlefield. Interestingly, the Israeli Supreme Court in 2006 observed that:

> It is difficult for us to see how a third category [of unlawful combatants] can be recognized in the framework of the Hague and Geneva Conventions. It does not appear to us that we were presented with data sufficient to allow us to say, at the present time, that such a third category has been recognized in customary international law.[90]

And in 1998, the ICTY held that:

> [i]f an individual is not entitled to the protections of the [GC III] as a prisoner of war (or of the First or Second Conventions) he or she necessarily falls within the ambit of Convention IV, provided that its Article 4 requirements are satisfied.[91]

While a majority of legal doctrine appears to support the ICRC approach, the controversy has not fully blown over yet.

d. *Nationals of neutral states and co-belligerent states* The following categories of persons cannot qualify as 'protected persons' in the sense of the GC IV (Article 4§2 GC IV): nationals of a state which is not bound by the Convention, nationals of a neutral state and nationals of a co-belligerent state. The first category bears little relevance since the Geneva Conventions are ratified universally. As for the two remaining categories, it must be specified that they are only excluded from qualification as protected persons in the sense of the GC IV provided that the state of which they are nationals has normal diplomatic representation in the state in whose hands they are. The underlying idea is that in such scenario states may use normal diplomatic channels, including consular visits, to protect the interests of their nationals with the

---

[87] For an overview, see Bellinger and Padmanabhan, *supra* n.4, at 215 *et seq.*

[88] For authors supporting this approach see, for example, I. Detter, *The Law of War* (Cambridge: Cambridge University Press, 2000), at 136; C. Greenwood, 'International Law and the "War against Terrorism"', (2002) *International Affairs* 316. Other authors apparently limit the scope of application of GC IV to unlawful combatants operating in occupied territory. See, for example, Baxter, *supra* n.26, at 343 *et seq.*; Dinstein, *supra* n.10, at 36.

[89] Sassoli and Bouvier (eds), *supra* n.68, Chapter 6, at 2.

[90] Israeli Supreme Court, *Public Committee against Torture in Israel v. the Government of Israel* (2006) HCJ 769/02, §28.

[91] ICTY, *Prosecutor v. Delalic et al.*, IT-96-21-T, T.Ch., 16 November 1998, at para. 271.

belligerent state.[92] Conversely, persons who, before the beginning of hostilities, were considered as stateless or refugees shall be protected persons in all circumstances.[93]

3. THE PROTECTIVE REGIMES

A. The Wounded, Sick and Shipwrecked

The central principle regarding the wounded, sick and shipwrecked is that they must be respected and protected in all circumstances and are to be treated humanely and cared for (Article 12, GC I; Article 12, GC II; Article 16, GC IV; Article 10, AP I).[94] This rule contains both a negative and a positive obligation. First, the duty to 'respect' implies that one should not willfully cause harm to the wounded, sick or shipwrecked (at least as long as they abstain from hostile acts). LOAC specifically prohibits attempts upon their lives, or violence to their persons (e.g., torture or biological experiments), yet the duty to respect should be interpreted broadly, as encompassing also threats and harassments.[95] The sick and wounded should not be the object of reprisals.[96] The 'duty to protect', on the other hand, is of a positive nature, and entails an obligation to protect the wounded and sick, for example from pillage and ill-treatment[97] – by use of force if need be – and to provide them with such care as their condition requires. While the obligation to protect applies 'in all circumstances', it must be read as an obligation of *means*, rather than result.[98] This implies that each Party to the conflict must use its best efforts (using the equipment and staff at its disposal) to provide protection and care for the wounded, sick and shipwrecked. Parties may do so by permitting humanitarian organizations, such as the ICRC, to intervene to this end (such permission should not arbitrarily be denied).

The civilian population is also under an obligation to 'respect' the wounded, sick and shipwrecked, and in particular to refrain from acts of violence against them.[99] By contrast, there is no positive obligation for civilians to assist a wounded person.[100]

---

[92] Bellinger and Padmanabhan, *supra* n.4, at 216 (n.76).
[93] Article 73, AP I. For refugees see also Article 44, GC IV.
[94] On the treatment of the wounded and sick see, for example, W.A. Solf, 'Development of the Protection of the Wounded, Sick and Shipwrecked under the Protocols Additional to the 1949 Geneva Conventions', in J. Pictet and C. Swinarski (eds), *Studies and Essays on International Humanitarian Law and Red Cross Principles in Honour of Jean Pictet* (The Hague: Martinus Nijhoff, 1984), 237; J.K. Kleffner, 'Protection of the Wounded, Sick and Shipwrecked', in Fleck *et al.* (eds), *supra* n.13, at 325.
[95] Y. Sandoz, C. Swinarski and B. Zimmerman (eds), *Commentaire des Protocoles additionnels du 8 juin 1977 aux Conventions de Genève du 21 août 1949* (The Hague: Martinus Nijhoff, 1986), No. 704.
[96] Article 46, GC I; Article 47, GC II; Article 20, AP I.
[97] Article 15, GC I; Article 18 GC II; Article 16, GC IV.
[98] ICRC Customary Study Vol. I, *supra* n.3, Rule 110.
[99] Article 17, AP I. See also ICRC Customary Study Vol. I, *supra* n.3, Rule 111.
[100] Civilians may of course do so on a voluntary basis. The Conventions assert in this context that no-one may be 'molested or convicted for having nursed' the wounded, sick or

When providing medical treatment, priority may only be given to certain wounded and sick on the basis of urgent medical reasons.[101] The prioritization of patients based on the gravity of their wounds or their chances of survival is a matter of medical ethics, not of law. Otherwise, it is prohibited to make adverse distinctions, for example on the basis of race or religion, albeit that women shall be treated with all consideration due to their sex.[102]

Article 11 of AP I explains in detail the conditions under which the sick, wounded and shipwrecked may be subjected to surgery and other medical treatment. Thus, it prohibits any medical procedure which is not indicated by the state of health of the person concerned and which is not consistent with generally accepted medical standards.[103] Patients have the right to refuse any surgical operation.

Apart from the obligation to respect and protect, the Parties to a conflict must, without delay, take 'all possible measures' to search for and collect the wounded, sick and shipwrecked (Article 15, GC I; Article 18, GC II).[104] As far as the civilian sick and wounded are concerned, the primary responsibility for their search and collection remains with the civilian authorities, albeit that the Parties to the conflict should 'facilitate the steps taken' to this end (Article 16, GC IV). Parties to the conflict should, 'whenever circumstances permit', arrange an armistice, suspension of fire, or conclude a local arrangement, to permit the removal, exchange and transport of the wounded left on the battlefield.[105] Obviously, the duty to evacuate those *hors de combat* does not prevent Parties from temporarily keeping persons in the danger zone, if evacuation would expose them to greater risks due to their wounds or sickness (Article 19, GC III).

In any armed conflict, people have the right to know what has happened to their missing relatives. To this end, the First and Second Geneva Conventions spell out a variety of obligations on the part of the Parties to a conflict. Thus, Parties should record as soon as possible certain information allowing for the identification of the wounded, sick or dead falling into their hands[106] and are expected to communicate this information between themselves via the Information Bureau set up under the GC III. For deceased members of the regular armed forces, the main instrument for identification is the so-called double identity disc, one half of which is to remain on the body. The Conventions prescribe that dead persons (including civilians that have died for reasons related to hostilities) be interred in graves that are properly marked so that they

---

shipwrecked. LOAC also provides for the possibility of calling on the civilian population to assist in the care of the wounded, sick and shipwrecked. See Article 18, GC I; Article 17, AP I.

[101] Article 12§3 GC I; Article 12§3, GC II.

[102] Article 12§4 GC I; Article 12§4 GC II.

[103] It is specifically prohibited to carry out physical mutilations, medical or scientific experiments or removal of tissue organs for transplantation, even where the person concerned consents. See, however, in respect of donations of blood for transfusion or of skin for grafting, Article 11§3, AP I.

[104] As for the involvement of civilians and relief organizations in the collection of the sick and wounded, see *supra* n.100 which applies *mutatis mutandis*.

[105] Article 15(3), GC I; Article 18(2), GC II; Article 17, GC IV. Article 17 GC IV makes explicit reference to the evacuation of aged persons, children and maternity cases.

[106] Article 16, GC I; Article 19, GC II.

may always be found.¹⁰⁷ The First Additional Protocol has also introduced a general obligation for each Party to the conflict to search for the persons who have been reported missing by an adverse Party, as soon as circumstances permit, and at the latest from the end of active hostilities.¹⁰⁸

In spite of the cited rules, many armed conflicts (especially internal armed conflicts) continue to be marred by mass executions and unmarked graves.¹⁰⁹ Thus, of the circa 140,000 people that lost their lives in the Balkans conflict in the 1990s, a quarter simply vanished and were reported missing. In 2010, almost 15,000 people remained unaccounted for. In order to draw attention to this 'hidden tragedy', the ICRC in 2003 organized an international Conference to tackle the problem of missing persons.¹¹⁰ In 2006, the UN General Assembly adopted the International Convention for the Protection of all Persons from Enforced Disappearances.¹¹¹ The first Article of this Convention holds that '[n]o one shall be subjected to enforced disappearance. No exceptional circumstance whatsoever, whether a state of war or a threat of war, internal political instability or any other public emergency, may be invoked as a justification for enforced disappearance.' As of December 2011, however, only thirty states had actually ratified the Convention.

A crucial corollary of the protective regime for the wounded, sick and shipwrecked is the protection of medical units and medical personnel. Such persons and objects are indeed protected from attack at all times. This immunity from attack would only cease if medical facilities were being used for military purposes such as sheltering unwounded soldiers or military intelligence activities. In order to enable the identification of medical personnel and objects and to ensure their immunity from attack, LOAC has introduced the red cross, red crescent and (most recently) the red crystal emblems.¹¹² The protection accorded to medical personnel, medical units and medical transports is regulated in great detail in the Geneva Conventions and in the First Additional Protocol.¹¹³

---

¹⁰⁷ Article 17, GC I; Article 20, GC II; Article 33(4), AP I. See, for example, ICRC, 'Iran/Iraq: Joint Mission to Clarify the Fate of Soldiers Missing Since 1980–1988 War', News Release 11/247, 29 November 2011.

¹⁰⁸ Article 33(1), AP I.

¹⁰⁹ On the issue of dead and missing persons, see the contributions of Sassoli, Tougas and others in (2002) 84 *IRRC* 720–902. See also the contributions of Crettol, La Rosa and Naqvi in (2006) 88 *IRRC* 245–273 and 355–362; T. Blumenstock, 'Legal Protection of the Missing and their Relatives: The Example of Bosnia and Herzegovina', (2006) 19 *LJIL* 773.

¹¹⁰ See (2003) 85 *IRRC* 185.

¹¹¹ International Convention for the Protection of all Persons from Enforced Disappearance, New York, 20 December 2006, entry into force 23 December 2010, GA Res. 61/177, UN Doc. A/61/488. See also T. Scovazzi and G. Citroni, *The Struggle against Enforced Disappearance and the 2007 United Nations Convention* (Leiden: Martinus Nijhoff, 2007); L. Ott, *Enforced Disappearance in International Law* (Cambridge: Intersentia, 2011).

¹¹² The red crystal was introduced as a result of the Third Additional Protocol to the Geneva Conventions, adopted in December 2005. The Protocol entered into force on 14 January 2007.

¹¹³ See, in particular, Articles 19–44, GC I; Articles 22–45, GC II; Articles 18–22, GC IV; Articles 12–16, 21–31 AP I. See also on this J. Pictet, 'The Medical Profession and International Humanitarian Law', (1985) 247 *IRRC* 191; J. Miné, 'The Geneva Conventions and Medical Personnel in the Field', (1987) 257 *IRRC* 180.

Although the protection of hospitals and medical personnel is a sacrosanct principle of the 'Geneva law', experience regrettably shows the cited rules are violated all too often. Thus, an ICRC study based on an analysis of reports collected over a two-and-a-half-year period describing 655 violent incidents in sixteen different countries revealed that in situations of armed conflict, countless people die, not simply as a direct result of injuries caused by hostilities, but because medical personnel are prevented from carrying out their tasks or are themselves the object of attack.[114] The sobering results have inspired the ICRC to set up the 'health care in danger' project, which aims at the adoption of specific measures designed to help ensure that the sick and wounded have safe access to effective and impartial health care in situations of armed conflict.

B. Prisoners of War

i. Introduction

Up until the late nineteenth century, prisoners of war were usually either killed or enslaved, without this being considered unlawful.[115] This dreadful practice was abandoned in the nineteenth century and was formally disavowed by the 1907 Hague Regulations and subsequent Conventions, which established the principle that POWs can merely be interned for the duration of the armed conflict and are to be repatriated afterwards.

In spite thereof, the Second World War saw large-scale violations of these rules. On numerous occasions were captured combatants summarily executed (cf. the notorious *Kommissar-Befehl* and the *Kommando-Befehl* that ordered the execution of political commissars of the Red Army and of ununiformed commando units respectively). Others were forced to undertake long 'death marches' in extreme conditions without adequate food, clothing or medical care (with many dying from exhaustion) or were subject to medical experiments. Reprisals against POWs (including group executions) were no exception. It is estimated that of the 5.7 million Soviet POWs in German captivity, 3.3 million died.[116] Of the 3 million German POWs in Soviet camps, approximately one third died during captivity. Thousands of POWs were not repatriated until many years after the end of the war.

The appalling abuses of the Second World War inspired an ambitious overhaul of the POW regime. The GC III now contains detailed provisions concerning *inter alia* the internment, prosecution and repatriation of POWs.[117] Below we provide a non-exhaustive overview of some key aspects of the POW regime.

---

[114] ICRC, 'Health Care in Danger: Making the Case. A Sixteen-Country Study', July 2011, available at http://www.icrc.org/eng/assets/files/reports/4073-002-16-country-study.pdf.

[115] See H. Fischer, 'Protection of Prisoners of War', in Fleck *et al.* (eds), *supra* n.13, 367, at 368.

[116] *Ibid.*, at 370.

[117] The First Additional Protocol has influenced the requirements for POW status, yet it has brought no substantive alterations to the protective regime itself (save perhaps with the exception of Article 41, AP I).

ii. General protection

As a general rule, POWs must at all times be humanely treated.[118] This implies that the Detaining Power should abstain from ill-treating them. Examples of ill-treatment that are explicitly outlawed include physical mutilation and medical experiments[119] that are not in the interest of the prisoner. Reprisals are also prohibited – ill-treatment of prisoners by the adverse Party can never justify infringements of the GC III. Detaining Powers also have a positive obligation to protect POWs against acts of violence or intimidation and against insults and 'public curiosity'.[120] The display of POWs for propaganda purposes – such as, for instance, the broadcasting on Iraqi television of 'confessions' of two downed RAF pilots in the First Gulf War – is a clear violation of LOAC. The transmission of photos of interned POWs is only permitted if the individual prisoners cannot be identified or if this is done for reporting purposes by the Protecting Power, the ICRC or other recognized organizations.[121] Discriminatory treatment of POWs is in principle prohibited, although exception is made for specific provisions relating to sex and rank.[122] Thus, female prisoners must be treated with due regard to their sex[123] and should, among other things, be housed in separate dormitories.[124] A number of provisions of the GC III, such as those relating to POW labour,[125] moreover provide for a differentiated treatment of POWs on the basis of their rank.

iii. Captivity

For those persons falling within the personal scope of application of the GC III (cf. *supra*), POW protection applies as soon as they (physically) fall in the hands of the adversary. Upon capture, POWs are required to provide certain information regarding their rank and identity.[126] Those refusing to do so may render themselves liable (only) to a restriction of the privileges normally accorded to their rank or status, but may not be subject to any form of coercion (physical or other). Certain items, such as arms or

---

[118] Article 13, GC III. See, for example, ICTY, Kordic and Cerkez, case No. IT-95/14/2-T, Judgment of 26 Feburary 2001, §256.

[119] For an account of the horrific experiments performed by Japanese physicians on POWS, see S.H. Harris, 'Medical Experiments on POWs', available at http://www.crimesofwar.org/a-z-guide/medical-experiments-on-pows/.

[120] See, for example, G. Risius and M.A. Meyer, 'The Protection of Prisoners of War against Insults and Public Curiosity', (1993) 295 *IRRC* 288.

[121] See Fischer, *supra* n.115, at 379.

[122] Article 14, GC III.

[123] Article 14(2), GC III. The Commentary refers to three elements that must be taken into account: 'weakness', 'honour and modesty' and 'pregnancy and child-birth'. Thus, female prisoners must be defended against rape and indecent assault, for example through the instalment of separate dormitories and sanitary installations. Mothers with infants should be granted early repatriation. See J. de Preux, *Geneva Convention Relative to the Treatment of Prisoners of War. Commentary* (Geneva: ICRC, 1960), at 144–147.

[124] Article 25(4), GC III.

[125] See, for example, Article 49, GC III.

[126] Article 17, GC III. Under LOAC, the POW is not required to provide information other than that explicitly mentioned in Article 17(1) of the GC III. National law may effectively impose a duty on POWs not to provide further information. On this see Levie, *supra* n.43, at 106–109.

objects that may be used for escape, can be taken away.[127] Otherwise, personal items, articles for personal protection (e.g., helmets and gas masks), articles used for clothing and feeding, and identity documents should normally remain with the POW.[128]

One of the first duties of the Detaining Power in respect of POWs' capture on the battlefield is to evacuate them to internment camps situated in an area far enough from the combat zone for them to be out of danger.[129] Indeed, POWs may not be detained in areas where they are exposed to the fire of the combat zone, nor may their presence be used to render certain areas immune from attack.[130] If need be, the Detaining Power must build shelters against air bombardment and other hazards of war.

Inspired by the 'death marches' of the Second World War, Article 20 GC III prescribes that evacuation must be effected humanely and in conditions similar to those for the forces of the Detaining Power. In particular, POWs must be supplied with sufficient food and potable water, and with the necessary clothing and medical attention. The 1929 Geneva Convention foresaw that POWs should not be required to march more than 20 miles per day (a provision that was all too often ignored in the Second World War). The GC III no longer spells out a maximum marching distance. Arguably, the distance POWs can be expected to march without giving rise to 'inhumane treatment' must be determined on a case-by-case basis, taking account *inter alia* of the physical conditions of the POWs, the available supplies, climatic conditions, and so on.[131]

When evacuation from the combat zone is hindered by logistical constraints – for example when large numbers of enemy soldiers surrender and there are insufficient transport facilities to ensure speedy evacuation, or when enemy soldiers are captured by commando units – this does not release the Detaining Power of its duties under the GC III. Where unusual conditions prevent evacuation, POWs must be released and all feasible precautions must be taken to ensure their safety (Article 41(3), AP I). In other words, POWs may not be released in the middle of the Sahara or the Siberian tundra without adequate food and clothing.

The GC III elaborates at length on the conditions of internment. The underlying idea is that POWs may temporarily be 'interned' to prevent their further participation in hostilities. Such internment must not be confused with 'imprisonment':[132] POWs may only be locked up in a cell as a result of disciplinary or penal measures (cf. *infra*).

---

[127] Article 18, GC III. On this see Levie, *supra* n.43, at 110–118.

[128] Sums of money and articles of value may only be taken away by order of an officer and after a receipt has been given. Such objects and sums of money shall be returned to the POW at the end of his/her captivity. Article 18(4)–(6), GC III.

[129] Article 19, GC III. As mentioned earlier, however, evacuation can be postponed if it would expose a sick or wounded POW to greater risks than if he were to remain in the danger zone.

[130] Article 23, GC III. Articles 22–23 GC III spell out basic requirements as to the location of POW camps and minimal hygienic and health conditions.

[131] Fischer, *supra* n.115, at 393.

[132] According to Article 22 of GC III, POWs may not normally be interned in penitentiaries. Furthermore, the tying up of POWs is in principle prohibited.

Articles 25–32 GC III explain to what extent POWs must be provided with adequate food, clothing and medical attention.[133] The relevant provisions often enter into considerable detail. For example, as far as food supplies are concerned, basic daily food rations should be 'sufficient in quantity, quality and variety' to keep POWs in good health. Apart from this, the 'use of tobacco shall be permitted'. Furthermore, the Detaining Power is bound to take sanitary measures in order to prevent the outbreak of epidemics in internment camps, which should moreover be equipped with an infirmary. More far-reaching obligations are imposed as well. Thus, medical inspections of POWs should be held once a month. For this purpose 'the most efficient methods available shall be employed, e.g. periodic mass miniature radiography for the early detection of tuberculosis'.[134]

The Third Geneva Convention contains numerous other provisions regulating, among other things, the right of POWs to practise their religion (Article 34, GC III); the possibility to use weapons (as a last resort) against POWs, for example to prevent escape (Article 42, GC III);[135] the extent to which the Detaining Power may utilize the labour of POWs and the conditions applicable thereto (Articles 49–57, GC III);[136] the possibility for POWs to communicate with the outside world (Articles 70–71, GC III) and the right to complain about the conditions of captivity (Article 78, GC III). For all their detail, when reading the provisions regulating the conditions of captivity, some of the positive obligations imposed on the Detaining Power may strike one as archaic, overly demanding or, perhaps, naïve. It must be kept in mind, however, that they must be applied having due regard to the context and, in particular, to the situation of the Detaining Power's own troops. It is interesting in this respect to read the two Partial Awards on the treatment of POWs issued by the Eritrea Ethiopia Claims Commission (hereinafter 'EECC') in 2003,[137] two decisions dealing with an international armed conflict between two of the world's poorest countries – and one taking place in extreme conditions (cf. heat, drought). Thus, when dealing with accusations that Eritrea had failed to provide the necessary medical attention by not cleaning and bandaging wounds of Ethiopian POWs at or shortly after capture, the Commission, taking account of evidence that Eritrea had provided rudimentary first aid as soon as possible, expressed the following statement:

---

[133] On this see Levie, *supra* n.43, at 126–137.

[134] Article 31, GC III.

[135] Thus, according to Article 42 of GC III, the use of force should always be preceded by 'warnings appropriate to the circumstances'. In light thereof, it is forbidden to establish so-called 'death lines', the crossing of which leads to immediate shooting of a POW without proper warning. A.H. Harvey, 'The Maintenance of Control over Prisoners of War', (1963) 2 *RDMDG* 127, at 137.

[136] For example, Article 52 of GC III states that POWs may not be employed for unhealthy or dangerous work (such as mine-clearing), unless they volunteer. The working pay due to POWs is regulated by Articles 54 and 62 of GC III. See, for example, H.S. Levie, 'The Employment of Prisoners of War', (1963) 57 *AJIL* 318.

[137] Eritrea Ethiopia Claims Commission, Partial Award Prisoners of War, Ethiopia's Claim 4, The Hague, 1 July 2003 (2003) 42 *ILM* 1056; Eritrea Ethiopia Claims Commission, Partial Award Prisoners of War, Eritrea's Claim 17, The Hague, 1 July 2003 (2003) 42 *ILM* 1083.

> The Commission believes that the requirement to provide POWs with medical care during the initial period after capture must be assessed in light of the harsh conditions on the battlefield and the limited extent of medical training and equipment available to front line troops. On balance, and recognizing the logistical and resource limitations faced by both Parties to the conflict, the Commission finds that Eritrea is not liable for failing to provide medical care to Ethiopian POWs at the front and during evacuation.[138]

Elsewhere, dealing with the medical care provided in the POW camps, the Commission recognized that Eritrea and Ethiopia could not be required 'to have the same standards for medical treatment as developed countries'. Nonetheless, 'scarcity of finances and infrastructure [could not] excuse a failure to grant the minimum standard of medical care required by international humanitarian law'.[139]

In a similar vein, in relation to allegations that Ethiopian POWs were 'forced to walk from the front for hours or days over rough terrain, often in pain from their own wounds, often carrying wounded comrades and Eritrean supplies, often in harsh weather, and often with little or no food and water', the Commission took note of the evidence presented by Eritrea that 'its soldiers faced nearly the same unavoidably difficult conditions, particularly given the lack of paved roads'.[140] Eritrea was, however, found liable for inhumane treatment for having seized the footwear of the Ethiopian POWs, thus unnecessarily compounding their misery.

On a more general note, the EECC construed the positive obligations of the Detaining Powers in light of the context at hand and also made a distinction between more serious violations (e.g., those relating to physical abuse or inadequate medical care in the camps) and those 'claims that loomed less large' (e.g., the failure to post camp rules and allow complaints by POWs).[141] Even if both countries were found liable for infringements of LOAC ('sometimes significant, occasionally grave'), the Commission took care to emphasize that 'although these cases involve two of the poorest countries in the world, both made significant efforts to provide for the sustenance and care of the POWs in their custody' and both 'endeavoured to observe their fundamental humanitarian obligations to collect and protect enemy soldiers unable to resist on the battlefield'.[142]

The Third Geneva Convention contains various provisions aimed at facilitating the implementation of the GC III. Thus, Detaining Powers are required to establish Information Bureaus for exchanging information on the POWs in their hands.[143] Within certain conditions, they are moreover required to allow relief societies and related organizations to, for example, provide relief supplies to POWs.[144] Last, but certainly not least, they are under an obligation to permit representatives or delegates of the Protecting Powers – in practice this role will usually be fulfilled by the ICRC – to visit

---

[138] Ethiopia's Claim 4, *ibid.*, at §70.
[139] *Ibid.*, at §125.
[140] *Ibid.*, at §§73–74.
[141] *Ibid.*, at §§142–143. See also §80 in respect of confiscation of personal property.
[142] *Ibid.*, at §§12–13.
[143] Article 122, GC III *et seq.*
[144] Article 125, GC III.

POW camps and to interview the prisoners.[145] This rule is of vital importance for purposes of monitoring compliance with the GC III. In spite of its customary nature,[146] it still happens on occasion that the ICRC is refused access.[147] In 2005 the US legal advisor first recognized that the US had not given the ICRC access to all detainees in its custody, whether in Iraq or elsewhere.[148]

iv. Punishment

As indicated earlier, captured combatants may not be prosecuted merely for having taken part in hostilities. They may, however, be prosecuted if they have committed for instance certain war crimes prior to capture.[149] Upon falling in the hands of the Detaining Power, POWs also become subject to the laws, regulations and orders in force in the armed forces of the Detaining Power.[150] When a POW commits an offence against these laws, regulations and orders (e.g., by murdering a fellow prisoner), judicial or disciplinary measures can under certain conditions be imposed by the Detaining Power.[151]

The Convention expresses a preference for disciplinary,[152] rather than judicial measures, and specifically prescribes for instance that a POW who attempts to escape but is recaptured shall in principle only be liable to disciplinary measures (except, for instance, if he were to commit violence against life or limb during his escape).[153] Penal sanctions can only be imposed following a trial before an independent and impartial court.[154] The Convention prohibits collective punishment for individual acts, corporal punishment and any form of torture or cruelty, and imposes additional safeguards in relation to offences punishable by penalty of death.[155] Article 105 of GC III describes in detail the rights and means of defence of POWs put on trial, including the right to defence by a qualified advocate or counsel of his own choice and the right to call witnesses. Article 106 GC III provides for a right of appeal.

---

[145] Article 126, GC III.
[146] See, for example, Ethiopia's Claim 4, *supra* n.137, at §60.
[147] See, for example, *ibid.*, at §62; Levie, *supra* n.43, at 312.
[148] BBC News, 'US Bars Access to Terror Suspects', 9 December 2005, available at http://news.bbc.co.uk/1/hi/world/americas/4512192.stm.
[149] See, for example, M.A. Meyer, 'Liability of POWs for Offences Committed Prior to Capture – the Astiz Affair', (1983) 32 *ICLQ* 848. See also Levie, *supra* n.43, at 315–342.
[150] Article 82, GC III.
[151] See Articles 82–108, GC III.
[152] Disciplinary sanctions can take the form of a fine, a loss of privileges, fatigue duties or (temporary) confinement (Article 89, GC III). Other sanctions (e.g., withholding of communication rights) are not permitted.
[153] Articles 92–93, GC III. Furthermore, acts that are punishable only when committed by POWs shall only entail disciplinary punishments (Article 82, GC III).
[154] In principle, trial must take place before a military court, except if civil courts would be competent if the act(s) concerned had been committed by members of the forces of the Detaining Power. Article 84, GC III.
[155] Article 87, GC III, Articles 100–101, GC III.

v. Repatriation

Belligerent Parties have the right to intern POWs to prevent their continued participation in hostilities. By way of exception, they must directly repatriate certain categories of wounded and sick persons, such as persons who are incurably wounded and sick, or who are unlikely to recover within one year (Article 110, GC III). Repatriated persons may not be employed on active military service.[156]

For those POWs not qualifying for direct repatriation, captivity may end as a result of the prisoner's successful escape (in the sense of Article 91, GC III) or as a result of his death in captivity (which triggers specific obligations under Articles 120–121, GC III). Otherwise, captivity will normally only end following the cessation of hostilities. Indeed, while (healthy) POWs *can* be repatriated on a voluntary basis, such demarche is rare in practice.[157] Only when active hostilities have actually ceased does a *duty* to repatriate arise.[158] Repatriation may be postponed in respect of POWs that are awaiting trial or that are serving a sentence following trial.[159]

C. Civilians

i. General protection

As a general rule, the treatment of civilians and the conditions of their internment are comparable to the regime applicable to POWs. Civilians shall at all times be humanely treated.[160] They shall be especially protected against all acts of violence or threats thereof and against insults and public curiosity.[161] Other protective measures of a general nature include the prohibition from taking any measure of such a character as to cause the physical suffering or extermination of protected persons,[162] the prohibition of collective punishments and all measures of intimidation or of terrorism, as well as the prohibition of pillage, the taking of hostages and reprisals against them and their property.[163]

---

[156] Article 117, GC III.
[157] Fischer, *supra* n.115, at 414–415.
[158] This duty goes beyond the mere 'release' of the prisoner, but requires a planned approach, in consultation with the adverse Party, and, as the case may be, the Protecting Powers and/or the ICRC. On the interpretation of the notion of 'cessation of hostilities' in this regard, see *ibid.*, at 415. There is some discussion as to the situation of POWs unwilling to be repatriated. Article 109 of GC III states that sick or injured POWs will not be repatriated during hostilities against their will. By contrast, no such rule is incorporated in the GC III with regard to repatriation after the cessation of hostilities. It is sometimes suggested that in such scenario the ICRC should be involved so as to attest that POWs are truly refusing repatriation (in order to avoid abuse). See *ibid.*, at 416–417. See also Y. Dinstein, 'The release of prisoners of war', in Pictet and Swinarski (eds), *supra* n.93, 37; M. Sassoli, 'The Status, Treatment and Repatriation of Deserters Under International Humanitarian Law', (1985) *Yb. of the International Institute of Humanitarian Law* 9; Levie, *supra* n.43, at 395–429.
[159] Article 119, GC III.
[160] Article 27, GV IV.
[161] *Ibid.* See also ICTY, *Prosecutor v. Tadic*, Opinion and Judgment, IT-94-1-T, 7 May 1997, at 154–179.
[162] Article 32, GC IV.
[163] Article 33, GC IV.

Civilians shall be entitled to leave the territory at the outset of, or during the armed conflict, unless their departure is contrary to the national interests of the state,[164] in which case they will be informed with the reasons for refusal.[165] With the exception of special measures, particularly measures of control and security as a result of the war and assigned residence and internment, the situation of protected persons must continue to be regulated by the legal regime concerning aliens in times of peace.[166] In other words, the normal legal regime relating to aliens is the rule, while assigned residence and internment remain the exceptions. In the latter case, civilians will be entitled to challenge their placing in assigned residence or internment as soon as possible and at least twice a year.[167] In case of belligerent occupation, civilians who are subject to assigned residence or internment have a right to appeal the decision. If the decision is upheld, it must be subject to periodical review, if possible every six months, by a competent body.[168] During the conflict in the former Yugoslavia, civilians were detained after initial arrest for longer periods, none of them being informed of the reason for detention, with no legal basis to justify their deprivation of liberty.[169] In other words, even an initially lawful internment becomes unlawful if the Detaining Party does not respect the basic procedural rights of the detained persons and does not establish an appropriate court or administrative board.[170]

ii. Internment

When civilians are interned for reasons pertaining to the armed conflict, the GC IV contains detailed provisions on the conditions the detention regime needs to fulfil (Articles 79–141, GC IV). As far as possible, internees shall be accommodated according to their nationality, language and customs. They shall be accommodated and administered separately from POWs and persons deprived of their liberty for any other reason.[171] The necessary safeguards as regards hygiene and health will be taken.[172] Places of internment must provide sufficient protection against the rigours of the climate. Consequently, they must not be denied the most basic protection against freezing temperatures in the winter.[173] Food rations shall be sufficient in quality and quantity in order to keep them in good state of health.[174] Particular care shall be given to expectant and nursing mothers, as well as to children under fifteen years of

---

[164] Article 35, GC IV. See also ICTY, *Prosecutor v. Delalic et al.*, supra n.91, at 564–578.
[165] Article 35, GC IV.
[166] Article 38, GC IV.
[167] Article 43, GC IV.
[168] Article 78, GC IV.
[169] ICTY, *Prosecutor v. Krnojelac*, Judgment, IT-97-25-T, T.Ch.II, 15 March 2000, at 116–124.
[170] ICTY, *Prosecutor v. Delalic et al.*, supra n.91, at 583.
[171] Article 84, GC IV.
[172] Article 85, GC IV. In *Aleksovski*, the Trial Chamber gave examples of the detention conditions in which detainees were held, such as inadequate space and heating, sanitary conditions, food and medical care: ICTY, *Prosecutor v. Aleksovski*, Judgment, IT-95-14/1-T, T.Ch.Ibis, 25 June 1999, at 154–182.
[173] *Prosecutor v. Aleskovski*, ibid., at 137–138.
[174] Article 89, GC IV.

age.[175] The GC IV also contains detailed provisions in relation to personal property and financial resources (Articles 97–98, GC IV), administration and discipline (Articles 99–104, GC IV) and the relations with the exterior (Articles 105–116, GC IV), and provisions with regard to criminal and disciplinary sanctions which apply to internees (Articles 117–126, GC IV). In general, the national legislation applicable in the territory in which they are detained will continue to apply.[176]

Finally, interned persons must be released as soon as the reasons which necessitated their internment no longer exist.[177] After the close of hostilities, the internment must cease as soon as possible.[178]

iii. Fundamental protection

Under the Geneva Conventions and Protocol I, only two categories are excluded from POW status in case of capture by the enemy: spies and mercenaries. By analogy with other 'unlawful combatants' or 'unprivileged combatants',[179] however, they remain under the protection regime provided by the minimum safeguards of Article 75 of GC I. It provides fundamental protections for any person who does not benefit from a more favourable treatment under the GC and AP I and who has fallen into the hands of the adverse Party to the conflict, such as spies and mercenaries.[180]

iv. Relief actions

The Parties to the conflict are obliged to facilitate and allow the free passage of all consignments of medical and hospital stores and objects necessary for religious worship.[181] AP I extended the scope of the relief goods to include clothing, bedding, means of shelter and other supplies essential to the survival of the civilian population in occupied territories.[182] If the civilian population is not adequately supplied with the aforementioned goods, relief actions which are impartial and humanitarian in character and conducted without any adverse distinction shall not be regarded as interference in the armed conflict or as unfriendly acts.[183] Priority shall be given to children and pregnant and nursing women, who are to be accorded privileged treatment or special protection.[184] It remains controversial if and to what extent Article 70 of AP I imposes

---

[175] Ibid.
[176] Article 117, GC IV.
[177] Article 132, GC IV.
[178] Article 133, AP I.
[179] On this see *supra* Section 2Ciiic.
[180] Article 46(1) and 47(1), AP I.
[181] Article 23, GC IV. On the legal regime governing starvation and relief actions see, for example, C.A. Allen, 'Civilian Starvation and Relief during Armed Conflict: The Modern Humanitarian Law', (1989) 19 *Georgia J. Int'l & Comp. L.* 1; P. Macalister-Smith, 'Protection of the Civilian Population and the Prohibition of Starvation as a Method of Warfare: Draft Texts on International Humanitarian Assistance', (1991) 31 *IRRC* 440; Y. Dinstein, 'Siege Warfare and the Starvation of Civilians', in A.J.M. Delissen and G.J. Tanja (eds), *Humanitarian Law of Armed Conflict: Challenges Ahead. Essays in Honour of Frits Kalshoven* (Dordrecht: Martinus Nijhoff, 1991), 145.
[182] Article 69, AP I.
[183] Article 70, AP I.
[184] Ibid.

a duty to organize relief actions when the civilian population is not adequately supplied with such goods, especially those supplies which are essential for the survival of the civilian population. Such relief actions shall only be undertaken 'subject to the agreement of the Parties concerned in such relief actions'.[185] The Parties to the conflict which allow the passage of relief consignments and equipment retain the right to prescribe the technical arrangements, including search, under which such passage is permitted and may make such permission conditional on the distribution thereof under local supervision of a Protecting Power.[186] GC IV devotes particular attention for the free passage of all consignments of essential foodstuffs, clothing and tonics intended for children under fifteen, expectant mothers and maternity cases.[187]

v. Transfer, evacuation and deportation

In occupied territories, mass forcible transfers, as well as deportations of protected persons from occupied territory to other states remain prohibited, regardless of the motive.[188] However, the Occupying Power may undertake total or partial evacuation of a given area if the security of the population or imperative military reasons so demand. A particular case is the evacuation of children to a foreign country. Such evacuation is only permitted where compelling reasons of the health or the medical treatment of the child so require.[189] In occupied territory, this evacuation can also be justified for compelling reasons of their safety.[190] Only when their parents (or in their absence, the legal representatives) expressly consent, can children be evacuated under the supervision of the Protecting Power.[191] AP I is thus more restrictive than GC IV, the latter providing that the Parties to the conflict shall facilitate the reception of orphaned children or children separated from their parents in neutral countries.[192]

D. Special Categories of Protected Persons

Developments in the protection of special categories of protected persons, such as women and children, must be seen within a broader framework of advancements in international law, particularly international human rights law, including the Convention on the Elimination of All Forms of Discrimination Against Women (1979) and its Optional Protocol,[193] the Declaration on the Elimination of Violence Against Women (1993),[194] the Convention on the Rights of the Child (1989)[195] (hereinafter 'CRC') and its Optional Protocols on the Involvement of Children in Armed Conflict, and on the

---

[185] *Ibid.*
[186] *Ibid.*
[187] Article 23, GC IV.
[188] Article 49, GC IV. On this see, for example, C. Mcindersma, 'Legal Issues Surrounding Population Transfers in Conflict Situations', (1994) 41 *NILR* 31.
[189] Article 78, AP I.
[190] *Ibid.*
[191] *Ibid.*
[192] Article 24, GC IV.
[193] UNGA Resolution A/Res/54/4 (1999).
[194] UNGA Resolution 48/104 (1993).
[195] UNGA Resolution 44/25 (1989).

Sale of Children, Child Prostitution and Child Pornography.[196] In the next paragraphs, special attention will be drawn to the situation of two vulnerable categories of persons, namely women and children.[197] Notwithstanding their special protection, women and children benefit of the general rules of international humanitarian law as members of the civilian population.

i. Women

Gender crimes are not a novelty in times of armed conflict: Ancient Greeks viewed rape as socially acceptable behaviour well within the rules of warfare; in Europe, during the Middle Ages, if a city refused to surrender upon the victors' demand for surrender, the rules of combat allowed soldiers to rape women occupants; in the First World War, invading armies used rape to subjugate the will of civilian populations.[198] Prior to the ICTY and the International Criminal Tribunal for Rwanda (hereinafter 'ICTR'), the International Military Tribunal for the Far East (hereinafter 'IMTFE') characterized rape as a form of 'inhumane treatment', 'mistreatment' and a 'failure to respect family honor and rights' in its Charter.[199] However, rape did not figure prominently at Nuremberg.[200]

The analysis and understanding of gender have advanced substantially in the context of human rights, refugee law and international humanitarian law, in particular the jurisprudence of the *ad hoc* tribunals for the former Yugoslavia and Rwanda.[201] When

---

[196] UNGA Resolution 54/263 (2000).

[197] The issue of children and women in the context of the sick, the shipwrecked and POWs has been discussed in previous sections.

[198] F. Bensouda, 'Gender and Sexual Violence Under the Rome Statute', in E. Decaux, A. Dieng and M. Sow (eds), *From Human Rights to International Criminal Law/Des droits de l'homme au droit international penal* (Leiden: Martinus Nijhoff, 2007), 401 (citing S. Drownmiller, *Against Our Will: Men, Women and Rape* (New York: Fawcett Books, 1975), 33; see also T. Meron, 'Editorial Comment. Rape as a Crime Under International Humanitarian Law', (1993) 87 *AJIL* 3, at 425; C.N. Niarchos, 'Women, War, and Rape: Challenges Facing The International Tribunal for the Former Yugoslavia', (1995) 17 *Human Rights Quarterly* 660; C. Chinkin, 'Rape and Sexual Abuse of Women in International Law', (1994) 5 *EJIL* 326.

[199] Article 5(g) of the ICTY Statute; Articles 3(h) and 4(g) of the ICTR Statute. Rape had also been listed as a crime against humanity in Article II(1)(c) of CCL No.10 (but no charges related to rape were brought under this law).

[200] According to J. Laber, this was due 'not because the Germans were not guilty of rape, but because the allied forces, especially the Russians and the Moroccan forces under French control, were also guilty of rape', in Laber, 'Bosnia: Questions About Rape', (1993) 40 *NY Rev* 3, cited in Chinkin, *supra* n.198, at 334.

[201] ICTR, *Prosecutor v. Akayesu*, ICTR-96-4-T, Judgment, 2 September 1998, at 688; ICTY, *Prosecutor v. Delalic and others*, supra n.91, at 495; ICTY, *Prosecutor v. Furundzija*, Judgment, 10 December 1998, IT-95-17/1-T, at 271; ICTY, *Prosecutor v. Kunarac*, Judgment, 22 February 2001, IT-96-23-T and IT-96-23/1-T, at 460 and 495; ICTY, *Prosecutor v. Kvocka*, Judgment, 2 November 2001, IT-98-30-T; ICTR, *Prosecutor v. Gacumbtsi*, ICTR-2001-64-T, Judgment, 17 June 2004, at 321–333; ICTR, *Prosecutor v. Musema*, Judgment, ICTR-96-13, at 962–966; ICTR, *Prosecutor v. Semanza*, Judgment, 15 May 2003, ICTR-97-20-I, at 477–479; ICTY, *Prosecutor v. Krstic*, Judgment, 2 August 2001, IT-98-33-T, at 617–618; ICTY, *Prosecutor v. Tadic*, Judgment, 7 May 1997, IT-94-1-T, at 715. With regard to gender-based crimes in the statutes of the *ad hoc* Tribunals, commentators criticized the 'prevalent use in international

the Security Council adopted the ICTY Statute, it expressed 'once again its grave alarm at continuing reports of widespread and flagrant violations of international humanitarian law ... including reports of ... organized and systematic detention and rape of women'.[202] The International Criminal Court (hereinafter 'ICC') Statute explicitly recognizes sexual violence as a crime against humanity and a war crime.[203]

Although gender-based violence against women has been addressed in international humanitarian law, their particular concerns have often been regarded as peripheral, that is to say, 'as an inevitable aspect of armed conflict'.[204] The special protection offered to women is no substitute to the general protection given generally. It follows from this that the special respect due to women cannot be considered to free the Belligerent Parties from their obligation to give the civilian population as a whole the respect and protection to which they are entitled.[205]

When detained, it is important that the detention facilities are adequate and provide for separate quarters under the direct supervision of women.[206] More specific provisions exist to regulate the situation of pregnant women and women with children.[207]

Women are more often subject to abuse, such as rape, sexual enslavement, forced pregnancy and other forms of ill treatment because

> although both men and women are subject to sexual assault, a distinction needs to be drawn between them. Sexual torture as such, particularly during interrogation, with its full spectrum of humiliation and violence can, and often does, culminate in the rape of the victim, and is more common with women prisoners.[208]

---

humanitarian law of imprecise and inappropriate language' and to 'end this practice of so referring to established or readily identifiable crimes and, instead, to use language that most accurately identifies the crime and its nature' (K.D. Askin, 'Sexual Violence in Decisions and Indictments of the Yugoslav and Rwandan Tribunals: Current Status', (1999) 93 *AJIL* 101.

[202] UNSCR 827 (1994).
[203] Articles 7(1)(g) and 8(2)(b) define 'crime against humanity' and 'war crime' as including 'rape, sexual slavery, enforced prostitution, forced pregnancy, enforced sterilization, or any other form of sexual violence of comparable gravity'. Article 8(2)(b)(xxii) differs slightly from Article 7(1)(g) in defining other forms of sexual violence as being those 'also constituting a grave breach of the Geneva Conventions'. Article 8(2)(e)(vi) gives the same list of war crimes except that 'any other form of sexual violence' is defined as one 'constituting a serious violation of article 3 common to the four Geneva Conventions'. Articles 7(1)(c) and 7(2)(c) further include 'enslavement' as a crime against humanity, with specific reference to trafficking in women and children.
[204] J. Garden and H. Charlesworth, 'Protection of Women in Armed Conflict', (2000) 22 *Human Rights Quarterly* 150. See also Chinkin, *supra* n.198, 326 and J. Gardam, 'Women and the Law of Armed Conflict: Why the Silence?', (1997) 46 *ICLQ* 55, at 59–61.
[205] Pictet, *supra* n.62, at 135.
[206] Article 76, GC IV and Article 75(5), AP I.
[207] Articles 89, 91, 98 and 127 GC IV. See also Article 76, AP I.
[208] P. Daudin and H. Reyes, 'How Visits by the ICRC Can Help Prisoners Cope with the Effects of Traumatic Stress', (2001) 83 *IRRC* 509. See also the Report of the Special Rapporteur on Torture and Other Cruel, Inhuman or Degrading Treatment or Punishment, M. Nowak, 15 January 2008, UN Doc. A/HRC/7/3, at 41–43.

As protected persons, women are entitled, in all circumstances, to respect for their persons and their honour. They shall be especially protected against any attack on their honour, in particular against rape,[209] enforced prostitution or any form of indecent assault.[210] This refers to acts which are aimed at humiliating and ridiculing them, or even forcing them to perform degrading acts. This provision was intended to denounce widespread abuse of women and children during the Second World War, including rape, mutilation and forced prostitution.[211]

The involvement of the UN Security Council with regard to the situation of women in armed conflicts helped to strengthen the process.[212] Having evidenced the sexual attacks on women during the conflicts in the former Yugoslavia and Rwanda, the UN adopted in 1993 the Declaration on the Elimination of Violence against Women, requiring states to 'exercise due diligence to prevent, investigate and, in accordance with national legislation, punish acts of violence against women'.[213] On 31 October 2000, the Security Council adopted UNSCR 1325. The resolution highlights the fact that threats to women are distinct from those facing the civilian population as a whole and expands on the provisions contained in its earlier resolution of 1999. In 2006, the Security Council delivered its In-depth Study on all Forms of Violence against Women.[214] Despite these efforts, the Security Council reiterated its concerns over the lack of progress on the issue of sexual violence in situations of armed conflict (in particular against women and children, notably against girls).[215]

ii. Children

Like women, children have become even more acutely vulnerable to abuse with the shift in armed violence to armed conflicts.[216] In more recent times, civilians have become primary targets and prizes of war. Children are forcibly recruited as child soldiers or sex slaves and are more vulnerable to death and starvation when access to medical help and food aid becomes a method of warfare. Children are also affected

---

[209] In *Akayesu* and *Furundzija*, the *ad hoc* tribunals took different approaches in defining rape. In *Akayesu*, the Trial Chamber of the ICTR stated that 'rape is a form of aggression and that the central elements of the crime of rape cannot be captured in a mechanical description of objects and body parts. [...] Sexual violence is not limited to physical invasion of the human body and may include acts which do not involve penetration or even physical contact' (*Prosecutor v. Akayesu*, supra n.201, at 687–688). In *Furundzija*, the Trial Chamber gave a more 'mechanical' definition of rape (*Prosecutor v. Furundzija*, supra n.201, at 185).

[210] Article 27, GC IV; Articles 75(2)(b) and 76(1), AP I.

[211] Pictet, *supra* n.62, at 205.

[212] On the Security Council and the role of women in armed conflict, see A.-G. Tachou-Sipowo, 'The Security Council on Women in War: Between Peacebuilding and Humanitarian Protection', (2010) 92 *IRRC* 197.

[213] UNGA Resolution 48/104 (1993), Article 4(c).

[214] In-depth Study on all Forms of Violence against Women, Report of the Secretary-General, 6 July 2006, UN Doc. A/61/122/Add1.

[215] UNSC Resolution 1888 (1999).

[216] Sandoz, Swinarski and Zimmerman (eds), *supra* n.95, at 4544. See also the Official Records of the Diplomatic Conference on the Reaffirmation and Development of International Humanitarian Law Applicable on Armed Conflicts, Geneva, 1974–1977, XV, CDDH/III/SR.45, at 3.

because 'disrupting the social networks and primary relationships that support children's physical, emotional, moral, cognitive and social development ... can have profound physical and psychological implications'.[217] International humanitarian law protects children in different ways. First, as a particularly vulnerable category of persons, they are accorded special protection. Secondly, it questions the use of children in operational engagements and, finally, it takes into consideration their immaturity when committing offences during armed conflicts. Today, the principle that children deserve special protection is a norm of customary international law, regardless of the classification of the armed conflict.[218] The Security Council reaffirmed its preoccupation on the situation of children in armed conflicts in several resolutions.[219]

Although international humanitarian law contains different provisions on children, different term are used to describe them: children,[220] children under fifteen,[221] minors,[222] children under seven,[223] protected persons who are under eighteen years of age,[224] young people,[225] children under twelve,[226] infants and young children.[227] Under the Convention on the Rights of the Child, a child means 'every human being below the age of eighteen years unless under the law applicable to the child, majority is attained earlier'.[228]

Of particular concern is the recruitment of child soldiers and their direct participation in the hostilities.[229] International human rights standards have been put in place to

---

[217] UNICEF, Impact of Armed Conflict on Children, Report of the Expert of the Secretary-General (A/62/228).

[218] ICRC Customary Study Vol. I, *supra* n.3, Rule 135.

[219] UNSC Resolution 1261 (1999), UNSC Resolution 1314 (2000), UNSC Resolution 1379 (2001), UNSC Resolution 1460 (2003), UNSC Resolution 1612 (2005), UNSC Resolution 1882 (2009) and UNSC Resolution 1998 (2011). On the policy and practice of the UN Security Council mechanisms, see V. Nyland, 'From Standard-Setting to Implementation: The Security Council's Thematical Focus on Children in Armed Conflict', (2001) 5 *HR&ILD* 101.

[220] Articles 17, 24, 50, 82, 94, 132, GC IV; Articles 77 (1), 77(4), 78, AP I.

[221] Articles 24, 50, 89, GC IV; Articles 77(2), 77(3), AP I.

[222] Article 76, GC IV.

[223] Article 50, GC IV.

[224] Article 68, GC IV ; Article 77(5), AP I.

[225] Article 94, GC IV.

[226] Article 24, GC IV.

[227] Article 132, GC IV.

[228] Article 1, CRC. This definition was also endorsed by the UN Special Representative of the Secretary-General for Children and Armed Conflict (Office of the Special Representative of the Secretary-General for Children and Armed Conflict, The Six Grave Violations against Children during Armed Conflict: The Legal Foundation, Working Paper No.1 (2009), 3.

[229] The notion 'recruitment' covers any means, formal or *de facto*, by which a person becomes a member of the armed forces or of an armed group (Sandoz, Swinarski and Zimmerman, *supra* n.94, at 380). In contrast with AP I and the CRC, the ICC Statute distinguishes between 'conscripting' and 'enlisting'. The term 'conscription' refers to all forms of coerced recruitment (whether lawful or not under national legislation). See also the judgment of the Special Court for Sierra Leone in the CDF case (SCSL, *Prosecutor v. Fofana and Kondewa*, T.Ch.I, Judgment, 2 August 2007, SCSL-04-14-T and SCSL, *Prosecutor v. Fofana and Kondewa*, A.Ch., Judgment, 28 May 2008, SCSL-04-14-A), at 1659. On the notion of 'use' and

protect children from being involved in hostilities or forcibly conscripted into the armed forces. Article 38 CRC provides that 'States Parties undertake to respect and to ensure respect for the rules of international humanitarian law applicable to them in armed conflicts which are relevant to the child'. It prohibits the use of children younger than fifteen years of age in armed conflicts, regardless of the classification of the conflict.[230] Article 38(2) CRC clearly states that 'States Parties shall take all feasible measures to ensure that persons who have not attained the age of fifteen years do not take a direct part in hostilities'.[231] Children who have not attained the age of fifteen years, take a direct part in hostilities and fall into the power of the enemy shall continue to benefit from the special protection accorded by Article 77(3) of AP I. Additionally, they should not be required to perform activities indirectly linked to the armed conflict and, consequently, the prohibition against using children to participate in hostilities should cover combatant and non-combatant children equally.[232]

The Optional Protocol on the Involvement of Children in Armed Conflict of the CRC provides that persons under eighteen years should not take part in direct hostilities and that states should take all feasible measures to ensure that children under eighteen years

---

'participation' in hostilities see the decision of the confirmation of the charges against Lubanga by Trial Chamber I:

> The Chamber finds that Articles 8(2)(b)(xxvi) and 8(2)(e)(vii) apply if children are used to guard military objectives, such as the military quarters of the various units of the parties to the conflict, or to safeguard the physical safety of military commanders (in particular, when children are used as bodyguards). These activities are indeed related to hostilities in so far as i) the military commanders are in a position to take all the necessary decisions regarding the conduct of hostilities, and ii) they have a direct impact on the level of logistics resources and the organisation of operations required by the other party to the conflict, whose aim is to attack such military objectives.

(ICC, *Prosecutor v. Lubanga*, Pre-Trial Chamber, Decision on the confirmation of charges, 21 January 2007, ICC-01/04-01/06, at 263. Compare with SCSL in the AFRC case (SCSL, *Prosecutor v. Brima, Kamara and Canu*, T.Ch.II, Judgment, 20 June 2007, SCSL-04-16-T, at 737) and the RUF case (SCSL, *Prosecutor v. Sesay, Kallon and Gbao*, T.Ch.I, Judgment, 2 March 2009, SCSL-04-15-T, at 1720).

[230] For a comprehensive critique on the age of fifteen years as the minimum age for children to participate in hostilities, see J. Kuper, 'Children and Armed Conflict: Some Issues of Law and Policy', in D. Fotrell (ed.), *Revisiting Children's Rights: 10 Years of the UN Convention on the Rights of the Child 107* (The Hague: Kluwer Law International, 2000). See also R. Brett, 'Child Soldiers: Law, Politics and Practice', (1996) 4 *The International Journal of Children's Rights* 117.

[231] See also F. Ang, *Children in Armed Conflicts, A Commentary on the United Nations Convention on the Rights of the Child* (Leiden: Martinus Nijhoff, 2005).

[232] Sandoz, Swinarski and Zimmerman (eds), *supra* n.95, at 3187. According to the Special Representative of the Secretary-General on children and armed conflict, this prohibition is justified because the criterion for the prohibition is not whether the child actually took part in military operations, but whether his or her participation 'served an essential support function to the armed force or armed group during the period of conflict' (written submission of the UN Special Representative of the Secretary-General on children and armed conflict, Situation in the Democratic Republic of the Congo in the case of 'Prosecutor v. Thomas Lubanga Dyilo', 2008) cited by S. Vite, 'Protecting Children During Armed Conflict: International Humanitarian Law', (2011) 5 *HR&ILD* 24.

are not *compulsorily* recruited.[233] For *voluntary* recruitment, states are required to raise the minimum age to over fifteen.[234] When states recruit persons between the age of fifteen and eighteen years, priority should be given to the oldest. In this sense, the CRC reiterates the obligation contained in Article 77 of AP I.[235] Article 8 of the ICC Statute lists 'conscripting or enlisting children under the age of fifteen years into armed forces or groups or using them to participate actively in hostilities' as a war crime.[236] These elements indicate that children who committed serious crimes in the course of armed conflicts are not only perpetrators of such crimes, but can equally be seen as 'victims' in the hands of those who enrolled them into their forces.[237]

When children are separated from their family, 'the Parties to the conflict shall take the necessary measures to ensure that children under fifteen, who are orphaned or are separated from their families as a result of the war, are not left to their own resources. Additionally, their maintenance, the exercise of their religion and their education shall be facilitated in all circumstances. In case of family dispersion, the Parties to the conflict shall facilitate enquiries and shall encourage the work of organizations engaged in this task (provided they are acceptable to it and conform to its security regulations)'.[238] In 2010, the United Nations General Assembly (hereinafter 'UNGA') issued Guidelines for the Alternative Care of Children, providing recommendations concerning children deprived of parental care.[239]

iii. Journalists

In situations of armed conflict, accurate and independent information becomes even more crucial. Contemporary conflicts have proven that truth is among the first victims in times of war. Therefore, the role of impartial and independent journalists cannot be

---

[233] Articles 1 and 2. The CRC Protocol amended thus the minimum age for recruitment of persons into their armed forces from fifteen to eighteen years of age. For a critical analysis on the minimum age which is set in international legal provisions, including the Optional Protocol, above which children may participate in armed conflicts and the inadequate protection of children, see C. Breen, 'When is a Child Not a Child? Child Soldiers in International Law', (2007) 8 *Human Rights Review* 71.

[234] Article 3, CRC Protocol. As this age was set at fifteen in the CRC, the wording 'to raise' implies that the minimum age for voluntary recruitment is set at sixteen years. On the difference between the French version of Article 3 ('relevant en années') and the English version ('to raise'), see M. Happold, 'The Optional Protocol to the Convention on the Rights of the Child on the Involvement of Children in Armed Conflict', (2000) 3 *YIHL*, 226–244, at 238.

[235] According to Vite, this provision is problematic because 'by not distinguishing between international and non-international armed conflict, it becomes applicable to armed conflict of all types. As a result, it provides for weaker standards than the corresponding rule under Additional Protocol II' (Vite, *supra* n.232, at 26).

[236] Article 8(2)(b)(xxvi) and 8(2)(e)(vii) of the ICC Statute. On the elements of crime of conscripting and enlisting, see K. Dörmann, *Elements of War Crimes under the Rome Statute of the International Criminal Court: Sources and Commentary* (Cambridge: Cambridge University Press, 2003), at 377.

[237] See also the convictions for child recruitment by the Special Court for Sierra Leone in the AFRC case (*supra* n.229, the CDF case (*supra* n.229) and the RUF case (*supra* n.229).

[238] Article, 26 GC IV.

[239] UNGA, Guidelines for the Alternative Care of Children, A/RES/64/142, 24 February 2010, Annex.

underestimated. International humanitarian law distinguishes between two types of journalists in international armed conflicts: war correspondents and other journalists. War correspondents are persons who accompany the armed forces without actually being members thereof, provided that they have received authorization from the armed forces which they accompany and who are provided with an identity card for that purpose.[240] In other words, war correspondents are civilians but are accorded POW treatment in case of capture by the enemy. The possession of the identity card is not conditional of their right to be treated as a POW, but merely a supplementary safeguard.[241] Consequently, they will benefit of the protection of GC III and AP I. The fact that war correspondents benefit from POW treatment does not imply they had combatant status prior to their capture. They remain civilian, but are accorded this status 'in recognition of their close association with the armed forces to which they are attached'.[242] According to the ICTY in the Randal case, the term 'war correspondents' means 'individuals who, for any period of time, report (or investigate for the purposes of reporting) from a conflict zone on issues relating to the conflict'.[243] The omission of any reference to authorization by the Appeals Chamber as laid down in GC III is surprising. In view of the recent practice of 'embedded journalists', it cannot be concluded that the formal accreditation to the armed forces is no more constitutive of the notion of 'war correspondents'.

Journalists not benefiting from protection as war correspondents enjoy special protection as 'journalists engaged in dangerous professional missions in areas of armed conflict'.[244] They are civilians and, consequently, they also enjoy the general protection regime of civilians. The term should be understood in its broadest sense in order to encapsulate those persons 'who go for professional purposes to the armed conflict and [report] on the conflict to individuals outside the battlefield'.[245] According to the ICRC Commentary, the word 'journalist' shall mean 'any correspondent, reporter, photographer, and their technical film, radio and television assistants who are ordinarily engaged in any of these activities as their principal occupation'.[246]

In the Gulf War of 1990 a new practice emerged, namely that of 'embedded journalists' with the armed forces.[247] This apparently new concept does not create a new category of persons under international humanitarian law. Embedded journalists,

---

[240] Article 4A(4), GC III. Compare with ICTY, *Prosecutor v. Brdjanin and Talic*, Decision on Interlocutory Appeal, A. Ch., IT-99-36-AR73.9, 11 December 2002, at 29.

[241] Sandoz, Swinarski and Zimmerman, *supra* n.95, at 65.

[242] B. Saul, 'The International Protection of Journalists in Armed Conflict and Other Violent Situations', (2008) 14 *Australian Journal of Human Rights* 101.

[243] See *supra* n.240.

[244] Article 79, AP I. Compare with ICRC Customary Study Vol. I, *supra* n.3, Rule 34: 'civilian journalists engaged in professional missions'.

[245] G. Verschingel, 'Towards a Better Protection for Journalists in Armed Conflicts', (2008) 45 *Jura Falconis* 36.

[246] Sandoz, Swinarski and Zimmerman, *supra* n.95, at 3260.

[247] J. Lewis, T. Threadgold, R. Brooks and N. Mosdell, *Too Close for Comfort? The Role of Embedded Reporting During the 2003 Iraq War: Summary Report*, November 2003, Cardiff School of Journalism for the BBC.

unless they are members of the armed forces in which case they are combatants and thus liable to attack, remain civilians.

The fact that embedded journalists accompany the armed forces is in itself insufficient to make them liable to attack. As civilians, they are protected against attack, unless they participate directly in the hostilities.[248] However, due to their close proximity with the armed forces, they share the same risks as the combatants they accompany and have to assume the risk of being killed on the battlefield, especially when they wear protective equipment that can hardly be distinguished from combatants' equipment.[249] This is not to say that journalists may be attacked, but the question remains whether journalists who voluntarily accompany the armed forces should be taken into consideration in the proportionality analysis when attacking a legitimate military objective. Unlike voluntary human shields who intentionally try to shield military objectives from enemy attack, journalists have no such intentions.

Journalists lose their civilian immunity when and for such time they participate directly to the hostilities.[250] This will be the case when they transmit military messages, in which case they and their equipment become liable to attack.[251] The mere transmission of propaganda is, however, not sufficient to lose protection, unless this propaganda amounts to incitement to commit grave crimes, such as the crime of genocide.[252] Undermining civilian morale by attacking media is also prohibited. Journalists transmitting messages to the adverse Party face the risk of being treated as spies. In such case, they remain under the protection of the fundamental guarantees of Article 75 AP I but can be tried for their activities.

iv. Private Military and Security Companies (hereinafter 'PM/SC')

The presence of new actors on the battlefield, such as PM/SC, raises some issues in relation to their status under international humanitarian law. Since the 1990s, private contractors have played an increasing role, for two main reasons. First, the end of the Cold War led to major financial reductions in defence budgets. Consequently, governments sought to make use of private companies in order to outsource multiple tasks which until recently were solely executed by the military. Secondly, having regard to the technological improvements in the military domain, private companies were gradually entrusted with the maintenance of this highly sophisticated weaponry.[253]

---

[248] Article 51(3), AP I.

[249] Sandoz, Swinarski and Zimmerman, *supra* n.95, at 3269. See also Gasser, *supra* n.65, at 229.

[250] The fact that journalists carry weapons for the sole purpose of self-defence is not contrary to their status as civilians: see H.-P. Gasser, 'The Journalist Right to Information in Time of War and on Dangerous Mission', (2003) *YIHL* 377. Cf A. Van Engeland, *Civilian or Combatant: A Challenge for the 21st Century* (Oxford: Oxford University Press, 2011), at 85.

[251] ICTY, *Final Report to the Prosecutor by the Committee Established to Review the NATO Bombing Campaign Against the Federal Republic of Yugoslavia*, 8 June 2000, at 78.

[252] *Ibid.*, at 55; ICTR, *Prosecutor v. Nahimana, Barayagwisza, Ngeze*, 3 December 2003, ICTR-99-52-T; ICTR, *Prosecutor v. Ruggiu*, 2000, ICTR-97-32-I.

[253] L. Balmond, 'Observations sur le Document de Montreux aux Obligations Juridiques et aux Bonnes Pratiques pour les Etats concernant les Activités des Sociétés Militaires Privés', (2009) 113 *RGDIP* 113. See also M. Caparini and F. Schreier, *Privatising Security: Law,*

PM/SC are private entities that provide military/and or security services, irrespective of how they describe themselves. Personnel of a PM/SC are persons employed by, through direct hire or under a contract with, a PM/SC.[254] Depending on their function, private contractors could fall under several categories: combatants, civilian contractors entitled to POW treatment or even mercenaries. Two main categories can be distinguished: first, PM/SC participating directly in hostilities (in the broad sense) and, secondly, PM/SC not involved in combat operations.

Members of PM/SC could qualify as combatants if they satisfy the criteria of Article 4, A, (1) or (2) GC III. This could be the case if they are incorporated into the armed forces or qualify as 'members of other militias or volunteer corps belonging to a Party to the conflict. Insofar as they are not incorporated in the armed forces, they need to fulfil the following obligations: being commanded by a person responsible for his subordinates, carrying arms openly, having a fixed distinctive sign recognizable at a distance, and respecting the laws and customs of war.[255] However, only in peculiar scenarios could PM/SC meet the four standards, even under the definition of 'armed forces' under Article 43 of AP I.

Civilian contractors could also fall under the scope of Article 4A(2)(4) of GC III and enjoy treatment as POW when captured by the enemy. However, the non-exhaustive list of this Article clearly restricts the list of persons who accompany the armed forces without actually being members thereof to 'supply contractors' (in French: *'fournisseur'*). It does not extend to contractors who conduct military operations on behalf of parties to the conflict.[256]

If persons qualify as mercenaries, they would only be entitled to the minimum safeguards of Article 75 of AP I. However, the definition of mercenaries is so rigid that in most cases it will be hard to prove that persons fulfil the six cumulative criteria of Article 47 of AP I.[257]

In sum, members of PM/SC engaged in combat operations and participating directly in hostilities could qualify as combatants if the criteria of Article 4 of GC III/Article 43 of AP I are met. Members of PM/SC not engaged in combat operations remain civilians. Only civilian supply contractors can enjoy POW treatment as persons accompanying the armed forces.

Practice and Governance of Private Military and Security Companies (Geneva: DCAF, 2005), Occasional Paper No. 6, 44.

[254] Montreux Document on Pertinent International Legal Obligations and Good Practices for States related to Operations of Private Military and Security Companies during Armed Conflict, 17 September 2008, Preface, para. 9 (2009) 13 *JCSL* 453.

[255] See also J. Cockanyne, 'Regulating Private Military and Security Companies: The Content, Negotiation, Weakness and Promise of the Montreux Document', (2009) 13 *JCSL* 401; S. Chesterman, 'We Can't Spy ... If We Can't Buy": The Privatization of Intelligence and the Limits of Outsourcing "Inherently Governmental Functions"', (2008) 19 *EJIL* 5, at 1055–1074.

[256] C. Hoppe, 'Passing the Buck: State Responsibility for Private Military Companies', (2008) 19 *EJIL* 989–1014, at 1007.

[257] L. Doswald-Beck, 'PMCs under International Humanitarian Law', in S. Chesterman and C. Lehnardt (eds), *From Mercenaries to Market: The Rise and Regulation of Private Military Companies* (Oxford: Oxford University Press, 2007), 122.

v. Peacekeepers

The growing number of peace operations in the 1990s saw also an increase of attacks against peacekeepers.[258] In order to improve the safety of peacekeeping forces, a multilateral treaty was adopted by the UNGA in 1994.[259] Under Article 8(2)(e)(iii) of the ICC Statute, intentionally directing attacks against personnel, installations, material, units or vehicles involved in a humanitarian assistance or peacekeeping mission in accordance with the Charter of the United Nations, as long as they are entitled to the protection given to civilians or civilian objects under the international law of armed conflict, is prohibited. This is also reflected in the Secretary-General's Bulletin,[260] providing that the promulgation thereof does not affect the protected status of members of peacekeeping operations under the aforementioned 1994 Convention or their status as non-combatants, as long as they are entitled to the protection given to civilians under the international law of armed conflict.[261]

The protection of peacekeepers raises questions as to the scope of application and their loss of protection. As UN personnel are defined by reference to the relevant operations, the key issue is to determine the scope of such peacekeeping operations. According to Article 1(c) of the UN Safety Convention, UN operations mean

> an operation established by the competent organ of the United Nations and conducted under UN authority and control: (i) where the operation is for the purpose of maintaining or restoring international peace and security; or (ii) where the Security Council or the General Assembly has declared for the purposes of this convention, that there exists an exceptional risk to the safety of the personnel participating in the operation.

In the conduct of such UN operations, 'United Nations and associated personnel, their equipment and premises shall not be made the object of attack or of any action that prevents them from discharging their mandate'.[262] However, 'UN operations authorized by the Security Council as an enforcement action under Chapter VII of the Charter of the United Nations in which any of the personnel are engaged therein as combatants against organized armed forces to which the law of international armed conflicts applies' are excluded from its scope of application.[263] This has been interpreted as excluding the protection and safety for UN personnel 'unless and for such time they

---

[258] B. Boutros-Ghali, *Agenda for Peace: Preventive Diplomacy, Peacemaking and Peacekeeping. Report of the Secretary-General pursuant to the statement adopted by the Summit Meeting of the Security Council on 31 January 1992*, UN Doc. A/47/277, S/24111,1992, (1993) 31 *ILM* 953, at 66–68.

[259] Convention on the Safety of United Nations and Associated Personnel, 1994 (1995) 34 *ILM* 482.

[260] Secretary-General's Bulletin: 'Observance by United Nations Forces of International Humanitarian Law', 6 August 1999, UN Doc. ST/SBG/1999/13.

[261] Article 1.2, UN Safety Convention.

[262] Article 7(1), UN Safety Convention.

[263] Article 2(2), UN Safety Convention.

take a direct part in hostilities'.²⁶⁴ The protection does not cease 'when such personnel only use armed force in exercise of their right to individual self-defense'.²⁶⁵

The protection of UN personnel in peacekeeping missions by reference to the 1994 UN Safety Convention is nevertheless problematic for two reasons.²⁶⁶ First, such '*renvoi*' reduces UN operations into two categories: UN peacekeeping operations in which UN personnel are immune from attack and UN enforcement operations in which their personnel are engaged as combatants and consequently liable to attack. However, it should be recalled that in most enforcement operations UN forces are not engaged therein as combatants and remain entitled to the protection of the UN Safety Convention. In other words, in enforcement operations where the threshold of armed conflict has not been reached, UN forces may under no circumstances be attacked. This is also the case even when the threshold of armed conflict is reached, but UN forces are not engaged therein as a Party to the conflict. Secondly, if UN forces are engaged in enforcement operations under Chapter VII of the UN Charter as combatants to which the law of international armed conflict applies, they are legitimate military objectives for the entire duration of the conflict, unless they become *hors de combat*. In such case, their exclusion from the scope of application of the UN Safety Convention is not connected to the loss of protection of civilians within the meaning of Article 51(3) of AP I, meaning 'unless and for such time they take a direct part in hostilities', but a direct consequence of being a Party to the conflict and their status as 'combatants' under international humanitarian law.

In the *Abu Garda* case, Pre-Trial Chamber I noted that three basic principles are accepted as determining whether a given mission constitutes a peacekeeping mission, namely (1) consent of the parties, (2) impartiality and (3) the non-use of force except in self-defence.²⁶⁷ According to the Pre-Trial Chamber, the distinction between peace-keeping and peace-enforcement missions lies in the fact that the use of force in the former case is limited to self-defence, while in the latter case there is a mandate to use force beyond self-defence to achieve the objective.²⁶⁸ While this is certainly the case, one cannot conclude from the above that UN forces automatically lose their protection against attack when they operate in a peace-enforcement mission. Only when they are

---

²⁶⁴ Dörmann, *supra* n.236, at 455.
²⁶⁵ *Ibid*. See also Section 1.1 of the Secretary-General's Bulletin stating that

the fundamental principles and rules of international humanitarian law set out at the present bulletin are applicable to United Nations when in situations of armed conflict they are actively engaged therein as combatants, to the extent and duration of their engagement. They are accordingly applicable in enforcement actions, or in peacekeeping operations when the use of force is permitted in self-defense.

²⁶⁶ See also K. Okimoto, 'Violations of IHL by UN Forces and Their Legal Consequences', (2003) 6 *YIHL* 199, at 209–216; C. Greenwood, 'International Humanitarian Law and United Nations Military Operations', (1998) 1 *YIHL* 3, at 30–32.
²⁶⁷ ICC, *Prosecutor v. Bahar Idriss Abu Garda*, ICC-02/05-02/09, 8 February 2010, at 71.
²⁶⁸ *Ibid.*, at 74. See also the Special Court for Sierra Leone, where the Court held that 'the use of force by peacekeepers in self-defense in the discharge of their mandate, provided that it is limited to such use, would not alter or diminish the protection afforded to peacekeepers'. SCSL, *Prosecutor v. Issa Hassan Sesay, Morris Kallon and Augustine Gbao*, Judgment, SCSL-04-15-T, 2 March 2009, at 233.

engaged therein as combatants against organized armed forces would the protection cease. Although the UN Safety Convention was 'a major advancement in the legal protection of UN forces, there still remain serious practical difficulties in its application, namely in relation to [international humanitarian law]'.[269]

4. CONCLUSION

Ever since the day Henri Dunant stood on the hills of Solferino, the international community has developed a broad array of treaty and customary rules providing for various degrees of protection for different categories of 'protected persons'. The essence of these protective regimes is that those persons who do not or no longer take an active part in the fighting, and those who are unable to fight because they are *hors de combat* because of wounds, illness or surrender, must be respected and protected from the dangers and the effects of hostilities in all circumstances. War victims must be aided and cared for without distinction based on sex, religion or creed. The most elaborate protective regime – inspired by the horrors of the Second World War – is undoubtedly the one enshrined in GC III, which prescribes in great detail the daily business at POW camps and all aspects related to the internment and repatriation of POWs. As for civilians, the protective regime is most detailed for those living in occupied territory. At the same time, the general protection of all civilians has been 'upgraded' substantially by the First Additional Protocol. In all, one may conclude that the substantive protection of protected persons has evolved considerably over time, and has by and large been adapted to do away with important legal lacunae, taking account of the atrocities of the past as well as the changing nature of warfare. One notable exception, where further clarification may be needed, concerns the conditions for interning and trying persons unlawfully taking direct part in hostilities and who are not entitled to POW status.

If the substantive regimes themselves are, in a sense, satisfactory to meet the needs of war victims, the question nonetheless arises to what extent the rules enshrined therein are properly abided by those Parties involved in international armed conflicts. Here, as, for instance, the Partial Award on the treatment of POWs in the conflict between Ethiopia and Eritrea illustrates (cf. *supra*), the balance is mixed. On the one hand, especially as regards *international* armed conflicts, there seems to be an improvement in terms of implementation of the Geneva law in comparison to past conflicts. Thus, summary executions of POWs and collective reprisals against civilians seem to have become less 'common', and certainly less 'accepted', than once they were. At the same time, as, for example, the Balkans War illustrates, in several armed conflicts, violence against civilians continues unabated. Of particular concern in this context is the situation of women and children, two categories which are particularly vulnerable in times of armed conflict. Another issue that merits special consideration, given its detrimental effect on the well-being of the broader population, is violence against medical personnel.

---

[269] Okimoto, *supra* n.266, at 216.

Apart from the question of implementation and enforcement, the main problem of modern-day 'Geneva law'– if we may use the term one last time – is not that the substantive rules fall short of what is needed, but that the demarcation of the personal scope of application of the protective regimes is fraught with controversy. Thus, for the past twelve years, legal advisors and scholars have consistently been caught up in, seemingly insoluble, debates over the proper interpretation of the notion of 'direct participation in hostilities', over the precise requirements for according POW status as well as over the inclusion in, or exclusion from, the (full) scope of application of the GC IV of so-called 'unlawful combatants'. Apart from the difficult textual compatibility of the relevant provisions of the Geneva Conventions, these debates are largely fuelled by the presence of new actors on the battlefield, such as civilian contractors hired to perform military tasks, and the increased participation in hostilities, in various forms, of ordinary civilians, which challenges the *'acquis'* of international humanitarian law. A related cause is the evolution from traditional intra-state wars to armed conflicts with an 'interethnic' dimension. These new types of conflict impact on the scope of applicability of the GC, in particular GC IV. A further clarification of the conditions for interning and trying persons unlawfully taking direct part in hostilities and who are not entitled to POW status may be key to 'defuse' the trench war that has been waged over the 'status question' in recent years. If anything recent events have demonstrated that a rash erosion of the personal scope of application of the GC III and GC IV is not the right way forward. Yet, it may take several more years for the dust kicked up by the '9/11 wars' to finally settle down.

12. Private military companies
*Chia Lehnardt**

1. INTRODUCTION

Private military companies have played a major role in conflict and post-conflict situations, most prominently in Iraq and Afghanistan. Hired by both governments and non-state actors, such as non-governmental organizations, companies or international organizations, they provide functions traditionally associated with the armed forces of a state, including logistic support, collection of intelligence at both the strategic and tactical levels, the training of troops and, importantly, activities including the potentially lethal use of force: the staffing of checkpoints, protection of personnel and military assets, and sometimes combat functions.[1]

Just like state armed forces, private military personnel are susceptible to both violating interests protected by international law and becoming targets of belligerent action. This raises the question of how international law regulates their use, protection and conduct. In general, international law makes a basic distinction between private and state use of force. The principle of non-use of force is addressed at states,[2] as is its exception, the right to self-defence.[3] By contrast, private use of force without any state involvement falls outside the scope of the prohibition on the use of force.[4] Similarly, international humanitarian law generally addresses states when providing that in an

---

* This chapter draws on text previously published by the author, for example C. Lehnardt, 'Private Military Companies', in R. Wolfrum (ed.), *Max Planck Encyclopedia of Public International Law* (Oxford: Oxford University Press, 2012); 'Private Military Personnel as Prisoners of War', in C. Scheipers (ed.), *Prisoners in War* (Oxford: Oxford University Press, 2009), 221; 'Peacekeeping', in S. Chesterman and A. Fisher (eds), *Private Security, Public Order: The Outsourcing of Public Services and its Limits* (Oxford: Oxford University Press, 2010), 197.

[1] Other terms used in the literature include 'private military and security companies' ('PMSCs') and 'private security companies' ('PSCs'), while the term 'private military companies' ('PMCs') is often defined much more narrowly than here and reserved for those companies that actually fight wars alongside or in place of national armed forces, as opposed to those firms providing 'security services' or 'support functions' only. The term 'private military companies' is used here more broadly and preferred over 'private security companies' as it points to the qualitative difference between firms operating in conflict zones in a military environment and 'security firms' that primarily guard premises in a stable environment.

[2] Article 2(4), UN Charter (1945). For more see chapters 3 and 4 in this volume by Nicholas Tsagourias and Mary Ellen O'Connell respectively.

[3] Article 51, UN Charter (1945). See chapter 6 in this volume by Dino Kritsiotis.

[4] See Declaration on Principles of International Law concerning Friendly Relations and Co-operation among States in accordance with the Charter of the United Nations, GA Res. 2625 (1970), first principle.

international armed conflict all measures must be taken to spare civilians.[5] Although there is no ban on civilians participating directly in hostilities, only combatants who belong to a state's armed forces can claim treatment as prisoners of war,[6] while other persons participating in hostilities lose their protection while doing so.[7] The prohibition of piracy is one of the oldest international law principles banning private use of force, and international legal conventions to counter terrorism impose obligations on states to prevent and to criminalize terrorist acts. All this suggests that international law, while not explicitly assigning the use of force exclusively to states, assumes that states are the only actors who can legitimately use force.

Consequently, like other non-state actors present in conflict or post-conflict areas and involved in the use of force, private military personnel pose challenges to key principles of international law, the underlying premise of which is that states are the primary actors on the battlefield. Thus there have been calls for an international convention specifically regulating the use and conduct of private military companies. In 2010 the Human Rights Council established an intergovernmental working group mandated to draft such a legally binding instrument.[8] Efforts to provide clarification of the existing regulatory framework include the 2008 *Montreux Document*, the end result of a consultation process launched by the Swiss federal government and the International Committee of the Red Cross (hereinafter 'ICRC').[9] The non-binding document purports to clarify and reaffirm international law obligations on the part of the home state, the host state and the contracting state, and sets out good practices for them in relation to private military companies during armed conflict. However, it is not always clear from its general wording under what circumstances an international law provision applies and to what effect. This chapter seeks to examine the legal regime that applies to the use and conduct of private military personnel in conflict and post-conflict situations in more detail.

2. PRIVATE MILITARY PERSONNEL: MERCENARIES?

The fact that private military personnel provide services involving the use of force in exchange for financial compensation has prompted claims that they are 'modern day mercenaries'.[10] Yet from an international law perspective it is very unlikely that they fall under the definition of a mercenary, as its scope is narrowly drawn. Article 47(2) of Additional Protocol I, the two definitions in the UN Convention against the Recruitment, Use, Financing and Training of Mercenaries, and the Organization of African Unity/African Union Convention for the Elimination of Mercenarism in Africa list six

---

[5] Articles 57, 58, Additional Protocol I.
[6] Article 4A(1), Geneva Convention III, Articles 43, 44(1), Additional Protocol I.
[7] Article 51(3), Additional Protocol I; Article 13(3), Additional Protocol II.
[8] UN Doc. A/HRC/RES/15/26 (2010).
[9] Montreux Document on Pertinent International Legal Obligations and Good Practices for States Related to Operations of Private Military and Security Companies During Armed Conflict, 8 October 2008, UN Doc. A/63/467/S/2008/636.
[10] See, for example, A. Musah and J.K. Fayemi (eds), *Mercenaries: An African Security Dilemma* (London: Pluto Press, 1999).

cumulative conditions that must be met for someone to be considered a mercenary, and thus excluded from the right to prisoner of war status[11] and criminalized (by the two Conventions). For example, Article 1 of the OAU/AU Convention reads:

A mercenary is any person who:

(a) is specially recruited locally or abroad in order to fight in an armed conflict;
(b) does in fact take a direct part in the hostilities;
(c) is motivated to take part in the hostilities essentially by the desire for private gain and in fact is promised by or on behalf of a party to the conflict material compensation;
(d) is neither a national of a party to the conflict nor a resident of territory controlled by a party to the conflict;
(e) is not a member of the armed forces of a party to the conflict; and
(f) is not sent by a state other than a party to the conflict on official mission as a member of the armed forces of the said state.

Each of these criteria can be problematic. For example, although private military personnel might ultimately take a direct part in hostilities, most contractors are not recruited specifically for that purpose, which would exclude them from the scope of the provision by virtue of condition a). Moreover, proving, in accordance with due process standards, that someone fights for financial gain can be difficult. Apart from these technical flaws that render the provision unworkable,[12] it is hard to see, as a matter of principle, why a contractor from state A, which is not a party to the conflict, should be treated differently from a colleague contracted by state B, which is a party to the conflict, provided both employees fight for money. The definition excludes the latter from its scope by virtue of condition d). In any case, there is broad consensus that due to the number of requirements to be met for anyone falling under this definition, and the fact that some of them can easily be circumvented, the two Conventions relating to mercenarism and Article 47 of Additional Protocol I have little practical relevance.[13]

3. 'REGULATION' THROUGH THE MARKET?

In the absence of a legal regime specifically dealing with private military contractors a considerable part of the discussion has revolved around non-international law mechanisms to regulate the conduct of private military personnel. One line of argument is that the market itself will 'regulate' the companies in that it would constitute a competitive advantage to be perceived as an ethical company whose conduct is compatible with human rights.[14] This argument has been presented not only by the companies and their

---

[11] Article 47, Additional Protocol I.
[12] F. Hampson, 'Mercenaries: Diagnosis before Prescription', (1991) 22 *NYIL* 31.
[13] E.C. Gillard, 'Business Goes to War: Private Military/Security Companies and International Humanitarian Law', (2006) 88 *IRRC* 525, at 561.
[14] B. Perrin, 'Promoting Compliance of Private Security and Military Companies with International Humanitarian Law', (2006) 88 *IRRC* 613, at 634; A. Bearpark and S. Schulz, 'The

industry associations, but also by the UK government.[15] It glosses over the fact that the market for defence services lacks the competition and transparency essential to a functioning market.[16] Crucially, it might well be that a contracting state expects the company to act in violation of its own obligations, as the examples of MPRI (Military Professional Resources Incorporated) in Croatia and Sandline International in Sierra Leone demonstrate.[17]

One tool for presenting companies as 'ethical' is codes of conduct. Codes of conduct have been articulated to 'translate' international law obligations for private companies operating in weak states.[18] Private military companies have either developed their own codes individually or collectively, including the International Code of Conduct for Private Security Service Providers, which has been signed by 307 companies.[19] Whether those codes amount to more than window-dressing is hard to substantiate. Anecdotal evidence points to the conclusion that they do not – the companies implicated in the abuses at Abu Ghraib and the shootings at Nasoor Square in 2007

Future of the Market', in S. Chesterman and C. Lehnardt (eds), *From Mercenaries to Market: The Rise and Regulation of Private Military Companies* (Oxford: Oxford University Press, 2007), 239.

[15] UK Foreign Commonwealth Office, Consultation on Promoting High Standards of Conduct by Private Military and Security Companies Internationally, London (2009), available at http://www.fco.gov.uk/en/publications-and-documents/publications1/consultations1/closed-consultations/.

[16] D.D. Avant, *The Market for Force: The Consequences of Privatizing Security* (Cambridge: Cambridge University Press, 2005), at 219.

[17] D. Thürer and M. MacLaren, 'Military Outsourcing as a Case Study in the Accountability and Responsibility of Power', in A. Reinisch and U. Kriebaum (eds), *The Law of International Relations: Liber amicorum Hanspeter Neuhold* (Utrecht: Eleven, 2007), 347, at 350. The Croatian army had, with the approval of the US government, contracted MPRI in the autumn of 1994, officially to teach leadership skills. Due to the existing arms embargo the company was precluded from advising the Croatian army on battlefield skills or tactics. Yet the Croatian 'Operation Storm' against the Serbs, launched in August 1995 – while MPRI personnel were still in the country – and involving war crimes and crimes against humanity (see ICTY (Trial Chamber), *Prosecutor v Gotovina, Čermak and Markač*, IT-06-90-T, Judgment, 15 April 2011), has been described as bearing the hallmarks of US army doctrine; see R. Cohen, 'US Cooling Ties with Croatia After Winking at its Buildup', *New York Times* online, 28 October 1995; http://www.nytimes.com/1995/10/28/world/us-cooling-ties-to-croatia-after-winking-at-its-buildup.html?pagewanted=all&src=pm. On how Sandline International violated the arms embargo on Sierra Leone with the knowledge of Foreign and Commonwealth Office officials see House of Commons, Foreign Affairs Committee, Second Report Sierra Leone, HC 116-I (London, 1999). See also J.C. Zarazate, 'The Emergence of a New Dog of War: Private International Security Companies, International Law, and the New World Disorder', in (1998) 34 *Stan JIL* 75.

[18] On business and human rights initiatives generally see S. MacLeod, 'The Role of International Regulatory Initiatives on Business and Human Rights for Holding Private Military and Security Contractors to Account', in F. Francioni and N. Ronzitti (eds), *War by Contract: Human Rights, Humanitarian Law, and Private Contractors* (Oxford: Oxford University Press, 2011), 343.

[19] As of February 2012. See http://www.icoc-psp.org/.

continued working for the US government.[20] While eventually such codes might evolve into an influence of their own, given the environment in which private military personnel operate, and the rights and interests at risk, it is difficult to see how they could replace externally imposed regulation.

4. INTERNATIONAL HUMANITARIAN LAW

More importantly, there is a comprehensive legal regime in place that regulates the context in which the companies operate, including international humanitarian law. In an international armed conflict this legal regime identifies essentially two categories of persons, each of which implies a distinct level of rights and protection. Members of armed forces are, as combatants, entitled to prisoner of war status[21] and may not be prosecuted for their participation in hostilities unless they violated the laws of war.[22] Generally they shall be released and repatriated after the cessation of active hostilities.[23] Civilians, by contrast, do not have the right to take direct part in hostilities and are protected from attack by enemy forces as long as they refrain from doing so.[24] According to Article 50(1) of Additional Protocol I, private military personnel who have not committed hostile acts shall in case of doubt be treated as civilians immune from attack. This immunity, however, may be forfeited if contractors take 'a direct part in the hostilities',[25] in which case, lacking combatant privilege, upon capture they may be treated as criminals under the domestic law of the captor.

A. Private Military Personnel: Civilians or Combatants?

The proximity of private military personnel to the armed forces, combined with an appearance that is often indistinguishable from their military counterparts, has sometimes led to the assumption that they are combatants. Yet from an international law perspective there are only two ways of acquiring combatant and prisoner of war status, both depending on the affiliation to a party of the conflict. Article 4A(1) of Geneva Convention III determines that the following category of persons is entitled to prisoner of war status as a consequence of *de iure* combatant status:

> Members of the armed forces of a Party to the conflict, as well as members of militias or volunteer corps forming part of such armed forces.

---

[20] P. Beaumont, 'Abu Ghraib Abuse Firms are Rewarded', *Observer* online, 16 January 2005, available at http://www.guardian.co.uk/world/2005/jan/16/usa.iraq; J. Warrick, 'GAO Blocks Contract to Firm Formerly Known as Blackwater to Train Afghan Police', *Washington Post* online, 16 March 2010, available at http://www.washingtonpost.com/wp-dyn/content/article/2010/03/15/AR2010031503289.html.
[21] Article 44(1), Additional Protocol I; Article 4, Geneva Convention III.
[22] Articles 99–105, Geneva Convention III.
[23] Article 118, Geneva Convention III.
[24] Articles 51(2), (3), Additional Protocol I.
[25] Article 51(3), Additional Protocol I.

whereas subparagraph (2) addresses *de facto* combatant and prisoner of war status:

> Members of other militias and members of other volunteer corps, including those of organized resistance movements, belonging to a Party to the conflict and operating in or outside their own territory, even if this territory is occupied, provided that such militias or volunteer corps, including such organized resistance movements, fulfil the following conditions:
>
> (a) that of being commanded by a person responsible for his subordinates;
> (b) that of having a fixed distinctive sign recognizable at a distance;
> (c) that of carrying arms openly;
> (d) that of conducting their operations in accordance with the laws and customs of war.

Article 43(1) of Additional Protocol I encompasses both categories of combatants (see Article 43(2) of Additional Protocol I) and supplements Article 4A of Geneva Convention III to the extent applicable:

> The armed forces of a Party to a conflict consist of all organized armed forces, groups and units which are under a command responsible to that Party for the conduct of its subordinates, even if that Party is represented by a government or an authority not recognized by an adverse Party. Such armed forces shall be subject to an internal disciplinary system which, inter alia, shall enforce compliance with the rules of international law applicable in armed conflict.

It should be noted that, although the wording of the requirements of 'belonging to a Party to the conflict' and 'armed forces of a Party' as such do not exclude contractors who are not contracted to fight but are nonetheless armed – as, for example, security guards – the provisions should be understood more narrowly. As stated above, classification as combatant implies authorization to fight.[26] Where a state has made it clear that a person is not entitled to fight, there is no room for considering that person a combatant. This is so because it is the sovereign right of states to organize their armed forces.[27] In most cases, private military personnel are excluded from combatant status on the ground that they were not contracted for that purpose. If contractors are given the status of civilians accompanying the armed forces,[28] or if the contracting state makes it otherwise clear that the company is contracted for 'defensive services' only, these are strong indications that the state did not authorize them to fight. While it is clear that contractors authorized to fight – for example, by contract or tacit agreement – can qualify as combatants regardless of the formal status given to them by

---

[26] Article 43(2), Additional Protocol I.
[27] M. Bothe, K.J. Partsch and W.A. Solf, *New Rules for Victims in Armed Conflict: Commentary on the Two 1977 Protocols Additional to the Geneva Conventions* (Dordrecht: Nijhoff, 1982), at 232; C. Schaller, 'Private Security and Military Companies Under the International Law of Armed Conflict', in T. Jäger and G. Kümmel (eds), *Private Military and Security Companies: Chances, Problems, Pitfalls and Prospects* (Wiesbaden: VS Verlag, 2007), 345, at 348. See also ICRC, 'Interpretative Guidance on the Notion of Direct Participation in Hostilities under International Humanitarian Law', (2008) 90 *IRRC*, 991, at 1011.
[28] Article 4A(4), Geneva Convention III.

the contracting state,²⁹ the fact alone that private military personnel ultimately do take part in hostilities does not make them combatants but is a separate question pertinent to their individual criminal accountability.

A further criterion, explicit in Article 4A(2) of Geneva Convention III and implicit in Article 43(1) of Additional Protocol I (armed forces 'of' a party to a conflict), is that the group must belong to a party to the conflict.³⁰ According to the ICRC's commentary, the crucial criterion for determining whether a group belongs to a state is a *de facto* relationship between the party to the conflict and the group, the threshold question being whether it is clear for whom the group is fighting.³¹ At the very least an organized armed group 'belongs' to a party to the conflict if its conduct is attributable to it on the basis of Article 8 of the International Law Commission Articles on Responsibility of States for Internationally Wrongful Acts (hereinafter 'ILC Articles', discussed below).³² However, to the extent attributability of their conduct is considered not only one example for private persons 'belonging' to a party to the conflict but a requirement,³³ this appears to contradict the purpose of the provisions granting *de facto* combatant status, which is meant to address persons who are not members of the official army but fighting for their nation, and who therefore should not be treated as common criminals.³⁴ Such persons were rarely controlled by the state they were fighting for in a manner that would satisfy the requirement of Article 8 of the ILC Articles.³⁵ Thus, in principle, given the historical origin of the provisions, the criterion of 'belonging to a Party to the conflict' should not be construed too narrowly. Tacit agreement would therefore suffice, and a contract between the state and the company is generally capable of meeting this requirement.

Furthermore, the employees must be under the command of a person, civilian or military,³⁶ responsible for his or her subordinates and in a position to ensure adherence to the rules applicable in armed conflict. Contractors must also have a fixed distinctive sign recognizable from a distance, and carry their arms openly. These requirements have been relaxed in Article 44(3) of Additional Protocol I. The last criterion is compliance with the laws of war, which does not require each individual to act lawfully in every instance, but does require the company or group to which the employee

---

²⁹ K. Ipsen, 'Combatant and Non-Combatants', in D. Fleck (ed.), *The Handbook of International Humanitarian Law* (Oxford: Oxford University Press, 2008), at 82.

³⁰ Article 4A(2), Geneva Convention III.

³¹ J. Pictet, *Commentary on the Third Geneva Convention Relative to the Treatment of Prisoners of War* (Geneva: ICRC, 1960), 57; ICRC, 'Interpretative Guidance', *supra* n.27, at 999.

³² ICRC, 'Interpretive Guidance', *supra* n.27, at 999–1000; Summary Report on the Fourth Expert Meeting on the Notion of Direct Participation in Hostilities, (Geneva, 2006), 16.

³³ See ICTY, *Prosecutor v. Tadić*, IT-94-1-A, Judgment, 15 July 1999, at paras 93 and 98 (n.117).

³⁴ L. Doswald-Beck, 'Private Military Companies under International Humanitarian Law', in Chesterman and Lehnardt (eds), *supra* n.14, 115, at 116–117.

³⁵ M. Schmitt, 'Humanitarian Law and Direct Participation in Hostilities by Private Contractors or Civilian Employees', (2005) 5 *Chi J Int'l L* 511, at 527–528.

³⁶ Pictet, *supra* n.31, at 59.

belongs to respect the law generally.[37] Private military personnel contracted to fight in a war are therefore likely to be considered *de facto* combatants and therefore benefit from prisoner of war status. Other contractors, according to Article 50(1) of Additional Protocol I, are considered civilians.

B. Private Military Personnel Participating Directly in the Hostilities

As civilians, private military personnel do not have the right to participate in the hostilities.[38] Moreover, they are not entitled to prisoner of war status.[39] However, Article 4A(4) of Geneva Convention III provides an exception from the principle that only combatants are entitled to prisoner of war status, stipulating that persons falling into the following category are prisoners of war:

> Persons who accompany the armed forces without actually being members thereof, such as civilian members of military aircraft crews, war correspondents, supply contractors, members of labour units or of services responsible for the welfare of the armed forces, provided that they have received authorization from the armed forces which they accompany, who shall provide them for that purpose with an identity card similar to the annexed model.

As civilians accompanying the armed forces contractors are still prohibited from participating directly in hostilities[40] and would, like other civilians, lose their immunity from attack if they did engage in fighting.

This raises the question of under what circumstances contractors are considered to take direct part in the hostilities. The clear-cut case of a contractor using conventional arms and weapons in order to cause direct harm to the enemy is likely to be rare. With the advent of high-tech weapon systems, however, states have begun to outsource not only their maintenance but also their operation to private military companies.[41] For example, contractors have operated US Global Hawks and Unmanned Aerial Vehicles in Afghanistan and Iraq.[42] Such activities would clearly result in loss of immunity.

If international humanitarian law is to keep pace with changes in warfare, however, the notion of direct participation cannot be limited to actual fighting, that is to those activities that are the immediate cause of harm inflicted upon a party to the conflict. The vagueness of the term makes it open to an interpretation that takes such changes into account. The flip side is that its ambiguity results in great uncertainty as to what activities short of actual fighting result in a loss of protection. Military operations depend on a multitude of activities from producing weapons and ammunitions or feeding and sheltering troops to the actual launching of the operation. While it is acknowledged that the first two do not amount to direct participation and the last one

---

[37] Schmitt, *supra* n.35, at 531.
[38] See Article 43(2), Additional Protocol I.
[39] See Article 44(1), Additional Protocol I.
[40] Articles 50(1), 51(3) and 43(2), Additional Protocol I.
[41] See US General Accounting Office, Military Operations: Contractors Provide Vital Services to Deployed Forces But Are Not Adequately Addressed in DoD Plans, GAP-03-695, 2003, 8–9, 16.
[42] J.R. Heaton, 'Civilians at War: Reexamining the Status of Civilians Accompanying the Armed Forces', (2005) 57 *Air Force Law Review*, 155, at 190.

does, there is disagreement over nearly every function in between.[43] Particularly problematic are two major sources of business for the private military services industry: so-called support functions – the provision of intelligence, technical support, and maintenance of military equipment and systems – and the provision of close security. The Conventions and Additional Protocols are silent on whether such activities are prohibited. The only textual clues can be found in Article 49(1) of Additional Protocol I and Article 4A(4) of Geneva Convention III.

With regard to security services provided by the companies, the first provision makes clear that both defensive and offensive actions can constitute an attack, meaning that such qualification is irrelevant for the purposes of determining what constitutes direct participation. If, however, private military personnel engage in conduct covered by the right to individual self-defence or help to others, they make use of a right they have regardless of status. The exercise of these rights therefore does not constitute 'direct participation'.[44] They presuppose an unlawful attack, the existence of which is determined by reference to international humanitarian law. The crucial distinction to be made here is based on the character of the guarded object. As international humanitarian law permits the targeting of military objects, including combatants,[45] the use of force against military operations attacking such targets would constitute direct participation. Accordingly, civilians defending military objects are precluded from relying on the right to self-defence or defence of others and can thus be considered to take part in the hostilities as long as there is a nexus between the hostile act and the armed conflict. With regard to the guarding of civilian objects or civilians, the line is between use of force that is necessary for the purposes of self-defence on the one hand, and what goes beyond the necessary on the other. This line can be difficult to establish, particularly in an environment of armed conflict.

The second textual hint can be found in the Third Geneva Convention. As Article 50(1) of Additional Protocol I stipulates that anyone not falling under Article 4A(1), (2), (3,) and (6) of Geneva Convention III is a civilian, and as civilians are not entitled to fight, the persons mentioned in the remaining paragraphs of Article 4A Geneva Convention III typically do not engage in fighting.[46] The list of activities provided for in Article 4A(4) of Geneva Convention III is not exhaustive. The ICRC commentary notes, somewhat unhelpfully, that the provision could also cover 'other categories of persons or services who might be called upon, in similar conditions, to follow the armed forces'.[47] Instructions issued by the US Department of Defense on the use of

---

[43] N. Melzer, *Targeted Killing in International Law* (Oxford: Oxford University Press, 2008), at 334; J.-M. Henckaerts and L. Doswald-Beck, *Customary International Humanitarian Law* (Cambridge: Cambridge University Press, 2005), at 23.
[44] Melzer, *ibid.*, at 343; ICRC, 'Interpretative Guidance', *supra* n.27, at 1028.
[45] Article 48(1), Additional Protocol I.
[46] Schmitt, *supra* n.35, at 532.
[47] Pictet, *supra* n.31, at 64. See also Article 3 of the Regulations Respecting the Laws and Customs of War on Land, Annexed to Hague Convention (II) of 1899 and Hague Convention (IV) of 1907, which reads: 'Individuals who follow an army without directly belonging to it, such as newspaper correspondents and reporters, sutlers and contractors, who fall into the enemy's hand and whom the latter thinks expedient to detain, are entitled to be treated as

contractors prohibit the hiring of contractors for 'unique military functions'.[48] Such references, however, beg the question.[49] In an attempt to provide an abstract definition, the ICRC characterizes direct participation as an act that is 'likely to adversely affect the military operations or military capacity of a party to an armed conflict or, alternatively, to inflict death, injury, or destruction on persons or objects protected against direct attack'. In addition, there must be 'a direct causal link between the act and the harm likely to result either from that act, or from a coordinated military operation of which that act constitutes an integral part', and the act must be 'specifically designed to directly cause the required threshold of harm in support of a party to the conflict and to the detriment of another'.[50]

Thus, if private military personnel carry out an activity which is an integral part of a military operation, intentionally causing direct harm to the other party to the conflict, they take a direct part in hostilities.[51] This would include technical support to the extent that advice is provided during ongoing operations in order to make a weapon system operable or more effective.[52] Similarly, while the collection and provision of intelligence on a strategic level merely contribute to the war effort, on the tactical level, where information provided is directly relied upon to direct attacks, it becomes an indispensable requirement for launching an operation.[53] In all these cases the contractors involved would lose their protection as civilians and, in the case of Article 4A(4) of Geneva Convention III, their entitlement to prisoner of war status.

C. Is a Re-interpretation and Re-drafting of International Humanitarian Law Necessary?

The above analysis has shown that the majority of contractors hired by states are not only protected from attack but can, as civilians accompanying the armed forces, also be entitled to prisoner of war status. It is sometimes suggested that their protection as civilians is inadequate and that private military personnel should be considered

---

prisoners of war, provided they are in possession of a certificate from the military authorities of the army which they were accompanying.'

[48] Department of Defense (hereinafter 'DoD') Instruction No. 3020.41, 20 December 2011, Enclosure 2, at 4.f.; DoD Instruction No. 1100.22, 12 April 2010, Enclosure 4, at 1.d.(1)(f).

[49] DoD Instruction No. 1100.22, Enclosure 4, at 1.d.(1)(a)–(e) excludes companies from providing security services for example 'in high-risk environments' and in operations that require 'discretionary latitude to engage in offensive actions' or that 'would require substantial discretion, the outcome of which could significantly affect U.S. objectives with regard to the life, liberty, or property of private persons, a military mission, or international relations'.

[50] ICRC, Interpretative Guidance', *supra* n.27, at 995–996. See also Y. Sandoz, C. Swinarski and B. Zimmermann (eds), *Commentary to the Additional Protocols of 8 June 1977 to the Geneva Conventions of 12 August 1949* (Geneva/Dordrecht: ICRC/Martinus Nijhoff, 1987), at 516, para. 1679.

[51] M.E. Guillory, 'Civilianizing the Force: Is the United States Crossing the Rubicon?', (2001) 51 *Air Force Law Review* 111, at 134. For the opposite view see L.L. Turner and L.G. Norton, 'Civilians at the Tip of the Spear', (2001) 51 *Air Force Law Review* 1, at 28.

[52] Guillory, *ibid.*, at 128.

[53] See ICRC, Interpretative Guidance', *supra* n.27, at 1021–1023; H.-P. Gasser, 'Protection of the Civilian Population', in Fleck (ed.), *supra* n.29, 237, at 262.

combatants, with the consequence that they are subject to attack at all times. For example, some commentators argue that combatant status should be determined on the basis of actual activity, and that anyone carrying out combat functions should be considered a combatant.[54] Another argument is that affording contractors, who are voluntarily close to the battlespace, the same level of protection against attack as ordinary civilians is unrealistic and in any case not deserved.[55] Although it is not always clear whether these authors argue for a re-reading of existing categories of international humanitarian law, or for their complete revision, it is important to bear in mind that while there are considerable uncertainties regarding the interpretation of key notions of the laws of war, in the case of armed conflict the application of international humanitarian law is not a matter of choice. The factual circumstances on which combatant and prisoner of war status can be based are listed in Article 4A(2) of Geneva Convention III and Article 43(1) of Additional Protocol I. To the extent that these provisions are deemed applicable in principle to private military personnel, it is doubtful, in the absence of additional arguments, how a determination of that status could be based on an entirely different criterion. Secondly, the right to fight follows from combatant status. To claim that combatant status should be based on actual fighting is a circular argument and neglects the clear wording of Articles 43(2) and 51(3) of Additional Protocol I. According to these provisions, while civilians do not have the right to take a direct part in hostilities, the consequence of their doing so is not a change of their status, but the temporary loss of certain protections civilians enjoy. The fact that they can no longer claim non-combatant immunity in such cases also demonstrates that concerns that private military personnel, as 'dangerous' individuals, are unduly protected are unwarranted: when they do become dangerous by participating directly in the fighting, they lose protection from attack and cannot claim prisoner of war status if captured.

5. INTERNATIONAL RESPONSIBILITY

Private military personnel are, particularly if they are armed, just like state armed forces in a position to violate interests protected by international law, especially international humanitarian law and human rights law. Thus, their use also raises issues of international responsibility of the states that contract them and that are bound by these legal regimes.

---

[54] N. Boldt, 'Outsourcing War: Private Military Companies and International Humanitarian Law', (2004) 47 *German Yearbook of International Law* 502, at 518; D. Richemond Barak, 'Private Military Contractors and Combatancy Status under International Humanitarian Law', S. 9, 13, available at http://law.huji.ac.il/upload/Richmond_Barak_Private_Military_Contractors.pdf; M. Saage-Maass and S. Weber, '"Wer sich in Gefahr begibt, kommt darin um ..." – zum Einsatz privater Sicherheits- und Militärfirmen in bewaffneten Konflikten', (2007) Humanitäres Völkerrecht – Informationsschriften 170, at 174, arguing that '(m)ore practical is a broader interpretation of the notion of combatant... If private military personnel carry their arms openly or wear uniforms, they should be treated as combatants until the opposite has been proven' [author's translation].

[55] Saage-Maass and Weber, *ibid.*, at 173–175.

The basic rule is that conduct of any state organ is considered an act of that state.[56] However, the law of state responsibility, while taking the formal organization of a state as a starting point, also takes into account how states actually organize themselves. This means that persons who are not part of a formal organ of the state can also trigger its responsibility, provided they act on behalf of the state. The contracting state may also be internationally responsible if it has failed to take appropriate measures to prevent the violation of international law, or to ensure that the wrongdoer makes reparation or is punished.

A. Attribution of Conduct of Private Military Personnel

On the basis of the 'complete dependence' test developed by the International Court of Justice (hereinafter 'ICJ'), private military personnel fall into the category of *de facto* organs of a state if the relationship between the contracting state and the personnel on the ground is 'so much one of dependence on the one side and control on the other' and if the state 'exercise[s] such a degree of control in all fields as to justify treating' the private military personnel 'as acting on its behalf'.[57] Whether these conditions are met must be examined for each case individually. As the employees are on the ground solely because of the contract between the company and the state, and as they typically leave upon termination of the contract, it could be argued that the high threshold established by the ICJ is typically met. If private military personnel appear as an instrument of the contracting state – their operations reflecting its strategy and tactics – their conduct can be attributed to the state on that basis. Conversely, if the employees are given considerable discretion in the conduct of day-to-day operations and act largely independently of officials of the contracting state this would militate against a classification as *de facto* organs.

In the context of violations of international humanitarian law in an international armed conflict, international responsibility may also be incurred on the basis of Article 91 of Additional Protocol I, according to which a 'Party to the conflict … shall be responsible for all acts committed by persons forming part of its armed forces', which are defined in Article 43(1) of Additional Protocol I and Article 4(A) of Geneva Convention III. These provisions have been discussed above.[58] However, here the fact should be taken into account that they not only determine state responsibility but also define whether an individual is entitled to prisoner of war status and, in the case of Article 43(1) of Additional Protocol I, establish organizational requirements for the armed forces. It would be contrary to the purpose of Article 91 of Additional Protocol I to ensure comprehensive responsibility if reference to these provisions results in a negative finding because one of these criteria – for instance adherence to the laws of

---

[56] Article 4(1), ILC Articles on Responsibility of States for Internationally Wrongful Acts (ILC Articles).

[57] *Case Concerning Military and Paramilitary Activities in and Against Nicaragua* (Nicaragua v. United States) (hereinafter '*Nicaragua* case'), Judgment (Merits), [1986] ICJ Rep., at paras 106, 110; *Case Concerning the Application of the Convention on the Prevention and Punishment of the Crime of Genocide* (Bosnia and Herzegovina v. Serbia and Montenegro) (hereinafter '*Bosnia Genocide* case'), Judgment, [2007] ICJ Rep., at para. 393.

[58] See *supra* section 4.

war, or an internal disciplinary system enforcing international law – is lacking. Therefore, the criteria and organizational requirements set out in Article 4(A)(4)(a)–(d) of Geneva Convention III and Article 43(1) of Additional Protocol I are not relevant for the purposes of state responsibility.[59]

Courts have attributed private conduct to the state also where the private entity was authorized to exercise elements of governmental authority.[60] The focus is on the nature of the activity involved; not decisive is the public or private character of the entity that exercises that function and its link to the state. The commentary of the ILC on its Articles on State Responsibility notes that the principle is, in fact, meant to address the phenomenon of public corporations that have been privatized yet continue to exercise public functions, as well as para-statal entities exercising 'state functions'.[61] This attribution occurs regardless of whether the non-state actor has exceeded its competences or contravened instructions.[62]

At first glance private military companies would be an obvious example of non-state actors exercising such functions. Yet the application of the principle of attribution is difficult because it centres on the notion of 'governmental authority' – the definition of which is inevitably political and thus not only varies from region to region but also evolves over time. It is therefore not surprising that there is no international consensus as to what constitutes the exercise of governmental authority. The ILC endeavoured to give some guidelines, noting that the content of the delegated powers, the way in which they were conferred, the purpose for which they are to be exercised, and the extent to which the non-state entity is accountable to government for their exercise, are of particular relevance.[63] These criteria are, however, only of limited use. The first criterion – content of the competence in question – is essentially circular. Similarly, it is unclear how the means by which the power was transferred should affect its classification as governmental: can it have an impact on the classification of a competence whether it was granted through contract, order or statute? Furthermore, taking into account the extent of accountability to the government as a pertinent factor could result in undesirable consequences. Where a company has been authorized to interrogate prisoners but is not held accountable by the government, it would appear that its misconduct would not be attributed to the state and consequently that the state is not responsible for it. As a result, the state would have no incentive to hold the company accountable – a result that would undermine one of the rationales of attribution of private conduct to the state. The criterion of the purpose for which the transferred competences are exercised seems to be more useful and is echoed in

---

[59] C. Hoppe, 'Passing the Buck: State Responsibility for Private Military Companies', (2008) 19 *EJIL* 989, at 1014. See also ICRC, 'Interpretative Guidance', *supra* n.27, at 999.
[60] Article 5, ILC Articles.
[61] J. Crawford, *The International Law Commission's Articles on State Responsibility. Introduction, Text and Commentaries* (Cambridge: Cambridge University Press, 2002), Article 5, para. 1.
[62] Article 7, ILC Articles; *Yeager v. Iran*, 17 Iran–USCTR 92, at 110–111 (1987-IV).
[63] Crawford, *supra* n.61, at Article 5, para. 6.

attempts by different US government agencies to circumscribe the notion of 'governmental authority' or 'governmental function'.[64]

Functions which, for example, the ILC, the Iran–United States Claim Tribunal and the Inter-American Court of Human Rights have identified as constituting the exercise of elements of governmental authority include the detaining and disciplining of individuals,[65] seizure of property[66] and the collection of military intelligence.[67] Consequently, although there is little prospect of a clear definition of the concept of governmental authority, some activities are arguably so commonly regarded as 'core governmental functions' that their performance by private companies can be said to constitute the exercise of governmental authority. As a result, the conduct of CACI personnel at Abu Ghraib, who were hired to conduct interrogations, of Executive Outcomes and Sandline International, who fought wars alongside or in place of the governments' armed forces in Angola, Sierra Leone and Papua New Guinea, and of the contractors guarding the Erez crossing in Gaza,[68] would be attributed to the states that had contracted them.

An important question is whether protection of persons or buildings constitutes the exercise of governmental authority. This field of activity constitutes a significant source of revenue for the companies, and most incidents in Iraq where civilians were harmed occurred in this context. The classification of individual or static protection as falling under the principle laid down in Article 5 of the ILC Articles is sometimes rejected because the exercise of the right to self-defence or help to others is a right anyone has regardless of status.[69] This is true in that the exercise of a right that anyone has is by definition not the exercise of governmental authority.[70] However, it appears necessary to determine what precisely it is that contractors engage in when defending a person or an object against attack. In particular, not only the activity leading directly to the damage as such should be examined, but also its broader function. If contractors are hired to protect a legitimate military target, they are hired to participate directly in the hostilities and their conduct will be attributed to the contracting state. This does not necessarily mean that the protection of civil persons and objects is excluded from the scope of the principle in Article 5 of the ILC Articles, however. If private military personnel provide protection services to a government official the latter is not only

---

[64] Government Accountability Office, 'Government Contractors – Are Service Contractors Performing Inherently Governmental Functions?', GAO-GGD92-11, November 1991, at 4; OMB Circular A-76 (revised), 'Performance of Commercial Activities', 29 May 2003.

[65] Crawford, *supra* n.61, at Article 5, para. 2.

[66] *Hyatt International Corporation v. Iran*, 9 Iran USCTR 72 (1985-II).

[67] Inter-American Court of Human Rights (IACtHR), *Case of the Rochela Massacre v. Columbia*, Judgment (Merits), 11 May 2007, Series C no. 163, at paras 101–102.

[68] See Program on Humanitarian Policy and Conflict Research (HPCR), 'Private Security Companies in the Occupied Palestinian Territory (OPT): An International Humanitarian Law Perspective', available at www.opt.ihlresearch.org/_data/n_0013/resources/live/briefing3734.pdf.

[69] Hoppe, *supra* n.59, at 992.

[70] Crawford, *supra* n.61, at Article 5, para. 7.

protected as a private individual but as a representative of his government.[71] Accordingly, in such cases protection services primarily serve the functioning of the state, which would militate in favour of classification of such activities as the exercise of governmental authority.

Another indication that international law considers certain functions as the exercise of governmental authority is that it specifically obliges or allows states to undertake certain activities. If oil pipelines are guarded by private military personnel in a situation of occupation, this can be seen as a means to fulfil the contracting state's obligation to restore and maintain law and order in the occupied territory.[72] Similarly, should states contract private military companies to hunt pirates operating off the coast of Somalia when this is likely to fall under Article 5 of the ILC Articles?[73]

Where the conduct in question cannot be said to constitute the exercise of governmental authority, or where no authorization exists, private conduct can also be attributed to the state when it is carried out on the instructions of the state or where the private actor is under state direction or control.[74] A state hiring a firm and instructing it to abuse prisoners is a fairly clear-cut case. Much more complex is the situation in which no such instructions exist, but where the state played a role in the preparation and in the implementation of the operation by directing or controlling it. The ILC noted that for the purpose of attribution a 'real link' between the private person or group and the state machinery is required.[75] Some commentators regard the contract between a private military company and a state as sufficient to establish such a link.[76] By contrast, the *Montreux Document* states that 'entering into contractual relations does not in itself engage the responsibility of' the contracting state.[77] The divergence of views on this question is symptomatic of the debate on the extent of state control over private actors required for attribution.

The ICJ considered this question in 1986 in the *Nicaragua* case:

> even the general control of the respondent State with a high degree of dependency on it, would not in themselves mean, without further evidence, that the United States directed or enforced the perpetration of the acts contrary to human rights and humanitarian law alleged by the applicant State. For this conduct to give rise to legal responsibility of the United States, it would in principle have to be proved that the State had effective control of the

---

[71] See also Articles 22(2), 29, Vienna Convention on the Law of Diplomatic Relations; Articles 31(3), 40 Vienna Convention on the Law of Consular Relations.
[72] Article 43, Hague Regulations.
[73] Article 105 Convention on the Law of the Sea. See N. Ronzitti, 'The Use of Private Contractors in the Fight Against Piracy: Policy Options', in Francioni and Ronzitti (eds), *supra* n.18, 37, at 42.
[74] Article 8, ILC Articles.
[75] Crawford, *supra* n.61, at Article 8, para. 1.
[76] K. Nieminen, 'The Rules of Attribution and the Private Security Contractors at Abu Ghraib: Private Acts or Public Wrongs?', (2004) 15 *Finnish Yearbook of International Law* 289, at 316; R. Wolfrum, 'State Responsibility for Private Actors: An Old Problem of Renewed Relevance', in M. Ragazzi (ed.), *International Responsibility Today: Essays in Memory of Oscar Schachter* (Dordrecht: Nijhoff, 2005), 423, at 434.
[77] *Montreux Document*, *supra* n.9, Part One, A.7.

military or paramilitary operations in the course of which the alleged violations were committed.[78]

Even though the Court acknowledged that the *Contras* were dependent, *inter alia*, on US funding, the lack of control on the part of the United States over the specific operations prevented the judges from attributing their activities to the United States. Under this reading, if a state contracted private military personnel but did not exercise control over all their operations, their conduct would not be deemed attributable to the contracting state. Even the fact that the contractors would have to discontinue an operation upon cessation of payment would not change this assessment.

In 1997 the ICTY revisited the question of attribution by virtue of control. In *Tadić*, the Trial Chamber admitted that the *Nicaragua* test was a 'particularly high threshold test' but ultimately applied a similarly restrictive method along the lines of the ICJ.[79] However, its decision was overturned by the Appeals Chamber, which was less favourably disposed towards the ICJ approach. The judges dismissed the, in their view, overly strict test and established a more flexible approach according to which requirements could vary under different circumstances.[80] Where the private actors in question are organized and hierarchically structured – as opposed to a single private individual – more lenient guidelines apply according to which 'overall control' over the group would suffice for attribution of conduct of individuals.[81] Under this test, which does not require the issuing of specific orders or its direction over individual operations, conduct can be attributed more readily to the contracting state, depending on the role it played in the planning and financing of the activities of private military personnel.

A few years later, however, the ICJ reaffirmed its strict approach[82] and found that the test established by the Appeals Chamber of the ICTY 'stretches too far, almost to breaking point, the connection which must exist between the conduct of a State's organs and its international responsibility'.[83] Yet the Court did not explain why only 'effective control' will result in attribution.

It could be argued that since the company is only on the ground because of the contract and because private military companies are different from the militias at the centre of the judgments of the ICJ and the ICTY in that they do not have a political agenda on their own, attribution should occur more readily.[84] Yet these facts alone

---

[78] *Nicaragua* case, *supra* n.57, at para. 115.
[79] ICTY (Trial Chamber) *Prosecutor v. Tadić*, Judgment, 7 May 1997, IT-94-1-T, at paras 588, 605, 606.
[80] ICTY (Appeals Chamber) *Prosecutor v. Tadić*, Judgment, 15 July 1999, IT-94-1-A, at para. 117.
[81] *Ibid.*, at para. 137.
[82] *Case Concerning Armed Activities in the Territory of the Congo* (Democratic Republic of the Congo v. Uganda) (hereinafter '*Armed Activities in the Congo*'), Judgment, [2005] ICJ Rep., at para. 160; *Bosnia Genocide* case, *supra* n.57, at paras 402–406.
[83] *Bosnia Genocide* case, *supra* n.57, at para. 406.
[84] On the following see C. Lehnardt, *Private Militärfirmen und völkerrechtliche Verantwortlichkeit. Eine Untersuchung aus humanitär-völkerrechtlicher und menschenrechtlicher Perspektive* (Tübingen: Mohr Siebeck, 2011), at 171 *et seq.*

appear insufficient for transforming their conduct leading to a violation of international law into state conduct. Rather, bearing in mind that a state is responsible only for its own conduct and, therefore, only for conduct that can be said to be at least predetermined by it, it is arguable that the focus should be on the question of whether the state used the company, which it controls through the contract, for its purposes. This would suggest that if the state deploys personnel who pursue, on their own motion, the same illegal strategy or objectives as the state, no control over the particular conduct is required to justify attribution. Not attributing such conduct and instead merely accusing the state for failing to stop the conduct would fail to capture its role in such a context; it is, after all, the initiator and sponsor of the company, the actions of which are known and approved of in this scenario. Vice-President Al-Khasawneh addressed this point in his separate opinion in the *Bosnia Genocide* case:

> Unfortunately, the Court's rejection of the standard in the *Tadić* case fails to address the crucial issue raised therein – namely that different types of activities, particularly in the ever-evolving nature of armed conflict, may call for subtle variations in the rules of attribution. In the *Nicaragua* case, the Court noted that the United States and the *Contras* shared the same objectives – namely the overthrowing of the Nicaraguan Government. These objectives, however, were achievable without the commission of war crimes or crimes against humanity. The *Contras* could indeed have limited themselves to military targets in the accomplishment of their objectives. As such, in order to attribute crimes against humanity in furtherance of the common objective, the Court *held that the crimes* themselves should be the object of control. When, however, the shared objective is the commission of international crimes, to require both control over the non-State actors and the specific operations in the context of which international crimes were committed is too high a threshold. The inherent danger in such an approach is that it gives States the opportunity to carry out criminal policies through non-state actors or surrogates without incurring direct responsibility therefore. The statement in paragraph 406 of the Judgment to the effect that the '"overall control" test is unsuitable, for it stretches too far, almost to a breaking point, the connection which must exist between the conduct of a State's organs and its international responsibility' is, with respect, singularly unconvincing because it fails to consider that such a link has to account for situations in which there is a common criminal purpose. It is also far from self-evident that the overall control is always not proximate enough to trigger State responsibility.[85]

Accordingly, where, for example, both the company and the state pursue a strategy of 'indiscriminate shooting' to deter potential insurgents, criminals or terrorists – although no such explicit instruction from the state exists – and where the state exercises general control over the company by virtue of the contract, this would suffice for making the contracting state responsible for any wrongdoing on the part of the company. Conversely, although the contract is a *conditio sine qua non* for the violation, causality as such does not suffice for the purpose of attribution. A mere contract does not transform conduct into state conduct where the wrongdoing is the result of an autonomous decision on the part of the private personnel. In such a scenario, the state has merely provided the opportunity to engage in misconduct. The realization of the risk was, while foreseeable, not in its interest nor otherwise a consequence of conduct

---

[85] *Bosnia Genocide* case, *supra* n.57, Dissenting Opinion of Vice-President Al-Khasawneh, at para. 39.

that was predetermined by it. Rather, the question turns on the examination of whether the contracting state should have taken certain measures to prevent the misconduct.

B. Due Diligence

Where conduct of private military personnel is not attributed to the state, it might still be taken into account in determining state responsibility if it is accompanied by certain actions or omissions on the part of the state, as established in the case law of human rights bodies. Human rights conventions oblige states to 'ensure', 'protect' or 'secure' human rights.[86] These obligations have been interpreted as requiring states to take positive steps in order to prevent the violation of rights through private actors or, if such a violation has occurred, to investigate and sanction the conduct.[87] With regard to international humanitarian law, on the basis of Article 43 of the Hague Regulations, the ICJ in 2006 found Uganda, as the occupying power in the Ituri district in the Democratic Republic of the Congo, responsible for its lack of vigilance in preventing the violation of human rights and international humanitarian law and its violation of the obligation not to tolerate such violence by any third party.[88] Outside situations of occupation, Article 1 of the Geneva Conventions and the First Additional Protocol establishes a positive obligation for states 'to ensure respect' for international humanitarian law. This could be interpreted as an obligation for contracting states to ensure that the companies they hire do not violate the laws of armed conflict.

What this suggests is that where private military personnel act in violation of human rights or international humanitarian law, their conduct can generate the responsibility of the contracting state for failure to prevent or adequately respond to such conduct even if it is not clear what role state organs have played in the specific operation. In determining what diligence is due it is possible to determine factors to be taken into account, such as the risk of violation of international law, which would be assessed, *inter alia*, on the basis of what private actors are in play – whether, for instance, they are armed or not, as well as the protected group. A crucial factor is the fact that the state contracts the company to carry out a potentially hazardous activity, putting it in a position to violate individual rights in the first place.

---

[86] See Article 1, European Convention on Human Rights, Article 2, International Covenant on Political and Civil Rights, Article 1, American Convention on Human Rights; Human Rights Committee, General Comment No. 20: Article 7 (Prohibition of torture, or the cruel, inhuman or degrading treatment or punishment) (1992), UN Doc. HRI/GEN/1/Rev.9 (Vol. I), 27 May 2008, at 214, at para. 8; General Comment No. 6 (Right to life) (1982), UN Doc. HRI/GEN.1.Rev.9 (Vol. I), 27 May 2008, at 190, at para. 3; General Comment No. 31 (The nature of the general legal obligation imposed on state parties to the Covenant) (2004), UN Doc. HRI/GEN/1/Rev.9 (Vol. I), 27 May 2008, at 260, at para. 7; European Court of Human Rights, *Costello-Roberts v. United Kingdom*, appl. no. 13134/87, Judgment, 25 March 1993, at para. 28; IACtHR, *Velásquez-Rodriguez v. Honduras*, Judgment (merits), 28 July 1988, Series C no. 4, at para. 172.

[87] See A. Reinisch, 'The Changing International Framework for Dealing with Non-State Actors', in P. Alston (ed.), *Non-State Actors and Human Rights* (Oxford: Oxford University Press, 2005), at 79–80.

[88] *Armed Activities in the Congo*, supra n.82, at paras 178, 179.

On that basis, the contracting state must comply with a particularly high standard of due diligence. To avoid responsibility, it does not have much discretion in determining what measures to take to protect individual rights. If its private military personnel are armed and deployed in an unstable environment, it must ensure oversight, adequate training and background vetting of private military personnel – and it might also be obliged to integrate them in the military chain of command if circumstances warrant the conclusion that such tight control is the only adequate means to prevent violations of international law. If a violation has occurred nonetheless, the state must investigate the case and, if necessary, sanction the person responsible for it.[89] However, in practice states might be reluctant to extend the extraterritorial reach of their criminal law and to commit resources to investigating cases in conflict zones. The lack of effective prosecution of crimes committed by personnel contracted by the US in Iraq has resulted in effective impunity of private military personnel.[90]

The practical effect of the duty to prosecute on the part of the host state is particularly limited. In principle, private military companies are subject to the law of the state in which they operate. In practice weak states – where the companies conduct much of their business – are likely to be reluctant to exercise jurisdiction on political grounds. Factual dependency severely compromises prospects of the host government enforcing criminal law against contractors. In addition, when contracted by a state different from the territorial state, contractors might benefit from an agreement between the contracting and the host state extending the immunity granted to state officials and troops to contractor personnel. In any case, grave breaches of the Geneva Conventions committed in an international conflict are excluded from such immunity agreements, as the obligation to investigate and to prosecute such cases is mandatory under international law.[91]

6. PEACEKEEPING

Private military companies have been involved in peacekeeping operations since the 1990s. The activities they undertake in the context of UN peacekeeping range from 'second rank' activities, such as the building of barracks or transport of supplies, to

---

[89] See Human Rights Committee, Concluding observations of the Human Rights Committee: Lesotho, UN Doc. CCPR/C/79/Add.106, 8 April 1999, at para. 19; Concluding observations of the Human Rights Committee: Guatemala, UN Doc. CCPR/C/79/Add.63, 3 April 1996, at para. 20; Inter-American Commission on Human Rights, *Eugénio da Silva v. Brazil*, Case no. 11.598, Report no. 9/00, 24 February 2000, at paras 33, 40.

[90] See Report of the Working Group on the use of mercenaries as a means of violating human rights and impeding the exercise of the right of peoples to self-determination, A/HRC/15/25/Add.3, 15 June 2010.

[91] Article 49, Geneva Convention I; Article 50, Geneva Convention II; Article 129, Geneva Convention III; Article 146, Geneva Convention I; Articles 85, 86, Additional Protocol I.

more sensitive tasks, including the provision of intelligence or training of militaries, to functions involving the use of force.[92]

Despite the mixed reputation private military companies have earned in Iraq, given the continuing discrepancy between operational requirements on the one hand and the willingness of member states to commit the necessary resources on the other, the idea that contractors should play a bigger role in peacekeeping is increasingly supported by academics and practitioners.[93] It is sometimes even suggested that private military companies should be deployed as UN blue helmets with a robust mandate, as a rapid deployment force immediately after the cessation of hostilities and before the arrival of UN blue helmets, or even as UN-mandated or UN-led troops carrying out military sanctions.[94] Greater military efficiency, reduction of costs and the circumvention of the political and procedural constraints of the UN are seen as the main arguments for such options, with Executive Outcome's intervention in Sierra Leone in 1996 frequently presented as an illustration of the advantages of private military companies replacing national troops.

Nonetheless, it is unlikely that such proposals would be realized in the near future. With regard to a UN force composed of private military personnel enforcing military sanctions it is very doubtful whether it would be permissible to substitute the standing force foreseen in Article 43 of the UN Charter with troops composed of private companies. Secondly, Article 48 of the UN Charter stipulates that Security Council decisions under Chapter VII of the Charter shall be carried out by member states. Given the wording and the purpose of the provision, and in view of the fundamental importance of the maintenance of international peace and security as the overarching purpose of the UN, it would be a long stretch to argue that states could delegate this task to private military companies. With regard to peacekeeping operations, it is important to consider the impact of a larger and more active presence of private military companies on the character of an operation that is, broadly speaking, based on the principle of minimum use of force. The mere fact that the companies are prepared to take a more aggressive posture against spoilers does not sidestep the political considerations that shape the formulation of the mandate through the Security Council and any agreement on rules of engagement.

Conversely, it is inconceivable to send a private force into the field with a vaguely worded mandate, leaving its interpretation partly or entirely to the companies. Regardless of the envisaged relationship between the Security Council and the private

---

[92] C. Lehnardt, 'Peacekeeping', in Chesterman and Fisher (eds), *Private Security, Public Order: The Outsourcing of Public Services and its Limits* (Oxford: Oxford University Press, 2010), 197, at 200.

[93] For example, K.A. O'Brien, 'What Should and What Should Not be Regulated', in Chesterman and Lehnardt (eds), *supra* n.14, 30, at 45; A. van den Berg, 'Effective Peacekeeping and the Privatization of Security', in Jäger and Kümmel (eds), *supra* n.27, 293; O. Bures, 'Private Military Companies: A Second Best Peacekeeping Option?', (2005) 12 *International Peacekeeping* 533.

[94] See M.H. Patterson, *Privatizing Peace: A Corporate Adjunct to United Nations Peacekeeping and Humanitarian Operations* (Abingdon: Routledge, 2009); J.K. Wither, 'European Security and Private Military Companies: The Prospects for Privatized "Battlegroups"', (2005) 4 *Connections Quarterly Journal* 107, at 117.

force and the command structure – an aspect not even mentioned by those advocating a greater role for contractors – the UN will in principle be responsible for peacekeeping operations and states for military interventions authorized by the Security Council.[95] This alone is reason enough for the Security Council to be wary of attempts on the part of private military companies to obtain a broader authorization to use force. If this is accepted, it is hard to see how the alleged comparative advantage of military efficiency is supposed to play out in a peacekeeping operation. Moreover, if the situation on the ground changes and the mandate must be modified accordingly – as was the case in 1999 in East Timor – it is questionable whether the presence of a company operating on a contract that must be renegotiated and adapted would be an asset or a burden – although it is not impossible to provide for these types of unforeseen events and to apportion the risks accordingly.

7. FOREIGN POLICY BY PROXY AND THE LACK OF EXPORT CONTROLS

The US maintained an unpopular presence in Iraq with the support of contractors, whose role might grow after the withdrawal of US troops, and seeks to influence the conflict in Somalia by sending a firm, rather than its own troops, to avoid 'American footprint or boot on the ground'.[96] In 2011, contractors appear to have supported both NATO and the rebels in Libya; the role of their home states, including France and Great Britain, is unclear.[97] The conflict in Somalia on land has produced a problem at sea which opens up new business opportunities for the companies: as states remain reluctant to commit their resources to the protection of commercial shipping from pirates operating off the coast of Somalia, the preferred option appears to be to allow ships to have armed security guards on board.[98] Given that private military companies open up foreign policy options to states that otherwise might not be available on

---

[95] G. Gaja, 'Second Report on the Responsibility of International Organizations', UN Doc. A/CN.4/541, 2 April 2004, para. 32; K. Schmalenbach, *Die Haftung Internationaler Organisationen* (Frankfurt a. M. u.a.: Peter Lang, 2004), at 202. For a different view see D. Sarooshi, *The United Nations and the Development of Collective Security: The Delegation by the UN Security Council of its Chapter VII Powers* (Oxford: Oxford University Press, 2000), at 163; European Court of Human Rights, *Behrami and Behrami v. France & Saramati v. France* et al., application nos. 71412/01 and 78166/01, Judgment, 2 May 2007, at para. 133.

[96] J. Gettleman, M. Mazzetti and E. Schmitt, 'US Relies on Contractors in Somali Conflict', *New York Times* online, 10 August 2011, available at http://www.nytimes.com/2011/08/11/world/africa/11somalia.html?pagewanted=all.

[97] K. Fahim and M. de la Baume, 'Head of French Company is Killed in Libyan City', *New York Times* online, 12 May 2011, available at http://www.nytimes.com/2011/05/13/world/africa/13benghazi.html; M. Hosenball, 'Mercenaries Joining Both Sides of the Conflict', 2 June 2011, *Reuters*, available at http://af.reuters.com/article/libyaNews/idAFN0229488620110602.

[98] International Maritime Organization, Revised Interim Recommendations for Flag States Regarding the Use of Privately Contracted Armed Security Personnel on Board Ships in the High Risk Area, MSC.1/Circ.1406/Rev.1, 16 September 2011; BBC News, 'Somalia's Piracy: Armed Guards to Protect British Ships', 30 October 2011, available at http://www.bbc.co.uk/news/uk-15510467; C. Bolsover, 'Germany is Close to Deploying "Mercenaries" to Protect

political or financial grounds, the absence of adequate control and clear regulation is not surprising. At the same time, considering the crucial impact the companies can have on a conflict or on a post-conflict situation, the current lack of control and oversight exercised by contracting states is stunning, resembling rather control over any commercial contractor than over the state military. Absence of control over military services is likely to result in violations of international law, including international humanitarian law, human rights law and arms embargos.[99] It is therefore important to ensure private military services, just like military goods, are under adequate control, in particular when provided in a weak state. A preventive and comprehensive export control system for private military services, along with a systematic follow-up procedure ensuring adequate monitoring, would be an important step towards such a legal regime placing private military services under adequate control. However, at present there is no international law obligation to such effect.[100] Under human rights law, the home state as such is not under an obligation to protect human rights outside its territory. In cases of serious violations of international humanitarian law through a private military company, common Article 1 of Geneva Conventions I–IV imposes an obligation on all states, including the home state, to prevent and prosecute such conduct, but not to put a systematic export control system in place.

8. CONCLUSION

While there is a comprehensive legal regime governing the use and conduct of private military companies, the informal ways in which compliance with it operates in practice should not be underestimated.[101] This is particularly true where there are numerous practical problems and uncertainties relating to its interpretation and application. Although there is no empirical evidence that private military personnel are more likely to violate international law than state armed forces, lack of institutional culture and hierarchical organization can contribute to a certain indifference towards the applicable

---

Ships from Pirates', *Deutsche Welle* online, 18 August 2011, available at http://www.dw.de/dw/article/0,,15325923,00.html.

[99] See also Report of the Monitoring Group on Somalia and Eritrea pursuant to Security Council Resolution 1916 (2010), UN Doc. S/2011/433, 18 July 2011 (referring to private military companies violating the arms embargo in Somalia and noting that the activities of one company constitute a threat to peace and security in Somalia, at para. 172).

[100] For the opposite view see F. Francioni, 'The Role of the Home State in Ensuring Compliance with Human Rights by Private Military Contractors', in Francioni and Ronzitti (eds), *supra* n.18, 93, at 104; O. de Schutter, 'The Responsibility of States', in Chesterman and Fisher (eds), *supra* n.92, 25; R. McCorquodale and P. Simons, 'Responsibility Beyond Borders: State Responsibility for Extraterritorial Violations by Corporations of International Human Rights Law', (2007) 70 *Modern Law Review* 598, at 618.

[101] L. Dickinson, 'Military Lawyers, Private Contractors, and the Problem of International Law Compliance', (2010) 42 *New York University Journal of International Law and Politics* 355, at 357.

legal regime.[102] Finally, in general it is much easier for a state to claim *plausible deniability* if it is a private entity, rather than a state organ, that is engaged in misconduct. For the conduct of a state's armed forces that state is internationally responsible by virtue of the mere fact that the conduct stems from its armed forces. For the conduct of private military personnel it is responsible only if and to the extent that certain factors can be established, such as control over the company or lack of due diligence. All these factors are likely to result in an undermining of international law principles when private military companies, rather than a state's armed forces, fulfil military functions.

---

[102] *Ibid.*, at 373; D. Muñoz-Rojas and J.-J. Frésard, 'The Roots of Behaviour in War: Understanding and Preventing IHL Violations', (2004) 86 *IRRC* 189, at 203.

ns law
13. International humanitarian law and human rights law
Matthew Happold

1. INTRODUCTION

The nature of the relationship between international humanitarian law and international human rights law remains a vexed one. In recent years, human rights lawyers and activists have sought to apply human rights norms to military conduct in international and internal conflicts, and during belligerent occupations. With varying degrees of success, complainants have brought their cases before international tribunals, such as the European Court of Human Rights and the Inter-American Commission and Court of Human Rights, and to national courts able to apply international human rights standards. Although there exist situations falling within a 'grey zone'[1] between peace and war where it can be unclear what law applies, this development has occurred largely because forums exist to hear human rights claims, whereas they do not for persons claiming individual redress for violations of international humanitarian law.[2] However, human rights norms have also been seen as more restrictive: as placing greater constraints on states' freedom to conduct hostilities, preventively detain, and administer occupied territories. It is for this reason that some states have resisted attempts to extend the reach of international human rights law into areas traditionally seen as governed by international humanitarian law.

This chapter will examine the relationship between those two bodies of law. It will seek to reprise the extensive debates on the subject and, in the light of recent developments, to present some conclusions. It will be argued that principles have now developed to govern the relationship between the two bodies of law. However, their application to different situations remains a work-in-progress and controversies are likely to persist.

2. INTERNATIONAL HUMANITARIAN LAW AND HUMAN RIGHTS LAW: TWO DIFFERENT HISTORIES

The laws of war, the traditional name for what is now known as international humanitarian law, have a good claim to be one of the oldest areas of international law. Throughout history states have sought to regulate their mutual conflicts. Thus, the laws

---

[1] A. Eide, A. Rosas and T. Meron, 'Combating Lawlessness in Gray Zone Conflicts Through Minimum Humanitarian Standards', (1995) 89 *AJIL* 215.
[2] See J. Kleffner and L. Zegveld, 'Establishing an Individual Complaints Procedure for Violations of International Humanitarian Law', (2000) 3 *YIHL* 384; and L. Zegveld, 'Remedies for Victims of Violations of International Humanitarian Law', (2003) 84 *IRRC* 497.

of war governed issues which have always fallen within the scope of international law, as traditionally defined as the law regulating inter-state relations. The laws of war sought to harmonize the dictates of humanity with military necessity, and founded themselves on reciprocity backed up by reprisals in case of breach. What this meant, however, is that international humanitarian law simply regulated states' rights vis-à-vis each other as belligerents.

This was clearly set out in the 1949 Geneva Conventions (hereinafter 'GCs'). With the exception of Common Article 3 (at the time a novelty), the GCs only apply in situations of 'declared war or of any other armed conflict which may arise between two or more of the High Contracting Parties' and to 'cases of partial or total occupation of the territory of a High Contracting Party'. In addition, the majority of their provisions apply only to 'protected persons'. The requirement for being a protected person was that one was not a national of the state the hands of which one finds oneself.[3] Pictet's Commentary put the matter clearly:

> The definition [of protected persons in Article 4(1) of GC IV[4]] has been put in a negative form; as it is intended to cover anyone who is *not* a national of the Party to the conflict or occupying Power in whose hands he is. The Convention thus remains faithful to a recognised principle of international law: it does not interfere in a State's relations with its own nationals.[5]

International human rights law, conversely, marked a departure in that it sought to regulate areas which traditionally fell outside the scope of international law as being within states' domestic jurisdiction. Previously, the rights states enjoyed over persons and property within their national territories were governed solely by national law, provided that they did not trespass on the rights of other states.[6] This principle also had consequences as regards international humanitarian law. As the laws of war traditionally only applied in situations of international armed conflict and governed only states' treatment of other states' nationals, states retained a free hand in how they suppressed rebellion and other unrest among their subjects. Save when states recognized rebels as belligerents,[7] international law left internal armed conflicts to be governed by states' national law.[8]

---

[3] At least until *Prosecutor v. Dusko Tadić*, Case No. IT-94-1-A, ICTY Appeals Chamber, Judgment, 15 July 1999, paras 163–169.

[4] Article 4(1) provides that: 'Persons protected by the Convention are those who, at a given moment and in any manner whatsoever, find themselves, in case of a conflict or occupation, in the hands of a Party to the conflict or Occupying Power of which they are not nationals.'

[5] J. Pictet (ed.), *Commentary on the Geneva Conventions of 12 August 1949*, vol. IV (ICRC: Geneva, 1955), at 46.

[6] For example, by acting unlawfully towards the property or persons of other states' nationals: see *Mavrommatis Palestine Concessions* (Greece v. United Kingdom), Judgment of 30 August 1924, PCIJ Series A, No. 2, 12.

[7] See A. Cassese, *International Law*, 2nd edn (Oxford: Oxford University Press, 2005), 125–126.

[8] Indeed, this view persisted well into the Post-World War II period. France, throughout the Algerian war of independence, consistently argued that the conflict was an internal matter governed by French criminal law, and carefully avoided making any statement which might be

From its beginnings, international human rights law was different. It sought to refigure the relationship between states and their own nationals. International law was used to limit states' sovereign rights, which had previously only been subject to limitation through the operation of national law. This is why the precursors of international human rights treaties are to be found at the national level, in national constitutions and bills of rights, providing protections for citizens against their governments; in contrast to international humanitarian law which has, from the beginning, existed as a body of rules within international law. As Bill Bowring has written, albeit with some hyperbole, whereas international humanitarian law, under various names, has existed throughout history and is 'intrinsically conservative, taking armed conflict as a given', international human rights law has its origins in the democratic revolutions of the late eighteenth century and 'has always been revolutionary, scandalous in its inception, inspired by collective action and struggle, and threatening to the existing state order'.[9]

This may not entirely be the case, international humanitarian law and international human rights law were not established on the same premise and, at least originally, were not considered to have much overlap. It will be recalled that the category of crimes against humanity was included in the Charter of the International Military Tribunal to cover atrocities which could not be categorized as war crimes, as they had been committed against German nationals.[10] By contrast, the 1948 Genocide Convention, which has a good claim to be the first human rights treaty,[11] concerned itself largely with how states treat their own nationals,[12] and went beyond the International Military Tribunal Charter in making it clear that genocide could be committed 'in time of peace or in time of war'.[13] Contracting states' obligations under the European Convention on Human Rights to 'secure to everyone ... the rights and freedoms defined in Section I of [the] Convention' were originally provided to only be with respect to 'all persons residing within their territories', and although the latter phrase was changed during the treaty negotiations to 'all within their jurisdiction', it was simply with a view to 'expanding the Convention's application to others who may not reside, in a legal sense, but who are, nevertheless, on the territory of the Contracting

---

interpreted as indicating that it recognized the Provisional Government of the Republic of Algeria as a belligerent: see Jean Charpentier, 'La reconnaissance du G.P.R.A.', (1959) *AFDI* 799.

[9] B. Bowring, 'Fragmentation, *Lex Specialis* and the Tensions in the Jurisprudence of the European Court of Human Rights', (2009) 14 *JCSL* 485, at 489–490.

[10] Article 6(c), Charter of the International Military Tribunal, annex to the London Agreement on the Prosecution and Punishment of the major War Criminals of the Axis Powers, 82 UNTS 297 (1945).

[11] See W.A. Schabas, *Genocide in International Law: The Crime of Crimes* (Cambridge: Cambridge University Press, 2000), at 6.

[12] Convention on the Prevention and Punishment of Genocide, 78 UNTS 277 (1948), in particular Articles V and VI.

[13] Article I, Genocide Convention (1948). Article 6(c) of the International Military Tribunal Charter, by requiring a connection between crimes against humanity and crimes against the peace or war crimes, imported a 'nexus' to armed conflict.

States'.[14] Similarly, each state party to the International Convention on Civil and Political Rights 'undertakes to respect and to ensure to all individuals within its territory and subject to its jurisdiction the rights recognized in the present Covenant',[15] a provision which would appear to be meant to be read conjunctively rather than disjunctively. Both provisions have been subject to expansive interpretations as a result of subsequent practice.[16] Nevertheless, it remains the case that the extraterritorial application of human rights treaties is the exception. Just as with national constitutions and bills of rights,[17] the norm is their application within states' national territories.

In the same period as international human rights law was being developed, however, the reach of international humanitarian law was being extended. Common Article 3 of the 1949 Geneva Conventions, which provided some protection in situations of armed conflict 'not of an international character occurring in the territory' of a High Contracting Party, was augmented by the 1977 Additional Protocol II. However, the definition of armed conflict in Additional Protocol II was narrow,[18] and it was initially unclear whether breaches of the international humanitarian law applicable in non-international armed conflict incurred individual criminal responsibility.[19] Even today, the rules governing non-international armed conflict, despite the valiant efforts of the International Committee of the Red Cross (hereinafter 'ICRC'),[20] can seem sparse in comparison with the rich and detailed provisions governing international armed conflicts. And, in contrast with international armed conflicts, there exists no 'combatant privilege' in internal armed conflicts, at least as regards insurgents, who can continue to be prosecuted and punished for their activities under national law. States (that is, governments) have retained their sovereign right to suppress rebellion, while gaining belligerent rights under international law when insurgencies reach a certain threshold of intensity, giving them the choice to treat insurgents as criminals, or as parties to an armed conflict, or both, as best suits their purposes.

Given this situation, and given that human rights law, as we have seen, *prima facie* governs a state's conduct within its national territory, the issue of its applicability in

---

[14] *Banković and others v. Belgium and others*, Appl. no. 52207/99, interlocutory decision of 12 December 2001, [2001] ECHR 890, para. 63: See also Council of Europe, *Collected Edition of the 'Travaux Préparatoires' of the European Convention on Human Rights*, Vol. III (The Hague: Martinus Nijhoff, 1976), at 260.

[15] Article 2(1), International Covenant on Civil and Political Rights (1966).

[16] See *infra* section 4.

[17] See recent cases such as *R v. Hape*, 2007 SCC 26, [2007] 2 SCR; and *Boumediene v. Bush*, 553 U.S. 723 (2008).

[18] Requiring that rebels exercise control over territory: Article 1(1), Additional Protocol II relating to the Protection of Victims of Non-International Armed Conflicts (1977).

[19] Not until 1995 was it confirmed that such conduct could amount to a war crime: see *Prosecutor v. Dusko Tadić*, Case No. IT-94-1-A, ICTY Appeals Chamber, Interlocutory decision on jurisdiction, 2 October 1995, paras 128–137.

[20] See J.-M. Henckaerts and L. Doswald-Beck, *Customary International Humanitarian Law* (Cambridge: Cambridge University Press, 2005). The extent to which the ICRC's codification reflects customary international law has been disputed: see J.B. Bellinger III and W.J. Haynes II, 'A US Government Response to the ICRC Study *Customary International Humanitarian Law*', (2007) 89 *IRRC* 443; and E. Wilmshurst and S. Breau (eds), *Perspectives on the ICRC Study on Customary International Humanitarian Law* (Cambridge: Cambridge University Press, 2007).

non-international armed conflict immediately comes into issue. And although it has been argued that international humanitarian law, as *lex specialis*, displaces human rights law,[21] such an opinion is contrary to the weight of opinion. The argument was put to the International Court of Justice during proceedings concerning the *Legality of the Threat or Use of Nuclear Weapons*.[22] In response, the Court stated that:

> the protection of the International Covenant on Civil and Political Rights does not cease in times of war, except by operation of Article 4 of the Covenant whereby certain provisions may be derogated from in a time of national emergency.[23]

Such has also been the consistent view of all human rights bodies.[24] Unfortunately for the advocates of an absolute distinction between the two regimes, states sold the pass long ago. Beginning with the 1968 Tehran Conference on Human Rights[25] and the subsequent General Assembly resolutions on the protection of human rights in armed conflict,[26] the United Nations has accepted that human rights law applies in situations of armed conflict. This view is regularly reiterated in resolutions of the Security Council, the General Assembly, the former Commission on Human Rights and the present Human Rights Council.[27] It is also reflected in international humanitarian law itself. Article 72 of Additional Protocol I makes specific reference to 'other applicable rules of international law relating to the protection of fundamental human rights during international armed conflict', while the preamble to Additional Protocol II recalls that 'international instruments relating to human rights offer a basic protection to the human person'. And the existence of derogation clauses in human rights treaties indicates that they too, explicitly or implicitly, admit their general application.

The conclusion must be that human rights law applies in situations of armed conflict, whether international or non-international, (i) insofar as there has not been a valid

---

[21] See M.J. Dennis, 'Application of Human Rights Treaties Extraterritorially in Times of Armed Conflict and Military Occupation', (2005) 99 *AJIL* 119, at 119–120.

[22] *Legality of the Threat or Use of Nuclear Weapons*, Advisory Opinion, ICJ Reports 1996, 226, at 239: 'It was suggested that the Covenant was directed to the protection of human rights in peacetime, but that questions relating to unlawful loss of life in hostilities were governed by the law applicable in armed conflict.'

[23] *Ibid.*, at 240.

[24] See the jurisprudence of the Human Rights Committee, the Committee on Economic and Social Rights, the Committee on the Elimination of Racial Discrimination, the Committee on the Elimination of Discrimination against Women, the European Court of Human Rights, and the Inter-American Court and Commission of Human Rights cited in C. Droege, 'Elective Affinities? Human Rights and Humanitarian Law', (2008) 90 *IRRC* 501, at 507–508.

[25] International Conference on Human Rights, Res. XXIII on human rights in armed conflicts, 12 May 1968, *Final Act of the International Conference on Human Rights*, UN Doc. A/Conf.32/41, at 18.

[26] GA Res. 2444 (XXIII): Respect for human rights in armed conflicts (19 December 1968), and GA Res. 2675 (XXV): Basic principles for the protection of civilian populations in armed conflicts (9 December 1970).

[27] See, recently, SC Res. 1970 (2011) on peace and security in Africa and SC Res. 1973 (2011) on Libya; GA Res. 253/66 (2012) on the situation in the Syrian Arab Republic; and Human Rights Council Res. S-18/1 (2011) on the human rights situation in the Syrian Arab Republic.

derogation; and (ii) to the extent that such situations fall within the relevant treaty's geographical scope.[28] In consequence, we will first consider the extent to which states can derogate from their human rights obligations and the extraterritorial scope of those obligations, before going on to consider the various situations which arise when international human rights law and international humanitarian law are concurrently applicable.

Before doing so, however, it should be recalled that the general view is that human rights law addresses only states.[29] The activities of non-state parties to conflicts are governed only by international humanitarian law. This has occasionally been advanced as a reason why human rights law should not govern the conduct of government forces during internal armed conflicts, on the basis that otherwise what is said to be 'one of the fundamental precepts of the law of armed conflict ... the legal equality of belligerent parties' would be undermined.[30] Legal equality in this context, however, simply means equality before the law; both parties are governed by the law applicable to the conflict (the *jus in bello*) regardless of the justice of their cause (in particular, whether they are in breach of the *jus ad bellum*).[31] Thus, in the context of an internal armed conflict, the principle prevents a government from disapplying rules of international humanitarian law on the grounds that the insurgents fighting against it have unlawfully taken up arms.[32] It does not prevent states from binding themselves to apply higher standards, albeit that non-state parties to such armed conflicts remain bound solely by international humanitarian law.[33] It should equally be recalled, however, that rebels can be punished not only for breaches of international humanitarian law but also for violations of national law, that is, for treason for taking up arms, and for murder for killing government soldiers.

---

[28] In addition, the fact of the existence of an armed conflict may be relevant as regards the application of human rights law. The existence of an ongoing armed conflict can affect the extent to which qualified rights can be restricted, both civil and political rights (freedom of speech, freedom of conscience and religion, freedom of association and assembly), and also economic, social and cultural rights, which are governed, in many cases, by the principle of 'progressive realization' subject to 'available resources': see Article 2(1) of the International Covenant on Economic, Social and Cultural Rights, and Committee on Economic, Social and Cultural Rights, General Comment 3: the nature of State Parties' obligations (Article 2, para. 1 of the Covenant), UN Doc. E/1991/23, 14 December 1990.

[29] See L. Zegveld, *The Accountability of Armed Opposition Groups in International Law* (Cambridge: Cambridge University Press, 2002). For arguments to the contrary, however, see A. Clapham, *Human Rights Obligations of Non-State Actors* (Oxford: Oxford University Press, 2006).

[30] J.K. Kleffner, 'Section IX of the ICRC Interpretative Guidance on Direct Participation in Hostilities: The End of *Jus in Bello* Proportionality as We Know It?', (2012) 45 *Israel LR* 35, at 49.

[31] See H. Meyrowitz, *Le principe de l'égalité des belligérants devant le droit de la guerre* (Paris: Pedone, 1970).

[32] See F. Bugnion, '*Jus ad Bellum, Jus in Bello* and Non-International Armed Conflicts', (2003) 6 *YIHL* 167.

[33] Although the mechanisms by which this occurs remain unclear: see S. Sivakumaran, 'Binding Armed Opposition Groups', (2006) 55 *ICLQ* 369.

3. DEROGATIONS FROM STATES' HUMAN RIGHTS OBLIGATIONS

Article 15(1) of the European Convention on Human Rights states that:

> In time of war or other public emergency threatening the life of the nation any High Contracting Party may take measures derogating from its obligations under this Convention to the extent strictly required by the exigencies of the situation, provided that such measures are not inconsistent with its other obligations under international law.

Similar provisions appear in the International Covenant on Civil and Political Rights and the American Conventions on Human Rights,[34] but not in the African Charter on Human and Peoples' Rights or other human rights treaties. Unlike the European or the American Conventions, the International Covenant does not specifically indicate war as a time of public emergency. However, situations of armed conflicts fit squarely within the category of public emergencies threatening the life of the nation,[35] and have consistently been held to do so by human rights bodies, as well as by the International Court of Justice.[36]

States do not benefit from a derogation from their relevant treaty obligations automatically upon the existence of a public emergency threatening the life of the nation. Derogations must be notified to be effective. Indeed, the International Covenant requires that a state party not only notifies the derogation itself to the UN Secretary-General but also proclaims a state of emergency under its national law,[37] while the American Convention requires notification of the date set for its termination.[38] It is unlawful for a state to derogate from its human rights obligations except in conformity with the procedural requirements imposed by the relevant treaty or treaties.[39]

The term 'public emergency threatening the life of the nation' extends far more widely, however, than just situations of armed conflict. In the first case when the legality of a derogation under Article 15 of the Convention was at issue, the European Court of Human Rights was willing to defer to the judgment of the Irish Government that a campaign by a terrorist group which, in a period of over six months, had resulted in the deaths of two policemen and the wounding of another, amounted to a such a situation.[40] Subsequent cases have confirmed this practice of deference of the judgment of the political branch of Government, which is said to be best fitted to making what is

---

[34] Article 4, International Covenant on Civil and Political Rights (1966); and Article 27, American Convention on Human Rights (1969).

[35] As expressly indicated by the wording of Article 15(1) of the European Convention on Human Rights (1950).

[36] See *Nuclear Weapons* Advisory Opinion, *supra* n.22; and *Legal Consequences of the Construction of a Wall in the Occupied Palestinian Territory*, Advisory Opinion, [2004] ICJ Rep. 2004 136, at 178.

[37] Article 4(1), International Covenant on Civil and Political Rights (1966).

[38] Article 27(3), American Convention on Human Rights (1969).

[39] More than one derogation may be necessary depending on the human rights treaties to which a state is party.

[40] *Lawless v Ireland*, Judgment of 1 July 1961, Series A no. 3.

seen as a political rather than a legal determination. As Lord Hope stated in the UK House of Lords in the *Belmarsh detainees* case:

> the questions whether there is an emergency and whether it threatens the life of the nation are pre-eminently for the executive and for Parliament. The judgment that has to be formed on these issues lies outside the expertise of the courts ... [41]

Voices have been raised against such a wide interpretation of the term, most eloquently that of Lord Hoffmann, also in the *Belmarsh detainees* case.[42] Such views, however, have not been followed at the national, let alone the international level. What this means is that situations of unrest and civil strife in response to which states can derogate from their human rights obligations exist below the threshold for the application of international humanitarian law.

This is not to say, however, that in such circumstances neither international humanitarian law nor human rights law governs. Article 15(2) of the European Convention on Human Rights provides that: 'No derogation from Article 2, except in respect of deaths resulting from lawful acts of war, or from Articles 3, 4 (paragraph 1) and 7 shall be made under this provision. Article 4(2) of the International Covenant on Civil and Political Rights states that: 'No derogation from articles 6, 7, 8 (paragraphs 1 and 2), 11, 15, 16 and 18 may be made under this provision.' The two lists are in substance the same: preventing derogation from the right to life; the prohibitions of torture and inhuman or degrading treatment and punishment, and of slavery and servitude; and the principle of non-retroactivity. The International Covenant includes the right to freedom of thought, conscience and religion in its list of non-derogable rights, which the European Convention does not.[43] It might be thought, however, that this is a distinction without a difference. Freedom of thought and religion is a qualified right, so it can be restricted according to the applicable circumstances, so the right can be subject to restrictions in emergency situations without derogation. Conversely and more generally, derogations to rights can only be to 'the extent strictly required by the exigencies of the situation', which limits the extent to which any derogable right can be restricted following derogation. This idea has been systematized by the Human Rights Committee, which has argued that a number of derogable rights have a non-derogable

---

[41] *A (FC) and others (FC) (Appellants) v. Secretary of State for the Home Department (Respondent)* [2004] UKHL 56, at para. 116. See also Lord Bingham's conclusion, at para. 29, that: 'great weight should be given to the judgment of the Home Secretary, his colleagues and Parliament on this question, because they were called on to exercise a pre-eminently political judgment'.

[42] 'When one speaks of a threat to the "life" of the nation, the word life is being used in a metaphorical sense. The life of the nation is not coterminous with the lives of its people ... I do not underestimate the ability of fanatical groups of terrorists to kill and destroy, but they do not threaten the life of the nation ... Terrorist violence, serious as it is, does not threaten our institutions of government or our existence as a civil community.' *Ibid.*, paras 91 and 96.

[43] The International Covenant also prohibits derogation from the right not to be imprisoned for failure to fulfil a contractual obligation, which does not appear in the European Convention, but this may simply be because the existence or not of an armed conflict is irrelevant to the enjoyment of the right.

core.[44] However, a derogation that complies with a state's obligations under international humanitarian law is unlikely to be considered to go beyond what a situation of armed conflict requires.

States' practice as regards derogations is inconsistent. Some states have made derogations when faced with situations of armed conflict. Others have not.[45] What is common, however, is for states facing insurgencies to avoid describing them as armed conflicts,[46] usually because they fear that such a categorization, by defining rebels as parties to an armed conflict (although it grants them no additional legal rights[47]) dignifies their struggle and detracts from their status as criminals. In such situations, human rights law continues to apply, as it were, by default, subject only to any lawful derogations. Nevertheless, there remains an overlap – whether or not a state takes advantage of its right of derogation or not – between the fields of application of human rights and humanitarian law, at least that applicable in non-international armed conflicts. This is unsurprising. As we have already seen, a number of human rights treaties predate the substantive application of international humanitarian law to non-international armed conflicts. At the time of the adoption of the European Convention on Human Rights and the International Covenant on Civil and Political Rights, only Common Article 3 governed 'conflicts not of an international character'. Save for imposing certain minimum guarantees, international humanitarian law refrained from regulating non-international armed conflict, seeing it as a matter within states' domestic jurisdiction governed by national, rather than international, law. Human rights law then began to regulate how states exercised their sovereign rights, including during civil wars, insurgencies and other situations of internal unrest.[48] To this extent, then, it cannot be said that human rights law has trespassed on the domain

---

[44] General Comment 29: States of Emergency (Article 4), UN Doc. CCPR/C/21/Rev.1/Add.11, 31 August 2001, paras 11–15.

[45] Russia has not derogated from either the European Convention or the International Covenant as regards the situation in Chechnya: see F. Hampson, 'The Relationship between International Humanitarian Law and Human Rights Law from the Perspective of a Human Rights Treaty Body', (2008) 871 *IRRC* 549, at 563 (n.59).

[46] As Françoise Hampson points out, the Northern Irish 'Troubles' may, at certain times, in certain places, have crossed the threshold for the application of Common Article 3: *ibid.*, at 555.

[47] Unless recognized as belligerents: *op cit.* n.7. Such recognition is, however, uncommon and it may be that the concept of belligerency is falling into *desuetude*: Patrick Daillier *et al.*, *Droit International Public*, 8th edn (Paris: LGDJ, 2009), at para. 371.

[48] Hence Article 56 ('the colonial clause') of the European Convention on Human Rights, ensuring that state parties could avoid the application of the Convention to their colonial possessions: see L. Moor and A.W.B. Simpson, 'Ghosts of Colonialism in the European Convention on Human Rights', (2005) 76 *BYIL* 121. At the time of the Convention's adoption, a number of states of the Council of Europe retained colonial empires, where they faced increasing resistance to their rule. Indeed, the two earliest inter-state cases before the European Commission on Human Rights concerned the UK's conduct in repressing the EOKA insurgency in Cyprus: see A.W.B. Simpson, *Human Rights and the End of Empire: Britain and the Genesis of the European Convention* (Oxford: Oxford University Press, 2001), at 924–1053.

of international humanitarian law; one might even argue the reverse.[49] The same cannot be said, however, as regards the extraterritorial application of human rights law.

4. THE EXTRATERRITORIAL SCOPE OF STATES' HUMAN RIGHTS OBLIGATIONS

Article 1 of the European Convention on Human Rights obliges Contracting Parties to 'secure to everyone within their jurisdiction the rights and freedoms defined in Section I of this Convention'. The International Covenant on Civil and Political Rights is, on the face of it, even more restrictive.[50] Some other human rights treaties have similar provisions.[51] Others have nothing on the subject at all.[52] However, although states' jurisdiction is primarily territorial, it can extend further, so that the extraterritorial application of human rights treaties, even to non-nationals, cannot be ruled out. Indeed, the term 'jurisdiction' is Janus-faced, being used to refer both to the extent to which states lawfully can legislate, adjudicate and enforce their national laws and regulations as a matter of international law, and to the extent to which they in fact do so. As will be seen, human rights bodies have consistently looked at the facts in order to determine whether jurisdiction has been exercised, as has the International Court of Justice.

The extraterritorial extent of states' human rights obligations has arisen in two contexts in particular: when a state is in belligerent occupation of foreign territory and when it undertakes military operations abroad. Whether a state is in occupation is a question of fact; a territory is occupied when it is 'actually placed under the authority of the hostile army'.[53]

> The question is whether in fact the armed forces that have invaded the adversary's territory have brought the area under their control through their physical presence, to the extent they

---

[49] Although account does need to be taken of the fact that the date of coming into force of human rights treaties has often been some years after their adoption; and individual states' adherence has sometimes been much later. For example, France, although an original signatory to the European Convention on Human Rights, did not become a party until 1974, nearly 21 years after the treaty's entry into force.

[50] See *supra* n.15. The jurisprudence of the Human Rights Committee, however, has consistently taken the view that the International Covenant has an extraterritorial application.

[51] Article 1(1) of the American Convention on Human Rights provides that: 'The States Parties to this Convention undertake to respect the rights and freedoms recognized herein and to ensure to all persons subject to their jurisdiction the free and full exercise of those rights and freedoms.' Article 2 of the Convention against Torture requires that: 'Each State Party shall take effective ... measures to prevent acts of torture in any territory under its jurisdiction.' Article 2(1) of the Convention on the Rights of the Child states that: 'States Parties shall respect and ensure the rights set forth in the present Convention to each child within their jurisdiction ... '.

[52] In particular, the International Covenant on Economic, Social and Cultural Rights; the International Convention on the Elimination of All Forms of Racial Discrimination; and the Convention on the Elimination of All Forms of Discrimination against Women.

[53] Article 42, Hague Regulations annexed to the 1907 Hague Convention (No. IV) respecting the Laws and Customs of War on Land.

can actually assume the responsibilities which attach to an occupying power. This includes the ability to issue directives to the inhabitants of the conquered territory and to enforce them.[54]

In brief, the occupier must have expelled the indigenous sovereign and established itself in its place. Moreover, an occupier not only is subject to obligations as such, but also enjoys rights, which arise by virtue of the effectiveness rather than the legality (or otherwise) of its occupation. Therefore, it might be thought, a state which claims to be in occupation of a particular territory (and, consequently, to benefit from the rights accorded to occupiers), should also have to bear the burdens, even if it does not satisfy the legal (that is, factual) criteria for being an occupier.

Although formally belligerent rights, granted by international law, the rights enjoyed by an occupier are, in their substance, sovereign rights; and the condition of their enjoyment is precisely that a state is able to act as a sovereign (at least to the exclusion of any other) in territory it has occupied. For these reasons, for the purpose of the applicability of human rights protections, human rights bodies have assimilated territory occupied by a state to its national territory. Human rights treaty monitoring bodies have consistently done so in their concluding observations to states parties' reports.[55] The same view has been taken by international courts. In *Loizidou v. Turkey*, the European Court of Human Rights explained that:

> Bearing in mind the object and purpose of the Convention, the responsibility of a Contracting Party may also arise when as a consequence of military action – whether lawful or unlawful – it exercises effective control of an area outside of its national territory. The obligation to secure, in such an area, the rights and freedoms set out in the Convention derives from the fact of such control ...[56]

In its Advisory Opinion on the *Legality of the Construction of a Wall in the Occupied Palestinian Territory*,[57] the International Court of Justice had to decide whether the human rights treaties to which Israel was a party (the International Covenant on Civil and Political Rights, the International Covenant on Economic, Social and Cultural Rights, and the Convention on the Rights of the Child) were applicable, in addition to international humanitarian law, to Israel's conduct as occupier of the Occupied Palestinian Territory. In answering the question, the Court simply adopted the views expressed by the treaties' monitoring bodies (the Human Rights Committee, the Committee on Economic, Social and Cultural Rights, and the Committee on the Rights of the Child), all of which had previously expressed the opinion that those treaties did apply to Israel's activities in the Territory.

This view, it must be admitted, has not always been shared by states. In the *Legality of the Wall* case it was adopted contrary to Israel's contentions. Famously, the USA did not accept the opinion of the Inter-American Commission on Human Rights that the

---

[54] H. Gasser, 'Protection of the Civilian Population', in D. Fleck (ed.), *Handbook of Humanitarian Law in Armed Conflicts* (Oxford: Oxford University Press, 1995), 243.
[55] See the examples cited in Droege, *supra* n.24, at 510–511 and 518; and Hampson, *supra* n.45, at 567–569.
[56] *Loizidou v. Turkey (Preliminary Objections)*, A 310 (1995), 20 EHRR 99, para. 62.
[57] *Supra* n.26.

provisions of the American Declaration on the Rights and Duties of Man applied to its activities in Guantanamo.[58] Indeed, both Israel and the USA have consistently argued that human rights treaties have no extraterritorial effect.[59] The United Kingdom, following the invasion and occupation of Iraq, argued that it was not bound to act in accordance with the European Convention on Human Rights as regards its activities as an occupier in Southern Iraq: in the first place because although the UK might be in effective control of the area for the purposes of being in occupation (and benefiting from the rights accruing to an occupier), it was not for the purposes of the European Convention; and, secondly, because the Convention is a European treaty, which applies in a European 'legal space', so that to apply to Iraq would amount to 'human rights imperialism'.[60] Both these arguments were successful in the English courts.[61] However, neither received the support of the European Court of Human Rights. In its judgment in *Al-Skeini and others v. United Kingdom*, the Court reiterated what it said in *Loizidou* (and other earlier cases):

> Another exception to the principle that jurisdiction under Article 1 is limited to a State's own territory occurs when, as a consequence of lawful or unlawful military action, a Contracting State exercises effective control of an area outside that national territory.[62]

The Court continued:

> It is a question of fact whether a Contracting State exercises effective control over an area outside its own territory. In determining whether effective control exists, the Court will primarily have reference to the strength of the State's military presence in the area.[63]

Applying the law to the facts of the case, the Court took note that the USA and UK had been occupying powers within the meaning of Article 42 of the Hague Regulations and had for a period assumed the government of Iraq until authority passed from their vehicle, the Coalition Provisional Authority, to the Interim Iraqi Government. Accordingly, the Court concluded:

> [F]ollowing the removal from power of the Ba'ath regime and until the accession of the Interim Government, the United Kingdom (together with the United States) assumed in Iraq the exercise of some of the public powers normally to be exercised by a sovereign government. In particular, the United Kingdom assumed authority and responsibility for the maintenance of security in South East Iraq. Under these exceptional circumstances, the Court

---

[58] Response of the United States to Request for Precautionary Measures – Detainees in Guantanamo Bay, Cuba, 15 April 2002 (2002) 41 *ILM* 1015.

[59] Although the US position appears to have softened recently: see Fourth Periodic Report of the United States of America to the United Nations Committee on Human Rights concerning the International Covenant on Civil and Political Rights, 30 December 2011, at paras 504–507.

[60] A phrase used by Lord Rodger of Earlsferry in his judgment in *Secretary of State for Defence v. Al-Skeini and others* [2007] UKHL 26, [2008] 1 AC 28, at para. 78.

[61] *Ibid.* See also *R(Al-Skeini) v. Secretary of State for Defence* [2006] EWCA Civ 1609, [2006] 3 WLR 508; and *R(Al-Skeini) v. Secretary of State for Defence* [2004] EWHC 2911 (Admin), [2005] 2 WLR 1401.

[62] Application no. 55721/07, judgment of the Grand Chamber of 7 July 2011, at para. 138.

[63] *Ibid.*, at para. 139.

considers that the United Kingdom through its soldiers engaged in security operations in Basrah during the period in question, exercised authority and control over individuals killed in the course of such security operations, so as to establish a jurisdictional link between the deceased and the United Kingdom for the purposes of Article 1 of the Convention.[64]

This is, perhaps, not as explicit as might be hoped, but the implication seems clear: that the UK was in effective control of Southern Iraq and, therefore, individuals within that area were within its jurisdiction under Article 1 of the European Convention. The contrast with the judgment of the UK House of Lords, which held that only persons in the custody of British forces in Southern Iraq, not those shot at checkpoints and during military operations, fell within the UK's jurisdiction for the purpose of the Convention,[65] is clear. However, the Court's emphasis on the particular facts of the case leaves open the possibility that some situations of belligerent occupation might fall outwith the scope of the Convention.

The argument concerning the essentially regional character of the European Convention was also rejected by the Court.[66] And in his Concurring Opinion, Judge Bonello tartly observed that:

> I confess myself to be quite unimpressed by the pleadings of the United Kingdom Government to the effect that exporting the European Conventions on Human Rights to Iraq would have amounted to 'human rights imperialism'. It ill behooves a State that imposed its military imperialism over another sovereign State without the frailest imprimatur from the international community, to resent the charge of having exported human rights imperialism to the vanquished enemy ... For my part, I believe that those who export war ought to see to the parallel export of guarantees against the atrocities of war.[67]

The European Court's judgment in *Al-Skeini*, and its earlier decision in *Banković*[68] also serve to delimit the extent to which the Contracting Parties' obligations under the European Convention extend extraterritorially in situations outside of occupation. In *Al-Skeini* the Court stated that, although as a rule jurisdiction was territorial:

> In certain circumstances, the use of force by a State's agents operating outside its territory may bring the individual thereby brought under the control of the State's authorities under the State's Article 1 jurisdiction. This principle has been applied where an individual is taken into the custody of State agents abroad.[69]

In support of this proposition, the Court referred to a number of its previous decisions, including that in *Issa v. Turkey*,[70] where the Court held admissible allegations that Turkish forces operating in Northern Iraq had detained, and subsequently killed, a

---

[64] Ibid., at para. 148.
[65] Supra n.60.
[66] Supra n.62, para. 142.
[67] Ibid., Concurring Opinion of Judge Bonello, at paras 37–38.
[68] Supra n.14.
[69] Supra n.62, para. 136
[70] Appl. no. 31821/96, decision on admissibility, 30 May 2000; Judgment, 16 November 2004.

number of Kurdish shepherds.[71] To similar effect, the Human Rights Committee, in its General Comment 31, stated that:

> a State party must respect and ensure the rights laid down in the Covenant to anyone within the power or effective control of that State Party, even if not situated within the territory of the State Party ... This principle also applies to those within the power or effective control of the forces of a State Party acting outside its territory, regardless of the circumstances in which such power or effective control was obtained, such as forces constituting a national contingent of a State Party assigned to an international peace-keeping or peace-enforcement operation.[72]

The European Court of Human Rights, however, has distinguished situations where there is an 'exercise of physical power and control over the person in question'[73] from cases such as that in *Banković*. That case concerned the bombing of the offices of Serbian television in Belgrade by NATO forces in 1999, resulting in the death of 16 persons and serious injury to another 16. The Court concluded it did not have jurisdiction to consider the application as there was no exercise of authority and control over the victims. They were simply unfortunate enough to be in a building which NATO forces bombed.

Such a view has been disputed. Françoise Hampson, in particular, has argued that *Banković* was wrongly decided and that the appropriate test should not be control over territory but 'control over the effects said to constitute a violation, subject to a foreseeable victim being foreseeably affected by the act'.[74] And although the European Court has subsequently gone some way to modifying its rather dogmatic position in *Banković*,[75] the distinction between exercises of authority and control, and acts of war remains. By contrast, the Inter-American Commission on Human Rights, applying the American Declaration on the Rights and Duties of Man, has been willing to exercise jurisdiction over acts of war committed by a state outside of its territory.[76] And in the *Armed Activities in the Territory of the Congo* case, the International Court of Justice found violations of the International Convention on Civil and Political Rights as

---

[71] The Turkish forces constituted an invading rather than an occupying army: see C. Antonopoulos, 'The Turkish Military Operation in Northern Iraq of March–April 1995 and the International Law on the Use of Force', (1996) 1 *JACL* 33.

[72] Human Rights Committee, General Comment 31: The Nature of the General Legal Obligation imposed on State Parties to the Covenant, UN doc. CCPR/C/21/Rev.1/Add. 13, 26 May 2004, at para. 10.

[73] *Supra* n.62, at para. 138.

[74] *Supra* n.45, at 570.

[75] Which did not, in any case, entirely reflect its earlier jurisprudence: see M. Happold, '*Banković v Belgium* and the Territorial Scope of the European Convention on Human Rights', (2003) 3 *HRLR* 77.

[76] *Disabled People International and others v. US*, Case 9.213, admissibility decision of 22 September 1987, Ann. Rep. IACHR 1986–1987; and *Salas and others v. US*, Report No. 31/93, Case 10.573, 14 October 1993, Ann. Rep. IACHR 1993, 312. The claims related, respectively, to the US invasions of Grenada and Panama. See also *Armando Alejandre Jr. and others v. Cuba*, Report No. 86/99, Case 11.589, 29 September 1999, Ann. Rep. IACHR 1999, 586, which concerned the shooting down of an unarmed civilian aircraft by a Cuban military aircraft in international airspace.

regards Uganda's conduct not only in territory which it had occupied but also in other parts of the Congo.[77] No legal reasons, however, were given by the Court for its doing so.[78] It is, of course, quite possible that the extraterritorial reach of some human rights treaties is broader than that of others. The main obstacle to a further extension of that of the European Convention on Human Rights would appear to be the European Court of Human Rights' view that the Convention applies in an 'all or nothing' fashion, so that it can only apply in situations where a Contracting Party can guarantee all the rights therein,[79] but *Al-Skeini* seems to have mitigated this rigid approach.[80] The matter is likely to come for determination again by the European Court of Human Rights in the context of the inter-state claim brought by Georgia against Russia concerning the latter's invasion of the former in August 2008.[81]

In consequence, it would seem that states' human rights obligations do apply to their extraterritorial conduct in at least two situations: when they are in effective control of areas outside of their national territory (which seems largely assimilable to whether the state was in belligerent occupation of the area); and when they have detained or taken into custody persons outside of their national territory. Arguments have also been made that international human rights law applies more widely, to all extraterritorial uses of force. The use in recent years of drones to undertake 'targeted killings' of terrorist suspects by Israel and the USA has increased support for such a view.[82] However, although it has some support in the jurisprudence of the International Court of Justice and the American Commission on Human Rights and in legal doctrine, the current case law of the European Court of Human Rights argues the contrary.

---

[77] [2005] ICJ Rep. 165, at 239 and 244–245. The tenor of the Court's *Nuclear Weapons* Advisory Opinion would also seem to support such a conclusion, given that it is difficult to imagine a state using nuclear weapons within its national territory or any area within its effective control.

[78] The Court simply stated (*ibid.*, at 243), with reference to its *Legality of the Wall* Advisory Opinion that: 'The Court further concluded that international human rights instruments are applicable "in respect of acts done by a State in the exercise of its jurisdiction outside its own territory", particularly in occupied territories', which entirely begs the question.

[79] *Banković*, *supra* n.14, at para. 75.

[80] *Al-Skeini*, *supra* n. 62, at para. 137.

[81] *Georgia v. Russia*, Appl. no. 38263/08. In its decision on admissibility of 13 December 2011, the Court reserved questions of Russia's 'jurisdiction' for the purposes of Article 1 of the European Convention in South Ossetia, Abkhazia and neighbouring regions, and the interplay of the provisions of the Convention with the rules of international humanitarian law to the merits stage of proceedings.

[82] In particular because otherwise extraterritorial uses of force (that is, 'targeted killings' using drones and airstrikes, etc.) would be outside of the ambit of international human rights law even if not committed during an armed conflict: see Report of the Special Rapporteur on extrajudicial, summary and arbitrary executions, Philip Alston. Addendum: Study on targeted killings, UN Doc. A/HRC/14/24/Add.6, 28 May 2010.

5. SITUATIONS OF THE SIMULTANEOUS APPLICABILITY OF INTERNATIONAL HUMANITARIAN LAW AND HUMAN RIGHTS LAW

To say that international humanitarian law and international human rights law are applicable simultaneously in situations of armed conflict cannot, however, be the end of the matter. In particular, how are potential conflicts to be avoided or resolved? In such situations the *lex specialis* principle is said to apply. Taken originally from Roman law, this principle provides that *lex specialis derogat legi generali*; that is, the more specific rule prevails over the more general.[83] However, precisely what the principle represents has not always been made clear and its application has been subject to cogent criticism.[84] Two issues seem particularly problematic: first, whether the principle applies at the level of legal regimes (in which case international humanitarian law might potentially displace human rights law entirely during situations of armed conflict) or as regards particular rules (which would open the possibility to holding that, in certain situations, human rights law is more specific than international humanitarian law); and, secondly, whether the principle is a method for avoiding conflicts of norms, for resolving them, or both.

The International Court of Justice has addressed the relationship between international humanitarian law and human rights law on several occasions and its jurisprudence provides a good starting point for discussion of the issues. As already mentioned, the Court did so first in relation to Article 6 of the International Covenant on Civil and Political Rights in its *Nuclear Weapons* Advisory Opinion. Article 6(1) provides that: 'Every human being has the inherent right to life... No one shall be arbitrarily deprived of his life.' International humanitarian law, by contrast, permits the taking of life in certain circumstances.[85] Having pointed out that Article 6 was non-derogable and that therefore, in principle, it continued to apply in hostilities, the Court continued to say:

> The test of what is an arbitrary deprivation of life, however, then falls to be determined by the applicable *lex specialis*, namely, the law applicable in armed conflict which is designed to regulate the conduct of hostilities. Thus whether a particular loss of life, through the use of a certain weapon in warfare, is to be considered an arbitrary deprivation of life contrary to Article 6 of the Covenant, can only be decided by reference to the law applicable in armed conflict and not deduced from the terms of the Covenant itself.[86]

---

[83] See R. Jennings and A. Watts (eds), *Oppenheim's International Law*, 9th edn (London: Longman, 1992), para. 636. See also J. Pauwelyn, *Conflict of Norms in Public International Law: How WTO Law Relates to Other Rules of International Law* (Cambridge: Cambridge University Press, 2003), at 385–415.

[84] See, in particular, N. Prud'homme, '*Lex Specialis*: Oversimplifying a More Complex and Multifaceted Relationship?', (2007) 40 *Israel LR* 356.

[85] See, in particular, C. Jochnick and R. Normand, 'The Legitimation of Violence: A Critical History of the Laws of War', (1994) 35 *Harvard ILJ* 35.

[86] *Supra* n.22, at 240.

The Court's statement has been viewed as supporting the view that the relationship between the two bodies of international human rights law and international humanitarian law is one, respectively, of *lex generalis* and *lex specialis*. However, in subsequent cases the Court was more nuanced. In its *Legality of the Wall* Advisory Opinion, the Court stated that:

> the protection offered by human rights conventions does not cease in case of armed conflict, save through the effect of provisions for derogation of the kind to be found in Article 4 of the International Covenant on Civil and Political Rights. As regards the relationship between international humanitarian law and human rights law, there are thus three possible situations: some rights may be exclusively matters of international humanitarian law; others may be exclusively matters of human rights law; yet others may be matters of both these branches of international law. In order to answer the question put to it, the Court will have to take into consideration both these branches of international law, namely human rights law and, as *lex specialis*, international humanitarian law.[87]

Finally, in the *Armed Activities* case the Court abandoned reference to international humanitarian law as *lex specialis*, reproducing the quote from its Opinion in the *Legality of the Wall* case set out above with the exception of its final sentence, and stating that: 'It [the Court in the *Legality of the Wall* case] thus concluded that both branches of international law, namely international human rights law and international humanitarian law, would have to be taken into consideration.'[88]

The International Court of Justice's statement in the *Legality of the Wall* Advisory Opinion highlights that even when international human rights law and international humanitarian law apply simultaneously they do not have the same scope and do not always regulate the same issues. International humanitarian law has little or nothing to say on some matters governed by human rights law, such as the right to education[89] and the right to marry. The reverse is also true. Whereas human rights law talks in broad generalities, particular issues such as the treatment of prisoners of war and of civilians in occupied territories are extensively regulated under international humanitarian law, often in great detail. Human rights law, for example, says nothing about the enlistment of children into formations or organizations subordinate to an occupying Power, nor prohibits propaganda aimed at encouraging Protected Persons' voluntary enlistment into the armed or auxiliary forces of an occupying Power.[90] Neither does it require that the canteens of civilian internment camps sell tobacco or soap 'at prices not higher than market prices'.[91]

But what about situations when both bodies of law apply? In its *Nuclear Weapons* Advisory Opinion, the International Court of Justice applied the principle in the context of interpreting a general norm (the prohibition of arbitrary killing in the International Covenant on Civil and Political Rights) by reference to more specific rules (those

---

[87] *Supra* n.36, at 178.
[88] *Supra* n.77, at 243.
[89] Although for obvious reasons, the conditions for the enjoyment of this right can be seriously affected in situations of conflict.
[90] Articles 50 and 51, Geneva Convention IV relative to the Protection of Civilian Persons in Time of War (1949).
[91] Article 96, *ibid*.

governing the use of lethal force in international humanitarian law). International humanitarian law did not displace the human rights treaty norm, which continued to apply; it simply defined the standard for its application in situations of armed conflict. The same, it is argued, can be done in relation to Article 9(1) of the International Covenant, which provides, *inter alia*, that: 'No one shall be subjected to arbitrary arrest or detention.' In that way, the legality of detention and internment in armed conflict can be assessed using the yardstick of international humanitarian law.[92]

Certainly, the Inter-American Commission and Court of Human Rights have interpreted the American Convention on Human Rights, as it applies in situations of armed conflict, by reference to the requirements of international humanitarian law.[93] Although originally the Commission maintained it could apply international humanitarian law directly, following the Court's admonitions, it now has accepted that humanitarian law can only be used in order to interpret the requirements of the American Convention in situations of conflict. As Judge Sergio Garcia Ramirez stated in the *Bámaca Velásquez* case:

> It is not an issue of directly applying [Common] Article 3 ... but of admitting the facts provided for this whole system of laws – to which this principle belongs – in order to interpret the meaning of a norm that the Court must apply directly.[94]

The European Convention on Human Rights, however, is said to be different. Article 2 of the Convention provides an exhaustive list of exceptions to the right to life, with Article 15 requiring derogation from Article 2 to legalize deaths resulting from lawful acts of war. Similarly, Article 5 provides an exhaustive list of exceptions to the right to liberty and security of the person, which do not include detention or internment during an armed conflict or belligerent occupation. Hence, the European Commission on Human Rights held that, in the absence of derogation, the detention of prisoners of war by Turkey during its 1974 invasion of Cyprus was unlawful.[95] However, there are signs that the Court's jurisprudence, at least regarding Article 2 of the European Convention, has developed so as to apply, when it considers appropriate, standards derived from international humanitarian law. In its 2009 judgment in *Varnava and others v. Turkey*, the Grand Chamber of the European Court of Human Rights stated in terms that:

> Article 2 must be interpreted in so far as possible in light of the general principles of international law, including the rules of international humanitarian law which play an

---

[92] Whether this is entirely correct, however, may be doubted.
[93] See L. Zegveld, 'The Inter-American Commission on Human Rights and International Humanitarian Law: A Comment on the *Tablada* Case', (1998) 324 *IRRC* 505; and L. Moir, 'International Humanitarian Law and the Inter-American Human Rights System', (2003) 25 *HRQ* 182.
[94] *Bámaca Velásquez* case, Judgment of 25 November 2000, Series C: Decisions and Judgments No. 70, Separate Opinion of Judge Sergio Garcia Ramirez, at para. 24.
[95] *Cyprus v. Turkey*, Appl. nos 6780/74 and 6950/75, Report of the Commission, 10 July 1976. Françoise Hampson calls this an 'absurd' result: *supra* n.45, at 565.

indispensable and universally-accepted role in mitigating the savagery and inhumanity of armed conflict.[96]

As Cordula Droege has shown, the European Court in practice distinguishes between killings by state agents committed in situations of normality and those of crisis,[97] a distinction made even more apparent in the Court's recent judgment in *Finogenov and others v. Russia*.[98]

However, the extent to which human rights law rules concerning the right to life should be interpreted according to international humanitarian law remains unclear. The cases decided by the European Court of Human Rights have dealt with deaths either as a result of combat between government forces and organized armed groups or of attacks on civilians or the civilian population. As yet, there have been few decisions concerning the killing of members (or suspected members) of organized armed groups when they were not taking a direct part in hostilities. Under international humanitarian law, it is argued, such persons can be targeted at all times if they are exercising a 'continuous combat function'.[99] In the *Targeted Killings* case, however, the Israeli Supreme Court, drawing on human rights law, did not take an absolute view but admitted their lawfulness in some circumstances.[100] International human rights bodies, faced with the necessity to decide individual complaints, may well take a similar view,[101] holding the killing of members of organized armed groups legally justified only when other methods of neutralizing them (in particular, through their capture and detention) are not available.

Even if human rights bodies use international humanitarian law to interpret human rights law, they may develop their own perceptions of what international humanitarian law permits. Two examples can be given. The first concerns the idea, advanced in the *Interpretative Guidance on the Notion of Direct Participation in Hostilities under International Humanitarian Law* published by the ICRC that members of organized

---

[96] *Varnava and others v. Turkey*, Appl. Nos 16064/90, 16065/90, 16068/90, 16070/90, 16072/90 and 16073, Judgment of 2009, para. 185.

[97] *Supra* n.24, at 530–533. The cases instanced by Droege where the latter approach prevailed are *Ergi v. Turkey*, Appl. No. 23818/94, Judgment of 28 July 1998, Reports 1998-IV; *Ahmet Özkan v. Turkey and others v. Turkey*, Appl. No. 21689/93, Judgment of 6 April 2004; *Isayeva, Yusopova and Bazayeva v. Russia*, Appl. Nos 57947/00, 57948/00 and 57949/00, Judgment of 24 February 2005; and *Isayeva v. Russia*, Appl. No. 57950/00, Judgment of 24 February 2005.

[98] Appl. Nos 18299/03 and 27311/03, Judgment of 20 December 2011, at paras 212–216. The Court specifically referenced *Isayeva* (*ibid.*), to justify its approach. It is highly doubtful that international humanitarian law applied to the siege of the Dubrovka Theatre but this does not negate the argument that the Court is now applying two standards according to the situation.

[99] ICRC, *Interpretative Guidance on the Notion of Direct Participation in Hostilities under International Humanitarian Law* (Geneva: ICRC, 2003), at 71–73.

[100] *Public Committee against Torture v. Government of Israel*, Judgment of 11 December 2006, HCJ 769/02.

[101] See *Guerrero v. Colombia*, Human Rights Committee, Communication No. R.11/45, UN Doc. Supp. No. 40 (A/37/40), 31 March 1992.

armed groups can have a 'continuous combat function' so that they are classed as participating directly in hostilities, and, as such, can be targeted at all times. This, it has been argued, is questionable as a matter of international humanitarian law insofar as it is contrary to specific treaty language.[102] A second example also concerns the *Interpretative Guidance*, which provides that:

> the kind and degree of force which is permissible against persons not entitled to protection against direct attack must not exceed what is actually necessary to accomplish a legitimate military purpose in the prevailing circumstances.[103]

This recommendation is justified by reference, not to human rights law, but to 'the fundamental principles of military necessity and humanity which underline and inform the entire normative framework of IHL'.[104] It has been the subject of considerable criticism,[105] in particular on the grounds that it has no basis in *lex lata* and that it seeks inappropriately to introduce human rights concepts in international humanitarian law. Nonetheless, it is likely to be attractive to human rights bodies, given its resemblance to the general rule under human rights law that the use of lethal force is only permitted when necessary to achieve a legitimate purpose.

6. CONCLUSION

By abandoning the idea that international humanitarian law, as a branch of law, is *lex specialis* to human rights law's *lex generalis*, the International Court of Justice opened the way to admitting that the relationship can run both ways. For example, torture is prohibited both as a matter of human rights and humanitarian law.[106] However, as none of the humanitarian law instruments defines what torture is, so the definition in human rights law has been used to define the extent of the prohibition in international humanitarian law.[107] What a 'regularly constituted court, affording all the judicial guarantees which are recognized as indispensable by civilized peoples' under Common Article 3 might entail has been defined by reference to Article 75 of Additional

---

[102] Report of the Special Rapporteur on extrajudicial, summary and arbitrary executions, *supra* n.68, at para. 65.
[103] *Supra* n.100, Recommendation IX, at 17.
[104] *Ibid.*, at 78.
[105] For a particularly intemperate example, see W.H. Park, 'Part IX of the ICRC "Direct Participation in Hostilities" Study: No Mandate, No Expertise and Legally Incorrect', (2010) 47 *NYUJILP* 769. A more measured critique is Kleffner, *supra* n.30.
[106] On the human rights side, see Article 3, European Convention on Human Rights; Article 7, International Covenant on Civil and Political Rights; Article 5, American Convention on Human Rights; and the Convention against Torture. As regards international humanitarian law, see Common Article 3 of the Geneva Conventions and Article 75, Additional Protocol I.
[107] See *Prosecutor v. Furundzija*, case no. IT-95-17/1, Judgment of the Trial Chamber, 10 December 1998, para. 159.

Protocol I, seen as reflecting customary international law.[108] The content of Article 75, however, was itself inspired by Article 14 of the International Covenant on Civil and Political Rights, so that reference to Article 14 can be made in order to elucidate the content of both Article 75 and Common Article 3 insofar as they relate to criminal proceedings.[109] In other words, when the same matter is governed by both human rights law and humanitarian law, the more general rule (whatever its origin) is interpreted by reference to the more specific. What is important is the relationship between particular norms in the context of their application. As Cordula Droege has put it: 'In determining which rule is the more specialized one, the most important indicators are the precision and clarity of a rule and its adaptation to the particular circumstances of the case.'[110]

Applied in such a manner, the *lex specialis* principle can be seen as an aspect of the 'principle of systemic integration' said to be inherent in international law.[111] Because treaties are creatures of international law, they cannot be viewed in isolation but, however wide their subject matter, are subject to limitation and interpretation by reference to the international legal system of which they form part,[112] including other applicable treaty rules.[113] From this perspective, the principle is, as Marko Milanović has put it, not a rule of norm conflict resolution but of norm conflict avoidance.[114] It certainly does not imply the disapplication of one body of law (human rights law) in favour of the other (international humanitarian law) when both govern a matter.

But what happens if the two bodies of law cannot be read together? If they do mandate – or permit – different outcomes? Milanović shows that there are only few rules of norm-conflict resolution in international law,[115] all of which have limited application in the context of the relationship between international humanitarian law and human rights law. However, most inconsistencies between the rules of the two bodies of law are not true conflicts at all, as they do not require states to conduct themselves in different ways. Rather, it is simply that international humanitarian law is the more permissive system; states' belligerent rights under international humanitarian law are wider than their sovereign rights as limited by human rights law. In such situations, to argue that the two bodies of law are 'complementary and mutually

---

[108] See *Hamdan v. Rumsfeld* 548 US 557 (2006), 633 (Opinion of Justice Stevens, joined by Justices Souter, Ginsburg and Breyer).

[109] *Ibid.* (albeit only in a footnote).

[110] *Supra* n.24, at 524.

[111] See International Law Commission, 'Conclusions of the work of the Study Group on the Fragmentation of International Law: Difficulties arising from the Diversification and Expansion of International Law' (2006), *Yearbook of the International Law Commission*, 2006, vol. II, Part Two, para. 19; and C. McLachlan, 'The Principle of Systemic Integration and Article 31(3)(c) of the Vienna Convention on the Law of Treaties', (2005) 54 *ICLQ* 279.

[112] McLachlan, *ibid.*, at 280.

[113] *Ibid.*, at 313–315.

[114] M. Milanović, 'A Norm Conflict Perspective on the Relationship between International Humanitarian and Human Rights Law', (2009) 14 *JCSL* 459. See also McLachlan, who states that: 'The principle of systemic integration in treaty interpretation operates before an irreconcilable conflict of norms has arisen.' See McLachlan, *supra* n.111, at 318.

[115] He instances *jus cogens*, Article 103 of the Charter of the United Nations, conflict clauses in treaties and *lex posterior*: *ibid.*, at 466.

reinforcing'[116] or, to put it another way, that they act as belt and braces,[117] is to do little more than issue a policy prescription.

In reality, in such cases states have to make a choice as regards which rules they wish to comply (a choice which is likely to be a political one) and take the consequences. There are fundamental incompatibilities between international humanitarian law and human rights law, not only as regards discrete rules but in their theoretical bases. Attempts can be made to reconcile them, to avoid conflicts, but they can only be provisional and on a case-by-case basis. The legal tools available cannot always provide an answer: with absent legislation, conflicts will remain. And in a world of states with differing interests and values, the adoption of new rules governing armed conflict and belligerent occupation will be difficult, if not impossible.

One difference between the two bodies of rules, in particular, remains fundamental. Despite developments over past decades which are said to indicate a 'humanization of humanitarian law',[118] international humanitarian law, in contrast to human rights law, is not based on an individual rights paradigm. Human rights treaties frequently require review of situations of possible human rights violations; for example, by requiring access to a court to challenge the legality of a person's detention[119] or obliging states to undertake effective investigations of allegations of torture and arbitrary killing.[120] When individuals consider their rights have been violated, they have an individual right to a remedy; that is, to have the matter adjudicated upon, either by a national court or some international body. And if a violation is found, they have an individual right to reparation.[121] This is not to argue that international humanitarian law does not provide for investigations, remedies or reparations; simply that it does not do so at the behest of individuals.[122] It is this difference, even excluding the differences in the substantive protections accorded individuals under the two bodies of law, which will ensure that

---

[116] Human Rights Council Res. 9/9: Protection of the human rights of civilians in armed conflict, 24 September 2008.

[117] W.A. Schabas, 'Lex Specialis? Belt and Suspenders? The Parallel Operation of Human Rights Law and the Law of Armed Conflict, and the Conundrum of Jus ad Bellum', (2007) 40 Israel LR 592.

[118] T. Meron, 'The Humanization of Humanitarian Law', (2000) 94 AJIL 243.

[119] Article 5(4), European Convention on Human Rights (1959); Article 9(4), International Covenant on Civil and Political Rights (1966); and Article 7(7), American Convention on Human Rights (1969).

[120] See McCann and others v. UK, Judgment of 27 September 1995, Series A No. 324, and Assenov v. Bulgaria, Judgment of 28 October 1998, Reports 1998-VIII (European Convention on Human Rights); Velásquez-Rodríguez v. Honduras, Judgment of 29July 1988, Series C No. 4 (American Convention on Human Rights); Human Rights Committee, General Comment No. 31, supra n.58, at para. 8 (International Covenant on Civil and Political Rights).

[121] Article 41, European Convention on Human Rights (1959); Article 2(3), International Covenant on Civil and Political Rights (1966); and Article 63, American Convention on Human Rights (1969). See also GA Res. 60/147 (2005): Basic Principles and Guidelines on the Right to a Remedy and Reparation for Victims of Gross Violations of International Human Rights Law and Serious Violations of International Humanitarian Law.

[122] See P. d'Argent, Les réparations de guerre en droit international public: la responsabilité internationale des États à l'épreuve de la guerre (Brussels: Bruylant, 2002); and E. Chiara-Gillard, 'Reparations for Violations of International Humanitarian Law', (2003) 85 IRRC 529.

individuals continue to bring complaints regarding their treatment in situations of armed conflict before human rights bodies. And even if human rights bodies take the view that states' human rights obligations in situations of armed conflict are to be interpreted using the yardstick of international humanitarian law, their interpretations of humanitarian law are likely to differ from lawyers advising states' defence ministries and armed forces, who are likely to continue to be unhappy with such trespasses into what they see as their *chasse gardée*.

14. War crimes
Robert Cryer

1. INTRODUCTION

War crimes are a criminalized sub-set of violations of the law of armed conflict. As such, given their link to armed conflict, the relationship of the law of war crimes to peace and security hardly needs explanation. The law of war crimes is an old area of international criminal law. Trials for what would now be called war crimes have been a frequent occurrence throughout history. That said, the majority of the developments in the law of war crimes occurred in the twentieth century. This chapter will begin with a discussion of the concept of war crimes and its development. It will then discuss the relationship that the modern law of war crimes has with the law of armed conflict. It will then move on to discuss the substantive norms that make up war crimes law, and the implementation of the rules in this area of law.

2. THE HISTORY AND DEVELOPMENT OF THE LAW OF WAR CRIMINALITY

Depending on how far back it is considered worthwhile looking, prosecutions for war crimes, or at least their analogues, can be traced back a long way in history.[1] Rather like the history of international humanitarian law, which can be traced back to practically all of the major world civilizations in some form or another,[2] the law of war crimes is both old and trans-civilizational.[3] Even if it is the case that the well-known von Hagenbach trial in 1474[4] was not really a precedent for modern war crimes trials,[5] at the very latest in the mid to late nineteenth century, the right of states to prosecute violations of the law of armed conflict was generally accepted. Perhaps the most notable examples of prosecutions for such violations then occurred in the American

---

[1] For a very useful history see, generally, T.L.H. McCormack, 'From Sun Tzu to the Sixth Committee: The Evolution of an International Criminal Law Regime', in T.L.H. McCormack and G.J. Simpson (eds), *The Law of War Crimes: National and International Approaches* (The Hague: Nijhoff, 1997), 31.

[2] See, for example, R. Cryer, *Prosecuting International Crimes: Selectivity and the International Criminal Law Regime* (Cambridge: Cambridge University Press, 2005), Chapter 1.

[3] See McCormack, *supra* n.1.

[4] G. Schwarzenberger, *International Law as Applied by International Courts and Tribunals; vol II: The Law of Armed Conflict* (London: Stevens and Sons, 1968), Chapter 39.

[5] McCormack, *supra* n.1, at 38.

Civil War, in particular the prosecution of Henry Wirtz with respect to the Andersonville Prisoner of War Camp.[6] Such prosecutions, though, gave rise to the interesting question, at least at the time, of whether international law directly provided for individual liability, or whether it simply provided for the lawful assertion of domestic jurisdiction over enemy belligerents.

The modern law of war crimes, in the sense that they are direct violations of international law, can be traced, if not before,[7] to the Report of the Commission on the Authors of the War and Enforcement that was set up in the aftermath of the First World War. The Commission, in spite of determining that aggression was not a crime in existing international law, said that there was responsibility under international law for violations of the laws and customs of war and the laws of humanity. They therefore recommended that prosecutions occurred on the basis of '[t]he principles of the law of nations as they result from the usages established among civilised peoples, from the laws of humanity and from the dictates of public conscience'.[8] This was subject to a dissent by the US members of the Commission, who said that they knew of 'no international statute or convention making violation of the laws and customs of war –not to speak of the laws or principles of humanity – an international crime'.[9] The Japanese members of the Commission felt similarly,[10] but these were, in the end, dissents rather than the view of the majority, who asserted that there was direct liability under international law for violations of the law of armed conflict.[11] The Majority gave a list of various war crimes, including rape and abduction of women and girls for enforced prostitution.[12]

The Report, however, did not lead to a large practical advance in the enforcement of the law of armed conflict. The attempts to bring the Kaiser to an 'arraignment' for a 'supreme offence against international morality and the sanctity of treaties' for starting the War, in the words of Article 227 of the Treaty of Versailles, led to nothing, owing to the refusal of the Netherlands to extradite him.[13] This was on the basis that the offence was a political, rather than a legal one, a position that was not fatuous. The prosecutions for war crimes *stricto sensu* in Article 228 of the Treaty of Versailles had little more success. Although that article envisioned prosecutions by the Allies, this did not come to pass. Of the close to 1000 suspects the Allies sought to prosecute, only

---

[6] L.L. Laska and J.M. Smith, '"Hell and the Devil", Andersonville and the Trial of Captain Henry Wirz, C.S.A., 1865', (1975) 68 *Mil L Rev* 77; McCormack, *supra* n.1, at 42.

[7] Which it well could be, even with regard to modern international criminal law, by reference to the first proposal for an international criminal court by Gustav Moynier in 1872. See C.K. Hall, 'The First Proposal for a Permanent International Criminal Court', (1998) 38 *IRRC* 57.

[8] Report of the Commission on the Responsibility of the Authors of the War and Enforcement, (1920) 14 *AJIL* 95, at 122.

[9] *Ibid.*, at 146. The American representatives considered the 'principles of humanity' to be too vague for criminal law. *Ibid.*, at 144–145.

[10] *Ibid.*, at 152.

[11] *Ibid.*, at 122.

[12] *Ibid.*, at 113–115.

[13] See, for example, M. Cherif Bassiouni, 'World War I: The War to End All Wars and the Birth of a Handicapped International Criminal Justice System', (2001–2002) 30 *Denv J Intl L & Pol* 244.

twelve were brought to trial before the *Lansdgericht* in Leipzig.[14] Although those people were prosecuted for violations of German law, the trials led to questionable acquittals and lenient sentences. The experience was perhaps best summed up by Leo Gross, who said that '[t]he Versailles experiment taught the Allies at least one lesson, namely how *not* to set about trying German war criminals'.[15]

In the inter-war period there were some limited developments in the law of war crimes; in particular there were some suggestions that there ought to be an international criminal court to prosecute war crimes. These suggestions, however, fell on the stony ground of state indifference, although the idea of direct individual responsibility for violations of the law of armed conflict was becoming increasingly accepted.[16] This tracked the increasing acceptance in the inter-war period that individuals could be the subject of rights and duties under international law irrespective of domestic law.[17] The development was not complete, however. Article 29 of the 1929 Geneva Convention on the Wounded and Sick required domestic legislation to repress violations.[18] Equally, this is not inconsistent with direct liability in international law, but relates more to the question of domestic application of international law.

Even during the Second World War, there were some questions about whether international law directly criminalized violations of the laws and customs of war, or whether prosecutions for war crimes were, in fact, internationally sanctioned prosecutions under domestic law. For example, even commentators such as Manfred Lachs equivocated on this point.[19] On the other hand, such *eminences grises* as Sir Hersch Lauterpacht and Quincy Wright, both of whom had a large influence on Allied policy on war crimes, took a strong line in favour of the view that war crimes were directly criminalized by international law.[20]

At the Nuremberg International Military Tribunal (hereinafter 'IMT') the Court determined, in probably its most famous holding, that:

> crimes against international law are committed by men, not abstract entities, and only by punishing individuals who commit such crimes can the provisions of international law be

---

[14] As McCormack notes, though the Allies, in the end, submitted forty-five names to the German authorities for prosecution. McCormack, *supra* n.1, at 49.

[15] L. Gross, 'The Punishment of War Criminals, The Nuremberg Trial', in L. Gross (ed.), *Selected Essays on International Law and Organisation* (Ardsley: Transnational, 1984), 133, at 136.

[16] See, for example, McCormack, *supra* n.1, at 51–55.

[17] See, somewhat sceptically, K. Parlett, *The Individual in the International Legal System: Continuity and Change in International Law* (Cambridge: Cambridge University Press, 2011), at 176–180.

[18] 118 LNTS 303.

[19] M. Lachs, *War Crimes: An Attempt to Define the Issues* (London: Stevens and Sons, 1944).

[20] H. Lauterpacht, 'The Law of Nations and the Punishment of War Crimes', (1944) 21 *BYIL* 58; Q. Wright, 'The Law of the Nuremberg Trial', (1947) 41 *AJIL* 38. Wright was the advisor to Robert Jackson, US Chief Prosecutor at Nuremberg. On Lauterpacht's influence see M. Koskenniemi, 'Hersch Lauterpacht and the Development of International Criminal Law', (2004) 2 *JICJ* 810.

enforced ... individuals have international duties which transcend the national obligations of obedience imposed by the individual state.[21]

With specific reference to the laws of armed conflict, the Nuremberg IMT opined that:

> the crimes defined by Article 6, section (b) were already recognized as war crimes under international law. They were covered by Articles 46, 50, 52 and 56 of the Hague Convention of 1907 and Articles 2, 3, 4, 46 and 51 of the Geneva Convention of 1929. That violation of these provisions constituted crimes for which the guilty individuals were punishable is too well settled to admit argument.[22]

Although many prosecutions (particularly in the civil law systems) after the War occurred on the basis of domestic law that required the relevant war crime to also be a violation of domestic law,[23] this was not considered necessary by many courts, including the Nuremberg 'subsequent proceedings' undertaken by the US.[24] The developments of the time were perhaps most accurately summarized by the Special Tribunal for Lebanon, which explained:

> [War crimes were] originally born at the domestic level: States began to prosecute and punish members of the enemy military (then gradually also of their own military) who had performed acts that were termed either as criminal offences perpetrated in time of war (killing of innocent civilians, wanton destruction of private property, serious ill-treatment of prisoners of war, and so on), or as breaches of the laws and customs of war. Gradually this domestic practice received international sanction, first through the Versailles Treaty (1919) and the following trials before the German Supreme Court at Leipzig (1921), then through the London Agreement of 1945 and the trials at Nuremberg. Thus, the domestic criminalisation of breaches of international humanitarian law led to the international criminalisation of those breaches and the formation of rules of customary international law authorising or even imposing their punishment.[25]

Even so it ought to be noted that when the Geneva Conventions of August 1949 (hereinafter 'GCs') were drafted, the famous grave breaches provisions, which quite clearly relate to war crimes, studiously avoided that terminology.[26] As has been said, '[o]riginally war crimes and grave breaches were distinct concepts in international law'.[27] It was only in 1977, in Additional Protocol I (hereinafter 'AP I'), that it was

---

[21] Nuremberg IMT, 'Judgment and Sentence', (1947) 41 *AJIL* 171, at 221.
[22] *Ibid.*
[23] For example, *Wagner* III LRTWC, 23, at 50–54.
[24] For a comprehensive analysis see K.J. Heller, *The Nuremberg Military Tribunals and the Origins of International Criminal Law* (Oxford: Oxford University Press, 2011).
[25] Special Tribunal for Lebanon, Interlocutory Decision on the Applicable Law: Terrorism, Conspiracy, Homicide, Perpetration, Cumulative Charging, STL-11-01-17*bis*, 16 February 2011, at para. 104.
[26] M.D. Öberg, 'The Absorption of Grave Breaches into War Crimes Law', (2009) 91 *IRRC* 163, at 163; H. Fischer, 'Grave Breaches of the 1949 Geneva Conventions', in G. Kirk-McDonald and O. Swaak-Goldman (eds), *Substantive and Procedural Aspects of International Criminal Law* (The Hague: Kluwer, 2000), 65, at 70–71.
[27] Fischer, *ibid.*

expressly accepted that grave breaches were, in fact, war crimes.[28] On the other hand, it was accepted in the 1968 Convention on the Non-applicability of Statutory Limitations to War Crimes and Crimes Against Humanity that war crimes were, *apropos* Nuremberg, international crimes *per se*.[29] By this time it was clear that war crimes were, in and of themselves, international crimes, albeit as with all international crimes, without international tribunals to enforce them, that job being delegated, for better or for worse, to domestic courts.

3. THE RELATIONSHIP OF WAR CRIMES LAW TO THE LAW OF ARMED CONFLICT

The above raises the question of the relationship of the law of war crimes and the law of armed conflict. Is a war crime any violation of the law of armed conflict, or is more required? This has been the subject of considerable debate. The Nuremberg IMT seemingly did not consider this an important issue, probably as the conduct for which the defendants were being tried would have fallen under any reasonable definition of war crimes.[30] There was more discussion of the matter in Tokyo, where one of the dissentients raised the issue of whether or not all violations of the law of armed conflict were criminalized. Speaking of certain violations of the law of war, especially the use of Allied Prisoners of War in work related to the Japanese war effort, Judge Pal asserted that he 'would consider this violation a mere delinquency on the part of the state. Those are mere acts of state. I would not make any of the accused criminally responsible for them.'[31] It ought to be noted, though, that Pal cited no authority for the distinction he suggested, and there is more than a little suspicion that he was making an argument that was convenient for his own purposes rather than one that was based on a coherent approach to the law, not least as they were serious violations of the laws of armed conflict at the time, as they are now.[32]

Nowadays there are three basic ideas about the way in which the law of war crimes and the law of armed conflict interrelate. The first is that any violation of humanitarian law is automatically a war crime. Although this has the advantage of simplicity, and

---

[28] Article 85(5), Protocol Additional to the Geneva Conventions of 12 August 1949, and relating to the Protection of Victims of International Armed Conflicts (Protocol I) (1977) 1125 UNTS 3. Although see Fischer, *ibid.*, at 167.

[29] Convention on the Non-Applicability of Statutory Limitations to War Crimes and Crimes Against Humanity, GA Res. 2931, 754 UNTS 73.

[30] Although with respect to unrestricted submarine warfare, the defence made a clever case about the lawfulness of that practice that led the Nuremberg IMT into an uncomfortable, and unconvincing, contortion. See T. Taylor, *The Anatomy of the Nuremberg Trials* (London: Bloomsbury, 1993), at 566–568.

[31] Dissenting Opinion of the Member from India, reprinted in N. Boister and R. Cryer (eds), *Documents on the Tokyo International Military Tribunal: Charter, Indictment, Judgments* (Oxford: Oxford University Press, 2009), 809, at 1396–1397.

[32] See N. Boister and R. Cryer, *The Tokyo International Military Tribunal: A Reappraisal* (Oxford: Oxford University Press, 2008), 188–189.

some support in practice,[33] it has been subjected to considerable criticism on the basis that there are certain technical aspects of humanitarian law (such as the requirement that Prisoners of War may purchase tobacco at local market prices) that do not readily or appropriately lend themselves to criminalization.[34] This is true, and leads to the better view, that all serious violations of humanitarian law are war crimes.[35]

This is not enough for some. George Abi-Saab, to take one example, has written that '[i]t is not enough, as is currently done, simply to use adjectives, by describing the violation as "serious" or "Grave" or the violated norm as "fundamental". Such a question-begging approach is neither valid nor operational as a distinguishing criterion.'[36] Some doubt may be expressed about the difficulty which actually arises in practice on this, but the International Criminal Tribunal for the Former Yugoslavia (hereinafter 'ICTY') has traditionally taken the view that more is required, opining in its classic *Tadić* Opinion that to prosecute a violation of humanitarian law as a war crime four criteria have to be fulfilled, which are that:

i. the violation must constitute an infringement of a rule of international humanitarian law;
ii. the rule must be customary in nature or, if it belongs to treaty law, the required conditions must be met;
iii. the violation must be 'serious,' that is to say, it must constitute a breach of a rule protecting important values, and the breach must involve grave consequences for the victim; and
iv. the violation must entail, under customary or conventional law, the individual criminal responsibility of the person breaching the rule.[37]

There is little authority for this last condition,[38] but it, as well as the requirement that the violation of humanitarian law must be 'serious' for it to amount to a war crime, might imply that there is a separate substantive regime between the law of armed conflict and the law of war crimes. In other words, the same general norms in humanitarian law and war crimes law might be interpreted or applied differently, or have a broader or narrower substantive content. Fortunately, since further fragmentation of international law in this area would be unfortunate, the ICTY, for the vast majority of cases, has taken the law of war crimes to contain a *renvoi* to the relevant humanitarian law, rather than to a separate general regime of humanitarian law to those

---

[33] For example, both the Nuremberg and Tokyo IMTs' Statutes defined war crimes as 'violations of the laws and customs of war'. See, for example, R. Cryer, '*Galić* and the War Crime of Terror Bombing', (2005–2006) 2 *IDF Law Review* 73, at 95–96.

[34] R. Cryer, H. Friman, D. Robinson and E. Wilmshurst, *An Introduction to International Criminal Law and Procedure*, 2nd edn (Cambridge: Cambridge University Press, 2010), at 225–226.

[35] See, for example, C. Greenwood, 'International Humanitarian Law and the *Tadić* Case', (1996) 7 *EJIL* 265, at 279–280.

[36] G. Abi-Saab, 'The Concept of War Crimes', in S. Yee and W. Tieya (eds), *International Law and the Post-Cold War World: Essays in Honour of Li Haopei* (London: Routledge, 2001), 99, at 112.

[37] *Prosecutor v. Tadić*, Decision on Interlocutory Appeal on Jurisdiction, IT-94-1-AR72, 2 October 1995, at para. 94.

[38] See Cryer, *supra* n.33.

underlying norms.[39] However, there are areas of dissonance which cannot be ignored. This issue can be seen quite clearly in certain provisions of the Rome Statute of the International Criminal Court (hereinafter 'ICC').[40]

Looking briefly to the relationship between international criminal law and human rights law, they have considerable overlaps,[41] but are, like human rights law and humanitarian law, subject to different interpretative principles. It is often taken as read that human rights law is subject to broad, relatively free interpretation.[42] International criminal law, on the other hand, under the influence of principles such as legality, *in dubio pro reo* and the prohibition of analogy, ought to warrant a more narrow interpretative stance, but in practice international criminal law sometimes falls short of fulfilling a strict interpretation of such principles.[43] In part for these reasons, Darryl Robinson is sceptical of this partial convergence between these areas of law, asserting that:

> The assumptions of human rights and humanitarian lawyers can also distort ICL [international criminal law] reasoning through substantive and structural conflation. Many of the prohibitions of ICL are drawn from, and similar to, prohibitions in human rights and humanitarian law. Faced with familiar-looking provisions, ICL practitioners often assume that the ICL norms are coextensive with their human rights or humanitarian law counterparts, and uncritically transplant concepts and jurisprudence from other domains to flesh out their content. Such assumptions overlook the fact that these bodies of law have different purposes and consequences and thus entail different philosophical commitments.[44]

On the other hand, Hans-Peter Gasser has said: 'international criminal law, human rights law and international humanitarian law have different origins. They have developed each in their own way – up to a certain point. Today the three domains meet together. Their principal legal instruments must be read in conjunction with each other.'[45] This position can be supported in relation to the ICTY as Article 13 of its Statute requires that when composing chambers, 'due account shall be had to the experience of the judges in criminal law, international law, including international

---

[39] There is one possible exception: the Trial Chamber's decision in the *Vasiljević* case, *Prosecutor v. Vasiljević*, Judgment, IT-98-32-T, 29 November 2002, at paras 193–204. See R. Cryer, 'Commentary: Prosecutor v Vasiljević', in G. Sluiter and A. Klip (eds), *Annotated Leading Cases of the International Criminal Tribunals: Volume XI* (Antwerp: Intersentia, 2007), 688.

[40] See *infra*, text accompanying notes 98 ff.

[41] See R. Cryer, 'The Interplay of Human Rights and Humanitarian Law: The Approach of the ICTY', (2009) 14 *JCSL* 511.

[42] Although for a contrary view see J. Christoffersen, 'Impact on General Principles of Treaty Interpretation', in M. Kamminga and M. Scheinen (eds), *The Impact of Human Rights Law on General International Law* (Oxford: Oxford University Press, 2009), 37.

[43] See D. Robinson, 'The Identity Crisis of International Criminal Law', (2008) 21 *LJIL* 925.

[44] *Ibid.*, at 946.

[45] H.-P. Gasser, 'The Changing Relationship Between International Criminal Law, Human Rights Law and Humanitarian Law', in M. Cherif Bassiouni *et al.* (eds), *The Legal Regime of the International Criminal Court: Essays in Memory of Igor Blischenko* (Leiden: Nijhoff, 2009), 1111, at 1117.

humanitarian law and human rights law'. In addition, looking to the ICC, Article 21 of the Rome Statute requires that its interpretation of the Statute must be consistent with human rights law, which gives the ICC quite a broad interpretative mandate on point.[46] This is not to say that the areas are fused. They are not.

4. THE SUBSTANTIVE LAW OF WAR CRIMES: THE CONTEXT

To move on to the substantive law of war crimes, much of what it covers involves a great deal of conduct that would also amount to domestic crimes. Not all such conduct amounts to a war crime, however, even when committed in times of armed conflict. Thefts by civilians in occupied territory, for example, are not transformed into war crimes simply because the law of armed conflict is applicable to the situation in general.[47] There has to be what is known as a nexus to the armed conflict. The most detailed jurisprudence on point has come from the ICTY, although for the ICC, the issue is dealt with in the Elements of Crimes.[48]

The international tribunals have consistently required that there be an armed conflict for a war crime to exist. This is, in some ways obvious, although it is rendered more complex in situations of low-level violence (such as that at the outset of the Libyan conflict in 2011) or where there is the possibility of internationalized armed conflicts. The authoritative pronouncement on the nexus in the ICTY is the *Kunarac* case.[49] In this case the Appeals Chamber explained (on the basis of the *Tadić* jurisdictional decision, which had determined the point) that there were two basic requirements: that there is an armed conflict, and that 'the acts of the accused must be closely related to' it.[50] Furthermore, it is not required that fighting is actually going on in the place where the conduct occurs as the laws of armed conflict apply:

> in the whole territory of the warring states or, in the case of internal armed conflicts, the whole territory under the control of a party to the conflict, whether or not actual combat takes place there, and continue to apply until a general conclusion of peace or, in the case of internal armed conflicts, until a peaceful settlement is achieved.[51]

---

[46] R. Young, 'Internationally Recognised Human Rights Before the International Criminal Court', (2011) 60 *ICLQ* 189. See also P. Rowe, 'War Crimes', in D. McGoldrick, P. Rowe and E. Donnelly (eds), *The Permanent International Criminal Court: Legal and Policy Issues* (Oxford: Hart, 2004), 203, at 212–217; Cryer, *supra* n.41.

[47] It ought to be noted that, in spite of some jurisprudence to the contrary, it is settled that war crimes can be committed by civilians as well as officials and rebels. See *Prosecutor v. Akayesu*, Judgment, ICTR-95-1-A, 1 June 2001, at paras 444–445.

[48] These are a detailed set of conditions of liability that are intended to guide the ICC in its interpretation of its substantive criminal law. See W. Schabas, *The International Criminal Court: A Commentary on the Rome Statute* (Oxford: Oxford University Press, 2010), 258.

[49] *Prosecutor v. Kunarac, Kovać and Vuković*, Judgment, IT-96-23-A, 12 June 2002, at para. 58.

[50] *Ibid.*, at para. 55.

[51] *Ibid.*, at para. 57.

From here the Appeals Chamber moved on to explain the nexus that is required, in a passage that is now considered the classic statement of the relevant customary law:

> What ultimately distinguishes a war crime from a purely domestic offence is that a war crime is shaped by or dependent upon the environment – the armed conflict – in which it is committed. It need not have been planned or supported by some form of policy. The armed conflict need not have been causal to the commission of the crime, but the existence of an armed conflict must, at a minimum, have played a substantial part in the perpetrator's ability to commit it, his decision to commit it, the manner in which it was committed or the purpose for which it was committed. Hence, if it can be established ... that the perpetrator acted in furtherance of or under the guise of the armed conflict, it would be sufficient to conclude that his acts were closely related to the armed conflict.[52]

The Chamber also set out some of the criteria that may be taken into account in determining the nexus. These are:

> the fact that the perpetrator is a combatant; the fact that the victim is a non-combatant; the fact that the victim is a member of the opposing party; the fact that the act may be said to serve the ultimate goal of a military campaign; and the fact that the crime is committed as part of or in the context of the perpetrator's official duties.[53]

Horst Fischer suggests that in five situations, a presumption can be made that there is a link to an armed conflict. These are where the conduct relates to:

> the exercise of a specific function, the exercise of specific war aims of the parties, the exploitation of the specific circumstances of the war, in particular the availability of specific weapons, the exploitation of internment circumstances and the exploitation of power given to an occupying force.[54]

These may be useful indicia, but are not self-applying (the concept of exploitation, for example, is a normative conception, that cannot be understood outside its interpretation), and it must be remembered that the presumption of innocence applies as much to war crimes trials as to other criminal trials, which makes presumptions against the defence perilous, although not inherently unlawful in all circumstances.

The ICTY has equivocated on the question of whether or not the perpetrator needs to have knowledge of the conflict. Initially the ICTY did not require it.[55] However, the jurisprudence is now settled that knowledge of the factual circumstances (although not a legal evaluation of those facts) is necessary to found a conviction for war crimes there.[56] Were the Tribunal to require a legal evaluation of the existence of an armed conflict, and its nature, it would be often very difficult to prove. The existence and nature of an armed conflict is a complex issue. For example, the ICTY itself has gone back and forward on the nature of the various conflicts, and if international tribunals

---

[52] *Ibid.*, at para. 58.
[53] *Ibid.*, at para. 59.
[54] Fischer, *supra* n.26, at 82–83.
[55] See, for example, *Prosecutor v. Tadić*, Judgment, IT-94-1-T, 7 March 1997, at para. 572.
[56] *Prosecutor v. Kordić and Čerkez*, Judgment, IT-95-14/2-A, 17 December 2004, at para. 311.

have found the question vexing most soldiers (and civilians) cannot be expected to make such a call in the heat of the moment.

The ICC Elements of Crimes require that the conduct be committed 'in the context of and associated with' an armed conflict. They also make clear that the legal evaluation is not required, either as to the existence of an armed conflict, or its nature. Furthermore, '[t]here is only a requirement for the awareness of the factual circumstances that established the existence of an armed conflict that is implicit in the terms "took place in the context of and was associated with"'.[57] So far, the application of these provisions by the ICC has been largely similar to that by the ICTY,[58] although, as William Schabas has pointed out, the focus on higher-level defendants at the ICC than the ICTY in its early practice has meant that the issue has not been so important in practical terms.[59] It is also fair to say that in most conflicts, the question of whether the fighting has reached the requisite level (rather than the nature of such an armed conflict) is fairly easy to answer.

5. THE MATERIAL CONTENT OF THE LAW OF WAR CRIMES

War crimes law is made up of both treaty and customary international law, which have considerable overlaps.[60] It would not be possible, for reasons of space, to cover all of either in the depth they deserve.[61] What must be borne in mind, however, is that the law of war crimes is parasitic on the law of armed conflict. This chapter will, therefore, concentrate more closely on where there are differences to the underlying substantive norms, or between tribunals, and the most important or innovative war crimes. Similarly, for reasons of space we will begin around the Second World War.

In addition, owing to the distinction in the law of armed conflict between international and non-international conflicts,[62] a similar split runs through the law of war crimes. We will deal with them separately, although, as we will see, there are considerable overlaps between the two, not least as the ICTY, in particular, has deliberately attempted to create a common law applicable to both types of conflict.[63] The ICC Statute maintains the distinction between the two types of conflict, even though, as we will see, there are identical or similar provisions applicable whichever the type of conflict in that treaty.

---

[57] Elements of Crimes, Article 8, introduction ICC-ASP/1/3/.
[58] Equally, see Cryer *et al.*, *supra* n.34, at 286 (n.123).
[59] Schabas, *supra* n.48, at 207.
[60] K. Roberts, 'The Contribution of the ICTY to the Grave Breaches Regime', (2009) 7 *JICJ* 743.
[61] The relevant chapter in Schabas, 'Article 8' *supra* n.48, which only covers the ICC Statute, runs to the best part of seventy pages. W. Fenrick *et al.*, 'Article 8', in Otto Triffterer (ed.), *Commentary on the Rome Statute of the International Criminal Court: Observer's Notes: Article by Article*, 2nd edn (Oxford: Hart, 2008), at 299, is almost 300 pages long.
[62] For more on this distinction see Chapter 8 in this volume by Marko Milanovic and Vidan Hadzi-Vidanovic.
[63] S. Boelaert-Suominen, 'The Yugoslavia Tribunal and the Common Core of Humanitarian Law Applicable to all Armed Conflicts', (2000) 13 *LJIL* 619.

A. International Armed Conflicts

i. Treaty law/international legislation

Although the 1919 Commission on the Responsibility of the Authors of the War referred to various violations of the law of armed conflict, the first instrument that dealt with direct liability for war crimes in treaty law was Article 6(a) of the Nuremberg IMT's Statute, which provided for liability for:

> War crimes: namely, violations of the laws or customs of war. Such violations shall include, but not be limited to, murder, ill treatment or deportation to slave labour or for any purpose of civilian populations of or in occupied territory, murder or ill-treatment of prisoners of war or persons on the seas, killing of hostages, plunder of public or private property, wanton destruction of cities, town or villages, or devastation not justified by military necessity.[64]

It is important to remember that Article 6 was a non-exclusive formula that, by treaty, gave the Nuremberg IMT jurisdiction over all violations of the applicable treaty-based and customary law of armed conflicts that occurred in the European sphere of the Second World War. The Tokyo IMT's provision on point (Article 5(b)) was even more brief, granting that Tribunal jurisdiction over all 'violations of the laws and customs of war' in the Pacific region.

a. The Geneva Conventions of 1949   In the post-war era the most important provisions that related to war crimes were the grave breaches provisions of the GCs.[65] These were usefully parsed in Article 8(2)(a) of the Rome Statute of the ICC (which is very similar to Article 2 of the ICTY Statute). The Rome Statute described grave breaches as follows:

> any of the following acts against persons or property protected under the provisions of the relevant Geneva Convention:
>
> (i) Wilful killing;
> (ii) Torture or inhuman treatment, including biological experiments;
> (iii) Wilfully causing great suffering, or serious injury to body or health;
> (iv) Extensive destruction and appropriation of property, not justified by military necessity and carried out unlawfully and wantonly;
> (v) Compelling a prisoner of war or other protected person to serve in the forces of a hostile Power;
> (vi) Wilfully depriving a prisoner of war or other protected person of the rights of fair and regular trial;
> (vii) Unlawful deportation or transfer or unlawful confinement;
> (viii) Taking of hostages.

Grave breaches of the GCs, as such, were not directly referred to as war crimes in the 1949 Conventions, but this is what they are.[66] They are a sub-category of war crimes that are subject to a specific regime of mandatory, essentially, universal jurisdiction,

---

[64] Nuremberg IMT Statute, at para. 6(b).
[65] See, generally, the symposium in (2009) 7 *JICJ* 653; Fischer, *supra* n.26, at 65.
[66] J.G. Stewart, 'Introduction', (2009) 9 *JICJ* 653, at 653.

owing to their particularly serious nature.[67] In other words, all parties are required to search for, and prosecute, all persons who violate the Conventions.[68] The extent to which that duty is territorially limited, in circumstances such as in peacekeeping operations and occupations, is a matter of considerable controversy. The latter situation is particularly complex, in part owing to the European Court of Human Rights' decision in the *al-Skeini* case that the European Convention on Human Rights applies in many such circumstances, which imposes obligations on parties to that treaty to investigate, if not prosecute, analogous violations of the European Convention.[69]

The grave breaches provisions, as well as the Statutes of international tribunals such as the ICTY (Article 2) or the ICC (Article 8(2)(a)) that have jurisdiction over such offences necessarily refer to the applicability of the Conventions and their protections.[70] These are limited to those persons and property protected by the Conventions.[71] In the *Tadić* jurisdictional decision, the Trial Chamber asserted that Article 2 of the ICTY's Statute (which provided for jurisdiction over Grave Breaches) applied irrespective of the conditions of applicability of the Conventions themselves.[72] At the Appeals level, the Majority were deeply critical of any such suggestion, stating that:

> the Trial Chamber's reasoning is based on a misconception of the grave breaches provisions and the extent of their incorporation into the Statute of the International Tribunal ... The Trial Chamber is right in implying that the enforcement mechanism has of course not been imported into the Statute of the International Tribunal, for the obvious reason that the International Tribunal itself constitutes a mechanism for the prosecution and punishment of the perpetrators of 'grave breaches.' However, the Trial Chamber has misinterpreted the reference to the Geneva Conventions contained in the sentence of Article 2: 'persons or property protected under the provisions of the relevant Geneva Conventions.' (Statute of the Tribunal, art. 2.) ... , this reference is clearly intended to indicate that the offences listed under Article 2 can only be prosecuted when perpetrated against persons or property regarded as 'protected' by the Geneva Conventions under the strict conditions set out by the Conventions themselves.[73]

---

[67] Y. Sandoz, 'The History of the Grave Breaches Regime', (2009) 7 *JICJ* 657, at 674.

[68] Articles 50, 51, 137 and 141 of the respective four Conventions. In spite of high authority to the contrary (B.V.A. Röling, 'The Law of War and the National Jurisdiction Since 1945', (1960-II) 100 *RdC* 329, at 359–363; D.W. Bowett, 'Jurisdiction: Changing Patterns of Authority Over Activities and Resources', (1982) 53 *BYIL* 1, at 12), this obligation is not limited to belligerents; see R. van Elst, 'Implementing Universal Jurisdiction Over Grave Breaches of the Geneva Conventions', (2000) 13 *LJIL* 815, at 821–823. The duty is probably customary. See, for example, C. Kress, 'Reflections on the *Iudicare* Limb of the Grave Breaches Regime', (2009) 7 *JICJ* 789, at 792–795.

[69] *Al-Skeini v. UK*, Judgment, Application no. 55721/07, 7 July 2011.

[70] See, for example, M. Bothe, 'War Crimes', in A. Cassese, P. Gaeta and J.R.W.D. Jones (eds), *The Rome Statute of the International Criminal Court: A Commentary* (Oxford: Oxford University Press, 2001), 379, at 390.

[71] Fischer, *supra* n.26 at 69.

[72] *Prosecutor v. Tadić*, Decision on the Defence Motion on Jurisdiction, IT-94-1-T, 10 August 1995.

[73] *Tadić, supra* n.55, at paras 80–81. See L. Moir, 'Grave Breaches and Internal Armed Conflicts', (2009) 8 *JICJ* 763. Although, as he notes, the grave breaches regime has had an

It is true that such an authority as Georges Abi-Saab has asserted that customary law has developed to encompass grave breaches in non-international armed conflicts.[74] This has, with rare exceptions,[75] been rejected as being beyond what states have accepted, which is that the grave breaches provisions only reflect customary international law for international armed conflicts.[76] The general practice of the ICTY is now only to apply Article 2 of its Statute to international armed conflicts,[77] and to refer to the relevant concepts that it includes to determine protected status. In some cases, such as *Delalić* and *Tadić*, the ICTY has taken a progressive, functional approach to what amounts to nationality for the purposes of the conventions, which has not gone uncommented upon.[78] On other matters, such as the existence of an occupation, the ICTY has also made interesting pronouncements, which deserve further study but which cannot be addressed here.[79]

b. Additional Protocol I [80] Before the grave breaches provisions were ever put into much effect, AP I to the GCs expanded the definition of grave breaches (and described them as war crimes in Article 85(5)). Article 85(1–2) simply expands the grave breaches regimes in the 1949 Conventions to aspects of the law relating to the protection of the wounded, sick and medical personnel which were expanded on in AP I (in ways which were not controversial),[81] and to conflicts included in Article 1(4), that is wars of national liberation (which was).[82] Outside of wars of national liberation, the most controversial aspects of the Protocol relate to the expansion of combatant

---

influence on prosecutions of offences in non-international armed conflicts which are not strictly covered by those provisions.

[74] *Tadić*, Dissenting Opinion of Judge Abi-Saab; discussed by Moir, *supra* n.73, at 772–775, 778ff.

[75] S. Boelaert-Suominen, 'Grave Breaches, Universal Jurisdiction and Internal Armed Conflicts: Is Customary Law Moving Towards a Uniform Enforcement Mechanism for all Armed Conflicts?', (2000) 5 *JCSL* 63.

[76] See, for example, J.-M. Henckaerts, 'The Grave Breaches Regime as Customary International Law', (2009) 7 *JICJ* 683.

[77] Although see A. Cassese, 'On the Current Trends Towards Criminal Prosecution and Punishment of Breaches of International Humanitarian Law', (1998) 9 *EJIL* 2, at 29; See also J. Stewart, 'The Future of the Grave Breaches Regime: Segregate, Assimilate, or Abandon?', (2009) 7 *JICJ* 855, at 861–863.

[78] Both positively and negatively. For an example of the former see T. Meron, 'War Crimes Tribunals: The Record and the Prospects', (1998) *Am U Intl L Rev* 1383, at 1509 as cited in Fischer, *supra* n.26, at 85; Moir, *supra* n.73, at 776–778; D. Fleck, 'Shortcomings of the Grave Breaches Regime', (2009) 7 *JICJ* 833, at 842–844. The latter view receives its most erudite expression in M. Sassoli and L. Olsen, 'The Judgment of the ICTY Appeals Chamber on the Merits in the *Tadić* Case', (2000) 82 *IRRC* 733.

[79] For discussion see Fleck, *ibid.*, at 845–846.

[80] On which see, generally, Y. Sandoz, C. Swiniarski and B. Zimmermann (eds), *Commentary on the Additional Protocols of 8 June 1977* (Geneva: ICRC/Martinus Nijhoff, 1987), 899 and M. Bothe, K.J. Partsch and W.A. Solf, *New Rules for Victims of Armed Conflicts* (The Hague: Martinus Nijhoff, 1982), 507.

[81] See Chapter 11 in this volume by Tom Ruys and Christian De Cock.

[82] As well as violations of Article 11 of AP I, which relates to medical aspects of the care of those in the hands of an adverse party, which was not controversial.

status to those referred to in Articles 44 and 45.[83] AP I goes beyond updating the 1949 grave breaches regime; Article 85(3–4) adds,[84] building upon the provisions in the Protocol itself (many, although not all, of which were already customary),[85] to provide that:

> 3. [in addition to those identified in Article 11] ... the following acts shall be regarded as grave breaches of this Protocol, when committed willfully, in violation of the relevant provisions of this Protocol, and causing death or serious injury to body or health:
>
> (a) Making the civilian population or individual civilians the object of attack;
> (b) Launching an indiscriminate attack affecting the civilian population or civilian objects in the knowledge that such attack will cause excessive loss of life, injury to civilians or damage to civilian objects ... ;
> (c) Launching an attack against works or installations containing dangerous forces in the knowledge that such attack will cause excessive loss of life, injury to civilians or damage to civilian objects ... ;
> (d) Making non-defended localities and demilitarized zones the object of attack;
> (e) Making a person the object of attack in the knowledge that he is *hors de combat*;
> (f) The perfidious use ... of the distinctive emblem of the red cross, red crescent or red lion and sun or of other protective signs recognized by the Conventions of this Protocol.
>
> 4. In addition to the grave breaches defined in the preceding paragraphs and in the Conventions, the following shall be regarded as grave breaches of this Protocol, when committed wilfully[86] and in violation of the Conventions of the Protocol;
>
> (a) The transfer by the Occupying Power of parts of its own civilian population into the territory it occupies, or the deportation or transfer of all or parts of the population of the occupied territory within or outside this territory, in violation of Article 49 of the Fourth Convention;
> (b) Unjustifiable delay in the repatriation of prisoners of war or civilians;
> (c) Practices of apartheid and other inhuman and degrading practices involving outrages upon personal dignity, based on racial discrimination;
> (d) Making the clearly-recognized historic monuments, works of art or places of worship which constitute the cultural or spiritual heritage of peoples and to which special protection has been given by special arrangement, for example, within the framework of a competent international organization, the object of attack, causing as a result extensive destruction thereof, where there is no evidence of the violation by the adverse Party of Article 53, sub-paragraph (b), and when such historic monuments, works of art and places of worship are not located in the immediate proximity of military objectives:
> (e) Depriving a person protected by the Conventions or referred to in paragraph 2 of this Article of the rights of fair and regular trial.

---

[83] Fischer, *supra* n.26, at 74–75.

[84] Fischer, *ibid.*, at 73. Some were unhappy about the fact that it did not add enough, see Sandoz *et al.*, supra n.80, at 991–993.

[85] Sandoz, *supra* n.67, at 676, 679.

[86] Which, according to the ICRC commentary 'encompasses the concepts of "wrongful intent" or "recklessness", *viz.*, the attitude of an agent who, without being certain of a particular result accepts the possibility of it occurring; on the other hand, ordinary negligence or lack of foresight is not covered'. Sandoz *supra* n.67, at 994.

Some of these new grave breaches were controversial, but it is difficult to see many of them as truly problematic.[87] Perhaps the most politically sensitive was 85(4)(a), which was considered by some to be directed against Israeli policies in the occupied territories. This may be the case, but it is notable that Article 49 of Geneva Convention IV had probably already covered the practices of encouraging people to settle in occupied territory, and the grave breach in the Protocol is linked to a violation of that Article.[88] The inclusion of *apartheid* was not uncontroversial, but there were two reasons for its inclusion. The first was that it was, by 1977, undoubtedly contrary to customary international law (and was an obligation South Africa was violating); the second was that in situations of international armed conflict, this actually added nothing to what would already be prohibited by the 1949 Conventions, so the provision was a clarification, rather than an extension of the pre-existing law.[89]

There are legitimate critiques of the grave breaches regime(s), in that they are far from complete.[90] However, it ought to be said that they were not intended to be; they were the violations of the Conventions that were intended to be subjected to a specific regime of mandatory prosecution, rather than exhaustive of what amount to war crimes. The grave breaches regime is not, nor should it be, the be all and end all of even the treaty law on point.[91] Other serious violations of the GCs and AP I are also war crimes, although they are not covered by the duty to criminalize them domestically and search for offenders.

c. The ICTY Statute The next provision that can be considered treaty-based[92] (although not a treaty *per se*) is the ICTY Statute. We have already discussed Article 2, which gave the ICTY jurisdiction over grave breaches of the GCs (although not AP I). Article 3 provides that:

> The International Tribunal shall have the power to prosecute persons violating the laws or customs of war. Such violations shall include, but not be limited to:
>
> (a) employment of poisonous weapons or other weapons calculated to cause unnecessary suffering;
> (b) wanton destruction of cities, towns or villages, or devastation not justified by military necessity;
> (c) attack, or bombardment, by whatever means, of undefended towns, villages, dwellings, or buildings;
> (d) seizure of, destruction or wilful damage done to institutions dedicated to religion, charity and education, the arts and sciences, historic monuments and works of art and science;
> (e) plunder of public or private property.

---

[87] Although the inclusion of offences based on 'Hague' law was controversial. See Bothe *et al.*, *supra* n.80, at 514–515.

[88] Sandoz *et al.*, *supra* n.80, at 1000.

[89] *Ibid.*, at 1001–1002.

[90] Fleck, *supra* n.78, at 836ff.

[91] Even within international humanitarian law there are also other treaties, such as the Chemical Weapons Convention and the Ottawa Convention on Anti-Personnel Landmines, that may be relevant. See also Stewart, *supra* n.77, at 863–870.

[92] I.e. Article 25 of the UN Charter, and for some time, if not the Charter for the Federal Republic of Yugoslavia, then the Dayton Agreement.

Although the examples given all refer to 'Hague' law prohibitions, the ICTY decided, in the seminal *Tadić* decision, that it referred to all of the relevant treaty-based and customary law of armed conflict not already referred to directly in the Article itself.[93] This has led the Tribunal into some less than satisfactory reasoning on whether or not a violation of treaty law sufficed, or whether such a violation also had to be a violation of customary law. There are reasons to understand why the Tribunal has been uncomfortable, in that the Secretary-General, in his report on the Statute, said that:

> [T]he application of the principle of *nullum crimen sine lege* requires that the international tribunal should apply rules of international humanitarian law which are beyond any doubt part of customary law so that the problem of adherence of some but not all States to specific conventions does not arise. This would appear to be particularly important in the context of an international tribunal prosecuting persons responsible for serious violations of international humanitarian law.[94]

Nonetheless, there is no conceptual reason why a crime needs to be based on customary, rather than treaty law, so long as the treaty was in force at the relevant time, a position which the ICTY has now largely, albeit not always unambiguously, accepted.[95]

d. The Rome Statute The most significant recent treaty-based statement of the law of war crimes is the Rome Statute of the International Criminal Court. Article 8(2)(a) provides for jurisdiction over grave breaches of the 1949 Conventions (although not AP I). Article 8(2)(b), though, sets out a partial list of '[o]ther serious violations of the laws and customs applicable in international armed conflict, within the established framework of international law' that are exhaustive for the purposes of the jurisdiction of the ICC (although, emphatically, not war crimes law more generally).[96] The list is as follows:

(i) Intentionally directing attacks against the civilian population as such or against individual civilians not taking direct part in hostilities;
(ii) Intentionally directing attacks against civilian objects, that is, objects which are not military objectives;
(iii) Intentionally directing attacks against personnel, installations, material, units or vehicles involved in a humanitarian assistance or peacekeeping mission in accordance with the Charter of the United Nations, as long as they are entitled to the protection given to civilians or civilian objects under the international law of armed conflict;
(iv) Intentionally launching an attack in the knowledge that such attack will cause incidental loss of life or injury to civilians or damage to civilian objects or widespread, long-term and severe damage to the natural environment which would be

---

[93] See *infra* pp. 488–489. It also included the law applicable owing to the agreements between the relevant belligerents in Bosnia.

[94] Report of the Secretary-General Pursuant to Paragraph 2 of Security Council Resolution 808, UN Doc. S/25704, at para. 34

[95] Cryer *et al.*, *supra* n.34, at 9–10.

[96] See, for example, Article 10 of the Rome Statute. *Prosecutor v. Furundžija*, Judgment, IT-95-17/1-T, 10 December 1998, at para. 227. *Prosecutor v. Tadić*, Judgment, 15 July 1999, IT-94-1-A, at para. 223. But see Separate Opinion of Judge Shahabuddeen, at para. 3.

clearly excessive in relation to the concrete and direct overall military advantage anticipated;
(v) Attacking or bombarding, by whatever means, towns, villages, dwellings or buildings which are undefended and which are not military objectives;
(vi) Killing or wounding a combatant who, having laid down his arms or having no longer means of defence, has surrendered at discretion;
(vii) Making improper use of a flag of truce, of the flag or of the military insignia and uniform of the enemy or of the United Nations, as well as of the distinctive emblems of the Geneva Conventions, resulting in death or serious personal injury;
(viii) The transfer, directly or indirectly, by the Occupying Power of parts of its own civilian population into the territory it occupies, or the deportation or transfer of all or parts of the population of the occupied territory within or outside this territory;
(ix) Intentionally directing attacks against buildings dedicated to religion, education, art, science or charitable purposes, historic monuments, hospitals and places where the sick and wounded are collected, provided they are not military objectives;
(x) Subjecting persons who are in the power of an adverse party to physical mutilation or to medical or scientific experiments of any kind which are neither justified by the medical, dental or hospital treatment of the person concerned nor carried out in his or her interest, and which cause death to or seriously endanger the health of such person or persons;
(xi) Killing or wounding treacherously individuals belonging to the hostile nation or army;
(xii) Declaring that no quarter will be given;
(xiii) Destroying or seizing the enemy's property unless such destruction or seizure be imperatively demanded by the necessities of war;
(xiv) Declaring abolished, suspended or inadmissible in a court of law the rights and actions of the nationals of the hostile party;
(xv) Compelling the nationals of the hostile party to take part in the operations of war directed against their own country, even if they were in the belligerent's service before the commencement of the war;
(xvi) Pillaging a town or place, even when taken by assault;
(xvii) Employing asphyxiating, poisonous or other gases, and all analogous liquids, materials or devices;
(xviii) Employing poison or poisoned weapons;
(xix) Employing bullets which expand or flatten easily in the human body, such as bullets with a hard envelope which does not entirely cover the core or is pierced with incisions;
(xx) Employing weapons, projectiles and material and methods of warfare which are of a nature to cause superfluous injury or unnecessary suffering or which are inherently indiscriminate in violation of the international law of armed conflict, provided that such weapons, projectiles and material and methods of warfare are the subject of a comprehensive prohibition and are included in an annex to this Statute, by an amendment in accordance with the relevant provisions set forth in articles 121 and 123;
(xxi) Committing outrages upon personal dignity, in particular humiliating and degrading treatment;
(xxii) Committing rape, sexual slavery, enforced prostitution, forced pregnancy, as defined in article 7, paragraph 2 (f), enforced sterilization, or any other form of sexual violence also constituting a grave breach of the Geneva Conventions;
(xxiii) Utilizing the presence of a civilian or other protected person to render certain points, areas or military forces immune from military operations;
(xxiv) Intentionally directing attacks against buildings, material, medical units and transport, and personnel using the distinctive emblems of the Geneva Conventions in conformity with international law;

(xxv) Intentionally using starvation of civilians as a method of warfare by depriving them of objects indispensable to their survival, including wilfully impeding relief supplies as provided for under the Geneva Conventions;

(xxvi) Conscripting or enlisting children under the age of fifteen years into the national armed forces or using them to participate actively in hostilities.

To draw out some of the most interesting issues in this provision,[97] and beginning with the Hague law side, Articles 8(2)(b)(i) and (ii) both reflect the basic principle of distinction which is fundamental to the law of armed conflict.[98] There is no doubt that they reflect long-standing war crimes, although the requirement that the attack be intentional may be more limited than customary law, which probably accepts that recklessness suffices.[99] Article 8(2)(b)(iii) may look innovative, in that it creates a crime, in essence, of attacking peacekeepers, a crime probably only accepted at the transnational level in 1994, in the Convention on Crimes Against Peacekeepers.[100] The crime raises difficult issues of participation in hostilities, and the status of those engaged in humanitarian assistance or peacekeeping, which are, however, to some extent avoided by the Rome Statute, as it only proffers protection to the extent to which those persons are entitled to civilian status in the law of armed conflict.[101] Hence the provision is really an application of Article 8(2)(b)(i) to a specific situation, rather than an expansion of liability.

Article 8(2)(b)(iv), which basically deals with issues of collateral damage to civilians, civilian objects and the environment, was a controversial provision at Rome and after. This is, in part, because the definition, in particular the inclusion of the words 'clearly' and 'overall', renders the crime narrower than that in customary law and AP I.[102] The Elements of Crimes which, while not binding on the ICC are intended to assist it in interpreting the crimes,[103] appear, although not unambiguously, to require the perpetrator to have made the subjective assessment that the relevant damage will have been clearly excessive, which will render the crime extremely difficult, if not impossible, to prove.[104]

Staying with the Hague law aspects, the Rome Statute has interesting inclusions and exclusions. Although there are prohibitions on dum-dum bullets, poison and gas weapons that are contrary to the 1925 Gas Protocol, these hardly exhaust weapons prohibited in armed conflict. For example, there is no reference to the weapons that have been completely banned under the relevant protocols to the 1980 Conventional

---

[97] As mentioned above, *supra* n.61, space constraints preclude a detailed review of all of the details of Article 8.

[98] See David Turns (Chapter 10) and Tom Ruys and Christian De Cock (Chapter 11) in this volume.

[99] See Dörmann, 'Article 8', in Triffterer, *supra* n.61 at 325–327. Although see Schabas, *supra* n.48, at 224.

[100] UN. Doc. A/RES/49/59 (Annex).

[101] See also Chapter 11 in this volume by Tom Ruys and Christian De Cock.

[102] Cryer, *supra* n.2, at 277–279.

[103] See Article 9 and Article 21 of the Rome Statute (1998). But see also *Prosecutor v. al-Bashir*, Decision on the Prosecution's Application for a Warrant of Arrest Against Omar al-Bashir, ICC-02/05-01/09, 4 March 2009, at paras 127–128.

[104] Cryer, *supra* n.2. Although see also Cryer *et al. supra* n.34, at 297–302.

Weapons Convention, such as those that injure by means of non-detectable fragments and blinding laser weapons.[105] There may be a question about whether or not the use of such weapons is contrary to the customary law of armed conflict, but the same does not apply to the absence of the prohibition of biological weapons, which were also covered by the 1925 Geneva Protocol. The reason for this was a discomforting compromise in the negotiations. There were a number of non-nuclear weapon states (and some non-declared in the Nuclear Non-Proliferation Treaty sense) that sought to have nuclear weapons prohibited, *per se*, in the Statute.[106] Nuclear weapon states, and those that shelter under the nuclear umbrella of those states, in addition to various other states, were unwilling to accept this, for reasons both legal and political. The compromise, therefore, was that nuclear weapons – the notional 'rich man's weapon of mass destruction – were not mentioned but nor were the 'poor man's' equivalent, biological weapons, or chemical weapons banned by the 1993 Chemical Weapons Convention but that do not come under the 1925 Gas Protocol.[107] This is unfortunate, and although the legality of nuclear weapons is hotly contested,[108] the same cannot be said of chemical and biological weapons, which are unambiguously prohibited by the 1925 Geneva Protocol, the 1972 Biological Weapons Convention and the 1993 Chemical Weapons Convention.

The nuclear weapons issue also partially explains Article 8(2)(b)(xx), which is intended to deal with weapons that cause superfluous injury or unnecessary suffering or are inherently indiscriminate. This provision, owing to the fact that for a crime to be committed under its provisions, such a weapon has to be subject to a comprehensive prohibition, and included in the Statute pursuant to its (onerous) amendment procedures is denuded of any independent force.[109] The reason for this was a compromise, as some states thought that the general principles would achieve their aim of rendering nuclear weapons unlawful by the back door, whereas other states disagreed, but were unwilling to run the risk of such arguments even being made. There were also concerns with the possibility that an open provision on weapons could be used to pronounce on the (possible il)legality of weapons such as landmines and cluster munitions on the basis of these general principles of the law of armed conflict.

On the 'Geneva' side there is probably only one major controversial provision in the Rome Statute, that is Article 8(2)(b)(vii), which deals with the transfer of people and populations into and out of occupied territory. This was very controversial at Rome, largely because some states on either side of the debate saw the provision as raising the issue of Israeli policies in the occupied territories. The debate raged around the inclusion of the words 'or indirect' in the definition of the offence. While it was probably not in advance of Article 49 of the Geneva Convention IV,[110] there were

---

[105] Which were also suggested for inclusion. See H. von Hebel and D. Robinson, 'Crimes Within the Jurisdiction of the Court', in R.S. Lee (ed.), *The International Criminal Court: The Making of the Rome Statute* (The Hague: Kluwer, 1999), 79, at 114.

[106] *Ibid.*, at 114–115.

[107] *Ibid.*

[108] See, for example, *Legality of the Threat or Use of Nuclear Weapons* Advisory Opinion, [1996] ICJ Rep. 226.

[109] Cryer, *supra* n.2 at 281.

[110] Cottier, 'Article 8', in Triffterer, *supra* n.61 at 362–375. Which was criminalized by Additional Protocol I see above at 481.

obvious political sensitivities surrounding the negotiations of both the Rome Statute and the Elements of Crimes, which provide for compromise language that the transfer must occur in violation of international law.[111] This does not alter the ambit of the offence, and was probably already implicit in the chapeau of Article 8(2)(b), which required that the offences occur 'within the established framework of international law'.[112]

Outside of the Rome Statute, there are also other treaty-based offences that look a lot like war crimes, such as, for their parties, the use of landmines or cluster munitions. For such offences to be committed, though, the relevant treaties have to be in force for the relevant parties (although this is also the case for some of the other war crimes mentioned above). The precise relationship between such offences and the general law of war crimes is an understudied, but complex, area. Furthermore, in addition to treaties, some of which reflect customary law, there is an additional body of customary war crimes law, that also applies, and, owing to its customary status, avoids the technical conditions of applicability that apply to those treaties other than to the requirement that there be an (international) armed conflict.

ii. Customary law

Treaties do not exhaust the list of possible war crimes. Treaties can, as is well known, codify customary law, crystallize it at the time of drafting or later come to reflect it.[113] It is generally accepted that the GCs, to all intents and purposes, reflect customary international law,[114] and the majority, although not all, of AP I does too.[115] Although the list of such offences is not uncontroversial, the ICRC Customary International Humanitarian Law Study postulated a list of customary war crimes, which includes grave breaches of AP I (as defined therein), and, *inter alia*, cannibalism, and using starvation or human shields as a means of warfare. Few would criticize such inclusion on moral grounds,[116] although there has been some scepticism about aspects of the ICRC study from some quarters,[117] in particular, although not solely, from the US.[118] It

---

[111] Elements of Crimes, Article 8(2)(b)(vii).

[112] Article 8(2)(b) chapeau.

[113] *North Sea Continental Shelf Case* (Denmark v. FRG, the Netherlands v. FRG), [1969] ICJ Rep. 3.

[114] T. Meron, 'The Geneva Conventions as Customary Law', (1987) 81 *AJIL* 78.

[115] C. Greenwood, 'Customary Status of the 1977 Geneva Protocols', in A.J.M. Delissen and G.J. Tanja (eds), *Humanitarian Law of Armed Conflict: Challenges Ahead* (Dordrecht: Martinus Nijhoff, 1991), 93.

[116] For an in-depth study of war crimes from the point of view of just war theory see L. May, *War Crimes and Just War* (Cambridge: Cambridge University Press, 2007).

[117] Garraway notes that the list included by the ICRC is remarkably similar to the list of crimes the ICRC was unsuccessful in including in the Rome Statute. See C. Garraway, 'War Crimes', in E. Wilmshurst and S. Breau (eds), *Perspectives on the ICRC Study on Customary International Humanitarian Law* (Cambridge: Cambridge University Press, 2007), 377, at 387. Equally, this does not mean that they were not customary, as the Rome Statute is not a complete codification of the law of war crimes, a point, to be fair, that Garraway accepts. See Garraway, *ibid.*, at 388.

[118] Y. Dinstein, *The Conduct of Hostilities under the Law of International Armed Conflict*, 2nd edn (Cambridge: Cambridge University Press, 2010), at 16. For a balanced critique see G.

is possible that not all grave breaches of AP I are customary to their full extent.[119] Even so, it bears remembering that with respect to most war crimes in customary law the question tends to be whether or not a specific treaty provision has come to reflect customary international law, so the question of ratification drops away; the vast majority of AP I has reached this status. The same cannot always be said for more modern weapons prohibitions such as those of anti-personnel landmines and cluster munitions. Indeed, in the latter case the treaty itself essentially accepts that this is the case.[120] In this context, treaty law tends to lead normative advancement and the question of an abstract evaluation of customary law in the absence of any treaty provisions on point, is rare, although perfectly possible.

B. Non-international Armed Conflicts[121]

In spite of the fact that much of the conduct that was prohibited by the law of armed conflict in non-international armed conflicts was criminal in international armed conflicts, and under domestic law, by the early 1990s there was still no consensus that there was a law of war crimes applicable to non-international armed conflict.[122] The grave breaches provisions, in spite of some judicial dicta to the contrary, were not considered to apply to non-international armed conflicts.[123] When it came to treaty law, Common Article 3 of the GCs was not considered to fall under the grave breaches provisions, and Additional Protocol II, quite deliberately, did not include any provisions on criminal liability for violations even of its most basic provisions. There was also before the 1990s by no means any agreement that there was customary international

---

Aldrich, 'Customary International Humanitarian Law: An Interpretation on Behalf of the International Committee of the Red Cross', (2005) 76 *BYIL* 503. Under the Obama administration there has been something of a return to an acceptance of much of Additional Protocol I, especially with respect to Article 75 of AP I. Article 75 is particularly important as it deals with people who, irrespective of nationality, are not entitled to any greater protection under the law of international armed conflict; therefore it operates as a default level of protection for all in such conflicts as customary.

[119] Garraway, *supra* n.117, at 388. But see, importantly, G. Aldrich, 'Violations of the Laws and Customs of War', in McDonald and Swaak-Goldman, *supra* n.26, at 102–103.

[120] Article 21, The Convention on Cluster Munitions (2008).

[121] For a detailed survey see E. La Haye, *War Crimes in Internal Armed Conflict* (Cambridge: Cambridge University Press, 2007).

[122] D. Plattner, 'The Penal Repression of Violations of International Humanitarian Law Applicable in Non-International Armed Conflicts', (1990) 30 *IRRC* 409, at 414; P. Rowe, 'War Crimes and the Former Yugoslavia: The Legal Difficulties', (1993) 32 *RDMDG* 317, at 328–333; Preliminary Remarks of the ICRC 25 March 1993, cited in La Haye, *ibid.*, at 131. It is a common misconception that the prosecutions in the American Civil War were an early example of war crimes law applying to non-international armed conflict. There had been a recognition of belligerency in that conflict, and as such, the conflict was, from a legal point of view, an international armed conflict.

[123] Tadić, *supra* n.37, at para. 84; Boelaert-Suominen, *supra* n.75, although see the Dissenting Opinion of Judge Abi Saab; Aldrich, *supra* n.119, at 110.

law applicable to non-international armed conflicts that did not find its genesis in those treaties.[124]

As discussed above, in international armed conflict the treaties have tended to be a prelude to custom, as responses to developments in armed conflicts. Therefore discussion tends to be whether or not those treaties, or specific provisions they contain, have entered into custom. The law of non-international armed conflicts has worked rather differently. In this context custom (or judicial decisions purporting to set out customary war crimes)[125] has tended to drive treaty-based developments. Hence this section will treat custom first, then look at treaties.

i. Customary law

The traditional position – that there was no war crimes law applicable to non-international armed conflicts – changed quite dramatically with the adoption of the ICTY and International Criminal Tribunal for Rwanda's Statutes. The former, although not referring to the law applicable to non-international armed conflict, was interpreted as doing so by virtue of Article 3 of that Tribunal's Statute. Article 3 provided the ICTY with jurisdiction over a non-exhaustive list of serious violations of the laws and customs of war.[126] The list was drawn from the Regulations attached to Hague Convention IV of 1907[127] and the Nuremberg IMT Statute, which only dealt with international armed conflicts.

That did not trouble the ICTY Appeals Chamber in the *Tadić* case. On the basis of comments made by some states before the Security Council when adopting the Statute, that it was intended to cover all serious violations of the law of armed conflict that occurred in former Yugoslavia, and a purposive interpretation of its Statute, it decided that Article 3 covered, *inter alia*, '(iii) violations of common Article 3 and other customary rules on internal conflicts;[128] (iv) violations of agreements binding upon the

---

[124] A. Cullen, *The Concept of Non-International Armed Conflict in International Humanitarian Law* (Cambridge: Cambridge University Press, 2010), at Chapter 4; La Haye, *supra* n.121, at 136. Although see A. Cassese, 'The Spanish Civil War and the Development of Customary International Law Concerning Internal Armed Conflict', in A. Cassese (ed.), *Current Problems of International Law* (Milan: Dott. I. Giuffre, 1975), reprinted in A. Cassese, *The Human Dimension of International Law* (Oxford: Oxford University Press, 2008), 128.

[125] For discussion see T. Meron, 'International Criminalization of Internal Atrocities', (1995) 79 *AJIL* 561. This article has proved highly influential, not least on the ICTY. The language it uses is very similar to that in the (later) *Tadić* decision, but it would be indelicate to make too much of it.

[126] See *supra* section 5Aib.

[127] *Tadić*, *supra* n.37 at para. 87.

[128] I.e:

any of the following acts committed against persons taking no active part in the hostilities, including members of armed forces who have laid down their arms and those placed *hors de combat* by sickness, wounds, detention or any other cause:

(i) Violence to life and person, in particular murder of all kinds, mutilation, cruel treatment and torture;

(ii) Committing outrages upon personal dignity, in particular humiliating and degrading treatment;

(iii) Taking of hostages;

parties to the conflict, considered qua treaty law, that is, agreements which have not turned into customary international law.'[129]

From here the Appeals Chamber engaged in a detailed (albeit *obiter*) discussion of what the customary law of non-international armed conflict looked like. In a discussion that was presentationally positivist but clearly influenced by a humanitarian agenda on the part of Antonio Cassese, the then President of the ICTY,[130] the Appeals Chamber determined that various aspects of the law of international armed conflict had entered into customary international law for non-international armed conflicts too. These were the prohibition of attacks on civilians, indiscriminate attacks, the protection of those not taking part in hostilities, the general principles of Additional Protocol II, and the prohibition of perfidy and of the use of gas weapons.[131] The level of evidence that was given for these positions was variable, in particular with respect to the case that their violation was customarily criminal, but the case was made with a keen eye to what would be acceptable, and in a sophisticated manner.[132] If a reader is willing to be convinced, the decision gives every reason to be taken along for the ride.

The Appeals Chamber, in spite of its notionally self-denying assertion that:

(i) only a number of rules and principles governing international armed conflicts have gradually been extended to apply to internal conflicts; and (ii) this extension has not taken place in the form of a full and mechanical transplant of those rules to internal conflicts; rather, the general essence of those rules, and not the detailed regulation they may contain, has become applicable to internal conflicts.[133]

made some very broad statements, intended to analogize, as much as possible, the law of international and non-international armed conflict.[134] Perhaps the Chamber's boldest statement was that:

(iv) The passing of sentences and the carrying out of executions without previous judgement pronounced by a regularly constituted court, affording all judicial guarantees which are generally recognized as indispensable.'

---

[129] *Tadić*, supra n.37, at paras 89, 92–93.
[130] T. Hoffmann, 'The Gentle Civilizer of Humanitarian Law – Antonio Cassese and the Creation of the Customary Law of Non-International Armed Conflicts', in C. Stahn and L. van den Herik (eds), *Future Perspectives on International Criminal Justice* (The Hague: MC Asser Press, 2010), 58; T. Meron, 'Cassese's Tadić and the Law of Non-International Armed Conflicts', in L. Chand Vohrah *et al.* (eds), *Man's Inhumanity to Man: Essays in Honour of Antonio Cassese* (The Hague: Kluwer, 2003), 533; B. van Schaack, 'Crimen Sine Lege: Judicial Lawmaking at the Intersection of Law and Morals', (2008–2009), 97 *Geo LJ* 119. For further discussion see R. Cryer, 'The Philosophy of International Criminal Law', in A. Orakhelashvili (ed.), *Research Handbook on the History and Theory of International Law* (Cheltenham: Edward Elgar, 2011), 232, at 244–247.
[131] *Tadić*, supra n.37, paras 100–124.
[132] C. Warbrick and P. Rowe, 'The International Criminal Tribunal for Yugoslavia: The Decision of the Appeals Chamber on the Interlocutory Appeal on Jurisdiction in the *Tadić* Case', (1996) 45 *ICLQ* 691.
[133] *Tadić*, supra n.37, at para. 126.
[134] Hoffmann, supra n.130 at 68. A. Cassese, 'The Judge: Interview With Antonio Cassese', in H.V. Stuart and M. Simons (eds), *The Prosecutor and the Judge: Benjamin Ferencz and Antonio Cassese: Interviews and Writings* (Amsterdam: Amsterdam University Press, 2009), 47, at 53.

> Since the 1930s, ... international legal rules have increasingly emerged or have been agreed upon to regulate internal armed conflict. ... A State-sovereignty-oriented approach has been gradually supplanted by a human-being-oriented approach. Gradually the maxim of Roman law *hominum causa omne jus constitutum est* (all law is created for the benefit of human beings) has gained a firm foothold in the international community as well. It follows that in the area of armed conflict the distinction between interstate wars and civil wars is losing its value as far as human beings are concerned. Why protect civilians from belligerent violence, or ban rape, torture or the wanton destruction of hospitals, churches, museums or private property, as well as proscribe weapons causing unnecessary suffering when two sovereign States are engaged in war, and yet refrain from enacting the same bans or providing the same protection when armed violence has erupted 'only' within the territory of a sovereign State? If international law, while of course duly safeguarding the legitimate interests of States, must gradually turn to the protection of human beings, it is only natural that the aforementioned dichotomy should gradually lose its weight. ... [E]lementary considerations of humanity and common sense make it preposterous that the use by States of weapons prohibited in armed conflicts between themselves be allowed when States try to put down rebellion by their own nationals on their own territory. What is inhumane, and consequently proscribed, in international wars, cannot but be inhumane and inadmissible in civil strife.[135]

This was, to say the least, a legal leap of faith, but one that has, on the whole, been on the positive end of the judgment of history.[136] It is now generally accepted that there is liability for war crimes committed in non-international armed conflict, although the ambit of the substantive customary norms on point is not always agreed upon.[137] The ICTY has, however, done its best to harmonize various areas of the law of armed conflict, by deciding that it is unnecessary to determine the nature of the conflict, on the basis that on many, perhaps most, issues, the law is the same whatever the nature of the conflict.[138] There are certain areas, such as the law of occupation, and combatant/Prisoner of War status that are difficult, if not impossible, to assimilate in this way.[139] It is testimony to the impact of the ICTY's jurisprudence on point that the *ICRC Customary Law Study* considers most of the rules of the law of armed conflict to be consistent, irrespective of the nature of the conflict, a position frequently supported by reference to that case-law.[140] States have, by a considerable majority, taken *Tadić* to heart, and accepted its findings on the law applicable to non-international armed conflicts.

---

[135] *Tadić, supra* n.37, at paras 97, 119.

[136] For discussion at the time see Greenwood, *supra* n.35; Warbrick and Rowe, *supra* n.132: G.R. Watson, 'The Humanitarian Law of the Yugoslavia War Crimes Tribunal: Jurisdiction in Prosecutor v Tadić', (1996) 36 *VJIL* 687, at 709–728. For an exemplary presentation of much of the relevant law see A.P.V. Rogers, *Law on the Battlefield*, 2nd edn (Manchester: Manchester University Press, 2004), Chapter 9.

[137] For one list see La Haye, *supra* n.121, at 172–176.

[138] Boelaert-Suominen, *supra* n.63.

[139] Although for an argument, in part on the basis of ICTY jurisprudence, that the standards of treatment for internees in international and non-international armed conflicts are now essentially the same (although the status of lawful combatancy remains different) see E. Crawford, *The Treatment of Combatants and Insurgents under the Law of Armed Conflict* (Oxford: Oxford University Press, 2010).

[140] R. Cryer, 'Of Custom, Treaties, Scholars and the Gavel: The Impact of the International Criminal Tribunals on the ICRC Customary Study', (2006) 11 *JCSL* 239.

ii. Treaties/international legislation

Although the law of war crimes in non-international armed conflict is often dated to 1995, and the *Tadić* Opinion, that development (if that is what it was) ought not solely be attributed to the ICTY and its case-law. After all, in 1994, a year before the *Tadić* decision, the International Criminal Tribunal for Rwanda (hereinafter 'ICTR') Statute criminalized violations of Common Article 3. The UN Secretary-General, commenting on this provision, noted that it was the first time that Common Article 3 had been expressly criminalized.[141] Although this was perhaps a surprise at the time, the position is now a commonplace. This is, in many respects, owing to the fact that (inspired by the *Tadić* case)[142] states, in drafting the Statute of the ICC in Rome, included in Article 8(2)(c) violations of Common Article 3 as war crimes in non-international armed conflict.[143] In addition to Common Article 3, Article 8(2)(e), again picking up, at least in part, on *Tadić*, included a list of other war crimes that states considered contrary to customary international law, and thus punishable by the Court. These are:

(i) Intentionally directing attacks against the civilian population as such or against individual civilians not taking direct part in hostilities;
(ii) Intentionally directing attacks against buildings, material, medical units and transport, and personnel using the distinctive emblems of the Geneva Conventions in conformity with international law;
(iii) Intentionally directing attacks against personnel, installations, material, units or vehicles involved in a humanitarian assistance or peacekeeping mission in accordance with the Charter of the United Nations, as long as they are entitled to the protection given to civilians or civilian objects under the international law of armed conflict;
(iv) Intentionally directing attacks against buildings dedicated to religion, education, art, science or charitable purposes, historic monuments, hospitals and places where the sick and wounded are collected, provided they are not military objectives;
(v) Pillaging a town or place, even when taken by assault;
(vi) Committing rape, sexual slavery, enforced prostitution, forced pregnancy, as defined in article 7, paragraph 2 (f), enforced sterilization, and any other form of sexual violence also constituting a serious violation of article 3 common to the four Geneva Conventions;
(vii) Conscripting or enlisting children under the age of fifteen years into armed forces or groups or using them to participate actively in hostilities;
(viii) Ordering the displacement of the civilian population for reasons related to the conflict, unless the security of the civilians involved or imperative military reasons so demand;
(ix) Killing or wounding treacherously a combatant adversary;
(x) Declaring that no quarter will be given;
(xi) Subjecting persons who are in the power of another party to the conflict to physical mutilation or to medical or scientific experiments of any kind which are neither justified by the medical, dental or hospital treatment of the person concerned nor carried out in his or her interest, and which cause death to or seriously endanger the health of such person or persons;
(xii) Destroying or seizing the property of an adversary unless such destruction or seizure be imperatively demanded by the necessities of the conflict.[144]

---

[141] Secretary-General's Report on the ICTR Statute, at para. 12.
[142] See *infra* p. 492.
[143] Cryer *et al.*, *supra* n.34, at 277.
[144] See, generally, La Haye, *supra* n.121, at 138–144.

This is, in many ways, a cut-down version of Article 8(2)(b) of the Rome Statute. There are important omissions though, such as any provision on collateral damage analogous to Article 8(2)(b)(iv) of the Statute, and any provision on prohibited weapons. The latter omission has been partially rectified by the Kampala Review Conference, which adopted an amendment (which is not yet in force) that bans the same weapons prohibited in Article 8(2)(b)(xvii–xix) in non-international armed conflicts, although with some slight caveats necessitated by the different circumstances that are likely to be at play in those conflicts.[145] Given that the purely positivist case that such weapons are prohibited in non-international armed conflicts is controversial, the impact of the moral imperative that the ICTY advanced in that case can be seen to have had an effect.[146]

Still, in other areas, the Rome Statute includes offences not mentioned in *Tadić*. Probably the most controversial was the inclusion of the prohibition of the recruitment, enlistment or use of child soldiers (that is, those under fifteen). In Rome there were some questions about whether or not the prohibition (which was considered customary) gave rise to criminal liability in customary law in either type of armed conflict.[147] The provision has, nonetheless, formed the basis of a number of charges before the ICC, in particular in the first case that came to trial.[148]

The question of the lawfulness of such charges reached a head before the ICC had an opportunity to pronounce on the relevant provisions when the Special Court for Sierra Leone (hereinafter 'SCSL') was faced with a jurisdictional challenge about prosecutions for recruiting and using child soldiers. This was because in addition to the jurisdiction the SCSL had been granted over serious violations of Common Article 3 and Additional Protocol II,[149] Article 4 of the SCSL Statute also gave jurisdiction over three violations of the law of armed conflict. These were:

(a) Intentionally directing attacks against the civilian population as such or against individual civilians not taking direct part in hostilities;
(b) Intentionally directing attacks against personnel, installations, material, units or vehicles involved in a humanitarian assistance or peacekeeping mission in accordance with the Charter of the United Nations, as long as they are entitled to the protection given to civilians or civilian objects under the international law of armed conflict;
(c) Conscripting or enlisting children under the age of fifteen years into armed forces or groups or using them to participate actively in hostilities.

---

[145] This is particularly the case with respect to expanding bullets which at times (in particular in aeroplanes) are a necessary part of law enforcement operations. See A. Alamuddin and P. Webb, 'Expanding Jurisdiction over War Crimes under Article 8 of the ICC Statute', (2010) 8 *JICJ* 1219.

[146] On the proof the ICRC made on this point see D. Turns, 'Weapons in the ICRC Customary Law Study', (2006) 11 *JCSL* 201.

[147] Von Hebel and Robinson, *supra* n.105, at 117–118.

[148] *Prosecutor v. Lubanga*, ICC-01/04-01/06. There is controversy on whether or not this should have been the only charge he faced, not least as there have been allegations that Lubanga was involved in mass killing and sexual offences.

[149] See Article 3, Statute of the Special Court for Sierra Leone (2007), which is, to all intents and purposes, identical to Article 4 of the ICTR Statute.

Subparagraphs (a) and (b) were uncontroversial retreads of Article 8(2)(e)(i) and (iii) of the Rome Statute, which were considered unambiguously customary. Subparagraph (c) was more complex. It was also drawn from the Rome Statute (Article 8(2)(e)(vii)), but the Special Court has jurisdiction going back to 1996, and so the Secretary-General, in his initial draft of the Statute, framed the offence more narrowly, as '[a]bduction and forced recruitment of children under the age of 15 years into armed forces or groups for the purpose of using them to participate actively in hostilities', so that it would fall under Common Article 3, to avoid any *nullum crimen* issues. The Security Council insisted on the Rome Statute language, which is what was eventually included in Article 4(c).

It was therefore no surprise that the defence in the *Norman* case sought to have some charges about child soldiers dismissed on the basis of the *nullum crimen sine lege* principle. The Appeals Chamber rejected the application, subject to a significant dissent by Judge Robertson, arguing that customary international criminal law contained such a prohibition as far back as at least 1996.[150] The evidence that the Majority brought to show that the prohibition was customary was rather stronger than that shown to prove that the prohibition was criminalized that far back,[151] although this is not infrequently the case in international criminal tribunals. Critiques of the decision rely on the proposition that for a war crime to exist, there has to be a separate rule criminalizing a serious violation of the law of armed conflict; a position that is not uncontroversial.[152]

6. ENFORCEMENT

As discussed earlier in this chapter, initially war crimes were considered internationally authorized exercises of domestic criminal law, but are now considered international crimes in the true sense of international law directly applying to individuals. War crimes can thus be prosecuted both domestically and by international criminal tribunals. This is not limited to grave breaches, which are war crimes, but are not exhaustive of that concept. Even in the absence of a treaty-based obligation to criminalize violations of the law of armed conflict, the GCs, as well as customary international law, permit states to domestically criminalize relevant war crimes.

For customary war crimes there is universal jurisdiction. In other words, any state can prosecute a customary war crime, wherever it was committed.[153] In addition, there is no material state immunity for war crimes (although personal immunities may still be an issue).[154] Whether or not a state requires domestic implementing legislation to do so

---

[150] *Prosecutor v. Norman*, Decision on Preliminary Motion Based on Lack of Jurisdiction (Child Recruitment), SCSL-04-14-AR72(e), 31 May 2004.

[151] For critique see M. Happold, 'International Humanitarian Law, War Criminality and Child Recruitment: The Special Court for Sierra Leone's Decision in *Samuel Hinga Norman*', (2005) 18 *LJIL* 258.

[152] See *supra* p. 471–73.

[153] J.-M. Henckaerts and L. Doswald-Beck, *Customary International Humanitarian Law* (Cambridge: Cambridge University Press, 2005), at 604–607.

[154] D. Akande and S. Shah, 'Immunities of State Officials, International Crimes and Foreign Domestic Courts', (2011) 21 *EJIL* 815.

is a matter of domestic constitutional law, although most states are wary of relying directly on customary international law to base criminality in the domestic legal order without some legislative nudging.[155]

Even so it is not a violation of the *nullum crimen sine lege* principle for a state to grant itself jurisdiction over customary war crimes committed prior to the passage of domestic implementing legislation. This is because the criminal prohibition was already binding on the person committing the offence as a matter of international law at the time of the conduct. The UK has done this, for example in the 1991 War Crimes Act and the 2009 Coroners and Justice Act.[156] The European Court of Human Rights has accepted that such practices are lawful, so long as they relate to customary law in force at the time of the relevant conduct.[157]

It must be said that, in general, state implementation of customary war crimes in domestic law tends to be unsatisfactory, and omits, or narrowly defines, many of the relevant rules.[158] Where such legislation defines war crimes more broadly than international law, such conduct can only be prosecuted on the basis of the traditional principles of jurisdiction such as territoriality and nationality, and retrospectivity is an issue.

With respect to treaty-based war crimes, much depends on the relevant treaty. The most famous example of these is the grave breaches regime of the GCs, which creates a duty to implement what is the functional equivalent to universal jurisdiction. Since practically every state in the world is a party to the GCs,[159] any state is entitled to exercise jurisdiction over any grave breach wherever it is committed.[160] The position with respect to some grave breaches of AP I is not so simple. As it is possible that some aspects may not be customary,[161] states are not entitled to assert universal jurisdiction over those aspects that are not customary offences. They can only be prosecuted where the Protocol is in force for the relevant parties to a conflict. Where this is the case though, any party to AP I is entitled to prosecute such violations. With respect to other treaties, much will depend on their terms. The Cluster Munitions Convention, for example, provides for jurisdiction to be asserted on the basis of territoriality and

---

[155] An example of which is section 4(4) of the Canadian Crimes Against Humanity and War Crimes Act (2000). In the UK, it would appear that implementing legislation is probably now required. See *R v. Jones et al.* [2006] UKHL 16.

[156] Section 70 Coroners and Justice Act. See R. Cryer and P.D. Mora, 'The Coroners and Justice Act 2009 and International Criminal Law: Backing Into the Future?', (2010) 59 *ICLQ* 803. On the 1991 Act see A.T. Williams, 'The War Crimes Act 1991', (1992) 55 *MLR* 73.

[157] *Kononov v. Latvia*, Judgment, Application No. 36376/04, 17 May 2010.

[158] Cryer et al., supra n.34, at 73–75.

[159] The only non-parties, Kosovo and the Palestinian Territories, are subject to serious doubts as to their status as states.

[160] See R. O'Keefe, 'The Grave Breaches Regime and Universal Jurisdiction', (2009) 7 *JICJ* 811. It is worth noting, though, that in 1949 national principles of liability were expected to be used for domestic prosecutions (Sandoz, *supra* n.67. at 675), which shows that the relationship between war crimes as national and international offences was still complex.

[161] There are significant non-parties to the Protocol, such as the US, Pakistan, India, China and France.

nationality.¹⁶² Where a treaty comes to reflect custom though, universal jurisdiction is acceptable, along the lines mentioned above with respect to customary war crimes.

Unfortunately, and in spite of an upswing in prosecutions in the last fifteen years, the domestic prosecution of war crimes has not proved to be a resounding success.¹⁶³ States' reluctance to condemn their own nationals (in particular their service members) as war criminals,¹⁶⁴ and the fact that prosecution of non-nationals is often seen as an unfriendly, or politically damaging, act (as Belgium found out to its chagrin)¹⁶⁵ have meant that prosecutions are relatively rare,¹⁶⁶ and have tended to centre on conflicts where there has also been an international tribunal prosecuting war crimes, thus legitimizing prosecutions at a political level (the Second World War, former Yugoslavia and Rwanda).¹⁶⁷

This is, in some ways, paradoxical, as reluctance to prosecute war crimes is often what has led to calls for international tribunals. There have been a number of such tribunals with jurisdiction over war crimes – the Nuremberg and Tokyo IMTs in the aftermath of the Second World War, the ICTY and ICTR in the 1990s, and the ICC and SCSL in the new millennium (the ICC Statute having come into force in 2002) are the most well-known examples.¹⁶⁸ Practical limitations do mean, however, that they can only prosecute a very small minority of the war crimes that are committed, so their role in encouraging domestic prosecutions (for the ICC, particularly through the mechanism of complementarity)¹⁶⁹ is particularly important.

Another very important role that international tribunals, in particular the ICTY, have taken on is the role of development of the law of armed conflict, both in terms of declaring (or, in truth, practically legislating) customary law, and interpreting the relevant norms in a detailed fashion. There is little doubt that the ICTY has done an

---

[162] Article 9, The Convention on Cluster Munitions (2008). See L. Maresca, 'Article 9: National Implementation Measures', in G. Nystuen and S. Casey-Maslem (eds), *Commentary on the Convention on Cluster Munitions* (Oxford: Oxford University Press, 2010), 473.

[163] La Haye, *supra* n.121, at 108.

[164] T.L.H. McCormack, 'Their Atrocities and Our Misdemeanours: The Reticence of States to Try Their Own Nationals for International Crimes', in P. Sands and M. Lattimer (eds), *Justice for Crimes Against Humanity* (Oxford: Hart, 2003), 107. This may explain why in some circumstances, most notably in the United States, prosecutions of nationals for acts that amount to war crimes are prosecuted as domestic offences. This is not necessarily unlawful, however. See W. Ferdinandausse, 'Prosecution of Grave Breaches Before National Courts', (2009) 7 *JICJ* 723, at 730–731.

[165] See S. Ratner, 'Belgium's War Crimes Statute: A Postmortem', (2003) 97 *AJIL* 888.

[166] Ferdinandausse, *supra* n.164.

[167] On the failings see K. Dörmann and R. Geiss, 'The Implementation of Grave Breaches into Domestic Legal Orders', (2009) 7 *JICJ* 703. See also Ferdinandausse, *supra* n.164, who argues that mild differences in application of the relevant rules are unproblematic, a position that is controversial, in particular with respect to the assertion of universal jurisdiction, which is not plenary, but over international crimes as defined in international law. See also A. Colangelo, 'The Legal Limits of Universal Jurisdiction', (2006–2007) 47 *VJIL* 149.

[168] For an overview see T. Meron, 'Reflections on the Prosecution of War Crimes by International Tribunals', (2006) 100 *AJIL* 551.

[169] K. Doherty and T.L.H. McCormack, 'Complementarity as a Catalyst for Comprehensive Domestic Penal Legislation', (1999) 5 *UC Davis J Intl L & Poly* 147.

extraordinary job of 'humanizing' the law of armed conflict,[170] although some question whether judges ought to take on such a role, particularly in a criminal context,[171] and query whether they have pushed the balance too far from military necessity, and what states will accept.[172] From the other side, though, the development of the law of armed conflict through international criminal law has also been critiqued on the basis that concentrating on the criminalized aspects of the law may lead to narrower interpretation of the primary norms of the law of armed conflict because of the principles of strict interpretation of criminal law and *nullum crimen sine lege*.[173]

7. CONCLUSION

At a legal level, there is no question that the law of war crimes has been at the forefront of many debates about the nature of international law, especially the relationship between state sovereignty and more communitarian ideals.[174] The ICTY has been at the forefront of such discussions, with respect, for example, to the sources doctrine, but also regarding the respective roles of international tribunals and states in the development of international law.

It is a frequent criticism of the law of armed conflict that it needs to be frequently updated to take into account modern developments in the nature and practices of armed conflict.[175] Even where this is accepted, the nature of the international legal system means that the multilateral treaty-making conference is unlikely to be quick or necessarily satisfactory. Against this background international criminal tribunals (especially the ICTY), whether they ought to have done so or not, have stepped into the gap, and given a modern twist to the existing and developing norms of the law. This has met with a perhaps surprising level of success, with the greatest jump being the *Tadić* decision, which was iconoclastic in all senses of the word, although by no means the

---

[170] A. Marston Danner, 'When Courts Make Law: How the International Criminal Tribunals Recast the Laws of War', (2006) 59 *Vand L Rev* 1; M. Swart, 'Judicial Lawmaking at the *ad hoc* Tribunals: The Creative Use of the Sources of International Law and "Adventurous Interpretation"', (2010) 70 *ZAöRV* 459; S. Darcy, 'The Reinvention of War Crimes by the International Criminal Tribunals', in S. Darcy and J. Powderly (eds), *Judicial Creativity at the International Criminal Tribunals* (Oxford: Oxford University Press, 2010), 106; A. Zahar, 'Civilizing Civil War: Rewriting Morality as Law', in B. Swart, A. Zahar and G. Sluuiter (eds), *The Legacy of the International Criminal Tribunal for the former Yuglsolavia* (Oxford: Oxford University Press, 2011), 469.

[171] For support of the tribunals on point, see Beth van Schaack, 'Crimen Sine Lege: Judicial Lawmaking at the Intersection of Law and Morals', (2008–2009) 97 *Georgetown LJ* 119.

[172] M.N. Schmitt, 'Military Necessity and Humanity in International Humanitarian Law: Preserving the Balance', (2010) 50 *VJIL* 795.

[173] S. Sivakumaran, 'Re-envisaging the Law of Internal Armed Conflict', (2011) 22 *EJIL* 219, at 238–240.

[174] See, for example, B. Simma, 'From Bilateralism to Community Interest in International Law', (1994–IV) 250 *RdC* 217. See also T. Meron, *The Humanization of International Law* (Leiden: Nijhoff, 2006).

[175] J. Kunz, 'The Chaotic Status of the Laws of War and the Urgent Necessity for Their Revision', (1951) 45 *AJIL* 37.

only time the ICTY has looked to develop the law.[176] On occasion the ICTY has also sought to delegitimize aberrant state practice, which perhaps reached its high-tide in the direct rejection of the US torture memoranda in the *Brdjanin* case.[177]

The substantive (treaty and customary) law of war crimes is now tolerably broad, even though it is by no means a panacea, and far from unimprovable. This is particularly the case if it is accepted that all serious violations of the law of armed conflict are war crimes. On the other hand, what amounts to a serious violation of the law of armed conflict raises interesting questions, both of what amounts to serious, and what is a violation of that law.[178]

Even if all of the above is accepted, it cannot be ignored that the issue of enforcement, especially criminal prosecution, only arises as a result of failure.[179] That is, a failure of the law to exert a sufficient deterrent function (although we should not overstate the extent to which international law has a lesser deterrent function than domestic criminal law, particularly as the relevant evidence is unclear at both levels). It is also, in the context of war crimes, which are usually committed by members of armed forces, be they state-based or rebels, often a failure of command and control. There is a reason military hierarchy exists, and international criminal law contains the principle of command responsibility, which renders superiors responsible for the offences of subordinates when they do not do what they can to prevent the commission of international crimes, and initiate proceedings against subordinates if they commit such crimes.[180]

Even against the background of all the problems mentioned above, it would be an error to dismiss the importance of the law of war crimes to the enforcement of the law of armed conflict. As Dieter Fleck notes, 'in the turmoil of armed conflicts, criminal courts may not be in the forefront of activities to ensure respect for international humanitarian law. ... But it is deploringly true that without an effective legal system for prosecution of war crimes, compliance with existing obligations under international humanitarian law would not be taken seriously enough.'[181]

The law of war crimes is therefore one of the various mechanisms that can lead to compliance with the law of armed conflict. There are many others, such as publicity of violations, the quiet diplomacy of the ICRC, and sanctions against states that commit or tolerate serious violations of the law of armed conflict. Compliance with the relevant rules is the overall goal of most enforcement mechanisms at both the domestic and international levels. Sadly, it is unlikely that war crimes law will be relegated to the

---

[176] See, for example, Roberts, *supra* n.60.
[177] *Prosecutor v. Brdjanin*, Judgment, IT-99-36-A, 3 April 2007, at paras 244–252.
[178] On the second point, whether or not certain arms control treaties fall under the regime of the law of armed conflict or not is an area of great importance, but little scholarship.
[179] H. McCoubrey, 'The Concept and Treatment of War Crimes', (1996) 1 *JACL* 121, at 121. For a more aggressive critique see S. Sur, *International Law, Power, Security and Justice* (Oxford: Hart, 2010), 486, 488–489.
[180] The issue is considerably more complex than can be discussed here. For further comment see, among a vast literature, G. Mettraux, *The Law of Command Responsibility* (Oxford: Oxford University Press, 2009).
[181] Fleck, *supra* n.78, at 848.

footnotes of history any time soon.[182] It is also the case that where, in spite of modern developments, the law of war crimes is at its weakest, that is in non-international armed conflicts, those conflicts are the norm, not the exception. What can be hoped is that non-selective, effective prosecutions help, to some extent, to deter future violations, continue to assist in developing the law, and reaffirm that war crimes are not acceptable on the part of anyone.

---

[182] There is also the fact that those who have committed such serious crimes as war crimes ought to be labelled as such.

15. Peace settlements and international law: from *lex pacificatoria* to *jus post bellum*
Christine Bell*

1. INTRODUCTION

This chapter will examine the ways in which peace settlements are producing a *lex pacificatoria*, a new 'law of the peacemakers', in a range of different areas relating to international conflict and security law.[1] The chapter considers the relationship between this 'lex pax' and proposals for re-invigorating a concept of *jus post bellum* which forms a theme of this collection.

The chapter illustrates how the practice of fashioning and implementing peace settlements is forcing a revision of relevant international law, as the traditional assumptions and boundaries of relevant legal regimes do not fit within post-settlement political landscapes, are inadequate for enabling and regulating peace settlement implementation, and do not contain guidance for the dilemmas faced post-settlement. The chapter sets out the relationship between peace agreements and international law, describing the ways in which a lack of fit between peace settlement dilemmas and international legal doctrines has generated new practices and new articulations of international law. Building on earlier arguments, I argue that these revisions constitute a new *lex pacificatoria*, or 'law of the peacemakers', in the form of a normativized practice of conflict resolution. The extent to which these new practices constitute 'law' at all is critically evaluated throughout the chapter. In conclusion, I consider whether it is possible, useful and desirable to frame and develop the 'new law' as a new *jus post bellum* that might supplement existing categories of *jus ad bellum* and *jus in bello*.

2. PEACE SETTLEMENTS AND INTERNATIONAL LAW

The contemporary peace settlement is a post-Cold War phenomenon. International law historically divided conflict into 'international' conflict, to which international law applied, and 'internal' conflict, to which it largely did not. This classification, never entirely satisfactory, faced a particular challenge post-Cold War where it appeared to reflect neither the factual situation of war, which itself appeared ever more fused in its

---

* I would like to thank Kasey L. McCall-Smith for research assistance.
[1] This chapter builds and develops arguments set out in C. Bell, *On the Law of Peace: Peace Agreements and the Lex Pacificatoria* (Oxford: Oxford University Press, 2008) and C. Bell, 'Post-conflict Accountability and the Reshaping of Human Rights and Humanitarian Law', in O. Ben-Naftali (ed.), *International Humanitarian Law and International Human Rights Law* (Oxford: Oxford University Press, 2011).

international and internal dimensions, nor to delimit appropriate boundaries with respect to international law's goals of maintaining international peace.

As the Cold War ended, an apparent post-Cold War rise in intrastate conflict appeared to constitute the main threat to international peace and so drew the attention and involvement of international actors acting within a framework of international law. Intrastate conflict, originating mainly within state borders, involving state forces and non-state armed opposition groups, for example, in former Yugoslavia, Sri Lanka, Sierra Leone and Liberia, increasingly had interstate repercussions. It spilt across borders, drew in regional actors as conflict-underwriters or mediators, created new states, and attracted the attention and intervention of international organizations, in particular the United Nations (hereinafter 'UN'), and relevant regional organizations.[2] In addition, new practices of terminating intrastate conflict through negotiated settlement came to constitute a key international response to conflict. New post-Cold War conflicts prompted the use of negotiation in an attempt to contain and divert conflict. Long-standing conflicts appeared to hold real possibilities for conflict resolution and to present needs and opportunities for international intervention – itself now free from Cold War strictures and able to experiment. From 1990 onwards, peace processes appeared to break out all over in contexts as diverse as South Africa, the Middle East, Central America, and Eastern, and even Western, Europe. Even in the most domestic of conflicts, international actors – states, coalitions of states and international organizations – became involved in conflict resolution efforts. Conflict resolution within state boundaries was also curiously generated by interstate conflict. Post-Cold War, 'international' armed conflict began to see international military intervention justified partly in terms of post-conflict outcomes for the state against which force was deployed. International use of force in Bosnia, Kosovo, Afghanistan, Iraq (2003) and Libya was articulated wholly, or in part, in terms of ambitions to change the government and constitutional order of the states in question.[3] These international interventions contemplated some type of post-conflict political and legal reconstruction, often to involve the accommodation of those sub-state groups involved in an internal conflict operating in parallel to the international conflict.

It is difficult to overestimate the scale of this landscape on conflicts from 1990 onwards. In the period between 1990 and 2010, over 600 peace agreements were signed in around 90 jurisdictions.[4] The types of conflict in which negotiated settlements were attempted were varied in terms of their scale, nature, geographical location, the degree of internationalization of conflict containment and conflict resolution efforts, and the constellation of international actors involved. However, settlement terms across conflicts indicated a common approach to conflict resolution, namely an attempt to negotiate a permanent ceasefire coupled with political and legal reforms, aimed at

---

[2] D. Wippman (ed.), *International Law and Ethnic Conflict* (Ithaca, NY: Cornell University Press, 1998).

[3] There have also been some 'pure' interstate conflicts involving two states and often revolving around border disputes, for example: Chad/Libya, Ethiopia/Eritrea, China/India, India/Pakistan and Ecuador/Peru. However, even many of these conflicts also had closely related intrastate dimensions. The first war with Iraq of 1991 forms a clearer exception as an interstate conflict with little (initial) relationship to events within the state.

[4] See Bell, *On the Law of Peace*, supra n.1, appendix.

restructuring the state to accommodate the state's dissenters in a revised state formation. Peace settlements also almost invariably contemplated some type of international involvement to secure implementation – from full-on international administration, such as in Bosnia or Kosovo, to *ad hoc* involvement of 'international figures' for one-off implementation tasks, such as the involvement of individuals in decommissioning in Northern Ireland.

3. INTERNATIONAL CONFLICT AND SECURITY LAW

This conflict and peace settlement landscape had an impact on international law even as international law attempted to regulate it. The assumptions of relevant international legal regimes – human rights law, humanitarian law, refugee law and even UN Charter law on the use of force – were often inapposite to peace process needs and dilemmas. The post-settlement environment defied distinctions between international/domestic spheres of action, between war and peace, and indeed between public (state) and private (non-state) actors, on which the boundaries of these legal regimes depended.

A. 'International–Domestic' Hybridity

Ending conflict required an internal political settlement that was inclusive of military opponents within the state and the external enforcement of that settlement.[5] The internal and external dimensions were linked: internal settlement and compromise on the nature of the state was necessary to stopping the fighting, while external actors were needed to reassure the state's opponents that the state would be held to its side of the bargain in a domestic political and legal order that was now every bit as 'anarchic' as the international legal system itself. Thus, the typical post-conflict political and legal landscape was characterized by 'international–domestic' hybridity with post-settlement implementation tasks undertaken by international and domestic actors together. Post-conflict, states became entities that were both a national jurisdiction, with technical continuity of statehood, and at the same time a space of transnational administration permeated by international actors and characterized by 'post-sovereign' elements, such as bi-nationalism and international administration. This international–domestic hybridity created difficulties for traditional understandings of sovereignty and accountability, as assuming an ability to categorize the connection between the governors and the population they govern.

B. War–Peace Hybridity

Post-conflict seldom is *post*-conflict – even when a conflict has been terminated through a formally agreed ceasefire. War–peace hybridity can be seen in the 'no-war-no-peace' situation that tends to prevail post-settlement. The move from war to not-war is seldom linear and forms of violence often mutate in complex ways, rather than being eliminated. In practice, the signing of a peace agreement was seldom the end of the

---

[5] *Ibid.*, Chapters 5 and 10.

matter. Parties to settlements often reneged on their commitments and, covertly or overtly, returned to violence. Parties outside the negotiations post-settlement acted as 'spoilers' and attempted to destabilize fragile accords through high-profile dramatic acts, such as the assassination of Rabin post-Oslo Accords in the Middle East (now clearly not 'post-conflict'), the Omagh Bomb by the 'real IRA' immediately after the Belfast Agreement in Northern Ireland, the post-Arusha Accord genocide in Rwanda, and on-going violence in Iraq and Afghanistan. On-going conflict violence typically continued and, in some situations, even increased. Or the conflict ostensibly ended to be replaced by the new, more amorphous violence of dissenters, 'organized criminals' or increased inter-personal violence: for example, the 'new' racist violence of South Africa, the 'new' organized criminality of erstwhile paramilitaries in Colombia or domestic violence. These 'new' forms of violence were at once different and yet linked to the past conflict in ways that were difficult to document and articulate, let alone legally categorize, again with implications as to the governing body of law.

In short, post-settlement environments were characterized by a complex mix of war-acts, human rights violations and 'ordinary' criminal law violations, perpetrated by a range of domestic and international, state and non-state actors. Clear categorization of either the type of violence or the status of the perpetrator became impossible. Traditional regime boundaries, determining which legal regime applied, to whom and when, simply did not seem to fit the facts. Similarly, shifting in and out of different legal regimes, as violence waxed and waned, did not service the need for a coherent peace settlement implementation capable of being sustained, often in the face of violent attempts to destabilize it. Rather, what implementation required of law was the steady guidance and regulation of a set of complex implementation tasks to be undertaken in a fluid and complex security situation.

C. State and Non-state Actors

Finally, post-conflict environments contained a complex mix of state and non-state actors, both of whom could be alleged to be acting in private interest while laying legitimate claim to be public actors. Indeed, the very distinction between public and private, state and non-state actors is complicated by the fact of political transition. Both state and non-state actors face charges from each other that they do not represent 'the public' while claiming such representation for themselves. During transition from conflict to peace, the nature of the state itself is in transition from an authoritarian, illegitimate, violent or exclusionary regime that has not been acting in the traditional 'public' role of the state, towards a less authoritarian, more legitimate, less violent and exclusionary future, where public actors are restrained by public law.[6] Non-state actors may also be transitioning from a role as a 'private' actor exercising private power, to a role as a public actor exercising public power and claiming a representative legitimacy, as politicians or army chiefs, for example. The post-conflict period is one of attempted transition to a new political and even constitutional framework aimed at creating a new 'public' in which both the 'old' state and the new non-state actors will participate,

---

[6] See, generally, C. Bell, 'Peace Agreements: Their Nature and Legal Status', (2006) 100 *AJIL* 373.

eventually under the legitimacy of a revised form of election. However, the period of transition is one in which the legitimacy of both state and non-state actors is constantly under question and where civil society actors and international actors (also operating without electoral mandates) are often given a role to supplement and supervise the role of state and non-state actors as authors and implementers of any new order.

In legal terms, this set of transitional political realities creates difficulties for deciding who constitutes 'the state' in the event that the new transitional arrangements for holding power start to fall apart. Given that international law distinguishes between public and private actors and draws its use of force boundaries with specific reference to concepts such as 'state consent', again a set of 'fit' dilemmas arises: if peacekeepers need to move from peaceful settlement of disputes to enforcement – whose consent is necessary? What do the traditional concepts of neutrality and impartiality between conflict parties mean in a context in which the fabric and legitimacy of the state are being re-constituted to include both former state officials and anti-state combatants as part of the new constitutional order? If part of the post-conflict business is accountability for past human rights abuses and violations, but any attempt to move from these patterns of abuses and violations depends on the on-going consent of both state and non-state actors to a new set of political and legal institutions, then who should hold whom accountable for what and under what legal regime?

4. A NEW *LEX PACIFICATORIA*

Over the last twenty years of peace settlement practice, the needs and dilemmas of that practice began to force an interpretive revision of international law. Elsewhere I have argued that these developments can best be understood as a new '*lex pacificatoria*' or 'law of the peacemakers'. This *lex* bears similarity to the concept of *lex mercatoria* in that it stands less as a fully fledged new legal regime and more as a set of practices moving in a normativized direction, that is: they are increasingly codified by soft law standards (as the 'industry standards' of peacemakers rather than merchants); shape, and are incorporated in, interpretations of binding legal instruments; and on occasion influence, or are determinative of, court judgments. However, the normativity of the new *lex* lies less in being able to point to normative impacts and more in the ways in which the practices can be articulated to be compliant with, and even creative extensions of, traditional legal doctrines. The *lex* as creative application of new law, creates an on-going normative expectation as to how the political and moral conundrums of post-conflict reconstruction should be handled, that give it a jurisgenerative quality. The broad rubric and dynamic of the emergent 'new *lex*' can be sketched in outline, focusing on how the doctrines of self-determination, gender equality, refugee return, use of force and international legal accountability have been revised.

5. A NEW LAW OF HYBRID SELF-DETERMINATION

A. Traditional Understandings

Self-determination law provides that '[a]ll peoples have the right of self-determination. By virtue of that right they freely determine their political status and freely pursue their economic, social and cultural development.'[7] A range of legal declarations (and indeed the UN Charter) make clear that states retain a right to territorial integrity.[8] Prior to 1990 it was a truism to state that the law on self-determination was unclear. Emerging in the de-colonization period as a legal norm, whether and how the norm applied post-decolonization was much debated. Outside the de-colonization context the norm's two pillars, respect for territorial integrity and a commitment to representative government for peoples, appeared to clash. Rather than resolving self-determination disputes, the norm stood accused of fuelling them by telling states and their secessionist opponents that they both had a right to the quite different territorial and political states to which they aspired.[9]

B. The *Lex Pacificatoria*

This relationship between peace processes, peace settlements and self-determination law produced a new concept of 'hybrid self-determination', which operated to transcend the apparent tension of the dual commitment to territorial integrity and representative government by incorporating dimensions of both external and internal self-determination into the framework for resolving conflict. Conflict resolution practices centred on negotiations that included state and non-state actors on an equal basis and brokered compromise agreements that split power through a range of innovative power-sharing mechanisms, but also split sovereignty – not territorially, but by internationalizing the new constitutional arrangements in innovative ways.

The hybrid self-determination solutions of peace settlement, in general terms, therefore had some, or all, of the following elements:

- a procedural right for peoples to be heard, as implemented through negotiations between the state and groups who can credibly claim to be excluded from the state's social contract;
- a substantive right to elections, to an individual rights framework and to additional constitutional arrangements aimed at *effective* participation of groups

---

[7] Article 1, International Covenant on Civil and Political Rights (1966).

[8] Declaration on Principles of International Law Concerning Friendly Relations and Co-operation Among States in Accordance with the Charter of the United Nations (1970), GA Res. 2625(XXV) (1970); Declaration on the Granting of Independence to Colonial Countries and Peoples (1960), GA Res. 1514(XV) (1960); Article 2(4), Charter of the United Nations (1945).

[9] See discussion in M. Weller, 'Settling Self-determination Conflicts: Recent Developments', (2009) 20 *EJIL* 111, initial pages dealing with three instances where the law was unclear; see generally, J. Crawford, *The Creation of States in International Law* (Cambridge: Cambridge University Press, 2006).

in public decision-making, through mechanisms such as power-sharing and/or territorial autonomy;
- a right to dislocated statehood, or 'fuzzy sovereignty', which dislocates the state's power from a territorially defined 'demos', through forms of bi-nationalism, the language of external self-determination and/or international supervision.

From one point of view, these second two elements were produced as a logical consequence of the commitment to negotiated solutions to conflict. The logical response to negotiating disputes over access to the symbolism, power and resources of the state is to find ways to 'split' them and give all contenders access. The attempt to 'dislocate' power, from a territorially defined 'demos' to a more fluid 'beyond-the-state' set of institutions and actors, further splits power between domestic and international actors. Even the commitment to elections – a legal requirement under international human rights law – is, at the same time, a practical political necessity for auto-implementation of the new order.

However, this new 'hybrid self-determination' did not present itself as a crude compromise, but also as a reconciliation of the conflicting legal claims that the parties had made as to the application of self-determination law. By incorporating elements of internal self-determination through changes in the nature of the state, to make it more representative of all its peoples, but also elements of external self-determination through a more fluid notion of the external territoriality of the state, hybrid self-determination could claim to be an innovative fulfilment of self-determination law, capable of transcending, and thereby reconciling, not just competing self-determination claims but the conflict itself. A range of soft law standards and court decisions began to both reflect and underwrite the development of the practice, adding to the norm's normative dimensions. These standards underwrote not just a 'right to be heard' but the second element of hybrid self-determination, namely a right to some substantive revision of state political and legal institutions to ensure an on-going 'right to be heard' that goes beyond a right to elections (legally guaranteed in human rights law), to ensure not just participation as representation but '*effective* participation'. The UN Declaration on the Rights of National Minorities, the UN Declaration on the Rights of Indigenous Peoples and the Council of Europe Framework Convention on Minority Rights developed the idea of 'effective participation' as a substantive legal requirement of domestic constitutional and legal processes.[10] In addition to these minority and

---

[10] Declaration on the Rights of Persons Belonging to National or Ethnic, Religious or Linguistic Minorities (1992), GA Res. 47/135, annex, UN Doc. A/47/49 (1993) (hereinafter referred to as 'UN Declaration on Minorities'), Articles 2(3) and 5 (effective participation); Declaration on Rights of Indigenous Peoples (2007), GA Res. 61/295, UN Doc. A/RES/61/295 (2007) (hereinafter referred to as 'UN Declaration on Indigenous Peoples'), Articles 18–20 (effective participation) and 38 (consultation with indigenous peoples to achieve goals of declaration); Council of Europe, Framework Convention on the Protection of National Minorities (1994) (hereinafter referred to as 'Framework Convention'), that draws on the Conference on Security and Cooperation in European (later OSCE) documents that preceded it; see for example, Report of the CSCE Committee of Experts on National Minorities (19 July 1991), (1991) 30 *ILM* 1692. The Convention Concerning Indigenous and Tribal Peoples in Independent Countries (ILO No. 169) (1989), adopted on 27 June 1989 by the General Conference of the

indigenous peoples' standards, a number of legal standards and international guidelines now also address the need for inclusion of other groups: participation of women (addressed further in Section 6 below), children and even groups, such as 'victims' or 'displaced persons', in political negotiations and legal processes that will affect them.[11] The endorsement of a 'right to be heard' can also be seen in decisions of international organizations and international courts and tribunals, which have emphasized a right to processes of resolution in self-determination cases, rather than deciding in favour of the status quo of the existing state, or secession in cases involving self-determination claims.[12]

International Labour Organization, similarly emphasizes recognition and the need to move beyond representative democracy to ensure participation: Article 2(1) provides that: 'Governments shall have the responsibility for developing, with the participation of the peoples concerned, co-ordinated and systematic action to protect the rights of these peoples and to guarantee respect for their integrity.' Article 6(1)(b) provides that Governments are to: 'Establish means by which these peoples can freely participate, to at least the same extent as other sectors of the population, at all levels of decision-making in elective institutions and administrative and other bodies responsible for policies and programmes which concern them.'

[11] Report of the Fourth World Conference on Women, Annex II, Beijing Platform for Action (1995), UN Doc. A/CONF.177/20 (1995) (hereinafter referred to as 'Beijing Platform for Action'), at paras 181–195 (women in power and decision-making); Article 68 (participation of victims), Rome Statute of the International Criminal Court (1998) (hereinafter referred to as 'Rome Statute'). New standards on impunity also provide for the participation of women, minorities and victims in the design of transitional justice mechanisms, and associated rule of law reform; see D. Orentlicher, Report of the Independent Expert to Update the Set of Principles to Combat Impunity, Addendum: Updated Set of Principles for the Protection and Promotion of Human Rights through Action to Combat Impunity, UN Commission on Human Rights, UN Doc. E/CN.4/2005/102/Add.1 (2005) (hereinafter referred to as 'Updated Set of Principles'), at paras 7(c) and 35. See also UN Secretary-General, Report on the Rule of Law and Transitional Justice in Conflict and Post-Conflict Societies (2004), UN Doc. S/2004/616 (2004), at para. 64(f), providing that participation of 'groups most affected by conflict and a breakdown of the rule of law, among them children, women, minorities, prisoners and displaced persons'. New standards on a right to return of refugees and displaced persons similarly note their right to 'participate in the return and restitution process and in the development of the procedures and mechanisms put in place to protect these rights'; see for example, Sub-Commission on the Promotion and Protection of Human Rights, The Right to Return of Refugees and Internally Displaced Persons (2002), UN Doc. E/CN.4/SUB.2/RES/2002/30 (2002), at para. 6.

[12] See, ICJ decisions cited in J. Klabbers, 'The Right to be Taken Seriously: Self-determination in International Law', (2006) 28 *HRQ* 286; see also, Opinions Nos. 1– 10 of the Arbitration Commission of the Peace Conference on Yugoslavia, published in (1992) 31 *ILM* 1494 (No. 1), 1497 (No. 2), 1499 (No. 3), 1501 (No. 4), 1503 (No. 5), 1507 (No. 6), 1512 (No. 7), 1521 (No. 8), 1523 (No. 9), 1525 (No. 10); Opinions 11–15 published in (1993) 32 *ILM* 1586 (No. 11), 1589 (No. 12), 1591 (No. 13), 1593 (No. 14), 1595 (No. 15) (collectively referred to as the 'Badinter Opinions'); European Community: Declaration on Yugoslavia and on the Guidelines on the Recognition of New States (16 December 1991), (1992) 31 *ILM* 1485. See R. Rich, 'Recognition of States: The Collapse of Yugoslavia and the Soviet Union', (1993) 4 *EJIL* 36; M. Weller, 'The International Response to the Dissolution of the Socialist Federal Republic of Yugoslavia', (1992) 86 *AJIL* 569, for discussion of the complex relationship between the Yugoslav Guidelines, the conflict in Yugoslavia and the Badinter Opinions issued with respect to it.

As regards the other innovative dimension of hybrid self-determination – 'fuzzy sovereignty', again this concept is promoted by international legal standards that contemplate that self-government can go 'beyond-the-state'.[13] As regards bi-nationalism, and group contacts and governance that go beyond the state's territory, the Council of Europe Framework Convention on National Minorities and the UN Declaration on National Minorities refer to the right of ethnic groups to maintain cross-border contacts with ethnic counterparts in other jurisdictions and for states even to sign bilateral agreements to this effect.[14] The Declaration on the Rights of Indigenous Peoples expressly provides that indigenous peoples divided by international borders 'have the right to maintain and develop contacts, relations and cooperation, including activities for spiritual, cultural, political, economic and social purposes, with their own members as well as other peoples across borders' and that states should take effective measures to 'facilitate the exercise and ensure the implementation of this right'.[15] These provisions parallel and underwrite self-determination settlement attempts to sever notions of 'nationhood' from territorially based notions of 'statehood'.

The second mechanism for dislocating power – international supervision – also has a tenuous legal basis. First and foremost, international administration and supervision can be authorized by the UN Security Council (hereinafter 'UNSC') in particular conflicts. More recently, however, there have been attempts to found a more general legal articulation of 'fuzzy' or 'contingent' sovereignty through the 'responsibility to protect' doctrine.[16] Attempts to rationalize and bound 'humanitarian interventions' (that is, military intervention justified as a response to violations of humanitarian law) have attempted a fundamental revision of state sovereignty at the international constitutional level by developing a concept of 'responsibility to protect'. The 'responsibility to protect' doctrine works by attempting to reframe military intervention away from a 'humanitarian' exception to state sovereignty and towards a new conceptualization of sovereignty that views sovereignty as contingent on the state's willingness and ability to protect its own citizens.[17] Of course, the attempt to formulate sovereignty as conditioned on 'the responsibility to protect' can be seen as not very bounded and merely a rhetorical flourish that mitigates and justifies foreign intervention almost at will. Nonetheless, cynical or not, the concept of 'responsibility to protect' illustrates an attempt to underwrite international intervention by revising the concept of sovereignty, rather than articulating intervention as an exception to it: sovereignty must be envisaged as justified by states in terms of the prior normative authority of 'the people', rather than claimed as a static attribute of states as black boxes and therefore confers

---

[13] See, generally, W. Kymlicka, *Multicultural Odysseys: Navigating the New International Politics of Diversity* (Oxford: Oxford University Press, 2007), at 3–55, *passim* (arguing that these are a key part of the 're-internationalization' of state–minority relations).

[14] UN Declaration on Minorities, *supra* n.10, Articles 2(5), 5(2) and 6; Framework Convention, *supra* n.10, Articles 17 and 18.

[15] UN Declaration on Indigenous Peoples, *supra* n.10, Article 36.

[16] See 2005 World Summit Outcome Document, UN Doc. A/60/L.1 (2005), at paras 138–139; International Coalition for the Responsibility to Protect, available at www.responsibilitytoprotect.org; Global Centre for the Responsibility to Protect, available at globalr2p.org.

[17] *Ibid.*

obligations as well as rights. Once sovereignty is reconceived as a 'relational', rather than an absolute, concept it becomes more 'fuzzy': degrees of sovereignty, shared sovereignty and 'earned' sovereignty all become possible and international organizations are legitimized as supervisors and enablers of sovereignty, rather than entities that transgress the sovereignty of states when they intervene.

C. Normative (In)Stability

Despite the emergence of a normativized practice of 'hybrid self-determination', its normative basis is unstable with regard to its two main innovations. Soft law standards, the practices of international organizations, and even international courts and tribunals, have all appeared to endorse the concept. However, as Kymlicka has pointed out, these normative developments remain *ad hoc*, unstable, patchy and difficult to roll out beyond a European context.[18] Kymlicka argues that there is a tension between an approach of general anti-discrimination norms and targeted norms that go beyond anti-discrimination to suggest substantive measures aimed at including particular kinds of minorities, such as national minorities or indigenous peoples. As Iorns Magallanes argues, this tension can also be viewed as a tension between 'democratization' standards and 'indigenous peoples' standards, which in practice comes down to a different stance on groups' rights.[19] In short, while indigenous peoples' standards and decisions involving such group dimensions appear to have moved towards requiring such mechanisms, in the realm of minority rights there appears to be a measure of retreat to a concept of individual equality and a classic 'liberal' framework for political participation and rights. As regards power-sharing, for example, some soft law standards, guidelines and commentators suggest that it constitutes good practice, its hybridity between representative and participative democracy constituting a form of 'responsible realism', which combines a commitment to individual rights with a commitment to the realities of the need for group accommodation for equality to be achieved and sustained in practice.[20] However, other international courts and commentators view such mechanisms as being of dubious international legality, at best to be tolerated as a temporary transitional device where they can be demonstrated to enable a move from conflict to peace, moving to unlawful once the situation has stabilized.[21]

Similarly, the post-state dimensions of hybrid self-determination also have an unstable normative basis. While international law shows some programmatic endorsement of extra-national mechanisms for creating beyond-the-state governance, and while

---

[18] Kymlicka, *supra* n.13, Chapter 8.
[19] C. Iorns Magallanes, 'Indigenous Rights and Democratic Rights in International Law: An "Uncomfortable Fit"?', (2010) 15 *UCLA J Int'l L & Foreign Affairs* 111.
[20] J. McGarry and B. O'Leary, *The Northern Ireland Conflict: Consociational Engagements* (Oxford: Oxford University Press, 2004), at 19–24. See Lund Recommendations on the Effective Participation of National Minorities in Public Life & Explanatory Note (September 1999), available at www.osce.org/hcnm/30325.
[21] *Case of Sejdić and Finci v. Bosnia and Herzegovina*, Applications Nos. 27996/06 and 34836/06, Eur. Ct. Hum. Rts. GC, Judgment of 22 December 2009; see also, S. Wheatley, *Democracy, Minorities and International Law* (Cambridge: Cambridge University Press, 2005), at 153, for arguments that power-sharing can violate international law.

there are attempts to justify international intervention on the grounds that claims of sovereignty must be connected to good government within the state, both constitute a radical revision of a system of international law based on the sovereign equality of states, about which there is little to no formal consensus. The 'right to protect', for example, is a new and controversial doctrine, and while some legal standards promote 'beyond-the-state' institutions, it is unclear that these are *required* of states. It is often claimed that 'self-determination law is not a suicide club for states', and neither is the new *lex* of 'hybrid self-determination'.

The instability of the norms underwriting hybrid self-determination appear to invite resolution in the direction of retreat to more traditional notions of participation and statehood, or advancement in the direction of solidifying and clarifying the boundaries of the new normative approach. Paradoxically, this normative instability is, to some extent, sustaining the hybridity of the new normative development as neither retreat nor development appear possible or desirable. There is little to retreat to in terms of self-determination law helpful to addressing conflict, while developing the norm would require state consensus that does not exist. Curiously, the capacity of hybrid self-determination arrangements to operate as a 'holding device' for disagreements between the domestic parties to a conflict over sovereignty also enables it to operate as a holding device at the international level, bridging competing conceptions of how sovereignty should be understood in a post-Westphalian international legal world. It is easier, for example, for states to live with a fluid and partial quasi-law of hybrid self-determination into which they can all read a version of self-determination law to which they can ascribe, than to embrace and support a move to international law as requiring, for example, liberal statehood or an accepted definitition of permissible humanitarian intervention.

6. A NEW LAW OF GENDER INCLUSION

A. Traditional Understandings

Traditionally, the process of negotiating an end to a conflict was a matter for the parties to the conflict and, to the extent that the conflict was viewed as an 'internal', the only thing constraining who came to the table, and what was discussed there, was the political will of the parties involved. Peace-making in non-international conflicts was a domestic political matter for those involved in the conflict and untouched by international legal frameworks. With the development of human rights law, equality for women became a matter of international concern. However, the Convention on the Elimination of All Forms of Discrimination Against Women, 1979 (hereinafter 'CEDAW') notoriously did not address violence against women, nor did it address violent conflict in which women were caught. The idea that equality for women should make demands on the process or substance of peace settlements required over a decade of exploring the gendered dynamics of conflict, a rise in the impact of human rights law more generally and experience of the gendered nature of peace negotiations.

B. The *Lex Pacificatoria*

The post-Cold War environment was one in which human rights and humanitarian law standards were understood to apply to both conflict and peace processes and were increasingly understood to constrain both the process and substance of negotiations. Moreover, the same post-Cold War years that witnessed a steady proliferation of peace processes and peace agreements aimed at bringing violent social conflict to an end[22] were also marked by the transnational mobilization of women to secure feminist-informed reform to international law and institutions.[23] Violence against women was itself defined as a form of discrimination[24] and increasingly international conferences and resolutions began to emphasize the need to consider the gendered dimensions of armed conflict and its impact on women and women's equality.[25] With the rise of peace processes and agreements, attention focused on the inclusion of women in peace processes, the gender impact of what the parties to conflict agreed to and post-conflict accountability for the abuse of women, in particular sexual violence.

It can also be argued that concern about the inclusiveness or non-inclusiveness of peace processes with regard to women also derived from the concept of hybrid self-determination. A concept that endorses a right to participate cannot draw the line at the participation of the ethnic protagonists to the conflict. As touched on in Section 2, processes aimed at linking ceasefires to constitutional revision raise questions as to the appropriate authors of such revision. In a context where neither state nor non-state actors can assert themselves as fully legitimate representatives of 'the people', and where issues of 'equality' and inclusion are central to conflict resolution, a question arises as to how widely the concepts of equality and inclusion should go.

Again it can be argued, both as a conflict resolution imperative and a response to international human rights standards relating to women, that a new law of gender inclusion began to be articulated and underwritten by new legal standards that specifically addressed peace processes. Most notably, marking the culmination of a series of resolutions and World Conference commitments, on the 31 October 2000 UNSC Resolution 1325 on Women, Peace and Security was passed.[26]

---

[22] For description of the rise in peace agreements, the reasons linking it to the end of the Cold War and the scale of the phenomenon, see Bell, *On the Law of Peace*, supra n.1.

[23] N. Reilly, *Women's Human Rights: Seeing Gender Justice in a Globalising Age* (Oxford: Polity, 2008); see also A. Boyle and C. Chinkin, *The Making of International Law* (Oxford: Oxford University Press, 2007), Chapter 2.

[24] Committee on the Elimination of all forms of Discrimination against Women, General Recommendation No. 19 (1992), UN Doc. CEDAW/C/1992/L.1/ Add.15 (1992), at para. 1: 'Gender-based violence is a form of discrimination that seriously inhibits women's ability to enjoy rights and freedoms on a basis of equality with men.'

[25] Windhoek Declaration and Namibia Plan of Action on Mainstreaming a Gender Perspective in Multidimensional Peace Support Operations (2000), UN Doc. A/55/138-S/2000/693, Annex I and II (2000); Bejing Platform for Action, *supra* n.11; Vienna Declaration and Programme of Action (1993), UN Doc. A/CONF.157/23 (1993), at para. 29.

[26] Resolution on Women, Peace and Security, UNSC Res. 1325 (2000), UN Doc. S/RES/1325 (2000).

Resolution 1325 called for women's equal participation with men and their full involvement in all efforts for the maintenance and promotion of peace and security. It reaffirmed the need to fully implement international humanitarian and human rights law to protect women and girls from human rights abuses, including gender-based violence.[27] It identified the need to mainstream gender perspectives in relation to conflict prevention, peace negotiations, peacekeeping operations, humanitarian assistance, post-conflict reconstruction and disarmament, demobilization and reintegration initiatives.[28] The resolution was addressed variously to UN institutions, member states and all parties to armed conflict. Of particular note here, the Resolution specifically targeted peace processes and agreements; paragraph 8:

Calls on all actors involved, when negotiating and implementing peace agreements, to adopt a gender perspective, including, inter alia:

(a) The special needs of women and girls during repatriation and resettlement and for rehabilitation, reintegration and post-conflict reconstruction;
(b) Measures that support local women's peace initiatives and indigenous processes for conflict resolution, and that involve women in all of the implementation mechanisms of the peace agreements;
(c) Measures that ensure the protection of and respect for human rights of women and girls, particularly as they relate to the constitution, the electoral system, the police and the judiciary.

The adoption of Resolution 1325 was significant on several grounds. The Resolution constituted the first time that the UNSC turned its full attention to the subject of women and armed conflict and acknowledged the role of women as active agents in the negotiation and maintenance of peace agreements, legalizing the issue.[29] The resolution symbolically marked the impact of war on women and provided formal, high-level acknowledgement that the exclusion of women from conflict resolution is a threat to peace. In practice, the Resolution automatically triggered on-going UN attention to women, peace and security, not least through creating the need for on-going UN Secretary-General reporting on its implementation.[30] The Resolution constituted a major victory for women's transnational mobilization in mainstreaming women's equality within the UN.[31] In the approach to its ten year anniversary, Resolution 1325

---

[27] *Ibid.*, at paras 9, 10, 11 and 12.
[28] *Ibid.*, at paras 1, 2, 5, 6, 7, 8 and 13.
[29] Resolution 1325 is a 'thematic' Resolution best understood as a Chapter VI UN Charter (non-binding) resolution. Its legal authority has been accentuated by the fact that it was passed unanimously, and that the Resolution uses the language of obligation. On the status and nature of Resolution 1325, see S. Anderlini, *Women Building Peace: What they Do, Why it Matters* (Boulder, CO and London: Lynne Reinner, 2004), at 196–199; on the background of Resolution 1325, see generally, Peace Women website, available at peacewomen.org/themes_theme.php?id=15&subtheme=true; UNIFEM Women War and Peace Portal, available at womenwarpeace.org/1325_toolbox.
[30] UNSC Res. 1325, *supra* n.26, at para. 17. For reports see tracking at www.womenwarpeace.org/1325_toolbox#tracking.
[31] See further, C. O'Rourke, 'Feminism v. Feminism: What is a Feminist Approach to Transnational Criminal Law?', (2008) *ASIL Proceedings of the 102nd Annual Meeting* 274.

was supplemented by additional UNSC resolutions aimed at strengthening and expanding its provisions and securing its implementation. UNSC Resolution 1820 (2008) continues and reinforces Resolution 1325's provisions on sexual violence against women in armed conflict and urges increased participation of women in peace talks.[32] UNSC Resolution 1888 (2009), focusing on the implementation of measures dealing with sexual violence, also notes in its preamble 'the underrepresentation of women in formal peace processes, the lack of mediators and ceasefire monitors with proper training in dealing with sexual violence, and the lack of women as Chief or Lead peace mediators in United Nations-sponsored peace talks.'[33] This Resolution was closely followed by UNSC Council Resolution 1889 (2009) aimed at increasing awareness and achieving the implementation of Resolution 1325 and affirming its key peace process dimensions.[34]

C. Normative (In)stability

Unlike the normative developments with relation to hybrid self-determination, the norm of gender inclusion appears to be fairly clearly articulated and established at least as nonbinding law. However, it remains sparsely implemented. Between 1990 and 2010, only 16 per cent of peace agreements mention women in any form, although these mentions rise from 11 per cent before the passing of UNSC Resolution 1325, to 25 per cent after.[35] Most of these references are isolated and, while perhaps of benefit to some women, do not evidence the adoption of a holistic 'gender perspective' that UNSC 1325 contemplates. Rather than normative instability, there is an 'under-enforcement'

---

[32] UNSC Res. 1820 (2008). Paragraph 12 urges 'the Secretary-General and his Special Envoys to invite women to participate in discussions pertinent to the prevention and resolution of conflict, the maintenance of peace and security, and post-conflict peacebuilding, and encourages all parties to such talks to facilitate the equal and full participation of women at decision-making levels'.

[33] Paragraph 17 urges that 'the issues of sexual violence be included in all United Nations-sponsored peace negotiation agendas', and also that 'the inclusion of sexual violence issues from the outset of peace processes in such situations, in particular in the areas of pre-ceasefires, humanitarian access and human rights agreements, ceasefires and ceasefire monitoring, DDR [demobilization, demilitarization and reintegration] and SSR [security sector reform] arrangements, vetting of armed security forces, justice, reparations, and recovery/development'.

[34] UNSC Res. 1889 recognizes in its preamble the under-representation of women 'at all stages of peace processes', and in particular at the level of mediators. The preamble also notes the particular exclusion from peace processes of refugees and internally displaced persons, both being groups where women tend to be over-represented. Paragraph 1 calls on member states, and international and regional organizations to improve the participation of women in peace processes; paragraph 4 calls on the Secretary-General to develop a strategy to increase the number of UN mediators who are women.

[35] C. Bell and C. O'Rourke, 'Peace Agreements of Pieces of Paper? The Impact of UNSC Resolution 1325 on Peace Processes and Their Agreements', (2010) 59 *ICLQ* 941.

issue.³⁶ The under-enforcement of UNSC Resolution 1325, however, raises a wider difficulty with the normativizing of peace processes and peace agreements. How far should normative standards dictate the substance of peace agreement texts and the make-up of peace agreement processes, and to what extent do the ideals which they articulate need to be balanced with the need to leave enough substance to negotiators, to enable them to reach agreements which they are capable and willing of implementing? The development of a norm of gender inclusion in peace processes and agreements points to a tension between using norms to shape, and even dictate, who and what gets included and the need to create a dynamic process, which has capacity to lead to a number of different outcomes and is thus capable of bringing fighting parties to the table – the conflict itself often forming a key barrier to any material gains for women.

7. A NEW LAW OF RETURN

A. Traditional Understandings

Traditionally international law did not address the right of refugees and displaced persons to return to their home country, less to the actual physical houses out of which they had been forced. Rather, refugee law was more concerned with the right of refugees *not* to return to homes where they would be persecuted.³⁷ The one conflict in which return was a political demand of refugees, the Israel–Palestine conflict, was excepted from the refugee convention regime and had its own UN agency.³⁸ A number of general human rights provisions, however, appear to support a right of refugees and displaced persons to return home at the end of conflict: namely, Article 12(4) of the International Covenant on Civil and Political Rights, 1966 (hereinafter 'ICCPR') provides that 'no one shall be arbitrarily deprived of the right to enter his own country'. Article 17 of the Universal Declaration of Human Rights provides for a right to own private property and not to be arbitrarily deprived of that property, which could be used to support a right to return to actual homes that were vacated or to be provided with compensation, although this right appears in neither the ICCPR nor the International Covenant on Economic, Social and Cultural Rights, 1966. The concept of 'refugee' is given a strict legal definition under the Refugee Convention 1951 as, 'people who have

---

³⁶ See Fionnuala Ní Aoláin for the concept of 'under-enforcement' in a gender context: F. Ní Aoláin, 'Gendered Under-enforcement in the Transitional Justice Context', in S. Buckley-Zistel and R. Stanley (eds), *Gender in Transitional Justice* (Basingstoke: Palgrave Macmillan, 2012); F. Ní Aoláin and E. Rooney, 'Underenforcement and Intersectionality: Gendered Aspects of Transition', (2007) 1 *Int'l J of Trans Justice* 338.

³⁷ Article 33(1), UN Convention on the Status of Refugees (1951) (hereinafter referred to as 'Refugee Convention').

³⁸ Refugee Convention, *ibid.*, provides in the introductory note that the Convention:

[D]oes not apply to those refugees who benefit from the protection or assistance of a United Nations agency other than UNHCR, such as refugees from Palestine who fall under the auspices of the United Nations Relief and Works Agency for Palestine Refugees in the Near East (UNRWA).

fled across an international boundary as a result of a well-founded fear of persecution for reasons of race, religion, nationality, membership of a particular social group, or political opinion'.[39] Those who have committed serious crimes are not included. The UN Convention therefore provides neither a right not to return, nor a right to return of 'non-status refugees' – those fleeing across state borders displaced by general armed conflict, or 'internally displaced persons' – those who flee homes and localities but do not cross international borders, neither of whom are caught by its definitions.

B. The *Lex Pacificatoria*

The post-Cold War conflict and post-conflict environment exposed a lack of fit between the coverage and concerns of refugee law and the political and material needs of all those displaced by the conflict and also third party states affected by flows of people. As regards fit, often the refugee law definitions of refugee do not fit those who flee as a result of conflict. People flee merely under well-founded fears of persecution, but also in anticipation of attack, meaning it can be unclear whether they satisfy the Convention definition. In practice, the scale of mass movement triggered by conflict post-1990 was often dealt with by third party countries bringing in 'temporary protection' regimes which enabled them to receive large numbers of people fleeing conflict without the need to avoid processing individual asylum claims, but also enabled them to keep post-conflict 'return' open both legally and politically.[40] The Refugee Convention itself does not provide a formal right to resettlement in the country of refuge, or a right of resettlement elsewhere; neither does it provide for a formal right not to be returned to the state of origin once the situation permits. However, the 1990s saw a concept of 'safe return' promoted by reception states as a mid-way measure between 'voluntary return' (the concept preferred by the UN High Commissioner on Refugees (hereinafter 'UNHCR')) and *de facto* expulsion, as debates over the temporary nature of protection, the extent of necessary protection from refoulement and the permissibility of mandatory return under the Convention gathered pace. For reasons of self-interest, displacement as a result of conflict focused international attention on the return of refugees and displaced persons as a post-conflict imperative. In terms of political and moral basis of the peace process, there were also reasons to make provision for return. Where displacement had been not just a consequence of conflict but a tool of the conflict, for example the ethnic cleansing of Bosnia, 'undoing' the expulsion of ethnic groups through return constituted a political demand of displaced constituencies and their representatives, while fitting with the interests of reception states. Return in this instance was also linked to the international community's preferred solution to the conflict of a unitary central state, in a context where this state had been given very little substance in preference to ethnically defined and segregated

---

[39] Regional conventions definitions are somewhat broader, see Organization of African Unity, Convention Governing the Specific Aspects of Refugee Problems in Africa (1969).

[40] See, generally, C. Bell, *Peace Agreements and Human Rights* (Oxford: Oxford University Press, 2000), at 235–242.

entities. Return therefore bore the burden of reversing over time what had been conceded at the peace negotiations, illustrating how return can link to self-determination questions: return of the displaced has capacity to change the balance of minorities and majorities in electoral units or even regions.

Return was often also viewed as part of a concept of reparation for victims of the conflict and an attempt to 'restore' them to their previous situation. From a purely pragmatic point of view, aggrieved displaced communities could sow the seeds of renewed conflict by creating an on-going perception that the conflict is not over by agitating as a diaspora against an indigenous leadership, and even by funding conflict. An unmanaged return and re-claiming of property, with no peace agreement provision for re-distribution or compensation, had a very direct capacity to re-ignite local conflicts and the central conflict itself. Dealing with the return of those displaced by the conflict became a peace agreement imperative because failing to do so would affect the sustainability of the settlement.

Even where displacement was a consequence, rather than a tool, of the conflict it was viewed as important to deal with issues of return in many peace agreements. People often start to return home if a situation is perceived to be safe, such as when a ceasefire or peace agreement is signed, even in the absence of a peace agreement commitment to return. A rapid return of a large number of people without the involvement of appropriate international and domestic agencies can create a host of social problems that a peace agreement can usefully anticipate and address. Management of return was understood to be crucial to post-conflict stability and the safety of returnees.

Again, provision of peace agreements bolstered by soft law standards began to address the relative silence of refugee law on questions of return, 'creating' law and fleshing out more detailed legal provision and new institutional mechanisms to facilitate a 'right to return'. In 1995, for example, the Dayton Peace Agreement (hereinafter 'DPA') made detailed provision for a 'right to return' for displaced persons. Annex 7 provided an Agreement on Refugees and Displaced Persons, Article 1 providing that:

> All refugees and displaced persons have the right freely to return to their homes of origin. They shall have the right to have restored to them the property of which they were deprived in the course of hostilities since 1991 and to be compensated for any property that cannot be restored to them.[41]

A set of positive obligations and mechanisms for giving effect to this right were then provided for: the UNHCR was called on to 'develop in close consultation with asylum countries and the parties [to the agreement] a repatriation plan' to allow for 'early' return of refugees and displaced persons; while the parties undertook to cooperate with, and give unrestricted access to, UNHCR, the International Committee of the Red Cross (hereinafter 'ICRC'), the UN Development Programme and other relevant international,

---

[41] General Framework Agreement for Peace in Bosnia and Herzegovina (14 December 1995) (hereinafter referred to as 'Dayton Peace Agreement'), Annex 7, 'Agreement on Refugees and Displaced Persons', Article 1.

domestic and non-governmental organizations.⁴² Similar provisions aimed at establishing and enabling a right to return can be found in a range of other peace agreements.⁴³

These types of mechanisms began also to be reflected in soft law standards, such as UN Guiding Principles on Internal Displacement and the Principles on Housing and Property Restitution for Refugees and Displaced Persons.⁴⁴ These standards specifically defined and addressed all forms of displaced persons, whether they satisfied Refugee Convention definitions or not, and started to flesh out a right to return, to include:

- a right to return to one's country and even locality;
- a right for return to be voluntary;
- a right not to be returned where conditions are not safe;
- a right to return to own homes or to be compensated where this is not possible;
- a right not to be discriminated against, having returned, and to political, legal and physical security;
- a requirement on parties to the conflict to cooperate with the relevant agencies to ensure safe and voluntary return;
- a right to be included as a group in decisions about return, including in the peace negotiations themselves.

These standards claimed to elucidate existing hard law standards, such as human rights law or international criminal law.⁴⁵ However, they have significantly developed the law even as they applied it to the post-settlement context, in a sense developing a quasi-specialist regime for refugees and displaced persons post-conflict.⁴⁶

C. Normative (In)stability

As with the area of gender inclusion, these norms are in place but without apparent moves to codify them as 'hard law'. In this area too they are 'under-enforced'. Further, as with the issue of gender, when taken cumulatively with other norms relating to peace settlement terms, these 'return' norms appear to further limit the realm of what can be freely negotiated, again indicating a dilemma over whether to adopt a maximalist approach to international legal regulation that attempts to ensure that return is dealt

---

⁴² *Ibid.*, Articles I, para. 5 and III, para. 2.

⁴³ See for example, Comprehensive Agreement concluded between the Government of Nepal and the Communist Party of Nepal (Maoist), 21 November 2006; Arusha Peace and Reconciliation Agreement for Burundi, 28 August 2000.

⁴⁴ UN Commission on Human Rights, Guiding Principles on Internal Displacement (1998), UN Doc. E/CN.4/1998/53/Add.2 (1998) (hereinafter referred to as 'Guidelines on the Internally Displaced'); P. Sérgio Pinheiro, Final Report of the Special Rapporteur, Principles on Housing and Property Restitution for Refugees and Displaced Persons, Annex: Principles on Housing and Property Restitution for Refugees and Displaced Persons, UN Doc. E/CN.4/Sub.2/2005/17 (2005).

⁴⁵ See W. Kälin, *Guiding Principles on Internal Displacement – Annotations* (Washington, DC: ASIL and Brookings Institutions, 2000).

⁴⁶ Guidelines on the Internally Displaced, *supra* n.44, Principle 28(2); see also, Addressing Internal Displacement in Peace Processes, Peace Agreements and Peace-Building, Brookings Institute–University of Bern (September 2007).

with, and dealt with in appropriate detail, and a more minimalist pragmatic approach that leaves room for pragmatic concerns of how best to get people to agree and to implement their agreement.[47]

8. A NEW LAW OF TRANSITIONAL JUSTICE

A. Traditional Understandings of Post-conflict Accountability

Traditionally, the ending of interstate conflict included broad amnesties for those waging the war aimed at the demobilization of troops and the return of prisoners taken during the war.[48] After the First World War, punitive reparations were imposed against Germany, which were later seen as having played a part in the political dynamics which led to the rise of Hitler. After the Second World War, an individual criminal justice approach was preferred, with the dedicated and temporal individual criminal law processes in the Nuremberg and Tokyo tribunals. In the period between 1945 and 1990, international responsibility for internationally wrongful acts continued to be developed but continued to view state-to-state reparations as the key remedy.[49]

As regards internal conflict, the question of how to deal with those who had been involved in the conflict was assumed to be a political matter, with the granting of domestic amnesty even a 'right' of states. Up until the early 1990s, the negotiated settlements of such conflicts typically viewed amnesty as a key tool in peace negotiations and the idea that there was a justice–peace dilemma implicating international law did not figure. For example, formal or *de facto* amnesties figured in attempts to end the conflict in Northern Ireland and the conflict with the Red Brigades in Italy in the 1980s. Concepts of reparations as applying between the state and individuals within the state were to depend on developments in human rights law.[50]

B. The *Lex Pacificatoria*

Again, it can be argued that the post-conflict landscape has significantly revised international law towards a partial and somewhat messy 'new law' of transitional justice. In this case, the new *lex* was a product of 'fitting' the accountability

---

[47] G. McHugh, *Integrating Internal Displacement in Peace Processes and Agreements* (Washington, DC: Brookings Institute, 2010).
[48] See further, A. Du Bois-Pedain, *Transitional Amnesty in South Africa* (Cambridge: Cambridge University Press, 2007), at 302.
[49] See for example, *Corfu Channel Case (United Kingdom v. Albania)*, Merits, Judgment of 9 April 1949, [1949] ICJ Rep. 4, 23; *Case concerning Military and Paramilitary Activities in and against Nicaragua (Nicaragua v. United States of America)*, Merits, Judgment of 27 June 1986 [1986] ICJ Rep. 14, at paras 283, 292; see further, Articles on Responsibility of States for Internationally Wrongful Acts, reproduced in UN Doc. A/56/49(Vol. I)//Corr.4 (2001), Article 1.
[50] For a history of development, see T. van Boven, 'The United Nations Basic Principles and Guidelines on the Right to a Remedy and Reparation for Victims of Gross Violations of International Human Rights Law and Serious Violations of International Humanitarian Law', available at untreaty.un.org/cod/avl/pdf/ha/ga_60-147/ga_60-147_e.pdf.

requirements of human rights and humanitarian law to post-conflict accountability demands, as mediated by the need to sustain the ceasefire. This process revised both regimes, while also shaping the development of international criminal law, to the point of a loose bottom common denominator. This common denominator established a normative imperative in the direction of a prohibition of broad amnesties that include serious war crimes, while leaving some (loosely identified) scope for negotiating partial accountability as not requiring full investigation, prosecution and punishment for all violators and violations. The new *lex* also requires the rights of victims to be addressed and has viewed reparations as the entitlement of victims and local communities, rather than states.[51]

The normative move towards prohibiting amnesties has been articulated as being required by the combined import of human rights and humanitarian law, as underwritten by international criminal law developments.[52] These new interpretations of the legal regimes are again underwritten by a range of soft law standards, by judicial decisions and by peace agreement practice.

i. Human rights law

At the end of the Cold War it was not initially apparent that human rights had any post-conflict regulatory claim over the conflict past. It was with respect to the resolution of conflicts in Central and South America that the argument first came to be made that human rights law had a post-conflict reach. Human rights commentary and advocacy from the early 1990s argued that human rights law did impose obligations on the post-settlement regime to account for the violations of the past regime.[53] The argument was that human rights standards imposed not just a negative obligation not to violate rights, but, in respect of serious human rights violations, such as arbitrary execution and torture, imposed positive obligations to investigate and, possibly, to prosecute and even punish those responsible, which constrained and outlasted any political settlement or change of regime. It was suggested that a balance with the political needs of transition were met by the fact that not all human rights violations had to be systematically investigated, prosecuted and punished, but rather international legal requirements could be met by focusing on grave human rights abuses.[54] Perhaps

---

[51] *Ibid.*

[52] For academic support, see H. Gropengießer and J. Meißner, 'Amnesties and the Rome Statute of the International Criminal Court', (2005) 5 *Int'l Crim L Rev* 267; R. O'Brien, 'Amnesty and International Law', (2005) 74 *Nordic J Int'l L* 261; J. Gavron, 'Amnesties in the Light of Developments in International Law and the Establishment of the International Criminal Court', (2002) 51 *ICLQ* 91; R.C. Slye, 'The Legitimacy of Amnesties Under International Law and General Principles of Anglo-American Law: Is a Legitimate Amnesty Possible?', (2002) 43 *Va J Int'l L* 172.

[53] See in particular the influential articles of D. Orentlicher, 'Settling Accounts: The Duty to Prosecute Human Rights Violations of a Prior Regime', (1991) 100 *Yale L J* 2537; N. Roht-Arriaza, 'State Responsibility to Investigate and Prosecute Grave Human Rights Violations in International Law', (1990) 78 *Cal L Rev* 449.

[54] See D. Orentlicher, '"Settling Accounts" Revisited: Reconciling Global Norms with Local Agency', (2007) 1 *Int'l J Tran Justice* 10, for an explanation of the context in which her 1991 article was written.

not surprisingly, these arguments were developed first in the context of Central and South America, where impunity was a key feature of the conflicts and the mechanism whereby such conflict was recycled. From this context the idea of an explicitly 'transitional' form of justice emerged as a form of justice that took place in, and responded to, a political transition from authoritarianism to democracy. The concept of 'transition to democracy' was understood to shape the type of accountability offered. Pursuit of democratic transition both underwrote arguments that human rights law's obligations had purchase and, paradoxically, also legitimated an approach whereby partial forms of accountability of those most responsible for the most serious violations would suffice.[55]

ii. Humanitarian law

Similar problems of fit and reinterpretation arose with regard to the application of humanitarian law. As with human rights law, towards the beginning of the 1990s humanitarian law's standards of accountability were not viewed as requiring post-conflict accountability for violence in intrastate conflicts. Although humanitarian law has provisions dealing with non-state as well as state action, and was specifically designed for situations of conflict, arguments that humanitarian law required post-conflict accountability again had to be asserted and required an interpretive shift, similar to that of human rights law.

Although from 1945 onwards there has been a clear legal framework in the Geneva Conventions imposing legal requirements on states to prosecute for grave breaches of international law taking place during international conflict, there has been no clear requirement of a duty to prosecute in internal armed conflict. Only a sub-section of intrastate armed conflict is covered by humanitarian law – conflicts involving national liberation movements (Protocol I) and conflicts meeting the threshold tests of Protocol II and Common Article 3 of the Geneva Conventions.[56] Even where an intrastate conflict does fall within humanitarian law's parameters, states are often reluctant to concede its application and (unlike with human rights treaties) there is no supervisory body to enforce the Conventions; rather, there is an obligation on all states to ensure

---

[55] See P. Arthur, 'How "Transitions" Re-shaped Human Rights: A Conceptual History', (2009) 31 *HRQ* 321, arguing that the concept of 'transition to democracy' prioritized legal–institutional reform also over social justice and re-distribution. *Cf.* R. Teitel, *Transitional Justice* (New York: Oxford University Press, 2000), addressing the broader lineage and application of the term 'transitional justice'.

[56] Protocol Additional to the Geneva Conventions of 12 August 1949, and Relating to the Protection of Victims of International Armed Conflicts (Protocol I) (1977); Protocol Additional to the Geneva Conventions of 1949, and Relating to the Protection of Victims of Non-international Armed Conflicts (Protocol II) (1977); Common Article 3 of the Geneva Convention for the Amelioration of the Condition of the Wounded and Sick in Armed Forces in the Field (1949), Geneva Convention for the Amelioration of the Condition of Wounded, Sick and Shipwrecked Members of Armed Forces at Sea (1949), Geneva Convention Relative to the Treatment of Prisoners of War (1949), and Geneva Convention Relative to the Protection of Civilian Persons in Time of War (1949) (collectively referred to as the 'Geneva Conventions').

implementation.[57] Moreover, what these texts require as regards post-conflict accountability in internal conflict is not spelt out. There is no equivalent to the explicit grave breaches regime relating to international conflict that imposes an obligation to prosecute grave breaches of humanitarian law in international armed conflict. The argument that humanitarian law required post-conflict individual liability to be imposed through criminal law process again required an interpretive revision.

Over time, the application of individual criminal accountability to violations of humanitarian law in non-international armed conflict came to be firmly accepted in a range of state practice and judgments of international courts and tribunals.[58] Moreover, the consequent duties to prosecute were understood to be on-going and therefore to have post-conflict application.[59] By 2005, international acceptance that humanitarian law imposed on-going accountability requiring individual criminal responsibility was apparently so comprehensive that the ICRC stated as customary law that:

- individuals are responsible for war crimes committed in both international and non-international armed conflict;
- states are required to investigate such war crimes and, if appropriate, prosecute;
- states have the right to vest universal jurisdiction in their national courts for such crimes.[60]

However, a further difficulty of fitting humanitarian law to intrastate conflict was Article 6(5) of Protocol II to the Geneva Conventions, which appears to require amnesty, providing that:

> At the end of hostilities, the authorities in power shall endeavour to grant the broadest possible amnesty to persons who have participated in the armed conflict, or those deprived of their liberty for reasons related to the armed conflict, whether they are interned or detained.

As the pressure for post-conflict accountability increased, states that had rejected the application of Protocol II during the conflict began to turn to it in peace negotiations.[61] This new-found attraction of states to Protocol II lay in its perceived capacity to demand accountability, not just of the state, but of its non-state armed opponents, while also promoting mutual amnesty as a conflict resolution tool. While peace settlements incorporated provisions taken from humanitarian law to non-state actors in conflicts,

---

[57] F. Ní Aoláin and O. Gross, *Law in Times of Crisis: Emergency Powers in Theory and Practice* (Cambridge: Cambridge University Press, 2007).

[58] See for example, *Prosecutor v. Dusko Tadić*, IT-94-AR72, Decision on the Defence Motion for Interlocutory Appeal on Jurisdiction of 2 October 1995, paras 96–127, available at www.icty.org.

[59] J.M. Henckaerts and L. Doswald-Beck, *International Committee of the Red Cross: Customary International Humanitarian Law* (Cambridge: Cambridge University Press, 2005).

[60] *Ibid.*

[61] See C. Campbell, 'Peace and the Laws of War: The Role of International Humanitarian Law in the Post-conflict Environment', (2000) 82 *Int'l Rev of the Red Cross* 627; see also N. Roht-Arriaza, 'Combating Impunity: Some Thoughts on the Way Forward', (1996) 59 *Law & Contemp Probs* 93.

domestic courts began relying on Article 6(5) to justify amnesties and truth commissions against human rights challenges.[62]

Combating this turn to humanitarian law as a justification for amnesty required an interpretive revision of humanitarian law as being consistent with human rights law. Faced with questions as to the scope of Article 6(5) in 1995 the ICRC produced an explanatory interpretation of international law's one provision requiring amnesty.[63] The ICRC argued that Article 6(5) had been designed to offer 'the equivalent of what in international armed conflicts is known as "combatant immunity"' that was implicitly limited by commitments to accountability:

> Article 6(5) attempts to encourage a release at the end of hostilities for those detained or punished for the mere fact of having participated in hostilities. It does not aim at an amnesty for those having violated international humanitarian law.[64]

While the ICRC's opinion clearly carries weight, the point remains that this opinion was driven by the need for internal regime coherence and also coherence with human rights law. The type of interpretation offered by the ICRC simply was not needed or given at the time of drafting (and does not appear in the contemporaneous commentary). The ICRC reading of Article 6(5) constituted an attempt to reconcile the Protocol's requirement of amnesty with the accountability requirements found in other parts of humanitarian law, and indeed human rights law, so as to further underwrite the emerging prohibition on amnesty, which is now being picked up on by human rights courts.[65]

iii. International criminal justice

Post-conflict revisions of international human rights and humanitarian law were also reinforced by moves towards the use of international criminal justice. In essence, international criminal law initiatives codified a merged regime of post-conflict accountability. The *ad hoc* tribunals in Rwanda and former Yugoslavia created definitions of crimes that drew on the crimes of humanitarian law, concepts of 'crimes against humanity' and of gross human rights violations, but in ways that clearly addressed both international and internal conflict.[66] A similar list of crimes was used by the Special Criminal Court of Sierra Leone.[67] These provisions added to developing arguments of universal jurisdiction for grave breaches of humanitarian law and a move towards

---

[62] See for example, *Azapo v. President of the Republic of South Africa* 1996 (4) SA 562 (CC). See also, Roht-Arriaza, *supra* n.61, at 96–98; N. Roht-Arriaza and L. Gibson, 'The Developing Jurisprudence on Amnesty', (1998) 20 *HRQ* 843.

[63] Letter of Dr. Toni Pfanner, Head of the Legal Division, ICRC Headquarters, to the Department of Law at the University of California of 15 April 1997 (referring to CDDH, Official Records, 1977, Vol. IX, p. 319), cited in Roht-Arriaza, *supra* n.61, at 97.

[64] *Ibid.*

[65] See recent decision of the Inter-American Court of Human Rights in I/A Court H.R., *Case of the Massacres of El Mozote and nearby places v. El Salvador*. Merits, Reparations and Costs. Judgment of October 25, 2012. Series C No. 252, at paras 284–296.

[66] See Updated Statute of the International Tribunal for Former Yugoslavia (2009); Statute for International Tribunal for Rwanda (2004).

[67] Statute of the Special Court for Sierra Leone (2002).

universal jurisdiction with respect to humanitarian law violations in internal conflict.[68] The merging of human rights and humanitarian law, with respect to defining international criminal law, was also followed by the Rome Statute of 1998 establishing the permanent International Criminal Court (hereinafter 'ICC').[69] While originally conceived as a response to interstate conflict, with antecedents that long preceded the peace agreement era,[70] the ICC's eventual establishment took place against a backdrop of intrastate conflict and associated transitional justice developments. The Rome Statute framework of criminal responsibility, like that of the *ad hoc* tribunals and hybrid tribunals, offered a merged set of humanitarian and human rights legal standards capable of applying over a range of conflict scales and, most importantly for current discussion, not limited to either 'internal' or 'international' conflict.[71] Importantly, the seismic normative development of a new international court and the lack of an explicit transitional justice exception, also spoke symbolically to amnesty of serious crimes as lifted out of the discretion of domestic and international mediators. Post-conflict accountability for serious international crimes now appeared to be a straightforward legal requirement of a hierarchical criminal justice regime, policed ultimately by the ICC.

However, the scope for compromise was not entirely eliminated. Prosecution strategies targeted only those most responsible and it soon became clear that very few perpetrators would ever see the inside of a court. As will be seen below, the application of international criminal law to intrastate conflict did not entirely eliminate scope for restorative justice mechanisms. Rather, international criminal law, particularly pre-ICC, can be viewed as creating a 'bifurcated approach', whereby international criminal justice was to hold those 'most responsible' to account, leaving more flexible quasi-law mechanisms to sweep up the rest.

iv. Regime merge?

Over time, therefore, a prohibition of a blanket amnesty in intrastate conflict that nonetheless tolerates some unspecified forms of amnesty has emerged as a common denominator in both human rights and humanitarian law, now supported by international criminal law. This common denominator does not find a positive law articulation in any regime, but must be 'read into' a unified narrative of what the differentiated regimes collectively require. As one court has put it, the prohibition is a 'crystallising' norm of international law derived from diverse legal sources.[72] The prohibition of a broad amnesty has been normatively endorsed in soft law standards

---

[68] T. Meron, *War Crimes Law Comes of Age: Essays* (Oxford: Clarendon Press, 1998), at 235–244.

[69] Rome Statute, *supra* n.11. The statute entered into force on 1 July 2002. See generally, W.A. Schabas, *An Introduction to the International Criminal Court* (Cambridge: Cambridge University Press, 2006); and on drafting history, M.C. Bassiouni, 'Negotiating the Treaty of Rome on the Establishment of an International Criminal Court', (1999) 32 *Cornell Int'l L J* 443.

[70] On these antecedents, see Schabas, *ibid.*, at 1–21.

[71] Article 5, Rome Statute, *supra* n.11.

[72] *Prosecutor v. Morris Kallon, Brima Bazzy Kamara*, Case No. SCSL-2004-15-AR72(E) and Case No. SCSL-2004-16-AR72(E) (Special Court for Sierra Leone) (13 March 2004), at para. 72. See also D. Orentlicher, Amicus Curiae *Brief Concerning the Amnesty Provided by the*

and UN policy statements and practice. Throughout the 1990s soft law standards articulating normative requirements of accountability for mass atrocity referencing both human rights and humanitarian law regimes were developed. The 1989 Principles on the Effective Prevention and Investigation of Extra-legal, Arbitrary and Summary Executions, prohibits blanket immunity from prosecution for extra-legal, arbitrary or summary executions in Article 19.[73] Similarly, the 1993 UN Declaration on the Protection of All Persons from Enforced Disappearances prevents special amnesty for disappearances.[74] In 1997 the Joinet Principles provided a 'Set of Principles for the Protection and Promotion of Human Rights Through Action to Combat Impunity'. Principle 25 sets out limits to amnesty, prohibiting its application to perpetrators of 'serious crimes under international law' while clearly contemplating that amnesty may be used nationally 'when intended to establish conditions conducive to a peace agreement or to foster national reconciliation'.[75]

These normative developments towards viewing forms of amnesty as unlawful were bolstered by UN practice and policy statements as the UN attempted to reconcile its peace-making practices with its norm-promotion role. In July 1999, the UN Secretary-General Representative in Sierra Leone, on the instruction of the UN Secretary-General, added a proviso to the UN signature on the Lomé Agreement, between the Sierra Leonean government and the Revolutionary United Front making it clear that the 'United Nations holds the understanding that the amnesty and pardon in Article IX of the agreement shall not apply to international crimes of genocide, crimes against humanity, war crimes and other serious violations of humanitarian law'.[76] This UN dissent served to 'normativize' and publicize its move towards a position as a

---

Lomé Accord in the case of the Prosecutor v. Morris Kallon, SCSL-2003–07 (27 October 2003). Cf. also *The Case of the Massacres of El Mozote*, supra n.65.

[73] UN Principles on the Effective Prevention and Investigation of Extra-legal, Arbitrary and Summary Executions (1984), ECOSOC Res. 1989/65, UN Doc. E/1989/89 (1989).

[74] UN Declaration on the Protection of All Persons from Enforced Disappearances (1993), GA Res. 47/133, UN Doc. A/47/687/Add.2 (1993).

[75] See Report of the Special Rapporteur Louis Joinet, The Administration of Justice and the Human Rights of Detainees, Question of the Impunity of Perpetrators of Human Rights Violations, Set of Principles for the Protection and Promotion of Human Rights through Action to Combat Impunity (1997), UN Doc. E/CN.4/Sub.2/1997/20/Rev.1, Annex II (1997); see also, UN Commission on Human Rights, Res. 2005/35, Basic Principles and Guidelines on the Rights to a Remedy and Reparation for Victims of Gross Violations of International Human Rights Law and Serious Violations of International Humanitarian Law, UN Doc. E/CN.4/2005/L.10/Add.1 (2005); UN Commission on Human Rights, Res. 2004/34, the Right to Restitution, Compensation and Rehabilitation for Victims of Grave Violations of Human Rights and Fundamental Freedoms, UN Doc. E/CN.4/2004/127 (2004).

[76] Seventh Report of the Secretary-General on the UN Observer Mission in Sierra Leone (1999), UN Doc. S/1999/836 (1999), at para. 7. Interestingly, the versions of the agreement available online do not record this disclaimer. The UN does not seem to be able to produce a copy of the disclaimer (correspondence on file with the author). The Secretary-General's report to the UNSC, while describing the rider, did not quote it, and subsequent citations of the rider seem to refer to this description, see for example, W.A. Schabas, 'Amnesty, the Sierra Leone Truth and Reconciliation Commission and the Special Court for Sierra Leone', (2004) 11 *UC Davis J Int'l L & Pol'y* 145, at 149; P. Hayner, *Negotiating Peace in Liberia: Preserving the Possibility for Justice* (Geneva: Henry Durant Centre for Humanitarian Dialogue, 2007).

'normative negotiator'. It can be argued that the Lomé rider, with its real-world impact in terms of UN signature and controversy, gave the prohibition on blanket amnesty instant legal effect in a way that statements of commitment and soft law standards could not. As will be seen, it also arguably paved the way for the UNSC to later establish a Special Criminal Court for Sierra Leone that operated contemporaneously with the Truth Commission.[77]

The new normative stance of the UN was reinforced on 10 December 1999 when the UN Secretary-General reported in a press release that he had issued guidelines addressing human rights and peace negotiations to his envoys.[78] These guidelines, at the time of writing, have not been made public.[79] The UN direction towards clear prohibition of amnesty was further consolidated by an intervention by the UN Secretary-General in his August 2004 report on *The Rule of Law and Justice in Conflict and Post-conflict Societies*, which reasserted a UN position of rejecting any endorsement of broad amnesty and capital punishment.[80] In 2005, Orentlicher updated the Joinet Principles and in Principle 24 reiterated Joinet's approach of prohibiting broad amnesties while contemplating some form of restricted amnesty as still possible.[81]

The corollary of a prohibition of blanket amnesty, as Orentlicher's principle suggested, is that some level of amnesty is permitted and even required. Here too, however, the permissibility of amnesty must again be garnered from a variety of legal doctrines.[82] The only direct treaty law provision for amnesty is Article 6(5) of Protocol II to the Geneva Conventions which only covers certain intrastate conflicts and which the ICRC contends does not apply to serious violations of humanitarian law. The international legality of limited amnesty is also supported by the view that some domestic amnesties are outside international law's reach and still constitute a political matter within the gift of the state. While the norms appear to articulate the two poles – accountability for serious violations of international law, and amnesty for lesser violations, there is little to no codification as to the grey area of permissible amnesty that lies in the middle.

---

[77] UNSC Res. 1315 (2000). Views are somewhat divided on how exactly the rider did this, and whether the rider created an impetus for accountability which was acted on once fighting was renewed, or whether the rider was in part responsible for the renewed fighting itself; see, for example, Schabas, *ibid*.

[78] UN Secretary-General, Press Release, Secretary-General Comments on Guidelines given to Envoys (10 December 1999).

[79] The rationale for privacy can be mooted to lie in the wish to keep the guidelines as an internal, almost bureaucratic, matter so as not to reveal the mediator's hand. In the interests of disclosure, the author has viewed the guidelines in the context of an expert meeting to advise on their updating.

[80] UN Secretary-General, Report at the Security Council, Report on the Rule of Law and Justice in Conflict and Post-conflict Societies (2004), UN Doc. S/2004/616 (2004), at para. 64(c).

[81] Updated Set of Principles, *supra* n.11.

[82] See Slye, *supra* n.52, who has attempted to conduct an even broader 'regime merge' so as to produce specific criteria for 'legitimate amnesty' which are similar to the stated 'new law'; Orentlicher, *supra* n.11.

C. Normative (In)stability

It can be argued that these standards operate to establish a broad and programmatic direction towards the prohibition of amnesty, which still leaves some, seemingly narrowing, room to manoeuvre. In practice, innovative institutional developments have attempted to work within these two poles. Thus, truth commissions that attempt to reconcile some amnesty with some accountability, or approaches that couple international criminal justice for the most serious offenders with some softer 'restorative justice' mechanism involving narratives of reconciliation rather than punishment for the majority of those involved in the conflict, have attempted to work within the normative poles of the new *lex*. However, as with the concept of hybrid self-determination, the compromise of the new law is apparently internally unstable. Neither human rights, nor humanitarian law, nor international criminal law have any explicit provisions that require or permit accountability for the past to be balanced against the wider social 'good' and even protection of rights that achieving 'peace' might bring. As in the area of self-determination, the new norm appears to try to hold together a middle ground that is squeezed by both ends: the desire to resolve the norm towards a more absolute and inflexible standard of prosecution and punishment in all cases on one hand, and the desire to retreat from it as unhelpful to peace negotiations on the other.

While there have been some attempts to provide a normative blueprint that would spell out the boundaries and conditions of an explicitly 'transitional' form of justice, it has proved impossible to articulate in general terms an appropriate relationship between accountability and amnesty.[83] It is suggested that it is impossible precisely because specification of the relationship would require an impossible-to-achieve shared understanding of the permissible goals of transition and consensus as to when these political considerations might attenuate the letter of human rights law. In the absence of such a shared understanding, any attempt to provide for an explicitly exceptional transitional justice runs the danger of undermining, rather than reinforcing, human rights and humanitarian law standards of accountability.

9. A NEW LAW OF THIRD PARTY INTERVENTION

A. Traditional Understandings

Chapter VI and Chapter VII of the UN Charter provide a formal legal basis for third party intervention in conflict and post-conflict settings. Chapter VI provides for Pacific Settlement of Disputes, Article 33 providing that:

---

[83] A series of UN Commission and UN Council Resolutions on Transitional Justice have avoided attempting to articulate a relationship emphasizing the need to provide for transitional justice and the rule of law and setting out some process matters. See for example, Human Rights Council, Human Rights and Transitional Justice, Res. 9/10 (2008); UN Human Rights Commission, Human Rights and Transitional Justice, Res. 2005/70 (2005).

1. The parties to any dispute, the continuance of which is likely to endanger the maintenance of international peace and security, shall, first of all, seek a solution by negotiation, enquiry, mediation, conciliation, arbitration, judicial settlement, resort to regional agencies or arrangements, or other peaceful means of their own choice.
2. The Security Council shall, when it deems necessary, call upon the parties to settle their dispute by such means.

Chapter VI additionally empowers the UNSC to become involved and make recommendations for resolution of the conflict. However, there is no provision for enforcing these recommendations.

Chapter VII provides for Action with Respect to Threats to the Peace, Breaches of the Peace and Acts of Aggression, Article 39 providing that:

> The Security Council shall determine the existence of any threat to the peace, breach of the peace, or act of aggression and shall make recommendations, or decide what measures shall be taken in accordance with Articles 41 and 42, to maintain or restore international peace and security.

Article 40 empowers the UNSC to call for provisional measures; Article 41 provides for enforcement not involving armed force, such as disruption of economic relations; Article 42 provides that where other measures have proved inadequate, action involving armed force can be taken to address the conflict.

As regards formally authorized intervention, under Chapter VI pacific resolution of the dispute can be taken with the consent of the parties in cases involving a threat or potential threat to international peace and security. Non-military and military actions can be taken without the consent of the party in the event that pacific resolution of the dispute fails and there is an actual threat to peace – by implication *international* peace. In practice, however, these chapters apply to formal UNSC authorized intervention. A range of other organizations can intervene as a matter of their own constitutions, provided they do not contravene the UN Charter.

B. The *Lex Pacificatoria*

The contemporary post-conflict environment relies heavily on a diverse range of international actors to carry out a diverse range of peace implementation functions. These functions can be categorized in terms of four broad tasks: policing demobilization and demilitarization; guaranteeing and implementing an internal constitutional settlement; mediating its development; and administering the transitional period in some form. The scale and nature of international intervention are varied, ranging from full administration, to forms of peacekeeping, to involvement in domestic institutions, such as hybrid courts.[84] Some forms of governance and peacekeeping are undertaken by the UN; some are UN authorized but conducted by regional groupings such as the North Atlantic Treaty Organization (hereinafter 'NATO'); some, such as those in Iraq, are performed by third party states; and some are undertaken by 'international'

---

[84] For a full picture of third party involvement see Bell, *On the Law of Peace*, supra n.1, at 175–195.

individuals with state endorsement but no clear representative capacity.[85] Discrete parts of the UN also become involved in separate issues, for example the UNHCR in return and repatriation of refugees and displaced persons.[86] Other international organizations can also find themselves with peace implementation roles; for example, the International Labour Organization (hereinafter 'ILO') has played a role in the implementation of the San Andreas Agreement between the Ejército Zapatista de Liberación Nacional (hereinafter 'EZLN') and the Mexican government, undertaken under the rubric of its treaty monitoring with relation to the ILO's Indigenous and Tribal Peoples Convention 1989 (169).[87] International 'individuals' and civil society actors can also be given third party implementation roles. The main regulatory framework for these tasks is often the internal constitution of the institutions undertaking these tasks.

Again, the assumptions of the traditional framework for regulating international intervention in conflicts appear inappropriate for the type of international intervention required and undertaken in pursuit of peace settlement implementation. The UN Charter framework does not envisage or address the broad range of possibilities for international involvement within states; for example, it does not provide a clear framework for the regulation of the intervention of regional organizations, now often equal or predominant players to the UN in mediation, peacekeeping and settlement implementation tasks. There are also further difficulties of 'fit' as regards Charter regulation of UNSC authorized intervention. In conflicts occurring largely within international state boundaries, it can sometimes be unclear when a threat constitutes a threat to *international* peace and security, and countries tend to resist the 'internationalization' of a conflict precisely because it puts their own sovereignty in question. Where a settlement framework is in place, and a tentative ceasefire holds, it can become even more difficult to justify post-conflict intervention in terms of a threat to international peace and security. Therefore, the legal boundary as to when international actors can forcibly intervene or not is not always appropriate to the nature of post-settlement implementation. Similarly, a distinction between consensual intervention and non-consensual intervention is difficult to apply in situations of political transition from one state structure to another, particularly when the new structures involve brokered compromise and power-sharing between former 'state' officials and their non-state opponents. In practice, consent may fluctuate and operations that were consent-based may need to move to a non-consensual basis very quickly. In the event that some parts of 'the state' withdraw their consent, but the state is being reconstructed, whose consent is relevant?

---

[85] For a full review of international territorial administration, see R. Wilde, *International Territorial Administration: How Trusteeship and the Civilizing Mission Never Went Away* (Oxford: Oxford University Press, 2008).

[86] See for example, Arusha Peace and Reconciliation Agreement for Burundi (28 August 2000), Protocol 4, Chapter 3, Article 17, available at www.usip.org/library/pa.html.

[87] See Report of the Committee set up to examine the representation alleging non-observance by Mexico of the Indigenous and Tribal Peoples Convention, 1989 (No. 169), made under Article 24 of the ILO Constitution by the Authentic Workers' Front (2004), available at www.ilo.org/ilolex/english/newcountryframeE.htm, in which the ILO examined the complaint as regards the Convention through the framework of the San Andrés Larraínzar Agreement between ELZN and the Mexican government, which was based on this Convention.

In short, the Charter framework contemplates a clear sovereign independent state, capable of giving or withholding consent, clear distinctions between peace and conflict and between international and non-international threats to peace. Post agreement, ambiguity over 'who' constitutes the state, and whether the war is over, means that such clarity seldom exists in periods of post-settlement transition. As regards other organizations and forms of intervention not requiring or having UNSC authorization, when and how they can intervene largely depend on the terms of their own constitutions, although at times interventions have been criticized for non-compliance with the Charter.

A practical pressure for the development of a *lex pacificatoria* to justify and govern third party intervention comes from the need for international actors, focused on 'implementing' democracy and the rule of law, to be able to articulate a legal basis for their own intervention. A legal grey zone relating to the basis and legality of the third party intervention can undermine third party implementation functions because it can be used by recalcitrant parties to the settlement to undermine those functions where they are resisting them. As Bertram notes with reference to the UN, legal challenges to third party implementation can:

> [c]reate serious problems on the ground, undermining the credibility and capability of UN peace builders to carry out their missions. Inevitably, groups that stand to lose as a result of UN intervention will claim – legitimately or not – infringement of state sovereignty and the perception of infringement may also trigger popular opposition.[88]

Again, the difficulty of lack of 'fit' of law to task and dilemmas has generated revisions in how the law applies. As regards UNSC authorized third party intervention, the authorizing resolutions tend to reference both consent and authorization and often remain silent and ambiguous as to whether they are Chapter VI or Chapter VII resolutions – the extension and development of a silent so-called VI ½ resolution as best suited to peace settlement enforcement. Interestingly, this development does not just involve international organizations being enabled to move from consent to use of force in Chapter VI-like initiatives, but also involves reaching back for consent in what are stated to be Chapter VII interventions. The use of international force in Kosovo, for example, was terminated by UNSC 1244, which made provision for international administration but attempted to build internal structures with reference to the Rambouillet Agreement.[89] This draft agreement had been negotiated with the parties to the conflict, under the threat of use of force, but ultimately failed to secure their agreement – triggering the NATO intervention. The attempt to incorporate Rambouillet, post-conflict in a UNSC resolution constituted an attempt to reach backwards for an element of consent from the recalcitrant parties in the state's transitional structures.

---

[88] E. Bertram, 'Reinventing Governments: The Promise and Perils of United Nations Peace Building', (1995) 39 *J of Conflict Resolution* 387.

[89] UNSC Res. 1244 (1999), at para. 11(a): 'Promoting the establishment, pending a final settlement, of substantial autonomy and self-government in Kosovo, taking full account of annex 2 and of the Rambouillet accords (S/1999/648).'

In many post-conflict situations, however, the UNSC is not involved. In these cases, as with both peacekeeping and the broader range of implementation functions undertaken by diverse third parties, the peace agreement itself often serves as a 'quasi-legal' basis for third party legitimacy and intervention – authorizing, defining and limiting third party tasks, effectively bypassing questions of consent. The constitutional and treaty-like nature of the hybrid self-determination settlement terms creates a situation in which the involvement of third parties can be presented not as an exception to sovereignty and self-determination, but part and parcel of achieving it. The necessary consent is of all the parties (domestic and international) to the peace settlement itself.

C. Normative (In)stability

The emergent *lex pacificatoria* in the area of third party intervention remains vague, general and operating at a political and programmatic level. It is difficult to imagine coherent reform of the UN Charter to enable authorization of a broader range of peace agreements. Developments in understandings of what the Charter permits have been addressed by consecutive UN Secretary-Generals in a series of 'lessons learned' reports that tried to grapple with, and revise, concepts of 'consent', 'neutrality' and 'impartiality' in the context of post-conflict reconstruction tasks that often required the redistribution of power within the state.[90]

10. A NEW LAW OF THIRD PARTY ACCOUNTABILITY

A. Traditional Understandings

Traditionally, the spheres of operation of international organizations and the sphere of operation of the state domestically were understood to be distinct: international organizations existed to pursue common state interests, such as taking collective action with respect to common or global problems. The accountability of state actors was through the framework of the state's institutions and accountability of international actors through the framework of the international organization's institutions. In so far as international organizations committed wrongs within states, any accountability was contemplated to flow from the international organization to the state; however, when and how accountability applied remained controversial, depending on matters such as the relationship between the organization and its member states and what acts were attributable to the organization.[91]

---

[90] See for example, United Nations (1995) 'Supplement to An Agenda for Peace, Position Paper of the Secretary-General on the Occasion of the Fiftieth Anniversary of the United Nations, Report of the Secretary-General', 3 January 1995, New York, United Nations. UN Soc A/50/60-S/1995/1; United Nations (2000) 'Report of the panel on United Nations Peace Operations', 21 August 2000, New York, United Nations. UN Doc A/55/305-S/2000/809.

[91] See J. Klabbers, *An Introduction to International Institutional Law*, 2nd edn (Cambridge: Cambridge University Press, 2009), at 271–293.

B. The *Lex Pacificatoria*

Again, these assumptions are inapposite to post-conflict scenarios and tasks. The tapestry of international involvement in peace settlement implementation tasks, as described in Section 9 above, gives rise to questions of third party accountability for violations of international law with respect to local populations. Two exercises of power in particular give rise to demands for accountability to local populations: the use of force and the exercise of what are normally the powers of government. When international implementers use force and exercise governmental functions they, in essence, carry out the business of the state. The exercise of what is normally conceived of as domestic government by international actors, like all use of public power, can give rise to human rights violations. Local populations have on occasion asserted that the third parties are themselves violating legal rights found in international human rights and humanitarian law and indeed the domestic framework of peace settlements: challenges to the actions of peacekeepers have included challenges to the use of force,[92] charges of sexual abuse,[93] use of administrative detention[94] and, in Bosnia, challenges to the constitutionality of the exercise of domestic legislative power by the Office of the High Representative. (hereinafter 'OHR')[95] Human rights challenges require a response from third parties because human rights abuses undermine peace settlement implementation efforts by undermining third party legitimacy in the eyes of the local population. Given that peace-building typically involves a re-allocation of power from one side in the conflict to another, challenges to third party legitimacy tend to be seized on by 'spoilers', that is, recalcitrant parties who view settlement failure as their desired outcome, to help build their political base locally.[96]

While the application of human rights and humanitarian law seems relevant, again both regimes have difficulties of fit. The post-conflict environment, with its hybrid international/domestic actors and ambiguous sovereignty, does not sit easily with the assumptions of either human rights or humanitarian law. The accountability offered by each regime is inadequate, both in reach and in enforcement mechanism, for dealing with the third party accountability issues that arise. The normal assumption that the state is able and capable of being the primary locus of human rights accountability does not prevail. As a result, the peculiarity of transitions from conflict gives rise to pressure

---

[92] Allegations of torture and execution against Belgian, Italian and Canadian UN troops in Somalia (1992–1995). See for example, Report of the Somalia Commission of Inquiry, available at www.dnd.ca/somalia/somaliae.htm.

[93] See UN Secretary-General, Special Measures for protection from sexual exploitation and sexual abuse (2007), UN Doc. A/61/957 (2007), detailing sexual exploitation and related offences in the UN system in 2006, including sexual assault and sex with a minor.

[94] See for example, *Al-Jedda v. Secretary of State for Defence* [2007] UKHL 58, *Al-Jedda v. United Kingdom*, ECHR Application No. 27021/08, 8 July 2011.

[95] See *Twenty-five Representatives of the People's Assembly of Republika Srpska*, Constitutional Court of Bosnia Herzegovina U-26/01 (28 December 2001), at para. 13, available at www.ccbh.ba/eng.

[96] S.J. Stedman, 'Spoiler Problems in Peace Processes', (1997) 22 *Int'l Sec* 5; Bertram, *supra* n.87.

for a form of regime merge that, in its broad dynamic, is similar to that described with reference to transitional justice.

i. Human rights law

Human rights law is acknowledged to apply in situations of conflict and of peace, and the standards it offers appear to have the capacity to hold international implementers to account, to the extent that they are using force or undertaking governmental-type roles. Human rights treaties impose a high standard of protection with regard to the right to life, capable of providing for accountability for killings by peacekeepers. Their strength, but also their weakness, is that they contemplate such killings as something other than potentially legitimate acts of war. As regards international governance, human rights standards are specifically designed to provide accountability for the exercise of government power, vis-à-vis the individual, and so would seem to be relevant to international administrators when they exercise the powers of the state. Finally, in the event that states fail to provide mechanisms for adjudicating on human rights breaches, unlike humanitarian law, there is international machinery, in the form of treaty mechanisms, capable of providing for some form of adjudication of a breach.

The difficulty in holding international implementors accountable is that human rights treaties regulate relationships between a state and the people within its borders, with the state obligated to deliver rights as minimum standards. As a technical matter, the rights contained in international conventions only apply to the state parties that sign the conventions, and so therefore do not apply directly to international organizations. The application of existing rights mechanisms to international organizations, including the UN, is not obvious and remains legally controversial.[97] While mission mandates and regulations can provide for international organizations to undertake duties in ways that protect and promote human rights,[98] these seldom provide for a clear mechanism through which victims of rights violations can pursue accountability. There are similar difficulties with the application of customary international law to international organizations. Although the state technically retains its on-going treaty and customary law human rights commitments, having abrogated its power to international organizations, and often having given them immunity at point of entry through status of forces agreements, it cannot effectively hold international actors to account.

---

[97] See generally, A. Devereux, 'Selective Universality? Human-rights Accountability of the UN in Post-conflict Operations', in B. Bowden, H. Charlesworth and J. Farfall (eds), *The Role of International Law in Rebuilding Societies after Conflict: Great Expectations* (Cambridge: Cambridge University Press, 2009), at 198; B. Kondoch, 'Human Rights Law and UN Peace Operations in Post-conflict Situations', in N.D. White and D. Klaasen (eds), *The UN, Human Rights and Post-conflict Situations* (Manchester: Manchester University Press, 2005), at 19; J. Cerone, 'Reasonable Measures in Unreasonable Circumstances: A Legal Responsibility Framework for Human Rights Violations in Post-conflict Territories under UN Administration', in White and Klaasen (eds), *ibid.,* , at 42, 68; G. Verdirame, 'UN Accountability for Human Rights Violations in Post-conflict Situations', in White and Klaasen (eds), *ibid.,* at 81; F. Mégret and F. Hoffman, 'The UN as a Human Rights Violator? Some Reflections on the United Nations Changing Human Rights Responsibilities', (2003) 25 *HRQ* 314.

[98] See for example, UNMIK Regulation 1/1991 (25 July 1999), available at www.unmikonline.org, discussed further below.

In response, commentators have posited a range of legal routes to finding the UN accountable.[99] Some commentators have contended that human rights apply directly to the UN by virtue of the constitutional standing of the UN Charter in combination with the International Covenants on Civil, Political and Economic, Social and Cultural Rights of 1966.[100] This argument views UN administrators as bound by human rights standards as part of its own constitution. Others have found *jus cogens* and customary law obligations to be directly applicable to UN administrators, given the UN's status as a subject of international law.[101] A third route to application finds the UN to be subject to human rights norms through its usurpation of the state's functions – either as surrogate state, or as derivative or successor of the state. Each line of argument could, in theory, apply also to regional peacekeeping in terms of the respective constitutional foundations of the relevant regional organization (which also have roots in the UN Charter framework). The very existence of these arguments, however, testifies to an unhelpful lack of clarity as to UN human rights obligations. Moreover, these UN accountability theories leave the accountability of non-state third parties, such as non-governmental organizations, private security contractors, companies and individual actors, virtually untouched.

Third party 'home' states would seem, in principle, to retain treaty responsibility to pursue the accountability of their own personnel. This form of accountability is unsatisfactory for local populations as it seems to deliver accountability to the wrong constituency. Nevertheless, it is a form of accountability. However, asserting home state accountability in practice has exposed clear limitations on when treaty obligations apply.[102] Cases asserted under the European Convention on Human Rights, for example, have determined that:

- the Convention is primarily applicable territorially but can apply to states acting extra-territorially when they 'exercise all or some of the public powers normally to be exercised' by governments; or exercise effective control over the area in which they operate;[103]

---

[99] For a full review, see Devereux, *supra* n.97.
[100] Kondoch, *supra* n.97, at 36; see also, White and Klaasen, *supra* n.97, at 7; N.D. White, *The United Nations System: Towards International Justice* (Boulder, CO: Lynne Rienner, 2002), at 14–17; P.-M. Dupuy, 'The Constitutional Dimension of the Charter of the UN Revisited', (1997) 1 *Max Planck UNYB* 1. For arguments on the UN Charter as constitutional law, see B. Fassbender, '"We the Peoples of the United Nations": Constituent Power and Constitutional Form in International Law', in M. Loughlin and N. Walker (eds), *The Paradox of Constitutionalism* (Oxford: Oxford University Press, 2007), at 269.
[101] Kondoch, *supra* n.97, at 36–37; White and Klaasen, *supra* n.97.
[102] See further, T. Hadden (ed.), *A Responsibility to Assist: Human Rights Policy and Practice in European Union Crisis Management Operations* (Oxford: Hart Publishing, 2009).
[103] *Banković and others v. Belgium and others*, Application No. 52207/88, [GC] (Dec.), no. 52207/99, ECHR 2001-XII; *Al-Skeini and others v. United Kingdom*, Application no. 55721/07, 7 July 2011.

- however, where the mission is formally authorized by the United Nations, UNSC authorization to carry out a specific operation or use 'all necessary measures' may legitimize actions which would otherwise violate human rights standards;[104]
- and where the operation is a UN one, responsibility lies with the UN rather than the contributing states.[105]

ii. Humanitarian law

Similar difficulties apply with reference to the application of humanitarian law. Once again, it is unclear that this body of law applies to the peacekeeping forces of international organizations. While most UN states are state parties to the Geneva Conventions, the UN itself is not and direct accession has apparently been ruled out.[106] As Cerone notes, a further query over application lies in 'the notion that operations undertaken pursuant to the Chapter VII power of the S[ecurity] C[ouncil] are somehow exempt from the ordinary application of international law, such that even the [international humanitarian law] obligations of the member states participating in the operation are inapplicable'.[107] International legal accountability for private actors, to whom third party states contract-out peace implementation duties, is even more unclear.[108] Moreover, the starting point of UN operations has been to provide for the immunity of peacekeeping and mission personnel from host jurisdiction. It has been standard practice for UN and regional terms of agreements between the international organization and the host state to include immunity for its personnel, and now often also for private contractors.[109]

Humanitarian law's standards also seem inappote to the type of accountability sought by local actors. As regards the use of force, humanitarian law authorizes the use of lethal force against enemy combatants and permits some margin of error with regard to the collateral killing of civilians. Military action involving large numbers of civilian casualties is legitimate, as long as the intention was to target enemy combatants, adequate planning and precautions were taken, and appropriate means used, even if large-scale civilian loss of life results. However, as Hadden writes, where peacekeepers are responsible for civilian deaths the result 'will often be to cause a substantial

---

[104] *Al-Jedda, supra* n.94 (although the Grand Chamber of the European Court of Human Rights found that there was no clear conflict between the UNSC resolution and the Convention, as the UNSC resolution did not require the use of detention such as was at issue in the current case).

[105] *Behrami and Behrami v. France and Saramati v. France, Germany and Norway*, Application Nos. 71412/01and 78166/01, Eur. Ct. Hum. Rts. GC, Judgment of 2 May 2007.

[106] See U. Palwankar, 'Applicability of International Humanitarian Law to United Nations Peacekeeping Forces', (1993) 294 *Int'l Rev of the Red Cross* 227; Cerone, *supra* n.97.

[107] Cerone, *supra* n.97.

[108] On issues of accountability raised by private contractors, see 'Symposium: Private Military Contractors and International Law', (2008) 19 *EJIL*; A. Faite, 'Accountability of Private Contractors in Armed Contract: Implications under Humanitarian Law', (2002) 4 *Defence Studies* 166.

[109] UN Model Agreement between the United Nations and Member State contributing personnel and equipment to the United Nations peace-keeping operations (1991), UN Doc. A/46/185, Annex (1991); Hadden, *supra* n.102, at 109.

reduction in the perceived legitimacy and acceptability of the international forces'.[110] Reliance on humanitarian law, which includes more scope for lawful killing than human rights law, undercuts the very concept of the political landscape as 'post-conflict'.

As regards the broader governance roles of international actors and violations of rights other than the right to life, again there is a mismatch between humanitarian law's rationale, assumptions and standards and the governance functions undertaken by third parties implementing contemporary transitions from conflict. For standards addressing the broader governance roles of third parties, one must look to humanitarian law's regulation of occupation. Geneva IV and the Hague Convention (IV) Respecting the Laws and Customs of War on Land of 1907, regulate an occupation, regardless of whether it is legal or not. Recourse to the law of occupation, however, is not automatic for international administrators. As Ratner notes, UN missions have tended to assume the priority of the human rights framework of accountability, while state-led international administrations have tended to view humanitarian law as the governing framework.[111] Ratner argues that regime choice is more a 'default position' that depends on the nature of the third party rather than a choice: international administrations tend to be run by civilians and so assume the primacy of human rights law, while state interventions run by military personnel tend to automatically turn to humanitarian law.[112]

Where humanitarian law is viewed as the appropriate framework there are further difficulties of fit, based on its lack of provision for a concept of 'transformative occupation'.[113] The underlying rationale driving the standards is an attempt to prevent the illegality of acquiring territory by force.[114] The law aims to protect the occupied state from being incorporated into the territory of the occupier. Therefore, 'the watchword is the legal maintenance of the status quo while protecting the basic welfare of the population, pending a final disposition of territory, typically a withdrawal from it'.[115] The difficulty for contemporary transitions is that rules designed to restrict an occupier's capacity to reshape the state's internal configuration also restrict third parties, whose implementation function under a peace agreement is precisely that of 'transforming' state structures. Geneva IV limits on occupiers preclude actions that peacekeepers undertake as a matter of practice, such as disapplying former laws, involvement in constitutional reform, and associated substantive reform of political and legal institutions.[116] The whole point of international implementation of contemporary

---

[110] Hadden, *ibid.*, at 118.
[111] S.R. Ratner, 'Foreign Occupation and International Territorial Administration: The Challenges of Convergence', (2005) 16 *EJIL* 695, at 702–703.
[112] *Ibid.*
[113] A. Roberts, 'Transformative Military Occupation: Applying the Law of War and Human Rights', (2006) 100 *AJIL* 580.
[114] *Ibid.*
[115] Ratner, *supra* n.111, at 700.
[116] A brief glance at the opening Article 47 of Section III of Geneva IV on occupation illustrates the mismatch between regime and contemporary transition: 'Protected persons who are in occupied territory shall not be deprived, in any case or in any manner whatsoever, of the benefits of the present Convention by any change introduced, as the result of the occupation of

transitions is to move away from the status quo associated with a war towards a situation in which the laws of war do not apply. International implementers aim to achieve this precisely by changing institutions and government by agreement. The assumptions and remit of the international humanitarian law of occupation and its modalities of accountability seem inapposite to the third party enforcement tasks of international organizations. This has led to alternative forms of legal authorization being sought post-conflict. In Iraq, for example, the move towards ending occupation led to UNSC resolutions being used to create extraordinary occupation powers, using the argument that Geneva IV did not provide for the needs of a gradual transition, such as the need for occupiers to engage in domestic constitutional reform, or management of oil resources.[117]

A third difficulty in fitting humanitarian law to post-conflict pressures for accountability is that it appears to offer accountability of international actors to the 'wrong' people. Accountability for third party actions is contemplated to lie with the domestic legal mechanisms of the third party state, with little formal international machinery to force states to comply and no treaty monitoring mechanism.[118] Whether use of force or other violations of rights are at issue, for local parties the perception, and mostly the reality, is that international actors have *de facto* immunity from the international norms that they promote locally.[119] In short, there is a perceived 'accountability gap' between local populations and international implementer that is not addressed by home state accountability in either principle or in practice.

The difficulty of fitting and applying either humanitarian law or human rights regime to the post-conflict tasks that third parties undertake again can be argued to be producing forms of regime merge and institutional innovation.

iii. Regime merge?

Post-conflict accountability pressures have forced attempts at new normative articulations. It can be argued that the hybrid international–domestic, war–no war, post-conflict environment prompts recourse to the provisions of both human rights and humanitarian law regimes. Again, this turn to both regimes is not a process of orderly harmonization with priority being given to the most appropriate *lex specialis* where standards cannot be reconciled. As Ratner, Roberts and Stahn have all pointed out (from slightly different perspectives), the political context of post-conflict peace-building efforts points towards the need to view the laws of occupation and human rights law as, in some sense, a harmonized regime capable of servicing the needs of the contemporary

---

a territory, into the institutions or government of the said territory, nor by any agreement concluded between the authorities of the occupied territories and the Occupying Power, nor by any annexation by the latter of the whole or part of the occupied territory.'

[117] UNSC Res. 1483 (2003); UNSC Res. 1511 (2004); UNSC Res. 1546 (2004). On the US justification for the need for these resolutions, see J. Bellinger, 'Summary of Remarks available at "State Department Legal Adviser Discusses U.S. Views on International Law, Security Council Powers under Chapter VII of the UN Charter"', (2005) 99 *AJIL* 891, at 892–893.

[118] Ratner, *supra* n.111, at 701. As Ratner notes, the international enforcement of state accountability is largely informal through lobbying, with only the Security Council or possibly the International Court of Justice being able to issue a binding directive to the state.

[119] Hadden, *supra* n.102, at 112–113.

transition.[120] In practice, regime merge has involved an attempt to eclectically draw on the 'spirit' or 'observance' of the regimes as both offering relevant standards, while mediating the strict legal application of those standards so as to balance it with peace-building imperatives.[121] The attempt at formulating new normative guidance is a complex effort to apply different standards to different third party functions by applying different standards to different actors, or different standards to the same actors when exercising different functions, but to bind them to the spirit rather than the letter of the law. This search for accountability reaches out to pluck from humanitarian law, human rights law and criminal law, eclectically and often simultaneously. The point can be illustrated by a glance at some of the attempts at norm-development, aimed at filling the accountability gap left by the lack of fit of human rights and humanitarian law. In 1999, for example, the UN Secretary-General issued a Bulletin providing for the 'Observance by United Nations forces of international humanitarian law'.[122] This Bulletin sets out a subset of humanitarian law provisions that are to apply to UN forces in situations of conflict when 'they are actively engaged therein as combatants'.[123] It provides that, in Status of Forces Agreements concluded between the UN and a host state, the UN will undertake to ensure that the force 'shall conduct its operations with full respect for the principles and rules of the general conventions applicable to the conduct of military personnel'.[124] However, violations of humanitarian law are to be prosecuted in the national courts of the contributing state.[125]

In 2000, UNSC Resolution 1325 stated the UN's willingness to incorporate a 'gender perspective' into peacekeeping operations and urged the Secretary-General 'to ensure that, where appropriate, field operations include a gender component'.[126] In 2006, a UN Group of Legal Experts, established in response to concerns about sexual violence committed by peacekeepers, submitted a report to the General Assembly on the Accountability of United Nations staff and experts on mission with respect to criminal

---

[120] Ratner does not aim to go so far as resolving the legal issues here, but states his purpose to be 'to show how any doctrinal approach, legal or political, must take account of the commonalities of these missions'; Ratner, *supra* n.111, at 697.

[121] See for example, UN Model Agreement between the United Nations and Member State contributing personnel and equipment to the United Nations peace-keeping operations (1991), UN Doc. A/46/185, Annex (1991), Article 28, which provides that UN peacekeeping operations 'shall observe and respect the principles and spirit of the general international conventions applicable to the conduct of military personnel'.

[122] UN Secretary-General's Bulletin (6 August 1999), UN Doc. ST/SGB/1999/13 (1999) (a Code of 'principles and rules of international humanitarian law applicable to United Nations forces conducting operations under United Nations' command and control', promulgated by then UN Secretary-General Kofi Annan. The Code does not provide for the direct application of humanitarian law; neither does it apply to peacekeeping forces under control other than that of the UN).

[123] *Ibid.*, Section 1.1.

[124] *Ibid.*, Section 3.

[125] *Ibid.*, Section 4. Moreover, it does not apply to peacekeeping organizations under the command and control of regional organizations, even when deployed under UN auspices.

[126] UNSC Res. 1325, *supra* n.26, at para. 5.

acts committed in peacekeeping operations.[127] The report's emphasis was on placing criminal law accountability with the host state; however, it also raised the possibility that hybrid domestic–international tribunals might be an innovative way to enable local justice, while responding to concerns of contributing states as to fair process and human rights protections for their staff.[128] The report's attempt to plug accountability gaps remained limited as it only contemplated criminal accountability in cases such as sexual abuse which by their nature fell outside the definition of 'acts performed in the exercise of their official functions'. For such acts an on-going backdrop of UN immunity was contemplated.[129] The Expert Group appended a Draft Convention on the criminal accountability of UN officials and experts on mission, which included these limitations,[130] and also the limitation that the convention 'not apply to military personnel of national contingents assigned to the military component of a United Nations peacekeeping operation' and to other persons who status-of-forces agreements stated were 'under the exclusive jurisdiction of a State other than the host state'.[131]

Regional organizations have also moved towards standard forms of codified application of international legal standards. For example, as Hadden documents, the European Union (hereinafter 'EU') has developed a series of documents providing for general standards of conduct for all EU Missions,[132] and guidelines for mainstreaming human rights and gender.[133] These documents set out principles aimed at 'behavioural' standards of conduct and procedures for implementation, which include a requirement that provision be made for procedures of complaints and reporting misconduct. While extending clarified standards for accountability to EU Missions, discipline remains to be provided for by 'national authorities', or heads of missions in the case of 'contracted personnel'.

In addition to codification, attempts have been made to provide a level of accountability through the legal instruments that establish the peace operation. In particular, since the 1990s, Status of Forces Agreements of the UN (hereinafter 'SOFAs'), while providing for immunity of troops from local state jurisdiction, have also begun to 'contract' some application of human rights and humanitarian law by including references in their provisions. Although these agreements reaffirm the immunity of UN Troops from local jurisdiction, they now also contain provision for 'full respect for the

---

[127] Report of the Group of Legal Experts on ensuring accountability of United Nations Staff and experts on mission with respect to criminal acts committed in peacekeeping operations (2006), UN Doc. A/60/980 (2006).

[128] *Ibid.*, Section C.

[129] *Ibid.*, at para. 9.

[130] Article 18, Draft Convention on the Criminal Accountability of the United Nations Officials and Experts on Mission, GA Res. 61/29 (2011), provides that the Convention does not confer any right or impose any obligation which is 'inconsistent with any immunity of a UN official or expert unless the competent organ of the UN has waived such immunity'.

[131] *Ibid.*, Article 2(2).

[132] Generic Standards of Behaviour for ESDP Operations (18 May 2005), CEU 8373/3/05 (2005).

[133] Mainstreaming Human Rights in ESDP Missions (7 June 2006), CEU 10076/06 (2006); Conclusions on Promoting Gender Equality and Gender Mainstreaming in Crisis Management (13 November 2006).

principles and spirit of conventions concerning military personnel'.[134] However, at the EU level the EU Model Status of Forces and EU Model Status of Mission Agreements, promulgated initially in 2005, have been criticized for conferring a more extensive set of privileges and immunities on EU operations than current international practice warrants.[135] Neither do these Model Agreements include any provision, similar to that of the UN Model Code, providing for 'full respect for the spirit and principles' of humanitarian law.

Civilian missions can similarly be contracted or regulated into some form of human rights commitment. In Kosovo, the Interim Administration Mission in Kosovo (hereinafter 'UNMIK') Regulation 1 provides that 'all persons undertaking public duties or holding public office in Kosovo shall observe internationally recognized human rights standards and shall not discriminate against any person on any ground'.[136] The limitation of these provisions is that it is somewhat unclear what respecting the 'principles and spirit' of the conventions, or 'observing' the standards, requires in practice and the mechanism for enforcement remains organizational disciplinary structures or home state criminal law jurisdiction, meaning that an accountability gap persists as regards local populations.[137]

The pressure for direct accountability to local populations has resulted in another route to third party accountability, through *ad hoc* institutional innovation. For example, an ombudsperson's office was set up in the UN Transitional Administration in East Timor and the UNMIK, with the ombudsperson authorized to receive complaints against all the people employed by the UN, as well as against personnel working for local authorities, but with no enforcement mechanism.[138] In Kosovo, for example, UNMIK has taken steps in effect to 'accede' to human rights conventions through technical agreements with the Council of Europe that bring them within the supervision mechanisms of the Convention on the Prevention of Torture and the Framework Convention on the Protection of National Minorities.[139] These agreements state that

---

[134] Agreement between the United Nations and the Government of the Republic of Rwanda on the Status of the United Nations Assistance Mission for Rwanda (5 November 1993), Article 7.

[135] Draft Model Agreement on the status of the European Union-led forces between the European Union and a Host State (20 July 2007), CEU 11894/07 (2007); Draft Model Agreement on the Status of the European Union Civilian Crisis Management Mission in a Host State (SOMA) (15 December 2008), CEU 17148/08 (2008). See further, A. Sari, 'Status of Forces and Status of Mission Agreements under the ESDP: The EU's Evolving Practice', (2008)19 *EJIL* 67, commenting on largely similar 2005 drafts of the Model Agreements.

[136] UNMIK Regulation 1/1991 (25 July 1999), available at www.unmikonline.org.

[137] See further, R. Kolb, S. Vité and G. Porretto, *L'application Du Droit International Humanitaire Et Des Droits De L'homme Aux Organisations Internationales: Forces De Paix Et Administrations Civiles Transitoires* (Brussels: Bruylant, 2005).

[138] See F. Hampson, Administration of Justice, Rules of Law and Democracy, Working paper on the Accountability of International Personnel Taking Part in Peace Support Operations Submitted by Françoise Hampson, UN Doc. E/CN.4/Sub.2/2005/42 (2005), at para. 79. A local ombudsperson's office was also set up in other Peace Support Operation missions, including in the United Nations Mission of Support in East Timor.

[139] See Agreement between the United Nations Interim Administration in Kosovo and the Council of Europe on technical arrangements related to the Framework Convention for the

UNMIK is to provide the relevant information through a specifically designed reporting mechanism and so bypass the difficulties of a technical accession to the Conventions. A further step towards accountability took place in 2006 when an international Human Rights Advisory Panel was established to 'examine complaints from any person or group of individuals claiming to be the victim of a violation by UNMIK of the human rights of [eight human rights conventions]'.[140] The crafting of the Advisory Panel's jurisdiction operates practically to incorporate the conventions domestically as regards UNMIK, by providing a domestic mechanism for their application.[141] Other *ad hoc* accountability mechanisms include a Personnel Conduct Committee in the United Nations Mission in Sierra Leone (hereinafter 'UNAMSIL'), and the Code of Conduct Committee in the United Nations Operation in Burundi. Both of these involved quasi-judicial mechanisms, with no enforcement arm, in response to well-publicized abuses.[142]

To this example an exceptional instance of host state accountability over international actors can be added.[143] In Bosnia, the DPA provision established the OHR as the 'theatre of final authority' for the entire agreements, and these powers were subsequently extended to include the power to legislate when the domestic legislature was log-jammed.[144] The Bosnian Constitutional Court was subsequently repeatedly asked to consider the constitutionality of this OHR-promulgated legislation. In response the

---

Protection of National Minorities (23 August 2004), available online at http://www.unhcr.org/refworld/country,,,MULTILATERALTREATY,SRB,,,0.html. For full body of reports and Committee of Ministers resolutions pursuant to this agreement, seehttp://www.cpt.coe.int/en/states/srb.htm. Agreement between the United Nations Interim Administration Mission in Kosovo and the Council of Europe on technical arrangements related to the European Convention on the Prevention of Torture and Inhuman and Degrading Treatment or Punishment (23 August 2004), available online at http://www.unhcr.org/refworld/country,,,MULTILATERALTREATY,SRB,,,0.html. See further, UNMIK, Press Release, UNMIK/PR/1216 (23 August 2004), available at www.unmikonline.org/press/2004/pressr/pr1216.pdf. These agreements expressly note in their preambles that they do not make UNMIK a 'party' to the treaty in question.

[140] See UNMIK Regulation No. 2006/12, On the Establishment of a Human Rights Advisory Panel, UNMIK/REG/2006/12 (2006), Chapter 1, Section 1.2, available at www.unmikonline.org/regulations/unmikgazette/02english/E2006regs/RE2006_12.pdf.

[141] The domestic incorporation had already happened through UNMIK Regulation No. 1001/9, Constitutional Framework for Provisional Self-government, UNMIK/REG/2001/9 (2001), Chapter 3, but appeared to apply only to the institutions of government listed in the constitution.

[142] UNAMSIL, Press Release, Special Representative of the Secretary-General launches UNAMSIL Personnel Conduct Committee (26 August 2002), available at http://www.un.org/depts/oios/reports/a57_465.htm; PeaceWomen website, Burundi: UN Mission Sets up Units to Check Sexual Abuse (15 November 2004), http://www.irinnews.org/report.aspx?reportid=52053. See further, Hampson, *supra* n.138, at paras 80–81.

[143] There is a partial example also in Northern Ireland, where the international Bloody Sunday Tribunal was repeatedly judicially reviewed by the English Court of Appeal so as to overturn venue and anonymity rulings of the Tribunal – raising the spectre of judicial review of the Tribunal's final findings. For judgments, seehttp://webarchive.nationalarchives.gov.uk/20101103103930/http://bloody-sunday-inquiry.org/rulings-and-judgments/index.html.

[144] These powers were provided in the Peace Implementation Conference, Bonn Conclusions (10 December 1997), Article XI(2), available at www.ohr.int/pic/default.asp?content_id=5183.

Court asserted that 'the mandate of the High Representative derives from Annex 10 of the [DPA], the relevant resolutions of the United Nations Security Council and the Bonn Declaration and that the mandate and the exercise of the mandate are not subject to the control of the Constitutional Court.'[145] Nevertheless, the Court simultaneously found that, 'in so far as the High Representative intervenes into the legal system of Bosnia and Herzegovina, the laws enacted by him are, by their nature, domestic laws of Bosnia and Herzegovina, whose conformity with the Constitution of Bosnia and Herzegovina can be examined by the Constitutional Court'.[146] In this move, the Constitutional Court, whose authority derives from one of the DPA's sub-Annexes, empowered itself to review the actions of the OHR, who is the 'final theatre of authority' for the whole agreement – enforcement inversion whereby international actors are held accountable through domestic institutions, rather than vice versa. This innovation illustrates the capacity of peace agreement dilemmas of fit to reshape and reconstruct both the international, and indeed the domestic legal order, established by the peace agreement. The Bosnian Constitutional Court's assumption of jurisdiction created a new relationship between international enforcer and domestic court (in this case itself an internationalized court), that domesticised the third party role as implementor of the peace agreement as treaty.

The above innovations illustrate the diversity of *ad hoc* attempts to respond to legitimacy crises which attempt to restore a connection between accountability mechanisms and those whose rights are violated. The mechanisms both respond to the mix of international and domestic actors in the post-conflict state and further construct the post-conflict state as a space of hybrid governance characterized by transnational legal pluralism.

C. Normative (In)stability

In the area of third party accountability, as with other areas, the development of a *lex pacificatoria* is incomplete and *ad hoc*. Some of the difficulties of applying norms to international organizations are a specific version of the broader difficulty with the accountability of international organizations under contemporary international law.[147] However, part of the difficulty in this context is the complex innovation as regards the use of international third parties in peace settlement implementation tasks, and the difficulty international law-making has with catching up. Moreover, the task of 'catching up' is difficult as it is unlikely that one instrument could ever capture the full range of third parties and third party functions that arise in practice. Third parties

---

[145] Twenty five Representatives of the People's Assembly of Republika Srpska, U-26/01 (28 December 2001), at para. 13; see also, *Trideset i četiri poslanika Narodne skupštine Republike Srpske*, U-25/00 (23 March 2001); Eleven members of the House of Representatives of the Parliamentary Assembly of Bosnia and Herzegovina, U-9/00 (3 November 2000); Eleven members of the House of Representatives of the Parliamentary Assembly of Bosnia and Herzegovina U-16/00 (2 February 2000), all available at http://www.ccbh.ba/eng.

[146] *Ibid.*

[147] See generally, Klabbers, *supra* n.91, at 271–293; see also reports of the International Law Commission, The Responsibility of International Organizations, available at www.un.org/law/ilc/.

include a range of other actors, private actors, judges, non-governmental organizations and donors, many of whom stand beyond international law's easy reach and whose functions would require specifically tailored standards.[148]

As a result, the very partial *lex pacificatoria* that has emerged can be conceived of as establishing a broad framework for accountability, namely that:

- international human rights law, humanitarian law, domestic constitutional law principles and the peace agreement itself, should all be understood to provide standards relevant to the accountability of third parties for their transitional actions; and that
- the more third party actors take on functions of governance, the more they should be accountable through international human rights commitments, however that accountability is achieved; and
- the longer third party actors undertake functions of governance, the more they should be accountable through domestic legal and political processes, however that accountability is achieved.

However, these principles must be drawn from across quite different existing legal standards, judgments and practices. A recent report by Hampson in 2005 illustrates the complexity of fashioning any accountability regime which would cut across the complexity of third party functions in this context. Tellingly, and perhaps ambiguously, entitled 'Administration of Justice, Rule of Law and Democracy', the report addresses the accountability of 'international personnel' taking part in peace support operations and aims to address a broad cross section of third party post-conflict roles: civilian and military personnel, international experts, international civil servants and others, such as the foreign staff of non-governmental organizations. It documents the complex, overlapping and chaotic types of immunity that pertain, and the equally complex, overlapping and chaotic range of constituencies to whom accountability is owed, all of which point to different venues for determining accountability.[149] As demonstrated above, in place of coherent formal legal accountability, soft law norms have been fashioned, providing for a range of different accountabilities for different types of actors, together with a set of *ad hoc* mechanisms providing for accountability of some actors in particular conflicts, or attempts to 'contract' such obligations into the legal instruments that 'contract' the international implementers into their tasks.

11. FROM *LEX PACIFICATORIA* TO *JUS POST BELLUM*?

The attempt to apply international law to transitions from conflict has produced reinterpretations of key international legal doctrines which operate to reshape what are understood to be the boundaries of international legal regimes and, indeed, international law itself. It has been argued throughout that the attempt to use international law to

---

[148] See for example, International Criminal Court, Code of Judicial Ethics, ICC-BD/02-01-05 (9 March 2005).
[149] Hampson, *supra* n.138.

regulate peace agreement settlements and their implementation has required new accounts of how international law applies and what it demands. These new accounts have re-worked the scope and concerns of core international legal regimes, such as refugee law, human rights law and humanitarian law, so as to address the peculiar political dilemmas of transition. I have termed these new developments a new *lex pacificatoria* or 'law of the peacemakers'.

In each case, however, any shift in international legal doctrine is partial and unstable and it is unclear whether the interpretations will be sustained, developed or rolled back. The new *lex* does not operate as a clear new legal regime establishing a set of legal obligations. Rather, it operates as a set of programmatic standards that provide guidance and, at times, go further in creating a normative expectation as to how the dilemmas of peace settlements can be resolved concomitantly with the requirements of international law.

The very partiality and instability of the *lex pacificatoria* means that it is tempting to view it as a *lex ferenda*, or 'developing law', whose natural trajectory would seem to be towards a more established, clearly legal, and fully worked out body of law capable of applying to transitions from conflict. Indeed, it has been argued that the types of developments outlined in this chapter point to a need for, and indeed the development of, a *jus post bellum* that extends and develops concepts of *jus ad bello* and *jus in bello* to provide a differentiated application of current legal regimes to the post-conflict phase; a 'post-conflict needs' argument has been central to driving discussion of a *jus post bellum* in recent years.[150] Lawyers dislike 'quasi' legal regimes, laws that do not contemplate or fit the facts, and radical legal pluralism, whereby it is constantly unclear which legal regime applies and has precedence. From this dislike derives an instinct to codify a *jus post bellum* that would regulate post-conflict dilemmas more clearly and more appropriately. If international law is now a law of regimes, and the post-conflict environment has no specific or appropriate regime, then, the argument runs, it now needs one.

A second driver for *jus post bellum* discourse, however, lies in the link between the waging of international armed conflict and a justificatory discourse rooted in the need to transform the targeted state, in particular to prevent human rights abuses.[151] In the international armed conflicts of recent years, the legality of intervention has been disputed in many key cases, namely Kosovo, Iraq and Afghanistan. Here, talk of a *jus post bellum* has been driven by attempts to link the practice of intervention to questions of the morality of war and just war theory, against a backdrop of questionable legality for the war itself. Where there are concerns over the legality of the war, arguments of the need for state transformation have been used either to bolster arguments of lawfulness or to suggest that 'technical' unlawfulness is overcome by a higher moral good. Both types of justification of armed intervention are undermined if the resultant state is not transformed. An illegal or unjust war can be legitimated retrospectively by achieving a measure of justice for the citizens of the country attacked, while a legal or just war it would seem should achieve a just result and can be understood as 'unjust' if

---

[150] See for example, C. Stahn, '"Jus ad Bellum", "Jus in Bello", "Jus post Bellum"? – Rethinking the Conception of the Law of Armed Force', (2006) 17 *EJIL* 921.
[151] *Ibid.*

it does not. To the extent the legal arguments are built on the case for humanitarian intervention, then the justice arguments and the legality arguments are connected.

Both these drivers indicate the practical political, legal and moral reasons to reach to a distinctive *jus post bellum*. In conclusion, however, this chapter will address whether a new and distinct *jus post bellum* is either possible or desirable.

A. Is a *Jus Post Bellum* Possible?

There are a number of practical problems impinging on whether a more fully fledged *jus post bellum* can be achieved. First, it is unclear who would design and sign up to any new regime. Practices of international law-making are complex and typically protracted. Multi-lateral treaties involve complex and lengthy interstate negotiations that increasingly involve a host of other actors. There is no clear will or capacity to agree a new 'fifth' Geneva Convention or suchlike.

Secondly, even if the will did exist it is unlikely that consensus could be reached on the content of any new regime. Attempts to codify, even in soft law standards, some of the 'new law's' current content have often foundered or produced very vague general principles. This failure is not a simple lack of commitment or will. There are real conceptual problems with designing a new 'hybrid' regime for post-conflict situations. Chief among these is the difficulty of containing the consequence of any new standard, for how we understand the underlying legal regimes to apply in less controversial settings. For example, will a new standard on transitional justice strengthen or water down existing human rights provision: is an explicitly *transitional* justice to be articulated as an exception to norms demanding accountability, or a differentiated application of them appropriate to the transitional state? What is the definition of 'transition' to which this 'different' form of justice would apply? Moreover, as regards the breadth of the *lex* as a whole, where soft law guidance currently exists it relates to one dimension of transition – refugees, transitional justice, gender or third party accountability. It is difficult to imagine how the developing soft law of these disparate areas could be woven into a coherent, unified formal legal regime capable of regulating all aspects of transition.

Thirdly, while the pressure for a new international legal regime arises in part to escape the boundary dilemmas of existing regimes, a new regime would merely present a new set of 'boundary' dilemmas. To which types and scales of conflict would the new regime apply? The very scale of peace agreement practice illustrates the diverse conflict situations to which a *jus post bellum* might be argued to apply: fully fledged international wars, Protocol II non-international armed conflict, conflict governed by Common Article 3 of the Geneva Conventions and conflict that falls outside humanitarian law definitions altogether. When is a conflict the type that triggers the *jus post bellum*? If the categories of humanitarian and human rights law are to be merged, then the concept of the relevant 'conflict' also becomes critical. Are there any limits to the situation in which a new *jus post bellum* would apply? What type of conflict and political transition suffices? How and when is it decided that a situation is 'post'-conflict? Peace settlements are often only partially implemented, with sporadic or sustained violence re-emerging. Post-settlement is not the same as 'post-conflict', although the literature often assumes that it is. Often, no consensus exists between any of the parties (including international third parties) as to whether a situation is 'post-conflict', or when a distinctive 'transition' begins and ends. Without a clear sense of such boundaries it is unclear when the differentiated standards of any *jus post bellum* would begin or end. The fluctuating nature of post-conflict violence indicates a difficulty in deciding when any new *jus post bellum* might apply.

B. Is a *Jus Post Bellum* Desirable?

These practical problems prompt the question of whether a new 'third way' post-conflict regime is desirable. It can be argued that the partial nature of the *lex pacificatoria* leaves vital room for negotiations. It can be argued that the consent of the parties to a conflict to new political and legal arrangements is vital to ending a conflict. Guidelines for what peace agreements should include, therefore, may be more appropriate to enabling negotiated solutions, rather than using international law to require particular substantive outcomes. A broad sketching of the possible parameters of amnesty, exhortations to include women, and 'best practice' guidance on the return of refugees and displaced persons leave some room for the parties to negotiate solutions with some flexibility. What is lost in the give and take of negotiations may be gained in the commitment and ability to implement whatever is agreed. Binding international legal standards making detailed provision on what is required in each area would effectively operate to require a particular blueprint of any political deal, narrowing the parties' room to manoeuvre. The more law specifies peace settlement terms, the less the parties are able to negotiate. Rather than guiding negotiations, a new regime would run the risk of effectively establishing legal pre-requisites for any end of the conflict.

More positively, the partially formed state of the *lex pacificatoria* may assist and enable agreement to some normative framework for resolving conflicts. At present, the 'new law' of peacemakers operates as a holding device for disagreement over what law and conflict resolution requires and should require. For example, in the area of transitional justice, it holds together the idea that both accountability and amnesty are useful and permissible and some sense of where the line should be drawn between them. In the undefined middle space lie possibilities for negotiated settlement. As the area of transitional justice illustrates, a project of bringing 'clarity' to a *jus post bellum* almost inevitably involves excluding the middle ground, the search for which has driven the new developments. This middle ground – the only ground on which international actors can find agreement – is often the same middle ground that enables the parties to a conflict to reach agreement.

A second danger to moving to a *jus post bellum* pertains. The new boundary disputes of a new *jus post bellum* regime create the possibility that, to the extent that a *jus post bellum* allows for an exceptional application of humanitarian or human rights law, this exceptionality would begin to creep through to all applications. The boundary disputes created by the category, in particular the difficulty of defining 'post-conflict' or 'transition', open up the possibility of attenuating human rights standards indefinitely, of using humanitarian law in times of peace and even the possibility of enabling international enforcers to self-servingly grab enabling provisions, such as 'administrative detention', cut free from their overarching framework of third party accountability.

12. CONCLUSION

Whether the *jus post bellum* is viewed as a useful development of international law will depend on what view is taken of the political import of any *jus post bellum*, with reference to the underlying justification for international law-making itself. The desirability and shape of any *jus post bellum* will depend on an account of the current situating of international law as post-Westphalian and whether this situation is viewed positively or negatively.

If the project of international law is seen as having moved from the 'international law' of states to the 'international law of regimes', then the creation of a new regime may perhaps be understood as inevitable, but will be evaluated differently by those who think specialist regimes are a useful development of international law and those who are concerned about international law's fragmentation. Beyond a general concern with fragmentation, sterner critiques of international law as the 'law of regimes' have been made, namely that understanding international law as a law of regimes repositions international lawyers as regime experts, and the politics and majesty of international law become lost in a series of inter-regime battles approached as technocratic projects.[152] From this point of view, even the technocratic project of 'fixing mess' by clarifying post-conflict soft law as a *jus post bellum* has a politics: the politics of obscuring what is at stake in regime disputes of experts.[153]

Alternatively, if the post-Westphalian project of international law is viewed as the international promotion, and even requirement, of liberal statehood, then one may view the current *lex pacificatoria*'s incomplete nature as a way-station towards achieving a clearer *jus post bellum*. However, the parameters of this *jus* will be set by the goal of achieving liberal democratic statehood. The project of embracing and building a new *jus post bellum* would, from this perspective, become very explicitly tied up with ensuring the emergence of a liberal democratic state and its components would be developed so as to ensure that such a state is delivered. Thus, some of the more fluid dimensions of the *lex pacificatoria* would be rejected in the codification, or tolerated only to the extent that they were expressly transitional. For example, power-sharing and group rights might be tolerated short term, but with pressure to move towards individual elections and rights, while short-term amnesties might be tolerated with a pressure to move to full human rights accountability for all. Moreover, a liberal international lawyer may be predisposed to reasserting the state as the only appropriate power-holder whose monopoly on the use of force must be bolstered to include the punishment of non-state actors all aimed at installing a standard set of legal and political institutions. However, if the development of liberal peace-making is viewed sceptically, these attempts may be resisted in favour of acknowledging and working with prevailing domestic power-structures – even when profoundly illiberal, while understanding the contingent nature of both state and non-state legitimacy. It can also

---

[152] See for example, M. Koskenniemi, 'The Fate of Public International Law: Between Technique and Politics', (2007) 70 *MLR* 1.

[153] D. Kennedy, 'The Mystery of Global Governance', in J.L. Dunoff and J.P. Tracthman (eds), *Ruling the World? Constitutionalism, International Law, and Global Governance* (Cambridge: Cambridge University Press, 2009).

be argued that such a project will inevitably result in any case. Case studies question whether what emerges from liberal peace-making practices is in fact 'liberal peace' or a hybrid variant where top-down imposition of liberal institutions competes with bottom-up resistance operating to preserve indigenous power structures, which often subvert the liberal peace-making project.[154] The role of law, from this perspective, should perhaps be one of a limited ambition aimed at constructive engagement with the dynamic of imposition and resistance, rather than an attempt to require, ever more militarily forcibly, a move towards Western liberal values and institutions.

Finally, there are those who may be sceptical of a *jus post bellum* on realist grounds, namely that its strong association with the justifications for international intervention means that it cannot be separated from uni-polar attempts to pursue the interests of the United States and its allies, and that its development and application cannot resist being subverted to those ends. From this perspective, the move from existing regimes of human rights and humanitarian law may be viewed suspiciously as enabling their selective application in pursuit of the ambitions of the international hegemon as the example of retaining administrative detention but lifted free from wider constraints on 'transformative occupation' illustrates.

The term *lex pacificatoria* in its allusion to the *lex mercatoria* has a descriptive accuracy in its allusion to a body of law that operates somewhere between binding international law and not law. It also points to the contingent nature of the developments and the possibility both for further development but also for retreat. It does not signal a fully fledged regime as a possible or desirable end point of current developments, as opposed to *jus post bellum*. Moreover, the term, in remaining open as to the future, does not automatically applaud resolution of the indeterminacy of current regulation of post-conflict dilemmas by international law as being 'a good thing'. Finally, the term *lex pacificatoria*, in contrast to the term *jus post bellum*, signals openness to the possibility that the useful purpose of international legal regulation of peace settlements is to set out broad normative parameters that support negotiated outcomes involving local parties to conflict, rather than to dictate outcomes.

For these reasons, I prefer the term *lex pacificatoria* as a way of capturing the current state of international law governing peace settlements and their implementation, not because it is important to have a battle over Latin terms, but because terms start to tell stories about the current state of play and the law's future directions and ambitions. The *lex pacificatoria* acknowledges that international law may usefully be shaped by conflict resolution innovations, even as it attempts to shape settlement terms, and that it is important to understand the two-way nature of the interface.

---

[154] R. MacGinty, 'Hybrid Peace: The Interaction between Top Down and Bottom Up Peace', (2010) 41 *Security Dialogue* 391.

16. Foreign territorial administration and international trusteeship over people: colonialism, occupation, the mandates and trusteeship arrangements, and international territorial administration
*Ralph Wilde**

1. INTRODUCTION

Colonialism, territorial administration by states under the Mandate and Trusteeship systems, occupation by states and territorial administration by international organizations are commonly treated as distinct activities in international law and public policy. Such treatment is helpful in understanding particular issues, for example on certain matters of legitimacy (consider the contrast between mainstream ideas associated with state-conducted colonialism and occupation, on the one hand, and international territorial administration (hereinafter 'ITA'), on the other), applicable law and mechanisms of accountability. However, a fundamental commonality also operates as between these activities, as a matter of international law and public policy: they are each manifestations of the international institution of trusteeship over people. This commonality is significant not only because it explains the similar nature of activities that tend to be regarded as entirely distinct from each other. Also, it is important because it foregrounds the relevance of an important norm in international law, self-determination, which potentially places the legitimacy of all these activities into question.

Although other normative ideas are also relevant to foreign territorial administration, the trusteeship and self-determination concepts are perhaps the most important: they speak to the fundamental question of whether trusteeship over people *per se* is legitimate as a matter of international law. A focus on them, therefore, is important in identifying how trusteeship over people has been treated normatively in the past and, because of this, how it might be treated in the future. This chapter analyses the contrasting fortunes of each normative vision in mediating the treatment of foreign territorial administration over the course of the 20th century and into the 21st century, and what is at stake in choosing between them when existing and new forms of foreign territorial administration are considered today.[1]

---

* Thanks are due to Dr Silvia Borelli for research assistance.
[1] This chapter draws on text and ideas set out in the following pages of R. Wilde, *International Territorial Administration: How Trusteeship and the Civilizing Mission Never Went Away* (Oxford: Oxford University Press, 2008): Chapter 6, pp. 229–232; Chapter 8, pp. 311–312, 317–318, 326, 335–343, 356–357, 360–363, 373–379, 381–382, 418, 422–423.

2. FOREIGN TERRITORIAL ADMINISTRATION: SIMILAR ACTIVITIES

Colonialism, territorial administration by states under the Mandate and Trusteeship systems, occupation and the administration of territory by international organizations – what I term 'international territorial administration' – share a common feature: in each case an important distinction is understood to operate between the identity of the administering entity or entities and that of the administered territorial unit.[2] The nature of this separation between the two is as different as between territorial administration by individual states under the Mandate and Trusteeship systems, occupation and ITA, on the one hand, and colonialism, on the other. In the former category, the administering entity is or was not understood to enjoy sovereignty in the sense of title/ownership (and, in the case of occupation, is legally prohibited from claiming such a privilege) with respect to the territory involved. In the latter category, by contrast, this form of sovereignty is or was sometimes considered to subsist. Even when such a situation prevailed, however, the territory and its people were treated in various ways as something 'other' than the territory and the population of the 'metropolis'; for example, as far as the population was concerned, in terms of differences in the enjoyment of legal rights and the operation of the franchise.[3] Because of the common feature of the existence of a degree of differentiation between the identity of the administering actors and that of the administered territories, the activities under consideration can be treated collectively; in doing so, they will be referred to as 'foreign territorial administration'. The common feature identified is, however, an elemental commonality rooted simply in the activity performed; in order to fully appreciate how the practices under evaluation have been treated normatively as far as the question of the basis on which they are introduced, what they seek to achieve, and when they should end, it is also necessary to consider the extent to which the purposes with which these practices have been associated also manifest commonality.

3. TRUSTEESHIP: COMMON PURPOSES

The wide-ranging history and instances of the various practices under evaluation reveal significant heterogeneity in terms of the purposes with which these practices were associated.[4] However, an overall concept, that of 'trusteeship', can be identified in many instances of foreign territorial administration, and has purchase in illuminating what the activities under evaluation have in common in their own terms, and also in

---

[2] On colonialism, see the sources cited in Wilde, *ibid.*, List of Sources, section 5.3, and the discussion and sources cited in *ibid.*, Chapter 5, section 5.3, and Chapter 8. On the Mandate and Trusteeship systems, see the discussion and sources cited in *ibid.*, Chapter 5, section 5.3 and Chapter 8. On occupation, see the discussion and sources cited in *ibid.*, Chapter 8. On international territorial administration, see *ibid.*, and the sources cited therein, List of Sources, sections 5.1 and 5.2.

[3] See further the discussion in *ibid.*, Chapter 8, section 8.2, and sources cited therein.

[4] See further the discussion in *ibid.*, Chapter 8, section 8.3, and sources cited therein.

explaining how they came to be treated in a common fashion in the second half of the twentieth century. The concept of 'trusteeship' is significant in explaining how the internal governance of the territories involved has been understood – the basis on which foreign rule was to operate and also, therefore, the basis on which it might be brought to an end.[5]

International trusteeship can be understood in terms of a response to two distinct conceptions of the pre-existing governance structure in the territory. In the first place, covering colonial trusteeship and state administration under the Mandate and Trusteeship systems, the racialized concept of a 'standard of civilization' was deployed to determine that certain peoples in the world were 'uncivilized', lacking organized societies, a position reflected and constituted in the notion that their 'sovereignty' was either completely lacking or at least of an inferior character when compared with that of 'civilized' peoples.[6] In the second place, also covering certain forms of colonial trusteeship, state administration under the Mandate and Trusteeship systems, occupation and ITA, foreign rule was or has been introduced after conflict, often in circumstances where governance in the territory has been degraded in some way by that conflict, for example through the collapse of a defeated government and the destruction of infrastructure.[7]

Understanding the exercise of administrative prerogatives over territory in these two circumstances as 'trusteeship' conceptualizes the relationship between the foreign actor and the territory and its people in a particular manner: the trustee/guardian state is controlling the beneficiary/ward territory, acting on behalf of the latter entity – the 'sacred trust of civilization' or the 'civilizing mission'.[8] The role of the trustee was often understood to have a two-part character: first, to care for the ward, and secondly, to exercise tutelage of the ward in order that it could mature and eventually care for itself. In the context of colonialism, then, the idea of the 'civilizing mission' was to govern in such a way as to address the perceived incapacity for self-government, or at least governance that met the standard of civilization, and also to build up local capacities, sometimes with the aim to render self-administration, meeting the standard, realizable.[9]

---

[5] For commentary on the concept of international trusteeship conducted by individual states, mostly concerned with either or both of colonialism and the League of Nations Mandate and United Nations Trusteeship systems, see the sources cited in Wilde, *ibid.*, Chapter 8 (nn. 104 and 107–108). For a discussion of the relevance of the trusteeship concept to the practices under evaluation, see *ibid.*, Chapter 8, section 8.3.2.

[6] See the sources cited in *ibid.*

[7] *Ibid.*

[8] *Ibid.*

[9] See generally the sources cited in *ibid.* For Bill Ashcroft, Gareth Griffiths and Helen Tiffin, through the civilizing mission, 'colonialism could be (re)presented as a virtuous and necessary civilizing task involving education and paternalistic nurture'; B. Ashcroft, G. Griffiths and H. Tiffin, *Post-Colonial Studies: The Key Concepts* (Abingdon: Routledge, 2000), at 47. Anthony Anghie describes the civilizing mission as the idea of 'extending Empire for the higher purpose of educating and rescuing the barbarian'; A. Anghie, *Imperialism, Sovereignty and the Making of International Law* (Cambridge: Cambridge University Press, 2005), at 96; see also *ibid.*, 96 *et seq.*; M. Koskenniemi, *The Gentle Civilizer of Nations* (Cambridge: Cambridge University Press, 2002), at 145, 147, 168.

The concept of 'trusteeship' is also relevant in the case of ITA, which has occurred since the creation of the League of Nations.[10] Although the word 'trusteeship' is not used officially in relation to this activity, the activity manifests the central elements of a trust relationship: a 'ward' people placed under the care of an international organization, which ostensibly performs administrative functions not for its own gain but in the ward's own interest, with the dual role of remedying perceived incapacities for governance and transforming the situation so that these incapacities no longer exist and the local population is able to run its own affairs.[11]

4. THE DURATION AND TERMINATION OF TRUSTEESHIP: PROGRESSIVE DEVELOPMENT TOWARDS SELF-ADMINISTRATION

A. Introduction

Focusing on the trust nature of many instances of foreign territorial administration is helpful in understanding the normative basis on which the duration and termination of these arrangements was, is and can be understood. The concept of trust foregrounds the key notions of incapacity for self-administration, building up local capacities and eventual self-administration that encapsulate the ideas with which the arrangements have been and are often associated. Within the common theme of trusteeship, there are significant differences across the different practices under evaluation in terms of the normative models adopted for duration and termination. In what follows, each practice will be evaluated in turn, and then comparative analysis between them will be offered.

B. Duration and Termination under Colonial Trusteeship

In some instances of colonialism, the introduction of foreign administration was viewed originally as being of indefinite duration.[12] As a result, the people of the territories involved were to be displaced from the role of territorial administration indefinitely – there was no exit in sight. As far as the status of the colonial territory was concerned, there was no suggestion, whether implicit or explicit, that the people would attain independence at some future date. In this model, then, the 'civilizing mission' was conceived to be exclusively palliative, not also remedial, as far as responding to perceived local deficiencies in self-administration was concerned. Colonial authorities would step in to provide a functioning administrative system; they were not, in the main, concerned with increasing the capacity of the people of the territory to govern in a particular manner so that the people would eventually be able to take over territorial administration directly.

---

[10] On the definition of 'International Territorial Administration', see Wilde, *supra* n. 1, Chapter 1, section 1.4.

[11] See *ibid.*, *passim* and in particular Chapter 6 and Chapter 8, section 8.3.3 and sources cited therein.

[12] See the works listed in *ibid.*, List of Sources, sections 5.3.1–5.3.3.

In some cases, in the latter stages of colonial rule, ideas concerning the possibility for progressive improvement in local capacities entered the discourse of colonial ideology.[13] Allied to such ideas was the notion that one of the objectives of colonial administration was to foster improvement through 'tutelage'.[14] This is evident in Article VI of Chapter I of the General Act of the Berlin Conference of 1884–1885, with its reference to an obligation to 'care for the improvement of the conditions of [the natives'] moral and material wellbeing'.[15] Similarly, Article 73 of the UN Charter obliges colonial states to 'promote... the well-being of the inhabitants' and:

> to ensure ... their political, economic, social, and educational advancement ...
>
> [and] to develop self-government, to take due account of the political aspirations of the peoples, and to assist them in the progressive development of their free political institutions.[16]

From the notion that improving local capacities for self-administration was one of the objectives of colonial rule came the idea that, within overall colonial control, the level of self-administration would be calibrated according to the capacity for self-administration of the local people. According to Frederick Lugard, explaining the 'dual mandate' of British colonialism in Africa:

> [t]he British Empire ... has only one mission – for liberty and self-development ... [which] can be best secured to the native population by leaving them free to manage their own affairs through their own rulers, proportionately to their degree of advancement, under the guidance of the British staff, and subject to the law and policy of the administration.[17]

Along the same lines, under Article 73 of the UN Charter the 'progressive development' of 'free political institutions' in Non-Self-Governing Territories is to be 'according to the particular circumstances of each territory and its peoples and their varying stages of advancement'.[18]

The next potential stage in this process is the idea that the people would become capable of the level of self-administration that would justify independence, thereby triggering a termination of the arrangement. Put differently, the people would attain a measure of progress that would bring the notion of foreign administration conceived on

---

[13] See the sources cited in *ibid.*, Chapter 8 (n. 183).
[14] See the sources cited in *ibid.*, Chapter 8 (n. 184).
[15] General Act of the Conference respecting (1) Freedom of Trade in the Basin of the Congo; (2) the Slave Trade; (3) Neutrality of the Territories in the Basin of the Congo; (4) Navigation of the Congo; (5) Navigation of the Niger; and (6) Rules for Future Occupation on the Coast of the African Continent, signed at Berlin, 26 February 1885, 165 CTS 485.
[16] Article 73 (a) and (b), UN Charter (1945). See also *ibid.*, para. (d).
[17] F.D. Lugard, *The Dual Mandate in British Tropical Africa*, 3rd edn (Edinburgh and London: Blackwood, 1926), 94, quoted in R.H. Jackson, *The Global Covenant: Human Conduct in a World of States* (Oxford: Oxford University Press, 2000), at 302. See also Wilde *supra* n. 1, Chapter 8 (n. 187).
[18] Article 73 (b), UN Charter (1945).

the basis of local incapacity into question. If this led to independence, the overall process would amount to what Robert Jackson terms 'evolutionary decolonization'.[19]

In the colonial context, states were divided as to whether full independence, or self-government within the framework of overall imperial rule, should be the end stage.[20] Notably, the relevant provision of the UN Charter concerning Non-Self-Governing Territories uses the phrase 'self-government or independence'.[21] William Bain reports that these differences in policy mapped onto general trends in attitudes towards colonial rule as between the USA, which took the 'full independence' position, and Britain, which took the 'self-government within imperial rule' position.[22] Bain states that:

> American scepticism of empire transformed trusteeship from a justification of empire, as it was in the British tradition, into an alternative to empire that was expressed concretely in the form of the League of Nations mandates system and the United Nations trusteeship system.[23]

C. Duration and Termination under the Mandate and Trusteeship Systems

As far as the Mandate and Trusteeship systems were concerned, provisions implicating the issues of progressive improvement, the role of the administering authority in fostering improvement and the prospects for eventual independence were explicitly included in the Covenant of the League of Nations and the Charter of the United Nations. Moreover, as will be explained below, the provisions conceived these issues in a variated fashion, both as between the two systems and, within the Mandate system, through the distinction between different 'classes' of Mandated territories. However, two of the leading scholars on these systems, Quincy Wright and Ramendra Nath Chowdhuri, argue that, despite this differential treatment within the Covenant and between the Covenant and the Charter, the two systems were generally understood at the time to operate on the basis that, in all cases, the developmental level was expected to improve, the administering authorities had a role in fostering this, and once improvements occurred, independence, and an exit for the foreign administering authorities, would be actualized.[24] The differentiated treatment of these issues within the Covenant and the Charter is still worth considering, however, because the arrangements represent two important and influential attempts to conceptualize tutelage, progress and potential exit by the administering authority.[25]

---

[19] R.H. Jackson, *Quasi-States: Sovereignty, International Relations and the Third World* (Cambridge: Cambridge University Press, 1990), at 86–91.

[20] On the idea of self-government within imperial rule, see, for example, H.D. Hall, *Mandates, Dependencies and Trusteeship* (London: Stevens & Sons, 1948), at 11, 95–97.

[21] Article 73 (b), UN Charter (1945).

[22] See W. Bain, *Between Anarchy and Society: Trusteeship and the Obligations of Power* (Oxford: Oxford University Press, 2003), Chapter 5, *passim*, and especially 117.

[23] *Ibid.*, 21. See also *ibid.*, 108.

[24] On these arguments, see further Wilde *supra* n. 1, Chapter 8 (n. 194).

[25] For other commentary on the relevant provisions of the League Covenant and the UN Charter, and the various agreements used to set up the arrangements, see the works cited in *ibid.*, Chapter 8 (n. 195).

For the League Mandate arrangements, although there were no provisions on termination, the use of the word 'yet' in the phrase 'not yet able to stand by themselves' at the beginning of Article 22 of the League of Nations Covenant suggested a possibility, indeed an expectation, that capacity for self-administration might arise in the future; thus the inability to 'stand by themselves' was not fixed, and might be remedied.[26] The conception of this capacity to 'stand by themselves' in terms of the 'strenuous conditions of the modern world' implied a notion of external freedom, something beyond internal self-administration within the overall framework of a colonial authority. This suggested that foreign administration was not to last indefinitely, but, rather, would operate until the people of the territory were deemed 'able to stand by themselves', an ability that might include the capacity to exist as an independent entity.[27]

However, the provisions of Article 22 arranged things in a fashion running counter to the idea that the suggestion made in the first paragraph applied to all Mandated territories equally. Paragraph 3 stated that:

> [t]he character of the mandate must differ according to the stage of the development of the people, the geographical situation of the territory, its economic conditions and other similar circumstances.[28]

So the developmental level, hitherto the sole principle governing the introduction of foreign administration, was now but one of several factors in operation. Placing a varied emphasis on these factors, the Covenant divided up the Mandated territories into three classes, later designated as classes 'A', 'B' and 'C'.[29] For classes 'A' and 'B', the 'stage of development' was seemingly determinative of the character of the Mandate. The people of 'A' class Mandates were deemed to have:

> reached a stage of development where their existence as independent nations can be provisionally recognized subject to the rendering of administrative advice and assistance by the Mandatory until such time as they are able to stand alone.[30]

Thus the people of the territory were judged to be almost capable of self-administration, requiring only an attenuated form of administrative involvement ('advice and assistance') of a finite duration, the end point being contingent on improvements in local capacity ('until such time as they are able to stand alone'). By contrast, 'B' class territories were deemed to be 'at such a stage' that the Mandatory

---

[26] Article 22, Covenant of the League of Nations (1919). See also the discussion in Wilde, *supra* n. 1, Chapter 8 (n. 196).
[27] See Wilde, *supra* n. 1, Chapter 8 (n. 198).
[28] Article 22, League Covenant (1919).
[29] *Ibid.*, Article 22, fourth, fifth and sixth paragraphs (corresponding to classes 'A', 'B' and 'C' respectively). The letters A, B and C are not found in the Covenant but were adopted by the League to denote the different classes of territory set out therein. For more detail on the particular territories covered, see, for example, the sources cited in Wilde, *supra* n. 1, Chapter 8 (n. 200).
[30] Article 22, League Covenant (1919).

power had to be responsible for plenary administration, and without any cut-off point.[31] Unlike 'A' and 'B' class Mandated territories, 'C' class Mandated territories were arranged according to factors other than the level of development:

> the sparseness of their population, or their small size, or their remoteness from the centers of civilization, or their geographical contiguity to the territory of the Mandatory, and other circumstances.[32]

For these Mandated territories, plenary administration 'under the laws of the Mandatory as integral portions of its territory' was in order, again without any suggestion of subsequent alteration.[33]

Taken together, these arrangements built on the trusteeship concept developed in the earlier colonial context, adopting the developmental level as the ostensible reason for the need for foreign administration and the ostensible grounds for ending it. As far as the end of foreign administration was concerned, this factor would also determine a possible change in territorial status, with the possibility, for example, of independent statehood. However, despite the suggestion made in the 'not yet able to stand by themselves' phrase of Article 22's opening paragraph, which is seemingly applicable to all territories, the Mandate system actually adopted a differentiated policy for the three classes of territory.[34] For 'C' class territories, external administration was set at an indefinite duration, as in certain forms of colonialism. The reasons for introducing external administration suggested somewhat unchangeable factors (for example, small size) and did not concern the level of development; this appeared to rule out the possibility that the need for administration may change in the future. By contrast, although trusteeship in 'B' class Mandated territories was similarly set at an indefinite duration, by making the reason for external administration the level of development, the contingent factor from the earlier phrase was picked up. However, this factor was only set as the basis for introducing external administration, not also for withdrawing it, and there was no explicit anticipation that, in fact, the level of development might improve in the future. This only suggested that the people were 'not able' to stand by themselves, rather than 'not yet' being able.[35]

Only 'A' class Mandated territories were conceived so that the duration was contingent on the same factor – the level of development – as the basis for the introduction of foreign administration; moreover, an express statement was made that the situation was expected to improve in the future.[36] Only with respect to this class of Mandated territories was there an implicit reference to a change in status – becoming

---

[31] Ibid.
[32] Ibid.
[33] Ibid.
[34] On this, see generally the discussion in Q. Wright, *Mandates Under the League of Nations* (Chicago: University of Chicago Press, 1930), at 232 *et seq.*
[35] See J.C. Hales, 'The Reform and Extension of the Mandate System', (1940) 26 *Transactions of the Grotius Society* 153, at 185.
[36] See *ibid*, at 185.

recognized as 'independent nations' on a non-provisional basis – if and when such improvement came about.[37]

Like the Mandate system, the Trusteeship system contained no explicit provisions on the termination of Trusteeship arrangements.[38] In contrast to the variations of the Mandate system, however, it adopted a simple, uniform approach for evolutionary developmental improvement echoing certain aspects of the formula adopted for 'A' class Mandates.[39] Administration in Trust territories was to:

> promote the political, economic, social and educational advancement of the inhabitants ... and their progressive development towards self-government or independence.[40]

The end goal, then – 'self-government or independence' – was clearer than the vague notion of being able to 'stand by themselves' applied to Mandated territories generally, but, conversely, was more equivocal, with its option of self-government without independence, than the provisions for 'A' class Mandated territories.[41]

It will be recalled that, with the Mandate arrangements, the level of development was explicitly invoked as the basis for introducing external administration (classes 'A' and 'B') and the reason for removing it (class 'A'). By contrast, in the Trusteeship arrangements it was invoked in a third sense: a positive alteration in the developmental level became one of the objectives for administration. Not only, then, was administration introduced because of the idea of a poor developmental level; it was also aimed at somehow improving this situation. Whereas an increase in development was seen as likely in 'A' class Mandated territories, and not ruled out in 'B' class Mandated territories, in neither class was the administering authority explicitly obliged to support such improvement, beyond the vague objective applicable to all Mandated territories that 'improvement' is part of the 'sacred trust'. Recalling the general policy objectives operating with respect to both the Mandate and Trusteeship arrangements, this difference between them in terms of a responsibility for enabling improvement indicated that, in the words of Ramendra Nath Chowdhuri:

> the emphasis ... shifted from the mere prohibition of abuses under the Mandate regime to the more positive aspect of constructive development in political, social, and educational spheres.[42]

As with 'A' class Mandated territories, the end of foreign administration in Trust territories was conceived to be contingent on an increase in the developmental level. Whereas this was explicit for 'A' class Mandated territories ('until such time as they are able to stand alone'), for Trust territories it was implicit as the negative outcome of the

---

[37] See Wilde, *supra* n. 1, Chapter 8 (n. 208).
[38] See the discussion in R.N. Chowdhuri, *International Mandates and Trusteeship Systems: A Comparative Study* (The Hague: Martinus Nijhoff, 1955), at 9, 62–63, 246.
[39] The territories were, however, divided into 'strategic' and 'non-strategic' Trust territories; see Wilde, *supra* n. 1, Chapter 8 (n. 98). See also *ibid.*, Chapter 8 (n. 210).
[40] Article 76 (b), UN Charter (1945).
[41] On the equivocal nature of this formulation for Trust territories in the Charter see, for example, Hall, *supra* n. 20, at 280.
[42] Chowdhuri, *supra* n. 38, at 11.

endpoint – 'self-government or independence' – towards which the progressive increase in development through external administration was aimed. Whereas the Mandate system only adopted this formula for territories understood to be the most highly developed, the Trusteeship system applied it across the board, to territories conceived as being at varying levels of development. It would be expected, then, that these territories would attain the enhanced developmental level at different stages.

Arguably, this difference between the Mandate and Trusteeship systems mediated the different formulae these two systems adopted in terms of changes in territorial status. For 'A' class Mandates, the level of development was such that independent statehood could be already 'provisionally recognized'; implicitly, this status was to operate on a provisional basis until development increased to a level where the people of the territory were 'able to stand alone'. For Trust territories, however, the starting point was merely the negative sovereignty outcome of detachment from the defeated powers, as in 'B' and 'C' class Mandates. A change in status – 'self-government or independence' – depended on developmental improvements. Given that such improvements would take place at different stages in different territories, the adoption of a formula for territorial status change that assumed a particular level of development, as was done in the case of 'A' class Mandates, was not followed.

D. Duration and Termination under Occupation

In the case of occupation, there is a general assumption that the arrangements are supposed to be temporary (even if some occupations have been, in fact, prolonged); the specific outcome of title vesting in the occupying state by virtue of its exercise of control is legally prohibited.[43] The obligation to preserve order and provide a system of administration in occupation law creates a possibility for improving local conditions for governance, and such improvement and an increase in development become clear objectives when occupations pursue a broader 'transformatory' agenda of economic and political reconstruction and transformation, often explicitly referencing some sort of aim at improvement to a level that will enable self-administration and the end of occupation.[44]

E. Duration and Termination under ITA

The introduction, and potential removal, of ITA in any given situation depends on two factors relating to how its operation is conceived. The first factor concerns whether administrative prerogatives are to be exercised 'reactively' or 'proactively', while the second factor concerns whether ITA is operating in a 'palliative' or 'remedial' fashion, or both.

---

[43] On the legal prohibition, see the sources cited in Wilde, *supra* n.1, Chapter 8 (n. 75). On the idea that occupation is a 'temporary' measure, see, for example, E. Benvenisti, *The International Law of Occupation*, paperback edn (Princeton, NJ: Princeton University Press, 2004), at xi.

[44] On the obligations of occupation law, see Wilde, *supra* n. 1, Chapter 8 (nn. 75 and 129 and sources cited therein).

With regard to the first factor, the 'reactive' use of administrative prerogatives occurs in some cases of 'partial' ITA – where the conduct of administration by international actors operates alongside the exercise of such activities by local actors.[45] In 'reactive' instances of 'partial' ITA, administrative prerogatives are exercised by the international actor only if some problem with local territorial administration is considered to be manifest; if not, the prerogatives of the international actor remain dormant. The League of Nations in Danzig and the Office of the High Representative (hereinafter 'OHR') in Bosnia and Herzegovina operated in this way.[46] For example, the OHR exercised its power to impose legislation and remove elected officials ostensibly on the basis that, respectively, the legislature had been deemed unwilling or incapable of passing such legislation itself, and there had been some problem with the officials in question (for example, corruption or nationalist extremism).[47]

As far as the end of the performance of this form of ITA is concerned it is a matter of the international actor declining to exercise its administrative prerogatives, and allowing the default activity of local territorial administration to operate. Authority is not transferred to local actors but, rather, those actors are able to exercise the authority they already possess, without interference. This is illustrated in the language used by the High Representative in Bosnia and Herzegovina when welcoming the 2001 adoption by the local legislature of an Electoral Law he deemed acceptable, thereby obviating the need for him to exercise his professed power to legislate:

> [t]he High Representative views the passage of the Election Law as a signal achievement of the elected representatives of Bosnia and Herzegovina and a very positive example of pragmatism and political maturity.[48]

In 'proactive' ITA projects, by contrast, the need for the exercise of administrative prerogatives is assumed from the beginning, and so this exercise, rather than administration by local actors, is the default. This occurs when plenary ITA operates, as in UN-run 'refugee' camps, the United Nations Transitional Administration for Eastern Slavonia, the EU Administration in Mostar (hereinafter 'EUAM'), the United Nations Interim Administration Mission in Kosovo (hereinafter 'UNMIK'), and the United Nations Transitional Administration in East Timor (hereinafter 'UNTAET');[49] or when particular administrative acts are performed because local actors are assumed to be unable or intrinsically unsuitable to perform them (for example, the conduct of

---

[45] On the definition of ITA, including partial ITA, see *ibid.*, Chapter 1, section 1.4.5. On 'reactive' partial ITA, see *ibid.*, Chapter 6, section 6.4.3.2, and sources cited therein.

[46] On the League of Nations in Danzig and OHR in Bosnia Herzegovina, see *ibid.*, *passim* (references contained in the Index pp. 589 and 588 respectively).

[47] See Wilde, *supra* n. 1, Chapter 1, at 15–16; on the OHR's powers to impose legislation and dismiss elected government officials, see *ibid.*, Chapter 2, section 2.3.3 and sources cited therein.

[48] OHR Press Release, 'High Representative Welcomes House of Peoples' Adoption of Election Law', 23 August 2001, available at http://www.ohr.int.

[49] On 'refugee' camp administration by the Office of the United Nations High Commissioner for Refugees (hereinafter 'UNHCR'), EUAM, UNMIK and UNTAET, see Wilde, *supra* n. 1, *passim* (references contained in the Index at pp. 604, 590, 590 and 589 respectively) and sources cited therein.

elections by the United Nations Transitional Authority in Cambodia (hereinafter 'UNTAC') in Cambodia).[50] Here, ITA does not operate alongside the existing governmental authority, performing the same activities as that authority reactively when the local authority is deemed somehow deficient. Rather, it takes over from this authority in the conduct of these activities at the outset. In consequence, the termination of the activity similarly involves the positive step of transferring authority to local actors.

The second factor influencing the end of the ITA form of trusteeship concerns the extent to which the ITA missions, like the other forms of trusteeship, are concerned not only with remedying problems with locally conducted governance through their own direct conduct of governance, but also with improving the situation with regard to the way governance is performed by local actors, so that the problems associated with this practice no longer prevail, and self-administration can therefore be actualized.

As with certain forms of colonialism, some instances of ITA have been understood only in terms of serving as the remedy themselves, without also addressing the underlying problem. UNHCR administration of 'refugee' camps in economically underdeveloped countries can be seen as a semi-permanent means of 'burden-sharing' between those host states and the relatively prosperous states that provide most of the funding for the agency.[51] This approach assumes the long-term incapacity of host states, transferring responsibility elsewhere rather than enhancing local capabilities. There is, thus, no exit anticipated.

In most ITA projects, however, a second approach is adopted in tandem with the first: changing the structural features of local governance to remove the supposed problem that led to the need for ITA in the first place. Here, the emphasis is on not administration for its own sake – what direct difference it makes in terms of governmental policy – but administration aimed at constructing or reconstructing institutions, broadly defined, including material infrastructure, public bodies, commercial enterprises, media and telecommunications, and civil-society organizations.[52] When there is supposedly a governmental vacuum, these initiatives are designed to enhance the possibility that governance can be conducted by local actors.[53] When there is a perceived absence of governance conforming to certain policy objectives, they seek to enhance the possibility that local actors will govern in a manner promoting these objectives.[54] So the people of the territories where the projects take place are being instructed by the staff of international organizations on how to be democratic, observe the rule of law, and so on.[55]

The general dual-track approach evident in other forms of trusteeship – being both palliative and remedial – is repeated, and so too, therefore, the same general basis on which the arrangements might come to an end. Within this, there are significant differences in the way arrangements are made to accommodate improvement and

---

[50] On UNTAC, see *ibid.*, *passim* (references contained in the Index, at 588–589). On the concept of 'proactive' ITA generally, see *ibid.*, Chapter 6, section 6.4.3.2, and sources cited therein.
[51] See the source cited *supra* n. 49.
[52] See Wilde, *supra* n. 1, Chapter 6, *passim* and in particular 6.4.3.4.
[53] See *ibid.*, Chapter 6, sections 6.4.1 and 6.4.3.4.
[54] See *ibid.*, Chapter 6, sections 6.4.2 and 6.4.3.4.
[55] See *ibid.*, Chapter 6 (n. 143).

transfer authority to local actors, and, more fundamentally, to prepare for and actualize independence where this does not already exist.

In the case of East Timor, there was a clear underlying commitment to eventual independence from the outset. Although this was not spelled out in UNTAET's original mandate under UN Security Council Resolution 1272, it was implicit in the preambular statement of that resolution, which took note of the outcome of the 'popular consultation':

> through which the East Timorese people expressed their clear wish to begin a process of transition under the authority of the United Nations towards independence, which it regards as an accurate reflection of the views of the East Timorese people.[56]

Subsequent resolutions made explicit references to the eventual outcome of independence, and tied the duration of the mission to this eventual outcome.[57] UNTAET's original mandate was fixed until the end of January 2001; at the expiry of that initial period, the mandate was renewed for a further year until the end of January 2002 and then again until 20 May 2002.[58] With this backdrop, the progressive transfer of authority to local actors over the course of UNTAET's mandate had as its end point completion by the fixed date of independence.[59]

In Kosovo, by contrast, not only was there no fixed date for independence determined at the start of the project; also, there was no guarantee of independence at all: instead, a commitment was made to the settlement of Kosovo's status, possibly, but not necessarily, involving independence. UNMIK's mandate did not have an explicit sunset-clause; its duration was, thus, open-ended. The end point of its general objective for governance was the occurrence of a particular event: a 'final settlement' on future status.[60] In the meantime, a progressive transfer of authority to local actors was to take place, but, at this stage, on the basis of implementing 'substantial autonomy', crucially short of the end point of independence that operated in the case of devolved authority in East Timor. Autonomy was actualized through the creation of the Provisional Institutions of Self-Government, authority being transferred progressively, ostensibly on the basis of capacity, to the level of substantial autonomy under overall UN control.[61] By itself, then, this process had no implication for the termination of UNMIK's mandate; it affected the degree to which UNMIK was involved directly in administration as opposed to exercising overall supervision of locally run institutions.

---

[56] SC Res. 1272 (1999), preamble. Whether or not the consultation result can be regarded as the expression of a 'clear wish' in favour of the interim period of UN administration is discussed further in Wilde, *supra* n. 1, text accompanying nn. 472 *et seq*.
[57] See the sources cited in Wilde, *ibid*, Chapter 8 (n. 293).
[58] See the sources cited in Wilde, *ibid*., Chapter 8 (n. 291).
[59] On the mandate to transfer authority, see, for example, the provisions in SC Res. 1338 (2001), at para. 3 concerning the progressive delegation of authority from UNTAET to the East Timorese.
[60] SC Res. 1244 (1999), at para. 11 (a); see also para. 11 (e).
[61] On these arrangements generally, see Wilde, *supra* n. 1, Chapter 1 (n. 1) and sources cited therein. This idea of transfer contingent on capacity is reflected in UNMIK's mandate; see SC Res. 1244 (1999), at para. 11 (d).

At the same time, over the course of the mission, UNMIK adopted a strategy for governance as conducted by the Provisional Institutions tied to the resolution of the status question: the 'standards before status' and later 'Standards for Kosovo' policy.[62] These standards included, first, the existence of effective, representative and functioning democratic institutions; secondly, respect for the rule of law; thirdly, freedom of movement; fourthly, the sustainable return of refugees and displaced persons, and respect for the rights of communities; fifthly, the creation of a sound basis for a market economy; and, sixthly, fair enforcement of property rights.[63] Although, then, the people of Kosovo had been deemed capable of self-administration to the point of substantial autonomy, they would have to meet further tests before Kosovo's eventual status could be resolved and independence potentially realized. This implicated UNMIK's existence in the sense that, if the status question were to be settled, then potentially UNMIK's mandate would come to an end. When the settlement was forthcoming, UNMIK was mandated to oversee the transfer of authority from provisional institutions of self-government to the institutions established under it.[64] In the event, when Kosovo declared independence without the agreement of Serbia in 2008, the question of whether this constituted a 'settlement' under the terms of Resolution 1244 was contested, placing the UN in a difficult position in terms of whether or not it could lawfully regard the situation as having terminated its administrative mandate in the territory.[65]

F. Comparisons Across All the Manifestations of Foreign Territorial Administration

Comparing these different arrangements concerning improvement of local capacities and/or termination of foreign territorial administration, one can see a progressive refinement of a common enterprise. In many instances of colonial trusteeship, external administration was introduced on a seemingly indefinite basis, vague notions of eventual improvement in the capacities for self-government of the local actors notwithstanding. Foreign administration was associated exclusively with the provision of governance. With no assumption that the people of the territories involved might become more capable of self-administration, there was no suggestion of future independence and thus a termination of the arrangement and a potential change in territorial status. As a matter of the provisions of the League Covenant, this model continued in the case of 'C' class Mandates, whereas with 'A' and 'B' class Mandates,

---

[62] On this policy, see UNMIK, *Standards for Kosovo*, presented on 10 December 2003, and endorsed by the Security Council in a Presidential Statement of 12 December 2003 (UN Doc. S/PRST/2003/26).
[63] *Ibid.*
[64] SC Res. 1244 (1999), at para. 11 (f).
[65] On the independence declaration, see Assembly of Kosovo, Kosovo Declaration of Independence, available at http://www.assembly-kosova.org/?krye=news&newsid=1635&lang=en and, for commentary, R. Wilde, 'Kosovo – Independence, Recognition and International Law', paper presented at Chatham House (the Royal Institute of International Affairs), London, 22 April 2008, contained in 'Kosovo: International Law and Recognition', Discussion Group Summary, Chatham House, 8–20, available at http://www.chathamhouse.org.uk/files/11547_il220408.pdf.

Trust territories in the Charter, and later forms of colonialism and occupation trusteeship were modified. In the case of 'A' and 'B' class Mandates under the Covenant, invoking the level of development as the basis for foreign administration and, with later ideas of colonialism, explaining the role for colonial administration in terms of local incapacities, the possibility of an end to administration, and so potentially a change in territorial status, was suggested.

A contingent developmental level and the idea of eventual independence were explicitly referenced by the Covenant in the case of 'A' class Mandated territories; the trusteeship model in the Charter supplemented this formula, introducing the missing element in terms of actualizing improvement (other than the vague objective of 'improvement' articulated in relation to all Mandated territories): the administering power was not only to provide governance until local capacities for self-government improved; it was also to attempt to foster such improvements itself. The later forms of colonial trusteeship lacked the clear commitment to independence as the eventual outcome (the phrase 'self-government or independence' is used in the UN Charter), but they did share the general notion of seeking to improve local conditions. The temporary conception of occupation trusteeship presupposes eventual independence from the control of the occupying authorities; whereas this is not necessarily tied to developmental improvement and initiatives are not always taken to promote improvement, when such initiatives are attempted – 'transformatory' occupations – the end of occupation may be tied to some sort of benchmark of improvement.

As far as a suggestion that self-administration may arise eventually and, where applicable, the territorial status may be altered in favour of the people of the territory (for example, through statehood) there are two models: (1) no such suggestion (certain forms of colonial trusteeship, 'C' class Mandates); and (2) the suggestion, either contingent on developmental improvements ('B' class Mandates by implication, 'A' class Mandates, all Trust territories and colonies under the UN Charter explicitly, 'transformatory' occupations) or not necessarily contingent in this way (non-'transformatory' occupations).

The Kosovo and East Timor models of ITA echo the model of trusteeship articulated in the League Covenant and the UN Charter for 'A' class Mandates and all Trust territories respectively: foreign administration due to the incapacity of local actors and the goal of eventual self-government. In being mandated to improve local conditions for governance and capacities for self-administration, the missions also manifest the additional element of effecting improvement vaguely articulated in the Covenant in relation to all Mandate territories and made a clear objective in relation to Trust territories. The Kosovo model echoes other forms of international trusteeship with the twin objectives of acting as a direct remedy for perceived incapacities for governance and building up local capacities for self-administration. Being committed from the outset to an end point of self-administration pending an eventual settlement on status, the Kosovo arrangement echoes the later forms of colonial trusteeship, notably the conception for Non-Self-Governing Territories in the UN Charter, and in failing to guarantee independence if local capacities are deemed to have improved sufficiently (although not ruling out its possibility). With Non-Self-Governing Territories, a guarantee of sorts arose through the self-determination entitlement (discussed further

562 *Research handbook on international conflict and security law*

below); in Kosovo, by contrast, whether independence was to be a possibility was conceived as contingent on the outcome of the political settlement.

5. THE REPUDIATION OF TRUSTEESHIP: SELF-DETERMINATION

It was suggested at the outset of this chapter that colonialism, the Mandate and Trusteeship systems, occupation and ITA are comparable because of the nature of the activity performed and the relationship between the administering actors and the administered territories. This commonality was deepened with the subsequent consideration of the trusteeship conception of foreign territorial administration evident in each activity, and the different but related bases for duration and termination provided by this general conception. In what follows, it will be suggested that a further basis for treating the activities collectively is provided by the self-determination entitlement that emerged after the Second World War.

As will be explained further in the following section, the call for self-determination in this period amounted to a repudiation of the system of foreign territorial administration that existed in the forms of colonialism, ITA, the Mandate and Trusteeship systems, and occupation.[66] Administration by an outside actor, necessarily preventing self-administration, was considered *ipso facto* objectionable, whether or not it operated on the basis of trust.[67] All the existing foreign territorial administration arrangements were treated together for the purposes of self-determination: they were all manifestations of 'alien subjugation, domination and exploitation'.[68]

6. DURATION AND TERMINATION UNDER THE SELF-DETERMINATION PARADIGM

> [i]nadequacy of political, economic, social or educational preparedness should never serve as a pretext for delaying independence.[69]

The effect of the self-determination entitlement was to render the continued duration of existing trusteeship arrangements contingent on the views of the people of the territories concerned (though not necessarily all these people), rather than, as before, on the policy objectives that had led to the introduction of foreign administration to begin with, and the determination of such objectives by the administering authorities. For example, with those arrangements introduced because of the perceived incapacity for

---

[66] On self-determination, see the discussion and sources cited in Wilde, *supra* n. 1, Chapter 5 section 5.2 and the academic commentary listed *ibid.*, List of Sources, section 5.4.

[67] On the different forms of anti-colonial argument, see the discussion in *ibid.*, section 8.7.1 and sources cited therein; and the works contained in *ibid.*, List of Sources, sections 5.3.1 and 5.3.3.

[68] The quote is taken from GA Res. 1514 (XV) (1960), at para. 1.

[69] *Ibid.*, para. 3.

self-administration, independence was no longer to be granted if and when the development of local capacity for governance had reached a certain stage; it was an automatic entitlement. So it made no difference whether the administration arrangement envisaged a contingent form of future independence (as with the treaty conceptions for 'A' class Mandated and Trust territories) or was indefinitely constituted (as in certain colonial arrangements); the arrangement was to end unless it was given the support of the people (as some arrangements were). Thus, even if there was not much local capacity for governance, self-administration would be actualized unless the people of the territory decided otherwise.[70] This idea is articulated in the passage from General Assembly Resolution 1514 cited above.

As Robert Jackson observes, 'independence was a matter of political choice and not empirical condition'.[71] In the words of William Bain:

> decolonization abolished the distinction upon which the idea of trusteeship depended. There were no more 'child-like' peoples that required guidance in becoming 'adult' peoples: everyone was entitled by right to the independence that came with adulthood. Thus it no longer made any sense to speak of a hierarchical world order in which a measure of development or a test of fitness determined membership in the society of states.[72]

Crucially for present purposes, these arguments amounted to a rejection of trusteeship *per se* – not merely trusteeship that was in some way flawed, for example because the states carrying it out breached their obligation to act on behalf of the local population, acting instead in their own interests.[73] As William Bain states:

> [t]he charge that European colonial rulers failed to fulfil their obligations as trustees of civilization provided a powerful argument in support of their claim of independence. But this argument did not discredit the idea of trusteeship itself; it merely undermined the justification of the means by which colonial powers attempted to carry out their obligations.
>
> The argument of self-determination achieved something quite different: self-determination rendered trusteeship an unsustainable practice by definition.[74]

In 1945, the international lawyer Philip Marshall Brown noted that:

> [t]he arguments now generally used in criticism of the colonial powers ... are not based so much on charges of unjust exploitation as on the abstract right of all peoples to attain self-government.[75]

Brian Simpson observes that:

---

[70] For Robert Jackson, decolonization thus shifted from being 'evolutionary', that is, depending on improvements in and capacity for self-administration (as mentioned above, text accompanying n. 189) to being 'accelerated' and 'precipitous'; Jackson, *supra* n. 19, at 95–102.
[71] *Ibid.*, at 95.
[72] Bain, *supra* n. 22, at 135.
[73] On the different critiques of trusteeship, see the discussion and sources cited in Wilde, *supra* n. 1, Chapter 8, section 8.7.1.
[74] Bain, *supra* n. 22, at 132–133.
[75] P.M. Brown, 'Editorial Comment: Imperialism', (1945) 39 *AJIL* 84, 85.

the main thrust of the anti-colonialist movement ... was simply to bring an end to foreign domination of government. It was about the legitimacy of the structures of government, about who should govern colonial peoples, not about how they should be governed.[76]

Equally, the oppressive forms of government within colonial administration, and the anti-colonial resistance to this oppression, 'did not affect the fact that the anti-colonial movement had as its principal aim simply the ending of foreign rule, not the imposition of restraints on the powers of government'.[77]

7. TRUSTEESHIP AND SELF-DETERMINATION RECONCILED?

A. Introduction

The absolutist version of self-determination as articulated during the post-Second World War era of decolonization cannot be reconciled with the model of introducing trusteeship over people, and making the duration and termination of such arrangements contingent on improvements in local capacities for governance. Freedom is absolute; no new trusteeships should be introduced and any existing arrangements should be dismantled. However, in other ways the trusteeship model has been understood to be compatible with self-determination, providing a normative basis for certain arrangements which amounts to a hybrid of the two visions.

In the first place, certain ITA projects created during the period of decolonization can be understood as means of performing certain administrative activities that were deemed necessary, paradoxically, to bring foreign territorial administration to an end. In the second place, many of the proposals since the end of the Cold War for reviving trusteeship have suggested that such arrangements can be legitimate if they are rooted in a clear commitment to eventual self-determination.

B. Trusteeship to Bring about the End of Trusteeship

Although the era of decolonization saw the repudiation of foreign territorial administration and so the de-legitimization of the idea of introducing new arrangements of this type, in some cases it was nonetheless deemed necessary, as an exceptional measure, to introduce ITA so as to implement the self-determination entitlement.[78] Before foreign territorial administration in general could be brought to an end (unless it was consented to) by the self-determination entitlement, then, its internationalized version was to be utilized for one final purpose.

---

[76] A.W.B. Simpson, *Human Rights and the End of Empire: Britain and the Genesis of the European Convention* (Oxford: Oxford University Press, 2001), at 300.
[77] *Ibid.*, at 301.
[78] Steven Ratner also identifies the connection between the objectives of the projects in Namibia, Cambodia and East Timor and the process of decolonization and self-determination; see S. Ratner, 'Foreign Occupation and International Territorial Administration: The Challenges of Convergence', (2005) 16 *EJIL* 695, at 696.

The *a priori* rejection of foreign territorial administration had the effect of transforming the policy objective of the existing trusteeship arrangements. Regardless of their original policy bases, their role now was to prosecute the decolonization agenda: to address the various aspects of this agenda that required certain administrative arrangements. As a result, the administering authority was obliged to promote a new territorial status for the territory. Since this status, if it were not to be independence, was to be validated by the people, the administering authority was also obliged to implement a particular governance policy: the conduct of a consultation. Overall, then, the decolonization agenda not only brought the colonial and Mandate and Trusteeship arrangements to an end; it also effected a temporary, uniform reorientation of the purposive framework of these institutions in order to achieve their demise.

At the time the push towards decolonization occurred, there were no inherited ITA projects that could be challenged, like colonialism and the Trusteeship arrangements, by the call for self-determination. The Saar (administered by the League from 1920) was assimilated into Germany in 1935, and the League administrative involvement in the Free City of Danzig ended with the German invasion of Poland in 1939.[79] The Free Territory of Trieste arrangement for an administrative role for the new United Nations was never implemented.[80] So ITA was not targeted, like colonialism and the Trusteeship system, as an existing phenomenon which, in the light of changing political circumstances, should be brought immediately to an end. That said, new ITA projects were conceived during this time in order to support the decolonization agenda.[81]

In all but one case, the new ITA projects introduced in this era – what might be called the 'decolonization projects' – involved performing the administrative activities incumbent on the existing administering authorities, in circumstances where those authorities were understood to be either unwilling or unable to do so, either at all, or in an acceptable fashion. The two projects in South West Africa/Namibia – the original United Nations Council for South West Africa/Namibia, which was never able to implement its mandate fully, and the later United Nations Transitional Assistance Group (hereinafter 'UNTAG') – epitomize the two different roles that ITA performed in this regard.[82] Originally, the perceived problem concerned South Africa's unwillingness to accept the policy of self-determination. Had the Council's mandate been implemented, it would have created an administrative structure willing to give up administrative control to whatever authority was agreed to under a self-determination consultation. South Africa's long-standing refusal to accept 'external' self-determination was unusual, and recourse to ITA in this context was unique. However,

---

[79] On the Saar and Danzig arrangements, see Wilde, *supra* n. 1, *passim* (references contained in the Index at 590 and 589).

[80] On the arrangements for the Free Territory of Trieste, see, for example, ibid., n. 47, sources cited therein and accompanying text.

[81] According to Robert Jackson, '[f]rom 1945 until the end of the cold war, legitimate and lawful international trusteeship was confined to [the] UN supervised transition of a small number of territories from quasi-colonial territories to independence'; Jackson, *supra* n. 17, at 305.

[82] On the UN Council for South West Africa/Namibia and UNTAG see Wilde, *supra* n. 1, *passim* (references contained in the Index at pp. 591 and 589 respectively).

when South Africa belatedly changed its position, the different problem its administration manifested, concerning the conduct of a consultation (in this case elections for government office), was common.

The UN began its involvement in the conduct of consultations before the creation of the UN Council for South West Africa/Namibia in 1967, ensuring that when they took place in Non-Self-Governing and Trust territories they were seen to be free and fair.[83] Although the organization's activity in this regard was pronounced in the main 'wave' of decolonization in the 1960s and 1970s, enduring disputes about certain territories meant that the activity was carried out as late as 1989–1990 (in Namibia) and 1999 (in East Timor). Given the unimplemented ITA mandate in Western Sahara at the time this chapter was completed, it may yet be used again in this regard.[84] In these missions, ITA was understood to be supporting the implementation of the self-determination agenda through the adoption of particular policies in the self-determination unit. Although this replicated the underlying activity that had been repudiated by the agenda of self-determination, it was not inconsistent with this agenda for that reason.

ITA responded to a paradoxical problem arising out of the decolonization process. Because of the historical denial of self-administration, peoples were entitled to decide how their internal administrative arrangements, and external status, were to operate in the future. However, the legacy of foreign administration also meant that they were not in a position to carry out the process through which their entitlement would be realized – they were not in control – and, moreover, the actors who had imposed external administration to begin with were in control. Thus, as an exceptional measure, a new phase of external administration was introduced, limited to the particular administrative activity necessary to bring an end to, or legitimize through some form of consent from the people, the externally imposed plenary arrangements that had operated hitherto, and/or to enable elections for the governments of the newly independent states.

In the case of self-determination consultations in particular, with the continuance of existing arrangements as one possible option for the realization of 'external' self-determination (the right of a people to determine their external status), the administering state had a clear interest in the outcome of the consultation (although not necessarily an outcome favouring maintenance of the status quo). Given that one of the bases for the self-determination agenda was that foreign administration had originally been imposed on the people concerned, having the administering authority carry out the process that would determine whether this arrangement continued was not considered appropriate in many cases.[85]

In general, the use of ITA to implement the obligations of the administering authority, enable the 'act of self-determination' and enable government elections is ultimately not inconsistent with the self-determination agenda of preventing a repeat of the trusteeship paradigm in the future. Involving, paradoxically, a form of trusteeship, ITA was necessary to bring the activity to a permanent end and set up an essential

---

[83] See *ibid.*, Chapter 2 (n. 31 and accompanying text).
[84] On the United Nations Mission for the Referendum in the Western Sahara (hereinafter 'MINURSO'), see *ibid.*, *passim* (references contained in Index, at p. 589).
[85] On the critique of colonial trusteeship concerning its 'imposed' character, see the discussion in Wilde, *supra* n. 1, at 386, and sources cited therein.

component of its replacement, a locally constituted government. Trusteeship to bring about trusteeship is necessarily limited to those situations where trusteeships already existed. Once the decolonization agenda had been fully prosecuted, there would be no more need for new arrangements to be created. However, a further paradigm developed after the Cold War, whereby the introduction of trusteeship with a clear commitment to eventual self-administration was again proposed and in some cases actualized. This time, the model was not limited to territories with pre-existing forms of foreign territorial administration but, rather, a more general prescription applicable to circumstances where governments had collapsed or were pursuing policies that were deemed objectionable, and sometimes in relation to existing states (where the introduction of trusteeship would therefore limit only internal, not also external self-determination) in addition to non-state entities.

C. Trusteeship Leading to Self-Determination, or Trusteeship Truly Realized

> [the guardian] … cannot stay on any longer in the territory than he is required, but must cause sovereignty to be recognized as existing in the government of the territory, as soon as the latter is suitably trained to take over control. The essence of a perfect trusteeship is the gradual training of backward peoples towards nationhood and sovereignty. It implies the faithful application of this principle by the guardian, and its strict respect by all other existing nations.[86]

The end of the Cold War saw proposals for reviving trusteeship as a legitimate feature of international public policy. Many of these proposals argued that decolonization had been actualized too quickly: the absolutist self-determination model of a precipitous exit was overhasty. For William Pfaff:

> [c]olonialism lasted long enough to destroy the preexisting social and political institutions, but not long enough to put anything solid and lasting in its place.[87]

David Helman and Steven Ratner, who advocated 'UN Conservatorship' for 'failed states', argued that the collapse of the state in Africa had its roots in decolonization, where 'self-determination, in fact, was given more attention than long-term survivability'.[88] Roland Paris, in his conceptualization of 'state building' generally, *inter alia* in terms of promoting the institution of the Westphalian state, suggests that this enterprise of modern state-building can be explained as addressing the missing component in an agenda of decolonization understood in terms of creating new states regardless of viability.[89] In seeking to prop up 'the institutional form of the Westphalian state in parts of the periphery where the state lacks firm roots', state-building is aimed at preventing

---

[86] Hales, *supra* n. 35, at 177.
[87] W. Pfaff, 'A New Colonialism? Europe Must Go Back Into Africa', (Jan./Feb. 1995) 74 *Foreign Affairs* 2, at 4.
[88] G.B. Helman and S.R. Ratner, 'Saving Failed States', (1992) 89 *Foreign Policy* 3, at 4. See also the discussion in Jackson, *supra* n. 17, at 304–305.
[89] R. Paris, 'International Peacebuilding and the Mission Civilisatrice', (2002) 28 *Review of International Studies* 637, at 655.

'a reversal in the historic expansion of the modern state from Europe to the rest of the world' as part of the 'ongoing reproduction of the Westphalian state model'.[90]

Some commentators seek to reconcile trusteeship with self-determination by holding that it can be legitimate if self-determination is the clear, exit end-game. Tom Parker defines international trusteeship in this manner, and on such a basis argues that UNMIK in Kosovo does not constitute a trusteeship because of the absence in UNMIK's mandate, as discussed earlier, of a clear commitment to independence as the eventual outcome.[91] UNTAET, by contrast, did constitute trusteeship because there was 'no limit to [the eventual goal of] self-administration and the clear goal' was to 'prepare for independence'.[92] On the basis that an obligation to end up with self-determination would operate if ITA projects were placed under the UN Trusteeship system, but not necessarily if they operated under the aegis of the Security Council, Parker argues that the Trusteeship system should be revived for future such projects.[93]

Henry Perritt, discussing both plenary ITA projects and the interventions in Afghanistan and Iraq, states that 'the intervening parties and sanctioning authorities justified the trusteeship explicitly in terms of governing for... the purpose of preparing the ... territory for eventual self-rule'.[94] Roland Paris distinguishes 'peacebuilding' missions generally from colonial rule on the grounds that the former are established 'with the goal of establishing conditions for war-shattered states to govern themselves'.[95] Under these approaches, trusteeship can be presented as compatible with the right to self-determination, because it is aimed at achieving self-determination as an end point. Richard Caplan states that '[t]he contradiction between executive international authority and local self-determination can only be overcome with the progressive transfer of responsibility to local authorities'.[96]

As the original theorists of colonial trusteeship sought to humanize existing and future arrangements through the idea of selfless administration and a general aspiration to improving local conditions, so commentators seek to humanize the ITA projects of the 21st century through a clear commitment to improvement leading to eventual independence. Although the foregoing analysis indicates that a commitment to independence was not evident in all instances of international trusteeship, even, it could be argued, the UN Trusteeship system prior to the advent of the post-Second World War self-determination entitlement, these arguments are illustrative of how some view the legitimacy of trusteeship and its relationship to the self-determination entitlement now.

---

[90] *Ibid.*, at 655.
[91] T. Parker, *The Ultimate Intervention: Revitalising the UN Trusteeship Council for the 21st Century* (Sandvika: Norwegian School of Management, 2003), at 36.
[92] *Ibid.*, at 36–37 (quotation from 37).
[93] Parker, *supra* n. 91, *passim* and especially 12, 50. Trust territories were, like colonies, entitled to external self-determination in international law. See the sources referred to above in n. 66.
[94] H.H. Perritt, 'Structures and Standards for Political Trusteeship', (2003) 8 *UCLA Journal of International Law & Foreign Affairs* 385, at 399.
[95] Paris, *supra* n. 89, at 652.
[96] R. Caplan, *International Governance of War-Torn Territories: Rule and Reconstruction* (Oxford: Oxford University Press, 2005), at 194.

Interventionists such as Michael Ignatieff and Gerhard Kreijen advocate new arrangements assuming an eventual reversion to independence, necessarily involving a revision of the non-intervention aspect of the self-determination entitlement, but only on a temporary basis.[97] Others, such as Parker, who wish to humanize existing and future projects without going into the question as to whether the projects themselves are legitimate, seek to affirm the position that existed in relation to colonial trusteeship on the emergence of the self-determination entitlement: preparation should be made for self-government meaning independence.[98] In both cases – creating new arrangements and reconstituting existing arrangements – trusteeship is legitimized and even reconciled with self-determination because of the clear commitment to eventual independence.

Whereas, as mapped out above, the notion of international trusteeship as temporary was articulated implicitly and explicitly in the different ways non-ITA international trusteeship arrangements were conceived, with the post-Cold War plenary ITA missions that notion is invoked explicitly in the name given to the missions (for example, 'The United Nations Interim Administration Mission in Kosovo'). For many commentators this reflects the idea that it is now beyond doubt, as was not the case with previous forms of international trusteeship, that the notion of progressive improvement leading to self-administration is both realizable and will be implemented in good faith by international administrators. The arrangements, then, are not portrayed as 'colonial' because the promise of eventual self-administration is seen as a genuine one; there will not be endless deferrals of independence as was the case with colonialism.[99]

This has purchase – temporary is seen as *really* meaning temporary – when it is coupled with the other legitimating ideas associated with international organization-conducted trusteeships.[100] Because the notion of governmental capacity seen as having created the need for ITA in some cases is supposedly based on a universal, universally realizable standard, not the racialized, culturally specific 'standard of civilization' posited as the basis for earlier forms of trusteeship, the underlying reason for conceiving the arrangements as temporary – that the people's capacities will improve – is now rooted in a standard represented as meaningful to and realizable by them.[101] Since the standard according to which improvement is judged is now seen as legitimate, so the prospects for meeting this standard, and the likelihood that the temporary projects will indeed be temporary, are enhanced. Equally, because the actor involved both in fostering improvement and judging whether development has occurred – the international organization – is conceived as selfless and humanitarian, critiques of colonial trusteeship based on the failure of the administering authorities to prepare

---

[97] M. Ignatieff, *Empire Lite: Nation-Building in Bosnia, Kosovo and Afghanistan* (London: Vintage, 2003); G. Kreijen, *State Failure, Sovereignty and Effectiveness: Legal Lessons from the Decolonization of Sub-Saharan Africa* (The Hague: Brill, 2004).
[98] Parker, *supra* n. 91.
[99] On such critiques of colonial trusteeship, see the discussion and sources cited in Wilde, *supra* n. 1, at Chapter 8, section 8.7.1.
[100] These other legitimating ideas are discussed in detail in Wilde, *ibid.*, at Chapter 8, section 8.7.2.
[101] On this idea of the legitimate basis for what ITA trusteeships are understood to be concerned with, see *ibid.*, at Chapter 8, section 8.7.2.2.

people adequately for self-administration and the corrupted nature of these authorities' judgments on whether local capacity for self-administration existed can be dismissed.[102] The 'international' in the form of both a universal normative framework that can serve as the legitimate basis for trusteeship and a responsible actor to act as trustee, has created the conditions for 'true' or, in the words of James Hales at the start of this section, 'perfect' temporary trusteeship to exist.

As previously mentioned, this vision is incompatible with the absolutist articulation of self-determination, with its affirmation of an automatic and immediate right to freedom from outside rule. It amounts to a return to the trusteeship basis for duration and termination – concerned with governance standards reaching a certain level – but, within the general trusteeship paradigm, a narrowing of the options within the original range mapped out earlier, in that external self-determination, for non-state entities, and the restoration of full internal self-determination (self-administration), for existing states, is the clear end point.

8. CONCLUSION

The fundamental axis of disagreement in current debates about the introduction, duration and termination of occupation, ITA or other forms of intervention is between those who insist that such arrangements can be legitimate provided they operate only until the local population are deemed ready to run their own affairs, and those who argue that foreign control is inherently unjust and a violation of the freedom of the population affected. In international law and public policy, the former argument, actualized through the concept of trusteeship administration functioning until a certain developmental level has been reached, was the orthodox position. By the time of the UN Charter, it existed as an international legal regime applicable to all forms of colonial administration. The post-Second World War call for self-determination led to a profound normative shift: the latter position of absolutist freedom from outside control became the orthodox position.

For many, the legitimacy of contemporary trusteeships over people hinges on a commitment to eventual self-determination as the end point for exits. However, this necessarily involves a step back from the absolutist vision of self-determination to the earlier trusteeship paradigm. The revival of trusteeship in fact since the end of the Cold War necessitates a consideration of whether or not the self-determination norm in international law has somehow become modified. Are those involved in contemporary trusteeships obliged to exit precipitously, or can they remain in control until they deem the local population capable of self-administration?

Within the UN system, ITA missions have been treated as *sui generis*, and created in an *ad hoc* fashion. There is no department of territorial administration within the UN; the Trusteeship Council was not revived to supervise the conduct of the missions and the Peacebuilding Commission does not perform an equivalent supervisory function;

---

[102] On these critiques of colonial trusteeship, see *ibid.*, at Chapter 8, section 8.7.1. On the idea that international organizations are legitimate actors as far as conducting trusteeships is concerned, see *ibid.*, at Chapter 8, section 8.7.2.3.

UN legal authority, when it has been forthcoming, has come from the Security Council not the General Assembly.[103] Given this, it is difficult to conclude that a general view has been taken by the majority of the world's states that trusteeship, even in its internationalized form, is back as a legitimate feature of international public policy. The absence of much objection to a few ITA projects created without any multilateral approval beyond the small membership of the UN Security Council falls far short of a clear, general affirmation that the self-determination norm in international law has been modified. Whereas it is possible, as illustrated earlier, to find general support for such a modification within the academy, such support derives mainly from commentators who come from states which would never be subject to trusteeship. Such commentators are, moreover, mostly advocating what the global normative regime should be, not describing how it is at present. The normative challenge for those who seek to implement the trusteeship vision of such advocates when conceiving exits in practice is to find a sound basis for the acceptance of this vision in globally accepted public policy.

---

[103] On the legal authority provided for the ITA projects, see for example the discussion in Wilde, *supra* n. 1, at Chapter 8, 346–347 and section 8.7.2.1. On the non-revival of the Trusteeship Council, see the discussion in *ibid.*, at 424–428. On the Peacebuilding Commission, see, for example, Hilary Charlesworth, 'Peacebuilding Commission', in Ralph Wilde (ed.), *United Nations Reform Through Practice: Report of the International Law Association Study Group on United Nations Reform* (December 2011), 28, and sources cited therein, available from http://ssrn.com/abstract=1971008 and http://www.ila-hq.org/en/committees/study_groups.cfm/cid/0.

17. Peacekeeping or war-fighting?
Nigel D. White

1. INTRODUCTION

The prevailing view in the negotiations that led to the UN Charter was that the UN needed a war-fighting capacity, so that aggression could be met, and peace maintained and restored, through collective counter-force.[1] The reality of the Cold War was that classic inter-state wars were less prevalent than internal, internationalised, increasingly asymmetrical wars, requiring the development of a range of military responses. The restrictions of the Cold War that in effect prevented the realisation of some form of UN army led to the development of peacekeeping which, though valuable, was rather limited, presenting a military image of the UN, but without real war-fighting competence or capability. There were exceptions in the form of a Coalition that fought under the UN flag in Korea in 1950–1953, and a belligerent version of the blue helmets that fought under UN command in the Congo (hereinafter 'ONUC') a decade later. The end of the Cold War saw an expansion in the range of responses by the UN and competent regional organisations from traditional peacekeeping through to war-fighting, but all relying on the contributions of member states. Although other organisations such as the African Union (hereinafter 'AU') and the Economic Community of West African States have undertaken peacekeeping tasks, the UN dominates practice in this area and UN peacekeeping doctrine and principles have contributed greatly to the development of peacekeeping law. That being said, the UN and competent regional organisations remain almost entirely dependent upon member states to deploy military forces. The UN relies on states to provide troops and other military resources for military actions taken under its name in Coalitions of the Willing (hereinafter 'CoWs'), or under its command and control in Peacekeeping Operations (hereinafter 'PKO'). States have maintained a virtual monopoly on the use of force in international relations though the growth of private military and security companies has led to calls for the outsourcing of peacekeeping to private contractors and not just states.[2]

Despite the exponential growth in the deployment of soldiers in the name of the UN, the problem of matching military responses to the gravity and nature of conflict or post-conflict situations remains; too often political, financial and other practical difficulties facing member states signify that the force sent is not adequate for the tasks required, epitomised by the inadequacies of the AU/UN response to the crisis in Darfur

---

[1] R.B. Russell and J.E. Muther, *A History of the United Nations Charter* (Washington, DC: Brookings Institute, 1958), 96, at 105.

[2] M. Patterson, 'A Corporate Alternative to United Nations *ad hoc* Military Deployments', (2008) 13 *JCSL* 215.

in the 21st century (2003–). Even worse are cases where member states are unwilling to send a force or an existing one is withdrawn, as in Rwanda in 1994 in the face of a ferocious genocide.

This chapter discusses the constitutional questions raised by the development and deployment of PKOs operating under a UN mandate, but also assesses the drift towards a more belligerent form of PKO, and asks whether this development undermines the legitimacy and indeed effectiveness of peacekeeping. Law is also important for our assessment of peacekeeping and its development. Oscar Schachter made clear, early in the development of UN peacekeeping, that law performs several important functions. First, law (in the form of the UN Charter and international law) provides authority for the intervention, additional to the consent of the host state. Secondly, law helps to constrain the behaviour of the parties by laying down prescribed standards. More broadly, international law provides a 'common frame of reference and the standards of mutual interest that are necessary for collective effort in today's divided world'.[3] Of course for CoWs acting under United Nations Security Council (hereinafter 'UNSC') authority to take military enforcement action under Chapter VII of the Charter, the legal framework is different from that governing peacekeeping in that intervention by CoWs is normally undertaken without consent and the legal framework governing hostilities is the law of war as opposed to the law of peace. However, Schachter's essential points about the importance of law remain.

In order to fulfil its functions to maintain or restore peace and security, the UN has both the competence to create consensual peacekeeping forces and to authorise military enforcement actions. For a number of reasons the UN needs to be clear as to the applicable legal frameworks and, moreover, the conditions of peace and security which necessitate peacekeeping and those which necessitate enforcement. All states, not only the host state and the troop-contributing nations (hereinafter 'TCNs'), need to know when a force is benign and impartial and when it is coercive and belligerent. The host state in particular will have anxieties that a peacekeeping force in its territory could become an enforcement action. Such sovereign concerns have to be balanced against the UN's growing concern that the behaviour within the host state has to conform to certain minimum standards of human rights compliance if any peace operation is to remain impartial and non-coercive. In essence the chapter explores the question of whether the UN has managed to reconcile these apparently conflicting aims.

2. THE FUNCTIONS OF PEACEKEEPING

Peacekeeping is a development of the Cold War. It was not envisaged in the UN Charter of 1945, but it is vital to securing a minimum level of peace and security in trouble spots around the world. In the case of UN PKO this ranged from the colonial and post-colonial conflicts in Indonesia, Kashmir and Palestine in the late 1940s, where unarmed observer forces were dispatched to provide the UNSC with a reliable account of the facts, to the fully fledged, several thousand-strong force United Nations

---

[3] See O. Schachter, 'The Uses of Law in International Peace-Keeping', (1964) 50 *Virginia LR* 1096.

Emergency Force (UNEF) deployed to secure the peace by acting as a buffer between formerly hostile nations, following the French/British/Israeli intervention in Suez in 1956.

Although new in its day this now 'traditional' type of peacekeeping reflects established principles of international law, in that it was based on the consent of the host state or states and, even though it appeared to constitute military intervention, its respect for sovereignty was reflected in the neutrality of such forces. Applicable norms were therefore those of established international law. The restrictions on the use of force to the defence of peacekeepers and their equipment meant that the trinity of peacekeeping principles of consent, impartiality and non-use of force very much reflected those fundamental principles of international law of sovereignty, non-intervention and non-use of force found in Article 2 of the UN Charter and located more specifically in Chapters IV and VI of the Charter, which contain the powers of the United Nations General Assembly (hereinafter 'UNGA') and the UNSC as regards the pacific settlement of disputes.

However, Article 2(7) and Chapter VII (Article 42) of the UN Charter both recognise that the UNSC has exceptional powers to undertake enforcement action, which has led to peacekeeping forces on occasions being given more coercive mandates. Thus while traditional consensual, inter-positional forces can be said to be constitutionally derived from Chapter VI of the Charter, those with Chapter VII elements are more properly based in Article 40, which empowers the UNSC to call or demand provisional measures such as cease-fires.

The dialectic between consensual peacekeeping and its more belligerent variant was established as early as the second full peacekeeping force in the Congo in 1960–1964, and was repeated, with less success, in the force in Somalia in 1993–1995; and is currently back on the agenda as the UN struggles to implement the 'human security' and 'responsibility to protect' agendas through 'protection' mandates given to UN forces. In general judges and jurists have still maintained that such mandates are compatible with the traditional principles of international law and peacekeeping,[4] and therefore do not constitute full-blown enforcement action on a par with the UN-authorised actions in Korea in 1950–1953 and the Gulf in 1991 (whose constitutional base in the Charter is Article 42 of Chapter VII), since they are not necessarily directed against the government of a state but also against rebel factions, armed groups, mercenaries or 'spoilers' (those non-state actors who seek to undermine the peace). Nevertheless, coercive mandates mean that peacekeepers are increasingly crossing the line to become war-fighters, or 'combatants' in the language of the law of war, causing confusion as to the legal status of peacekeepers who were traditionally not seen as legitimate targets (indeed attacks on them are prohibited under the UN Safety Convention of 1994).[5] Furthermore, the development of more aggressive peacekeeping

---

[4] *Certain Expenses of the United Nations*, Advisory Opinion, [1962] ICJ Rep. 151, at 163–164; A. Orakhelashvili, 'The Legal Basis of the United Nations Peace-Keeping Operations', (2003) 43 *Virginia Journal of International Law* 485. For a more realistic analysis see D.W. Bowett, *United Nations Forces: A Legal Study of United Nations Practice* (London: Stevens, 1964), at 274–312.

[5] Convention on the Safety of United Nations and Associated Personnel 1994.

forces calls into question the competence of regional organisations to mandate such forces given the limitations of Chapter VIII of the Charter, especially its injunction in Article 53 against regional enforcement action that has not been authorised by the UNSC. Though not without controversy, there is a trend in the literature towards accepting that regional organisations can undertake belligerent peacekeeping if force is used against non-state actors, but if force is used against the state (the government and its forces) then it is, in effect, enforcement action requiring UNSC approval.[6] Even post-Cold War peacekeeping forces which have remained mainly consensual have developed a long way away from the traditional buffer forces of the Cold War in the Middle East and Cyprus (hereinafter 'UNFICYP'), evolving in the early 1990s towards complex civilian–military operations designed to build the peace as well as keep it, and including within their structures military, police, humanitarian and other civilian elements. Sometimes these take on state-building functions, as in Kosovo and East Timor.[7] Arguably the developing nature and function of modern complex peace operations reflects changes in international and UN law, where the drive for external self-determination in the period of decolonisation and independence of new states has been replaced to a large extent by concerns for internal self-determination within existing states, and the protection and enhancement of human rights and security has supplemented the traditional concern for security between states. This has led to 21st century peace operations being furnished as a matter of course with Chapter VII elements in their mandates, enabling them to protect the peace process and civilians under threat of attack, while still being based on the consent of the host state. Thus the move towards greater coercion by UN peace operations has continued apace with the end of the Cold War, though they are still distinct from military enforcement action taken by CoWs under UN authority but not under its command and control.

Though peacekeeping realises UN goals of maintaining a basic level of peace in the world's flash points and prevents the collapse of states, the UNSC system has as a core goal the confrontation of threats to peace and security, and of aggression and other breaches of peace and security. To do this it needs to be able to take military enforcement action without the agreement of the target state or states. Thus there is no contradiction in the UNSC having both a 'police' function (in the form of peacekeeping) and a 'military' function (in the shape of military enforcement). However, instead of the envisaged centralised UN commanded and controlled military option found in the Charter, the UN and member states have shaped a decentralised model of non-consensual enforcement action. In this model a member state or groups of states take coercive military action under the authority of the UNSC to tackle a specified aggressor or threat to the peace. Being dependent upon contributions from member states such a system does not therefore guarantee that all the most serious threats to, or breaches of, the peace are met or confronted with military responses.

When the UN was trying to gather enough military forces to address a deteriorating situation in Somalia in late 1992, the decentralised enforcement model that had

---

[6] For discussion see E.P.J. Myjer and N.D. White, 'Peace Operations Conducted by Regional Organizations and Arrangements', in T.D. Gill and D. Fleck (eds), *The Handbook of the International Law of Military Operations* (Oxford: Oxford University Press, 2010), 163.

[7] UNSC Res. 1244 (1999) and 1272 (1999).

emerged from the Korean war of the 1950s and the Iraq war of 1991 was likened to the 'posse' depicted in so many Hollywood Westerns, in which the local Sherriff has to rely on a mixture of bounty-hunters and good citizens to assemble enough firepower to deal with outlaws.[8] UN Secretary-General Boutros-Ghali invoked the posse model in 1992 in the face of famine and state collapse in war-torn Somalia, where the lack of vested interests did not prevent the US, to its great credit, stepping forward to offer troops in order to ensure the delivery of humanitarian aid.[9]

The failure by 1994–1995 of what became a mixture of belligerent UN peacekeeping in Somalia (UNOSOM II),[10] operating alongside a US force whose aim was the defeat of Somali warlords, marked the end of the 'new world order' optimistically invoked by President George Bush in 1991 with the defeat of Iraq. In truth this ended in mid 1994 when a UN peacekeeping force in Rwanda (UNAMIR) proved unsuitable and incapable of preventing a genocide of over 800,000 people (mainly Tutsis) in that country,[11] followed by the failure of the UN Protection Force in Bosnia (UNPROFOR) contingents to protect the UNSC-designated Muslim safe areas in Bosnia from vicious genocidal attacks by the Bosnian Serb army, culminating in the massacre of approximately 8,000 unarmed men and boys in Srebrenica in July 1995.[12] In the face of such unimaginable violence traditional peacekeeping forces are clearly inadequate, but the experience of Somalia shows that overwhelming force may have to be authorised by the UN to stop it, necessitating fully equipped armies of 100,000 and more to be assembled, not lightly armed peacekeeping forces of, at best, 20,000.

Though UN peacekeeping forces still outnumber the UN-authorised CoWs, since 1990 there has been an increasing number of such military operations. Furthermore, it must not be forgotten that CoWs require much greater resources (in terms of troops, equipment and support) than peacekeeping operations, with forces in Korea and Kuwait being in excess of 100,000, while the smaller observer forces number less than 100 (though typically peacekeeping force numbers are in the region of 5000–10,000 troops).

3. CONSENT AND IMPARTIALITY

A. Consent

Peacekeeping forces are deployed and emplaced on the basis of having the consent of the host state; reflected in the negotiation and putting in place of a Status of Forces Agreement (hereinafter 'SOFA') between the UN and the host state, governing such

---

[8] S. Peterson, *Me against my Brother: At War in Somalia, Sudan and Rwanda* (Abingdon: Routledge, 2002), at 95; M.W. Doyle and N. Sambanis, *Making War and Building Peace: United Nations Peace Operations* (Princeton, NJ: Princeton University Press, 2006), at 144.
[9] UNSC Res. 794 (1992).
[10] UNSC Res. 814 (1993).
[11] Report of the Independent Inquiry into the Actions of the United Nations During the 1994 Genocide in Rwanda, UN Doc. S/1999/1257.
[12] Report of the Secretary-General pursuant to General Assembly Resolution 53/35: The Fall of Srebrenica, UN Doc. A/54/549 (1999).

matters as the legal status of military and police contingents, communications, freedom of movement, use of flags, uniforms and weaponry, disciplinary jurisdiction over peacekeepers (which is with the TCN), privileges and immunities of the force, and any claims procedures allowing access to justice for the local population. SOFAs are based on the 1990 model UN SOFA,[13] a revision of which is long overdue in order to reflect changes in function and to engender greater accountability.[14]

In the case of an inter-state PKO, then, for the force to operate on both sides of the border it must have the agreement of both states (for example, Israel did not consent to UNEF's presence in 1956), and if either state withdraws its consent the force must be withdrawn, repositioned or re-mandated (Egypt's withdrawal of consent to UNEF's presence in 1967 led to its withdrawal by order of the UN Secretary-General (hereinafter 'UNSG').[15] As Tsagourias writes: 'states cannot be compelled to accept the [continued] deployment of a PKO. If this is the case, then it is an enforcement action.'[16] The first full PKO, UNEF I (1956–1967) established the principles underpinning peacekeeping. UNEF I was created in 1956 in spite of a UNSC deadlocked by French and British vetoes cast to protect their involvement in the joint plan with Israel to secure the Suez Canal from Egypt. In the space of a few days in November the UNGA called for a cease-fire and then for the UNSG to establish an emergency force to secure the cease-fire when it had been agreed, and then to supervise a withdrawal of Israeli, French and British forces from Egyptian territory.[17] Thus in relation to PKO, the UNGA has exceptional competence to mandate such forces when the UNSC is deadlocked by the veto; enabling the UN to respond even when permanent members are involved. In 1950, in the Uniting for Peace Resolution,[18] the UNGA claimed exceptional powers to recommend enforcement action by military forces when the UNSC was deadlocked. The process envisaged in the Uniting for Peace Resolution of transferring competence from the UNSC to the UNGA was used in 1956 to enable the UNGA to mandate a consensual peacekeeping operation, though the International Court recognised that the UNGA had existing competence to authorise peacekeeping under Articles 10 and 14 of the UN Charter.[19]

The UNSG Dag Hammarskjold was instrumental in establishing the basis of UN PKO and so his description of UNEF is part of UN peacekeeping doctrine. First, he made clear the neutrality of the force, there being 'no intent in the establishment of the Force to influence the military balance in the present conflict and, thereby, the political balance affecting efforts to settle the conflict'. Secondly, he made clear the consensual basis of the force:

---

[13] UN Doc. A/45/594 (1990).
[14] For efforts to promote a 'human rights' revision of the UN's standard SOFA see a project based at Essex University, available at www.essex.ac.uk/.../model_sofa_peliminay_report_august_2010.pdfwww.essex.ac.uk/.../model_sofa_peliminay_report_august_2010.pdf.
[15] Report of the UNSG on withdrawal of UNEF, UN Doc. A/6730 (1967).
[16] N. Tsagourias, 'Consent, Neutrality/Impartiality and the Use of Force in Peacekeeping: Their Constitutional Dimension', (2006) 11 *JCSL* 465, at 469.
[17] UNGA Res. 997-1001 (1956).
[18] UNGA Res. 377 (1950).
[19] *Certain Expenses* Advisory Opinion, *supra* n. 4.

while the General Assembly is enabled to *establish* the Force with the consent of those parties which contributed units to the Force, it could not request the Force to be *stationed* or *operate* on the territory of a given country without the consent of the Government of that country.

Thirdly, he distinguished UNEF from the UN-authorised enforcement action in Korea, by pointing out the 'obvious difference between establishing the Force in order to secure the cessation of hostilities, with a withdrawal of forces, and establishing such a Force with a view to enforcing a withdrawal of forces'. UNEF was to secure the cease-fire and withdrawal on the basis that the parties had agreed to do so, and agreed to its implementation under supervision of UNEF. Thus UNEF was not an enforcement action, nor an occupying force.[20] It effectively served the function of an inter-state buffer force between Egypt and Israel until it was withdrawn in 1967 following Egypt's withdrawal of its consent.

B. Doctrine: From Neutrality to Impartiality

For a peacekeeping force to be placed within a state following an intra-state conflict, it only formally requires the consent of the government of the host state, but for it to be able to act effectively it needs the cooperation of all parties. As peacekeeping has become more complex it remains difficult for the force to be completely neutral, and the doctrine has been modified so that it must be impartial in the implementation of its mandate, enabling it to take coercive action against spoilers and others trying to undermine the peace process and the force's wider peace-building mandate. This is reflected in the latest version of UN peacekeeping doctrine (the so-called 'Capstone Doctrine' produced by UNPKO in 2008).[21] In that document the UN distinguishes impartiality from neutrality by declaring that UN peacekeepers should be 'impartial in their dealings with the parties to the conflict, but not neutral in the execution of their mandate'. Further, Capstone declares that the 'need for even-handedness towards the parties should not become an excuse for inaction in the face of behaviour that clearly works against the peace process ... or the international norms and principles that a United Nations peacekeeping operation upholds'.[22] Thus UN PKOs are bound to uphold fundamental human rights and humanitarian norms.

Dominick Donald provides an excellent critique of the difficult change in peace-keeping doctrine from neutrality to impartiality over the decades since 1956.[23] In the UNEF-type interpositionary model of peacekeeping, envisaged by UNSG Hammarsk-jold, impartiality and neutrality were essentially the same, but once the ONUC type of force was created in the 1960s within a deteriorating intra-state conflict, strict neutrality could not be maintained in the face of violence by certain parties. In these circumstances, if the peacekeeping force is to fulfil its mandate, it must be active but impartial

---

[20] UNSG Second and Final Report on UNEF, UN Doc. A/3302 (1956).
[21] United Nations Peacekeeping Operations: Principles and Guidelines (Capstone Doctrine) available at http://pbpu.unlb.org/pbps/Library/Capstone_Doctrine_ENG.pdf.
[22] *Ibid.*, at 33.
[23] D. Donald, 'Neutrality, Impartiality and UN Peacekeeping at the Beginning of the 21st Century', (2002) 9 *International Peacekeeping* 21.

in that its judgment on decisions to act is based on an unbiased application of its mandate within the wider frameworks of applicable international and UN law, whether that be to keep the country from breaking up, as in the case of ONUC in the 1960s, or to protect civilians, as with UNAMID in Darfur in the 21st century.[24]

While modern peacekeeping doctrine, encapsulated in the Brahimi Report of 2000[25] and in the Capstone Doctrine of 2008, seems to have accepted this move from neutrality to impartiality, the change does not appear to have been fully matched by actions on the ground or in the understandings of their obligations by TCNs or even the UNSG and UN officers.[26] While the intention is that peacekeepers should not again stand by in the face of genocide (as they did in Rwanda and Srebrenica in 1994–1995), the practical problems of establishing a credible gap between neutrality and impartiality have led to instances of peacekeepers remaining passive in the face of violence against civilians. Problems with consent and impartiality were present early in the evolution of peacekeeping, which is not surprising when one considers that the second full peacekeeping force in the Congo (ONUC 1960–1964) was placed in a hostile environment with the agreement of a government that only controlled a (diminishing) part of the country, and was struggling to cope with independence following the rapid departure of Belgium and the failure of that country to develop any indigenous governmental infrastructure. As the crisis deepened in the Congo, and the presence of mercenaries and secessionists in the province of Katanga threatened the territorial integrity of the country, both the UNSC and (when it became deadlocked) the UNGA adopted increasingly coercive measures in order to preserve the territorial integrity and political independence of the state. The UNSG strove to keep ONUC within the bounds of peacekeeping,[27] reflected in its original consensual mandate,[28] so that in the face of Belgian refusal to withdraw from Katanga the UNSC declared that ONUC would enter Katanga but would 'not be a party to or in any way influence the outcome of any internal conflict'.[29] The issue was then passed to the UNGA under the Uniting for Peace Procedure, and that organ adopted a resolution which was premised on support for the government and requested the UNSG to take 'vigorous action' to restore law and order and to preserve the unity of the Congo.[30] When the matter returned to the UNSC it hardened this mandate further by clarifying ONUC's functions to include maintaining the integrity of the Congo, assisting the central government to restore order, preventing the occurrence of a civil war, and securing the withdrawal of foreign forces and mercenaries.[31] Clearly ONUC was fighting on the side of the government, so not falling fully on the Chapter VII enforcement side of the line where coercive action is taken against a government, but it was clearly not a classical peacekeeping

---

[24] See further Tsagourias, *supra* n. 16, at 478–481.
[25] Report of the Panel on United Nations Peace Operations (Brahimi Report), UN Doc. A/55/305, S/2000/809, at paras 48–50.
[26] Donald, *supra* n. 23, at 23–25, 31–33.
[27] G. Abi-Saab, *The UN Operation in the Congo* (Oxford: Oxford University Press, 1978), at 13.
[28] UNSC Res. 143 (1960).
[29] UNSC Res. 146 (1960).
[30] UNGA Res. 1474 (1960).
[31] UNSC Res. 169 (1961).

force either. Such interventions are more akin to intervention at the request of the government, when outside states send forces to prop up a beleaguered government, such as those undertaken by the UK in Jordan in 1958 and the US in Lebanon the same year. Significant military support for the government has been provided by the AU peacekeeping mission in Somalia – AMISOM, a UNSC-authorised regional peacekeeping force,[32] which has fought alongside the Somali National Army against factions opposing the transitional federal government, including al-Shabab. Clearly, in these operations, the rules of international humanitarian law are more likely to be applicable, permitting significantly greater levels of force and use of weaponry than in normal peacekeeping operations. It is worth noting that AMISOM personnel received pre-deployment training in international humanitarian law in May 2012.[33] Though official AU/UN reports on the fighting lack detail, it is clear that UNISOM forces were involved in heavy street-to-street fighting against al-Shabab in Mogadishu in 2011–2012 and, after forcing the insurgents' withdrawal, were engaging them in open fighting where the greater firepower of AMISOM troops brought further military successes.[34]

C. The Certain Expenses Advisory Opinion

The International Court of Justice's opinion of 1962 in *Certain Expenses* concerning peacekeeping was arguably a little disingenuous in failing to distinguish the two forms of peacekeeping, but it clearly places peacekeeping within the Charter. In this opinion, the Court found that both the UNSC and the UNGA could mandate consensual peacekeeping forces, and that therefore the expenses of the operations in the Middle East (UNEF I) and the Congo (ONUC) were lawfully incurred by the UN. France and the Soviet Union had refused to pay for these forces, arguing that their creation/mandating by the UNGA was *ultra vires*, but the Court found that since UN PKOs fulfilled the purposes of the UN and did not violate any express limitation found in the Charter, it was not *ultra vires*.[35]

The main objection from the non-paying states was that only the UNSC was empowered to mandate military forces, thereby rendering the creation of both UNEF and ONUC unconstitutional in that they had received mandates from the UNGA. The Court responded by declaring that the UNSC only had primary, not exclusive, responsibility for peace and security under the UN Charter,[36] and that while only the Security Council could 'order coercive action',[37] there was nothing in the Charter to prevent the Assembly recommending the deployment of consensual peacekeeping operations.[38] Clearly the Assembly had come perilously close to recommending

---

[32] UNSC Res. 1744 (2007).
[33] AMISOM Press Release, 13 May 2012, available at http://amisom-au.org/2012/05/amisom-peacekeepers-successfully-complete-an-advanced-course-on-international-humanitarian-law-and-the-rules-of-conduct.
[34] A. Harding, 'On Somalia's Front Line', BBC News, available at http://www.bbc.co.uk/news/world-africa-17115579, 22 February 2012.
[35] *Certain Expenses* Advisory Opinion, *supra* n. 4.
[36] Article 24(1), UN Charter (1945).
[37] Article 11(2), UN Charter (1945).
[38] *Certain Expenses* advisory opinion, *supra* n. 4, at 163–164.

coercive action, but the Court was content to judge ONUC by its consensual nature and not by its use of coercive measures. While legally speaking, ONUC did seem to stop short of full-blown enforcement action under Article 42 of the Charter, it did amount, at times, to enforcement of pretty widely drawn provisional measures under Article 40 of the Charter.[39]

D. Pressure of a Hostile Environment on the Notion of Consent

We will turn to the more recent peacekeeping force in the Congo (MONUC – first emplaced in 1999 and replaced in 2010) in discussions below, though there is a certain element of *déjà vu*, given that in implementing its increasingly widely drawn mandate to protect civilians from attacks by non-state actors MONUC, like its predecessor (ONUC), ended up fighting on the government's side. As Christine Gray points out in the context of the UN's force in Bosnia (UNPROFOR) in the period 1992–1995, peacekeeping in a hostile environment places considerable pressure on the consensual nature of peacekeeping.[40] While it is desirable to obtain the agreement of all the parties to the presence of a peacekeeping force to oversee a cease-fire and other provisional measures agreed to by the parties, the legal requirement is that only the government of the host state needs to agree to the establishment of such a force on its territory.[41] This, of course, increases the chances of the force encountering resistance by factions that refuse to cooperate with it, but it at least helps to ensure that it does not take coercive action against the state (though this in turn might lead to the possibility of the peacekeepers siding with the government against the rebels, as it has done in the Democratic Republic of the Congo in the past and in recent years). While the Bosnian government agreed to the presence of UNPROFOR in Bosnia in 1992,[42] the Bosnian Serbs did not, leading first of all to problems of delivering humanitarian aid and then to protecting the safe areas created by the UNSC (which were Muslim-populated enclaves within Bosnian Serb-held territory – such as Srebrenica).

Gray's analysis makes it clear that negotiations with the host state not only cover the presence of the force but also the terms of the mandate and the composition of the force.[43] After agreement is reached on these issues, consent to the detailed rights and duties of the UN and the host state follow and a SOFA is adopted, though this may not occur until after the force has been dispatched (a SOFA was not agreed until May 1993 in the case of Bosnia).[44] In subsequent situations where no SOFA is agreed, the UNSC has increasingly deemed the model UN SOFA to be in force until a specific one is

---

[39] R. Higgins, *United Nations Peacekeeping: Documents and Commentary, Vol. 3: Africa* (Oxford: Oxford University Press, 1980), at 54; Bowett, *supra* n. 4, at 176; G. Abi-Saab, *supra* n. 27, at 105.

[40] C. Gray, 'Host-State Consent and United Nations Peacekeeping in Yugoslavia', (1996) 7 *Duke JILP* 241, at 241.

[41] *Ibid.*, at 244.

[42] UNSC Res. 758 (1992).

[43] Gray, *supra* n. 40, at 249.

[44] *Ibid.*, at 252.

agreed.⁴⁵ This practice shows that the UNSC treads the line between what is consensual and what is coercive even in the negotiation of the SOFA, by relying on its mandatory decision-making powers where necessary to ensure that the model SOFA is applicable. In the development of the mandate of a peacekeeping force the UNSC also often crosses the line from a purely consensual (Chapter VI) operation to one with Chapter VII elements. While the first 16 UNSC resolutions on UNPROFOR made no reference to Chapter VII at all,⁴⁶ in the face of Bosnian Serb intransigence and increasing violence against civilians in 1992–1993 the UNSC stepped into Chapter VII in its instructions to UNPROFOR, for instance in the delivery of humanitarian aid,⁴⁷ and then eventually in the protection of the safe areas.⁴⁸ The invocation by the UNSC of Chapter VII in the preamble of its resolutions starting in 1993⁴⁹ meant that all factions in Bosnia were bound to comply with the terms of those resolutions, even though the force was still based on consent. However, despite this Gray argues convincingly that consent is still the basis for the continuing presence of a peacekeeping force on the territory since force was not directed against the government, and therefore the force did not amount to a non-consensual enforcement action. This means that the host state still has the right to withdraw its agreement from the PKO, as shown by Croatia's withdrawal of consent to UNPROFOR in 1995 leading to the renegotiation of a new force on Croatian territory (UNCRO).⁵⁰

Thus in both the negotiation of the SOFA and in the application of the mandate the UNSC is prepared to use some form of coercion (even if it is just the adoption of a binding decision), but the presence of that original consent given by the host state is still the legal factor that distinguishes peacekeeping from military enforcement, so that a peacekeeping force has to be withdrawn if that consent is retracted. However, the wavering on the line between peacekeeping and a more coercive variant can only create confusion, or even deliberate misunderstanding on the part of the parties within a state and the TCNs, who may choose to stick to a purely consensual interpretation of the mandate, eschewing any coercive action as being against their own interests. This has been exacerbated by statements coming from the UN itself, statements which hark back to the neutral starting point of peacekeeping, such as that made by the UNSG, Boutros Boutros Ghali in July 1994 – that UNPROFOR was 'deployed to work with the parties in a transparent and impartial mode; it is not a combat force and it is not equipped or deployed to take offensive action against any of the parties'.⁵¹ This was despite the fact that, by this time, the UNSC had already mandated UNPROFOR under Chapter VII to take 'necessary measures, including the use of force, in reply to bombardments against

---

⁴⁵ See for example UNSC Res. 1159 (1998), at para. 19 (MINURCA); UNSC Res. 1320 (2000), at para. 6 (UNMEE); UNSC Res. 1528 (2004), at para. 9 (ONUCI); UNSC Res. 1590 (2005), at para. 16 (UNMIS).
⁴⁶ Gray, *supra* n. 40, at 258.
⁴⁷ UNSC Res. 776 (1992).
⁴⁸ First to NATO in UNSC Res. 816 (1993) and then to UNPROFOR in UNSC Res. 836 (1993).
⁴⁹ UNSC Res. 807 (1993).
⁵⁰ Gray, *supra* n. 40, at 265.
⁵¹ Cited in M. Rose, *Fighting for Peace: Lessons from Bosnia* (London: Sphere, 1998), at 14.

the safe areas by any of the parties or to armed incursion into them or in the event of any deliberate obstruction in and around those areas to the freedom of movement of UNPROFOR or of protected humanitarian convoys'.[52] The same resolution requested that the UNSG reinforce UNPROFOR accordingly in consultation with the TCNs. The failure to implement this mandate properly led to the over-running of the safe areas by the Bosnian Serbs and the massacre at Srebrenica; events which finally led to a more coercive UNSC-mandated Rapid Reaction Force and UNSC-authorised NATO bombardments of Bosnian Serb positions.[53] This, combined with a successful Croatian offensive, led to the leaders of Bosnia, Serbia and Croatia agreeing to the Dayton Peace Accords of 1995, which endorsed a federally structured Bosnian state.

4. PEACEKEEPING AND PEACE ENFORCEMENT

The line between consensual and coercive UN military operations has become blurred but the distinction can still be made that consensual PKOs, though mandated increasingly to use coercion, employ it to further specific aims – to deliver humanitarian aid, or to protect safe areas, and so generally against non-state actors, and are present with the consent of the host government; while coercive military enforcement action entails action against states or governments, classically exemplified by the UN-sanctioned military campaigns against North Korea in 1950 and Iraq in 1991.

When turning to CoWs authorised to respond to threats to the peace, such as that arising from events in Libya during the 'Arab Spring' of 2011, we also see that the military action is largely directed at the government of Colonel Gaddafi, although the mandate was to use 'all necessary measures ... to protect civilians and civilian populated areas under threat of attack' in Libya,[54] and therefore action could have been taken against rebels if they were attacking civilians.

However, when we consider CoWs authorised to respond to threats to the peace in post-conflict countries such as Bosnia and Kosovo, then the line between peacekeeping and enforcement is narrowed. The UNSC authorised NATO-led forces in Bosnia (IFOR) in 1995 after the Dayton Peace Accords, and Kosovo (KFOR) in 1999 following Serb withdrawal in the face of NATO bombing. These forces appear to be peacekeepers, though they do not wear blue helmets, since most of the time they operate in peaceful conditions and their role is to oversee the implementation of the peace agreement (through, for example, facilitating the return of refugees). However, the idea is that the forces are sufficiently armed and powerful to deter any breaches of the accords, and to act coercively (against state or non-state actors) if any breaches occur. Thus IFOR was mandated to 'take all necessary measures to effect the implementation of and to ensure compliance with' the relevant parts of the Dayton Accords.[55] The resolution stressed that the provision applied to all parties, which, at Dayton, were the governments of Bosnia, Croatia and Serbia, though they were also

---

[52] UNSC Res. 836 (1993).
[53] UNSC Res. 998 (1995).
[54] UNSC Res. 1973 (2011).
[55] UNSC Res. 1031 (1995).

deemed to represent the factions in Bosnia. The point is that potential enforcement measures undertaken by IFOR would apply to state and non-state actors alike. In the case of Kosovo, KFOR was created to deter renewed hostilities in Kosovo and ensure (by coercion if necessary) the withdrawal of Serb forces and demilitarisation of the Kosovo Liberation Army and other armed Kosovo Albanian groups.[56]

Coming from the perspective of peacekeeping, the line between it and enforcement has been narrowed by the increasing inclusion of protection mandates in modern operations, whereby peacekeepers are mandated to protect civilians within their areas of deployment, reviewed more fully below. UNAMID was a joint UN/AU force in Darfur, deployed to a region of Sudan where crimes against humanity were being committed against the people of Darfur by a government-backed militia known as the Janjaweed.[57] Despite the complicity of the government in the abuse of civilians, the mandate of UNAMID attempted to keep on the peacekeeping side of the line by being a blue-helmeted force present with the consent of the government of Sudan. Its mandate included an authorisation to 'take the necessary action, in the areas of deployment of its forces and as it deems within its capabilities' in order to protect civilians 'without prejudice to the responsibility of the Government of Sudan'.[58] Despite the fact that there were direct parallels between the situation in Darfur and that in Libya, with both the leaders of those countries (Al-Bashir of Sudan and Gaddafi of Libya) being investigated by the International Criminal Court for ongoing crimes against humanity involving systematic attacks on their own citizens,[59] one situation was responded to by military enforcement action by a UN-authorised CoW, while the other merited the deployment of a peacekeeping force, albeit one including an enforcement element to protect civilians. Whether such mandates work will be examined below, though, in the Darfur situation, the conflict between UNAMID's consensual peacekeeping character and the necessity of it taking action against government-backed militia is an unlikely recipe for success.

Coming from the perspective of a Chapter VII enforcement action, some of the mandates that have been granted to CoWs in the past show that the line between peacekeeping and enforcement is not always clear. In a desperate attempt to do something about the genocide in Rwanda in 1994, the UNSC authorised a French force to intervene under Chapter VII of the Charter, but stressed its humanitarian purposes be conducted in an 'impartial and neutral fashion'.[60] Three years later, in authorising an Italian-led force to intervene in Albania in the face of the growing anarchy in that country following the collapse of a national pyramid-selling scheme, the UNSC also stated that the force should be both 'neutral and impartial'.[61] These limitations were included by the UNSC because, as Donald points out, 'both resolutions were drawn up in haste, in the face of considerable Security Council suspicion, to authorize actions

---

[56] UNSC Res. 1244 (1999).
[57] Report of the International Commission of Inquiry on Darfur to the UN Secretary General Pursuant to UNSC Resolution 1564 (2005).
[58] UNSC Res. 1769 (2007).
[59] USC Res. 1593 (2005) (Sudan); UNSC Res. 1970 (2011) (Libya).
[60] UNSC Res. 929 (1994).
[61] UNSC Res. 1101 (1997).

that the French and Italian governments had already indicated they would take regardless', despite the fact that 'neutrality is incompatible with true impartiality; it is doubly incompatible with Chapter VII of the UN Charter'.[62]

Despite this blurring of peacekeeping and peace enforcement, Tsagourias provides a useful analysis of the main differences between peacekeeping with Chapter VII elements and peace enforcement mandated entirely under Chapter VII. The latter 'designates a culpable [state] party that is treated as the enemy' against whom coercive action, that is neither neutral nor impartial, is taken. That action is aimed at forcing a political solution not at facilitating one. In peacekeeping with Chapter VII elements, however, 'coercion is not the primary aim of the mission but incidental thereto. Furthermore, no enemy is designated and no solution is imposed, instead all parties are treated evenhandedly against the mission's mandate and are encouraged to reach a mutually agreed settlement.'[63] He does concede, however, that sometimes the dividing line is fine, particularly from the perspective of those on the ground.

An ideal collective security system would aim to respond to threats and aggressions in a proportionate and calibrated way. UNSC practice does follow this principle in a loose way in that aggressions have been met by massive military enforcement responses (Korea and Iraq); lesser threats by CoWs performing peace support functions (Bosnia and Kosovo); and post-conflict duties by PKOs. However, there is no guarantee that the deployment of different types of forces matches the gravity of the threat or the nature of the aggression. The move towards greater coercion by peacekeeping forces has suggested that this might not be such a problem, but, in truth, peacekeeping is still a much more limited operation. This leads us on to a more detailed discussion of the levels of force permitted and used by peacekeepers.

5. THE USE OF FORCE BY PEACEKEEPERS

Though there has been an increase in outsourcing of military functions by some states, in general terms states maintain a monopoly on military force so that both defensive and offensive actions in the international arena are essentially taken by the militaries of states, though if military enforcement action is contemplated in the absence of an armed attack then UNSC authority is needed. When that authority is granted the armed forces of a state can use significant levels of force, but when the mandate is for a PKO the levels of force are much reduced, though there has been a lack of clarity on this since the inception of peacekeeping in 1956.

A. Personal Self-defence

The reasons for confusion are due to the fact that PKOs are seen as 'UN' forces rather than states' forces that are authorised by the UNSC. This raises the question as to whether the UN has the same rights and duties as a state to act in self-defence and, indeed, to take enforcement action. Doctrine has generally fallen short of this, initially

---

[62] Donald, *supra* n. 23, at 28–29.
[63] Tsagourias, *supra* n. 16, at 471–472.

at least limiting peacekeepers to a form of self-defence more akin to that of personal self-defence than the defence of a state or organisation. Arguably, however, PKOs should have wider rights to use force in pursuit of UN goals and to uphold international and UN norms, though because of its nature it will fall short of full enforcement. Historically, the acceptability of a PKO lies in the fact that it usually has limited objectives, normally helping to maintain a cease-fire and a separation of the belligerents, not by means of enforcement but by consent and cooperation. Hence peacekeeping is still stated by the General Assembly's Special Committee on Peacekeeping to be based on a trinity of virtues – consent, impartiality and restrictions on the use of force.[64] The restricted nature of the latter was established by the basic principles guiding UNEF I. In the UNSG's 'Summary Study' of UNEF in 1958, he stated that while there is some margin for judgement on the level of force to be used by peacekeepers, they should not become combat operations, and should be limited to the right of self-defence.[65] He warned that 'a wide interpretation of the right of self-defence might well blur the distinction between [peacekeeping] operations ... and combat operations, which would require a decision under Chapter VII of the Charter'. A 'reasonable definition' used by UNEF is,

> where the rule is applied that men engaged in the operation may never take the initiative in the use of armed force, but are entitled to respond with force to an attack with arms, including attempts to use force to make them withdraw from positions they occupy under orders from the Commander, acting under the authority of the Assembly and within the scope of its resolutions.

The essence is a prohibition on the use of offensive force in which the initiative would be taken by the PKO, thereby restricting it to defensive, reactive force.[66] Though Findlay points out this was a somewhat retroactive construction of the rules governing UNEF,[67] it has become UN doctrine, and was applied, at least initially, even to ONUC which was deployed to the Congo in 1960 in very different circumstances from UNEF. UNEF was imaginatively described by Finn Seyersted as 'acting like a plate-glass window', incapable of withstanding any significant assault upon it but nevertheless acting as a 'lightly armed barrier that all see and tend to respect'.[68]

At its core the limited use of force available to peacekeepers means self-defence, interpreted narrowly to cover a peacekeeper using force in defence of his own life, his 'comrades and any person entrusted in [his] care, as well as defending [his] post, convoy, vehicle or rifle'.[69] Beyond this there has been a continuing lack of clarity as to whether the force could also 'defend' its mandate. As UNSG Hammarskjold recognised

---

[64] Special Committee on Peacekeeping, 'Comprehensive Review of the Whole Question of Peacekeeping Operations in all their Aspects', Report UN Doc. A/56/767 (2003), at para. 46.
[65] UNSG Report, UN Doc. A/3943 (1958).
[66] UNSG Report, UN Doc. A/3943 (1958).
[67] T. Findlay, *The Use of Force in UN Peace* (Oxford: Oxford University Press, 2002), at 22–23.
[68] F. Seyersted, *United Nations Forces in the Law of Peace and War* (Leiden: Sijthoff, 1966), at 48.
[69] *General Guidelines for Peace-Keeping Operations*, UN Doc. UN/210/TC/CG95 (1995).

in 1956, the wider the right of self-defence is drawn the more blurred the distinction between peacekeeping and enforcement action under Chapter VII becomes.[70] UNSG Waldheim's 1973 guideline, which stated that 'self-defence would include resistance to attempts by forceful means to prevent the force from discharging its duties under the mandate of the Security Council',[71] seemed to raise the prospect of a widely drawn mandate giving rise to enforcement action, though in practice rules of engagement (hereinafter 'RoE') were drawn quite conservatively.[72] In general, peacekeeping was acceptable during the Cold War because it was kept distinct from enforcement action. Such a limited military operation not only suited the veto-wielding powers in the UNSC, but it also met with the approval of the Non-Aligned states. It is no coincidence that the major troop contributors to peacekeeping forces during the Cold War were smaller volunteer states drawn from outside the five permanent members of the UNSC and their immediate allies (with the exception of Britain in Cyprus).

B. Defence of Mandate

Early in the development of peacekeeping, an exception to the view that limited peacekeeping force to self-defence was to be found in the Congo operation (ONUC) of 1960–1964. In his first statement to the UNSC on the creation of ONUC UNSG Hammarskjold stated that it was to have the same basis as, and would operate in the manner of, UNEF.[73] But Draper points out that 'in relation to their respective constitutional bases, their essential nature and the tasks they were called upon to perform, the differences between these two United Nations Forces were so great that it could only be a matter of time before the precedents afforded by UNEF would prove inadequate, if not inapplicable' for ONUC.[74] 'This is particularly true in the matter of the quality and quantity of the armed force that would have to be used' by ONUC, due to the formidable amount of force opposing it.[75] Draper does not see this change from UNEF as being as constitutionally problematic since ONUC had the backing of the UNSC (he virtually ignores the contribution of the UNGA), which has Chapter VII enforcement powers at its disposal (though the UNSC did not expressly invoke Chapter VII), while UNEF was the creation of the UNGA and UNSG.[76]

One problem is that the RoE and directives issued to UN forces are stated by the UN to be strictly confidential and therefore difficult to ascertain.[77] Despite this, it is clear from its actions that ONUC did use mortars, fighter and bomber aircraft, light

---

[70] Report of the Secretary General on UNEF I, UN Doc. A/3943 (1956), at para. 179.
[71] UN Doc. S/11052/Rev.1 (1973).
[72] M. Goulding, 'The Evolution of United Nations Peacekeeping', (1993) 69 *Int Affairs* 451, at 455. See also R. Zacklin, 'The Use of Force in Peacekeeping Operations', in N. Blokker and N. Schrijver (eds), *The Security Council and the Use of Force* (The Hague: Martinus Nijhoff, 2005), at 100.
[73] UNSC 873rd meeting (1960), UN Doc. S/4387 (1960).
[74] G.I.A.D. Draper, 'The Legal Limitations Upon the Employment of Weapons by the United Nations Force in the Congo', (1963) 12 *ICLQ* 387, at 391.
[75] *Ibid.*
[76] *Ibid.*, at 392.
[77] *Ibid.*, at 395.

armoured vehicles, rifles, light automatic weapons and bayonets, as well as anti-tank and anti-aircraft weapons.[78] This flowed from the resolutions adopted by the UNSC and UNGA, as interpreted by the UNSG. However, at the outset of the operation, the UNSG clearly viewed ONUC's right to use force as being the same as UNEF's, that is, being based on self-defence.[79] Draper states that this was probably sufficient to justify the force used by ONUC when it was concerned with overseeing the withdrawal of Belgian troops, but was inadequate when its task became the elimination of the mercenaries supporting the Katangese secession, who, in November in 1961, were considered by the UNSC to be the main threat to international peace and security, a threat that could widen to suck in the superpowers.[80]

Certainly, in the early period of ONUC's presence, the doctrine was one of reactive self-defence. In his first report on ONUC of September 1960 the UNSG referred to the problems for a highly trained soldier of reconciling his training with the strictures of being part of a UN peace force: 'He is allowed the right to use force in the last resort of legitimate self-defence. The troops are also compelled by the demands of non-intervention not to resort to military initiative in situations which would normally call for a strong reaction from courageous and responsible troops.'[81] All ONUC troops received the following press release:

> You serve as members of an international force. It is a peace force not a fighting force ... Protection against acts of violence is to be given to all the people, white and black. You carry arms, but they are to be used *only* in self-defence. You are in the Congo to help *everyone*, to harm no one.[82]

It is possible, as Draper points out, to argue that the host state's agreement that ONUC should have freedom of movement throughout the Congo could have been combined with self-defence to justify ONUC protecting itself when asserting its freedom of movement in Katanga, but this 'telling example of the expanding nature of the right of self-defence' provokes speculation as to the point at which 'that right has yielded up all that it can properly provide and the moment when it becomes necessary to' mandate the force with Chapter VII authorisation to use all necessary means. Draper also suggests that the line between peacekeeping and war-fighting is not passed until the force ceases to react in a defensive way and starts to take the initiative; in other words, it starts to enforce the peace.

Anticipatory action, Draper suggests, is often undertaken in wartime by military commanders, but could not be justified in conditions short of that.[83] This contrasts with the UNSG's Bulletin of 1999, which states that the law of war applies when the UN is engaged in enforcement actions or in self-defence in the context of peacekeeping.[84] The

---

[78] *Ibid.*, at 396.
[79] UNSC 873rd meeting, *supra* n. 73.
[80] Draper, *supra* n. 74, at 398. See UNSC Res. 169 (1961).
[81] UN Doc. S/4531 (1960).
[82] UN Press Release CO/15 (1960).
[83] Draper, *supra* n. 74, at 400–402.
[84] UNSG's Bulletin, 'Observance by United Nations Forces of International Humanitarian Law', 1999, section 1.1.

higher threshold of force suggested by Draper, to mark the line between peacekeeping and peace enforcement, would have the benefit over the 1999 Bulletin in that peacekeepers would not be subject to the laws of war whenever they engage in defensive action – preventing the impracticality of peacekeepers stepping in and out of the laws of war.

In February 1961 the UNSC widened ONUC's mandate considerably to 'take immediately all appropriate measures to prevent the occurrence of civil war in the Congo, including arrangement for cease-fires, the halting of all military operations, the prevention of clashes and the use of force, if necessary in the last resort'.[85] Initially, in the period after this resolution was adopted, ONUC responded by using force as a last resort in a defensive way, responding to mercenary attacks against it, but then it had to cross the line into offensive action in order to achieve such a wide mandate so that it became 'heavily engaged in normal combat activities in which all force is used which is necessary to secure military objectives'. The severest fighting, which led to the elimination of the mercenary elements in Katanga, followed a later UNSC resolution adopted in November 1961, which authorised the UNSG to take vigorous action, including force, to tackle the mercenaries in Katanga.[86]

C. A Broader Concept of Self-defence

Interestingly, the UN's Office of Legal Affairs in 1993 explained the right of self-defence in the context of peacekeeping as something belonging to the UN, not just to individual peacekeepers. According to this view, the right of self-defence is not 'limited to States and applies as an inherent right also to the United Nations'.[87] There is potentially a vast difference between recognising that peacekeepers have the right to personal self-defence and equating the UN's right to self-defence with states under Article 51. The statement seems to go against UN practice, but given the UN's international personality such an argument can be supported, although this does not mean that it necessarily has the same rights and duties as those of a state when defending its territorial integrity and political independence, existential elements the UN manifestly does not have. Nonetheless, if the UN deploys forces around the world then such an international actor should have the right to defend its functionality as a security organisation as well as defend the components of the peace operation.

Tsagourias' explanation of why the UN sticks to the mantra of self-defence, even with PKOs moving towards having enforcement elements to protect the peace process and civilians, is that it makes them more acceptable to the host state and the parties within it.[88] The Brahimi Report of 2000 extended the language of self-defence from individual self-defence to defence of the mission.[89] As Tsagourias states, this follows the 'gradual expansion of the meaning of self-defence in PKOs, from individual self-defence inherent to military personnel, to freedom of movement and defence of

---

[85] UNSC Res. 161 (1961).
[86] Draper, *supra* n. 74, at 406. UNSC Res. 169 (1961).
[87] UN Juridical Yearbook, 1993, at 371–372.
[88] Tsagourias, *supra* n. 16, at 473.
[89] Brahimi Report, 2000, *supra* n. 25, at paras 48–51.

positions, to the defence of the mandate and the protection of third parties'.[90] However, the reality is that once self-defence is so-expanded it is no longer individual self-defence, but is a mandate that permits a certain amount of enforcement (of measures of the type envisaged by Article 40 of Chapter VII), though short of full peace-enforcement under Article 42 of Chapter VII. Ultimately, if peacekeepers' right to use force was based solely on self-defence there would be no need for the mandate of modern peace operations to contain Chapter VII elements.[91]

A common criticism is that peacekeeping, developed during the Cold War as a limited military option, has been used out of context and contrary to its limited functions, in more violent post-Cold War situations.[92] A former UN peacekeeping official in Bosnia has argued that there should be no creep ('upgrade') from Chapter VI to Chapter VII; if extensive coercion is required then the Chapter VI peacekeeping operation should be withdrawn and replaced with a Chapter VII CoW.[93] Thus it is important for the UN to clarify the nature and extent of force that can be used by peacekeepers; in other words how far self-defence can be lawfully extended. Given that it is not an easy task either legally, politically or indeed practically to move from peacekeeping to enforcement,[94] it is important for the UN to be clear on the levels of force appropriate to each, and to deploy the right type of force to meet the force, or threat of force, deployed against it. This section will show that it has done this to some extent, when looking at the RoE of modern peace operations, contrasting them with those given to soldiers fighting within a military enforcement operation.

D. Rules of Engagement

Each mission's RoE govern the use of force by military peacekeepers,[95] and Directives on the Use of Force (hereinafter 'DUF') govern the use of force by any police contingent to the mission. Both are developed by the Department of Peacekeeping Operations (hereinafter 'DPKO') in New York. Oswald, Durham and Bates state that 'the legal framework for ROE is a combination' of international humanitarian law and international human rights law, 'whereas the legal foundation for DUF is primarily' international human rights law, though TCNs may well also give directives to their contingents to ensure that their domestic laws are complied with. The UN's DPKO will

---

[90] Tsagourias, *supra* n. 16, at 473.
[91] *Ibid.*, at 473.
[92] K.E Cox, 'Beyond Self-Defense: United Nations Peacekeeping Operations & the Use of Force', (1998–99) 27 *Denver JILP* 239, at 240.
[93] Y. Akashi, 'The Use of Force in a United Nations Peace-Keeping Operation: Lessons Learnt from the Safe Areas Mandate', (1995) 19 *Fordham ILJ* 312, at 321.
[94] O. Schachter, 'Authorized Uses of Force by the United Nations and Regional Organizations', in L.F. Damrosch and D.J. Scheffer (eds), *Law and Force in the New International Order* (Boulder, CO: Westview, 1991), at 65 and 84.
[95] H. McCoubrey and N.D. White, *The Blue Helmets: The Legal Regulation of United Nations Military Operations* (Aldershot: Dartmouth, 1996), at 146; P. Rowe, 'The United Nations Rules of Engagement and the British Soldier in Bosnia', (1994) *ICLQ* 946, at 947.

then draft a mission-specific 'Soldier's Pocket Card', though there does not appear to be a similar card for UN police.[96]

An examination of an example of the Soldier's Pocket Card of 2005 developed by the UN for a modern peace operation – UNMIS in Sudan – shows that in reality peacekeepers are still operating from the basis of self-defence, but within that notion is included the protection of civilians within their areas of deployment and subject to the threat of imminent violence. It has been argued that defence of third parties can be brought within the concept of self-defence. For example, under French domestic law the concept of legitimate defence includes defence of others, actions that are not dependent upon the consent of those being aided.[97]

The UNMIS Pocket Card states that minimum and proportionate force should be used. Force must be limited in intensity and duration to achieve the authorised objective and must be commensurate with the level of the threat. Deadly force is justified in some cases but the overriding principle is that force should be used 'only when absolutely necessary to achieve [the] immediate aim, to protect yourself, your soldiers, UN or other designated personnel, installations, equipment and civilians under imminent threat of physical violence'. Safeguards provide that the 'decision to open fire shall only be made by order of the on-the-scene commander', 'unless there is insufficient time to obtain an order'; and further, 'before opening fire, give a final warning at least three times', either in Arabic or English. Fire 'must be aimed and controlled – automatic fire will be opened only as a last resort'; 'if possible, a single shot should be aimed at non-vital parts of the body in order not to kill'; and 'indiscriminate fire is not permitted'. Fire 'for effect must not last longer than is necessary to achieve the immediate aim', and collateral damage must be avoided or minimised. Above all, peacekeepers must 'when in doubt, always seek clarification from higher command'. Subject to these conditions the Pocket Card allows peacekeepers to use force (up to and including deadly force) 'to defend oneself, other UN personnel, individuals designated by the Head of Mission or other international personnel against a hostile act or a hostile intent'; to resist attempts to abduct the above people; to protect designated installations, facilities and equipment from hostile acts or hostile intent; 'to protect civilians under imminent threat of physical violence, when competent local authorities are not in a position to render immediate assistance'; and to 'resist attempts by any person or group that limits or intends to limit the freedom of movement of UN personnel, humanitarian workers or individuals designated by the Head of Mission'. 'Hostile act' is defined as 'an action where the intent is to cause death, bodily harm or destruction of designated property'; and 'hostile intent' is defined as the 'threat of imminent use of force, demonstrated through an action which appears to be preparatory to a hostile act. Only a reasonable belief in the hostile intent is required, before the use of force is authorized.' Force, excluding deadly force, is allowed to prevent the escape of any apprehended or detained individual, to prevent forcible passage of individuals or groups through checkpoints, and to detain those who try to effect forcible passage. Thus the

---

[96] B. Oswald, H. Durham and A. Bates (eds), *Documents on the Law of UN Peace Operations* (Oxford: Oxford University Press, 2010), at 562.

[97] G.P. Fletcher and J.D. Ohlin, *Defending Humanity: When Force is Justified and Why* (Oxford: Oxford University Press, 2008), at 67–76.

on-the-ground interpretation of the broader discussion of the use of force for peace operations shows a fair degree of caution as to when lethal and non-lethal force can be utilised, and although it does go beyond a strict reading of self-defence, it falls a long way short of military enforcement action.

Contrast this with RoE for UN-authorised military enforcement actions, shown by the Pocket Card given to US troops containing a summary of the RoE to be followed by those troops when fighting in Operation Desert Storm against Iraq under a UN mandate in 1991. The rules open with a general statement that 'all enemy military personnel and vehicles transporting the enemy or their supplies may be engaged', but then it lists a number of prohibitions upon the use of force against enemy combatants that are rendered *hors de combat*, civilians and their property (unless necessary to save US lives) and protected targets such as hospitals and churches, unless force is necessary in self-defence.[98] Thus under the RoE in military enforcement operations self-defence is the exception to the norm of using whatever force is necessary to achieve the objectives of the mission, which in the case of Operation Desert Storm was to force Iraqi troops and armour out of Kuwait.[99] Thus there remains qualitative and quantitative differences between peacekeeping and its emphasis on self-defence (though increasingly widely drawn), and military enforcement action with its emphasis on engaging the enemy as effectively as possible. The problem is that while the UNSC might not be willing or able (due to lack of volunteers) to authorise full enforcement action, it may be able to persuade states to contribute to a peace operation with a more coercive mandate. This tension is brought to a head by the development of 'protection' mandates for peace operations.

6. PROTECTION MANDATES

Ultimately, as international and UN law turn towards the protection of human security as well as the traditional concern for national and international security, the mandates of both PKOs and CoWs have changed. Originating in ideas of human security and the responsibility to protect,[100] the protection of civilians has become the focus of attention in peace operations at the turn of the century, especially those located in the Democratic Republic of the Congo and Darfur, where human rights abuse, systematic rape and killings, and other war crimes and crimes against humanity have been committed, often on an unimaginable scale.

The UNSC, in adopting Resolutions 1296 (2000) and 1674 (2006), has created the expectations that peacekeepers will protect civilians, and has included protection mandates in almost all of its recently mandated peace operations. Though force sizes have increased, the ineffectiveness of lightly armed peace operations of up to 20,000

---

[98] In A. Roberts and R. Guelff (eds), *Documents on the Laws of War*, 3rd edn (Oxford: Oxford University Press, 2000), at 362–363.
[99] UNSC Res. 678 (1990).
[100] S. Hassler, 'Peacekeeping and the Responsibility to Protect', (2010) 14 *J Int Peacekeeping* 134.

troops spread across large countries is a huge impediment to fulfilling these expectations and protecting civilians from arbitrary violence. The alternative is to protect civilians through CoWs, as evidenced most recently in the NATO air campaign over Libya in 2011 (authorised by the UNSC),[101] and more controversially over Kosovo in 1999 (unauthorised by the UNSC).

This section critically evaluates whether peacekeeping forces are capable of delivering these goals; bearing in mind the legal, political and military limitations placed upon them. While such lofty ideals as the 'responsibility to protect' may be readily criticised as not having a clear legal content,[102] there can be no doubt that a basic human right – to life – is in issue here, and if peacekeepers have only a basic human rights obligation, it should be to protect life.

The turn of the 21st century seemed to be the start of a new approach to UN peacekeeping. In the Report of the Panel on United Nations Peace Operations of August 2000, commonly known as the Brahimi Report after its chair, Lakhdar Brahimi, there were clear expressions of dissatisfaction with the inability of peacekeepers to prevent violence and protect civilians, combined with a recognition that in the future most, if not all, peace operations should not only have protection mandates, but also the ability to carry them out. The Report identified both the desire to increase the protection of civilians but also very clearly outlined the difficulties that would be present in mandating under-equipped and under-trained peace operations to protect hundreds of thousands of civilians in their areas of deployment.[103] The message was clear: peace operations should be given mandates that include the protection of civilians within their areas of deployment – but only if they have the capability of so doing. Looking at the mandates granted by the UNSC to numerous operations deployed after the turn of the century, there seems to be a near universal move towards accepting the need for protection mandates.[104] In contrast none of the currently deployed PKOs, whose creation dates back to before Brahimi, possess protection mandates.[105]

In an unstable post-conflict environment the Brahimi Report recommended that peace operations be bigger and better equipped, so that they can deal with 'spoilers' and also protect civilians where necessary. The idea was that such forces would act as a credible deterrent, in contrast to traditional peacekeeping forces, which were more symbolic and non-interventionist. In these circumstances it is necessary for TCNs to be prepared to allow their troops to operate under RoE and run the risk of casualties, while

---

[101] UNSC Res. 1973 (2011).
[102] C. Focarelli, 'The Responsibility to Protect Doctrine and Humanitarian Intervention: Too Many Ambiguities for a Working Doctrine', (2008) 13 *JCSL* 191.
[103] Brahimi Report, *supra* n. 25, at paras 62–63, 108–109.
[104] For example SC Res. 1279 (1999) and SC Res. 1565 (2004) (MONUC in the Congo); SC Res. 1509 (2003) (UNAMIL in Liberia); SC Res. 1528 (2004) (UNOCI in Cote d'Ivoire); SC Res. 1542 (2004) (MINUSTAH in Haiti); SC Res. 1590 (2005); SC Res. 1706 (2006) (UNMIS in Sudan); SC Res. 1769 (2007) (UNAMID in Darfur); SC Res. 1778 (2007) (MINURCAT in Chad and the Central African Republic).
[105] UNTSO in the Middle East created in 1948; UNMOGIP in Kashmir created in 1951; UNFICYP in Cyprus created in 1964; UNDOF in the Golan Heights created in 1974; UNIFIL in Lebanon created in 1978; MINURSO in Western Sahara created in 1991; and UNOMIG in Georgia created in 1993.

still supporting the peacekeeping principles of consent, impartiality and the use of force only in self-defence. In this way the Brahimi Report represented an attempt to draw the peacekeeping line nearer to Chapter VII than Chapter VI.[106] Overall, the function of the peacekeeping element of the peace operation is to provide security. It does this primarily by overseeing a cease-fire, and then by protecting human rights,[107] by demobilising the armed factions, by disarming and de-mining, and by police and army reform. The peacekeeping force should not only protect the human rights of individuals within its area of deployment (which might require forceful intervention on occasions), but must be human rights compliant in its own activities (for example when detaining spoilers), and when engaged in conflict it must respect the principles of international humanitarian law contained in the Geneva Conventions (including distinguishing between combatants and non-combatants, and distinguishing between military and civilian targets).[108]

Arguments have been made that this reflects an emerging wider norm of a collective responsibility to protect in the event of genocide and other large-scale killings, ethnic cleansing or serious violations of international humanitarian law which sovereign governments have proved powerless or unwilling to prevent.[109] Again, though, caution must be exercised due to the potential for disconsonance between the mandate given to peace operations and the reality on the ground. In the Democratic Republic of the Congo in 2001, a wholly inadequate UN force (MONUC) of 5,500 was unable to prevent horrific violence in the Bunia region, despite a mandate that contained a provision under Chapter VII, which enabled necessary action to be taken to protect civilians.[110] Indeed, an EU force (CoW) was required in 2003 to tackle the violence in that region. With the UN peace operation in the Congo (MONUC) struggling to maintain order, especially in the Ituri Province centred around the town of Bunia, the EU decided to send a 1,800-strong French-led force to that area, acting under a mandate from the UNSC.[111] Although the operation was stated to be humanitarian or crisis management within the Petersberg tasks of the EU,[112] the line between such operations and war-fighting was not entirely clear, as shown by the clashes between French troops and rival militias shortly after the EU force's deployment. Having restored some calm, EU Operation Artemis was withdrawn on 1 September 2003. Another temporary EU force was sent in mid to late 2006 to support MONUC while elections were held in the country.[113] These temporary deployments were only sufficient to quell the violence for a while and in the interim violence flared again

---

[106] Brahimi Report, *supra* n. 25, at paras 48–52.
[107] See Memorandum of Understanding between UN High Commissioner for Human Rights and UN DPKO.
[108] Secretary General's Bulletin, 'Observance by the United Nations Forces of International Humanitarian Law', UN Doc. ST/SGB/1999/13.
[109] High Level Panel Report on Threats, Challenges and Change, *A More Secure World: Our Shared Responsibility* (2004), at para. 203. See a more qualified version in the World Summit Outcome document, GA Res. 6/1 (2005), at para. 139.
[110] UNSC Res. 1291 (2000), at para. 8.
[111] UNSC Res. 1484 (2003).
[112] Article 17, Treaty on European Union.
[113] UNSC Res. 1671 (2006).

despite significant increases in the size and mandate of MONUC.[114] Ultimately, MONUC was involved in fighting rebels alongside government troops.[115] It was replaced by MONUSCO in 2010 but the new force still had a mandate to support the government in providing security and consolidating the peace, and in protecting civilians.[116] UNOCI in the Ivory Coast has also been in action alongside French troops in supporting the democratically elected government in 2010–2011.[117] Though the AU and the UN cooperated and coordinated their efforts in response to the crisis in Darfur caused by the crimes against humanity being committed there since 2003, the hybrid UN/AU force (UNAMID 2007–)[118] had only deployed 7,000 troops by January 2008, far short of the 26,000 required, thus restricting the initial impact of peacekeepers on preventing attacks on civilians. However, by the end of 2008 UNAMID had increased in size to 15,000. Despite this, there has been limited evidence of it carrying out its protection mandate. In February 2009 the UNSG reported that the security situation had deteriorated and that UNAMID 'will continue its efforts to systematically monitor, report and investigate attacks in accordance with its mandate', noting a number of attacks against civilians that had occurred. The UNSG appealed for the promised troops from a number of countries to be deployed which 'would constitute a significant increase in the mission's troop strength and thus its protection capability and ability to implement its core mandated tasks'.[119] In 2011 the UNSC underlined the need for UNAMID to use its full resources to prioritise the protection of civilians,[120] reflecting the on-going violence directed against them.[121]

In practice, the Congo (MONUC) and Darfur (UNAMID) forces have not implemented the Chapter VII elements of their mandates sufficiently to adequately protect civilians. This is due in part to TCNs (largely drawn from the South) being unable or unwilling to provide sufficiently equipped and trained troops, and moreover those troops and their military and political leaders still tend to follow the UNEF/UNPROFOR model and stick to traditional peacekeeping doctrine and adopt national RoE accordingly, no matter that they are operating under protection mandates. Peacekeeping contingents may also be faced with other obstacles in the way of protecting civilians. If a contingent does intervene to protect civilians or to confront spoilers it is unlikely to have the resources or mechanisms to protect the human rights of any detainees in accordance with the TCN's human rights obligations. The TCN has to balance these issues against the consequences of any failure to intervene to protect civilians, which, as the experience of Dutchbat at Srebrenica shows, can be devastating. In addition, the gap between the political decision by the UNSC and the practical

---

[114] Initially MONUC consisted of 5,500 troops (UNSC Res. 1291, 2000); in 2002 it was increased to 8,700 (UNSC Res. 1445, 2002); UNSC Res. 1493 (2003) increased it to 10,800; UNSC Res. 1565 of 2004 increased it to 16,700.
[115] UNSC Res. 1856 (2008). UNSG's Report, UN Doc. S/2009/303, at 19.
[116] UNSC Res. 1925 (2010).
[117] See UN Press Release SG/SM/13503 (2011).
[118] UNSC Res. 1769 (2007).
[119] Report of the Secretary-General on the deployment of the African Union–United Nations Hybrid Operation, UN Doc. S/2009/83, at paras 10, 31 and 44.
[120] UNSC Res. 2003 (2011).
[121] Secretary-General s Report, UN Doc. S/2011/643, at para. 49.

implementation of the mandate by the UN force is not only due to TCNs' reluctance but must also be due to inadequate direction from the UN's DPKO. The Capstone Doctrine may show a change of attitude at the UN, but it still needs to be translated into practice.

There is no real conceptual or legal impediment to the successful development of more robust peacekeeping,[122] empowered to protect civilians, thus fulfilling the human security agenda. Peacekeepers cannot stand by when civilians are under attack. The impediments are not legal but practical and could be overcome by better-provisioned and trained forces. Such forces can still respect the principles of consent (minimally of the government), impartiality (if the force protects all groups of civilians and confronts any attack on them), and the use of force in self-defence (if the force recognises that self-defence not only covers defence of peacekeepers but also defence of civilians in imminent danger). Of course if, as is arguably the situation in Darfur, the government is wholly or partly responsible for attacks against civilians then the legal and conceptual basis of peacekeeping and peace operations is undermined, since to protect civilians in these circumstances is to confront the government and the state. In these circumstances enforcement action is necessary; a robust peace operation is insufficient both legally and practically. The need to authorise a CoW in the case of Libya in 2011 is evidence of this.[123] On the other side of the coin, if the PKO becomes an arm of the government and uses force to fight alongside governmental forces to suppress a rebellion, then it has lost its impartiality and has gone far beyond the protection of civilians; and, although not a fully fledged enforcement action, it amounts to a more aggressive type of peace support operation more appropriate for CoWs under a general Chapter VII mandate.[124]

7. DEVELOPMENT AND REFORM

There is no doubt that the UN security system has a long way to go in developing and regulating its military options (whether PKOs or CoWs, or more integrated operations of the future). It remains possible to distinguish PKOs from CoWs, although they both perform a significant role in fulfilling UN goals and values, even as these develop to include human security alongside national and international security. Though the UN security system has the *de jure* monopoly on military enforcement action, the *de facto* monopoly on force in the international system still rests with states. The fact that the UN has to rely on TCNs in order to assemble a PKO or a CoW signifies that states still have a great deal of influence over the actions of those peacekeepers and soldiers. States may decide not to contribute forces, but even if they do they can divert the forces from the tasks given to them. For instance, the government of a TCN to a UN PKO can

---

[122] But see J. Sloan, *The Militarisation of Peacekeeping in the Twenty-First Century* (Oxford: Hart, 2011), at 291–295.
[123] UNSC Res. 1973 (2011).
[124] On peace support or stabilisation operations see N.D. White, 'Peace Operations', in V. Chetail (ed.), *Post-Conflict Peacebuilding: A Lexicon* (Oxford: Oxford University Press, 2009), at 221–222.

play the 'red card', thereby preventing its troops from undertaking what it considers to be too dangerous or risky elements of the force's mandate.[125] This is despite the fact that UN PKOs are subject to a UN command and control structure. Such state interventions impinge severely on a PKO's ability to protect civilians, as this will mean putting peacekeepers in harm's way. In the case of a CoW, the TCN's control is so much greater, given that command and control is delegated to the TCNs, and so inevitably leads those states to interpret the mandate in ways that serve their purposes and not always the goals as set down by the mandating organ within the UN.

PKOs have greater legitimacy in that they are subject to greater UN control and accountability (with their mandates being subject to regular renewal), and responsibility (where the UN normally accepts responsibility for wrongful acts committed within UN commanded and controlled peacekeeping operations, but not for UN-authorised CoWs).[126] However, the limited military capabilities of peacekeepers in the face of increasing violence against them and civilians within their areas of deployment means that the UN and TCNs have to ensure that they are properly equipped and trained to uphold the mandate, including the protection of civilians. Though by no means easy to assemble, UN PKOs can be established more readily than CoWs. CoWs are very difficult to assemble and depend upon a confluence of UN goals and state interests. In order to prevent the latter prevailing, the use of open-ended, vague mandates such as found in Resolution 678 of 1990 in the case of Iraq, and Resolution 1973 of 2011 in the case of Libya, should give way to more precise, renewable and accountable mandates. Only in these ways can the UN move towards a predictable and reliable collective security system, where force is only used where absolutely necessary, and at a level of intensity and duration to meet the specific threat or aggression being confronted.

---

[125] T. Thakur and D. Banerjee, 'India: Democratic, Poor, Internationalist', in C. Ku and H. Jacobson (eds), *Democratic Accountability and the Use of Force in International Law* (Cambridge: Cambridge University Press, 2003), 176, at 198.

[126] I. Scobbie, 'International Organizations and International Relations', in R.J. Dupuy (ed.), *A Handbook on International Organizations* (The Hague: Martinus Nijhoff, 1998), at 891; G. Gaja, Second Report on Responsibility of International Organizations, UN Doc. A/CN.4/541, 2 April 2004, 16–19. While this is the practice there is a lack of clarity at the doctrinal level – contrast Draft Article 7 of the International Law Commission's Draft Articles of the Responsibility of International Organisations 2011 (ILC Report of 63rd session (2011), UN Doc. A/66/10), which adopts a narrow 'effective control of conduct' test for attribution of state organs or agents (such as peacekeepers from TCNs) to the UN; with the European Court of Human Rights in the case of *Behrami and Saramati v. France, Germany and Norway*, Judgment (App. Nos 71412/01 and 78166/01) 2007, which adopts a broader 'ultimate authority and control' test to attribute conduct of state agents to the UN.

18. Human rights protection during extra-territorial military operations: perspectives at international and English law

Alexander Orakhelashvili

1. INTRODUCTION

Over the past decade the issue of human rights protection has acquired an unprecedented intensity in terms of regulating the conduct of states parties to human rights treaties when conducting military operations abroad. The classical philosophical meaning of human rights has historically concerned the relationship between the government and the governed. Yet the letter and spirit of human rights treaties have also led to governments being held accountable for what they do abroad and to non-nationals. This issue has received the most intensive treatment in the jurisprudence of the European Court of Human Rights, which interprets and applies Article 1 of the European Convention on Human Rights (hereinafter 'ECHR') requiring the protection of the rights of those who find themselves under the jurisdiction of states parties. The Strasbourg Court (and the European Commission on Human Rights at earlier stages) had to examine this issue in its multiple aspects, ranging from rather trivial and mundane situations relating to the conduct of consular officials to more extraordinary situations, including the wars in Cyprus, Yugoslavia and Iraq. Given that the Strasbourg Court's jurisdiction is meant to complement the jurisdiction of national courts, the latter, especially in England, have encountered cases where the identification of the precise scope of Article 1 was required.

This contribution examines this process by primarily focusing upon the international legal technique of interpretation as applied to Article 1 of the ECHR. Before proceeding to specific questions of interpretation, section 2 will examine the preliminary questions that share a common underlying theme, namely the possibility of legal obstacles restricting the effective extra-territorial application of human rights treaties: the applicability of humanitarian law in the same situation where human rights law applies and the question of the attribution of wrongful acts in situations where multiple entities are active. Section 3 will then proceed to identify the precise meaning of Article 1 and how it has been applied in judicial practice. Section 4 will examine the implications for the English legal system when issues are raised under Article 1. Section 5 will focus on situations where human rights treaties apply extra-territorially in principle but a resolution adopted by the UN Security Council is invoked to supersede their effect. Section 6 will focus on further obstacles to the effective application of human rights treaties presented by litigation in England, such as Act of State and justiciability. Section 7 will then offer general conclusions.

2. PRELIMINARY QUESTIONS: OBSTACLES TO THE EFFECTIVE EXTRA-TERRITORIAL APPLICATION OF HUMAN RIGHTS TREATIES

A. The Relationship between Human Rights and Humanitarian Law

The basic position regarding the relationship between human rights and humanitarian law is that both bodies of law apply to armed conflict and belligerent occupation.[1] Where humanitarian law applies as a more specialised body of law (*lex specialis*), it provides specific, not inherently less beneficial, legal regulation. In addition, the practice of the relevant international tribunals lacks any reference to any inherent normative conflict between the two bodies of law to the effect that the lower protection under humanitarian law prevails. In some cases there may be a conflicts-of-law type of reference from the relevant human rights rule to humanitarian law because the latter is specifically designed to apply to armed conflict situations,[2] but the ultimate effect normally is not to curtail the human rights protection but to complement and reinforce it, and at times even provide a higher degree of protection to individuals under humanitarian law than would be available under human rights law.[3] In some armed conflict situations human rights norms will be applied only to the relevant conduct and humanitarian law will not play a limiting role.[4] The speciality of humanitarian law means that it offers a specialised protection, not that it lowers the otherwise available protection.

This should be enough to dispel the assumption that, wherever human rights treaties such as the ECHR apply extra-territorially in situations of armed conflict and occupation, their effect could be curtailed by the more limited humanitarian law protection. Admittedly in line with previous jurisprudence, in *Al-Skeini* the European Court of Human Rights, having ascertained that the British troops' presence in Basra was covered by the ECHR, addressed the issue of violation of Article 2 (freedom from arbitrary deprivation of life) on the basis of the ECHR only, even though the situation in question was also governed by humanitarian law. The issue of lowering protection of

---

[1] This has been repeatedly confirmed in the International Court's jurisprudence; see *Legal Consequences of the Construction of a Wall in the Occupied Palestinian Territory*, Advisory Opinion, [2004] ICJ Rep. 136, at para. 106; *Case Concerning the Armed Activities on the Territory of the Congo* (Democratic Republic of the Congo v Uganda) [2005] ICJ Rep. 168, at para. 216. For a detailed analysis see A. Orakhelashvili, 'The Interaction between Human Rights and Humanitarian Law: Fragmentation, Conflict, Parallelism or Convergence?', (2008) 19 *EJIL* 161. Lord Bingham acknowledged in *Al-Skeini* that even as in his view the Human Rights Act was not extra-territorial, the 1907 Hague Convention still applied to the UK 'in a situation such as prevailed in Iraq'. *Al-Skeini v UK* (GC), No. 55721/07, 7 July 2011 (hereinafter '*Al-Skeini* (GC)'), at para. 26 (*per* Lord Bingham).

[2] *Legality of the Threat or Use of Nuclear Weapons*, Advisory Opinion, [1996] ICJ Rep. 226, at 240.

[3] *Juan Carlos Abella v Argentina*, Case 11.137, 18 November 1997, OEA/Ser.L/V/II.98, at paras 159–165.

[4] See, for example, *Issayeva, Yusupova & Bazayeva v Russia*, Judgment, 24 February 2005, Nos 57947/00, 57948/00 & 57949/00.

individuals because *jus in bello* also applied simply did not arise.[5] The parallel applicability of the two sets of rules was also confirmed in *Al-Jedda v UK*, where the European Court, having concluded that humanitarian law treaties do not envisage detention of the kind to which *Al-Jedda* was subjected, found that Article 5 of the European Convention was violated.[6] This again confirms that human rights law and humanitarian law effectively shadow each other for the protection of individuals during an armed conflict and belligerent occupation.

B. The Allocation of Responsibility to the Entities Involved

In several situations where human rights treaties apply extra-territorially, it may be the case that the relevant state, to which the conduct in question is imputed, acts in concert with other entities or under the mandate of the UN, NATO or EU.[7] The ways in which the peace operation mandate approved by international organisations can be claimed to prevent extra-territorial state responsibility for human rights violations are twofold. In the *Behrami* case, the European Court of Human Rights adopted the approach that the mere fact that the respondent state acted under the mandate of the UN Security Council (hereinafter 'UNSC') transferred, allegedly *in toto*, the responsibility from that state to the UN.[8] The acts committed by KFOR national contingents in Kosovo (Federal Republic of Yugoslavia (hereinafter 'FRY')) were not attributable to the relevant states parties to which the contingents belonged. The Court asserted that 'the key question is whether the UNSC retained ultimate authority and control so that operational command only was delegated'.[9] But this refers to mandate, delegation and formal authority, as opposed to the actual commission of the wrongful act and the actual effective control over it.

When addressing the Responsibility of International Organisations, the UN International Law Commission has distanced itself from *Behrami* and subscribed to the approach that national governments bear responsibility for what their military contingents do.[10] The same approach has been upheld by national courts. The English High Court in *Bici* and the Dutch Court of Appeal in the *Dutchbat* case specified that the

---

[5] Deprivation of life should therefore be 'absolutely necessary' to meet purposes stated in Article 2. This was due not least to the fact that the Convention's safeguards should be applied as practical and effective in protecting individuals. See *Al-Skeini*, *supra* n.1, at paras 161ff.

[6] *Al-Jedda v UK* (GC), No. 27021/08, 7 July 2011, at para. 107 (further referring to the ICJ's relevant pronouncements in *DRC/Uganda* regarding the applicability of human rights law where humanitarian law also applies) (hereinafter '*Al-Jedda* (GC)').

[7] For detail see A. Orakhelashvili, *Collective Security* (Oxford: Oxford University Press, 2011), at Chapter 8.

[8] *Behrami and Behrami v France & Saramati v France, Germany, Norway* (GC), Nos 71412/01 & 78166/01, Admissibility Decision, 2 May 2007 (hereinafter '*Behrami* (GC)').

[9] *Ibid.*, at paras 133–136.

[10] International Law Commission Articles on the Responsibility of International Organisations and the Commentary thereto, Articles 6 and 7, adopted at second reading 2011.

British and Dutch Governments retained command of their forces and were responsible for their conduct notwithstanding that they were acting under the auspices of the UN.[11]

Curiously and problematically enough, the House of Lords in *Al-Jedda* has distinguished *Behrami* rather than disapproving it as the Multi-National Force (hereinafter 'MNF') operating in Iraq under UN Security Council resolution 1546 (2004) as it was not institutionally part of the UN.[12] The Grand Chamber judgment in *Al-Jedda* also distinguished *Behrami* on the basis that the UN had no security chain in Iraq and referred to the factual distinction between the UNMIK/KFOR situation in Kosovo and the position of MNF in Iraq.[13] Against this background, the fact remains that neither the House of Lords nor the Strasbourg Court have so far addressed the need to identify the genuine difference between the delegation of mandate to conduct peace operations and the actual commission of wrongful acts during those operations. If responsibility goes with the former, then the ECHR should apply neither to the situation in Kosovo nor that in Iraq; if it goes with the latter, then it should apply to both. The Grand Chamber's hesitation to expressly distance itself from *Behrami* is unsettling because some potential still remains for a continuing obstacle to inhibit ensuring accountability for extra-territorial violations of the ECHR, as far as litigation before the Strasbourg Court is concerned, although it is far from certain that the *Behrami* approach, so far isolated, will prevail in the long run.

As for the position under general international law, the rule of primary attribution to individual states remains, in line with the ILC's Articles, based on a rather simple and straightforward question of who actually performs the relevant act. General Comment 31 of the UN Human Rights Committee adopts a similar stance.[14] The overall conclusion should therefore be that the fact that the relevant state may be acting under the Security Council mandate does not affect the attribution to that state of acts that it has performed.

3. THE EXTRA-TERRITORIAL APPLICATION OF THE ECHR UNDER ARTICLE 1

A. The Principal Controversies

Judicial treatment of the territorial scope of the ECHR manifests some degree of turbulence, expressed through the contestable use of concepts on which the application of Article 1 is premised. To illustrate, in *Banković v Belgium et al.* the Strasbourg Court declared the complaints that the NATO bombings of Belgrade in 1999 violated Article

---

[11] *Bici v MOD*, High Court, EWCH 786, 7 April 2004, para. 2; the Hague Court of Appeal judgment on *Dutchbat*, 5 July 2011, available at http://zoeken.rechtspraak.nl.

[12] *R (on the application of Al-Jedda) (FC) (Appellant) v Secretary of State for Defence (Respondent)*, Appellate Committee, [2007] UKHL 58, Judgment, 12 December 2007, at paras 23–24 (*per* Lord Bingham) (hereinafter '*Al-Jedda* (HL)').

[13] *Al-Jedda* (GC), *supra* n.6, at para. 84.

[14] General Comment No. 31, Nature of the General Legal Obligation on States Parties to the Covenant, UN Doc. CCPR/C/21/Rev.1/Add.13 (2004), at para. 10.

2 of the Convention inadmissible. The Court's principal findings were threefold: (a) the NATO bombings were not covered by 'jurisdiction' under Article 1, which is essentially territorial; (b) the situation was not under the 'effective control' of the states whose air forces conducted the bombing; and (c) the regional European nature of the Convention (*espace juridique*) prevented its application to the events in the territory of FRY that was at that time not a state party to the Convention.[15] This case gave impetus to intensive discussions regarding the scope of Article 1 and the factors that make it apply, or not, to the relevant extra-territorial military action.[16] Clarity of the underlying concepts is an indispensable requirement both for courts to apply Article 1 properly and for writers to consistently evaluate courts' jurisprudence.

This problem has been obvious in subsequent litigation. The *Al-Skeini* litigation before the UK House of Lords concerned the deaths of six Iraqi civilians, one of whom (Baha Mousa) died as a consequence of brutal maltreatment by members of British armed forces in Iraq. The claims were based on the Human Rights Act (hereinafter 'HRA') 1998 and so needed to demonstrate that the rights of the victims were violated by the unlawful acts of public authorities, as specified in section 6. The House of Lords decided that none of the civilians, apart from Baha Mousa, came within Britain's jurisdiction under Article 1. The Grand Chamber of the Strasbourg Court overturned these findings and held that all six applicants were covered by Article 1.

The *Smith* case before the UK Supreme Court arose out of the death of Private Jason Smith, who was mobilised for service in Iraq in June 2003. On 9 August he reported sick, complaining of heat that exceeded 50 degrees; on 13 August he was found collapsed, rushed to hospital and died almost immediately. The inquest into his death suffered from procedural shortcomings and his mother brought a claim under the HRA 1998, arguing that throughout the time Private Smith was on service in Iraq the UK Government owed to him a duty to respect his right to life under Article 2 of the European Convention. Lord Phillips identified the basic issue of jurisdiction, namely whether 'a soldier on military service abroad in Iraq [is] subject to the protection of the HRA 1998 when outside his base'. For deciding this question, the scope of jurisdiction under Article 1 ECHR was crucial;[17] the question posed was answered in the negative.

---

[15] *Banković et al. v Belgium et al.* (GC), No. 52207/99, Admissibility Decision, 12 December 2001 (hereinafter '*Banković* (GC)').

[16] See, for example, J. Williams, '*Al-Skeini*: A Flawed Interpretation of *Bankovic*', (2007) 23 *Wisconsin JIL* 687; K.M. Larsen, 'Territorial Non-application of the ECHR', (2009) 78 *Nordic JIL* 73; E. Berry, 'Extra-territorial Reach of the ECHR', (2006) 12 *EPL* 629; R. Wilde, 'Legal "Black Hole"? Extraterritorial State Action and International Treaty Law on Civil and Political Rights', (2005) 26 *MJIL* 739; R. Wilde, 'The Extraterritorial Application of the Human Rights Act', (2005) 58 *CLP* 47; M. Gondek, *The Reach of Human Rights in a Globalising World: Extraterritorial Application of Human Rights Treaties* (Dordrecht: Intersentia, 2009); M. Milanović, *Extra-territorial Application of Human Rights Treaties: Law, Principles and Policy* (Oxford: Oxford University Press, 2011).

[17] *R (on the application of Smith) (FC) (Respondent) v Secretary of State for Defence (Appellant) and another*, [2010] UKSC 29, 30 June 2010, at paras 1–2, 5 (*per* Lord Phillips) (hereinafter '*Smith*').

B. Interpretation of Article 1 ECHR: The Ordinary Meaning of 'Jurisdiction'

Article 1 focuses upon the 'jurisdiction' of states parties, not their territory, which indicates that it inherently incorporates an extra-territorial element. If, then, the balance struck by Article 1 is assessed on its merit, the occurrence of the act in question under the jurisdiction of one of the states parties can be covered by Article 1, whether or not that act takes place within the relevant state's territory. There is no inherent presumption for or against extra-territoriality.

This is how the early case-law such as *Drozd* and *Loizidou* addressed this issue. The Strasbourg Court in *Drozd* viewed 'jurisdiction' under Article 1 not as jurisdiction in the ordinary sense of international law, but in the sense of what the respondent state had actually done in whatever location.[18] The *Loizidou* case followed this approach by stating that 'the responsibility of Contracting Parties can be involved because of acts of their authorities, whether performed within or outside national boundaries, which produce effects outside their own territory', and then citing *Drozd*. After this, the European Court proceeded to add that 'the responsibility of a Contracting Party may *also* arise when as a consequence of military action – whether lawful or unlawful – it exercises effective control of an area outside its national territory.'[19]

Banković, however, settled for a hitherto unprecedented restrictive understanding of the scope of Article 1 that 'jurisdiction' is primarily territorial and only exceptionally extends to acts performed outside the territory of the state party.[20] The lasting legacy of *Banković* has been a judicially introduced ill-conceived presumption, defying the balance struck through the wording of Article 1, that the locus of the act in question can determine whether Article 1 will cover that act.[21] To illustrate, in *Al-Skeini* Lord Bingham followed the *Banković* presumption, asserting that 'the focus of the Convention is primarily on what is done or not done within the borders of contracting states and not outside'. As the claimants relied on 'special circumstances in which British troops were operating in Basra', they had to substantiate their situation under one of those exceptions.[22]

The *Al-Skeini* litigation witnessed a further interpretative presumption, notably by Lord Rodger, to the effect that 'an act which would engage the Convention if committed on the territory of a contracting state does not *ipso facto* engage the Convention if carried out by that contracting state on the territory of another state

---

[18] *Drozd and Janousek v France & Spain*, No. 12747/87, Judgment, 26 June 1992, at paras 91–96.

[19] *Loizidou v Turkey* (GC), Preliminary Objections, No. 15318/89, Judgment, 23 March 1995, at para. 62 (emphasis added) (hereinafter '*Loizidou* (GC) (Preliminary Objections)').

[20] This contribution will not examine *Banković* in great detail; see instead A. Orakhelashvili, 'Restrictive Interpretation of Human Rights Treaties in the Recent Jurisprudence of the European Court of Human Rights', (2003) 14 *EJIL* 529.

[21] See for example, *Medvedyev v France* (GC), No. 3394/03, Judgment, 29 March 2010, at para. 64 (hereinafter '*Medvedyev* (GC)').

[22] *Al-Skeini and Others v Secretary of State for Defence*, [2007] UKHL 26, Judgment, 13 June 2007, at paras 3–4, 14 (*per* Lord Bingham) (hereinafter '*Al-Skeini* (HL)'); *Smith, supra* n.17, at para. 47 (*per* Lord Phillips).

outside the Council of Europe'.²³ This rather blanket statement reveals that *Banković* is in stark contrast to the European Court's other decisions. In *Issa v Turkey*, the Strasbourg Court observed that 'Article 1 of the Convention cannot be interpreted so as to allow a state party to perpetrate violations of the Convention on the territory of another State, which it could not perpetrate on its own territory', and admitted the possibility that Turkey could be held responsible for the conduct of its armed forces on the territory of Iraq.²⁴ The same approach has been used by the UN Human Rights Committee in *Lopez Burgos*, which observed that the right approach relates 'not to the place where the violation occurred, but rather to the relationship between the individual and the State in relation to a violation of any of the rights set forth in the Covenant, wherever they occurred'.²⁵ The *Issa* principle is an important statement of the object and purpose of the ECHR as a human rights treaty and substantiates that object and purpose specifically in relation to Article 1.

The 'primary territorial with limited/special exceptions' approach suffers from methodological and logical incoherence. The ordinary meaning of Article 1 does not warrant distinguishing between primary (or mainline) and exceptional (or special) headings of 'jurisdiction'. What Article 1 instead requires is that once the exercise of state jurisdiction is demonstrated on whatever basis, the Convention must be applied to the act in question. If, as Lord Bingham suggested, 'jurisdiction' under Article 1 referred to acts performed within the territory of the respondent state, it would not be primarily territorial but exclusively territorial, for that would then be what states parties have agreed upon, and it would be plainly inappropriate for courts to admit extra-territorial exceptions to such territorial 'jurisdiction'. The bulk of the existing Article 1 jurisprudence would then be *ultra vires* of the Strasbourg Court's powers.

But this far-reaching possibility does not have to materialise, for there are other ways to construe the Article 1 'jurisdiction' through the use of ordinary means of treaty interpretation, among which the plain and ordinary meaning of treaty provisions, in accordance with the treaty's object and purpose, has to be prioritised pursuant to Article 31 of the 1969 Vienna Convention on the Law of Treaties. In this sense, Lord Phillips in *Smith* specified that the natural meaning of Article 1 'jurisdiction' could refer to: (a) substantive state competence to affect persons or things through administrative or judicial action; and (b) geographical ambit to which the state's laws and administration extends, its legal system. It could thus mean '"subject to the authority of" but can equally bear the natural meaning "within the territory over which authority is exercised"'.²⁶

In principle there is no cardinal distinction between these two options. If the state's laws extend to X, then that state's courts and administration ordinarily have jurisdiction over that X, whether or not X is situated or takes place within or outside its borders.

---

²³ *Al-Skeini* (HL), *ibid.*, at para. 71 (*per* Lord Rodger), see also at para. 75, further elaborating on incompatibility between *Issa v Turkey*, No. 31821/96, Judgment, 16 November 2004 (hereinafter '*Issa*') and *Banković*.

²⁴ *Ibid., Issa*, at paras 71–81.

²⁵ *Delia Saldias de Lopez v Uruguay*, UN Human Rights Committee, Communication No. 52/1979, U.N. Doc. CCPR/C/OP/1 at 88 (1984), at para. 12.3.

²⁶ *Smith, supra* n.17, at paras 36, 39 (*per* Lord Phillips).

By deploying troops, officials and agents abroad, the state inherently extends its laws and administrative orders to those troops, officials and agents; therefore it extends to them its extra-territorial jurisdiction in both senses above. All those agents and forces obtain instructions from the sending state and carry out its legislative and executive prescriptions; they are also under that state's judicial jurisdiction in both a criminal and disciplinary sense. Therefore, whenever these agents, officials or troops are on duty or encounter individual victims, they treat them through the exercise of jurisdiction of the sending state. Understanding 'jurisdiction' literally in either sense does not trim down the scope of Article 1; it only emphasises that when states extend their sovereign action extra-territorially Article 1 will *ipso facto* accompany that extension.

Furthermore, if 'jurisdiction' under Article 1 mirrors the general concept of state jurisdiction under international law, then Article 1 cannot, as a matter of principle, be 'primarily territorial' but must have regular and inherent extra-territorial elements, namely through the exercise of the extra-territorial jurisdiction that international law allows states, or through the extra-territorial executive action that may be internationally illegal yet be premised on the state party's exercise of its executive jurisdiction. Article 1 is then merely an umbrella clause that attributes violations of the Convention to its states parties to the extent that they exercise their jurisdiction extra-territorially.

At first sight, this approach could emphasise that Article 1 can extend only to such acts of contracting states that take place in situations in relation to which states are entitled to exercise jurisdiction under general international law or under a specific treaty that confers such jurisdiction. This would arguably exclude situations where the state acts unlawfully in the first place, for instance through the unlawful incursion into or presence in the relevant foreign territory, because such situations would fall outside that state's jurisdiction. Such narrow reading of Article 1 is unsustainable, given that Article 1 has been used to cover situations where the state acted despite a manifest lack of ordinary jurisdiction under international law (for example *Drozd* and *Loizidou*). In *Banković* the relevant NATO states had no ordinary jurisdiction over the territory of FRY. The acts concerned were still performed by those under the jurisdiction of those states even if the ultimate effect of those acts was displayed where the NATO states had no obvious and lawful jurisdictional reach.

In other words, the approach that even if individuals are encountered in situations where the state party in question has no obvious jurisdiction on lawful grounds applying its jurisdiction and authority through those acts relating to victims, is more plausible. The alternative approach, reducing 'jurisdiction' under Article 1 to situations where states have lawful jurisdiction over individuals, territory or situation, is simply unworkable and has been repeatedly dismissed in the European Court's jurisprudence.[27]

---

[27] To illustrate further, diplomatic personnel are obviously exempted from the host state's jurisdiction; yet by violating their ECHR rights the host state undoubtedly and indisputably exercises jurisdiction over them and brings them within Article 1.

C. Application in Judicial Practice

Once the ordinary meaning of 'jurisdiction' under Article 1 is identified, we need to verify how its treatment has evolved in the Strasbourg jurisprudence. The early case of *W.M.* has identified Article 1 'jurisdiction' with the actual impact on the relevant individuals. As the European Commission on Human Rights observed,

> these complaints are directed mainly against Danish diplomatic authorities in the former DDR. It is clear, in this respect, from the constant jurisprudence of the Commission that authorised agents of a State, including diplomatic or consular agents, bring other persons or property within the jurisdiction of that State to the extent that they exercise authority over such persons or property. In so far as they affect such persons or property by their acts or omissions, the responsibility of the State is engaged.[28]

Thus, 'jurisdiction' derives from no more than the actual impact over individuals, whether lawful or not. In that case the ambassador had exercised executive jurisdiction over the individual in question by transferring them from the embassy premises to GDR authorities. Even though the matter took place on embassy premises, the Commission did not rely on the locus factor. Instead it relied on the broader factor of affecting persons and their property.

The merits decision in the *Loizidou* case confirmed that the extra-territorial element in Article 1 is its regular, not exceptional, aspect. The Court treated this as a question of imputability and emphasised, pursuant to the preliminary objections judgment in the same case, that:

> under its established case-law the concept of 'jurisdiction' under Article 1 of the Convention is not restricted to the national territory of the Contracting States. Accordingly, the responsibility of Contracting States can be involved by acts and omissions of their authorities which produce effects outside their own territory.[29]

The exceptionality argument emerged later in the case-law, especially in *Banković*, and this confirms that this argument is not an inherent part of the reasoning regarding Article 1. The *Loizidou* approach was reiterated in *Issa*, which specified in a comprehensive manner that 'a State may also be held accountable for violation of the Convention rights and freedoms of persons who are in the territory of another State but who are found to be under the former State's authority and control through its agents operating – whether lawfully or unlawfully – in the latter State'.[30] The exercise of jurisdiction then inherently, almost definitionally, arises from the exercise of a state's authority through its agents, officials and officers.

---

[28] *W.M. v Denmark*, No. 17392/90, Commission Decision, 14 October 1992, *Decisions and Reports* (DR) 73, 'The Law' section, at para. 1.

[29] *Loizidou v Turkey* (GC) (Merits) Judgment, 18 December 1996, at para. 52 (hereinafter '*Loizidou* (GC) (Merits)') (referring to para. 62 of the preliminary objections judgment).

[30] *Issa*, supra n.23, at para. 71. In *Smith* Lord Phillips observed that *Issa* 'clearly advances state agent authority as an alternative to effective territorial control as a basis of Article 1 jurisdiction'. *Smith*, supra n.17, at para. 20 (*per* Lord Phillips).

The post-*Banković* jurisprudence reveals a rather inconvenient trend to accommodate the *Banković* limitation on 'jurisdiction' while trying not to accord too much effect to *Banković* because, as presumably realised within the Strasbourg Court, it could limit the Convention's scope so as to make it virtually impossible to apply to extra-territorial situations. The *Medvedyev* case, which involved an enforcement operation conducted by French naval authorities on the high seas against those who were not nationals of states parties to the ECHR, illustrates the uneasy compromise of seeking a middle way. The *Medvedyev* Court summarised the approach as follows:

> In its first Loizidou judgment (*preliminary objections*), for example, the Court found that bearing in mind the object and purpose of the Convention, the responsibility of a Contracting Party might also arise when as a consequence of military action – whether lawful or unlawful – it exercised effective control of an area outside its national territory (see *Loizidou v. Turkey* (*preliminary objections*) [GC], 23 March 1995, 62, Series A no. 310). This excluded situations, however, where – as in the Banković case – what was at issue was an instantaneous extraterritorial act, as the provisions of Article 1 did not admit of a 'cause-and-effect' notion of 'jurisdiction' (*Banković*, § 75).[31]

But this is not a completely accurate reading of *Loizidou* as it did not include that which was later considered outside the scope of Article 1 in *Banković*. *Loizidou* did not restrict the *Drozd* principle, but actually expanded it to include the acts of subordinate administrations, like that of the Turkish Republic of Northern Cyprus (hereinafter 'TRNC'), even if their acts were not strictly the acts of the respondent state within Article 1.[32] *Banković*, however, approached this in reverse order and found 'effective control' to be a precondition for, not one of the implications of, the attributability of the relevant act to the relevant state party. Therefore, *Banković* contradicted the previous case-law without explaining the reasons for this contradiction, and so treating it as a leading case is unsound.

The *Medvedyev* Court also alluded to France's 'full and exclusive' control over the victims in order to include the relevant acts within the scope of Article 1. Under this restrictive approach, if the French forces had simply shot the victims Article 1 would not have covered that situation. Alternatively, if the French forces had intercepted a neutral civilian ship on the high seas, without any entitlement to do so under general international law, they could potentially exercise full and effective control over the victims but no lawful jurisdiction under the law of the sea or any relevant principle of international law. Effective and full control would then create responsibility in the absence of state jurisdiction.[33] How the complex and nuanced qualification of 'jurisdiction' can be read into the text of Article 1 remains a mystery that so far neither courts nor academic commentators have succeeded to explain and substantiate. For if unlawful occupation of territory, as per *Loizidou*, can fall within Article 1, so can an unlawful interception of a ship. In both cases the agents of the state are under that

---

[31] *Medvedyev* (GC), *supra* n.21, at para. 64.
[32] Regarding the 'effective control' aspect see sub-section 'E' below.
[33] There still would, as per above, be French jurisdiction exercised over its own naval forces. It is this, as opposed to 'full control', that has really brought the situation within Article 1.

state's jurisdiction. Even if French naval forces were to have no lawful jurisdiction over the relevant individuals, their own action would be an exercise of the French executive jurisdiction and that jurisdiction, and *a fortiori* Article 1, would then also cover the victims.

To illustrate this process even further, the *Pad v Turkey* case deviates from the *Banković* 'exceptional extra-territoriality' approach to an important extent. The applicants, predictably enough, argued '[r]elying on the Court's established case-law relating to the exceptional circumstances capable of extending jurisdiction extraterritorially', and submitted that 'the Turkish Government should be held accountable for violations of the Convention rights and freedoms of their relatives who were found to have been under the authority and control of the Turkish army forces operating within the territory of Iran'.[34] The Turkish Government asserted that the acts in question took place on Turkish territory.[35] There was thus a disagreement as to the locus of the act. The Court declined to become entangled in that disagreement, instead pointing out, in more categorical terms, that:

> While the applicants attached great importance to the prior establishment of the exercise by Turkey of extraterritorial jurisdiction with a view to proving their allegations on the merits, the Court considers that it is not required to determine the exact location of the impugned events, given that the Government had already admitted that the fire discharged from the helicopters had caused the killing of the applicants' relatives.[36]

Jurisdiction under Article 1 would be present whether the killing took place in Turkey or Iran as soon as it was actually performed by Turkish authorities. In other words, the Court admits here that once a state's armed forces fly over foreign territory and kill civilians, Article 1 is engaged without any further requirements of effective control needing to be satisfied. The Court therefore once again subscribes to the agency and cause-and-effect approach and effectively, even if impliedly, overrules *Banković*, which similarly involved the actions of the air force over foreign territory.[37]

This brings us to the question as to what would be the scope of Article 1 in relation to an 'instantaneous extra-territorial act', such as an abduction or assassination, which by definition constitutes an exercise of regular jurisdiction by the state party. It would be against both the ordinary meaning of 'jurisdiction' under Article 1 and the object and purpose of the Convention to exclude such instantaneous acts from the scope of this instrument. Yet this is what *Banković* has done in relation to aerial bombardment and is what again makes *Banković* incompatible with the object and purpose of the Convention, as on face value acts like assassination and abduction would also be placed outside the Convention's scope.

On balance, the notion of 'instantaneous act' is not an independent criterion but an element of a broader state agency test, focusing on the latter's one particular category.

---

[34] *Mansur Pad and others v Turkey*, No. 60167/00, Admissibility Decision, 28 June 2007, at para. 48 (hereinafter '*Pad*').

[35] *Ibid.*, at para. 51.

[36] *Ibid.*, at para. 54.

[37] The case was dismissed for non-exhaustion of local remedies, but for which it would have proceeded to merits on the above terms.

The only standard that can make sense across the board is the cause-and-effect standard underlying the state agency test, even though some judicial decisions have distanced themselves from it. It is worth emphasising that the reluctance of some judicial decisions to accept this standard casts doubt on the credibility of those decisions, not on the validity of the cause-and-effect standard, for those decisions have excluded those acts to which it obviously applies, through its ordinary meaning, object and purpose, from the Convention's scope.

A straightforward and reliable approach, then, is to follow the wording of Article 1 and apply it to situations where the relevant state exercises its own jurisdiction one way or another. Article 1 offers no categorisation of those situations such as mainstream, regular, special or exceptional. Once the exercise of jurisdiction by the state party is ascertained, its 'regular' or 'exceptional' nature can only be descriptive and have merely semantic importance. The 'exceptions' to the 'territorial' nature of Article 1 are not in reality exceptional, but are inherent in this provision. In other words, the extra-territorial effect of Article 1 can be exceptional only in empirical terms, in the sense that the number of cases where states parties are held responsible for acts committed outside their territory will be far less than the instances of violation of the Convention within their territories; exceptionality is, however, not a categorical requirement that can be superimposed on individual cases where Article 1 'jurisdiction' will be found to exist on regular grounds.

D. Specific Headings of 'Exceptionality'

Once we have ascertained that the 'exceptionality' approach to the extra-territorial nature of Article 1 lacks merit, we have to examine some judicial pronouncements as to how that 'exceptionality' is apparently manifested in specific situations. To illustrate this narrow approach, Lord Brown suggested in *Al-Skeini* that Baha Mousa fell within Article 1 on the narrow basis of extra-territorial exception applicable to embassies,[38] which presumably applied by analogy to army bases.

But such isolated extra-territorial extensions do not make sense unless they are substantiated by reference to broader concepts and principles that justify the extra-territorial approach as such and on its own. To illustrate, it would be meaningless to argue that the Convention is primarily territorial but exceptionally extends specifically to ships or embassies. Exceptionality of that kind cannot be constituted by ship, army base or embassy, and the Convention simply cannot extend to these beyond the contracting state's territory unless some broader underlying principle built in Article 1 takes it there. This was not how the Supreme Court approached the matter in *Smith*. Lord Phillips saw the task as identifying whether Article 1 provided an extra-territorial exception specifically for armed forces deployed abroad:

> The question then is whether, applying the original meaning principle, it is right to include a State's armed forces abroad as falling within the jurisdiction of the State for purposes of article 1 by reason of the special status that they enjoy ... as the Grand Chamber pointed out

---

[38] *Al-Skeini* (HL), *supra* n.22, at para. 132 (*per* Lord Brown).

in *Bankovic*, [this proposition was] not reflected by State practice. It is, furthermore, almost wholly unsupported by Strasbourg jurisprudence.

Lord Phillips was likewise unconvinced with the argument that diplomatic and consular

> officials were themselves within the jurisdiction of their States and that the same principle should apply to the armed forces. ... The question [was] whether, in concluding the Convention, the contracting States agreed that article 1 jurisdiction should extend to armed forces when serving abroad as an exception to the essentially territorial nature of that jurisdiction.[39]

But this confuses the matter. It is, quite simply, moot to enquire into whether states parties have agreed that armed forces, embassies or ships specifically fall within Article 1. Through Article 1 states parties agreed that situations involving state jurisdiction are covered, but they did not agree a definition or limit on this jurisdiction. When armed forces are abroad, it is plainly absurd to say that the sending state stops having control, command, direction and personal jurisdiction over them, or that the lawfulness of their conduct is no longer controlled by the sending state's legal system. Under Lord Phillips' two concepts of jurisdiction examined above, armed forces abroad remain firmly within the scope of Article 1.

As Lord Brown 'recognised at the outset, our armed forces abroad *are* subject not only to UK military law but also to the UK's general criminal and civil law'.[40] However, Lord Hope agreed with Lord Phillips on armed forces, adding that '[t]o hold otherwise would be to go beyond the categories that have hitherto been recognised by the Strasbourg Court in cases that do not arise from the effective control of territory within the Council of Europe area'.[41] More significantly, Lord Hope's approach is premised on the thesis that even though armed forces are under the sending state's jurisdiction in the first place, *prima facie* at least falling within Article 1, the 'effective control' and *espace juridique* factors as developed in *Banković* reverse this presumption and exempt armed forces from the ambit of Article 1. Lord Hope further stated that there are no policy grounds for extending Article 1 to armed forces,[42] which is premised on perceiving Article 1 as having no independent content and is instead only informed by Courts' decisions. This approach runs counter to the legal framework of treaty interpretation.

The principal problem with the decision in *Banković*, and the adherence to it in subsequent House of Lords decisions, has been the failure to acknowledge that Article 1 ECHR is an independent treaty provision whose content and scope are not contingent on gradual case-by-case formulation and extension by international and national courts. Its content and scope should instead be ascertained through the use of regular methods of treaty interpretation under the 1969 Vienna Convention, among which the ordinary and natural meaning of 'jurisdiction' under Article 1 and the purposes it serves as part

---

[39] *Smith*, *supra* n.17, at paras 46, 50–53 (*per* Lord Phillips).
[40] *Smith*, *supra* n.17, at para. 143 (*per* Lord Brown); *ibid.*, at para. 191 (*per* Lord Mance).
[41] *Ibid.*, at para. 90 (*per* Lord Hope). This projects the *espace juridique* thesis and does not accord with most of the Strasbourg jurisprudence. On *espace juridique* see sub-section F below.
[42] *Smith*, *supra* n.17, at para. 91 (*per* Lord Hope); *ibid.*, at para. 308 (*per* Lord Collins).

of the overall ECHR framework are most prominent. This approach, as opposed to the case-by-case approach, is the only one that acknowledges the relevance of Article 1 as states parties have agreed upon it, rather than regarding its content and scope as being dependent on occasional judicial pronouncements. The latter approach essentially subverts the nature of ECHR as an agreement among states by imagining it as part of judge-made law, which is both intellectually unconvincing and practically inconsistent. To an important extent, the Grand Chamber decision in *Al-Skeini* has rectified the outcomes of this misunderstanding by distancing itself from the approach that projects abstract limitations onto the concept of jurisdiction.[43] The distinctive virtue of *Al-Skeini* (GC) is precisely its abstraction from individual instances of past jurisprudence and the grounding of its approach into what Article 1 suggests when properly interpreted pursuant to the rules of treaty interpretation.

E. 'Effective Control'

As the previous section demonstrated, the Strasbourg jurisprudence initially postulated the notion of the 'primarily territorial' jurisdiction but then allowed the extra-territorial exceptions to effectively swallow up the 'primary territorial' postulate. The rather diverse application of the notion of 'effective control' has also been part of that process. After *Banković*, the 'effective control' requirement was used by the House of Lords in *Al-Skeini* to the effect that Baha Mousa was found to have died under the effective control of British troops and so was covered by Article 1. It is not immediately clear how other applicants in *Al-Skeini* or the troops themselves, as in *Smith*, were beyond the reach of Article 1. Lord Rodger in *Al-Skeini* suggested that pursuant to *Banković* 'the obligation under article 1 can arise only where the contracting state has such effective control of the territory of another state that it could secure to everyone in the territory all the rights and freedoms in Section 1 of the Convention'.[44] This treats effective control as a separate factual requirement that needs to be satisfied before the legal regime established by the Convention can be brought into play at all. The duty under Article 1 depends, then, on the factual ability to secure the relevant rights. However, even under that approach the factual ability to kill or not to kill is actually the ability to secure or not to secure the freedom from arbitrary deprivation of life and the result is the same whether the killing in question is committed within or outside the state's territory.

Lord Rodger then alluded to *Issa* and specified in relation to five applicants other than Baha Mousa that 'the facts would not justify the conclusion that the deceased were, in any real sense, under the control of the particular British soldiers who were, or

---

[43] Mainly through the treatment of the 'effective control' and *espace juridique* issues; see below sub-sections E and F.

[44] *Al-Skeini* (HL), *supra* n.22, at para. 79 (*per* Lord Rodger); further observing that 'even applying the approach in *Issa*, I would not consider that the United Kingdom was in effective control of Basra and the surrounding area for purposes of jurisdiction under article 1 of the Convention at the relevant time', at para. 83. But nothing in *Issa* requires control of territory as such.

may have been, responsible for their deaths'.[45] But this is a rather curious result, as it essentially contends that if an individual is taken into custody by a state and then killed, the act falls within that state's jurisdiction; however, if that individual is killed instantly then the state has no jurisdiction over the act.

In principle, it would be right to suggest that if the basic requirement of Article 1 remains jurisdiction as an entitlement to act, as a matter of general international law, then 'effective control' can no longer be a crucial requirement. 'Effective control', 'full control', 'control and authority' are not terms enshrined in Article 1, nor do they possess any authority greater than a court's occasional pronouncement would have on its own. Therefore the meaning of these concepts has to be identified as part of the interpretation of Article 1 in terms of its ordinary meaning and the object and purpose of the Convention.

First, it should be specified whether it is about the 'effective control' of the act and conduct in question, or of the territory on which it is committed. Usually, under general international law 'effective control' is relevant only as control over the actor and the wrongful act is then attributed to the relevant state.[46] The ECHR-specific treatment of this notion does not, in principle, contradict this perspective, although Strasbourg jurisprudence has developed its further features. One aspect of this is the negative effect that without having effective control as a matter of fact the state party cannot exercise Article 1 'jurisdiction' over the events in question, even if the area in question may officially be under its sovereign jurisdiction of 'effective control', to the effect that its absence can be a valid defence if the state party cannot, as a matter of fact, exercise 'jurisdiction' over the events in question, even if the area in question may officially fall under its sovereign jurisdiction.[47] The lack of 'effective control' will prevent attribution along similar lines to the way attribution operates as a matter of general law on state responsibility. However *Ilaşcu v Moldova & Russia* illustrates, problematically, that Article 1 has been applied even where the 'effective control' by a state party is plainly lacking and the matter cannot be attributable to the state party under general international law.[48]

Another important question is whether all that matters is the actual exercise of 'effective control', or whether the way in which 'effective control' was obtained over the victims is also relevant. In practice, differentiating between these two aspects may not be practicable. The *Medvedyev* decision, for instance, refers to the 'total and

---

[45] *Al-Skeini* (HL), *supra* n.22, at para. 82 (*per* Lord Rodger).

[46] *Military and Paramilitary Activities in and against Nicaragua* (Nicaragua v United States of America), Merits, [1986] ICJ Rep. 14, at 61–65; Article 8 on State Responsibility and its commentary, Report of the International Law Commission on the work of its Fifty-third Session (2001), *Official Records of the General Assembly, Fifty-sixth Session, Supplement No. 10* (A/56/10).

[47] *An v Cyprus*, 13 *HRLJ*, 153 (hereinafter '*An*').

[48] *Ilaşcu and Others v Moldova and Russia* (GC), No. 48787/99, Judgment, 8 July 2004 (hereinafter '*Ilaşcu* (GC)'). For a detailed analysis see A. Orakhelashvili, 'Division of Reparation between Responsible Entities', in J. Crawford, A. Pellet and S. Olleson (eds), *The Law of International Responsibility* (Oxford: Oxford University Press, 2010), 647, at 659–660.

exclusive' control over relevant individuals by French authorities,[49] but is silent as to the ways in which such 'effective control' was obtained. This partial evaluation of the underlying facts and the consequent basing of the decision on the fact that the violations in question occurred *while* France was exercising effective control over the relevant individuals, allowed the Strasbourg Court to present its findings as being in line with the decision in *Banković*. However, the question of the means of obtaining that 'effective control' is still part of the picture and while in *Medvedyev* the facts were such as to not necessitate the examination of those means, in other cases it may be more pressing to do so. What needs to be understood is whether the methods and means of obtaining 'effective control' over persons, situations or territory are also part of that 'effective control'. That initial process of obtaining 'effective control' can be displayed by the relevant State party either within or without its own national territory. There is substantial evidence to suggest that 'effective control' is not an indispensable requirement for the application of Article 1, as several cases did not treat it as such. In the early case of *X v UK* (1979),[50] a British employee of the European Commission in Brussels was found to be within the jurisdiction of the UK under Article 1. Due to a British domestic decision the applicant, while abroad, could not vote in British elections although UK diplomatic representatives could. If there was any 'effective control' it was over the act that this domestic decision constituted, not over the individual in question. The individual was merely affected by the decision.

The case of *Stephens v Malta* further illustrates that violations of the Convention can be attributed to the state notwithstanding the lack of effective control over the applicant. The Court encountered a situation where one state acted at the request or instigation of another state, and noted that:

> the applicant was under the control and authority of the Spanish authorities in the period between his arrest and detention in Spain on 5 August 2004 and his release on bail on 22 November 2004. In so far as the alleged unlawfulness of his arrest and detention is concerned, it cannot be overlooked that the applicant's deprivation of liberty had its sole origin in the measures taken exclusively by the Maltese authorities pursuant to the arrangements agreed on by both Malta and Spain under the European Convention on Extradition.[51]

Therefore, the applicant's complaints under Article 5 were held to engage the responsibility of Malta under the Convention. This demonstrates a line of reasoning regarding Article 1, independent of any effective control requirements. The instigation of the acts causing the violation of the Convention brings the matter within the 'jurisdiction' of the state that instigated it, even though it did not physically perform

---

[49] It was similarly specified in *Al-Saadoon*, that 'given the total and exclusive *de facto*, and subsequently also *de jure*, control exercised by the United Kingdom authorities over the premises in question, the individuals detained there, including the applicants, were within the United Kingdom's jurisdiction', *Al-Saadoon & Mufdhi v UK*, No. 61498/08, Judgment, 2 March 2010, at para. 88. Note however that the European Court adopted this approach by expressly following the House of Lords approach in *Al-Skeini*, which was later overruled in *Al-Skeini* (GC) in favour of a more relaxed and dynamic understanding of 'effective control'.

[50] *X v United Kingdom* (1979) 15 *DR* 137.

[51] *Stephens v Malta*, No. 11956/07, Judgment, 21 September 2009, at para. 51.

it.⁵² The threshold is thus far lower than requiring actual effective control over the act in question, let alone over the underlying situation.

First mentioned in *Loizidou*,⁵³ 'effective control' came to supplement, not displace, the agency and cause-and-effect approach. In principle, any act committed by state agents of whatever description and covered by that state's 'effective control' of the territory can be attributed to that state as an act of its agents without 'effective control' being of crucial importance. The only independent relevance 'effective control' may have, and why it was introduced in *Loizidou*, is to create a presumption of attributability for acts performed in the territory where the state in question exercises that 'effective control', even if those acts are not technically performed by that state's agents. The underlying message to the state in question is: 'you are now in effective control and thus responsible for more than just your agent's actions.' This was demonstrated by *Loizidou*, attributing the conduct performed by the unrecognised entity of TRNC to Turkey. As the *Loizidou* merits judgment observed,

> It is not necessary to determine whether, as the applicant and the Government of Cyprus have suggested, Turkey actually exercises detailed control over the policies and actions of the authorities of the 'TRNC'. It is obvious from the large number of troops engaged in active duties in northern Cyprus that her army exercises effective overall control over that part of the island. Such control, according to the relevant test and in the circumstances of the case, entails her responsibility for the policies and actions of the 'TRNC'. Those affected by such policies or actions therefore come within the 'jurisdiction' of Turkey for the purposes of Article 1 of the Convention. Her obligation to secure to the applicant the rights and freedoms set out in the Convention therefore extends to the northern part of Cyprus.⁵⁴

Turkey was thus responsible, over and above its own deeds, for acts performed by the TRNC administration, despite the individual acts of that administration not, strictly speaking, being attributable to Turkey. This approach is further reaffirmed by the Grand Chamber in *Al-Skeini*, specifying that,

> Where the fact of such domination over the territory is established, it is not necessary to determine whether the Contracting State exercises detailed control over the policies and actions of the subordinate local administration. The fact that the local administration survives as a result of the Contracting State's military and other support entails that State's responsibility for its policies and actions.⁵⁵

---

⁵² This could differ from *An* and *Ilaşcu* (GC), *supra* nn.47, 48 because in those cases Cyprus and Moldova did not instigate the violation nor did anything to aid, support or sustain it.

⁵³ *Loizidou* (GC) (Preliminary Objections), *supra* n.19.

⁵⁴ *Loizidou* (GC) (Merits), *supra* n.29, at para. 56; this writer has repeatedly pointed to these considerations: see A. Orakhelashvili, 'Restrictive Interpretation of Human Rights Treaties in the Recent Jurisprudence of the European Court of Human Rights, (2003) 14 *EJIL* 529; A. Orakhelashvili, *The Interpretation of Acts and Rules in Public International Law* (Oxford: Oxford University Press, 2008), Chapter 5 (hereinafter 'Orakhelashvili, *Interpretation*'); A. Orakhelashvili, *Governmental Activities on Foreign Territory*, Max-Planck Encyclopaedia of Public International Law, available at www.mpepil.com.

⁵⁵ *Al-Skeini* (GC), *supra* n.1, at para. 138.

As for the application of the 'effective control' factor in *Al-Skeini*, the Grand Chamber observed that:

> in *Medvedyev and Others v. France* the Court held that the applicants were within French jurisdiction by virtue of the exercise by French agents of full and exclusive control over a ship and its crew from the time of its interception in international waters. The Court does not consider that jurisdiction in the above cases arose solely from the control exercised by the Contracting State over the buildings, aircraft or ship in which the individuals were held. What is decisive in such cases is the exercise of physical power and control over the person in question.[56]

This is also in line with the above point regarding the commencement of 'effective control' and the means through which it has been obtained. Physical control and power, which as a matter of fact was exercised in a building or on a ship, has effectively amounted to effective control. This is not to say that it was effective control because it was exercised in a building or on a ship as an extension of the British or French public authority in the first place. Therefore, *Al-Skeini* (GC) essentially associates 'effective control' with the implications of state agency action and the consequent causal impact on victims. Even after *Al-Skeini* (GC), 'effective control' is not a separate condition of applicability of Article 1, but merely an interpretative tool to describe how, in the relevant case, Article 1 'jurisdiction' has come to be exercised on the ground. *Loizidou*, by emphasising that effective control is only one of several ways to identify the applicability of Article 1 (by using the word 'also'), has reinforced the relativity of the distinction between state agency and 'effective control'. The later *Solomou v Turkey* judgment treats these matters in reverse order; it mentions that responsibility arises in the case of effective control, and then adds that,

> Moreover, a State may *also* be held accountable for a violation of the Convention rights and freedoms of persons who are in the territory of another State but who are found to be under the former State's authority and control through its agents operating – whether lawfully or unlawfully – in the latter State. Accountability in such situations stems from the fact that Article 1 of the Convention cannot be interpreted so as to allow a State party to perpetrate violations of the Convention on the territory of another State which it could not perpetrate on its own territory. In addition, the acquiescence or connivance of the authorities of a Contracting State in the acts of private individuals which violate the Convention rights of other individuals within its jurisdiction may engage that State's responsibility under the Convention. Any different conclusion would be at variance with the obligation contained in Article 1 of the Convention.[57]

This is a rather broad, but necessary, statement reflecting the categorical nature of human rights obligations under the European Convention, linking its applicability to what states actually do, largely ignoring the context in which the act in question was performed, or of how state agents got to the point of performing it. Further, following *Loizidou*, *Solomou* specifies that:

---

[56] *Ibid.*, at para. 136.
[57] *Solomou v Turkey*, No. 36832/07, Judgment, 24 June 2008, at paras 45–46 (emphasis added) (hereinafter '*Solomou*').

since [Turkey] had effective overall control over northern Cyprus, Turkey's responsibility could not be confined to the acts of its own soldiers or officials in northern Cyprus but had also to be engaged by virtue of the acts of the local administration which survived by virtue of Turkish military and other support. It follows that, in terms of Article 1 of the Convention, Turkey's jurisdiction must be considered to extend to securing the entire range of substantive rights set out in the Convention and those additional Protocols which it has ratified, and that violations of those rights are imputable to Turkey.[58]

This illustrates an additional point, despite Lord Phillips suggesting, well after *Solomou*, in *Smith* that 'effective control' is premised on the actual ability to safeguard all Convention rights to the individual in question in the relevant territory: jurisdiction, as part of responsibility, will be present whenever 'effective control' exercised by the respondent state over the relevant entity is demonstrated. This effectively negates Lord Phillips' point that 'effective control', in the sense of factual ability to secure the range of Convention rights, is a necessary precondition for 'jurisdiction' under Article 1 to exist. *Solomou* treats the matters in reverse order, specifying that wherever as a matter of fact the state has effective control over the situation or entity, it will be covered by Article 1 'jurisdiction', including acts that are not strictly its own if the state agency test alone were to be applied. Accordingly, as far as action by state agents as such is concerned, 'effective control' is not a strict requirement.

Capitalising on previous jurisprudence and having analysed relevant evidence, including Security Council resolutions, the European Court of Human Rights observed in *Al-Skeini* that:

> following the removal from power of the Ba'ath regime and until the accession of the Interim Government, the United Kingdom (together with the United States) assumed in Iraq the exercise of some of the public powers normally to be exercised by a sovereign government. In particular, the United Kingdom assumed authority and responsibility for the maintenance of security in South East Iraq. In these exceptional circumstances, the Court considers that the United Kingdom, through its soldiers engaged in security operations in Basrah during the period in question, exercised authority and control *over individuals* killed in the course of such security operations, so as to establish a jurisdictional link between the deceased and the United Kingdom for the purposes of Article 1 of the Convention.[59]

Therefore, British forces were in 'effective control' of the relevant situation in Basra, triggered Article 1 and thus had jurisdiction over the victims under that clause, regardless of the way in which they got to Basra and then ended up engaging people in security operations. The principle is understandably broader than the set of facts to which it has been applied by the Grand Chamber and the 'exceptionality' of that approach appears to be a mere façade. The *Al-Skeini* (GC) decision thus moves on from the previous *Al-Saadoon* and *Medvedyev* decisions which alluded to the notion of 'total' control. *Al-Skeini* comes closer to viewing effective control as a relative concept,

---

[58] *Ibid.*, at para. 47. Furthermore, given that 'the bullets which had hit Mr Solomou had been fired by the members of the Turkish-Cypriot forces', it was their act as an entity controlled by Turkey, and through these acts the firing has become attributable to Turkey in terms of its jurisdiction and effective control. *Ibid.*, at paras 50–51.

[59] *Al-Skeini* (GC), *supra* n.1, at para. 149 (emphasis added).

effectively associating it with impact on individuals, rather than a broader notion of control covering a particular area or territory.

In applying this approach to individual victims the Grand Chamber noted that:

> the deaths of the first, second, fourth, fifth and sixth applicants' relatives were caused by the acts of British soldiers during the course of or contiguous to security operations carried out by British forces in various parts of Basrah City. It follows that in all these cases there was a jurisdictional link for the purposes of Article 1 of the Convention between the United Kingdom and the deceased. The third applicant's wife was killed during an exchange of fire between a patrol of British soldiers and unidentified gunmen and it is not known which side fired the fatal bullet. The Court considers that, since the death occurred in the course of a United Kingdom security operation, when British soldiers carried out a patrol in the vicinity of the applicant's home and joined in the fatal exchange of fire, there was a jurisdictional link between the United Kingdom and this deceased also.[60]

Therefore, a sustainable version of 'effective control' regards it as one of the incidences of extra-territorial 'jurisdiction' existing pursuant to Article 1 rather than as its necessary precondition. Consequently, when a state agent encounters an individual the state is deemed to have 'effective control' over any act perpetrated by the agent against the individual.

F. Object and Purpose of a Treaty: *Espace Juridique* and the Regional Nature of the ECHR

It will be recalled that one of the principal bases of reasoning in *Banković* was that the European Convention is a regional treaty primarily designed to apply in Europe as its *espace juridique*, because Article 1 requires that no vacuum should exist in places to which the Convention already applies within the Council of Europe's membership.[61] A fundamental problem with the approach projecting the regional nature of the Convention is that, if applied as a straightforward principle, it will totally negate the liability of states parties for their extra-territorial acts. Another problem with the regional nature approach is that it is inconsistent with the principle that the Convention imposes objective obligations assumed by states parties towards individuals whether or not they are nationals of states parties. In the early case of *Austria v Italy* the attribution of acts to the respondent took place on the basis that it was a party to the Convention when those acts were committed, even though Austria was not. The European Commission explained that in becoming a party to the Convention a state undertakes to secure the Convention rights and freedoms 'not only to its own nationals and those of other High Contracting Parties but also to nationals of States not parties to the Convention and to stateless persons'.[62] If the conduct of NATO states were not covered by the Convention

---

[60] *Ibid.*, at para. 150.
[61] *Banković* (GC), *supra* n.15, at para. 80.
[62] *Austria v Italy*, 4 *YB ECHR* (1961), at 136–140; see further *Ireland v UK*, 58 ILR 188, at 291; *Cyprus v Turkey*, 8007/77, 13 *DR*, 147; A. Orakhelashvili, *Peremptory Norms in International Law* (Oxford: Oxford University Press, 2004), at Chapter 4; A. Orakhelashvili, 'Commentary to Article 30 of the 1969 Vienna Convention on the Law of Treaties (Application of Successive Treaties relating to the Same Subject Matter)', in P. Klein and O. Corten (eds),

because FRY nationals are not nationals of an ECHR state party, then the applicability of the Convention would be differentiated depending on whose national the victim is; this approach is fundamentally inimical to the Convention's legal order. The Convention's territorial scope is thus inseparable from the objective nature of its obligations.

Furthermore, the 'regional' approach almost definitionally stumbles at the 'essentially territorial' nature of jurisdiction under general international law and manifests the internal inconsistency in the reasoning of the *Banković* decision. For, even if *Banković* were correct in adopting the 'primarily' or 'essentially' territorial nature of state jurisdiction that then gets incorporated from general international law into Article 1, the territoriality of jurisdiction also relates to the place where the relevant act was commenced, not just to where its final effect was displayed. Therefore, even if the 'regional' approach is strictly applied, states parties should be held responsible for acts that have been committed from within their 'essentially territorial' jurisdictional space under Article 1.

For these reasons, the *espace juridique* thesis essentially exists to reflect some ideological perceptions as to what the European Convention is for, but never to make substantial impacts in subsequent cases. Several cases, such as *Medvedyev*, *Issa*, *Pad* and *Al-Saadoon*, are related to extra-territorial violations, but have arrived at their outcomes without the 'regional' argument standing in the way. The fact that in *Al-Skeini* Lord Rodger articulated the difficulty in reconciling *Issa* with the regional character of the Convention and with its application to events in Iraq,[63] is yet another confirmation that the House of Lords has afforded far greater weight to the 'regional' approach than it has been given in Strasbourg's jurisprudence. The Grand Chamber in *Al-Skeini* also declined to treat the 'regional' approach as determinative of the merit of Article 1 claims, specifying that 'the importance of establishing the occupying State's jurisdiction in such cases does not imply, *a contrario*, that jurisdiction under Article 1 of the Convention can never exist outside the territory covered by the Council of Europe Member States'.[64]

It appears that, in the majority of cases, both the requirements of 'effective control' and *espace juridique* are attempts to read restrictions into Article 1 that are not there. As the Permanent Court specified in *Acquisition of Polish Nationality*, when the text of a treaty clause is clear, the Court 'is bound to apply this clause as it stands, without considering whether other provisions might with advantage have been added to or substituted for it. ... To impose an additional condition not provided for [in the Treaty text], would be equivalent not to interpreting the Treaty, but to reconstructing it'.[65] Most importantly, the European Convention is there not to provide enhanced protection of human rights to people within its member states as compared to the protection people outside the ECHR region enjoy. It is there instead to ensure that states parties

---

Commentary to the Vienna Convention of the Law of Treaties (Oxford: Oxford University Press, 2011), 764, at 777–780.

[63] *Al-Skeini* (HL), *supra* n.22, at paras 76–77 (*per* Lord Rodger); see also Lord Hope, above notes 41–42.

[64] *Ibid.*, at para. 142.

[65] *Acquisition of Polish Nationality*, Advisory Opinion of 15 September 1923, PCIJ Series B, No. 7, 6, at 20.

are held accountable for violating basic human rights that all individuals enjoy, wherever those violations should take place and whoever's nationals they are. The effect of the ECHR goes by the identity of the respondent state, not by the locus of the violation. The Convention's regional character only means that it applies to states of the region that signed and ratified it, not that it cannot apply to their action outside that region.

G. Subsequent Practice within the ECHR Framework

Under Article 31(3)(b) of the 1969 Vienna Convention, for the purposes of treaty interpretation, 'any subsequent practice in the application of the treaty which establishes the agreement of the parties regarding its interpretation … shall be taken into account'. 'Subsequent practice' is a popular concept raised in multiple adjudications, yet its strict requirements are rarely satisfied, there being very few cases where the meaning of treaty provisions has been identified by reference to it.[66] The inter-state agreement underlying 'subsequent practice' is qualitatively and evidentially the same as that amounting to the conclusion of the original treaty, or to the creation of a new customary norm. Therefore it makes perfect sense to assume that presumption should ordinarily be against the existence of 'subsequent practice', for states should not, in the absence of a clear and affirmative indication, be thought to have modified the treaty they themselves signed and ratified. The above 'classical' version of 'subsequent practice' does not apply to its full extent to treaties where a supervisory organ has been established to interpret and apply the treaty in question. Similarly, all Strasbourg jurisprudence examined above effectively amounts to the ECHR's subsequent practice under Article 31(3)(b) of the 1969 Vienna Convention. States parties must be deemed to have accepted that the European Court's practice as to the meaning of the Convention provisions is a better indication of 'subsequent practice' than isolated unilateral statements by states parties themselves. Nevertheless, there is no evidence that the practice of states parties themselves has ever been displayed or developed with the intention or the means of satisfying the requirements in order to amount to 'subsequent practice' under Article 31(3)(b), and all we are left with is the practice of Strasbourg organs.

This approach is substantiated if the treatment of the 'subsequent practice' argument in the House of Lords decision on *Al-Skeini* is considered, in relation to the Resolution of the Council of Europe Parliamentary Assembly that 'call[ed] upon those of its member states that are engaged in the MNF [in Iraq] to accept the full applicability of the ECHR to the activities of their forces in Iraq, in so far as those forces exercised effective control over the areas in which they operated'.[67] In *Al-Skeini*, Lord Bingham used this as evidence that the Convention did not, on its own, apply to Iraq. Lord Rodger, however, considered that this resolution was 'irrelevant to any decision of the

---

[66] See for detail Orakhelashvili, *Interpretation*, supra n.54, at Chapter 10; A. Orakhelashvili, 'Recent Practice on the Principles of Treaty Interpretation', in A. Orakhelashvili and S. Williams (eds), *40 Years of the Vienna Convention on the Law of Treaties* (London: British Institute of International and Comparative Law, 2010), 117, at 140–141.

[67] Resolution 1386 (2004), at para. 18.

European Court, or indeed of this House, on the proper interpretation of Article 1'. For, 'nothing said or done by the contracting states could make the Convention apply to the activities of their forces in Iraq if, on a proper judicial construction and application of article 1, it did not apply to those activities'.[68]

Lord Rodger's approach is methodologically correct, with the substantive outcome that the Assembly's resolution cannot be seen as either denying the Convention's applicability to actions in Iraq if Article 1 envisages otherwise, or as requiring states parties to extend the Convention's ambit further than Article 1 takes it. The phrase 'accept the full applicability' refers to the effect that the Convention already has and requires taking such action and attitude as conforms to that effect and requires acting accordingly.

H. The Use of Preparatory Work

Pursuant to the framework of treaty interpretation under Articles 31 and 32 of the 1969 Vienna Convention, preparatory work possesses merely supplementary relevance and so is irrelevant once an interpretative outcome has been arrived at through any of the methods available under Article 31. It has been shown above that the use of Article 31 alone is sufficient to establish a consistent meaning of Article 1. However, when judicial practice regarding the scope of Article 1 is examined it appears that the resort to preparatory work is aimed at presenting the scope of Article 1 as narrower than it actually is. *Banković* used preparatory work to support its *espace juridique* argument and restrict the scope of Article 1. In *Al-Skeini*, Lord Phillips similarly placed heavy reliance on *travaux* to prioritise the *Banković* approach.[69] On the other hand, preparatory work was not used in the Grand Chamber decision on *Al-Skeini*. It is a generally accepted position that preparatory work cannot be a primary way of interpreting treaties and with the ECHR this approach is even more compelling. In *Loizidou*, the European Court determined the role of preparatory work by reference to the objective character of the Convention obligations, and stated that the Convention cannot solely be interpreted in accordance with the intentions of its authors as expressed more than forty years ago.[70] In sum, '[t]he special nature of the European Convention means that particular caution is necessary in relying on the preparatory work of the Convention. Preparatory work is notoriously unreliable as a general guide to treaty interpretation.'[71]

---

[68] *Al-Skeini* (HL), *supra* n.22, at para. 65 (*per* Lord Rodger).
[69] *Al-Skeini* (HL), *supra* n.22, at paras 48 ff. (*per* Lord Phillips).
[70] *Loizidou* (GC) (Preliminary Objections), *supra* n.19, at paras 70–71.
[71] F. Jacobs and R. White, *The European Convention on Human Rights*, 5th edn (Oxford: Oxford University Press, 2010), at 66; *travaux* are not often helpful also according to D. Harris, M. O'Boyle and C. Warbrick, *Law of the European Convention on Human Rights*, 2nd edn (Oxford: Oxford University Press, 2009), at 17.

4. EXTRA-TERRITORIAL EFFECT OF THE ECHR IN ENGLISH LAW

A. Constitution, Parliamentary Sovereignty and Statutory Interpretation

If we follow the doctrine of Parliamentary Sovereignty, then the effect of the Convention rights in English law is not automatic but depends on the decision of Parliament when it adopted the HRA 1998. Consequently, as Lord Brown suggested, the extent of the Convention rights, 'created [in English law] as they were by the 1998 Act, depends upon the proper interpretation of that Act'.[72] But then, the meaning of the Act also depends on the fact that it is meant to give effect to the Convention as an international treaty. The Act and the Convention thus end up in a circular relationship. This dilemma, combining constitutional factors with statutory interpretation, received comprehensive treatment in *Al-Skeini* (HL). The claimants had to demonstrate that their claims fell not just within the Convention, but also within the Act as a domestic statute. For Lord Bingham, the principal question was that the acts complained of were not committed within the borders of the UK and thus fell outside the protection of the Act. Lord Bingham's approach was that, pursuant to the dualistic regime in relation to the transformation of treaties into English law, 'the claimants may have a claim which would succeed against the UK at Strasbourg but they have none against the Secretary of State under the Act'.[73] This mirrors the radical dualist approach taken previously by the House of Lords in *Brind* that projected a principled and systemic dichotomy of international and English law revealing that an option of tolerating, and even fostering, violations of international obligations of the United Kingdom is systemically embedded in the basic constitutional foundations of the UK.[74] Indeed, Lord Bingham reiterated this approach in *Al-Skeini*:

> A decision to give no directly enforceable domestic right to persons claiming to be victims of violations of Convention rights by UK authorities outside the UK, leaving such persons to pursue any such claim against the UK in Strasbourg, would have involved no breach of any obligation binding on the UK in international law. In argument before the House, the claimants did not seek to attach great weight to this presumption.[75]

The argument is thus made that a domestic decision to stick to a violation of the ECHR and deny domestic remedies to victims is not a breach of international obligations. But in reality such a breach would be there on account of the violation of the specific Convention right involved and also of the obligation under Article 13 ECHR to provide individuals with effective remedy wherever a breach of Convention rights is alleged to have been committed. On a broader plane, such dualistic separation can result in pedantic rhetoric, for if the Strasbourg Court can declare that a breach of the Convention has been committed through an act that an upper national Court has upheld, how is the decision of that very Court not a violation of international obligations?

---

[72] *Al-Skeini* (HL), *supra* n.22, at para. 134 (*per* Lord Brown).
[73] *Ibid.*, at para. 4 (*per* Lord Bingham).
[74] *R v Home Secretary, ex p Brind* (CA), 1 AC (1991), 696.
[75] *Al-Skeini* (HL), *supra* n.22, at para. 12 (*per* Lord Bingham).

622 *Research handbook on international conflict and security law*

The Secretary of State argued in *Al-Skeini* that '[u]nless the contrary intention appears, Parliament is taken to intend an Act to extend to each territory of the United Kingdom but not to any territory outside the United Kingdom', and that on this basis extra-territorial military operations are outside the Act, even if they are covered by Article 1 of the Convention. If we approach this issue from the viewpoint of statutory interpretation, the query should begin by focusing on the meaning of the relevant statute, by reaching a conclusion as to the interpretative outcome on the basis of generalised presumptions.

Focusing on the approaches to statutory interpretation, Lord Bingham suggested that:

> the House must employ the familiar tools of statutory interpretation. The starting point is the language of the Act, from which the court seeks to derive the meaning of what Parliament has enacted. Significance may be attached not only to what Parliament has said but also, on occasion, to what it has not said. Attention may be paid to presumptions applicable to the drafting of statutes, since these are rules which expert professional draftsmen may ordinarily be expected to follow in the absence of reason to conclude that they may not have done so or an indication in the statute that they have not done so. While the express terms of a statute are always crucial, the courts will eschew an overly literal construction, taking account of the purpose of the statute, the mischief sought to be remedied and other circumstances relevant to interpretation.[76]

If the range of available methods of statutory interpretation is that broad and enables judges to select interpretative factors with this degree of freedom, then it can be said without hesitation that the buck always stops with the courts. This is especially true here as there is ultimately no one, apart from judges, to ascertain, in relation to specific cases, what rules and approaches 'expert professional draftsmen may ordinarily be expected to follow'.

Proceeding on that basis, Lord Bingham suggested that:

> Parliament intended the effect of the Act to be governed by its terms and not, save by reference, the Convention. ... Had article 1 been included in section 1 and the Schedule, this would have assisted the claimants, since by 1997–1998 the Strasbourg jurisprudence had recognised some limited exceptions to the territorial focus of the Convention, and it could have been said that Parliament intended the territorial scope of the Act to be subject to the same limited exceptions. As it is, the omission of any reference to article 1 is of some negative assistance to the Secretary of State.[77]

This is a 'negative' textual approach under which Parliamentary intention is established by reference to what is or is not expressly said, as opposed to other factors such as general background and mischief. Everything, then, becomes a matter of choice between inferences derivable from silences that are allegedly competing. As Lord Bingham continued in pursuit of this approach, '[he did] not, overall, find these textual indications very compelling in favour of one side or the other ... More compelling in [the Secretary of State's] favour is the absence of any clear pointer in the claimants'

---

[76] *Ibid.*, at para. 9 (*per* Lord Bingham).
[77] *Ibid.*, at para. 14 (*per* Lord Bingham).

favour.'⁷⁸ The claimants allegedly needed clear pointers in their favour, while the respondent was fine with the absence of such to their detriment. The silence thus interpreted could amount to an essentially arbitrary choice in favour of the respondent who benefits from that silence, and against the applicant who does not, which outcome has been arrived through the exercise of interpretative freedom of judges that has been described above.

The above arguments regarding statutory interpretation reveal a substantial difference between presuming the territoriality of statutes and identifying their actual scope. The overall presumption of territoriality is an implication of the limits of sovereignty, and thus of the legislative competence of the UK, pursuant to the requirements of comity and non-interference with other states' domestic affairs.⁷⁹ But with the HRA no such interference with their domestic affairs takes place and no comity is infringed upon because the government only submits to accountability for its own acts and conduct; it does not assert its competence in the domestic realm of other states. Lord Rodger has demonstrated that the presumption of territoriality is neither comprehensive nor irrefutable, observing that:

> this rule of construction has to be seen against the background of international law. One state is bound to respect the territorial sovereignty of another state. So, usually, Parliament will not mean to interfere by legislating to regulate the conduct of its citizens in another state. Such legislation would usually be unnecessary and would often be, in any event, ineffective. But sometimes Parliament has a legitimate interest in regulating their conduct and so does indeed intend its legislation to affect the position of British citizens in other states.⁸⁰

The whole framework then becomes relative, because Parliament, on Lord Rodger's approach, can indeed legislate extra-territorially and this can be seen as an implication of the traditional understanding of what Parliamentary Sovereignty means. Lord Rodger then develops a very important presumption that, although not expressly but inevitably in essence, operates to favour the interpretation of statutes so that they are seen to incorporate the requirements of international law. Thus,

> the burden of the legislation falls on public authorities, rather than on private individuals or companies. Most of the functions of United Kingdom public authorities relate to this country and will therefore be carried out here. Moreover, exercising their functions abroad would often mean that the public authorities were encroaching on the sovereignty of another state. Nevertheless, where a public authority has power to operate outside of the United Kingdom and does so legitimately – for example, with the consent of the other state – in the absence of any indication to the contrary, when construing any relevant legislation, it would only be sensible to treat the public authority, so far as possible, in the same way as when it operates at home.⁸¹

---

⁷⁸ *Ibid.*, at para. 16 (*per* Lord Bingham).
⁷⁹ See, for example, an earlier case of *Le Louis* (1817) 2 *Dods* 210 (even though this presumption is a limit on the Parliamentary Sovereignty thesis).
⁸⁰ *Al-Skeini* (HL), *supra* n.22, at para. 49 (*per* Lord Rodger).
⁸¹ *Ibid.*, at para. 53 (*per* Lord Rodger).

The burden falling on the authorities entails a presumption, consistent with the Rule of Law, that Parliament does not intend to exempt extra-territorial executive action from legal limits and scrutiny. Contrary to Lord Bingham's approach, Lord Rodger's approach is premised on the need to examine every statute on its merit in order to identify whether or not it has extra-territorial scope, as opposed to superimposing abstract presumptions of how Parliament is supposed to exercise its Sovereignty. Imposing a generally applicable presumption of territoriality would run contrary to the essential nature of the statutory interpretation process. First, it would elevate a principle of interpretation to the level of a fixed constitutional principle, with the counter-factual implication of diminishing the role of courts. Secondly, it would override considerations of Parliamentary intention by superimposing the abstract requirement of territoriality over and above the principle that the reach of an Act of Parliament has to be clarified by reference to what Parliament intended while enacting that specific piece of legislation. This problem would be further exacerbated if this requirement were to be applied in the context not just of express phrases, but also of silences in the statutory text of the type that Lord Bingham placed emphasis upon and that each litigant will be inclined to construe to their own benefit.

The intention of Parliament can be identified in various ways, either on the basis of express wording or in terms of the socio-political background against which the statute was adopted and that did not require express emphasis. For example, the European Convention, being the motivating factor behind the adoption of the HRA 1998, clearly qualifies as circumstances requiring little emphasis. A key question is at what level must Parliament be deemed to have expressed its intention as to the territorial scope of the 1998 Act, at the level of its overall decision to legislate for giving domestic effect to the Convention; or at the level of the use or non-use of specific words in specific places of the statutory text? If, moreover, the presumption is that Parliament would not legislate in defiance of international law, why would its failure expressly to mention Article 1 amount to its intention to exclude its operation from English law?

Lord Rodger and Baroness Hale observed in *Al-Skeini* that the Act gave effect to the Convention, which is extra-territorial, and therefore section 6 was meant to give remedy to individuals who can access the Strasbourg Court, whenever the ECHR would allow, in relation to extra-territorial violations.[82] Lord Bingham's approach, on the other hand, is that, whatever the scope of the Convention, the Act is a product of Parliamentary Sovereignty and its scope depends upon what Parliament adopted, again doing all this through inferences. On what basis can it be said that one of these interpretative policies is better than the other? Presumably on terms of consistency with Parliament's overall intention to implement the Convention in English law, because this very factor yields contextual significance clarifying that the inferences Lord Bingham advanced do not operate in a vacuum. On that account the approach of Lord Rodger and Baroness Hale has greater merit and does not confront or refute Lord Bingham's above argument of territoriality, either in principle or by evidence. What matters here is the level at which judges should concentrate their efforts of statutory interpretation. By opting to focus on the parameters of Parliamentary intention *in casu*, rather than general presumptions derivable from constitutional principles, such as Parliamentary

---

[82] *Ibid.*, at para. 88 (*per* Baroness Hale).

Sovereignty, Lord Rodger and Baroness Hale have adopted an approach to the statutory effect of Article 1 that is correct both as a matter of international and English law.

In practical terms, the question is precisely where the essential difference between the approaches of Lord Bingham and the rest of the House of Lords lies. The question is whether the majority's treatment of section 6 reveals more evidence in favour of the extra-territoriality of the 1998 Act than Lord Bingham was prepared to admit when he denied the Act's extra-territorial effect. It seems that it does not, the majority in *Al-Skeini* merely used section 6 as a gateway to the extra-territorial application of the Act without requiring additional proof of such extra-territoriality in any other provision. The use of section 6 was meant to transfer the Parliamentary intention issue from the level of words and phrases to the level of the Act's overall design and intention. The need to adduce the proof of 'clear pointers' and dispel the implications of silence of the text, as Lord Bingham insisted upon, simply did not arise. This approach seems to acknowledge that the overall intention behind the statute to respect and incorporate international law acquires enhanced importance, with the need to evidence the specific intention of the legislator precisely to that extent becoming less stringent. The overall background of legislating in relation to the field covering international law should suffice for that purpose.

B. Effect of Strasbourg Court Decisions in English Law

After the Grand Chamber decision in *Al-Skeini*, those who decided *Al-Skeini* and *Smith* in the House of Lords and Supreme Court respectively, had reasonable grounds on which to wonder why the Strasbourg Court moved away from its previous approach and disapproved their decisions based on the earlier Grand Chamber decision in *Banković*. The problem was initially produced by *Banković*, which presented the scope of Article 1 in a clearly restrictive way. That said, however, it was plainly obvious in the Strasbourg Court's pre-*Al-Skeini* jurisprudence that the *Banković* approach was not the only one. *Banković* was, to say the least, implicitly disapproved if not overruled, in post-*Banković* decisions on *Solomou*, *Pad*, *Issa* and *Ilascu*. These latter cases created at least a reasonable possibility that the Strasbourg Court would not be indefinitely prepared to stick to *Banković*.

Section 2(1) HRA 1998 requires that, 'A court or tribunal determining a question which has arisen in connection with a Convention right must take into account any judgment, decision, declaration or advisory opinion of the European Court of Human Rights', as well as decisions by the European Commission and the Committee of Ministers.[83] Even if section 2(1) is read as not making Strasbourg judgments strictly binding in English courts, it still produces a strong presumption – rebuttable only

---

[83] See also S.H. Bailey, J.P.L. Ching and N.W. Taylor, *The Modern English Legal System* (London: Thomson-Sweet & Maxwell, 2007), at 527 (referring to 'any judgment'). It should be added that when an English court engages with any issue relating to the HRA, it in essence interprets the ECHR, for which purpose dealing with Strasbourg decisions amounts to examining 'subsequent practice' under Article 31(3)(b) of the 1969 Vienna Convention, and ultimately bears on the correctness of the interpretation by an English court. See also above sub-section 3G.

through consistent and persuasive demonstration that the decision in question contradicts the Convention – that these judgments must be followed. The cautious language deployed in section 2(1) is understandable, given that the Strasbourg Court decisions, just like any other international judgment or award, are not meant to be binding beyond the scope of the case and parties to which they relate. In that sense Strasbourg judgments do not produce free-standing obligations and the HRA does not pretend that they do. However, section 2(1) operates on the plane of interpretation of the Convention and is premised on the principle that, while the Strasbourg Court has been designated as the organ to safeguard the Convention, its interpretation is better and more authoritative than that performed by national authorities. Section 2(1) HRA reflects just that. The English courts have a duty to follow interpretations placed upon the ECHR by the European Court of Human Rights, despite a lack of emphasis on the strict binding force of the decisions.

This international legal side of the question is further reinforced by systemic preconditions under English law. In the English legal system, which is based on the system of precedent, it makes perfect sense to also regard Strasbourg decisions as such. The system of judicial precedents as part of common law was introduced when Royal courts emerged after the 1066 Norman Conquest. This system was meant to streamline judicial practice through publishing and prioritising decisions of upper courts. Those decisions would then provide the guidance to indicate how upper courts would be deciding the case if it got there by appeal.[84] The role of the Strasbourg Court in relation to English courts' decisions fits perfectly with this picture. Strasbourg decisions, or Strasbourg jurisprudence as a whole, should be seen before English courts as precedent in relation to every issue that may eventually be submitted to the Strasbourg Court and decided there with binding force. From here, the next step involves identifying how various Strasbourg decisions should be prioritised, which cannot be done through the use of the doctrine of precedent. Instead, this has to be done the way the Strasbourg Court would do it itself, namely by addressing the systemic factors of interpretation of ECHR as required under the 1969 Vienna Convention. The ECHR is an international treaty and it is on these conditions that HRA 1998 incorporates ECHR into English law, as opposed to subjecting the ECHR and Strasbourg Court decisions to the interpretation process that applies to national, as opposed to international, law.

The practice of English courts has elaborated on the effect of Strasbourg Court decisions on several occasions. Lord Slynn pointed out in *Alconbury* that:

> Although the Human Rights Act 1998 does not provide that a national court is bound by these decisions it is obliged to take account of them so far as they are relevant. In the absence of some special circumstances it seems to me that the court should follow any clear and constant jurisprudence of the European Court of Human Rights. If it does not do so there is at least a possibility that the case will go to that court which is likely in the ordinary case to follow its own constant jurisprudence.[85]

---

[84] Bayley, Ching and Taylor, *supra* n.83, at 475.
[85] *R (on the application of Alconbury Developments Ltd) v Secretary of State for the Environment, Transport and the Regions*, [2003] 2 AC 295, at para. 26.

However, in relation to Article 1 it is difficult to find jurisprudence that is clearly consistent, which places English courts in a position where they can unilaterally choose which part of Strasbourg jurisprudence should be preferred to another.

Accordingly, it is submitted that the Strasbourg Court's jurisprudence must be taken as a consistent whole and there is no reasonable basis for regarding one particular decision as having greater importance than others. Given that this jurisprudence is not free-standing but merely a part of the overall treaty framework of the European Convention, that part of jurisprudence which endorses the letter and objectives of the Convention has to be given priority over that which curtails those, as this responds to principles of interpretation applicable to the ECHR under Articles 31 and 32 of the Vienna Convention on the Law of Treaties.

A further interpretative policy was stated by Lord Bingham in *Anderson*, to the effect that:

> While the duty of the House under section 2(1)(a) of the Human Rights Act 1998 is to take into account any judgment of the European Court, whose judgments are not strictly binding, the House will not without good reason depart from the principles laid down in a carefully considered judgment of the court sitting as a Grand Chamber.[86]

Again, this falls short of providing an intelligible principle and adds an element of judicial creativity to the HRA section 2(1) requirement that *any* decision of Strasbourg organs, not just Grand Chamber decisions, must be taken into account. This discrepancy in reasoning is further corroborated by the uncertainty as to what a 'carefully considered' judgment means, whether there is 'good reason' to depart from it, and whether national courts ought to have the final word on those asserted categories that carry with them the risk of subjective appreciation and subjective manipulation.

This approach of relativity accounts for much of the treatment of Strasbourg's decisions in the *Al-Skeini* and *Smith* judgments of English courts. Lord Phillips agreed with Lord Brown in *Al-Skeini* that Strasbourg jurisprudence should be taken as a guideline as to how far Article 1 jurisdiction extends.[87] The *Al-Skeini* decision was essentially based on the decision made by the House of Lords that between *Issa* and *Banković* the latter had to be followed, and a 'primarily territorial' approach to Article 1 had to be applied instead of the cause-and-effect approach.[88] However, the House of Lords did not explain how the previous decision on *Banković* could supersede the later one in *Issa*, if moreover it was acknowledged that at the time when *Banković* was decided *Issa* was still in judicial consideration.[89] Also, according to Lord Brown in *Smith*, *Banković* 'must be regarded as Strasbourg's ruling judgment on the point' and *Issa* 'should not be understood to detract in any way from the clearly restrictive

---

[86] *R v Secretary of State ex parte Anderson*, [2002] UKHL 46, at para. 18.
[87] *Smith*, supra n.17, at para. 60 (*per* Lord Phillips); *ibid.*, at para. 93 (*per* Lord Hope); *ibid.*, at para. 147 (*per* Lord Brown); *Al-Skeini* (HL), supra n.22, at para. 107 (*per* Lord Brown).
[88] As confirmed by Lord Phillips in *Smith*, supra n.17, at paras 23–25.
[89] As acknowledged in *Smith*, *ibid.*, at para. 16 (*per* Lord Phillips); *ibid.*, at para. 265 (*per* Lord Collins).

approach to article 1 jurisdiction adopted in *Banković*.[90] Lord Phillips in *Smith* recognised the discrepancies between various decisions of the Strasbourg Court and effectively acknowledged that, to say the least, the issue remained open. In *Medvedyev*,

> The court held at para 67 that as the vessel and its crew were, at least *de facto*, under the control of France, they were effectively under France's jurisdiction for the purposes of article 1. This decision, when added to that in *Issa* suggests that the Strasbourg Court may be prepared to found article 1 jurisdiction on state agent authority, even though this principle does not seem consistent with the approach in *Bankovic*.[91]

Lord Collins was, however, more categorical in submitting that, '[n]ot only is there no firm basis in authority for the notion of authority and control as a basis of jurisdiction under article 1, *Issa* is also inconsistent with the notion of the regional nature of the Convention'.[92] Overall it seems that the Law Lords' reasoning in both *Al-Skeini* and *Smith* singles out those elements within Strasbourg cases that could be interpreted as conducive to their pro-*Banković* attitude, while disregarding elements that would be problematic to it. Consequently, Lord Brown's assertion that 'holding the UK's armed forces abroad to be within the state's article 1 jurisdiction ... would be to go further than the [European Court of Human Rights] has yet gone, to construe article 1 as reaching further than the existing Strasbourg jurisprudence clearly shows it to reach'[93] is plainly counter-factual. Both *Al-Skeini* (HL) and *Smith* thus fall considerably short of the full use of the jurisdictional resource that Article 1 and its application in the Strasbourg jurisprudence offer. That much was perfectly clear at the time when the House of Lords and Supreme Court were deciding *Al-Skeini* and *Smith*, for they expressly professed that they chose to prioritise the previous decision on *Banković*, rejected the subsequent decision on *Issa*, and hardly gave due consideration to *Solomou* and *Pad*. There must, therefore, have been a reasonable degree of certainty at that point that the Strasbourg Court was likely to disagree with English courts' decisions. The only sensible and sustainable solution to the dilemmas in *Al-Skeini* and *Smith* was to recognise that *Banković* was an incorrect decision adopted under the pressure of political considerations of the day and thus defying both ordinary meaning and the purpose and object of the Convention.

Overall, as also the Grand Chamber judgment in *Al-Skeini* demonstrates, the European Court of Human Rights is not subjected to the system of judicial precedent, which does not operate within the international legal system as it is inimical to its consensual underpinnings. If the Strasbourg Court's previous decision appears unjustified, this Court can subsequently adopt a different decision, each decision being applicable to its own situation, and the one which reflects the requirements of the

---

[90] *Smith*, ibid., at paras 141–142 (*per* Lord Brown); having earlier suggested, in para. 127 of *Al-Skeini*, that the *Issa* reasoning was mostly *obiter dicta*. In para. 149 of *Smith* Lord Brown was 'confident, the Parliamentary Assembly's exhortation of 24 June 2004 notwithstanding, that the Strasbourg court will continue to maintain the *Bankovic* approach which seems to me only logical'.
[91] *Smith*, *supra* n.17, at para. 30 (*per* Lord Phillips).
[92] *Ibid.*, at para. 289 (*per* Lord Collins); on *espace juridique* see section 3F above.
[93] *Smith*, *supra* n.17, at para. 147 (*per* Lord Brown).

ECHR as properly interpreted pursuant to Articles 31 and 32 of the 1969 Vienna Convention should be prioritised whenever this issue arises in subsequent litigation. This is actually how the Grand Chamber decision in *Al-Skeini* dealt with the discrepancy between *Issa* and *Banković*.

5. THE INTERPRETATION OF SECURITY COUNCIL RESOLUTIONS CLAIMED TO AUTHORISE EXTRA-TERRITORIAL VIOLATIONS OF HUMAN RIGHTS

English courts and the European Court in *Al-Jedda* have examined the legality of Mr Al-Jedda's effectively indefinite detention in Iraq without access to judicial review. As Elias LJ specified in *Al-Jedda II*, there was a conflict between Resolution 1546 (2004) and Article 5 of the European Convention (right to liberty) because paragraph 10 of this Resolution arguably allowed detention for security reasons which was not among the grounds on which Article 5 allows detention.[94] Thus, English courts have essentially approved an indefinite detention even though it breaches Article 5. Little was said in the judgments to confront and explain this problem. Lord Bingham merely pointed out that Al-Jedda's detention is lawful only to the extent that is 'inherent in that detention',[95] which is not only circular but also contradicts the fundamental standard of protection under Article 5, which requires assessing the legality and rationale of that very detention in terms of its compliance with the fundamental right to liberty and security of the person that this Article is meant to protect.[96]

In *Al-Jedda II* before the Court of Appeal, Arden LJ followed the same approach by suggesting that, 'even if the present claim cannot be used to determine the lawfulness of the detention of Mr Al-Jedda, there would not be as a result a complete "legal black hole" as he is not completely deprived of protection under the Convention'.[97] This, again, rang hollow, as Al-Jedda's protection was in fact completely taken away, and he did not continue to enjoy any viable human rights protection while in detention.

As to the nature of the freedom from arbitrary detention and deprivation of liberty, Arden LJ suggested that:

> the essence of a right is not immovable and inflexible, or unresponsive to the circumstances. In a normal state of affairs, a person who has been arrested can be brought before a judge in very short order. It may be different if there is a national emergency: see, for example,

---

[94] *Al Jedda v Secretary of State for Defence*, Court of Appeal – Civil Division, 8 July 2010, [2010] EWCA Civ. 758 (hereinafter '*Al-Jedda II*'), at paras 62, 181–182; see also, to the same effect, *Al-Jedda* (HL), *supra* n.12.

[95] *Al-Jedda* (HL), *supra* n.12., at para. 39.

[96] A. Orakhelashvili, 'Case Review on *Al-Jedda* (HL)', (2008) 103 *AJIL* 337. This author has earlier observed that the House of Lords approach in *Al-Jedda* essentially attempts to legitimise detentions such as those practised by the US Government in Guantanamo if covered by a Security Council resolution. See A. Orakhelashvili, 'Threat, Emergency and Survival: The Legality of Emergency Action in International Law', (2010) 9 *Chinese JIL* 345, at 373.

[97] *Al-Jedda II*, *supra* n.94, at para. 17 (*per* Arden LJ).

Brogan v United Kingdom, Application no. 11209/84, 29 November 1988. It follows that regard can also be had to the fact that the Iraqi political situation is in transition.[98]

But this uses a false premise to reach the conclusion as to the flexibility of rights under Article 5. The *Brogan* case is an exemplary illustration of the rigidity of the Article 5 safeguards. The European Court interpreted the 'promptness' rigidly. In doing so it has overruled the objections advanced by dissenting judges who pointed to the need of flexible interpretation of this provision to enable governments to cope with the challenges of terrorism. In any case, the suggestion that 'regard can also be had to the fact that the Iraqi political situation is in transition' is too broad to be entertained by any intelligible legal standard, and opens the door for restricting Article 5 rights on the basis of subjective policy preferences in the infinite variety of situations.

However, Arden LJ then observed that, even though detention was authorised by Resolution 1546,

> the loss of liberty was indefinite and, however regular the review, the fact remained that release was discretionary. It does not seem to me that a court using its judicial experience even in Iraq would reach the conclusion that the essence of the right to liberty is preserved in those circumstances where a person has so little control over his own freedom and dignity. There was no judicial process to enable it to be determined, for example, whether 'imperative reasons of security' in fact continued. The crucial role of judicial safeguards is obvious in this situation.[99]

This is an accurate description of interests and imperatives involved where the freedom from arbitrary deprivation of liberty is involved.

As a starting point, Security Council resolutions have to be interpreted pursuant to interpretation rules applicable to treaties under the 1969 Vienna Convention. The *sui generis* nature of resolutions has been advanced doctrinally and judicially. But it has hardly ever been demonstrated how that alleged *sui generis* nature could impact interpretative outcomes where the interpreter's sole task is to identify the parameters of the agreement between states that underlies every single resolution the Council adopts. To illustrate, the International Court suggested in the *Kosovo* Advisory Opinion that:

> While the rules on treaty interpretation embodied in Articles 31 and 32 of the Vienna Convention on the Law of Treaties may provide guidance, differences between Security Council resolutions and treaties mean that the interpretation of Security Council resolutions also requires that other factors be taken into account. Security Council resolutions are issued by a single, collective body and are drafted through a very different process than that used for the conclusion of a treaty.[100]

---

[98] *Ibid.*, at para. 61 (*per* Arden LJ).
[99] *Ibid.*, at para. 62 (*per* Arden LJ).
[100] *Accordance with International Law of the Unilateral Declaration of Independence in Respect of Kosovo*, Advisory Opinion of 22 July 2010, General List No. 141, at para. 94 (hereinafter '*Kosovo* Advisory Opinion').

The Court does not specify what these 'other factors' are, and how the drafting process of resolutions is 'very different' from that of treaties. In reality both these processes relate to reaching agreement between states, enshrining that agreement in the text and enabling the relevant states to place reliance upon it whenever their rights and obligations are at stake. In general, it is not uncommon in the Court's jurisprudence to pay lip-service to the 'special' nature of certain 'non-treaty' acts, but ultimately interpret them in compliance with the Vienna Convention regime.[101] Resolutions are consensual instruments and international law is well equipped with rules to interpret them, above all under the Vienna Convention. Although not formally applicable to resolutions, Articles 31 and 32 of the Convention constitute the customary law on interpretation which, given that there is no alternative set of interpretative rules, must be deemed to apply to resolutions.

It is suggested that the drafting of resolutions is a complex process of which some aspects are known publicly and others are not, and that the 'overall political background' has to be considered in interpreting resolutions. Arguably, then, 'it becomes highly artificial, and indeed to some extent simply not possible, to seek to apply all the Vienna Convention rules *mutatis mutandis* to [Security Council resolutions]'.[102] But the argument about the political nature of resolutions leads nowhere. Resolutions are not more or less political than treaties. Many bilateral and multilateral treaties carry major political importance, yet they are fully subjected to the interpretation regime under the Vienna Convention. On balance, neither doctrinal suggestions nor the *Kosovo* Opinion offer sufficient grounds for moving the interpretation of Security Council resolutions away from Articles 31 and 32 of the Vienna Convention, or for distorting the sequence of methods of interpretation as prescribed by those provisions.

The European Court of Human Rights in *Al-Jedda* had to focus on the interpretation of Resolution 1546, and in doing so it did not accord any relevance to either the political or the *sui generis* nature of that resolution. Instead, the Grand Chamber went on to identify what precisely was agreed in that resolution and whether the outcome of that covered the detention to which Al-Jedda was subjected. The Court observed that:

> In the event of any ambiguity in the terms of a Security Council Resolution, the Court must therefore choose the interpretation which is most in harmony with the requirements of the Convention and which avoids any conflict of obligations. In the light of the United Nations' important role in promoting and encouraging respect for human rights, it is to be expected

---

[101] In *Fisheries Jurisdiction* (Spain/Canada) the International Court stated that the Optional Clause declarations of the acceptance of the Court's jurisdiction are *sui generis* instruments. However, the actual process of interpretation in this case was conducted in the same way as the faithful application of the 1969 Vienna Convention would require, by reliance on the textual meaning of the Canadian declaration as the crucial factor in ascertaining its meaning. *Fisheries Jurisdiction* (Spain v Canada) (Jurisdiction of the Court), Judgment, [1998] ICJ Rep. 432, especially at paras 61–80.

[102] M. Wood, 'The Interpretation of Security Council Resolutions', (1998) 2 *Max-Plank YBUNL* 74, at 79–81, 95, although in principle accepting the law of treaties analogy as per Lord McNair, *ibid.*, 95.

that clear and explicit language would be used were the Security Council to intend States to take particular measures which would conflict with their obligations under international human rights law.[103]

Three main points need to be made in relation to this passage. First, the Grand Chamber pointed out by reference to the International Court's Advisory Opinion in *Namibia* that 'a Security Council resolution should be interpreted in the light not only of the language used but also the context in which it was adopted'.[104] The US Secretary of State's letter to the President of the Security Council, attached to Resolution 1546 and pledging that the presence of the MNF in Iraq contemplated no detentions defying the Fourth Geneva Convention, even if not expressly mentioned in the Grand Chamber decision, crucially provided part of that context. Secondly, 'harmonious' interpretation does not operate as a free-standing method of interpretation. The Grand Chamber decision on *Al-Jedda* placed the prevailing emphasis on clear and express words of Resolution 1546. The lack of clear words to authorise the detentions of a certain kind entailed the outcome of harmony of Resolution 1546 with international law. It was the Security Council itself that adopted the decision that is in harmony with the ECHR, not that the Strasbourg Court would harmonise the Council's decision with the Convention even if the Council's decision was not in such harmony in the first place. Once it is established that the resolution's text does not reveal any contradiction with the ECHR, the need for reading the resolution in harmony with the ECHR simply does not arise. There is no ambiguity in the first place for the need for its 'harmonisation' to arise. If this was not the case, then potentially nearly all silences in Security Council resolutions would have to be qualified as ambiguity, thus producing risks to impute to the Council decisions it has not really adopted.[105] Conversely, had the Council expressly purported to override the ECHR, no harmonious interpretation would have helped to secure a human rights-friendly interpretation. Therefore, the conclusion that:

> In the absence of clear provision to the contrary, the presumption must be that the Security Council intended States within the Multi-National Force to contribute towards the maintenance of security in Iraq while complying with their obligations under international human rights law[106]

means that it is the absence of clear words that produces the presumption referred to, not that such presumptions constitute an independent factor of interpretation to be superimposed on the general framework of interpretation of Security Council resolutions.

Thirdly, the interpretation of resolutions has also to deal with the *vires* of the Security Council and the limits of its decision-making. The Strasbourg Court manifested the position that the Council's potential decision to contravene the ECHR amounts to contravening the principles and purposes of the UN Charter that are binding

---

[103] *Al-Jedda* (GC), *supra* n.6, at para. 102.
[104] *Ibid.*, at para. 76.
[105] See for detail and more examples, A. Orakhelashvili, *Collective Security* (Oxford: Oxford University Press, 2011), Chapters 2 and 5.
[106] *Al-Jedda* (GC), *supra* n.6, at para. 106.

on the Council.¹⁰⁷ The European Court therefore rejects the approach that considerations of peace and security can prevail over human rights, or that there is some kind of invisible hierarchy among the purposes of the UN Charter. It is therefore doubtful whether the European Court would have given effect to a Security Council resolution if its contradiction with the purposes and principles of the UN Charter could be demonstrated. The House of Lords in *Al-Jedda* denied that a national court can refuse to implement a Security Council resolution, even if it contradicts the standards that the Council is obliged to obey. Yet in the subsequent case of *Jabar*, the UK Supreme Court admitted such a possibility,¹⁰⁸ and if the Strasbourg Court were to override a Security Council resolution contradicting the UN Charter and/or the Convention, that very course of action would necessarily imply that the relevant national court both can and must disregard the relevant resolution to remain within the bounds of the Convention and applicable international law.¹⁰⁹

The *Al-Jedda* litigation process also illustrates some issues regarding the standing of agencies that interpret Security Council resolutions.¹¹⁰ The House of Lords had effectively upheld the unilateral interpretation of Resolution 1546 by the Executive conducted in defiance of the governing regime of interpretation under Articles 31 and 32 of the Vienna Convention.¹¹¹

Similar to the approach in the *Kosovo UDI* Advisory Opinion of the International Court of Justice,¹¹² the European Court in *Al-Jedda* follows, and consolidates, the approach that any international tribunal can interpret Security Council resolutions if this issue matters for the case brought before it, nor are there inherent limits as to non-justiciability. Furthermore, the Grand Chamber judgment in *Al-Jedda* also implies that the House of Lords should have engaged with proper interpretation of Resolution 1546 when deciding on this case, for this was indispensable for properly applying Article 5 of the European Convention to underlying facts. Following this approach, in *Al-Jedda v UK*, the Strasbourg Court corrected the unilateral interpretation placed by the government upon Resolution 1546, and upheld the one that follows from the ordinary meaning of the resolution in the light of its context and object and purpose, as required under Article 31 of the Vienna Convention.

---

¹⁰⁷ For a similar approach voiced earlier see Orakhelashvili, *Peremptory Norms*, *supra* n.62, at Chapter 12.
¹⁰⁸ *HM Treasury v Mohammed Jabar Ahmed and Others*, [2010] UKSC 2, 27 January 2010, at para. 151.
¹⁰⁹ For detail regarding the refusal by states to implement illegal resolutions of the Security Council, see Orakhelashvili, *supra* n.105, at Chapter 8.
¹¹⁰ On the agencies of interpretation see Orakhelashvili, *Interpretation*, *supra* n.54, at Chapter 16.
¹¹¹ See Orakhelashvili, *supra* n.96; A. Orakhelashvili, 'Unilateral Interpretation of UN Security Council Resolutions: UK Practice', (2010) 2 *GoJIL* 823, at 833–835; Orakhelashvili, *supra* n.105, at Chapter 5.
¹¹² *Kosovo* Advisory Opinion, *supra* n.100, at para. 46; see for a detailed analysis A. Orakhelashvili, 'The International Court's Advisory Opinion on the UDI in respect of Kosovo: Washing Away the "Foam on the Tide of Time"', (2011) 15 *Max-Planck YB UN Law* 65.

6. FURTHER QUESTIONS OF ENGLISH LAW: CONFLICT OF LAWS, PUBLIC POLICY, ACT OF STATE AND NON-JUSTICIABILITY

In *Al-Jedda* the question arose before English courts as to whether the legality of Al-Jedda's detention under Iraqi law and Constitution impacted upon the ability of English courts to examine the situation. As the Court of Appeal judgment in *Al-Jedda II* demonstrates, the conflicts of law and public policy approach can be used to upset the domestic effect of Security Council resolutions in English law. Arden LJ, initially proceeding from the premise that Resolution 1546 authorised Mr Al-Jedda's detention,

> attach[ed] weight to the fact that the Constitution of Iraq is stated to be the supreme law without exception. We have, moreover, not been shown any provision of the Constitution which states that compliance with international law [that is Security Council Resolution 1546] overrides the rights conferred by it. ... I respectfully doubt therefore the utility of praying in aid the turmoil in Iraq: if there was a state of emergency there were other provisions in the Constitution which authorised the taking of other powers which could have been but which were not used.[113]

Therefore, the requirements under the Iraqi Constitution remained unaffected by Resolution 1546, and continued to be opposable before English courts. It will be recalled that in *Kuwait Air Corp.* public international law, not Iraqi law, was used to determine the applicable law to judge the legality of the seizure of the aircraft by Iraq from the territory of Kuwait. But in *Al-Jedda II* the Iraqi law was not as such considered to be objectionable or inopposable; it merely had to be examined to identify the basis of Al-Jedda's private law claims.

Elias LJ also suggests that there is no general principle requiring the compliance of national law with international law, unless the latter is expressly incorporated into the former, and 'there would seem to be no basis for asserting that the UK courts should refuse to give effect to the national law of another state on the grounds that they are incompatible with international obligations undertaken by the UK'.[114] So then foreign

---

[113] *Al-Jedda II, supra* n.94, at paras 64, 66 (*per* Arden LJ). It has to be noted that Sir John Dyson thought the detention to be in compliance with the applicable law in Iraq, but did not suggest any conclusion going further than (unclear) enabling the detaining authority to decide whether continuous detention is warranted or not, and to do so without any meaningful judicial supervision, see paras 112–127. Elias LJ adopted the same line of reasoning, arguing that the purpose of Article 5 is 'to prevent arbitrary detention taken without legal authority. The judicial role is to provide an independent and objective review of the material evidence, made in good faith, and to determine whether it is in accordance with the law. The reference to judicial authority or a judicial decision is intended to secure the adoption of procedures which will encompass these characteristics. On this analysis the essence of the right conferred by these Articles requires not the involvement of a judge; rather it requires that the decision displays the essential features of these typically judicial characteristics' (paras 148–150). But who is going to decide whether those 'essential features' of non-judicial organs are 'typically judicial'? This invests too much discretion in authorities and enables them to unilaterally determine when Article 5 applies and when it does not.

[114] *Ibid.*, at para. 178 (*per* Elias LJ).

law, too, could be applied in England if that would engage the UK's international responsibility. This approach somewhat endangers the overriding force of Security Council resolutions, seemingly across the board, and enables domestic courts to evade the effect of those resolutions.

The ordinary relevance of public policy in private international law is to offset the domestic effect of foreign law that is immoral or objectionable from the viewpoint of the domestic legal system. The parameters of English public policy in the face of the applicable Iraqi and international law also focus, as per *Al-Jedda II*, on whether the possibility of the MNF being under Iraqi law liable for Al-Jedda's detention contradicted public policy in England. Arden LJ in *Al-Jedda II* explained the relevance of public policy in terms that are very much in point to address the very essence of public policy in international law cases:

> the effect of applying Iraqi law to Mr Al Jedda's claim to determine the lawfulness of his detention is that the British government is at risk of liability for doing no more than carrying out its international obligations, in circumstances where its obligations under the UN Charter have been sufficient to qualify protection for Mr Al Jedda under the Convention. Nonetheless, in my judgment, that does not mean that it is appropriate to invoke the public policy exception. That exception fails to be applied if the relevant law of Iraq is in some way in itself offensive or objectionable. It does not apply simply because a remedy exists in Iraqi law which would not be available under domestic law. There is nothing inherently offensive or objectionable about the Iraqi law on which Mr Al Jedda relies. A failure by the MNF (subject to Coalition Provisional Authority 17) to obtain immunity from Iraqi law would not of itself make it contrary to public policy to apply Iraqi law.[115]

Elias LJ made similar observations regarding public policy:

> The [Iraqi] law in issue is one which requires judicial oversight of the detention of any person. In my judgment that law does not remotely begin to engage the public policy principle. Plainly, if this provision were part of the law of the United Kingdom it is inconceivable that it could be said to be contrary to public policy. The purpose of the particular provision is to ensure that basic human liberties are properly protected. It is impossible to contend that it is an affront to fundamental principles of fairness and justice.[116]

To conceptualise this further, the two judges' conclusion means that public policy cannot be used to shield British authorities from accountability whenever they break foreign law; it can only be used if foreign law itself is inadmissible within the English legal system. On this vision, conflict of laws operates as a transparent system under which public authorities are judged on the legality of their acts wherever they perform those acts.

The next issue to be considered in *Al-Jedda II* was the Act of State doctrine, with its origins in English law in the case of *Luther v Sagor*, where the Court of Appeal declined to challenge the Soviet Russian expropriation decree, suggesting that judging the acts of a sovereign government performed within its territorial realm would offend

---

[115] *Ibid.*, at para. 86 (*per* Arden LJ).
[116] *Ibid.*, at para. 174 (*per* Elias LJ).

the comity of nations.[117] The Act of State doctrine is not applicable to serious violations of international law and to human rights violations, as was confirmed in *Oppenheimer v Cattermole*;[118] and further in *Kuwait Air Corp.*, that qualified the doctrine by fundamental legal standards including *jus cogens*.[119] In *Al-Jedda II*, it was acknowledged that the standard of non-justiciability of foreign sovereign action was not to upset the outcome in *Kuwait Air Corp.*, for 'it was open to the court in other cases to consider whether the acts of a foreign state violated international law, or were contrary to public policy'.[120]

That much is commonly accepted, but in *Al-Jedda II* the Act of State doctrine was used in a reverse manner, proceeding from the premise that the acts committed by British authorities gave effect to international obligations and therefore were covered by this doctrine. Arden LJ affirmatively linked the relevance of the Act of State doctrine to the overriding force of Resolution 1546, stating that 'internment was part of the role which the British contingent of the MNF were specifically required to carry out',[121] even though this resolution did not in fact possess such overriding effect. As for the conceptual and policy basis for Arden LJ's approach,

> If courts hold states liable in damages when they comply with resolutions of the UN designed to secure international peace and security, the likelihood is that states will be less ready to assist the UN to achieve its role in this regard, and this would be detrimental to the long-term interests of the states. The individual is sufficiently protected in this situation by compliance with Geneva 4.[122]

The overall reasoning of Arden LJ in *Al-Jedda II* is that Act of State doctrine works because there is an overriding legal basis for Al-Jedda's detention, a Security Council resolution, not – presumably at least – because the Act of State doctrine can shield even the acts that violate the applicable law.[123]

Al-Jedda II thus projected a policy in relation to the Act of State doctrine as informed by Security Council resolutions, without ascertaining the proper effect of the relevant Council resolution; nor was it enquired into what precisely the requirements of the IV Geneva Convention were in relation to *Al-Jedda* and how Resolution 1546 interacted with it. Without adducing evidence that the Security Council has positively authorised an essentially extra-judicial and semi-permanent detention of the kind that was practised in relation to Al-Jedda – which it had not – it could not be sensibly argued that the Act of State doctrine operated on the basis of the Security Council's involvement. Furthermore, the Grand Chamber decision in *Al-Jedda* obviously upsets the *Al-Jedda II* findings regarding the Act of State doctrine, for to remain within the

---

[117] *Luther v Sagor*, 3 *KB* (1921), 558; further mirrored in the House of Lords decision in *Buttes*, AC 1982, 938, and the US Supreme Court decision in *Sabbatino*, 36 US 428 (1964).
[118] *Oppenheimer v Cattermole* (HL), AC 1976, 283.
[119] *Kuwait Air Co.*, House of Lords, [2002] UKHL 19, [2002] 2 AC 883; for detailed analysis of the relevant judicial practice see Orakhelashvili, *Peremptory Norms*, *supra* n.62, at Chapter 19.
[120] *Al-Jedda II*, *supra* n.94, at para. 74 (*per* Arden LJ).
[121] *Ibid.*, at paras 108, 110 (*per* Arden LJ); *ibid.*, para. 195 (*per* Elias LJ).
[122] *Ibid.*, at para. 108 (*per* Arden LJ).
[123] *Ibid.*, at para. 109 (*per* Arden LJ).

proper bounds of ECHR, English courts had to decline applying the Act of State doctrine. In addition, the finding on and interpretation of Resolution 1546 is inconsistent with the earlier finding that Resolution 1546 did not produce, in relation to the Iraqi law, the effect it allegedly purported to produce. How, it must be asked, can Resolution 1546 inform the Act of State doctrine if it did not extend to the 'Act' in question, and even if it had, its international effect would have been dubious for its conflict with the Fourth Geneva Convention and the ECHR?

7. CONCLUSION

This analysis has covered the national and international judicial practice regarding the extra-territorial effect of human rights treaties and the obstacles that can be posed to that effect before national courts. There are two principal issues arising specifically in relation to the ECHR: the interpretation of treaties and the rules governing normative conflicts, the former being a precondition to establishing whether the latter has materialised. What this analysis has demonstrated is that straightforward normative requirements supported by the ordinary meaning of treaties are of primary importance. The Grand Chamber's landmark decision in *Al-Skeini* has moved the notions of 'jurisdiction' and 'effective control' back closer to their normal meaning under general international law. National and international courts can develop concepts, notions and doctrines that enable them to give proper effect to treaties in relation to specific situations, or to adopt strategies to balance multiple interests and priorities. But the common feature of those notions, doctrines and strategies is their relativity. They can have legitimacy only as far as they accord with the parameters of inter-state agreement under treaties adopted within the consensual system of international law; apart from that, their significance is merely episodic.

19. Reparation and compensation
Natalino Ronzitti

1. VIOLATION OF *JUS AD BELLUM* AND VIOLATION OF *JUS IN BELLO*: INTERNATIONAL AND NON-INTERNATIONAL ARMED CONFLICT

There is no formal definition of *jus post bellum*. Generally it can be said that *jus post bellum* is the body of law that applies when hostilities end after peace has been restored through a peace treaty or a general armistice. The transition from war to peace is often blurred and a distinctive border is difficult to identify. Often the situation is neither peace nor war, rendering it difficult to determine the correct law to be applied. In a number of instances there is no formal cessation of hostilities and the very existence of a situation of armed conflict is denied. Be that as it may, it is expedient to say that *jus post bellum* applies when peace is restored or, at least, hostilities are terminated. If *jus post bellum* relies on a legal process, the relevant norms may be determined, the violation of which entails the responsibility of States. Two sets of norms come into consideration: those related to *jus ad bellum* and those related to *jus in bello*.

In relation to the first category, the rules governing State responsibility are those related to the violation of the prohibition of the use of force in international relations, in particular those prohibiting waging an aggressive war. These are enshrined in Article 2(4) of the United Nations Charter and in the customary norm prohibiting aggression. For the second category, the law to be considered is that contained in the Hague Convention No. IV of 1907 and in Protocol I of 1977, additional to the Four Geneva Conventions, which states that a belligerent is responsible for the conduct of its armed forces. Until recently, only violations of law in international armed conflicts came into consideration. *Jus ad bellum* is properly concerned with inter-State violence, while the use of force against rebels during a civil war is not regarded as a violation of international law.[1] *Jus in bello* rules relate both to international and non-international armed conflicts. However, the codification of rules on reparations for violations of *jus in bello* has, until now, only dealt with international armed conflict. For non-international armed conflict there is no general rule and norms regulating reparations

---

[1] Scholars are divided on the legal qualification of the struggle for self-determination from the point of view of *jus ad bellum*. It has been submitted that the government in power repressing self-determination violates the principle forbidding the use of force in international relations. However, this opinion has been subject to criticism and struggles for self-determination are not discussed here. They may be considered from the standpoint of *jus in bello*, since Protocol I additional to the Geneva Conventions qualifies self-determination struggles as international armed conflicts and thus Article 91 on compensation may be applied.

should be extracted from State practice or from general principles of law. Separate sections will be dedicated to the violation of *jus ad bellum* and to the violation of *jus in bello*.

2. FROM WAR INDEMNITIES TO WAR REPARATIONS

The Hague Convention No. IV of 1907 codified the rules regarding reparations for violations of the law of war. However, the Hague provisions do not cover damage caused by States having made recourse to an illegal war. This is understandable as prior to the entry into force of the League of Nations Covenant resort to force was generally understood as lawful independent from the existence of legal cause. Usually the victor imposed an indemnity to the vanquished to be paid, even if the vanquished did not commit any wrong in terms of a violation of international law.[2]

The first manifestation of a transformation of the 'victor–vanquished' relationship into a legal process was the Versailles Peace Treaty of 1919, where the victorious Powers sanctioned Germany's illegal resort to force. The Versailles Treaty is the cornerstone of a process that has since been incrementally developed. This process is marked by the League of Nations Covenant (1919), the Kellogg–Briand Pact (1928) and the entry into force of the United Nations Charter (1945).

3. VIOLATION OF *JUS AD BELLUM*

A. The Treaty of Versailles

The Treaty of Versailles, concluded in 1919 and entered into force in 1920, is the first manifestation of a practice which relied on a violation of international law for imposing a system of reparation to the vanquished. The relevant provision is Article 231, which states:

> The Allied and Associated Governments affirm and Germany accepts the responsibility of Germany and her allies for causing all the loss and damage to which the Allied and Associated Governments and their nationals have been subjected as a consequence of the war imposed upon them by the aggression of Germany and her allies.

---

[2] On the State practice before and after the two World Wars see specifically P. d'Argent, *Les réparations de guerre en droit international public: La responsabilité internationale des Etats à l'épreuve de la guerre* (Bruxelles: Bruylant, 2002); and A. Gattini, *Le riparazioni di guerra nel diritto internazionale* (Padova: Cedam, 2003). Old and contemporary practice is also reviewed by H. Van Houtte, B. Delmartino and I. Yi (eds), *Post-War Restoration of Property Rights under International Law, Volume 1: Institutional Feature and Substantive Law* (Cambridge: Cambridge University Press, 2008); and H. Das and H. Van Houtte, *Post-War Restoration of Property Rights under International Law, Volume 2: Procedural Aspects* (Cambridge: Cambridge University Press, 2008).

The Versailles Treaty established that, due to its aggression, Germany owed a reparation. The difficulty is whether in 1914, when the Central Empires entered war, aggression was a violation of international law. This is doubtful.

B. The World War II Settlements

From the perspective of international law, the situation was completely different at the beginning of World War II. The Covenant of the League of Nations limited the recourse to force and the Kellogg–Briand Pact outlawed war as an instrument of national policy and, according to many commentators, outlawed wars of aggression. Between the two World Wars aggression became a violation of international law and the process was sanctioned by Article 39 of the United Nations Charter. It is doubtful whether the Nuremberg trial applied *ex post facto* criminal law in inflicting punishment to the major war criminals as aggression was not yet considered an international crime. In contrast, it is less doubtful that aggression was a violation of international law, for which the State launching an aggressive war should be held responsible.

The reparations imposed on Germany consisted first of all in dismantling industrial assets, which were transferred to the victorious Powers and in particular to the Soviet Union, which had suffered the most severe losses. The apportionment was made in accordance with the part of the territory of the German Reich occupied by the victorious Powers and substantiated in the 1946 Agreement on Reparation from Germany on the Establishment of an Inter-Allied Reparation Agency and on the Restitution of Monetary Gold. A final settlement had to be made through a formal peace treaty. This was concluded later when circumstances were completely changed and close to Germany's reunification, when it regained its status as a great economic power. The former four occupying Powers made the Treaty on the Final Settlement with respect to Germany in 1990, renouncing all rights towards the former enemy State. For its part Germany declared itself ready to compensate the victims of the Nazi regime on a voluntary basis. Compensations were also given to Israel, even though it did not exist at the end of World War II and had never become a belligerent State against Germany.

The concept of reparation and war damages as means for redressing a violation committed by vanquished belligerents may be found in numerous post-war settlements. On 10 February 1947 the Allied and Associated Powers concluded separate peace treaties in Paris with Bulgaria, Italy, Finland, Hungary and Romania. The Peace Treaty with Italy served as a model for other treaties with the defeated States. The source of the liability is, according to the Preamble, the war of aggression started by Italy together with the other two Axis Powers (Germany and Japan): Italy 'bears her share of responsibility for the war'. The Treaty sets out three categories of obligation:

(a) war reparations (Art. 74), i.e. a sum of money and other assets to be delivered to the victorious Powers;
(b) restitution (Art. 75), i.e. returning property taken in the territory of the victorious Powers; and
(c) confiscation, i.e. the liberty to seize Italian property held in the territory of the victorious Power, including private property and without any compensation.

The San Francisco Peace Treaty of 1951 was made by Japan and a number of Allied Powers (48 out of 55 and not including the USSR). The principle of paying reparation was recognized even though the amount due was to be substantiated in separate bilateral treaties to be concluded later. The Treaty was created six years after the surrender of Japan when the country was already fully integrated into the West. This explains why the reparations imposed on Japan were not so harsh. It is interesting to note that Article 14(a) of the Treaty contained the principle of the capacity to pay:

> It is recognized that Japan should pay reparations to the Allied Powers for the damage and suffering caused by it during the war. Nevertheless it is also recognized that the resources of Japan are not presently sufficient, if it is to maintain a viable economy, to make complete reparation for all such damage and suffering and at the same time meet its other obligations.

C. The UN Era: Unlawful Use of Force and War of Aggression

The entry into force of the UN Charter has completely changed the system of *jus ad bellum* and of the resort to force in international relations. Article 2(4) made any resort to force by an individual State, unless justified under self-defence or authorized by the UN Security Council (as shown by subsequent practice), an international wrong. Article 2(4) contains an absolute prohibition and any uncertainty among writers is related to the exceptions and whether there are other lawful uses of force in addition to self-defence, such as humanitarian intervention or intervention to protect nationals abroad. The content of the right of self-defence is also the object of differing interpretations. The division among legal scholars is related to the notions of pre-emption, anticipatory self-defence and self-defence exercisable only after an armed attack has occurred. The notion of armed attack, which triggers the right of self-defence, is also the object of different interpretations.

The Charter has also made certain that aggression is outlawed by the system and Article 39 enables the Security Council to authorize action when aggression threatens international peace and security. Article 39 does not define aggression or war of aggression. Aggression and acts constituting aggression are defined by United Nations General Assembly (hereinafter 'GA') Resolution 3314 (XXIX), which can only act as a guide to the Security Council for determining if an act of aggression has been committed. The amendment adopted at Kampala in 2010, by the Conference of Review and amendment of the International Criminal Court (hereinafter 'ICC'), incorporated the GA definition of aggression.[3] The amendment, which has not yet entered into force, regards aggression as an international crime and therefore related to the *jus in bello* and not to *jus ad bellum*, even though aggression may not have a substantially different meaning according to the two sectors of law.

Even more difficult is defining what constitutes a 'war of aggression': Article 6 of the 1945 London Agreement and the Nuremberg Judgment might offer assistance. However, the relevance for the purpose of distinguishing a war of aggression from an act of aggression is relative and is mainly related to the level of State responsibility and

---

[3] Cf. Stefan Barriga and Leena Grover, 'A Historic Breakthrough on the Crime of Aggression', (2011) 105 *AJIL* 517.

the amount of reparation due. It is important to affirm that every violation of *jus ad bellum* gives rise to State responsibility and that international law imposes on the wrongdoer the duty to redress the violation it has committed.

D. The UN Security Council and Judicial Practice

Prior to the UN Charter, the only practice available for war reparations for violations of *jus ad bellum* was that related to the Versailles Treaty and to peace treaties concluded after World War II. After the Charter came into force a number of judicial and arbitral decisions may also be considered. In addition, in the Iraq–Kuwait affair the Security Council made clear that the violation of *jus ad bellum* entails State responsibility that the violator is obliged to repair. The difference between the practice developed by the judicial and arbitral bodies and that of the Security Council is clear. While the Security Council is a political organ and its decisions obey political considerations, which may in some cases derogate from international law, the conduct of judicial and arbitral institutions is confined to the application of international law. In other words, while the practice of the Security Council may be reminiscent of the victor–loser relationship of the two World Wars, the findings by judicial and arbitral institutions are dictated by legal reasoning and are based on international legal principles. Thus, the practice of the Eritrea–Ethiopia Commission is very important as it laid out a set of principles that may be of guidance for future cases. The following precedents may be enumerated:

- The *Corfu Channel* case is the first judgment of the International Court of Justice (hereinafter 'ICJ') related to the use of force.[4] In its judgment of 9 April 1949 the Court found that the British incursion into Albanian waters, in order to sweep mines disseminated along the Corfu Channel, constituted a violation of international law and stated that the declaration on the illegality of intervention constituted appropriate satisfaction for Albania. Satisfaction is a means of repairing an international wrong and the ICJ made clear that it constitutes an appropriate means of reparation in connection with a wrongful act concerning the violation of territorial integrity through military means.
- In the *Nicaragua/United States* case the ICJ was confronted with an extensive policy of intervention by the United States in Nicaragua that lasted for a considerable period of time and was carried out using war material and covert operations.[5] After affirming that the United States was responsible for having violated, *inter alia*, the territorial integrity of Nicaragua and the obligation, stemming from customary international law, not to use force, the Court stated, in its judgment of 27 June 1986, that the United States was obliged to make reparation, the form and amount of which should be settled by the Court failing an agreement between the parties. The US contested the ICJ dictum as a political judgment which did not have any legal foundation and did not comply with the obligation to repair. After having tried in vain to oblige the US to comply with the

---

[4] *Corfu Channel* case (Albania v. United Kingdom) [1949] ICJ Rep. 3.
[5] *Case Concerning Military and Paramilitary Activities in and Against Nicaragua* (Nicaragua v. United States of America), [1986] ICJ Rep. 14.

judgment, a change of government in Nicaragua prompted the Central American State to cease its attempts to enforce the judgment.

- Security Council Resolution 687 (1991) and the United Nations Compensation Commission (hereinafter 'UNCC') are a new development in the practice of post-conflict reparations.[6] Resolution 687, enacted at the end of the Iraqi war between the coalition of States and Iraq, is a type of peace treaty and has been formally accepted by Iraq. Paragraph 16 states that Iraq is 'liable under international law for any direct loss, damage, including environmental damage and the depletion of natural resources, or injury to foreign Governments, nationals and corporations, as a result of Iraq's unlawful invasion and occupation of Kuwait'. Even though the resolution does not formally qualify Iraq as an aggressor, its violation of *jus ad bellum* is clearly established. The wording 'unlawful invasion and occupation of Iraq' is the language also employed in the decision of the Governing Council, that is the body created by Resolution 687 for directing the Commission entrusted with the task of processing claims submitted by those (individuals and corporations) who suffered damages as a result of the Gulf war. The practice of the UNCC is of utmost importance for establishing international responsibility for the violation of *jus ad bellum*. The UNCC adjudicated claims for damages caused to States. Claims were usually submitted by Governments on behalf of individuals and corporations, which had suffered damage, asking for proper compensation.
- In the *Democratic Republic of Congo v. Uganda* case the ICJ, in its judgment of 1 December 2005, determined that Uganda had violated the norm on the prohibition of the use of force and consequently held that the Congo was entitled to reparation, the amount of which should be established in a separate proceeding, should the parties fail to agree on their content.[7]
- The Claims Commission between Eritrea and Ethiopia was established by the 2000 Algiers Agreement. It acted as an arbitral tribunal and its findings are of utmost importance for determining the responsibility deriving from violations of *jus ad bellum*.[8] It established principles for assessing the quality and quantum of reparations and in Decision No. 7 of 27 July 2007 it gave the parties 'guidance regarding *jus ad bellum* liability'. The starting point is that Eritrea bears responsibility for a violation of *jus ad bellum*, even though the Commission finding is not that Eritrea initiated an aggressive war against Ethiopia. The significant point is that compensation can only be awarded once a causal link between the violation of international law and the harm suffered has been established. Thus, for the Commission legal causation should be proved between the unlawful action and the resulting damage and the criteria for determining the causal link should be established before evaluating the amount of compensation

---

[6] Cf. M.F. di Rattalma and T. Treves (eds), *The United Nations Compensation Commission: A Handbook* (The Hague: Kluwer Law International, 1999).

[7] *Armed Activities on the Territory of the Congo* (Democratic Republic of the Congo v. Uganda), Judgment, [2005] ICJ Rep. 2005, 280–281.

[8] Cf. A. de Guttry, H.H.G. Post and G. Venturini (eds), *The 1998–2000 War between Eritrea and Ethiopia: An International Legal Perspective* (The Hague: T.M.C. Asser Press, 2009).

for the damages. On this point the Commission makes similarities and distinctions with the conduct of other international tribunals or claims commissions, including that established under Resolution 687 (1991) on Iraq. It is noteworthy to recall what the Commission stated on the law relating to compensation for war damages:

> there have been few modern instances in which a State has been determined to bear responsibility for damages resulting from a war as a matter of international law. Throughout history, indemnities frequently have been exacted from the losing parties in wars, but this has resulted from the exercise of power by the victor, not the application of the international law of State responsibility. (page 9 para. 21)[9]

In its Final Award on Damages of 1 August 2009 the Commission gave Ethiopia substantial monetary compensation for Eritrea's violation of *jus ad bellum*.[10]

E. Reparation/Compensation and the Re-establishment of Peace: The Recovery of the Defeated State

War is often a source of economic poverty for belligerent States, both for the victor and the loser. In the end an enormous quantity of resources are destroyed. Harsh conditions for peace imposed on the loser impede reconstruction and may produce instability, paving the way for dictatorial regimes, as happened in Germany after World War I and the severe reparations imposed by the Versailles Treaty.

World War II ended with the dismantling of German industry and the transfer of industrial assets mainly to the Soviet Union, the country which had suffered the biggest losses.

The recovery of the defeated State is often a condition for a lasting peace. There are various modes for pursuing that goal. A regime change and the establishment of a democratic government are often imperative. The victorious Powers may renounce war damages, in whole or in part, negotiated in the peace treaty and a programme of economic aid may be established in order to benefit all countries within a region affected by the war, including the loser. An example is post-war Germany. The United States declined to claim a part of the total amount of war damages. A similar policy was followed with regard to Italy. At the same time, a plan for Europe's economic recovery was promoted by the United States: the Marshall Plan.[11] It lasted four years (1948–1951) and a conspicuous amount of resources were channelled to the UK and Western Continental countries, including the two former enemy States, Italy and the Federal Republic of Germany. Even though the Marshall Plan was originally designed to aid all European countries destroyed by the war, the Soviet Union and its satellites did not accept the offer. The Marshall Plan became an instrument of the European

---

[9] Eritrea–Ethiopia Claims Commission, Decision Number 7, Guidance Regarding Jus ad Bellum Liability, available at www.pca-cpa.org.

[10] Eritrea Ethiopia Claims Commission, Final Award, Eritrea's Damages Claims; Eritrea–Ethiopia Claims Commission, Final Award, Ethiopia's Damages Claims (17 August 2009), available at www.pca-cpa.org.

[11] See A. de Zajas, 'Marshall Plan (European Economic Recovery)', in *Max Planck Encyclopedia of Public International Law*, available at www.mpepil.com.

democracies to cope with the threat represented by the Communist parties (namely in France and Italy) and to reinforce the links with the United States in the first years of the Cold War.

Nowadays, the *jus post bellum* should be anchored within the United Nations. Two organs come into consideration: the Security Council and the newly established Peace-building Commission. The policy of the Security Council is to act as a stabilizer after the cessation of hostilities. It can act under Article 39 of the UN Charter on the premise that the situation constitutes a threat to international peace, notwithstanding the cessation of hostilities. The Security Council can act on its own with a post-conflict mission or may authorize a coalition of States to do so. The war against Iraq in 2003 was not authorized by the Security Council. However, immediately after the cessation of hostilities the Security Council took the (nominal) lead. After the Iraq *debellatio* by the Anglo-American coalition, the Security Council enacted Resolution 1483 (2003), legitimizing the presence of the occupying Powers and of those countries which offered to send troops to Iraq. Thereafter, the Security Council endorsed the Coalition Provisional Authority, the real governing institution of occupied Iraq. The occupying forces and the forces of other countries stationed in Iraq were transformed into a multinational force under US command and authorized to maintain peace and security by Security Council Resolution 1511. Resolution 1546 (2004) blessed the establishment of an Iraqi provisional government and the multinational force remained in Iraq with the consent of the newly established Iraqi Government.

The Peace-building Commission was created after the New York Summit at the level of heads of State and Government in 2005 and started to operate in 2006. The Peace-building Commission is a subsidiary organ of the Security Council and of the GA and its mandate is broad enough to encompass conciliation and reconstruction. The main problem of the Commission is its funding, which is made of voluntary contributions to a Peace-building Fund. The record of the Commission is recent and its work has been devoted to intra-State conflict, such as in Liberia, Sierra Leone and Burundi.

4. WAR REPARATIONS AND HUMAN RIGHTS

A harsh policy imposing extreme war reparations on the defeated State may endanger the basic needs of its population and create a sense of resentment that inhibits the restoration of peace. The human rights of individuals and populations should be taken into account. Human rights concerns have been developed since World War II; thus those treaties concluded at the end of the two World Wars did not take this issue into account.

Nowadays the protection of human rights in war reparation cannot be ignored. For instance, war reparations in the form of forced labour of the population of the defeated country would be contrary to the International Labour Organization Convention on the prohibition of forced labour and to a number of other conventions.[12] It may also be said

---

[12] See F. Domb, 'Human Rights and War Reparation', (1993) 23 *IsrYHR*, at 94–95.

that a clause imposing forced labour as war reparation would be contrary to *jus cogens* and thus void, or should be terminated if stipulated before the birth of such a *jus cogens* norm.

Additionally, Article 42, paragraph 3 of the 1996 International Law Commission (hereinafter 'ILC') Draft Articles on State Responsibility affirmed that 'In no case shall reparation result in depriving the population of the State of its own means of subsistence'. In the commentary it was explained that full reparation cannot be taken to such a point as to endanger the whole social system of the State concerned, for example in a peace treaty following the defeat of a particular State.

Article 1, paragraph 2 of the 1966 International Covenant on Civil and Political Rights also affirms that 'in no case may a people be deprived of its own means of subsistence'.

Article 42, paragraph 3 was not retained in the ILC final Draft Articles on State Responsibility (2001). However, it took into account the principle of proportionality that inspires each form in which reparation is articulated (restitution, compensation or satisfaction): proportionality may safeguard human rights. Proportionality should be assessed not only against the gains of the victorious party, but also (and foremost) against the need of the population that might starve because of the imposition of extensive war damages.[13]

5. WAR REPARATIONS: COMPENSATION, RESTITUTION, SATISFACTION AND THE QUANTUM OF COMPENSATION

Article 31 of the Draft Articles on State Responsibility affirms that the responsible State is under an obligation to make full reparation for the injury caused by the international wrongful act. Article 34 sets out the following methods for full reparation of the injury caused by an international wrong: restitution, compensation and satisfaction. They may be granted either singly or in combination. The point is that while it is certain that a violation of *jus ad bellum* is an international wrong it is less certain that the obligation to repair the damages caused by the wrongdoer 'puisse être adéquatement régie par les dispositions normalement applicables à la responsabilité en droit international'.[14] This pessimistic evaluation derives from the practice of the peace treaties after the two World Wars, and even Security Council Resolution 687, terminating the Iraq–Kuwait conflict, is not perfectly in line with the law of international responsibility and the consequences deriving from an international wrongful act.

Decision No. 7 of the Eritrea–Ethiopia Claims Commission contains guidance regarding *jus ad bellum* liability. The starting point is that 'Compensation can only be awarded in respect of damages having a sufficient causal connection with conduct violating international law'. However, the degree of remoteness to establish the causal link varies and this is reflected in the amount of compensation to be given. Legal

---

[13] Cf Y. Dinstein, *War, Aggression and Self-Defence*, 3rd edn (Cambridge: Cambridge University Press, 2001), at 100.

[14] J. Verhoeven, 'Preface to d' Argent', *supra* n.2, at xiii.

causation is explained as a reasonable connection between the violation and the damage, or, as proximate cause. All these criteria entail a measure of discretion. Another distinction is between direct and indirect damages, or damage foreseeable by the wrongdoer, or, at least, reasonably foreseeable, and damage that is unforeseen and unforeseeable.

The Claim Commission opted for the criterion of proximate cause, which best describes the connection between the wrong and the damage:

> In assessing whether this test [that is the 'proximate cause'] is met, and whether the chain of causation is sufficiently close in a particular situation, the Commission will give weight to whether particular damage reasonably should have been foreseeable to an actor committing the international delict in question. The element of forseeability, although not without its own difficulties, provides some discipline and predictability in assessing proximity. Accordingly, it will be given considerable weight in assessing whether particular damages are compensable.[15]

The Commission made a distinction between aggressive war and a mere violation of the rule on prohibiting the use of force. While the former entails extensive financial responsibility and full reparation for war damages, the latter renders the financial responsibility less serious. However, there is no mathematical formula and the proximity criteria should be substantiated by an appropriate finding of a claim commission or a tribunal or through a negotiating process. Note that damages to be compensated from an illegal resort to the use of force are also those provoked by a lawful action according to the *jus in bello*, for instance the aerial bombardment of a lawful target, such as an airfield. This was the finding of the Eritrea–Ethiopia Claim Commission in its Final Award of 17 August 2009. The Commission awarded compensation to Ethiopia for the attack on Mekele airport, which the Commission found in conformity with the law of war but was nevertheless an action arising from the context of Eritrea's illegal recourse to violence.[16] This finding is in accordance with the opinion rendered by a number of learned writers.[17] To argue otherwise, that is to endorse the contrary opinion, according to which the wrongdoer would not be responsible for that conduct which is in keeping with the law of war, would render the responsibility for violation of *jus ad bellum* an empty rule. At most, it can be concluded that respect for *jus in bello* is a kind of extenuating circumstance, influencing the quantum of compensation. If a belligerent violates *jus ad bellum* and simultaneously commits a violation of the law of war, it will be responsible for the violation of both *jus ad bellum* and *jus in bello*. If, on the contrary, it violates the *jus ad bellum* but abides by the law of war, it will be held responsible only for the violation of *jus ad bellum*, according to the meaning described above. This would act as an incentive to

---

[15] Eritrea–Ethiopia Claims Commission, *supra* n.9
[16] Ethiopia's Damages Claims, *supra* n.10, at paras 426–427.
[17] See, for instance, G. Fitzmaurice, 'The Juridical Clauses of the Peace Treaties', (1948) 73 *Hague Recueil*, at 325–326; H. Lauterpacht, 'The Limits of the Operation of the Laws of War', (1953) 30 *BYIL* 254; and the authors quoted by Erik V. Koppe, 'Compensation for War Damages under *Jus ad Bellum*', in de Guttry *et al.*, *supra* n.8, at 427–429, who criticizes the above opinion. Cf. also the remarks by Vera Gowlland-Debbas, *ibid.*, at 440–448.

respect the laws of war. It is necessary to note that the Draft Articles on the Law of State Responsibility demand that the responsible State terminates the international wrongful act, if it is continuing, and offer assurances and guarantees of non-repetition 'if circumstances so require'. Assurances and guarantees of non-repetition are typical of peace treaties, and other international acts imposed by the victorious party, to prevent the loser from resuming its aggressive policy. For instance, the 1947 Peace Treaty with Italy imposed a vast programme of demilitarization. Security Council Resolution 687 (1991) did the same with Iraq.

The practice of peace treaties concluded after World War II reveals that the victorious Powers confiscated assets belonging to the defeated State and to its citizens. A limit to the type of property that may be seized is now established by Article I, paragraph 3 of the Protocol to the Hague Cultural Property Convention of 1954, which prohibits the seizure of moveable cultural property as war reparation.

6. COLONIALISM AND REPARATION: THE UNIQUE CASE OF THE 2008 ITALIAN–LIBYAN TREATY

The Treaty on Friendship, Partnership and Cooperation between Italy and Libya of 30 August 2008 is unique among the relationships between a colonial Power and its former colony, an example that was not followed by other European Powers.[18] The Treaty, signed in Benghazi, was meant to put an end to the dispute between the two countries and Libya's claims relating to Italian colonialism. In greeting Colonel Muammar Gaddafi at the time of the signing ceremony, the Italian Prime Minister expressed his regret for the colonial period in the following very strong terms: 'In the name of the Italian people, as head of the government, I feel it my duty to apologize and express my sorrow for what happened many years ago and left a scar on many of your families.' As a matter of fact, the normalization of Italian–Libyan relations with the conclusion of the Treaty of Benghazi was preceded by a number of bilateral agreements, which nevertheless left many questions unanswered, including the Libyan request for reparations for the damages caused by colonialism.

The Treaty consists of three parts: general principles; closing with the past and ending the disputes; and partnership. It begins with a long Preamble that sets down, among other things, the will to close the 'painful "chapter of the past" for which Italy has already expressed its regret for the suffering that Italian colonization caused the Libyan people'. In this way, Libya has managed to receive a 'condemnation' of Italian colonialism, which is reflected in several of the Treaty's provisions. The colonialism reparations are included in the second part of the Treaty and commit Italy to building basic infrastructure for a total of $5 billion. The annual expenditure will amount to $250 million over 20 years. Less onerous, but still Italy's responsibility, are the 'special initiatives' for 'the benefit of the Libyan people', such as scholarships, the rehabilitation of victims of mine explosions and the return of archeological artefacts shipped to Italy during the colonial period.

---

[18] See the text in (2009) 92 *Rivista di Diritto Internazionale* 633–640.

The Benghazi Treaty sets out the manifold form of the reparation for an international wrong: compensation, restitution and satisfaction. The difficulty is that colonialism was not an international wrong at the time it was committed, yet the parties acted as though it was in order to set out reparations.

7. THE VIOLATION OF *JUS IN BELLO*: THE 1907 HAGUE CONVENTION NO. IV AND PROTOCOL I OF 1977 ADDITIONAL TO FOUR GENEVA CONVENTIONS

The responsibility for violations of *jus in bello*, that is for violations of the law regulating armed conflict, is enshrined both in Article 3 of Hague Convention No. IV of 1907 and in Article 91 of Protocol I additional to the Geneva Conventions. Both state that a party to the conflict is obliged to pay compensation for violations of the Regulation appended to Hague Convention No. IV and of the provisions of the Geneva Conventions or of the Additional Protocol respectively. Both provisions add that the compensation is due 'if the case demands'. However, this formulation does not set out a limit on State responsibility; it means only that compensation is due if other forms of reparation, for instance restitution, are not possible. The belligerent is responsible for all acts committed by persons forming part of its armed forces, including acts committed *ultra vires*. The responsibility for violations of the law of war is also established in connection with the rules on the protection of cultural property, as demonstrated by Article 38 of the 1999 Protocol II to the Hague Convention of 1954 for the Protection of Cultural Property in the Event of Armed Conflict, which states that the criminal responsibility of an individual does not prejudice the responsibility of States, according to international law, including the duty of reparation. The rule on responsibility for violations of the law of war and the obligation to pay compensation belong to customary international law.

Both Article 3 of the Hague Convention No. IV and Article 91 of Protocol II only concern international armed conflict. The central issue is determining whether they only regulate State-to-State relations or if they may also be invoked by an individual victim before a domestic tribunal. The case-law, primarily from the Japanese courts, indicates that the Hague Convention does not contain self-executing provisions and that an individual does not have any right to claim damages before a domestic tribunal. This opinion was followed by the US and German Tribunals, which had the occasion to judge claims by individuals.

A different stance was taken by the Greek Court of Cassation in the *Distomo* affair (a decision later reversed) and by the Italian Military Tribunals, which condemned German nationals who committed war crimes during World War II. The Italian courts, in addition to inflicting penalties, also required the wrongdoer to pay compensation in conjunction with Germany.[19]

---

[19] See next paragraph and P. Gaeta, 'Are Victims of Serious Violations of International Humanitarian Law Entitled to Compensation?', in O. Ben-Naftali (ed.), *International Humanitarian Law and International Human Rights Law* (Oxford: Oxford University Press, 2011), at 308–311.

The ICJ Advisory Opinion on the Legal Consequences of the Construction of a Wall in Palestine is also relevant here. The Court affirmed that Israel had violated a number of rules of international law and was under the obligation 'to make reparation for the damages caused to all natural or legal persons concerned'.[20]

8. THE DECLARATION ADOPTED BY THE INTERNATIONAL LAW ASSOCIATION AT THE HAGUE (2010)

As discussed above, reparation and compensation for war damages, and in particular for violation of the rules on armed conflict, is a State-to-State matter and an individual has no *locus standi* to enforce State responsibility and obtain redress for a violation. In order to remedy this situation the International Law Association in 2010 enacted a Declaration of International Law Principles on Reparation for Victims of Armed Conflict.[21] Although the Declaration is soft law, it may still influence the work of international bodies, including international tribunals. It may also be relevant for domestic tribunals that have to judge claims by individuals who have been the victim of a violation of the law of war.

The Declaration addresses violations of both international and non-international armed conflicts and affirms that the victim, that is the natural or legal person who has suffered harm, has a right to reparation, the form of which may consist of restitution, compensation, satisfaction, and guarantees and assurances of non-repetition – either singly or in combination.

The responsible party is the author of the violation, which may be a State or an international organization responsible for a violation of the law of armed conflict. Non-State actors may also be included in the category of responsible party. It is of utmost importance that the responsible party establish programmes and maintain institutions to give effect to reparations and that States ensure that victims have a right to reparation under national law. The statutes of limitation may frustrate the right of the individual to reparation. It is thus recommended that the statutes should not unduly impact the exercise of the victim's ability to exercise their rights and claim for reparation.

9. INDIVIDUAL CLAIMS FOR VIOLATIONS OF *JUS IN BELLO*: THE IMMUNITY OF STATES FROM FOREIGN JURISDICTION HURDLES

The main obstacle for individual claims for reparation is the principle of immunity of States from jurisdiction. Action by the victim is often defeated since the immunity of

---

[20] *Legal Consequences of the Construction of a Wall in the Occupied Palestinian Territory*, Advisory Opinion, [2004] ICJ Rep., at para. 152.

[21] The Declaration is available at www.ila-hq.org.

the responsible State from jurisdiction in national courts is well established under international law.

The distinction between absolute and relative immunity from civil jurisdiction in foreign countries is a well-settled principle of international law. Since military activities are, by definition, a manifestation of a State's sovereignty, they fall squarely within the principle of absolute immunity, namely concerning combat activities.

The law of State immunity has been the object of two Conventions: the 1972 Council of Europe Basle Convention and the 2005 UN Convention on the Jurisdictional Immunities of States and Their Property. Both Conventions follow the method of lists. They affirm the principle of State immunity (Article 15 of the Basle Convention and Article 5 of the UN Convention). Article 5 is paradigmatic: 'A state enjoys immunity, in respect of itself and its property, from the jurisdiction of the courts of another state subject to the provision of the present Convention.'

The list enumerates the instances in which a State may be submitted to the jurisdiction of another State, for example in cases of commercial transactions or contracts of employment with local manpower. Military activities are excluded from the jurisdiction of foreign States. This principle is expressly stipulated in Article 31 of the Basle Convention and is also affirmed, albeit implicitly, by the UN Convention.[22]

How can the rule on sovereign immunity be removed? There are two ways: the tort exception and the *jus cogens* argument:

(a) The tort exception is established in both Article 11 of the Basle Convention and Article 12 of the UN Convention. A number of conditions are required to nullify the rule on sovereign immunity. First, the damage should occur in the forum State; secondly, the author of the damage should be present in the territory of the forum State when the damage occurred. The action should be aimed at recovering pecuniary compensation for death or injury, or damage or loss of property.

In the *Distomo* case, the Greek Areios Pagos (Supreme Court) decided, in November 2000, that Germany could not invoke immunity from jurisdiction for atrocities committed during the occupation of Greece at the time of World War II.[23] The Greek Special Supreme Court reversed the Areios Pagos decision in 2002.[24] It stated that the Basle Convention was not applicable, since Greece was not a State party, and that it is not declaratory of customary international law, nor was the tort exception retained by the European Court of Human Rights in the judgment *McElhinney v. Ireland*.[25]

While Article 31 of the European Convention states that the Convention cannot prejudice the actions of armed forces stationed in foreign territory, such a clause is not contained in the UN Convention. Although a number of scholars believe that it is

---

[22] G. Hafner and L. Lange, 'La Convention des Nations Unies sur les Immunités Juridiction-nelles des Etats et de leurs biens', (2004) 50 *AFDI* (2004), 75.

[23] *Prefecture of Voiotia v. Federal Republic of Germany*, 4 May 2000, reproduced in (2001) 95 *AJIL* 198.

[24] M. Panezi, 'Sovereign Immunity and Violation of Jus Cogens Norms', (2003) 58 *RHDI*, 199.

[25] *McElhinney v. Ireland* [GC], No. 31253/96, 21 November 2001, ECHR 2001-XI. McElhinney was fired upon by a British policeman when passing the border with Northern Ireland. The Supreme Court of Ireland (1985) stated that the UK was entitled to immunity from jurisdiction. The Irish judgment was confirmed by the ECHR.

implied, this opinion is untenable as the drafter of the UN Convention was very familiar with the Basle Convention and did not feel the necessity of excluding the acts of armed forces from the tort exception.

(b) According to a doctrinal construction, *jus cogens* norms are hierarchically superior to all other provisions of international law. If a State infringes a *jus cogens* norm, it implicitly forfeits its right to immunity from jurisdiction. The *jus cogens* exception was recognized, together with other lines of reasoning, by the Court of Cassation of Italy in the *Ferrini* case. Mr Ferrini was deported to Germany during the occupation of Italy by Germany after 8 September 1943 and the Court said that Germany was not entitled to sovereign immunity since Germany had violated fundamental principles of international law.[26] The *Ferrini* finding has been followed in a number of judgments by Italian tribunals. The issue is now (end of 2011) pending before the ICJ, since Germany instituted proceedings against Italy on 23 December 2008.[27] Greece applied to intervene, stating that it had a legal interest, due to the *Distomo* affair, and its request was accepted by the Court in its order of 4 July 2011.[28] It is worth noting that the drafters of the 2005 UN Convention knew the *jus cogens* exception argument and it was not taken into account in completing the list of exceptions to sovereign immunity.[29] However, this does not prove that the *jus cogens* exception might not be part of the exception to sovereign immunity. The Preamble of the New York Convention clearly states that the rules of customary international law continue to govern matters not regulated by the Convention. Since the *jus cogens* exception is part of customary international law and since that matter is not regulated by the New York Convention it is possible to conclude that this exception is still valid, notwithstanding the silence of the Convention on this point.

The Institut de Droit International, in its 2009 Naples session, passed a resolution on international law and State immunity, and the immunity of State agents. However, it did not take a stance on the issue of violations of a *jus cogens* norm and State immunity before foreign jurisdictions and it only affirmed, in Article IV of the resolution, that the provisions on agents' immunity 'are without prejudice to the issue whether and when a State enjoys immunity from jurisdiction before the national courts of another State in civil proceedings relating to an international crime committed by an agent of the former State'.

---

[26] *Ferrini c. Repubblica federale di Germania* (Cass. Sez. Un. No. 5044/04), 11 March 2004, reproduced in (2004) 87 *RDI* 539.

[27] The controversy was settled by the ICJ in its judgment of 3 February 2012. The judgment rejected all the Italian defences and found that Italy violated the customary norm on the jurisdictional immunity of States by allowing civil claims to be brought against Germany: *Jurisdictional Immunity of the State (Germany v. Italy): Greece Intervening*, ICJ Judgment, 3 February 2012.

[28] *Jurisdictional Immunity of the State* (Germany v. Italy), *Application by the Hellenic Republic for Permission to Intervene*, ICJ, Order, 4 July 2011.

[29] Hafner and Lange, *supra* n.22, at 67.

10. REMEDIES FOR VIOLATION OF HUMAN RIGHTS LAW

It is important to point out that remedies for violations of human rights law are at the disposal of the individuals who suffered harm during the hostilities, or after they have ended. For harms suffered during the hostilities the remedies available under the law of war are not the only tools at the disposal of individuals. One has to point out that human rights law applies during hostilities unless derogated as *lex specialis* by humanitarian law. This is particularly true for non-international armed conflict, unless the derogation clause which is inserted in human rights treaties has been activated by the responsible government. However, even in this case the core provisions cannot be derogated from, such as the prohibition of torture.

The second point to be mentioned concerns the extra-territorial application of human rights treaties. Their provisions apply to foreign territory in so far as they are under the control of the army belonging to a State that has ratified the relevant human rights treaty.[30]

Even remedies under human rights law may be barred by the doctrine of sovereign immunity, but are not usually subject to the exception of the non self-executing nature of the provisions giving rights to individuals.

Human rights law should be applied, in its entirety, within the territories formerly involved in war and thereafter freed from hostilities. Again, the extra-territorial application of human rights treaties should protect individuals against troops stationed in the territory. In this case the main hurdles are the following:

- the stipulation of a Status of Forces Agreement with the host country, which usually exempts the stationed troops from the local jurisdiction;
- the unwillingness of the international organizations dispatching soldiers or other officials in the host country to be held accountable for their conduct before the local jurisdiction. Claims commissions are, in some cases, instituted and this may provide some remedy against a situation which is not consistent with human rights law and the right to access to justice. Usually the State of nationality of the officials dispatched abroad under the banner of an international organization is not held responsible, but the situation is changing, as shown by the judgment of 5 July 2011 of The Hague Court of Appeal, which held the Dutch Government responsible for not having given protection to three Bosnian men who had taken refuge with the Dutch contingent serving as members of the UN peace-keeping forces.[31]

---

[30] See for instance A. Gioia, 'The Role of the European Court of Human Rights in Monitoring Compliance with Humanitarian Law in Armed Conflict', in Ben-Naftali (ed.), *supra* n.19, at 207–212.

[31] Cf. Cees van Dam 'Netherlands Found Liable for Srebrenica Deaths', *ASIL Insight*, 19 September 2011, Vol. 15, Issue 27.

11. INTERNATIONAL CRIMINAL TRIBUNALS AND COMPENSATION FOR THE VICTIMS

If the violation of the law of war amounts to the commission of an international crime, the international tribunals are entitled to deal with reparations.[32] They may be granted by the ICC in application of Article 75 of its Statute. The Court may award reparation to the victim upon request or, in exceptional circumstances, on its own motion. The Court is empowered to adjudicate claims against individuals, but not against the State to which the individual belongs, even though the State bears international responsibility. It is logical that the victim has the right to claim reparation from the State bearing international responsibility.[33] However, as has already been noted, under the present ICC Statute the Court cannot adjudicate a claim against the responsible State. Reparation may consist of:

(a) restitution, for instance restoration of property;
(b) compensation, i.e. a sum of money for any economically assessable damage;
(c) rehabilitation, which 'should include medical and psychological care as well as legal and social services'.

The three kinds of reparation are listed in Article 75, while the examples given are drawn from Human Rights Resolution 2005/35 on Basic Principles for Remedying Gross Violations of Human Rights. According to Article 75, the Court should establish principles relating to reparations. This proposition is rather obscure since the Court has not been endowed with the power to change the Statute. At the end of 2011 these principles had yet to be drafted and the Court is still working on them. On 12 December 2011 the Assembly of States Parties passed a resolution on reparations requesting the Court to adopt coherent principles for reparations, including the identification and freezing of assets of convicted individuals and pointing out that liability for reparations is based on the individual criminal responsibility of convicted persons.

Article 75's content has been spelled out by the ICC Rules of Procedure and Evidence. While Article 94 deals with requests for reparation by the victim, Article 95 deals with the case in which the Court proceeds on its own motion.

Article 97 of the Rules of Procedure and Evidence specifies how reparation is given. Reparation may be awarded on an individual basis, on a collective basis, or both. Reparation on a collective basis means that a sum is awarded for all victims, should reparation take the form of compensation. Reparation on a collective basis may be awarded through the Trust Fund, as explained below. The ICC makes an order which is pronounced against the convicted person or executed through the Trust Fund, allowing the victim to recover compensation. The Court may also order interim measures, for instance freezing of property of the convicted person. The decision of the Court should be implemented in the domestic order of the relevant State party and enforced under

---

[32] See generally L. Zegveld, 'Victims Reparations Claims and International Criminal Courts', (2010) 8 *J Int Criminal Justice*, at 75–79.
[33] Gaeta, *supra* n.19, at 321–322.

Article 109 of the Rome Statute. The enforcement procedure is that of the State party. This rule is customary for proceedings of this nature.

The Trust Fund is governed by Article 79 of the Statute. The Fund was established by a decision of the Assembly of States Parties and is made up of the fines and forfeitures ordered by the Court and also voluntary contributions. The Trust Fund has already been set up and its governing board named.

Article 75, paragraph 6 contains a saving clause. It is stated that 'nothing in this Article shall be interpreted as prejudicing the rights of victims under national or international law'. This clause is also difficult to interpret and should be clarified with respect to the Court's case-law. It could mean that the victim can avail him/herself of a court's judgment before a domestic tribunal. Is it the same for an international tribunal? Can the victim seek compensation before an international tribunal availing him/herself of the Court judgment, provided he/she has a right of access? A couple of issues come into consideration. The first is raised by the exhaustion of local remedies. Are proceedings before the ICC considered equivalent to the exhaustion of local remedies? The second is raised by the issue of complementarity. Supposing that the national tribunal delivers a judgment establishing a penalty for the guilty without awarding any compensation (or only nominal compensation) – can the ICC be activated under the principle of complementarity to obtain full compensation? What about the principle of complementarity between the ICC, on the one hand, and *ad hoc* international tribunals and hybrid tribunals, on the other? This issue is not resolved by the ICC Statute.

As concerns access to justice, the ICC raises the following issues:

- the individual cannot start a criminal proceeding (only a State party, the Security Council or the Prosecutor are entitled to trigger the Court's jurisdiction);
- the ICC is competent for war crimes committed on a large scale. Isolated crimes are not within the ICC's reach;
- under Article 94 of the Rules of Procedure and Evidence a victim may request reparation under Article 75. This means that criminal proceedings are triggered by a State party, the Prosecutor or the Security Council, but once the proceedings are initiated, the victim has some power.

Since its inception to the end of 2011, the ICC has not rendered any judgment.[34] A few cases are still pending and the prospects of the Court are rather gloomy (in the first ten years since its inception the ICC rendered just one verdict and cost about $900 million), rendering its effectiveness uncertain. It is still to be discovered whether the Court will ever fulfil the promise embodied in its Preamble in which the States parties are 'determined to put an end to impunity for the perpetrators of these crimes [that is the crimes envisaged by the Statute] and thus to contribute to the prevention of such crimes'.

The Statute of the International Criminal Tribunal for the Former Yugoslavia (hereinafter 'ICTY') does not contain any specific rule on compensation. It has only

---

[34] Since the completion of this chapter we should note the first verdict has been delivered, on 14 March 2012, against Thomas Lubanga Dyilo, who was found guilty of crimes of war committed in the Democratic Republic of Congo.

one provision (Article 24(3)) that states that the Trial Chamber can order restitution of property, as an additional penalty for the guilty. Restitution is regulated by Article 105 of the Rules of Procedure and Evidence. The request is formulated by the Prosecutor or if the Tribunal, of its own volition, orders the restitution. The victim is not a party to the proceedings (unlike the ICC procedure, where the victim, as well as the convicted person, may be invited by the Court to make observations).

Compensation is possible only through indirect means. Article 106 of the Rules of Procedure, under the title 'Compensation to victims', states that the Registrar transmits the guilty judgment to the competent national authorities. The victim may bring an action to a national court. The provision states that the claim can also be brought before any other 'competent body'. What does this mean? Rule 106 of the Rules of Procedure and Evidence states that for the purpose of obtaining reparation, the Tribunal's judgment shall be considered 'final and binding'. In other words, Article 106 does not give a right to compensation; this can only be obtained through national tribunals.

The same considerations concerning the ICTY equally apply to the International Criminal Tribunal for Rwanda (hereinafter 'ICTR'). Article 23, paragraph 3 of the ICTR Statute is drafted in the same way as Article 24, paragraph 3 of the ICTY Statute. There is also a provision of the Rules of Procedures and Evidence (Article 106) drafted in the same way as the corresponding provision of the Rules of Procedure and Evidence of the ICTY.

The internationalized or hybrid criminal tribunals are those courts of law established under an agreement between the United Nations and a specific State, or under a resolution by the International Authority mandated by the United Nations to administer a country. The Special Court for Sierra Leone and the Extraordinary Chambers in the Courts of Cambodia are examples of the former, while the Special Panels for Serious Crimes of Dili District (Timor Leste) and 'Regulation 64' Panels in the Courts of Kosovo are examples of the latter. The basic instruments contain provisions on compensation, the confiscation and restitution of property, and pecuniary penalties. Article 19, paragraph 3 of the Statute of the Special Court for Sierra Leone states that 'in addition to imprisonment, the Trial Chamber may order the forfeiture of the property, proceeds and any assets acquired unlawfully or by criminal conduct, and their return to their rightful owner or to the State of Sierra Leone'. Article 39, paragraphs 2 and 3 of the Law on the Establishment of Extraordinary Chambers in the Courts of Cambodia for the Prosecution of Crimes Committed During the Period of Democratic Kampuchea states that 'in addition to imprisonment, the Extraordinary Chamber of the trial court may order the confiscation of personal property, money, and real property acquired unlawfully or by criminal conduct'. Strangely enough, the individual does not come into consideration, as the Cambodian Law goes on to affirm that 'the confiscated property shall be returned to the State'. For Timor Leste, Section 10, paragraph 1 of Regulation No. 2000/15 on the Establishment of Panels with Exclusive Jurisdiction over Serious Criminal Offences establishes that a Panel may impose a fine of up to a maximum of US$ 500,000 and the forfeiture of proceeds, property and assets derived from the crime, in addition to imprisonment for a specified number of years. The same regulation, under Section 25, provides for the possible constitution of a Trust Fund for the benefit of the victims of crimes. The Trust Fund should be endowed through fines collected, property confiscated and foreign donations.

The Trust Fund is an appropriate mechanism for providing victims with reparation when it is impossible to recover damages from those responsible for serious crimes. The Trust Fund could be a useful tool for those situations in which it is materially impossible to find a responsible entity for crimes.

While Hague Convention No. IV and Protocol I additional to the Geneva Conventions only deal with international armed conflicts, the international criminal tribunals also deal with crimes committed during a non-international conflict. This depends on the statute of the tribunal.

12. THE TRUTH AND RECONCILIATION COMMISSIONS

Commissions of enquiry were established after both World War I and II in order to uncover crimes committed by the Axis Powers immediately before and during the hostilities. Those Commissions are completely different from the truth and reconciliation commissions instituted in Latin America, Africa and also Asia after a period of protracted civil war or a decolonization conflict. War-torn societies (or simply countries where freedom and democratic liberties have been re-established) need their system of justice to be renovated and the aim of the commission is to find the truth and to promote reconciliation within the society. As a rule, the commissions are not a legal tool and cannot be considered a judicial body. They may be established autonomously by the Government in power or recommended with a resolution by an international organization, such as the African Union or the United Nations. The commission may also recommend reparations. These may take the form of individual reparation (indemnity or monetary compensation), but often collective reparation to benefit a community, such as building hospitals or schools, is preferred. The commission may also recommend amnesty as an element of reconciliation. Article 6, paragraph 5 of the Additional Protocol II, for instance, encourages granting 'the broadest possible amnesty' at the end of hostilities. An amnesty may raise the issue of criminal accountability for those who have committed an international crime, such as war crimes, genocide and crimes against humanity, including the competence of the ICC and the power of the Security Council (according to Article 16 of the ICC Statute) to ask the Court to suspend the penal prosecution for a 12 month period (renewable) with a resolution under Chapter VII. Article 16 allows for the striking of a balance between the need for pacification and the quest for criminal accountability.[35]

Truth and reconciliation commissions, or simply truth commissions, have been established in Peru (2001), Guatemala (1994), El Salvador (1992), Argentina (1983) and Mexico (2001) in Latin/Central America, and in South Africa (1995) and Liberia (2006) in Africa. The truth and reconciliation commission in Timor-Leste (2001) was mandated by the United Nations Transitional Administration in East Timor. While truth and reconciliation commissions may be established after an international or an internal armed conflict, recent practice shows that they are a characteristic of post-conflict society at the end of an internal conflict and are an important element of transitional

---

[35] Cf. C. Bell, 'Post-conflict Accountability and the Reshaping of Human Rights and Humanitarian Law', in Ben-Naftali (ed.), *supra* n.19, 345.

justice. They may continue to work notwithstanding the establishment of an *ad hoc* criminal tribunal, as happened in Sierra Leone, where the commission was not discontinued after the setting up of the Special Criminal Court. The establishment of facts and the discovery of abuses may be a powerful means for restoring society and preventing abuses from happening again. Forgiving, instead of punishment and revenge, may be an ingredient of transitional justice and it leaves the door of criminal tribunals open for the most heinous crimes.

The International Law Association Hague Declaration of International Law Principles on Reparation for Victims of Armed Conflict, cited above, recommends in Article 12, *Promotion of Justice, Peace and Reconciliation*, intervention by the international community, which is called upon to provide assistance in the larger process of promoting justice, peace and reconciliation during and after armed conflict. To this end the international community should foster a culture of obedience to the rule of law, including respect for victims' rights and trust in government institutions.

13. CONCLUDING REMARKS

The above analysis shows that the distinction between *jus ad bellum* and *jus in bello* still holds good for reparation and compensation at the end of hostilities. From the perspective of international law progress has been made as far as reparation and compensation for violations of *jus ad bellum* are concerned. Reparation and compensation are now anchored in legal standards and are heading in the right direction, in the sense that recent settlements have tended to be free from the historical victor/loser relationship. The two main obstacles slowing the process are represented by those States that do not comply with the decisions of international bodies, and the paucity of *post bellum* reparation practice. As a matter of fact, not all conflicts have been brought before a judicial or arbitral body charged with the task of ensuring an impartial system of reparation/compensation. An alternative may be to allow individual claims against the responsible State. However, the immunity of foreign States before domestic tribunals and/or political considerations leave little scope for the success of individual claims.

By definition *jus ad bellum* reparation/compensation relates only to international armed conflict, even though non-international armed conflicts have become the major instances of violence within the international system in recent years. The situation appears more promising when viewed from the perspective of reparation/compensation for violations of *jus in bello*.

Both Article 3 of the IV Hague Convention and Article 91 of Additional Protocol I offer a textual element for claiming reparations for violations of the law of war. The two provisions are not self-executing and regard only inter-State claims. However, recent case-law developed by the Italian Tribunals goes in the direction of giving the individual a right to claim reparation if a serious violation has been committed. The ICJ should clarify whether it is possible to overcome the obstacle of State immunity and the international community is currently waiting for the judgment on the controversy between Germany and Italy.³⁶ The trend appears to be heading towards giving individuals a remedy for violations of the law of war, as demonstrated by the International Law Association 2010 Declaration. The human rights conventions and their extra-territorial application in a number of specific instances are of paramount importance for developing the law of reparation/compensation. Accountability for war crimes is now established by the Statutes of international tribunals. Moreover, criminal responsibility is established not only in connection with international armed conflict but also for internal conflict. Accountability for the most heinous crimes does not exclude pacification, and truth and reconciliation commissions are called to play a role, as illustrated by the success story of South Africa and other countries in which they have been established.

The international community may now count on the United Nations, which has developed new instruments for regulating a true *jus post bellum*. The Security Council is deeply involved in post-conflict situations and the post-conflict Peace-building Commission may become a useful tool for constructing peace, if it is appropriately funded.

---

³⁶ As said earlier (*supra* n.27), the ICJ affirmed that the sovereign immunity of the State cannot be disregarded even if serious violations of the law of war had been committed. And this runs counter to the trend that has been highlighted in this chapter.

Index

9/11
  impact of
    on combatants, interpretation of 384
    on protected persons, status of 390–92
    on right to self-defence 105, 112–13
    on use of force, legality 1, 74–5, 81, 105, 118
    whether events were armed attacks 205–7

Abi-Saab, Georges 472, 479
accountability, of third parties 111
  under Geneva Conventions 534–5
  under international criminal law 536–7
  of international organizations
    for human rights violations 530–32
    for humanitarian law violations 533–5
    peacekeepers 533–4, 539–41
  and post conflict justice 529–41
  of United Nations 531–3, 536–9
Acquisition of Polish Nationality, Advisory Opinion (1923) 618–19
Act of State doctrine 635–7
Additional Protocols *see under* Geneva Conventions (1949)
aerial warfare
  developments in 336–8, 349–50
  regulation 348–54, 371–2
  unmanned combat aerial vehicles 336–8
Afghanistan
  sanctions 35–6
  Soviet intervention 226–7
  state representation concerns 279–80
  terrorism
    Taliban, as combatants 378
    whether armed attack 205–7
  use of force, as self-defence 105, 112–13
African Union 28
  Constitutive Act (2000) 144, 147, 237, 246
  Darfur, intervention in 147, 237, 241–2
  on humanitarian intervention 237, 241–2, 246
  on recruitment of mercenaries 422–3
Agenda for Peace (1992) 27–9
aggression
  accountability for 111, 641
  meaning 109–10, 197–8, 200–201, 230
    war of aggression 641–2

  reparations for wars of 641–2
  vs. defensive actions 82–3, 114
aircraft
  as targets, legality 347–9
  war role, development 348–54
Al-Firdus bunker 368–9
Al-Jedda v. UK (2011) 600, 629–34
Al-Jedda II v. UK (2011) 634–7
Al-Saadoon and Mufdhi v. UK (2010) 616–17
Al-Skeini v. UK (2006) 455–6, 599–600, 602–4, 609, 611, 614–17, 619–21, 624–5, 627–9
Alabama Claims arbitration (1872) 95–6
Albania 584–5
Algiers Agreement (2000) 643–4
'all necessary means,' interpretation 73, 83–4, 135–6, 150, 163–5, 221–2, 252–3
American Convention on Human Rights (1992) 460
amnesties, prohibition 522–5
Antarctic Treaty (1959) 47
Anti-Personnel Landmines Convention (1997) 47, 317–18, 321, 328, 333, 341
anti-vehicle mines 333–4
apartheid 480–81
Arab League 147
Arab Spring (2011-2012) 118–19, 583
Argentina, invasion of Falkland Islands 81–2, 223, 225, 348
Aristotle 92
armed attack
  interpretation of
    acts of terrorism 203–10
    and aggression, meaning of 197–8, 200–201
    judicial interpretation, by ICJ 196–203, 207, 212–13
    non-state actors, action by 204–10
    offensive *vs.* defensive actions 429
    possibility of armed attack 200–201
    UN General Assembly Resolution 3314 on 197–8, 201, 641
  use of force in self-defence
    armed attack requirement 80–81, 127–8, 159–60, 187–8

imminence of attack criteria 160–62, 192–6
armed conflict, generally *see also* international armed conflict; non-international/ internal armed conflict; transnational armed conflict
　classification and interpretation
　　challenges 256–7, 269–72, 275–9
　　different categories, need for 272–3
　　international armed conflict 256, 261–2, 267–8, 272–3
　　and international personality 275–9
　　jus ad bellum and *jus in bello*, role in 266–7
　　multilateral conflicts 275–6
　　non-international/ internal armed conflict 256, 261–4, 266–9, 272–3
　　redefinition 298–300
　　transnational armed conflict 303–12
　　war on terror 269–70, 289, 303–4, 307–8
　　whether generic concept 269–72
　and international humanitarian law 256–7, 284–9, 304–8
　post conflict justice
　　broad amnesties, prohibition of 522–5
　　and human rights law 518–19, 530–32
　　international criminal law 521–2
　　and international humanitarian law 519–21, 533–5
　　and *lex pacificatoria* 517–25, 541–6
　　regime overlaps 522–5, 535–40
　　third party accountability 529–41, 536–7
　　third party intervention 525–9
　　trends 517
　state responsibility, derogation of 450–53
　thresholds
　　international armed conflict 273–82
　　internationalized non-international armed conflict 292–302
　　non-international armed conflict 282–92
　　parallel/ mixed armed conflicts 302–3
　and war crimes
　　international armed conflict 477–87
　　non-international armed conflict 487–93
　　relationship between 471–4
arms control 2, 11–12, 42, 53–7, 339–40 *see also* disarmament
Articles on Responsibility of States for Internationally Wrongful Acts (1996, ILC) 427, 433–5, 646, 648
atomic bombs 351–2
Atomic Energy Commission 44
Austria v. Italy (1961) 617

Balkan Wars (First, 1912-1913) 349
Bámaca Velásquez case (2000) 461
Bankovic v. Belgium (2001) 456–7, 601–3, 606–8, 610–11, 620, 625, 627–8
Behrami v. France (2007) 600–601
belligerency, recognition and regulation of 262–4
biological and toxic weapons
　Conventions on 49, 51–3, 55, 62
　riot control agents 51–2
　verification mechanisms 52, 54–5
black market, in weapons and nuclear materials/ technology 43, 59–61
Blair, Tony 194–5, 238
Boer Wars 346
Bosnia 539–40, 557, 576, 581–4
Bowett, Derek 115–16
Brahimi Report (2000) 42, 579, 589, 593–4
Brogan v. UK (1988) 629–30
Brownlie, Ian 91, 115–16
Burma 154

Cambodia 558, 656
Capstone Doctrine 578–9
Caroline correspondence 95, 177–9, 189–91, 207–9, 211, 214, 227–8
Certain Expenses Advisory Opinion (1962, ICJ) 140–41, 580–81
chaplains, military, status of 379, 387
chemical weapons
　Conventions on 36, 41, 47, 51–6, 62, 65, 328
　and customary international law 46–7
　riot control agents 51–2
　white phosphorus 334–6
　World War II, use in 351
Chemical Weapons Convention (1993) 36, 41, 47, 62, 65
　limitations 52–3
　prohibitions under 51–3, 328
　verification mechanisms 54–6
children
　convention protections 405–8, 410–13
　involvement in hostilities 412–13, 492
　war crimes against 492
China 76–7, 82, 242
Chowdhuri, Ramendra 552, 555–6
civil war, recognition and regulation 262–4
　see also non-international/ internal armed conflict
civilians, protection of 419–20
　children 405–8, 410–13
　civilian contractors 382–3, 416, 428–30
　co-belligerent states, nationals of 394–5

Index 663

collateral damage 368–71, 382, 484, 492
Convention protections 353–4
definition 348
direct participation in hostilities 357–62, 420
distinction, principle of 320–21, 344, 355–62, 484
in hands of enemy 389–91
identification of civilians 377–8
international organization personnel 417–19
journalists 413–15
liability to attack 382–3
medical personnel 397–8
neutral states, nationals of 394–5
in occupied territories 389–90
    human rights 406–7
    internment rules 405–6
    relief actions 406–7
    transfer, evacuation and deportment 407
    treatment 404–5
by peacekeepers 417–19, 584–5, 589–90, 592–6
private military company personnel 415–16, 425–8
protected persons
    hostile activity, engagement in 391–2
    identification 389–92
    nationality requirement 390–92
    right to knowledge of 396–7
targeting, precautionary measures 369–70
unlawful combatants 357–8, 384, 390–94, 406, 420
women 405–10
wounded, sick or shipwrecked persons 375–6, 389, 395–8, 479–80
cluster munitions 47, 65, 317–18, 328, 330–32, 341, 494–5
Cold War
collective security functions during 7–8
influences of
    on disarmament/ arms control 42–3
    on peacekeeping 572–4
    on UN functions and officers 130–35, 572
collateral damage 343, 352, 368–71, 382, 492
collective security
concept development 5–9, 171–3
and disarmament 11–12, 36–8, 46
dispute settlement obligations 9–11
functions 5–7
interpretation challenges 7–8
legal basis 5–7
legal framework 9–12
and right to self-defence 171–4

UN Security Council, role and powers 5–9, 120–22, 171–3
    changing emphasis 7–9, 39–40
    enforcement powers 84–8, 143–4
colonialism
civilizing mission 550–51
decolonization 552, 564–6
features 547–8
reparations for 648–9
stages 550–52
and trusteeship
    administrative prerogative 549, 556–7
    duration and termination 550–52
    reconciliation between 568–9
    self-determination 547, 551–2, 563–9
UN Charter obligations 551–2
combatants
battlefield status
    excluded military personnel 379, 387
    identification 345–7, 377–8
    and irregular armed forces 379–80, 392–5
    persons *levée en masse* 380–81
    private military company personnel 416, 425–8
combatant privilege 377–81
direct participation in hostilities 381–5
    recognition criteria 385–6
    withdrawal from hostilities 382
liability to attack 381–4
missing or dead, right to knowledge of 396–8
peacekeeping *vs.* peace-enforcement 418–19, 572–5, 577
prisoners of war
    captivity, procedures following 399–403
    combatant status 384–7
    evacuation 400–402
    excluded persons 387–8, 393
    information exchange 402–3
    mercenaries 388
    protection, development of 346, 398
    punishment 403
    repatriation 404
    rights of 400–402
    spies 387–8
    status, determination 384–7
    status, loss of 385–6
    treatment 399–403, 419–20
unlawful combatants, protection 357–8, 384, 390–94, 406, 420
wounded, sick and shipwrecked combatants
    protection 375–6, 388–9, 479–80
    treatment 395–8

Commission on the Responsibility Authors of the War and Enforcement (1920) 468–9, 477
compensation *see* reparations
'complete dependence test' 432
Comprehensive Test Ban Treaty (1996) 48, 54
Conference on Disarmament 44–6
confidence-building measures 56–7
conflict prevention 2 *see also* collective security
  coercive mechanisms 31–8
  conflict management and resolution 19–22
  definitions 5–6, 8–9
  disarmament 36–8
  operational/ direct prevention 8–9
  powers of recommendation 31–3
  preventative deployment 28–31
  referrals procedures 19–20
  Regional Arrangements/ Initiatives 25–8, 126–7
  sanctions 34–6
  timing, relevance of 19–22
  UN Secretary General, role 22–5
  UN Security Council, role 5–9, 120–22, 171–3
    changing emphasis in 7–9, 39–40
    discretionary powers 6–7, 31–2
    limitations 39–40
    and unilateral threats 84–8
conflict resolution *see* peace settlements
Congo, Democratic Republic of
  cluster munitions, disarmament 65
  DRC v. Uganda (2005, ICJ) 111–12, 161, 199–200, 215–16, 457–8, 643
  UN operations in
    consent challenges 581–2
    enforcement actions 133–4
    limitations 594–5
    and prevention of genocide 579–80, 594–5
    and protection of mandate 587–9
    and use of force by peacekeepers 587–9
  war reparations 643
Conventions *see also* Treaties
  on Anti-Personnel Landmines (1997) 47, 317–18, 321, 328, 333, 341
  on Biological and Toxic Weapons (1972) 49, 51, 55, 62, 327–8
  on Certain Conventional Weapons (1980) 321, 484–5
  on Chemical Weapons (1993) 36, 41, 47, 51–6, 62, 65, 328
  on Cluster Munitions (2008) 47, 65, 317–18, 328, 330–32, 341, 494–5
  on Crimes Against Peacekeepers (1994) 484
  on the Criminal Accountability of UN Officials and Experts (Draft, 2011) 536–7
  on Discrimination Against Women (1979) 407
  on the Jurisdictional Immunities of States and their Property (1972) 651–2
  on the Law of the Sea (1982) 61
  on the Law of Treaties (1969) 52, 604–5, 610–11, 619–20, 626–33
  on Minority Rights (1994) 505–6
  for the Protection of Civilian Populations Against New Engines of War (Draft, 1938) 353–4
  on the Rights of the Child (1989) 407–8, 411–13
  on the Suppression of Acts of Nuclear Terrorism (2005) 43
  on Use of Environmental Modification (1976) 325–6
  on the Use of Mercenaries (1989) 422–3
Corfu Channel case *(1949, ICJ)* 69, 102–3, 135, 230–31, 642
Côte d'Ivoire 251–3, 254, 280–81
Council of Europe 121
  on minority rights 505–6
  on state immunity 651–2
crimes against humanity 446, 521–2
Croatia 582–4
Cuba 83, 96
cultural property, protection of 649
Customary Humanitarian Law Study
  on military *vs.* civilian distinction 320–21
  on use of weapons 322–3, 325–6
  on war crimes 486–7
customary international law
  and human rights law 236, 463–4, 645–6
  and humanitarian intervention 236, 253–4, 463–4
  right to self-defence 179–81
  use of force, prohibition of 90–91, 113–14
  on use of weapons
    chemical weapons 46–7
    environmental damage 325–6
    nuclear weapons 46–7
    superfluous injury/ unnecessary suffering 322–3
  and war crimes 479, 486–90, 493–4
cyber warfare 338–40
Cyprus 82

Darfur *see* Sudan

Dayton Peace Agreement (1995) 515, 583–4
dead persons, right to knowledge of 396–7
Declarations
    on Fact-Finding by the UN in the field of
        maintenance of international peace and
        security (1991) 16, 18–19
    Paris Declaration on Marine Law (1856) 95
    on Principles of International Law
        Concerning Friendly Relations among
        States (1970) 230
    on the Rights of Indigenous Peoples (2007,
        UN) 505–6
    on the Rights of National Minorities (1992)
        505–6
decolonization 552, 564–6
Dinstein, Y. 152, 160
direct participation in hostilities
    by civilians 357–62, 420
    and combatant status 381–4
    connection with armed conflict criteria 361–2
    direct causal link with harm 361–2, 429–30
    by heads of state 360–61
    human shields 362–4
    under international humanitarian law 357–62,
        428–30
    and liability to attack 381–4
    military support functions 429–30
    private military companies 428–30
    withdrawal from hostilities 382
disarmament *see also* non-proliferation
    and arms control 42, 53–7
    and collective security 46
    and conflict prevention 36–8
    conventional weapons, use restrictions 42,
        48–50
    counter-proliferation 43
    de-militarized areas 47
    disarmament, demobilization and
        reintegration regime (DDR) 42, 65–6
    humanitarian policies, conflicts between 41,
        65–6
    influences on 42–3, 63
    international treaties on 36–7, 41
    of non-state actors/ terrorists 43, 63
    nuclear disarmament 47–51, 55
        ICJ Advisory Opinion on 49, 66, 70–71,
            329
        nuclear materials and technology,
            availability 42–3
        nuclear-weapons-free-zones 48
        of Outer Space 316–17
        START Treaty (2010) 46, 51, 330
    objectives 41–4
    Review Conferences 57–8
    small arms proliferation 33, 37
    sources of law 46–9
    UN Charter obligations 11–12, 36–8, 43–7
    UN sanctions
        imposition 37–8
        legality 45–6
    UN Security Council role 62–4
    verification mechanisms 53–7
    weapons of mass destruction, restrictions on
        biological and chemical weapons 51–3
        nuclear weapons 49–51
    withdrawal clauses 58–9
displaced persons 515–16 *see also* refugee
    law
dispute resolution *see also* peace settlements
    dispute *vs.* situation, meaning 13–14
    regional arrangements and initiatives 25–8,
        126–7
    UN Charter principles and obligations 14–15
distinction, principle of 320–21, 344–5,
    355–6, 357–62, 484
Distomo case (2011) 651–2
Donald, Dominick 578–9, 584–5
Douhet, Giulio 350–51
Draper, G. 587–9
drones 336–8
*Drozd and Janousek v. France and Spain
    (1992)* 603, 607
Dunant, Henry 375
Dunlop, Charles 339–40
Dutchbat case (2011) 600–601

East Timor 559, 561, 657
economic sanctions 34–6, 101, 113
Egypt 112, 114–15, 577
environmental protection, and use of weapons
    324–6
Eritrea-Ethiopia Claims Commission 643–4,
    646–8
espionage 387–8, 391–2
Ethiopia 643–4, 646–8
European Convention on Human Rights
    (1952)
    Article 1, Basic rights 598, 601–9
    Article 2, Right to life 599–600
    Article 5, Right to liberty and security 599,
        629–30, 633
    on derogation of State obligations 450–52
    on extra-territorial application, and foreign
        military operations 599–600
    challenges 601–2
    conflicts with UN Resolutions 629–30

effective control 611–17
and *espace juridique* thesis 617–19
exceptionality approach 609–11
and instantaneous acts 608–9
judicial interpretation, generally 601–9
judicial interpretation, Strasbourg rulings 625–9
judicial interpretation, under English law 621–9
jurisdiction, interpretation 603–5
and purpose of treaty 617–19
regional applicability 617–19, 627–8
and subsequent practice 619–20
on international humanitarian law 461–2
on third party accountability 532
European Union
  collective security enforcement powers 147–8
export controls, and non-proliferation of weapons 59–60

fact-finding missions 16, 18–19, 21, 77
Falkland Islands invasion
  defensive counter-attack, legality 81–2, 223, 225, 348
Ferrini v. Germany (2004) 652
Finogenov v. Russia (2011) 462
force *see* threat of force; use of force
forced labour, prohibition 645–6
Franck, Thomas 134, 213–14
Franco-Prussian War (1870-1871) 346
francs-tireurs 345–6
Friendly Relations Declaration (1970) 10

gas, use as weapon 59, 323–4, 327, 351, 484–5
Gasser, Hans-Peter 473–4
gender
  gender-based violence, protections against 408–10
  inclusion, in peace settlements 509–13, 536
General Belgrano (ship) 348
General Report of the Commission of Jurists (1922-1923) 352–3
Geneva Convention on the Protection of War Victims (1864) 95–6
Geneva Conventions (1949) 212
  Additional Protocols 284–8, 325–6, 329
  on aerial warfare 352, 354
  on children, protection of 412–13
  on civilian *vs.* military distinction 320–21, 355–6
  and collateral damage 368–9, 382–3
  on combatant privilege 377–81
  criticisms 356–7
  and customary international law 376
  on direct participation in hostilities 358, 361, 382–4, 429
  on environmental protection 324–5
  on grave breaches 479–81, 519–20
  and human rights/ humanitarian rights violations 447
  on human shields 362–3
  on liability to attack 383–4
  on post conflict justice 520–21
  on private military company personnel 415–16, 425–8, 432–3
  on reparations 638
  on superfluous injury/ unnecessary suffering 322–3
  on targeting principles 354–5, 364–6
  on unlawful combatants 394
  on war crimes 470–71, 479–81, 487–8
  on wounded, sick and shipwrecked combatants 388–9, 395–6, 479–80
armed conflict thresholds 267–9
  cross-border spillovers, interpretation 288–92
  international armed conflict 267–70, 273–5, 293–4, 298–9, 301, 307, 314
  and international criminal law 287–8
  internationalization 293–302
  non-international armed conflict 268–9, 282–90, 293–9, 305, 314, 447
  non-state actors, applicability to 284–8
  transnational armed conflicts 304–5
on civilians, protection
  civilian contractors 416, 428–30
  eligibility criteria 389–91
  in occupied territories 404–7
human rights law, applicability to 445–7
international humanitarian law, applicability to 445–6
on prisoners of war, protection of 348, 384–8, 399–403
on private military company personnel, protection of 416, 425–6
on third party accountability 534–5
on unlawful combatants, protection of 357–8, 384, 390–94, 406, 420
on war crimes 470–71
  grave breaches 477–81, 487–8
  prosecution obligations 477–8
on war reparations 649–50
weapons, regulation
  and environmental damage 324–6

and superfluous injury/ unnecessary
    suffering 322–3
  on wounded, sick and shipwrecked
    combatants 375, 388–9, 395–6
Geneva Protocol for the Prohibition of the
    Use in War of Asphyxiating, Poisonous
    or other Gases and of Bacteriological
    Methods of Warfare (1925) 59, 327, 351,
    484–5
genocide
  and human rights law 446–7
  prevention of, UN peacekeeping *vs.* peace
    enforcement role 579–80
  and use of force in humanitarian intervention
    239–40
  in Congo 579–80
  in Côte d'Ivoire 251–3
Genocide Convention (1949) 268–9
Gentili, Alberico 93
Georgia 77, 275
Germany 351–2, 640–41
Global Threat Reduction Initiative 60–61
globalization, and collective security 8, 307–8
Gray, Christine 581–2
Greece 76, 82, 651–2
Grotius, Hugo 93–4
Guyana 78

Hague Conventions
  on the Laws and Customs of War on Land
    (1899) 320, 327, 347, 351–2
  on the Pacific Settlement of Disputes (1899)
    90, 97, 327
  on the Protection of Cultural Property (1954)
    649
Hague Declaration on Reparation of Victims
    of Armed Conflict (2010) 650, 658–9
Hague Peace Conference (1907) 97–8, 351–2,
    639, 649–50
Hague Rules for Aerial Warfare (1923) 352–3
Haiti 28, 33, 138
Hamdan v. Rumsfeld (2006) 269, 387
Hammerskjold, Dag 577–9, 586–7
Helman, David 567
High-Level Panel on Threats, Challenges and
    Change (2004) 20–21, 153, 161, 168,
    195–6
Hiroshima 351–2, 370
HIV/ AIDS, as generic threat to peace 33
hostage situations, use of force in
  legality 106–7, 112
  whether armed attack 203–4, 208
Human Rights Act 1988 (UK)

judicial interpretation, European Court
    influences on 625–9
human rights law
  applicability beyond armed conflict 445–7,
    599
  and customary international law 236, 463–4,
    645–6
  definitions 598
  extra-territorial application, during military
    operations 599–600
    and Act of State doctrine 635–6
    allocation of responsibilities 600–601
    challenges 601–2
    conflict of laws 634–7
    'effective control' 611–17
    espace juridique thesis 617–19
    under European Convention on Human
      Rights 601–29
    exceptionality approach 609–11
    and instantaneous acts 608–9
    judicial interpretation, European rulings
      625–9
    judicial interpretation, generally 601–9
    judicial interpretation, under English law
      621–9
    jurisdiction, conflicts between 629–30
    jurisdiction, interpretation 603–5
    public policy conflicts 635–7
    and purpose of treaty 617–19
    regional applicability 617–19, 627–8
    and subsequent practice 619–20
    UNSC Resolutions 629–33
  genocide 446–7
  historical development 445–7
  and international humanitarian law 256–7,
    305–8
    customary international law interpretations
      463–4
    overlaps and conflicts 444–9, 464–6,
      599–600
    small arms proliferation, influence on 37
  and peace, conflicts between goals of 114
  post conflict justice
    third part accountability 530–32
    third party intervention 526–9
    transitional justice 518–19
  remedies, for violations of 653
  right to be heard 505–6
  right to democratic governance 33
  right to life 461–2, 599–600
  rights of children 410–13
  rights of refugees 513–17
  rights of return 513–17

and self-determination 505–6
state obligations
　challenges 454–5
　derogations from 450–53
　extra-territorial scope 453–8
　during military operations abroad 454–9
　of occupying state 453–9
　and public emergencies 450–53
treaties, jurisdictional scope 446–7
and war crimes, relationship between 473–4
and war reparations 645–6
human shields 362–4
humanitarian intervention *see also*
　Responsibility to Protect (R2P)
and customary international law 236, 253–4
intervention by invitation 116–17, 150–51, 229
and military necessity 2, 463
UN Security Council powers 148–56
　inter-organisational challenges 150–51
　interpretation challenges 137–8
　Responsibility to Protect (R2P) 2, 117, 153–6
　and unilateral enforcement of collective will 151–3
　use of force authorisations 137–8, 533
unilateral right of
　challenges 253–5
　framework 237–40
　and genocide 239–40
　legality 148–9, 152–3
　UK proposal for 238–9
　vs. self-defence 148
use of force in, legality 79–80, 116–17, 150–51, 229
　in Darfur 147, 237, 241–2
　in Iraq 231–3
　in Kosovo 233–7
　legal basis 229–31, 527–8, 533–4
　opposition to 229
　under UN Charter Article 2(4) 229–31, 234–7
humanity, principle of 344
Hungary 108

IEDs 332–4
Ilaşcu v. Moldova and Russia (2004) 612
Implementing the Responsibility to Protect 243
improvised explosive devices 332–4
In Larger Freedom (2005) 161, 196
India 60
indigenous peoples, rights of 505–6, 649

injured and sick combatants
　protection 375–6, 388–9
　treatment 395–8
insurgency, recognition and regulation 262–4
　see also non-international/ internal armed conflict
Interim Administration Mission in Kosovo (UNMIK) 538–9, 557, 559–60
internal armed conflict *see* non-international/ internal armed conflict
international armed conflict
　categorisation, reasons for 272–3
　challenges 275–82
　combatant privilege 345–8, 377–81
　conflict status changes 281–2
　cross-border requirement 274–5
　internal conflicts, cross-border spillovers 288–92, 300–301
　internalization/ de-internationalization 281–2, 288–302
　and international personality 275–9
　interpretation 256, 261–2, 267–8, 298–300
　non-state actors, role in 277–9, 449
　reparations rules 638–9, 649–50, 657
　and state responsibility 277–82
　status of individual during 377–95
　thresholds 267–70, 273–5, 293–4, 298–9, 301, 307, 314
　transnational conflicts, as separate category 303–12
　and war crimes 477–87
　and wars of national liberation 298–300
International Atomic Energy Agency 36–8, 54–5, 60–61, 63
International Code of Conduct for Private Security Service Providers 424–5
International Commission on Intervention and State Sovereignty 117, 153, 240
International Committee of the Red Cross
　on cyberwarfare 339–40
　on direct participation in hostilities 358–9, 362–4, 383–4, 429–30
　establishment 375
　on human rights law, interpretation under international humanitarian law 462–3
　on missing or dead persons, right to knowledge of 397
　on post conflict justice 520–21
　on refugees right of return 515–16
　role in development of international humanitarian law 256–7, 283
　on unlawful combatants 393

international conflict and security law, general
    trends 501–3
  inclusiveness 505–6, 510–13
  international -domestic hybridity 501, 536–7
  minorities and indigenous peoples 505–6
  post-conflict justice 517–25
  state and non-state actors 502–3
  war-peace hybridity 501–2
  women, role in 510–13
International Court of Justice (ICJ)
  Advisory Opinions
    on certain expenses (1962) 140–41,
      580–81
    on construction of a wall in Occupied
      Palestinian Territory (2004) 173–4,
      204–5, 454–5, 460–61, 650
    on nuclear weapons (1996) 49, 66, 70–71,
      174, 176–7, 329, 448, 459–60
    on reparations for Injuries (1949) 140
  'complete dependence' test, private military
    companies 432
  Corfu Channel case *(UK v. Albania)* 69,
    102–3, 135, 230–31, 642
  DRC v. Uganda (2005) 111–12, 161,
    199–200, 215–16, 457–8
  on human rights obligations
    extra-territorial scope 457–8
    and relationship with international
      humanitarian law 459–61
  on humanitarian intervention, legality of use
    of force 230–31
  on international disarmament obligations 47
  Nicaragua case (1986)
    on dispute settlement obligations 10–11,
      47
    on humanitarian intervention 231
    on intervention by invitation 104–5, 116
    on meaning of armed attack 104–5,
      196–201, 207
    on parallel/ mixed armed conflicts 302–3
    on private conduct, government authority
      for 435–6
    on proportionality 210–11, 214–15
    on reporting requirement 225–7
    on right to collective self-defence 69–70,
      179–87
    on use of force, interpretation 77, 104–5,
      116, 165–6
    on war reparations 642–3
  Oil Platforms case *(Iran v. USA, 2003)* 104,
    181–2, 201–3, 212–13
  on private conduct, governmental authority
    for 433–8

Red Crusader incident (1962) 104–5
on threat of force 69–71
  and actual use of force, legality of 85
  and self-defence 82, 104
International Covenant on Civil and Political
  Rights (1996) 446–7, 450–53, 457–8,
  531, 646
International Covenant on Economic, Social
  and Cultural Rights (1996) 454, 531
International Criminal Court (ICC)
  and compensation of victims 654–7
  crimes covered by 46
  and post conflict justice 521–2
  Trust Fund 655–7
  on war crimes 477–8, 482–6, 492–3
international criminal law *see also*
  International Criminal Tribunals
  post conflict justice 521–2, 536–7
  third party accountability 536–7
  and war crimes, relationship between 473–4
International Criminal Tribunals
  for Rwanda (ICTR) 491, 656
  for Yugoslavia (ICTY)
    on compensation of victims 655–6
    jurisdiction 478–9, 488–9
    powers 481–2
    on war crimes 478–9, 481–2, 488–90,
      495–7
international humanitarian law
  application of 256–7
    to acts by non-state actors 278–9, 284–8,
      449
    in armed conflict, generally 444–6
    cross-border spillover of internal armed
      conflicts 290–91, 300–301
    and derogation of state responsibility
      450–53
    in internationalized non-international
      armed conflicts 292–303
    in non-international armed conflict
      284–9, 303, 447–9
    and state representation 279–80
    in transnational armed conflict 303–8
    in wars of national liberation 299–300
  disarmament principles, conflict between 41,
    65–6
  gender-based violence 408–10
  historical development 444–5
  and human rights law
    customary international law interpretations
      463–4
    influence on 256–7, 305–8

overlaps and conflicts 444–9, 464–6, 599–600
simultaneous applicability 459–63
small arms proliferation, influence on 37
individual violation claim forums 444
as *lex specialis,* challenges of 459–63
occupying powers obligations 406–7
post conflict justice
   third party accountability 533–5
   third party intervention 526–9
   transitional justice 519–22
private military company personnel, protection 415–16
state obligations
   derogation from 450–53
   extra-territorial scope 453
and targeting rules
   and direct participation in hostilities 357–62, 428–30
   legality 343–4
   military objectives, limitation to 355, 364–8
war crimes, violations as 471–3
International Labour Organization 527
International Law Association
   on protection of civilians 353–4
   on reparation of victims 650, 658–9
International Law Commission
   on responsibility of states for internationally wrongful acts 427, 433–5, 646, 648
international law, generally
   development, influences on 258–9
   law of war and law of peace, influences on 258–9
   law of war crimes, relationship with 469
   public policy, conflicts with 635–6
international legal personality
   armed conflict, challenges for 275–9
international organizations
   accountability
      for human rights violations 530–32, 600–601
      for international humanitarian law violations 533–5
      of peacekeepers 539–41
   peace implementation roles 276–8, 500, 526–9, 539–41
international territorial administration
   administrative prerogatives
      proactive use 557–8
      reactive use 556–7
   challenges 564–7, 570–71
   common features 548–50, 560–62

   duration and termination 556–60
      influences on 557–8
      and local governance 557–60
      reconstructive purpose of 558–9
   interpretation 547–8, 560–62
   legitimacy 570–71
   purpose of, trends 560–62
   refugee camps 558
   and self-determination 547, 560–62
      humanization 568–9
      as interim/ temporary enabling mechanism 564–70
      interventionists role 569–70
      purpose, changes in 565–7
      and state building, purpose of 567–8
      and trusteeship, common purpose 548–50
intervention *see also* humanitarian intervention
   by invitation 107–9, 116–17, 119, 150–51, 229
   in non-international/ internal armed conflict 291–2
   non-intervention principle 101
   and post conflict justice 525–9
   UN Security Council powers 137–8
investigation, UN powers of 15–16
invitation, use of force by
   legality 107–9, 116–17
   in Kosovo 116, 150–51, 229
   as self-defence 107–8, 116, 119
Iran
   disarmament and non-proliferation position 38
   Oil Platforms case *(2003, ICJ)* 104, 181–2, 201–3, 212–13
   Resolution 1696 (2006) 63, 84
   Resolution 1737 (2006) 63–4
   threat of force, coercion element 76–8
Iraq
   disarmament
      obligations 37–8, 164–5
      verification mechanisms 55, 62
   economic sanctions 34–5
   international armed conflict in
      conflict status changes 281–2
      human rights obligations, extra-territorial scope 455–7
      state representation issues 280
   invasion of Kuwait
      cease-fire resolution 223
      human shields 362–3
      self-defence and proportionality 215–16

UN Security enforcement powers,
    influence on 135–8
Resolution 661 (1990) 221
Resolution 678 (1990) 83–5, 135–7, 163–5, 216
Resolution 687 (1991) 37–8, 56, 62, 73–5, 84–5, 164, 643–4
Resolution 688 (1991) 85
Resolution 1154 (1998) 74, 84
Resolution 1199 (1998) 84
Resolution 1284 (1999) 62
Resolution 1441 (2002) 62, 75, 84, 164–5
Resolution 1483 (2003) 645
Resolution 1546 (2004) 601, 629–34, 636–7, 645
threat of force
    attitudes after 9/11 74–5
    and collective security obligations 84–5, 87–8
    defensive actions *vs.* aggression 83
    legality of actions 73–5, 82, 87–8
use of force against
    human rights law, extra-territorial application 599–600
    as humanitarian intervention 231–3
    legality, international endorsement 117–18
    post-authorisation control of action 163–5, 167
    Rules of Engagement for, US 592
    and self-defence 112–13, 117
war reparations and recovery plans 644–5
irregular armed forces
    identification 379–80
    and unlawful combatants 392–5
Israel
    Advisory Opinion on Construction of a Wall in Occupied Palestinian Territory (2004, ICJ) 173–4, 204–5, 454–5, 460–61, 650
    hostage situations 106–7, 112, 203–4, 208
    human shields 362–3
    Iran, threat of force from 76–8
    Lebanon, actions against 208–10, 216–18, 223
    peacekeepers, consent for 577
    Resolution 487 (1981) 191
    self-defence 112, 191, 208–9
    war of national liberation 298–300
Issa v. Turkey (2000) 456–7, 604, 606, 611–12, 627–8
Italian Turkish War (1911) 348
Italy 640–41, 648–9

journalists, protection of 413–15

jurisdiction
    extra-territorial application of European Convention of Human Rights 599–600
    challenges 601–2
    effective control 611–17
    and *espace juridique* thesis 617–19
    exceptionality approach 609–11
    and instantaneous acts 608–9
    judicial interpretation, generally 601–9
    judicial interpretation, Strasbourg rulings 625–9
    judicial interpretation, under English law 621–9
    and judicial precedent 628–9
    jurisdiction, interpretation 603–5
    preparatory work 620
    and purpose of treaty 617–19
    regional applicability 617–19, 627–8
    and subsequent practice 619–20
    of International Criminal Tribunals 478–9, 488–9
    state immunity, law of 650–52, 658–9
    of treaties, interpretation 446–7, 604–5, 610–11, 619–20
    of UN Security Council 13–15
jus ad bellum
    aggression, accountability for 111
    concept of 'war' in
        development 264–5
        replacement for 265–7
    and cyber warfare 340
    jus in bello, separation from 264–5
    non-state actors, applicability to 118–19
    proportionality 211–12, 345
    weapons, role in 316–18
jus cogens norms *see* customary international law
jus in bello
    concept of 'war' in
        development of 264–5
        replacement of 265–7
    crimes prohibited under 46–7
    and customary international law 46–7
    general principles 1–2, 41
    and human rights law 2, 109
    jus ad bellum, separation from 264–5
    proportionality 211–12, 345
    reparations rules 638–9, 650–52
    targeting rules, development 342–4
    weapons, role in
        definitions 318–19
        and environmental protection 324–6
        military *vs.* civilian distinction 320–22

prohibited weapons 46–7, 322–4
regulation 320–26, 340–41
and superfluous injury/ unnecessary
    suffering 322–4
temporal limitations 324–6
jus post bellum 2 *see also* reparations
challenges 638–9
definition 638
disarmament role 42
legacy weapons, injury to civilians from
    331–2
and *lex pacificatoria* 517–25, 541
advantages and challenges 543–6
post conflict justice
    broad amnesties, prohibition of 522–5
    development trends 517
    and human rights law 518–19, 530–32
    and international humanitarian law
        519–21, 533–5
    punitive reparations 517
    regime overlaps 522–5, 535–40
    third party accountability 529–41
    third party intervention 525–9
weapons control 327–8
Just War Doctrine 89–95
justice *see* transitional justice

Kadi and Al Barakaat v. Council (2008, ECJ)
    35–6
Kampala Review Conference 46
Kassen case (2004) 380
Kellogg-Briand Pact (1928) 90, 98–9, 639–40
Kenya 290–91
KFOR *see* Kosovo
The Koran, on prohibition of weapons 320
Korea 572, 574
Kosovo
    armed conflict, categorisation of 275
    international territorial administration
        559–62
    legality of actions in
        human rights law, extra-territorial
            application 600, 633
        humanitarian intervention 150–51, 233–7
        intervention by invitation 116, 150–51, 229
        threat of force 71–2, 85–6
        UN Security Council enforcement
            competence 149–51
        use of force 106
    NATO role in 145–6, 149–51
    peacekeeping *vs.* peace enforcement 583–4
    Resolution 1244 (1999) 72, 235, 528
    UN role in (UNMIK) 538–9, 557, 559–60

Kuwait
    invasion by Iraq
        cease-fire resolution 223
        Resolution 678 (1990) 83–5, 135–7,
            163–5, 216
        Resolution 687 (1991) 37–8, 56, 62, 73–5,
            84–5, 164, 643–4
        self-defence, and proportionality 215–16
        threat of force, and legality of actions 73–5,
            82, 84–5, 117–18
        UN Security enforcement powers 135–8
Kuwait Air Corp case *(2002)* 636

landmines 47, 317–18, 321, 328, 333, 341
The Law of Nations (1758) 94–5, 175
Law of the Sea 61
League of Arab States 74, 246
League of Nations
    on aerial warfare 354
    collective security role 121
    Covenant (1919) 44, 121
    on mandate and trusteeship arrangements
        552–3, 560–62
    on prohibition of use of force 67–8, 90, 98
    on reparations 639
Lebanon 208–10, 216–18, 223
legacy weapons 331–2
levée *en masse* 380–81
lex pacificatoria (law of peacemakers)
    characteristics of 504–8
    jus post bellum, transition from 517–25, 541,
        543–6
    and law of war, conflict between 258–9
    and peace settlements
        characteristics 499, 503–8
        inclusiveness 510–13
        right of refugees to return 514–16
        women, equal participation of 510–13
    and post conflict justice 517, 541–6
        broad amnesties, prohibition of 522–5
        and human rights law 518–19, 530–32
        and international criminal law 521–2
        and international humanitarian law
            519–21, 533–5
        regime overlaps 522–5, 535–40
        third party accountability 540–41
        third party intervention 525–9
Liberia 108–9, 119
Libya
    colonial reparations 648–9
    head of state, targeting 360–62
    international armed conflict
        interpretation difficulties 276–8

and state representation 281
statements on 248–9
international organizations role in 276–8
Italian Turkish War (1911) 348
Lockerbie hijack 105
post-authorisation control of actions 165–6
Resolution 1970 (2011) 166, 244–5, 247
Resolution 1973 (2011) 165–6, 246–51
and Responsibility to Protect (R2P) 154–5, 244–51
sanctions 34–5
use of force in, legality of 1–2, 106
and humanitarian intervention 154–5, 244–51, 254–5
peacekeeping *vs.* peace-enforcement 583–4, 593
Lieber Code for Governing Conduct of Union forces (1863) 95
Lockerbie 105
Loizidou v. Turkey (1995) 454–5, 603, 606–7, 614, 620
Lopez Burgos v. Uruguay (1984) 604
Luther v. Sagor (1921) 635–6

Macedonia, Former Republic of 29–30, 576, 581–3
Machiavelli, Niccolo 93
'Manchurian crisis' 260–61
mandate and trusteeship arrangements
administrative prerogative 549, 556–7
classes of mandated territories 552–6, 560–62
features 548–50
League of Nations Covenant on 552–5
and self-determination 545–7, 552–4
trusteeship, duration and termination 552–6
Manila Declaration on the Peaceful Settlement of Disputes (1982) 10
Manu, Law of 320
Marshall Plan 644–5
Massive Ordnance Air Blast (MOAB) 317
media
facilities, targeting of 366–7
misinterpretation/ misreporting by 343
medical personnel
protection 397–8, 479–80
status 379, 387
Medvedyev v. France (2010) 607–8, 612–13, 615–17, 628
mercenaries 388, 416, 422–3
Milanović, Marco 464
military necessity
and humanitarian intervention 2, 463
and public emergency 450–53

and self-preservation 174–5
and state responsibility for human rights 450–53
military objectives
broadcasting facilities 366–7
defining 364–6
dual use objects 367–8
economic targets as 366
targeting limitations 355, 364–8
military support functions, as direct participation in hostilities 429–30
minority peoples, rights of 505–6
Missile Technology Control Regime 59
missing persons, right to knowledge of 396–7
Model Status of Mission Agreements (EU) 537
Montreux Document (2008) 422
MONUC *see* Congo
A more secure world (2004) 81, 161, 240

Nagasaki 351–2, 370
Namibia 565–6
NATO
collective self-defence obligations 183–5
enforcement powers, compared with UN 144–7, 150–51
international legal personality of 276–8
powers of intervention 526–7
on right of humanitarian intervention 149, 233–4
role in Kosovo 145, 149–51, 233–7
role in Libya 154–5, 276–8
neutrality, law of 259, 262–4
civilians from neutral states, protection of 394–5
and peacekeeping operations 578–80
Nicaragua v. USA (1986, ICJ)
on dispute settlement obligations 10–11, 47
on humanitarian intervention 231
on intervention by invitation 104–5, 116
on meaning of armed attack 104–5, 196–201, 207
on parallel/ mixed armed conflicts 302–3
on private conduct, government authority for 435–6
on proportionality 210–11, 214–15
on reporting requirement 225–7
on right to collective self-defence 69–70, 179–87
on use of force, interpretation 77, 104–5, 116, 165–6
on war reparations 642–3
Non-Alignment Movement 229, 236

non-international/ internal armed conflict
  challenges 282–4
  cross-border spillovers 288–92, 300–301
  and foreign intervention 291–2
  human rights violations, derogation of state responsibility 450–53
  internal nature, relevance of 288–92
  and international criminal law 287–8
  and international humanitarian law 284–9, 447–9, 519–20
  internationalization of 291–302
  interpretation 256, 261–4, 266–9, 272–3, 282–4
  nexus requirement 291–2
  and non-state actors 284–8, 295–8
  parallel/ mixed armed conflicts 302–3
  political context, importance of 283–4
  post conflict justice 519–21
  recognition and regulation 107–10, 262–4
    costs of 308–9
  reparations rules 638–9, 649–50, 657–9
  thresholds 282–92
  violence element 285
  and war crimes 487–93
non-intervention, principle of 101, 103, 111, 138
non-proliferation, of weapons
  obligations 37, 42, 49–51
  transfer controls 59–61
Non-Proliferation Treaty (1968) 37, 42, 50
  chemical and biological weapons 52
  non-compliance implications 64–5
  nuclear weapons 49–51, 329
  Review Conferences 51
non-state actors *see also* private military companies
  in armed conflict 118–19
    categorisation 284–8
    international humanitarian law, applicability to 278–9, 284–8, 449
    legal personality 277–9
    in non-international armed conflicts 284–8, 295–8, 300–302, 447–9
  changing role of 502–3
  disarmament 43, 63
  peace settlements, influence on 502–3
  in transition state 502–3
  use of force by
    private military companies 421–2
    and right to self-defence 105
    terrorism 156–8
    whether armed attack 204–10
North Korea 37–8, 62–3, 106, 131–2

North Sea Continental Shelf cases 10–11
nuclear energy, peaceful use of 42
nuclear materials
  availability 42–3
  transfer controls and agreements 59–60
Nuclear Posture Review (2010) 50
Nuclear Security Summit (2010) 51
Nuclear Suppliers Group 59–60
nuclear weapons
  black market 43, 59
  disarmament 47–51, 55
    nuclear-weapons-free-zones 48
    of Outer Space 316–17
    START Treaty (2010) 46, 51, 330
  ICJ Advisory Opinion on (1996) 49, 66, 70–71, 174, 176–7, 329, 448, 459–60
  international law obligations 46–7, 49–51, 324
  and *jus ad bellum* 316–17
  non-proliferation treaty provisions 49–51, 61, 329
  nuclear materials/ technology, availability 42–3
  nuclear testing ban treaties 48, 54
  regulation 329–30
  for self-defence/ self-preservation 176–7
  as strategic deterrent 317
  verification mechanisms 54–5
  and war crimes law 485
nullum crimen sine lege principle 493–4, 496
Nuremberg International Military Tribunal 469–71, 477

occupied territories
  civilians, protection in 389–90
    human rights 406–7
    internment rules 405–6
    relief actions 406–7
    transfer, evacuation and deportment 407
  occupying powers
    accountability 533–6
    human right obligations 404–9, 454–9
    rights of, under international law 454
    and war crimes 480–86
  territorial administration
    common features 547–50
    duration and termination 556
    and self-determination 556
  treaty regulation of 533–4
    regime overlaps 535–6
Office of the High Representative (Bosnia) 557

Oil Platforms case *(Iran v. USA, 2003, ICJ)* 104, 181–2, 201–3, 212–13
On the Law of War and Peace (1625) 94
Oppenheimer v. Cattermole (1976) 636
Orakhelashvili, A. 143, 145, 148
Organization for the Prohibition of Chemical Weapons 36, 52, 54
Organization of American States (OAS) 28
Outer Space Treaty (1967) 47, 316–17

pacifism, Christian principles of 91–3
Pact of Paris (1928) 68, 98–9
Pad v. Turkey (2007) 608
Palestine
   Advisory Opinion on Construction of a Wall in Occupied Palestinian Territory (2004, ICJ) 173–4, 204–5, 454–5, 460–61, 650
   human shields 362–3
   UN peacekeeping force, consent for 577–8
Panama 108–9
Paris, Roland 567–8
Partial Test Ban Treaty (1963) 48
peace *see also lex pacificatoria*
   conflicts
     with human rights 114
     with law of war 258–9
   international obligations
     disarmament 11–12, 36–8, 43–7
     not to endanger 9–11
     prevention of threats to 5–6
   threats to
     changing nature 7–8, 31–2
     concept of endangerment 15
     determination of, UNSC role in 124–8
     generic threats 33, 159
     intrastate threats 137–8
     refusal to implement UNSC resolutions as 32–3
     sanctions, as artificial form of 35
     terrorism 33, 159
     weapons of mass destruction 33, 37, 45–6
peace-making *see also* peace settlements
   influences on 545–6
   law of, development 499, 503
   meaning 19–20
   and responsibility to protect (R2P) 507
Peace of Westphalia (1648) 94
peace settlements
   approaches to
     attitude changes 501–2
     common themes 500–502
     gender inclusion 509–13, 536
     hybrid self-determination 504–9

   international supervision 507–8
   Responsibility to Protect (R2P) 507
international law, influences on
   Cold War 499–500, 572
   international intervention 500–501
   intrastate conflict trends 500–501
   non-state actors, involvement of 502–3
and *lex pacificatoria*
   characteristics 504–8
   creation 499, 503
   inclusiveness, developments in 510–13
   and post conflict justice 517–25, 541–6
   refugees rights under 514–17
   women, equal participation 510–13
post conflict justice 517
   broad amnesties, prohibition 522–5
   and human rights law 518–19, 530–32
   international criminal law 521–2, 536–7
   and international humanitarian law 519–21, 533–5
   international organization roles 500, 526–9
   punitive reparations 517
   regime overlaps 522–5, 535–40
   third party accountability 529–41
   third party intervention 525–9
trends in
   international-domestic hybrids 501, 536–7
   reasons for 499–501
   war-peace hybrids 501–2
and violence, returns to/ changes in nature of 501–2
peacekeeping *see also* humanitarian intervention
   accountability of peacekeepers 533–4, 539–41
   attacks against peacekeepers, as criminal acts 278–9, 484
   Brahimi Report (2000) 42, 579, 589, 593–4
   challenges 572–3, 594–7
   civilian protection mandate 592–6
   and consent of host state
     challenges 578–83
     hostility, influence on 581–3
     need for 576–8
     withdrawal of consent 582–3
   functions 573–6, 586
     changes in 592–6
   and international law, relationship between 573–4
   law, importance of 573
   legal personality challenges 278–9
   neutrality and impartiality, importance 578–80

and post conflict justice 528–9
private military companies' role 439–41
protection of peacekeepers 417–19
state-building role 575
and Status of Force Agreements (SOFA), of the UN 536–7, 576–7, 581–3, 653
UN policy on
  aggressive focus, emergence of 574–6
  Cold War influence on 572–4
  development 572–3, 577–8, 596–7
  limitations 575–6
  police and military functions, relationship between 575–6
use of force by peacekeepers
  concept development 589–90
  in defence of mandate 587–90
  limitations, reasons for 585–7
  personal self-defence 585–7
  rules of engagement 587, 590–92
vs. peace-enforcement
  Capstone Doctrine 578–9
  Certain Expenses Advisory Opinion (1962, ICJ) 140–41, 580–81
  debate over 418–19, 572–5, 577
  hostility, influence of 581–3
  operational trends 574–6
  protection of civilians mandate 417–19, 584–5, 589–90, 592–6
  and UN enforcement powers 574–5
Permanent Court of International Justice 98
Pictet, J. 273–4
Pocket Card 591–2
poison, use as weapon 323–4
precision-guided munitions 317–18
preventative deployment 28–31
principle of subsidiarity 151
prisoners of war
  legal status
    combatants 384–6
    determination of 386–7
    excluded persons 387–8, 393, 422
    loss of status 385–6
    mercenaries 388
    private military company personnel 422
    spies 387–8
  rights of 400–402
  treatment of 419–20
    evacuation 400–402
    following captivity 399–403
    information exchange 402–3
    protection, development of 346, 398
    punishment 403
    repatriation 404

private military companies
  as civilian contractors 428–30
  codes of conduct for 424–5
  complete dependence test 432
  conduct, responsibility for 431–9
  due diligence 438–9
  foreign policy implications of use 441–2
  governmental authority 433–6
  and international humanitarian law
    protections under 415–16, 425–31
    violations, responsibility for 432–3, 438–9
  law, development of 1, 95
  legal status
    civilians *vs.* combatants 425–8
    direct participation in hostilities 428–30
    under international humanitarian law 425–31
    under international law 421–2
    POW status 422
    right to self-defence 421
    and use of force 421–2
    whether mercenaries 422–3
  market regulation of 423–5
  role of
    criticisms 441–3
    development 421, 441–2
    peacekeeping 439–41
privateers *see* private military companies
Proliferation Security Initiative 61
proportionality
  and collateral damage 368–71
  and distinction, principle of 345
  and use of force in self-defence 115, 129, 210–19
  and war reparations 645–6
Prosecutor v. Bahar Idriss Abu Garda (2010, ICC) 418–19
Prosecutor v. Norman (2004) 493
Prosecutor v Tadić (1995, ICTY)
  on armed conflict thresholds 268–9, 271, 282–3, 288, 291, 293–5, 323, 391
  on private conduct, government authority for 436–7
  on UNSC powers 128
  on war crimes 488–90, 496–7
protected persons *see* civilians; prisoners of war; wounded combatants
Public Committee against Torture in Israel v. Government of Israel (2007) 273–4, 301–2
public emergencies, and derogation of human rights obligations 450–53

Index 677

R v. Home Sec ex p. Brind (1991) 621
rebellion, recognition and regulation 107–10, 262–4 *see also* non-international/internal armed conflict
Red Crusader incident (1962, ICJ) 104–5
refugee law
  hard *vs.* soft law developments 515–17
  internal displacement guidelines 515–16
  refugee camps, as burden-sharing 558
  refugees right of return 513–17
religious military personnel, status of 379, 387
reparations and compensation 517
  amnesties, broad, prohibition of 522–5
  under customary international law 652
  Eritrea-Ethiopia Claims Commission 643–4, 646–8
  Geneva Conventions on 649, 657
  Hague Convention on 649, 657
  and human rights law 645–6, 653
  ICJ Advisory Opinion on (1949) 140
  individual claims for 650–52
  influences on 646–8
  and international criminal law 654–7
  judicial practice regarding 642–4
  and *jus ad bellum* 658–9
  and *jus in bello* 650–52, 658–9
  and non-international armed conflict 638–9, 649–50, 657–9
  proportionality 645–6
  recovery of defeated state 644–5
  Resolution 687 (1991) 643–4
  state immunity from 650–52, 658–9
  Truth and Reconciliation Commissions 657–8
  World War I 639–40
  World War II 640–41
Repertoire of the Practice of the UNSC 18–19, 25–6
reprisals 162–3
Resolutions, of UN Security Council
  on equal participation of women 510–13
  extra-territorial applicability to human rights violations 629–33
  non-compliance implications 32–3
  Resolution 487 (1981) 191
  Resolution 661 (1990) 222
  Resolution 678 (1990) 83–5, 135–7, 163–5, 216
  Resolution 687 (1991) 37–8, 56, 62, 73–5, 84–5, 164, 643–4
  Resolution 688 (1991) 85
  Resolution 1154 (1998) 74, 84

Resolution 1199 (1998) 84
Resolution 1244 (1999) 72, 235, 528
Resolution 1284 (1999) 62
Resolution 1296 (2000) 592–3
Resolution 1325 (2000) 510–13, 536
Resolution 1368 (2001) 105
Resolution 1373 (2001) 35–6
Resolution 1441 (2002) 62, 75, 84, 164–5
Resolution 1483 (2003) 645
Resolution 1514 (1960) 563
Resolution 1540 (2004) 36–8, 45–6, 64
Resolution 1546 (2004) 601, 629–34, 636–7, 645
Resolution 1556 (2004) 241
Resolution 1564 (2004) 241
Resolution 1674 (2006) 241, 592–3
Resolution 1695 (2006) 38
Resolution 1696 (2006) 63, 84
Resolution 1737 (2006) 63–4
Resolution 1887 (2009) 46, 50–51, 58–9
Resolution 1962 (2010) 252–3
Resolution 1970 (2011) 166, 244–5, 247
Resolution 1973 (2011) 165–6, 246–51
Resolution 1975 (2011) 252
on restoration of peace requirement 221–4
Responsibility to Protect (R2P)
  development 240–43
  and humanitarian intervention 240–43, 507
    beyond-the-state protection 507–9
  in Côte d'Ivoire 251–3, 254
  criticisms 244, 247–9, 253–4
  in Darfur 241–2
  implementation 244–53
  in Libya 154–5, 244–51, 254–5
  in Syria 254–5
  UN Secretary General Reports on 243–4
  UN Security Council powers 2, 117, 153–6
right to be heard 505–6
right to democratic governance 33
right to knowledge, of missing/ dead combatants 396–8
right to liberty and security 599, 629–30, 633
right to life 461–2, 599–600
riot control agents 51–2
robots 336–8
Rome Statute of the ICC
  on compensation of victims 654–5
  on war crimes 477–8, 482–6, 492–3
Roosevelt, Theodore 97, 99
Rules of Engagement, in peacekeeping operations 591–2
Russia 108, 226–7
Rwanda 8

gender crimes against women 408
International Criminal Tribunal (ICTR) 491, 656
UN involvement in 20, 576, 584–5

St Augustine of Hippo 91–2
St Petersburg Declaration (1868) 322, 327, 340
St Thomas Aquinas 92
San Andreas Accords (1996) 527
San Francisco Peace Treaty (1951) 641
sanctions
  economic sanctions 34–6, 101, 113
  UN sanctions
    imposition 37–8
    legality 45–6
self-defence
  individual and collective rights 181–2, 227–8
    acts of terrorism 105, 112–13, 156–9, 205–7
    anticipatory self-defence 188–91
    duration 219–24
    nature 182–5
    peacekeepers 585–7
    pre-emptive self-defence 191–6
    regulation 185–7
    reporting requirement 224–7
  unilateral right to
    Caroline correspondence on 95, 177–9, 189–91, 207–9, 211, 214, 227–8
    historical development 174–9
    inherent and customary right 179–81
    non-forcible measures 173–4
    self-preservation and necessity 174–9
    'until clauses' 170, 219–24
  use of force, legality of 1, 80–83, 100, 104, 115–17, 160, 193
    anticipatory self-defence 111–13, 115, 159–62, 187–91
    armed attack requirement 80–81, 127–8, 159–60, 187–8
    imminence of attack criteria 160–62, 192–6
    intervention by invitation 107–8, 116, 119
    by peacekeepers 585–7
    pre-emptive self-defence 80–81, 85, 115, 159–62, 191–6
    proportionality 115, 129, 210–19
    reprisals 162–3
    and terrorism 105, 112–13, 156–9, 205–7
self-determination, law of
  hybrid self-determination 504–9
    features of 505–6

peace settlement process, role in 504
Resolution 1514 (1960, UNSC) 563
and territorial trusteeship/ administration arrangements 547, 560–62
  automatic right to 562–4
  challenges 564–7
  colonial territories 547, 551–2, 563–9
  humanization in 568–9
  as interim/ temporary enabling mechanism 564–70
  interventionists, role in 569–70
  mandated territories 545–7, 552–4
  termination arrangements 562–4
Serbia, NATO use of force against
  collateral damage 370
  human rights law, extra-territorial application 457
  legality 106, 116–17
  peacekeeping *vs.* peace enforcement 582–3
  proportionality 370
serious violations, meaning 109–10
sexual violence, protections against 408–10
shipwrecked combatants, protection of 375–6, 388–9
sick and injured combatants
  protection 375–6, 388–9
  treatment 395–8
Sierra Leone
  hostage situations, use of force in 106–7
  Special Court 492–3, 656, 658
Simpson, Brian 563–4
situation, meaning 13–14
Six Day War (1967) 112
Smith v. Sec of State for Defence (2010) 602, 609–10, 616, 625, 627–8
soldiers *see* combatants
Solomou v. Turkey (2008) 615–16
Somalia 290–91, 575–6, 580
South East Asia Collective Defence Treaty (1954) 184
South Vietnam 116
South West Africa 565–6
sovereignty
  Act of State doctrine 635–7
  and responsibility to protect (R2P) 507–9
  and self-determination 506–8, 547, 560–62
  and state immunity, law of 650–52, 658–9
  and territorial trusteeship/ administration arrangements 547, 560–62
Spanish Civil War 351
spies, status of 387–8, 391–2
START Treaty (2010) 46, 51, 330

state immunity, from war reparations 650–52, 658–9
state responsibility, legal principles of *see also* Responsibility to Protect (R2P)
  derogation of 450–53
  in international armed conflict 277–82
  for internationally wrongful acts 427, 433–5, 646, 648
  private military companies 431–8
Status of Force Agreements (SOFA), of the UN 536–7, 576–7, 581–3, 653
Stephens v. Malta (2009) 613–14
subsidiarity, principle of 151
Sudan
  humanitarian intervention 147, 237, 241–2
  peacekeeping *vs.* peace enforcement 584
  sanctions, role of 35
  UN role in 154, 241, 572–3, 578–9, 584, 591–2
Suez Crisis (1956) 114–15, 577
Suriname 78
Syria 254–5

Taiwan 76–7, 82
Taliban, identification as combatants 378
Targeted Killings case (2007) 273–4, 301–2, 462
targeting, law relating to
  aerial warfare 347–52, 371–2
  applicable objects 348–56
  applicable persons 345–8
  atomic bombs 351–2
  authorised Target Sets 373–4
  broadcasting facilities 366–7
  campaign details, publication of 372–3
  challenges 356–71
  civilian heads of state 360–62
  collateral damage 343, 352, 368–71, 484
  combatants, identification of 345–7, 377–8
  deliberate *vs.* dynamic targeting 372–3
  direct participation in hostilities
    by civilians 357–62, 420
    connection with armed conflict, need for 361–2
    direct causal link with harm 361–2, 429–30
    withdrawal from hostilities 382
  distinction, principle of 320–21, 344, 355–6, 484
  dual use objects 367–8
  economic targets 366
  historical development 342–56
  human rights law, extra-territorial application 458
  human shields 362–4
  land warfare 352
  maritime warfare 352
  military objectives, limitation to 355, 364–8
  principle of humanity *vs.* law of armed conflict 343–4
  and proportionality 345, 368–71, 369–71
  public opinion, influences on 343
  rules, generally 354–6
  targeting processes, modern 371–4, 458
territorial administration *see* international territorial administration
terrorism *see also* 9/11
  acts of
    and derogation of human rights obligations 450–53
    as generic threat to peace 33, 159
    as public emergency 450–53
    whether armed attack 203–10
  by civilians, and protected status 391–2
  and disarmament 43, 63
  financing of, UN Resolution on 35–6
  nuclear materials/ weapons, availability 43
  preventative enforcement mechanisms 35–6
  and right to self-defence 105, 112–13, 156–9, 205–7
  war on terror
    targeted killings, legality 309–12
    US policy development 307–8
    whether armed conflict 269–70, 289, 303–4
Thirty Years War 93–4
threat of force
  to avert humanitarian catastrophe 79–80
  changing attitudes towards 67–8, 87–8
  coercion element 76–7
  credibility 77–8, 86
  definition 76–8, 86
  legality of actions 1, 67–9
    counter-threats *vs.* aggression 82–3, 114
    defensive counter-threats 80–83, 87–8
    ICJ rulings on 10–11, 47, 69–71, 87
    in Iraq (1991-2003) 73–5
    in Kosovo (1998-1999) 71–2
    pre-emptive attacks 80–81, 85, 159–62, 191–6
  subjectivity *vs.* objectivity 77–8
  under UN Charter
    collective security obligations 84–8
    institutional threats of force 83–4
    lawful threats 83–7
    prohibitions 67–8, 76
    unilateral threats 84–8

Threshold Ban Treaty (1974) 48
Timor-Leste 559, 561, 656–8
Tokyo International Military Tribunal 471, 477
toxic weapons *see* biological and toxic weapons; chemical weapons
transitional justice, law of
  development 517–18
  and human rights law 518–19
  and international criminal law/justice 521–2
  and international humanitarian law 519–21
  regime overlaps 522–5, 535–40
  and third party accountability 537–40
transnational armed conflicts
  legal interpretation 303–4
  recognition costs 308–9
  as separate category 304–12
  targeted killings, legality 309–12, 462
Treaties
  Bangkok (1995) 48
  on Conventional Armed Forces in Europe (1990) 42, 48–9
  on Friendship and Cooperation between Italy and Libya (2008) 648–9
  on Joint Defense and Economic Cooperation (1950, Arab League) 147
  Pelindaba (1996) 48
  Rarotonga (1985) 48
  Semipalatinsk (2006) 48
  START Treaty (2010) 46, 51, 330
  Tlatelolco (1967) 48
  Versailles (1919) 98, 468, 639–40
trusteeship, over foreign territories 570–71
  administrative prerogative 549, 556–7
  challenges 564–7, 570–71
  common purposes 548–50
  duration and termination
    under colonialism 547, 551–2, 563–6
    dual track approach 558–9
    under mandate and trusteeship arrangements 547, 552–6
  legitimacy 570–71
  meaning 547
  and self-determination 547, 560–64
    challenges 564–7
    humanization 568–9
    as interim/temporary enabling mechanism 564–70
    interventionists' role 569–70
    of Non-Self-Governing and Trust territories 556–7
  and state building, purpose of 567–8
Truth and Reconciliation Commissions 657–8

Tsagourias, Nicholas 139, 577, 585, 589–90
Turkey 76, 82

Uganda
  DRC v. Uganda (2005, ICJ) 111–12, 161, 199–200, 215–16
  hostage situations 106–7, 203–4
  UN involvement in 20
UN Charter
  Article 1, Prevention of threats to peace 5–6
  Article 2, Purposes and principles 9–11, 67–71, 77, 79
  Article 2(4) Use of force, prohibition
    basis for 89–91
    challenges of 114–17
    Cold War influences on interpretation 130–35, 572
    criticism of 113–14, 134–5
    and customary international law 90–91, 113–14
    force other than armed force 101
    hostage situations, applicability to 106–7, 112
    and humanitarian intervention 229–31, 234–7
    impact 113–18
    interpretation debates 105, 113–17, 130–35
    intervention by invitation 107–9, 116–17, 119
    and Just War Doctrine 89–95
    meaning 99–113
    minimal force, meaning 102–7
    and rebellion 109–10
    scope 99–101, 113–14, 638–9
    self-defence 100, 104, 111–13, 115–16
    serious violations and aggression 110–14
    successes of 117–18
    territorial integrity and independence 100, 134–5
    terrorism, applicability to 105
  Article 2(7) Intervention, prohibition of 137–8, 574
  Article 24, Security Council powers 171
  Article 26, Member State armament obligations 11–12, 45, 62
  Article 27, Member State voting 129
  Article 33, Member State dispute resolution obligations 6, 9–11, 13–19, 14, 525–6
  Article 34, UNSC investigation powers 15–16
  Article 35, Dispute referral procedures 18–19

Article 36, UNSC dispute resolution powers 13–14, 16–17, 26
Article 37, Terms of settlement 13–14, 16–18, 26
Article 39, UNSC recommendation powers 16, 31–4, 45, 125, 526, 645
Article 40, Provisional enforcement measures 526, 590
Article 41, Enforcement measures, non-forcible 34–5, 45, 125
Article 42, Enforcement measures, forcible 125, 129, 140–41, 526, 574, 590
Article 43, Member State enforcement obligations 125–6, 130, 139–40
Article 47, Military Staff Committees 141
Article 48, Member State direct actions 140
Article 51, Right of self-defence 100, 107–8, 111–13, 115–17
  and armed attack 80–81, 127–8, 159–62, 187–8
  collective self-defence 171–2, 182–4, 227–8
  and customary law 179–81
  and imminent threat of attack 195–6
  implied purpose 170–71
  and meaning of 'war' 266–7
  and peacekeepers, personal self-defence of 589–90
  reporting requirement 170, 224–7
  until clause 219–24
Article 52, Regional Arrangements 26, 126–7
Article 53, Regional Arrangements 127, 140, 575
Article 73, Non-self-governing territories 551–2
Article 98, Secretary General's powers 23
Article 99, Secretary General's powers 23
Article 103, Conflict of laws 146
diplomatic powers of UNSC 12–19
  dispute resolution procedures 16–17, 29
  investigations 15–16
  jurisdiction 13–15
  terms of settlement 17–18
disarmament obligations 11–12, 36–8, 43–6
preventative deployment 29–31
purpose 122–3
on reparations 641–2
on third party intervention 525–9
UN Department of Peacekeeping Operations, Rules of Engagement 590–92
UN Disarmament Commission 44
UN General Assembly
  Resolution 3314 197–8, 201, 641

  role of 132–3, 168–9
  Uniting for Peace resolution 132–3, 151
UN, generally
  accountability 531–3, 536–9
  establishment 122–3
  purpose and functions 122–3
  and right of self-defence 589–90
UN Human Rights Committee 601
UN Military Staff Committee 126, 130–31
UN Panel of Government Experts on Verification 53–4
UN Register of Conventional Arms 59–60
UN Secretary General, role of 22–5, 40
UN Security Council *see also* Resolutions
  coercive prevention mechanisms 34–6
    disarmament 11–12, 36–8
    powers of recommendation 31–3
  Cold War influences on 130–35, 572
  complaints against 62
  diplomatic powers
    adjustment procedures 16–17, 29
    discretionary powers 6–7, 31–2
    dispute settlement 14–17
    investigations 15–16, 18–19, 21–2
    jurisdiction 13–15
    terms of settlement 17–18
    timing of involvement 19–22
  enforcement powers
    'all necessary means,' interpretation 73, 83–4, 135–6, 150, 163–5, 221–2, 252–3
    armed attack requirement 80–81, 127–8, 159–62, 187–8
    authorisation of use of force 137–42
    'autonomy thesis' 143
    challenges to 142–67
    and collective security 143–4
    exclusive responsibility, interpretation 144–7, 149–51
    humanitarian intervention, challenges 142–56, 527–8
    implied powers 138–42
    and international law norms 129–30
    interpretation challenges 126–8, 137–42
    limitations 128–35
    Members States obligations under 125–6
    NATO powers, compared with 144–7, 150–51
    non-forcible measures 125
    post-authorisation control of actions 163–7
    post-Cold War developments 135–42
    pre-emptive attacks, legality of 80–81, 85, 159–62

primary responsibility, exclusivity 141,
   144–5, 150–51
primary responsibility, failure to act 132–3
purpose of 123–4
regional arrangements 25–8, 126–7
and reprisals 162–3
and responsibility to protect (R2P) 2, 117,
   153–6, 507
scope of 124–8
secondary responsibility, invocation of
   149–51
'subsequent practice,' relevance 140–42
threat of force, 83–4
unilateral enforcement of collective will
   151–3
veto, influence of 131, 135
reform of 168–9
restrictions on 31–2, 39–40
role of
   collective security obligations 5–9,
      120–21, 171–3
   disarmament/ arms control 64–7
   maintenance of international peace and
      security 123–4
   Regional Arrangements and Initiatives
      25–8, 126–7
   threats to peace, determination 124–8
UN Transitional Assistance Group (UNTAG)
   565–6
UNAMID *see* Sudan
United Kingdom
   decolonialization practices 552
   human rights law, extra-territorial
      applicability 599–600, 621–9
   and Act of State doctrine 635–6
   conflicts of law and public policy 634–7
   criticisms 455–7
   European Court of Human Rights rulings,
      impact of 625–9
   judicial rulings on 600–601, 603–4,
      609–11, 614–17, 619–29
   statutory interpretation approach 621–9
National Security Strategy (2010) 239
on pre-emptive self-defence, in Iraq 84–5,
   87–8, 194–5
on use of force in humanitarian assistance
   238–9, 245
on use of weapons, and superfluous injury/
   unnecessary suffering 322–3
United States
   actions in Cuba
      whether defensive or aggressive 83
   actions in Iraq

civilian contractors role 441–2
   legality of threats against 84–5, 87–8
actions in Panama
   by invitation, legality 108–9
colonialism
   decolonialization practices 552
   use of force, justification for 96–7
Global Threat Reduction Initiative 60–61
human rights obligations, extra-territorial
   application 455–7
on humanitarian assistance framework
   239–40
international peace movement, role in
   development 97–9
National Security Strategy 159–60, 239–40,
   242
on Responsibility to Protect (R2P) 242
war on terror, policy development 307–8
weapons strategy and policy 317
   nuclear weapons 50–51
Uniting for Peace resolution 132–3, 151,
   577–9
unmanned combat aerial vehicles 336–8
UNMIK 538–9, 557, 559–60
UNPREDEP 29–31
UNPROPFOR 29–30, 576, 581–3
use of force
   de minimis use 102–7, 274
   force other than armed force 101
   under international law 89, 118–19
   measures not involving 45–6
   against peaceful protesters 118–19
   by peacekeepers
      in defence of mandate 587–90
      personal self-defence 585–7
      rules of engagement 587, 590–592
   by private military companies 421–2
   prohibition of
      under customary international law 90–91,
         113–14
      historical basis 89–90
      and Just War Doctrine 89–95
      League of Nations on 67–8, 90, 98
      under UN Charter 67, 89–91
   and self-defence, legality of 1, 80–83, 100,
      104, 115–17
      anticipatory self-defence 111–13, 115,
         159–62, 187–91
      armed attack requirement 80–81, 127–8,
         159–62, 187–8
      imminence of attack criteria 160–62,
         192–6

intervention by invitation 107–8, 116, 119, 527–8
by peacekeepers 585–7
pre-emptive self-defence 80–81, 85, 115, 159–62, 191–6
proportionality 115, 129, 210–19
reprisals 162–3
terrorism, relevance to 105, 112–13, 156–9
under UN Charter Article 2(4) 67, 89–91, 638–9
  applicability to terrorism 105
  force other than armed force 101
  hostage situations, legality in 106–7, 112
  interpretation challenges 114–17, 128–30
  intervention by invitation 107–9, 116–17, 119, 527–8
  minimal force 102–7
  and rebellion 109–10
  scope of prohibition 99–101, 113–14
  self-defence 100, 104, 111–13, 115–16
  serious violations and aggression 110–14
  territorial integrity and independence 100, 134–5

Varnava v. Turkey (2009) 461–2
Vattel, Emmerich de 94–5, 175
veto, influences of 131, 135
Vietnam 116, 224–5

Waldheim, Kurt 107, 587
Waldock, Humphrey 175–6
war *see also* armed conflict
  collateral damage 343, 352, 368–71, 484
  interpretation
    challenges 256–7, 260–61
    as inter-state conflict 256, 261–2
    and non-state actors 256, 261–2
    as subjective legal concept 259–61
    war of aggression 641–2
  justification for
    Alabama Claims arbitration *(1872)* 95–6
    Christian views on 91–4
    Just War Doctrine 89–95
    legal rules, development of 94–8
    Machiavellian views on 93
    objective tests 93–4
    philosophy of 91–2
    State leaders, right to wage war 93–5
  law of
    civil war, rebellion and belligerency 262–4
    classification 256–7
    conceptual evolution 264–7
    criticism of 496–7

and international humanitarian law 256–7
jus ad bellum and *jus in bello,* role in 264–7
and law of peace, conflict between 258–9
and neutrality 259, 262–4
recognition 260–61
and war crimes 471–4, 497–8
methods of, historical development 345–7
and principle of humanity, balance between 344
war crimes
  apartheid, inclusion of 480–81
  challenges 496–8
  collateral damage 484, 492
  in context 474–6
  conventional weapons, relevance to 484–5
  customary law treatment 479, 486–90, 493–4
  definitions 467, 477, 480–81
  domestic prosecutions 493–5
  Elements of Crimes 484
  enforcement 493–6, 497–8
  exclusions 484–6
  under Geneva Convention and Protocols 477–81
  grave breaches provisions 477–81
  historical development 467–71, 493
  and human rights law 473–4
  under ICTR 491
  under ICTY 478–9, 481–2, 488–90, 495–7
  under international criminal law 473–4
  under international humanitarian law 471–3
  and law of armed conflict, generally 471–4, 477–8, 497–8
  limitations of 478–9, 484–6, 497–8
  in non-international armed conflicts 487–93
  nuclear weapons, relevance to 485
  nullum crimen sine lege principle 493–4, 496
  in occupied territories 480–86
  prosecution obligations 478–9
  under Rome Statute of ICC 477, 482–6
  Special Court for Sierra Leone 492–3
  superfluous injury/ unnecessary suffering 485
  treaty provisions 477–86, 491–3
  and wounded, sick and medical personnel 479–80
war indemnities 639 *see also* reparations
war on terror
  combatants, interpretation 384
  US policy development 307–8
  whether armed conflict 269–70, 289, 303–4, 307–8
war victims *see* civilians; reparations and compensation; wounded combatants
Warsaw Pact (1955) 184

Wassenaar Arrangement on Export Controls for Conventional Arms and Dual-Use Goods and Technologies (2004) 59
weapons *see also* disarmament; nuclear weapons; weapons of mass destruction
　anti-materiel use 324
　anti-vehicle mines 333–4
　biological and toxic weapons
　　Conventions on 49, 51–3, 55, 62
　　riot control agents 51–2
　　verification mechanisms 52, 54–5
　chemical weapons
　　Conventions on 36, 41, 47, 51–3, 54–6, 62, 65, 328
　　and customary international law 46–7
　　riot control agents 51–2
　　verification mechanisms 54–6
　　white phosphorus 334–6
　　World War II, use in 351
　classification 47
　cluster bombs 47, 65, 317–18, 328, 330–32, 341, 494–5
　conventional weapons
　　non-transference obligations 49–50
　　treaty provisions regulating 321–2
　　use restrictions 42, 48–9
　　war crimes, relevance to 484–5
　and customary international law 46–7, 322–3, 325–6
　cyber warfare 338–40
　drones and robots 336–8
　and environmental protection 324–6
　improvised explosive devices 332–4
　incendiary weapons 324
　under *jus ad bellum* 316–18, 340
　under *jus in bello*
　　definitions 318–19
　　distinction, principle of 320–22
　　prohibited weapons 46–7, 322–4
　　regulation 320–26, 340–41
　　use of, prohibited outcomes 322–6
　under *jus post bello* 327–8, 331–2
　landmines 47, 317–18, 321, 328, 333, 341
　legacy weapons 331–2
　'means and methods of warfare' 318–19
　non-proliferation 52, 64–5, 329
　　obligations 37, 42, 49–51
　　transfer controls 59–61
　poison 323–4
　precision-guided munitions 317–18
　regulation
　　challenges 315
　　historical development 320, 327–8, 340–41

　role in war, generally 315–18
　small arms proliferation, influences of 33, 37
　smart weapons 317–18
　and superfluous injury/ unnecessary suffering 322–4, 485
　and technological developments 315
　white phosphorus 334–6
weapons of mass destruction
　biological and chemical weapons 51–6, 328
　definition 47
　disarmament, UN Security Council role in 63, 67
　and non-state actors, availability to 42–3, 63
　nuclear weapons 329–30
　　black market 43, 59
　　ICJ Advisory opinion on (1996) 49, 66, 70–71, 174, 176–7, 329, 448, 459–60
　　nuclear-weapons-free-zones 48
　　Resolution 687 (1991) 36–7, 56, 62, 73–5, 84–5, 164
　　Resolution 1540 (2004) 36–8, 45–6, 64
　　Review Conferences 57–8
　　as threat of force 78, 83
　　as threat to peace 33, 37, 45–6
　　verification mechanisms 54–5
　　withdrawal clauses 58–9
White, Nigel 131–2
white phosphorus 334–6
Wilmshurst, Elizabeth 111–12
withdrawal clauses 58–9
W.M. v. Denmark (1992) 606
women
　convention protections 405–10
　equal participation 510–13, 536
World Summit Outcome (2005) 21, 153–4, 161, 168–9, 240–44, 254
World War I
　aerial warfare developments 349–50
　international law development, influences on 97–8, 376, 468–9
　reparations 639–40
World War II
　aerial warfare developments 350–52, 371
　international law development, influences on 68–9, 398, 469–71
　post conflict justice 517
　reparations 640–41, 644–5
wounded combatants
　protection 375–6, 388–9, 479–80
　treatment 395–8

X v. UK (1979) 613

Yugoslavia
  International Criminal Tribunal (ICTY)
    on compensation of victims 655–6
    jurisdiction 478–9, 488–9
    powers 481–2
    on war crimes 478–9, 481–2, 488–90, 495–7
  NATO threat of force against
    collateral damage 370
    extra-territoriality of human rights law 601–2
    as humanitarian intervention 233–7
    legality 85–8, 106, 601–2
    proportionality 370
  Prosecutor v Tadić (1995, ICTY)
    on armed conflict thresholds 268–9, 271, 282–3, 288, 291, 293–5, 323, 391
    on private conduct, government authority for 436–7
    on UNSC powers 128
    on war crimes 488–90, 496–7
    UN involvement in 20, 600

Zangger Committee 59
zeppelins 349–50
Zimbabwe 28